ScottForesman
LITERATURE
AND INTEGRATED STUDIES

Annotated Teacher's Edition
Volume Two

English Literature

ScottForesman

Editorial Offices: Glenview, Illinois
Regional Offices: San Jose, California • Tucker, Georgia
Glenview, Illinois • Oakland, New Jersey • Dallas, Texas

Visit ScottForesman's Home Page at http://www.scottforesman.com

acknowledgments

Cover (detail): Dante Gabriel Rossetti, *The Beloved*/ Tate Gallery,
London/Bridgeman Art Library, London/Superstock, Inc. **853e(t)** UPI-
Corbis/Bettmann **853f(t)** Walt Disney/Photofest

ISBN: 0-673-29467-6

Copyright © 1997
Scott, Foresman and Company, Glenview, Illinois
All Rights Reserved. Printed in the United States of America.

1.800.554.4411
http://www.scottforesman.com

1 2 3 4 5 6 7 8 9 10 DR 03 02 01 00 99 98 97 96

ScottForesman
LITERATURE
AND INTEGRATED STUDIES

Middle School: Grade Six

Middle School: Grade Seven

Middle School: Grade Eight

Forms in Literature

World Literature

American Literature

English Literature

The cover features a detail of Dante Gabriel Rossetti's *The Beloved,* which also appears on this page. Rossetti (1828–1882), who achieved equal fame as a painter and a poet, is known for the sensuousness and exoticism of his works in both areas. *Tate Gallery, London*

ScottForesman
LITERATURE
AND INTEGRATED STUDIES

English Literature

Senior Consultants

Alan C. Purves
State University of New York at Albany

Carol Booth Olson
University of California, Irvine

Carlos E. Cortés
University of California, Riverside (Emeritus)

ScottForesman

Editorial Offices: Glenview, Illinois
Regional Offices: San Jose, California • Tucker, Georgia
Glenview, Illinois • Oakland, New Jersey • Dallas, Texas

Visit ScottForesman's Home Page at http://www.scottforesman.com

Acknowledgments

Texts

8 Reuse of abridgment of *Beowulf: The Oldest English Epic,* translated by Charles W. Kennedy from pages 3-101. Reprinted by permission. **35** From *Grendel,* by John Gardner. Copyright © 1971 by John Gardner. Reprinted by permission of Alfred A. Knopf Inc. **47–48** "The Prologue" and "The Pardoner's Prologue and Tale" from *The Canterbury Tales* by Geoffrey Chaucer, translated by Nevill Coghill (Penguin Classics 1951, Fourth revised edition, 1977). Copyright © 1951, 1958, 1960, 1975, 1977 by Nevill Coghill. Reproduced by permission of Penguin Books Ltd. **61** From *Sir Gawain And The Green Knight,* translated by M. R. Ridley. Reprinted by permission of Reed Consumer Books. **88** From *A Distant Mirror* by Barbara W. Tuchman. Copyright © 1978 by Barbara W. Tuchman. Reprinted by permission of Random House, Inc. **92** From *The Once and Future King* by T.H. White. Reprinted by permission. **192** From *Ancient Egyptian Literature, Three Volumes,* by Miriam Lichtheim, pp. 125-126. Copyright © 1973-1980 by The Regents of the University of California. Reprinted by permission of The University of California Press. **193** "Aeschylus" from *The Eumenides,* translated by Richmond Lattimore. Copyright © 1953 by The University of Chicago. Reprinted by permission. **194** From *Crime And Punishment* by Feodor Dostoevski. Reprinted by permission. **211** "Summer is Gone" from *A Book Of Ireland,* edited by Frank O'Connor. Reprinted by permission. **212** "Fern Hill" by Dylan Thomas from *The Poems Of Dylan Thomas.* Copyright 1952 by The Trustees for the Copyrights of Dylan Thomas. Reprinted by permission of New Directions Publishing Corporation and David Higham Associates Limited. **219** "Lineage" from *Crow* by Ted Hughes. Reprinted by permission. **239** From "David's Story" and "The Bubble Boy" by Carol Ann with Kent Demaret in *People Weekly,* October 29, 1984 and November 5, 1984. Copyright © 1984 by Time, Inc. Reprinted by permission. **241** From *Six Degrees Of Separation* by John Guare. Copyright © 1990 by John Guare. Reprinted by permission of Vintage Books, a Division of Random House Inc. **244** Lyrics only of "We Are The World" by Michael Jackson and Lionel Richie. Reprinted by permission. **280** "Postcard from Paradise" by Chris Williamson. Copyright ©1993 by Bird Ankles Music (BMI). Reprinted by permission of Chris Williamson. **369** Excerpts from *Fame In The 20th Century* by Clive James. Reprinted by permission. **389** Excerpt from A Room of One's Own by Virginia Woolf. Reprinted by permission. **394** Lyrics only of "London Pride" by Noel Coward. Reprinted by permission. **394** "October 10, 1940" from *This Is London* by Edward R. Murrow. Reprinted by permission. **434** Abridgment of "The Power Of Dreams" by George Howe Colt in *Life,* September 1995. Reprinted by permission. **507** From "The Monster's Human Nature" by Stephen Jay Gould in *Natural History,* July 1994. Copyright © 1994 by the American Museum of Natural History. Reprinted by permission.

continued on page 1017

ISBN: 0-673-29450-1

Copyright © 1997
Scott, Foresman and Company, Glenview, Illinois
All Rights Reserved. Printed in the United States of America.

1.800.554.4411
http://www.scottforesman.com

1 2 3 4 5 6 7 8 9 10 DR 03 02 01 00 99 98 97 96

Senior Consultants

Alan C. Purves

Professor of Education and Humanities, State University of New York at Albany; Director of the Center for Writing and Literacy. Dr. Purves developed the concept and philosophy of the literature lessons for the series, consulted with editors, reviewed tables of contents and lesson manuscript, wrote the Assessment Handbooks, and oversaw the development and writing of the series testing strand.

Carol Booth Olson

Director, California Writing Project, Department of Education, University of California, Irvine. Dr. Olson conceptualized and developed the integrated writing strand of the program, consulted with editors, led a team of teachers in creating literature-based Writing Workshops, and reviewed final manuscript.

Carlos E. Cortés

Professor Emeritus, History, University of California, Riverside. Dr. Cortés designed and developed the multicultural strand embedded in each unit of the series and consulted with grade-level editors to implement the concepts.

Series Consultants

Visual and Media Literacy/Speaking and Listening/Critical Thinking

Harold M. Foster. Professor of English Education and Secondary Education, The University of Akron, Akron. Dr. Foster developed and wrote the Beyond Print features for all levels of the series.

ESL and LEP Strategies

James Cummins. Professor, Modern Language Centre and Curriculum Department, Ontario Institute for Studies in Education, Toronto.

Lily Wong Fillmore. Professor, Graduate School of Education, University of California at Berkeley.

Drs. Cummins and Fillmore advised on the needs of ESL and LEP students, helped develop the Building English Proficiency model for the program, and reviewed strategies and manuscript for this strand of the program.

Fine Arts/Humanities

Neil Anstead. Coordinator of the Humanitas Program, Cleveland Humanities Magnet School, Reseda, California. Mr. Anstead consulted on the fine art used in the program.

Reviewers and Contributors

Pupil and Teacher Edition

Jay Amberg, Glenbrook South High School, Glenview, Illinois **Edison Barber,** St. Anne Community High School, St. Anne, Illinois **Lois Barliant,** Albert G. Lane Technical High School, Chicago, Illinois **James Beasley,** Plant City Senior High School, Plant City, Florida **Linda Belpedio,** Oak Park/River Forest High School, Oak Park, Illinois **Richard Bruns,** Burges High School, El Paso, Texas **Kay Parks Bushman,** Ottawa High School, Ottawa, Kansas **Jesús Cardona,** John F. Kennedy High School, San Antonio, Texas **Marlene Carter,** Dorsey High School, Los Angeles, California **Patrick Cates,** Lubbock High School, Lubbock, Texas **Timothy Dohrer,** New Trier Township High School, Winnetka, Illinois **Margaret Doria,** Our Lady of Perpetual Help High School, Brooklyn, New York **Lucila Dypiangco,** Bell Senior High School, Bell, California **Judith Edminster,** Plant City High School, Plant City, Florida **Mary Alice Fite,** Columbus School for Girls, Columbus, Ohio **Montserrat Fontes,** Marshall High School, Los Angeles, California **Diane Fragos,** Turkey Creek Middle School, Plant City, Florida **Joan Greenwood,** Thornton Township High School, Harvey, Illinois **William Irvin,** Pittsfield Public Schools, Pittsfield, Massachusetts **Carleton Jordan,** Montclair High School, Montclair, New Jersey **Mark Kautz,** Chapel Hill High School, Chapel Hill, North Carolina **Elaine Kay,** Bartow High School, Bartow, Florida **Roslyn Kettering,** West Lafayette Junior/Senior High School, West Lafayette, Indiana **Kristina Kostopoulos,** Lincoln Park High School, Chicago, Illinois **Julia Lloyd,** Harwood Junior High School, Bedford, Texas **John Lord,** Ocean Township High School, Oakhurst, New Jersey **Dolores Mathews,** Bloomingdale High School, Valrico, Florida **Jim McCallum,** Milford High School, Milford, Massachusetts **Monette Mehalko,** Plant City Senior High School, Plant City, Florida **Lucia Podraza,** DuSable High School, Chicago, Illinois **Frank Pool,** Anderson High School, Austin, Texas **Alice Price,** Latin School, Chicago, Illinois **Anna J. Roseboro,** The Bishop's School, La Jolla, California **Peter Sebastian,** Granite Hills High School, El Cajon, California **Rob Slater,** East Forsyth High School, Winston Salem, North Carolina **Catherine Small,** Nicolet High School, Glendale, Wisconsin **Dennis Symkowiak,** Mundelein High School, Mundelein, Illinois **Rosetta Tetteh,** Senn High School, Chicago, Illinois **Pamela Vetters,** Harlandale High School, San Antonio, Texas **Polly Walwark,** Oak Park High School, Oak Park, Illinois **Karen Wrobleski,** San Diego High School, San Diego, California **Dru Zimmerman,** Chapel Hill High School, Chapel Hill, North Carolina

Contents

Unit 1 Medieval Literature

Part 1: Getting Even

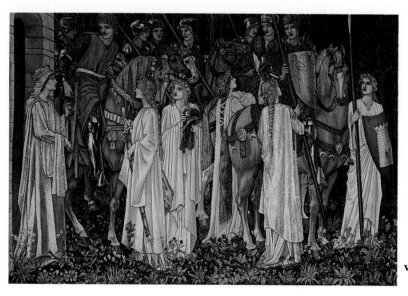

Part 2: Codes of Honor

Unit 2 The Elizabethan Era
The Lure of Ambition

Unit 3   The Seventeenth Century
Part 1: The Meaning of Life

Part 2: The Fall from Grace

Unit 4 The Age of Reason

Part 1: A Focus on Society

Part 2: Other People's Lives

xiii

THEMES IN ENGLISH
LITERATURE: LONDON

Unit 5 The Romantic Era

Part 1: Visions and Dreams

Part 2: The Outsider

Part 3: Exceeding Human Limits

Unit 6 The Victorians

Part 1: The Struggle to Understand

Part 2: Hope and Despair

Unit 7 The Early Twentieth Century

Part 1: Upward Mobility

Part 2: War and Aftermath

Part 3: The Search for Identity

Unit 8 The Later Twentieth Century

Part 1: The Passing of Empire

xxi

Part 2: The Slant View

Glossaries, Handbooks, and Indexes

Genre Overview

Short Stories

Novel Excerpts

Tales, Romances, and Narratives

Poetry

Feature Overview

Planning Unit 6: The Victorians

Literature

Integrated Language Arts

	Literary	Writing/Grammar, Usage and Mechanics	Reading, Thinking, Listening, Speaking	Vocabulary/Spelling
The Lady of Shalott *by Alfred, Lord Tennyson* Poem *(average)* p. 528 **Ulysses** *by Alfred, Lord Tennyson* Poem *(average)* p. 531 **Lyric 106 from In Memoriam** *by Alfred, Lord Tennyson* Poem *(easy)* p. 534 **Crossing the Bar** *by Alfred, Lord Tennyson* Poem *(easy)* p. 535	Rhyme Mood Imagery Symbol Meter Characterization Draw conclusions Theme Metaphor	Description Dialogue Editorial Verb pair *lie* and *lay*	Find the main idea Analyze Draw conclusions Recognize values	Using a dictionary
Sonnet 43 *by Elizabeth Barrett Browning* Poem *(easy)* p, 539 **Porphyria's Lover** *by Robert Browning* Poem *(average)* p. 539 **My Last Duchess** *by Robert Browning* Poem *(average)* p. 542	Dramatic monologue Mood Characterization	Brief description Dramatic monologue Essay Irregular verbs	Recognize values Find the main idea Draw conclusions	Using the dictionary
A Mad Tea-Party **from Alice's Adventures in** **Wonderland** *by Lewis Caroll* Novel Excerpt *(easy)* p. 547	Pun Connotation/denotation Personification	Write a brief scene Feature story Write riddles Compound sentences	Inference Literal and figurative language Synthesize Compare and contrast	Puns
Dover Beach *by Matthew Arnold* Poem *(average)* p. 555	Connotation/denotation Theme	Impressions Paragraph on symbolism Personal letter Using hyphens		

Meeting Individual Needs

Multi-modal Activities	Mini-Lessons
Create a fictitious place	Verb pair *lie* and *lay*
Illustrated oral report	Using reference materials
Musical show	
Understanding inverted word order	Using a dictionary
Comparing details	
Making personal connections	
Presenting a poem	

Oral reading	Using the dictionary
Illustrated report	Irregular verbs
Create an artwork	
Dramatizing the poem	
Exploring contractions	

Tell the story	Pun
Reader's theater performance	Compound sentences
Improving comprehension	
Linking past and present	

Picture book	Using hyphens
Videotape	
Contrasting images	

Interdisciplinary Studies
The Crystal Palace

Format	Content Area	Highlights	Skill
Diary: **The Great Exhibition** *from Queen Victoria's Journal*	History	Queen Victoria's account of the first World's Fair.	Using primary and secondary sources Using an almanac
Picture Essay: **Touring the Crystal Palace**	History	Pictures of the types of things on display at the Crystal Palace.	

Writing Workshop

Mode	Writing Format	Writing Focus	Proofreading Skills
Expository writing	A comparison/contrast essay	Guiding the reader	Avoiding run-on sentences

Program Support Materials

For Every Selection	For Every Writing Workshop
Unit Resource Book Graphic Organizer Study Guide Vocabulary Worksheet Grammar Worksheet Spelling, Speaking and Listening, or Literary Language Worksheet Alternate Check Test Vocabulary Test Selection Test	**Unit Resource Book** Prewriting Worksheet Revising Strategy Worksheet Editing Strategy Worksheet Presentation Worksheet Writing Rubric **Transparency Collection** Fine Art Transparency Student Writing Model Transparencies

For Every Interdisciplinary Study	Assessment
Unit Resource Book Study Guide Mini-Lesson Skill Worksheet	**Unit Resource Book** TE Check Tests Alternate Check Test (blackline master) Vocabulary Test (blackline master) Selection Test (blackline master) **Test Generator Software** **Assessment Handbook**

Planning Unit 6: The Victorians

Literature

Integrated Language Arts

Literature	Literary	Writing/Grammar, Usage and Mechanics	Reading, Thinking, Listening, Speaking	Vocabulary/Spelling
Poems by Thomas Hardy **The Darkling Thrush** *(average)* p. 574 **The Man He Killed** *(average)* p. 576 **"Ah, Are You Digging on My Grave?"** *(average)* p. 577	Assonance Point of view Irony Dialect Dialogue	Compare and contrast Analytic essay Personal journal entry Forming singular and plural possessives	Compare and contrast Draw conclusions Understand sequence	
Poems by Gerard Manley Hopkins **Pied Beauty** *(average)* p. 581 **Spring and Fall: To a Young Child** *(average)* p. 582	Alliteration Theme	Use alliteration Poetic stanza Short essay Recognizing sentence fragments	Compare and contrast Find the main idea	

The Lagoon
    by Joseph Conrad
Short Story
(average)
p. 586
	Setting, foreshadowing
	Imagery
	Characterization
	Alliteration
	Flashback
	Irony, theme
		Analytic essay
		Write a story
		Understanding active and
		    passive verbs
		Imagery and figurative
		    language
			Draw conclusions
			Detect bias
			Find the main idea
			Recognize cause and effect
			Recognize values
			Synthesize
				Etymology

Poems by A. E. Housman **To an Athlete Dying Young** *(average)* p. 599 **When I Was One-and-Twenty** **Loveliest of Trees** *(easy)* p. 601	Anastrophe	Words of wisdom Thank-you letter Poem Analytic essay Adjective forms—positive, comparative, superlative	Find the main idea	Word map
Poems by William Butler Yeats **When You Are Old** **The Wild Swans at Coole** *(average)* p. 605 **The Second Coming** *(average)* p. 607 **Sailing to Byzantium** *(challenging)* p. 608	Consonance Theme Allusions	Paragraph Description Editorial Using adverbs	Find the main idea Compare and contrast	

The Star
    by H. G. Wells
Short Story
(average)
p. 612
	Point of view
	Irony
	Imagery
		Characteristics
		Headlines
		Simple, compound and
		    complex sentences
			Draw conclusions
			Infer
			Recognize cause and effect
			Find the main idea
			Compare and contrast	

Poems by Rudyard Kipling
Tommy
(average) p. 624
If-
(average) p. 626
	Synecdoche
	Dialect
	Theme
		Letter of recommendation
		Short poem
		Recognize colloquialisms,
		    slang, idioms, and
		    jargon
				Etymology

Meeting Individual Needs

Multi-modal Activities	Mini-Lessons
Writing a dialogue Artistic treatment of confrontation Musical composition Exploring metaphor and simile Making cultural connections	Forming singular and plural possessives
Creating a video Illustrated story Musical piece Exploring imagery	Recognizing sentence fragments

Debate
Analyzing setting and mood
Contrasting point of view
Describing a place
Analyzing cultural distinctives
Expanding vocabulary notebooks
	Setting
	Understanding active
	  and passive verbs
	Imagery and figurative
	  language
	Etymology

Speech
Radio show
Chart pros and cons
Making personal connections
	Adjective forms—posi-
	  tive, comparative,
	  superlative

Oral report Composite collage Analyzing imagery	Using adverbs Consonance

Oral report
Sequencing events
Visualizing the cosmic
Exploring key events
Responding to key events
	Point of view
	Simple, compound
	  and complex
	  sentences
	Map skills
	Pace

Oral reading
Collage
Oral report
Exploring dialect
	Recognize
	  colloquialisms,
	  slang, idioms, and
	  jargon

Interdisciplinary Studies
Century's End

Format	Content Area	Highlights	Skill
Excerpt: **The War of the Worlds** by H. G. Wells	Popular Culture	An exploration of the possibility of a Martian invasion.	Recognize graphic art styles
Article: **Counting the Years** by Lance Morrow	Mathematics	A discussion of multi-cultural views of the beginning of a new millennium.	
Poll: **The Future Poll**	Future	A poll of what is thought to be in store for future generations.	Communicate clearly and effectively

Writing Workshop

Mode	Writing Format	Writing Focus	Proofreading Skills
Narrative/expository writing	A found poem and an explanation	Development by detail	Spelling homophones correctly

Program Support Materials

For Every Selection	For Every Writing Workshop
Unit Resource Book Graphic Organizer Study Guide Vocabulary Worksheet Grammar Worksheet Spelling, Speaking and Listening, or Literary Language Worksheet Alternate Check Test Vocabulary Test Selection Test	**Unit Resource Book** Prewriting Worksheet Revising Strategy Worksheet Editing Strategy Worksheet Presentation Worksheet Writing Rubric **Transparency Collection** Fine Art Transparency Student Writing Model Transparencies

For Every Interdisciplinary Study	Assessment
Unit Resource Book Study Guide Mini-Lesson Skill Worksheet	**Unit Resource Book** TE Check Tests Alternate Check Test (blackline master) Vocabulary Test (blackline master) Selection Test (blackline master) **Test Generator Software** **Assessment Handbook**

Media and Technology

Part One Selections

The Lady of Shalott/Ulysses/Lyric 106/Crossing the Bar

Audiotape *Treasury of Alfred Lord Tennyson*, Spoken Arts, includes "Ulysses."

Videotape *Victorian Poetry*, 28 minutes, Films for the Humanities & Sciences, includes the work of Tennyson, Browning, and others.

Home Connection Many people, Tennyson included, look with interest or nostalgia on a certain place in a period of history that existed before they were born. Students might like to query older adults or family members about what period or place from the past they would like to visit if they had a time machine.

Sonnet 43/Porphyria's Lover/My Last Duchess

Audiotape *Sonnets from the Portuguese:* Elizabeth Barrett Browning, Spoken Arts, includes Browning's complete cycle of love sonnets. *Treasury of Robert Browning,* Spoken Arts, includes "My Last Duchess," and other poems.

Community Resources Browning's dramatic monologues contain murder and some violence.

Should they be R-rated? You might invite one or two speakers to class to talk about viewpoints on censorship and to discuss such questions as these: Should nothing be censored? Should some things be censored, and if so, what? Who has a right to censor material and for whom?

A Mad Tea Party

Audiotape Christopher Plummer reads *The Complete Alice in Wonderland*, 6 hours, Caedmon/Harper Audio, 1993.

Videotape *Original Alice,* 23 minutes, Britannica, 1989, traces the life of the original Alice in Wonderland. Consider showing *Alice in Wonderland,* 90 minutes, Library Video Company, 1985, starring Red Buttons and others.

Computer Software Consider using the CD-ROM program *Alice in Wonderland,* for IBM, Macintosh, and Windows, from Queue.

Home Connection Although Carroll's book about Alice was intended for children, many adults confess that they did not appreciate it until they were grown up. Students might like to discuss with adults what their favorite childhood stories were. Were they stories they were "supposed" to listen to, watch, or read, or were they off the recommended list?

Dover Beach

Audiotape *Treasury of Matthew Arnold,* Spoken Arts, includes "Dover Beach" and other poetry.

Community Resources Arnold speaks of the "Sea of Faith" in his poem. Some students might like to research, perhaps in a book of quotations or in a religious work, what various people have said about faith.

Part Two Selections

The Darkling Thrush/The Man He Killed/"Ah, Are You Digging on My Grave?"

Videotape *Thomas Hardy*, 30 minutes, Britannica, documents the author's life, as does *Thomas Hardy and Dorset*, 15 minutes, Films for the Humanities & Sciences. Students may want to experience Hardy's *Far From the Madding Crowd*, 2 hours 46 minutes, MGM/UA Home Video, 1990.

Pied Beauty/Spring and Fall: To a Young Child

Videotape *Gerard Manley Hopkins,* 58 minutes, Films for the Humanities & Sciences, is a picture of the first modern English poet.

Connections to
Custom Literature Database

For Part One "The Struggle to Understand" Selections with Lessons

• from "In Memoriam" by Alfred, Lord Tennyson

• "Andrea del Sarto" by Robert Browning

Additional theme-based selections can be accessed on the ScottForesman database.

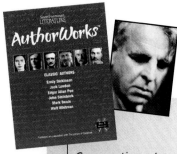

Connections to
Author works

Information about the life and times of Thomas Hardy, W. B. Yeats, and Joseph Conrad is available on ScottForesman's AuthorWorks CD-ROM.

Home Connection Hopkins was undoubtedly a nonconformist. Do some people set out to be nonconformists, or can't they help themselves? Is it good or bad not to be like everyone else? Who is happier in life–a conformist or a nonconformist? Some students might like to elicit the views of older adults on these questions.

The Lagoon

Audiotape *Heart of Darkness and Other Stories*, Listening Library, includes Conrad's "The Lagoon."

Videotape *An Outpost of Progress*, 45 minutes, from The American Short Story Collection, Library Video Company, 1982, is based on a short story by Conrad.

Community Resources Joseph Conrad was well traveled before he sat down to write. (In fact his first book was not published until the year he was 37.) If someone in the community has come from or visited Malaysia, you might invite them to speak to the class and/or show a video or pictures of their experiences.

To an Athlete Dying Young/When I Was One-and-Twenty/Loveliest of Trees

Audiotape *A Shropshire Lad and Other Poetry*, Caedmon/Harper Audio, read by James Mason, features the work of A. E. Housman.

Community Resources Since two of Housman's poems are about making choices, you may want to ask several people to speak to the class about decision-making. The popularity of the Ann Landers and Dear Abby columns are evidence that many people seek help in making decisions. There may be experts in your community who can provide assistance on how to go about making a decision.

When You Are Old/The Wild Swans at Coole/The Second Coming/Sailing to Byzantium

Audiotape *Poems and Memories: William Butler Yeats*, Spoken Arts, presents poems of the author and a discussion of his work. *The Poetry of William Yeats*, Caedmon/Harper, features Siobhan McKenna reading.

Community Resources "We are not a normal family," Yeats once said. In *Family Secrets: William Butler Yeats and His Relatives* (Syracuse, 1995), William Murphy writes of the Yeats family—sisters Susan and Elizabeth, a textile designer and printer respectively, and brother Jack, a painter, as well as other family members. Students interested in Yeats will enjoy the book.

The Star

Audiotape "The Star" is included on *The Time Machine and Other Stories*, Listening Library. Ben Kingsley reads an unabridged version of Wells's *Time Machine*, 2 hours 30 minutes, Dove Audio, 1994.

Videotape Rod Taylor and Yvette Mimieux star in Wells's *Time Machine*, 103 minutes, Library Video Company, 1960. *The Magic Shop*, 12 minutes, Britannica, filmed in a contemporary setting, is based on a short story by Wells.

Tommy/If

Audiotape *Kipling Short Stories and Poems*, 3 hours, is available through Audio Book Contractors, 1994.

Videotape Flashbacks recreate a day in the life of Kipling in *Rudyard Kipling –The Road from Mandalay*, 30 minutes, Centron Educational Films, 1978.

Home Connection Someone once made a poster containing the first two lines of "If" and irreverently adding a third : "You just don't understand the situation." But in fact, many people of an earlier generation memorized all or some of "If," in part because it contains valuable advice. Students might be interested in asking older adults whether they memorized poetry in school, and if so, what they now remember of it.

Connections to
Custom Literature Database

For Part Two "Hope and Despair" Selections with Lessons

• "In Time of "The Breaking of Nations"' and "Hap" by Thomas Hardy
• "The Scrupulous Father" by George Gissing

Additional theme-based selections can be accessed on the ScottForesman database.

Connections to
NovelWorks

Audiotapes of Thomas Hardy's *The Mayor of Casterbridge* and Joseph Conrad's *Lord Jim* are among the many teaching tools included in the ScottForesman NovelWorks kits.

The Victorians

 Art Study

George William Joy painted *The Bayswater Omnibus* in 1895. The omnibus, invented in mid-nineteenth century, derives its name from the Latin word for "all" (omni) and means "carriage for everyone." The introduction of the omnibus corresponds with the rising middle-class population and the blurring of distinction between members of different classes. Anyone who could afford to pay the fare could ride side by side with other citizens, regardless of one's class. The passengers in the painting, from the left, are a poor woman with her children, a fashionable woman, a city man, and a nursemaid.

Visual Literacy *The Bayswater Omnibus* comes from the tradition of narrative painting, which illustrated historical or literary events. Later, narrative paintings were any pictures that told a story with the setting, costumes, and facial expressions. The viewers were invited to create a story based on the image.

Question What story might this narrative painting tell? *(Students' responses will vary greatly. Encourage students to do some research that may help them understand each person's possible circumstances. Students may want to devise possible connections between the characters and their circumstances.)*

UNIT **6**

The Victorians

The Struggle to Understand
Part One, pages 524–569

Hope and Despair
Part Two, pages 570–642

THEMES IN ENGLISH LITERATURE

Rule, Britannia!
Theme Portfolio, pages 643–655

523

THEMATIC CONNECTIONS

The scientific advances of the nineteenth century challenged the soul of the British populace, who found the contradictions between democracy, class conflict, progressive humanism, and imperialist warfare to pose a cultural dilemma.

Part One:
The Struggle to Understand

The writers in Part One question how the changing world will affect their values, experiences, dreams, and mythologies.

Ideas to Explore

- How does the literature reflect the effect of material progress on the nature of interpersonal relationships?
- How do these writers represent the desire to cling to the past even while embracing the future?

Part Two:
Hope and Despair

With a mixture of hope and despair, the authors attempt to reconcile themselves to the cultural upheaval in Victorian England.

Ideas to Explore

- How do the social beliefs of the authors surface in their writing?
- Which of the writers seem optimistic? pessimistic? both?

🎨 Art Study

The icon for Part One is the March Hare from John Tenniel's illustrations for *Alice's Adventures in Wonderland*. The second icon is Ernst Ludwig Kirchner's *Bildnis des Dichters Frank (Portrait of the Poet Frank)*. The contrast of bright colors with the melancholy expression suggests the tension between hope and despair.

Part One: The Struggle to Understand
Historical Overview

EXPLORING CONCEPTS

- During the sixty-three-year reign of Queen Victoria, the British empire reached its height of global power.
- Social unrest caused by oppressive environmental and economic conditions created a domestic atmosphere of dispute and uncertainty.
- Devoted to progress, British explorers, engineers, and scientists overturned traditional notions of nature: its boundaries and practical applications, as well as its creation and evolution.
- Cultural trends kept up with the pace of science and industry as writers such as George Eliot sought to break free from the conservative limitations of tradition.

Research Activity   In the 1860s social theorists began to borrow heavily from Darwin's biological theories to support Britain's imperialist policy. Have students research this political trend.

Questions

- How was the theory of "survival of the fittest" applied to Britain's international policy?
- How did British diplomats use Social Darwinism to justify their racial oppression in India, South Africa, and other countries?
- How is the imperialist thinking of Victorian Great Britain reflected in the literature?
- How has modern literature from around the world reevaluated British imperialism?
- How did Great Britain's imperialist policy contribute to the economic growth of England?

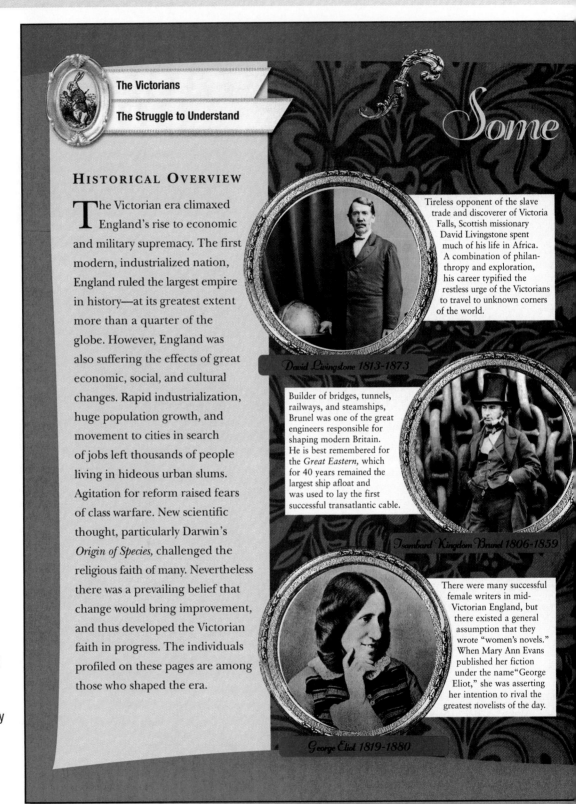

The Victorians

The Struggle to Understand

HISTORICAL OVERVIEW

The Victorian era climaxed England's rise to economic and military supremacy. The first modern, industrialized nation, England ruled the largest empire in history—at its greatest extent more than a quarter of the globe. However, England was also suffering the effects of great economic, social, and cultural changes. Rapid industrialization, huge population growth, and movement to cities in search of jobs left thousands of people living in hideous urban slums. Agitation for reform raised fears of class warfare. New scientific thought, particularly Darwin's *Origin of Species,* challenged the religious faith of many. Nevertheless there was a prevailing belief that change would bring improvement, and thus developed the Victorian faith in progress. The individuals profiled on these pages are among those who shaped the era.

Some

Tireless opponent of the slave trade and discoverer of Victoria Falls, Scottish missionary David Livingstone spent much of his life in Africa. A combination of philanthropy and exploration, his career typified the restless urge of the Victorians to travel to unknown corners of the world.

David Livingstone 1813-1873

Builder of bridges, tunnels, railways, and steamships, Brunel was one of the great engineers responsible for shaping modern Britain. He is best remembered for the *Great Eastern,* which for 40 years remained the largest ship afloat and was used to lay the first successful transatlantic cable.

Isambard Kingdom Brunel 1806-1859

There were many successful female writers in mid-Victorian England, but there existed a general assumption that they wrote "women's novels." When Mary Ann Evans published her fiction under the name "George Eliot," she was asserting her intention to rival the greatest novelists of the day.

George Eliot 1819-1880

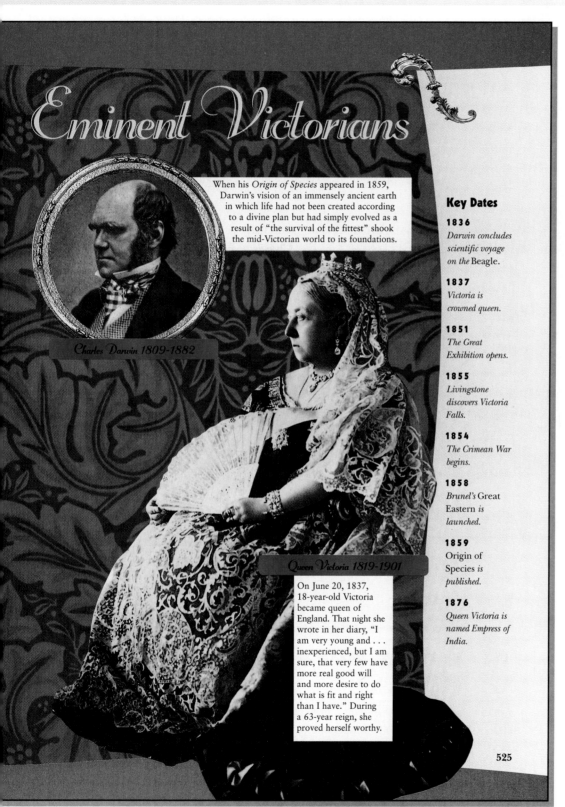

Eminent Victorians

When his *Origin of Species* appeared in 1859, Darwin's vision of an immensely ancient earth in which life had not been created according to a divine plan but had simply evolved as a result of "the survival of the fittest" shook the mid-Victorian world to its foundations.

Charles Darwin 1809-1882

Queen Victoria 1819-1901

On June 20, 1837, 18-year-old Victoria became queen of England. That night she wrote in her diary, "I am very young and . . . inexperienced, but I am sure, that very few have more real good will and more desire to do what is fit and right than I have." During a 63-year reign, she proved herself worthy.

Key Dates

1836
Darwin concludes scientific voyage on the Beagle.

1837
Victoria is crowned queen.

1851
The Great Exhibition opens.

1855
Livingstone discovers Victoria Falls.

1854
The Crimean War begins.

1858
Brunel's Great Eastern *is launched.*

1859
Origin of Species is published.

1876
Queen Victoria is named Empress of India.

525

Key Dates

1833 The Factory Bill of 1833 outlaws the employment of children under nine.

1847 The Ten Hours Act of 1847 limits work hours for women and children.

1854 Dickens publishes *Hard Times.*

1865 The open-hearth steel-processing method is first used.

1867 Karl Marx publishes the first volume of *Das Kapital.*

MATERIALS OF INTEREST
Books

- *Charles Darwin: A New Life* by John Bowlby (W.W. Norton, 1991).
- *Middlemarch* (1872), *Mill on the Floss* (1860), *Silas Marner* (1861), by George Eliot.
- *The Travels of Livingstone* by Richard Humble (F. Watts, 1991).
- *What Jane Austen Ate and Charles Dickens Knew: From Fox Hunting to Whist—the Facts of Daily Life in Nineteenth-Century England* by Daniel Pool (Simon & Schuster, 1993).

Multimedia

- *Victoria Regina* [videotape] Showcase Theater presentation for the play by Laurence Housman (Films for the Humanities: 1983).
- *George Eliot, Novelist* [videotape] (Encyclopaedia Britannica Educational Corporation, Famous Author's Series, 1987).

Connections to
Custom Literature Database

For further historical background, under **Background Articles,** see **Early Victorian England 1830–1880.**

The Struggle to Understand

FOR ALL STUDENTS

Have students read the first two paragraphs.

- What happens when the rich and the poor are "not governed by the same laws"?
- Why do people resist cultural or social change?
- Who is most likely to embrace change?

To further explore the theme, use the transparency noted below.

Transparency Collection
Fine Art Writing Prompt 11

For At-Risk Students

Ask students to create a poster about one of the following topics:

- the coronation of Queen Victoria
- the working conditions in factories
- the "underworld" of London

For Students Who Need Challenge

Have students research the Victorian Age and discuss the connotation and the denotation of the word *Victorian*.

For Kinesthetic and Social Learners

Students might host a high tea for the entire class. They can provide information about the kinds of food and tea served and a brief history of the tradition.

🐾 MULTICULTURAL CONNECTION

As an imperialist nation, Great Britain borrowed from the cultures that they oppressed. Even things such as tea that are considered very "English" came into popularity after the expansion of British rule. Most teas were imported from China, India, and Ceylon. Students might research how the large import market from the British colonies affected their economies and cultures.

Part One

The Struggle to Understand

The Victorian age was one of strong contrasts. Depending on your focus (and sometimes your control of power), you might describe the nation as proof of the blessing of "the Ordering and Creating God" (Charles Kingsley) or as a split nation, with rich and poor "formed by a different breeding . . . [and] not governed by the same laws" (Benjamin Disraeli).

🐾 **Multicultural Connection** The Industrial Revolution brought about many **changes,** both economic and social. Typically, people responded either by embracing those changes or by rejecting them with anger or despair. How do the characters in the following selections struggle to understand and to respond to the changes that are occurring in their culture?

IDEAS THAT WORK

Motivating with Art

I would ask the students to write a brief character sketch for each of the people in *The Bayswater Omnibus.* To help them develop the characters further, I would have them do a "Dickens" and write the characters into a single story, even if the coincidences seem a bit forced.

Their characters could then serve as a means to respond to the literature. The students could write a brief response to each of the works from the point of view of two of the people in the painting.

For example, the poor woman and the well-off man will hold different views about what the "newer world" in "Ulysses" is. The fashionable woman and the working nurse may react differently to the Mad Hatter's tea party: the first may find it too foolish, and the latter may find it not nearly as foolish as a real tea.

You could compile the responses into a publication at the end of this section and call the collection "The Best of the Bayswater Literary Omnibus."

Rosemary Baker,
Chicago, Illinois

The Lady of Shalott
Lyric 106 from In Memoriam

Ulysses
Crossing the Bar

by Alfred, Lord Tennyson

Alfred, Lord Tennyson
1809–1892

Alfred Tennyson's closest friend at Cambridge University was Arthur Henry Hallam, and it was he who urged Tennyson to publish his first volume, *Poems, Chiefly Lyrical* in 1830. When Hallam died suddenly on a trip to Vienna, Tennyson was devastated. In the months following Hallam's death, Tennyson crafted "Ulysses" and some of the lyrics that were to become *In Memoriam, A. H. H.* This volume brought enormous critical and public success and profits that enabled Tennyson to marry Emily Sellwood, to whom he had long been engaged. Many more volumes of poetry were to follow. Tennyson became poet laureate of England in 1850, meaning that he was officially recognized for his work, and Queen Victoria made him a nobleman in 1884, thus entitling him to be called, like Byron, a lord.

Building Background

A Source of Inspiration Camelot and the legendary King Arthur are a constant source of inspiration for writers, musicians, movie makers, and artists, and Tennyson was no exception. His interest in Arthur began in his childhood, and "The Lady of Shalott" was his first poem based on the Arthurian legends. Shalott is the same place as Astolat, where, according to Malory's *Morte Darthur,* Lancelot (see page 88 and 90–91) meets a lady known as the Fair Maid of Astolat. Tennyson frequently had disagreements with artists hired to depict his Arthurian scenes. According to biographer Robert Barnard Martin, after an illustrated edition of his poems was published, he confronted artist Holman Hunt, demanding to know why "the Lady of Shalott in the illustration had 'her hair wildly tossed about as if by a tornado.' Hunt mildly explained that he wanted to convey the idea of the catastrophe that had overtaken her, but Tennyson insisted, 'I didn't say her hair was blown about like that.'" Tennyson later wrote *Idylls of the King,* twelve connected poems based on Arthurian legend.

Literary Focus

Rhyme **Rhyme** is the exact repetition of sounds in at least the final accented syllable of two or more words. If the rhyme occurs at the ends of lines, it is called **end rhyme.** If the rhyme occurs within the line, it called **internal rhyme.** A **rhyme scheme** is any pattern of rhyme in a stanza or poem. The scheme of the first stanza of "The Lady of Shalott," for example, is *aaaabcccb.* The first rhyme and all the words rhyming with it are labeled *a;* the second rhyme is labeled *b;* the third rhyme is labeled *c;* and so on.

Writer's Notebook

Victoria and Victorias Because of Queen Victoria's long and influential reign, a number of places and things were named for her: an open carriage for two; a genus of water lilies; a lake and a waterfall in Africa; an island in the Arctic; a region in Antarctica; a mountain in New Guinea; and the Victoria Cross, awarded to British soldiers and sailors for extreme valor. Jot down some American places or things named for people. Are any of them named for women?

The Lady of Shalott **527**

Building Background

The class might brainstorm books, poems, plays, or movies that have been inspired by Arthurian legends. You might get things started by reminding students of the *Morte Darthur* excerpt from Unit 1.

Literary Focus

You might note that most rhymed poetry is written with end rhyme. Examples of internal rhyme include Poe's "The Raven"
—Once upon a midnight *dreary* while I pondered weak and *weary*—
and Coleridge's "Rime of the Ancient Mariner"
—We were the *first* that ever *burst* into that silent sea—

Writer's Notebook

Note that the American equivalent of Britain's Victoria in quantity of place names is most probably George Washington. Students may be hard-pressed for places named for women. You might discuss reasons for this.

More About Tennyson

Tennyson's poetry reflected the values of his day. As a result, he became the target of a generation of poets rebelling against Victorian standards. "Rehabilitated" by yet a later generation, he is again appreciated for his craftsmanship.

SUPPORT MATERIALS OVERVIEW

Unit 6 Resource Book
- Graphic Organizer, p. 1
- Study Guide, p. 2
- Vocabulary, p. 3
- Grammar, p. 4
- Alternate Check Test, p. 5
- Vocabulary Test, p. 6
- Selection Test, pp. 7–8

Building English Proficiency
- Selection Summaries
- Activities, p. 235

Reading, Writing & Grammar SkillBook
- Grammar, Usage, and Mechanics, pp. 197–198

Technology
- Audiotape
- Personal Journal Software
- Custom Literature Database: Additional selections by Alfred, Lord Tennyson can be found on the database.
- Test Generator Software

Selection Objectives

- to identify rhyme schemes
- to identify mood and imagery
- to apply standard usage to verb pairs

 Unit 6 Resource Book
Graphic Organizer, p. 1
Study Guide, p. 2

Theme Link

Tennyson's struggle to understand is reflected in the themes of loneliness and the clash between personal hopes and the limitations of a material existence.

 ## Art Study

Responses to Caption Questions The stained glass, wallpaper, Gothic arches, cut of the dress, burning lamp, and dark interior lend a medieval quality. The pose suggests that she is weary—of needle-work and, perhaps, of life in general.

1 Literary Element
Mood

Questions What is the mood of Part 1? *(lonely, gray)* What images convey the mood? *(gray walls, gray towers; the silent isle embowers; heavy barges, slow horses, reaper weary)*

THE LADY OF SHALOTT

ALFRED, LORD TENNYSON

Mariana, painted in 1871 by Sir John Everett Millais (1829–1896), was inspired by a Tennyson poem of the same title. What elements of the painting give it a romantic, medieval quality? What might the woman's pose suggest about her state of mind?

528 UNIT SIX: THE VICTORIANS

PART 1

On either side the river lie
Long fields of barley and of rye,
That clothe the wold[1] and meet the sky;
And through the field the road runs by
5   To many-towered Camelot;[2]
And up and down the people go,
Gazing where the lilies blow
Round an island there below,
   The island of Shalott.

10 Willows whiten, aspens quiver,
Little breezes dusk and shiver
Through the wave that runs for ever
By the island in the river
   Flowing down to Camelot.
15 Four gray walls, and four gray towers,
Overlook a space of flowers,
And the silent isle embowers[3]
   The Lady of Shalott.

By the margin, willow-veiled
20 Slide the heavy barges trailed
By slow horses; and unhailed
The shallop[4] flitteth silken-sailed
   Skimming down to Camelot:
But who hath seen her wave her hand?
25 Or at the casement[5] seen her stand?
Or is she known in all the land,
   The Lady of Shalott?

---

1. **wold** (wōld), *n.* high, rolling country, bare of woods.
2. **Camelot,** the place of King Arthur's court.
3. **embower** (em bou′ər), *v.* enclose in a shelter of leafy branches.
4. **shallop** (shal′əp), *n.* a small boat with a sail or oars.
5. **casement** (kās′mənt), *n.* window that opens on hinges.

SELECTION SUMMARY

The Lady of Shalott; Ulysses; Lyric 106; Crossing the Bar

The Lady of Shalott Under a curse, the Lady of Shalott may not look directly to Camelot and views the world only in the reflection of a mirror. The reflected sight of the shining knight Lancelot finally brings her out of her tower. On a boat bound for Camelot, she succumbs to the curse.

Ulysses The hero of ancient lore laments the inactivity of his declining years and resolves to set sail for one more adventure.

Lyric 106 The narrator, on the New Year, expresses sadness at the ills of society and his hopes for a better world.

Crossing the Bar Completed late in the poet's life, the short poem is an extended metaphor in which Tennyson anticipates "putting out to sea" to meet his Pilot face to face.

 *For summaries in other languages, see the **Building English Proficiency** book.*

Only reapers, reaping early
In among the bearded barley,
30 Hear a song that echoes cheerly
From the river winding clearly,
    Down to towered Camelot:
And by the moon the reaper weary,
Piling sheaves in uplands airy,
35 Listening, whispers "'Tis the fairy
    Lady of Shalott."

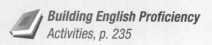

PART 2

There she weaves by night and day
A magic web with colors gay.
She has heard a whisper say,
40 A curse is on her if she stay
    To look down to Camelot.
She knows not what the curse may be,
And so she weaveth steadily,
And little other care hath she,
45   The Lady of Shalott.

And moving through a mirror clear
That hangs before her all the year,
Shadows of the world appear,
There she sees the highway near
50   Winding down to Camelot:
There the river eddy whirls,
And there the surly village churls,[6]
And the red cloaks of market girls,
    Pass onward from Shalott.

55 Sometimes a troop of damsels[7] glad,
An abbot on an ambling pad,[8]
Sometimes a curly shepherd lad,
Or long-haired page in crimson clad,
    Goes by to towered Camelot;
60 And sometimes through the mirror blue
The knights come riding two and two:
She hath no loyal knight and true,
    The Lady of Shalott.

But in her web she still delights
65 To weave the mirror's magic sights,
For often through the silent nights

A funeral, with plumes and lights
    And music, went to Camelot:
Or when the moon was overhead,
70 Came two young lovers lately wed;
"I am half sick of shadows," said
    The Lady of Shalott.

PART 3

A bow-shot from her bower eaves,
He rode between the barley sheaves,
75 The sun came dazzling through the leaves,
And flamed upon the brazen[9] greaves
    Of bold Sir Lancelot.
A red-cross knight for ever kneeled
To a lady in his shield,
80 That sparkled on the yellow field,
    Beside remote Shalott.

The gemmy bridle glittered free,
Like to some branch of stars we see
Hung in the golden Galaxy.[10]
85 The bridle bells rang merrily
    As he rode down to Camelot:
And from his blazoned baldric[11] slung
A mighty silver bugle hung,
And as he rode his armor rung,
90   Beside remote Shalott.

All in the blue unclouded weather
Thick-jewelled shone the saddle leather,
The helmet and the helmet feather
Burned like one burning flame together,
95   As he rode down to Camelot.
As often through the purple night,
Below the starry clusters bright,

---

6. **churl** (chèrl), *n.* a freeman of the lowest rank.
7. **damsel** (dam′zəl), *n.* a young girl.
8. **pad,** a slow riding horse.
9. **brazen** (brā′zn) **greave** (grēv), brass armor for the leg below the knee.
10. **Galaxy,** the Milky Way.
11. **blazoned baldric** (bôl′drik), an ornamental (emblazoned) belt hung from one shoulder to the opposite side to support the wearer's bugle or sword.

The Lady of Shalott   **529**

BUILDING ENGLISH PROFICIENCY

ESL
LEP
ELD
SAE
LD

Understanding Inverted Word Order

Help students recognize inverted word order in a poem.

1. Point out that normal word order in English is subject-verb-complement. (A complement completes the meaning of a verb: They seemed <u>tired</u>. We ran <u>up the hill</u>.) Have volunteers describe normal order in other languages.

2. Explain that we call a sentence inverted when the subject follows the verb instead of preceding it—for example, <u>To school went I</u>.

3. Ask students to consider why inverted word order often appears in poems with regular rhyme scheme or regular rhythm pattern. *(It helps the rhymes and rhythm patterns "fit.")*

4. Invite pairs of students to find examples of inverted word order in "The Lady of Shallott." Have them turn the sentence around, read it aloud in normal word order, and compare the effect.

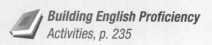

Building English Proficiency
Activities, p. 235

6 Literary Element
Mood

Question How does Lancelot's appearance change the mood of the poem? (*The mood becomes sunny, bright, shining.*)

7 Literary Element
Symbol

Questions What do you think the cracking of the mirror symbolizes? (*Possible response: that the lady has looked directly at the world, at reality, and can never return to seeing only its reflection*)

8 Reading/Thinking Skills
Draw Conclusions

Questions Why do you think the lady, knowing she is under a curse, looks to Camelot? (*Possible responses: She is "half-sick of shadows"; she wants to experience life, not a reflection of it.*)

Some bearded meteor, trailing light,
    Moves over still Shalott.

100 His broad clear brow in sunlight glowed;
On burnished hooves his war horse trode;[12]
From underneath his helmet flowed
His coal-black curls as on he rode,
    As he rode down to Camelot.
105 From the bank and from the river

6

He flashed into the crystal mirror,
"Tirra lirra," by the river
    Sang Sir Lancelot.

She left the web, she left the loom,
110 She made three paces through the room,
She saw the water lily bloom,
She saw the helmet and the plume,
    She looked down to Camelot.
Out flew the web and floated wide;

7 115 The mirror cracked from side to side;
"The curse is come upon me," cried

8   The Lady of Shalott.

PART 4

In the stormy east wind straining,
The pale yellow woods were waning,
120 The broad stream in his banks
      complaining.
Heavily the low sky raining
    Over towered Camelot;
Down she came and found a boat
Beneath a willow left afloat,
125 And round about the prow she wrote
    The Lady of Shalott.

And down the river's dim expanse
Like some bold seer in a trance,
Seeing all his own mischance—
130 With a glassy countenance
    Did she look to Camelot.
And at the closing of the day
She loosed the chain, and down she lay;
The broad stream bore her far away,
135   The Lady of Shalott.

Lying, robed in snowy white
That loosely flew to left and right—
The leaves upon her falling light—
Through the noises of the night
140   She floated down to Camelot:
And as the boathead wound along
The willowy hills and fields among,
They heard her singing her last song,
    The Lady of Shalott.

145 Heard a carol, mournful, holy,
Chanted loudly, chanted lowly,
Till her blood was frozen slowly,
And her eyes were darkened wholly,
    Turned to towered Camelot.
150 For ere she reached upon the tide
The first house by the water-side,
Singing in her song she died,
    The Lady of Shalott.

Under tower and balcony,
155 By garden wall and gallery,
A gleaming shape she floated by,
Dead-pale between the houses high,
    Silent into Camelot.
Out upon the wharfs they came,
160 Knight and burgher,[13] lord and dame,
And round the prow they read her name,
    The Lady of Shalott.

Who is this? and what is here?
And in the lighted palace near
165 Died the sound of royal cheer;
And they crossed themselves for fear,
    All the knights at Camelot:
But Lancelot mused a little space;
He said, "She has a lovely face;
170 God in his mercy lend her grace,
    The Lady of Shalott."

---

12. **trode** (trōd), *v.* an archaic past tense of *tread*, step.
13. **burgher** (bėr′gər), *n.* citizen.

530   UNIT SIX: THE VICTORIANS

MINI-LESSON: GRAMMAR

Verb Pair Lie and Lay

Teach The verbs *lie* and *lay,* seemingly close in meaning, are often confused. *Lie* means "to rest or remain in a prone position." Its principal parts are *lie, lay, (have) lain, (is) lying.* *Lay* means "to put down or place." Its principal parts are *lay, laid, (have) laid, (is) laying.*

    Ask students to skim the poem for use of any principal part of *lie* or *lay.* Ask students

• What meaning does the word have?

• What part is it—present tense, past tense, past participle, or present participle? (*line 1:* lie *meaning "rest," present tense; line 133:* lay *meaning "rest," past tense; line 136:* lying *meaning "in a prone position," present participle*)

Activity Ideas

• Generate sentences that require use of *lie* or *lay* or one of its parts. Read them aloud and have students complete the sentences.

• Have students write a paragraph or a tongue-twister using as many parts of each verb as possible.

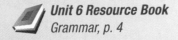
Unit 6 Resource Book
Grammar, p. 4

ULYSSES

ALFRED, LORD TENNYSON

In the legendary Trojan War, the Greeks besieged Troy for ten years to win back the beautiful queen Helen. After their victory the warrior king Ulysses (yü-lis′ēz), a victim of hostile gods, wandered for ten more years, sailing unknown seas, battling with monsters, and even journeying to the land of the dead, before he reached his island home of Ithaca. There, he had to kill a band of rivals who wished to seize his wife Penelope (pə nel′ə pē) and his lands. Homer's Odyssey *comes to an end there, but Tennyson concludes that after such adventures Ulysses could not rest content at home.*

It little profits that an idle king,
By this still hearth, among these barren crags,
Matched with an agèd wife, I mete and dole
Unequal laws unto a savage race,
5 That hoard, and sleep, and feed, and know not me.
I cannot rest from travel: I will drink
Life to the lees: all times I have enjoyed
Greatly, have suffered greatly, both with those
That loved me, and alone; on shore, and when
10 Through scudding drifts the rainy Hyades
Vexed the dim sea: I am become a name;
For always roaming with a hungry heart
Much have I seen and known; cities of men
And manners, climates, councils, governments,
15 Myself not least, but honored of them all;
And drunk delight of battle with my peers,
Far on the ringing plains of windy Troy.
I am part of all that I have met;
Yet all experience is an arch wherethrough
20 Gleams that untraveled world whose margin fades
Forever and forever when I move.
How dull it is to pause, to make an end,
To rust unburnished, not to shine in use!
As though to breathe were life! Life piled on life
25 Were all too little, and of one to me
Little remains: but every hour is saved
From the eternal silence, something more,

3 mete and dole, distribute and give in small portions.

7 lees (lēz), *n. pl.* dregs; the least desirable part.

10 Hyades (hī′ə dēz′), cluster of stars in the constellation Taurus, supposed by the ancients to be a sign of rain when they rose with the sun.

27 eternal silence, death.

Ulysses   **531**

9 Reading/Thinking Skills
Analyze

Question What does Ulysses think of the people he rules? *(that they are a "savage race" with petty concerns, guided by greed or fear)*

10 Literary Element
Meter

You might note to the class that "Ulysses" is written in unrhymed iambic pentameter, i.e., blank verse.

11 Reading/Thinking Skills
Recognize Values

Questions What does Ulysses state is the purpose of life? *(Possible responses: to live life to the fullest right up to the end, including all its joys and suffering; to experience, learn, travel, and see.)* What does he mean by "As though to breathe were life"? *(There is more to life than just existing.)*

12 Reading/Thinking Skills
Analyze

Question What do you think the line "every hour is saved/From the eternal silence" might mean? *(Possible response: Every hour of life is an hour snatched away from the eternity of death.)*

BUILDING ENGLISH PROFICIENCY

Comparing Details

Use discussion and a T-chart to help students understand why Ulysses wants to leave his homeland.

1. Ask volunteers to locate Greece on the map and share what they recall about the *Odyssey*.

2. Have students work together in groups to complete a T-chart, listing phrases that Ulysses uses to describe his boring present and his exciting past.

Present	Past
idle king	roaming with a hungry heart
still hearth	Much have I seen . . .
aged wife	

13 Literary Element
Characterization

Questions How does Ulysses characterize his son Telemachus? *(Possible responses: prudent, centered, responsible, conservative, unadventurous, blameless, decent)* How is the son different from his father? *(Possible responses: Telemachus is content to stay at home, play by the rules; Ulysses is restless, in need of adventure, even scornful of his people.)*

14 Literary Element
Mood

Question What is the mood after Ulysses reaches the ship? *(dark, gloomy)* How is the mood fostered? *(through such images as "gloom the dark, broad seas" and "the deep/Moans with many voices"; and with Ulysses's talk of old age and death—"you and I are old"; "Death closes all"; "The long day wanes")*

15 Literary Element
Draw Conclusions

Question How will the old, weakened Ulysses achieve great things on his final voyage? *(Possible response: by substituting strength of will for a body weakened by time and fate)*

A bringer of new things; and vile it were
For some three suns to store and hoard myself,
30 And this gray spirit yearning in desire
To follow knowledge like a sinking star,
Beyond the utmost bound of human thought.
This is my son, mine own Telemachus,
To whom I leave the scepter and the isle—
35 Well-loved of me, discerning to fulfill
This labor, by slow prudence to make mild
A rugged people, and through soft degrees
Subdue them to the useful and the good.
Most blameless is he, centered in the sphere
40 Of common duties, decent not to fail
In offices of tenderness, and pay
Meet adoration to my household gods,
When I am gone. He works his work, I mine.
There lies the port; the vessel puffs her sail:
45 There gloom the dark, broad seas. My mariners,
Souls that have toiled, and wrought, and thought with me—
That ever with a frolic welcome took
The thunder and the sunshine, and opposed
Free hearts, free foreheads—you and I are old;
50 Old age hath yet his honor and his toil;
Death closes all: but something ere the end,
Some work of noble note, may yet be done,
Not unbecoming men that strove with gods.
The lights begin to twinkle from the rocks:
55 The long day wanes: the slow moon climbs: the deep
Moans round with many voices. Come, my friends,
'Tis not too late to seek a newer world.
Push off, and sitting well in order smite
The sounding furrows; for my purpose holds
60 To sail beyond the sunset, and the baths
Of all the western stars, until I die.
It may be that the gulfs will wash us down:
It may be we shall touch the Happy Isles,
And see the great Achilles, whom we knew.
65 Though much is taken, much abides; and though
We are not now that strength which in old days
Moved earth and heaven; that which we are, we are;
One equal temper of heroic hearts,
Made weak by time and fate, but strong in will
70 To strive, to seek, to find, and not to yield.

33 Telemachus (tə lem′ə kəs).

42 meet (mēt), *adj.* fitting. [Archaic]

46 wrought (rôt), *v.* worked. [Archaic]

49 you, Ulysses' companions.
60–61 baths . . . stars. In ancient belief, the stars literally plunge into the sea at the edge of the earth.
63 Happy Isles, a paradise for dead heroes like Achilles (ə kil′ēz), who fought beside Ulysses at Troy.

In *The King* by Max Beckmann, the hooded, mysterious-looking woman standing behind the king seems to have his ear, while the young woman kneeling and embracing him seems to have his heart. The hooded woman's left hand is raised in a gesture that suggests she is at odds with the other woman. Like Ulysses, the king seems to feel the pull of two opposing forces. Which one do you think might ultimately triumph? Why? ➤

MINI-LESSON: STUDY SKILLS

Using Reference Materials

Teach In Greek mythology, the Hyades (line 10 of "Ulysses") were the daughters of Atlas. They were placed in the sky by Zeus. To learn more about them, students could do research in a library. An encyclopedia might have information (key words: *mythology, constellation,* or *star),* but students may need to use the card catalog or library's database to find more information.

Activity Ideas

• Have students look up the story of the Hyades in a book on Greek mythology. Allow students to retell or express the myth in poetry or in an art medium of their choice.

• Have students research the origins of heavenly bodies based on the mythology of ancient Greeks, Native Americans, or any other people that interest them.

Response to Caption Question
Student responses will depend on how they interpret the painting.

Visual Literacy   Beckmann's dark colors, deep shadows, and hooded figure give the painting an ominous mood. If the figure before the king is young and innocent, is the hooded figure behind him old and knowing? While the king wears a crown, his clothes, particularly the collar, suggest the traditional outfit of a harlequin or clown.

Questions   What do you think the two figures on either side of the king might suggest? *(Possible responses: youth and old age; life and death; an emotional response* vs. *a rational response)* What do you think the clown outfit might suggest about the king? *(Possible response: that he is or feels foolish in this conflict between the two figures)*

BUILDING ENGLISH PROFICIENCY

Making Personal Connections

Help students understand that Ulysses and Telemachus stand for different character types. One type craves adventure, as Ulysses does here. Telemachus, however, is cautious; he represents another type.

Activity Idea   Ask students to consider if they are more like Ulysses or Telemachus. To discuss which type they might prefer to be, urge them to complete the chart shown.

	Advantages of being . . .	Disadvantages of being . . .
Ulysses		
Telemachus		

Questions What is the scheme of the
end rhyme in the first stanza? *(abba)* Can
you find an example of internal rhyme in
the first stanza? *(flying and dying in line 3)*

17 Reading/Thinking Skills
Recognizing Values

Questions What higher values does the
poet call for with the new year? *(redress to
all mankind, sweeter manners, purer laws,
love of truth and right, common love of
good)* What problems of the time are identified? *(feuds between rich and poor; the
dying cause and party strife; grief, want,
care, and sin; faithlessness and mournful-
ness; false pride; slander and spite)*

Literary Criticism

"Few poets have been gifted with greater
sensibility of eye and ear [than Tennyson];
none ever labored more diligently at his
art. He was not a great original thinker,
but through a long life he kept abreast of
the thought of his time. He remains the
representative poet of the Victorian Age."

Herbert Grierson
J.C. Smith
A Critical History of English Poetry

LYRIC 106

ALFRED, LORD TENNYSON

16
Ring out, wild bells, to the wild sky,
    The flying cloud, the frosty light:
    The year is dying in the night;
Ring out, wild bells, and let him die.

5 Ring out the old, ring in the new,
    Ring, happy bells, across the snow:
    The year is going, let him go;
Ring out the false, ring in the true.

17
Ring out the grief that saps the mind,
10   For those that here we see no more;
    Ring out the feud of rich and poor,
Ring in redress to all mankind.

Ring out a slowly dying cause,
    And ancient forms of party strife;
15   Ring in the nobler modes of life,
With sweeter manners, purer laws.

Ring out the want, the care, the sin,
    The faithless coldness of the times;
    Ring out, ring out my mournful rhymes,
20 But ring the fuller minstrel in.

Ring out false pride in place and blood,
    The civic slander and the spite;
    Ring in the love of truth and right,
Ring in the common love of good.

12 redress (re dres′), *n.* a
setting right; relief.

14 strife (strīf), *n.* a quarrel-
ing; fighting.

20 minstrel (min′strel), *n.*
musician, singer, or poet.

MINI-LESSON: VOCABULARY

Using a Dictionary

Some words in Tennyson's poetry are probably unfamiliar to most
students. A dictionary can guide students to their meanings.

Teach Some of Tennyson's words aren't used often now. Point out that
to find out their meanings, students can use the context to figure out a
likely meaning, but to be sure of knowing the meaning, they need to use
a dictionary. They should look up the word in alphabetical order, read the
definitions, and figure out which one makes the most sense in the poem.

Activity Ideas

• Ask students to use a dictionary or thesaurus to suggest more familiar
or modern equivalents for these words:

"The Lady of Shallot": *wold, embower, shallop, casement, churl,
damsel, pad, trode, burgher*

"Ulysses": *mete*

"Lyric 106": *redress*

"Crossing the Bar": *bourne*

• Have students write sentences using modern words for *churl, damsel,
pad, burgher, mete,* and *bourne.*

25   Ring out old shapes of foul disease;
      Ring out the narrowing lust of gold;
      Ring out the thousand wars of old,
    Ring in the thousand years of peace.

    Ring in the valiant man and free,
30   The larger heart, the kindlier hand;
      Ring out the darkness of the land,
    Ring in the Christ that is to be.

29 valiant (val′yənt), *adj.*
brave; courageous.

CROSSING THE BAR

ALFRED, LORD TENNYSON

    Sunset and evening star,
      And one clear call for me!
  And may there be no moaning of the bar,
     When I put out to sea,

5 But such a tide as moving seems asleep,
     Too full for sound and foam,
  When that which drew from out the boundless deep
     Turns again home.

    Twilight and evening bell,
10   And after that the dark!
  And may there be no sadness of farewell,
     When I embark;

    For though from out our bourne of Time and Place
     The flood may bear me far,
15 I hope to see my Pilot face to face
    When I have crossed the bar.

bar, sandbar; an underwater
ridge of sand across a harbor.

13 bourne (bôrn), *n.* bound-
ary; limit.
15 Pilot. The word has the
double meaning of one who
steers a ship in or out of a
harbor, and God.

Crossing the Bar   **535**

535

After Reading

MAKING CONNECTIONS

1. Possible responses: She commits suicide because she is tired of being isolated; she is killed by an outside force—the curse.

2. Possible responses: to examine a universal theme; to examine how knowledge of death influences the meaning of life

3. Possible response: The medieval setting evokes a romantic and otherworldly mood; descriptions of the seasons initially contribute to a peaceful, bucolic mood; at the end, description contributes to a mood of sadness as the lady dies.

4. Possible response: Ulysses feels that life is dull and that he is useless; he no longer shines as a great hero.

5. Possible response: Both structure and repetition replicate the ringing of bells at the New Year.

6. "Crossing the Bar" is an extended metaphor for death.

7. "Lady," "Lyric," and "Crossing" are written with end rhyme; the "Lyric" rhyme scheme is *abba;* the "Crossing" scheme is *abab;* repetition is employed in "Lady" and "Lyric"; "Ulysses" is in blank verse. The dreamy, medieval setting and imagery of "Lady" evoke a melancholic mood. The "Ulysses" setting is both ancient and nautical; the mood is quiet, but defiant. The "Lyric" imagery evokes a cold New Year night; the mood is sad, but hopeful. The "Crossing" mood is hopeful.

8. Students might list changes in race relations, social classes and lack of opportunity for some, AIDS, or other contemporary problems.

9. Possible responses: yearning for a land ruled by chivalry, for a time of ideals, for a romanticized past

---

After Reading

Shaping Your Response

Making Connections

1. What do you think kills the Lady of Shalott? Is she responsible for her own death?

2. In your opinion, why do people write poetry about old age and death?

Analyzing the Poems

3. Explain how the **setting,** both the place and the season, contributes to the **mood** of "The Lady of Shalott."

4. How do lines 22 and 23 in "Ulysses" help to explain his decision?

5. Explain how the structure and **repetition** in Lyric 106 reflect the topic of bells.

6. What is the extended **metaphor** in "Crossing the Bar"?

7. Compare and contrast the **rhythms** and **style** (including mood, imagery, and repetition) of Tennyson's poems.

Extending the Ideas

8. 🐾 If you were to make your own list of hopes for the future, what things would be different from the speaker's hopes for **changes** to come in Lyric 106?

9. In your opinion, what is it about the Arthurian legends that continues to fascinate writers and movie makers even today?

Literary Focus: Rhyme

Rhyme is the exact repetition of sounds in at least the final accented syllables of two or more words. **Rhyme scheme** is any pattern of rhyme in a stanza or poem. Chart the rhyme scheme in the first three stanzas of "Lyric 106." Does the poem have **end rhyme** or **internal rhyme**?

More About the Author

Poet Laureate To the ancient Greeks, laurel was a symbol of distinction and was used to form a crown of honor for poets and heroes. In England's Middle Ages, the title *poet laureate* was applied to any eminent poet. The office became official when Charles II appointed John Dryden poet laureate in 1670. The duties of poet laureate have included producing verses on birthdays and court occasions, but William Wordsworth accepted the laureateship on the condition that he would not necessarily have to do so, and the office became an honorary one. Tennyson, who followed Wordsworth into the office, did much to elevate the office in the eyes of his fellow poets.

536 UNIT SIX: THE VICTORIANS

LITERARY FOCUS: RHYME

The rhyme scheme of the first three stanzas is *abba cddc effe.* The poem has both end rhyme and internal rhyme.

Expressing Your Ideas

Writing Choices

Writer's Notebook Update Can you imagine an automobile, flower, lake, or product named for you? Suppose that you are forty years older than you are now and have become famous. Describe the things and places that bear your name.

What Happens Next? Novelists and poets often write sequels to classic or traditional stories, as Tennyson did in "Ulysses." Sometimes a sequel deals with the fortunes of a minor character in the original work. Write a **dialogue** between Ulysses' wife Penelope or his son Telemachus and Ulysses when he announces that he is leaving again. Or, you might write a dialogue between Ulysses and his companions prior to their setting out on the proposed voyage.

Righting Old Wrongs In Lyric 106, Tennyson mentions a number of wrongs, such as "the feud of rich and poor," that he wants to see ended with the old year. Review the poem, choose three of these wrongs, and write an **editorial** in which you demonstrate whether there is or is not still evidence of them in the U. S. today.

Other Options

A Far Country Fictitious places such as Camelot, Xanadu, or Shalott seem more appealing sometimes than actual places. In a small group, create a **fictitious place** that you would find appealing. Choose among the following:

- Name and map the country and its geography.
- Using graphics, outline the type of government and the economy.
- Describe the characteristics and beliefs of the people, using illustrations when possible.
- Identify the chief leisure-time interests of the inhabitants.
- Create an illustrated history of the country.

Show-and-Tell Research the personal life and career of any Victorian artist, such as those whose works illustrate the early Victorian writers in this part, and give an **illustrated oral report** to the class. Show examples of your chosen artist's work and discuss especially elements of his or her artisitc style.

"So Long, It's Been Good to Know You" Folk songs, cowboy songs, blues, rock lyrics, and much country and western music deal with the theme of restlessness and moving on. Compile your own **musical show** by playing some songs for the class that could depict Ulysses' urge to leave home again—and his wife's possible reactions.

WRITING CHOICES
Writer's Notebook Update

Before students begin, you might lead a discussion of possibilities other than city or state names: buildings, parks, playgrounds, plazas, streets and highways, theaters, philosophies, scientific ideas, and even flowers, e.g., the Audrey Hepburn rose.

What Happens Next?

Stress that this is a dialogue, as in a play or movie. Pairs of students might volunteer to perform their dialogues.

Righting Old Wrongs

Remind students to back up their statements with examples or evidence. You might also ask students to find newspaper editorials as examples.

Selection Test

Unit 6 Resource Book,
pp. 7–8

OTHER OPTIONS
A Far Country

Ask students to be as vivid as possible. Have each group choose a spokesperson to present descriptions of their fictitious place.

Musical Show

You may suggest that students work in small groups to select musical pieces. You might also select a student crew to decide how such a show would be staged, the order of songs, and so on.

Before Reading

Building Background

You might ask students if they have ever written a fan letter. Could a romance by letter be kindled today? Could such a romance be kindled by e-mail or over the Internet?

Literary Focus

You might note that readers often assume that a narrator, especially a first-person narrator, is the voice of the author. Writers, however, often create fictional characters to tell a story. Ask students, as they read Browning's dramatic monologues, to decide if the narrator is a fictional character or the voice of the poet.

Writer's Notebook

Urge students to use colorful adjectives: for example, words such as *gangly* or *towering,* rather than *tall.*

More About the Brownings

Before meeting Robert Browning, Elizabeth Barrett, who believed herself to be a hopeless invalid, spent much of her time in a darkened room. Their courtship and elopement is one of history's most famous romances, subject of books, plays, and movies. Browning referred to his wife as "my little Portuguese"— hence the title *Sonnets from the Portuguese.*

Before Reading

Sonnet 43 by Elizabeth Barrett Browning
Porphyria's Lover by Robert Browning
My Last Duchess by Robert Browning

Elizabeth Barrett Browning
1806–1861

Elizabeth Barrett published her first collection of verse at twenty, but illness made her a recluse. In 1846 she married Robert Browning. *Sonnets from the Portuguese,* in which Sonnet 43 appeared, chronicles her love for him.

Robert Browning
1812–1889

Robert Browning decided early to become a poet and worked at his craft diligently. In 1855 he published a collection of dramatic monologues titled *Men and Women* and in 1868–9 published *The Ring and the Book,* a lengthy poem about an obscure Roman murder.

Building Background

Love and Letters One of the world's most famous courtships began with the letters between two poets, Elizabeth Barrett and Robert Browning. At age thirty-nine Elizabeth was the better known of the two. She had referred to his collection, *Bells and Pomegranates,* in her *Poems* (1844). An admirer of her work for several years, Robert began his first letter (January 10, 1845) with the words "I love your verses with all my heart, dear Miss Barrett." Then, as if carried away by his feelings, after several lines he wrote: "I do, as I say, love these verses with all my heart—and I love you too." Elizabeth, then an invalid, replied the next day, though with somewhat more reserve. Eventually they wrote each other 574 letters, including one that she asked him to burn. They did not meet in person until May 20, 1845, when Robert visited her. Despite some misgivings, Elizabeth eventually came to love Robert too. Because her father had forbidden any of his children to marry, Elizabeth and Robert were wed secretly in St. Marylebone Church in London on September 12, 1846, with two witnesses only— his cousin and her maid. The couple fled to Italy, and Mr. Barrett refused to see the Brownings or their son (born in 1849) ever again.

Literary Focus

Dramatic Monologue A **dramatic monologue** is a poem in which a fictional character speaking in the first person reveals details of dramatic situation, characterization, and setting. A silent listener or audience is often, but not always, assumed to be present. Since the speaker's thoughts are subjective—and frequently self-serving—readers must watch for hints as to the true situation. As you read Robert Browning's two poems, both dramatic monologues, be ready to make some inferences about the speakers and the events described.

Writer's Notebook

Characterize a Person Think of a person you know well and jot down some adjectives that describe that person. Think of words that describe physical characteristics or actions as well as words that describe the person's character and personality.

SUPPORT MATERIALS OVERVIEW

Unit 6 Resource Book
- Graphic Organizer, p. 9
- Study Guide, p. 10
- Vocabulary, p. 11
- Grammar, p. 12
- Alternate Check Test, p. 13
- Vocabulary Test, p. 14
- Selection Test, pp. 15–16

Building English Proficiency
- Selection Summaries
- Activities, p. 236
- "Sonnet 43" in Spanish

Reading, Writing & Grammar SkillBook
- Writing, pp. 117–118
- Grammar, Usage, and Mechanics, pp. 193–196

Technology
- Audiotape
- Personal Journal Software
- Custom Literature Database: Additional selections by Elizabeth Barrett Browning and Robert Browning can be found on the database.
- Test Generator Software

Sonnet 43

Elizabeth Barrett Browning

1 How do I love thee? Let me count the ways.
I love thee to the depth and breadth and height
My soul can reach, when feeling out of sight
For the ends of Being and ideal Grace.
5 I love thee to the level of everyday's
Most quiet need, by sun and candlelight.
I love thee freely, as men strive for Right;
I love thee purely, as they turn from Praise.
I love thee with the passion put to use
10 In my old griefs, and with my childhood's faith,
I love thee with a love I seemed to lose
With my lost saints—I love thee with the breadth,
Smiles, tears, of all my life!—and, if God choose,
I shall but love thee better after death.

Porphyria's Lover

Robert Browning

The rain set early in tonight,
  The sullen wind was soon awake,
It tore the elm-tops down for spite,
  And did its worst to vex the lake:
5   I listened with heart fit to break
When glided in Porphyria; straight
  She shut the cold out and the storm,
And kneeled and made the cheerless grate
  Blaze up, and all the cottage warm;
10   Which done, she rose, and from her form
Withdrew the dripping cloak and shawl,
  And laid her soiled gloves by, untied
Her hat and let the damp hair fall,
  And, last, she sat down by my side
2 15   And called me. When no voice replied,

Porphyria (pôr fir′ē ə).

4 vex (veks), *v.* disturb; agitate.

Porphyria's Lover   **539**

3 **Reading/Thinking Skills**
Find the Main Idea

Questions Why do you think Porphyria will not "give herself . . . forever"? *(Possible response: She may be unwilling to give up wealth or social position.)* What phrase suggests this response? *("Pride, and vainer ties" [line 24] suggests her social position is higher than his.)*

4 **Reader's Response**
Making Personal Connections

Questions Why do you think the narrator strangles Porphyria? *(Possible responses: He is insane; he is in a jealous rage; if he can't have her, no one will have her; by killing her, she will be his forever.)* Do you think this poem accurately reflects certain aspects of human behavior? *(Answers will vary, but some might note that murders of this type seem to occur all too often.)*

5 **Literary Focus**
Dramatic Monologue

Questions What is the verb tense of the final 10 lines? *(present tense)* What do you think this change in verb tense suggests? *(It suggests the presence of a "silent listener.")* You might note that this monologue was originally paired with another poem under the title "Madhouse Cells." How did the original title change this poem? *(At the change of verb tense, the reader discovers that setting and time have changed, revealing that setting and time will never change for the narrator, who is quite mad.)* Which title do you think is more effective? *(While responses will vary, it might be noted that the original title does compound the horror of the tale.)*

She put my arm about her waist,
 And made her smooth white shoulder bare,
And all her yellow hair displaced,
 And stooping, made my cheek lie there,
20 And spread, o'er all, her yellow hair,
Murmuring how she loved me—she
 Too weak, for all her heart's endeavor,
To set its struggling passion free
 From pride, and vainer ties dissever,
3 25 And give herself to me forever.
But passion sometimes would prevail,
 Nor could tonight's gay feast restrain
A sudden thought of one so pale
 For love of her, and all in vain:
30 So, she was come through wind and rain.
Be sure I looked up at her eyes
 Happy and proud; at last I knew
Porphyria worshiped me: surprise
 Made my heart swell, and still it grew
35 While I debated what to do.
That moment she was mine, mine, fair,
 Perfectly pure and good: I found
A thing to do, and all her hair
 In one long yellow string I wound
40 Three times her little throat around,
4 And strangled her. No pain felt she;
 I am quite sure she felt no pain.
As a shut bud that holds a bee,
 I warily oped her lids: again
45 Laughed the blue eyes without a stain.
And I untightened next the tress
 About her neck; her cheek once more
Blushed bright beneath my burning kiss:
 I propped her head up as before,
50 Only, this time my shoulder bore
5 Her head, which droops upon it still:
 The smiling rosy little head,
So glad it has its utmost will,
 That all it scorned at once is fled,
55 And I, its love, am gained instead!
Porphyria's love: she guessed not how
 Her darling one wish would be heard.
And thus we sit together now,
 And all night long we have not stirred,
60 And yet God has not said a word!

540 Unit Six: The Victorians

24 dissever (di sev′ər), v. separate.

46 tress (tres), n. lock, curl, or braid of hair.
53 utmost (ut′mōst), adj. greatest; highest.

In *The Kiss,* a 1908 oil painting by Viennese artist Gustav Klimt (1862–1918), the two lovers have skin that appears lushly sensual. What elements of the painting contrast with the lovers' skin, making it appear even more sensual? ➤

MINI-LESSON: VOCABULARY
Using the Dictionary

The dictionary is a major tool with which writers enrich their understanding and use of the language.

Teach A dictionary entry provides pronunciation, part of speech, etymology, primary meaning, secondary meanings, and sometimes synonyms.

Activity Idea Instruct students to use the dictionary to look up the answers to these questions:

• List two other definitions for *vex* besides "disturb, agitate." *(to anger or annoy; to worry or trouble)*

• What Latin word does *dissever* come from? *(disseparare, to sever apart)*

• Find a definition for *utmost* as a noun. *(the most that is possible; extreme limit)*

• Find the adjective form of *munificence* and its definition. *(munificent, extremely generous)*

Response to Caption Question The enveloping metallic gold and the highly abstract patterns enhance the sensual quality of the lovers' skin.

Visual Literacy Gustav Klimt's *The Kiss* may be less sensual and more scientific than it first appears. The woman, who seems to grow out of a precipice on the very edge of the earth, is covered, like the earth, with abstract flower patterns. She is embraced from above by a man in a robe that is covered on one side by radiating sun patterns and shines with the golden radiance of the sun.

Questions What do you think these flower and sun details might suggest about the nature of this kiss? *(Possible response: The details suggest that this "kiss" may be a metaphor for the interconnection of the sun and life on earth; the earth is embraced by the sun's radiating energy, which seems to flow through the female figure, giving life to the flowers.)*

BUILDING ENGLISH PROFICIENCY

Dramatizing the Poem

Because of the violent subject matter of "Porphyria's Lover," you might want to read it aloud to the class (or use the Audiotape) and discuss the speaker's motivation and sanity. Paraphrasing and dramatizing the poem in groups will also help students respond to its characters and subject.

1. Divide the poem into eight-line sections. (The last section will be four lines.) Have each three-student group paraphrase its section and then rehearse to present it to the class.

2. Suggest that two students mime the action while one reads the lines. Remind readers to look carefully at the punctuation and to

work with the next group so that the reading and miming will flow smoothly.

3. Encourage students to read expressively, communicating emotion and heightening suspense by pausing, changing from loud to soft, slowing down or speeding up, and so on.

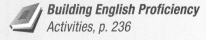

Building English Proficiency
Activities, p. 236

7 **Literary Element**

Characterization

Questions How does the Duke characterize his wife? *(Possible response: She "had a heart too soon made glad"—she liked everything and everybody that she saw, and her eyes roved too far; too many people pleased her, to the point of producing a characteristic blush on her cheek.)* How would you characterize her husband the Duke? *(Possible response: jealous and proud)*

My Last Duchess

Robert Browning

The place is the city of Ferrara in northern Italy. The time is the 1500s. The speaker is the Duke of Ferrara, who is negotiating for a marriage with a count's daughter.

> That's my last duchess painted on the wall,
> Looking as if she were alive. I call
> That piece a wonder, now: Frà Pandolf's hands
> Worked busily a day, and there she stands.
> 5 Will 't please you sit and look at her? I said
> "Frà Pandolf" by design, for never read
> Strangers like you that pictured countenance,
> The depth and passion of its earnest glance,
> But to myself they turned (since none puts by
> 10 The curtain I have drawn for you, but I)
> And seemed as they would ask me, if they durst,
> How such a glance came there; so, not the first
> Are you to turn and ask thus. Sir, 'twas not
> Her husband's presence only, called that spot
> 15 Of joy into the Duchess' cheek: perhaps
> Frà Pandolf chanced to say, "Her mantle laps
> Over my lady's wrist too much," or "Paint
> Must never hope to reproduce the faint
> Half-flush that dies along her throat": such stuff
> 20 Was courtesy, she thought, and cause enough
> For calling up that spot of joy. She had
> A heart—how shall I say?—too soon made glad,
> Too easily impressed; she liked whate'er
> She looked on, and her looks went everywhere.
> 25 Sir, 'twas all one! My favor at her breast,
> The dropping of the daylight in the West,
> The bough of cherries some officious fool
> Broke in the orchard for her, the white mule
> She rode with round the terrace—all and each
> 30 Would draw from her alike the approving speech,
> Or blush, at least. She thanked men—good! but thanked
> Somehow—I know not how—as if she ranked
> My gift of a nine-hundred-years-old name
> With anybody's gift. Who'd stoop to blame

3 Frà Pandolf, the painter, a monk.

11 durst (dèrst), *v.* a past tense of *dare*. *[Archaic]*

16 mantle (man′tl), *n.* cloak.

27 officious (ə fish′əs), *adj.* meddlesome.

MINI-LESSON: GRAMMAR

Irregular Verbs

Many languages have verbs that change to express tense or number in ways that differ from the dominant patterns of the language.

Teach An irregular verb does not form the past tense or past participle by adding -*d* or -*ed* to the present tense. Instead, the past tense and participle may be formed by changing a vowel (and sometimes other letters) in the word, adding -*en,* or making no change at all.

Activity Ideas

- Ask students to find as many irregular verbs as possible (in any form) in "Porphyria's Love" or "My Last Duchess" and give the present, past, and participle for them.

- Ask students to give examples of regular verbs in present, present participle, past, and past participle. *(for example, want, is wanting, wanted, have wanted)*

- Ask students to write sentences using some of the irregular verbs from the poems.

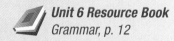

Unit 6 Resource Book
Grammar, p. 12

35 This sort of trifling? Even had you skill
In speech—which I have not—to make your will
Quite clear to such an one, and say, "Just this
Or that in you disgusts me; here you miss,
Or there exceed the mark"—and if she let
40 Herself be lessoned so, nor plainly set
Her wits to yours, forsooth, and made excuse—
E'en then would be some stooping; and I choose
Never to stoop. Oh sir, she smiled, no doubt,
Whene'er I passed her; but who passed without

8
45 Much the same smile? This grew; I gave commands;
Then all smiles stopped together. There she stands
As if alive. Will 't please you rise? We'll meet
The company below, then. I repeat,
The Count your master's known munificence
50 Is ample warrant that no just pretense
Of mine for dowry will be disallowed;
Though his fair daughter's self, as I avowed
At starting, is my object. Nay, we'll go

9
Together down, sir. Notice Neptune, though,
55 Taming a sea-horse, thought a rarity,
Which Claus of Innsbruck cast in bronze for me!

41 forsooth (fôr sŭth′), *adv.*
in truth; indeed. *[Archaic]*

49 munificence (myŭ nif′ə-
səns), *n.* very great generosity.
50 pretense (prē′tens), *n.*
claim.
51 dowry (dou′rē), *n.*
money or property that a
woman brings to the man she
marries.
52 avow (ə vou′), *v.* declare
openly; admit.
54 Neptune, the Roman god
of the sea.
56 Claus of Innsbruck, a
fictitious sculptor.

My Last Duchess **543**

Questions Why couldn't the Duke stoop
to discussing his feelings with his wife?
*(Possible response: Pride—he feels it
would have been a weakness, a loss of
face that would lower him to her level.)*
What does "I gave commands" suggest?
(He ordered his wife's murder.)

9 Literary Element
Characterization

Questions The Duke progresses from
discussing murder to a new wife's dowry
to a statue of Neptune. What does the
progression suggest about his character?
*(Possible response: He thinks of people as
possessions, to be displayed or disposed of
as he pleases; the late Duchess has been
reduced to a work of art.)* Considering the
Duke's character, why do you think he reveals
the portrait and the story to the Count's
envoy? *(Possible responses: to show his
strength, pride, and ruthlessness; to be
sure his new wife behaves to his liking)*

Check Test

1. How would you describe the love
Elizabeth Barrett Browning describes?
*(Possible responses: timeless, without
limit, free, pure)*

2. Who narrates "Porphyria's Lover?
(the nameless lover)

3. How does Porphyria become his
forever? *(He kills her.)*

4. What has happened to the Duke's
former wife in "My Last Duchess?"
(He had her killed.)

5. To whom does the Duke address his
monologue? *(an ambassador from a
Count with a marriageable daughter)*

Unit 6 Resource Book
Alternate Check Test p. 13

BUILDING ENGLISH PROFICIENCY

Exploring Contractions

Help students distinguish between poetic
and modern contractions in this poem.

1. Explain that Victorians used poetic
contractions like *'twas* to make the line's
syllables fit a rhythm pattern.

2. Ask pairs of students to find five poetic
and three modern contractions.

Contraction	Poetic or Modern	Shortened form
that's	modern	that is
will't	poetic	will it

MAKING CONNECTIONS

1. Responses might vary from flattery, to embarrassment, to annoyance.

2. Responses will vary, but the obvious defense is insanity.

3. Browning describes "passions of old griefs" and loss of "old saints" and "childhood's faith." She states that she loves with the innocent love of a child; she then describes love in the present and in the future, i.e., beyond death.

4. Students may respond that the climax is reached in lines 40–41, when he confesses he strangled her to hold on to the moment.

5. Students may infer that the Duke was so jealous that he mistook his wife's kind and gentle nature for sexual overtures. While he is proud of the Fra Pandolf portrait, his jealousy has persuaded him that the painted smile and blush must be the result of a relationship between his wife and the artist.

6. The Duke ordered her murder.

7. Accept all reasonable answers. Decisions about casting could create interesting discussion about the appearance and personality of each of the main characters: the Duke, the envoy to whom he speaks, as well as characters in flashback, such as the last duchess and the painter Fra Pandolf.

8. Students might reasonably respond that both Porphyria's lover and the Duke would resist change with equal ferocity: the lover's refusal to accept reality leads to murder; and the Duke would obviously go to any lengths to avoid loss of family prestige or personal power. The narrator of Sonnet 43 would be most accepting of change; the poem is filled with inevitability of change, from loss of childhood innocence to death.

Making Connections

Shaping Your Response

1. How would you respond if Sonnet 43 had been written for you?

2. If you had to defend Porphyria's lover in a court of law, what would your defense be?

Analyzing the Poems

3. In Sonnet 43, what details imply a former life, and what do they add to the feelings expressed?

4. In your opinion, which lines in "Porphyria's Lover" contain the **climax** or emotional peak of the poem?

5. What can you **infer** about the Duke's feelings for his wife and for Frà Pandolf in "My Last Duchess" and the reasons for those feelings?

6. What sort of "commands" (line 45) do you infer the Duke gave?

Extending the Ideas

7. Suppose that the story of "My Last Duchess" is expanded and about to be made into a film, and you are in charge of setting up a casting call. List the characters' names, their descriptions (some of which you will have to make up), and then suggest suitable actors for the roles.

8. 👥 Which of the speakers in these three poems do you think would be most resistant to **changes** in society or in his or her personal circumstances and which of the speakers would be most accepting? Explain your choices.

Literary Focus: Dramatic Monologue

In a **dramatic monologue** a fictional character reveals a dramatic situation and, often, details of characterization and setting. If a listener is present within the dramatic situation, he or she is silent. Since the speaker may not be entirely objective, readers must usually make inferences about a situation and about the speaker's true feelings.

1. Describe the setting of "Porphyria's Lover."

2. How does the speaker try to justify his murder to himself? Is there an audience or a listener?

3. When the Duke in "My Last Duchess" insists that he is primarily interested in the Count's "fair daughter's self" (line 52), what inference can you draw?

4. What sort of report do you think the listener, the Count's envoy or representative, will deliver to the Count?

LITERARY FOCUS: DRAMATIC MONOLOGUE

1. Accepting the poem at face value, the setting is a lakeside cottage on a cold, stormy night. The fire has nearly gone out until Porphyria rekindles it.

2. He justifies the murder by stating that she felt no pain, her "utmost will" has been achieved, and God's silence is a sign of approval. Although it is not stated, the change from past to present verb tense suggests that there may be a "silent listener."

3. Students may speculate that the Duke "protests too much," and that he is really most interested in the dowry.

4. Responses will vary. At the time of this poem, women were considered first the property of fathers and then of husbands; the Duke's easy candor suggests that an alliance with a duke may be too valuable to bother much over the fate of a daughter.

Expressing Your Ideas

Writing Choices

Writer's Notebook Update Review the adjectives you jotted down to describe someone you know. Then write a brief description of that person in the form of a poem, using rhyme if you can. Here is an example:

> Blue-eyed, curly-haired, not too proud;
> Anxious, careful, but somewhat loud.

My Husband the Duke Write a **dramatic monologue** from the young Duchess's point of view. Make the setting the room where she is having her portrait painted. The listener could then be Fra Pandolf. The dramatic situation might begin when footsteps are heard. You might consider beginning with this answer to a question from Fra Pandolf: "That's my husband, passing in the hall. . . ."

How He Does It Write an **essay** in which you analyze how Browning employs the technique of dramatic monologue in "My Last Duchess." First define the term. Then describe how the words of the Duke create a sense of place and time, a specific listener, and a dramatic situation. Last, analyze the discrepancy between what the Duke says and what you infer about him and what you infer about what actually happened before these negotiations for a new wife.

Other Options

Thus We Sit Together Now Prepare an **oral reading** of either of Browning's dramatic monologues printed here. For greatest effectiveness, think of them not just as poems to be recited but as scripts to be acted. Consider details of voice, gesture, and facial expression. Rehearse until you are satisfied you're communicating the character and the ideas, and perform your reading for the class.

Looking As If They Were Alive Bring to class a number of library books that have color reproductions of portraits from the past. Divide into small groups and examine some of these pictures together. What can you tell about the subjects from their facial expressions, posture, dress, and pictured possessions? What can you tell about the painters' eras from their subjects and styles of painting? (See also Looking at a Portrait on page 851.) Make each group member responsible for a brief **illustrated report** of the group's conclusions.

How Do I Love Thee? Imagine that someone has just asked you a question like the one that prompts Sonnet 43 (except that you can substitute another emotion if you wish). Create an **artwork,** such as a painting, collage, or paper sculpture, that expresses the extent of your emotion or else "counts the ways," as Elizabeth Barrett Browning does.

WRITING CHOICES
Writer's Notebook Update

If students are having trouble composing rhymes, suggest the use a rhyming dictionary or thesaurus.

My Husband the Duke

Remind students that in a dramatic monologue, the listener is silent. You might note that a dramatic monologue can be prose as well as poetry.

How He Does It

Student essays should discuss how setting and situation are established and what words or lines provide clues. The essay might also provide a short character study of the Duke.

Selection Test

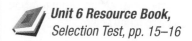

Unit 6 Resource Book,
Selection Test, pp. 15–16

OTHER OPTIONS
Looking As If They Were Alive

Students will be exercising their "visual literacy" skills in this activity. If you have used some of the Art Study notes from this text, remind students of how color, form, structure, and seemingly extraneous objects can offer clues to an artist's ideas and intentions.

How Do I Love Thee?

Remind students that they could answer one of these questions, How do I fear thee? admire thee? resent thee? Note that artwork should exhibit strong emotion, so that others can comprehend it.

Before Reading

Building Background

You might also ask students if they are in any way familiar with *Alice in Wonderland*—through films such as the 1951 Disney animated version, or even through the name of a ride at Disney theme parks.

Literary Focus

You might note examples of Carroll's puns: e.g., *beat* as in "beating time" or "beating a person"; and *draw* as in "drawing water from a well" or "drawing a picture."

Writer's Notebook

Remind students that these characters and situations can be humorous or frightening. In *Alice in Wonderland,* characters and situations may change from funny to frightening to funny again.

More About Lewis Carroll

Lewis Carroll published under a pseudonym. He created his pen name by translating his two first names, Charles Lutwidge, into Latin, *Carolus Lodovicus;* he then reversed the names and Anglicized them into Lewis Carroll. The author enjoyed the creation of such inventions. His poem "Jabberwocky" is filled with new words, including *chortle*—a Carroll combination of *chuckle* and *snort* that has become part of the language.

Before Reading

A Mad Tea-Party from Alice's Adventures in Wonderland

by Lewis Carroll

Lewis Carroll (Charles Lutwidge Dodgson)
1832–1898

Charles Lutwidge Dodgson was a college lecturer in mathematics and also wrote works on mathematics and logic, booklets of games and puzzles, some light poetry, and a variety of witty pamphlets. He is best known, however, for *Alice's Adventures in Wonderland* (1865), *Through the Looking-Glass* (1872), and *The Hunting of the Snark* (1876), all of which he published under the pen name Lewis Carroll. Though a serious academic, there was in him a vein of childlike playfulness. He once wrote to a friend, a young girl: "I had just time to look into the kitchen and saw your birthday feast getting ready, a nice dish of crusts, bones, pills, cotton-bobbins, and rhubarb and magnesia. 'Now,' I thought, 'she will be happy!'"

Building Background

The Adventures Begin Alice's adventures in Wonderland grow out of Dodgson's affection for a little girl, Alice Liddell, daughter of the Dean of Christ Church. On July 4, 1862, Dodgson and a friend take the three Liddell girls, Alice among them, boating on the Thames. As they row along, Dodgson begins to tell extemporaneous stories of Alice's adventures underground—how Alice dreams that she chases a White Rabbit down a rabbit hole to a world filled with such characters as the Cheshire Cat, the Mad Hatter, the March Hare, the Duchess, the King and Queen of Hearts, and the Mock Turtle. Among Alice's adventures are her discovery that eating from one side of a curious mushroom will make her shrink, and eating from the other side will make her grow. At the end of the day, Alice Liddell asks him to write out the adventures for her. He does, and the book has been enjoyed by young and old alike ever since. Before "A Mad Tea-Party" begins, Alice has just come in sight of the the March Hare's house, which has chimneys shaped like ears and a roof thatched with fur.

Literary Focus

Pun A **pun** is a humorous use of a word that can have different meanings, or of two or more words with the same or nearly the same sound but different meanings. A pun is also called a play on words. The old riddle, "What has four wheels and flies?" uses a pun based on two definitions of *fly,* one meaning "housefly" and the other meaning "to move through the air." Since the answer to the riddle is "a garbage truck," one can see how puns also came to be known as the lowest form of humor. As you read, look for Carroll's clever use of puns.

Writer's Notebook

A World of Dreams Carroll once wrote: "We often dream without the least suspicion of unreality: 'sleep hath its own world,' and it is often as lifelike as the other." Much of "A Mad Tea-Party" is like a dream. In your notebook, jot down some unreal characters and situations one might meet in a dream but not in real life.

546 UNIT SIX: THE VICTORIANS

SUPPORT MATERIALS OVERVIEW

Unit 6 Resource Book
- Graphic Organizer, p. 17
- Study Guide, p. 18
- Vocabulary, p. 19
- Grammar, p. 20
- Alternate Check Test, p. 21
- Vocabulary Test, p. 22
- Selection Test, pp. 23–24

Building English Proficiency
- Selection Summaries
- Activities, p. 237

Reading, Writing & Grammar SkillBook
- Grammar, Usage, and Mechanics, pp. 165–166

World of Work
- Toy Designer, p. 21
- Activity, p. 22

Technology
- Personal Journal Software
- Custom Literature Database: Additional excerpts from *Alice's Adventures in Wonderland* and other selections by Lewis Carroll can be found on the database.
- Test Generator Software

The Mad Hatter, the Dormouse, and the March Hare have tea with Alice in *Dreamchild*, a film about the real-life Alice Liddell, for whom Charles Dodgson created *Alice's Adventures in Wonderland*. Does this scene match his description of the mad tea party? Why or why not?

A MAD TEA-PARTY

LEWIS CARROLL

There was a table set out under a tree in front of the house, and the March Hare and the Hatter were having tea at it: a Dormouse[1] was sitting between them, fast asleep, and the other two were using it as a cushion, resting their elbows on it, and talking over

---

1. **dormouse,** not a mouse but a kind of rodent that resembles a squirrel.

A Mad Tea-Party   **547**

SELECTION SUMMARY

A Mad Tea-Party

Alice comes upon three "fellows," the March Hare, the Hatter, and a Dormouse, seated at one end of a tea table. The Hatter and March Hare are rude to Alice, who finds herself being rude in return. The Dormouse sleeps. The Hatter poses a riddle, for which he has no answer. He also has a watch that once told the day of the month, but is now gummed up with bread crumbs and butter. Eventually, the Dormouse tells a story about three girls in a well; they live on treacle and draw treacle, as well as things that begin with the letter *m*, such as muchness. Alice can make little sense of the story or of the party, which she judges "the stupidest tea-party I ever was at in all my life!" After leaving, she enters a tree through a door and eats a bit of mushroom to shrink herself sufficiently to enter a garden.

 For summaries in other languages, see the Building English Proficiency book.

During Reading

Selection Objectives

- to identify examples of puns
- to discover playful uses of language
- to appreciate fantasy in a children's story
- to apply conventional standards of English to hyphens

Unit 6 Resource Book
Graphic Organizer, p. 17
Study Guide, p. 18

Theme Link

The Industrial Revolution turned 19th-century Britain upside down. Carroll's work expresses his struggle to understand a world in which the same language is spoken, but what is said doesn't make sense.

Art Study

Responses to Caption Questions
Most students will note the scene does not exactly match the description. Carroll describes the Hatter and March Hare as leaning against a sleeping Dormouse.

Historical Note
Mad as a Hatter

Carroll may have made his character a hatter because the profession was already identified with madness. Hat makers of this time often suffered from mental problems due to handling mercury, a poisonous metal used in the creation of men's hats.

Connections to
AuthorWorks

Charles Dickens, who Struggled to Understand his times, is a featured author in the AuthorWorks CD-ROM series.

Connections to
NovelWorks

NovelWorks: Great Expectations offers a rich variety of unique materials for teaching the novel.

Questions   Do the phrases "I say what I mean" and "I mean what I say" denote the same thing? connote the same thing? *(Possible responses: It could be argued that both phrases denote expressing oneself in a precise and clear manner. However, they have different connotations. "I mean what I say" is generally a warning of firmness of purpose; imagine a parent saying, "Now, I mean what I say!" "I say what I mean" usually connotes frankness.)*

Dipping one's watch in tea does make a weird kind of sense. The English, on occasion, dip bread-and-butter tea sandwiches into their tea, rather as Americans dunk donuts into coffee. As the bread-crumb and butter-filled watch is now useless as a watch, might it be put to use as a tea sandwich? After dipping it in tea, the March Hare decides, alas, it won't do.

THE HATTER'S REMARK SEEMED TO HER TO HAVE NO SORT OF MEANING IN IT, AND YET IT WAS CERTAINLY ENGLISH.

its head. "Very uncomfortable for the Dormouse," thought Alice; "only, as it's asleep, I suppose it doesn't mind."

The table was a large one, but the three were all crowded together at one corner of it. "No room! No room!" they cried out when they saw Alice coming. "There's *plenty* of room!" said Alice indignantly, and she sat down in a large armchair at one end of the table.

"Have some wine," the March Hare said in an encouraging tone.

Alice looked all round the table, but there was nothing on it but tea. "I don't see any wine," she remarked.

"There isn't any," said the March Hare.

"Then it wasn't very civil of you to offer it," said Alice angrily.

"It wasn't very civil of you to sit down without being invited," said the March Hare.

"I didn't know it was *your* table," said Alice; "it's laid for a great many more than three."

"Your hair wants cutting," said the Hatter. He had been looking at Alice for some time with great curiosity, and this was his first speech.

"You should learn not to make personal remarks," Alice said with some severity: "it's very rude."

The Hatter opened his eyes very wide on hearing this; but all he *said* was, "Why is a raven like a writing-desk?"

"Come, we shall have some fun now!" thought Alice. "I'm glad they've begun asking riddles—I believe I can guess that," she added aloud.

"Do you mean that you think you can find out the answer to it?" said the March Hare.

"Exactly so," said Alice.

"Then you should say what you mean," the March Hare went on.

"I do," Alice hastily replied; "at least—at least I mean what I say—that's the same thing, you know."

2

"Not the same thing a bit!" said the Hatter. "Why, you might just as well say that 'I see what I eat' is the same thing as 'I eat what I see'!"

"You might just as well say," added the March Hare, "that 'I like what I get' is the same thing as 'I get what I like'!"

"You might just as well say," added the Dormouse, who seemed to be talking in his sleep, "that 'I breathe when I sleep' is the same thing as 'I sleep when I breathe'!"

"It *is* the same thing with you," said the Hatter, and here the conversation dropped, and the party sat silent for a minute, while Alice thought over all she could remember about ravens and writing-desks, which wasn't much.

The Hatter was the first to break the silence. "What day of the month is it?" he said, turning to Alice: he had taken his watch out of his pocket, and was looking at it uneasily, shaking it every now and then, and holding it to his ear.

Alice considered a little, and said, "The fourth."

"Two days wrong!" sighed the Hatter. "I told you butter wouldn't suit the works!" he added, looking angrily at the March Hare.

"It was the *best* butter," the March Hare meekly replied.

"Yes, but some crumbs must have got in as well," the Hatter grumbled: "you shouldn't have put it in with the bread-knife."

The March Hare took the watch and looked at it gloomily: then he dipped it into his cup of tea, and looked at it again: but he could think of nothing better to say than his first remark, "It was the *best* butter, you know."

3

Alice had been looking over his shoulder with some curiosity. "What a funny watch!" she

MINI-LESSON: LITERARY FOCUS

Pun

The pun is the foundation of all wit; it is, at least, the most common form.

Teach   A pun is a play on words that takes a word with more than one meaning and deliberately confuses its usage. To create puns, you first need to understand the meanings of a word. For example: "A farmer is a person who is outstanding in his field." This double pun uses the meanings of "outstanding" (very good) and "out standing" (standing somewhere outside) and two meanings of "field" (a person's chosen profession; a plot of land where crops are grown).

Activity Idea   Make a class list of all the puns that students can recall or invent.

remarked. "It tells the day of the month, and doesn't tell what o'clock it is!"

"Why should it?" muttered the Hatter. "Does *your* watch tell you what year it is?"

"Of course not," Alice replied very readily: "but that's because it stays the same year for such a long time together."

4 "Which is just the case with *mine*," said the Hatter.

5 Alice felt dreadfully puzzled. The Hatter's remark seemed to her to have no sort of meaning in it, and yet it was certainly English. "I don't quite understand you," she said as politely as she could.

"The Dormouse is asleep again," said the Hatter, and he poured a little hot tea on to its nose.

The Dormouse shook its head impatiently, and said, without opening its eyes, "Of course, of course: just what I was going to remark myself."

"Have you guessed the riddle yet?" the Hatter said, turning to Alice again.

"No, I give it up," Alice replied: "what's the answer?"

"I haven't the slightest idea," said the Hatter. "Nor I," said the March Hare.

Alice sighed wearily. "I think you might do something better with the time," she said, "than wasting it in asking riddles that have no answers."[2]

6 "If you knew Time as well as I do," said the Hatter, "you wouldn't talk about wasting *it*. It's *him*."

"I don't know what you mean," said Alice.

"Of course you don't!" the Hatter said, tossing his head contemptuously. "I dare say you never even spoke to Time!"

"Perhaps not," Alice cautiously replied: "but I know I have to beat time when I learn music."

7 "Ah! that accounts for it," said the Hatter. "He won't stand beating. Now, if you only kept on good terms with him, he'd do almost anything you liked with the clock. For instance, suppose it were nine o'clock in the morning, just

time to begin lessons: you'd only have to whisper a hint to Time, and round goes the clock in a twinkling! Half-past one, time for dinner!"

("I only wish it was," the March Hare said to itself in a whisper.)

"That would be grand, certainly," said Alice thoughtfully: "but then—I shouldn't be hungry for it, you know."

"Not at first, perhaps," said the Hatter: "but you could keep it to half-past one as long as you liked."

"Is that the way *you* manage?" Alice asked.

The Hatter shook his head mournfully. "Not I!" he replied. "We quarreled last March—just before *he* went mad, you know—" (pointing with his teaspoon at the March Hare) "—it was at the great concert given by the Queen of Hearts, and I had to sing

> '*Twinkle, twinkle, little bat!*
> *How I wonder what you're at!*'

You know the song, perhaps?"

"I've heard something like it," said Alice.

"It goes on, you know," the Hatter continued, "in this way—

> '*Up above the world you fly,*
> *Like a teatray in the sky.*
> *Twinkle, twinkle—*'"

Here the Dormouse shook itself, and began singing in its sleep, "*Twinkle, twinkle, twinkle, twinkle—*"and went on so long that they had to pinch it to make it stop.

"Well, I'd hardly finished the first verse," said the Hatter, "when the Queen bawled out, 'He's murdering the time! Off with his head!'"

"How dreadfully savage!" exclaimed Alice.

8 "And ever since that," the Hatter went on in a mournful tone, "he won't do a thing I ask! It's always six o'clock now."

---

2. **no answers.** Carroll later supplied this answer: "Because it can produce a few notes, though they are very flat; and it is never put with the wrong end in front." Among other popular suggestions is this one: Because they both stand on legs, and should be made to shut up.

A Mad Tea-Party **549**

4 Literary Focus
Pun

Question Can students find a pun in the Hatter's remark on his watch? *(Possible response: A case is both "an instance of something" and "the outer covering of a watch.")*

5 Reading/Thinking Skills
Infer

Question What can students infer about the Hatter's "puzzling" remarks about his watch? *(that time now "stays the same for such a long time")*

6 Literary Element
Personification

Questions What literary device does the Hatter use when he refers to Time as "he"? *(personification)*

7 Literary Focus
Pun

Question How does the Hatter's response affect the meaning of Alice's "I have to beat time when I learn music"? *(Possible response: It twists the meaning of beat from "count" to "strike" or "hit.")*

8 Reading/Thinking Skills
Literal and Figurative Language

Questions How does "It's always six o'clock" affect the meaning of "murdering the time"? *(Possible responses: The original meaning, which plays on the "beating time" pun, is figurative—the Hatter does not keep the proper musical beat. That it's now "always six o'clock" suggests Time, personified, is literally dead, i.e., stopped.)*

BUILDING ENGLISH PROFICIENCY

Improving Comprehension

Help students appreciate Carroll's sly "digs" at Victorian values.

1. Explain: Upper-class Victorians believed strongly in good manners and reason; Alice, a polite, rational Victorian child, keeps trying to make sense of the rude, "crazy" world she has fallen into; hares, related to rabbits, seemed to go crazy in March, the start of the breeding season; hatters sometimes went mad (insane) because of a chemical used in the hat-blocking process.

2. Divide students into groups of five (a narrator, Alice, March Hare, Mad Hatter, and Dormouse), and have them practice reading this scene as Reader's Theater.

3. Ask: What might Carroll be saying about manners, "small talk," "rational argument," and social occasions?

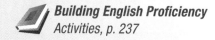

Building English Proficiency
Activities, p. 237

9 Literary Focus
Pun

Point out that "things between whiles" contains a pun on *while*, "a period of time," and *wile*, "to pass time agreeably."

Question Besides creating another pun, why do you think the author uses *while* instead of the word *time*? *(Possible response: If it's always six o'clock, there can be no period of time to pass agreeably.)*

10 Literary Element
Connotation/Denotation

You might point out that the word *treacle* denotes "molasses," but connotes *a* "cloying speech" or "sentimentality."

11 Reading/Thinking Skills
Synthesize

Question If *nothing* is equated with a zero bank account, can one have less than nothing? *(Possible response: One can have less than nothing in the bank, i.e., be "in the hole," in debt.)*

12 Literary Focus
Pun

Question What is the pun on *draw*? *(While Alice assumes* draw *to mean "to make a likeness on paper," the Dormouse means "to take or pull out.")*

A bright idea came into Alice's head. "Is that the reason so many tea-things are put out here?" she asked.

"Yes, that's it," said the Hatter with a sigh: "it's always tea-time, and we've no time to wash the things between whiles."

"Then you keep moving round, I suppose?" said Alice.

"Exactly so," said the Hatter: "as the things get used up."

"But when you come to the beginning again?" Alice ventured to ask.

"Suppose we change the subject," the March Hare interrupted, yawning. "I'm getting tired of this. I vote the young lady tells us a story."

"I'm afraid I don't know one," said Alice, rather alarmed at the proposal.

"Then the Dormouse shall!" they both cried. "Wake up, Dormouse!" And they pinched it on both sides at once.

The Dormouse slowly opened his eyes. "I wasn't asleep," he said in a hoarse, feeble voice: "I heard every word you fellows were saying."

"Tell us a story!" said the March Hare.

"Yes, please do!" pleaded Alice.

"And be quick about it," added the Hatter, "or you'll be asleep again before it's done."

"Once upon a time there were three little sisters," the Dormouse began in a great hurry; "and their names were Elsie, Lacie, and Tillie;[3] and they lived at the bottom of a well—"

"What did they live on?" said Alice, who always took a great interest in questions of eating and drinking.

"They lived on treacle,"[4] said the Dormouse, after thinking a minute or two.

"They couldn't have done that, you know," Alice gently remarked: "they'd have been ill."

"So they were," said the Dormouse; "*very* ill."

Alice tried a little to fancy to herself what such an extraordinary way of living would be like, but it puzzled her too much, so she went on: "But why did they live at the bottom of a well?"

"Take some more tea," the March Hare said to Alice, very earnestly.

"I've had nothing yet," Alice replied in an offended tone, "so I can't take more."

"You mean, you can't take *less*," said the Hatter: "It's very easy to take *more* than nothing."

"Nobody asked *your* opinion," said Alice.

"Who's making personal remarks now?" the Hatter asked triumphantly.

Alice did not quite know what to say to this: so she helped herself to some tea and bread-and-butter, and then turned to the Dormouse, and repeated her question.

"Why did they live at the bottom of a well?"

The Dormouse again took a minute or two to think about it, and then said, "It was a treacle-well."

"There's no such thing!" Alice was beginning very angrily, but the Hatter and the March Hare went "Sh! sh!" and the Dormouse sulkily remarked, "If you can't be civil, you'd better finish the story for yourself."

"No, please go on!" Alice said very humbly: "I won't interrupt you again. I dare say there may be *one*."

"One, indeed!" said the Dormouse indignantly. However, he consented to go on. "And so these three little sisters—they were learning to draw, you know—"

"What did they draw?" said Alice, quite forgetting her promise.

"Treacle," said the Dormouse, without considering at all this time.

"I want a clean cup," interrupted the Hatter: "let's all move one place on."

He moved on as he spoke, and the Dormouse followed him: the March Hare moved into the Dormouse's place, and Alice rather unwillingly took the place of the March

---

3. **Elsie, Lacie, and Tillie,** a reference to the Liddell sisters. *Elsie* stands for L. C. or Lorina C.; *Lacie* is an anagram for Alice; *Tillie* is a form of Matilda, Edith's nickname.

4. **treacle** (trē′kəl), *n.* molasses.

MINI-LESSON: GRAMMAR

Compound Sentences

Teach A simple sentence, while it need not be short, has a subject and predicate. (Example: Alice, the Hatter, and two animals were at a tea party.) A compound sentence consists of two or more sentences joined by a coordinating conjunction, such as *and, but,* or *or.* (Example: Three of them were discussing a variety of topics, and the Dormouse was sleeping.) A complex sentence includes one independent clause and at least one subordinate clause. (Example: Although at a glance the party seemed calm, underneath there was an air of tension, hostility, and rudeness.)

Activity Ideas

• Write the story of Elsie, Lacie, and Tillie, using at least one simple sentence, one compound sentence, and one complex sentence.

• Rewrite the paragraph in column 2 that begins "Alice did not quite know what to say. . . . " Use only simple sentences.

• Identify as simple, compound, or complex the sentences from the bottom of the first column of page 551 through the end of the selection.

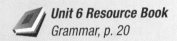

Unit 6 Resource Book
Grammar, p. 20

Hare. The Hatter was the only one who got any advantage from the change: and Alice was a good deal worse off than before, as the March Hare had just upset the milk-jug into his plate.

Alice did not wish to offend the Dormouse again, so she began very cautiously: "But I don't understand. Where did they draw the treacle from?"

"You can draw water out of a water-well," said the Hatter: "so I should think you could draw treacle out of a treacle-well—eh, stupid?"

"But they were *in* the well," Alice said to the Dormouse, not choosing to notice this last remark.

13 "Of course they were," said the Dormouse, "—well in." This answer so confused poor Alice, that she let the Dormouse go on for some time without interrupting it.

"They were learning to draw," the Dormouse went on, yawning and rubbing its eyes, for it was getting very sleepy; "and they drew all manner of things—everything that begins with an M—"

"Why with an M?" said Alice.

"Why not?" said the March Hare.

Alice was silent.

The Dormouse had closed its eyes by this time, and was going off into a doze, but on being pinched by the Hatter, it woke up again with a little shriek, and went on: "—that begins with an M, such as mousetraps, and the moon, and memory, and muchness—you know you say things are 'much of a muchness'[5]—did you ever **14** see such a thing as a drawing of a muchness?"

"Really, now you ask me," said Alice, very much confused, "I don't think—"

"Then you shouldn't talk," said the Hatter.

This piece of rudeness was more than Alice could bear: she got up in great disgust, and walked off: the Dormouse fell asleep instantly, and neither of the others took the least notice of her going, though she looked back once or twice, half hoping that they would call after her: the last time she saw them, they were trying to put the Dormouse into the teapot.

"At any rate I'll never go *there* again!" said Alice as she picked her way through the wood. "It's the stupidest tea-party I ever was at in all my life!"

Just as she said this, she noticed that one of the trees had a door leading right into it. "That's very curious!" she thought. "But everything's curious today. I think I may as well go in at once." And in she went.

Once more she found herself in the long hall, and close to the little glass table. "Now, I'll manage better this time," she said to herself, and began by taking the little golden key, and unlocking the door that led into the garden. Then she set to work nibbling at the mushroom (she had kept a piece of it in her pocket) till she was about a foot high: then she walked down the little passage: and *then* she found herself at last in the beautiful garden, among the bright flowerbeds and the cool fountains.

---

5. **much of a muchness.** This British phrase means "things are pretty much the same."

"IT'S THE STUPIDEST TEA-PARTY I EVER WAS AT IN ALL MY LIFE!"

---

13 Literary Focus
Pun

Question What is the pun in *well in*? (Possible response: The Dormouse switches the meaning of well from "a hole in the earth" to "the utmost extent.")

14 Reading/Thinking Skills
Compare and Contrast

Question Can you think of any phrase in "A Mad Tea-Party" that compares to or contrasts with "drawing of a muchness"? (Possible response: "taking more than nothing")

Check Test

1. Who are the three characters that Alice meets at the Tea-Party? *(the March Hare, the Dormouse, and the Hatter)*

2. What is the unsolved riddle? *(Why is a raven like a writing desk?)*

3. What does Alice eat and drink at the Tea-Party? *(bread and butter and tea)*

4. What do the three girls in the well eat? *(treacle)*

5. What does Alice eat to change size? *(a bit of a mushroom)*

Unit 6 Resource Book
Alternate Check Test, p. 21

BUILDING ENGLISH PROFICIENCY

Linking Past and Present

Help students relate Carroll's Victorian times to their own world.

Activity Ideas

• Have groups of students brainstorm a list of things Carroll might think "mad" about today's world.

• Ask students to imagine that Carroll or one of his "mad" characters could send an e-mail message to their school. Ask them to compose, in less than 50 words, the message that he might send.

• Have students who are interested in art draw a cartoon strip featuring a twentieth-century person who suddenly shrinks to a tiny size (six inches, for example). Ask students to show what might happen to this person.

After Reading

MAKING CONNECTIONS

1. Students may label their "mad scale" with markers such as "slightly off," "mildly weird," or "completely bonkers."

2. Responses will vary, but should be supported by reasons and examples from the selection.

3. Changing the word order changes the object of the sentence and the verb that defines the relationship of the subject and object.

4. Alice and the Hatter speak the same language but exist in different realities.

5. Possible responses: The author enjoys playing with words and their meanings and entertaining his audience; the multiple meanings of words may suggest multiple meanings of other things, including differing realities.

6. Responses will vary.

7. Change is frightening, exciting, and sometimes mysterious, threatening, and desirable.

After Reading

Making Connections

Shaping Your Response

1. How mad is the tea-party? Devise a mad scale to measure its madness. Go mad with it.

2. Who is the craziest character? the wittiest character?

Analyzing the Novel Excerpt

3. Why isn't "I like what I get" the same as "I get what I like" when both sentences have the same words?

4. Alice is puzzled by the fact that she doesn't understand a remark by the Hatter even though it is spoken in English. What might account for her failure to understand?

5. What can you conclude about the **author's purpose** in including all the passages having to do with language, such as Alice's confusion about "drawing treacle"?

Extending the Ideas

6. Have you ever listened to or taken part in a conversation during which you felt as confused as Alice? Explain.

7. Dreams are often characterized by strange **changes** in characters, settings—even cultural conditions. What are some possible explanations for the fact that people so often dream about change?

Literary Focus: Pun

A **pun** is the humorous use of a word that can have different meanings, or of two or more words with the same or nearly the same sound but different meanings.

1. Alice says she has to "beat time" when she learns music. What does the Hatter think she means?

2. What is the pun on the word *draw*?

Vocabulary Study

Puns are based on **homophones** like *eight* and *ate,* which sound the same but are spelled differently, and **homonyms** like *mail* meaning "letters" and *mail* meaning "armor." Each item below contains two definitions. One of the words defined is shown. You are to provide the other word, which will sometimes have the same spelling and sometimes a different spelling as the word shown.

1. "a long cry of grief or pain" and "a ridge in the weave of corduroy": ____/wale

2. "the first whole number" and "the past tense of *win*": one/____

LITERARY FOCUS: PUN

Possible Responses

1. The Hatter thinks that she means she is striking Time, a person.

2. "Draw" means both "to extract or take out," as in drawing water from a well, and "to inscribe with a pencil," as in drawing a picture.

3. "a short sleep" and "the short woolly threads on the surface of cloth": ____/nap

4. "the sweet fruit of a palm" and "a particular day, month, or year": date/____

5. "a female sheep" and "a singular or plural pronoun": ewe/____

6. "things arranged in a straight line" and "use oars to move a boat": ____/row

7. "vein of metal ore" and "a burden": lode/____

8. "what we breathe" and "a person who inherits property": ____/heir

9. "time between evening and morning" and "a medieval man pledged to do good deeds": night/____

10. "from a higher to a lower place" and "soft feathers": ____/down

The first letters in each pair combine to spell a place. What is it?

Expressing Your Ideas

Writing Choices

Writer's Notebook Update Use your notes on unreal characters and situations to write a brief scene that might take place in Wonderland or some other fantastic setting.

Riddle Me This Try your hand at writing a few **riddles** based on words in the Vocabulary Study or on other homographs or homophones. Here is an example:

Q. Why did Queen Victoria want to move to sunny Italy?
A. She was tired of the reign.

Alice's Illustrator John Tenniel was the first artist to illustrate Alice's adventures, and his illustrations became so widely known that it is almost impossible to think of Carroll's characters without recalling Tenniel's artwork. Research Tenniel's life and his troubles with Carroll and write a **feature story** that could be printed on the anniversary of Carroll's or Tenniel's birth.

Other Options

More Curious Adventures How are you at storytelling? Read at least one other chapter from *Alice's Adventures in Wonderland* or *Through the Looking Glass* and **tell the story** for the rest of the class.

Act Out With a group, prepare a **reader's theater performance** of "A Mad Tea-Party." Reader's theater requires no costumes or props, and the actors work with scripts. Actors may stand or be seated, and they act with a minimum of physical movement. If you wish, use a narrator to read descriptions; for example, the first sentences of paragraphs 1 and 2 on pages 547–548.

A Mad Tea-Party **553**

WRITING CHOICES
Writer's Notebook Update
Students should describe the setting and use dialogue to move the action. They might try using puns in the Carroll style.

Riddle Me This
Additional Examples
Q. What happened to the farmer on *Wheel of Fortune?*

A. He found two ewes.

Q. What was the size of Aladdin's army?

A. *A Thousand and One Arabian Knights*

Alice's Illustrator

You might suggest to students that the necessary information is available in major encyclopedias.

Selection Test

Unit 6 Resource Book
pp. 23–24

OTHER OPTIONS
More Curious Adventures

You might suggest certain passages, e.g., the Queen of Hearts' croquet game.

Act Out

You might also encourage students to hold Readers Theater performances of some of the fantasy scenes written for Writer's Notebook Update.

Building Background

You might ask students if they have ever visited the sea shore. What effect did the motion and sound of the tides, the light, and the smells have on their feelings or mood?

Literary Focus

Possible Responses

- sailor: ship; adventure; ports of call
- fisherman: fish; a great catch; danger
- surfer: surf board; the beach; the "great wave"

Writer's Notebook

Encourage students to look for preoccupations and stylistic traits that these Victorian writers have in common.

More About Matthew Arnold

Arnold, a leading social critic of Victorian Britain, referred to the aristocracy as the "barbarians," to the commercial middle class as the "philistines," and to the rest as the "populace." Other important poems include

- "Sohrab and Rustum"
- "The Scholar Gypsy"
- "Thyrsis"

Dover Beach

by Matthew Arnold

Matthew Arnold
1822–1888

Matthew Arnold felt intensely the confusion of the modern world. "Everything is against one," he wrote in 1849. He tried to write poetry that would "not only . . . interest, but also . . . inspirit and rejoice the reader." His first volume, *The Strayed Reveller,* was published in 1849. To support himself and his family he worked as an inspector of private schools for poor children—an exhausting job, which required extensive travel—for thirty-five years. The job did permit Arnold direct involvement in some of the social problems of his day, however, and more and more he turned to writing prose. His range expanded from essays on literature to books on theology, education, and political issues.

Building Background

Channel Watch The town of Dover, sheltered by the towering chalk cliffs of the English south coast, lies within sight of France. For centuries it has served as a port for travelers bound across the English Channel for the continent. Arnold and his wife Fanny Lucy visited Dover twice in 1851: in June just after their wedding and in October on their way to a continental vacation. He almost certainly wrote "Dover Beach" during this period, and he clearly poured into this relatively short poem, which seems to be addressed to his wife, the ideas and feelings of the moment.

Literary Focus

Connotation/Denotation Connotation refers to the emotional associations surrounding a word, as opposed to the word's literal meaning, or **denotation.** A connotation may be personal, or it may have universal associations. The denotation of *sea,* for example, is "a great body of salt water." The connotations, however, may well depend on one's experience with the sea. Copy this chart and complete it with words and phrases you think each person might associate with the sea. Add other people to the chart if you can think of some. Look for the speaker's connotations of various key words in "Dover Beach," which help to enrich the meaning of the poem.

sea	
Denotation	**Connotations**
a great body of salt water	1. sailor
	2. fisherman
	3. surfer

Writer's Notebook

What is your impression of the Victorian era so far? Jot down a few comments based on your reading in this part.

SUPPORT MATERIALS OVERVIEW

Unit 6 Resource Book
- Graphic Organizer, p. 25
- Study Guide, p. 26
- Vocabulary, p. 27
- Grammar, p. 28
- Alternate Check Test, p. 29
- Vocabulary Test, p. 30
- Selection Test, pp. 31–32

Building English Proficiency
- Selection Summaries
- Activities, p. 238

Reading, Writing & Grammar SkillBook
- Writing, pp. 119–120, 121–122
- Grammar, Usage, and Mechanics, pp. 247–248

Technology
- Audiotape
- Personal Journal Software
- Custom Literature Database: Additional selections by Matthew Arnold can be found on the database.
- Test Generator Software

DOVER BEACH

MATTHEW ARNOLD

▲ *Fingall's Cave, Island of Staffa, Scotland* (Thomas Moran, 1884–5) captures conditions of weather and light. What elements give it an almost cinematic quality?

The sea is calm tonight,
The tide is full, the moon lies fair
Upon the straits; on the French coast the light
Gleams and is gone; the cliffs of England stand,
5 Glimmering and vast, out in the tranquil bay,
Come to the window, sweet is the night air!

Dover Beach   **555**

Selection Objectives

- to distinguish between the denotation and connotation of words
- to identify Arnold's focus on the confusion of the world of his time
- to apply standard usage to hyphenation

 Unit 6 Resource Book
Graphic Organizer, p. 25
Study Guide, p. 26

Theme Link

The poet's work integrates his struggle to understand himself and his times during a period of great change.

Vocabulary Preview

tremulous, quivering
cadence, rhythm
turbid, confused; disordered
drear, gloomy; sad; sorrowful
certitude, certainty; sureness
Students can add the words and definitions to their Writer's Notebooks.

 **Art Study**

Response to Caption Question   The rich colors, sense of motion, and intense atmosphere of drama and expectation create a cinematic quality.

SELECTION SUMMARY

Dover Beach

The narrator describes a calm, moonlit sea from the English coast at Dover. He calls a companion to the window to enjoy the view and calls attention to the sound of the waves and the movement of the tide. He remembers Sophocles listening to the same roar of the sea, and he, like Sophocles, hears in the ebb and flow sounds of human misery. The narrator then speaks of the Sea of Faith, once at so high a tide, but now ebbed into the dark of night. He pledges his fidelity and asks that his love do the same. While the world looks wonderfully new and beautiful, it is in fact a dark, confusing place filled with the ceaseless conflict of the ignorant and faithless.

 *For summaries in other languages, see the **Building English Proficiency** book.*

1 Literary Focus
Connotation/Denotation

Questions What does the word "sea" denote? *(The body of salt water that covers much of the earth's surface.)* Combed with "faith," what does "sea" connote? *(Possible response: something that compares with the ocean in its overwhelming scope or vastness)*

2 Literary Element
Theme

Question Keeping in mind the poet's use of connotative words and the previous stanza dealing with the ebb of Christian faith, what do you think the poem's final stanza suggests? *(Possible response: The poet pledges faithfulness and asks his love to do the same for they exist in a dark, joyless place, where much of humanity struggles and battles in ignorance and without faith.)*

Check Test

1. What are the two countries that are visible from Dover Beach? *(France and England)*

2. What sea did Sophocles know? *(the Aegean)*

3. What do the waves fling up on the beach? *(pebbles)*

4. Is Dover Beach in the northern or southern hemisphere? *(northern)*

5. What is the metaphoric "sea" to which the poem refers? *(Sea of Faith)*

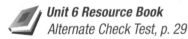
Unit 6 Resource Book
Alternate Check Test, p. 29

Only, from the long line of spray
Where the sea meets the moon-blanched land,
Listen! you hear the grating roar
10 Of pebbles which the waves draw back, and fling,
At their return, up the high strand,
Begin, and cease, and then again begin,
With <u>tremulous</u> <u>cadence</u> slow, and bring
The eternal note of sadness in.

15 <u>Sophocles</u> long ago
Heard it on the <u>Aegean</u>, and it brought
Into his mind the <u>turbid</u> ebb and flow
Of human misery; <u>we</u>
Find also in the sound a thought,
20 Hearing it by this distant northern sea.

1 The Sea of Faith
Was once, too, at the full, and round earth's shore
Lay like the folds of a bright <u>girdle</u> furled.
But now I only hear
25 Its melancholy, long, withdrawing roar,
Retreating, to the breath
Of the night wind, down the vast edges <u>drear</u>
And naked shingles of the world.

Ah, love, let us be true
30 To one another! for the world, which seems
To lie before us like a land of dreams,
So various, so beautiful, so new,
Hath really neither joy, nor love, nor light,
Nor <u>certitude</u>, nor peace, nor help for pain;
35 And we are here as on a darkling plain
Swept with confused alarms of struggle and flight,
2 Where ignorant armies clash by night.

13 tremulous (trem′yə ləs), *adj.* quivering.
13 cadence (kād′ns), *n.* rhythm.
15 Sophocles (sof′ə klēz′), a Greek dramatist (495?–406? B.C.)
16 Aegean (i jē′ən), a sea between Greece and Turkey.
17 turbid (tèr′bid), *adj.* confused; disordered.

23 girdle (gèr′dl), *n.* a garment that encircles, or girds, the body.

27 drear (drir), *adj.* gloomy; sad; sorrowful.
28 shingle, pebble beach.

34 certitude (sèr′tə tyūd), *n.* certainty; sureness.

MINI-LESSON: GRAMMAR
Using Hyphens

Teach A hyphen is a punctuation mark used between parts of a compound word *(tea-party, right-wing)* or name *(Jean-Bertrand Aristide)* or between the syllables of a word divided at the end of a line of text. The writer must know how to divide the word into syllables in order to properly place the hyphen.

Activity Idea Assign students the task of properly hyphenating the following words: tremulous *(trem-u-lous)*, cadence *(ca-dence)*, girdle *(gir-dle)*, certitude *(cer-ti-tude)*, melancholy *(mel-an-chol-y)*, ignorant *(ig-nor-ant)*, withdrawing *(with-draw-ing)*, various *(var-i-ous)*, beautiful *(beau-ti-ful)*

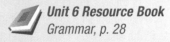
Unit 6 Resource Book
Grammar, p. 28

After Reading

Making Connections

Shaping Your Response

1. Do you think the speaker's solution (in lines 29–30) to life in a world that only *seems* beautiful and new is a good one?

Analyzing the Poem

2. Trace the way in which Arnold develops his **imagery** of the sea to lead finally to a philosophical conclusion.

3. Explain the ways in which both Sophocles and the modern speaker find **symbolism** in the ocean's roar. Does it mean the same to both or something different?

4. Summarize the speaker's vision of the human condition.

5. ✊ What major **change** has occurred in the speaker's world? How does he feel about it?

Extending the Ideas

6. Does Arnold's use of the word *ignorant* to describe armies seem appropriate in the 1900s? Why or why not?

Literary Focus: Connotation/Denotation

Connotation is the personal or emotional association surrounding a word, as opposed to a word's literal meaning or **denotation.**

1. What connotation does the "grating roar of pebbles" have for the speaker?

2. What does the "ebb and flow" of the tide connote in the third stanza?

3. Choose another word from the poem and explain its denotation and connotation.

Vocabulary Study

Write the letter of the situation that best demonstrates the meaning of the numbered word.

1. tremulous   **a.** a math teacher explaining an algebra problem
                    b. a small child explaining that she is lost
                    c. a coach explaining how to hold a golf club

2. cadence   **a.** a band marching briskly down the street
                    b. clouds drifting overhead
                    c. the flight of a butterfly

3. drear   **a.** an unexpected present
                 b. a dark, gloomy day
                 c. a get-well card from a friend

Dover Beach   **557**

After Reading

MAKING CONNECTIONS

1. Students' answers will vary, but may include their personal conclusions about whether the world really is, or only seems, beautiful and new.

2. Arnold first focuses on his view of the sea from a window, then shifts to a discussion of the Aegean and Sophocles's vision of human misery; he compares the vastness of the sea to a time of over-whelming human faith, a time that has now ebbed; he concludes by stating that the beauty they see from their window masks a dark and confusing place of ignorance and conflict.

3. Sophocles is reminded of the ebb and flow of human misery; Arnold hears an "eternal note of sadness" and the ebb of faith.

4. The speaker believes that the world lacks joy, love, light, certitude, peace, and help for pain, and that it is filled with con-fusion, struggle, ignorance, and conflict.

5. The religious faith of his world has diminished, resulting in a dark, dangerous place of conflict.

6. While responses will vary, students should note that the poet's use of *ignorant* connotes a state of "unenlightenment," rather than "illiteracy."

LITERARY FOCUS: CONNOTATIONS/ DENOTATION

1. the eternal note of sadness

2. eternal human misery

3. Possible response: "clash by night" from line 37—the inevitable conflict of an existence lived without faith

BUILDING ENGLISH PROFICIENCY

ESL
LEP
ELD
SAE
LD

Contrasting Images

Help students see that the contrasting images in Arnold's poem show two different ways of looking at a scene. Review the meaning of *image*—a phrase that appeals to the senses. Then ask students to complete the T-chart shown here.

"Happy" Images	"Sad" Images
calm sea	grating roar
fair moon	turbid ebb and flow
tranquil bay	naked shingles

📖 *Building English Proficiency*
Activities, p. 238

557

VOCABULARY STUDY

1. b
2. a
3. b
4. a
5. a

Unit 6 Resource Book
Vocabulary, p. 27
Vocabulary Test, p. 30

WRITING CHOICES
Writer's Notebook Update

Again, remind students to look for similarities among Victorian writers and to note significant differences in their attitudes toward their world.

Probing Symbolism

You might note to the class that religion was a much more significant and widely shared part of the culture and daily life of people in Arnold's time than it is for many people today.

Let Us Be True

In making this assignment, be clear about whether the letters will be read by the teacher, by the class, posted on a bulletin board, and so on.

Selection Test

Unit 6 Resource Book,
pp. 31–32

Transparency Collection
Fine Arts Writing Prompt p. 11

---

4. certitude
   a. the rising of the sun
   b. a phone call from your boyfriend or girlfriend
   c. rain on graduation day

5. turbid
   a. gate crashers at a rock concert
   b. actors on-stage taking a bow
   c. a person operating a construction crane

Expressing Your Ideas

Writing Choices

Writer's Notebook Update Look back at the impressions of the Victorian era that you wrote in your notebook. Have your impressions changed or grown after reading "Dover Beach"? If so, jot down some different or additional impressions.

Probing Symbolism The "Sea of Faith" (line 21) in Arnold's poem can have several meanings. In a **paragraph,** explain what you think it means to Arnold as expressed in this poem and what it means to you.

Let Us Be True Arnold apparently addressed "Dover Beach" to his new wife, Fanny Lucy. Write a **personal letter** to your love or to someone who means a great deal to you. In your letter describe a scene from nature or a scene from your everyday surroundings and then explain what that scene suggests to you about how you should live your life.

Other Options

The Way We Are The struggle to understand can affect anyone at any age, but it may show most strongly when people try to communicate across generations. Choose an aspect of teenage life, such as dating, hanging out, after school jobs, and so on. Write and illustrate a **picture book** appropriate for first-grade children about how teenagers behave and why, focusing on the aspect you have chosen. Share your book with some children.

Welcome to My World Arnold chose a beach at night as a point of departure for his thoughts about society and the world of his time. Which images would best express the world of your time? Prepare a **videotape** showing scenes from your school, your neighborhood, your community, or the surrounding countryside that you feel are typical examples of your world and that express the way you feel about it.

OTHER OPTIONS
The Way We Are

Students should keep in mind that the images they use should be sharp and clear and be consistent with the message that they wish to communicate. A picture book focusing on after-school jobs should contain pictures of teens serving hamburgers at a restaurant or bagging groceries. Photographs of the outside of a restaurant or of grocery-store customers would not effectively communicate the message.

Welcome to My World

Video shots should include action, not just "talking heads." However, action shots should express what is typical about the subject matter, not what is unusual or the atypical.

A Visit to THE GREAT EXHIBITION

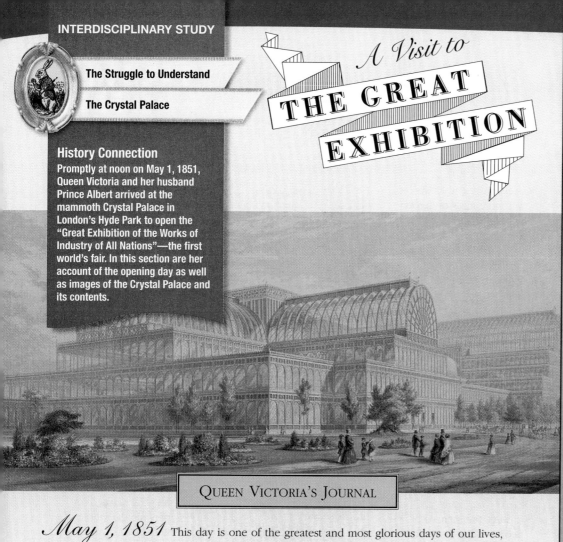

History Connection

Promptly at noon on May 1, 1851, Queen Victoria and her husband Prince Albert arrived at the mammoth Crystal Palace in London's Hyde Park to open the "Great Exhibition of the Works of Industry of All Nations"—the first world's fair. In this section are her account of the opening day as well as images of the Crystal Palace and its contents.

QUEEN VICTORIA'S JOURNAL

May 1, 1851 This day is one of the greatest and most glorious days of our lives, with which to my pride and joy, the name of my dearly beloved Alfred is for ever associated! It is a day which makes my heart swell with thankfulness. We began the day with tenderest greetings and congratulations on the birth of our dear little Arthur. He was brought in at breakfast and looked beautiful with blue ribbon on his frock. Mama and Victor were there, as well as all the children and our dear guests. Our little gifts of toys were added to by ones from the P[rin]ce and P[rin]cess [of Prussia].

The Park presented a wonderful spectacle, crowds streaming through it,—carriages and troops passing, quite like the Coronation, and for *me*, the same anxiety. The day was bright and all bustle and excitement. At 1/2 p. 11 the whole procession in 9 State carriages was set in motion. Vicky and Bertie were in our carriage (the other children and Vivi did not go).

Interdisciplinary Study **559**

Interdisciplinary Study

Theme Link

Queen Victoria's journal entry reflects the mood of confidence and faith in progress, exemplified by the Great Exhibition, which glorified the public's struggle to understand technology as well as the effect of Britain's imperialist expansion.

Curricular Connection: History

Use the information in this interdisciplinary study to explore not only the first world's fair, but more importantly, the intriguing perspective of Britain's longest-reigning monarch.

Terms to Know

highland, pertaining to the Highlands of Scotland, characterized by Gaelic culture.

transept, in a cross-shaped church or building, one of the two shorter arms of the cross.

prefabricated, manufactured in parts in advance of final construction.

mandarin (man′dər ən), an official of any of nine ranks under the Chinese empire.

obeisance (ō bā′sns, ō bē′sns), movement of the body expressing deep respect or reverence; deep bow or curtsy.

nave (nāv), the main room of a church.

howdah (hou′də), a seat, usually canopied, for riding on the back of an elephant.

 Unit 6 Resource Book
Interdisciplinary Study Guide, p. 33

BUILDING ENGLISH PROFICIENCY

Linking Past and Present

The headnote describes the Great Exhibition as "the first world's fair." Preface the reading by having students reflect upon similar exhibitions today.

Activity Ideas

• Some students have attended or participated in school or community multicultural festivals. Invite them to comment upon what they saw and learned there.

• If any students have visited Epcot Center in Florida, have them talk about the exhibitions. Ask: What were the most interesting things that you saw? What did you learn about at least one culture that was different from your own?

• Ask: Suppose that a TV documentary today attempted to show both the "typical" and the "best" of every country in the world. What would you expect to see? Have groups of students create and share a list of ten such items and the country that each item would represent.

Art Study

The Crystal Palace, designed by Sir Joseph Paxton, was built like a cathedral, with a high central hall flanked by two symmetrical wings. Since it consisted of prefabricated elements with bolted connections, workers were able to disassemble and rebuild it after the exhibition. The Crystal Palace was the first great iron-framed, glass-walled building, and an early achievement in large-scale prefabrication. It clearly served as a precursor to the glass-walled skyscrapers of the contemporary urban landscape.

Question How do the architecture, the name of the building, and the elaborate decoration inside the Crystal palace symbolize the mood of England in the middle of the nineteenth century? *(Possible response: These elements symbolize the extravagant wealth, the importance of the monarchy and the empire, the influence of the Christian religion in the English culture, and the optimism of the time.)*

*V*icky was dressed in lace over white satin, with small wreath of pink wild roses in her hair, and looked very nice. Bertie was in full Highland dress. The Green Park and Hyde Park were one mass of densely crowded human beings, in the highest good humor and most enthusiastic. I never saw Hyde Park look as it did, being filled with crowds as far as the eye could reach. A little rain fell, just as we started, but before we neared the Crystal Palace, the sun shone and gleamed upon the gigantic edifice, upon which the flags of every nation were flying. We drove up Rotten Row and got out of our carriages at the entrance on that side. The glimpse, through the iron gates of the Transept, the waving palms and flowers, the myriads of people filling the galleries and seats around, together with the flourish of trumpets as we entered the building, gave a sensation I shall never forget, and I felt much moved. We went for a moment into a little room where we left our cloaks and found Mama and Mary. Outside, all the princes were standing. In a few seconds we proceeded, Albert leading me, having Vicky at his hand and Bertie holding mine. The sight as we came to the

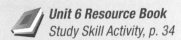
(PRECEEDING PAGE) LONDONERS WERE AS FASCINATED BY THE BUILDING THAT HOUSED THE GREAT EXHIBITION AS BY ITS CONTENTS. THE CRYSTAL PALACE WAS COMPOSED OF A PREFABRICATED WOOD AND IRON FRAMEWORK CONTAINING NEARLY A MILLION SQUARE FEET OF GLASS. MANY VISITORS FELT THEY WERE GETTING A GLIMPSE OF A FUTURE IN WHICH EVERYONE WOULD BE HOUSED UNDER GLASS.

LIVING TREES AND A 27-FOOT CUT-GLASS FOUNTAIN DECORATED THE ENTRANCE TO THE CRYSTAL PALACE.

center where the steps and chair (on which I did *not* sit) was placed, facing the beautiful crystal fountain was magic and impressive. The tremendous cheering, the joy expressed in every face, the vastness of the building, with all its decoration and exhibits, the sound of the organ (with 200 instruments and 600 voices, which seemed nothing) and my beloved husband, the creator of this peace festival "uniting the industry and art of all nations of the earth," all this was indeed moving, and a day to live forever. God bless my dearest Albert, and my dear country, which has shown itself so great to-day. One felt so grateful to the great God, whose blessing seemed to pervade the whole undertaking. After the National Anthem had been sung, Albert left my side and at the head of the Commissioners,—a curious assemblage of political and distinguished men—read the report to me, which is a long one, and I read a short answer. After this the Archbishop of Canterbury offered up a short and appropriate prayer, followed by the singing of Handel's "Hallelujah Chorus," during which time the Chinese Mandarin came forward and made his

MINI-LESSON: STUDY SKILLS

Use Primary and Secondary Sources

Teach Explain that Queen Victoria's journals are considered primary sources, as are her letters, the letters of her close associates and children, and the transcriptions of her speeches. Primary sources such as letters and journals offer a direct and often surprising perspective on the thoughts and experiences of historical figures. Secondary sources include the chronicles of Victoria's contemporaries, historical criticism, and biographical sources.

Apply Have students research the opening of the Great Exhibition using secondary sources such as encyclopedia articles, history books, and old newspaper articles. Compare the focus of these sources to the focus that is presented by Victoria's journal—her children, her husband, the pomp and circumstance, and the love of the English people.

Activity Idea Suggest that students research Queen Victoria's letters and journals and conduct further comparative analysis.

Unit 6 Resource Book
Study Skill Activity, p. 34

obeisance. This concluded, the Procession of great length began, which was beautifully arranged, the prescribed order being exactly adhered to. The Nave was full of people, which had not been intended, and deafening cheers and waving of handkerchiefs continued the whole time of our long walk from one end of the long building to the other. Every face was bright and smiling, and many had tears in their eyes. Many Frenchmen called out "Vive la Reine." One could, of course, see nothing but what was high up in the Nave, and nothing in the Courts. The organs were but little heard, but the Military Band at one end had a very fine effect, playing the march from *Athalie* as we passed along. The old Duke of Wellington and L[or]d. Anglesey walked arm in arm, which was a touching sight. I saw many acquaintances amongst those present. We returned to our place and Albert told L[or]d. Breadalbane to declare the Exhibition to be opened, which he did in a loud voice saying "Her Majesty commands me to declare this Exhibition open," when there was a flourish of trumpets, followed by immense cheering. We then made our bow and left.

THIS VIEW OF THE MAIN AVENUE OF THE CRYSTAL PALACE SHOWS HOW THE EXHIBITS WERE ORGANIZED.

Interdisciplinary Study   **561**

Historical Note

The mood and political stance of Queen Victoria and her court changed greatly when she married her first cousin, Prince Albert of Saxe-Coburg, in 1840. Although the name "Victorian" has come to represent prudishness, it was actually Albert who was concerned with maintaining strait-laced behavior, and he introduced a strict decorum in court. He also influenced Victoria to become more politically conservative.

Victoria's influence extended beyond her role as monarch of the British Empire. She was the mother of nine children, and many of her descendants eventually ended up on the thrones of Europe.

BUILDING ENGLISH PROFICIENCY

Exploring Key Thoughts

Teach   Queen Victoria's thoughts about the Great Exhibition wander from one topic to the next rather freely, as most people's thoughts do when they keep journals. As readers of someone else's journal, we sometimes have to sort through these thoughts and organize them ourselves.

Activity Idea   To help your students sort through the variety of information, suggest that they make an outline as if they were going to prepare the information for a more formal presentation than a journal entry. Students could use any of the following headings:

- information about her family
- descriptions of the Great Exhibit
- descriptions of the ceremonies
- reflections about the significance of the exhibit
- thoughts about her husband

Interdisciplinary Activity Ideas

- Have students create the Great Exhibition that might have occurred if the roles were reversed and India or another country ruled England. How would the exhibit hall be designed? What treasures from England would be displayed?
- Students could diagram Victoria and Albert's family tree, tracing the family's influence throughout Europe.
- Students could present a display of the houses of Queen Victoria. They could include floor plans, photographs of the interiors, and anecdotes associated with each home.

Responding

1. Possible Response She seems innocent and good-hearted, religious, devoted to her husband, and grateful for the gifts that accompany her position in life. Students may find her to have these qualities to a fault, to the extent that she doesn't seem aware of much beyond the ceremony of the occasion. For example, she is not too concerned that she really doesn't get to see any of the exhibit at the opening, and she doesn't recognize that the exhibit represents the destruction of some cultures.

2. Possible Response Answers will vary but should reflect an ability to make judgments based on the contents of the photographs.

3. Possible Response The exhibit might also have served to encourage international trade, to generate revenue, to educate the public, and to demonstrate national pride.

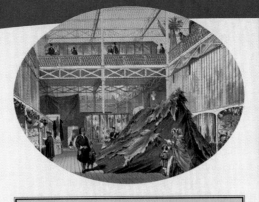

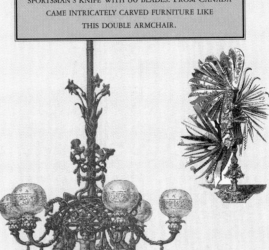

(BELOW) AMONG THE EXHIBITS OF BRITISH WORKMAN-SHIP WERE AN ELABORATE GAS CHANDELIER AND A SPORTSMAN'S KNIFE WITH 80 BLADES. FROM CANADA CAME INTRICATELY CARVED FURNITURE LIKE THIS DOUBLE ARMCHAIR.

(LEFT) A NOMAD'S TENT DRAPED WITH LION SKINS WAS SURROUNDED BY A TUNISIAN BAZAAR. ALTHOUGH THE EXOTIC GOODS DISPLAYED THERE WERE NOT SUPPOSED TO BE SOLD, VISITORS OFTEN BOUGHT THEM ILLEGALLY.

(ABOVE) AFTER THE GREAT EXHIBITION CLOSED IN 1852, THE CRYSTAL PALACE AND ITS CONTENTS WERE MOVED TO A PARK AT SYDENHAM IN SOUTHEAST LONDON (WHERE IT REMAINED UNTIL DESTROYED BY A FIRE IN 1936). AMONG THE EXHIBITS ON ITS GROUNDS WERE THE FIRST MODELS OF DINOSAURS.

Responding

1. What kind of person does Victoria's account of her visit to the Great Exhibition reveal her to be?

2. Which of these exhibits do you think you would have most enjoyed visiting?

3. The official goal of the Great Exhibition was to promote industry and world peace. What other purposes would such an event serve?

MINI-LESSON: STUDY SKILLS

Using an Almanac

Teach The Great Exhibition was an opportunity for countries from all over the world to present a small sample of their culture: religious artifacts, arts and crafts, cultural achievements, animal life, and more. If you wanted to find out the main characteristics of a culture without attending a world's fair you might consult an almanac.

Apply Explain that there are various kinds of almanacs, for example, an astronomical almanac, *The Farmer's Almanac, The World Almanac,* the *African-American Almanac, The Facts on File World Almanac,* and *The World Almanac Book of Inventions.*

Question Which of the above almanacs might tell you about a foreign country? *(Possible response: Facts on File, World Almanac)*

Activity Idea Assign a country to each student and have them plan an exhibition booth, using almanacs to provide them with facts and statistics about their country. Encourage students to use photographs, models, drawings, and diagrams to illustrate the design of their booth.

THE GREAT EXHIBITION

A STUFFED INDIAN ELEPHANT WAS BORROWED FROM A MUSEUM TO DISPLAY AN ELABORATE GOLD AND SILVER HOWDAH WITH A FRINGED AWNING.

Research Topics

- British reformer Henry Cole and his connection to the Great Exhibition of 1851
- Sir Joseph Paxton and the team of architects that designed the Crystal Palace
- The life and work of Prince Albert, Prince Consort of England
- The conditions in the colonies that were represented at the Great Exhibition

Historical Note

The elephant pictured on page 563 represents the British rule of India. The colonizing of India, as well as other countries around the world, allowed some British people to move up in society. Officers in the British army had to pay for their commissions. An officer was also expected to maintain his good standing among other officers by entertaining. Consequently, they were usually from wealthy families—often the younger sons who would not inherit family property. India, however, was a less expensive place to live and entertain, so middle-class men could afford to purchase commissions in the army.

BUILDING ENGLISH PROFICIENCY

Responding to Visual Cues

A variety of sights greeted visitors to the Great Exhibition. Invite students to focus on the sights depicted here.

1. Give students a few minutes to work in their reading journals, jotting down notes about the items displayed and their reactions to them.

2. Tell students to imagine themselves as tour guides for the Great Exhibition. Divide them into six groups and assign each group one of the pictures. Have them write a description of the item pictured as if they were talking about it to a group of visitors.

3. Have group representatives read aloud the descriptions, following an order that parallels the sequence of pictures on these pages as if they were following the progress of a tour group through the exhibits.

Writing Workshop

WRITER'S BLUEPRINT
Specs

The Specs in the Writer's Blueprint address these writing and thinking skills:

- orienting the reader
- characterization
- setting
- drawing conclusions
- comparing and contrasting
- supporting a position
- using quotations
- making judgments
- avoiding run-on sentences

These Specs serve as your lesson objectives, and they form the basis for the **Assessment Criteria Specs** for a superior paper, which appear on the final TE page for this lesson. You might want to read through the Assessment Criteria Specs with students when you begin the lesson.

Linking Literature to Writing

Even though these two poems were written by the same author, students could generate a list of differences in style and substance between the two, since they focus on two very different characters. Focusing on these differences should help students get started analyzing the characters.

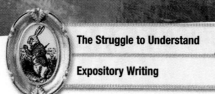

The Struggle to Understand

Expository Writing

Writing Workshop

What's Your Attitude?

Assignment In Tennyson's "The Lady of Shalott" and "Ulysses," the title characters live in two very different worlds—one of magic, one of legend; and they live their lives in very different ways. Compare and contrast what their actions and words tell you of their attitudes toward how life ought to be lived, and decide which comes closer to your own attitude.

WRITER'S BLUEPRINT

Product	A comparison/contrast essay
Purpose	To explore attitudes about how to live
Audience	People who are not familiar with the literature
Specs	As the writer of a successful essay, you should:

❏ Begin by introducing your readers to the two characters and the settings for the poems. Give your readers enough background to enable them to follow your train of thought.

❏ Go on to discuss what both characters' actions and words tell you about their attitudes on how to live life. Are the characters outgoing and adventurous, or repressed and cautious?

❏ Include a discussion of how the unique worlds the characters inhabit influence those attitudes. Do they feel comfortable in their worlds? Are they free to reach out and meet new challenges?

❏ Present your conclusions in a clear compare-and-contrast format. Use specific details and quotes from the poems to support your conclusions.

❏ End by explaining which character's attitude comes closer to your own attitude about how to live life, and why.

❏ Follow the rules of grammar, usage, spelling, and mechanics. Avoid run-on sentences.

WRITING WORKSHOP OVERVIEW

Product
Expository writing: A comparison/contrast essay

Prewriting
Revisit the poems—Try a quickwrite—Discuss your ideas—Make a writing plan
Unit 6 Resource Book
Prewriting Worksheets pp. 35–36

Drafting
As you draft
Transparency Collection
Student Models for Writing Workshop 21, 22

Revising
Ask a partner—Strategy: Guiding the Reader
Unit 6 Resource Book
Revising Worksheet p. 37

Editing
Ask a partner—Strategy: Avoiding Run-on Sentences
Unit 6 Resource Book
Grammar Worksheet p. 38
Grammar Check Test p. 39

Presenting
Read Aloud
Perform
Save

Looking Back
Self-evaluate—Reflect—For Your Working Portfolio
Unit 6 Resource Book
Assessment Worksheet p. 40
Transparency Collection
Fine Art Writing Prompt 11

STEP 1 PREWRITING

Revisit the poems. Study each character and the world he or she inhabits. What can you find out about the characters' attitudes toward living life? Make notes in a chart like the one shown.

Ulysses

Things Character Does and Says	What This Reveals About the Character's Attitude	Setting: What His World Is Like	How This Might Influence the Character's Attitude
"I cannot rest from travel"		islands, stormy seas	

LITERARY SOURCE
"I cannot rest from travel: I will drink
Life to the lees: all times I have enjoyed
Greatly, have suffered greatly, both with those
That loved me, and alone; on shore, and when
Through scudding drifts the rainy Hyades
Vexed the dim sea: . . . ."
from "Ulysses" by Alfred, Lord Tennyson

Try a quickwrite. Based on your charts, imagine the kind of advice Ulysses and the Lady of Shalott would offer students today about how to live life. Quickwrite two brief monologues in which each character gives advice. Use modern American speech if you wish.

Discuss your ideas. With a partner, discuss the characters' views on how life should be lived. Which character's viewpoint comes closer to your own? Jot down some notes about your discussion to use when you make your writing plan.

Make a writing plan. Use an outline like this one.

- **Introduction** (Introduce characters and settings)
  First character and setting
  Second character and setting
- **Body** (Compare and contrast attitudes of characters and influence of settings, including details and quotes from the poems)
  First character
  —words and actions
  —influence of setting
  Second character
  —words and actions
  —influence of setting
- **Conclusion** (Compare and contrast attitudes)
  Similarities
  Differences
  Which attitude is closer to mine and why

OR . . .
Work with a partner to improvise a dialogue between the two characters in which they argue about how one should approach life. Tape-record your dialogue.

OR . . .
Do a point-by-point comparison of the subjects and their attitudes about how life should be lived.

Writing Workshop **565**

STEP 1 PREWRITING
Revisit the poems

Ask students to discuss gender in relation to the author's treatment of the two title characters in these poems. For additional support, see the feature at the bottom of page 565 and the worksheets referenced below.

Unit 6 Resource Book
Prewriting Worksheet, p. 35
Prewriting Worksheet, p. 36

Try a quickwrite

Remind students to think and write as the characters. Students should not be concerned with writing complete sentences, but work to get the character's thoughts down on paper.

Discuss your ideas

Have students pair up with someone who holds opinions different from their own. Remind students to take notes as they discuss different ideas.

Make a writing plan

Discuss with students the strengths and weaknesses of writing a comparison-and-contrast essay point by point as opposed to dealing with all of one position and then all of the opposite position. For additional support, see the mini-lesson at the bottom of page 566.

Connections to
Writer's Notebook
For selection-related prompts, refer to Writer's Notebook.

Connections to
Writer's Resource
For additional writing prompts, refer to Writer's Resource.

BUILDING ENGLISH PROFICIENCY

Exploring Setting

Help students understand that the setting is composed not only of surroundings (seas, a tower), but of the culture and beliefs that exist in those surroundings. Ask students to create a collage to explore the setting.

1. Have students draw or write the name of the character in the middle of their paper.

2. Ask them to draw or describe the physical surroundings around the character.

3. Have students add other details about the character's world (such as Ulysses' duty) that might influence his or her behavior or views.

4. Ask students to circle the details that they think would support their ideas best.

STEP 2 DRAFTING
As you draft

Remind students that they should take on a persuasive tone as they write. For students who plan on following the first drafting tip, suggest they first visualize the characters and make rough sketches of them.

The Student Models

The **transparencies** referenced below are authentic student models. Review them with the students before they draft. These questions will help:

1. How does the writer of model 21 use compare-and-contrast signal words to guide the reader?

2. How does the writer of model 22 explain his own attitude about how to live life in relation to the characters' attitudes?

3. Which model do you think does a better job of explaining how the worlds the characters live in influence them?

Transparency Collection
Student Models for Writing Workshop 21, 22

STEP 3 REVISING
Ask a partner
(Peer assessment)

Have students take notes of their peer's most effective arguments in order to ensure constructive feedback.

Revising Strategy: Guiding the Reader

Before students read the Revising Strategy, ask them to list ways in which they believe a good writer guides readers.

For additional support, see the mini-lesson at the bottom of this page and the worksheet referenced below.

Unit 6 Resource Book
Revising Worksheet, p. 37

Connections to
Writer's Resource

Refer to the Grammar, Usage, and Mechanics Handbook on Writer's Resource.

As you draft, remember that your primary objective is to show the similarities and differences between the characters' attitudes. The following tips may help you get started:

- Begin your essay with a dramatic firsthand description of the two characters in their worlds, as if you, the writer, were there watching them. You might even imagine the two characters side by side in their settings, like a split-screen shot in a movie, and move back and forth between the two characters as you introduce them.

- Use ideas from the monologue or dialogue material you created in "Try a quickwrite" when you write your conclusion.

STEP **3** REVISING

Ask a partner for comments on your draft before you revise it.

✔ Have I given readers unfamiliar with the poems enough information to be able to follow my train of thought?

✔ Have I used specific details and quotes from the poems to support my conclusions?

✔ Do I state comparisons and contrasts clearly?

Revising Strategy

Guiding the Reader

Words or phrases that set up compare-and-contrast statements act as signals, guiding the reader through the argument. Consider using some of these signal words and phrases as you revise.

To signal similarities: similarly, in much the same way, just as, like, alike, likewise, same, along the same lines, by comparison

To signal differences: however, as opposed to, in contrast, inversely, but, instead of, on the other hand, unlike, while, by contrast

Notice how comparison-contrast signals were added to the student model that follows.

MINI-LESSON: WRITING STYLE
Guiding the Reader

Teach   Review with students the words and phrases from the lesson that signal similarities and differences. Encourage students to add to the list.

Activity Idea   Put a chart on the board that shows the two methods of organizing a comparison-and-contrast essay. Then ask students to put in transitional words or phrases to guide a reader through each method of organization.

Apply   Have students look at their drafts according to the organizational method they used and put in necessary transitional words and phrases to guide the reader from from point to point.

In contrast to the Lady of Shalott,   *,not by walls.*
My view on life is like Ulysses'. He is held in by a duty.

He does not give into his restrictions, though. He takes steps to break

free of his duty by giving the kingdom to his son.

STUDENT MODEL

STEP 4 EDITING

Ask a partner to review your revised draft before you edit. When you edit, look for mistakes in grammar, usage, spelling, and mechanics. Look closely for errors with run-on sentences.

Editing Strategy

Avoiding Run-on Sentences

Proofread your essay for any run-on sentences. Run-on sentences are two or more independent clauses strung together with little or no punctuation. If the clauses are loosely related, separate them into different sentences:

Run-on Ulysses is an adventurous man Ithaca is his true home, the place he loves more than all the others.

Corrected Ulysses is an adventurous man. Ithaca is his true home, the place he loves more than all the others.

If the clauses are closely related, join them with a comma and coordinating conjunction:

Run-on Everything for which she had lived before—her weaving, her mirror—was gone she could have begun anew.

Corrected Everything for which she had lived before—her weaving, her mirror—was gone, but she could have begun anew.

> **FOR REFERENCE**
> You'll find more guidelines for avoiding run-on sentences in the Language and Grammar Handbook in the back of this book.

STEP 4 EDITING
Ask a partner
(Peer assessment)

Have students note and discuss any patterns of error that their partners seem to be having trouble with.

Editing Strategy: Avoiding Run-on Sentences

Have volunteers read aloud a passage from a newspaper or magazine article without stopping to pause for periods, thereby running the sentences together. This should serve as a good demonstration of the confusion run-ons can cause.

For additional support, see the mini-lesson at the bottom of this page and the worksheets referenced below.

Unit 6 Resource Book
Grammar Worksheet, p. 38
Grammar Check Test, p. 39

Connections to
Writer's Resource

Refer to the Grammar, Usage, and Mechanics Handbook on Writer's Resource.

MINI-LESSON: GRAMMAR

Avoiding Run-on Sentences

One way to correct run-ons is to use a semicolon to connect two independent clauses into one sentence. Have students correct the following run-ons with the use of semicolons.

Example:

Many liberals would disagree, they think the senator is doing a fine job.

Many liberals would disagree; they think the senator is doing a fine job.

• Waist tackling is legal, "clotheslining" is a foul.

• She was a tough legal opponent, her wit was as sharp as her mind.

• A politician makes promises about what he will get done if elected, a leader gets things done.

Have volunteers create other sentences in which two closely related clauses could be connected by a semicolon.

Unit 6 Resource Book
Grammar Worksheet, p. 38
Grammar Check Test, p. 39

STEP 5 PRESENTING
Read Aloud

After students present and discuss their essays, ask them if this assignment has had any effect on their thoughts on representations of gender in literature. Have males tended to react in different ways from females in the class? If so, why do students think this has happened?

Perform

You might pick the best performances and videotape or audiotape them for use in future years.

Save

If students have a reflective piece they wrote in middle school, encourage them to bring it to compare to this essay.

STEP 6 LOOKING BACK
Self-evaluate

The *Assessment Criteria Specs* at the bottom of this page are for a superior paper. You might want to post these in the classroom. Students can then evaluate themselves based on these criteria. For a complete scoring rubric, use the *Assessment Worksheet* referenced below.

Unit 6 Resource Book
Assessment Worksheet, p. 40

Reflect

This assignment could lead very easily into a composition in which students explore more fully their own attitudes on living life.

To further explore the theme, use the Fine Art Transparency referenced below.

Transparency Collection
Fine Art Writing Prompt 11

 **STEP 5 PRESENTING**

Consider these ideas for presenting your essay:

- Read each other's essays in a small groups. Then pick the essay that most closely matches your attitude and explain why.

- Work with a group of classmates to write and perform monologues and dialogues based on your essays.

- Save this essay. Years from now you can look back to see how your attitudes about living life have developed over time.

 **STEP 6 LOOKING BACK**

Self-evaluate. What grade would *you* give your paper? Look back at the Writer's Blueprint and give your paper a score for each separate item, from 6 (superior) to 1 (inadequate).

Reflect. Think about what you have learned from doing this comparison/contrast essay as you write answers to these questions.

✔ What thoughts prompted by this assignment will help you plan the next few years of your life?

✔ Based on comments from peers and your own assessment, which do you think was your greatest area of strength in this paper: being clear, being insightful, or being technically correct? Which area were you weakest in? How could you improve in your next paper?

For Your Working Portfolio Add your essay and your reflection responses to your working portfolio.

ASSESSMENT CRITERIA SPECS

Here are the criteria for a superior paper. A full six-level rubric for this paper appears on the *Assessment Worksheet* referenced below.

6 Superior The writer of a 6 paper impressively meets these criteria:

- Provides an introduction that successfully orients the reader unfamiliar with the poems and vividly identifies the characters and settings.

- Describes each character's attitude by citing specific actions and words that exemplify it.

- Insightfully explains the influence of the worlds the characters inhabit, using specific examples and quotations where appropriate.

- Uses a clear comparison-and-contrast format to present these attitudes.

- Closes by comparing and contrasting the writer's own attitude toward living life with those of the characters.

- Has few, if any, errors in the conventions of standard written English. Avoids run-on sentences.

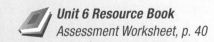 **Unit 6 Resource Book**
Assessment Worksheet, p. 40

Beyond Print

Multimedia Presentations

Step up to the Information Age: an age in which you can use modern technology—computers, VCRs, CD-ROMs, and programs such as HyperCard—to energize traditional speeches and transform them into exciting media events. Whenever you use a combination of media to communicate to an audience, you are making a multimedia presentation. This includes speeches, posters, slides, video, projected images, graphs, computers, recordings, or even skits.

The computer is a powerful tool in producing any multimedia presentation. You can hook up the computer to a projection unit in order to use the program during an oral presentation and provide animation, special effects, sound, and video. You might engage your audience with an interactive program in which viewers manipulate the type and order of information they receive by clicking a button.

Since each piece of media you add makes the presentation more complex, be thoughtful and organized in preparing your materials. Save only the most important information for posters or computer screens. Make sure the type size is legible for your audience. Avoid materials that are cluttered or confusing.

Here are some hints for using multimedia in oral presentations.

- Use pictures and music that will supplement the information, not distract the audience.
- Use large type (for readability) and important heads (for emphasis) in projections. Present additional details orally or in handouts.
- Apply your writing skills to ensure concise, clear, and correctly spelled text.
- Plan, organize, and practice presenting your material.
- Project your voice so that everyone can hear.

Activity Option

Prepare a multimedia presentation based on a selection, an author, or a theme related to the selections in this part. Prepare a speech; then add a simple graphic, such as a poster, graph, transparency, or computer image, along with music or special sound effects.

Beyond Print   **569**

Historical Overview

EXPLORING CONCEPTS

- The turn of the century in England was a time of political turmoil, as many citizens reconsidered the value of imperialism.
- The socialist movement gained a foothold among the dissatisfied and under-appreciated working classes.
- Artists and writers focused on the dark side of industrial and scientific progress.
- The suffragette movement symbolized the growing demand for equal rights in Britain's outdated political structure.

Art Study

Walter Crane (1845–1915) was a prominent English painter, designer, and illustrator, who was connected with the British arts and crafts movement, a reaction to the decline in craftsmanship caused by cheap mass-production technologies. Crane dedicated his 1895 work *A Garland for May Day* (p. 571) to the workers in Great Britain. The nymph-like figure set against a decorative frame reflects the style of art nouveau (new art), a movement which sought to break away from traditional styles in art.

Question How does Crane's drawing embody his socialist beliefs? *(Possible response: The use of the female figure holding up a vine interlaced with socialist slogans may be celebrating the life of the working people. By making written texts a part of the art, Crane may be demonstrating the power of art to influence and to teach people.)*

Research Activity

Students may want to conduct further research into the arts and crafts movement, William Morris, art nouveau, and Aubrey Beardsley.

The Victorians

Hope and Despair

HISTORICAL OVERVIEW

By 1880 opinion was strongly divided between imperialists, who advocated expanding the British empire, and those who saw this as dangerous. There was also conflict over England's domestic politics. The British working class was still overworked, underpaid, poorly fed, clothed, housed, and educated. Radical intellectuals such Bernard Shaw saw socialism as a cure for these ills. At the same time, British suffragettes were waging a campaign to gain women the vote. English culture expressed a less confident outlook than it had at the height of the Victorian era. Thomas Hardy's pessimistic rural novels and H. G. Wells's scientific fantasies disturbed many readers. There were also disturbing trends in the visual arts, such as impressionism, with its experimental approach to rendering the effects of light.

In his painting *The Old Bedford* (1897–98), British painter Walter Sickert depicts an audience at a music-hall. Both his subject matter and technique show the influence of French Impressionism.

The most prominent British imperialist of the 1880s and '90s was Cecil Rhodes (1853–1902), shown in this cartoon bestriding the continent of Africa, where he had made a fortune in the diamond mines.

The most famous literary periodical of the 1890s was *The Yellow Book*, which was notorious for the decadent art and literature that appeared in it.

Mrs. Emmeline Pankhurst (1858–1928), leader of the British women's suffrage movement, appears third from the left in this photograph of a rally during an election campaign in 1907.

THE END OF AN ERA

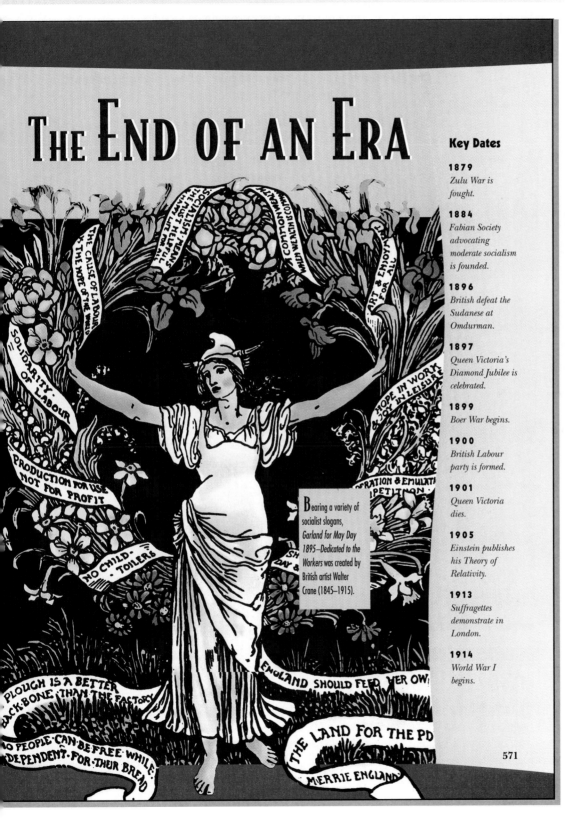

Bearing a variety of socialist slogans, *Garland for May Day 1895–Dedicated to the Workers* was created by British artist Walter Crane (1845–1915).

MATERIALS OF INTEREST
Books

- *Pax Britannica: The Climax of an Empire* by James Morris (Harvest Books, 1980)
- *Dreadnought: Britain, Germany, and the Coming of the Great War* by Robert K. Massie (Ballantine, 1992)
- *The Intelligent Woman's Guide to Socialism and Capitalism*, by Bernard Shaw (Transaction Books, 1984)

Multimedia

- *The Landscape of Pleasure—The Shock of the New: Episode 3* (Time-Life, 1980)
- *Sylvia Pankhurst—Shoulder to Shoulder: Episode 6;* Masterpiece Theater (PBS Video, 1988)
- *Breaker Morant,* court martial during the Boer War (International Video Entertainment, 1979)

Connections to
Custom Literature Database

For further historical background, under **Background Articles,** see **Late Victorian and Edwardian England 1830–1880.**

FOR ALL STUDENTS

Ask students to create collages that show how the following quotation demonstrates the state of the British Empire:

> There is no certainty that a woman will lose her son if he goes to the front; in fact, coal mines and the shunting yard are more dangerous places than the camp." Bernard Shaw, 1902

To further explore the theme, use the transparency referenced below.

Transparency Collection
Fine Art Writing Prompt 12

For At-Risk Students

Have students make a map of the British Empire. Students can research literature that represents the British presence in different countries and add titles or quotations to the map.

For Students Who Need Challenge

Students can analyze the portrayal of the characters that appear in both *Jane Eyre* and *Wide Sargasso Sea*.

✋ MULTICULTURAL CONNECTION

Use the quotation from Finlay Peter Dunne's *Mr Dooley's Philosophy* (1910) to discuss the meaning of western civilization.

> Whin ye get among th' Chinee . . . says (the emperor of Germany) 'raymimber that ye ar-re the van gaurd iv Christyanity'. . . an' stick ye'er baynet through ivry hateful infidel you see. . . .Lave him understand what our westhern civilization means . . . An if by chance ye shud pick up a little land be th'way, don't lave e'er a Frinchman or Rooshan take it from ye.'

Part Two

Hope and Despair

Some Victorians hoped that every problem had a solution; others despaired that their religious or cultural beliefs might not be valid after all.

✋ Multicultural Connection Culture has a great influence on the **perspective** that a person brings to viewing the basic and universal aspects of life.

IDEAS THAT WORK

Motivating with Word Studies

Although my students are unaware, I make the concepts in the "Prayer of St. Francis of Assisi" the focal point of this unit. We discuss how authors use the technique of posing opposites in order to illustrate the complexities of life. I have my students write definitions of *hatred* and *love; injury* and *pardon; doubt* and *faith; despair* and *hope; darkness* and *light;* and *sadness* and *joy.* As we read the selections from this part, my students look for symbols and ideas which represent these abstractions. Encouraging students to relate these concepts to their lives gives us fuel for long discussions and good essays. What fun! What discussions! What essays! What education! What better way of learning that all literature is about the loss of innocence, and that the literary experience can help assuage the guilt of experience.

Peter R. Sebastian
El Cajon, California

Before Reading

The Darkling Thrush
The Man He Killed
"Ah, Are You Digging on My Grave?" by Thomas Hardy

Thomas Hardy
1840–1928

After beginning a career in church architecture, Thomas Hardy tried writing poetry. When he could not get his poems published, he switched to the more profitable writing of fiction. After his first major success, *Far From the Madding Crowd* (1874), came *The Return of the Native* (1878), *The Mayor of Casterbridge* (1885), and *Tess of the D'Urbervilles* (1891) — all about the farmers and working-class people of his boyhood area, the Dorset countryside. Often criticized for rejecting middle-class moral values, Hardy nonetheless gained popularity. However, in 1895 *Jude the Obscure* was attacked so harshly that Hardy decided to give up writing novels and return to poetry. In 1898, at age 58, he published his first volume of poetry. Over the next 29 years Hardy completed over 900 lyrics.

Building Background

"A Poet's Power to Feel . . ." Poet and critic Mark Van Doren explains the special essence of Hardy's poetry: "A poet's power to feel is best proved in the stories he tells, provided he can tell stories. Hardy could; that was where his genius lay . . . Hardy's stories are little melodramas, sensational, unrelenting, and if need be mournful beyond bearing, as the great ballads are." Doubtless it was Hardy's many years of melodramatic storytelling in his novels that influenced the stories of his poetry. In both novels and poetry Hardy was able to take the small, almost insignificant, events of ordinary daily life, infuse them with details and emotion, and thereby relate them not only to the individual experience but to the whole of human experience.

Literary Focus

Assonance The repetition of similar vowel sounds followed by different consonant sounds in stressed words or syllables is called **assonance.** It is often used instead of rhyme. *Hate / great* is an example of rhyme; *hate / grade* is an example of assonance. In ". . . that hoard, and sleep, and feed, and know not me," from Tennyson's "Ulysses," the words *sleep, feed,* and *me* are assonant. As you read Hardy's poems, look for examples of assonance.

Writer's Notebook

War Words When you think of war, what descriptive words come to your mind? Jot down a list of five to ten words and phrases to describe war.

The Darkling Thrush **573**

Before Reading

Building Background

Ask students to recall poems they have read, either from the text or outside of class, that tell stories. You might begin by mentioning Browning's dramatic dialogues.

Literary Focus

Assonance is the repetition of vowel sounds followed by different consonant sounds in *stressed* words or syllables of a line or couplet, e.g., I arise from dreams of thee/In the first sweet sleep of night.

Writer's Notebook

Have students think about the sensory details that would be involved in a war, paying attention to specific sounds, smells, and sights that would surround them.

More About Thomas Hardy

While Hardy's ashes were placed in Westminster Abbey, his heart was buried near his birthplace in Stinsford, Dorset.

Connections to AuthorWorks

Thomas Hardy is a featured author in the AuthorWorks CD-ROM series.

Connections to NovelWorks

NovelWorks: The Mayor of Casterbridge offers a rich variety of unique materials for teaching the novel.

SUPPORT MATERIALS OVERVIEW

Unit 6 Resource Book
- Graphic Organizer, p. 41
- Study Guide, p. 42
- Vocabulary, p. 43
- Grammar, p. 44
- Alternate Check Test, p. 45
- Vocabulary Test, p. 46
- Selection Test, pp. 47–48

Building English Proficiency
- Selection Summaries
- Activities, p. 239

Reading, Writing & Grammar SkillBook
- Grammar, Usage, and Mechanics, pp. 175–177

Technology
- Audiotape
- Personal Journal Software
- Custom Literature Database: Additional selections by Thomas Hardy can be found on the database.
- Test Generator Software

Selection Objectives

- to examine how Hardy uses assonance in his poetry
- to analyze his exploration of hope and despair
- to practice using singular and plural possessives

 Unit 6 Resource Book
Graphic Organizer, p. 41
Study Guide, p. 42

Theme Link

As in all of Hardy's work, the theme of hope and despair is central to these poems, which explore the positive and negative contrasts of human existence.

Vocabulary Preview

spectre, ghost

crypt, burial vault

ecstatic, full of joy

terrestrial, earthly

fidelity, faithfulness

Students can add the words and definitions to their Writer's Notebooks.

1 Literary Focus

Assonance

Question What are examples of assonance in the first couplet? *(Possible responses: upon/coppice/Frost and gate/gray)*

2 Reading/Thinking Skills

Compare and Contrast

Questions How are the settings and themes of "The Darkling Thrush" and Keats's "Ode to a Nightingale" similar? *(Both describe an experience in a natural setting in which a bird's song transforms a narrator's mood from despair to hope.)* How do the settings differ? *(Keats's poem is set in lush summer, Hardy's in winter.)*

The Darkling Thrush

Thomas Hardy

1

I leaned upon a coppice¹ gate
    When Frost was specter²-gray,
And winter's dregs made desolate
    The weakening eye of day.
5 The tangled bine-stems³ scored the sky
    Like strings of broken lyres,
And all mankind that haunted nigh
    Had sought their household fires.

The land's sharp features seemed to be
10   The Century's corpse outleant,⁴
His crypt⁵ the cloudy canopy,⁶
    The wind his death-lament.
The ancient pulse of germ and birth
    Was shrunken hard and dry,
15 And every spirit upon earth
    Seemed fervorless⁷ as I.

At once a voice arose among
    The bleak twigs overhead
In a full-hearted evensong
20   Of joy illimited;
An agèd thrush, frail, gaunt, and small,

In blast-beruffled plume,
    Had chosen thus to fling his soul
Upon the growing gloom.

25 So little cause for carolings
    Of such ecstatic⁸ sound
Was written on terrestrial⁹ things
    Afar or nigh around,
That I could think there trembled through
30   His happy good-night air
Some blessèd Hope, whereof he knew
    And I was unaware. **2**

---

darkling (därk′ling), *adj.* dim; obscure.
1. **coppice** (kop′is), *n.* a thicket of small trees or shrubs.
2. **specter** (spek′tər) -**gray,** ghost-gray.
3. **bine-stems,** climbing vines.
4. **outleant** (out′lent′), *adj.* laid out.
5. **crypt** (kript), *n.* burial vault.
6. **canopy** (kan′ə pē), *n.* rooflike covering.
7. **fervorless** (fėr′vər lis), *adj.* emotionless.
8. **ecstatic** (ek stat′ik), *adj.* full of joy.
9. **terrestrial** (tə res′trē əl), *adj.* earthly.

This work by Samuel Palmer, entitled *A Hilly Scene,* dates to about 1826. What is the mood of this work? How does the artist's choice of detail help to create that mood? ➤

SELECTION SUMMARY

The Darkling Thrush; The Man He Killed; Ah, Are You Digging on My Grave?

The Darkling Thrush The speaker gazes upon a barren landscape, which he compares to the corpse of the last century. The ecstatic song of a thrush interrupts, and he is surprised by the hope that he hears in this desolate place.

The Man He Killed The narrator muses that he might have shared a drink with the enemy soldier he has killed and wonders if the man, like himself, enlisted because he was out of work; he finds it "quaint and curious" that he should kill a man to whom he might have stood a drink or made a loan.

Ah, Are You Digging on My Grave? The speaker asks who visits her grave—lover, relative, old rival? The visitor, her pet dog, replies that he buries a bone, having forgotten this is her grave.

 For summaries in other languages, see the Building English Proficiency book.

 **Art Study**

Responses to Caption Questions
Students might note that while the painting is dark in color and autumnal in detail, the mood is hopeful. The earth is bountiful with wheat; the sheep on the hill suggest plenty as well as peace and serenity; the church steeple, light above the hill, bright star, and crescent moon seem to promise spiritual transformation.

Visual Literacy The arching tree branches, open gate, and path through the wheat field give the painting dimension and depth.

Question How might these structural elements add to the spiritual feeling of the painting? *(Possible response: The arching branches suggest the arches of a Gothic church, adding to the spiritual feeling; the open gate and path seem to suggest "the way," i.e., a path to peace and serenity.)*

BUILDING ENGLISH PROFICIENCY

Exploring Metaphor and Simile

ESL LEP ELD SAE LD

Use the following activity to help students grasp the figures of speech in "The Darkling Thrush."

1. Give a short refresher on simile (one thing likened in some way to another dissimilar thing by the use of *like* or *as*—for example, *like a bird on the wing*) and metaphor (an implied comparison, in which a word or phrase normally used of one thing is applied to another—for example, *all the world's a stage*).

2. Ask students to choose an example of each figure of speech from the selection. Have them write a few lines in their journals, describing the meaning or image pictured.

3. Divide the class into small groups to share their comments.

4. Challenge students to invent original similes and metaphors to share with the class.

 Building English Proficiency
Activities, p. 239

3 Literary Element
Point of View

Question What is the point of view from which "The Man He Killed" is written? *(first person)*

4 Literary Element
Irony

Question What is ironic about "That's clear enough"? *(Possible response: that it is not at all clear that these two men are foes)*

5 Literary Element
Dialect

Questions What do the speaker's dialect and his comment about work suggest about his station in life? *(Possible response: that he comes from a working-class background and that he enlisted because he was out of work)*

6 Reading/Thinking Skills
Draw Conclusions

Question What conclusions can you draw about the poet's attitude toward war and the common soldier? *(Possible responses: The poem suggests that Hardy was against the war and in sympathy with the common soldier, who had no real reason to be fighting.)*

The Man He Killed

Thomas Hardy

> "Had he and I but met
> By some old ancient inn,
> We should have sat us down to wet
> Right many a nipperkin!¹

3

> 5 "But ranged as infantry
> And staring face to face,
> I shot at him as he at me,
> And killed him in his place.

> "I shot him dead because—
> 10 Because he was my foe,
> Just so: my foe of course he was;
> That's clear enough; although

4

> "He thought he'd 'list,² perhaps,
> Off-hand like—just as I—
> 15 Was out of work—had sold his traps³—
> No other reason why.

5

> "Yes; quaint and curious war is!
> You shoot a fellow down
> You'd treat if met where any bar is,
> 20 Or help to half-a-crown."⁴

6

---

1. **to wet . . . nipperkin,** to drink many half-pints of ale.
2. **'list,** enlist, as in the army.
3. **traps,** personal belongings.
4. **half-a-crown,** an English coin worth about sixty cents at the time of the poem, though far more in purchasing power.

MINI-LESSON: GRAMMAR

Forming Singular and Plural Possessives

Have students read through "The Darkling Thrush," identifying the possessive nouns in the poem (winter's, land's, Century's). Explain that these are singular possessives—the nouns are singular, and therefore the correct possessive form is an apostrophe followed by an *s*. Remind them that a plural form of the noun that ends in an *s* is formed by adding an apostrophe (e.g., boys') but a plural noun that does not end in *s* (e.g., women) would be punctuated with an apostrophe and *s* (e.g., women's).

Activity Ideas

- Have students find singular and plural nouns in the poems and punctuate them as possessives.
- Have students come up with their own examples of singular and plural nouns and discuss how they should be punctuated as possessives.

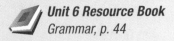
Unit 6 Resource Book
Grammar, p. 44

"Ah, Are You Digging on My Grave?"

Thomas Hardy

7 "Ah, are you digging on my grave
    My loved one?—planting rue?"[1]
"No: yesterday he went to wed
One of the brightest wealth has bred.
5 'It cannot hurt her now,' he said,
    'That I should not be true.' "

"Then who is digging on my grave?
    My nearest dearest kin?"
"Ah, no: they sit and think, 'What use!
10 What good will planting flowers produce?
No tendance[2] of her mound can loose
    Her spirit from Death's gin.' "[3]

"But some one digs upon my grave?
    My enemy?—prodding sly?"
15 "Nay: when she heard you had passed the
    Gate
That shuts on all flesh soon or late,
She thought you no more worth her hate,
    And cares not where you lie."

"Then, who is digging on my grave?
20   Say—since I have not guessed!"

"O it is I, my mistress dear,
Your little dog, who still lives near,
And much I hope my movements here
    Have not disturbed your rest?"

25 "Ah, yes! *You* dig upon my grave . . .
    Why flashed it not on me
That one true heart was left behind!
What feeling do we ever find
To equal among human kind
30   A dog's fidelity!"[4]

"Mistress, I dug upon your grave
    To bury a bone, in case
I should be hungry near this spot
When passing on my daily trot.
35 I am sorry, but I quite forgot
    It was your resting-place."

9

---

1. **rue** (rü), *n.* a woody herb, often used as a symbol of sorrow or regret.
2. **tendance** (ten'dəns), *n.* attention; care.
3. **gin** (jin), *n.* snare or trap.
4. **fidelity** (fə del'ə tē), *n.* faithfulness.

"Ah, Are You Digging on My Grave?" **577**

7 Literary Element

Dialogue

You might note to the class that the poem is written in dialogue, that is, conversation between two or more characters. Ask students to be on the lookout for the identities of the speakers.

8 Reading/Thinking Skills

Understand Sequence

Questions What is the order of the speaker's questions? What might this sequence suggest about the theme of the poem? *(Possible response: She asks after her loved one, then her nearest relative, and finally her rival. The descending order may suggest the futility of putting one's trust in love.)*

9 Literary Element

Irony

Question What is ironic about the dog's final response? *(Possible response: Even the dog has forgotten her and the location of her grave.)*

Check Test

1. How does the thrush affect the narrator of "The Darkling Thrush?" *(It gives him hope.)*

2. Why does the narrator of "The Man He Killed" kill another man? *(He is a soldier in battle.)*

3. In another situation, what would the speaker in "The Man He Killed" have done with the dead man? *(bought him a drink; loaned him money)*

4. Where is the speaker in "Ah, Are You Digging on My Grave?" *(in her grave)*

5. Why is the dog digging on her grave? *(to bury a bone)*

Unit 6 Resource Book
Alternate Check Test, p. 45

BUILDING ENGLISH PROFICIENCY

Making Cultural Connections

The question of how the dead are (or should be) remembered is universal. Encourage students to draw upon their various cultural traditions to discuss questions such as the following:

- Who should visit the graves of the dead, and how often?

- What, if anything, should be left at a grave site?

- What is an appropriate length of time for family and friends to mourn?

- What sorts of thoughts help comfort those who grieve?

After Reading

MAKING CONNECTIONS

1. One possible response: I found "The Man He Killed" most touching because the speaker, trapped in a life-and-death situation not of his own making, is very aware that the "enemy" is not the person he has killed.

2. Possible responses: Such phrases as "spectre gray," "strings of broken lyres," "the wind his death-lament" contribute to a grim mood of gloom and resignation.

3. Possible response: The barren, winter landscape is compared to the old, dead century, presumably the nineteenth century.

4. Possible response: The narrator discerns hope in the thrush's song, although he does not understand the source of that hope.

5. The speaker, without work or belongings, has no attachment to a "cause"; he sees the man he killed as a person, not unlike himself.

6. Possible response: It suggests hesitation and doubt; the narrator does not know why he kills.

7. Possible response: The speaker lists the people in the order of their importance to her—her lover, nearest relative, enemy.

8. The answers suggest that the woman's affections were wasted on insensitive, selfish people.

9. Even her dog, an animal known for its loyalty and affection, has forgotten where she is buried.

10. Students' comparisons should reflect the perception that the Romantic poets found positive affirmation in nature; Hardy's landscapes are hard and bleak.

After Reading

Making Connections

Shaping Your Response

1. In which of the three poems do you believe Hardy tells the most touching story? Explain your response.

Analyzing the Poems

2. How would you describe the **mood** in "The Darkling Thrush"? Cite some phrases that contribute to that mood.

3. What **metaphor** dominates the second stanza?

4. What influence does the thrush seem to have on the speaker? Why?

5. In "The Man He Killed" what influence does the speaker's occupation and social class seem to have on his **perspective?**

6. What does the punctuation of stanzas 3 and 4 suggest about the speaker's thoughts?

7. In "Ah, Are You Digging on My Grave?" how do you interpret the guesses the speaker makes about who is digging on her grave and the order in which she makes them?

8. What **main idea** is suggested by the answers the speaker gets?

9. Explain what you find **ironic** about the last stanza?

Extending the Ideas

10. Compare Hardy's natural **settings** with those in the poems of Wordsworth and Coleridge.

Literary Focus: Assonance

Assonance, a kind of near rhyme, is the repetition of similar vowel sounds followed by different consonant sounds in stressed words or syllables. Hardy uses both rhyme and assonance in these poems to achieve strong, emphatic sounds. Find at least five examples of assonance in "A Darkling Thrush."

Vocabulary Study

Write the letter of the best answer for each question.

1. Who would display *ecstatic* behavior?

  a. a losing team   **b.** a crying baby
  c. an engaged couple   **d.** a comforting doctor

2. If you had just seen a *specter,* what would you have been looking at?

  a. a bird   **b.** a ghost
  c. a teacher   **d.** a soldier

LITERARY FOCUS: ASSONANCE

Possible Responses

Lines 1–2: upon/coppice/Frost and gate/gray

Line 3: dreg/desolate

Lines 5–6: bine/sky/lyres

Lines 7–8: mankind/nigh/fires

Line 9: features/seemed

Line 14: germ/birth

Lines 16–20: voice/joy and arose/overhead

Lines 21–22: thrush/beruffled

Lines 23–24: chosen/soul/growing

Line 27: written/things

3. *Fidelity* is a characteristic that might describe which of these?

    a. a late employee   **b.** a jilted lover

    c. a long-time pet   **d.** a maid who has just been fired

4. The animal was described as a *terrestrial* being. Where would it live?

    a. on the land   **b.** in the sea

    c. in the heavens   **d.** in trees

5. Where would you be most likely to find a *crypt*?

    a. on a beach   **b.** in an apartment building

    c. in a restaurant   **d.** in a church

Expressing Your Ideas

Writing Choices

Writer's Notebook Update Compare your list of adjectives with Hardy's choice of "quaint and curious" in "The Man He Killed." In a brief paragraph compare and contrast the attitudes implied by your words and Hardy's words.

A Century Ends Hardy's "The Darkling Thrush" is an *elegy,* a solemn, reflective poem, usually about death. In this poem he laments the end of the nineteenth century, the 1800s. Write an **analytic essay** in which you compare and contrast the reactions of the speaker and the thrush to the century's end.

 **A Different View of the World** W. H. Auden said that Thomas Hardy wrote with a "hawk's vision, his way of looking at life from a very great height." If you could choose to look at life from a **perspective** different from your own, what perspective would you choose and why? Defend your choice in a **personal journal entry.**

Other Options

A Dialogue Between Living and Dead Working with a classmate, prepare a **dialogue** between two characters—both alive, both dead, or one alive and one dead. In your dialogue one speaker should reveal an insight or "truth" to the other speaker. That revelation could be ironic (as in "Ah, Are You Digging on My Grave?") or humorous, or serious, or whatever you like. Perform your dialogue for your class.

War Everywhere In "The Man He Killed" Hardy presents a touching picture which takes war from the general to the specific, to two human beings confronting each other. Create an **artistic treatment of confrontation** involving two soldiers, a soldier and a civilian, two civilians, a protester and a politician, and so on. War is an especially effective background for confrontation, but, of course, confrontation is not confined to wartime.

Fling Your Soul to the World Hardy's aged thrush, although frail, gaunt, and small, "flings his soul" to the world in ecstatic sound. Create a **musical composition** in which you fling your soul to the world. Your composition can be just music, or it can be words and music both. Perform your composition for your class, perhaps as part of a musical program with other similar compositions.

 Unit 6 Resource Book
Vocabulary, p. 43
Vocabulary Test, p. 46

VOCABULARY STUDY

1. c

2. b

3. c

4. a

5. d

WRITING CHOICES
Writer's Notebook Update

Students should note that "quaint and curious" are quaint and curious adjectives to describe war; they are odd, unexpected, and ironic.

A Century Ends

Before students begin writing, they might set up a two-column chart listing concrete examples of how the speaker and thrush are alike and how they are different.

A Different View of the World

Students might brainstorm various perspectives before they begin their personal journal entries.

Selection Test

Unit 6 Resource Book
pp. 47–48

OTHER OPTIONS
A Dialogue Between Living and Dead

You might suggest that brevity is one key to a successful and insightful dialogue. Students should try to write revealing dialogues in as few lines as possible.

War Everywhere

You might suggest that students search their own lives for examples of interesting conflict.

Building Background

You might write the word *inscape* on the board and then list students' responses to what individuals find most vivid in music, painting, and poetry.

Literary Focus

You might ask students if they can think of particularly vivid examples of "a succession of similar sounds" in advertising jingles.

Writer's Notebook

Suggest that students be as creative as possible, and remind them that they will share their efforts with the class at the end of the lesson.

More About Gerard Manley Hopkins

Hopkins's poetry was not well-received when it was initially published. A second edition, published in 1930, found a larger and more appreciative audience, including such twentieth-century poets as T. S. Eliot, Dylan Thomas, and Stephen Spender.

Before Reading

Pied Beauty
Spring and Fall: To a Young Child by Gerard Manley Hopkins

Gerard Manley Hopkins
1844–1889

Eldest of nine children in a family devoted to the Church of England, Gerard Manley Hopkins joined the Roman Catholic Church at age 22. When he began to train for the priesthood in the Jesuit order, he dramatically and symbolically burned all of his youthful poems. After his ordination in 1877 Hopkins served as a parish priest and as a teacher of Classical languages. In the last years of his life Hopkins became haunted by the suicides of several Oxford friends and overwhelmed by a "constant, crippling" melancholy which, he confessed, "is much like madness." He died in an outbreak of typhoid fever in 1889. A friend and fellow writer, the poet laureate Robert Bridges, saved Hopkins's poems and published them 29 years later, in 1918.

Building Background

"On the Side of Oddness" In a letter to Robert Bridges, who was often highly critical of his friend's poetry, Hopkins tried to explain his poetic technique: "No doubt my poetry errs on the side of oddness. I hope in time to have a more balanced and Miltonic style. But as air, melody, is what strikes me most of all in music, and design in painting, so design, pattern, or what I am in the habit of calling **inscape** is what I above all aim at in poetry." Hopkins created his inscape by experimenting with language, by adding new life to ordinary words, by combining words in unusual ways to suggest new possibilities of meaning, by choosing only concrete words of vigor and action. He also sought to re-create the natural rhythms of speech by using what he called **sprung rhythm.** Although he wrote in the Victorian age, his poetic works reflect little of the Victorian tradition; rather they are forerunners of twentieth-century verse.

Literary Focus

Alliteration The easiest way to remember **alliteration** is to memorize this definition, itself an example of alliteration: a succession of similar sounds. Look for Hopkins's skillful use of alliteration as you read his poems.

Writer's Notebook

A Lovely, Languid Lagoon Try your hand at the use of alliteration. For each of the following words write one example of a very alliterative phrase: shore, field, mountain, cottage, river.

SUPPORT MATERIALS OVERVIEW

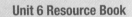

Unit 6 Resource Book
- Graphic Organizer, p. 49
- Study Guide, p. 50
- Vocabulary, p. 51
- Grammar, p. 52
- Alternate Check Test, p. 53
- Vocabulary Test, p. 54
- Selection Test, pp. 55–56

Building English Proficiency
- Selection Summaries
- Activities, p. 240

Reading, Writing & Grammar SkillBook
- Grammar, Usage, and Mechanics, pp. 149–152

Technology
- Audiotape
- Personal Journal Software
- Custom Literature Database: Additional selections by Gerard Manley Hopkins can be found on the database.
- Test Generator Software

Pied Beauty

Gerard Manley Hopkins

Glory be to God for dappled[1] things—
    For skies of couple-color as a brinded[2] cow;
      For rose-moles all in stipple[3] upon trout that swim;
Fresh-firecoal chestnut-falls;[4] finches' wings;
5   Landscape plotted and pieced[5]—fold, fallow, and plow;
      And all trades, their gear and tackle and trim.[6]

All things counter,[7] original, spare, strange;
    Whatever is fickle, freckled (who knows how?)
      With swift, slow; sweet, sour; adazzle, dim;
10 He fathers-forth whose beauty is past change:
                       Praise him.

---

pied (pīd), *adj.* variegated; streaked with many colors.
1. **dappled** (dap′əld), *adj.* spotted.
2. **brinded** (brin′did), *adj.* streaked with different colors.
3. **stipple** (stip′əl), *n.* In art, areas of color or shade are sometimes represented by masses of tiny dots, called *stipples.*
4. **fresh-firecoal chestnut-falls.** Newly fallen nuts stripped of their husks look like glowing coals.
5. **plotted and pieced,** laid off into plots and fields.
6. **trim,** equipment.
7. **counter,** contrary to expectation.

"Pure color over pure color" is the way William Henry Hunt described the method he used to create paintings such as this one, entitled *Primroses and Bird's Nest.* What objects in this painting might be considered as examples of "Pied Beauty"?

SELECTION SUMMARY

Pied Beauty; Spring and Fall: To a Young Child

Pied Beauty   The narrator thanks God for the richness and complexity of the world: the beauty of the colors of the sky; the flesh of fish; the wings of birds; the contrasts of humanity and the opposites of life. All is different; yet all is God's creation, immutable and the same.

Spring and Fall: To a Young Child   The narrator addresses a child who grieves for autumn's falling leaves. He tells her that as she gets older, the pain will lessen; and yet, she will continue to weep because the source of all sorrow is the same: change and decay. So the child grieves not just for the falling leaves, but for her own inevitable fate.

 *For summaries in other languages, see the **Building English Proficiency** book.*

During Reading

Selection Objectives

- to examine Hopkins's use of alliteration
- to analyze Hopkins's exploration of hope and despair
- to practice finding sentence fragments

Unit 6 Resource Book
Graphic Organizer, p. 49
Study Guide, p. 50

Theme Link

"Pied Beauty" celebrates the beauty, complexity, and hope inherent in the totality of life. "Spring and Fall: To a Young Child," concludes with a young girl's despair for the fate of all living things—including her own.

1 Literary Focus
Alliteration

Question What are examples of alliteration in the first stanza?

Possible Responses
- line 1—Glory/God
- line 2—couple-color/cow
- line 3—moles/stipple/swim and stipple/trout
- lines 4–5—Fresh-firecoal/falls/ finches'/fold/fallow
- line 5—plotted/pierced/plow
- line 6—trades/tackle/trim
- between lines—dapple/couple/stipple and couple/color/cow/coal/tackle

 ## Art Study

Response to Caption Question
Nearly everything pictured in the painting could be listed: bird's eggs, bird's nest, flowers, leaves, mosses, lichens, and so on.

2 Reading/Thinking Skills
Compare and Contrast

Questions How would you contrast "Goldengrove" with "world of wanwood"? *(Possible response: "Goldengrove" suggests beauty, value; "wanwood" suggests sorrow, blight, physical decline.)*

3 Reading/Thinking Skills
Find the Main Idea

Questions What might the phrase "sorrow's springs" mean? *(the source of all sorrow)* According to the narrator, what is the source of all sorrow? *(change, i.e., all earthly things, particularly living things, eventually decay)*

4 Literary Element
Theme

Questions What other meanings besides spring and autumn might the title suggest? Connect responses to specific phrases. *(Possible responses: birth and death—"the blight man was born for"; innocence and loss of innocence—"fresh thoughts" that "as the heart grows older" will greet "such sights colder")*

Check Test

1. What does the title "Pied Beauty" mean? *(the beauty of spotted or different things)*

2. Who is offered thanks for the beauty of pied things? *(God)*

3. Who is the young child in "Spring and Fall"? *(Margaret)*

4. Over what does Margaret grieve? *(falling leaves)*

5. According to the narrator, what is the source of all sorrow? *(change; disintegration)*

 **Unit 6 Resource Book**
Alternate Check Test, p. 53

Spring and Fall: to a Young Child

Gerard Manley Hopkins

Márgarét, are you gríeving
Over Goldengrove unleaving?
Leáves, líke the things of man, you
With your fresh thoughts care for, can you?
5 Áh! ás the heart grows older
It will come to such sights colder
By and by, nor spare a sigh
Though worlds of wanwood leafmeal¹ lie;
And yet you wíll weep and know why.
10 Now no matter, child, the name:
Sórrow's spríngs áre the same.
Nor mouth had, no nor mind, expressed
What heart heard of, ghost guessed:
It ís the blight² man was born for,
15 It is Margaret you mourn for.

---

1. **wanwood leafmeal,** pale ("wan") colored autumn leaves have fallen to the ground where they lie matted and disintegrating ("leafmeal").
2. **blight** (blīt), *n.* decay; deterioration.

MINI-LESSON: GRAMMAR

Recognizing Sentence Fragments

Teach Explain to students that a complete sentence has a subject and a predicate. Remind them that a complete sentence expresses a complete thought, while a sentence fragment will sound like an incomplete thought. Some of the unusual (perhaps even wrong-sounding) sentences in "Spring and Fall: To a Young Child" are merely inverted, with subject, verb, and direct object in unusual order, but there are some fragments also, such as "Now, no matter, child, the name." Ask students if they can find other sentence fragments in this poem or in "Pied Beauty."

Activity Ideas

- Have students complete each sentence fragment (in their own words) so it sounds like a complete sentence.
- Have students read completed sentences to the class. Have the class identify whether it is a sentence fragment or a complete sentence.

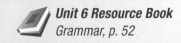 **Unit 6 Resource Book**
Grammar, p. 52

After Reading

Making Connections

Shaping Your Response

1. In which of Hopkins's poems are you more conscious of the **rhythm** and the **rhyme?**

Analyzing the Poems

2. What do you think is the **main idea** of "Pied Beauty"? Why do you select that idea?

3. Why do you think Hopkins concludes his list of dappled things with the phrase "all trades"?

4. In stanza 2 Hopkins speeds up the rhythm of the poem by moving to a string of contrasting adjectives. What do you think he accomplishes with these contrasts?

5. Which of your senses are stimulated by Hopkins's word choices in "Pied Beauty"? Supply specific examples.

6. Why do you think Hopkins entitled the poem about falling leaves "Spring and Fall"? Is the title an integral part of the poem?

7. Why do you think Hopkins capitalized the combination-word *Goldengrove?*

8. What comment do you think Hopkins is making by using the **hyperbole** "worlds of wanwood leafmeal"?

9. How does the speaker relate Margaret's present grief to the sorrow she will feel in the future?

Extending the Ideas

10. Which of these poems seems closer in spirit to the nature poetry of the Romantics? Explain your answer.

11. How does knowing that Hopkins is writing from the **perspective** of the priesthood help you understand his attitude toward the subject matter?

Literary Focus: Alliteration

Alliteration is a succession of similar sounds. Point out several instances of alliteration in Hopkins's poems. Why do you think Hopkins uses alliteration in addition to rhyme?

After Reading

MAKING CONNECTIONS

1. Students may respond that the rhythm of "Pied Beauty" is more noticeable because it is less natural than the rhythm of "Spring and Fall"; the less complex rhyme of "Spring and Fall" may be more noticeable.

2. Possible response: that we should appreciate the beauty of all life, including that which is different and subtle. Students' opinions should be supported with examples.

3. He extends his praise to humanity.

4. The contrasts point the reader's attention toward what is unseen, overlooked, or under appreciated.

5. Possible responses: sight—nearly all images; taste—"sweet, sour"; touch—"rose-moles," "trout that swim," "Fresh-firecoal chestnut-fall," "gear and tackle"; sound—"trout/swim," "finches' wings," "fold, fallow, and plow"; smell—indirectly in "cow," "trout," "fallow and plow"

6. The integral title, Spring and Fall, suggests other meanings than spring and autumn, including birth and death and innocence and its loss.

7. The capitalization suggests a particular place and gives emphasis.

8. The hyperbole suggests the decay of all things of this world.

9. He equates her present sorrow with "the blight man was born for," i.e., death and decay.

10. Responses may vary. "Pied Beauty" is an affirmation of nature; "Spring and Fall" explores the universality of nature's lessons.

11. While responses will vary, students might note that the priesthood requires the belief and expression of prescribed views.

LITERARY FOCUS: ALLITERATION

Alliteration is used to enrich imagery, foster new rhythms, and trigger the reader's imagination.

BUILDING ENGLISH PROFICIENCY

Exploring Imagery

Students, especially urban students, may have a hard time understanding the imagery in Hopkins's poem "Pied Beauty" because they are not familiar with the things described. This activity may help.

1. Using the footnotes, confirm that students understand the word definition of each image.

2. Ask students to scour nature magazines for pictures of things in "Pied Beauty."

3. The second stanza of the poem becomes more general. Discuss and clarify the meaning of "All things counter, original, spare, strange . . . " and ask students to build a collection of photos that show things that have these qualities.

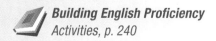
*Building English Proficiency
Activities, p. 240*

Writer's Notebook Update

To stimulate student ideas before they try writing again, go around the class and ask each student to add a word to an alliterative phrase. The goal is to demonstrate how one can explore one's imagination.

Strange Things

Encourage students to use words that engage as many senses—smell, sight, touch, taste, and sound—as possible.

Spring, Summer, Fall, Winter

Before students begin writing, you might encourage them to remember that seasons vary considerably from one place to another. For example, summers in San Francisco are quite different from summers in Miami. Descriptions should be specific.

Selection Test

Unit 6 Resource Book
pp. 55–56

Expressing Your Ideas

Writing Choices

Writer's Notebook Update Look back at the alliterative phrases you created. Are your alliterations unique or commonplace? To answer that question, compare your alliterations with those of your classmates. Did several of you come up with the same or similar phrases? Try, this time, to use ordinary words in uncommon ways or to think of unusual word associations. Maybe you can even invent some new words.

Strange Things . . . In the first stanza of "Pied Beauty" Hopkins lists the dappled things for which he praises God. Following Hopkins's style, write a **poetic stanza** in which you list strange things or sweet / sour things or swift / slow things. Be very specific with the images you create. Try to use unusual word combinations, like *couple-color,* and alliteration, like *fresh-firecoal chestnut falls.*

Spring, Summer, Fall, Winter Select a season, perhaps your favorite season, and write a **short story** in which a character gains an understanding about himself or mankind from his observations of the season.

Other Options

Captured Images Critic John Wain says that Hopkins's imagination is "performing one of the chief functions for which we now use the cinema and television—that of presenting an image which moves and takes form while it is focused." Create a **video** or a series of slides in which you try to capture the feeling created by the images Hopkins presents in "Pied Beauty." You might even use the poem in your sound track.

Loss of Innocence In "Spring and Fall" Margaret is experiencing a loss of innocence as she comes to accept the inevitability of death. Recall a situation in your life in which you lost your innocence about the harsh realities of life. Perhaps a pet died or a family member or personal hero you admired turned out to be less than perfect. Tell about your loss of innocence in an **illustrated story** suitable for students in the fourth or fifth grade.

Unity in Variety A possible theme for Hopkins's "Pied Beauty" is unity in variety or changelessness in change. Select a topic other than nature, and develop this theme in a **musical piece** or a **dance.** Your notes or your movements should be concrete and powerful, just as Hopkins's words are.

OTHER OPTIONS
Captured Images

As an alternative project, students might create collages from magazine images.

Loss of Innocence

Some students may prefer to present their story in a cartoon format, including dialogue for each of the characters. (You may want to point out that in addressing fourth- or fifth-grade children, high school students face the same conflict of values—truth versus illusion—that Hopkins faced in addressing Margaret.)

Unity in Variety

Some students may want to pair up; one student may set a dance to a piece of music composed by another student.

Before Reading

The Lagoon

by Joseph Conrad

Joseph Conrad
1857–1924

Teodor Józef Konrad Korzeniowski was born in the Polish Ukraine. Because of the political activities of his father, a Polish noble, the family was exiled to Russia. At age 11 Józef was orphaned and was placed in the guardianship of his uncle. At 17 he joined the French merchant marine and later the British merchant navy. He worked his way up to the rank of ship's captain, changed his name to Joseph Conrad, and became a naturalized British subject. When his first novel was published in 1894, Conrad shifted his energies to literature. In the next 29 years he wrote 31 volumes of fiction and reminiscence, tales of the sea, such as *Lord Jim* (1900); of adventure, such as *Heart of Darkness* (1902); and of politics, such as *Nostromo* (1904).

Building Background

True to Himself As a sailor in the British merchant navy, Joseph Conrad traveled to the African Congo, the Indian Ocean, the China seas, and the Malay Peninsula. The peninsular states of Malaysia, the setting of Conrad's "The Lagoon," had become part of the British Empire in the mid 1800s. The British, seeking to protect their trade interests in the region and to control disputes between the Malay rulers and the Chinese immigrants who labored in the tin mines, had sent in resident advisers who dictated policy. Thus, there were a few white men who moved with ease among the Malaysian natives. Conrad was one who quickly gained the confidence of the natives, thereby also gaining the opportunity to share in their culture and their experiences. Those experiences he later examined with the eye of an older, more thoughtful man. Conrad says: ". . . I need not point out that I had to make material from my own life's incidents arranged, combined, colored for artistic purposes. . . . What I claim as true are my mental and emotional reactions to life, to men, to their affairs and passions as I have seen them. I have in that sense kept always true to myself."

Literary Focus

Setting The time and place in which the action of a narrative takes place is its **setting.** Setting can contribute strongly to the mood or atmosphere of a work as well as to its believability. Sometimes a setting plays a role in influencing events of the plot; at other times it is unimportant, merely a background. As you read this story, consider how important the setting is. How does the setting influence the plot?

Writer's Notebook

Out of Your Element Recall a situation in which you were out of your "natural element," among people (or even with just one person) very different from yourself. Jot down a few words to describe the differences you were aware of; then list some words that describe your feelings about those differences.

The Lagoon **585**

Before Reading

Building Background

Ask students to share what they know about the geography and history of Malaysia and its capital, Kuala Lumpur.

Literary Focus

Suggest that the class look around the school room and list what is part of the setting. They might consider light, time of year, weather, sounds, smells, architecture, other students, including how they talk and are dressed.

Writer's Notebook

Have students ask themselves what surprised them about the situation?

More about Joseph Conrad

As a ship's steward, Conrad probably smuggled guns, which he describes in Nostromo. His adventures commanding a steamboat on the Congo inspired the novella "Heart of Darkness," which in turn inspired the film *Apocalypse Now*.

Connections to
AuthorWorks

Joseph Conrad is a featured author in the AuthorWorks CD-ROM series.

Connections to
NovelWorks

NovelWorks: Lord Jim offers unique materials for teaching the novel.

SUPPORT MATERIALS OVERVIEW

Unit 6 Resource Book
- Graphic Organizer, p. 57
- Study Guide, p. 58
- Vocabulary, p. 59
- Grammar, p. 60
- Alternate Check Test, p. 61
- Vocabulary Test, p. 62
- Selection Test, pp. 63–64

Building English Proficiency
- Selection Summaries
- Activities, p. 241

Reading, Writing & Grammar SkillBook
- Reading, pp. 45–46, 47–48
- Writing, pp. 111–112
- Grammar, Usage, and Mechanics, pp. 203–204

Technology
- Audiotape
- Personal Journal Software
- Custom Literature Database: Additional selections by Jospeh Conrad can be found on the database.
- Test Generator Software

Selection Objectives

- to examine how Conrad uses setting in his fiction
- to analyze Conrad's exploration of hope and despair
- to learn about active and passive verbs

Unit 6 Resource Book
Graphic Organizer, p. 57
Study Guide, p. 58

Theme Link

In "The Lagoon," Conrad examines hope and despair by exploring connections between love, alienation, and the individual.

Vocabulary Preview

entice, tempt

impenetrable, unable to pass through

stagnant, still; not flowing

propitiate, win the favor of

demeanor, behavior

ominous, unfavorable; threatening

audacious, bold

abysmal, bottomless

infamous, disgraceful

plaintive, mournful

stealthy, secret

incomprehensible, impossible to understand

Students can add the words and definitions to their Writer's Notebooks.

Art Study

Response to Caption Question   In general, the illustration conforms to details given on page 588 of the text—"rude ladder giving access to the bamboo platform" and "the low door of the hut."

◄ Does this 19th-century engraving of a chief's house on New Guinea convey the same mood as Conrad's description of Arsat's dwelling? Why or why not?

The Lagoon

Joseph Conrad

The white man, leaning with both arms over the roof of the little house in the stern of the boat, said to the steersman— "We will pass the night in Arsat's clearing. It is late."

The Malay only grunted, and went on looking fixedly at the river. The white man rested his chin on his crossed arms and gazed at the wake of the boat. At the end of the straight avenue of forests cut by the intense glitter of the river, the sun appeared unclouded and dazzling, poised low over the water that shone smoothly like a band of metal. The forests, sombre and dull, stood motionless and silent on each side of the broad stream. At the foot of big, towering trees, trunkless nipa palms rose from the mud of the bank, in bunches of leaves enormous and heavy, that hung unstirring over the brown swirl of eddies. In the stillness of the air every tree, every leaf, every bough, every tendril of creeper and every petal of minute blossoms seemed to have been bewitched into an immobility perfect and final. Nothing moved on the river but the eight paddles that rose flashing regularly, dipped together with a single splash; while the steersman swept right and left with a periodic and

SELECTION SUMMARY

The Lagoon

A white man visits an old friend, Arsat, a Malaysian man who lives in isolation on a remote lagoon. The visitor finds his friend upset because his love, Diamelen, is very ill. Sitting up through the night with the woman, Arsat tells his friend how he and his brother abducted Diamelen from the court of their ruler and employer. When the ruler's men followed, the brother told Arsat that he would remain behind to fend off the pursuers, then follow. Beset by the men, the brother cried out for aid, but Arsat ignored the cries and escaped with his love on the river. The brother was killed. While Arsat tells the story, the woman dies. Arsat states that all is dark, but when he again is able to see, he will revenge his brother's death. When the white man leaves, Arsat sits before the hut—alone, staring into his own darkness.

*For summaries in other languages, see the **Building English Proficiency** book.*

1 sudden flourish of his blade describing a glinting semicircle above his head. The churned-up water frothed alongside with a confused murmur. And the white man's canoe, advancing upstream in the short-lived disturbance of its own making, seemed to enter the portals of a land from which the very memory of motion had forever departed.

> **PREDICT:** The white man is entering "a land from which the very memory of motion had forever departed." What kind of a land might that be?

2

The white man, turning his back upon the setting sun, looked along the empty and broad expanse of the sea-reach. For the last three miles of its course the wandering, hesitating river, as if enticed[1] irresistibly by the freedom of an open horizon, flows straight into the sea, flows straight to the east—to the east that harbors both light and darkness. Astern of the boat the repeated call of some bird, a cry discordant[2] and feeble, **3** skipped along over the smooth water and lost itself, before it could reach the other shore, in the breathless silence of the world.

The steersman dug his paddle into the stream, and held hard with stiffened arms, his body thrown forward. The water gurgled aloud; and suddenly the long straight reach seemed to pivot on its center, the forests swung in a semicircle, and the slanting beams of sunset touched the broadside of the canoe with a fiery glow, throwing the slender and distorted shadows of its crew upon the streaked glitter of the river. The white man turned to look ahead. The course of the boat had been altered at right-angles to the stream, and the carved dragon-head of its prow was pointing now at a gap in the fringing bushes of the bank. It glided through, brushing the overhanging twigs, and disappeared from the river **4** like some slim and amphibious[3] creature leaving the water for its lair[4] in the forests.

The narrow creek was like a ditch: torturous,

fabulously deep; filled with gloom under the thin strip of pure and shining blue of the heaven. Immense trees soared up, invisible behind the festooned draperies of creepers. Here and there, near the glistening blackness of the water, a twisted root of some tall tree showed amongst the tracery of small ferns, black and dull, writhing and motionless, like an arrested snake. The short words of the paddlers reverberated loudly between the thick and somber walls of vegetation. Darkness oozed out from between the trees, through the tangled maze of the creepers, from behind the great fantastic and unstirring leaves; the darkness, mysterious and invincible; the darkness scented and poisonous of impenetrable[5] forests. **5**

The men poled in the shoaling[6] water. The creek broadened, opening out into a wide sweep of a stagnant[7] lagoon. The forests receded from the marshy bank, leaving a level strip of bright green, reedy grass to frame the reflected blueness of the sky. A fleecy pink cloud drifted high above, trailing the delicate coloring of its image under the floating leaves and the silvery blossoms of the lotus. A little house, perched on high piles, appeared black in the distance. Near it, two tall nibong palms, that seemed to have come out of the forests in the background, leaned slightly over the ragged roof, with a suggestion of sad tenderness and care in the droop of their leafy and soaring heads.

The steersman, pointing with his paddle, said, "Arsat is there. I see his canoe fast between the piles."

The polers ran along the sides of the boat glancing over their shoulders at the end of the day's journey. They would have preferred to

---

1. **entice** (en tīs′), *v.* tempt.
2. **discordant** (dis kôrd′nt), *adj.* harsh; clashing.
3. **amphibious** (am fib′ē əs), *adj.* of land and water.
4. **lair** (ler), *n.* hideaway.
5. **impenetrable** (im pen′ə trə bəl), *adj.* unable to be passed through.
6. **shoaling** (shō′ling), *adj.* shallow.
7. **stagnant** (stag′nənt), *adj.* still; not flowing.

The Lagoon **587**

BUILDING ENGLISH PROFICIENCY

Analyzing Setting and Mood

As "The Lagoon" opens, Conrad describes the natural environment of his story. Help students appreciate this section not only as simple description but as a way of setting mood.

1. Before they begin the selection, ask students to read the definitions for vocabulary words—the words in blue in the footnotes. Then have students use each word in short sentences of their own and share their sentences with the class.

2. Ask students to predict the nature of the setting, based on the vocabulary words alone.

3. Students could draw an abstract or expressionistic picture of the setting. The artistic quality isn't important; students just should express the feelings evoked by Conrad's description.

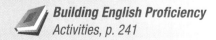
Building English Proficiency Activities, p. 241

---

1 Literary Focus
Setting

Question What specific passages of the opening description of the setting seem particularly evocative? *(Possible responses: "the intense glitter of the river"; "water that shone . . . like a band of metal"; "The forest, somber and dull, stood motionless and silent"; every tree, leaf, bough, tendril, petal "seemed to have been bewitched into an immobility perfect and final.")*

2 Active Reading
Predict

Possible Responses a place where time has stopped; a place that is changeless, eternal

3 Literary Element
Foreshadowing

Question What might the bird's "discordant" cry foreshadow? *(Possible response: that some conflict, harsh and clashing, may take place)*

4 Literary Element
Imagery

Question What do you think the imagery of the "dragon headed" canoe that "disappeared . . . like some slim and amphibious creature" suggests? *(a swimming water snake that slithers ashore)*

5 Literary Element
Foreshadowing

Question What mood is evoked by the description of the passage up the narrow creek? *(Possible responses: dark and ominous*

587

The terrain of Malaysia, where this story is set, includes mountain ranges, extending south from Thailand, and swamp forests, such as those described in "The Lagoon." The climate of Malaysia is hot and humid: daily minimum temperature in Kuala Lumpur, the capital, is 73° F; maximum temperature is about 90° F; annual rainfall is approximately 100 inches.

6 Literary Focus

Setting

Question   At what setting does the canoe finally stop? (*Possible response: a lagoon of weird aspect and ghostly reputation*)

7 Active Reading

Clarify

Possible response   The boatsmen initially view Arsat as a stranger; they also dislike that he has repaired an abandoned house. The white man views Arsat without superstition.

8 Reading/Thinking Skills

Draw Conclusions

Question   What do you think is the relationship between the white man and the boatsmen? (*Possible response: The boatsmen are in the employ of the white man; they respond "sulkily" to his orders; he speaks "curtly" in return.*)

---

6 spend the night somewhere else than on this lagoon of weird aspect and ghostly reputation. Moreover, they disliked Arsat, first as a stranger, and also because he who repairs a ruined house, and dwells in it, proclaims that he is not afraid to live amongst the spirits that haunt the places abandoned by mankind. Such a man can disturb the course of fate by glances or words; while his familiar ghosts are not easy to propitiate[8] by casual wayfarers upon whom they long to wreak[9] the malice of their human master. White men care not for such things, being unbelievers and in league with the Father of Evil, who leads them unharmed through the invisible dangers of this world. To the warnings of the righteous they oppose an offensive pretence of disbelief. What is there to be done?

> **CLARIFY: From what perspective do the boatsmen view Arsat? the white man?**

7 So they thought, throwing their weight on the end of their long poles. The big canoe glided on swiftly, noiselessly, and smoothly, towards Arsat's clearing, till, in a great rattling of poles thrown down, and the loud murmurs of "Allah be praised!" it came with a gentle knock against the crooked piles below the house.

The boatmen with uplifted faces shouted discordantly, "Arsat! O Arsat!" Nobody came. The white man began to climb the rude ladder giving access to the bamboo platform before the house. The juragan[10] of the boat said sulkily, "We will cook in the sampan,[11] and sleep on the water."

"Pass my blankets and the basket," said the **8** white man, curtly.

He knelt on the edge of the platform to receive the bundle. Then the boat shoved off, and the white man, standing up, confronted Arsat, who had come out through the low door of his hut. He was a man young, powerful, with broad chest and muscular arms. He had nothing on but his sarong.[12] His head was bare. His big, soft eyes stared eagerly at the white man,

but his voice and demeanor[13] were composed as he asked, without any words of greeting—

"Have you medicine, Tuan?"[14]

"No," said the visitor in a startled tone. "No. Why? Is there sickness in the house?"

"Enter and see," replied Arsat, in the same calm manner, and turning short round, passed again through the small doorway. The white man, dropping his bundles, followed.

In the dim light of the dwelling he made out on a couch of bamboos a woman stretched on her back under a broad sheet of red cotton cloth. She lay still, as if dead; but her big eyes, wide open, glittered in the gloom, staring upwards at the slender rafters, motionless and unseeing. She was in a high fever, and evidently unconscious. Her cheeks were sunk slightly, her lips were partly open, and on the young face there was the ominous[15] and fixed expression—the absorbed, contemplating expression of the unconscious who are going to die. The two men stood looking down at her in silence.

"Has she been long ill?" asked the traveler.

"I have not slept for five nights," answered the Malay, in a deliberate tone. "At first she heard voices calling her from the water and struggled against me who held her. But since the sun of today rose she hears nothing—she hears not me. She sees nothing. She sees not me—me!"

He remained silent for a minute, then asked softly—

"Tuan, will she die?"

"I fear so," said the white man, sorrowfully. He had known Arsat years ago, in a far country

---

8. propitiate (prə pish′ē āt), v. win the favor of.
9. wreak (rēk), v. inflict.
10. juragan (ju′rä gän), n. the rower responsible for steering the boat.
11. sampan (sam′pan), n. small boat.
12. sarong (sə rông′) n. a brightly colored cloth, wrapped around the waist and worn as a skirt by both men and women in the Malay Archipelago and the Pacific Islands.
13. demeanor (di mē′nər), n. behavior.
14. Tuan (tü än′), n. "Lord," a Malay term of respect.
15. ominous (om′ə nəs), adj. unfavorable, threatening.

MINI-LESSON: LITERARY FOCUS

Setting

Teach   Setting is the time and place in which the action of a narrative occurs. Setting may be established through dialogue and action, or it may be described by the narrator or one of the characters. Setting is an important part of the mood and atmosphere of a work. Have students find examples of elements that make up the setting in "The Lagoon." Some examples are

- page 587: the description of the creek and forest
- page 588: the description of the hut
- page 588, column 1: the polers' thoughts on Arsat and his house
- page 589, column 1: the description of the sunset

Questions   Why is the setting, the lagoon, important in this story? Could the story have been set anywhere else? (*The setting of the lagoon is crucial because it sets up an eerie mood that parallels the theme of the story. The setting could have been elsewhere—other authors have written about mortality and guilt in other settings—but Conrad uses this setting very effectively.*)

Activity Idea   Have students write a paragraph describing a setting with which they are familiar. They should be as precise and descriptive as possible.

in times of trouble and danger, when no friend-ship is to be despised. And since his Malay friend had come unexpectedly to dwell in the hut on the lagoon with a strange woman, he had slept many times there, in his journeys up and down the river. He liked the man who knew how to keep faith in council and how to fight without fear by the side of his white friend. He liked him—not so much perhaps as a man likes his favorite dog—but still he liked him well enough to help and ask no questions, to think some-times vaguely and hazily in the midst of his own pursuits, about the lonely man and the long-haired woman with audacious[16] face and triumphant eyes, who lived together hidden by the forests—alone and feared.

The white man came out of the hut in time to see the enormous conflagration[17] of sunset put out by the swift and stealthy shadows that, rising like a black and impalpable[18] vapor above the treetops, spread over the heaven, extinguishing the crimson glow of floating clouds and the red brilliance of departing daylight. In a few moments all the stars came out above the intense blackness of the earth and the great lagoon gleaming suddenly with reflected lights resem-bled an oval patch of night sky flung down into the hopeless and abysmal[19] night of the wilder-ness. The white man had some supper out of the basket, then collecting a few sticks that lay about the platform, made up a small fire, not for warmth, but for the sake of the smoke, which would keep off the mosquitos. He wrapped him-self in the blankets and sat with his back against the reed wall of the house, smoking thoughtfully.

Arsat came through the doorway with noise-less steps and squatted down by the fire. The white man moved his outstretched legs a little.

"She breathes," said Arsat in a low voice, anticipating the expected question. "She breathes and burns as if with a great fire. She speaks not; she hears not—and burns!"

He paused for a moment, then asked in a quiet, incurious[20] tone—

"Tuan . . . will she die?"

The white man moved his shoulders uneasily and muttered in a hesitating manner—

"If such is her fate."

"No, Tuan," said Arsat, calmly. "If such is my fate. I hear, I see, I wait. I remember . . . Tuan, do you remember the old days? Do you remem-ber my brother?"

"Yes," said the white man. The Malay rose suddenly and went in. The other, sitting still out-side, could hear the voice in the hut. Arsat said: "Hear me! Speak!" His words were succeeded by a complete silence. "O Diamelen!" he cried, suddenly. After that cry there was deep sigh. Arsat came out and sank down again in his old place.

They sat in silence before the fire. There was no sound within the house, there was no sound near them; but far away on the lagoon they could hear the voices of the boatmen ringing fit-ful and distinct on the calm water. The fire in the bows of the sampan shone faintly in the dis-tance with a hazy red glow. Then it died out. The voices ceased. The land and the water slept invisible, unstirring and mute. It was as though there had been nothing left in the world but the glitter of stars streaming, ceaseless and vain, through the black stillness of the night.

The white man gazed straight before him into the darkness with wide-open eyes. The fear and fascination, the inspiration and the wonder of death—of death near, unavoidable, and unseen, soothed the unrest of his race and stirred the most indistinct, the most intimate of his thoughts. The ever-ready suspicion of evil, the gnawing sus-picion that lurks in our hearts, flowed out into the stillness round him—into the stillness profound and dumb, and made it appear untrustworthy

---

16. **audacious** (ô dā′shəs), *adj.* bold.
17. **conflagration** (kon′flə grā′shən), *n.* fire.
18. **impalpable** (im pal′pə bəl), *adj.* not capable of being touched.
19. **abysmal** (ə biz′məl), *adj.* bottomless.
20. **incurious** (in kyùr′ē əs), *adj.* unquestioning.

The Lagoon **589**

9

10

11

12

---

9 **Literary Element**
Characterization

Questions How is Arsat characterized? *(as a man who is caring toward his female companion; loyal to his friends; hospitable; able to keep his mouth shut; and brave)* By whom is Arsat characterized? *(both by the third-person narrator and by the white man through the omniscient narrator)*

10 **Reading/Thinking Skills**
Detect Bias

Question What do you detect from the white man's musing about his affection for Arsat? *(The musing reveals how he views Arsat—not as his equal. It may also reveal how the author—Conrad—views Arsat.)*

11 **Literary Element**
Imagery

Question Note that Conrad has used contrasting light and dark imagery from the beginning of the story. What might the setting sun imagery foreshadow? *(Possible responses: that the rest of the story will be dark, hopeless, abysmal, wild; that the sick woman will die, as the day has died)*

12 **Reading/Thinking Skills**
Find the Main Idea

Question What do you think has hap-pened? *(The woman, apparently, has lapsed into unconsciousness.)*

BUILDING ENGLISH PROFICIENCY

Contrasting Points of View

The white man and the Malay boatmen have very different images of Arsat. Help students clarify these differing points of view.

1. Ask students to make a T-chart like the one shown. In the left-hand column, they should write the feelings of the boatmen about Arsat; in the right-hand column, they should note the feelings of the white man.

2. Have students discuss why these characters see the same man so differently.

MALAYS	WHITE MAN
• afraid of Arsat • think Arsat has supernatural powers	• likes Arsat well enough • finds Arsat useful

13 Reading/Thinking Skills

Recognize Cause and Effect

Question How is the white man affected by the sense that death is near? *(Possible response: It both soothes and stirs his emotions. He projects internalized fears onto the dark of the jungle; he associates death with strife and violence, feelings that are both "terrible and charming, august or ignoble.")*

14 Literary Element

Alliteration

Question What do the alliterative *s* sounds in this sentence suggest? *(Possible response: Their repetition suggests the sibilant sounds of whispering, as if one could hear the "plaintive murmur" of the night.)*

15 Literary Element

Flashback

Question You might remind students that *flashback* is a literary device in which an earlier event is inserted into the normal chronological order of a narrative. Why do you think Conrad inserts the flashback tale of Arsat and his brother? *(Possible response: to reveal necessary information in an interesting, dramatic fashion)*

---

and infamous,[21] like the placid and impenetrable mask of an unjustifiable violence. In that fleeting and powerful disturbance of his being the earth enfolded in the starlight peace became a shadowy country of inhuman strife, a battlefield of phantoms terrible and charming, august or ignoble,[22] struggling ardently[23] for the possession of our helpless hearts. An unquiet and mysterious country of inextinguishable desires and fears.

A plaintive[24] murmur rose in the night; a murmur saddening and startling, as if the great solitudes of surrounding woods had tried to whisper into his ear the wisdom of their immense and lofty indifference. Sounds hesitating and vague floated in the air round him, shaped themselves slowly into words; and at last flowed on gently in a murmuring stream of soft and monotonous sentences. He stirred like a man waking up and changed his position slightly. Arsat, motionless and shadowy, sitting with bowed head under the stars, was speaking in a low and dreamy tone—

". . . for where can we lay down the heaviness of our trouble but in a friend's heart? A man must speak of war and of love. You, Tuan, know what war is, and you have seen me in time of danger seek death as other men seek life! A writing may be lost; a lie may be written; but what the eye has seen is truth and remains in the mind!"

"I remember," said the white man, quietly. Arsat went on with mournful composure—

"Therefore I shall speak to you of love. Speak in the night. Speak before both night and love are gone—and the eye of day looks upon my sorrow and my shame; upon my blackened face; upon my burnt-up heart."

A sigh, short and faint, marked an almost imperceptible[25] pause, and then his words flowed on, without a stir, without a gesture.

"After the time of trouble and war was over and you went away from my country in the pur-

. . . what the eye has seen is truth and remains in the mind!

suit of your desires which we, men of the islands, cannot understand, I and my brother became again, as we had been before, the sword-bearers of the Ruler. You know we were men of family, belonging to a ruling race, and more fit than any to carry on our right shoulder the emblem of power. And in the time of prosperity Si Dendring showed us favor, as we, in time of sorrow, had showed to him the faithfulness of our courage. It was a time of peace. A time of deer-hunts and cock-fights; of idle talks and foolish squabbles between men whose bellies are full and weapons are rusty. But the sower watched the young rice-shoots grow up without fear, and the traders came and went, departed lean and returned fat into the river of peace. They brought news, too. Brought lies and truth mixed together, so that no man knew when to rejoice and when to be sorry. We heard from them about you also. They had seen you here and had seen you there. And I was glad to hear, for I remembered the stirring times, and I always remembered you, Tuan, till the time came when my eyes could see nothing in the past, because they had looked upon the one who is dying there—in the house."

He stopped to exclaim in an intense whisper, "O Mara bahia! O Calamity!" then went on speaking a little louder:

"There's no worse enemy and no better friend than a brother, Tuan, for one brother knows another, and in perfect knowledge is

---

21. **infamous** (in′fə məs), *adj.* disgraceful.
22. **august** (ô gust′), *adj.* **or ignoble** (ig nō′bəl), *adj.* majestic or humble.
23. **ardently** (ärd′nt lē), *adv.* eagerly.
24. **plaintive** (plān′tiv), *adj.* mournful.
25. **imperceptible** (im′pər sep′tə bəl), *adj.* that cannot be noticed; slight.

MINI-LESSON: GRAMMAR

Understanding Active and Passive Verbs

Explain to students that in the active voice, the pattern of the sentence is subject, verb, object. (Example: *He* threw *the ball*.) But when a writer uses the passive voice, the pattern of the sentence is reversed and the preposition *by* is necessary: object, verb, by subject. (Example: *The ball* was thrown *by him*. Even though *The ball* is now the subject of the sentence, it is the object, the receiver, of the action.) In the active voice, the feeling of action is stronger and more direct. Some examples of sentences written in the active or passive voice are

- p. 589: "His words were succeeded by a complete silence." (passive)
- p. 590: "But the sower watched the young rice-shoots grow up without fear . . ." (active)

- p. 590: ". . . I remembered the stirring times . . ." (active)

Activity Ideas

- Have students find other sentences in the story that are in either the active or the passive voice. Have them rewrite the sentences in the opposite voice to see the effect of the change.
- Students can write their own sentences in the active or passive voice.

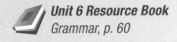 **Unit 6 Resource Book**
Grammar, p. 60

16 strength for good or evil. I loved my brother. I went to him and told him that I could see nothing but one face, hear nothing but one voice. He told me: 'Open your heart so that she can see what is in it—and wait. Patience is wisdom. Inchi Midah may die or our Ruler may throw off his fear of a woman!' . . . I waited! . . . You remember the lady with the veiled face, Tuan, and the fear of our Ruler before her cunning and temper. And if she wanted her servant, what could I do? But I fed the hunger of my heart on short glances and stealthy²⁶ words. I loitered on the path to the bath-houses in the daytime, and when the sun had fallen behind the forest I crept along the jasmine hedges of the women's courtyard. Unseeing, we spoke to one another through the scent of flowers, through the veil of leaves, through the blades of long grass that stood still before our lips; so great was our prudence, so faint was the murmur of our great longing. The time passed swiftly . . . and there were whispers amongst women—and our enemies watched—my brother was gloomy, and I began to think of killing and of a fierce death

17 . . . . We are of a people who take what they want—like you whites. There is a time when a man should forget loyalty and respect. Might and authority are given to rulers, but to all men is given love and strength and courage. My brother said, 'You shall take her from the midst. We are two who are like one.' And I answered, 'Let it be soon, for I find no warmth in sunlight that does not shine upon her.' Our time came when the Ruler and all the great people went to the mouth of the river to fish by torchlight. There were hundreds of boats, and on the white sand, between the water and the forests, dwellings of leaves were built for the households of the Rajahs. The smoke of cooking-fires was like a blue mist of the evening, and many voices rang in it joyfully. While they were making the boats ready to beat up the fish, my brother came to me and said, 'To-night!' I looked to my weapons, and when the time came our canoe took its place in the circle of boats carrying the torches. The lights blazed on the water, but behind the boats there was darkness. When the shouting began and the excitement made them like mad we dropped out. The water swallowed our fire, and we floated back to the shore that was dark with only here and there the glimmer of embers. We could hear the talk of slavegirls amongst the sheds. Then we found a place deserted and silent. We waited there. She came. She came running along the shore, rapid and leaving no trace, like a leaf driven by the wind into the sea. My brother said gloomily, 'Go and take her; carry her into our boat.' I lifted her in my arms. She panted. Her heart was beating against my breast. I said, 'I take you from those people. You come to the cry of my heart, but my arms take you into my boat against the will of the great!' 'It is right,' said my brother. 'We are men who take what they want and can hold it against many. We should have taken her in daylight.' I said, 'Let us be off'; for since she was in my boat I began to think of our Ruler's many men. 'Yes. Let us be off,' said my brother. 'We are cast out and this boat is our country now—and the sea is our refuge.' He lingered with his foot on the shore, and I entreated²⁷ him to hasten, for I remembered the strokes of her heart against my breast and thought that two men cannot withstand a hundred. We left, paddling downstream close to the bank; and as we passed by the creek where they were fishing, the great shouting had ceased, but the murmur of voices was loud like the humming of insects flying at noonday. The boats floated, clustered together, in the red light of torches, under a black roof of smoke; and men talked of their sport. Men that boasted, and praised, and jeered—men that would have been our friends in the morning, but on that night were already our enemies. We paddled swiftly past. We had no more friends in the country of our birth. She sat in the middle of the canoe with covered face; silent as she is now; unseeing

26. **stealthy** (stelʹthē), *adj.* secret.
27. **entreat** (en trētʹ), *v.* beg.

The Lagoon **591**

---

16 Literary Element
Characterization

Question What do you think Arsat's comment about brothers reveals about his character? *(Possible responses: that he is a realist, i.e., he loves his brother, but knows his brother's faults; or that he is very cynical about human nature)*

17 Reading/Thinking Skills
Recognize Values

Questions What do you think the statement about "taking . . . like you whites" reveals about Arsat? *(Possible responses: It reveals his admiration for strength and courage; it suggests that he is ruthless.)* What do you think it reveals about his attitude toward Europeans? *(Possible response: He admires their drive and ruthlessness.)*

BUILDING ENGLISH PROFICIENCY

Describing a Place

One way to get students to connect to the detailed descriptions found in Conrad is to have them try creating their own.

1. Using photos (and perhaps videotape), inspire students to write a paragraph of their own describing a forest, river, or lagoon. (You may choose another scene as well, as long as all students write about the same one.)

2. Challenge students to use special descriptive adjectives and verbs by referring to a thesaurus. Set a minimum number of words to use (perhaps five to ten) that students either didn't know before or seldom use.

3. After you return their papers, have students volunteer words to write on the board for a class list of descriptive words.

Reading/Thinking Skills
Draw Conclusions

Question What can you conclude about the brother's attitude from "There is half a man in you now . . . When you are a whole man again, you will . . . shout defiance." *(Instead of skulking, the brother wants to openly defy authority. He thinks Arsat's courage has been displaced by love, which has made him cautious, unmanly.)*

Literary Element
Foreshadowing

Question What might the simile comparing the canoe to a poison arrow foreshadow? *(Possible responses: Their fate is poisoned; they rush forward to their doom.)*

Reader's Response
Making Personal Connections

Question Does Conrad accurately capture the sensation of physical exhaustion? *(Students who disagree might suggest additional details.)*

Literary Focus
Setting

Question Why does Conrad interrupt the flashback and return the narrative to the lagoon setting? *(As the exhausted brothers take a breather, so does the text—a device that increases suspense.)*

---

as she is now—and I had no regret at what I was leaving because I could hear her breathing close to me—as I can hear her now."

He paused, listened with his ear turned to the doorway, then shook his head and went on:

"My brother wanted to shout the cry of challenge—one cry only—to let the people know we were freeborn robbers who trusted our arms and the great sea. And again I begged him in the name of our love to be silent. Could I not hear her breathing close to me? I knew the pursuit would come quick enough. My brother loved me. He dipped his paddle without a splash. He only said, 'There is half a man in you now—the other half is in that woman. I can wait. When you are a whole man again, you will come back with me here to shout defiance. We are sons of the same mother.' I made no answer. All my strength and all my spirit were in my hands that held the paddle—for I longed to be with her in a safe place beyond the reach of men's anger and of women's spite. My love was so great, that I thought it could guide me to a country where death was unknown, if I could only escape from Inchi Midah's fury and from our Ruler's sword. We paddled with haste, breathing through our teeth. The blades bit deep into the smooth water. We passed out of the river; we flew in clear channels amongst the shallows. We skirted the black coast; we skirted the sand beaches where the sea speaks in whispers to the land; and the gleam of white sand flashed back past our boat, so swiftly she ran upon the water. We spoke not. Only once I said, 'Sleep, Diamelen, for soon you may want all your strength.' I heard the sweetness of her voice, but I never turned my head. The sun rose and still we went on. Water fell from my face like rain from a cloud. We flew in the light and heat. I never looked back, but I knew that my brother's eyes, behind me, were looking steadily ahead, for the boat went as straight as a bushman's dart, when it leaves the end of the sumpitan.[28] There was no better paddler, no better steersman than my

brother. Many times, together, we had won races in that canoe. But we never had put out our strength as we did then—then, when for the last time we paddled together! There was no braver or stronger man in our country than my brother. I could not spare the strength to turn my head and look at him, but every moment I heard the hiss of his breath getting louder behind me. Still he did not speak. The sun was high. The heat clung to my back like a flame of fire. My ribs were ready to burst, but I could no longer get enough air into my chest. And then I felt I must cry out with my last breath, 'Let us rest!' . . . 'Good!' he answered; and his voice was firm. He was strong. He was brave. He knew not fear and no fatigue . . . My brother!"

A murmur powerful and gentle, a murmur vast and faint; the murmur of trembling leaves, of stirring boughs, ran through the tangled depths of the forests, ran over the starry smoothness of the lagoon, and the water between the piles lapped the slimy timber once with a sudden splash. A breath of warm air touched the two men's faces and passed on with a mournful sound—a breath loud and short like an uneasy sigh of the dreaming earth.

Arsat went on in an even, low voice.

"We ran our canoe on the white beach of a little bay close to a long tongue of land that seemed to bar our road; a long wooded cape going far into the sea. My brother knew that place. Beyond the cape a river has its entrance, and through the jungle of that land there is a narrow path. We made a fire and cooked rice. Then we lay down to sleep on the soft sand in the shade of our canoe, while she watched. No sooner had I closed my eyes than I heard her cry of alarm. We leaped up. The sun was halfway down the sky already, and coming in sight in the opening of the bay we saw a prau[29] manned by many pad-

---

28. **sumpitan** (sum′pi tan), *n.* a type of blowgun used by the natives of Borneo and nearby islands to propel a poisoned dart.
29. **prau** (prou), *n.* a swift Malay sailing boat.

MINI-LESSON: WRITING STYLE

Imagery and Figurative Language

Teach Conrad's writing style provides an example of rich, lyrical, sensuous prose. The descriptions of the lagoon are full of dense imagery and figurative language. The sentences themselves are structured in a complex and elegant way.

Question Ask students why they think Conrad wrote "The Lagoon" in this rich, sensuous prose style. *(Possible responses: Conrad's prose style, with his rich descriptions, enables the reader to fully experience the world of the lagoon; his complex sentences parallel the lagoon's twisting, eerie world.)*

Activity Ideas

- Have students use Conrad's writing style to describe a journey they have taken.
- Have students attempt to rewrite a paragraph in "The Lagoon" with simple, declarative sentences. How does this change the mood?

This engraving shows a lakatoi (lä′kä tō′ē), a double-hulled dugout canoe used by the islanders of Indonesia. What is the first impression you get from the image of this boat?

Art Study

Response to Caption Question   The boat looks like a dragon: the prow is carved to replicate the head of a dragon; the sails give the impression of dragon wings.

22 **Literary Element**
Characterization

Question   What does the brother's plan of defense suggest about his character? *(Possible response: He is brave, willing to take risks, and willing to sacrifice himself for Arsat.)*

dlers. We knew it at once; it was one of our Rajah's praus. They were watching the shore, and saw us. They beat the gong, and turned the head of the prau into the bay. I felt my heart become weak within my breast. Diamelen sat on the sand and covered her face. There was no escape by sea. My brother laughed. He had the gun you had given him, Tuan, before you went away, but there was only a handful of powder. He spoke to me quickly: 'Run with her along the path. I shall keep them back, for they have no firearms, and landing in the face of a man with a gun is certain death for some. Run with her. On the other side of that wood there is a fisherman's house—and a canoe. When I have fired all the shots I will follow. I am a great runner, and before they can come up we shall be gone. I will hold out as long as I can, for she is but a woman—that can neither run nor fight, but she has your heart in her weak

hands.' He dropped behind the canoe. The prau was coming. She and I ran, and as we rushed along the path I heard shots. My brother fired—once—twice—and the booming of the gong ceased. There was silence behind us. That neck of land is narrow. Before I heard my brother fire the third shot I saw the shelving[30] shore, and I saw the water again; the mouth of a broad river. We crossed a grassy glade. We ran down to the water. I saw a low hut above the black mud, and a small canoe hauled up. I heard another shot behind me. I thought, 'That is his last charge.' We rushed down to the canoe; a man came running from the hut, but I leaped on him, and we rolled together in the mud. Then I got up, and he lay still at my feet. I don't know whether I had killed him or not. I and Diamelen pushed the canoe

---

30. **shelving** (shel′ving), *adj.* sloping.

The Lagoon   **593**

BUILDING ENGLISH PROFICIENCY

Analyzing Cultural Distinctives

Arsat and his brother belonged to a warrior culture with a system of values very different from those generally held in the United States. Confirm students' understanding of these cultural distinctives.

1. Have students list details from Arsat's narrative on pages 590–592 that define his culture for the reader.

2. Divide the class into small discussion groups and have students share their lists. Ask each group to create a master list to form a more comprehensive picture of this culture.

3. After a spokesperson from each group shares the group's list with the class, discuss Arsat's cultural mores.

Earlier in the story, Arsat states, "There's no worse enemy and no better friend than a brother . . ." At this point in the story, who do you think Arsat was referring to when he said, "no worse enemy"? and when he said, "no better friend"? *(The "worse enemy" is Arsat; the "no better friend" is the brother.)*

Possible response Diamelen meets Arsat and his brother by the shore. They escape by canoe. Eventually, they stop to rest. When one of the Rajah's boats turns into the bay, the brother tells Arsat to run ahead; the brother will fend off the others with his gun, and then will join them. When Arsat hears his brother being attacked, hears his brother's cry for help, he runs on, thinking only of Diamelen.

Question How does this change in the setting affect the mood? *(Possible responses: The fog erases the stars, turns everything gray and cold, seems to set the hut into a dark, pitiless sea; the mood is forlorn and lonely.)*

Question What is ironic about this statement? *(The statement seems offhanded and banal, an inadequate response; it suggests that we don't all love our brothers or that we don't love them sufficiently to stop "denying" them, i.e., sacrificing them for our own gain. It also suggests that the white man knows from personal experience what Arsat feels.)*

---

afloat. I heard yells behind me, and I saw my brother run across the glade. Many men were bounding after him. I took her in my arms and threw her into the boat, then leaped in myself. When I looked back I saw that my brother had fallen. He fell and was up again, but the men were closing round him. He shouted, 'I am coming!' The men were close to him. I looked. Many men. Then I looked at her. Tuan, I pushed the canoe! I pushed it into deep water. She was kneeling forward looking at me, and I said, 'Take your paddle,' while I struck the water with mine. Tuan, I heard him cry. I heard him cry my name twice; and I heard voices shouting, 'Kill! Strike!' I never **23** turned back. I heard him calling my name again with a great shriek, as when life is going out together with the voice—and I never turned my head. My own name! . . . My brother! Three times he called—but I was not afraid of life. Was she not there in that canoe? And could I not with her find a country where death is forgotten—where death is unknown!"

24 **SUMMARIZE: Summarize the events of the stealing of Diamelen.**

The white man sat up. Arsat rose and stood, an indistinct and silent figure above the dying embers of the fire. Over the lagoon a mist drifting and low had crept, erasing slowly the glittering images of the stars. And now a great expanse of white vapor covered the land; it flowed cold and gray in the darkness, eddied in noiseless whirls round the tree-trunks and about the platform of the house, which seemed to float upon a restless and impalpable illusion of a sea. Only far away the tops of the trees stood outlined on the twinkle of heaven, like a somber and forbidding shore—a coast deceptive, **25** pitiless and black.

What did I care who died? I wanted peace in my own heart.

Arsat's voice vibrated loudly in the profound peace.

"I had her there! I had her! To get her I would have faced all mankind. But I had her—and——"

His words went out ringing into the empty distances. He paused, and seemed to listen to them dying away very far—beyond help and beyond recall. Then he said quietly—

"Tuan, I loved my brother."

A breath of wind made him shiver. High above his head, high above the silent sea of mist the drooping leaves of the palms rattled together with a mournful and expiring sound. The white man stretched his legs. His chin rested on his chest, and he murmured sadly without lifting his head—

"We all love our brothers." **26**

Arsat burst out with an intense whispering violence—

"What did I care who died? I wanted peace in my own heart."

He seemed to hear a stir in the house—listened—then stepped in noiselessly. The white man stood up. A breeze was coming in fitful puffs. The stars shone paler as if they had retreated into the frozen depths of immense space. After a chill gust of wind there were a few seconds of perfect calm and absolute silence. Then from behind the black and wavy line of the forests a column of golden light shot up into the heavens and spread over the semicircle of the eastern horizon. The sun had risen. The mist lifted, broke into drifting patches, vanished into thin flying wreaths; and the unveiled lagoon lay, polished and black, in the heavy shadows at the foot of the wall of trees.

A white eagle rose over it with a slanting and ponderous flight, reached the clear sunshine and appeared dazzlingly brilliant for a moment,

---

MINI-LESSON: VOCABULARY

Etymology

Teach Learning origins of words by looking up their etymologies can help students understand a word's meaning today.

Activity Idea Divide the class into groups and assign each group three words from the vocabulary list from this selection. Then ask each group to pick out another word they may not understand from the selection. They will track down the etymology of each word. Ask students to

- check a dictionary to see if each word is in its most basic form, free of added prefixes or suffixes
- find the word's etymology in the dictionary
- brainstorm other words that share the same root as the word
- give a report to the class on etymologies and links to other words

then soaring higher, became a dark and motionless speck before it vanished into the blue as if it had left the earth forever. The white man, standing gazing upwards before the doorway, heard in the hut a confused broken murmur of distracted words ending with a loud groan. Suddenly Arsat stumbled out with outstretched hands, shivered, and stood still for some time with fixed eyes. Then he said—

"She burns no more."

Before his face the sun showed its edge above the tree-tops rising steadily. The breeze freshened; a great brilliance burst upon the lagoon, sparkled on the rippling water. The forests came out of the clear shadows of the morning, became distinct, as if they had rushed nearer—to stop short in a great stir of leaves, of nodding boughs, of swaying branches. In the merciless sunshine the whisper of unconscious life grew louder, speaking in an incomprehensible[31] voice round the dumb darkness of that human sorrow. Arsat's eyes wandered slowly, then stared at the rising sun.

"I can see nothing," he said half aloud to himself.

"There is nothing," said the white man, moving to the edge of the platform and waving his hand to his boat. A shout came faintly over the lagoon and the sampan began to glide towards the abode of the friend of ghosts.

"If you want to come with me, I will wait all the morning," said the white man, looking away upon the water.

27 EVALUATE: Judge the way the white man responds to Arsat's story and to the death of Diamelen.

"No, Tuan," said Arsat, softly. "I shall not eat or sleep in this house, but I must first see my road. Now I can see nothing—see nothing! There is no light and no peace in the world; but there is death—death for many. We are sons of the same mother—and I left him in the midst of enemies; but I am going back now."

He drew a long breath and went on in a dreamy tone:

"In a little while I shall see clear enough to strike—to strike. But she has died, and . . . now . . . darkness."

He flung his arms wide open, let them fall along his body, then stood still with unmoved face and stony eyes, staring at the sun. The white man got down into his canoe. The polers ran smartly along the sides of the boat, looking over their shoulders at the beginning of a weary journey. High in the stern, his head muffled up in white rags, the juragan sat moody, letting his paddle trail in the water. The white man, leaning with both arms over the grass roof of the little cabin, looked back at the shining ripple of the boat's wake. Before the sampan passed out of the lagoon into the creek he lifted his eyes. Arsat had not moved. He stood lonely in the searching sunshine; and he looked beyond the great light of a cloudless day into the darkness of a world of illusions. **28**

---

31. incomprehensible (in′kom pri hen′sə bəl), *adj.* impossible to understand.

The Lagoon **595**

---

27 Active Reading
Evaluate

Possible response His response, "We all love our brothers," seems banal, but may be a connection through personal revelation. His response to the death is in keeping with their kind of friendship: there is no display of emotion; help is offered with sincerity; the refusal of help is accepted without further comment because nothing more needs saying.

28 Literary Element
Theme

Questions At the end of the story, Arsat, who plans to revenge his brother's death, looks beyond the light into the "darkness of a world of illusions." What do you think Conrad means by "world of illusions"? *(Possible response: that revenge will not make him a "full man" again; the betrayal of his brother has exiled him into permanent darkness.)* When Arsat states that he can see nothing, the white man replies "There is nothing." What do you think is meant by the reply? *(Possible response: It suggests that Arsat will never find his way out; and it suggests that the white man, who "takes what he wants," knows this from experience.)*

Check Test

1. What is the relationship between the white man and Arsat? *(They are friends from long ago.)*

2. What is wrong with the woman? *(She is dying.)*

3. Why does Arsat want to abduct the woman? *(He is in love with her, and she, apparently, is unavailable.)*

4. Why does the brother tell Arsat to run ahead when the Rajah's soldiers arrive? *(to escape)*

5. How does brother betray brother? *(When the brothers calls for help, Arsat chooses the woman.)*

Unit 6 Resource Book
Alternate Check Test, p. 61

BUILDING ENGLISH PROFICIENCY

Expanding Vocabulary Notebooks

Encourage students to continue to add to their vocabulary notebooks as they read. As "The Lagoon" concludes, for example, you might suggest that students define and create original sentences for the following adjectives from pages 590–593: freeborn, profound, wooded, expiring, indistinct, fitful, impalpable, ponderous, somber, stony, forbidding, searching.

After Reading

MAKING CONNECTIONS

1. Most students will sympathize with either Arsat or his brother.

2. Students will probably feel the tone is pessimistic, based on prevalent mood and the final image.

3. The white man is used as a basis of comparison. Both men are cut off from their own kind; both "take what they want"; both live in darkness.

4. While the depth of the friendship is unequal, both share in a bond that allows Arsat to relate his tale.

5. He admires their ruthlessness at "taking what they want."

6. He speaks of romantic love and brotherly love. Outside forces oppose the romantic love; interior forces destroy brotherly love.

7. Arsat's punishment for betraying his brother is to find himself forever "outside," alone in the dark.

8. to make himself "whole" again through revenge

9. Conrad introduces light and dark imagery, and the concept of hope and despair, with his description of the river flowing "to the east that harbors both light and darkness." Other examples are numerous: "streaked glitter of the river" contrasted to "the darkness . . . of impenetrable forests"; "conflagration of sunset" put out by "black and impalpable vapor"; "white eagle" soars over "the black lagoon"; in the end, this imagery reflects the state of the two men's souls.

10. Conrad may be suggesting that certain actions can isolate one until "there is nothing." Student responses will vary.

11. One possible response: It would be a good movie: it would have beauty, action, adventure, a serious theme, and a love interest. The story would best be told in the same flashback sequence as the original.

After Reading

Making Connections

Shaping Your Response

1. For which character in the story do you feel the greatest sympathy? Why?

2. Do you feel that Conrad's general **tone** in this story is optimistic or pessimistic? Explain your response.

Analyzing the Story

3. Why do you think the author includes a white man in this story of Malay natives?

4. How close are the white man and Arsat, and how does their relationship affect Arsat's situation?

5. What is Arsat's **perspective** of the culture of the white man?

6. Arsat speaks repeatedly of "love." What is the nature of love in this story? What forces arise in opposition to it?

7. In your opinion, what is the connection between Arsat's crime and his punishment?

8. Why do you think Arsat decides to return to the kingdom from which he has escaped?

9. Trace the **images** of darkness and light throughout the story. Discuss the symbolism of each image.

Extending the Ideas

10. In the story of Arsat, what comment does Conrad seem to make about the way words and actions influence a person's life? Do you agree with him?

11. If you were writing the movie script for this story, where would you begin the story and where would you end it? Is the whole interest in the movie contained in the long **flashback?**

Literary Focus: Setting

Setting is the time (both time of day and period in history) and place in which the action of a story takes place. Could this story have taken place in England? in America? What is important about this particular setting? How does the setting influence the plot?

Vocabulary Study

Write the word from the list that best completes the meaning of each sentence. You will not use all the words.

1. The dark and mysterious forests along the river loomed so thick and imposing that they appeared to be _____.

2. The black waters of the hidden lagoon were still and _____.

596   UNIT SIX: THE VICTORIANS

LITERARY FOCUS: SETTING

Possible Responses

- The story could be set in England or America if it were placed in a location of similar physical and metaphorical mystery and isolation, such as a heath in England or the Everglades or Great Dismal Swamp in the United States.

- The physical setting of the lagoon is important because the dense, dark, lush flora of the lagoon parallels the theme of the story—the certainty of mortality and the power of love and passion.

- The isolated setting mirrors the emotional isolation of the characters.

abysmal
audacious
demeanor
enticed
impenetrable
incomprehensible
infamous
ominous
plaintive
propitiate
stagnant
stealthy

3. The night was so black and dark that it seemed like an _____ pit.

4. Arsat had been so _____ by the beauty and charm of Diamelen that he had to have her for his own.

5. The _____ meetings between Arsat and Diamelen were held at night in remote places.

6. The stealing of Diamelen by Arsat and his brother was an _____ move since they were just two against more than one hundred.

7. Arsat knew that stealing Diamelen had made him _____ among his people.

8. As soon as the white man saw how ill Diamelen was, he knew that the situation was _____.

9. As Arsat realized that Diamelen was indeed going to die, his cries became more _____.

10. Although at times Arsat found Diamelen's death _____, at other times he felt her death was a result of his treatment of his brother.

Expressing Your Ideas

Writing Choices

Writer's Notebook Update Look back at your notes about being out of your element. Think about what you learned or how you changed as a result of your encounter. Write a paragraph or so about your experience.

Analyze Conrad's Style The American writer H. L. Mencken once said, "Conrad may not have been the greatest novelist, but he was the greatest artist who wrote novels." Write an **essay** in which you analyze the artistic style of Joseph Conrad's writing. You might consider his use of simile, metaphor, repetition, imagery, and parallel structure.

Home Again Write the story of Arsat's return to the kingdom from which he stole Diamelen and where he abandoned his brother. First consider what characters to include. (Is there any way to work in the white man?) Then

decide what the main actions will be. Be sure you know the ending before you start to write.

Other Options

Debate Arsat's Dilemma Work with a partner to prepare an informal **debate** on the following question: Should Arsat have left his brother behind or should he have gone back to rescue him? Among the factors you may want to consider are the depth of Arsat's love, the importance of family, the time frame in which Arsat had to make his decision, the power of the men chasing his brother, and Arsat's current situation.

Diamelen Remembered Imagine how Arsat would want to remember Diamelen. Create a **marker and its inscription** for Diamelen's grave. Accompany your creation with a description of the memorial service you think Arsat would hold.

The Lagoon   **597**

VOCABULARY STUDY

1. impenetrable
2. stagnant
3. abysmal
4. enticed
5. stealthy
6. audacious
7. infamous
8. ominous
9. plaintive
10. incomprehensible

 Unit 6 Resource Book
Vocabulary, p. 59
Vocabulary Test, p. 62

WRITING CHOICES
Writer's Notebook Update

In looking at their notes, students might want to identify the strongest feeling or reaction they had, and begin their paragraph with that.

Analyze Conrad's Style

You might ask students to find an example of each before they begin writing.

Home Again

Before students begin their stories, they might brainstorm a variety of opening sentences, which students could "borrow" to begin their stories.

Selection Test

 Unit 6 Resource Book
pp. 63–64

OTHER OPTIONS
Debate Arsat's Dilemma

Before they split up into pairs to prepare a debate, have the class brainstorm possible answers to the questions.

Diamelen Remembered

Arsat's religious background is not clear. You might suggest that students research Islam, Buddhism, and animism to find out what an appropriate memorial service might be like in these religions. Or, students could make the memorial service nonreligious.

Before Reading

Building Background

Ask students to consider why people write, when they write, and under what circumstances they might feel inspired to write their best work.

Literary Focus

After explaining the concept of *anastrophe*, you might ask students to examine the rhythmic impact and imagery of the following lines:

—The night air is sweet
Sweet is the night air—

Writer's Notebook

As you write, consider what the advice was, who gave it, and why the advice appealed to you. Would the same advice have seemed different if it had come from someone else?

More About A. E. Housman

Housman, whose initials stood for Alfred Edward, never married; he lived a secluded life within Trinity College, Cambridge. His last poems were published after his death, under the title *More Poems,* by his brother, Lawrence Housman, a playwright.

Before Reading

When I Was One-and-Twenty
Loveliest of Trees
To an Athlete Dying Young by A. E. Housman

A. E. Housman
1859–1936

A. E. Housman was a promising scholar of classical languages, but he failed his Oxford comprehensive examination through inadequate preparation. For ten years, while he held a dreary civil service job in London, he spent his free time studying the classics and publishing scholarly essays. In 1893 his stature as a scholar helped him earn the post of Professor of Latin at the University of London. That success seemed to inspire his poetic spirit and within two years he had assembled a collection of 58 poems. At his own expense he published *A Shropshire Lad,* also called *Poems by Terence Hearsay.* Although he published another collection, *Last Poems,* in 1922, most of those lyrics were from the time of his first book.

Building Background

The Bubbling Spring A. E. Housman describes how his poems often began: "Having drunk a pint of beer at luncheon—beer is a sedative to the brain, and my afternoons are the least intellectual portion of my life—I would go out for a walk of two or three hours. As I went along, thinking of nothing in particular, only looking at things around me and following the progress of the seasons, there would flow into my mind, with sudden and unaccountable emotion, sometimes a line or two of verse, sometimes a whole stanza at once, accompanied, not preceded, by a vague notion of the poem which they were destined to form a part of. Then there would usually be a lull of an hour or so, then perhaps the spring would bubble up again. . . When I got home I wrote them down, leaving gaps, and hoping that further inspiration might be forthcoming another day."

Literary Focus

Anastrophe The technique of inverting the normal, customary, or logical sequence of words in a sentence to achieve greater dramatic emphasis or to create particular rhythms or rhymes is called **anastrophe** (ə nas′trə fē). For example, Tennyson's "The Lady of Shalott" begins, "On either side the river lie / Long fields of barley and of rye. . . ." in which *fields* and *lie* are inverted from normal subject-verb order. Look for anastrophe in each of Housman's poems.

Writer's Notebook

Good Advice Think about all of the people who have given you advice—your parents, your teachers, your friends, your coaches, your pastor. Jot down the best piece of advice you have received in your life so far.

SUPPORT MATERIALS OVERVIEW

Unit 6 Resource Book
- Graphic Organizer, p. 65
- Study Guide, p. 66
- Vocabulary, p. 67
- Grammar, p. 68
- Alternate Check Test, p. 69
- Vocabulary Test, p. 70
- Selection Test, pp. 71–72

Building English Proficiency
- Selection Summaries
- Activities, p. 242

Reading, Writing & Grammar SkillBook
- Grammar, Usage, and Mechanics, pp. 214–217

Technology
- Audiotape
- Personal Journal Software
- Custom Literature Database: Additional selections by Housman can be found on the database.
- Test Generator Software

To an Athlete Dying Young

A. E. HOUSMAN

The time you won your town the race
We chaired you through the market place;
Man and boy stood cheering by,
And home we brought you shoulder-high.

1

5 Today, the road all runners come,
Shoulder-high we bring you home,
And set you at your threshold down,
Townsman of a stiller town.

2

Smart lad, to slip betimes[1] away
10 From fields where glory does not stay,
And early though the laurel[2] grows
It withers quicker than the rose.

Eyes the shady night has shut
Cannot see the record cut,[3]
15 And silence sounds no worse than cheers
After earth has stopped the ears.

Now you will not swell the rout[4]
Of lads that wore their honors out,
Runners whom renown[5] outran
20 And the name died before the man.

So set, before its echoes fade,
The fleet foot on the sill of shade,
And hold to the low lintel up
The still-defended challenge cup.

25 And round that early-laureled head
Will flock to gaze the strengthless dead,
And find unwithered on its curls
The garland briefer than a girl's.

---

1. **betimes** (bi tīmz′), *adv.* early.
2. **laurel.** In Greek and Roman times victorious athletes and celebrated poets would be crowned with a wreath of laurel leaves.
3. **cut,** improved upon; broken.
4. **swell the rout,** increase the crowd.
5. renown (ri noun′), *n.* fame.

To an Athlete Dying Young   **599**

During Reading

Selection Objectives

- to analyze the use of anastrophe to add impact and enhance rhyme
- to assess the use of poetry in the telling of a story or the conveying of values
- to use adjective forms effectively

Unit 6 Resource Book
Graphic Organizer, p. 65
Study Guide, p. 66

Theme Link

In Housman's lifetime, almost all aspects of life, from economic and industrial to family and class structure, changed with great rapidity, creating a national mood of hope and despair. Burdened with a dark view of human prospects, Housman was prey to the unsettling doubts of his times.

Vocabulary Preview

renown, fame

Students can add the word and its definition to their Writer's Notebooks.

1 ## Multicultural Note
Pallbearers

The phrase "home we brought you shoulder-high" refers to a corpse in a coffin; the "we" refers to pallbearers. In the British Isles, coffins were (and in some places still are) transported on the shoulders of pallbearers, who walk slowly and with great dignity.

2 ## Literary Focus
Anastrophe

Question   What are examples of anastrophe in the first two stanzas? *(line 1—"won your town the race"; line 3—"stood cheering by"; line 4—"home we brought you shoulder-high"; line 5—"the road all runners come"; line 6—"Shoulder-high we bring you home"; line 7—"set you at your threshold down")*

SELECTION SUMMARY

To an Athlete Dying Young; When I Was One-and-Twenty; Loveliest of Trees

To an Athlete Dying Young   In this elegy, a young man, who had won a race as a younger person, has died and is being brought back to his hometown for burial. Housman explores the benefits of an early death in allowing one to avoid weakening and disillusionment.

When I Was One-and-Twenty   A twenty-two-year-old looks back on the advice received at twenty-one. He was told not to give his heart away in love, and he now regrets that he did not heed the advice.

Loveliest of Trees   The speaker, a twenty-year-old, considers a cherry tree in bloom and decides to pay attention to the blossoming of things, having only fifty more springs to enjoy them.

*For summaries in other languages, see the **Building English Proficiency** book.*

🎨 Art Study

Response to Caption Question   He takes the time now "to look at things in bloom" because he is aware of his mortality; if he lives a normal life span, he will only have 50 more springs in which to view the cherry blossoms.

Visual Literacy   No cherry trees in bloom and no spring day ever looked like this painting. And yet, *Trees in Bloom, Souvenir of Mauve* exactly captures the ecstatic feelings one can experience on such a day: the unearthly beauty of spring flowers; the light and its warmth after a long, gray winter. By using broad brush strokes of many colors, the artist has rendered the orchard ground into a churning sea, not of water, but of mud.

Questions   Where does the movement of the brush strokes lead your eye? *(Possible response: The brush strokes seem to lead one out of the mud and up the tree, into the beauty of the flowers and sky.)* What might this suggest? *(Possible response: The artist's intentions may be similar to Housman's in "Loveliest of Trees"; there are only so many springs in one's life.)*

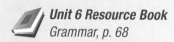

MINI-LESSON: GRAMMAR

Adjective Forms—Positive, Comparative, Superlative

Teach   Adjectives modify nouns or pronouns. When one thing is described, the form of the adjective is called the *positive*. If two things are compared, the form is called the *comparative,* and if three or more things, the form is called the *superlative*. Most adjectives form the comparative by adding *-er* (or the word *more* for a longer adjective) and the superlative by adding *-est* (or the word *most* for a longer adjective). *Less* and *least* with positive adjectives show lesser degrees. For irregular adjectives, the whole word may change. (Examples: tall, taller, tallest; shady, shadier, shadiest; frequent, more frequent, most frequent; far, less far, least far; bad, worse, worst; good, better, best)

Activity Idea   Ask students to locate several adjectives in the poems, identify the nouns that the adjectives modify, and then state whether they are the positive, comparative, or superlative form.

📖 *Unit 6 Resource Book*
Grammar, p. 68

When I Was One-and-Twenty

A. E. HOUSMAN

3 When I was one-and-twenty
　　I heard a wise man say,
　"Give crowns and pounds and guineas
　　But not your heart away;
5　Give pearls away and rubies
　　But keep your fancy free."
　But I was one-and-twenty,
　　No use to talk to me.
　When I was one-and-twenty
10　I heard him say again,
　"The heart out of the bosom
　　Was never given in vain;
　'Tis paid with sighs a plenty
　　And sold for endless rue."[1]
15 And I am two-and-twenty,
　　And oh, 'tis true, 'tis true.

---

1. **rue** (rü), *n.* sorrow.

Loveliest of Trees

A. E. HOUSMAN

◄ *Trees in Bloom, Souvenir of Mauve* (1888), is an oil painting created by Vincent van Gogh (1853–1890). Why does the speaker in "Loveliest of Trees" take the time now "to look at things in bloom"?

　Loveliest of trees, the cherry now
　Is hung with bloom along the bough,
　And stands about the woodland ride,
　Wearing white for Eastertide.

5　Now, of my threescore years and ten,
　Twenty will not come again,
　And take from seventy springs a score,
　It only leaves me fifty more.

　And since to look at things in bloom
10　Fifty springs are little room,
　About the woodlands I will go
　To see the cherry hung with snow.

4

Loveliest of Trees　**601**

Questions　About what does the wise man warn? *(the emotional costs of love)* What does the narrator mean when he states, "No use to talk to me"? *(The young do not listen to the voice of experience.)* What is the narrator's attitude at the end? *(Possible response: that the price of love is indeed dearer than jewels)*

4 Literary Focus
Anastrophe

Questions　If the first couplets of stanzas 1 and 3 were prose, how might word order differ? *(Possible response: The boughs of the cherry, loveliest of trees, are now hung with bloom; Since fifty springs are little room to look at blooming things.)* Why do you think these couplets were written with similar anastrophes? *(Possible responses: to give parallel structures to the beginning and ending; to lead the reader into comparing images and rhythms)*

Check Test

1. Under what two circumstances was the athlete carried? *(in victory and in death)*

2 Why does the narrator think it wise for a hero to die young? *(to avoid seeing his records broken, his fame fade, and his body weaken)*

3. What advice was the narrator given at age 21? *(He was advised not to give his heart away.)*

4. In these poems, what physical and emotional characteristics of the young does Housman describe? *(Possible responses: beauty, grace, strength, and headstrong attitude)*

5. In "Loveliest of Trees," how many springs does the narrator believe he has left? *(50)*

Unit 6 Resource Book
Alternate Check Test, p. 69

BUILDING ENGLISH PROFICIENCY

Making Personal Connections

ESL
LEP
ELD
SAE
LD

The tone in these poems by A. E. Housman is ironic, suffused with the sadness and short-ness of life. His speakers always seem to view youth from the vantage point of old age.

　Suggest that students write or dictate short passages about their lives now, written from the imagined perspective of an elderly person. Afterward, discuss how this activity has helped them understand Housman's poems better.

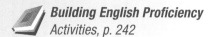
Building English Proficiency
Activities, p. 242

After Reading

MAKING CONNECTIONS

1. Responses will vary but should be substantiated with ideas from the Housman quote.

2. He is smart to die in his prime, untouched by time and disillusionment.

3. He compares laurel and roses, cheers and silence, and suggests that the result of a long life would be the fading of fame and physical ability.

4. that decisions of the heart can and should be made logically, like financial decisions

5. Presumably, his heart has been broken by someone.

6. Yes, in the future he will be more careful to protect his emotions.

7. In stanza one, the tree is dressed for Easter—symbolic of spring and resurrection. In the third stanza, it is covered in snow—symbolic of winter and death.

8. He's figuring out how much longer he has to live based on the biblical promise that each man has three score years and ten to live.

9. Possible responses: that the young must figure things out for themselves and cannot rely on the experiences of others; that all humans learn best by experience.

After Reading

Making Connections

Shaping Your Response

1. Reread Housman's description of how his poems began in Building Background on page 598. Select two or three lines from Housman's poetry that you think might have flown into his mind as inspiration.

Analyzing the Poems

2. In "To an Athlete Dying Young" why does the speaker consider the athlete a "smart lad" (line 9)?

3. Explain the various **images** Housman uses to suggest death and the final resting place.

4. In "When I Was One-and-Twenty" what do you think is suggested by the verbs the wise man uses: *give, keep, paid,* and *sold?*

5. 🐾 What do you infer has happened to the speaker to cause him to change his **perspective** and finally to agree (in line 16) with the wise man?

6. Do you think that the speaker will live his life differently now that he is twenty-two?

7. In "Loveliest of Trees" compare and contrast the tree as described in stanza 1 and in stanza 3.

8. Why do you think the speaker is doing arithmetic in stanza 2?

Extending the Ideas

9. Why do you think boys and girls—indeed men and women—so often do not follow the advice they receive from others?

Literary Focus: Anastrophe

Anastrophe, the inversion of the usual order of the parts of a sentence, is used to emphasize a word or idea or to achieve a certain rhythm or rhyme. Find at least one example of anastrophe in each of Housman's poems. For each example explain why you think he chose to use this inversion.

Vocabulary Study

Create a word map of synonyms for *renown.* Then create a word map of adjectives that might describe someone who has achieved renown.

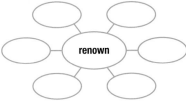

LITERARY FOCUS: ANASTROPHE

Possible Responses

- "To an Athlete Dying Young": "home we brought you"—for rhythm; "And round that early-laureled head/Will flock to gaze the strengthless dead"—for rhyme

- "When I Was One-and-Twenty": one-and-twenty, two-and-twenty—both for rhythm

- "Loveliest of Trees": "And since to look at things in bloom/Fifty springs are little room"—for rhyme; "About the woodlands I will go"—for rhythm

Expressing Your Ideas

Writing Choices

Writer's Notebook Update You've thought about advice given to you. Now write down two or three important "words of wisdom" you would like to share with a younger brother or sister or cousin.

Thanks to You Write a **thank-you letter** to someone who has given you some wise advice. Tell how you reacted to the advice initially, how you incorporated that advice into your life, and how following that advice has changed you. If you don't have such a person in your life, invent a wise character to write to.

Carpe Diem Revisited The speaker in "Loveliest of Trees" decides to "seize the day" and spend time looking at the cherry trees in full bloom. Write a **poem** in which you describe a scene or situation which would cause you to alter your schedule and *carpe diem.*

Carried Shoulder-high Write an **analytic essay** in which you compare and contrast the athlete at the height of his glory with the athlete in death. Use specific images from the poem.

Other Options

Join the Team! In his poem "To an Athlete Dying Young," Housman seems to suggest that the goal of competitive athletics is victory, the laurel wreath. Prepare a **speech** in which you talk about the importance of winning but put it in perspective with other values that can be gained from participating in sports activities. Your audience for your speech will be incoming freshmen and their parents.

Advice from an Upperclassman As an upperclass student you have a wealth of wisdom to share with the underclass students in your school. Prepare a **radio show** in which you answer questions you know are on the minds of many younger students. Your answers can be serious, or maybe you would prefer to write something humorously "tongue in cheek." If you can, record your talk show to play for your class or over the school's public-address system.

How to Decide Some of Housman's poems confront the choices that we must often make in life. Think about a major choice which you will have to make within the next year; for example: Will you attend college, work, or travel? Which college will you choose? What will you select as your major? First identify each of your alternatives; then, draw a **chart** like the following on which you list the pros and cons for each choice. What decision will you make, based on this analysis?

The Question		
Alternative 1	Pros	Cons
Alternative 2	Pros	Cons
Alternative 3	Pros	Cons
My Decision		

To An Athlete Dying Young **603**

VOCABULARY STUDY

Possible synonyms: fame, reputation, honor, name, respectability, credit, esteem, regard, favor, approval

Possible adjectives: superior, star, achiever, celebrity, notorious, immortal

Unit 6 Resource Book
Vocabulary, p. 67
Vocabulary Test, p. 70

WRITING CHOICES
Writers Notebook Update

Suggest to students that the advice given should be appropriate to children of a particular age.

Thanks to You

Some students may prefer to write about advice they wish they had received—and to consider whether they would have heeded it.

Carpe Diem Revisited

Ask students to consider how the decisions a person makes every day about how to spend his or her time on Earth can make a difference.

Carried Shoulder-high

Writing this essay will require students to consider when they think death is most welcome: on the way up, at the peak, or on the way down.

Selection Test

Unit 6 Resource Book
pp. 71–72

OTHER OPTIONS
Join the Team!

Students have probably heard many such speeches about values other than winning. They should make their speeches fresher by enlivening their opinions with anecdotes about real-life athletes and events.

How to Decide

As students think about their future and choices, you may want to discuss the euphemistic phrase "inadequate preparation" in the note about Housman on page 598. Do students think Housman may have regretted not having studied enough for his Oxford comprehensive exam? What might he have been doing instead of studying? How did he pay for his "inadequate preparation"?

Before Reading

Building Background

Theosophy, a system of philosophic and religious thought, is based on the idea that truth and real insight come not through the senses or by reason, but by direct communion of the soul with divine reality. As students read Yeats's work, they should look for evidence of his mystical beliefs.

Literary Focus

Suggest to the class that consonance, also called slant rhyme, is an effective device for linking sound, mood, and meaning.

Writer's Notebook

Ask students to imagine themselves as much older. What would be their concerns about social security? taxes? health care? home security and safety of the streets?

More About Yeats

Yeats spent part of his later life living on the Irish coast in a tower, which appears as a symbol in his poetry of this period. He died and was buried in France during World War II. After the War, his body was returned to Ireland. Poet W. H. Auden wrote

"Earth, receive an honored guest:
William Yeats is laid to rest."

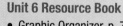

Connections to
AuthorWorks

W. B. Yeats is a featured author in AuthorWorks CD-ROM series.

Before Reading

When You Are Old   The Second Coming
The Wild Swans at Coole   Sailing to Byzantium by William Butler Yeats

William Butler Yeats
1865–1939

As a child W. B. Yeats (yāts) lived part-time in Dublin and London with his father, a portrait painter, and part-time in County Sligo, Ireland, where he lived with his mother's family. Yeats attended art school, but then he turned his energies to writing romantic lyrics and studying Irish myth and folklore. In 1905 Yeats and his friend Lady Augusta Gregory cofounded the Abbey Theatre in Dublin. Writing for the stage impressed Yeats with the importance of precise, lean language. His later poems show his evolution into a leader in modernist, experimental poetry. In 1923 Yeats received the Nobel Prize for literature. From 1922 to 1928 he served as a senator in the newly founded Irish Free State. He lived his remaining years in Italy and France.

Building Background

Metaphors from the Spirits Dissatisfied both with his father's atheism and with orthodox religion, yet wanting to believe in something, Yeats searched continuously for a hidden supernatural dimension in life. As a young man he became interested in the mystical occult philosophy of Helena Blavatsky and the Theosophical Society. He joined secret groups, attended seances, and studied alchemy. In 1917 he married Georgie Hyde-Lees, a woman half his age, who had the medium's gift for automatic writing, receiving written messages from spirits called Instructors. After several sessions Yeats offered to devote his life to interpreting the Instructors' communications. They responded, "No, we have come to give you metaphors for poetry." Shortly thereafter, Yeats began to develop a body of symbolic images that gave coherence to his beliefs and power to his writings. In *A Vision,* first published in 1925, Yeats tried to explain his understanding of the relationship between the occult and the imagination.

Literary Focus

Consonance Consonance is the use of words in which the final consonant sounds in stressed syllables are the same, but the vowel sounds that precede them differ; for example, *sad* and *reed* or *born* and *burn.* Keats used consonance along with rhyme to achieve a melancholy feeling in "Ode to a Nightingale":

Forlorn! the very word is like a *bell*
To *toll* me back from thee to my *sole self.*

Look for examples of consonance in Yeats's poetry.

Writer's Notebook

The Older Generation When you think of older people, what pictures come to your mind? What kinds of problems or issues are peculiar to the older generation? Jot down a few ideas.

SUPPORT MATERIALS OVERVIEW

Unit 6 Resource Book
- Graphic Organizer, p. 73
- Study Guide, p. 74
- Vocabulary, p. 75
- Grammar, p. 76
- Alternate Check Test, p. 77
- Vocabulary Test, p. 78
- Selection Test, pp. 79–80

Building English Proficiency
- Selection Summaries
- Activities, p. 243
- "When You Are Old," "The Wild Swans at Coole," "The Second Coming," and "Sailing to Byzantium" in Spanish

Reading, Writing & Grammar SkillBook
- Writing, pp. 125–126
- Grammar, Usage, and Mechanics, pp. 211–213

Technology
- Personal Journal Software
- Custom Literature Database: Additional selections by Yeats can be found on the database.
- Test Generator Software

When You Are Old

William Butler Yeats

1

When you are old and gray and full of sleep
And nodding by the fire, take down this book,
And slowly read, and dream of the soft look
Your eyes had once, and of their shadows deep;

5 How many loved your moments of glad grace,
And loved your beauty with love false or true,
But one man loved the pilgrim soul in you,
And loved the sorrows of your changing face;

And bending down beside the glowing bars,
10 Murmur, a little sadly, how Love fled
And paced upon the mountains overhead
And hid his face amid a crowd of stars.

The Wild Swans at Coole

William Butler Yeats

The trees are in their autumn beauty,
The woodland paths are dry,
Under the October twilight the water
Mirrors a still sky;
5 Upon the brimming water among the stones
Are nine-and-fifty swans.

The nineteenth autumn has come upon me
Since I first made my count;
I saw before I had well finished,
10 All suddenly mount

Coole (kūl). Coole Park was the country estate of Yeats's
wealthy friend Lady Augusta Gregory
(1852–1932), the Irish playwright and folklorist.

The Wild Swans at Coole **605**

During Reading

Selection Objectives

- to understand one man's view of life through his poetry
- to analyze the use of consonance to add musical repetition of sound
- to learn to use adverbs effectively

Unit 6 Resource Book
Graphic Organizer, p. 73
Study Guide, p. 74

Theme Link

Yeats's poetry is unusual in its grasp of the struggle between hope and despair in old age—a time when memory becomes the dominant source of meaning.

Vocabulary Preview

anarchy, absence of a system of government and law
conviction, firm belief
revelation, disclosure of divine truth
indignant, angry at something unjust
paltry, worthless
artifice, skillful construction

   Students can add the words and definitions to their Writer's Notebooks.

1 Literary Focus
Consonance

Question   What is the dominant use of consonance in "When you are Old"? Give examples. *(The* d *consonant sound [in stanza 1] of old, nodding, read, shadows; [in stanza 2] of loved, loved, loved, loved; [in stanza 3] of bending, beside, sadly, fled, paced, overhead, hid, amid, crowd.)*

SELECTION SUMMARY

When You Are Old; The Wild Swans at Coole; The Second Coming; Sailing to Byzantium

When You Are Old   An old woman is urged to read a book and remember the man who loved her "pilgrim soul" and her sorrows, and who is now (implicitly) dead.

The Wild Swans at Coole   This poem presents the metaphor of a flock of swans that represent the fleeting challenges and changes of mortal life.

The Second Coming   The speaker questions the anarchy and loss of innocence in the world and longs for the Second Coming. And yet, before the Second Coming, will come the horror of the beast, which may already "slouch towards Bethlehem to be born."

Sailing to Byzantium   Haunted by mortality, the narrator makes a spiritual quest and arrives at the "holy city," the spiritual perfection, of Byzantium.

 *For summaries in other languages, see the **Building English Proficiency** book.*

Art Study

Response to Caption Question
The curves of the swans' bodies, particularly their necks, wings, and tails, are repeated in the heads and leaves of the stylized cattails.

Visual Literacy   The design is an early example of a style later called art nouveau. Characterized by sinuous curves, interlacing patterns, and highly stylized images of plants, birds, and women, art nouveau reached the height of its popularity in turn-of-the-century graphics and interior design.

2 Literary Element
Theme

Questions   Why is the narrator sore at heart? *(Possible response: Seeing the swans unchanged reminds him that "all's changed" in his life.)* What emotions and attributes does the narrator assign to the swans? *(They love and are companionable; their hearts remain young; they have passions and conquests; they wander freely.)* What might these emotions and characteristics suggest about the narrator? *(Possible responses: that he no longer has passions, conquests, a life companion, or freedom; that his heart has grown old)* What do you think the swans might symbolize? *(Possible response: eternal youth and beauty; enduring love and passion)*

◄ Walter Crane created this wallpaper design, called "Swan, Rush, and Iris," in 1877. What details in the design help to convey the grace and beauty of these majestic creatures?

And scatter wheeling in great broken rings
Upon their clamorous wings.

I have looked upon those brilliant creatures,
And now my heart is sore.
15 All's changed since I, hearing at twilight,
The first time on this shore,
The bell-beat of their wings above my head,
Trod with a lighter tread.

Unwearied still, lover by lover,
20 They paddle in the cold
Companionable streams or climb the air;
Their hearts have not grown old;
Passion or conquest, wander where they will,
Attend upon them still.
25 But now they drift on the still water,
Mysterious, beautiful;
Among what rushes will they build,
By what lake's edge or pool
Delight men's eyes when I awake some day
30 To find they have flown away?

MINI-LESSON: GRAMMAR

Using Adverbs

Teach   Remind students that an adverb is a modifier of a verb, adjective, or another adverb. The ending *-ly* is generally the sign of an adverb, but there are many, many adverbs that do not end in *-ly*. Ask students to locate several adverbs on pages 606–607 and identify the word and its part of speech that the adverb modifies.

Activity Idea   Choose one verb from a Yeats poem, and have students brainstorm a list of adverbs for it. Use this opportunity to help students become aware of adverbs that *do not* end in *-ly*.

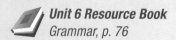
Unit 6 Resource Book
Grammar, p. 76

The Second Coming

William Butler Yeats

Turning and turning in the widening gyre[1]
The falcon cannot hear the falconer;[2]
Things fall apart; the center cannot hold;
Mere anarchy[3] is loosed upon the world,
5 The blood-dimmed tide is loosed, and everywhere
The ceremony of innocence is drowned;
The best lack all conviction,[4] while the worst
Are full of passionate intensity.

Surely some revelation[5] is at hand;
10 Surely the Second Coming is at hand.
The Second Coming! Hardly are those words out
When a vast image out of *Spiritus Mundi*[6]
Troubles my sight: somewhere in sands of the desert
A shape with lion body and the head of a man,
15 A gaze blank and pitiless as the sun,
Is moving its slow thighs, while all about it
Reel shadows of the indignant[7] desert birds.
The darkness drops again; but now I know
That twenty centuries of stony sleep
20 Were vexed[8] to nightmare by a rocking cradle,
And what rough beast, its hour come round at last,
Slouches towards Bethlehem to be born?

---

1. **gyre** (jīr), *n.* a spiral motion.
2. **falcon cannot . . . . falconer,** hawk trained to hunt other birds and small animals cannot hear his trainer's instructions.
3. anarchy (an'ər kē), *n.* absence of a system of government and law.
4. conviction (kən vik'shən), *n.* firm belief.
5. revelation (rev'ə lā'shən), *n.* disclosure of divine truth.
6. *Spiritus Mundi,* "soul of the world." *[Latin]* Yeats believed in the existence of a "Great Memory," a collective unconscious that connects individuals with the Spiritus Mundi and serves as a reservoir of symbolic images from the past.
7. indignant (in dig'nənt), *adj.* angry at something unjust.
8. **vex** (veks), *v.* provoke.

---

3 Historical Note
War and Aftermath

"The Second Coming" was written in 1919 soon after the end of World War I. The war had toppled the "old order" of Europe, including the monarchies of Russia, Germany, and the Austro-Hungarian Empire. Yeats rightly saw that the new order created by the Treaty of Versailles would eventually lead to chaos. Twenty years after the creation of the treaty, World War II broke out.

4 Literary Element
Allusions

While the poet uses *revelation* to mean "a disclosure of divine truth," the word also alludes to the New Testament's The Revelation of Saint John the Divine, an apocalyptic vision of the Second Coming. According to Revelation, the presence on earth of the Antichrist, a satanic figure who denies the incarnation and role of Jesus, will precede the Second Coming of Christ. Thus, the poet exclaims in line 11 "The Second Coming!"; for if the Second Coming is near, then so is the dreaded arrival of the Antichrist. In lines 21–22, the "rough beast" who "slouches towards Bethlehem to be born" alludes to this figure, who is described in Revelation as a blasphemous beast with seven heads and ten horns. In Revelation, the Antichrist is ultimately destroyed before the Last Judgment.

BUILDING ENGLISH PROFICIENCY

Analyzing Imagery

"The Second Coming" is filled with strange, mystical images that may confuse students at first. Help students to appreciate the power of these images.

1. Divide students into small groups; assign each group one or two images from the poem.

2. Have each group make a list of events from the news that illustrate each image in terms of real life. (For example, have them consider how "the ceremony of innocence" is "drowned" in today's world.) The associations do not have to be literal. Anything that is brought to mind by the images is fair game.

3. Have each group share their responses with the class, and have the class discuss them.

Building English Proficiency
Activities, p. 243

Reading/Thinking Skills
Find the Main Idea

Questions What do the fish and fowl commend? *(mortal life, that which begets, is born and dies)* What do they neglect? *(intellectual achievement, that which does not age and die)*

Reading/Thinking Skills
Compare and Contrast

Questions How does Byzantium contrast with "That country" of the first two stanzas? *(Possible response: It is eternal, an artificial place of unaging intellect.)* How would you contrast the golden bird singing "of what is past, or passing, or to come" with the fowl commending what is "begotten, born, and dies"? *(Possible response: The song of the golden bird, "an artifice of eternity," is both eternal and about immortality; the fowl commends what is living, and, therefore, what will die.)*

Check Test

1. In "When You Are Old," what does the narrator regret about the loss of youth? *(the loss of the soft look of eyes, i.e., innocence; the admiration of others; beauty; and love, whether false or true)*

2. What happens before the narrator can complete his count of "The Wild Swans"? *(They fly away.)*

3. What falls apart in "The Second Coming?" *(the natural order; the conventions of government and leadership; these are symbolized by the falcon that cannot hear the falconer and the undirected bloodshed that results.)*

4. What will come before the Second Coming? *(the beast)*

5. What is it about Byzantium that the narrator seeks? *(Possible response: that which is eternal)*

Unit 6 Resource Book
Alternate Check Test, p. 77

Sailing to Byzantium
William Butler Yeats

That is no country for old men. The young
In one another's arms, birds in the trees,
—Those dying generations—at their song,
The salmon-falls, the mackerel-crowded
    seas,
5 Fish, flesh, or fowl, commend[1] all summer
    long
Whatever is begotten, born, and dies.
Caught in that sensual music all neglect
Monuments of unaging intellect.

An aged man is but a <u>paltry</u>[2] thing,
10 A tattered coat upon a stick, unless
Soul clap its hands and sing, and louder
    sing
For every tatter in its mortal dress,
Nor is there singing school but studying
Monuments of its own magnificence;
15 And therefore I have sailed the seas and
    come
To the holy city of Byzantium.

O sages[3] standing in God's holy fire
As in the gold <u>mosaic</u>[4] of a wall
Come from the holy fire, perne in a gyre,[5]
20 And be the singing-masters of my soul.
Consume my heart away; sick with desire
And fastened to a dying animal
It knows not what it is; and gather me
Into the <u>artifice</u>[6] of eternity.

25 Once out of nature I shall never take
My bodily form from any natural thing,
But such a form as Grecian goldsmiths
    make[7]
Of hammered gold and gold enameling
To keep a drowsy Emperor awake;
30 Or set upon a golden bough to sing
To lords and ladies of Byzantium
Of what is past, or passing, or to come.

Byzantium (bi zan′shē əm), an ancient name for the city that became Constantinople and later Istanbul, Turkey. For Yeats it was a symbol for the timeless world of art and intellect as opposed to the natural world of biological change. It was a "holy city"—literally, because it was the center of Eastern Christendom; symbolically, because it fostered the development of intellect and imagination that produces artistic perfection.
1. **commend** (kə mend′), *v.* praise.
2. **paltry** (pôl′trē) *adj.* almost worthless.
3. **sage** (sāj), *n.* wise person.
4. **mosaic** (mō zā′ik), *n.* picture made of small pieces of different colored stone, glass, or wood inlaid in a design.
5. **perne in a gyre.** A perne (or pirn) is a spool or bobbin; a gyre is a spiraling motion. The image seems to be of a long file of sages, spiraling down like the thread flying off a spinning bobbin, forming ever tighter circles that narrow to a single point.
6. **artifice** (är′tə fis), *n.* skillful construction.
7. **such a form . . . make,** an artificial singing bird. Yeats commented, "I use it as a symbol of the intellectual joy of eternity, as contrasted with the instinctive joy of human life."

MINI-LESSON: LITERARY FOCUS

Consonance

Teach Remind students of the definition of consonance on page 604. Use two consonant words, such as "Fish, flesh" on this page, to start a brainstorming session of other words that are consonant with them.

Activity Idea Invite students to write a poem of their own, using unrhymed couplets that have consonant words at the ends of the lines.

After Reading

Making Connections

Shaping Your Response

1. What question would you most like to ask Yeats about his metaphors or about his poetry in general?

Analyzing the Poems

2. In "When You Are Old" what kind of a person do you think the speaker is describing when he says she has a "pilgrim soul" and a "changing face"?

3. Contrast the speaker and his beloved. Which one may really have the "pilgrim soul" after all?

4. In "The Wild Swans at Coole" compare the changes in the speaker's life with the changes in the lives of the swans.

5. Although he asks where the swans will alight, what question do you think the speaker is really asking in the last stanza?

6. In "The Second Coming" what do you think the **images** of the falcon and the falconer and the half-man / half-lion beast reveal about Yeats's view of civilization?

7. Describe the lives of those who dwell in the speaker's homeland in "Sailing to Byzantium." What qualities seem to be missing from their lives?

8. What do you think the speaker hopes to accomplish by going on a journey to Byzantium?

9. Why do you think the speaker chooses to take the form of a golden bird?

Extending the Ideas

10. 👣 Yeats wrote "The Second Coming" right after World War I. Do you think he would have cause to write from a similar **perspective** today?

Literary Focus: Consonance

Consonance, sometimes called half rhyme or near rhyme, is the repetition of consonant sounds that are preceded by different vowel sounds.

1. Find at least one example of consonance in each of Yeats's poems.

2. What other sound devices can you find in his poems?

3. Why do you think poets spend so much time searching for the exact words in order to achieve rhyme or assonance or consonance?

After Reading

MAKING CONNECTIONS

1. Responses will vary, but should relate to metaphors in these poems.

2. someone who is striving toward her own ideals and who is deeply affected by her experiences

3. Possible response: the narrator; he is returning into the deeper meanings of the experience of the beloved.

4. While the swans appear to remain unchanged and eternal, the narrator has lost the things that make life meaningful for him.

5. Possible response: what his own fate will be

6. The images suggest that the poet believes that civilization is breaking down and will be overtaken by chaos and savagery.

7. They are interesting only in the ordinary process of "whatever is begotten, born, and dies"; they are not interested in "monuments of unaging intellect."

8. He hopes to achieve immortality through the composition of songs that will be listened to forever.

9. It is an artifice of eternity, a monument of unaging intellect, something that cannot die.

10. Yes; in many ways civilization and civility seem more endangered today than in 1919.

LITERARY FOCUS: CONSONANCE

1. Possible responses:

- "When You Are Old": loved, glad; hid, amid, crowd
- "The Wild Swans of Coole": autumn, come; head, trod, tread
- "The Second Coming": turning, widening; hear, falconer; loosed, world; blood-dimmed tide; Second, hand
- "Sailing to Byzantium": fish, flesh; begotten, born; Monuments, magnificence

2. repetition, alliteration, assonance

3. Students may respond that poets try to achieve pleasing sounds, flowing words, and images that are strengthened by the right words.

VOCABULARY STUDY

1. revelation
2. anarchy
3. conviction
4. indignant
5. paltry

WRITING CHOICES

Writers Notebook Update

Before students begin, you might ask the class to brainstorm various contemporary political issues that affect the lives and welfare of the elderly.

Traveling to . . .

Remind students that such places as Byzantium and Bethlehem are symbolic both for individuals and for society. Encourage students to consider what their destinations might symbolize.

Slouching Towards Bethlehem

To complete this assignment, students will need to review the symbolism of the poem and, then, re-interpret it in their own place and times and with reference to the issue they choose.

Selection Test

Unit 6 Resource Book
pp. 79–68

Vocabulary Study

Write the word from the list that best completes the meaning of the sentence. You will not use all the words.

anarchy
artifice
conviction
indignant
paltry
revelation

1. Yeats trusted in mystical sources to provide him with _____ and inspiration for his poetry.
2. Yeats believed that a nation without a strong sense of values was destined to end in _____.
3. Yeats held the strong _____ that the Irish people needed to become more aware of their national culture.
4. Yeats was _____ about the way the Irish were treated by the English.
5. Yeats's poetry suggests that he was worried that as an old man he would be considered _____.

Expressing Your Ideas

Writing Choices

Writer's Notebook Update Select one of the problems of older people you identified and write a brief paragraph about how effectively you think the younger generation is dealing with this issue.

Traveling to . . . In "Sailing to Byzantium" an aging man wishes to sail to Byzantium, maybe the real place, maybe the spiritual ideal, maybe both. Select a place, real, imaginary, or spiritual, to which you would like to travel. Write a **description** of your chosen destination, telling what hopes and dreams you believe this place will help you to realize.

Slouching Towards Bethlehem Select one of the images of the world in "The Second Coming" and develop that image into a commentary on some aspect of modern day society. Prepare your commentary as an **editorial** for your school or community newspaper. Use a quotation from the poem as the title of your editorial.

Other Options

Not At All Tattered Yeats describes the aged man as "A tattered coat upon a stick." Think of an older person who is quite the opposite of a "tattered coat." You might choose someone whom you know in your personal life or who has been prominent in the world of politics or sports or entertainment. Research that person's life to determine what has prevented him or her from becoming a "tattered coat" with age. Present your results as an **oral report** to your class.

What Rough Beast Make a composite **collage** of a beast that represents your vision of today's world. Include parts of as many animals as you wish, but use them for their symbolic, not their literal, attributes. For example, usually an owl represents wisdom and doves represent peace or love. Give your modern beast a symbolic name and write a descriptive caption.

610   UNIT SIX: THE VICTORIANS

What Rough Beast

You may want to provide a variety of magazines and newspapers for students to cut apart. You might also encourage students to creatively use such objects as feathers, stones, candy, flowers, and so on—three-dimensional objects that can symbolize their vision of the world.

Before Reading

The Star

by H. G. Wells

H. G. Wells
1866–1946

In his youth Herbert George Wells drifted from one dreary job to another. Eventually he became a science teacher, but after four years, when he had to stay in bed because of tuberculosis, he turned to writing short essays on science for popular magazines. In 1895 he became a full-time writer. Over the next fifty years Wells wrote 114 books, among them science fantasies, novels about contemporary society, satires, and philosophic commentaries. After World War I, stating that the future would be "a race between education and catastrophe," Wells wrote a very popular and influential historical work, *The Outline of History.* Said fellow writer George Orwell, "The minds of all of us, and therefore the physical world, would be perceptibly different if Wells had never existed."

Building Background

"Exercises of the Imagination" Building upon a base of scientific knowledge, H. G. Wells let his imagination carry science to unusual yet logical, terrifying yet hopeful, conclusions. In the preface to a collection of his scientific fantasies Wells said that his stories "do not pretend to deal with possible things; they are exercises of the imagination." He imagined traveling into the past and future (*The Time Machine,* 1895). He imagined a sinister doctor transforming beasts into men (*The Island of Dr. Moreau,* 1896). He imagined an ambitious scientist discovering how to make himself invisible (*The Invisible Man,* 1897). He imagined the earth being invaded by Martians (*The War of the Worlds,* 1898). He imagined men from earth landing on the moon (*The First Men in the Moon,* 1901). Through all of his tales, Wells mixed science and technology with adventure and social commentary. He predicted the hopes and the dangers of the technological revolution of the twentieth century. Although he became more pessimistic near the end of his life, in most of his books Wells retained a belief in the positive aspects of human nature. Wells was an immensely popular writer; his popularity was enhanced because many of his novels were made into movies.

Literary Focus

Point of View The vantage point from which an author presents the actions and characters in a story is called **point of view.** The story may be told by a character (**first-person** point of view) or by a narrator who does not participate in the action (**third-person** point of view). Further, the third-person narrator may be **omniscient**—able to see into the minds of all characters; **limited**—confined to a single character's perceptions; or **objective**—describing only what can be seen. Determine what point of view Wells uses in "The Star."

Writer's Notebook

Science Fact or Fiction? Wells was one of the first writers of science fiction. What characteristics come to your mind when you think of a science-fiction story? What expectations do you have when you pick up a science-fiction tale? Look at the picture on page 617. Jot down your expectations for "The Star."

The Star **611**

Before Reading

Building Background

You might begin by asking students if they have ever seen movie versions of *The Time Machine, The Island of Dr. Moreau, The Invisible Man,* or *The War of the Worlds.* What do the plots of such films suggest about the author's imagination?

Literary Focus

You might discuss with the class how some stories are told from multiple points of view, i.e., the same story is told from the point of view of different characters. Ask students what effect multiple points of view might have on plot or theme.

More About H.G. Wells

Wells was badly shaken by the senseless carnage of World War I and saw its aftermath as the beginning of worldwide instability. Known and respected around the world, Wells interviewed Franklin D. Roosevelt and Soviet leader Joseph Stalin in an effort to establish some middle ground between capitalism and communism. Other works include

- *Kipps* (1905)
- *The History of Mr. Polly* (1909)
- *Outline of History* (1920)
- *The Shape of Things to Come* (1933)

SUPPORT MATERIALS OVERVIEW

Unit 6 Resource Book
- Graphic Organizer, p. 81
- Study Guide, p. 82
- Vocabulary, p. 83
- Grammar, p. 84
- Alternate Check Test, p. 85
- Vocabulary Test, p. 86
- Selection Test, pp. 87–88

Building English Proficiency
- Selection Summaries
- Activities, p. 244

Reading, Writing & Grammar SkillBook
- Reading, pp. 79–80
- Writing, pp. 117–118
- Grammar, Usage, and Mechanics, pp. 147–148, 163–164, 165–166

The World of Work
- Astronomer, p. 23
- Activity, p. 24

Technology
- Audiotape
- Personal Journal Software
- Test Generator Software

Selection Objectives

- to understand a character through his actions and the response of other characters
- to understand point of view and how it affects a reader's attitude and response
- to master the writing of compound and complex sentences

Unit 6 Resource Book
Graphic Organizer, p. 81
Study Guide, p. 82

Theme Link

Wells, in this story, explores the hope and despair of people in different locations, situations, and walks of life responding to the news of impending doom.

Vocabulary Preview

erratic, irregular

unprecedented, never done before; never known before

apparition, something strange, **remarkable,** or unexpected

imminent, about to happen

agape, open-mouthed with wonder

centrifugal, moving away from a center

luminous, shiny; bright

obdurate, stubborn

devastating, very destructive

inexplicable, mysterious; unable to be explained

Students can add the words and definitions to their Writer's Notebooks.

 Art Study

Response to Caption Question
Students may respond that the mood is space-like, eerie, mysterious, but strangely hopeful.

THE STAR
H.G. WELLS

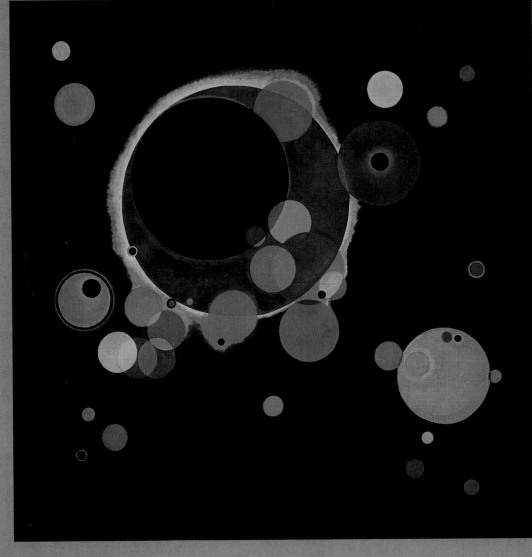

SELECTION SUMMARY

The Star

On New Year's Day, scientists become aware that a star they have been watching is causing erratic movement in the orbit of Neptune. Before long, the star collides and combines with Neptune before continuing its gravitational fall toward the sun. As the star nears Earth, a mathematician calculates that it is bound to affect, if not obliterate, Earth. People calmly go about their business until disaster is imminent. Earthquakes, storms, floods, and volcanic eruptions wreak havoc on the planet and its population. When at last the star is absorbed into the sun and survivors on Earth find their way to newly changed land masses, Martian astronomers assess the damage to Earth based on what they can see—"not much damage done."

 For summaries in other languages, see the Building English Proficiency book.

1 t was on the first day of the new year that the announcement was made, almost simultaneously[1] from three observatories, that the motion of the planet Neptune, the outermost[2] of all the planets that wheel about the sun, had become very <u>erratic</u>.[3] Ogilvy had already called attention to a suspected retardation in its velocity in December. Such a piece of news was scarcely calculated to interest a world the greater portion of whose inhabitants were unaware of the existence of the planet Neptune, nor outside the astronomical profession did the subsequent discovery of a faint remote speck of light in the region of the perturbed[4] planet cause any very great excitement. Scientific people, however, found the intelligence remarkable enough, even before it became known that the new body was rapidly growing larger and brighter, that its motion was quite different from the orderly progress of the planets, and that the deflection[5] of Neptune and its satellite was becoming now of an <u>unprecedented</u>[6] kind.

Few people without a training in science can realize the huge isolation of the solar system. The sun with its specks of planets, its dust of planetoids, and its impalpable comets, swims in a vacant immensity that almost defeats the imagination. Beyond the orbit of Neptune there is space, vacant so far as human observation has penetrated, without warmth or light or sound, blank emptiness, for twenty million times a million miles. That is the smallest estimate of the distance to be traversed before the very nearest of the stars is attained. And, saving a few comets more unsubstantial than the thinnest flame, no matter had ever to human knowledge crossed this gulf of space, until early in the twentieth century this strange wanderer appeared. A vast mass of matter it was, bulky, heavy, rushing with-

out warning out of the black mystery of the sky into the radiance of the sun. By the second day it was clearly visible to any decent instrument, as a speck with a barely sensible diameter, in the constellation Leo near Regulus. In a little while an opera glass could attain it.

On the third day of the new year the newspaper readers of two hemispheres were made aware for the first time of the real importance of this unusual <u>apparition</u>[7] in the heavens. "A Planetary Collision," one London paper headed the news, and proclaimed Duchaine's opinion that this strange new planet would probably collide with Neptune. The leader writers enlarged upon the topic. So that in most of the capitals of the world, on January 3rd, there was an expectation, however vague, of some <u>imminent</u>[8] phenomenon in the sky; and as the night followed the sunset round the globe, thousands of men turned their eyes skyward to see—the old familiar stars just as they had always been. **2**

Until it was dawn in London and Pollux setting and the stars overhead grown pale. The winter's dawn it was, a sickly filtering accumulation of daylight, and the light of gas and candles shone **3** yellow in the windows to show where people were astir. But the yawning policeman saw the thing, the busy crowds in the markets stopped <u>agape</u>,[9] workmen going to their work betimes,[10] milkmen,

---

Several Circles, No. 323, painted in 1926 by Vasily Kandinsky (1866–1944), may reflect the Russian artist's interest in the interaction of galaxies. What mood does Kandinsky create with his floating, overlapping circles?

1. **simultaneously** (sī′məl tā′nē əs lē), *adv.* at the same time.
2. **outermost.** When Wells wrote "The Star," Neptune was the outermost known planet. The planet Pluto was not discovered until 1930.
3. erratic (ə rat′ik), *adj.* irregular.
4. **perturbed** (pər térbd), *adj.* caused to be irregular in movement by the gravitational attraction of another body.
5. **deflection** (di flek′shən), *n.* changing of direction.
6. unprecedented (un pres′ə den′tid), *adj.* never done before; never known before.
7. apparition (ap′ə rish′ən), *n.* something strange, remarkable, or unexpected.
8. imminent (im′ə nənt), *adj.* about to happen.
9. agape (ə gāp′), *adj.* open-mouthed with wonder.
10. **betimes** (bi tīmz′), *adv.* early. [archaic]

The Star **613**

BUILDING ENGLISH PROFICIENCY

Sequencing Events

This story contains a great deal of information. Students can isolate and focus on its key events if they work, in groups, to create a time line for the story. An example appears here. If necessary, place one or two events on the time line to spark students' thinking.

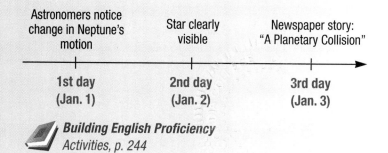

Astronomers notice change in Neptune's motion	Star clearly visible	Newspaper story: "A Planetary Collision"
1st day (Jan. 1)	**2nd day** (Jan. 2)	**3rd day** (Jan. 3)

Building English Proficiency Activities, p. 244

ESL LEP ELD SAE LD

the drivers of news-carts, dissipation[11] going home jaded and pale, homeless wanderers, sentinels on their beats, and in the country, laborers trudging afield, poachers slinking home, all over the dusky quickening country it could be seen—and out at sea by seamen watching for the day—a great white star, come suddenly into the westward sky!

Brighter it was than any star in our skies; brighter than the evening star at its brightest. It still glowed out white and large, no mere twinkling spot of light, but a small round clear shining disc, an hour after the day had come. And where science has not reached, men stared and feared, telling one another of the wars and pestilences that are foreshadowed by these fiery signs in the Heavens. **4** Sturdy Boers, dusky Hottentots, Gold Coast Negroes, Frenchmen, Spaniards, Portuguese, stood in the warmth of the sunrise watching the setting of this strange new star.

And in a hundred observatories there had been suppressed excitement, rising almost to shouting pitch, as the two remote bodies had rushed together, and a hurrying to and fro to gather photographic apparatus and spectroscope, and this appliance and that, to record this novel astonishing sight, the destruction of a world. For it was a world, a sister planet of our earth, far greater than our earth indeed, that had so suddenly flashed into flaming death. Neptune it was, had been struck, fairly and squarely, by the strange planet from outer space and the heat of the concussion had incontinently turned two solid globes into one vast mass of incandescence.[12] Round the world that day, two hours before the dawn, went the pallid great white star, fading only as it sank westward and the sun mounted above it. **5** Everywhere men marveled at it, but of all those who saw it none could have marveled more than those sailors, habitual watchers of the stars, who far way at sea had heard nothing of its advent and saw it now rise like a pigmy moon and climb zenithward and hang overhead and sink westward with the passing of the night.

And when next it rose over Europe everywhere were crowds of watchers on hilly slopes, on house-roofs, in open spaces, staring eastward for the rising of the great new star. It rose with a white glow in front of it, like the glare of a white fire, and those who had seen it come into existence the night before cried out at the sight of it. "It is larger," they cried. "It is brighter!" And, indeed the moon a quarter full and sinking in the west was in its apparent size beyond comparison, but scarcely in all its breadth had it as much brightness now as the little circle of the strange new star.

"It is brighter!" cried the people clustering in the streets. But in the dim observatories the watchers held their breath and peered at one another. *"It is nearer,"* they said. *"Nearer!"*

And voice after voice repeated, "It is nearer," and the clicking telegraph took that up, and it trembled along telephone wires, and in a thousand cities grimy compositors fingered the type. "It is nearer." Men writing in offices, struck with a strange realization, flung down their pens; men talking in a thousand places suddenly came upon a grotesque possibility in those words, "It is nearer." It hurried along awakening streets, it was shouted down the frost-stilled ways of quiet villages, men who had read these things from the throbbing tape stood in yellow-lit doorways shouting the news to the passers-by.

PREDICT: What is the "grotesque possibility" in the words "It is nearer"?   **6**

"It is nearer." Pretty women, flushed and glittering, heard the news told jestingly between the dances, and feigned[13] an intelligent interest they did not feel. "Nearer! Indeed. How curious! How very, very clever people must be to find out things like that!"

Lonely tramps faring through the wintry night murmured those words to comfort themselves—

---

11. **dissipation** (dis/ə pā′shən), *n.* people who indulge excessively in foolish pleasures.
12. **incandescence** (in/kən des/ns), *n.* shining brilliance.
13. **feign** (fān), *v.* pretend.

MINI-LESSON: LITERARY FOCUS

Point of View

Teach   Refer to the definitions on page 611 of first-person point of view, third-person point of view, and (for the third-person point of view) omniscient, limited, and objective narrator. Encourage students to think of stories or books they have read for each kind of point of view.

Questions
- What point of view does this story, "The Star," employ? *(third-person omniscient)*
- What are some of the things this narrator knows that let you know the point of view is omniscient? *(what people in different parts of the world are thinking, doing, and feeling)*

Activity Ideas
- Ask students to imagine other points of view from which this story might be written and to show how the narration—and the events described—would have to change because of the change in point of view.
- Ask students to improvise narrations of some familiar stories such as "Little Red Riding Hood," using different points of view.

looking skyward. "It has need to be nearer, for the night's as cold as charity. Don't seem much warmth from it if it *is* nearer, all the same."

"What is a new star to me?" cried the weeping woman kneeling beside her dead.

The schoolboy, rising early for his examination work, puzzled it out for himself—with the great white star, shining broad and bright through the frost-flowers of his window. "Centrifugal, centripetal,"[14] he said, with his chin on his fist. "Stop a planet in its flight, rob it of its centrifugal force, what then? Centripetal has it, and down it falls into the sun! And this—!"

"Do *we* come in the way? I wonder—"

It is larger . . . It is brighter . . . It is nearer!

The light of that day went the way of its brethren, and with the later watches of the frosty darkness rose the strange star again. And it was now so bright that the waxing moon seemed but a pale yellow ghost of itself, hanging huge in the sunset. In a South African city a great man had married, and the streets were alight to welcome his return with his bride. "Even the skies have illuminated," said the flatterer. Under Capricorn, two Negro lovers daring the wild beasts and evil spirits, for love of one another, crouched together in a cane brake where the fire-flies hovered. "That is our star," they whispered, and felt strangely comforted by the sweet brilliance of its light.

The master mathematician sat in his private room and pushed the papers from him. His calculations were already finished. In a small white phial there still remained a little of the drug that had kept him awake and active for four long nights. Each day, serene, explicit, patient as ever, he had given his lecture to his students, and then had come back at once to this momentous calculation. His face was grave, a little drawn and hectic from his drugged activity. For some time

he seemed lost in thought. Then he went to the window, and the blind went up with a click. Half way up the sky, over the clustering roofs, chimneys and steeples of the city, hung the star.

He looked at it as one might look into the eyes of a brave enemy. "You may kill me," he said after a silence. "But I can hold you—and all the universe for that matter—in the grip of this little brain. I would not change. Even now."

He looked at the little phial. "There will be no need of sleep again," he said. The next day at noon, punctual to the minute, he entered his lecture theater, put his hat on the end of the table as his habit was, and carefully selected a large piece of chalk. It was a joke among his students that he could not lecture without that piece of chalk to fumble in his fingers, and once he had been stricken to impotence[15] by their hiding his supply. He came and looked under his gray eyebrows at the rising tiers of young fresh faces, and spoke with his accustomed studied commonness of phrasing. "Circumstances have arisen—circumstances beyond my control," he said and paused, "which will debar[16] me from completing the course I had designed. It would seem, gentlemen, if I may put the thing clearly and briefly, that—Man has lived in vain."

CLARIFY: What do you think the mathematician means when he tells his students, "Man has lived in vain"?

The students glanced at one another. Had they heard aright? Mad? Raised eyebrows and grinning lips there were, but one or two faces remained intent upon his calm gray-fringed face. "It will be interesting," he was saying, "to devote

---

14. **centrifugal** (sen trif′yə gəl), *adj.* . . .**centripetal** (sentrip′ə təl), *adj.* Centrifugal means moving away from a center; centripetal means moving toward a center.
15. **impotence** (im′pə təns), *n.* condition of helplessness.
16. **debar** (di bär′), *v.* prevent.

The Star **615**

BUILDING ENGLISH PROFICIENCY

Visualizing the Cosmic

ESL
LEP
ELD
SAE
LD

The events in this story are of such mammoth scale that it might be difficult for students to grasp the cosmic forces involved. Use this activity to help them do so.

1. You might obtain *Nova* videotapes, or other movies and filmstrips available through the school or local library, that show the power of stars, planets, and comets. (There is an exciting music video made of Gustav

Holst's composition *The Planets* that convincingly depicts the gigantic majesty of planets in space.)

2. Ask students, after viewing these materials, to write or dictate a short fictional narrative about the moment of impact when (assuming) the star collides with the Earth. Have them compare their narratives with Wells's (pages 616–618).

---

7 Literary Focus
Point of View

Question What do the words of a lonely tramp tell you about the point of view? *(Possible response: that the third-person narration is omniscient; the narrator knows what is going in places that an ordinary person could not know)*

8 Geographical Note
Under Capricorn

Under Capricorn refers to south of the Tropic of Capricorn. In the nineteenth century, the term was generally used to refer to Australia.

9 Reading/Thinking Skills
Find the Main Idea

Question What does he mean by "I can hold the entire universe in the grip of this little brain"? *(Possible response: that the human mind's capacity for understanding is as vast as the universe)*

10 Reading/Thinking Skill
Infer

Question What can you infer from this statement about sleep? *(Possible response: If one is going to die, there is no need to sleep; the mathematician has calculated that the star will hit Earth or the sun.)*

11 Active Reading
Clarify

Response The comment suggests that everything that humanity has achieved over thousands of years will be obliterated.

12 Literary Element
Irony

Question What is ironic about the mathematician turning to the blackboard and meditating? *(After saying that all human knowledge will be destroyed, he continues his calling, i.e., to teach, to disseminate human knowledge.)*

13 Active Reading
Predict

Response Most students will predict that the star will crash into Earth or the sun.

14 Reading/Thinking Skills
Compare and Contrast

Question What might this comparison between the brightness of the star and the wan, yellow lamp light suggest? *(the insignificance of human endeavor compared to the forces of the universe)*

15 Literary Focus
Point of View

Question How does the narrator, referring to the reader as "you" and to himself as "I," change point of view? *(Point of view changes from omniscient third-person to first-person.)* Why do you think Wells switches point of view? *(Possible response: to create a sense of immediacy and intimacy)*

---

this morning to an exposition, so far as I can make it clear to you, of the calculations that have led me to this conclusion. Let us assume—"

12 He turned towards the blackboard, meditating a diagram in the way that was usual to him. "What was that about 'lived in vain'?" whispered one student to another. "Listen," said the other, nodding towards the lecturer.

And presently they began to understand.

> **13** PREDICT: At this point in the story what do you predict will happen to the star?

That night the star rose later, for its proper eastward motion had carried it some way across Leo towards Virgo, and its brightness was so great that the sky became a luminous[17] blue as it rose, and every star was hidden in its turn, save only Jupiter near the zenith, Capella, Aldebaran, Sirius and the pointers of the Bear. It was very white and beautiful. In many parts of the world that night a pallid halo encircled it about. It was perceptibly larger; in the clear refractive sky of the tropics it seemed as if it were nearly a quarter the size of the moon. The frost was still on the ground in England, but the world was as brightly lit as if it were midsummer moonlight. One could see to read quite ordinary print by that cold clear light, **14** and in the cities the lamps burned yellow and wan.

And everywhere the world was awake that night, and throughout Christendom a somber murmur hung in the keen air over the countryside like the belling of bees in the heather, and this murmurous tumult grew to a clangor in the cities. It was the tolling of the bells in a million belfry towers and steeples, summoning the people to sleep no more, to sin no more, but to gather in their churches and pray. And overhead, growing larger and brighter as the earth rolled on its way and the night passed, rose the dazzling star.

And the streets and houses were alight in all the cities, the shipyards glared, and whatever roads led to high country were lit and crowded all night long. And in all the seas about the civilized lands, ships with throbbing engines, and ships with bellying sails, crowded with men and living creatures, were standing out to ocean and the north. For already the warning of the master mathematician had been telegraphed all over the world, and translated into a hundred tongues. The new planet and Neptune, locked in a fiery embrace, were whirling headlong, ever faster and faster towards the sun. Already every second this blazing mass flew a hundred miles, and every second its terrific velocity increased. As it flew now, indeed, it must pass a hundred million of miles wide of the earth and scarcely affect it. But near its destined path, as yet only slightly perturbed, spun the mighty planet Jupiter and his moons sweeping splendid round the sun. Every moment now the attraction between the fiery star and the greatest of planets grew stronger. And the result of that attraction? Inevitably Jupiter would be deflected from his orbit into an elliptical path, and the burning star, swung by his attraction wide of its sunward rush, would "describe a curved path" and perhaps collide with, and certainly pass very close to, our earth. "Earthquakes, volcanic outbreaks, cyclones, sea waves, floods, and a steady rise in temperature to I know not what limit"—so prophesied the master mathematician.

And overhead, to carry out his words, lonely and cold and livid, blazed the star of the coming doom.

To many who stared at it that night until their eyes ached, it seemed that it was visibly approaching. And that night, too, the weather changed, and the frost that had gripped all Central Europe and France and England softened towards a thaw.

But you must not imagine because I have spoken of people praying through the night and people going aboard ships and people fleeing towards mountainous country that the whole world was already in a terror because of the star. **15** As a matter of fact, use and wont[18] still ruled the

---

17. **luminous** (lū′mə nəs), *adj.* shining; bright.
18. **wont** (wunt), *n.* custom.

MINI-LESSON: GRAMMAR

Simple, Compound, and Complex Sentences

Teach Help students differentiate between simple, compound, and complex sentences and find examples of each in the story.

- Simple (has a subject and predicate, which may be compound): The students glanced at one another. (p. 615, column 2)
- Compound (two or more sentences joined by a coordinating conjunction): Already every second this blazing mass flew a hundred miles, and every second its terrific velocity increased. (p. 616, column 2)
- Complex (one independent clause and at least one subordinate clause): He looked at it as one might look into the eyes of a brave enemy. (p. 615, column 2)

Students may even find compound-complex sentences (at least two independent clauses and at least one subordinate clause).

Activity Ideas

- Have students identify simple subjects and predicates in each sentence.
- Have students consider Wells's use of different sentence structures, and even sentence fragments, in his story. What was his purpose? What is the effect?

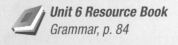

Unit 6 Resource Book
Grammar, p. 84

◄ This picture, which appeared in a magazine in 1908, shows the supposed destruction that would occur if a comet passed too close to the earth. "Buildings and human beings would be scorched to cinders in a second," said the caption that accompanied the picture. Compare the scene depicted here with the descriptions of destruction and death in "The Star." Why do you suppose their details are so similar?

Art Study

Response to Caption Question   The illustration and the story were both completed in approximately the same period; both artist and writer shared similar scientific sources.

Question   Do you find anything strange or unconvincing about the illustration? *(Possible response: Heat of this intensity would kill human beings before it would melt structural iron and steel.)*

16   Reader's Response
Making Personal Connections

Questions   Do you believe that people would really keep going about their business in the way Wells describes? Why or why not? *(Some students might note that human beings tend to find comfort in daily routine, even when the routine is absurd.)* What would you do if you thought the end of the world would come in a couple of days? Would you do your homework? go to school? wash dishes? *(Responses will vary.)*

The World of Work
Astronomer

For a real-life discussion of the stars, use the pages referenced below.

The World of Work pp. 23–24

world, and save for the talk of idle moments and the splendor of the night, nine human beings out of ten were still busy at their common occupations. In all the cities the shops, save one here and there, opened and closed at their proper hours, the doctor and the undertaker plied their trades, the workers gathered in the factories, soldiers drilled, scholars studied, lovers sought one another, thieves lurked and fled, politicians planned their schemes. The presses of the newspapers roared through the nights, and many a priest of this church and that would not open his

The Star   **617**

BUILDING ENGLISH PROFICIENCY

ESL
LEP
ELD
SAE
LD

Exploring Key Events

Wells provides a convincing and exciting (sometimes horrifying) portrait of global disaster. Invite students to respond in one or both of the following ways.

Activity Ideas

• Have students keep a dialog journal as they read. In the left-hand column, they should note details and images that catch their attention; in the right-hand column, they should jot down personal responses. Allow for optional, voluntary sharing.

• Have students select various people described in the story, and allow students to speak spontaneously in character, describing their lives and how they reacted to their impending doom.

17 Reading/Thinking Skills
Draw Conclusions

Question How do you explain the behavior of people who deny that anything unusual is taking place? *(Possible responses: It is sometimes easier to pretend something is not happening than to deal with the truth; many people distrust scientists and/or the media.)*

18 Reader's Response
Challenging the Text

Question Do you think Wells's description of how such great heat would affect Earth is accurate? *(While responses will vary, students should note that polar ice would melt, causing devastating flooding; and weather would be violent.)*

19 Literary Element
Imagery

You might point out how the imagery of "the star, with the wan moon in its wake" parallels earlier imagery of the yellow, wan light of lamps. Moonlight has become as insignificant as lamplight.

---

holy building to further what he considered a foolish panic. The newspapers insisted on the lesson of the year 1000—for then, too, people had anticipated the end. The star was no star—mere gas—a comet; and were it a star it could not possibly strike the earth. There was no precedent for such a thing. Common sense was sturdy everywhere, scornful, jesting, a little inclined to persecute the obdurate[19] fearful. That night, at seven-fifteen by Greenwich time, the star would be at its nearest to Jupiter. Then the world would see the turn things would take. The master mathematician's grim warnings were treated by many as so much mere elaborate self-advertisement. Common sense at last, a little heated by argument, signified its unalterable convictions by going to bed. So, too, barbarism and savagery, already tired of the novelty, went about their mighty business, and save for a howling dog here and there, the beast world left the star unheeded.

. . . it grew with a terrible steadiness hour after hour. . . .

And yet, when at last the watchers in the European States saw the star rise, an hour later it is true, but no larger than it had been the night before, there were still plenty awake to laugh at the master mathematician—to take the danger as if it had passed.

But hereafter the laughter ceased. The star grew—it grew with a terrible steadiness hour after hour, a little larger each hour, a little nearer the midnight zenith, and brighter and brighter, until it had turned night into a second day. Had it come straight to the earth instead of in a curved path, had it lost no velocity to Jupiter, it must have leapt the intervening gulf in a day, but as it was it took five days altogether to come by our planet. The next night it had become a third the size of the moon before it set to English eyes,

and the thaw was assured. It rose over America near the size of the moon, but blinding white to look at, and *hot;* and a breath of hot wind blew now with its rising and gathering strength, and in Virginia, and Brazil, and down the St. Lawrence valley, it shone intermittently through a driving reek of thunder-clouds, flickering violet lightning, and hail unprecedented. In Manitoba was a thaw and devastating[20] floods. And upon all the mountains of the earth the snow and ice began to melt that night, and all the rivers coming out of high country flowed thick and turbid,[21] and soon—in their upper reaches—with swirling trees and the bodies of beasts and men. They rose steadily, steadily in the ghostly brilliance, and came trickling over their banks at last, behind the flying population of their valleys.

And along the coast of Argentina and up the South Atlantic the tides were higher than had ever been in the memory of man, and the storms drove the waters in many cases scores of miles inland, drowning whole cities. And so great grew the heat during the night that the rising of the sun was like the coming of a shadow. The earthquakes began and grew until all down America from the Arctic Circle to Cape Horn, hillsides were sliding, fissures were opening, and houses and walls crumbling to destruction. The whole side of Cotopaxi[22] slipped out in one vast convulsion, and a tumult of lava poured out so high and broad and swift and liquid that in one day it reached the sea.

So the star, with the wan moon in its wake, marched across the Pacific, trailed the thunderstorms like the hem of a robe, and the growing tidal wave that toiled behind it, frothing and eager, poured over island and island and swept them clear of men. Until that wave came at last—in a blinding light and with the breath of a fur-

---

19. obdurate (ob′dər it), *adj.* stubborn.
20. devastating (dev′ə stā′ting), *adj.* very destructive.
21. turbid (tėr′bid), *adj.* muddy.
22. Cotopaxi, the highest active volcano in the world, in the Andes of northern Ecuador.

MINI-LESSON: GEOGRAPHY

Using Latitude, Longitude, and Elevation on a Map

Teach Ask students to combine their knowledge and resources to make a set of rules for determining the climate of a place based on its latitude, longitude, and elevation. What is the climate like, for example, at sea level near the equator? in high mountains halfway to the South Pole?

Activity Ideas

- Have pairs of students choose one of the places described in the story and determine what its normal (pre-star) climate and geography are like. How would this place be changed by the coming of the star? Students can use atlases and other reference books to find more information.

- Ask students to compare notes about different places and to speculate as to where the safest place on Earth might be were an event like the coming of the star to take place.

nace, swift and terrible it came—a wall of water, fifty feet high, roaring hungrily, upon the long coasts of Asia, and swept inland across the plains of China. For a space the star, hotter now and larger and brighter than the sun in its strength, showed with pitiless brilliance the wide and populous country; towns and villages with their pagodas and trees, roads, wide cultivated fields, millions of sleepless people staring in helpless terror at the incandescent sky; and then, low and growing, came the murmur of the flood. And thus it was with millions of men that night—a flight nowhither, with limbs heavy with heat and breath fierce and scant, and the flood like a wall swift and white behind. And then death.

China was lit glowing white, but over Japan and Java and all the islands of Eastern Asia the great star was a ball of dull red fire because of the steam and smoke and ashes the volcanoes were spouting forth to salute its coming. Above was the lava, hot gases and ash, and below the seething floods, and the whole earth swayed and rumbled with the earthquake shocks. Soon the immemorial snows of Tibet and the Himalaya were melting and pouring down by ten million deepening converging channels upon the plains of Burma and Hindustan. The tangled summits of the Indian jungles were aflame in a thousand places, and below the hurrying waters around the stems were dark objects that still struggled feebly and reflected the blood-red tongues of fire. And in a rudderless confusion a multitude of men and women fled down the broad river-ways to that one last hope of men—the open sea.

Larger grew the star, and larger, hotter and brighter with a terrible swiftness now. The tropical ocean had lost its phosphorescence, and the whirling steam rose in ghostly wreaths from the black waves that plunged incessantly, speckled with storm-tossed ships.

And then came a wonder. It seemed to those who in Europe watched for the rising of the star

that the world must have ceased its rotation. In a thousand open spaces of down and upland the people who had fled thither from the floods and the falling houses and sliding slopes of hill watched for that rising in vain. Hour followed hour through a terrible suspense, and the star rose not. Once again men set their eyes upon the old constellations they had counted lost to them forever. In England it was hot and clear overhead, though the ground quivered perpetually, but in the tropics, Sirius and Capella and Aldebaran showed through a veil of steam. And when at last the great star rose near ten hours late, the sun rose close upon it, and in the center of its white heart was a disc of black.

Over Asia it was the star had begun to fall behind the movement of the sky, and then suddenly, as it hung over India, its light had been veiled. All the plain of India from the mouth of the Indus to the mouths of the Ganges was a shallow waste of shining water that night, out of which rose temples and palaces, mounds and hills, black with people. Every minaret was a clustering mass of people, who fell one by one into the turbid waters, as heat and terror overcame them. The whole land seemed a-wailing, and suddenly there swept a shadow across that furnace of despair, and a breath of cold wind, and a gathering of clouds, out of the cooling air. Men looking up, near blinded, at the star, saw that a black disc was creeping across the light. It was the moon, coming between the star and the earth. And even as man cried to God at this respite, out of the East with a strange inexplicable[23] swiftness sprang the sun. And then star, sun, and moon rushed together across the heavens.

So it was that presently, to the European watchers, star and sun rose close upon each other, drove headlong for a space and then slower, and at last came to rest, star and sun merged into one glare of flame at the zenith of the sky. The moon

23. **inexplicable** (in′ik splik′ə bəl), *adj.* mysterious; unable to be explained.

20 **Geographical Note**
Hindustan

Hindustan is that part of northern India, roughly the Ganges plain from the Punjab to Assam, where the predominate languages are Indic.

21 **Literary Element**
Imagery

Question   To what senses do Wells's images of the disasters befalling Earth appeal? Give an example for each.

Possible Responses
- sight—"people staring in helpless terror at the incandescent sky"; "the Indian jungles were aflame"; "the whirling steam rose in ghostly wreaths"
- sound—"a wall of water . . . roaring hungrily"; "murmur of the flood"; "the whole earth swayed and rumbled"
- touch—"limbs heavy with heat"; "the whole earth swayed"
- taste—indirectly by "smoke and ashes the volcanoes were spouting" on lips and tongues
- smell—"lava, hot gases and ash"

BUILDING ENGLISH PROFICIENCY

Responding to Key Events

Invite students to explore their feelings about the story's climax and to imagine a sequel to its catastrophe.

1. Brainstorm with students about what survivors would be facing in putting the world back together. Point out real-life disasters, such as hurricanes and floods, as models on which to base their speculations.

2. Divide students into "think tank" committees that will formulate a response to the crisis.

3. Have students publish a post-apocalypse edition of the local newspaper. Have students contribute "articles" about the steps that government officials are taking to restore food, shelter, medical services, and so on.

Literary Focus
Point of View

Question What is the point of view at this point of the story? *(omniscient third-person)* How do you know the narrator is omniscient, i.e., that the narrator "has total knowledge"? *(He is describing Martian astronomers and their reactions to the event.)*

23
Active Reading
Clarify

Response All the Martians know about Earth is what they can see from Mars: geographic formations, polar ice caps, but nothing of humanity.

Check Test

1. What path did the star take on its route through the solar system? *(It collided with Neptune; intersected with the orbit of Jupiter; came close, but bypassed Earth; was sucked into the sun.)*

2. Why does the mathematician take a drug? *(to stay awake to complete calculations about the path of the star)*

3. Why do temperatures go up as the star nears Earth? *(Heat from the star raises temperatures on Earth.)*

4. How did life on Earth change as a result of the catastrophe? *(The sun was larger and the moon smaller, so temperatures were warmer; previously cold places became temperate; population was smaller, and there was a new sense of brotherhood; people migrated to cooler climates.)*

5. Who studies Earth at the end of the story? *(Martian astronomers)*

Unit 6 Resource Book
Alternate Check Test, p. 85

---

no longer eclipsed the star but was lost to sight in the brilliance of the sky. And though those who were still alive regarded it for the most part with that dull stupidity that hunger, fatigue, heat and despair engender, there were still men who could perceive the meaning of these signs. Star and earth had been at their nearest, had swung about one another, and the star had passed. Already it was receding, swifter and swifter, in the last stage of its headlong journey downward into the sun.

And then the clouds gathered, blotting out the vision of the sky, the thunder and lightning wove a garment round the world; all over the earth was such a downpour of rain as men had never before seen, and where the volcanoes flared red against the cloud canopy there descended torrents of mud. Everywhere the waters were pouring off the land, leaving mud-silted ruins, and the earth littered like a storm-worn beach with all that had floated, and the dead bodies of the men and brutes, its children. For days the water streamed off the land, sweeping away soil and trees and houses in the way, and piling huge dykes and scooping out titanic gullies over the country side. Those were the days of darkness that followed the star and the heat. All through them, and for many weeks and months, the earthquakes continued.

But the star had passed, and men, hunger-driven and gathering courage only slowly, might creep back to their ruined cities, buried granaries, and sodden fields. Such few ships as had escaped the storms of that time came stunned and shattered and sounding their way cautiously through the new marks and shoals of once familiar ports. And as the storms subsided men perceived that everywhere the days were hotter than of yore, and the sun larger, and the moon, shrunk to a third of its former size, took now fourscore days between its new and new.

But of the new brotherhood that grew presently among men, of the saving of laws and books and machines, of the strange change that had come over Iceland and Greenland and the shores of Baffin's Bay, so that the sailors coming there presently found them green and gracious, and could scarce believe their eyes, this story does not tell. Nor of the movement of mankind now that the earth was hotter, northward and southward towards the poles of the earth. It concerns itself only with the coming and the passing of the Star.

The Martian astronomers—for there are astronomers on Mars, although they are very different beings from men—were naturally profoundly interested by these things. They saw them from their own standpoint of course. "Considering the mass and temperature of the missile that was flung through our solar system into the sun," one wrote, "it is astonishing what a little damage the earth, which it missed so narrowly, has sustained. All the familiar continental markings and the masses of the seas remain intact, and indeed the only difference seems to be a shrinkage of the white discoloration (supposed to be frozen water) round either pole." Which only shows how small the vastest of human catastrophes may seem, at a distance of a few million miles.

22

CLARIFY: What do you think the conclusion the Martian astronomers draw from their different **perspective** indicates about their knowledge of the earth?

23

MINI-LESSON: AUTHOR'S CRAFT

Pace

Teach Invite a student volunteer to read aloud one or more paragraphs from this page. Encourage dramatic reading, and when the reading is through, ask students to discuss the methods by which Wells conveys the mood and pace of the story. Ask how quickly things are happening at this point in the story. *(quickly, but things are now relative to the universe, rather than to people's lives—it could actually be years described here)*

Activity Idea Ask students to compare the sentences on this page with those that appear earlier in the story. What stands out? Elicit that the use of conjunctions *(and, but, so, nor)* keep the sentences rolling along with hardly a pause from the periods that separate them. The result is an almost musical inevitability of events following events that ends when the narrative at last moves to the viewpoint of the Martian astronomers.

After Reading

Making Connections

Shaping Your Response

1. What emotions do you feel as the star grows larger and brighter? What emotions do you feel when the earth is spared?

2. With what tone of voice do you imagine the mathematician would deliver his final lecture? Choose a passage and read it in this tone.

Analyzing the Short Story

3. Why do you think Wells chooses to begin his story on the first day of the new year?

4. Trace the progress of the star from a "faint remote speck of light" (paragraph 1) to a "great white star" (paragraph 4). What do you think Wells achieves by describing the star in so many different ways throughout?

5. In presenting the different ways people react to the star, Wells is commenting on various elements of society. Draw a chart like the one shown. List several types of people, their reactions, and the commentary you think Wells is making about them.

Type of Person	Reaction to Star	Commentary

6. Why do you think Wells chooses a mathematician to be the one **character** he develops fully in this story?

7. Why do you think the mathematician looks at the star "as one might look into the eyes of a brave enemy"?

8. What do you think the prediction of a "new brotherhood" indicates about Wells's attitude toward mankind?

9. How does the last paragraph about the Martian astronomers cast an entirely different light on the events?

Extending the Ideas

10. Wells writes his tale from the **perspective** of a scientist. How do you think the story would be different if it had been written from the perspective of a politician or a clergyman?

Literary Focus: Point of View

Point of view is the vantage point from which an author presents the actions and characters in a story. What point of view does Wells use in "The Star"? What advantage does Wells gain by selecting this point of view? How might the story change if he were to select a different point of view?

The Star   **621**

LITERARY FOCUS: POINT OF VIEW

Possible Responses

- third-person omniscient point of view; at one point, he does switch in and out of first-person point of view

- The advantage is that the narrator can tell what is happening around the world and in people's minds—their reactions to the impending disaster.

- With a different point of view, the reader would not be able to enter the lives of as many people and experience their reactions and fear about the disaster.

MAKING CONNECTIONS

1. Student responses will vary.

2. The text indicates a serious, but detached tone.

3. Possible response: From this point in time, nothing will be the same.

4. The star, at first, is visible only to scientists in an observatory; then it can be seen through opera glasses; finally by the naked eye. Wells shows the relationship between awareness, attitude, and proximity.

5. Possible responses:

- The mathematician calculates the star's path; thinking life is doomed, he continues to study and teach.

- Lovers believe the star is a personal sign; their reality is clouded by emotion.

- Newspaper editors discount the danger; they are cynical and publish stories to sell papers to the deluded.

6. The mathematician serves as a plot device, i.e., he provides vital information; he exemplifies reason and human knowledge.

7. He is aware of the star's power and is respectful of forces beyond human control.

8. He believes that people can be united by common needs and experiences.

9. It shows importance of the event relative to the universe; even man's nearest neighbors have little idea of the star's impact on life on Earth.

10. It could have been less objective and more subjective; a politician might have written about dealing with the human toll or finding some advantage in the situation; a clergyman might have written about how people in difficult times turn to religion.

VOCABULARY STUDY

1. apparition
2. erratic
3. unprecedented
4. imminent
5. obdurate
6. agape
7. luminous
8. impotence
9. devastating
10. inexplicable

Unit 6 Resource Book
Vocabulary, p. 83
Vocabulary Test, p. 86

WRITING CHOICES
Writer's Notebook Update

If time allows, you might lead a discussion on how superior fiction often transcends genre, whether science fiction, mystery, or even romance.

It's Headline News

Remind students that a headline always contains a verb and that it must encapsulate the event in the briefest, most vivid way possible to make readers pick up the paper.

Selection Test

Unit 6 Resource Book
pp. 87–88

Vocabulary Study

Select the word from the list that best completes the meaning of each sentence. You will not use all the words.

agape
apparition
centrifugal
devastating
erratic
imminent
impotence
inexplicable
luminous
obdurate
unprecedented

1. All the world is stunned by the _____ in the sky of a new star.
2. Because the strange star veers off its expected course, its movements are called _____.
3. Scientists think the star's behavior _____ because the star moves in a way they have never seen before.
4. When the mathematician predicts that the star will collide with the earth, the students believe that the end of the world is _____.
5. Some call the mathematician a fool for being _____ in his belief.
6. Fascinated by the brightness of the star, the people stand _____.
7. The star is so _____ that at night people are able to read without using lamplight.
8. People feel their complete _____ at not being able to do anything whatsoever about the approaching star.
9. Given the closeness of the star to the earth, it is amazing that the damage is not more _____.
10. Why the star collides with the sun rather than with the earth remains a(n) _____ mystery.

Expressing Your Ideas

Writing Choices

Writer's Notebook Update Look back at your expectations for this story. How many of the characteristics that you mentioned did you actually find in the story? What characteristics did you notice that you had not thought of?

It's Headline News Write the **headlines,** beginning with January 3, the day the story of the star first breaks in the newspapers. Continue with daily headlines until the star has passed. Conclude with headlines for a special edition summarizing the destruction.

Other Options

The Survival Lecture Assume that the mathematician and his class are among those who survive the star. Prepare the first five minutes of his opening **lecture** on the first day of class. Deliver the lecture in character as you imagine the mathematician might do it.

The War of the Worlds On October 30, 1938, the actor Orson Welles caused near panic with a radio broadcast of Wells's *The War of the Worlds* (see page 629). Many listeners believed that Martians were actually invading the earth. Research the event in books and old newspapers and prepare an **oral report** for your class.

OTHER OPTIONS
The Survival Lecture

Students may consider the challenges facing the survivors of such a disaster and what their attitude would be, given what they have seen. Encourage students to practice their lectures before delivering them in class.

The War of the Worlds

You might play a recording of the Welles broadcast of "The War of the Worlds," which may be available on tape or record in public library collections.

Before Reading

Tommy

If— by Rudyard Kipling

Rudyard Kipling
1865–1936

Rudyard Kipling was born in Bombay, when England ruled the entire subcontinent of India. From age 6 on his parents sent him to school in England. At 17 he returned to India where he worked as an editorial assistant for a newspaper and began to write stories and poems, some of which served as newspaper fillers. In his first book of poetry, *Departmental Ditties* (1886), he described colonial society. Gaining great popularity as a writer, he moved to England where he published the two *Jungle Books* (1894, 1895) and the sea tale *Captains Courageous* (1897). In 1901 appeared his finest novel, *Kim,* the adventures of an orphan living in the streets of India. Kipling became the respected confidant of heads of state and military leaders, and he was the first English writer to win the Nobel Prize for literature (1907).

Building Background

Kipling's India During Kipling's lifetime India was part of the massive British Empire. In fact, in 1876 Queen Victoria was declared Empress of India. The masses in India, however, were living in poverty, and famines contributed to a general spirit of unrest. In 1885 the Indian National Congress raised the political consciousness of many Indians and called for national unification. Throughout many uprisings Kipling remained a solid supporter of British rule and the use of force. He believed that it was the duty of every Englishman to bring European culture to the uncivilized world; he once called that duty "the white man's burden." Even though his enthusiasm for war and power and imperialistic control made him controversial and isolated, Kipling retained his popularity as a writer.

Literary Focus

Synecdoche A figure of speech in which a part stands for the whole is called **synecdoche** (si nek′də kē). For example, in "hired hands" *hands* (the part) stands for the workers (the whole), those who labor with their hands. Synecdoche also refers to an expression in which the whole stands for a part, as in "call the law." Here, *law* (the whole) represents the police (a part of the whole system of law). Try to find examples of synecdoche in Kipling's poems.

Writer's Notebook

Adult Virtues As a typical Victorian, Kipling believed in a number of "manly virtues" that a successful, responsible man ought to possess. (Women would have been considered separately.) Make a list of ten or twelve virtues or characteristics that you think are important for a responsible adult to possess.

Tommy   **623**

Before Reading

Building Background

You might begin by asking students if they have ever seen movies set in India under British, colonial rule, (e.g., *Gunga Din, The Jewel in the Crown,* and *Passage to India*), or if they have seen a film based upon a Kipling story, such as *Jungle Book.*

Literary Focus

You might note that synecdoche comes from two ancient Greek words meaning "to take up with another," i.e., to take or understand in a certain sense.

Writer's Notebook

Encourage students to think of virtues that are of equal value to men and women.

More About Rudyard Kipling

In 1892, Kipling married Caroline Balustier, an American, and the couple moved to Vermont, where Kipling wrote *Jungle Books, Captains Courageous,* and *Kim.* Unpopular with their neighbors, the Kiplings eventually resettled in England. Other works include

- *The Light That Failed* (1890)
- *Puck of Pook's Hill* (1906)
- *Rewards and Fairies* (1910)

SUPPORT MATERIALS OVERVIEW

Unit 6 Resource Book
- Graphic Organizer, p. 89
- Study Guide, p. 90
- Vocabulary, p. 91
- Grammar, p. 92
- Alternate Check Test, p. 93
- Vocabulary Test, p. 94
- Selection Test, pp. 95–96

Building English Proficiency
- Selection Summaries
- Activities, p. 245

Reading, Writing & Grammar SkillBook
- Reading, pp. 67–68

Technology
- Audiotape
- Personal Journal Software
- Custom Literature Database: Additional selections by Kipling can be found on the database.
- Test Generator Software

Selection Objectives

- to identify the historical and social context of a poem
- to analyze the use of synecdoche as figurative language in a poem
- to recognize dialect

Unit 6 Resource Book
Graphic Organizer, p. 89
Study Guide, p. 90

Theme Link

Kipling's works reflect his hope in the civilizing influence of Western culture and his despair at all humanity's capacity for brutality.

Vocabulary Preview

red-coats, British soldiers

blackguard, scoundrel

Students can add the words and definitions to their Writer's Notebooks.

1 Historical Note

Tommies

Nineteenth-and twentieth-century British soldiers were called *Tommies*, which derived from the fictitious name Tommy Atkins. The John Doe-like name was used on army sample forms.

2 Literary Element

Dialect

Questions Note that dialect is a speech form characteristic of a region or class, differing from the standard language in pronunciation and vocabulary. What examples of dialect can you find in the first stanza? *("public-'ouse," "pint o' beer," "publican 'e," "be'ind," "I outs into the street," "sez I")* What is characteristic of this dialect? *(dropped h's; dropped consonants from ends of words)* What effects does the dialect lend? *(a unique sound and rhythm; authenticity and poignancy)*

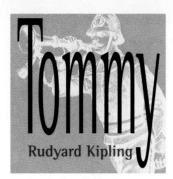

Tommy

Rudyard Kipling

I went into a public-'ouse to get a pint o' beer,
The publican[1] 'e up an' sez, "We serve no red-coats[2] here."
The girls be'ind the bar they laughed an' giggled fit to die,
I outs into the street again an' to myself sez I:
5   O it's Tommy this, an' Tommy that, an' "Tommy, go away";
      But it's "Thank you, Mister Atkins," when the band begins to play—
      The band begins to play, my boys, the band begins to play,
      O it's "Thank you, Mister Atkins," when the band begins to play.

I went into a theater as sober as could be,
10 They gave a drunk civilian room, but 'adn't none for me;
They sent me to the gallery or round the music-'alls,
But when it comes to fightin', Lord! they'll shove me in the stalls![3]
      For it's Tommy this, an' Tommy that, an' "Tommy, wait outside";
      But it's "Special train for Atkins" when the trooper's on the tide—
15   The troopship's on the tide, my boys, the troopship's on the tide,
      O it's "Special train for Atkins" when the trooper's on the tide.

Yes, makin' mock o' uniforms that guard you while you sleep
Is cheaper than them uniforms, an' they're starvation cheap;
An' hustlin' drunken soldiers when they're goin' large a bit
20 Is five times better business than paradin' in full kit.
      Then it's Tommy this, an' Tommy that, an' "Tommy, 'ow's yer soul?"
      But it's "Thin red line of 'eroes" when the drums begin to roll—
      The drums begin to roll, my boys, the drums begin to roll,
      O it's "Thin red line of 'eroes" when the drums begin to roll.

25 We aren't no thin red 'eroes, nor we aren't no blackguards[4] too,
But single men in barricks, most remarkable like you;
An' if sometimes our conduck isn't all your fancy paints,[5]
Why, single men in barricks don't grow into plaster saints;
      While it's Tommy this, an' Tommy that, an' "Tommy, fall be'ind,"
30   But it's "Please to walk in front, sir," when there's trouble in the wind—
      There's trouble in the wind, my boys, there's trouble in the wind,
      O it's "Please to walk in front, sir," when there's trouble in the wind.

SELECTION SUMMARY

Tommy; If—

Tommy A British infantry soldier complains that he is looked down on by society off the battlefield—in bars, in theaters, in general. However, when trouble arises and there are battles to be fought, he is treated with deference and respect—and is called on to go to the front lines. He observes, "Tommy ain't a bloomin' fool"; he is aware of the hypocrisy.

If— The narrator describes the characteristics that qualify a male for manhood.

*For summaries in other languages, see the **Building English Proficiency** book.*

You talk o' better food for us, an' schools, an' fires, an' all:
We'll wait for extry rations if you treat us rational.[6]
35 Don't mess about the cook-room slops, but prove it to our face
The Widow's[7] uniform is not the soldier-man's disgrace.
　　For it's Tommy this, an' Tommy that, an' "Chuck him out, the brute!"
　　But it's "Saviour of 'is country" when the guns begin to shoot;
　　An' it's Tommy this, an' Tommy that, an' anything you please;
40 　　An' Tommy ain't a bloomin' fool—you bet that Tommy sees!

---

1. **publican** (pub′lə kən), *n.* keeper of the pub, or tavern.
2. **red-coats,** British soldiers.
3. **stalls,** seats in the front part of the theater; here, referring to the front lines on a battlefield.
4. **blackguard** (blag′ärd), *n.* scoundrel.
5. **fancy paints,** imagination pictures.
6. **rational** (rash′ə nəl), *adv.* rationally; reasonably.
7. **Widow,** Queen Victoria.

This illustration appeared on the cover of the sheet music for the song "The Queen's Own Little Box of Soldiers." In depicting real-life English soldiers as toys that spring out of a box, what attitude toward those soldiers does this illustration imply? How is this attitude similar to the one the speaker finds so offensive in the poem "Tommy"? ▼

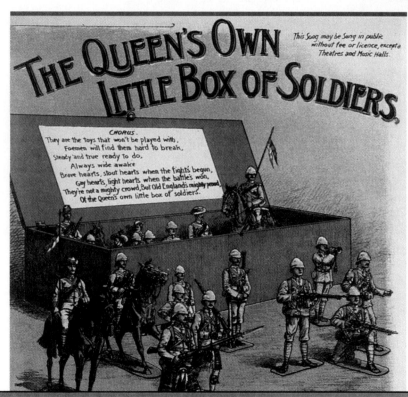

Tommy　625

Synecdoche

You might review the meaning of synecdoche with students.

Questions　Is the title "Tommy" an example of synecdoche? *(Possible response: No; it is a symbol, but bears no small-to-large relationship to the whole.)* Is "red-coat" a synecdoche? *(Possible response: Yes; originally a piece of the British uniform, the red coat represented the uniform, then the soldier, and by extension all British soldiers.)*

 Art Study

Responses to Caption Questions
The illustration suggests the attitude that soldiers should stay in their place, that is, out of sight, when they are unneeded. The narrator of the poem describes the same attitude; soldiers are second-class citizens, unwelcome in public places and condemned for their morals and rough ways, until they are needed in time of war.

BUILDING ENGLISH PROFICIENCY

Exploring Dialect

Point out to students that Kipling's poem "Tommy" is written in Cockney dialect, necessitating the frequent use of apostrophes for contractions. Help students focus on this colorful dialect.

1. Discuss with students the Cockney dialect. If possible, play a recording of a Cockney speaking, or use the recording of this poem on the Audiotape.

2. Have students make a log of words that are unfamiliar or that are spelled in unusual ways (such as *paradin'* and *conduck*) and collaborate on determining the meanings.

3. Have students experiment with capturing in writing an accent or dialect with which they are familiar.

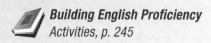 **Building English Proficiency**
Activities, p. 245

4 Literary Focus
Synecdoche

Question Can you find an example of synecdoche in the first stanza? *(Possible response: In "If you can keep your head when all about you/Are losing theirs . . .," head is a synecdoche for temper, cool thinking, intelligence, values, and calm. By using synecdoche, he reduces this large cache of virtues to one manageable idea.)*

5 Literary Element
Theme

Question Write a description of Kipling's ideal man. *(Possible responses: cool under pressure; self-confident; patient; honest; above petty hatreds; modest; imaginative; moderate; thoughtful, but active; realistic; forbearing; resourceful; uncomplaining; brave; self-controlled; self-disciplined; affectionate, but controlled and self-reliant; dependable)*

Check Test

1. In "Tommy," what is the soldier's complaint? *(Soldiers are given no respect, except when they're needed.)*

2. What do civilians seem to think of soldiers? *(that they're blackguards, scoundrels, rascals)*

3. How do politicians think of soldiers? *(They are a burden requiring food, shelter, and education; a necessary evil and a nuisance, except in war time.)*

4. According to the ideas in "If," what should a man's truth be? *(his own ideas and thoughts, uninfluenced by others)*

5. What are two big impostors of life? *(triumph and disaster)*

Unit 6 Resource Book
Alternate Check Test, p. 93

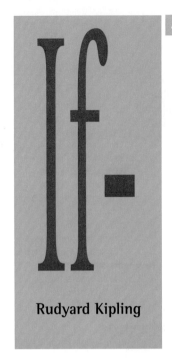

If

Rudyard Kipling

4

If you can keep your head when all about you
    Are losing theirs and blaming it on you,
If you can trust yourself when all men doubt you,
    But make allowance for their doubting too;
5 If you can wait and not be tired by waiting,
    Or being lied about, don't deal in lies,
Or being hated, don't give way to hating,
    And yet don't look too good, nor talk too wise:

If you can dream—and not make dreams your master;
10   If you can think—and not make thoughts your aim;
If you can meet with Triumph and Disaster
    And treat those two impostors[1] just the same;
If you can bear to hear the truth you've spoken
    Twisted by knaves[2] to make a trap for fools,
15 Or watch things you gave your life to, broken,
    And stoop and build 'em up with worn-out tools:

If you can make one heap of all your winnings
    And risk it on one turn of pitch-and-toss,
And lose, and start again at your beginnings
20   And never breathe a word about your loss;
If you can force your heart and nerve and sinew[3]
    To serve your turn long after they are gone,
And so hold on when there is nothing in you
    Except the Will which says to them: "Hold on!"

25 If you can talk with crowds and keep your virtue,
    Or walk with Kings—nor lose the common touch,
If neither foes nor loving friends can hurt you,
    If all men count with you, but none too much;
If you can fill the unforgiving minute
30   With sixty seconds' worth of distance run,
Yours is the Earth and everything that's in it,
5
    And—which is more—you'll be a Man, my son!

---

1. **impostor** (im pos′tər), *n.* pretender; deceiver.
2. **knave** (nāv), *n.* dishonest man; rascal.
3. **sinew** (sin′yū), *n.* tendon; here, body.

MINI-LESSON: GRAMMAR

Recognizing Colloquialisms, Slang, Idioms, and Jargon

Teach The footnotes to "Tommy" are full of definitions of words whose meaning and usage are particular to Tommy's class, culture, and experience. Review these terms: *colloquialism*—word or phrase used in everyday speech but unacceptable in formal speech (e.g., *close call* for "narrow escape"); *slang*—word or phrase with a meaning different from its literal meaning, often popular for a short time (e.g., 1990s word *cool* meaning "great, remarkable"); *idiom*—phrase or expression with a figurative meaning that cannot be understood from the ordinary meaning of the words (e.g., *hold your tongue* for "be quiet"); *jargon*—specialized language of a certain group (e.g., *stat* meaning "immediately" among medical people).

Activity Idea Ask students to suggest words that they might use if they were Tommy, instead of the colloquialisms in this poem.

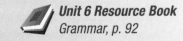
Unit 6 Resource Book
Grammar, p. 92

After Reading

After Reading

Making Connections

Shaping Your Response

1. Do you think the virtues extolled in "If—" can be realistically attained? Explain your response.

Analyzing the Poems

2. Why do you think Kipling chose to write "Tommy" in **dialect**?

3. Whom or what do you think Tommy represents?

4. 👁 How does the **perspective** of the narrator help to convey a message about the contrasting treatment of soldiers on the battlefront and the home front? What is that message?

5. Explain the last line of the poem "Tommy."

6. Why do you think the speaker in "If—" pictures other people as he does?

7. In times of trouble what does the speaker seem to think is the most important characteristic to possess?

8. What importance do you think the speaker sees in the Will?

9. What skill is suggested by lines 29 and 30?

Extending the Ideas

10. Think back over those authors you have read who have used dialect—Burns, Hardy, Kipling. Why do you suppose these authors used dialect to represent speakers of the lower class?

Literary Focus: Synecdoche

In the figure of speech **synecdoche,** a part can stand for a whole, or a whole can stand for a part. For each sample word that is a part, tell what whole the words could represent. For each sample word that is a whole, tell what part the word could represent.

Sample Words		Sample Words	
Parts	**Wholes**	**Parts**	**Wholes**
wave			school
sail			government
stars			music
petal			forest
roof			church

What do you think the following Kipling synecdoches stand for? From "If—": *head* (line 1); *heart and nerve and sinew* (line 21); from "Tommy": *red-coats* (line 2); *uniforms* (line 16); *fires* (line 31).

If—   627

MAKING CONNECTIONS

1. Answers will vary, but should be substantiated by examples from experience.

2. Possible response: to establish the character's background and to establish a sense of realism

3. Possible response: the common British soldier

4. He is resentful of the different treatment he gets at home and at the front and thinks that soldiers willing to risk their lives for their country should receive respect in times of peace as well as war.

5. Kipling makes the point that soldiers are aware that they are valued only in times of war; and that soldiers are more intelligent than they are given credit for.

6. Possible response: He compares positive characteristics to negative human traits; human beings are capable of both extremes.

7. a cool head

8. The will to keep going and to stick to your principles is vitally important.

9. time management and going the extra mile

10. Possible response: to create a realistic picture; to show that speech reflects background, location, and social status, and perhaps to challenge social stereotypes

---

LITERARY FOCUS: SYNECDOCHE

Possible Responses

Parts: wave—ocean; sail—ship; stars—galaxy; petal—field of flowers; roof—city

Wholes: classroom—school; judge—government; note—music; tree—forest; one congregant—church

Kipling's Synecdoches

- head: grace under pressure, intelligence, common sense
- heart and nerve and sinew: body
- red-coats: British soldiers, army
- uniforms: British soldiers
- fires: barracks

VOCABULARY STUDY

Sample responses *bluebeard:* a man who is thought to be a wife-killer or murderer of women [from Bluebeard, a folk tale character who murdered one wife after another] *bluestocking:* a pedantic woman [from a derogatory name, Blue Stocking Society, for an eighteenth-century English organization that included a member well known for wearing odd, blue stockings]

Unit 6 Resource Book
Vocabulary, p. 91
Vocabulary Test, p.94

WRITING CHOICES
Writer's Notebook Update

Ask students to make their own judgments about each of these virtues or characteristics. Which one thing is most important overall—to them and to Kipling?

I Recommend

Remind students that letters of recommendation may be written for people trying to get jobs, into college, or admission to special organizations such as the National Honor Society.

Little Words That Count

Other little words to consider: *so, why, who, try, do, don't, of*

Selection Test

Unit 6 Resource Book
pp. 95–96

Transparency Collection
Transparency Collection Fine Arts Writing Prompt p. 12

Vocabulary Study

Redcoats were British soldiers; *blackguards* are scoundrels. There are many other instances of color adjectives being added to nouns to help define a particular kind of person. Look up one or more of the following words and explain its meaning and its etymology to your class: *black belt, black sheep, bluebeard, bluecollar, bluestocking, graybeard, greengrocer, greenhorn, Orangeman, redcap, redneck, white knight, Yellow Belly.*

Expressing Your Ideas

Writing Choices

Writer's Notebook Update Reread "If —" and make a list of the virtues or characteristics that Kipling suggests are important to possess in order to be a Man (with a capital letter). Compare Kipling's list with the list you wrote in your notebook.

I Recommend You may have observed someone—a friend, a relative, a public figure—who has exhibited one or more of the moral characteristics described by Kipling in "If—." Write a personal **letter of recommendation** for this person, discussing in depth a situation in which moral characteristics were displayed and why these virtues are important to explaining this person's approach to life.

Little Words That Count Kipling uses the repetition of a little but powerful word, *If,* to provide the structure for his poem of advice to the young. Find a little word of your own—such as *but* or *then* or *when*—and write a short **poem** using that word to give both structure and meaning to your ideas.

Other Options

Story Time Most of Kipling's books will be found in the children's section of your local library. Look through the many collections of Kipling's tales and select one you would like to prepare for reading to a class of second graders. Prepare an **oral reading** of the story complete with illustrations.

Perfect—and Then Some Create a **collage** of a character that embodies several of the virtues you consider important to be a Man or a Woman. You might combine features from magazine photos of various people in the news who display one virtue or another, along with other pictures that symbolize the virtues you have chosen. Label your collage with the people and qualities you have combined.

Kipling's India Select one of the following topics for research about Kipling's India: British colonial rule, India's struggle for independence, the culture of India. Prepare an **oral report** for your class. If possible, illustrate your report with pictures or with charts.

OTHER OPTIONS
Story Time

As students look through Kipling's stories, encourage them to note the use of the second person address (e.g., "Oh best beloved . . . "). What does this say about Kipling's understanding of what it means to be a storyteller? Encourage them to incorporate this understanding of the teller/listener relationship in their retellings of Kipling's stories.

Kipling's India

Encourage an understanding of India as a nation made up of a great many small cultures and an enormous number of languages. What would it mean to such a place to be under the control of one power?

Hope and Despair

Century's End

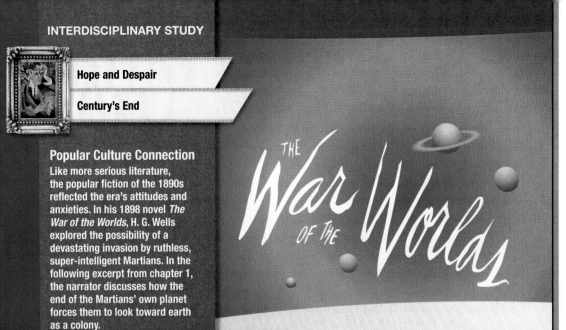

Popular Culture Connection

Like more serious literature, the popular fiction of the 1890s reflected the era's attitudes and anxieties. In his 1898 novel *The War of the Worlds*, H. G. Wells explored the possibility of a devastating invasion by ruthless, super-intelligent Martians. In the following excerpt from chapter 1, the narrator discusses how the end of the Martians' own planet forces them to look toward earth as a colony.

BY H. G. WELLS

No one would have believed in the last years of the nineteenth century that this world was being watched keenly and closely by intelligences greater than man's and yet as mortal as his own; that as men busied themselves about their various concerns they were scrutinized and studied, perhaps almost as narrowly as a man with a microscope might scrutinize the transient creatures that swarm and multiply in a drop of water. With infinite complacency men went to and fro over this globe about their little affairs, serene in their assurance of their empire over matter. It is possible that the infusoria under the microscope do the same. No one gave a thought to the older worlds of space as sources of human danger, or thought of them only to dismiss the idea of life upon them as impossible or improbable. It is curious to recall some of the mental habits of those departed days. At most, terrestial men fancied that there might be other men upon Mars, perhaps inferior to themselves and ready to welcome a missionary enterprise. Yet across the

gulf of space, minds that are to our minds as ours are to those of the beasts that perish, intellects vast and cool and unsympathetic, regarded this earth with envious eyes, and slowly and surely drew their plans against us. And early in the twentieth century came the great disillusionment.

The planet Mars, I scarcely need remind the reader, revolves around the sun at a mean distance of 140,000,000 miles, and the light and heat it receives from the sun is barely half of that received by this world. It must be, if the nebular hypothesis has any truth, older than our world; and long before this earth ceased to be molten, life upon its surface must have begun its course. The fact that it is scarcely one-seventh of the volume of the earth must have accelerated its cooling to the temperature at which life could begin. It has air and water and all that is necessary for the support of animated existence.

Yet so vain is man and so blinded by his vanity, that no writer, up to the very end of the nineteenth century, expressed any idea that

Interdisciplinary Study   **629**

Theme Link

The War of the Worlds suggests the parallel between a Martian invasion and European imperialism, pointing out that the conqueror's hope of greener pastures causes despair for the civilizations whose resources, culture, and lives are sacrificed to accommodate that hope.

Curricular Connection: Popular Culture

You can use this interdisciplinary study to explore the potential that science fiction offers for social criticism, by allowing the author to create an alternate reality through which to explore the folly or injustice of humanity's interactions.

Terms to Know

infusoria (in⁄fyə sôr⁄ē ə), microscopic organisms that often develop in decaying matter and stagnant water.

nebular (neb⁄yə lər) **hypothesis,** the theory that the solar system developed from the cooling and contracting of a hot, rotating mass of dust particles and gases.

Tasmanian, inhabitant of Tasmania, an island off the coast of Australia, especially one of the extinct aborigines.

 Unit 6 Resource Book
Interdisciplinary Study Guide,
p. 97

BUILDING ENGLISH PROFICIENCY

Expanding Vocabulary Notebooks

Wells's vocabulary can be challenging, so encourage students to build their own word resources as they read this excerpt from *The War of the Worlds*.

1. Offer examples of words that may be completely new to them (such as *scrutinize* and *infusoria*) and words that may have a different meaning here (such as *curious* and *mean*).

2. Have students note these or other words, define each word, and then use it in an original sentence.

Word	Definition	Sentence
scrutinize	examine carefully or in great detail	You won't find anything wrong with this shirt, no matter how long you scrutinize it.

Art Study

Possible Response   Answers will vary. Students might argue that as the poster was used for advertising purposes, it was wise to spark people's curiosity by withholding the gory details until they had paid for their tickets. However, other students might say that a depiction of the grotesque Martians would have drawn even larger crowds.

Visual Literacy   The term *poster* was coined in England around the year 1838. The mass production of posters was aided by technological developments like the power press, which by 1848 could print as many as ten thousand sheets an hour.

Additional Background

In 1938, Orson Wells broadcast a realistic adaptation of *The War of the Worlds* over the radio. Some residents of New Jersey, where the Martian ships were supposed to be landing, panicked and fled their homes in terror.

Responding

1. Possible response   He sees it as natural and logical that there is a species more highly evolved than humans who treat humans as cruelly as they have treated the people of different races that the Europeans considered "lower."

2. Possible Response   He considers imperialism cruel, greedy, and unjustifiable.

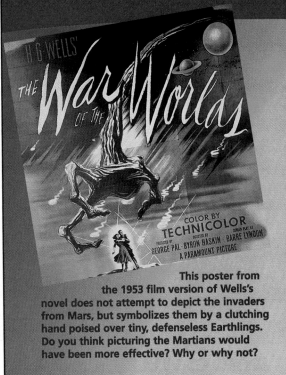

This poster from the 1953 film version of Wells's novel does not attempt to depict the invaders from Mars, but symbolizes them by a clutching hand poised over tiny, defenseless Earthlings. Do you think picturing the Martians would have been more effective? Why or why not?

intelligent life might have developed there far, or indeed at all, beyond its earthly level. Nor was it generally understood that since Mars is older than our earth, with scarcely a quarter of the superficial area and remoter from the sun, it necessarily follows that it is not only more distant from life's beginning but nearer its end.

The secular cooling that must some day overtake our planet has already gone far indeed with our neighbor. Its physical condition is still largely a mystery, but we know now that even in its equatorial region the mid-day temperature barely approaches that of our coldest winter. Its air is much more attenuated than ours, its oceans have shrunk until they cover but a third of its surface, and as its slow seasons change huge snow-caps gather and melt about either pole and periodically inundate its temperate zones. That last stage of exhaustion, which to us is still incredibly remote, has become a present-day problem for the inhabitants of Mars. The immediate pressure of necessity has brightened their intellects,

enlarged their powers, and hardened their hearts. And looking across space with instruments, and intelligences such as we have scarcely dreamed of, they see, at its nearest distance only 35,000,000 of miles sunward of them, a morning star of hope, our own warmer planet, green with vegetation and gray with water, with a cloudy atmosphere eloquent of fertility, with glimpses through its drifting cloud-wisps of broad stretches of populous country and narrow, navy-crowded seas.

And we men, the creatures who inhabit this earth, must be to them at least as alien and lowly as are the monkeys and lemurs to us. The intellectual side of man already admits that life is an incessant struggle for existence, and it would seem that this too is the belief of the minds upon Mars. Their world is far gone in its cooling and this world is still crowded with life, but crowded only with what they regard as inferior animals. To carry warfare sunward is, indeed, their only escape from the destruction that generation after generation creeps upon them.

And before we judge of them too harshly we must remember what ruthless and utter destruction our own species has wrought, not only upon animals, such as the vanished bison and the dodo, but upon its own inferior races. The Tasmanians, in spite of their human likeness, were entirely swept out of existence in a war of extermination waged by European immigrants, in the space of fifty years. Are we such apostles of mercy as to complain if the Martians warred in the same spirit?

Responding

1. How does Darwinism, with its belief in the "survival of the fittest," affect the narrator's attitude toward the Martian invasion?

2. Judging by the narrator's comment on the extermination of the Tasmanians, what is his attitude toward European imperialism?

MINI-LESSON: VISUAL LITERACY

Recognize Graphic Art Styles

Teach   The graphic style of the movie poster on page 628 is typical of the science fiction book jacket style of the Pulp Era. Inexpensive "pulp" fiction magazines, printed on pulpwood paper and sold only on newsstands, achieved mass circulation at the beginning of the twentieth century. Although pulp magazines like *Amazing Stories* reprinted stories by Wells and other authors, they also printed lurid adventure tales, likened to soap operas set in outer space. Their covers featured fantastic sensational illustrations that were often far more explicit than the stories inside.

Questions

- What elements of this movie poster make it "sensational"? *(Possible response: the attractive young couple in a tragic embrace and the huge, wrinkled hand.)*
- How does the mood of the poster contrast with the mood of Wells's introductory remarks? *(Possible response: Wells is serious and socially conscious; the poster is fantastic and commercially seductive.)*

Activity Idea   Suggest that students rent the 1953 movie version of *The War of the Worlds* and compare the film to its poster. How do they match up?

INTERDISCIPLINARY STUDY

Mathematics Connection
Regardless of whether we believe the new century actually begins on January 1, 2000, or January 1, 2001, it is sure to bring with it changes that turn today's dreams into tomorrow's reality. It is a reality that will be created by the people who live it, for better or worse. Will we be able to make it better?

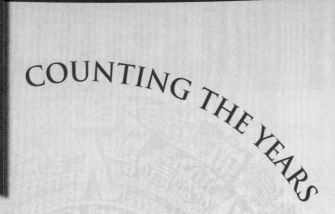

COUNTING THE YEARS

BY LANCE MORROW

urists like to point out that, technically speaking, the beginning of the new millenium does not really occur on January 1, 2000, but on January 1, 2001. This is because there is no year zero in the Christian era, on which historical calendars are calculated. The first year of the era is called A.D. 1, and the one immediately preceding is 1 B.C. Therefore, by the time the calendar reaches January 1, 2000, only 1,999 years will have elapsed since A.D.'s starting point. The same phenomenon occurs as each new century is recorded. In popular observance, however, the simultaneous turning of the zeros marks the beginning of each new century, and very few of the world's citizens will wait for January 1, 2001, to mark the millenium's beginning. In fact, numerous other systems have been devised to keep track of the passage of the years. The oldest in continuous use, China's lunisolar cycle, assigns an animal to each year based on the Chinese zodiac: the Year of the Tiger, Horse and so on. One of the longest counts is Judaism's reckoning of time from the creation of the world, by which the year 2000 will begin during 5760. For the world's Muslims, it will be the year 1420, counted from the Prophet Muhammad's Hegira (migration) to Medina.

All countries will join in using the year 2000 on their civil calendars, despite the number's Christian basis. Paradoxically, although Jesus' actual birth date is unknown, it is almost certain that he was born several years "before Christ." This anomaly occurred because of an error in the calculations of Denis the Little, the 6th century monk who decided that history should be split into B.C. and A.D.

Interdisciplinary Study

Theme Link
The beginning of the twenty-first century may raise similar questions that the writers at the beginning of the twentieth century asked.

Curricular Connection: Mathematics
You can use this interdisciplinary study to discuss the imprecision of mathematical timekeeping, due to human miscalculation and conflicting cultural traditions.

Terms to Know
lunisolar, relating or attributed to the moon and the sun.

hegira (hi jī′rə, hej′ər ə), the migration of the Prophet Muhammad from Mecca to Medina in A.D. 622

anomaly (ə nom′ə lē) peculiarity, deviation from the expected.

Interdisciplinary Activity Ideas
- Have students design their own movie posters for *The War of the Worlds*, adapting its imagery to fit the end of the twentieth century.
- Have students research and report on the planet Mars. Which of H. G. Wells's assertions are accurate, and which have been disproved since he wrote his book?
- Have students find out which year of the Chinese Zodiac each member of their family was born, and research the symbolic significance of the zodiac sign for each year. Have class members compile their reports into a Zodiac Log Book.

BUILDING ENGLISH PROFICIENCY

Making Personal Connections

No matter which reckoning of time one uses, the start of a new year—and, even more, a new millenium—symbolizes a new beginning or fresh start. People often use these markers as points from which to evaluate the past and speculate about the future.

Activity Ideas
- Invite students to respond to "Counting the Years" by creating a details web. In it they can record personal resolutions, hopes for the world, or other thoughts about the character of the twentieth century.
- Ask students to imagine what kind of web H. G. Wells (or one of the other writers from this unit) might generate if he were alive today. Students could work in groups to create the author's web.

Art Study

Cartoon artists, like science fiction writers, can take advantage of an entertaining and popular genre to convey social commentary or political satire. Comic strips, which date from the 1890s, often satirize characters by exaggerating their weaknesses and lampooning their interactions with slapstick and irony.

Questions Who or what is Chast making fun of in this comic strip? *(Possible response: people who worry too much about manners, futurists who fantasize about how technologically advanced life will be in the future, our frequent inability to determine what are appropriate ways to interact in our present age)*

Research Topics

- works by other late Victorian science fiction writers: *Across the Zodiac* by Percy Greg, *A Plunge Into Space* by Robert Cromie, and *The Martian,* by George Du Maurier

- the term fin-de-siècle and its historical and cultural significance

Responding

The ages, occupations, and geographic locations of the magazine's poll respondents covers a wide spectrum of individuals. The class members, who, despite their diversity, may have many of these crucial factors in common.

The Future Poll

In Which Various Intriguing Questions are Posed to the Great American Public

1. If you had to predict, which of the following do you think are likely to occur in the 21st century? (Percentages indicate which portion of those responding thought which events were likely to occur.)

Scientists will find a cure for AIDS	75%
Scientists will find a cure for cancer	80%
Scientists will find a cure for the common cold	39%
The average American will live to be a hundred	57%
A woman will be president of the U. S.	76%
A black will be president of the U. S.	76%
Automobiles will no longer run on gasoline	75%
Computers will be as smart as humans and have personalities like humans	44%
Humans will make regular trips to other planets	43%
Beings who live on other planets will come in contact with us	32%

2. Do you think the world will be in better shape at the end of the 21st century than it is today?

Better	41%
Worse	32%
About the same	15%

3. Compared with the 20th century, do you think the 21st century will have more:

Wars	32%
Environmental Disasters	59%
Poverty	61%
Disease	53%
Hope for the Future	62%

From a telephone poll of 800 adult Americans taken for *Time/CNN* on July 22-23, 1995 by Yankelovich Inc. Sampling error ± 3.5%

Manners of Tomorrow

© 1992 Roz Chast

Responding
Run the Future Poll in your class. Determine the percentages for each response. Calculate the difference in the percentages listed in the chart to those in your class. How might you account for any great ranges in responses?

MINI-LESSON: SPEAKING AND LISTENING SKILLS

Communicate Clearly and Effectively

Teach Point out that the Future Poll was taken over the telephone by a polling corporation. Ask students if they have ever responded to a poll on the telephone or been asked to perform telemarketing services for a job or for an organization.

Apply Take this opportunity to review the following methods of effective communication, stressing that over the telephone, these skills are even more important.

- State the questions clearly and without biased overtones.
- Speak slowly enough to be clear, but not so slow that the respondent loses interest or focus.

- Volume should be appropriate to the needs of the interviewee.
- Clear enunciation is crucial in order to ensure accurate poll results.

Activity Idea Divide students into groups and have them design a training program for telemarketers. Students might create several scenarios that may occur when a telemarketer is taking a poll. Also, they might present scenes that demonstrate what to do and what to avoid.

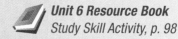

Unit 6 Resource Book
Study Skill Activity, p. 98

Language History

The Language of the Victorians

 . . . a man who labors under the pressure of pecuniary embarrassments, is, with the generality of people, at a disadvantage.
Charles Dickens, *David Copperfield* (1850)

Polite English of the Victorian period—especially the early years—was extremely formal. Men addressed their wives as "Mrs." and husbands were treated with equal courtesy. The utmost formality was extended to strangers, thereby implying they were solemn and important people. Certain classes of people—the ambitious businessman, the newly rich, the aspiring student—carried this formality to absurd lengths, as does Mr. Micawber in the example above, explaining that he is broke. They spoke an exaggerated English of their own called *genteelism*.

The first and most important rule of genteelism was to avoid the common word and use instead a learned, bookish synonym. The advocates of genteelism did not begin a meal—they commenced a collation; they did not use a toothpowder—they employed a dentifrice; and they never used *before, except,* or *about*—it was *ere, save,* and *anent*.

Other Victorians had more serious concerns with regard to the English language. One such group was the Philological Society, which in 1858 resolved to prepare a new dictionary that would display the entire history of every word that was or had been in the English language. The Society's monumental dictionary project produced the *Oxford English Dictionary,* published in ten volumes from 1884 to 1928.

As American English grew, it often used different words from British English for the same things. For example, Britishers were *ill, clever,* and *homely;* Americans were *sick, smart,* and *friendly.* Compare the following American and British words pertaining to the railroad industry: *railroad, railway; conductor, guard; fireman, stoker; car, carriage; track, line; freight, goods; trunk, box;* and *check, register.*

The rapid advance of invention and mechanization all during the Victorian Age created a need for many new words. Grammarians protested the forming of such words as *telegraph* and *typewriter* by scientists, inventors, and manufacturers, and felt that the making of words should be left to the etymologists. Nevertheless, people used or invented words as needed, with little regard for "correctness."

Language History **633**

Language History

Teaching Objectives

- to examine the "politics" of language usage
- to understand that changes in language are inevitable despite resistance to change
- to evaluate how concerns about language usage reflect other concerns of the Victorian Age

Introduce

Discuss the implications of the following quotation, from H. W. Fowler's *A Dictionary of Modern English Usage* (1926). "By *genteelism* is here to be understood the substituting, for the ordinary natural word that first suggests itself to the mind, of a synonym that is thought to be less soiled by the lips of the common herd, less familiar, less plebeian, less vulgar, less improper."

- How does Fowler use irony to demonstrate the attitude of people who speak genteelism?
- What does Fowler's definition reveal about the Victorian concern over keeping clear lines between the classes and about the superficiality of class distinction?

Follow Up

Have students write a script for a classroom discussion about one of the literature selections in which all of the students speak in genteelism. Students can consider the following questions as they write their scripts.

- What does each student want to communicate about himself or herself?
- What does each student think of the others, and how does he or she demonstrate that attitude?
- What breakdowns in communication are likely to occur?

CONTENT AREA READING

Use a Dictionary

All of the language of the Victorian age may strike the modern reader as genteelism. Students need to understand the difference between the use of words to create a certain image of the speaker or writer (genteelism) and usage that is simply no longer used or is peculiar to a region.

Several dictionaries can help students understand the unfamiliar usage of words that may have meant something different in the past or may have a different meaning in another English-speaking country:

- *Dictionary of Americanisms*
- *Dictionary of Regional English* (available for many countries, including Jamaica and Canada)
- *Oxford English Dictionary*

Activity Idea Using the resources above, students can create dialogues between two English speakers from different periods of times or different geographical regions. Ask them to demonstrate the possible confusion that may result.

Writing Workshop

WRITER'S BLUEPRINT
Specs

The Specs in the Writer's Blueprint address these writing and thinking skills:

- comparing and contrasting
- organizing information
- synthesizing
- generalizing
- development by detail
- recognizing values
- making judgments
- spelling homophones correctly

These Specs serve as your lesson objectives, and they form the basis for the **Assessment Criteria Specs** for a superior paper, which appear on the final TE page for this lesson. You might want to read through the Assessment Criteria Specs with students when you begin the lesson.

Linking Literature to Writing

Ask students to discuss some of the elements of writing—ideas or techniques—that they might like to borrow from the authors in this unit for their own composing.

Hope and Despair

Narrative/Expository Writing

Writing Workshop

Found Images

Assignment A found poem is created by collecting favorite lines and phrases from other writers' works and knitting them together with words of your own. Using the literature in this part of the unit, create a found poem and then explain what your poem has to say about the themes of hope and despair.

> ## WRITER'S BLUEPRINT
>
> Product   A found poem and an explanation
> Purpose   To explore the themes of hope and despair
> Audience   Other people who have read the literature
> Specs   To write a successful poem and explanation, you should:
>
> ❏ Collect ten lines or phrases from the literature that you think best illustrate the theme of hope. Look for strong images. Do the same for despair.
>
> ❏ Create a found poem, using some or all of the images you've collected and knitting them together with words of your own. Your goal is to make a powerful statement about hope and despair.
>
> ❏ Write a short, informal essay that contains:
> —an opening statement summing up what your poem has to say about the themes of hope and despair
>
> —comments on how some of the individual images in the poem illustrate this statement
>
> —a closing statement that leaves the reader with your single, most important message about hope and despair
>
> ❏ Follow the rules of grammar, usage, spelling, and mechanics. Take care to spell homophones correctly.

WRITING WORKSHOP OVERVIEW

Product
Narrative/Expository writing: A found poem and an explanation

Prewriting
Review the literature—Compose your poem—Try a quickwrite—Exchange poems—Plan your explanation
Unit 6 Resource Book
Prewriting Worksheets pp. 99–100

Drafting
Start writing
Transparency Collection
Student Models for Writing Workshop 23, 24

Revising
Ask a partner—Strategy: Development by Detail
Unit 6 Resource Book
Revising Worksheet p. 101

Editing
Ask a partner—Strategy: Spelling Homophones Correctly
Unit 6 Resource Book
Grammar Worksheet p. 102
Grammar Check Test p. 103

Presenting
Group Poem
Collage

Looking Back
Self-evaluate—Reflect—For Your Working Portfolio
Unit 6 Resource Book
Assessment Worksheet p. 104
Transparency Collection
Fine Art Writing Prompt 12

Review the literature for lines and phrases about hope and despair that create strong images for you. Record these images in two charts, one for hope and one for despair. Include your reactions to these images. For example:

Despair

Images from the Literature	Reactions
"a cry discordant and feeble" (from "The Lagoon")	This could be a sound that Despair would make if it could speak.
"anarchy is loosed upon the world" (from "The Second Coming")	I see Despair as a raging beast. Despair can lead a person to anger, to violence.

Then circle the ten images in each chart that seem strongest to you.

Compose your poem. Begin by writing each of the circled images from your charts onto a separate note card. Then start grouping and arranging them, deleting some, if you wish. You might end up using all the images, or just a few. Experiment with different arrangements until you find the order that works best. As you proceed, jot down words and phrases on the cards that will help you knit these images together into a poem.

OR . . .
Try a quickdraw. Draw the images you circled to create a rich mental picture. Use this drawing for inspiration when you write your poem.

Then write your final draft. Here are parts of two writers' poems. (The lines from the literature have been underlined so that you can more easily see the different ways these writers have knitted them together.)

I close my eyes and hear
<u>a cry discordant and feeble.</u>
I look up and see a star,
<u>the sweet brilliance of its light.</u>
I look out to see that
<u>anarchy is loosed upon the world,</u>
and I tell myself:
<u>If you can keep your head
when all about you
are losing theirs . . .</u>

 STUDENT MODEL

<u>A cry discordant and feeble</u>
announces that
<u>anarchy is loosed upon the
world.</u>
<u>If you can keep your head
when all about you
are losing theirs . . .</u>

STUDENT MODEL

Writing Workshop **635**

STEP 1 PREWRITING
Review the literature

Remind students that the images they chart need not directly address hope or despair, but may be related in some more general way. Urge students to jot down any and all of their reactions, even the ones that don't seem especially pertinent at the time. Later, looking over their notes, they may see connections that weren't immediately apparent. For additional support, see the worksheet referenced below.

Unit 6 Resource Book
Prewriting Workshop, p. 99

Compose your poem

Encourage students to read their poems aloud to themselves as they draft, to help get a feel for the sound of the language.

 **ESL LEP ELD SAE LD**

BUILDING ENGLISH PROFICIENCY

Using Grammar Creatively

Make sure students understand that the phrases that connect the found pieces of the poem must not only join the ideas but make grammatical sense.

1. Show students parts of two poems that use different verb tenses. Have them work in groups to produce sentences that connect the parts in a way that makes the shift in tense reasonable. Be prepared to model an example.

2. Give students found phrases that have no verbs. Challenge groups to put them into complete sentences.

Try a quickwrite

Suggest that students read their poems several times to get a feel for the rhythm and message. Then they can quickwrite about the images that come to mind.

Exchange poems

Students may want to quickwrite for a few minutes as they read their partner's poem line by line. Partners may also need time to discuss their reactions to each other's poems.

Plan your explanation

Students can view this activity as if they are analyzing their own work as they would a published piece by another writer. Urge them to be as detached as possible from the fact that they wrote the poem they are now interpreting. For additonal support, see the worksheet referenced below.

Unit 6 Resource Book
Prewriting Worksheet, p. 100

Connections to
Writer's Notebook

For selection-related prompts, refer to Writer's Notebook.

Connections to
Writer's Resource

For additional writing prompts, refer to Writer's Resource.

STEP 2 DRAFTING
Start writing

Discuss with students the strengths and weaknesses of writing about a poem line by line and from a holistic perspective.

Try a quickwrite. For five minutes, write about your poem. Jot down whatever comes to mind as you ask yourself: *What do these images seem to say about the nature of hope and despair?*

Exchange poems with a partner and react to your partner's poem with a quickwrite like the one you wrote in reaction to your own poem. Then return quickwrites and poems. Use your partner's reactions to help you write your essay of explanation.

Plan your explanation. Review your poem, quickwrites, and charts as you plan your essay of explanation. Make notes on these points:

* An opening statement about hope and despair

* How specific images illustrate the general statement

* A closing statement of your most important message about hope and despair

STEP **2** DRAFTING

OR . . .
Group similar images and deal with one group at a time.

Start writing. Here are some drafting tips to consider:

* Choose the strongest three or four images of hope and of despair and deal with them one at a time.

* For your closing statement, return to your single strongest image and focus on its significance.

* Take care that you develop your general ideas with specific details. See the Revising Strategy in Step 3 of this lesson.

STEP **3** REVISING

Ask a partner to react to your draft before you revise it. Make sure your partner has a copy of your poem to refer to. Use this checklist as a guide.

✔ Does the essay address the poem?

✔ Does the essay develop the opening statement with specific details?

MINI-LESSON: WRITING STYLE

Development by Detail

Teach Ask students to envision the general statement of their essay as a pencil outline of a picture that must be shaded in with the colors and textures of all of the various details.

Activity Idea For each of these general statements, have students develop a paragraph that contains three specific details to complete the picture in the reader's mind.

Despair comes easily; hope is hard to come by.

Hope is an elephant; despair is a mole.

Fear cannot be without hope nor hope without fear.—Benedict Spinoza

Apply Have students search their partner's essay for general statements that need further development.

Revising Strategy

Development by Detail

Good explanatory writing demands that each general idea be developed by specific details. The reader can't be expected to know specifically what the writer means by such a general term as *hope* or *despair*. The reader needs to see specific details that clearly illustrate what this particular writer is getting at. If the reader can't see the connection, the writing loses focus.

Notice how the student model was revised to make it clearer how the details relate to the general statement they are meant to illustrate.

> My poem shows hope and despair as opposites but as existing simultaneously. Each opposite is seen in terms of the other. They are two sides of the same coin. One leads directly to the other. I see hope in terms of clarity and despair as confusion. Before looking up at the star I hear a "cry discordant and feeble." The ~~star~~ *star's clear, brilliant light* represents hope, while the *confusing, discordant* cry stands for despair.

STUDENT MODEL

STEP 4 EDITING

Ask a partner to review your revised draft before you edit. When you edit, look for errors in grammar, usage, spelling, and mechanics. Pay special attention to the spellings of short, simple words that you may otherwise overlook. Look over each sentence to make sure you have used homophones correctly.

MINI-LESSON: GRAMMAR

Spelling Homophones Correctly

Have students work in teams to create humorous sentences with homophone errors. For example:

"Theirs know better weigh two seek piece than threw hour strength."

From these sentences, develop a class list of homophones to watch for.

Unit 6 Resource Book
Grammar Worksheet, p. 102
Grammar Check Test, p. 103

The Student Models

The **transparencies** referenced below are authentic student models. Review them with the students before they draft. These questions will help:

1. Notice the statements of the essay part of model 23. What details could be added to develop good explanations rather than general statements?

2. How could the writer of model 24 improve her summary statement about the themes of hope and despair?

3. Which model do you think does a better job of interpreting the accompanying poem and why?

Transparency Collection
Student Models for Writing Workshop 23, 24

STEP 3 REVISING
Ask a partner (Peer assessment)

Have students list the specific details that support the writer's opening statement.

Revising Strategy: Development by Detail

For additional support, see the mini-lesson at the bottom of page 636 and the worksheet referenced below.

Unit 6 Resource Book
Revising Worksheet, p. 101

Connections to
Writer's Resource

Refer to the Grammar, Usage, and Mechanics Handbook on Writer's Resource.

STEP 4 EDITING
Ask a partner (Peer assessment)

Remind students to check their peer's spelling as well as grammar and mechanics.

Editing Strategy: Spelling Homophones Correctly

For additional support, see the mini-lesson at the bottom of page 637 and the worksheets referenced below.

Unit 6 Resource Book
Grammar Worksheet, p. 102
Grammar Worksheet, p. 103

Connections to
Writer's Resource

Refer to the Grammar, Usage, and Mechanics Handbook on Writer's Resource.

STEP 5 PRESENTING
Group Poem

Have students illustrate their group poems and use them for a bulletin board display.

STEP 6 LOOKING BACK
Self-evaluate

The *Assessment Criteria Specs* at the bottom of this page are for a superior paper. You might want to post these in the classroom. Students can then evaluate themselves based on these criteria. For a complete scoring rubric, use the *Assessment Worksheet* referenced below.

Unit 6 Resource Book
Assessment Worksheet, p. 104

Reflect

Students may want to extend this writing project further into more personal reflections about their feelings of hope and despair.

To further explore the theme, use the Fine Art Transparency referenced below.

Transparency Collection
Fine Art Writing Prompt 12

Spelling Homophones Correctly

Homophones sound alike but have different spellings and meanings. The key to spelling homophones correctly is paying close attention to their meaning within the context of a passage. For example:

There are three key images in the first stanza. **They're** the strongest images in the poem. I hope readers feel **their** strength. **It's** a difficult task to bring abstract concepts like these to life. A concept like *hope* has **its** own special meaning for each of us, and **it's** the poet's task to narrow all those meanings down to one. As a poet, you know that **your** personal meaning is what **you're** out to communicate.

When you edit for spelling, don't overlook short, simple words like these.

COMPUTER TIP
If your computer has a spell checker, use it—but don't rely on it to give your perfect spelling. A spell checker won't catch a homophone mistake or a mistake like the one with *your* in the preceding sentence.

STEP 5 PRESENTING

- Form groups of three and read your poems to each other. As a group, choose what you feel are the four best lines in each poem and combine them to create a new, group poem.

- Make a collage to accompany your poem.

STEP 6 LOOKING BACK

Self-evaluate. Look back at the Writer's Blueprint and give yourself a score on each point, from 6 (superior) to 1 (inadequate).

Reflect. Respond to these items in writing:

✔ Think back to the literature in this part of the unit. Of all the writers you read, which one most closely reflects the ideas about hope and despair in your poem and why?

✔ Give an example of how the general statement in your explanation applies to an experience from your own life.

For Your Working Portfolio Add your poem, essay, and reflection responses to your working portfolio.

ASSESSMENT CRITERIA SPECS

Here are the criteria for a superior paper. A full six-level rubric for this paper appears on the Assessment Worksheet referenced below.

6 Superior The writer of a 6 paper impressively meets these criteria:

- Creates a found poem that gives genuine insights into the nature of hope and despair.

- Creates an accompanying essay that summarizes these insights in a skillfully phrased general statement.

- Elaborates on this general statement with specific images drawn from the poem.

- Closes by citing the single most important insight on hope and despair drawn from the poem.

- Has few, if any, errors in grammar, usage, mechanics, or spelling.

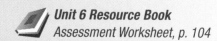

Unit 6 Resource Book
Assessment Worksheet, p. 104

Beyond Print

Images of the Future

Every generation tries to predict the future. H. G. Wells, whose story "The Star" appears in this part, was one of the best futurists ever. A surprising number of the technological innovations he created for his stories and novels have actually been developed in this century. Polls, like the Future Poll on page 632, show that everyone has opinions about the future. But how can we tell what is true?

We can't. The future hasn't happened yet. That hasn't stopped innumerable writers, movie and television designers and technicians, and science-fiction illustrators from making the attempt. The interesting thing is that you can often tell more about the artists and the times in which they live than you can tell about the future. For example, the movie *2001* presented a finely detailed picture of space flight (one famous detail: the instructions posted on a spaceship wall on how to use a zero-gravity toilet), but the movie ended with a light show and surrealistic images that strongly hinted at the movie maker's optimism. The movie *Blade Runner* presented a future society that is corrupt and disintegrating, and the sets and costumes supported that viewpoint.

Look closely at the illustration, a comic book cover by Frank R. Paul, created in 1928. Consider these points.

The Technology Much science fiction is dependent upon believable future technology. How is this man flying?

Beyond Print

Teaching Objectives

- to evaluate the visual elements that accompany the genre of science fiction
- to examine how art and literature can reflect a political and social context

Curricular Connection: Visual Skills

You can use the material in this article to help students hone their visual evaluation skills as they examine this illustration.

Introduce

- The "golden age" of science fiction, from 1937–1950, explored themes like robots, undiscovered worlds, traveling faster than light, galaxy battles, encounters with aliens, and, beginning in the late 1940s, the possibilities of nuclear power.
- The "New Wave" of science fiction, from around 1950–1970, dealt with themes such as ecology, drugs, overpopulation, disasters, and sexuality, often incorporating theories from anthropology, psychology, and sociology.
- Contemporary science fiction, often satirical and pessimistic, has incorporated computer technology and a cast of cyber-heroes, whose adventures occur inside the virtual reality of the computer, while the actual world shrinks and deteriorates.

BUILDING ENGLISH PROFICIENCY

Expanding upon Key Ideas

Teach As this feature points out, futuristic tales often tell more about the people who created them and the culture of the present time than they do about the future. Consequently, science fiction can give us an opportunity to look at ourselves from a creative and perhaps "safe" perspective.

Activity Idea Students can explore this idea about the possible value of science fiction stories by evaluating a current television show, such as one of the *Star Trek* series. Ask the students to consider the following questions as they evaluate the show.

- How does the show portray the roles of men and women? What kind of hope does it offer regarding issues of equality?

- What solutions does the show offer regarding relationships among different races and cultures?

- What conflicts do the characters face? How are these conflicts similar to those in our society today?

- What conflicts seem to be timeless—as likely 300 years from now or 300 hundred years ago? What new insights does the show offer about these conflicts?

Responding

The Technology

Possible Response: The man is flying with a jet pack, propelled by a combustion engine mounted on his back. Although military agencies have invented one-man helicopters and crude solo-flight devices, none have been made available for commercial use.

The Costumes

Possible Response: No, it looks more like scuba diving gear. The other costumes seem plausible, considering the landscape. They seem fairly similar to today's clothes.

The Setting

Possible Response: It appears to be a lush, warm climate. The houses, which seem like modified versions of the houses of the 1920s, do not seem as futuristic as the flying man.

The Relationships

Possible Response: No, the relationship seems stereotypical with the man going off to be a hero and the woman staying at home, waving good-bye with a handkerchief.

The Artistic Style

Possible Response: It is an optimistic, rose-colored vision of a peaceful and prosperous future.

Activity Options

Activity 1 Suggest that students gather magazine photographs and book illustrations of different models of this item throughout the years. They can pick interesting features and variations to emphasize in their own futuristic versions.

Activity 2 To help students develop a focus for their stories, suggest that they use one of the common science fiction themes described on page 639.

Can you imagine the technology that enables him to do so? To your knowledge, has a device for individual flight ever been invented in this century? If so, can you describe the technology involved?

The Costumes Is the man's outfit believable as a costume for flying? Are the costumes of the other characters believable as futuristic at-home wear? How do they differ from costumes you might actually see people wearing today?

The Setting What do the houses and the countryside tell you about the climate? Do the houses seem appropriately futuristic? Why or why not?

The Relationships Consider who is doing the flying and who is waving good-bye. Do you think this 1928 artist could have imagined the relative equality of the sexes that has evolved through the later part of the twentieth century?

The Artistic Style Consider the poses of the characters, the lines and colors employed, and the overall composition. What vision of the future do you think this comic book cover was apparently intended to convey?

Activity Options

1. Choose an area of technology, such as transportation, entertainment, or household upkeep, and create a picture that shows what you think one item will look like at a specific time in the future. You might choose 10 years, 100 years, or 1000 years—and your technological innovation is limited only by your imagination.

2. Write a short science-fiction story in which your main character makes use of some futuristic technology. Describe in detail what it looks like and what it does. (You don't, however, have to explain *how* it works.)

ANOTHER APPROACH

Science Fiction in the Movies

Discuss how technological advances have changed the special effects used in science fiction films. You might compare vintage science fiction films, like *The War of the Worlds* or *The Day the Earth Stood Still,* which use models, miniature sets, and projection tricks, to more contemporary films, like *Waterworld, Stargate,* and *Jurassic Park,* which use computer animation to create realistic futuristic images.

Activity Ideas

- Discuss whether students feel that computer technology has made the possibility of futuristic reality seem more plausible to moviegoers.

- Have students work in groups to create a Top Ten Sci-Fi Movie list, writing a brief synopsis of the plot and the special effects that make each film worth seeing.

Multicultural Connections

Change

Part One: The Struggle to Understand Understanding the world can be difficult enough to start with, but changes can make such understanding even more difficult. The characters in these selections see their world changing in bewildering ways—as Alice does in Wonderland—or in sad, frightening ways—as the speaker does in "Dover Beach." Depending on their perspectives, they respond with action, with violence, or with love.

■ Do you think that simply knowing that change is coming is enough to help a person cope with it? Are there other, more specific methods that can help a person deal with change?

Perspective

Part Two: Hope and Despair The particular viewpoint, or perspective, that a person applies to his or her life and the changes that occur in it can influence to a large extent whether that person will respond with positive or negative emotions, with hope or despair. Falling in love, growing old, dying—all such life experiences can be looked upon as either obstacles or challenges.

■ Which of the fictional characters in this part seems to be regarding life with most hope? with most despair? Is that character's response an appropriate one, in your opinion?

Activities

1. Work in a small group to list the major changes in technology, economy, world politics, and so on that have happened during your lifetime. Poll your group members for their opinions on whether each of these changes is good or bad, a challenge or an obstacle. Then devise some sort of graphic organizer to display the results of your poll.

2. Attempt to summarize your perspective—your view of the world— in no more than three sentences. Compare your summary with those of one or more classmates. To what extent can your personal experiences account for any differences among them?

641

Unit Wrap-Up

MULTICULTURAL CONNECTION

Students may have trouble understanding the psychological dimensions of the upheaval that shook European society during this era. The following ideas and questions may facilitate discussion.

Change

Point out that group identity often affects an individual's response to change: for example, Alice, lost in a strange world, is alone in her bewilderment, and everyone else is accustomed to the violence and absurdity.

• How might the feeling of alienation result from rapid social change?

• How much is an individual able to resist the forces of social change?

Possible Responses There is no way to predict the emotional effects of change, even when it is fully expected. However expecting change may help someone accept it. As with the writers in this unit, talking and writing about the changes that one is experiencing may help one to think more carefully about the changes and invite responses from other people.

Perspective

Point out that perspective is strongly influenced by group identity. You might discuss the group identities that influenced the authors in this part: nation, class, religion, and gender.

Possible Responses The most hopeful character might be the narrator of "The Star," who draws optimism from the earth's ability to survive catastrophe. His conclusion, that a distant perspective can make vast problems seem minute, is helpful in times of struggle. The most despairing character may be Arsat, who has lost his two loved ones. His response—threats of violent revenge—although understandable, show an inability to accept change.

Activities

Activity 1 Students might consult magazines like *Time* and *Newsweek* to research the events of the last decade as well as to find ideas for visual representations of poll results.

Activity 2 Have students imagine that they are writing these summaries in the 1890s: first, as a British citizen; next, as an Indian citizen living under British rule; and last, as Queen Victoria. You might experiment further with perspective by having students pretend they are of a different gender, age, religious affiliation, and so on.

UNIT 6 OPTIONS

Art

- Students might wish to stage a video of a scene from one of the works, or write a screen adaptation that includes camera shots, sets, and costumes.
- Suggest that students display their artwork in the classroom without revealing their literary sources. Can other students identify the literary selection which inspired the art?

History

Students might change the perspective of their time line, and make the events of Victorian England subordinate to the history of another culture. For example, students could write a time line on the history of India. Ask students to discuss how the different perspective helps us understand the impact of Great Britain.

Literature

You might suggest that students research the life of the author who wrote the novel they selected. How might social and economic circumstances, education, environment, and gender have affected the novelist's perspective on the changing world?

Connections to AuthorWorks

Data for completing this project can be found on AuthorWorks CD-ROM: Jane Austen, Emily and Charlotte Brontë, Charles Dickens, Thomas Hardy, Joseph Conrad, and George Orwell.

Unit Test

Unit 6 Resource Book
New Selection
Test 1
Test 2

Independent and Group Projects

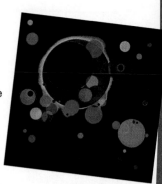

Art

"To Make You See" Joseph Conrad described his task as a writer: "By the power of the written word, to make you hear, to make you feel—it is, before all, to make you see." Which of the writers in this unit created a literary work that made you hear, feel, and see? Create an **artistic work**—a painting, a sculpture, a collage, a photograph—that depicts what your chosen writer made you hear, feel, and see.

History

Victorian Time Line Queen Victoria was a remarkable ruler, and a remarkable period of history is named after her. With a group, create a **time line** of the Victorian Age (1837–1901) in which you put what was happening in Great Britain into context with what was happening in the United States and around the world. In your time line include the following: political leaders; historical events; figures in literature, art, and music; advances in science and medicine; inventions.

Literature

The English Novel During the nineteenth century the English novel developed into an important source of entertainment as well as a commentary on the social conditions and the cultural and moral values of the English people. Read one of the following novels of this period: *Pride and Prejudice* by Jane Austen, *David Copperfield* by Charles Dickens, *Wuthering Heights* by Emily Brontë, *Jane Eyre* by Charlotte Brontë, *The Mill on the Floss* by George Eliot, or *Tess of the D'Urbervilles* by Thomas Hardy. Prepare an **oral report** for your class in which you introduce the important characters, summarize the main plot, and comment on the picture of English life that is presented. You might include several quotations from the novel.

Music

Sing Out in Praise What can you find to celebrate about the last century or this century? Write an **anthem**—a song of praise—for the centennial, the movement from the 1800s (nineteenth century) to the 1900s (twentieth century). Or, if you prefer, write an anthem for the millennium, the movement to the year 2000. Your anthem can include praise for past achievements and perhaps a vision of the future.

Music

Students might work in groups and perform their anthems before the class. Students who play the piano or the guitar might accompany the choral arrangement. Student may write their anthem to fit a pre-existing tune, perhaps a well-known anthem such as "The Star Spangled Banner," "Oh Canada," or "America."

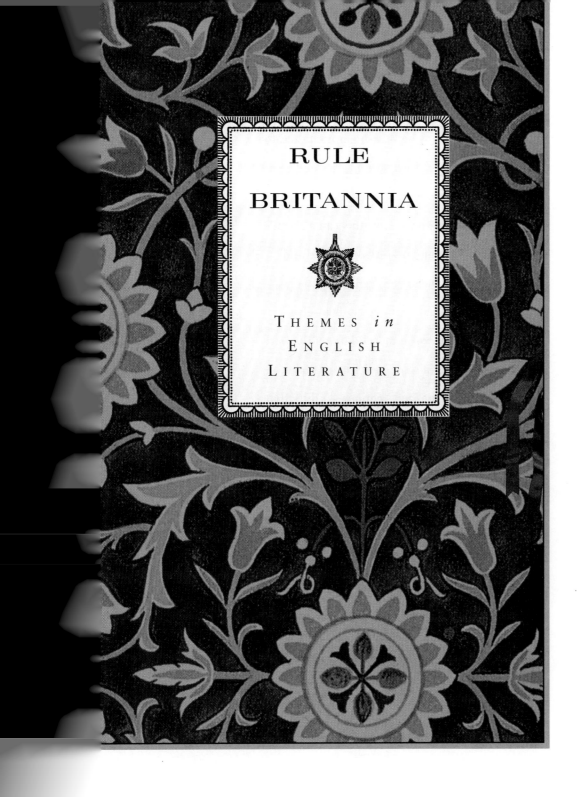

RULE
BRITANNIA

THEMES *in* ENGLISH LITERATURE

The phrase was first used at the close of the 1898 Spanish-American War, describing the responsibility of the United States in caring for Cuba and the Philippines. It soon became the watchword of imperialism. Kipling's poem with this title begins thus:

Take up the White Man's burden—
    Send forth the best ye breed—
Go bind your sons to exile
    To serve your captives' need;
To wait in heavy harness,
    On fluttered folk and wild—
Your new-caught, sullen peoples,
    Half-devil and half-child

Take up the White Man's burden—
    In patience to abide,
To veil the threat of terror
    And check the show of pride;
By open speech and simple,
    An hundred times made plain,
To seek another's profit,
    And work another's gain.

R U L E ,

The British empire lasted for several centuries and at its greatest extent covered one-fourth of the world. How this came about is a complex story of politics and economics, but English people managed to convince themselves that it was a moral duty on the part of England to guide the destinies of less "civilized" nations—a duty that Rudyard Kipling once called the "white man's burden." Needless to say, this position had its detractors as well as its adherents.

✳

*The sun never sets
on the British Empire.*

popular saying

✳

THEME LINK TO THE LITERATURE

Some other selections in the text that deal with the themes of the journey are the following:

B R I T A N N I A !

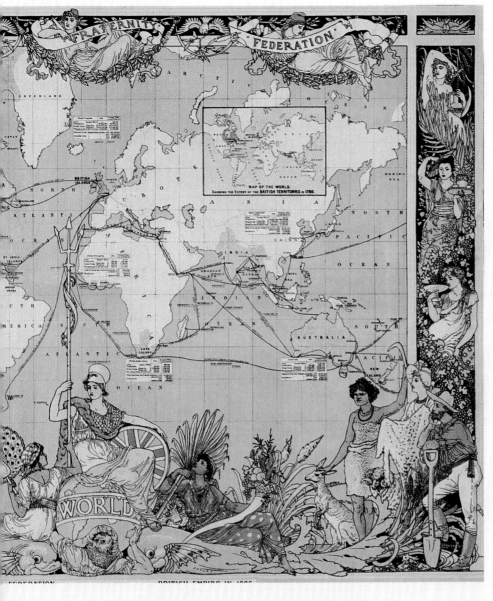

British possessions appear in pink on this 1886 map of the world.

645

Visual Literacy It was an artistic convention to include various decorative elements on maps, especially older maps of the world. Such elements might include ships, winds, sea-monsters, and (what the artist thought were) indigenous peoples, flora, and fauna of the countries represented.

Question What nationality or population group do you think is represented by each of the figures surrounding the map? *(Possible response: Native North Americans, Canadian immigrants of English descent, English sailors, soldiers, and officers in India, Indians, Africans, Native Australians, and Australian immigrants of English descent)*

BUILDING ENGLISH PROFICIENCY

Exploring Key Concepts

ESL
LEP
ELD
SAE
LD

Explain to students that the name *Britannia* refers both to the British Empire and to a symbolic figure.

1. The British Empire refers to England and the other countries of the British Isles—Scotland, Ireland, and Wales—and to all the other countries or possessions that England controlled at one time. Have students point these out on the map (shown in pink), and, if necessary, refer to a larger map to identify the countries.

2. Britannia is also the figure of a woman symbolizing Britain or the British Empire. She is shown here in the center, sitting on a globe, wearing a helmet, and carrying a trident (three-pointed spear) and a shield.

Question What human figure symbolizes the United States? *(Uncle Sam)*

About James Thomson

James Thomson (1700–1748), Scottish-born British poet, is best known for *The Seasons*, in which he repopularized blank verse and introduced nature as a self-sufficient theme in English literature. This song is from his masque (a musical court entertainment with elaborate costumes and scenery), *Alfred.*

About Richard II

In Act Two, Scene 1, old John of Gaunt, suffering on his death bed because Richard has banished his son Bolingbroke, speaks these famous lines, concluding, "this England / . . . Is now leased out . . . / Like to a tenement or pelting [paltry] farm." He warns Richard that his reputation is waning. As if to prove Gaunt right, Richard seizes all his possessions when he dies.

Oh, England.
Sick in head and sick in heart,
Sick in whole and every part,
And yet sicker thou art still
For thinking, that thou art not ill.

Anonymous (1600s)

RULE, BRITANNIA

When Britain first, at Heaven's command,
Arose from out the azure main,[1]
This was the charter of the land,
And guardian angels sung the strain:
Rule Britannia, rule the waves,
Britons never will be slaves.

The nations not so blessed as thee
Must, in their turns, to tyrants fall,
Whilst thou shalt flourish, great and free,
The dread and envy of them all.

Still more majestic shalt thou rise,
More dreadful from each foreign stroke;
As the loud blast that tears the skies
Serves but to root thy native oak.

Thee haughty tyrants ne'er shall tame;
All their attempts to bend thee down
Will but arouse thy generous flame,
But work their woe, and thy renown. . . .
Rule, Britannia, rule the waves,
Britons never will be slaves.

James Thomson (1740)

from
THE TRAGEDY OF KING RICHARD II

This royal throne of kings, this sceptered isle,
This earth of majesty, this seat of Mars,[1]
This other Eden, demi-paradise,
This fortress built by Nature for herself
Against infection and the hand of war,
This happy breed of men, this little world,
This precious stone set in the silver sea,
Which serves it in the office of a wall
Or as a moat defensive to a house,
Against the envy of less happier lands,
This blessed plot, this earth, this realm, this England. . . .

William Shakespeare (1597)

1. **main,** sea; ocean.   1. **Mars,** Roman god of war.

A 1900 Dutch cartoon presents a hostile view of British imperialism in the Boer War, showing Queen Victoria, like Pilate in the New Testament, attempting to cleanse herself of guilt.

MINI-LESSON: READING/THINKING SKILLS

Identify Assumptions

An assumption is an unstated belief that underlies an argument or piece of writing.

Teach   The writers of imperialist Britain, no less than the colonizers themselves, operated on a set of assumptions about who the English were and what their place was in the world.

Activity Idea   Have students discuss the beliefs behind these statements:

1. Britain arose "at Heaven's command."

2. Britain's charter was to "rule the waves."

3. Guardian angels sang that charter.

4. Other nations, "not so blessed" as England, must fall to tyrants.

5. Blasts loud enough to tear the skies only serve "to root thy native oak."

6. Tyrants' attempts to conquer Britain will "work their woe, and thy renown."

IMPERIALISM

The following excerpt advocating colonization is from a speech given to the House of Commons by Charles Buller, a member of Parliament.

I think, sir, that we cannot contemplate the conditions of this country without coming to the conclusion that there is a permanent cause of suffering in the constant accumulation of capital[1] and the constant increase of population within the same restricted field of employment. Every year adds its profits to the amount of capital previously accumulated; and certainly leaves the population considerably larger at its close than at its commencement. This fresh amount both of capital and population have to be employed, they must compete for a share of the previous amount of profits and wages. . . .

I propose that you should investigate the efficacy[2] of colonization as a remedy against the distress of the country. . . . I propose colonization as subsidiary[3] to free trade; as an additional mode of carrying out the same principles and attaining the same object. You advocates of free trade wish to bring food to the people. I suggest to you at the same time to take your people to the food. You wish to get the fresh markets by removing the barriers which now keep you from those that exist throughout the world. . . .

But the whole, nay the main advantage of colonization, is not secured by that mere removal of the laborer from the crowded mother country. . . His absence is only the first relief which he affords you. You take him hence to place him on a fertile soil, from which a very small amount of labor will suffice to raise the food which he wants. He soon finds that by applying his spare time and energies to raising additional food, or some article of trade or material of manufacture, he can obtain that which he can exchange for luxuries of which he never dreamed at home. He raises some article of export and appears in your market as a customer. He who a few years ago added nothing to the wealth of the country, but received all from charity . . . comes, after providing his own food, to purchase from you a better quality and a larger quantity of the clothing, and other manufactures which he used to take as a dole,[4] and to give employment and offer food to those on whose energies he was a burden before. . . .

It seems a paradox to assert that removing a portion of your population enables a country to support more inhabitants than it could before; and that the place of every man who quits his country because he cannot get a subsistence[5] may speedily be filled up by another whom that very removal will enable to subsist there in comfort. But the assertion is as true as it is strange.

Charles Buller (1843)

---

1. **capital,** wealth; money invested.
2. **efficacy** (ef′ə kə sē), *n.* effectiveness.
3. **subsidiary** (səb sid′ē er′ē), *n.* supplement.
4. **dole** (dōl), *n.* money, food, etc. given in charity.
5. **subsistence** (səb sis′təns), *n.* means of keeping alive.

647

About Imperialism

Much of world history is written in the rise and decline of vast empires. Egypt, Assyria, Babylon, and Persia established large empires from 2,000–4,000 years ago. Rome created a great empire from Asia Minor to what is now France and Great Britain. The new European nations of the 1400s–1500s acquired colonial possessions as they spread Christianity and searched for markets and raw materials. During the late 1800s, Belgium, France, Germany, Great Britain, Italy, Portugal, and Spain divided up nearly all of Africa and large sections of Southeast Asia and many islands in the South Pacific.

BUILDING ENGLISH PROFICIENCY

Imperialism

Have students use a large or unabridged dictionary to analyze the word *imperialism.*

1. What is the meaning and origin of *imperial?* *("Of or having to do with an empire"; it is from the Latin* imperium *meaning "empire.")*

2. What is the function of the suffix *-ism?* *(It forms a noun from other nouns and from adjectives and verbs. Here, it creates the meaning "policy or system of dominating another nation's economic, political, and even military structure without actually taking governmental control.")*

About Mutesa I

Mutesa Walugembe Mukaabya was the autocratic but progressive *kabaka* (ruler) of the African kingdom of Buganda. Under his rule Buganda's wealth came chiefly from raids into neighboring states, although he did not extend direct political control. When extensive contacts with Arabs and Europeans began, he was apparently influenced enough by Islam to observe some of its customs, but he also welcomed Christian missionaries, wishing to use European influence as a counter to threats from Egypt.

STANLEY MEETS MUTESA

Welsh-born Henry Morton Stanley (1841–1904) explored Africa over the course of many years. He found the explorer David Livingstone, who was presumed lost; traced the course of the Congo River, helped establish the Congo Free State; and aided colonial ruler Emin Pasha.

Such a time of it they had;
The heat of the day
The chill of the night
And the mosquitoes that followed.
Such was the time and
They bound for a kingdom.

The thin weary line of carriers
With tattered dirty rags to cover their backs;
The battered bulky chests
That kept on falling off their shaven heads.
Their tempers high and hot
The sun fierce and scorching
With it rose their spirits
With its fall their hopes
As each day sweated their bodies dry and
Flies clung in clumps on their sweat-scented
      backs.
Such was the march
And the hot season just breaking.

Each day a weary pony dropped,
Left for the vultures on the plains;
Each afternoon a human skeleton collapsed,
Left for the Masai[1] on the plains;
But the march trudged on
Its Khaki[2] leader in front
He the spirit that inspired.
He the light of hope.

Then came the afternoon of a hungry march,
A hot and hungry march it was;
The Nile and the Nyanza[3]
Lay like two twins
Azure across the green countryside.
The match leapt on chanting
Like young gazelles to a water hole.
Hearts beat faster
Loads felt lighter
As the cool water lapped their sore soft feet.
No more the dread of hungry hyenas
But only tales of valor when
At Mutesa's court fires are lit.
No more the burning heat of the day
But song, laughter and dance.

The village looks on behind banana groves,
Children peer behind reed fences.
Such was the welcome
No singing women to chant a welcome
Or drums to greet the white ambasador;
Only a few silent nods from aged faces
And one rumbling drum roll
To summon Mutesa's court to parley[4]
For the country was not sure.

The gate of reeds is flung open,
There is silence
But only a moment's silence—
A silence of assessment.
The tall black king steps forward,
He towers over the thin bearded white man
Then grabbing his lean white hand
Manages to whisper
"Mtu mweupe karibu"
White man you are welcome.
The gate of polished reed closes behind them
And the West is let in.

James D. Rubadiri

Mutesa (1838?–1884), king of the African kingdom of Buganda (now in Uganda), who welcomed Christian missionaries in 1877.
1. **Masai** (mä sī′), *n.* member of a tribe of tall people of East Africa, noted as hunters and as cattle raisers.
2. **Khaki** (kak′ē), *n.* a heavy twilled cloth of yellowish brown; here, a uniformed officer.
3. **Nile . . . Nyanza.** Uganda lies between the Nile River and Lake Nyanza.
4. **parley** (pär′lē), *v.* speak; talk.

MINI-LESSON: LITERARY ELEMENT

Free Verse

Free verse differs from conventional verse forms in that it is "free" from a fixed pattern of meter and rhyme, but uses rhythm and other poetic devices.

Teach First have students examine the poem for meter or rhyme. If necessary, teach the term free verse. (Free verse is not taught as a Literary Focus until p. 769 of this text.)

Activity Idea Ask students to identify other poetic devices they find in "Stanley Meets Mutesa." *(Rhythm: throughout, with good examples in lines 1–6 and 45–50; repetition: lines 2–3, 19–22, and 25–26; figurative language: lines 24, 25–26, 30, and 33; imagery: lines 2–4, 7–16, 36, 40–41, 42–43, and 45–48; alliteration: lines 9, 11, 28, and 29)*

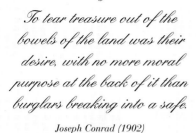

To tear treasure out of the bowels of the land was their desire, with no more moral purpose at the back of it than burglars breaking into a safe.

Joseph Conrad (1902)

A TREATY BETWEEN QUEEN VICTORIA AND THE KING OF MELLELLA
River Congo, March 19, 1877

1. The export of slaves to foreign countries is forever abolished in my territory.

2. No European or other person whatever shall be permitted to reside in my territories or those of my heirs or successors for the purpose of carrying on in any way the traffic in slaves; and no houses, stores, or buildings of any kind whatsoever shall be erected for the purpose of the slave trade.

3. If at any time it shall appear that the slave trade is being carried on through or from any part of my territories, the slave trade may be put down by force.

4. The subjects of Her Britannic Majesty and all white foreigners may always trade freely with my people. I, for myself, my heirs or successors, pledge myself to show no favor and to give no privilege to the ships and trade of other countries which I do not show to those of Great Britain. . . .

ENGLAND, MY ENGLAND

What have I done for you,
　　England, my England?
What is there I would not do,
　　England, my own?
With your glorious eyes austere,[1]
As the Lord were walking near,
Whispering terrible things and dear
　　As the Song on your bugles blown,
　　　England—
　　Round the world on your bugles blown!

Where shall the watchful sun,
　　England, my England,
Match the master-work you've done,
　　England, my own?
When shall he rejoice again
Such a breed of mighty men
As come forward, one to ten,
　　To the Song on your bugles blown,
　　　England—
　　Down the years on your bugles blown?. . .

They call you proud and hard,
　　England, my England:
You with worlds to watch and ward,
　　England, my own!
You whose mailed hand keeps the keys
Of such teeming[2] destinies
You could know nor dread nor ease
　　Were the Song on your bugles blown,
　　　England—
　　Round the Pit on your bugles blown!

William Ernest Henley (1889-92)

1. **austere** (ô stir′), *adj.* severe in self-discipline.
2. **teeming** (tē′ming), *adj.* full; alive.

649

About African Slavery

The beginnings of slavery are ancient. Wars and conquests often served to increase the power and wealth of a kingdom by increasing its human power and diminishing that of its rivals. Early in history some people started treating others as property, to be bought, sold, and exploited. Africa had a thriving slave trade centuries before European countries exported slaves to work in the Americas.

About William Ernest Henley

William Ernest Henley (1849–1903) was a British editor, critic, and poet. A friend and collaborator of Robert Louis Stevenson, Henley, it has been said, served as the model for Stevenson's famous pirate, Long John Silver. Like the pirate character, Henley was an amputee.

BUILDING ENGLISH PROFICIENCY

Doublets

A doublet is one of two or more words in a language, derived from the same original source, but coming by different routes.

1. Have students use a dictionary to look up *parley* (footnote 4 in "Stanley Meets Mutesa") and note its derivation.

2. Have students also look up these words, doublets of *parley:* palaver, parable, parabola, parole. After they have noted their derivations, students could discuss what these words have in common and how the original meaning has been modified by multiple borrowings.

About "England, Your England"

George Orwell (see p. 859) wrote this lengthy essay between 1940 and 1941, during a time when "highly civilized human beings [the Germans] are flying overhead, trying to kill me." In it, he talks of his country as "two [or more] nations," but also as one. He recognizes the exploitation of the poor, yet he knows the importance of ownership. In this time of immense national danger, he sees that a kind of family solidarity—one formed of the conservatism of rich and poor coming together—might be what saves the country.

England Your England

Yes, there is something distinctive and recognisable in English civilisation. It is a culture as individual as that of Spain. It is somehow bound up with solid breakfasts and gloomy Sundays, smoky towns and winding roads, green fields and red pillar-boxes.[1] It has a flavor of its own. Moreover it is continuous, it stretches into the future and the past, there is something in it that persists, as in a living creature. What can the England of 1940 have in common with the England of 1840? But then, what have you in common with the child of five whose photograph your mother keeps on the mantelpiece? Nothing, except that you happen to be the same person.

And above all, it is your civilisation, it is you. However much you hate it or laugh at it, you will never be happy away from it for any length of time. The suet puddings and the red pillar-boxes have entered into your soul. Good or evil, it is yours, you belong to it, and this side the grave you will never get away from the marks that it has given you.

Meanwhile England, together with the rest of the world, is changing. And like everything else it can change only in certain directions, which up to a point can be foreseen. That is not to say that the future is fixed, merely that certain alternatives are possible and others not. A seed may grow or not grow, but at any rate a turnip seed never grows into a parsnip. It is therefore of the deepest importance to try and determine what England is, before guessing what part England can play in the huge events that are happening. . . .

National characteristics are not easy to pin down, and when pinned down they often turn out to be trivialities[2] or seem to have no connection with one another. Spaniards are cruel to animals, Italians can do nothing without making a deafening noise, the Chinese are addicted to gambling. Obviously such things don't matter in themselves. Nevertheless, nothing is causeless, and even the fact that Englishmen have bad teeth can tell one something about the realities of English life. . . .

The gentleness of the English civilisation is perhaps its most marked characteristic. You notice it the instant you set foot on English soil. It is

a land where the bus conductors are good-tempered and the policemen carry no revolvers. In no country inhabited by whitemen is it easier to shove people off the pavement. And with this goes something that is always written off by European observers as "decadence"[3]

---

1. **pillar-boxes,** mailboxes.
2. **triviality** (triv′ē al′ə tē), *n.* small, unimportant thing.
3. **decadence** (dek′ədəns), *n.* decline; decay.
4. **hypocrisy** (hi pok′rə sē), *n.* a pretending to be what one is not.
5. **redcoat,** British soldier.

MINI-LESSON: READING/THINKING SKILLS

Generalize

To generalize is to express in a brief form the main idea of a piece of writing and several of the most important details.

Teach   Have students point out statements from the essay in which Orwell appears to be expressing a main idea. Have a volunteer write these on the chalkboard. Then have students work from the written statements to create a new statement that generalizes all Orwell's ideas.

Activity Idea   Give students practice in writing a traditional outline. They can copy the statements from the chalkboard as main (and perhaps secondary) heads; then on their own papers they can add supporting details.

or hypocrisy,[4] the English hatred of war and militarism. It is rooted deep in history, and it is strong in the lower-middle class as well as the working class. Successive wars have shaken it but not

A British family in India shown in front of their bungalow with their servants.

destroyed it. Well within living memory it was common for "the redcoats"[5] to be booed at in the street and for the landlords of respectable public-houses[6] to refuse to allow soldiers on the premises.

In peace-time, even when there are two million unemployed, it is difficult to fill the ranks of the tiny standing army, which is officered by the county gentry[7] and a specialized stratum[8] of the middle class, and manned by farm laborers and slum proletarians[9]. The mass of the people are without military knowledge or tradition, and their attitude towards war is invariably defensive. No politician could rise to power by promising them conquest of military "glory," no Hymn of Hate has ever made any appeal to them. In the 1914-18 war the songs which the soldiers made up and sang of their own accord were not vengeful but humorous and mock-defeatist. The only enemy they ever named was the sergeant-major.

In England all the boasting and flag-wagging, the "Rule Britannia" stuff, is done by small minorities. . . .

The reason why the English anti-militarism disgusts foreign observers is that it ignores the existence of the British Empire. It looks like sheer hypocrisy. After all, the English absorbed a quarter of the earth and held on to it by means of a huge navy. How dare they then turn round and say that war is wicked?

It is quite true that the English are hypocritical about their Empire. In the working class this hypocrisy takes the form of not knowing that the Empire exists. But their dislike of standing armies is a perfectly sound instinct. A navy employs comparatively few people, and it is an external weapon which cannot affect home politics directly. Military dictatorships exist everywhere, but there is no such thing as a naval dictatorship. What English people of nearly all classes loathe from the bottom of their hearts is the swaggering officer type, the jingle of spurs and the crash of boots. Decades before Hitler was ever heard of, the word "Prussian" had much the same significance in England as "Nazi" has today. So deep does this feeling go that for a hundred years past the officers of the British Army, in peace-time, have always worn civilian clothes when off duty. . . .

George Orwell (1953)

6. **public house,** tavern.
7. **gentry** (jen′trē), *n.* the upper class.
8. **stratum** (strā′təm), *n.* layer.
9. **proletarian** (prō′lə ter′ē ən), *n.* lower-class worker.

651

BUILDING ENGLISH PROFICIENCY

ESL
LEP
ELD
SAE
LD

Prefixes

Orwell writes of English anti-militarism. Explain that *anti-* is a prefix meaning "against." The word *anti-militarism,* then, means "policy or spirit of not using strong military organization."

1. Ask if any student knows a prefix that is the opposite to anti-. (*pro-*)

2. Have students brainstorm *pro-* and *anti-* words and list them on the chalkboard. They can supply the meanings of the words or guess at them, based on the meanings of the parts.

3. Make each student responsible for looking up one or more words in a dictionary to make sure that they do in fact contain the prefixes. *(Sample response: pro- is a Latin prefix in* proletarian, *another word Orwell uses, but it is not in* prong.*)* Then students can share or confirm the definition of each word.

About the Raj

The Indian Political Service were agents or residents who represented Her Majesty's Government in the more important native states and principalities scattered throughout India, as well as in the frontier districts. A Resident's power, exercised independently and much dependent on influence and personality, could be very great indeed. As a last resort he might even bring about the deposition of a prince or a rajah. As representative of the Viceroy, he moved in atmospheres thick with protocol and formality.

The Englishman in India has no home and leaves no memory.

Sir William Hunter (1895)

from PLAIN TALES FROM THE RAJ

If pomp[1] and ceremony dominated the native court it was no less in evidence in the higher circles of the British Raj. The Prince of Wales[2] was reported to have said that he had never realized what royalty really was until he stayed at Government House, Bombay, during his tour of India in 1920–1: "If the Governor was entertaining, all the guests would be arranged in a circle and he and his lady would be led round the circle and each would be introduced. The ladies would bob to him and the men would bow their heads, and the Governor and his lady would then lead the way into the meal." Here, too, hierarchy was clearly displayed. "At any formal dinner at Government House the precedence[3] was of the utmost importance," explains Christopher Masterman. "I once attended three dinners running at Government House and got the same lady beside me each time, strictly according to precedence. I was in the secretariat, he was a fellow secretary, so his wife was always invited to the same dinner as myself and I always got her as a partner. I really got very knowledgeable about her family."

To assist in the proper ordering of official society the Government published a warrant of precedence which was added to from time to time as new posts were created. This Civil List, variously known as the Blue, Green or even the Red Book, was to be found on every civil official's desk. "The Warrant of Precedence," declares David Symington, "was a very humorous document if read in the right spirit. It occupied about ten closely printed pages and showed the relative precedence of various jobs. If you

wanted to know whether an Inspector of Smoke Nuisances was a bit higher than a Junior Settlement Officer you had only to look it up and you'd find out what their relative position was." Armed with his book the junior official or the ADC[4] could plan the seating for a burra-khana[5] in full confidence. Only those outside the system created problems, Christopher Masterman once discovered: "A Mr. Abrahams had written his name in the Governor's book and the police reported to me that he was a very important international financier who was making a tour of India. So Mr. and Mrs. Abrahams were invited to a state dinner. As Collector I was also invited and when I arrived I was greeted by a member of the staff who said, "You must go and see your Mr. and Mrs. Abrahams." So I went to see them and I found they were very black, and he was improperly dressed in a blue serge suit. So I had the rather difficult job of telling them we were very sorry but they couldn't come into dinner, but they could be invited to the garden party. They took it very well."

Charles Allen (1975)

Raj, British rule in India.
1. **pomp** (pomp), *n.* a stately display.
2. **Prince of Wales,** the heir to the British throne.
3. **precedence** (pres′ə dəns), *n.* a putting in order by rank.
4. **ADC,** aide-de-camp; secretary to a superior officer.
5. **burra-khana** (bėr′ə kä′nə), *n.* meeting of native leaders.

MINI-LESSON: READING/THINKING SKILLS

Make Judgments

To make judgments is to evaluate the truth, effectiveness, or relevance of something, based on specified criteria.

Teach   Discuss with students the kinds of criteria that would lead to the creation of such a reference as "The Warrant of Precedence." List these on the chalkboard.

Activity Idea   Set up a two-column graphic organizer on the chalkboard. As students go through the selection sentence by sentence, list those items that seem to fit the 1920 criteria you have listed. In the second column, evaluate the item according to students' own modern criteria. Lastly, have students make a judgment about the criteria themselves.

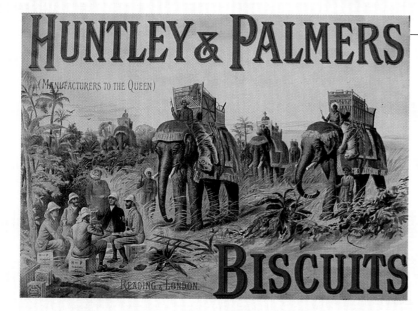

An 1884 advertising poster shows a British hunting party in India.

Art Study

Visual Literacy Images from the far-flung colonies enjoyed widespread use in advertisements in newspapers, magazines, and posters.

Questions   What do you imagine elephants have to do with biscuits [crackers]? Why do you imagine this picture was used to advertise them? *(Possible response: Nothing, really; except as an attention getter. The ad may suggest that the British hunters are enjoying a little bit of home comfort even during the stresses of hunting abroad.)*

RECESSIONAL

God of our fathers, known of old,
Lord of our far-flung battle line,
Beneath whose awful hand we hold
Dominion[1] over palm and pine
Lord God of Hosts, be with us yet,
Lest we forget—lest we forget!

The tumult[2] and the shouting dies;
The captains and the kings depart:
Still stands Thine ancient sacrifice,
A humble and a contrite[3] heart.
Lord God of Hosts, be with us yet,
Lest we forget—lest we forget!

Far-called, our navies melt away;
On dune and headland sinks the fire:
Lo, all our pomp of yesterday
Is one with Nineveh and Tyre![4]

Judge of the Nations, spare us yet,
Lest we forget—lest we forget!

If, drunk with sight of power, we loose
Wild tongues that have not Thee in awe,
Such boastings as the Gentiles[5] use,
Or lesser breeds without the Law—
Lord God of Hosts, be with us yet,
Lest we forget—lest we forget!

For heathen[6] heart that puts her trust
In reeking tube and iron shard,
All valiant dust that builds on dust,
And guarding, calls not Thee to guard,
For frantic boast and foolish word—
Thy Mercy on Thy People, Lord!

Rudyard Kipling (1897)

About "Recessional"

Rudyard Kipling (see p. 623) published this poem in 1897, near the close of Queen Victoria's Diamond Jubilee celebration. High government officials and troops, as well as kings and representatives of all the important nations of the world, were assembled for the ceremonies. In almost an Old Testament manner, Kipling sounds a warning to his nation, dazzled by the pomp and splendor of the occasion.

---

recessional (ri sesh′ə nəl), *n.* a hymn sung as the clergy and the choir leave the church at the end of a service.
1. **dominion** (də min′yən), *n.* rule; control.

2. **tumult** (tü′mult), *n.* noise; commotion.
3. **contrite** (kən trīt′), *adj.* showing deep regret and sorrow.
4. **Nineveh** (nin′ə və) . . . **Tyre** (tīr), two ancient cities, capitals of empires that no longer exist.

5. **Gentile** (jen′tīl), *n.* heathen; pagan; here, anyone not English.
6. **heathen** (hē′ᴛʜən), *adj.* referring to someone who does not believe in God or the Bible.

653

BUILDING ENGLISH PROFICIENCY

Pairing for Emphasis

Putting items into pairs is a time-honored device of poetry, rhetoric, advertising, and other forms of writing. Kipling uses several such pairs.

1. Point out the phrase *palm and pine* in line 4 and ask what it means. *(Possible response: It is meant to suggest the extent of the empire—from tropics [palm] to northern regions [pine].)* You may wish to point out that the phrase is alliterative, as are some other of Kipling's phrases. This phrase is also an example of metonymy, which Kipling uses along with synecdoche (see the Glossary of Literary Terms).

2. Have students point out other pairs in this poem, explain what they mean, and identify (if you choose) the alliteration, metonymy, or synecdoche. *(Possible response: tumult and shouting [noise associated with war or conflict]; captains and kings [armies and the countries they represent, alliteration, synecdoche]; dune and headland [all parts of a land, synecdoche]; Nineveh and Tyre [ancient power and glory, synecdoche]; reeking tube and iron shard [military action, metonymy]; frantic boast and foolish word [meaningless language, alliteration].)*

About
The Crack in the Teacup

Marina Warner's cultural study traces Great Britain's path in this century through the attitudes of British artists and writers toward society and modern life.

from THE CRACK IN THE TEACUP

The transition from a great empire to a commonwealth was achieved with remarkable ease and some harmony, but British citizens from commonwealth countries have experienced prejudice and tension here, which political parties of the right, notably the National Front and even some irresponsible members of the Conservatives, have exploited for their own ends. The popularity of the monarchy, and of the Queen herself, seems to have little power to alleviate[1] these problems though she visits commonwealth countries regularly, and recognizes, by bestowing official honors on individual leaders, their contribution to the position of Britain in the world. Mahatma Gandhi, for instance, the pacifist[2] leader of Indian nationalism, was first treated disgracefully by the British, harassed, and even imprisoned. But his wisdom, integrity and justice were at last recognized, and he is now honored by a statue in Russell Square, Bloomsbury. . . .

One of the worst prevalent contemporary attitudes is the ignorance shown, even by people who are not prejudiced, about the benefits Britain draws from the heterogeneousness[3] of its society. Citizens who came originally from former colonies or dominions, from India, Pakistan, the West Indies, Africa, or from Hong Kong, which is still under British rule, have enriched the country, not only by their invaluable labor, but also by the different cultural and religious and philosophical and social attitudes with which they broaden and enliven English life. Insularity[4] has been a British curse, xenophobia[5] a national illness, and it is time for this to pass, and for it to be understood that a nation withers at its roots if it does not receive continual stimulus from outside influences. The Press, in race questions, is usually excitable.

An abiding problem, which makes such changes in attitudes difficult to achieve, is the quality of the country's leadership. . . . But the chief source of disillusion has been the ever-fugitive vision of the successful and just society. Taxes rise, wages lose value, crime increases, poverty refuses to disappear. On the other hand, some causes, the rights of workers and the equality of women, have made progress.

Progress has also been made, most significantly, in the attitudes to social inequality, not in the inequality itself. It is no longer acceptable behavior to flaunt social divisions of class or wealth. But England remains a divided nation. The top 10 percent who owned 92 percent of the national capital in 1911–13 still own 83 percent today. It is an astonishing figure.

Marina Warner (1979)

> THE CONQUEST OF THE EARTH, WHICH MOSTLY MEANS THE TAKING IT AWAY FROM THOSE WHO HAVE A DIFFERENT COMPLEXION OR SLIGHTLY FLATTER NOSES THAN OURSELVES, IS NOT A PRETTY THING WHEN YOU LOOK INTO IT TOO MUCH.
>
> *Joseph Conrad (1902)*

1. **alleviate** (ə lē′vē āt), *v.* relieve.
2. **pacifist** (pas′ə fist), *adj.* peaceful; opposed to violence.
3. **heterogeneousness** (het′ər ə jē′nē əs-nis), *n.* mixture of unlike parts.
4. **insularity** (in′sə lar′ə tē), *n.* condition of living on an island
5. **xenophobia** (zen′ə fō′bē ə), *n.* hatred or fear of foreigners or strangers.

654

MINI-LESSON: LITERARY ELEMENT

Theme

The underlying meaning of a literary work is its theme. A theme may be directly stated or simply implied.

Teach   In an essay such as this, theme is usually stated directly. Ask students to identify some of Warner's statements that are representative of her theme. *(Possible response: Britain has successfully changed from an empire to a commonwealth, but problems remain in national prejudice and in quality leadership.)*

Activity Idea   Warner states that Britain draws benefits "from the heterogeneousness of its society." Have students work in small groups to discuss what benefits Britain or any other country might get from "different cultural and religious and philosophical and social attitudes." Encourage them to draw on their own experiences and to be as specific as possible. Finally, have each group report its conclusions.

Alfonse de Neuville's painting shows a famous episode from the Zulu War. On January 22, 1879, a British regiment was overwhelmed by a Zulu force at the Battle of Isandhlwana. Two officers, Lieutenants Melvill and Coghill, were killed attempting to save the regimental flag.

GOD SAVE THE QUEEN

God save our gracious Queen,
Long live our noble Queen,
God save the Queen!
Send her victorious,
Happy and glorious,
Long to reign over us
God save the Queen!

O Lord our God, arise,
Scatter her enemies
And make them fall!
Confound their politics,
Frustrate their knavish tricks,
On thee our hopes we fix,
God save the Queen!

Thy choicest gifts in store,
On her be pleased to pour,
Long may she reign!
May she defend our laws,
And ever give us cause,
To sing with heart and voice,
God save the Queen!

attributed to Henry Carey (about 1692)

RESPONDING

1. Summarize the viewpoint expressed in "Rule, Britannia" and the other pro-colonialist writing in this section.
2. In your opinion, what is the harshest criticism expressed?
3. Compare the rise and decline of the British empire with what you know of other colonizing countries.

About "God Save the Queen"

The words of Britain's national anthem first appeared in 1745 in *Gentleman's Magazine;* the tune appeared about the same time in an anthology. The origins of the words and music are obscure; Henry Carey (1687?–1743) may be the most likely author of both. Sung in the U.S. with different lyrics as "My Country, 'Tis of Thee," the song during the reign of a king is, of course, "God Save the King."

Responding

1. Colonialism is mutually beneficial: the colony benefits from economic stimulation of increased trade, superior political and military administration, and higher standards of morality and civilization. The colonizing country benefits from the extra room for an expanding population, access to raw materials, increased markets, and increased opportunity for its citizens.

2. Conrad quote (p. 649), in which colonizers are compared to burglars

3. Belgium, France, Germany, Italy, Portugal, and Spain all had colonies. Spain once controlled all of Central and South America (except for Brazil); all of these countries are independent, as are most of the areas that formed the British Empire. Of the U.S.'s former possessions, Hawaii and Alaska are states, Puerto Rico is a protectorate, and the Philippines are independent.

655

Planning Unit 7: The Early Twentieth Century

Literature

Integrated Language Arts

	Literary	Writing/Grammar, Usage and Mechanics	Reading, Thinking, Listening, Speaking	Vocabulary/Spelling
Pygmalion *by Bernard Shaw* Play *(average)* **Act 1** p. 662	Inference Characterization Dialect, theme Setting Figurative language Allusion, irony	Relative pronouns	Predict Make judgments Recognize values	
Act 2 p. 670	Inference Characterization Irony, theme Dialogue Stereotype Alliteration	Sentence complexity in speaking and in writing	Visualize Compare and contrast Understand sequence Make judgments Evaluate Recognize the use of persuasion Predict	Shades of meaning
Act 3 p. 686	Inference Plot and characterization Theme Satire	Colloquialisms, slang, idioms, jargon	Compare and contrast Summarize Analyze Clarify Understand sequence Make judgments	
Act 4 p. 696	Symbolism Plot Characterization Irony	Compound sentences	Make judgments Compare and contrast Clarify Analyze	
Act 5 p. 702	Inference Irony Theme	Paragraph Essay Editorial Consistent verb tense	Recognize values Draw conclusions Detect bias Distinguish between fact and opinion Compare and contrast Analyze Make judgments Find the main idea	Actual and figurative comparisons

Meeting Individual Needs

Multi-modal Activities	Mini-Lessons
Analyzing exposition Exploring dialect Analyzing main ideas	Relative pronouns
Exploring character and setting Analyzing character Exploring key passages Expanding vocabulary notebooks Analyzing contrasting views Exploring dramatic emotion Sequencing key events	Pitch, modulation, volume and inflection Sentence complexity in speaking and in writing Shades of meaning Researching using periodicals
Exploring parent-child relationships Exploring key ideas Analyzing relationships among characters Exploring adjectives and adverbs	Colloquialisms, slang, idioms, jargon Communicating clearly and effectively
Analyzing key statements Understanding a character	Identifying alternatives Compound sentences
Analyze different versions Newspaper ad Design and sketch costumes Exploring a subplot Supporting an opinion Tracking changes in character Exploring apostrophe usage Checking comprehension Analyzing the title	Summarizing Using appropriate speaking behavior for a variety of purposes Actual and figurative comparisons Consistent verb tenses

Interdisciplinary Studies
The English Class System

Format	Content Area	Highlights	Skill
Photo Essay and Articles: **The rich man at his castle, the poor man at his gate...** **The Upper Class** **The Lower Class**	History	Descriptions of how the rich and poor lived in Edwardian England.	Social history and statistics Photography and social class
Poem: **Burlington Bertie from Bow** *by William Hargreaves*	Popular Culture	The British class system has been used in theater as well as television	Video: fictional versus factual

Writing Workshop

Mode	Writing Format	Writing Focus	Proofreading Skills
Expository writing	An article for a consumer magazine	Avoiding overstatement	Using apostrophes correctly

Program Support Materials

For Every Selection	For Every Writing Workshop
Unit Resource Book Graphic Organizer Study Guide Vocabulary Worksheet Grammar Worksheet Spelling, Speaking and Listening, or Literary Language Worksheet Alternate Check Test Vocabulary Test Selection Test	**Unit Resource Book** Prewriting Worksheet Revising Strategy Worksheet Editing Strategy Worksheet Presentation Worksheet Writing Rubric **Transparency Collection** Fine Art Transparency Student Writing Model Transparencies

For Every Interdisciplinary Study	Assessment
Unit Resource Book Study Guide Mini-Lesson Skill Worksheet	**Unit Resource Book** TE Check Tests Alternate Check Test (blackline master) Vocabulary Test (blackline master) Selection Test (blackline master) **Test Generator Software** **Assessment Handbook**

Planning Unit 7: The Early Twentieth Century

Literature

Integrated Language Arts

	Literary	Writing/Grammar, Usage and Mechanics	Reading, Thinking, Listening, Speaking	Vocabulary/Spelling

The Soldier
    by Rupert Brooke
Poem
(average)
p. 735
Suicide in the Trenches
    by Siegfried Sassoon
Poem
(easy)
p. 737
Dulce et Decorum Est
    by Wilfred Owen
Poem
(average)
p. 738
Disabled
    by Wilfred Owen
Poem
(average)
p. 739
	Tone
	Theme
	Hyperbole
	Point of view
		Idealism versus realism
		Essay—comparison and
		    contrast
		Editorial
		Dangling modifiers
			Infer
			Recognize use of
			    persuasion
			Compare and contrast
			Recognize cause and effect
				Word web

from Testament of Youth *by Vera Brittain* Autobiography *(average)* p. 743	Mood Characterization Symbolism Theme, irony Imagery, tone	Short essay Description Journal entry Using indefinite pronouns	Synthesize, infer Visualize, analyze Compare and contrast Apply Recognize cause and effect Recognize values	Use a thesaurus Understand analogies

Tickets, Please
    by D. H. Lawrence
Short Story
(average)
p. 758
	Idiom, setting
	Style, characterization
	Alliteration
	Diction, tone
		Expository essay
		Descriptive paragraphs
		Compound-complex
		    sentences
			Draw conclusions
			Make analogies
			Point of view
			Predict, clarify
			Synthesize
			Infer	

The Hollow Men
    by T. S. Eliot
Poem
(challenging)
p. 769
	Free verse poem
	Informal essay
	Letter
	Standard sentence
	    punctuation
		Recognize values		

Meeting Individual Needs

Multi-modal Activities	Mini-Lessons
Oral reading	Dangling modifiers
Type of therapy	Tone
Bulletin board display	
Relating imagery and language	
Linking past and present	
Musical piece	Using a thesaurus
Script of conversation	Using indefinite
Planning a reading strategy	pronouns
Exploring character	Using multimedia
Tracking narrative events	Creating graphic
Using a map	organizers
	Understanding
	analogies
	Relating literature to
	personal experience
Dramatic monologue	Compound-complex
Oral report	sentences
Relating setting and mood	Idioms
Noticing character details	Foreshadowing
Dramatizing key events	
Exploring motivation	
Choral reading	Standard sentence
Illustrated oral report	punctuation
Improving comprehension	

Interdisciplinary Studies
Wasteland: Battlefield and Spirit

Format	Content Area	Highlights	Skill

Article:
The Horror at Ypres
  by L.B. Taylor, Jr.
  and C.L. Taylor
	History	The introduction of poison gas as a weapon in World War I.	Analyzing documentaries

Article: **The Boneyard** by Paul Fussell	History	The devastation of WWI remains visible even today.	Using primary and secondary sources

Writing Workshop

Mode	Writing Format	Writing Focus	Proofreading Skills
Persuasive writing	To sell an idea	Using an appropriate tone	Using a consistent teleplay format

Program Support Materials

For Every Selection	For Every Writing Workshop
Unit Resource Book	**Unit Resource Book**
Graphic Organizer	Prewriting Worksheet
Study Guide	Revising Strategy Worksheet
Vocabulary Worksheet	Editing Strategy Worksheet
Grammar Worksheet	Presentation Worksheet
Spelling, Speaking and Listening, or Literary Language Worksheet	Writing Rubric
Alternate Check Test	**Transparency Collection**
Vocabulary Test	Fine Art Transparency
Selection Test	Student Writing Model Transparencies

For Every Interdisciplinary Study	Assessment
Unit Resource Book	**Unit Resource Book**
Study Guide	TE Check Tests
Mini-Lesson Skill Worksheet	Alternate Check Test (blackline master)
	Vocabulary Test (blackline master)
	Selection Test (blackline master)
	Test Generator Software
	Assessment Handbook

Planning Unit 7: The Early Twentieth Century

Literature

Integrated Language Arts

Literature	Literary	Writing/Grammar, Usage and Mechanics	Reading, Thinking, Listening, Speaking	Vocabulary/Spelling
Eveline *by James Joyce* Short Story *(easy)* p. 790	Epiphany Mood Imagery	Paragraph Essay Write a review Using semicolons	Draw conclusions	
A Cup of Tea *by Katherine Mansfield* Short Story *(average)* p. 797	Stereotype Diction Irony Dialect	Character sketch Write a letter Essay Recognizing phrases	Find the main idea Compare and contrast Synthesize Infer	Using context clues
The Unknown Citizen *by W. H. Auden* Poem *(average)* p. 806 **Musée des Beaux Arts** *by W. H. Auden* Poem *(average)* p. 808 **Who's Who** *by W. H. Auden* Poem *(average)* p. 810	Satire Allusion	Claim to fame Biographical entry Analytical essay Commas	Infer Analyze	
Shakespeare's Sister **from A Room of One's Own** *by Virginia Woolf* Essay *(average)* p. 814	Paradox Theme	Endings Informal essay Letter to Woolf Punctuating multiple adjec- tives	Find the main idea Draw conclusions Infer	
Do Not Go Gentle into That **Good Night** *by Dylan Thomas* Poem *(average)* p. 823 **A Child's Christmas in Wales** by Dylan Thomas Autobiography *(average)* p. 825	Imagery Alliteration Figurative language Mood	Favorite holiday List of compounds Describe individuality Write a villanelle Using colons	Literal and figurative language Find the main idea Visualize	

Studies in the Park
by Anita Desai
Short Story
(average)
p. 833
	Simile
	Setting
	Point of view
	Theme
		Similes
		Essay
		Write a newspaper column
		Quotation marks and
		    dialogue
			Literal and figurative
			    language
			Draw conclusions
				Recognize multiple-
				    meaning words

Meeting Individual Needs

Multi-modal Activities	Mini-Lessons
Illustration Oral report Perform a section Analyzing reasons Exploring key statements	Using semicolons
Radio play Interview Exploring symbols Responding to characters	Recognize phrases Using context clues Analyzing a character
Debate Statistical report Making real-life connections Linking past and present	Comas Satire
Discussion summary Design a mural Exploring poetic device Expanding vocabulary notebooks Making cultural connections	Punctuating multiple adjectives Paradox
Greeting card Photo competition Exploring style Exploring compound words Making personal connections	Imagery Using colons
Oral review Play a recording Exploring synonyms Exploring connotation Summarizing a story	Quotation marks and dialogue Recognize multiple- meaning words Infer

Interdisciplinary Studies
Modern Faces

Format	Content Area	Highlights	Skill
Art: **Modern Faces**	Fine Art	Portraits created by artists who were contemporaries of Woolf.	Multimedia presentations

Writing Workshop

Mode	Writing Format	Writing Focus	Proofreading Skills
Expository writing	An interpretive essay	Writing an effective thesis statement	Avoiding sentence fragments

Program Support Materials

For Every Selection	For Every Writing Workshop
Unit Resource Book Graphic Organizer Study Guide Vocabulary Worksheet Grammar Worksheet Spelling, Speaking and Listening, or Literary Language Worksheet Alternate Check Test Vocabulary Test Selection Test	**Unit Resource Book** Prewriting Worksheet Revising Strategy Worksheet Editing Strategy Worksheet Presentation Worksheet Writing Rubric **Transparency Collection** Fine Art Transparency Student Writing Model Transparencies

For Every Interdisciplinary Study	Assessment
Unit Resource Book Study Guide Mini-Lesson Skill Worksheet	**Unit Resource Book** TE Check Tests Alternate Check Test (blackline master) Vocabulary Test (blackline master) Selection Test (blackline master) **Test Generator Software** **Assessment Handbook**

Media and Technology

Part One Selections

Pygmalion

Audiotape *Pygmalion*, Caedmon/Harper Audio, is a dramatization of Shaw's play performed by Michael and Lynn Redgrave and others.

Videotape Consider showing *Pygmalion*, 96 minutes, Library Video Company, 1938, starring Leslie Howard, and *My Fair Lady*, 170 minutes, CBS/Fox, 1964, a musical version starring Audrey Hepburn.

Home Connection One of the staple episodes in popular fiction, from folktales such as Cinderella to today's Hollywood movies, is the big makeover, where the heroine—less frequently the hero—is transformed from an ugly duckling into a beautiful swan. You might invite someone who deals professionally with makeovers—such as a hair stylist, dietician, physical trainer, and so on—to visit the class and talk about what they do.

Part Two Selections

The Soldier/Suicide in the Trenches/Dulce et Decorum Est/Disabled

Audiotape *Intrepid Birdmen*, 45 minutes, Syd Lieberman Prods, is the true story of World War I fighter pilots. *Diaries 1915-1918,* 12 hours, Recorded Books, is the reading of Sassoon's diaries written at the front during World War I.

Videotape *Poetry of World War II*, 20 minutes, Britannica, 1991, provides a look at poems that express different attitudes towards war. *Bronx Cheers*, 30 minutes, Carousel, 1991, is an award-winning film about a World War II veteran. Students might enjoy *Ashpet: An American Cinderalla*, 45 minutes, Davenport, 1991, set in the South in the early years of World War II. *Wilfred Owen: The Pity of War*, 58 minutes, Films for the Humanities & Sciences, is drawn from Owen's poems, diaries, and letters.

from Testament of Youth

Community Resources British composer Benjamin Britten wrote his *War Requiem* in 1961. First performed at Coventry Cathedral in 1962 and at Tanglewood in 1963, it consists of a Latin text interspersed with nine war poems of Wilfred Owen. Some students might like to listen to a recording of the requiem.

Tickets, Please

Videotape *D. H. Lawrence: The Rocking Horse Winner*, 90 minutes, Films for the Humanities & Sciences, is a film version of one of Lawrence's short stories. *Whispers on the Wind*, 45 minutes, The Heritage Poetry Series, Library Video Company, 1990, features LeVar Burton and others performing the work of D. H. Lawrence and other poets. *D. H. Lawrence*, 30 minutes, Britannica, chronicles the life of the author, as does *D. H. Lawrence as Son and Lover,* 52 minutes, Films for the Humanities & Sciences.

Home Connection Gender issues in school and the workplace are much discussed today. For an at-home activity, students might discuss with family members what standards should govern the conduct of men and women toward each other as fellow-students or fellow-workers.

Connections to
Custom Literature Database

For Part One "Upward Mobility" Selections with Lessons

- from *The Importance of Being Earnest,* Act One by Oscar Wilde
- "The Signalman" by Charles Dickens

Additional theme-based selections can be accessed on the ScottForesman database.

Connections to
Custom Literature Database

For Part Two "War and Aftermath" Selections with Lessons

- "Anthem for Doomed Youth" by Wilfred Owen
- "Peace" by Rupert Brooke and "In Flanders Fields" by John McCrae

Additional theme-based selections can be accessed on the ScottForesman database.

The Hollow Men

Community Resources Depression affects people in different ways. Some people experience frequent mood swings; others get the blues at particular times of year, such as holidays or at mid-winter. You might invite someone who deals professionally with those suffering from depression, such as a doctor or counselor, to visit the class and discuss what can be done to deal with such problems.

Part Three Selections

Eveline

Audiotape *Dubliners,* 8 hours, Books on Tape, 1992, is a collection of stories including "Eveline." "Eveline" is included on *Dead and Other Stories from 'Dubliners,'* 2 hours 30 minutes, Audio Partners, 1989.

Videotape *James Joyce,* 80 minutes, Films for the Humanities & Sciences, is an authoritative documentary of the author's life.

Home Connection What's the hardest thing about leaving home and starting a new life? separation from family and friends? getting used to a new school or job? For an at-home activity, students might discuss with family members the difficulties experienced by people beginning a new life in new surroundings.

A Cup of Tea

Videotape *A Portrait of Katherine Mansfield,* 54 minutes, Filmakers Library, 1988, offers a glimpse into the author's life.

The Unknown Citizen/Who's Who/Musee des Beaux Arts

Audiotape The author reads his work in *W. H. Auden: Selected Poems*, Spoken Arts.

Videotape *The Earlier Twentieth Century*, 28 minutes, Films for the Humanities & Sciences, 1989, includes the work of Auden and others.

Home Connection "The Unknown Citizen" imagines a public monument to an average person. In one of Auden's essays, he sketches his view of of paradise, where the public monuments are statues of great dead chefs. For an at-home activity, students might discuss with family members what people should have public monuments erected to them and what form these monuments should take.

Shakespeare's Sister

Audiotape Consider using *A Portrait and Moments of Being*, containing the only surviving recording of Woolf herself, available from BBC/American Audio Prose Library.

Videotape *Virginia Woolf,* 30 minutes, Britannica, documents the author's life. Student's may enjoy Woolf's *To the Lighthouse,* 115 minutes, Magnum Entertainment, 1983.

Do Not Go Gentle/A Child's Christmas

Audiotape The author reads poems and "A Child's Christmas in Wales," in *Dylan Thomas Reads*, 60 minutes, Caedmon/Harper Audio.

Videotape *Dylan Thomas: A Portrait,* 26 minutes, Films for the Humanities & Sciences, includes a reading of "Do Not Go Gentle," and background for "A Child's Christmas in Wales."

Home Connection Dylan Thomas creates delightful catalogues of "useful" and "useless" Christmas gifts in his essay. For an at-home activity, students and family members might list and compare their "Top-10" favorite presents—both useful and useless—from birthdays and holidays in the past.

Studies in the Park

Audiotape *In Custody*, 7 hours, Recorded Books, is based on a novel by Anita Desai.

Home Connection What contributes to making a good place for study? For an at-home activity, students might work with family members to help set up a good study area.

Connections to
Custom
Literature Database
For Part Three "The Search for Identity" Selections with Lessons
- "No worst, there is none" and "Carrion Comfort" by Gerard Manley Hopkins
- *Youth* by Joseph Conrad

Additional theme-based selections can be accessed on the ScottForesman database.

Connections to
AuthorWorks
Information about the life and times of D. H. Lawrence and Bernard Shaw is available on ScottForesman's AuthorWorks CD-ROM.

The Early Twentieth Century

 Art Study

Piccadilly Circus, a detail of which is shown on pages 656–657, was painted in 1912 by English painter Charles Ginner (1878–1952). Born in Cannes, Ginner was expert in the techniques of French Postimpressionism. He was one of the founders of the Camden Town Group and is best-known for his work showing city life. His unique brush stroke style set off his work.

Point out to students that Piccadilly Circus, an intersection in downtown London, is an area of restaurants, theaters, and shops very near the fashionable area of West End. Hyde Park, where the bus is headed, is a stylish district. This painting shows the contrast between the lower-class flower girl and the affluence around her.

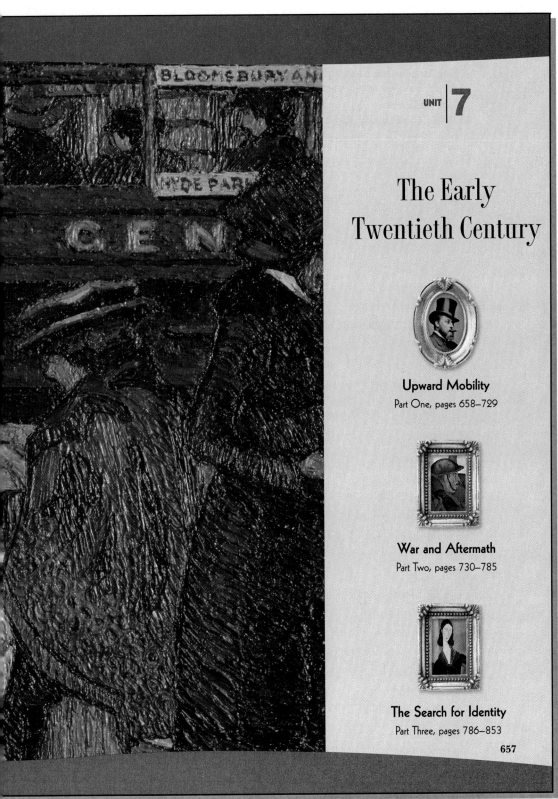

UNIT 7

The Early Twentieth Century

Upward Mobility
Part One, pages 658–729

War and Aftermath
Part Two, pages 730–785

The Search for Identity
Part Three, pages 786–853

657

The early twentieth century was a time of social and political change.

Part One
Upward Mobility

Part One features literature that explores a poor, uneducated woman's climb up the social ladder in London.

Ideas to Explore

• What defines social class?
• How is social class related to identity?

Part Two
War and Aftermath

The literature in Part Two includes works that show the effects of the war on people and their times.

Ideas to Explore

• Is war noble and heroic, terrible and destructive, or both?
• What are the effects of war on the human spirit?

Part Three
The Search for Identity

The literature in Part Three explores different conceptions of individuality.

Ideas to Explore

• How is each individual both unique and very much like other people?
• What shapes identity? How is identity expressed?

 Art Study

A photo of the Prince of Wales, a detail from *Over the Top* by John Nash, and the painting *Jeunne Femme* by Amedeo Modigliani (1884–1920) are shown on page 657.

EXPLORING CONCEPTS

- England consisted of two nations— "the rich" and "the poor." Each group had its own ways of speaking, dressing, and behaving.
- The early twentieth century was a time of reform, with attempts made to ease the life of those in poverty.

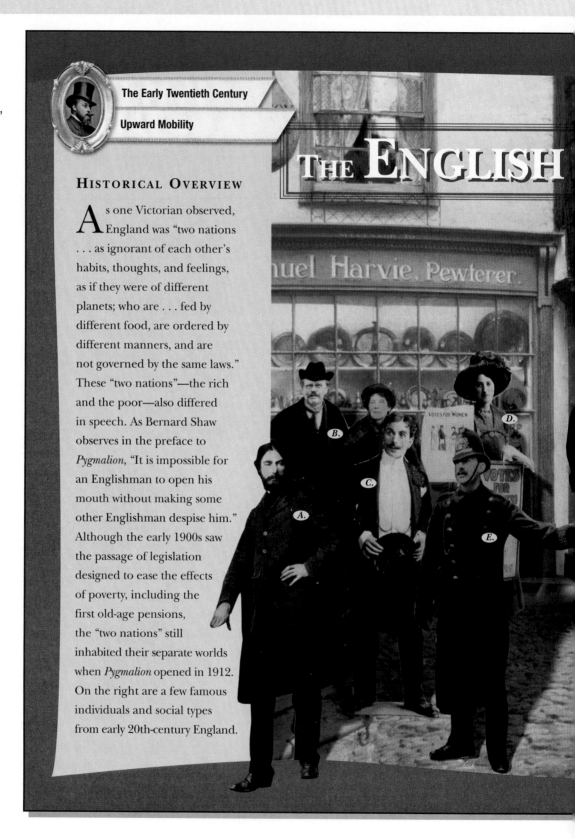

The Early Twentieth Century

Upward Mobility

THE ENGLISH

HISTORICAL OVERVIEW

As one Victorian observed, England was "two nations . . . as ignorant of each other's habits, thoughts, and feelings, as if they were of different planets; who are . . . fed by different food, are ordered by different manners, and are not governed by the same laws." These "two nations"—the rich and the poor—also differed in speech. As Bernard Shaw observes in the preface to *Pygmalion*, "It is impossible for an Englishman to open his mouth without making some other Englishman despise him." Although the early 1900s saw the passage of legislation designed to ease the effects of poverty, including the first old-age pensions, the "two nations" still inhabited their separate worlds when *Pygmalion* opened in 1912. On the right are a few famous individuals and social types from early 20th-century England.

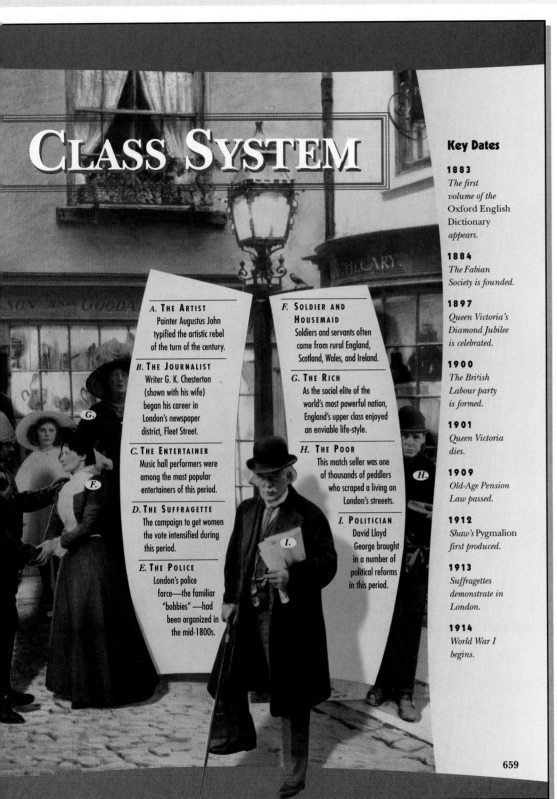

CLASS SYSTEM

A. THE ARTIST
Painter Augustus John typified the artistic rebel of the turn of the century.

B. THE JOURNALIST
Writer G. K. Chesterton (shown with his wife) began his career in London's newspaper district, Fleet Street.

C. THE ENTERTAINER
Music hall performers were among the most popular entertainers of this period.

D. THE SUFFRAGETTE
The campaign to get women the vote intensified during this period.

E. THE POLICE
London's police force—the familiar "bobbies"—had been organized in the mid-1800s.

F. SOLDIER AND HOUSEMAID
Soldiers and servants often came from rural England, Scotland, Wales, and Ireland.

G. THE RICH
As the social elite of the world's most powerful nation, England's upper class enjoyed an enviable life-style.

H. THE POOR
This match seller was one of thousands of peddlers who scraped a living on London's streeets.

I. POLITICIAN
David Lloyd George brought in a number of political reforms in this period.

Key Dates

1883
The first volume of the Oxford English Dictionary appears.

1884
The Fabian Society is founded.

1897
Queen Victoria's Diamond Jubilee is celebrated.

1900
The British Labour party is formed.

1901
Queen Victoria dies.

1909
Old-Age Pension Law passed.

1912
Shaw's Pygmalion first produced.

1913
Suffragettes demonstrate in London.

1914
World War I begins.

659

Key Dates

1884 The Fabians, a group of British socialists, taught that socialism could be achieved gradually, through a series of reforms. Notable Fabians included G. Bernarrd Shaw and H. G. Wells.

1897 Having ascended the throne at the age of 18, Victoria celebrates 60 years as Queen of England, giving her name to an age.

1901 Queen Victoria dies at age 81, having had the longest reign in British history. She is succeeded by Edward VII. During her reign the British Empire included about 25% of the world's population.

MATERIALS OF INTEREST
Books

- *Bernard Shaw: The Pursuit of Power* by Michael Holroyd (Vintage, 1989).
- *Bernard Shaw: The Search for Love* by Michael Holroyd (Vintage, 1990).
- *Divided Britain,* 2nd ed. by Ray Hudson and Allan M. Williams (John Wiley and Sons, 1995).
- *Pygmalion* by Charles A. Berst (Macmillan Publishing Company, Inc., 1995).
- *Shaw's People: Victoria to Churchill* by Stanley Weintraub (Pennsylvania State University Press, 1996).

Connections to
Custom Literature Database

For further historical background, under **Background Articles,** see **Late Victorian and Edwardian England 1830–1880.**

FOR ALL STUDENTS

- What personal qualities can help people improve their social or economic situations?
- What external factors can help people improve their social or economic situations?

Read the first paragraph on page 660 and explain to students that the play they will read is about changing lifestyles and opportunities.

To further explore the theme, use the transparency noted below.

Transparency Collection
Fine Art Transparency 13

For At-Risk Students

Ask students to

- recall stories, movies, and TV shows in which the main characters made drastic improvements in their lives
- tell what they most admire in the characters

For Students Who Need Challenge

Students might research the first production of *Pygmalion* or read another play, such as *Major Barbara.*

For Visual Learners

Rent the video of the Leslie Howard–Wendy Hiller version of *Pygmalion.*

MULTICULTURAL CONNECTION

Have students set up situations, acting out how their language might change with different people.

660

Part One

Upward Mobility

Everyone wants to get ahead, to rise in the world, to become better off, to *arrive.* Not everyone has the opportunity, however, to move up. Some people must make great efforts, it seems, just to maintain their lifestyle and not actually decline. For those people, upward mobility may seem like a cruel and unattainable dream.

Most everyone who does achieve success knows one secret: **communication.** The more adept a person is at communicating with people on a certain level of society, the more likely that person is to be accepted by those people. It is a secret that is intuitively grasped by the main character of the play *Pygmalion,* and it is a secret that changes her life.

Literature

IDEAS THAT WORK

Establishing Relevance

"Reading the play aloud highlights Shaw's satirical wit. Through cooperative group activities, journals, essay responses, and discussions, students can analyze serious themes: women's rights, love and marriage, and the importance of language.

Instruction can conclude with students viewing either the movie or the musical version to select their preference for an ending. They can also experiment with language by rewriting a scene into a contemporary setting, using appropirate dialect.

Such activities allow students to see the relevance of the play to their lives and to reinforce the concept that great literature is timeless and applicable."

Joan Greenwood
Lockport, Illinois

Before Reading

Pygmalion

by Bernard Shaw

Bernard Shaw
1856–1950

Bernard Shaw was born in Dublin. His father drank and, seeking a way to help support the family, his mother and older sister took vocal lessons from a local musician, George Vandaleur Lee. In 1872 Lee went to London, and Mrs. Shaw and her daughter followed. Shaw joined them in 1876 and wrote music criticism, sold telephones, and wrote five novels that no one would publish. In 1884, along with friends, he helped found the Fabian Society, Socialists committed to the peaceful redistribution of wealth. Shaw came to think he might make the theater a vehicle for his ideas, and he eventually wrote over fifty plays, including *Major Barbara* (1905), *Pygmalion* (1912), *Heartbreak House* (1919), and *Saint Joan* (1923). He received a Nobel Prize in 1925.

Building Background

An Old Story Updated In the original story of Pygmalion (pig mā′lē ən) told by the Roman poet Ovid (43 B.C.–A.D. 17?), Pygmalion is a sculptor who carves a statue of a woman so beautiful and so irresistible that he falls in love with her. Venus, the goddess of love, takes pity on him and brings the statue to life. Pygmalion names his love Galatea (gal′ə tē′ə), and Venus is present at their marriage. Many authors have written works on this theme, but one, Tobias Smollett (1721–1777), altered the story in an incident in his novel *Peregrine Pickle*. An early critic of Shaw's play, which opened in Vienna in 1913 and in London in 1914, recognized the similarity between this incident and Shaw's *Pygmalion*. When Shaw was questioned about this, he irritably admitted having read Smollett's work in his Dublin boyhood but not since and said he had not realized that "Smollett had got hold of my plot." Regardless of Shaw's source, his play contains some reversals of the original story. Since no character in the play is named Pygmalion, readers and playgoers must understand the **allusion** for themselves. The person who seems to be a Pygmalion expects far different things from his creation, who in turn expects much from him. And whether or not Shaw's comedy, set in London in the early twentieth century, has a happy ending, which a comedy is supposed to have, depends on your viewpoint.

Literary Focus

Inference An **inference** is a reasonable conclusion based on hints and clues. The characters in *Pygmalion* make inferences about each other, their backgrounds, their feelings, and their intentions. In turn, readers and playgoers must make inferences about characters, relationships, and motivations when they are not expressly mentioned.

Writer's Notebook

Dressing the Actors Costumes tell a great deal about characters in a play, and they are especially important in *Pygmalion*. As you read the play, make notes on any mention of clothing or accessories, either by the characters themselves or in the stage directions.

Pygmalion   **661**

Before Reading

Building Background

Students can find the Pygmalion myth in books such as *Mythology* by Edith Hamilton (various editions).

Literary Focus

As students read the play, they might make a chart on which they record their inferences and the clues that led to them.

Writer's Notebook

Students should note changes of costume. Scenes concerning Eliza's old and new clothes are significant.

More About Bernard Shaw

In 1879, feeling embarrassed by his Irish accent, Shaw hired a voice teacher to train him in pronunciation and articulation. He drew on this experience to portray the voice teacher Higgins. Higgins also is based on the phonetician Henry Sweet, as Shaw noted in his *Preface to Pygmalion*.

Connections to
AuthorWorks

Bernard Shaw is a featured author in the AuthorWorks CD-ROM series.

SUPPORT MATERIALS OVERVIEW

Unit 7 Resource Book
- Graphic Organizers, pp. 1, 9, 17, 25, 33
- Study Guides, pp. 2, 10, 18, 26, 34
- Vocabulary, pp. 3, 11, 19, 27, 35
- Grammar, pp. 4, 12, 20, 28, 36
- Alternate Check Tests, pp. 5, 13, 21, 29, 37
- Vocabulary Tests, pp. 6, 14, 22, 30, 38
- Selection Tests, pp. 7–8, 15–16, 23–24, 31–32, 39–40

Building English Proficiency
- Selection Summaries
- Activities, pp. 246, 247, 248, 249, 250

Reading, Writing & Grammar SkillBook
- Writing, pp. 109–110, 127–128, 131–133, 134–137
- Grammar, Usage, and Mechanics, pp. 147–148, 149–152, 165–166, 180–182, 205–206, 207–208

The World of Work
- Speech Therapist, p. 25
- Activity, p. 26

Technology
- Personal Journal Software
- Test Generator Software

During Reading

Selection Objectives

- to consider the themes of social status and conventions and appearance versus reality
- to make inferences and identify the role of inferences in drama
- to analyze the use of colloquialisms in a comedy

Unit 7 Resource Book
Graphic Organizer, p. 1
Study Guide, p. 2

Theme Link

Henry Higgins defies the accustomed modes of upward mobility when he decides to raise Eliza from flower girl to princess by voice lessons alone.

Vocabulary Preview

plinth, the lower, square part of the base of a column

deprecate, express strong disapproval of; belittle

sensibility, tendency to be hurt or offended too easily

staid, having a settled, quiet character; sober; sedate

mendacity, untruthfulness; lie

Students can add the words and definitions to their Writer's Notebooks.

Art Study

To many movie viewers, Audrey Hepburn captured the character of Eliza, who begins the play identified as the "Flower Girl." *My Fair Lady* (1964) is a musical based on Shaw's *Pygmalion,* and it is available in video formats.

Question What do you think is the major difference between the character on the left and on the right in these pictures? *(Possible response: The figure on the right has self confidence and a different outlook than the figure on the left.)*

PYGMALION
BERHARD SHAW

Audrey Hepburn as Eliza Dooliittle—before and after—in the film My Fair Lady.

All subsequent illustrations for *Pygmalion* (except the ones on pages 696–697 are photographs of a 1987 New York production starring Peter O'Toole as Henry Higgins, Amanda Plummer as Eliza Doolittle, Lionel Jeffries as Colonel Pickering, and John Mills as Alfred Doolittle.

ACT ONE SUMMARY

Pygmalion

Freddy, rushing to get a cab for his mother and sister at St. Paul's Church, collides with a flower girl, knocking down her basket of flowers. The flower girl tries to sell flowers to a gentleman, when a bystander warns her that a note taker is copying down her words. Afraid he is a policeman planning to arrest her, she loudly proclaims her innocence. The note taker says he amuses himself by identifying people's places of origin by their dialect. The note taker and the gentleman realize they've been searching for each other. The note taker is Professor Higgins, a voice teacher who claims he could pass the flower girl off as a duchess with a few months of instruction. The gentleman is Colonel Pickering, a Sanskrit specialist. They go off together, and Higgins tosses the flower girl a handful of money so she can ride home in a taxi.

  *For summaries in other languages, see the **Building English Proficiency** book.*

ACT ONE

Covent Garden[1] at 11:15 P.M. Torrents of heavy summer rain. Cab whistles blowing frantically in all directions. Pedestrians running for shelter into the market and under the portico of St. Paul's Church, where there are already several people, among them a LADY and her DAUGHTER in evening dress. They are all peering out gloomily at the rain, except one man with his back turned to the rest, who seems wholly preoccupied with a notebook in which he is writing busily.

The church clock strikes the first quarter.

THE DAUGHTER *(in the space between the central pillars, close to the one on her left).* I'm getting chilled to the bone. What can Freddy be doing all this time? He's been gone twenty minutes.

THE MOTHER *(on her DAUGHTER's right).* Not so long. But he ought to have got us a cab by this.

A BYSTANDER *(on the LADY's right).* He won't get no cab not until half-past eleven, missus, when they come back after dropping their theater fares.

THE MOTHER. But we must have a cab. We can't stand here until half-past eleven. It's too bad.

THE BYSTANDER. Well, it ain't my fault, missus.

THE DAUGHTER. If Freddy had a bit of gumption, he would have got one at the theater door.

THE MOTHER. What could he have done, poor boy?

THE DAUGHTER. Other people got cabs. Why couldn't he?

(FREDDY rushes in out of the rain from the Southampton Street side, and comes between them closing a dripping umbrella. He is a young man of twenty, in evening dress, very wet round the ankles.)

THE DAUGHTER. Well, haven't you got a cab?

FREDDY. There's not one to be had for love or money.

THE MOTHER. Oh, Freddy, there must be one. You can't have tried.

THE DAUGHTER. It's too tiresome. Do you expect us to go and get one ourselves?

FREDDY. I tell you they're all engaged. The rain was so sudden: nobody was prepared; and

everybody had to take a cab. I've been to Charing Cross one way and nearly to Ludgate Circus the other; and they were all engaged.

THE MOTHER. Did you try Trafalgar Square?

FREDDY. There wasn't one at Trafalgar Square.

THE DAUGHTER. Did you try?

FREDDY. I tried as far as Charing Cross Station. Did you expect me to walk to Hammersmith?

THE DAUGHTER. You haven't tried at all.

THE MOTHER. You really are very helpless, Freddy. Go again; and don't come back until you have found a cab.

FREDDY. I shall simply get soaked for nothing.

THE DAUGHTER. And what about us? Are we to stay here all night in this draft, with next to nothing on? You selfish pig—

FREDDY. Oh, very well: I'll go, I'll go. *(He opens his umbrella and dashes off Strandwards,[2] but comes into collision with a FLOWER GIRL, who is hurrying for shelter, knocking her basket out of her hands. A blinding flash of lightning, followed instantly by a rattling peal of thunder, orchestrates the incident.)*

THE FLOWER GIRL. Nah then, Freddy: look wh' y' gowin, deah.

FREDDY. Sorry. *(He rushes off.)*

THE FLOWER GIRL *(picking up her scattered flowers and replacing them in the basket).* There's manners f' yer! Te-oo banches o voylets trod into the mad. *(She sits down on the plinth[3] of the column, sorting her flowers, on the LADY's right. She is not at all an attractive person. She is perhaps eighteen, perhaps twenty, hardly older. She wears a little sailor hat of black straw that has long been exposed to the dust and soot of London and has seldom if ever been brushed. Her hair needs wash-*

1. **Covent Garden.** At the time of the play, the chief fruit, vegetable, and flower market district of London. The area also contains the Covent Garden Opera House and St. Paul's Church, designed by architect Inigo Jones (1573–1652).
2. **Strandwards,** toward the Strand, the main thoroughfare between the West End—the fashionable residential area—and the business and commercial center of London.
3. plinth (plinth), *n.* the lower, square part of the base of a column.

Pygmalion—Act One **663**

---

1 Literary Element
Characterization

Point out how gradually Shaw introduces the characters: first he refers to "people"; then a "lady" and her "daughter." None of the characters, except Freddy, is named until late in Act One. The mother is not named even then.

2 Literary Focus
Inference

Questions

• What does the daughter mean when she says they have "next to nothing on"? *(Possible response: She means that they are wearing light dresses or not enough coverings for the weather.)*

• Freddy runs off without helping the flower girl. Does she seem to be a person who demands respect from the others under the church portico? *(Possible response: No; she seems poor and of little importance to the others.)*

3 Literary Element
Dialect

Translation "There's manners for you! Two bunches of violets trod into the mud."

BUILDING ENGLISH PROFICIENCY

Analyzing Exposition

Use one or more of the following activities to help students grasp the information introduced on this page.

Activity Ideas

• Have students list the characters, identifying each one with a descriptive phrase.

• If possible, bring in a tourist map of London. Have volunteers find the places mentioned.

• Explain that stage directions usually describe the setting and characters and tell what the characters do and how they sound. In this play, Shaw's directions also comment upon characters and social conditions of the day. Ask students to look for examples of each kind of stage direction as they read.

Building English Proficiency
Activities, p. 246

ESL
LEP
ELD
SAE
LD

4

ing rather badly: its mousy color can hardly be natural. She wears a shoddy black coat that reaches nearly to her knees and is shaped to her waist. She has a brown skirt with a coarse apron. Her boots are much the worse for wear. She is no doubt as clean as she can afford to be; but compared to the ladies she is very dirty. Her features are no worse than theirs; but their condition leaves something to be desired; and she needs the services of a dentist.)

THE MOTHER. How do you know that my son's name is Freddy, pray?

5

THE FLOWER GIRL. Ow, eez ye-ooa san, is e? Wal, fewd dan y' de-ooty bawms a mather should, eed now bettern to spawl a pore gel's flahrzn than ran awy athat pyin. Will ye-oo py me f'them? *(Here, with apologies, this desperate attempt to represent her dialect without a phonetic alphabet must be abandoned as unintelligible outside London.)*

6

THE DAUGHTER. Do nothing of the sort, mother. The idea!

THE MOTHER. Please allow me, Clara. Have you any pennies?

THE DAUGHTER. No. I've nothing smaller than a sixpence.

THE FLOWER GIRL *(hopefully).* I can give you change for a tanner,[4] kind lady.

THE MOTHER *(to CLARA).* Give it to me. *(CLARA parts reluctantly.)* Now *(to the GIRL)* this is for your flowers.

THE FLOWER GIRL. Thank you kindly, lady.

THE DAUGHTER. Make her give you the change. These things are only a penny a bunch.

THE MOTHER. Do hold your tongue, Clara. *(To the GIRL.)* You can keep the change.

THE FLOWER GIRL. Oh, thank you, lady.

THE MOTHER. Now tell me how you know that young gentleman's name.

THE FLOWER GIRL. I didn't.

7

THE MOTHER. I heard you call him by it. Don't try to deceive me.

THE FLOWER GIRL *(protesting).* Who's trying to deceive you? I called him Freddy or Charlie same as you might yourself if you was talking

to a stranger and wished to be pleasant. *(She sits down beside her basket.)*

THE DAUGHTER. Sixpence thrown away! Really, mamma, you might have spared Freddy that. *(She retreats in disgust behind the pillar.)*

(An elderly GENTLEMAN of the amiable military type rushes into the shelter, and closes a dripping umbrella. He is in the same plight as FREDDY, very wet about the ankles. He is in evening dress, with a light overcoat. He takes the place left vacant by the DAUGHTER's retirement.)

8

THE GENTLEMAN. Phew!

THE MOTHER *(to the GENTLEMAN).* Oh, sir, is there any sign of its stopping?

THE GENTLEMAN. I'm afraid not. It started worse than ever about two minutes ago. *(He goes to the plinth beside the FLOWER GIRL; puts up his foot on it; and stoops to turn down his trouser ends.)*

THE MOTHER. Oh dear! *(She retires sadly and joins her DAUGHTER.)*

THE FLOWER GIRL *(taking advantage of the military GENTLEMAN's proximity to establish friendly relations with him).* If it's worse, it's a sign it's nearly over. So cheer up, Captain; and buy a flower off a poor girl.

THE GENTLEMAN. I'm sorry. I haven't any change.

THE FLOWER GIRL. I can give you change, Captain.

THE GENTLEMAN. For a sovereign?[5] I've nothing less.

THE FLOWER GIRL. Garn! Oh do buy a flower off me, Captain. I can change half-a-crown. Take this for tuppence.

THE GENTLEMAN. Now don't be troublesome: there's a good girl. *(Trying his pockets.)* I really haven't any change—Stop: here's three hapence, if that's any use to you. *(He retreats to the other pillar.)*

THE FLOWER GIRL *(disappointed, but thinking three half-pence better than nothing).* Thank you, sir.

---

4. **tanner** (tan′ər), *n.* sixpence (six pennies). [*Slang*]
5. **sovereign** (sov′rən), *n.* former British gold coin; the crown, worth much less, is also a former British coin.

THE BYSTANDER (*to the girl*). You be careful: give him a flower for it. There's a bloke here behind taking down every blessed word you're saying. (*All turn to the man who is taking notes.*)

THE FLOWER GIRL (*springing up terrified*). I ain't done nothing wrong by speaking to the gentleman. I've a right to sell flowers if I keep off the curb. (*Hysterically.*) I'm a respectable girl: so help me, I never spoke to him except to ask him to buy a flower off me. (*General hubbub, mostly sympathetic to the* FLOWER GIRL, *but deprecating[6] her excessive sensibility.[7] Cries of* Don't start hollerin. Who's hurting you? Nobody's going to touch you. What's the good of fussing? Steady on. Easy easy, etc., *come from the elderly staid[8] spectators, who pat her comfortingly. Less patient ones bid her shut her head, or ask her roughly what is wrong with her. A remoter group, not knowing what the matter is, crowd in and increase the noise with question and answer:* What's the row? What she do? Where is he? A tec[9] taking her down. What! Him? Yes, him over there. Took money off the gentleman, etc. *The* FLOWER GIRL, *distraught and mobbed, breaks through them to the* GENTLEMAN, *crying wildly.*) Oh, sir, don't let him charge me. You dunno what it means to me. They'll take away my character and drive me on the streets for speaking to gentlemen. They—

THE NOTE TAKER (*coming forward on her right, the rest crowding after him*). There, there, there, there! Who's hurting you, you silly girl? What do you take me for?

THE BYSTANDER. It's all right: he's a gentleman: look at his boots. (*Explaining to the* NOTE TAKER.) She thought you was a copper's nark, sir.

THE NOTE TAKER (*with quick interest*). What's a copper's nark?

THE BYSTANDER (*inapt at definition*). It's a—well, it's a copper's nark, as you might say. What else would you call it? A sort of informer.

THE FLOWER GIRL (*still hysterical*). I take my Bible oath I never said a word—

THE NOTE TAKER (*overbearing but good-humored*). Oh, shut up, shut up. Do I look like a policeman?

THE FLOWER GIRL (*far from reassured*). Then what did you take down my words for? How do I know whether you took me down right? You just show me what you've wrote about me. (*The* NOTE TAKER *opens his book and holds it steadily under her nose, though the pressure of the mob trying to read it over his shoulders would upset a weaker man.*) What's that? That ain't proper writing. I can't read that.

THE NOTE TAKER. I can. (*Reads, reproducing her pronunciation exactly.*) "Cheer ap, Keptin; n' baw ya flahr orf a pore gel."

THE FLOWER GIRL (*much distressed*). It's because I called him Captain. I meant no harm. (*To the* GENTLEMAN.) Oh, sir, don't let him lay a charge agen me for a word like that. You—

THE GENTLEMAN. Charge! I make no charge. (*To the* NOTE TAKER.) Really, sir, if you are a detective, you need not begin protecting me against molestation by young women until I ask you. Anybody could see that the girl meant no harm.

THE BYSTANDERS GENERALLY (*demonstrating against police espionage*). Course they could. What business is it of yours? You mind your own affairs. He wants promotion, he does. Taking down people's words! Girl never said a word to him. What harm if she did? Nice thing a girl can't shelter from the rain without being insulted, etc., etc., etc. (*She is conducted by the more sympathetic demonstrators back to her plinth, where she resumes her seat and struggles with her emotion.*)

THE BYSTANDER. He ain't a tec. He's a blooming busybody: that's what he is. I tell you, look at his boots.

---

6. deprecate (dep′rə kāt), *v.* express strong disapproval of; belittle.
7. sensibility (sen′sə bil′ə tē), *n.* tendency to be hurt or offended too easily.
8. staid (stād), *adj.* having a settled, quiet character; sober; sedate.
9. tec (tek), *n.* short for "detective." [*Slang*]

Pygmalion—Act One   665

BUILDING ENGLISH PROFICIENCY

ESL LEP ELD SAE LD

Exploring Dialect

Help students hear how the flower girl's dialect sounds.

1. Explain that the flower girl speaks cockney, a dialect of a poor section of London. The note taker uses phonetics, an alphabet of speech sounds, to record her pronunciation.

2. Have students in groups say and translate the speech in column 1 of page 664 with words spelled the way that the dialect sounds.

Dialect	Translation
1. Ow, eez ye-ooa san, is e?	1. Oh, he's your son, is he?
2. Wal, fewd dan y' de-ooty	2. Well, if you'd done your duty
3. bawms a mather should,	3. by him as a mother should,
4. eed now bettern to spawl	4. he'd know better than to spoil
5. a pore gel's flahrzn than	5. a poor girl's flowers and then
6. ran awy athat pyin.	6. run away without paying.

12 Literary Focus
Inference

Question How do you think the note taker knows that the bystander came from Selsey? (*Possible responses: probably from the bystander's style of speaking; possibly because he knows who the man is*)

13 Literary Element
Figurative Language

Point out the colorful and expressive speech of "lower-class" Londoners.

14 Literary Element
Theme

The note taker openly laughs at the name of the mother's home. His apology for this inappropriate behavior helps introduce the theme of social conventions—speaking and behaving in ways that fit the situation and company. This theme will take on increasing significance as the play's story develops and this character's behavior is further explored.

The World of Work

Speech Therapist

For the real-life experiences of a speech thearapist, use the pages referenced below.

The World of Work
pp. 25–26

12

THE NOTE TAKER (*turning on him genially*). And how are all your people down at Selsey?

THE BYSTANDER (*suspiciously*). Who told you my people come from Selsey?

THE NOTE TAKER. Never you mind. They did. (*To the* GIRL.) How do you come to be up so far east? You were born in Lisson Grove.

THE FLOWER GIRL (*appalled*). Oh, what harm is there in my leaving Lisson Grove? It wasn't fit for a pig to live in; and I had to pay four-and-six[10] a week. (*In tears.*) Oh, boo—hoo—oo—

THE NOTE TAKER. Live where you like; but stop that noise.

THE GENTLEMAN (*to the girl*). Come, come! He can't touch you: you have a right to live where you please.

A SARCASTIC BYSTANDER (*thrusting himself between the* NOTE TAKER *and the* GENTLEMAN). Park Lane, for instance. I'd like to go into the Housing Question with you, I would.

THE FLOWER GIRL (*subsiding into a brooding melancholy over her basket, and talking very low-spiritedly to herself*). I'm a good girl, I am.

THE SARCASTIC BYSTANDER (*not attending to her*). Do you know where *I* come from?

THE NOTE TAKER (*promptly*). Hoxton.

(*Titterings. Popular interest in the* NOTE TAKER'S *performance increases.*)

THE SARCASTIC ONE (*amazed*). Well, who said I didn't? Bly me! You know everything, you do.

THE FLOWER GIRL (*still nursing her sense of injury*). Ain't no call to meddle with me, he ain't.

THE BYSTANDER (*to her*). Of course he ain't. Don't you stand it from him. (*To the* NOTE TAKER.) See here: what call have you to know about people what never offered to meddle with you? Where's your warrant?

SEVERAL BYSTANDERS (*encouraged by this seeming point of law*). Yes, where's your warrant?

THE FLOWER GIRL. Let him say what he likes. I don't want to have no truck with him.

13 THE BYSTANDER. You take us for dirt under your feet, don't you? Catch you taking liberties with a gentleman!

THE SARCASTIC BYSTANDER. Yes: tell him where

---

he come from if you want to go fortune-telling.

THE NOTE TAKER. Cheltenham, Harrow,[11] Cambridge, and India.

THE GENTLEMAN. Quite right. (*Great laughter. Reaction in the* NOTE TAKER'S *favor. Exclamations of* He knows all about it. Told him proper. Hear him tell the toff[12] where he come from? *etc.*) May I ask, sir, do you do this for your living at a music hall?

THE NOTE TAKER. I've thought of that. Perhaps I shall some day.

(*The rain has stopped, and the persons on the outside of the crowd begin to drop off.*)

THE FLOWER GIRL (*resenting the reaction*). He's no gentleman, he ain't, to interfere with a poor girl.

THE DAUGHTER (*out of patience, pushing her way rudely to the front and displacing the* GENTLEMAN, *who politely retires to the other side of the pillar*). What on earth is Freddy doing? I shall get pneumonia if I stay in this draft any longer.

THE NOTE TAKER (*to himself, hastily making a note of her pronunciation of "monia"*). Earlscourt.

THE DAUGHTER (*violently*). Will you please keep your impertinent remarks to yourself?

THE NOTE TAKER. Did I say that out loud? I didn't mean to. I beg your pardon. Your mother's Epsom; unmistakeably.

THE MOTHER (*advancing between her* DAUGHTER *and the* NOTE TAKER). How very curious! I was brought up in Largelady Park, near Epsom.

THE NOTE TAKER (*uproariously amused*). Ha! ha! What a devil of a name! Excuse me. (*To the* DAUGHTER.) You want a cab, do you? 14

THE DAUGHTER. Don't dare speak to me.

THE MOTHER. Oh, please, please, Clara. (*Her* DAUGHTER *repudiates her with an angry shrug and retires haughtily.*) We should be so grateful to you, sir, if you found us a cab. (*The* NOTE

---

10. **four-and-six,** British money: four pounds and six shillings.
11. **Cheltenham, Harrow,** exclusive preparatory schools.
12. **toff** (tôf), *n.* dandy; well-to-do person. [*Slang*]

MINI-LESSON: GRAMMAR

Relative Pronouns

Teach Read aloud this sentence from column 1, page 668:

"I could even get her a place as lady's maid or shop assistant, which requires better English."

Point out that in this sentence Higgins uses the clause beginning with the relative pronoun *which* to add additional, but nonessential, information to the sentence. Since the information is nonessential, it is set off by a comma. Explain that *that* and *which* are relative pronouns that introduce subordinate clauses. Subordinate clauses can be either *restrictive* (essential to the meaning of the sentence) or *nonrestrictive* (nonessential—merely adding additional information). It is customary in formal English to use *that* for restrictive clauses and *which* for nonrestrictive clauses.

Activity Idea Have students write one sentence with a relative clause introduced by *that* or *which* describing each of the characters introduced in Act One.

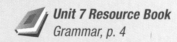

Unit 7 Resource Book
Grammar, p. 4

TAKER *produces a whistle.*) Oh, thank you. (*She joins her* DAUGHTER.)

(*The* NOTE TAKER *blows a piercing blast.*)

THE SARCASTIC BYSTANDER. There! I knowed he was a plain-clothes copper.

THE BYSTANDER. That ain't a police whistle: that's a sporting whistle.

THE FLOWER GIRL (*still preoccupied with her wounded feelings*). He's no right to take away my character. My character is the same to me as any lady's.

THE NOTE TAKER. I don't know whether you've noticed it, but the rain stopped about two minutes ago.

THE BYSTANDER. So it has. Why didn't you say so before? And us losing our time listening to your silliness! (*He walks off towards the Strand.*)

THE SARCASTIC BYSTANDER. I can tell where you come from. You come from Anwell.[13] Go back there.

THE NOTE TAKER (*helpfully*). Hanwell.

THE SARCASTIC BYSTANDER (*affecting great distinction of speech*). Thenk you, teacher. Haw haw! So long! (*He touches his hat with mock respect and strolls off.*)

THE FLOWER GIRL. Frightening people like that! How would he like it himself?

THE MOTHER. It's quite fine now, Clara. We can walk to a motor bus. Come. (*She gathers her skirts above her ankles and hurries off towards the Strand.*)

THE DAUGHTER. But the cab— (*Her* MOTHER *is out of hearing.*) Oh, how tiresome! (*She follows angrily.*)

(*All the rest have gone except the* NOTE TAKER, *the* GENTLEMAN, *and the* FLOWER GIRL, *who sits arranging her basket and still pitying herself in murmurs.*)

THE FLOWER GIRL. Poor girl! Hard enough for her to live without being worrited and chivied.

THE GENTLEMAN (*returning to his former place on the* NOTE TAKER'S *left*). How do you do it, if I may ask?

THE NOTE TAKER. Simply phonetics. The science of speech. That's my profession: also my hobby. Happy is the man who can make

a living by his hobby! You can spot an Irishman or a Yorkshireman by his brogue. *I* can place any man within six miles. I can place him within two miles in London. Sometimes within two streets.

THE FLOWER GIRL. Ought to be ashamed of himself, unmanly coward!

THE GENTLEMAN. But is there a living in that?

THE NOTE TAKER. Oh yes. Quite a fat one. This is an age of upstarts. Men begin in Kentish Town with £80 a year, and end in Park Lane with a hundred thousand. They want to drop Kentish Town, but they give themselves away every time they open their mouths. Now I can teach them—

THE FLOWER GIRL. Let him mind his own business and leave a poor girl—

THE NOTE TAKER (*explosively*). Woman: cease this detestable boohooing instantly; or else seek the shelter of some other place of worship.

THE FLOWER GIRL (*with feeble defiance*). I've a right to be here if I like, same as you.

THE NOTE TAKER. A woman who utters such depressing and disgusting sounds has no right to be anywhere—no right to live. Remember that you are a human being with a soul and the divine gift of articulate speech: that your native language is the language of Shakespeare and Milton and The Bible: and

---

13. **Anwell,** Hanwell, an insane asylum.

Pygmalion—Act One   **667**

don't sit there crooning like a bilious pigeon.

THE FLOWER GIRL (*quite overwhelmed, looking up at him in mingled wonder and deprecation without daring to raise her head*). Ah-ah-ah-ow-ow-ow-oo!

THE NOTE TAKER (*whipping out his book*). Heavens! What a sound! (*He writes; then holds out the book and reads, reproducing her vowels exactly.*) Ah-ah-ah-ow-ow-ow-oo!

THE FLOWER GIRL (*tickled by the performance, and laughing in spite of herself*). Garn!

THE NOTE TAKER. You see this creature with her curbstone English: the English that will keep her in the gutter to the end of her days. Well, sir, in three months I could pass that girl off as a duchess at an ambassador's garden party. I could even get her a place as lady's maid or shop assistant, which requires better English. That's the sort of thing I do for commercial millionaires. And on the profits of it I do genuine scientific work in phonetics, and a little as a poet on Miltonic lines.

THE GENTLEMAN. I am myself a student of Indian dialects; and—

THE NOTE TAKER (*eagerly*). Are you? Do you know Colonel Pickering, the author of *Spoken Sanskrit?*

THE GENTLEMAN. I am Colonel Pickering. Who are you?

THE NOTE TAKER. Henry Higgins, author of *Higgins's Universal Alphabet.*

PICKERING (*with enthusiasm*). I came from India to meet you.

HIGGINS. I was going to India to meet you.

PICKERING. Where do you live?

HIGGINS. 27A Wimpole Street. Come and see me tomorrow.

PICKERING. I'm at the Carlton. Come with me now and let's have a jaw over some supper.

HIGGINS. Right you are.

THE FLOWER GIRL (*to* PICKERING, *as he passes her*). Buy a flower, kind gentleman. I'm short for my lodging.

PICKERING. I really haven't any change. I'm

sorry. (*He goes away.*)

HIGGINS (*shocked at the girl's* mendacity).[14] Liar. You said you could change half-a-crown.

THE FLOWER GIRL (*rising in desperation*). You ought to be stuffed with nails, you ought. (*Flinging the basket at his feet.*) Take the whole blooming basket for sixpence.

(*The church clock strikes the second quarter.*)

HIGGINS (*hearing in it the voice of God, rebuking him for his Pharisaic*[15] *want of charity to the poor girl*). A reminder. (*He raises his hat solemnly, then throws a handful of money into the basket and follows* PICKERING.)

THE FLOWER GIRL (*picking up a half-crown*). Ah-ow-ooh! (*Picking up a couple of florins.*) Aah-ow-ooh! (*Picking up several coins.*) Aaaaah-ow-ooh! (*Picking up a half-sovereign.*) Aaaaaaaaaaaaah-ow-ooh!!!

FREDDY (*springing out of a taxicab*). Got one at last. Hallo! (*To the* GIRL.) Where are the two ladies that were here?

THE FLOWER GIRL. They walked to the bus when the rain stopped.

FREDDY. And left me with a cab on my hands! Damnation!

THE FLOWER GIRL (*with grandeur*). Never mind, young man. *I'm going home in a taxi.* (*She sails off to the cab. The* DRIVER *puts his hand behind him and holds the door firmly shut against her. Quite understanding his mistrust, she shows him her handful of money.*) Eightpence ain't no object to me, Charlie. (*He grins and opens the door.*) Angel Court, Drury Lane, round the corner of Micklejohn's oil shop. Let's see how fast you can make her hop it. (*She gets in and pulls the door to with a slam as the taxicab starts.*)

FREDDY. Well, I'm dashed!

---

14. mendacity (men das′ə tē), *n.* untruthfulness; lie.
15. **Pharisaic** (far′ə sā′ik), *adj.* self-righteous. The Pharisees were a strict Jewish sect at the time of Jesus.

After Reading

Act 1

Shaping Your Response

Making Connections

1. A playwright must capture and hold an audience's attention just as soon as the curtain goes up. How effective is the opening scene in your opinion?

Analyzing the Play

2. **Dialect** is a variety of language characteristic of a particular region or class. It is different from the standard language in pronunciation, usage, and vocabulary. What seems to be Shaw's purpose in emphasizing dialect here?

3. What—if anything—proves a hindrance to **communication** in this act? Explain.

4. Rank the characters according to how the Note Taker treats them, starting with the character he treats best. (You might list the bystanders as one character.) What can you conclude from this ranking?

5. How important is the **setting** to act 1? Explain.

Extending the Ideas

6. If such a varied gathering of people took place in your community, where would it be?

Literary Focus: Inference

An **inference** is a reasonable conclusion about the behavior of a character or the meaning of events drawn from limited information. Characters in a play, as well as readers and playgoers, must continually make inferences.

1. What do the Bystanders and then the Flower Girl infer about the Note Taker?

2. What can you infer about the Flower Girl from her speech to the Mother, her persistence in not moving on after the rain ends, and her reaction to Higgins's coins?

3. What can you infer about Freddy's character?

Vocabulary Study

Use the listed words in sentences that show you understand the meaning of the words.

deprecate
mendacity
plinth
sensibility
staid

After Reading

MAKING CONNECTIONS

1. Students who understand the tensions felt by poor people in a class-conscious England, or the flower girl's fear of being taken for a criminal, may sense great drama, while any student may appreciate humorous bits.

2. Possible responses: He is showing connections between dialect and social class; developing the character of Higgins, a language expert; and contrasting people who are different.

3. Possible responses: the characters' inferences about each other, such as the flower girl's suspicion of the note taker's motives; different uses of language, as in the mother's misunderstanding of the flower girl's random use of the name Freddy

4. Possible response: He treats Pickering best, the Mother next, bystanders not very well, and the flower girl worst.

5. Possible responses: It is primarily important as a shelter from the rain and a gathering place for people of all classes; it is a church, and this inspires Higgins to give the flower girl money; interestingly, people have come from the theater, and they are in a play, so there is a juxtaposition of real life and art.

6. Possible responses: at a church, park, beach, school, mall, voting place, holiday celebration, or some other place where people gather

VOCABULARY STUDY

Vocabulary words, as used in context, should reflect correct meanings and connotations.

Unit 7 Resource Book
Vocabulary, p. 3
Vocabulary Test, p. 6

Selection Test

Unit 7 Resource Book
pp. 7–8

LITERARY FOCUS: INFERENCE

Possible Responses

1. Students may say that at first they all think the note taker is spying and ill-intentioned toward the flower girl.

2. She has a sense of right and wrong; she is interested in the conversation between Higgins and Pickering; she is poor.

3. Freddy seems rather weak and easily swayed.

Selection Objectives

robust, strong and healthy; sturdy

genial, cheerful and friendly; kindly

stupent, dumbfounded; amazed

genteel, polite; well-bred

zephyr, mild breeze; gentle wind

strew, scatter or sprinkle

remonstrance, protest; complaint

diffident, lacking in self-confidence; shy

unabashed, not ashamed or embarrassed

booty, money, especially seized illegally; gains; winnings

Students can add the words and definitions to their Writer's Notebooks.

 ## Art Study

The picture shows actors Dora Bryan as Mrs. Pearce, Amanda Plummer as Eliza, Peter O'Toole as Higgins, and Lionel Jeffries as Pickering.

Eliza's clothes may look fancy to students, but compared to the gentlemen's clothing her garments are vulgar.

Question   How does Higgins's action suggest that he does not consider the young woman his social equal? *(Possible response: He is holding her chin the way a person might examine a horse.)*

1 **Reading/Thinking Skills**
Visualize

Encourage students to draw or diagram the room as it is described in the stage directions, to understand the setting and the action.

 Unit 7 Resource Book
Graphic Organizer, p. 9
Study Guide, p. 10

ACT TWO

Next day at 11 A.M. HIGGINS'S laboratory in Wimpole Street. It is a room on the first floor, looking on the street, and was meant for the drawing room. The double doors are in the middle of the back wall, and persons entering find in the corner to their right two tall file cabinets at right angles to one another against the walls. In this corner stands a flat writing table, on which are a phonograph, a laryngoscope,[1] a row of tiny organ pipes with bellows, a set of lamp chimneys *for singing flames with burners attached to a gas plug in the wall by an india-rubber tube, several tuning forks[2] of different sizes, a life-size image of half a human head, showing in section the vocal organs,*

---

1. **laryngoscope** (lə ring′gə skōp), *n.* instrument with a mirror for examining the larynx, including the vocal cords.
2. **tuning fork,** a small two-pronged steel instrument used for finding the standard pitch and for tuning musical instruments.

ACT TWO SUMMARY

Pygmalion

The following day, Eliza comes to Higgins's residence wanting lessons. Pickering, also visiting, bets Higgins that he can't pass Eliza off as a duchess at the ambassador's party. Higgins accepts. An argument ensues over how Eliza is to be treated, with Higgins making outrageous comments, Eliza reacting to them, and Pickering and Mrs. Pearce, the housekeeper, trying to keep peace. Finally Mrs. Pearce takes Eliza off to bathe and returns to lecture Higgins on his behavior. Eliza's father arrives, claiming to want his daughter but actually seeking money. He doesn't recognize Eliza, bathed and wrapped in a kimono, until she identifies herself. As the act ends, Eliza rushes out of the room to see her new clothes, and Higgins and Pickering conclude that they have a difficult job before them.

 *For summaries in other languages, see the **Building English Proficiency** book.*

and a box containing a supply of wax cylinders for the phonograph.

Further down the room, on the same side, is a fireplace, with a comfortable leather-covered easy chair at the side of the hearth nearest the door, and a coal scuttle. There is a clock on the mantelpiece. Between the fireplace and the phonograph table is a stand for newspapers.

On the other side of the central door, to the left of the visitor, is a cabinet of shallow drawers. On it is a telephone and the telephone directory. The corner beyond, and most of the side wall, is occupied by a grand piano, with the keyboard at the end furthest from the door, and a bench for the player extending the full length of the keyboard. On the piano is a dessert dish heaped with fruit and sweets, mostly chocolates.

The middle of the room is clear. Besides the easy chair, the piano bench, and two chairs at the phonograph table, there is one stray chair. It stands near the fireplace. On the walls, engravings: mostly Piranesi and mezzotint portraits.[3] No paintings.

PICKERING *is seated at the table, putting down some cards and a tuning fork which he has been using.* HIGGINS *is standing up near him, closing two or three file drawers which are hanging out. He appears in the morning light as a* robust,[4] *vital, appetizing sort of man of forty or thereabouts, dressed in a professional-looking black frock coat with a white linen collar and black silk tie. He is of the energetic, scientific type, heartily, even violently interested in everything that can be studied as a scientific subject, and careless about himself and other people, including their feelings. He is, in fact, but for his years and size, rather like a very impetuous baby "taking notice" eagerly and loudly, and requiring almost as much watching to keep him out of unintended mischief. His manner varies from* genial[5] *bullying when he is in a good humor to stormy petulance when anything goes wrong; but he is so entirely frank and void of malice that he remains likeable even in his least reasonable moments.*

HIGGINS (*as he shuts the last drawer*). Well, I think that's the whole show.
PICKERING. It's really amazing. I haven't taken half of it in, you know.

HIGGINS. Would you like to go over any of it again?
PICKERING (*rising and coming to the fireplace, where he plants himself with his back to the fire*). No, thank you; not now. I'm quite done up for this morning.
HIGGINS (*following him, and standing beside him on his left*). Tired of listening to sounds?
PICKERING. Yes. It's a fearful strain. I rather fancied myself because I can pronounce twenty-four distinct vowel sounds; but your hundred and thirty beat me. I can't hear a bit of difference between most of them.
HIGGINS (*chuckling, and going over to the piano to eat sweets*). Oh, that comes with practice. You hear no difference at first, but you keep on listening, and presently you find they're all as different as A from B. (MRS. PEARCE *looks in: she is* HIGGINS'S *housekeeper.*) What's the matter?
MRS. PEARCE (*hesitating, evidently perplexed*). A young woman wants to see you, sir.
HIGGINS. A young woman! What does she want?
MRS. PEARCE. Well, sir, she says you'll be glad to see her when you know what she's come about. She's quite a common girl, sir. Very common indeed. I should have sent her away, only I thought perhaps you wanted her to talk into your machines. I hope I've not done wrong; but really you see such queer people sometimes—you'll excuse me, I'm sure, sir—
HIGGINS. Oh, that's all right, Mrs. Pearce. Has she an interesting accent?
MRS. PEARCE. Oh, something dreadful, sir, really. I don't know how you can take an interest in it.

---

3. **Piranesi and mezzotint portraits.** Giovanni Battista Piranesi (1720–1778) was an Italian graphic artist known for his large prints of buildings of classical and post-classical Rome. A mezzotint is a picture engraved on a roughened copper or steel plate.
4. robust (rō bust´), *adj.* strong and healthy; sturdy.
5. genial (jē´nyəl), *adj.* cheerful and friendly; kindly.

2 Reading/Thinking Skills
Compare and Contrast

Point out that Higgins was not described in Act One. Here Shaw provides a detailed description.

Question Why do you think Shaw did not include this description in Act One when the character first appears? (*Possible responses: Shaw wanted the note taker to be mysterious in the opening scene; he gradually reveals most characters and lets the audience or reader form impressions, rather than being told.*)

3 Literary Focus
Inference

Question What do you think this dialogue suggests about Higgins? (*Possible responses: He is tireless; he doesn't understand that other people may not share his fervor and interest in the details of his topic.*)

BUILDING ENGLISH PROFICIENCY

Exploring Character and Setting

Help students use the stage directions, as well as songs from the soundtrack of *My Fair Lady,* to understand character and setting.

Activity Ideas

• Explain that a "drawing room" (from *withdrawing room*) in England was the room where hosts and guests went (withdrew) after dinner. Ask students to draw Higgins's laboratory, following the description in the stage directions. Have them label any 10 items in their drawing. Ask students to tell what the laboratory reveals about Higgins's character.

• If possible, obtain a CD, tape, or record of songs from *My Fair Lady.* Ask volunteers to explain, after hearing each song, how it develops a character, situation, or idea, and where it might fit in the play.

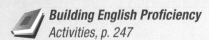
Building English Proficiency
Activities, p. 247

Literary Focus

Inference

Students may not know that "enters in state" refers to the flower girl's cere-monial manner of walking into the room.

Question What can you gather from the description of the flower girl's hat? (*Possible response: The bright colors of the feathers indicate that her taste is not sophisticated.*)

5 Reading/Thinking Skills

Understand Sequence

Question What can you infer about the chain of events that led to the flower girl's arrival at Higgins's house? (*Students may mention that before leaving St. Paul's the previous night, she apparently overheard Higgins's remark to Pickering about giving lessons, and took it seriously. She then decided she had found a use for the money that Higgins tossed to her. She may have been looking for an opportunity to better her position for some time.*)

HIGGINS (*to* PICKERING). Let's have her up. Show her up, Mrs. Pearce. (*He rushes across to his working table and picks out a cylinder to use on the phonograph.*)

MRS. PEARCE (*only half resigned to it*). Very well, sir. It's for you to say. (*She goes downstairs.*)

HIGGINS. This is rather a bit of luck. I'll show you how I make records. We'll set her talk-ing; and I'll take it down first in Bell's Visible Speech; then in broad Romic; and then we'll get her on the phonograph so that you can turn her on as often as you like with the writ-ten transcript before you.

MRS. PEARCE (*returning*). This is the young woman, sir.

(*The* FLOWER GIRL *enters in state. She has a hat with three ostrich feathers, orange, sky-blue, and red. She has a nearly clean apron, and the shoddy coat has been tidied a little. The pathos of this deplorable figure, with its innocent vanity and consequential air, touches* PICKERING, *who has already straightened himself in the presence of* MRS. PEARCE. *But as to* HIGGINS, *the only distinction he makes between men and women is that when he is neither bullying nor exclaiming to the heavens against some feather-weight cross, he coaxes women as a child coaxes its nurse when it wants to get anything out of her.*)

HIGGINS (*brusquely, recognizing her with uncon-cealed disappointment, and at once, babylike, making an intolerable grievance of it*). Why, this is the girl I jotted down last night. She's no use. I've got all the records I want of the Lisson Grove lingo; and I'm not going to waste another cylinder on it. (*To the* GIRL.) Be off with you: I don't want you.

THE FLOWER GIRL. Don't you be so saucy. You ain't heard what I come for yet. (*To* MRS. PEARCE, *who is waiting at the door for further instructions.*) Did you tell him I come in a taxi?

MRS. PEARCE. Nonsense, girl! What do you think a gentleman like Mr. Higgins cares what you came in?

THE FLOWER GIRL. Oh, we are proud! He ain't above giving lessons, not him: I heard him say so. Well, I ain't come here to ask for any compliment; and if my money's not good enough I can go elsewhere.

HIGGINS. Good enough for what?

THE FLOWER GIRL. Good enough for ye-oo. Now you know, don't you? I'm come to have lessons, I am. And to pay for em too: make no mistake.

HIGGINS (*stupent*[6]). Well!!! (*Recovering his breath with a gasp.*) What do you expect me to say to you?

THE FLOWER GIRL. Well, if you was a gentleman, you might ask me to sit down, I think. Don't I tell you I'm bringing you business?

HIGGINS. Pickering: shall we ask this baggage to sit down, or shall we throw her out of the window?

THE FLOWER GIRL (*running away in terror to the piano, where she turns at bay*). Ah-ah-oh-ow-ow-ow-oo! (*Wounded and whimpering.*) I won't be called a baggage when I've offered to pay like any lady.

(*Motionless, the two men stare at her from the other side of the room, amazed.*)

PICKERING (*gently*). What is it you want, my girl?

THE FLOWER GIRL. I want to be a lady in a flower shop stead of selling at the corner of Tottenham Court Road. But they won't take me unless I can talk more genteel.[7] He said he could teach me. Well, here I am ready to pay him—not asking any favor—and he treats me as if I was dirt.

MRS. PEARCE. How can you be such a foolish ignorant girl as to think you could afford to pay Mr. Higgins?

THE FLOWER GIRL. Why shouldn't I? I know what lessons cost as well as you do; and I'm ready to pay.

HIGGINS. How much?

THE FLOWER GIRL (*coming back to him, tri-umphant*). Now you're talking! I thought you'd come off it when you saw a chance of getting back a bit of what you chucked at me

---

6. **stupent** (stŭp′nt), *adj.* dumfounded; amazed.
7. **genteel** (jen tēl′), *adj.* polite; well-bred.

MINI-LESSON: SPEAKING AND LISTENING

Pitch, Modulation, Volume, and Inflection

Teach Draw student's attention to Higgins's line in column 2 above: "Well!!!" Point out the triple exclamation mark, and explain that part of the excitement that Shaw generates comes through the rise and fall of the human voice engaged in various kinds of communication. Remind students that we use our voices differently for declarative sentences, questions, imperatives, and exclamations. Have students find examples of each of the four sentence types in the dialogue on pages 672 and 673. (*Students should recognize a good mix of sentences.*)

Activity Idea Have students compare the kinds of sentences on this spread with sentences in a spread from *Macbeth*. Have students note how Shaw and Shakespeare use sentence types differently. Then have them read the dialogue aloud, paying attention to the way they use their voices.

last night. *(Confidentially.)* You'd had a drop in,[8] hadn't you?

HIGGINS *(peremptorily).* Sit down.

THE FLOWER GIRL. Oh, if you're going to make a compliment of it—

HIGGINS *(thundering at her).* Sit down.

MRS. PEARCE *(severely).* Sit down, girl. Do as you're told.

(She places the stray chair near the hearthrug between HIGGINS *and* PICKERING, *and stands behind it waiting for the* GIRL *to sit down.)*

THE FLOWER GIRL. Ah-ah-ah-ow-ow-ee! *(She stands, half rebellious, half bewildered.)*

PICKERING *(very courteous).* Won't you sit down?

THE FLOWER GIRL *(coyly).* Don't mind if I do. *(She sits down.* PICKERING *returns to the hearthrug.)*

HIGGINS. What's your name?

THE FLOWER GIRL. Liza Doolittle.

HIGGINS *(declaiming gravely).*

Eliza, Elizabeth, Betsy, and Bess,
They went to the woods to get a bird's nes':

PICKERING. They found a nest with four eggs in it:

HIGGINS. They took one apiece, and left three in it.

(They laugh heartily at their own wit.)

LIZA. Oh, don't be silly.

MRS. PEARCE. You mustn't speak to the gentleman like that.

LIZA. Well, why won't he speak sensible to me?

HIGGINS. Come back to business. How much do you propose to pay me for the lessons?

LIZA. Oh, I know what's right. A lady friend of mine gets French lessons for eighteenpence an hour from a real French gentleman. Well, you wouldn't have the face to ask me the same for teaching me my own language as you would for French; so I won't give more than a shilling. Take it or leave it.

HIGGINS *(walking up and down the room, rattling his keys and his cash in his pockets).* You know, Pickering, if you consider a shilling, not as a simple shilling, but as a percentage of this girl's income, it works out as fully equivalent to sixty or seventy guineas[9] from a millionaire.

PICKERING. How so?

HIGGINS. Figure it out. A millionaire has about £150[10] a day. She earns about half-a-crown.

LIZA *(haughtily).* Who told you I only—

HIGGINS *(continuing).* She offers me two-fifths of her day's income for a lesson. Two-fifths of a millionaire's income for a day would be somewhere about £60. It's handsome. By George, it's enormous! It's the biggest offer I ever had.

LIZA *(rising, terrified).* Sixty pounds! What are you talking about? I never offered you sixty pounds. Where would I get—

HIGGINS. Hold your tongue.

LIZA *(weeping).* But I ain't got sixty pounds. Oh—

MRS. PEARCE. Don't cry, you silly girl. Sit down. Nobody is going to touch your money.

HIGGINS. Somebody is going to touch you, with a broomstick, if you don't stop snivelling. Sit down.

LIZA *(obeying slowly).* Ah-ah-ah-ow-oo-o! One would think you was my father.

HIGGINS. If I decide to teach you, I'll be worse than two fathers to you. Here! *(He offers her his silk handkerchief.)*

LIZA. What's this for?

HIGGINS. To wipe your eyes. To wipe any part of your face that feels moist. Remember: that's your handkerchief; and that's your sleeve. Don't mistake the one for the other if you wish to become a lady in a shop.

*(*LIZA, *utterly bewildered, stares helplessly at him.)*

MRS. PEARCE. It's no use talking to her like that, Mr. Higgins: she doesn't understand you. Besides, you're quite wrong: she doesn't do it that way at all. *(She takes the handkerchief.)*

LIZA *(snatching it).* Here! You give that handkerchief. He give it to me, not to you.

---

8. **had a drop in,** had been drinking.
9. **guinea** (gĭn′ē), *n.* a British gold coin. It was discontinued in 1813, but the word continued in use for stating prices and fees.
10. **£150.** £ is the symbol for *pound,* a unit of British money.

---

6 **Literary Focus**

Inference

Question How does Mrs. Pearce perceive her role? *(Possible response: Here she seems to be echoing Higgins, acting as a go-between for him and the flower girl.)*

7 **Literary Element**

Characterization

Students will note that the flower girl now becomes Liza, once the character has identified herself. Higgins often calls her Eliza, and Shaw uses the name Eliza in some stage directions. The two forms of her name often are used interchangeably in discussions of the play.

Students should know that Shaw uses the words *lady* and *gentleman* in the traditional English manner, to refer to people of elevated social position. He does not intend the American meanings, in which the terms can refer to any woman or man.

8 **Literary Element**

Irony

Question What is ironic about Liza's estimation here? *(Possible response: Her estimation of the value of French lessons versus English lessons doesn't rest on the quality of the instruction, but rather on the perception that the subject—English—is already familiar to her.)*

BUILDING ENGLISH PROFICIENCY

Analyzing Character

To help students understand Higgins's character, use discussion and a graphic organizer.

1. Ask students to compare Higgins's treatment of Eliza on pages 672–673 with Pickering's treatment of her.

2. Have students develop a character traits web for Higgins. Ask them to begin with information from pages 672–673.

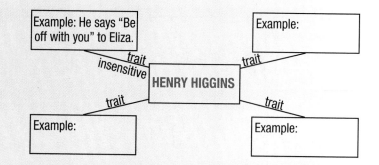

9

Reading/Thinking Skills
Compare and Contrast

Students might compare and contrast how Pickering and Higgins discuss the bet. Pickering offers the challenge to Higgins as a chance to prove himself the "greatest teacher alive," but he also offers to pay for the lessons—a kind gesture to Eliza. Higgins focuses on the professional challenge and insults Eliza in the process.

Question How do Liza's responses to Pickering and Higgins differ? *(She is grateful to Pickering and feels insulted by Higgins.)*

Literary Focus
Inference

Question What personal characteristic is exhibited in Higgins's statement about changing Liza? *(Possible response: His claim shows egotism. He speaks as if he can train her and disguise her identity with little contribution on her part.)*

Historical Note
Monkey Brand

Monkey Brand household cleanser came in a container with a picture of a monkey on it. It was never intended for use on human beings. Higgins thus insults Liza.

Literary Focus
Inference

Question What do Mrs. Pearce and Colonel Pickering find so funny? *(Higgins's lack of self-knowledge and absurd rationalizations)*

PICKERING (*laughing*). He did. I think it must be regarded as her property, Mrs. Pearce.

MRS. PEARCE (*resigning herself*). Serve you right, Mr. Higgins.

PICKERING. Higgins: I'm interested. What about the ambassador's garden party? I'll say you're the greatest teacher alive if you make that good. I'll bet you all the expenses of the experiment you can't do it. And I'll pay for the lessons.

LIZA. Oh, you are real good. Thank you, Captain.

HIGGINS (*tempted, looking at her*). It's almost irresistible. She's so deliciously low—so horribly dirty—

LIZA (*protesting extremely*). Ah-ah-ah-ah-ow-ow-oo-oo!!! I ain't dirty: I washed my face and hands afore I come, I did.

PICKERING. You're certainly not going to turn her head with flattery, Higgins.

MRS. PEARCE (*uneasy*). Oh, don't say that, sir: there's more ways than one of turning a girl's head; and nobody can do it better than Mr. Higgins, though he may not always mean it. I do hope, sir, you won't encourage him to do anything foolish.

HIGGINS (*becoming excited as the idea grows on him*). What is life but a series of inspired follies? The difficulty is to find them to do. Never lose a chance: it doesn't come every day. I shall make a duchess of this draggletailed guttersnipe.

LIZA (*strongly deprecating this view of her*). Ah-ah-ah-ow-ow-oo!

HIGGINS (*carried away*). Yes: in six months—in three if she has a good ear and a quick tongue—I'll take her anywhere and pass her off as anything. We'll start today: now! This moment! Take her away and clean her, Mrs. Pearce. Monkey Brand, if it won't come off any other way. Is there a good fire in the kitchen?

MRS. PEARCE (*protesting*). Yes; but—

HIGGINS (*storming on*). Take all her clothes off and burn them. Ring up Whiteley or some-

body for new ones. Wrap her up in brown paper till they come.

LIZA. You're no gentleman, you're not, to talk of such things. I'm a good girl, I am; and I know what the like of you are, I do.

HIGGINS. We want none of your Lisson Grove prudery here, young woman. You've got to learn to behave like a duchess. Take her away, Mrs. Pearce. If she gives you any trouble, wallop her.

LIZA (*springing up and running between* PICKERING *and* MRS. PEARCE *for protection*). No! I'll call the police, I will.

MRS. PEARCE. But I've no place to put her.

HIGGINS. Put her in the dustbin.

LIZA. Ah-ah-ah-ow-ow-oo!

PICKERING. Oh come, Higgins! Be reasonable.

MRS. PEARCE (*resolutely*). You must be reasonable, Mr. Higgins: really you must. You can't walk over everybody like this.

(HIGGINS, *thus scolded, subsides. The hurricane is succeeded by a zephyr*[11] *of amiable surprise.*)

HIGGINS (*with professional exquisiteness of modulation*). *I* walk over everybody! My dear Mrs. Pearce, my dear Pickering, I never had the slightest intention of walking over anyone. All I propose is that we should be kind to this poor girl. We must help her to prepare and fit herself for her new station in life. If I did not express myself clearly it was because I did not wish to hurt her delicacy, or yours.

(LIZA, *reassured, steals back to her chair.*)

MRS. PEARCE (*to* PICKERING). Well, did you ever hear anything like that, sir?

PICKERING (*laughing heartily*). Never, Mrs. Pearce: never.

HIGGINS (*patiently*). What's the matter?

MRS. PEARCE. Well, the matter is, sir, that you can't take a girl up like that as if you were picking up a pebble on the beach.

HIGGINS. Why not?

MRS. PEARCE. Why not! But you don't know any-

---

11. *zephyr* (zef′ər), *n.* mild breeze; gentle wind.

thing about her. What about her parents? She may be married.

LIZA. Garn!

HIGGINS. There! As the girl very properly says, Garn! Married indeed! Don't you know that a woman of that class looks a worn out drudge of fifty a year after she's married!

LIZA. Who'd marry me?

HIGGINS (*suddenly resorting to the most thrillingly beautiful low tones in his best elocutionary style*). By George, Eliza, the streets will be strewn[12] with the bodies of men shooting themselves for your sake before I've done with you.

MRS. PEARCE. Nonsense, sir. You mustn't talk like that to her.

LIZA (*rising and squaring herself determinedly*). I'm going away. He's off his chump, he is. I don't want no balmies teaching me.

13

HIGGINS (*wounded in his tenderest point by her insensibility to his elocution*). Oh, indeed! I'm mad, am I? Very well, Mrs. Pearce: you needn't order the new clothes for her. Throw her out.

LIZA (*whimpering*). Nah-ow. You got no right to touch me.

MRS. PEARCE. You see now what comes of being saucy. (*Indicating the door.*) This way, please.

LIZA (*almost in tears*). I didn't want no clothes. I wouldn't have taken them. (*She throws away the handkerchief.*) I can buy my own clothes.

HIGGINS (*deftly retrieving the handkerchief and intercepting her on her reluctant way to the door*). You're an ungrateful wicked girl. This is my return for offering to take you out of the gutter and dress you beautifully and make a lady of you.

MRS. PEARCE. Stop, Mr. Higgins. I won't allow it. It's you that are wicked. Go home to your parents, girl; and tell them to take better care of you.

LIZA. I ain't got no mother. Her that turned me out was my sixth stepmother. But I done without them. And I'm a good girl, I am.

HIGGINS. Very well, then, what on earth is all this fuss about? The girl doesn't belong to anybody— is no use to anybody but me. (*He goes to* MRS. PEARCE *and begins coaxing.*) You can

adopt her, Mrs. Pearce: I'm sure a daughter would be a great amusement to you. Now don't make any more fuss. Take her downstairs; and—

MRS. PEARCE. But what's to become of her? Is she to be paid anything? Do be sensible, sir.

HIGGINS. Oh, pay her whatever is necessary: put it down in the housekeeping book. (*Impatiently.*) What on earth will she want with money? She'll have her food and her clothes. She'll only drink if you give her money.

LIZA (*turning on him*). Oh you are a brute. It's a lie: nobody ever saw the sign of liquor on me. (*She goes back to her chair and plants herself there defiantly.*)

PICKERING (*in good-humored remonstrance*).[13] Does it occur to you, Higgins, that the girl has some feelings?

HIGGINS (*looking critically at her*). Oh no, I don't think so. Not any feelings that we need bother about. (*Cheerily.*) Have you, Eliza?

14

LIZA. I got my feelings same as anyone else.

HIGGINS (*to* PICKERING, *reflectively*). You see the difficulty?

PICKERING. Eh? What difficulty?

HIGGINS. To get her to talk grammar. The mere pronunciation is easy enough.

15

LIZA. I don't want to talk grammar. I want to talk like a lady.

MRS. PEARCE. Will you please keep to the point, Mr. Higgins? I want to know on what terms the girl is to be here. Is she to have any wages? And what is to become of her when you've finished your teaching? You must look ahead a little.

HIGGINS (*impatiently*). What's to become of her if I leave her in the gutter? Tell me that, Mrs. Pearce.

MRS. PEARCE. That's her own business, not yours, Mr. Higgins.

HIGGINS. Well, when I've done with her, we can throw her back into the gutter; and then it

---

12. strew (strū), *v.* scatter or sprinkle.
13. remonstrance (ri mon′strəns), *n.* protest; complaint.

13

Writing Style
Slang

Students may gather from context that Liza is saying Higgins is crazy. Shaw has made a noun from the British slang word *balmy*, meaning "loony" or "somewhat crazy."

14 ## Literary Element
Theme

Students should recognize that Higgins suggests a woman of Liza's social class— or at least someone who speaks as she does—is not worthy of courtesy and respect. Ask if students think Shaw saw great humor or serious importance—or both—in the relations between people of different social classes.

15 ## Literary Element
Irony

Question   Why is this passage humorously ironic? (*Possible response: Higgins responds to Liza's emotionally charged statement about her feelings with a comment on her grammar. She doesn't recognize that she proves Higgins's point about her grammar as she speaks, and he doesn't recognize that grammar and social status are not the primary determiners of personal worth. Liza also doesn't understand that "talk grammar" is how "ladies" speak.*)

BUILDING ENGLISH PROFICIENCY

Exploring Key Passages

Read aloud Pickering's second speech on page 674. Identify this as a key speech, for it describes the terms of the bet between Pickering and Higgins and sets in motion the conflict that will drive the play. The bet also develops a key idea—that the way in which one speaks determines one's "place" in life.

1. Have students note a significant question that rises from the bet. Mrs. Pearce asks at the top of column 2 on page 675, "But what's to become of her?"

2. Ask questions such as the following to encourage students to react to the bet and to the key ideas:

• How realistic is this bet? Would it happen in real life?

• What do you think will become of Eliza?

• What do you think of Higgins's idea? If speech does not determine one's place in life today, what does?

• When is it important to speak correctly?

16 Reading/Thinking Skills
Make Judgments

Question Do you think Liza is correct in her judgment of Higgins? *(Some students may agree with Liza, based on Higgins's egotistical comments. Others may think that it isn't so much that he cares about himself as that he cares about his field of study and the language, and he pays little attention to human beings—himself or anyone else.)*

17 Literary Element
Theme

Equality, social rights, and personal dignity are important themes in this play, on a variety of levels.

18 Literary Element
Dialogue

Higgins's comments show his quick wit, wily thinking, and prejudice. He interrupts Pickering's point with a bigoted remark apparently based on Liza's class or gender and then leaps to a philosophical questioning of perception. Pickering is not fooled. His point concerned Liza's rights and Higgins's responsibilities.

---

will be her own business again; so that's all right.

16 LIZA. Oh, you've no feeling heart in you: you don't care for nothing but yourself. *(She rises and takes the floor resolutely.)* Here! I've had enough of this. I'm going. *(Making for the door.)* You ought to be ashamed of yourself, you ought.

HIGGINS *(snatching a chocolate cream from the piano, his eyes suddenly beginning to twinkle with mischief).* Have some chocolates, Eliza.

LIZA *(halting, tempted).* How do I know what might be in them? I've heard of girls being drugged by the like of you.

(HIGGINS whips out his penknife; cuts a chocolate in two; puts one half into his mouth and bolts it; and offers her the other half.)

HIGGINS. Pledge of good faith, Eliza. I eat one half: you eat the other. (LIZA *opens her mouth to retort: he pops the half chocolate into it.*) You shall have boxes of them, barrels of them, every day. You shall live on them. Eh?

LIZA *(who has disposed of the chocolate after being nearly choked by it).* I wouldn't have ate it, only I'm too ladylike to take it out of my mouth.

HIGGINS. Listen, Eliza. I think you said you came in a taxi.

17 LIZA. Well, what if I did? I've as good a right to take a taxi as anyone else.

HIGGINS. You have, Eliza; and in future you shall have as many taxis as you want. You shall go up and down and round the town in a taxi every day. Think of that, Eliza.

MRS. PEARCE. Mr. Higgins: you're tempting the girl. It's not right. She should think of the future.

HIGGINS. At her age! Nonsense! Time enough to think of the future when you haven't any future to think of. No, Eliza: do as this lady does: think of other people's futures; but never think of your own. Think of chocolates, and taxis, and gold, and diamonds.

LIZA. No: I don't want no gold and no diamonds. I'm a good girl, I am. *(She sits down again, with an attempt at dignity.)*

HIGGINS. You shall remain so, Eliza, under the care of Mrs. Pearce. And you shall marry an officer in the Guards, with a beautiful mustache: the son of a marquis, who will disinherit him for marrying you, but will relent when he sees your beauty and goodness—

PICKERING. Excuse me, Higgins; but I really must interfere. Mrs. Pearce is quite right. If this girl is to put herself in your hands for six months for an experiment in teaching, she must understand thoroughly what she's doing.

18 HIGGINS. How can she? She's incapable of understanding anything. Besides, do any of us understand what we are doing? If we did, would we ever do it?

PICKERING. Very clever, Higgins; but not sound sense. *(To* ELIZA.*)* Miss Doolittle—

LIZA *(overwhelmed).* Ah-ah-ow-oo!

HIGGINS. There! That's all you'll get out of Eliza. Ah-ah-ow-oo! No use explaining. As a military man you ought to know that. Give her orders: that's what she wants. Eliza: you are to live here for the next six months, learning how to speak beautifully, like a lady in a florist's shop. If you're good and do whatever you're told, you shall sleep in a proper bedroom, and have lots to eat, and money to buy chocolates and take rides in taxis. If you're naughty and idle you will sleep in the back kitchen among the black beetles, and be walloped by Mrs. Pearce with a broomstick. At the end of six months you shall go to Buckingham Palace in a carriage, beautifully dressed. If the King finds out you're not a lady, you will be taken by the police to the Tower of London, where your head will be cut off as a warning to other presumptuous flower girls. If you are not found out, you shall have a present of seven-and-sixpence to start life with as a lady in a shop. If you refuse this offer you will be a most ungrateful and wicked girl; and the angels will weep for you. *(To* PICKERING.*)* Now are you satisfied, Pickering? *(To* MRS. PEARCE.*)* Can I put it more plainly and fairly, Mrs. Pearce?

MINI-LESSON: GRAMMAR

Sentence Complexity in Speaking and in Writing

Teach Tell students that when people speak, they often use a different sentence complexity than when they write. Shaw has captured the style of spoken sentences—often long and complex, with several sentences or thoughts strung together. Point out this sentence in column 2 above:

"And you shall marry an officer in the Guards, with a beautiful mustache: the son of a marquis, who will disinherit him for marrying you, but will relent when he sees your beauty and goodness—"

In formal writing, this may have been several sentences with different punctuation for easier readability, such as:

"Then you shall marry an officer in the Guards with a beautiful mustache. He will be the son of a marquis, who will disinherit him for marrying you. But the marquis will relent when he sees your beauty and goodness."

Question Why might Shaw have made Higgins speak this way? *(Possible response: to make him a distinctive character)*

Activity Idea Have students look for other long sentences of Higgins and rewrite them for formal writing.

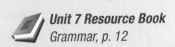
Unit 7 Resource Book
Grammar, p. 12

MRS. PEARCE (*patiently*). I think you'd better let me speak to the girl properly in private. I don't know that I can take charge of her or consent to the arrangement at all. Of course I know you don't mean her any harm; but when you get what you call interested in people's accents, you never think or care what may happen to them or you. Come with me, Eliza.

HIGGINS. That's all right. Thank you, Mrs. Pearce. Bundle her off to the bathroom.

LIZA (*rising reluctantly and suspiciously*). You're a great bully, you are. I won't stay here if I don't like. I won't let nobody wallop me. I never asked to go to Bucknam Palace, I didn't. I was never in trouble with the police, not me. I'm a good girl—

MRS. PEARCE. Don't answer back, girl. You don't understand the gentleman. Come with me. (*She leads the way to the door, and holds it open for* ELIZA.)

LIZA (*as she goes out*). Well, what I say is right. I won't go near the King, not if I'm going to have my head cut off. If I'd known what I was letting myself in for, I wouldn't have come here. I always been a good girl; and I never offered to say a word to him; and I don't owe him nothing; and I don't care; and I won't be put upon; and I have my feelings the same as anyone else—

(MRS. PEARCE *shuts the door; and* ELIZA's *plaints are no longer audible.* PICKERING *comes from the hearth to the chair and sits astride it with his arms on the back.*)

19 **PICKERING.** Excuse the straight question, Higgins. Are you a man of good character where women are concerned?

HIGGINS (*moodily*). Have you ever met a man of good character where women are concerned?

PICKERING. Yes: very frequently.

HIGGINS (*dogmatically, lifting himself on his hands to the level of the piano, and sitting on it with a bounce*). Well, I haven't. I find that the moment I let a woman make friends with me, she becomes jealous, exacting, suspi-cious, and a damned nuisance. I find that the moment I let myself make friends with a woman, I become selfish and tyrannical. Women upset everything. When you let them into your life, you find that the woman is driving at one thing and you're driving at another.

PICKERING. At what, for example?

HIGGINS (*coming off the piano restlessly*). Oh, Lord knows! I suppose the woman wants to live her own life; and the man wants to live his; and each tries to drag the other on to the wrong track. One wants to go north and the other south; and the result is that both have to go east, though they both hate the east wind. (*He sits down on the bench at the keyboard.*) So here I am, a confirmed old bachelor, and likely to remain so. **20**

PICKERING (*rising and standing over him gravely*). Come, Higgins! You know what I mean. If I'm to be in this business I shall feel responsible for that girl. I hope it's understood that no advantage is to be taken of her position.

HIGGINS. What! That thing! Sacred, I assure you. (*Rising to explain.*) You see, she'll be a pupil; and teaching would be impossible unless the pupils were sacred. I've taught scores of American millionairesses how to speak English: the best looking women in the world. I'm seasoned. They might as well be blocks of wood. *I* might as well be a block of wood. It's— **21**

(MRS. PEARCE *opens the door. She has* ELIZA's *hat in her hand.* PICKERING *retires to the easy chair at the hearth and sits down.*)

HIGGINS (*eagerly*). Well, Mrs. Pearce: is it all right?

MRS. PEARCE (*at the door*). I just wish to trouble you with a word, if I may, Mr. Higgins.

HIGGINS. Yes, certainly. Come in. (*She comes forward.*) Don't burn that, Mrs. Pearce. I'll keep it as a curiosity. (*He takes the hat.*)

MRS. PEARCE. Handle it carefully, sir, please. I had to promise her not to burn it; but I had better put it in the oven for a while.

19 Literary Focus

Inference

Questions

- What does Pickering mean when he asks about Higgins's character? (*Possible response: He wants to know if Higgins is planning to take advantage of Liza's position in the household in order to coerce her into a sexual relationship.*)

- How does Higgins sidestep the issue? (*He changes the question to a general philosophical consideration, rather than a question of his values.*)

A little later in the conversation, Higgins responds to Pickering's concern with the word *sacred*, assuring Pickering that he will act honorably as Liza's teacher.

20 Literary Element

Stereotype

Students may wish to discuss Higgins's generalizations about women, whom he blames for his own responses to women.

21 Literary Element

Characterization

Point out how Higgins dehumanizes relationships as he speaks about them. Note that this is consistent with an interpretation of his character as totally devoted to his work but careless of the persons involved.

BUILDING ENGLISH PROFICIENCY

Expanding Vocabulary Notebooks

ESL
LEP
ELD
SAE
LD

Suggest that students record unfamiliar terms as they read. Entries for these pages might include *resolutely, bolts, marquis, relent,* and *presumptuous* on page 676, and *plaints, dogmatically,* and *exacting* on page 677.

1. Encourage students to try using context clues first to figure out a word's meaning.

2. Have them verify their guesses by checking the meaning of the words in a dictionary or thesaurus.

Word	Meaning from Context	Actual Meaning
resolutely	bravely	in a determined way
bolts	swallows	swallows quickly

22 Reader's Response

Making Personal Connections

Questions Does Higgins's comment reveal that he knows himself accurately? *(It shows a lack of self-knowledge.)* Have you ever known someone like Higgins who has definite ideas about the behavior of others but inaccurate knowledge of his own behavior? How might you deal with such a person? *(Responses will vary based on personal experiences. Students might ignore, avoid, or help such a person.)*

23 Literary Element

Irony

Question How does Shaw inject humor into Higgins's denial? *(Higgins uses an expression about the devil; he thus swears in his denial of swearing.)*

24 Historical Note

Bloody

Bloody is the word that Mrs. Pearce is encouraging Higgins to avoid. The word is thought to be a contraction of the oath "By our Lady" (a reference to the Virgin Mary) or the oath "By Christ's blood." Secular use of such religious oaths was considered blasphemous or at least vulgar.

25 Literary Element

Alliteration

Here Higgins comes up with an odd excuse for swearing—poetic license in creating alliteration, using words beginning with the letter *b*.

HIGGINS *(putting it down hastily on the piano)*. Oh! Thank you. Well, what have you to say to me?

PICKERING. Am I in the way?

MRS. PEARCE. Not at all, sir. Mr. Higgins: will you please be very particular what you say before the girl?

HIGGINS *(sternly)*. Of course. I'm always particular about what I say. Why do you say this to me?

MRS. PEARCE *(unmoved)*. No, sir; you're not at all particular when you've mislaid anything or when you get a little impatient. Now it doesn't matter before me: I'm used to it. But you really must not swear before the girl.

HIGGINS *(indignantly)*. *I* swear! *(Most emphatically.)* I never swear. I detest the habit. What the devil do you mean?

MRS. PEARCE *(stolidly)*. That's what I mean, sir. You swear a great deal too much. I don't mind your damning and blasting, and what the devil and where the devil and who the devil—

HIGGINS. Mrs. Pearce: this language from your lips! Really!

678   UNIT SEVEN: THE EARLY TWENTIETH CENTURY

MRS. PEARCE *(not to be put off)*.—but there is a certain word I must ask you not to use. The girl has just used it herself because the bath was too hot. It begins with the same letter as bath. She knows no better: she learned it at her mother's knee. But she must not hear it from your lips.

HIGGINS *(loftily)*. I cannot charge myself with having ever uttered it, Mrs. Pearce. *(She looks at him steadfastly. He adds, hiding an uneasy conscience with a judicial air.)* Except perhaps in a moment of extreme and justifiable excitement.

MRS. PEARCE. Only this morning, sir, you applied it to your boots, to the butter, and to the brown bread.

HIGGINS. Oh, that! Mere alliteration, Mrs. Pearce, natural to a poet.

MRS. PEARCE. Well, sir, whatever you choose to call it, I beg you not to let the girl hear you repeat it.

HIGGINS. Oh, very well, very well. Is that all?

MRS. PEARCE. No, sir. We shall have to be very particular with this girl as to personal cleanliness.

HIGGINS. Certainly. Quite right. Most important.

MRS. PEARCE. I mean not to be slovenly about her dress or untidy in leaving things about.

HIGGINS *(going to her solemnly)*. Just so. I intended to call your attention to that. *(He passes on to* PICKERING, *who is enjoying the conversation immensely.)* It is these little things that matter, Pickering. Take care of the pence and the pounds will take care of themselves is as true of personal habits as of money. *(He comes to anchor on the hearthrug, with the air of a man in an unassailable[14] position.)*

MRS. PEARCE. Yes, sir. Then might I ask you not to come down to breakfast in your dressing-gown, or at any rate not to use it as a napkin to the extent you do, sir. And if you

---

14. **unassailable** (un ə sāl′ə bəl), *adj.* untroubled by doubt; unconquerable.

678

would be so good as not to eat everything off the same plate, and to remember not to put the porridge saucepan out of your hand on the clean tablecloth, it would be a better example to the girl. You know you nearly choked yourself with a fishbone in the jam only last week.

HIGGINS *(routed from the hearthrug and drifting back to the piano).* I may do these things sometimes in absence of mind; but surely I don't do them habitually. *(Angrily.)* By the way: my dressing-gown smells most damnably of benzine.

MRS. PEARCE. No doubt it does, Mr. Higgins. But if you will wipe your fingers—

HIGGINS *(yelling).* Oh very well, very well: I'll wipe them in my hair in the future.

MRS. PEARCE. I hope you're not offended, Mr. Higgins.

HIGGINS *(shocked at finding himself thought capable of an unamiable[15] sentiment).* Not at all, not at all. You're quite right, Mrs. Pearce: I shall be particularly careful before the girl. Is that all?

MRS. PEARCE. No, sir. Might she use some of those Japanese dresses you brought from abroad? I really can't put her back into her old things.

HIGGINS. Certainly. Anything you like. Is that all?

MRS. PEARCE. Thank you, sir. That's all. *(She goes out.)*

HIGGINS. You know, Pickering, that woman has the most extraordinary ideas about me. Here I am, a shy, <u>diffident</u>[16] sort of man. I've never been able to feel really grown-up and tremendous, like other chaps. And yet she's firmly persuaded that I'm an arbitrary overbearing bossing kind of person. I can't account for it.

*(*MRS. PEARCE *returns.)*

MRS. PEARCE. If you please, sir, the trouble's beginning already. There's a dustman[17] downstairs, Alfred Doolittle, wants to see you. He says you have his daughter here.

PICKERING *(rising).* Phew! I say! *(He retreats to the hearthrug.)*

HIGGINS *(promptly).* Send the blackguard[18] up.

MRS. PEARCE. Oh, very well, sir. *(She goes out.)*

PICKERING. He may not be a blackguard, Higgins.

HIGGINS. Nonsense. Of course he's a blackguard.

PICKERING. Whether he is or not, I'm afraid we shall have some trouble with him.

HIGGINS *(confidently).* Oh no: I think not. If there's any trouble he shall have it with me, not I with him. And we are sure to get something interesting out of him.

PICKERING. About the girl?

HIGGINS. No. I mean his dialect.

PICKERING. Oh!

MRS. PEARCE *(at the door).* Doolittle, sir. *(She admits* DOOLITTLE *and retires.)*

*(*ALFRED DOOLITTLE *is an elderly but vigorous dustman, clad in the costume of his profession, including a hat with a back brim covering his neck and shoulders. He has well marked and rather interesting features, and seems equally free from fear and conscience. He has a remarkably expressive voice, the result of a habit of giving vent to his feelings without reserve. His present pose is that of wounded honor and stern resolution.)*

DOOLITTLE *(at the door, uncertain which of the two gentlemen is his man).* Professor Higgins?

HIGGINS. Here. Good morning. Sit down.

DOOLITTLE. Morning, Governor. *(He sits down magisterially.)* I come about a very serious matter, Governor.

HIGGINS *(to* PICKERING*).* Brought up in Hounslow. Mother Welsh, I should think. *(*DOOLITTLE *opens his mouth, amazed.* HIGGINS *continues.)* What do you want, Doolittle?

DOOLITTLE *(menacingly).* I want my daughter: that's what I want. See?

---

15. **unamiable** (un ā′mē ə bəl), *adj.* unpleasant; disagreeable.
16. **diffident** (dif′ə dənt), *adj.* lacking in self-confidence; shy.
17. **dustman,** a trash or garbage collector.
18. **blackguard** (blag′ärd), *n.* low, contemptible person; scoundrel.

26 Literary Focus
Inference

Question What does the stage direction suggest about how the argument is going? *(Possible response: Higgins is losing the argument.)*

27 Literary Element
Characterization

Again, Higgins shows that his language studies take precedence over people in his dealings.

BUILDING ENGLISH PROFICIENCY

Analyzing Contrasting Views

Help students see that Shaw keeps the audience from disliking Higgins by making him a humorous character. Ask them to notice that on these two pages, Mrs. Pearce treats Higgins like a child and that he reacts as a child might. Ask students to contrast Higgins's view of himself with Mrs. Pearce's view of him.

Higgins's View	Mrs. Pearce's View
I never swear.	You swear a great deal.
I'm occasionally untidy due to absent-mindedness.	You're slovenly and you have bad manners.
I'm a shy poet.	You're bossy and difficult.

Question What is the rhetorical effect of this speech? *(Possible responses: Higgins gains an advantage by not only insisting that Doolittle is morally right, but also hinting that Doolittle has been slow in asserting his parental claims. Higgins is deflating any trouble or possible claims that Doolittle might try to make.)*

29 Historical Note
Public House

Public house is a British term for a bar or tavern, particularly the portion of a tavern open to the general public. (Many taverns in Britain also have or had private rooms for club members or other clientele.) Today public houses usually are called by the shortened term *pub*.

HIGGINS. Of course you do. You're her father, aren't you? You don't suppose anyone else wants her, do you? I'm glad to see you have some spark of family feeling left. She's upstairs. Take her away at once.

DOOLITTLE *(rising, fearfully taken aback)*. What!

HIGGINS. Take her away. Do you suppose I'm going to keep your daughter for you?

DOOLITTLE *(remonstrating)*. Now, now, look here, Governor. Is this reasonable? Is it fairity to take advantage of a man like this? The girl belongs to me. You got her. Where do I come in? *(He sits down again.)*

HIGGINS. Your daughter had the audacity to come to my house and ask me to teach her how to speak properly so that she could get a place in a flower-shop. This gentleman and my housekeeper have been here all the time. *(Bullying him.)* How dare you come here and attempt to blackmail me? You sent her here on purpose.

DOOLITTLE *(protesting)*. No, Governor.

HIGGINS. You must have. How else could you possibly know that she is here?

DOOLITTLE. Don't take a man up like that, Governor.

HIGGINS. The police shall take you up. This is a plant—a plot to extort money by threats. I shall telephone for the police. *(He goes resolutely to the telephone and opens the directory.)*

DOOLITTLE. Have I asked you for a brass farthing? I leave it to the gentleman here: have I said a word about money?

HIGGINS *(throwing the book aside and marching down on* DOOLITTLE *with a poser)*. What else did you come for?

DOOLITTLE *(sweetly)*. Well, what would a man come for? Be human, Governor.

HIGGINS *(disarmed)*. Alfred: did you put her up to it?

DOOLITTLE. So help me, Governor, I never did. I take my Bible oath. I ain't seen the girl these two months past.

HIGGINS. Then how did you know she was here?

DOOLITTLE *("most musical, most melancholy")*. I'll tell you, Governor, if you'll only let me get a word in. I'm willing to tell you. I'm wanting to tell you. I'm waiting to tell you.

HIGGINS. Pickering: this chap has a certain natural gift of rhetoric. Observe the rhythm of his native woodnotes wild. "I'm willing to tell you: I'm wanting to tell you: I'm waiting to tell you." Sentimental rhetoric! That's the Welsh strain in him. It also accounts for his mendacity and dishonesty.

PICKERING. Oh, please, Higgins: I'm west country[19] myself. *(To* DOOLITTLE.) How did you know the girl was here if you didn't send her?

DOOLITTLE. It was like this, Governor. The girl took a boy in the taxi to give him a jaunt. Son of her landlady, he is. He hung about on the chance of her giving him another ride home. Well, she sent him back for her luggage when she heard you was willing for her to stop here. I met the boy at the corner of Long Acre and Endell Street.

HIGGINS. Public house. Yes?

DOOLITTLE. The poor man's club, Governor: why shouldn't I?

PICKERING. Do let him tell his story, Higgins.

DOOLITTLE. He told me what was up. And I ask you, what was my feelings and my duty as a father? I says to the boy, "You bring me the luggage," I says—

PICKERING. Why didn't you go for it yourself?

DOOLITTLE. Landlady wouldn't have trusted me with it, Governor. She's that kind of woman: you know. I had to give the boy a penny afore he trusted me with it, the little swine. I brought it to her just to oblige you like, and make myself agreeable. That's all.

HIGGINS. How much luggage?

DOOLITTLE. Musical instrument, Governor. A few pictures, a trifle of jewelry, and a birdcage. She said she didn't want no clothes.

---

19. **west country,** the counties in the southwest of England, especially Devon and Cornwall, which are near Wales.

MINI-LESSON: VOCABULARY

Shades of Meaning

Teach Point out the words *mendacity* and *dishonesty* in Higgins's first speech in column 2 on this page. Explain that while the words are close in meaning, *mendacity* refers to lying or untruthfulness, while *dishonesty* is a broader term and refers not only to lying and dishonesty but also to cheating, defrauding, and deceiving.

Question Why might Shaw have included both words? *(Possible response: Neither one alone fully describes Doolittle's approach.)*

Activity Idea Have students write a description of one of the characters. They should choose words with fine shades of meaning to make their description precise.

What was I to think from that, Governor? I ask you as a parent what was I to think?

HIGGINS. So you came to rescue her from worse than death, eh?

DOOLITTLE (*appreciatively, relieved at being so well understood*). Just so, Governor. That's right.

PICKERING. But why did you bring her luggage if you intended to take her away?

DOOLITTLE. Have I said a word about taking her away? Have I now?

HIGGINS (*determinedly*). You're going to take her away, double quick. (*He crosses to the hearth and rings the bell.*)

DOOLITTLE (*rising*). No, Governor. Don't say that. I'm not the man to stand in my girl's light. Here's a career opening for her, as you might say; and—

(MRS. PEARCE *opens the door and awaits orders.*)

HIGGINS. Mrs. Pearce: this is Eliza's father. He has come to take her away. Give her to him. (*He goes back to the piano, with an air of washing his hands of the whole affair.*)

DOOLITTLE. No. This is a misunderstanding. Listen here—

MRS. PEARCE. He can't take her away, Mr. Higgins: how can he? You told me to burn her clothes.

DOOLITTLE. That's right. I can't carry the girl through the streets like a blooming monkey, can I? I put it to you.

HIGGINS. You have put it to me that you want your daughter. Take your daughter. If she has no clothes go out and buy her some.

DOOLITTLE (*desperate*). Where's the clothes she come in? Did I burn them or did your missus here?

MRS. PEARCE. I am the housekeeper, if you please. I have sent for some clothes for your girl. When they come you can take her away. You can wait in the kitchen. This way, please.

(DOOLITTLE, *much troubled, accompanies her to the door; then hesitates; finally turns confidentially to* HIGGINS.)

DOOLITTLE. Listen here, Governor. You and me is men of the world, ain't we?

HIGGINS. Oh! Men of the world, are we? You'd better go, Mrs. Pearce.

MRS. PEARCE. I think so, indeed, sir. (*She goes, with dignity.*)

PICKERING. The floor is yours, Mr. Doolittle.

DOOLITTLE (*to* PICKERING). I thank you, Governor. (*To* HIGGINS, *who takes refuge on the piano bench, a little overwhelmed by the proximity of his visitor; for* DOOLITTLE *has a professional flavor of dust about him.*) Well, the truth is, I've taken a sort of fancy to you, Governor; and if you want the girl, I'm not so set on having her back home again but what I might be open to an arrangement. Regarded in the light of a young woman, she's a fine handsome girl. As a daughter she's not worth her keep and so I tell you straight. All I ask is my rights as a father; and you're the last man alive to expect me to let her go for nothing; for I can see you're one of the straight sort, Governor. Well, what's a five-pound note to you? And what's Eliza to me? (*He returns to his chair and sits down judicially.*)

PICKERING. I think you ought to know, Doolittle, that Mr. Higgins's intentions are entirely honorable.

DOOLITTLE. Course they are, Governor. If I thought they wasn't, I'd ask fifty.

HIGGINS (*revolted*). Do you mean to say, you callous rascal, that you would sell your daughter for £50?

DOOLITTLE. Not in a general way I wouldn't; but to oblige a gentleman like you I'd do a good deal, I do assure you.

PICKERING. Have you no morals, man?

DOOLITTLE (*unabashed*).[20] Can't afford them, Governor. Neither could you if you was as poor as me. Not that I mean any harm, you know. But if Liza is going to have a bit out of this, why not me too?

HIGGINS (*troubled*). I don't know what to do, Pickering. There can be no question that as

───────────────

20. **unabashed** (un′ə basht′), *adj.* not ashamed or embarrassed.

30

31

---

30 Multicultural Note
Class Differences

Doolittle refers to Mrs. Pearce as Higgins's "missus," or wife, before he learns that she is the housekeeper, a servant. Mrs. Pearce regards this error as a social blunder. Students may cite comparable first impressions that anyone might make when encountering people of another social or economic class or cultural group. Various cultural and language groups also have different customary titles for wives, husbands, parents, and people in other household relations.

31 Reading/Thinking Skills
Compare and Contrast

Questions Does this exchange change your view of Higgins? How? (*Possible response: It shows the limits to Higgins's carelessness about other people. Although he has talked freely about beatings and such, he is surprised by Doolittle's cavalier or selfish attitude about moral values and social decorum.*) This dialogue concerns serious moral issues, but Shaw plays it for humor and irony. Doolittle often is regarded by theater audiences as laughably candid about his self-interests and cynical ethics.

BUILDING ENGLISH PROFICIENCY

Exploring Dramatic Emotion

Help students grasp this scene's emotions by role-playing.

1. Choose volunteers to play the roles on these two pages: Doolittle, Higgins, Pickering, and Mrs. Pearce.

2. Give students time to rehearse. Let other students help by looking up the meaning of unfamiliar words.

3. Have students act their roles in front of the class.

4. Afterwards, discuss which emotions best describe what happens here. (It might be interesting to have the actors and the audience jot down their responses separately and then see how close a match they have.) Record responses on a web, which may include *surprise, fear, anger, confidence, excitement, desperation, relief, revulsion.*

ESL
LEP
ELD
SAE
LD

32

Reading/Thinking Skills

Recognize the Use of Persuasion

Question What are the main ideas in Doolittle's argument? *(Possible response: Doolittle claims that he is discriminated against because he is a poor man honestly seeking selfish enjoyment rather than following the morality of the middle class.)*

33

Reading/Thinking Skills

Predict

Question Note that Higgins, again, looks at someone in terms of language. How do you think Doolittle will respond to this idea? *(Some students may say that Doolittle has made it fairly clear that he likes things the way they are. Others may think that he, like Liza, will leap at the opportunity to rise.)*

34

Literary Element

Characterization

Question How do Pickering's and Doolittle's ideas of "bad use" of money compare or contrast? *(Possible response: Pickering probably is afraid Doolittle will get drunk or otherwise waste the five pounds. Doolittle thinks that quickly spending it on a spree for himself and his woman is a good use; to him, bad use is to save money as the middle class does, making it a burden and a care.)*

---

a matter of morals it's a positive crime to give this chap a farthing. And yet I feel a sort of rough justice in his claim.

DOOLITTLE. That's it, Governor. That's all I say. A father's heart, as it were.

PICKERING. Well, I know the feeling; but really it seems hardly right—

32 **DOOLITTLE.** Don't say that, Governor. Don't look at it that way. What am I, Governors both? I ask you, what am I? I'm one of the undeserving poor: that's what I am. Think of what that means to a man. It means that he's up agen middle class morality all the time. If there's anything going, and I put in for a bit of it, it's always the same story: "You're undeserving; so you can't have it." But my needs is as great as the most deserving widow that ever got money out of six different charities in one week for the death of the same husband. I don't need less than a deserving man: I need more. I don't eat less hearty than him; and I drink a lot more. I want a bit of amusement, cause I'm a thinking man. I want cheerfulness and a song and a band when I feel low. Well, they charge me just the same for everything as they charge the deserving. What is middle class morality? Just an excuse for never giving me anything. Therefore, I ask you, as two gentlemen, not to play that game on me. I'm playing straight with you. I ain't pretending to be deserving. I'm undeserving; and I mean to go on being undeserving. I like it; and that's the truth. Will you take advantage of a man's nature to do him out of the price of his own daughter what he's brought up and fed and clothed by the sweat of his brow until she's growed big enough to be interesting to you two gentlemen? Is five pounds unreasonable? I put it to you; and I leave it to you.

33 **HIGGINS** (*rising, and going over to* PICKERING). Pickering: if we were to take this man in hand for three months, he could choose between a seat in the Cabinet and a popular pulpit in Wales.

PICKERING. What do you say to that, Doolittle?

DOOLITTLE. Not me, Governor, thank you kindly. I've heard all the preachers and all the prime ministers—for I'm a thinking man and game for politics or religion or social reform same as all the other amusements—and I tell you it's a dog's life any way you look at it. Undeserving poverty is my line. Taking one station in society with another, it's—it's—well, it's the only one that has any ginger in it, to my taste.

HIGGINS. I suppose we must give him a fiver.

PICKERING. He'll make a bad use of it, I'm afraid.

DOOLITTLE. Not me, Governor, so help me I won't. Don't you be afraid that I'll save it and **34** spare it and live idle on it. There won't be a penny of it left by Monday: I'll have to go to work same as if I'd never had it. It won't pauperize me, you bet. Just one good spree for myself and the missus, giving pleasure to ourselves and employment to others, and satisfaction to you to think it's not been throwed away. You couldn't spend it better.

HIGGINS (*taking out his pocket book and coming between* DOOLITTLE *and the piano*). This is irresistible. Let's give him ten. (*He offers two notes to the dustman.*)

DOOLITTLE. No, Governor. She wouldn't have the heart to spend ten; and perhaps I shouldn't neither. Ten pounds is a lot of money: it makes a man feel prudent[21] like; and then goodbye to happiness. You give me what I ask you, Governor: not a penny more, and not a penny less.

PICKERING. Why don't you marry that missus of yours? I rather draw the line at encouraging that sort of immorality.

DOOLITTLE. Tell her so, Governor: tell her so. *I'm* willing. It's me that suffers by it. I've no hold on her. I got to be agreeable to her. I got to give her presents. I got to buy her clothes something sinful. I'm a slave to that

---

21. **prudent** (prüd′nt), *adj.* sensible; discreet.

woman, Governor, just because I'm not her lawful husband. And she knows it too. Catch her marrying me! Take my advice, Governor: marry Eliza while she's young and don't know no better. If you don't you'll be sorry for it after. If you do, she'll be sorry for it after; but better her than you, because you're a man, and she's only a woman and don't know how to be happy anyhow.

HIGGINS. Pickering: if we listen to this man another minute, we shall have no convictions left. (*To* DOOLITTLE.) Five pounds I think you said.

DOOLITTLE. Thank you kindly, Governor.

HIGGINS. You're sure you won't take ten?

DOOLITTLE. Not now. Another time, Governor.

HIGGINS (*handing him a five-pound note*). Here you are.

DOOLITTLE. Thank you, Governor. Good morning. (*He hurries to the door, anxious to get away with his booty.*[22] *When he opens it he is confronted with a dainty and exquisitely clean young* JAPANESE LADY *in a simple blue cotton kimono printed cunningly with small white jasmine blossoms.* MRS. PEARCE *is with her. He gets out of her way deferentially and apologizes.*) Beg pardon, miss.

THE JAPANESE LADY. Garn! Don't you know your own daughter?

DOOLITTLE.	(*exclaiming*	Bly me! It's Eliza!
HIGGINS.	*simul-*	What's that! This!
PICKERING.	*taneously*)	By Jove!

LIZA. Don't I look silly?

HIGGINS. Silly?

MRS. PEARCE (*at the door*). Now, Mr. Higgins, please don't say anything to make the girl conceited about herself.

HIGGINS (*conscientiously*). Oh! Quite right, Mrs. Pearce. (*To* LIZA.) Yes: damned silly.

MRS. PEARCE. Please, sir.

HIGGINS (*correcting himself*). I mean extremely silly.

LIZA. I should look all right with my hat on. (*She takes up her hat; puts it on; and walks across the room to the fireplace with a fashionable air.*)

HIGGINS. A new fashion, by George! And it ought to look horrible!

DOOLITTLE (*with fatherly pride*). Well, I never thought she'd clean up as good looking as that, Governor. She's a credit to me, ain't she?

LIZA. I tell you, it's easy to clean up here. Hot and cold water on tap, just as much as you like, there is. Woolly towels, there is; and a towel horse so hot, it burns your fingers. Soft brushes to scrub yourself, and a wooden bowl of soap smelling like primroses. Now I know why ladies is so clean. Washing's a treat for them. Wish they saw what it is for the like of me!

HIGGINS. I'm glad the bathroom met with your approval.

LIZA. It didn't: not all of it; and I don't care who hears me say it. Mrs. Pearce knows.

HIGGINS. What was wrong, Mrs. Pearce?

MRS. PEARCE (*blandly*). Oh, nothing, sir. It doesn't matter.

LIZA. I had a good mind to break it. I didn't know which way to look. But I hung a towel over it, I did.

HIGGINS. Over what?

MRS. PEARCE. Over the looking-glass, sir.

HIGGINS. Doolittle: you have brought your daughter up too strictly.

DOOLITTLE. Me! I never brought her up at all, except to give her a lick of a strap now and again. She ain't accustomed to it, you see: that's all. But she'll soon pick up your free-and-easy ways.

LIZA. I'm a good girl, I am; and I won't pick up no free-and-easy ways.

HIGGINS. Eliza: if you say again that you're a good girl, your father shall take you home.

LIZA. Not him. You don't know my father. All he come here for was to touch you for some money to get drunk on.

DOOLITTLE. Well, what else would I want money for? To put into the plate in church, I suppose. (*She puts out her tongue at him. He is so incensed by this that* PICKERING *presently finds it*

---

22. booty (bū′tē), *n.* money, especially seized illegally; gains; winnings.

35 Reading/Thinking Skills
Evaluate

Students may realize that Shaw is presenting Doolittle as a comic scoundrel. His comments about Higgins marrying Liza show that he does not believe Higgins's statements about his intentions concerning Liza. Doolittle, however, is not too concerned about her fate. Discuss how the playwright pokes fun at Doolittle's views.

Question   Do you think Shaw succeeds in making Doolittle's approach to life funny? (*Possible responses: Yes; Doolittle is ridiculous. Yes; he is a scoundrel but he's honest about it, to a funny degree. No; it would be funny if he got his just desserts.*)

36 Literary Element
Theme

Liza's comments shed light on the difference between a flower girl and a lady—the lady has access to the implements that allow her to create an attractive personal appearance.

BUILDING ENGLISH PROFICIENCY

Sequencing Key Events

The following activity will help students keep track of important events in Shaw's plot.

1. Assign a group of students to make up a sentence or two summarizing key events in Acts One and Two. Ask them to write their sentences on large index cards, one card per event.

2. Collect and shuffle the cards. Then ask other groups to put the cards in the order of the events in Acts One and Two.

3. At the end of each act, choose different groups to write sentences and sequence the cards. Number and post the cards in correct sequence on the walls of your classroom for reference.

🐾 MULTICULTURAL NOTE

Students may contrast Doolittle's attitudes with approaches that people of various cultures use to guide their children, encourage achievement in education or advancement in life, and discipline their daughters and sons.

---

37 Reader's Response

Making Personal Connections

Question How do you feel about Liza's wish that she could show up her recent friends or fellow flower girls at Tottenham Court Road? *(Some students may blame Liza for planning to snub those whom she may be fortunate enough to leave behind socially and economically. Other students may understand her desire to show off, while others may find it humorous.)*

Check Test

1. Why does Liza come to Higgins's house? *(She wants speaking lessons to help her become a lady in a flower shop.)*

2. Why is Higgins at first disappointed to see Liza? *(He already has recorded her accent.)*

3. What plan do Higgins and Pickering develop for Liza? *(Higgins will try to teach her upper-class language and make her appear to be a "duchess.")*

4. Who is Doolittle? *(Liza's father)*

5. What does Doolittle convince Higgins to give him? *(five pounds)*

Unit 7 Resource Book
Alternate Check Test, p. 13

---

necessary to step between them.) Don't you give me none of your lip; and don't let me hear you giving this gentleman any of it neither, or you'll hear from me about it. See?

HIGGINS. Have you any further advice to give her before you go, Doolittle? Your blessing, for instance.

DOOLITTLE. No, Governor: I ain't such a mug as to put up my children to all I know myself. Hard enough to hold them in without that. If you want Eliza's mind improved, Governor, you do it yourself with a strap. So long, gentlemen. *(He turns to go.)*

HIGGINS *(impressively).* Stop. You'll come regularly to see your daughter. It's your duty, you know. My brother is a clergyman; and he could help you in your talks with her.

DOOLITTLE *(evasively).* Certainly. I'll come, Governor. Not just this week, because I have a job at a distance. But later on you may depend on me. Afternoon, gentlemen. Afternoon, ma'am. *(He takes off his hat to* MRS. PEARCE, *who disdains the salutation and goes out. He winks at* HIGGINS, *thinking him probably a fellow-sufferer from* MRS. PEARCE'S *difficult disposition, and follows her.)*

LIZA. Don't you believe the old liar. He'd as soon you set a bull-dog on him as a clergyman. You won't see him again in a hurry.

HIGGINS. I don't want to, Eliza. Do you?

LIZA. Not me. I don't want never to see him again, I don't.

PICKERING. What is his trade, Eliza?

LIZA. Taking money out of other people's pockets into his own. His proper trade's a navvy;[23] and he works at it sometimes too—for exercise—and earns good money at it. Ain't you going to call me Miss Doolittle any more?

PICKERING. I beg your pardon, Miss Doolittle. It was a slip of the tongue.

LIZA. Oh, I don't mind; only it sounded so genteel. I should just like to take a taxi to the corner of Tottenham Court Road and get out there and tell it to wait for me, just to put the girls in their place a bit. I wouldn't speak to them, you know.

PICKERING. Better wait till we get you something really fashionable.

HIGGINS. Besides, you shouldn't cut[24] your old friends now that you have risen in the world. That's what we call snobbery.

LIZA. You don't call the like of them my friends now, I should hope. They've took it out of me often enough with their ridicule when they had the chance; and now I mean to get a bit of my own back. But if I'm to have fashionable clothes, I'll wait. I should like to have some. Mrs. Pearce says you're going to give me some to wear in bed at night different to what I wear in the daytime; but it do seem a waste of money when you could get something to show. Besides, I never could fancy changing into cold things on a winter night.

MRS. PEARCE *(coming back).* Now, Eliza. The new things have come for you to try on.

LIZA. Ah-ow-oo-ooh! *(She rushes out.)*

MRS. PEARCE *(following her).* Oh, don't rush about like that, girl. *(She shuts the door behind her.)*

HIGGINS. Pickering: we have taken on a stiff job.

PICKERING *(with conviction).* Higgins: we have.

---

23. **navvy** (nav′ē), *n.* unskilled laborer, especially one doing excavation or construction work.

24. **cut,** snub; refuse to recognize socially.

MINI-LESSON: STUDY SKILLS

Researching Periodicals

Teach Draw students' attention to Eliza's reference in column 2 to fashionable clothes. Explain that if students wanted to find out about fashions in the second decade of this century, they could consult advertisements in periodicals from the appropriate years. Periodicals are stored on microfilm or microfiche and are available to view on special viewing equipment, usually in a special room of a library or resource center. Reference librarians can help with equipment instructions.

Activity Idea Have students research British fashion in 1911–1912 by using periodicals from the time. They can draw or describe various fashions of the time.

After Reading

Act 2

Shaping Your Response

Making Connections

1. Do you agree more with Doolittle's characterization of himself as one of the "undeserving poor" or with Liza's description of him as a liar and a disgrace? Explain.

Analyzing the Play

2. What can you **infer** about the way Higgins lives from Mrs. Pearce's instructions to him?

3. In your opinion, is Higgins a gentleman? Explain.

4. Both Doolittle and Higgins threaten Liza with violence. Why do you think they feel free to make these threats?

5. Explain how the inferences Higgins and Pickering make about Doolittle and the inferences he makes about them get in the way of their **communication.**

6. Explain how Doolittle redefines conventional ideas about a father's rights, morals, and the life of the undeserving poor.

Extending the Ideas

7. In turning Liza's plans into a bet, Higgins and Pickering assume their right to take over her life. Does this assumption of the rights of one class or gender over another occur in the U.S. today? Explain.

8. If you wanted to improve your life, what would you change about yourself?

Vocabulary Study

For each phrase in the first column, choose the phrase in the second column that is closest in meaning.

1. astounded and dumfounded
2. sturdy birdie
3. faint complaint
4. battered and scattered
5. famed, not ashamed
6. polite fight
7. seize a breeze
8. cheerful earful
9. shy guy
10. obtains gains

a. *unabashed* celebrity
b. *stupent* and overwhelmed
c. *genteel* argument
d. quiet *remonstrance*
e. *diffident* male
f. *genial* announcement
g. beaten and *strewn*
h. gets *booty*
i. *robust* canary
j. catch a *zephyr*

Pygmalion—Act Two   **685**

After Reading

MAKING CONNECTIONS

1. Students may be put off by his attitude toward Liza and agree with her view.

2. He has no manners and little self-knowledge and is disorderly.

3. While Higgins was born a gentleman, i.e., to a certain social position, he does not behave as a gentleman might; he does not adapt his behavior to fit the social situation or company, as a gentleman would.

4. Doolittle feels justified because he is her father. Higgins may feel justified threatening a person of a "low" social class. (Higgins's threats seem rhetorical.) Both may consider it acceptable to make threats against a poor, young woman.

5. Students should recognize that miscommunications come mainly from assumptions that differ, Doolittle's surprising ethics, and Higgins's presumptive attitudes.

6. Doolittle presents himself as a victim of other people's moral values. He claims they prevent him from getting basic necessities to enjoy life. He claims a right to make money from his daughter's success and a right to be "undeserving."

7. Students may cite examples of people forcing their will on others, such as on their employees, their children, or their loved ones.

8. Students may wish to change their appearance, habits, financial status, or skills.

VOCABULARY STUDY

1. b   **6.** c
2. i   **7.** j
3. d   **8.** f
4. g   **9.** e
5. a   **10.** h

Unit 7 Resource Book
Vocabulary, p. 11
Vocabulary Test, p. 14

Selection Test

Unit 7 Resource Book,
pp. 15–16

685

ACT THREE

It is MRS. HIGGINS'S *at-home day.[1] Nobody has yet arrived. Her drawing room, in a flat on Chelsea Embankment,[2] has three windows looking on the river; and the ceiling is not so lofty as it would be in an older house of the same pretension. The windows are open, giving access to a balcony with flowers in pots. If you stand with your face to the windows, you have the fireplace on your left and the door in the right-hand wall close to the corner nearest the windows.*

MRS. HIGGINS *was brought up on Morris and Burne Jones;[3] and her room, which is very unlike her son's room in Wimpole Street, is not crowded with furniture and little tables and nick-nacks. In the middle of the room there is a big ottoman; and this, with the carpet, the Morris wallpapers, and the Morris chintz window curtains and brocade covers of the ottoman and its cushions, supply all the ornament, and are much too handsome to be hidden by odds and ends of useless things. A few good oil-paintings from the exhibitions in the Grosvenor Gallery thirty years ago (the Burne Jones, not the Whistler side of them) are on the walls. The only landscape is a Cecil Lawson on the scale of a Rubens.[4] There is a portrait of* MRS. HIGGINS *as she was when she defied fashion in her youth in one of the beautiful Rossettian[5] costumes which, when caricatured by people who did not understand, led to the absurdities of popular estheticism in the eighteen-seventies.*

In the corner diagonally opposite the door MRS. HIGGINS, *now over sixty and long past taking the trouble to dress out of the fashion, sits writing at an elegantly simple writing table with a bell button within reach of her hand. There is a Chippendale chair further back in the room between her and the window nearest her side. At the other side of the room, further forward, is an Elizabethan chair roughly carved in the taste of Inigo Jones. On the same side a piano in a decorated case. The corner between the fireplace and the window is occupied by a divan cushioned in Morris chintz.*

It is between four and five in the afternoon.

The door is opened violently; and HIGGINS *enters with his hat on.*

MRS. HIGGINS *(dismayed).* Henry! *(Scolding him.)* What are you doing here today? It is my at-home day: you promised not to come. *(As he bends to kiss her, she takes his hat off, and presents it to him.)*

HIGGINS. Oh bother! *(He throws the hat down on the table.)*

MRS. HIGGINS. Go home at once.

HIGGINS *(kissing her).* I know, Mother. I came on purpose.

MRS. HIGGINS. But you mustn't. I'm serious, Henry. You offend all my friends: they stop coming whenever they meet you.

HIGGINS. Nonsense! I know I have no small talk; but people don't mind. *(He sits on the settee.)*

2

MRS. HIGGINS. Oh! Don't they? Small talk indeed! What about your large talk? Really, dear, you mustn't stay.

HIGGINS. I must. I've a job for you. A phonetic job.

MRS. HIGGINS. No use, dear. I'm sorry; but I can't get round your vowels; and though I like to get pretty postcards in your patent shorthand, I always have to read the copies in ordinary writing you so thoughtfully send me.

HIGGINS. Well, this isn't a phonetic job.

---

1. **at-home day,** the day a person in society receives callers.
2. **drawing room . . . Chelsea Embankment.** A drawing room is used mostly for entertaining guests. Chelsea is a pleasant residential district along the bank of the Thames.
3. **Morris and Burne-Jones.** William Morris (1834–1896) and Edward Burne-Jones (1833–1898) were members of a decorating firm noted for fine carvings, stained glass, metalwork, wallpapers, chintzes, tiles, and carpets. (See page 1 for a painting by Burne-Jones. The theme portfolio covers on pages 207, 383, 643, and 955 are designs by Morris.)
4. **Cecil Lawson . . . Rubens.** Cecil Lawson (1851–1882) was an English landscape painter. Peter Paul Rubens (1577–1640) was a Flemish painter known for his large canvases.
5. **Rosettian,** inspired by the paintings of Dante Gabriel Rosetti (1828–1882), whose work often pictures women in flowing robes. (See pages 90–91.)

ACT THREE SUMMARY

Pygmalion

Higgins comes to his mother's house to wait for her visitors, informing her that Eliza is coming too. He explains the bet and says Eliza's pronunciation is now fine, but he has restricted her to talk only about weather and health. The Eynsford Hills and Colonel Pickering arrive, but Higgins's own lack of social grace makes the conversation difficult. Eliza arrives and performs beautifully until the subject of influenza comes up. Eliza tells of her aunt's death, lapsing into slang, bad grammar, and topics shocking to Mrs. Eynsford Hill and fascinating to Freddy, even using the expletive "bloody." Higgins follows Eliza out, urging Clara to use the "new small talk." Clara does so, saying "bloody" herself and shocking her mother. Higgins's mother tries to talk with Higgins and Pickering about Eliza's situation, but they miss every point she makes.

For summaries in other languages, see the Building English Proficiency book.

MRS. HIGGINS. You said it was.

HIGGINS. Not your part of it. I've picked up a girl.

MRS. HIGGINS. Does that mean some girl has picked you up?

HIGGINS. Not at all. I don't mean a love affair.

MRS. HIGGINS. What a pity!

HIGGINS. Why?

MRS. HIGGINS. Well, you never fall in love with anyone under forty-five. When will you discover that there are some rather nice-looking young women about?

HIGGINS. Oh, I can't be bothered with young women. My idea of a lovable woman is something as like you as possible. I shall never get into the way of seriously liking young women: some habits lie too deep to be changed. *(Rising abruptly and walking about, jingling his money and his keys in his trouser pocket.)* Besides, they're all idiots.

MRS. HIGGINS. Do you know what you would do if you really loved me, Henry?

HIGGINS. Oh bother! What? Marry, I suppose?

MRS. HIGGINS. No. Stop fidgeting and take your hands out of your pockets. *(With a gesture of despair, he obeys and sits down again.)* That's a good boy. Now tell me about the girl.

HIGGINS. She's coming to see you.

MRS. HIGGINS. I don't remember asking her.

HIGGINS. You didn't. *I* asked her. If you'd known her you wouldn't have asked her.

MRS. HIGGINS. Indeed! Why?

HIGGINS. Well, it's like this. She's a common flower girl. I picked her off the curbstone.

MRS. HIGGINS. And invited her to my at-home!

HIGGINS *(rising and coming to her to coax her).* Oh, that'll be all right. I've taught her to speak properly; and she has strict orders as to her behavior. She's to keep to two subjects: the weather and everybody's health—Fine day and How do you do, you know—and not to let herself go on things in general. That will be safe.

MRS. HIGGINS. Safe! To talk about our health! About our insides! Perhaps about our outsides! How could you be so silly, Henry?

HIGGINS *(impatiently).* Well, she must talk about something. *(He controls himself and sits down again.)* Oh, she'll be all right; don't you fuss. Pickering is in it with me. I've a sort of bet on that I'll pass her off as a duchess in six months. I started on her some months ago; and she's getting on like a house on fire. I shall win my bet. She has a quick ear; and she's been easier to teach than my middle-class pupils because she's had to learn a complete new language. She talks English almost as you talk French.

MRS. HIGGINS. That's satisfactory, at all events.

HIGGINS. Well, it is and it isn't.

MRS. HIGGINS. What does that mean?

HIGGINS. You see, I've got her pronunciation all right; but you have to consider not only how a girl pronounces, but what she pronounces; and that's where—

(They are interrupted by the PARLOR MAID, *announcing guests.)*

THE PARLOR MAID. Mrs. and Miss Eynsford Hill. *(She withdraws.)*

HIGGINS. Oh Lord! *(He rises; snatches his hat from the table; and makes for the door; but before he reaches it his mother introduces him.)*

(MRS. *and* MISS EYNSFORD HILL *are the mother and daughter who sheltered from the rain in Covent Garden. The mother is well bred, quiet, and has the habitual anxiety of straitened means.[6] The daughter has acquired a gay air of being very much at home in society; the bravado of genteel poverty.)*

MRS. EYNSFORD HILL *(to* MRS. HIGGINS*).* How do you do? *(They shake hands.)*

MISS EYNSFORD HILL. How d'you do? *(She shakes.)*

MRS. HIGGINS *(introducing).* My son Henry.

MRS. EYNSFORD HILL. Your celebrated son! I have so longed to meet you, Professor Higgins.

HIGGINS *(glumly, making no movement in her direction).* Delighted. *(He backs against the piano and bows brusquely.)*

---

6. **straitened means,** limited financial resources.

Pygmalion—Act Three   **687**

| 3 | **Literary Focus**
Inference

Question   What light do these comments shed on Higgins's relationship with Liza? *(Possible responses: Higgins considers it an impersonal relationship. He is not romantically inclined, and even if he were, he would not likely be romantically interested in Liza, who is uncultured and young. He fails to understand people's ideas about him.)*

| 4 | **Reading/Thinking Skills**
Summarize

Question   According to his statement, what do you think Higgins expects will happen at his mother's "at-home"? *(He expects Liza to speak properly, in terms of pronunciation and social acceptability.)*

| 5 | **Literary Elements**
Plot and Characterization

Shaw uses dramatic coincidences to develop plot. Higgins accidentally meeting the Eynsford Hills twice in key encounters would be unlikely in London, except in a play. If necessary, help students understand the meaning of "the bravado of genteel poverty." Bravado is a show of boldness by someone who is not feeling brave. Genteel poverty is the economic hardship of people who are without much money, but who move in upper-class social circles, perhaps because of noble rank or former wealth.

BUILDING ENGLISH PROFICIENCY

Exploring Parent-Child Relationships

Help students relate to the idea that parents and children may be quite different and yet still alike in important ways.

1. Have groups of students create Venn diagrams that record ways in which Higgins and his mother are different and three ways in which they are alike.

2. Ask students to write in their private journals about how they and their parents are different and alike.

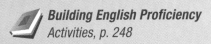

Building English Proficiency Activities, p. 248

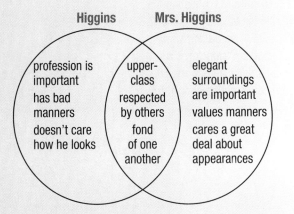

Higgins | Mrs. Higgins

profession is important / has bad manners / doesn't care how he looks

upper-class / respected by others / fond of one another

elegant surroundings are important / values manners / cares a great deal about appearances

ESL
LEP
ELD
SAE
LD

687

MISS EYNSFORD HILL *(going to him with confident familiarity)*. How do you do?

6 **HIGGINS** *(staring at her)*. I've seen you before somewhere. I haven't the ghost of a notion where; but I've heard your voice. *(Drearily.)* It doesn't matter. You'd better sit down.

MRS. HIGGINS. I'm sorry to say that my celebrated son has no manners. You mustn't mind him.

MISS EYNSFORD HILL *(gaily)*. I don't. *(She sits in the Elizabethan chair.)*

MRS. EYNSFORD HILL *(a little bewildered)*. Not at all. *(She sits on the ottoman between her daughter and MRS. HIGGINS, who has turned her chair away from the writing-table.)*

HIGGINS. Oh, have I been rude? I didn't mean to be.

(He goes to the central window, through which, with his back to the company, he contemplates the river and the flowers in Battersea Park on the opposite bank as if they were a frozen desert. The PARLOR MAID returns, ushering in PICKERING.)

THE PARLOR MAID. Colonel Pickering. *(She withdraws.)*

PICKERING. How do you do, Mrs. Higgins?

7 **MRS. HIGGINS.** So glad you've come. Do you know Mrs. Eynsford Hill—Miss Eynsford Hill? *(Exchange of bows. The COLONEL brings the Chippendale chair a little forward between MRS. HILL and MRS. HIGGINS, and sits down.)*

PICKERING. Has Henry told you what we've come for?

HIGGINS *(over his shoulder)*. We were interrupted: damn it!

MRS. HIGGINS. Oh Henry, Henry, really!

MRS. EYNSFORD HILL *(half rising)*. Are we in the way?

MRS. HIGGINS *(rising and making her sit down again)*. No, no. You couldn't have come more fortunately: we want you to meet a friend of ours.

HIGGINS *(turning hopefully)*. Yes, by George! We want two or three people. You'll do as well as anybody else.

(The PARLOR MAID returns, ushering FREDDY.)

THE PARLOR MAID. Mr. Eynsford Hill.

HIGGINS *(almost audibly, past endurance)*. God of Heaven! Another of them.

FREDDY *(shaking hands with MRS. HIGGINS)*. Ahdedo?

MRS. HIGGINS. Very good of you to come. *(Introducing.)* Colonel Pickering.

FREDDY *(bowing)*. Ahdedo?

MRS. HIGGINS. I don't think you know my son, Professor Higgins.

FREDDY *(going to HIGGINS)*. Ahdedo?

8 **HIGGINS** *(looking at him much as if he were a pickpocket)*. I'll take my oath I've met you before somewhere. Where was it?

FREDDY. I don't think so.

HIGGINS *(resignedly)*. It don't matter, anyhow. Sit down.

(He shakes FREDDY's hand, and almost slings him on to the ottoman with his face to the windows; then comes round to the other side of it.)

HIGGINS. Well, here we are, anyhow! *(He sits down on the ottoman next MRS. EYNSFORD HILL, on her left.)* And now, what the devil are we going to talk about until Eliza comes?

MRS. HIGGINS. Henry: you are the life and soul of the Royal Society's soirées;[7] but really you're rather trying on more commonplace occasions.

HIGGINS. Am I? Very sorry. *(Beaming suddenly.)* I suppose I am, you know. *(Uproariously.)* Ha, ha!

MISS EYNSFORD HILL *(who considers HIGGINS quite eligible matrimonially)*. I sympathize. *I* haven't any small talk. If people would only be frank and say what they really think!

9 **HIGGINS** *(relapsing into gloom)*. Lord forbid!

MRS. EYNSFORD HILL *(taking up her daughter's cue)*. But why?

HIGGINS. What they think they ought to think is bad enough, Lord knows; but what they really think would break up the whole show.

---

7. **Royal Society . . . soirée** (swä rä′), *n.* The Royal Society is a well-known scientific society in England. A soirée is an evening social gathering.

Do you suppose it would be really agreeable if I were to come out now with what *I* really think?

MISS EYNSFORD HILL (*gaily*). Is it so very cynical?

HIGGINS. Cynical! Who the dickens said it was cynical? I mean it wouldn't be decent.

MRS. EYNSFORD HILL (*seriously*). Oh! I'm sure you don't mean that, Mr. Higgins.

HIGGINS. You see, we're all savages, more or less. We're supposed to be civilized and cultured—to know all about poetry and philosophy and art and science, and so on; but how many of us know even the meanings of these names? (*To* MISS HILL.) What do you know of poetry? (*To* MRS. HILL.) What do you know of science? (*Indicating* FREDDY.) What does he know of art or science or anything else? What the devil do you imagine I know of philosophy?

10

MRS. HIGGINS (*warningly*). Or of manners, Henry?

THE PARLOR MAID (*opening the door*). Miss Doolittle. (*She withdraws.*)

HIGGINS (*rising hastily and running to* MRS. HIGGINS). Here she is, Mother. (*He stands on tiptoe and makes signs over his mother's head to* ELIZA *to indicate to her which lady is her hostess.*)

(ELIZA, *who is exquisitely dressed, produces an impression of such remarkable distinction and beauty as she enters that they all rise, quite fluttered. Guided by* HIGGINS's *signals, she comes to* MRS. HIGGINS *with studied grace.*)

LIZA (*speaking with pedantic correctness of pronunciation and great beauty of tone*). How do you do, Mrs. Higgins? (*She gasps slightly in making sure of the* H *in Higgins, but is quite successful.*)

11

Mr. Higgins told me I might come.

MRS. HIGGINS (*cordially*). Quite right: I'm very glad indeed to see you.

PICKERING. How do you do, Miss Doolittle?

LIZA (*shaking hands with him*). Colonel Pickering, is it not?

MRS. EYNSFORD HILL. I feel sure we have met before, Miss Doolittle. I remember your eyes.

LIZA. How do you do? (*She sits down on the ottoman gracefully in the place just left vacant by* HIGGINS.)

MRS. EYNSFORD HILL (*introducing*). My daughter Clara.

LIZA. How do you do?

CLARA (*impulsively*). How do you do? (*She sits down on the ottoman beside* ELIZA, *devouring her with her eyes.*)

12

FREDDY (*coming to their side of the ottoman*). I've certainly had the pleasure.

MRS. EYNSFORD HILL (*introducing*). My son Freddy.

LIZA. How do you do?

(FREDDY *bows and sits down in the Elizabethan chair, infatuated.*)

HIGGINS (*suddenly*). By George, yes: it all comes back to me! (*They stare at him.*) Covent Garden! (*Lamentably.*) What a damned thing!

MRS. HIGGINS. Henry, please! (*He is about to sit on the edge of the table.*) Don't sit on my writing table: you'll break it.

HIGGINS (*sulkily*). Sorry.

(*He goes to the divan, stumbling into the fender and over the fire-irons on his way; extricating himself with muttered imprecations; and finishing his disastrous journey by throwing himself so impatiently on the divan that he almost breaks it.* MRS. HIGGINS *looks at him, but controls herself and says nothing. A long and painful pause ensues.*)

MRS. HIGGINS (*at last, conversationally*). Will it rain, do you think?

13

LIZA. The shallow depression in the west of these islands is likely to move slowly in an easterly direction. There are no indications of any great change in the barometrical situation.

FREDDY. Ha! ha! How awfully funny!

LIZA. What is wrong with that, young man? I bet I got it right.

FREDDY. Killing!

MRS. EYNSFORD HILL. I'm sure I hope it won't turn cold. There's so much influenza about. It runs right through our whole family regularly every spring.

---

10 **Reader's Response**

Making Personal Connections

Question   What do you think of Higgins's analysis of society, as expressed here? *(Some students may agree that people pretend to be more cultured than they are or that society relies on pretense. Other students may think that Higgins is too cynical, disparaging, and rude.)*

11 **Reading/Thinking Skills**

Compare and Contrast

Question   How do Liza's appearance and speech contrast with her previous appearance and language in the play? *(Here Liza is speaking in careful, refined, and formal English, in contrast to her former informal, "ungrammatical" dialect. Her dress and appearance are more elegant.)*

12 **Reading/Thinking Skills**

Clarify

Question   What is Clara's attitude toward Liza here? *(She is fascinated by Eliza, taking her for a real lady of higher social rank.)*

13 **Literary Focus**

Inference

Question   Why do you think Mrs. Higgins asks about the weather? *(to give Liza an opening for the conversational topic she has prepared)*

BUILDING ENGLISH PROFICIENCY

Exploring Key Ideas

Higgins's remarks to the guests reveal Shaw's opinions on "society" manners and ideas. Have students relate Shaw's ideas about his world to their ideas about their world.

Activity Ideas

- Work with students to list Higgins's reasons for disliking people like the Eynsford Hills.

- On this page, Eliza's beautiful speech and clothes overwhelm the guests. Ask: Do you think that people today continue to be impressed by "image"? Invite students to examine newspapers and magazines for stories and pictures that show people being valued solely for their appearance.

- Have groups of students act out the kind of social gatherings and parties that they like and dislike.

Art Study

Visual Literacy This picture clearly illustrates a convention of the theater. In a play on a proscenium stage, a group of characters talking usually do not all face one another, as in a circle. Instead, they face the audience.

You might ask a volunteer to explain why the characters are conversing in this lined-up arrangement. Students who have not seen many plays probably will recognize the kind of arrangement from television shows, in which groups of characters face the camera.

14 **Reading/Thinking Skills**
Understand Sequence

Question What changes occur in Liza's speaking style and topics from the beginning of page 690 to the end of the page? Explain this dialogue sequence. *(Possible response: First she innocently mentions her aunt's death. Then she slips into slang and suggests that her aunt was murdered. To support her claim, she reveals that her father had fed the aunt gin. Liza elaborates, slipping into dialect more and more, and revealing details about theft and drinking in her family. Before she finishes, she depicts drinking as a healthy habit for husbands. She doesn't recognize how outrageous her account is to this audience.)*

LIZA *(darkly)*. My aunt died of influenza: so they said.

MRS. EYNSFORD HILL *(clicks her tongue sympathetically)*. !!!

LIZA *(in the same tragic tone)*. But it's my belief they done the old woman in.

MRS. HIGGINS *(puzzled)*. Done her in?

LIZA. Y-e-e-e-es, Lord love you! Why should she die of influenza? She come through diphtheria right enough the year before. I saw her with my own eyes. Fairly blue with it, she was. They all thought she was dead; but my father he kept ladling gin down her throat till she came to so sudden that she bit the bowl off the spoon.

MRS. EYNSFORD HILL *(startled)*. Dear me!

LIZA *(piling up the indictment)*. What call would a woman with that strength in her have to die of influenza? What become of her new straw hat that should have come to me? Somebody pinched it; and what I say is, them as pinched it done her in.

MRS. EYSNSFORD HILL. What does doing her in mean?

HIGGINS *(hastily)*. Oh, that's the new small talk. To do a person in means to kill them.

MRS. EYNSFORD HILL *(to ELIZA, horrified)*. You surely don't believe that your aunt was killed?

LIZA. Do I not! Them she lived with would have killed her for a hatpin, let alone a hat.

MRS. EYNSFORD HILL. But it can't have been right for your father to pour spirits down her throat like that. It might have killed her.

LIZA. Not her. Gin was mother's milk to her. Besides, he'd poured so much down his own throat that he knew the good of it.

MRS. EYNSFORD HILL. Do you mean that he drank?

LIZA. Drank! My word! Something chronic.

MRS. EYNSFORD HILL. How dreadful for you!

LIZA. Not a bit. It never did him no harm what I could see. But then he did not keep it up regular. *(Cheerfully.)* On the burst, as you might say, from time to time. And always more agreeable when he had a drop in. When he was out of work, my mother used to give him fourpence and tell him to go out and not come back until he'd drunk himself cheerful and loving-like. There's lots of women has to make their husbands drunk to make them fit to live with. *(Now quite at her ease.)* You see, it's like this. If a man has a bit of a conscience, it always takes him when he's sober; and then it makes him low-spirited. A drop of booze just takes that off and makes him happy. *(To* FREDDY, *who is in convulsions of suppressed laughter.)* Here! What are you sniggering at?

14

MINI-LESSON: GRAMMAR

Colloquialisms, Slang, Idioms, Jargon

Teach Read aloud these phrases that Eliza says on page 690: "done her in," "pinched it," "on the burst." Explain that the first two are slang—examples of language used by a group in informal speech to replace standard terms. The first means "killed her." The second means "stole it." The third is a colloquialism—an expression used in ordinary conversation as opposed to formal speech. Remind students that other kinds of specialized language found in informal speech are idioms (phrases or expressions with a figurative meaning that cannot be understood from the ordinary meaning of the words) and jargon (specialized language of a certain group).

Question Why might Shaw have included these informal usages? *(Possible response: to give character and authenticity to Eliza's discourse)*

Activity Idea Using an unabridged dictionary, have students review some of Eliza's speeches from Acts One and Two and make a chart of the examples of slang, colloquialisms, idioms, and jargon that they find.

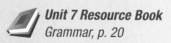 *Unit 7 Resource Book*
Grammar, p. 20

FREDDY (*opening the door for her*). Are you walking across the Park, Miss Doolittle? If so—

LIZA. Walk! Not bloody[8] likely. (*Sensation.*) I am going in a taxi. (*She goes out.*)

(PICKERING *gasps and sits down.* FREDDY *goes out on the balcony to catch another glimpse of* ELIZA.)

MRS. EYNSFORD HILL (*suffering from shock*). Well, I really can't get used to the new ways.

CLARA (*throwing herself discontentedly into the Elizabethan chair*). Oh, it's all right, Mamma, quite right. People will think we never go anywhere or see anybody if you are so old-fashioned.

MRS. EYNSFORD HILL. I daresay I am very old-fashioned; but I do hope you won't begin using that expression, Clara. I have got accustomed to hear you talking about men as rotters, and calling everything filthy and beastly; though I do think it horrible and unladylike. But this last is really too much. Don't you think so, Colonel Pickering?

PICKERING. Don't ask me. I've been away in India for several years; and manners have changed so much that I sometimes don't know whether I'm at a respectable dinner-table or in a ship's forecastle.

CLARA. It's all a matter of habit. There's no right or wrong in it. Nobody means anything by it. And it's so quaint, and gives such a smart emphasis to things that are not in themselves very witty. I find the new small talk delightful and quite innocent.

FREDDY. The new small talk. You do it so awfully well.

LIZA. If I was doing it proper, what was you laughing at? (*To* HIGGINS.) Have I said anything I oughtn't?

MRS. HIGGINS (*interposing*). Not at all, Miss Doolittle.

LIZA. Well, that's a mercy, anyhow. (*Expansively.*) What I always say is—

HIGGINS (*rising and looking at his watch*). Ahem!

LIZA (*looking round at him; taking the hint; and rising*). Well: I must go. (*They all rise.* FREDDY *goes to the door.*) So pleased to have met you. Goodbye. (*She shakes hands with* MRS. HIGGINS.)

MRS. HIGGINS. Goodbye.

LIZA. Goodbye, Colonel Pickering.

PICKERING. Goodbye, Miss Doolittle. (*They shake hands.*)

LIZA (*nodding to the others*). Goodbye, all.

---

8. **bloody,** British slang for "cursed" or "confounded" but considered so improper in Shaw's day that he was urged to remove the word from the play. Audiences gasped and then laughed uproariously when they heard it.

Pygmalion—Act Three **691**

Mrs. Higgins's perfectly ladylike response—responding to an extended and potentially embarrassing faux pas with a calm reply—demonstrates how unflappable and graceful she is.

16 Literary Element
Plot

Question Why do you think Shaw chose to use this as Liza's exit line? (*Possible responses: It punctuates the scene's drama, as Liza says her most outrageous thing and leaves the room, totally unaware of having been improper. It is funny.*)

17 Reader's Response
Making Personal Connections

Question Which character's views on slang and informal language are closest to yours? Explain. (*Some students may side with Clara, while others may agree with Mrs. Eynsford Hill.*)

BUILDING ENGLISH PROFICIENCY

Analyzing Relationships Among Characters

Creating a character sociogram is one way to help students explore how people in a group relate to one another.

1. Ask students to copy the chart shown here.

2. Wherever they see an arrow between the boxes, tell them to write one word that describes the dominant feeling that one person has for the other on pages 688–691. For example, Clara's feeling for Eliza might be described as pitying, admiring, jealous, shocked, angry, or fearful.

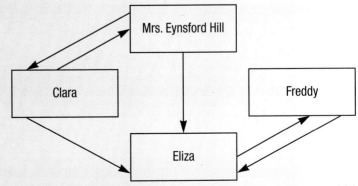

Inference

Given the customs and expectations of "ladylike" behavior in early twentieth-century England, Clara's expression is even more shocking than Higgins's harsher curse.

Question   Why might Clara have used such a term in this company? *(Possible responses: Liza had introduced the term into the conversation; Clara is following Higgins's lead and may wish to impress him; she also may feel such language is newly in style, rather than vulgar.)*

Make Judgments

Question   Henry and Mrs. Higgins seem to have different impressions of Liza's "performance." Who do you think has a more accurate or reasonable view of Liza's readiness to converse in "polite society"? *(Possible response: Mrs. Higgins is more aware of Liza's inappropriate language for a garden party; Henry Higgins's judgment may be skewed by how much he wants to think Liza is ready.)*

MRS. EYNSFORD HILL (*rising*). Well, after that, I think it's time for us to go. (PICKERING *and* HIGGINS *rise.*)

CLARA (*rising*). Oh yes: we have three at-homes to go to still. Goodbye, Mrs. Higgins. Goodbye, Colonel Pickering. Goodbye, Professor Higgins.

HIGGINS (*coming grimly at her from the divan, and accompanying her to the door*). Goodbye. Be sure you try on that small talk at the three at-homes. Don't be nervous about it. Pitch it in strong.

CLARA (*all smiles*). I will. Goodbye. Such nonsense, all this early Victorian prudery!

HIGGINS (*tempting her*). Such damned nonsense!

CLARA. Such bloody nonsense!

MRS. EYNSFORD HILL (*convulsively*). Clara!

CLARA. Ha! ha! (*She goes out radiant, conscious of being thoroughly up to date, and is heard descending the stairs in a stream of silvery laughter.*)

FREDDY (*to the heavens at large*). Well, I ask you— (*He gives it up, and comes to* MRS. HIGGINS.) Goodbye.

MRS. HIGGINS (*shaking hands*). Goodbye. Would you like to meet Miss Doolittle again?

FREDDY (*eagerly*). Yes, I should, most awfully.

MRS. HIGGINS. Well, you know my days.

FREDDY. Yes. Thanks awfully. Goodbye. (*He goes out.*)

MRS. EYNSFORD HILL. Goodbye, Mr. Higgins.

HIGGINS. Goodbye. Goodbye.

MRS. EYNSFORD HILL (*to* PICKERING). It's no use. I shall never be able to bring myself to use that word.

PICKERING. Don't. It's not compulsory, you know. You'll get on quite well without it.

MRS. EYNSFORD HILL. Only, Clara is so down on me if I am not positively reeking with the latest slang. Goodbye.

PICKERING. Goodbye (*They shake hands.*)

MRS. EYNSFORD HILL (*to* MRS. HIGGINS). You mustn't mind Clara. (PICKERING, *catching from her lowered tone that this is not meant for him to hear, discreetly joins* HIGGINS *at the window.*) We're so poor! And she gets so few par-

ties, poor child! She doesn't quite know. (MRS. HIGGINS, *seeing that her eyes are moist, takes her hand sympathetically and goes with her to the door.*) But the boy is nice. Don't you think so?

MRS. HIGGINS. Oh, quite nice. I shall always be delighted to see him.

MRS. EYNSFORD HILL. Thank you, dear. Goodbye. (*She goes out.*)

HIGGINS (*eagerly*). Well? Is Eliza presentable? (*He swoops on his mother and drags her to the ottoman, where she sits down in* ELIZA's *place with her son on her left.* PICKERING *returns to his chair on her right.*)

MRS. HIGGINS. You silly boy, of course she's not presentable. She's a triumph of your art and of her dressmaker's; but if you suppose for a moment that she doesn't give herself away in every sentence she utters, you must be perfectly cracked about her.

PICKERING. But don't you think something might be done? I mean something to eliminate the sanguinary[9] element from her conversation.

MRS. HIGGINS. Not as long as she is in Henry's hands.

HIGGINS (*aggrieved*). Do you mean that my language is improper?

MRS. HIGGINS. No, dearest: it would be quite proper—say on a canal barge; but it would not be proper for her at a garden party.

HIGGINS (*deeply injured*). Well I must say—

PICKERING (*interrupting him*). Come, Higgins: you must learn to know yourself. I haven't heard such language as yours since we used to review the volunteers in Hyde Park twenty years ago.

HIGGINS (*sulkily*). Oh, well, if you say so, I suppose I don't always talk like a bishop.

MRS. HIGGINS (*quieting* HENRY *with a touch*). Colonel Pickering: will you tell me what is the exact state of things in Wimpole Street?

PICKERING (*cheerfully: as if this completely changed the subject*). Well, I have come to live there

---

9. **sanguinary** (sang′gwə ner′ē), *adj.* with much blood, a reference to Liza's use of the word *bloody*.

with Henry. We work together at my Indian Dialects; and we think it more convenient—

MRS. HIGGINS. Quite so. I know all about that: it's an excellent arrangement. But where does this girl live?

HIGGINS. With us, of course. Where should she live?

MRS. HIGGINS. But on what terms? Is she a servant? If not, what is she?

PICKERING (*slowly*). I think I know what you mean, Mrs. Higgins.

HIGGINS. Well, dash me if *I* do! I've had to work at the girl every day for months to get her to the present pitch. Besides, she's useful. She knows where my things are, and remembers my appointments and so forth.

MRS. HIGGINS. How does your housekeeper get on with her?

HIGGINS. Mrs. Pearce? Oh, she's jolly glad to get so much taken off her hands; for before Eliza came, she used to have to find things and remind me of my appointments. But she's got some silly bee in her bonnet about Eliza. She keeps saying "You don't think, sir": doesn't she, Pick?

PICKERING. Yes: that's the formula. "You don't think, sir." That's the end of every conversation about Eliza.

HIGGINS. As if I ever stop thinking about the girl and her confounded vowels and consonants. I'm worn out, thinking about her, and watching her lips and her teeth and her tongue, not to mention her soul, which is the quaintest of the lot.

MRS. HIGGINS. You certainly are a pretty pair of babies, playing with your live doll.

HIGGINS. Playing! The hardest job I ever tackled: make no mistake about that, Mother. But you have no idea how frightfully interesting it is to take a human being and change her into a quite different human being by creating a new speech for her. It's filling up the deepest gulf that separates class from class and soul from soul.

PICKERING (*drawing his chair closer to* MRS. HIG-

GINS *and bending over to her eagerly*). Yes: it's enormously interesting. I assure you, Mrs. Higgins, we take Eliza very seriously. Every week—every day almost—there is some new change. (*Closer again.*) We keep records of every stage—dozens of gramophone disks and photographs—

HIGGINS (*assailing her at the other ear*). Yes, by George: it's the most absorbing experiment I ever tackled. She regularly fills our lives up: doesn't she, Pick?

PICKERING. We're always talking Eliza.

HIGGINS. Teaching Eliza.

PICKERING. Dressing Eliza.

MRS. HIGGINS. What!

HIGGINS. Inventing new Elizas.

HIGGINS.	*(speaking together)*	You know, she has the most extraordinary quickness of ear. I assure you, my dear Mrs. Higgins, that girl
PICKERING.		
HIGGINS.		Just like a parrot. I've tried her with every
PICKERING.		is a genius. She can play the piano quite beautifully.
HIGGINS.		possible sort of sound that a human being can make—
PICKERING.		We have taken her to classical concerts and to music
HIGGINS.		Continental dialects, African dialects, Hottentot
PICKERING.		halls; and it's all the same to her: she plays everything
HIGGINS.		clicks, things it took me years to get hold of; and
PICKERING.		she hears right off when she comes home, whether it's

20 **21**

20

Literary Focus

Inference

Question   What is Mrs. Higgins wondering about here? (*She seems shocked at the men's reference to dressing Eliza, by which they mean they plan the clothing she will wear. Mrs. Higgins wonders what they mean, and she probably hopes it is not meant literally.*)

21

Reading/Thinking Skills

Clarify

Shaw mixes what Pickering and Higgins are saying simultaneously. Here are their speeches, separated:

HIGGINS: You know, she has the most extraordinary quickness of ear. Just like a parrot. I've tried her with every possible sort of sound that a human being can make—Continental dialects, African dialects, Hottentot clicks, things it took me years to get hold of; and she picks them up like a shot, right away, as if she had been at it all her life.

PICKERING: I assure you, my dear Mrs. Higgins, that girl is a genius. She can play the piano quite beautifully. We have taken her to classical concerts and to music halls; and it's all the same to her: she plays everything she hears right off when she comes home, whether it's Beethoven and Brahms or Lehar and Lionel Monckton: though six months ago, she'd never as much as touched a piano—

BUILDING ENGLISH PROFICIENCY

Exploring Adjectives and Adverbs

Use the stage directions to extend students' understanding of adverbs and adjectives.

1. Point out that stage directions often tell how an actor is to speak or act (adverb) or what the condition of the speaker is (adjective). The stage directions also include verb forms ending in *-ing;* these are present participles, which do what verbs can do (take objects and so on) but which act as adjectives telling what the speaker is doing.

2. Work with students to develop a T-chart that lists various stage directions and classifies each as adverb or adjective. (Examples of each type from pages 692–693 are shown.)

Stage Directions	Adjective or Adverb?
eagerly	adverb
aggrieved	adjective
rising	adjective
tempting	adjective
convulsively	adverb

ESL
LEP
ELD
SAE
LD

Reader's Response

Making Personal Connections

Question The only women who were expected to work at jobs in Shaw's time were poor women who had to work. Mrs. Higgins recognizes that her son and Pickering are giving Liza manners that will mark her as a woman of an economic class in which she will be unable to work—yet she will not have money. Do you think that today a woman of refined manners would have a similar problem? *(Students are likely to think that times have changed, and women of all social classes today have opportunities to work.)*

Check Test

1. Why does Higgins take Liza to his mother's home? *(to test her ability to converse in polite society)*

2. Where had the Eynsford Hills and Higgins met before? *(at St. Paul's in Act One)*

3. What, according to Liza, ended her aunt's life? *(She was "done in," or murdered.)*

4. Besides Higgins, what two men come to Mrs. Higgins's "at-home"? *(Freddy and Pickering)*

5. What is a new skill that Liza has acquired, according to Higgins and Pickering? *(Possible responses: piano playing, excellent English pronunciation, mimicry, and helping Higgins keep track of things)*

Unit 7 Resource Book
Alternate Check Test, p. 21

HIGGINS.	*(speaking together)*	she picks them up like a shot, right away, as if she had Beethoven and Brahms or Lehar and Lionel Monckton:[10]
PICKERING.		
HIGGINS.		been at it all her life. though six months ago, she'd never as much as touched a piano—
PICKERING.		

MRS. HIGGINS (*putting her fingers in her ears, as they are by this time shouting one another down with an intolerable noise*). Sh-sh-sh—sh! (*They stop.*)

PICKERING. I beg your pardon. (*He draws his chair back apologetically.*)

HIGGINS. Sorry. When Pickering starts shouting nobody can get a word in edgeways.

MRS. HIGGINS. Be quiet, Henry. Colonel Pickering: don't you realize that when Eliza walked into Wimpole Street, something walked in with her?

PICKERING. Her father did. But Henry soon got rid of him.

MRS. HIGGINS. It would have been more to the point if her mother had. But as her mother didn't something else did.

PICKERING. But what?

MRS. HIGGINS (*unconsciously dating herself by the word*). A problem.

PICKERING. Oh, I see. The problem of how to pass her off as a lady.

HIGGINS. I'll solve that problem. I've half solved it already.

MRS. HIGGINS. No, you two infinitely stupid male creatures: the problem of what is to be done with her afterwards.

HIGGINS. I don't see anything in that. She can go her own way, with all the advantages I have given her.

MRS. HIGGINS. The advantages of that poor woman who was here just now! The manners and habits that disqualify a fine lady from earning her own living without giving her a fine lady's income! Is that what you mean?

PICKERING (*indulgently, being rather bored*). Oh, that will be all right, Mrs. Higgins. (*He rises to go.*)

HIGGINS (*rising also*). We'll find her some light employment.

PICKERING. She's happy enough. Don't you worry about her. Goodbye. (*He shakes hands as if he were consoling a frightened child, and makes for the door.*)

HIGGINS. Anyhow, there's no good bothering now. The thing's done. Goodbye, Mother. (*He kisses her, and follows* PICKERING.)

PICKERING (*turning for a final consolation*). There are plenty of openings. We'll do what's right. Goodbye.

HIGGINS (*to* PICKERING *as they go out together*). Let's take her to the Shakespeare exhibition at Earls Court.

PICKERING. Yes: let's. Her remarks will be delicious.

HIGGINS. She'll mimic all the people for us when we get home.

PICKERING. Ripping. (*Both are heard laughing as they go downstairs.*)

MRS. HIGGINS (*rises with an impatient bounce, and returns to her work at the writing table. She sweeps a litter of disarranged papers out of her way; snatches a sheet of paper from her stationery case; and tries resolutely to write. At the third line she gives it up; flings down her pen; grips the table angrily and exclaims*). Oh, men! Men!!! Men!!!

---

10. **Beethoven . . . Monckton,** all composers, the last two of light music.

MINI-LESSON: SPEAKING AND LISTENING

Communicating Clearly and Effectively

Teach Have pairs of students try to deliver the simultaneous speeches of Higgins and Pickering in a way that is intelligible. Discuss why Shaw might have written these lines in this way. What could he count on the audience grasping? *(Possible response: that Eliza consumes both men's time and attention; that Eliza has skills in speech and piano playing)* Help students draw the conclusion that clear, effective communication requires taking turns.

Activity Idea Have students work on developing techniques that will help them remember the points they want to make, examples they want to give, facts they want to mention, and so on, when another person is speaking. Encourage them to try different mnemonic devices, as well as note-taking, to keep track of what they want to say next.

Act 3

Making Connections

Shaping Your Response

1. What do you think of Liza's "performance" in Mrs. Higgins's drawing room?

2. What advice could you give her to help improve her conversation?

Analyzing the Play

3. During Mrs. Higgins's at-home, who has better manners, Higgins or Liza? What is the point of this contrast?

4. Why do you think Clara chooses to say "bloody nonsense!" at the end of her visit?

5. Higgins and Pickering praise Liza's ability to imitate sounds "just like a parrot" and to play the piano by ear. What might such abilities have to do with **communication** using language?

6. What insights have you gained so far into possible reasons why Higgins is a bachelor?

Extending the Ideas

7. In your opinion, how important are good manners today, and who defines good or bad manners?

Literary Focus: Inference

An **inference** is a reasonable conclusion based on hints and clues. The characters in *Pygmalion* make many inferences about each other, and we, in turn, make inferences about them.

1. What inference does Mrs. Higgins make when Higgins tells her he has picked up a girl?

2. What inferences do Mrs. Eynsford Hill, Clara, and Freddy make about Liza? Upon what clues do they base their inferences?

3. What inference does Mrs. Higgins make about possible problems inherent in the situation?

4. From Mrs. Eynsford Hill's admission to Mrs. Higgins about how poor they are and how few parties Clara gets, what do you infer about the Eynsford Hills' position in society?

Pygmalion—Act Three **695**

After Reading

MAKING CONNECTIONS

1. Students may find it funny, absurd, or a "nice try." They may wonder why Higgins thought she was ready.

2. Students may wish to inform her about choosing suitable topics of conversation, formal or customary language, or substitutes for some of her coarse expressions.

3. Possible response: Liza has better (although not cultured) manners than Higgins. Students may think the point is that simply being cultured doesn't make a person a lady or gentleman; that some things cannot be taught; that good manners depend on personality, not social class.

4. She may be trying to impress Higgins or trying to appear up-to-date. She may just be caught up in the language of the conversation.

5. Liza's gift might lead her to be sensitive to how people communicate to her. Alternately, it may mean that human speech sometimes is not so much about communicating as about following customs.

6. Possible responses: He says he only likes older women and women who are like his mother. His manners make it seem likely that women in whom he would be interested would not be interested in him.

7. Some students may feel that good manners are always important because they show respect or they smooth social interactions. Others may feel that some behavior regarded as good manners is too restrictive. Students may feel that individual communities and cultures define good manners, or they may feel that the majority population defines good manners.

LITERARY FOCUS: INFERENCE

Possible Responses

1. Mrs. Higgins thinks Higgins has fallen in love.

2. Possible responses: Mrs. Eynsford Hill infers that they have met before, based on the look in Eliza's eyes. Clara infers that Eliza is a real society lady, based on her dress and initial conversation. Freddy infers that she might be interested in him, from her age and responses to him.

3. Mrs. Higgins infers that teaching Eliza speech and manners will remove her from her social class without giving her the means to live as a member of the social class for which her manners and speech fit her.

4. Possible response: They used to be wealthier but have fallen on hard times.

Selection Test

Unit 7 Resource Book
pp. 23–24

Vocabulary Preview

purgatory, any condition of temporary suffering

presumptuous, too bold; forward

writhe, twist and turn; suffer mentally

subjective, existing in the mind

cant, insincere talk

dudgeon, feeling of anger or resentment

perfunctorily, mechanically; indifferently

infamous, shamefully bad

lavish, give or spend freely

decorum, proper behavior

Students can add the words and definitions to their Writer's Notebooks.

Literary Focus
Inference

Questions

- What emotions is Eliza feeling? *(Possible response: She is worn out and depressed.)*

- Why might she feel this way? *(Possible responses: because the bet is over; because she doesn't know what will happen to her now)*

Literary Focus
Inference

Question   Why did Eliza leave the room? *(Possible responses: She can't stand to be with Higgins any more; she's going to get his slippers.)*

Unit 7 Resource Book
Graphic Organizer, p. 25
Study Guide, p. 26

ACT FOUR

The Wimpole Street laboratory. Midnight. Nobody in the room. The clock on the mantelpiece strikes twelve. The fire is not alight: it is a summer night. Presently HIGGINS *and* PICKERING *are heard on the stairs.*

HIGGINS (*calling down to* PICKERING). I say, Pick: lock up, will you? I shan't be going out again.

PICKERING. Right. Can Mrs. Pearce go to bed? We don't want anything more, do we?

HIGGINS. Lord, no!

(ELIZA *opens the door and is seen on the lighted landing in opera cloak, brilliant evening dress, and diamonds, with fan, flowers, and all accessories. She comes to the hearth, and switches on the electric lights there. She is tired: her pallor contrasts strongly with her dark eyes and hair; and her expression is almost tragic. She takes off her cloak; puts her fan and flowers on the piano; and sits down on the bench, brooding and silent.* HIGGINS, *in evening dress, with overcoat and hat, comes in, carrying a smoking jacket which he has picked up downstairs. He takes off the hat and overcoat; throws them carelessly on the newspaper stand; disposes of his coat in the same way; puts on the smoking jacket; and throws himself wearily into the easy chair at the hearth.* PICKERING, *similarly attired, comes in. He also takes off his hat and overcoat, and is about to throw them on* HIGGINS'S *when he hesitates.*)

PICKERING. I say: Mrs. Pearce will row if we leave these things lying about in the drawing room.

HIGGINS. Oh, chuck them over the bannisters into the hall. She'll find them there in the morning and put them away all right. She'll think we were drunk.

PICKERING. We are, slightly. Are there any letters?

HIGGINS. I didn't look. (PICKERING *takes the overcoats and hats and goes downstairs.* HIGGINS *begins half singing half yawning an air from* La Fanciulla del Golden West.[1] *Suddenly he stops and exclaims.*) I wonder where the devil my slippers are!

(ELIZA *looks at him darkly; then rises suddenly and leaves the room.* HIGGINS *yawns again, and resumes his song.* PICKERING *returns, with the contents of the letterbox in his hand.*)

PICKERING. Only circulars, and this coroneted billet-doux[2] for you. (*He throws the circulars into the fender, and posts himself on the hearthrug, with his back to the grate.*)

HIGGINS (*glancing at the billet-doux*). Money-

---

1. **La Fanciulla del Golden West,** a combination of two titles. *La Fanciulla del West* is an opera by Giacomo Puccini that opened in New York in 1910 and is based on *The Girl of the Golden West,* a play by David Belasco.

2. **coroneted billet-doux.** *Billet-doux* (bil'ē dü') is French for "love letter," but Pickering is using the word ironically. This one bears a coronet, or crown, indicating that it is from someone of noble birth, but Higgins's response seems to indicate he feels the writer is an upstart.

ACT FOUR SUMMARY

Pygmalion

Higgins and Pickering return home late at night. Eliza is with them, but they do not speak to her. They discuss their day, and Pickering congratulates Higgins on winning the bet. As Eliza listens, distraught, Higgins disparages the deed and complains of being bored. The men decide to go to bed. Higgins, speaking to Eliza for the first time, tells her to put out the lights and asks where his slippers are. Eliza hurls them at him, and he finally realizes she is upset. She tells him she doesn't know what will happen to her now. Eliza is angered when he makes light of her concerns. She asks which of her clothes belong to her and returns a ring Higgins had bought her. Higgins, "wounded . . . to the heart," hurls the ring at the fireplace, and Eliza expresses her joy. Higgins goes out very upset, and Eliza, smiling, searches for the ring.

For summaries in other languages, see the Building English Proficiency book.

Other actresses who have portrayed Liza on stage or screen are shown in their formal gowns. The actresses are (from the left): Diana Wynard, Diana Rigg, Cathy Tyson, and Audrey Hepburn. What special qualities do you imagine each of these actresses brought to the role of Eliza?

3

lender. (*He throws the letter after the circulars.*) (ELIZA *returns with a pair of large-down-at-heel slippers. She places them on the carpet before* HIGGINS, *and sits as before without a word.*)

HIGGINS (*yawning again*). Oh Lord! What an evening! What a crew! What a silly tomfoolery! (*He raises his shoe to unlace it, and catches sight of the slippers. He stops unlacing and looks at them as if they had appeared there of their own accord.*) Oh! They're here, are they?

PICKERING (*stretching himself*). Well, I feel a bit tired. It's been a long day. The garden party, a dinner party, and the opera! Rather too much of a good thing. But you've won your bet, Higgins. Eliza did the trick, and something to spare, eh?

HIGGINS (*fervently*). Thank God it's over!

(ELIZA *flinches violently; but they take no notice of her; and she recovers herself and sits stonily as before.*)

PICKERING. Were you nervous at the garden party? *I* was. Eliza didn't seem a bit nervous.

HIGGINS. Oh, she wasn't nervous. I knew she'd be all right. No: it's the strain of putting the job through all these months that has told on me. It was interesting enough at first, while we were at the phonetics; but after that

I got deadly sick of it. If I hadn't backed myself to do it I should have chucked the whole thing up two months ago. It was a silly notion: the whole thing has been a bore.

PICKERING. Oh come! The garden party was frightfully exciting. My heart began beating like anything.

HIGGINS. Yes, for the first three minutes. But when I saw we were going to win hands down, I felt like a bear in a cage, hanging about doing nothing. The dinner was worse: sitting gorging there for over an hour, with nobody but a damned fool of a fashionable woman to talk to! I tell you, Pickering, never again for me. No more artificial duchesses. The whole thing has been simple purgatory.[3]

PICKERING. You've never been broken in properly to the social routine. (*Strolling over to the piano.*) I rather enjoy dipping into it occasionally myself: it makes me feel young again. Anyhow, it was a great success: an immense success. I was quite frightened

---

3. **purgatory** (pėr′gə tôr′ē), *n.* any condition of temporary suffering.

Pygmalion—Act Four   **697**

4

5

3
Literary Element
Symbolism

Question What personal quality or characteristic might Higgins's reaction to the slippers symbolize? (*Possible responses: his removal from things around him; his inattention to people*)

4
Reading/Thinking Skills
Make Judgments

Question To whom does Pickering credit with the successful winning of the bet? (*both Higgins and Eliza*)

5
Reading/Thinking Skills
Compare and Contrast

Question How would you compare and contrast Eliza's and Higgins's reactions? (*Possible response: Higgins is wrapped up in his own feelings; Eliza is terribly hurt by his expression of relief.*)

 Art Study

Response to Caption Question
Each of the actresses brought a unique brand of glamour to the role, a quality that is necessary for the character's transformation from "guttersnipe" to "duchess."

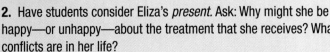
BUILDING ENGLISH PROFICIENCY

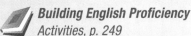

Analyzing Key Statements

As Eliza enters the laboratory, the stage directions tell us that "her expression is almost tragic" (middle of column 1, p. 696). Encourage students to consider the significance of this statement.

1. Have students consider Eliza's *past.* Ask: What has she had to go through to get to this point? Do you think she ever imagined being in this position?

2. Have students consider Eliza's *present.* Ask: Why might she be happy—or unhappy—about the treatment that she receives? What conflicts are in her life?

3. Have students consider Eliza's *future.* Ask: What kind of future did Eliza once want for herself? How well has this experiment prepared her for that future? What is to become of her?

4. As students read on, urge them to consider how that last question motivates Eliza.

Building English Proficiency Activities, p. 249

697

Question What does Pickering mean? *(Many people who belong by right to high society do not have the style associated with their position because they assume that they have it by birth and so pay no attention to it. Eliza, who has learned it all in six months, does it almost naturally.)*

7 Literary Element
Plot

Point out to students that these are the first words that Higgins speaks to Eliza in this act. You may also wish to point out that although the stage directions say "Liza," she is always referred to as "Eliza." Students might speculate on why.

8 Reading/Thinking Skills
Compare and Contrast

Question Compare this with Eliza's previous expressions of anger. *(Students should note that Eliza's whole way of expressing herself has changed, even when she's angry.)*

9 Literary Element
Characterization

Question Why does Higgins correct Eliza's grammar here? *(He is always guided by his profession and ignores the emotional import of the communication.)*

---

once or twice because Eliza was doing it so well. You see, lots of the real people can't do it at all: they're such fools that they think style comes by nature to people in their position; and so they never learn. There's always something professional about doing a thing superlatively well.

HIGGINS. Yes: that's what drives me mad: the silly people don't know their own silly business. *(Rising.)* However, it's over and done with; and now I can go to bed at last without dreading tomorrow.

(ELIZA's beauty becomes murderous.)

PICKERING. I think I shall turn in too. Still, it's been a great occasion: a triumph for you. Goodnight. *(He goes.)*

HIGGINS *(following him).* Goodnight. *(Over his shoulder, at the door.)* Put out the lights, Eliza; and tell Mrs. Pearce not to make coffee for me in the morning: I'll take tea. *(He goes out.)*

(ELIZA tries to control herself and feel indifferent as she rises and walks across to the hearth to switch off the light. By the time she gets there she is on the point of screaming. She sits down in HIGGINS's chair and holds on hard to the arms. Finally she gives way and flings herself furiously on the floor, raging.)

HIGGINS *(in despairing wrath outside).* What the devil have I done with my slippers? *(He appears at the door.)*

LIZA *(snatching up the slippers, and hurling them at him one after the other with all her force).* There are your slippers. And there. Take your slippers; and may you never have a day's luck with them!

HIGGINS *(astounded).* What on earth—? *(He comes to her.)* What's the matter? Get up. *(He pulls her up.)* Anything wrong?

LIZA *(breathless).* Nothing wrong—with you. I've won your bet for you, haven't I? That's enough for you. I don't matter, I suppose.

HIGGINS. You won my bet! You! Presumptuous⁴ insect! I won it. What did you throw those slippers at for me for?

LIZA. Because I wanted to smash your face. I'd like to kill you, you selfish brute. Why didn't

---

you leave me where you picked me out of—in the gutter? You thank God it's all over, and that now you can throw me back again there, do you? *(She crisps her fingers⁵ frantically.)*

HIGGINS *(looking at her in cool wonder).* The creature is nervous, after all.

LIZA *(gives a suffocated scream of fury, and instinctively darts her nails at his face).* !!

HIGGINS *(catching her wrists).* Ah! Would you? Claws in, you cat. How dare you show your temper to me? Sit down and be quiet. *(He throws her roughly into the easy chair.)*

LIZA *(crushed by superior strength and weight).* What's to become of me? What's to become of me?

HIGGINS. How the devil do I know what's to become of you? What does it matter what becomes of you?

LIZA. You don't care. I know you don't care. You wouldn't care if I was dead. I'm nothing to you—not so much as them slippers.

HIGGINS *(thundering).* Those slippers.

LIZA *(with bitter submission).* Those slippers. I didn't think it made any difference now.

(A pause. ELIZA hopeless and crushed. HIGGINS a little uneasy.)

HIGGINS *(in his loftiest manner).* Why have you begun going on like this? May I ask whether you complain of your treatment here?

LIZA. No.

HIGGINS. Has anybody behaved badly to you? Colonel Pickering? Mrs. Pearce? Any of the servants?

LIZA. No.

HIGGINS. I presume you don't pretend that *I* have treated you badly?

LIZA. No.

HIGGINS. I am glad to hear it. *(He moderates his tone.)* Perhaps you're tired after the strain of the day. Will you have a glass of champagne? *(He moves towards the door.)*

9

---

4. **presumptuous** (pri zump′chŭ əs), *adj.* too bold; forward.

5. **crisps her fingers,** clenches and relaxes her fists.

MINI-LESSON: READING/THINKING SKILLS

Identifying Alternatives

Teach Point out that on this page, Higgins, in his thoughtless, impersonal, self-centered way, still tries to think and react in cold, logical terms. He tries to come up with logical alternative explanations for Eliza's discouragement and feelings of abandonment. He first sees her emotional reaction as sub-human—animalistic—calling her a cat (column 2). Then he tries to think of logical explanations—someone has treated her badly. Then he thinks that she is merely tired and offers her champagne. He doesn't see himself as a cause for her feelings of abandonment.

Activity Idea As this act continues, have students make a list of more alternatives Higgins comes up with for Eliza's feelings and a list of his alternatives for making her feel better about her future.

LIZA. No. *(Recollecting her manners.)* Thank you.

HIGGINS *(good-humored again).* This has been coming on for some days. I suppose it was natural for you to be anxious about the garden party. But that's all over now. *(He pats her kindly on the shoulder. She writhes.[6])* There's nothing more to worry about.

LIZA. No. Nothing for you to worry about. *(She suddenly rises and gets away from him by going to the piano bench, where she sits and hides her face.)* Oh God! I wish I was dead.

HIGGINS *(staring after her in sincere surprise).* Why? In heaven's name, why? *(Reasonably, going to her.)* Listen to me, Eliza. All this irritation is purely subjective.[7]

LIZA. I don't understand. I'm too ignorant.

HIGGINS. It's only imagination. Low spirits and nothing else. Nobody's hurting you. Nothing's wrong. You go to bed like a good girl and sleep it off. Have a little cry and say your prayers: that will make you comfortable.

LIZA. I heard your prayers, "Thank God it's all over!"

HIGGINS *(impatiently).* Well, don't you thank God it's all over? Now you are free and can do what you like.

LIZA *(pulling herself together in desperation).* What am I fit for? What have you left me fit for? Where am I to go? What am I to do? What's to become of me?

HIGGINS *(enlightened, but not at all impressed).* Oh that's what's worrying you, is it? *(He thrusts his hands into his pockets, and walks about in his usual manner, rattling the contents of his pockets, as if condescending to a trivial subject out of pure kindness.)* I shouldn't bother about it if I were you. I should imagine you won't have much difficulty in settling yourself somewhere or other, though I hadn't quite realized that you were going away. *(She looks quickly at him: he does not look at her, but examines the dessert stand on the piano and decides that he will eat an apple.)* You might marry, you know. *(He bites a large piece out of the apple and munches it noisily.)* You see, Eliza, all men are not confirmed old bachelors like me and the Colonel. Most men are the marrying sort (poor devils!); and you're not bad-looking: it's quite a pleasure to look at you sometimes—not now, of course, because you're crying and looking as ugly as the very devil; but when you're all right and quite yourself, you're what I should call attractive. That is, to the people in the marrying line, you understand. You go to bed and have a good nice rest; and then get up and look at yourself in the glass; and you won't feel so cheap.

(ELIZA again looks at him, speechless, and does not stir. The look is quite lost on him: he eats his apple with a dreamy expression of happiness, as it is quite a good one.)

HIGGINS *(a genial afterthought occurring to him).* I daresay my mother could find some chap or other who would do very well.

LIZA. We were above that at the corner of Tottenham Court Road.

HIGGINS *(waking up).* What do you mean?

LIZA. I sold flowers. I didn't sell myself. Now you've made a lady of me I'm not fit to sell anything else. I wish you'd left me where you found me.

HIGGINS *(slinging the core of the apple decisively into the grate).* Tosh, Eliza. Don't you insult human relations by dragging all this cant[8] about buying and selling into it. You needn't marry the fellow if you don't like him.

LIZA. What else am I to do?

HIGGINS. Oh, lots of things. What about your old idea of a florist's shop? Pickering could set you up in one: he's lots of money. *(Chuckling.)* He'll have to pay for all those togs you have been wearing today; and that, with the hire of the jewelry, will make a big hole in two hundred pounds. Why, six months ago you would have thought it the millennium to have a flower shop of your own. Come! You'll be all

---

6. **writhe** (rīтн), *v.* twist and turn; suffer mentally.
7. **subjective** (səb jek′tiv), *adj.* existing in the mind.
8. **cant** (kant), *n.* insincere talk.

Pygmalion—Act Four **699**

---

10 **Literary Element**

Irony

Question Why is Eliza's claim ironic? *(Possible response: because Higgins had claimed in Act Two that Eliza couldn't understand anything, and now he speaks to her as if she were an equal and expects her to understand)*

11 **Reading/Thinking Skills**

Make Judgments

Question Is it true that Eliza is free? Explain. *(Possible response: In the historical situation of the play, Eliza was by no means free; on the contrary, she was more dependent now than ever—her training had disqualified her from earning her own living in the job she knew.)*

12 **Literary Focus**

Inference

Question What is Eliza searching for when she looks at Higgins? *(Possible response: some sign that he really cares about her as a human being, not just a linguistics experiment)*

13 **Literary Focus**

Inference

Question What does Eliza mean? *(Possible response: She would not have consented to marry for money even when she was desperately poor.)*

14 **Reading/Thinking Skills**

Compare and Contrast

Question Compare and contrast Eliza's and Higgins's understandings of Eliza's current situation. *(Possible response: Eliza feels that the only thing she has of value is herself, so that is all she has with which to earn a living. Higgins feels that Eliza is being prudish and that there is nothing wrong with the kind of arranged marriage that he is suggesting.)*

BUILDING ENGLISH PROFICIENCY

Understanding a Character

Creating an "open-mind" diagram for Eliza, as shown, will help students grasp what is shaping her thoughts during the conflict with Higgins that takes place on these pages. You might suggest these topics:

- her success at the garden party
- Higgins
- her past as a flower-seller
- her happiness

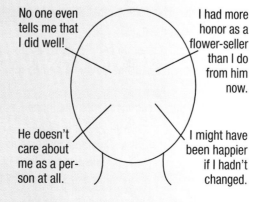

No one even tells me that I did well!

I had more honor as a flower-seller than I do from him now.

He doesn't care about me as a person at all.

I might have been happier if I hadn't changed.

15 Reading/Thinking Skills
Clarify

Question Why does Eliza call Higgins "sir"? *(Possible response: She has decided to treat him with the distance and reserve with which she feels that he treats her.)*

16 Reading/Thinking Skills
Analyze

Question What is Eliza doing here? *(Possible response: She is asserting her power over Higgins by treating him as coldly as he treats her and forcing him to respond to her emotionally rather than rationally.)*

17 Literary Focus
Inference

Question Why does Eliza smile? *(Possible response: She has proved to herself that Higgins does care about her.)*

Check Test

1. Where were Higgins and Pickering? *(at the garden party, a dinner party, and the opera)*

2. Why did Higgins dislike the dinner party so much? *(He didn't like having only a fashionable woman to speak to.)*

3. What is Eliza worried about? *(what will happen to her)*

4. What does Higgins suggest that Eliza do with her life? *(marry or open a florist shop)*

5. What does Eliza give back to Higgins? *(the hired jewels and the ring he bought for her)*

 Unit 7 Resource Book
Alternate Check Test, p. 29

---

right. I must clear off to bed: I'm devilish sleepy. By the way, I came down for something: I forget what it was.

LIZA. Your slippers.

HIGGINS. Oh yes, of course. You shied them at me. (*He picks them up, and is going out when she rises and speaks to him.*)

LIZA. Before you go, Sir—

HIGGINS. (*dropping the slippers in his surprise at her calling him Sir*). Eh?

LIZA. Do my clothes belong to me or to Colonel Pickering?

HIGGINS. (*coming back into the room as if her question were the very climax of unreason*). What the devil use would they be to Pickering?

LIZA. He might want them for the next girl you pick up to experiment on.

HIGGINS. (*shocked and hurt*). Is that the way you feel towards us?

LIZA. I don't want to hear anything more about that. All I want to know is whether anything belongs to me. My own clothes were burned.

HIGGINS. But what does it matter? Why need you start bothering about that in the middle of the night?

LIZA. I want to know what I may take away with me. I don't want to be accused of stealing.

HIGGINS. (*now deeply wounded*). Stealing! You shouldn't have said that, Eliza. That shows a want of feeling.

LIZA. I'm sorry. I'm only a common ignorant girl; and in my station[9] I have to be careful. There can't be any feelings between the like of you and the like of me. Please will you tell me what belongs to me and what doesn't?

HIGGINS. (*very sulkily*). You may take the whole damned houseful if you like. Except the jewels. They're hired. Will that satisfy you? (*He turns on his heel and is about to go in extreme dudgeon.*)[10]

LIZA (*drinking in his emotion like nectar, and nagging him to provoke a further supply*). Stop, please. (*She takes off her jewels.*) Will you take these to your room and keep them safe? I don't want to run the risk of their being missing.

HIGGINS (*furious*). Hand them over. (*She puts them into his hands.*) If these belonged to me instead of to the jeweler, I'd ram them down your ungrateful throat. (*He perfunctorily[11] thrusts them into his pockets, unconsciously decorating himself with the protruding ends of the chains.*)

LIZA (*taking a ring off*). This ring isn't the jeweler's: it's the one you bought me in Brighton. I don't want it now. (HIGGINS *dashes the ring violently into the fireplace, and turns on her so threateningly that she crouches over the piano with her hands over her face, and exclaims.*) Don't you hit me.

HIGGINS. Hit you! You infamous[12] creature, how dare you accuse me of such a thing? It is you who have hit me. You have wounded me to the heart.

LIZA (*thrilling with hidden joy*). I'm glad. I've got a little of my own back, anyhow.

HIGGINS (*with dignity, in his finest professional style*). You have caused me to lose my temper: a thing that has hardly ever happened to me before. I prefer to say nothing more tonight. I am going to bed.

LIZA (*pertly*). You'd better leave a note for Mrs. Pearce about the coffee; for she won't be told by me.

HIGGINS (*formally*). Damn Mrs. Pearce; and damn the coffee; and damn you; and damn my own folly in having lavished[13] hard-earned knowledge and the treasure of my regard and intimacy on a heartless guttersnipe. (*He goes out with impressive decorum,[14] and spoils it by slamming the door savagely.* ELIZA *smiles for the first time; expresses her feelings by a wild pantomime in which an imitation of* HIGGINS's *exit is confused with her own triumph; and finally goes down on her knees on the hearthrug to look for the ring.*)

---

9. **station,** social position.
10. dudgeon (duj′ən), *n.* feeling of anger or resentment.
11. perfunctorily (pər fungk′tər i lē), *adv.* mechanically; indifferently.
12. **infamous** (in′fə məs), *adj.* shamefully bad; disgraceful.
13. lavish (lav′ish), *v.* give or spend freely.
14. decorum (di kôr′əm), *n.* proper behavior.

MINI-LESSON: GRAMMAR

Compound Sentences

Teach Point out the following sentences in the first column on page 700:

I must clear off to bed: I'm devilish sleepy.

By the way, I came down for something: I forget what it was.

I'm only a common ignorant girl; and in my station I have to be careful.

Note that these are all compound sentences, the first two having no conjunction, the third using the coordinating conjunction *and*. Explain that Shaw frequently uses compound sentences in his dialogue and tends to punctuate them with semicolons and colons rather than commas. Discuss why Shaw might have done this rather than writing separate short sentences.

Activity Idea Have students search this page for three more compound sentences.

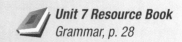 **Unit 7 Resource Book**
Grammar, p. 28

After Reading

Act 4

Shaping Your Response

Making Connections

1. Have your expectations about Higgins and Liza changed or remained about the same? Explain.

Analyzing the Play

2. Mrs. Patrick Campbell, the first actress to play Liza in London, complained about not having any lines in the first part of act 4 and said that the audience would think she had gone to sleep. In your opinion, whose instincts were right, hers or Shaw's? Explain.

3. When Higgins suggests that his mother could find a husband for Liza, her response is, "We were above that at the corner of Tottenham Court Road." What does she mean?

4. Liza insists that "in my station I have to be careful. There can't be any feelings between the like of you and the like of me." Why not?

5. Do you think the gap between social classes has been bridged in any way in this act? If so, what has achieved this bridge? If not, what has prevented it?

6. The 1938 film of *Pygmalion* includes a scene at the party although Shaw never intended it to be part of the play. Why do you think Shaw did not include the scene of Liza's triumph? Why might a film maker insist on inserting this scene?

Extending the Ideas

7. Do differences in language separate people today? How much do they affect **communication** between people? Are there other factors that divide people? Explain.

Vocabulary Study

cant
decorum
dudgeon
lavish
perfunctorily
presumptuous
purgatory
subjective
writhe

Create a dialogue between Liza and Freddy or some other character in which you use at least five of the listed words in such a way that you demonstrate your understanding of their meanings.

Pygmalion—Act Four **701**

After Reading

MAKING CONNECTIONS

1. Students' answers will vary.

2. Possible response: Shaw was right; if she were to read and follow Shaw's stage directions, no one would think she had fallen asleep.

3. Eliza would not have "sold herself" by marrying a man simply to gain financial support.

4. Students may say that neither of them can ever forget the differences in their backgrounds; that society wouldn't let them forget the differences; or that their upbringings have made them too different to ever really understand each other.

5. Students may say that, without acknowledging it, Higgins has begun to treat Eliza in some ways as an equal. They may also point out that Eliza has forced Higgins to admit that he does have some feelings about her. Thus, he has brought her into his world, and she has brought him into hers.

6. Possible response: Act Four is stronger if the triumph is unseen by the audience; the argument over who is triumphant is, thus, more dramatic and bittersweet.

7. Students will likely agree that, with the number of different languages and dialects spoken in America today, language differences do separate people. Their explanations may be affected by their experience and the regions in which they live.

VOCABULARY STUDY

Vocabulary words, as used in context, should reflect correct meanings and connotations.

 Unit 7 Resource Book
Vocabulary, p. 27
Vocabulary Test, p. 30

Selection Test

Unit 7 Resource Book
pp. 31–32

701

Vocabulary Preview

repudiate, reject

provocation, something that stirs up or irritates

incorrigible, too firmly fixed in bad ways to be changed

demean, lower in dignity; degrade

brougham, a closed carriage or automobile, having an outside seat for the driver

magnanimous, generous in forgiving

Students can add the words and definitions to their Writer's Notebooks.

1 Literary Focus
Inference

Question Why might they be calling the police? *(Possible responses: because Eliza left; because something may have been stolen)*

2 Literary Focus
Inference

Question What did the inspector suspect? *(Possible responses: that the relationship between Eliza and Pickering and Higgins might have been physical)*

 Unit 7 Resource Book
Graphic Organizer, p. 33
Study Guide, p. 34

ACT FIVE

MRS. HIGGINS'S *drawing room. She is at her writing-table as before. The* PARLOR MAID *comes in.*

THE PARLOR MAID (*at the door*). Mr. Henry, ma'am, is downstairs with Colonel Pickering.

MRS. HIGGINS. Well, show them up.

THE PARLOR MAID. They're using the telephone, ma'am. Telephoning to the police, I think.

MRS. HIGGINS. What?

THE PARLOR MAID (*coming further in and lowering her voice*). Mr. Henry is in a state, ma'am. I thought I'd better tell you.

MRS. HIGGINS. If you had told me that Mr. Henry was not in a state it would have been more surprising. Tell them to come up when they've finished with the police. I suppose he's lost something.

THE PARLOR MAID. Yes, ma'am. (*Going.*)

MRS. HIGGINS. Go upstairs and tell Miss Doolittle that Mr. Henry and the Colonel are here. Ask her not to come down till I send for her.

THE PARLOR MAID. Yes, ma'am.

(HIGGINS *bursts in. He is, as the* PARLOR MAID *has said, in a state.*)

HIGGINS. Look here, Mother: here's a confounded thing!

MRS. HIGGINS. Yes, dear. Good morning. (*He checks his impatience and kisses her, whilst the* PARLOR MAID *goes out.*) What is it?

HIGGINS. Eliza's bolted.

MRS. HIGGINS (*calmly continuing her writing*). You must have frightened her.

HIGGINS. Frightened her! Nonsense! She was left last night, as usual, to turn out the lights and all that: and instead of going to bed she changed her clothes and went right off: her bed wasn't slept in. She came in a cab for her things before seven this morning; and that fool Mrs. Pearce let her have them without telling me a word about it. What am I to do?

MRS. HIGGINS. Do without, I'm afraid, Henry. The girl has a perfect right to leave if she chooses.

HIGGINS (*wandering distractedly across the room*). But I can't find anything. I don't know what appointments I've got. I'm— (PICKERING *comes in.* MRS. HIGGINS *puts down her pen and turns away from the writing-table.*)

PICKERING (*shaking hands*). Good morning, Mrs. Higgins. Has Henry told you? (*He sits down on the ottoman.*)

HIGGINS. What does that ass of an inspector say? Have you offered a reward?

MRS. HIGGINS (*rising in indignant amazement*). You don't mean to say you have set the police after Eliza.

HIGGINS. Of course. What are the police for? What else could we do? (*He sits in the Elizabethan chair.*)

PICKERING. The inspector made a lot of difficulties. I really think he suspected us of some improper purpose.

MRS. HIGGINS. Well, of course he did. What right have you to go to the police and give the girl's name as if she were a thief, or a lost umbrella, or something? Really! (*She sits down again, deeply vexed.*)

HIGGINS. But we want to find her.

PICKERING. We can't let her go like this, you know, Mrs. Higgins. What were we to do?

MRS. HIGGINS. You have no more sense, either of you, than two children. Why—

(*The* PARLOR MAID *comes in and breaks off the conversation.*)

THE PARLOR MAID. Mr. Henry: a gentleman wants to see you very particular. He's been sent on from Wimpole Street.

HIGGINS. Oh, bother! I can't see anyone now. Who is it?

THE PARLOR MAID. A Mr. Doolittle, sir.

PICKERING. Doolittle. Do you mean the dustman?

THE PARLOR MAID. Dustman! Oh no, sir: a gentleman.

HIGGINS (*springing up excitedly*). By George, Pick, it's some relative of hers that she's gone to. Somebody we know nothing about. (*To the* PARLOR MAID.) Send him up, quick.

ACT FIVE SUMMARY

Pygmalion

Eliza has come to Mrs. Higgins for help. Higgins, Pickering, and Mr. Doolittle arrive. Doolittle chastises Higgins for forcing him into the middle class. Eliza enters and thanks Pickering for treating her like a lady—to her, *the* essential part of her education. Higgins says Eliza will relapse in three weeks without him. Doolittle tells Eliza he is going to marry her stepmother; Eliza, Pickering, and Mrs. Higgins decide to attend the wedding. Eliza and Higgins are left together, and they argue. Eliza announces that she'll marry Freddy Hill.

Higgins congratulates himself for making a woman of her. Eliza leaves for the wedding, saying she won't see Higgins again. Higgins replies by telling her to buy him a ham, a cheese, gloves, and a tie. The play ends as Higgins affirms to his mother that Eliza will buy them and chuckles to himself.

 *For summaries in other languages, see the **Building English Proficiency** book.*

THE PARLOR MAID. Yes, sir. *(She goes.)*

HIGGINS *(eagerly, going to his mother).* Genteel relatives! Now we shall hear something. *(He sits down in the Chippendale chair.)*

MRS. HIGGINS. Do you know any of her people?

PICKERING. Only her father: the fellow we told you about.

THE PARLOR MAID *(announcing).* Mr. Doolittle. *(She withdraws.)*

(DOOLITTLE enters. He is brilliantly dressed in a new fashionable frock coat, with white waistcoat and gray trousers. A flower in his buttonhole, a dazzling silk hat, and patent leather shoes complete the effect. He is too concerned with the business he has come on to notice MRS. HIGGINS. He walks straight to HIGGINS, and accosts him with vehement reproach.)

3

DOOLITTLE *(indicating his own person).* See here! Do you see this? You done this.

HIGGINS. Done what, man?

DOOLITTLE. This, I tell you. Look at it. Look at this hat. Look at this coat.

PICKERING. Has Eliza been buying you clothes?

DOOLITTLE. Eliza! Not she. Not half. Why would she buy me clothes?

MRS. HIGGINS. Good morning, Mr. Doolittle. Won't you sit down?

DOOLITTLE *(taken aback as he becomes conscious that he has forgotten his hostess).* Asking your pardon, ma'am. *(He approaches her and shakes her proffered hand.)* Thank you. *(He sits down on the ottoman, on PICKERING's right.)* I am that full of what has happened to me that I can't think of anything else.

HIGGINS. What the dickens has happened to you?

DOOLITTLE. I shouldn't mind if it had only happened to me: anything might happen to anybody and nobody to blame but Providence, as you might say. But this is something that you done to me: yes, you, Henry Higgins.

HIGGINS. Have you found Eliza? That's the point.

DOOLITTLE. Have you lost her?

HIGGINS. Yes.

DOOLITTLE. You have all the luck, you have. I ain't found her; but she'll find me quick enough now after what you done to me.

MRS. HIGGINS. But what has my son done to you, Mr. Doolittle?

DOOLITTLE. Done to me! Ruined me. Destroyed my happiness. Tied me up and delivered me into the hands of middle class morality.

HIGGINS *(rising intolerantly and standing over DOOLITTLE).* You're raving. You're drunk. You're mad. I gave you five pounds. After that I had two conversations with you, at half a crown an hour. I've never seen you since.

DOOLITTLE. Oh! Drunk! am I? Mad! am I? Tell me this. Did you or did you not write a letter to an old blighter in America that was giving five millions to found Moral Reform Societies all over the world, and that wanted you to invent a universal language for him?

HIGGINS. What! Ezra D. Wannafeller! He's dead. *(He sits down again carelessly.)*

4

DOOLITTLE. Yes: he's dead; and I'm done for. Now did you or did you not write a letter to him to say that the most original moralist at present in England, to the best of your knowledge, was Alfred Doolittle, a common dustman.

HIGGINS. Oh, after your last visit I remember making some silly joke of the kind.

DOOLITTLE. Ah! You may well call it a silly joke. It put the lid on me right enough. Just give him the chance he wanted to show that Americans is not like us: that they recognize and respect merit in every class of life, however humble. Them words is in his blooming will, in which, Henry Higgins, thanks to your silly joking, he leaves me a share in his Pre-digested Cheese Trust worth three thousand a year on condition that I lecture for his Wannafeller Moral Reform World League as often as they ask me up to six times a year.

5

HIGGINS. The devil he does! Whew! *(Brightening suddenly.)* What a lark!

PICKERING. A safe thing for you, Doolittle. They won't ask you twice.

DOOLITTLE. It ain't the lecturing I mind. I'll lecture them blue in the face, I will, and not turn a hair. It's making a gentleman of me that I

3

Critical Thinking

Predict

Question How might Doolittle's claim be possible? *(Responses will vary. Students may think that Higgins got him a position.)*

4

Historical Note

The American Millionaire

Shaw combined the names of two American philanthropists and industrialists —John Wanamaker (1838–1922) and John D. Rockefeller (1839–1937)—to create an imaginary American millionaire who supposedly left money to Alfred Doolittle.

5

Reader's Response

Challenging the Text

Question Do you think this is an accurate description of the American outlook? *(Students will probably see America as less class conscience than England, but some students may note that there are still class distinctions and high society here.)*

BUILDING ENGLISH PROFICIENCY

Exploring a Subplot

Help students understand the subplot of this play.

1. Explain that a subplot is a story within the main plot, with its own conflicts and resolution. In this case, the subplot focuses on the story of Alfred Doolittle.

2. Have students consider how the conflict between Doolittle and Higgins is resolved. Ask: According to Doolittle, who has won?

3. Help students see what the subplot adds to this play: opportunities for comic dialogue and statements of Shaw's ideas about society, middle-class morals, and appearance versus reality. On the following pages, Shaw uses Doolittle as a mouthpiece for his ideas on women and marriage.

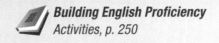
Building English Proficiency
Activities, p. 250

object to. Who asked him to make a gentleman of me? I was happy. I was free. I touched pretty nigh everybody for money when I wanted it, same as I touched you, Henry Higgins. Now I am worried; tied neck and heels; and everybody touches me for money. It's a fine thing for you, says my solicitor.[1] Is it? says I. You mean it's a good thing for you, I says. When I was a poor man and had a solicitor once when they found a pram in the dust cart, he got me off, and got shut of me and got me shut of him as quick as he could. Same with the doctors: used to shove me out of the hospital before I could hardly stand on my legs, and nothing to pay. Now they finds out that I'm not a healthy man and can't live unless they looks after me twice a day. In the house I'm not let do a hand's turn for myself: somebody else must do it and touch me for it. A year ago I hadn't a relative in the world except two or three that wouldn't speak to me. Now I've fifty, and not a decent week's wages among the lot of them. I have to live for others and not for myself: that's middle class morality. You talk of losing Eliza. Don't you be anxious: I bet she's on my doorstep by this: she that could support herself easy by selling flowers if I wasn't respectable. And the next one to touch me will be you, Henry Higgins. I'll have to learn to speak middle class language from you, instead of speaking proper English. That's where you'll come in; and I daresay that's what you done it for.

MRS. HIGGINS. But, my dear Mr. Doolittle, you need not suffer all this if you are really in earnest. Nobody can force you to accept this bequest. You can repudiate[2] it. Isn't that so, Colonel Pickering?

PICKERING. I believe so.

DOOLITTLE (*softening his manner in deference to her sex*). That's the tragedy of it, ma'am. It's easy to say chuck it; but I haven't the nerve. Which of us has? We're all intimidated. Intimidated, ma'am: that's what we are. What is there for me if I chuck it but the work-

house in my old age? I have to dye my hair already to keep my job as a dustman. If I was one of the deserving poor, and had put by a bit, I could chuck it; but then why should I, acause the deserving poor might as well be millionaires for all the happiness they ever has. They don't know what happiness is. But I, as one of the undeserving poor, have nothing between me and the pauper's uniform but this here blasted three thousand a year that shoves me into the middle class. (Excuse the expression, ma'am: you'd use it yourself if you had my provocation.[3]) They've got you every way you turn: it's a choice between the Skilly of the workhouse and the Char Bydis[4] of the middle class; and I haven't the nerve for the workhouse. Intimidated: that's what I am. Broke. Bought up. Happier men than me will call for my dust, and touch me for their tip; and I'll look on helpless, and envy them. And that's what your son has brought me to. (*He is overcome by emotion.*)

MRS. HIGGINS. Well, I'm very glad you're not going to do anything foolish, Mr. Doolittle. For this solves the problem of Eliza's future. You can provide for her now.

DOOLITTLE (*with melancholy resignation*). Yes, ma'am: I'm expected to provide for everyone now, out of three thousand a year.

HIGGINS (*jumping up*). Nonsense! He can't provide for her. He shan't provide for her. She doesn't belong to him. I paid him five pounds for her. Doolittle: either you're an honest man or a rogue.

---

1. **solicitor** (sə lis′ə tər), *n.* in Britain, a lawyer.
2. repudiate (ri pyü′dē āt), *v.* reject.
3. provocation (prov′ə kā′shən), *n.* something that stirs up or irritates.
4. **Skilly . . . Char Bydis.** Doolittle is referring to Scylla (sil′ə) and Charybdis (kə rib′dis). In the narrow strait that separates Italy and Sicily there is a dangerous rock and a whirlpool, which the ancient Greeks named Scylla and Charybdis. The expression "to be between Scylla and Charybdis" means to be between two evils, either one of which can be safely avoided only by risking the other.

MINI-LESSON: READING/THINKING SKILLS

Summarizing

Teach Remind students that a summary is a short statement—no more than several sentences—that gives the main idea of an article or tells what happened in a story. It is different from a paraphrase in that a paraphrase is a retelling in different words, and so it may be almost the same length as the original, whereas a summary is always much shorter than the original. Summarizing requires mentally sorting what is most important and necessary from what is detail that can be omitted.

A good example of a summary is Mrs. Higgins's long speech in column 1 of page 706, where she summarizes the previous evening's events and conversation, which take up several pages in Act Four.

Activity Idea Students might summarize Doolittle's two long speeches on this page, in which he relates his predicament with many details. Then have students compare their summaries for inclusion of important ideas and brevity.

DOOLITTLE (*tolerantly*). A little of both, Henry, like the rest of us: a little of both.

HIGGINS. Well, you took that money for the girl; and you have no right to take her as well.

MRS. HIGGINS. Henry: don't be absurd. If you want to know where Eliza is, she is upstairs.

HIGGINS (*amazed*). Upstairs!!! Then I shall jolly soon fetch her downstairs. (*He makes resolutely for the door.*)

MRS. HIGGINS (*rising and following him*). Be quiet, Henry. Sit down.

HIGGINS. I—

MRS. HIGGINS. Sit down, dear; and listen to me.

HIGGINS. Oh very well, very well, very well. (*He throws himself ungraciously on the ottoman, with his face towards the windows.*) But I think you might have told us this half an hour ago.

MRS. HIGGINS. Eliza came to me this morning. She passed the night partly walking about in a rage, partly trying to throw herself into the river and being afraid to, and partly in the Carlton Hotel. She told me of the brutal way you two treated her.

HIGGINS (*bounding up again*). What!

9

9 **Literary Focus**
Inference

Question Why might Eliza have behaved that way? (*Possible responses: Because she was so frightened about the future; because she was so angry with Higgins; because she felt so alone*)

 Art Study

Questions What differences do you note between Higgins's and Doolittle's manner of dress? (*Possible response: Doolittle is rather overdressed, compared to Higgins.*) What does this difference in dress suggest? (*Possible response: that Doolittle has acquired the funds, but not the polish of a gentleman; it subtly plays up the contrasts upon which the entire play is based.*)

BUILDING ENGLISH PROFICIENCY

Supporting an Opinion

Help students learn how to support an opinion.

1. Write these two sentences on the chalkboard:

- I think that *Pygmalion* would be a better play without the long speeches.
- I think that the speeches about Shaw's ideas help to make *Pygmalion* an outstanding play.

2. Let students hear each other expressing different opinions and reasons. Then ask students to copy the diagram shown here and the opinion above that they agree with and to write three reasons supporting their opinion.

My Opinion
1.
2.
3.

Irony

Question How is Pickering's statement, "We hardly said a word to her" ironic? *(because this was precisely the problem—neither man paid attention to Eliza after her triumph)*

Compare and Contrast

Questions Is Mrs. Higgins's description consistent with what happened in Act Four? Explain. *(Possible response: Students may say that Mrs. Higgins's explanation of Eliza's motivation and behavior complements what came out in Act Four, helps complete the picture, and is also consistent with what Eliza says to Higgins and with Higgins's and Pickering's treatment of her.)*

Detect Bias

What might Higgins's behavior suggest about any future relationship with Eliza? *(Possible response: that he will always be biased toward her and treat her as a flowergirl that he picked up out of the mud)*

PICKERING (*rising also*). My dear Mrs. Higgins, she's been telling you stories. We didn't treat her brutally. We hardly said a word to her; and we parted on particularly good terms. (*Turning on* HIGGINS.) Higgins: did you bully her after I went to bed?

HIGGINS. Just the other way about. She threw my slippers in my face. She behaved in the most outrageous way. I never gave her the slightest provocation. The slippers came bang into my face the moment I entered the room—before I had uttered a word. And used perfectly awful language.

PICKERING (*astonished*). But why? What did we do to her?

MRS. HIGGINS. I think I know pretty well what you did. The girl is naturally rather affectionate, I think. Isn't she, Mr. Doolittle?

DOOLITTLE. Very tender-hearted, ma'am. Takes after me.

MRS. HIGGINS. Just so. She had become attached to you both. She worked very hard for you, Henry. I don't think you quite realize what anything in the nature of brain work means to a girl like that. Well, it seems that when the great day of trial came, and she did this wonderful thing for you without making a single mistake, you two sat there and never said a word to her, but talked together of how glad you were that it was all over and how you had been bored with the whole thing. And then you were surprised because she threw your slippers at you! *I* should have thrown the fire-irons at you.

HIGGINS. We said nothing except that we were tired and wanted to go to bed. Did we, Pick?

PICKERING (*shrugging his shoulders*). That was all.

MRS. HIGGINS (*ironically*). Quite sure?

PICKERING. Absolutely. Really, that was all.

MRS. HIGGINS. You didn't thank her, or pet her, or admire her, or tell her how splendid she'd been.

HIGGINS (*impatiently*). But she knew all about that. We didn't make speeches to her, if that's what you mean.

PICKERING (*conscience stricken*). Perhaps we were a little inconsiderate. Is she very angry?

MRS. HIGGINS (*returning to her place at the writing-table*). Well, I'm afraid she won't go back to Wimpole Street, especially now that Mr. Doolittle is able to keep up the position you have thrust on her; but she says she is quite willing to meet you on friendly terms and to let bygones be bygones.

HIGGINS (*furious*). Is she, by George? Ho!

MRS. HIGGINS. If you promise to behave yourself, Henry, I'll ask her to come down. If not, go home; for you have taken up quite enough of my time.

HIGGINS. Oh, all right. Very well. Pick: you behave yourself. Let us put on our best Sunday manners for this creature that we picked out of the mud. (*He flings himself sulkily into the Elizabethan chair.*)

DOOLITTLE (*remonstrating*). Now, now, Henry Higgins! Have some consideration for my feelings as a middle class man.

MRS. HIGGINS. Remember your promise, Henry. (*She presses the bell-button on the writing-table.*) Mr. Doolittle: will you be so good as to step out on the balcony for a moment. I don't want Eliza to have the shock of your news until she has made it up with these two gentlemen. Would you mind?

DOOLITTLE. As you wish, lady. Anything to help Henry to keep her off my hands. (*He disappears through the window.*)

(*The* PARLOR MAID *answers the bell.* PICKERING *sits down in* DOOLITTLE's *place.*)

MRS. HIGGINS. Ask Miss Doolittle to come down, please.

THE PARLOR MAID. Yes, ma'am. (*She goes out.*)

MRS. HIGGINS. Now, Henry: be good.

HIGGINS. I am behaving myself perfectly.

PICKERING. He is doing his best, Mrs. Higgins. (*A pause.* HIGGINS *throws back his head; stretches out his legs; and begins to whistle.*)

MRS. HIGGINS. Henry, dearest, you don't look at all nice in that attitude.

MINI-LESSON: SPEAKING AND LISTENING

Using Appropriate Speaking Behavior for a Variety of Purposes

Teach Remind students of the ways in which Higgins's speaking behavior has been inappropriate in earlier acts:

- unacceptable language
- inappropriate tone
- socially unacceptable topics
- insults

Tell students that this behavior is highlighted by the contrast when Higgins is at his mother's house, because she is a perfect lady.

Activity Idea Have students identify inappropriate aspects of Higgins's speaking behavior in this scene. Then divide the class into small groups, and have them each rewrite a few of his speeches to make them appropriate. Give students the opportunities to read their revisions to the class.

HIGGINS (*pulling himself together*). I was not trying to look nice, Mother.

MRS. HIGGINS. It doesn't matter, dear. I only wanted to make you speak.

HIGGINS. Why?

MRS. HIGGINS. Because you can't speak and whistle at the same time.

(HIGGINS *groans. Another very trying pause.*)

HIGGINS (*springing up, out of patience*). Where the devil is that girl? Are we to wait here all day?

(ELIZA *enters, sunny, self-possessed, and giving a staggeringly convincing exhibition of ease of manner. She carries a little workbasket, and is very much at home.* PICKERING *is too much taken aback to rise.*)

LIZA. How do you do, Professor Higgins? Are you quite well?

HIGGINS (*choking*). Am I—(*He can say no more.*)

LIZA. But of course you are: you are never ill. So glad to see you again, Colonel Pickering. (*He rises hastily; and they shake hands.*) Quite chilly this morning, isn't it? (*She sits down on his left. He sits beside her.*)

13 HIGGINS. Don't you dare try this game on me. I taught it to you; and it doesn't take me in. Get up and come home; and don't be a fool.

(ELIZA *takes a piece of needlework from her basket, and begins to stitch at it, without taking the least notice of this outburst.*)

MRS. HIGGINS. Very nicely put, indeed, Henry. No woman could resist such an invitation.

14 HIGGINS. You let her alone, Mother. Let her speak for herself. You will jolly soon see whether she has an idea that I haven't put into her head or a word that I haven't put into her mouth. I tell you I have created this thing out of the squashed cabbage leaves of Covent Garden; and now she pretends to play the fine lady with me.

MRS. HIGGINS (*placidly*). Yes, dear; but you'll sit down, won't you?

(HIGGINS *sits down again, savagely.*)

LIZA (*to* PICKERING, *taking no apparent notice of* HIGGINS, *and working away deftly*). Will you drop me altogether now that the experiment is over, Colonel Pickering?

PICKERING. Oh don't. You mustn't think of it as an experiment. It shocks me, somehow.

LIZA. Oh, I'm only a squashed cabbage leaf—

PICKERING (*impulsively*). No.

LIZA (*continuing quietly*). —but I owe so much to you that I should be very unhappy if you forgot me.

PICKERING. It's very kind of you to say so, Miss Doolittle.

LIZA. It's not because you paid for my dresses. I know you are generous to everybody with money. But it was from you that I learned really nice manners; and that is what makes one a lady, isn't it? You see it was so very difficult for me with the example of Professor Higgins always before me. I was brought up to be just like him, unable to control myself, and using bad language on the slightest provocation. And I should never have known that ladies and gentlemen didn't behave like that if you hadn't been there. **15**

HIGGINS. Well!!

PICKERING. Oh, that's only his way, you know. He doesn't mean it.

LIZA. Oh, *I* didn't mean it either, when I was a flower girl. It was only my way. But you see I did it; and that's what makes the difference after all.

PICKERING. No doubt. Still, he taught you to speak; and I couldn't have done that, you know.

LIZA (*trivially*). Of course: that is his profession.

HIGGINS. Damnation!

LIZA (*continuing*). It was just like learning to dance in the fashionable way: there was nothing more than that in it. But do you know what began my real education?

PICKERING. What?

LIZA (*stopping her work for a moment*). Your calling me Miss Doolittle that day when I first came to Wimpole Street. That was the beginning of self-respect for me. (*She resumes her stitching.*) And there were a hundred little things you never noticed, because they came naturally to you. Things **16**

Pygmalion—Act Five **707**

13 Reading/Thinking Skills
Draw Conclusions

Question What game does Higgins mean? (*Possible response: the game of society manners*)

14 Reading/Thinking Skills
Distinguish Between Fact and Opinion

Question Is Higgins's claim fact or opinion? Explain. (*Possible response: Opinion; it has been clear from the outset that Eliza does not just parrot Higgins's ideas and that she has talents and abilities that she did not get from him.*)

15 Literary Element
Theme

Question What theme does this speech address? (*Possible response: the theme of contrasts between what constitutes a lady or a gentleman: position by birth or position by demeanor and behavior*)

16 Reader's Response
Making Personal Connections

Question In your opinion, where does self-respect come from and how does it arise? (*Students may or may not agree with Eliza's idea that we learn self-respect from the respect we receive from others.*)

BUILDING ENGLISH PROFICIENCY

Tracking Changes in Character

Eliza's reappearance surprises Higgins and Pickering alike. Help students grasp how Eliza has changed since Act One.

Activity Ideas

- Ask students to draw two pictures of Eliza, one "before" and one "after" her transformation.
- Have students discuss who and what caused the changes in Eliza.
- Have students complete the chart shown.

	Act One	Act Five
Appearance		
Speech		
Behavior		

ESL LEP ELD SAE LD

17 Reading/Thinking Skills
Compare and Contrast

Question   How would you compare
Eliza's statement here with her comment
on page 707 on the difference between a
flower girl and a lady. (*Possible response:
They are different ways of saying the same
thing.*)

18 Literary Focus
Inference

Question   What does this passage mean?
(*Possible response: Eliza has taken steps
that cannot be reversed—she can never
be an untutored Cockney flower girl
again—there is no going back for her.*)

19 Literary Element
Irony

Question   Why is Eliza's speech ironic?
(*Possible response: because just as she is
declaring that she can never relapse, she
utters one of her old Cockney cries*)

about standing up and taking off your hat
and opening doors—

PICKERING. Oh, that was nothing.

LIZA. Yes: things that showed you thought and
felt about me as if I were something better
than a scullery maid; though of course I
know you would have been just the same to
a scullery maid if she had been let into the
drawing room. You never took off your boots
in the dining room when I was there.

PICKERING. You mustn't mind that. Higgins
takes off his boots all over the place.

LIZA. I know. I am not blaming him. It is his way,
isn't it? But it made such a difference to me
that you didn't do it. You see, really and truly,
apart from the things anyone can pick up
(the dressing and the proper way of speaking,
and so on), the difference between a lady and
a flower girl is not how she behaves, but how
she's treated. I shall always be a flower girl to
Professor Higgins, because he always treats
me as a flower girl, and always will; but I know
I can be a lady to you, because you always treat
me as a lady, and always will.

MRS. HIGGINS. Please don't grind your teeth,
Henry.

PICKERING. Well, this is really very nice of you,
Miss Doolittle.

LIZA. I should like you to call me Eliza, now, if
you would.

PICKERING. Thank you. Eliza, of course.

LIZA. And I should like Professor Higgins to call
me Miss Doolittle.

HIGGINS. I'll see you damned first.

MRS. HIGGINS. Henry! Henry!

PICKERING (*laughing*). Why don't you slang back
at him? Don't stand it. It would do him a lot
of good.

LIZA. I can't. I could have done it once; but now I
can't go back to it. Last night, when I was wandering about, a girl spoke to me; and I tried to
get back into the old way with her; but it was
no use. You told me, you know, that when a
child is brought to a foreign country, it picks
up the language in a few weeks, and forgets its

own. Well, I am a child in your country. I have
forgotten my own language, and can speak
nothing but yours. That's the real break-off
with the corner of Tottenham Court Road.
Leaving Wimpole Street finishes it.

PICKERING (*much alarmed*). Oh! But you're coming back to Wimpole Street, aren't you?
You'll forgive Higgins?

HIGGINS (*rising*). Forgive! Will she, by George!
Let her go. Let her find out how she can get
on without us. She will relapse into the gutter in three weeks without me at her elbow.

(DOOLITTLE *appears at the center window. With a
look of dignified reproach at* HIGGINS, *he comes slowly
and silently to his daughter, who, with her back to the
window, is unconscious of his approach.*)

PICKERING. He's incorrigible,[5] Eliza. You won't
relapse, will you?

LIZA. No: not now. Never again. I have learned my
lesson. I don't believe I could utter one of
the old sounds if I tried. (DOOLITTLE *touches
her on her left shoulder. She drops her work, losing
her self-possession utterly at the spectacle of her
father's splendor.*) A-a-a-a-a-ah-ow-oh!

HIGGINS (*with a crow of triumph*). Aha! Just so. A-
a-a-a-ahowooh! A-a-a-a-ahowooh! A-a-a-a-
ahowooh! Victory! Victory! (*He throws himself
on the divan, folding his arms, and spraddling
arrogantly.*)

DOOLITTLE. Can you blame the girl? Don't look
at me like that, Eliza. It ain't my fault. I've
come into some money.

LIZA. You must have touched a millionaire this
time, Dad.

DOOLITTLE. I have. But I'm dressed something
special today. I'm going to St. George's,
Hanover Square.[6] Your stepmother is going
to marry me.

LIZA (*angrily*). You're going to let yourself down
to marry that low common woman!

---

5. **incorrigible** (in kôr′ə jə bəl), *adj.* too firmly fixed in
bad ways to be changed.
6. **St. George's, Hanover Square,** a church where many
fashionable weddings took place.

PICKERING *(quietly)*. He ought to, Eliza. (*To* DOOLITTLE.) Why has she changed her mind?

DOOLITTLE *(sadly)*. Intimidated, Governor. Intimidated. Middle class morality claims its victim. Won't you put on your hat, Liza, and come and see me turned off?

LIZA. If the Colonel says I must, I—I'll *(almost sobbing)* I'll <u>demean</u>[7] myself. And get insulted for my pains, like enough.

DOOLITTLE. Don't be afraid: she never comes to words with anyone now, poor woman! Respectability has broke all the spirit out of her.

PICKERING *(squeezing* ELIZA's *elbow gently)*. Be kind to them, Eliza. Make the best of it.

LIZA *(forcing a little smile for him through her vexation)*. Oh well, just to show there's no ill feeling. I'll be back in a moment. *(She goes out.)*

DOOLITTLE *(sitting down beside* PICKERING*)*. I feel uncommon nervous about the ceremony, Colonel. I wish you'd come and see me through it.

PICKERING. But you've been through it before, man. You were married to Eliza's mother.

DOOLITTLE. Who told you that, Colonel?

PICKERING. Well, nobody told me. But I concluded—naturally—

DOOLITTLE. No: that ain't the natural way, Colonel: it's only the middle class way. My way was always the undeserving way. But don't say nothing to Eliza. She don't know: I always had a delicacy about telling her.

PICKERING. Quite right. We'll leave it so, if you don't mind.

DOOLITTLE. And you'll come to the church, Colonel, and put me through straight?

PICKERING. With pleasure. As far as a bachelor can.

MRS. HIGGINS. May I come, Mr. Doolittle? I should be very sorry to miss your wedding.

DOOLITTLE. I should indeed be honored by your condescension, ma'am; and my poor old woman would take it as a tremenjous compliment. She's been very low, thinking of the happy days that are no more.

MRS. HIGGINS *(rising)*. I'll order the carriage and get ready. (*The men rise, except* HIGGINS.) I shan't be more than fifteen minutes. (*As she goes to the door* ELIZA *comes in, hatted and buttoning her gloves.*) I'm going to the church to see your father married, Eliza. You had better come in the <u>brougham</u>[8] with me. Colonel Pickering can go on with the bridegroom.

(MRS. HIGGINS *goes out.* ELIZA *comes to the middle of the room between the center window and the ottoman.* PICKERING *joins her.*)

DOOLITTLE. Bridegroom! What a word! It makes a man realize his position, somehow. *(He takes up his hat and goes towards the door.)*

PICKERING. Before I go, Eliza, do forgive him and come back to us.

LIZA. I don't think Papa would allow me. Would you, Dad?

DOOLITTLE *(sad but* <u>magnanimous</u>*)*.[9] They played you off very <u>cunning</u>, Eliza, them two sportsmen. If it had been only one of them, you could have nailed him. But you see, there was two; and one of them chaperoned the other, as you might say. (*To* PICKERING.) It was artful of you, Colonel; but I bear no malice: I should have done the same myself. I been the victim of one woman after another all my life; and I don't grudge you two getting the better of Eliza. I shan't interfere. It's time for us to go, Colonel. So long, Henry. See you in St. George's, Eliza. *(He goes out.)*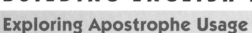

PICKERING *(coaxing)*. Do stay with us, Eliza. (*He follows* DOOLITTLE.)

(ELIZA *goes out on the balcony to avoid being alone with* HIGGINS. *He rises and joins her there. She immediately comes back into the room and makes for the door; but he goes along the balcony quickly and gets his back to the door before she reaches it.*)

---

7. **demean** (di mēn′), *v.* lower in dignity; degrade.
8. **brougham** (brŭm′), *n.* a closed carriage or automobile, having an outside seat for the driver.
9. **magnanimous** (mag nan′ə məs), *adj.* generous in forgiving.

---

20 Reading/Thinking Skills
Recognize Values

Question   What does Doolittle suggest about the relativity of values? *(Possible response: that marriage and legitimacy are middle-class constructs, about which there is nothing "natural")*

21 Reading/Thinking Skills
Recognize Values

Question   How do Doolittle's values cloud his understanding of the relationship between Eliza and the two men? *(Possible response: He sees all single women in search of a husband; he sees all single men doing their best to remain unattached.)*

BUILDING ENGLISH PROFICIENCY

Exploring Apostrophe Usage

You can use pages 708–709 to help students recognize the difference between commonly confused contractions and possessives.

1. Explain that a contraction replaces one or more letters with an apostrophe *(mustn't/must not; you'll/you will)*.

2. Explain that pronoun possessive forms may be confused with contractions. Possessives of pronouns, such as *its, your, their,* and *whose,* don't have apostrophes.

3. Ask students to copy examples based upon the dialogue from these pages:

- <u>Your</u> stepmother is going to marry me. <u>You're</u> going to let yourself down . . .
- Middle-class morality claims its victim. <u>It's</u> only the middle-class way.

4. Ask students in pairs to make up one sentence for each possessive form and contraction: their/they're; whose/who's.

Reading/Thinking Skills

Compare and Contrast

Question How would you compare and contrast what Higgins says here with how he has behaved throughout the play. *(Possible response: Higgins does treat everyone equally; however, his manners are not like Pickering's. Higgins treats everyone as if they were third-class carriage passengers, while Pickering treats everyone as if they were first-class carriage passengers.)*

Literary Focus

Inference

Question What is Higgins's motivation for saying this? *(Possible responses: He wants to reassert his power over Eliza; Eliza has pushed him to the point where he can actually acknowledge that he has some feelings for her, although he communicates it awkwardly and imperiously.)*

Reading/Thinking Skills

Analyze

Question How does Higgins's explanation help you understand Higgins? *(Possible response: He has a philosophical rather than a personal and social approach to life and seems to have few friends and personal connections—even his relationship with Pickering is about language and phonetics. This explains why he doesn't relate to Eliza the way she expects him to; he cannot.)*

HIGGINS. Well, Eliza, you've had a bit of your own back, as you call it. Have you had enough? And are you going to be reasonable? Or do you want any more?

LIZA. You want me back only to pick up your slippers and put up with your tempers and fetch and carry for you.

HIGGINS. I haven't said I wanted you back at all.

LIZA. Oh, indeed. Then what are we talking about?

HIGGINS. About you, not about me. If you come back I shall treat you just as I have always treated you. I can't change my nature; and I don't intend to change my manners. My manners are exactly the same as Colonel Pickering's.

LIZA. That's not true. He treats a flower girl as if she was a duchess.

HIGGINS. And I treat a duchess as if she was a flower girl.

LIZA. I see. *(She turns away composedly, and sits on the ottoman, facing the window.)* The same to everybody.

HIGGINS. Just so.

LIZA. Like Father.

HIGGINS *(grinning, a little taken down)*. Without accepting the comparison at all points, Eliza, it's quite true that your father is not a snob, and that he will be quite at home in any station of life to which his eccentric destiny may call him. *(Seriously.)* The great secret, Eliza, is not having bad manners or good manners or any other particular sort of manners, but having the same manner for all human souls: in short, behaving as if you were in Heaven, where there are no third-class carriages, and one soul is as good as another.

LIZA. Amen. You are a born preacher.

HIGGINS *(irritated)*. The question is not whether I treat you rudely, but whether you ever heard me treat anyone else better.

LIZA *(with sudden sincerity)*. I don't care how you treat me. I don't mind your swearing at me. I don't mind a black eye: I've had one before

this. But *(standing up and facing him)* I won't be passed over.

HIGGINS. Then get out of my way; for I won't stop for you. You talk about me as if I were a motor bus.

LIZA. So you are a motor bus: all bounce and go, and no consideration for anyone. But I can do without you: don't think I can't.

HIGGINS. I know you can. I told you you could.

LIZA *(wounded, getting away from him to the other side of the ottoman with her face to the hearth)*. I know you did, you brute. You wanted to get rid of me.

HIGGINS. Liar.

LIZA. Thank you. *(She sits down with dignity.)*

HIGGINS. You never asked yourself, I suppose, whether *I* could do without you.

LIZA *(earnestly)*. Don't you try to get round me. You'll have to do without me.

HIGGINS *(arrogant)*. I can do without anybody. I have my own soul: my own spark of divine fire. But *(with sudden humility)* I shall miss you, Eliza. *(He sits down near her on the ottoman.)* I have learned something from your idiotic notions: I confess that humbly and gratefully. And I have grown accustomed to your voice and appearance. I like them, rather.

LIZA. Well, you have both of them on your gramophone and in your book of photographs. When you feel lonely without me, you can turn the machine on. It's got no feelings to hurt.

HIGGINS. I can't turn your soul on. Leave me those feelings; and you can take away the voice and the face. They are not you.

LIZA. Oh, you are a devil. You can twist the heart in a girl as easy as some could twist her arms to hurt her. Mrs. Pearce warned me. Time and again she has wanted to leave you; and you always got round her at the last minute. And you don't care a bit for her. And you don't care a bit for me.

HIGGINS. I care for life, for humanity; and you are a part of it that has come my way and

---

MINI-LESSON: VOCABULARY

Actual and Figurative Comparisons

Teach Remind students that similes and metaphors are comparisons of unlike things that are alike in one way. Sometimes a phrase may sound like a simile or a metaphor, but if it compares similar things, it is merely a comparison. Eliza makes several comparisons on this page, which you can discuss.

- "You are a born preacher."—may be merely a comparison because Higgins and a preacher are both humans, but could also be considered a metaphor because perhaps they are alike in only a few ways, in this case, the ability to make an inspiring speech

- "So you are a motor bus."—a metaphor; Higgins is like a bus in only one way—all bounce and go

- "Oh, you are a devil."—a common figure of speech, since one meaning of *devil* is "a cruel or wicked person"

- "You can twist the heart in a girl as easy [easily] as some could twist her arms to hurt her."—though a comparison using *as,* it is a comparison of like things. A simile would compare unlike things—"as easy as taking candy from a baby"

Activity Idea Have students find comparisons in this act of similar things and of dissimilar things in the form of similes and metaphors.

been built into my house. What more can you or anybody ask?

LIZA. I won't care for anybody that doesn't care for me.

HIGGINS. Commercial principles, Eliza. Like *(reproducing her Covent Garden pronunciation with professional exactness)* s'yollin voylets [selling violets], isn't it?

LIZA. Don't sneer at me. It's mean to sneer at me.

HIGGINS. I have never sneered in my life. Sneering doesn't become either the human face or the human soul. I am expressing my righteous contempt for Commercialism. I don't and won't trade in affection. You call me a brute because you couldn't buy a claim on me by fetching my slippers and finding my spectacles. You were a fool: I think a woman fetching a man's slippers is a disgusting sight: did I ever fetch your slippers? I think a good deal more of you for throwing them in my face. No use slaving for me and then saying you want to be cared for: who cares for a slave? If you come back, come back for the sake of good fellowship; for you'll get nothing else. You've had a thousand times as much out of me as I have out of you; and if you dare to set up your little dog's tricks of fetching and carrying slippers against my creation of a Duchess Eliza, I'll slam the door in your silly face.

LIZA. What did you do it for if you didn't care for me?

HIGGINS *(heartily).* Why, because it was my job.

LIZA. You never thought of the trouble it would make for me.

HIGGINS. Would the world ever have been made if its maker had been afraid of making trouble? Making life means making trouble. There's only one way of escaping trouble; and that's killing things. Cowards, you notice, are always shrieking to have troublesome people killed.

LIZA. I'm no preacher: I don't notice things like that. I notice that you don't notice me.

HIGGINS *(jumping up and walking about intolerantly).* Eliza: you're an idiot. I waste the trea-

sures of my Miltonic mind by spreading them before you. Once for all, understand that I go my way and do my work without caring twopence what happens to either of us. I am not intimidated, like your father and your stepmother. So you can come back or go to the devil: which you please.

LIZA. What am I to come back for?

HIGGINS *(bouncing up on his knees on the ottoman and leaning over it to her).* For the fun of it. That's why I took you on.

LIZA *(with averted face).* And you may throw me out tomorrow if I don't do everything you want me to?

HIGGINS. Yes; and you may walk out tomorrow if I don't do everything you want me to.

LIZA. And live with my stepmother?

HIGGINS. Yes, or sell flowers.

LIZA. Oh! If I only could go back to my flower basket! I should be independent of both you and Father and all the world! Why did you take my independence from me? Why did I give it up? I'm a slave now, for all my fine clothes.

HIGGINS. Not a bit. I'll adopt you as my daughter and settle money on you if you like. Or would you rather marry Pickering?

LIZA *(looking fiercely round at him).* I wouldn't marry you if you asked me; and you're nearer my age than what he is.

HIGGINS *(gently).* Than he is: not "than what he is."

LIZA *(losing her temper and rising).* I'll talk as I like. You're not my teacher now.

HIGGINS *(reflectively).* I don't suppose Pickering would, though. He's as confirmed an old bachelor as I am.

LIZA. That's not what I want; and don't you think it. I've always had chaps enough wanting me that way. Freddy Hill writes to me twice and three times a day, sheets and sheets.

HIGGINS *(disagreeably surprised).* Damn his impudence! *(He recoils and finds himself sitting on his heels.)*

Pygmalion—Act Five   711

25 Reader's Response
Making Personal Connections

Question What do you think of the views expressed here? *(Responses will vary: Some students may agree that women shouldn't be servile, but disagree that the kind of impersonal relationship Higgins wants is possible between men and women. Some students may think that, although he does not communicate it very civilly or loftily, Higgins is describing the way people should relate to each other.)*

26 Reading/Thinking Skills
Make Judgments

Question Do you agree with Higgins's assessment? *(Possible responses: Some are likely to agree. Others may say that he has just not admitted the professional pride and personal enjoyment he has had from Eliza's company, while the benefits to her have been more obvious.)*

27 Literary Focus
Inference

Question Eliza claims she didn't want Higgins to fall in love with her. What did she want? *(Possible response: his respect and esteem)*

BUILDING ENGLISH PROFICIENCY

Checking Comprehension

Have students evaluate their reading by asking questions of the characters.

1. Have students write on separate slips of paper one question they would like to ask Eliza and one question they would like to ask Higgins at this point in the play. Ask them to write "For Eliza" or "For Higgins" on each question.

2. Put the questions in a box, shake it, and have each student draw two questions.

3. Have students answer the questions that they have received as they think the questioned character would answer them, as in this example:

<u>Question:</u> Higgins, what kind of marriage do you expect to have if neither person does anything for the other?

<u>Answer:</u> I never, never want to get married.

LIZA. He has a right to if he likes, poor lad. And he does love me.

HIGGINS *(getting off the ottoman)*. You have no right to encourage him.

LIZA. Every girl has a right to be loved.

HIGGINS. What! By fools like that?

LIZA. Freddy's not a fool. And if he's weak and poor and wants me, maybe he'd make me happier than my betters that bully me and don't want me.

HIGGINS. Can he make anything of you? That's the point.

LIZA. Perhaps I could make something of him. But I never thought of us making anything of one another; and you never think of anything else. I only want to be natural.

HIGGINS. In short, you want me to be as infatuated about you as Freddy? Is that it?

LIZA. No I don't. That's not the sort of feeling I want from you. And don't you be too sure of yourself or of me. I could have been a bad girl if I'd liked. I've seen more of some things than you, for all your learning. Girls like me can drag gentlemen down to make love to them easy enough. And they wish each other dead the next minute.

HIGGINS. Of course they do. Then what in thunder are we quarrelling about?

LIZA *(much troubled)*. I want a little kindness. I know I'm a common ignorant girl, and you a book-learned gentleman; but I'm not dirt under your feet. What I done *(correcting herself)* what I did was not for the dresses and the taxis: I did it because we were pleasant together and I come—came—to care for you; not to want you to make love to me, and not forgetting the difference between us, but more friendly like.

HIGGINS. Well, of course. That's just how I feel. And how Pickering feels. Eliza: you're a fool.

LIZA. That's not a proper answer to give me. *(She sinks on the chair at the writing-table in tears.)*

HIGGINS. It's all you'll get until you stop being a common idiot. If you're going to be a lady,

you'll have to give up feeling neglected if the men you know don't spend half their time snivelling over you and the other half giving you black eyes. If you can't stand the coldness of my sort of life, and the strain of it, go back to the gutter. Work till you are more a brute than a human being; and then cuddle and squabble and drink till you fall asleep. Oh, it's a fine life, the life of the gutter. It's real: it's warm: it's violent: you can feel it through the thickest skin: you can taste it and smell it without any training or any work. Not like Science and Literature and Classical Music and Philosophy and Art. You find me cold, unfeeling, selfish, don't you? Very well: be off with you to the sort of people you like. Marry some sentimental hog or other with lots of money, and a thick pair of lips to kiss you with and a thick pair of boots to kick you with. If you can't appreciate what you've got, you'd better get what you can appreciate.

LIZA *(desperate)*. Oh, you are a cruel tyrant. I can't talk to you: you turn everything against me: I'm always in the wrong. But you know very well all the time that you're nothing but a bully. You know I can't go back to the gutter, as you call it, and that I have no real friends in the world but you and the Colonel. You know well I couldn't bear to live with a low common man after you two: and it's wicked and cruel of you to insult me by pretending I could. You think I must go back to Wimpole Street because I have nowhere else to go but Father's. But don't you be too sure that you have me under your feet to be trampled on and talked down. I'll marry Freddy, I will, as soon as he's able to support me.

HIGGINS *(sitting down beside her)*. Rubbish! You shall marry an ambassador. You shall marry the Governor-General of India or the Lord-Lieutenant of Ireland, or somebody who wants a deputy-queen. I'm not going to have my masterpiece thrown away on Freddy.

MINI-LESSON: GRAMMAR

Consistent Verb Tense

Teach Read Eliza's speech on page 712 near the bottom of column 1 beginning, "I want a little kindness." Point out that Eliza uses the past participle of *do* instead of the past tense, and corrects herself. Tell students that when words have a past participle that is different from the past tense form, care must be taken not to confuse them.

Question What does Eliza's self-correction convey? *(Possible response: that she has internalized Higgins's standards so that even in times of emotional distress she tries to speak properly)*

Activity Idea Have students work in groups to make a chart of verbs with differing past tense and past participles. Challenge the groups to see which one can identify the greatest number of verbs.

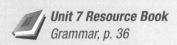

Unit 7 Resource Book
Grammar, p. 36

Art Study

Questions Do you think this photograph is actually part of a scene or is it a publicity still? Why? *(Possible response: It is a publicity still. Higgins and Eliza are dressed in their opera clothes; at this point in the play, Eliza was furious with the professor and would not have sat this closely next to him.)*

BUILDING ENGLISH PROFICIENCY

Analyzing the Title

As the play draws to its close, ask students to grasp the significance of its title.

1. Review the classic myth (very briefly summarized on page 661), in which the sculptor Pygmalion creates a statue so beautiful that he falls in love with it. The goddess of love pities him and brings the statue to life. Ask: Who is Pygmalion in this play? How is what happens in the play a reversal (the opposite) of what happens in the myth?

2. Ask students to predict what will happen at the end of the play.

3. Invite students to imagine that they meet someone who wants (and has the power) to change them into an amazingly attractive person. Have them weigh the pros and cons of agreeing to the transformation.

30 Literary Element
Theme

Higgins claims that independence is another middle class idea that is untrue to human nature. You might lead the class in a discussion of whether he is turning a practical issue into a philosophical issue for the sake of not being trapped by a strong opposing argument, or whether his comment is valid and relevant.

31 Literary Element
Theme

Question This is the most explicit statement of the Pygmalion theme. How does this relate it to the title? *(Possible response: Higgins believes he has created a creature that is both elegant and well-spoken, but also independent and thoughtful; believing her to be totally his creation, he is free to love her.)*

Check Test

1. Why does Higgins call the police? *(Eliza is missing.)*

2. What made Alfred Doolittle a middle-class man? *(Higgins's letter to an American millionaire who left Doolittle a bequest)*

3. What does Eliza want Higgins to call her? *(Miss Doolittle)*

4. What does Eliza plan to do to support herself? *(teach phonetics)*

5. What does Higgins think Eliza will do? *(return to Wimpole St.)*

Unit 7 Resource Book
Alternate Check Test, p.37

LIZA. You think I like you to say that. But I haven't forgot what you said a minute ago; and I won't be coaxed round as if I was a baby or a puppy. If I can't have kindness, I'll have independence.

HIGGINS. Independence? That's middle class blasphemy. We are all dependent on one another, every soul of us on earth.

LIZA *(rising determinedly).* I'll let you see whether I'm dependent on you. If you can preach, I can teach. I'll go and be a teacher.

HIGGINS. What'll you teach, in heaven's name?

LIZA. What you taught me. I'll teach phonetics.

HIGGINS. Ha! ha! ha!

LIZA. I'll offer myself as an assistant to Professor Nepean.

HIGGINS *(rising in a fury).* What! That impostor! That humbug! That toadying ignoramus! Teach him my methods! My discoveries! You take one step in his direction and I'll wring your neck. *(He lays hands on her.)* Do you hear?

LIZA *(defiantly non-resistant).* Wring away. What do I care? I knew you'd strike me some day. *(He lets her go, stamping with rage at having forgotten himself, and recoils so hastily that he stumbles back into his seat on the ottoman.)* Aha! Now I know how to deal with you. What a fool I was not to think of it before! You can't take away the knowledge you gave me. You said I had a finer ear than you. And I can be civil and kind to people, which is more than you can. Aha! That's done you, Henry Higgins, it has. Now I don't care that *(snapping her fingers)* for your bullying and your big talk. I'll advertize it in the papers that your duchess is only a flower girl that you taught, and that she'll teach anybody to be a duchess just the same in six months for a thousand guineas. Oh, when I think of myself crawling under your feet and being trampled on and called names, when all the time I had only to lift up my finger to be as good as you, I could just kick myself.

HIGGINS *(wondering at her).* You damned impudent slut, you! But it's better than snivelling; better than fetching slippers and finding spectacles, isn't it? *(Rising.)* By George, Eliza, I said I'd make a woman of you; and I have. I like you like this.

LIZA. Yes: you turn round and make up to me now that I'm not afraid of you, and can do without you.

HIGGINS. Of course I do, you little fool. Five minutes ago you were like a millstone round my neck. Now you're a tower of strength: a consort battleship. You and I and Pickering will be three old bachelors together instead of only two men and a silly girl.

(MRS. HIGGINS returns, dressed for the wedding. ELIZA instantly becomes cool and elegant.)

MRS. HIGGINS. The carriage is waiting, Eliza. Are you ready?

LIZA. Quite. Is the Professor coming?

MRS. HIGGINS. Certainly not. He can't behave himself in church. He makes remarks out loud all the time on the clergyman's pronunciation.

LIZA. Then I shall not see you again, Professor. Goodbye. *(She goes to the door.)*

MRS. HIGGINS *(coming to HIGGINS).* Goodbye, dear.

HIGGINS. Goodbye, Mother. *(He is about to kiss her, when he recollects something.)* Oh, by the way, Eliza, order a ham and a Stilton cheese, will you? And buy me a pair of reindeer gloves, number eights, and a tie to match that new suit of mine, at Eale & Binman's. You can choose the color. *(His cheerful, careless, vigorous voice shows that he is incorrigible.)*

LIZA *(disdainfully).* Buy them yourself. *(She sweeps out.)*

MRS. HIGGINS. I'm afraid you've spoiled that girl, Henry. But never mind, dear: I'll buy you the tie and gloves.

HIGGINS *(sunnily).* Oh, don't bother. She'll buy em all right enough. Goodbye.

(They kiss. MRS. HIGGINS runs out. HIGGINS, left alone, rattles his cash in his pocket; chuckles; and disports himself in a highly self-satisfied manner.)

Act 5

Shaping Your Response

Analyzing the Play

Making Connections

1. Are you satisfied with the ending of the play? Why or why not?

2. Many comedies end with a wedding or, at the least, a happy reunion of lovers. How has Shaw both followed this tradition and turned it upside down?

3. Compare Liza's entrance in act 5 to her appearance after a bath in act 2 and her introduction to Mrs. Higgins's at-home. What levels of development are apparent in each case?

4. What is the central **conflict** in Pygmalion? Is it resolved?

5. What are the differences in the causes and results of both Liza's and her father's transformations?

6. What details support Liza's claim that "the difference between a lady and a flower girl is not how she behaves, but how she's treated"?

7. Throughout the play, almost everyone has been trying to instruct the teacher, Henry Higgins. Do you think he learns anything? Explain.

8. 👣 Do you think there is genuine **communication** between Higgins and Liza in act 5? Does communication imply agreement between people? Explain.

9. In your opinion, is there anything in the play that serves as convincing evidence about what Liza will do next? Explain.

10. What **main idea** do you think Shaw wanted the audience to carry home from *Pygmalion*?

Extending the Ideas

11. Americans have always boasted that there is no class system in the United States. Is this true in your opinion? Explain.

Literary Focus: Inference

An **inference** is a reasonable conclusion about the behavior of a character or the meaning of events. Characters in a play as well as readers and playgoers must make inferences.

1. What inference might the audience make when Doolittle first appears in act 5, and what might that inference be based on?

2. Does Liza make any incorrect inferences in the play? Does Higgins? Explain.

3. What inferences do you make about Shaw's views in general about a class system?

LITERARY FOCUS: INFERENCE

1. Possible response: Students might infer that Doolittle changed his mind and decided to take lessons from Higgins. This inference could be based on the obvious change in his social and economic class implied by his attire and Higgins's offer in Act Two to teach him.

2. Students may mention the incorrect inference Eliza makes about Higgins in Act One and the incorrect inferences Higgins makes in Act Two about Eliza's understanding and capabilities.

3. Students should infer that Shaw was opposed to the class system and thought that people should be treated equally.

MAKING CONNECTIONS

1. Students may compare the ending of the play to the ending of "The Lady or the Tiger?" in which the audience is left to infer the outcome.

2. He ends with Doolittle's wedding and a prediction that Eliza will marry; but the former holds little interest for the audience, and the later is unsatisfactory because the audience, like Higgins, believes Eliza would be wasted on Freddy.

3. In Act Two, Eliza shows an understanding of how ladies take care of their appearance; when she appears at Mrs. Higgins's, she has acquired pronunciation and articulation; by Act Five she has acquired the bearing of a lady and the ability to think independently.

4. Students may respond that the central conflict is between how a person is defined by himself, others, and society.

5. Eliza's transformation is caused by serendipity laid on the foundation of desire to change. Doolittle's transformation is triggered by a joke. Eliza's transformation results in a change in social status and in how she views the world. Doolittle enters the middle class, but as an interloper with great reluctance.

6. It was Pickering's treatment of her that began her transformation.

7. Higgins may have learned to express his feelings in a limited way; he seems to believe that human feelings are slightly more important than he had believed.

8. Students may agree that they continue to miscommunicate until the end. Students are likely to agree that people do not need to agree to communicate, but rather understand each other's position.

9. Students may point out that there is little reason to doubt that she will marry Freddy and teach phonetics.

10. Possible response: that the class system is artificial and needs to be replaced by equality between and among classes and genders

11. While responses may vary, students might note that a class system exists.

VOCABULARY STUDY

1. repudiate
2. demean
3. magnanimous
4. incorrigible
5. provocation

WRITING CHOICES
Writer's Notebook Update

Before students begin, you might lead a discussion on differences in levels of formality in dress between the time of the play and today.

Classtime?

You might discuss with students interested in this project the basic difference between classes in Britain and the United States: that the class system is built into the British system of government, through the monarchy; that the U.S. class system, divorced from government, is based almost solely on money.

Unit 7 Resource Book
Vocabulary, p. 35
Vocabulary Test, p. 38

Selection Test

Unit 7 Resource Book
pp. 39–40

Transparency Collection
Fine Art Writing Prompt 13

Vocabulary Study

Match each example with the most appropriate word from the list. You will not use all the words.

demean
brougham
incorrigible
magnamimous
provocation
repudiate

1. refusing to accept someone's opinion
2. making fun of someone's appearance
3. writing a kind letter to someone who insulted you
4. being convicted of a crime for the third time
5. throwing stones to tease a dog

Expressing Your Ideas

Writing Choices

Writer's Notebook Update Review your notes on costumes throughout the play. Write a paragraph or so in which you discuss the importance of clothes and accessories in *Pygmalion* and the relation of clothes to themes in the play.

Protagonist / Antagonist Write an **essay** in which you analyze the characterization of Liza. Skim the play to find examples of what she says about herself, what others say about her, how she treats others and is treated by others, and her emotional reactions as suggested in the stage directions. You might devote one paragraph to the best examples you can find of each of these, concluding with a summary of what kind of person she seems to be. As an alternative, write about Higgins, following the same pattern, and attempting to answer some of these questions: Is he truly a confirmed bachelor? What does he want from Liza? Why does he seem to despise the Eynsford Hills?

Classtime? Expand your answer to question 11 into a community or school newspaper **editorial.** Be sure to include supporting examples for your opinions and to anticipate and rebut the arguments for the other side.

You might conclude with a plan of action for people in the U. S.

Other Options

Spinoffs Obtain copies of the 1938 film of *Pygmalion,* starring Wendy Hiller and Leslie Howard, and the film of the musical *My Fair Lady,* based on *Pygmalion* and starring Audrey Hepburn and Rex Harrison. In small groups **analyze these different versions** and compare them with Shaw's play. Have Shaw's chief ideas been retained?

Shaw Revival! Suppose that a new movie or stage production of *Pygmalion* is going to open. Design a full-page **newspaper ad** for the production. Decide what modern actors would best fit these roles, and also choose a producer and director if you wish. Include artwork as well as type in your ad.

Dressing Eliza You are the costume designer for a new production of *Pygmalion.* **Design and sketch costumes** for at least two of the characters throughout the play. Use clues from the text, but when Shaw says nothing, rely on your imagination. If possible, consult some library books on clothing of the period.

OTHER OPTIONS
Spinoffs

You may also want to have students study the script or the movie *Educating Rita* by Willy Russell, which has a similar plot and themes.

Upward Mobility

The English Class System

History Connection

In the following passages, two social historians describe how England's "two nations"—the rich and the poor—lived their very different lives during the Edwardian period (1901–1910, the reign of Victoria's son, King Edward VII) that forms the background of Bernard Shaw's *Pygmalion*.

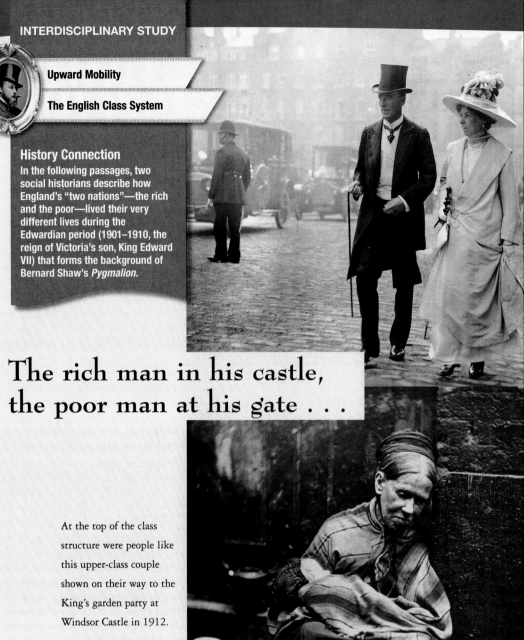

The rich man in his castle, the poor man at his gate . . .

At the top of the class structure were people like this upper-class couple shown on their way to the King's garden party at Windsor Castle in 1912.

At the bottom of the social pyramid were slum-dwellers like this mother and her child.

Interdisciplinary Study **717**

Interdisciplinary Study

Theme Link

Upward mobility was almost impossible for England's oppressed lower class, who could not even reach the bottom rung of the social ladder from which a few lucky middle-class individuals might rise to financial success.

Curricular Connection: History

You can use the information in this interdisciplinary study to offer students a historical perspective on the harsh social conditions that inspired Shaw to write his satire of the British class structure.

Terms to Know

hierarchical (hī′ə rär′kə kəl), of or having to do with a person who holds a high position.

death duties, taxes charged by a government at the time of a person's death.

inequity (in ek′wə tē), injustice.

hedonism (hēd′n iz′əm), living only for pleasure.

prodigiously (prə dij′ē əs lē), greatly, hugely.

philanthropic (fil′ən throp′ik), charitable, kindly.

demur (di mèr′), show disapproval, object.

stinted (stint′əd), restricted, limited.

palliative (pal′ē ā′tiv), something that lessens, softens, or excuses.

 Unit 6 Resource Book
Interdisciplinary Study Guide, p. 81

BUILDING ENGLISH PROFICIENCY

Responding to a Theme

Before students read the articles on pages 718–719, have them use the photographs above to prompt their memories about what they already have learned about the English class system.

1. Direct students' attention to the couple shown in the picture at the top of the page. Ask: What do you think the lives of these two people are like? What do you think the expression *upper class* means to them? Which characters in *Pygmalion* do you think

they resemble? How did you feel about those characters, and why?

2. Discuss similar questions as you focus on the slum-dwellers. Ask: How might this woman look at her own future and the future of her child? What did Eliza Doolittle want for her own future? How did her life change when she began associating with the rich instead of the poor?

Research Topics

- Karl Marx: his life and his writings on class struggle
- Photojournalism as social criticism
- The political reforms of David Lloyd George
- The formation of Britain's Labor party
- The Fabian Society's social platform

MULTICULTURAL NOTE

Although Britain's factories and mines had initially made it the financial giant of the world during the second half of the nineteenth century, the United States experienced its own industrial boom. Britain, with its older plants and equipment, began to fall behind in the international race for economic supremacy. Britain's miserable industrial workers found that the skills that they had learned in British mills and mines were useful in the growing United States. In the United States, wages were higher, and a laborer might work his way up the social ladder and become a foreman or even start his own business. Factory workers could cherish the hope that their children might become teachers or lawyers. The possibilities offered by American industries lured a new wave of British citizens to the United States.

The Upper Class

by Marina Warner

Britain was a narrow world, with its own hard and fast rules. The most important code of all concerned class. The chief ingredient in any man's personality, when assessed by anyone else at that time, was his social position—his class. Society was stratified very clearly and it was an expected form of behavior for everyone, at each level, to lord it over anyone beneath. This hierarchical instinct sometimes took subtler forms—a gentleman would not for instance be rude to a servant—but it was deeply ingrained, so ingrained in fact that the inequity was considered inevitable, natural, insurmountable.

The class in power was the rich, often synonymous with the old landed aristocracy. When a man of humbler birth became rich through business and industry—not uncommon then and earlier—he usual-

ly copied the behavior of the aristocracy, followed its traditions, and did not seek to change the customs of the upper classes. A successful factory-owner for instance would often bring up his son to pursue one of the "gentlemanly" professions—the Empire, Politics, the Church—rather than let him remain in trade like his own father. So although Edwardian society was mobile, in the sense that some individuals did move up the social ladder, it was at the same time stagnant, because their advancement did not cause any ripple in the calm lake of Edwardian self-assurance.

The wealth was fabulous. There was hardly any tax, and no death duties. Estates passed intact from father to son. From the evidence of wills, it has been estimated that 1 percent of the population over 25 owned 67 percent of the wealth of the country. . . . The gap between rich and poor was wider than it had been since the days of serfs.

The life of the wealthy was pure pleasure, and was enjoyed openly, with conspicuous display. The King himself, Edward VII, personified the age: jolly,

The Lower Classes

by Mary Cathcart Borer

All sections of the community, from the lowest of the middle classes upward, strove to copy, to the best of their ability, the manners and customs, the dress and household furnishings of the class immediately above them, for "keeping up with the Joneses" was a national pastime. At the bottom of this social structure, however, well below any real human contact and understanding, existed the bulk of England's population. They were the untouchables, the unconsidered poor, whose numbers were so vast that some foretold that, if they were not kept in their place, they might one day threaten the financial security of the entire country.

These lower classes were the artisans, the factory workers, the miners and industrial workers, the fishermen, the farm hands, the dockers, the seamstresses and domestic servants, the shop assistants and a large and murky residue of casual laborers and vagrants.

They worked incredibly long hours for starvation wages, they had little or no education and were appallingly badly housed. When they fell out of work there was no unemployment pay. They had little money for medical attention and there were no pensions for old age.

The consciences of many Victorians had been roused by the terrible inequalities in the distribution of wealth, and throughout the nineteenth century reforms had been made, not only by philanthropic individuals and societies, but also by succeeding governments, both Conservative and Liberal, which were to lead in time to the establishment of the Welfare State of today. Nevertheless, there were many from all walks of life, from the rich to the working classes themselves, who accepted the state of the poor unquestioningly, believing that the position in life to which one was born was part of the plan of an all-wise God, whose ways should not be questioned. Wealth was regarded as almost a divine right and poverty and misfortune a burden to be borne without demur, tempered by the debatable solace that things might be better in the next world. There had been a strong

MINI-LESSON: STUDY SKILLS

Social History and Statistics

Teach   Draw students' attention to places where Warner uses numbers and percentages to support her arguments.

Question   How does the inclusion of hard facts influence your impression of Warner's argument? *(Possible response: It makes you agree with her by lending credibility to her assertions.)*

Apply   An entire branch of sociology is devoted to demography, the scientific study of the characteristics and facts about human population. Sociologists use statistics, a branch of mathemat-

ics, to collect, organize, and interpret their data.

Activity Ideas

- Have students research other statistics from England at the turn of the century.
- Have students draw a graph (a pie graph, a line graph, or a bar graph) that organizes either the statistics in Warner's article or the statistics that they found through independent research.

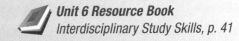

Unit 6 Resource Book
Interdisciplinary Study Skills, p. 41

sensual, rough and ready when it came to anything like the appreciation of music and poetry. His aristocratic subjects were idle, fun-loving, hearty as himself; there was a wide distrust of the arts, as if they were somehow unrespectable, and a corresponding confidence in the "manly" pursuits: huntin', shootin', fishin'. The families of substance followed the racing season around Britain. . . .

Edwardian hedonism was only made possible by the work of others, less advantaged. Everything a rich man required was provided by servants. A country house, visited only once a year for a month at the right time of the shooting season, might need fifty servants to keep it up. For these enormous establishments were without gas, electricity or running water. Servants carried coal down long corridors, up long flights of stairs to each bedroom at dawn so that the room might be warm when the gentleman or lady rose; later they brought hot water up from the kitchen hob—so that they could wash in comfort. For a bath, several journeys with kettles and buckets had

to be made. Edwardians of the upper class also ate prodigiously: sideboards at breakfast would be laden with hams, porridge, poached eggs, muffins, sausages, boiled plovers' eggs, tea, milk, coffee. They also dressed themselves elaborately, so that every lady needed a maid to help pull her stays tighter and button her up, and more servants behind the green baize door to wash, iron, crimp and goffer the starched and lacy undergarments she wore. She needed help to wash her long hair—never cut from birth—and dress it in the high voluptuous styles of the period. The daughter of a woman who had been "in service" remembered that one of her mother's employers, at the age of 30, had still never washed herself. Children too were waited upon: taught by governesses or sometimes private tutors, washed and walked and fed by maids. Forty-six percent of the population—most of them women—worked in domestic situations in 1911. For this they were poorly rewarded financially, and, at a broader level, emotionally. It was a life of complete poverty of spirit for most people.

---

religious revival in the mid-nineteenth century and people were still singing with fervent conviction:

The rich man in his castle,
The poor man at his gate,
God made them high and lowly,
And ordered their estate.

In his book *The Condition of England*, published in 1909, C. F. G. Mastermen wrote of Britain's laboring population: "They work in unventilated rooms. They are stinted of holidays. They are compelled to work overtime. They endure accident and disease. They are fined and cheated in innumerable ways. Their life is often confined to a mere routine of work and sleep. Yet they endure; and even at the heart of foul and impossible conditions retain always some rags of decency and honor."

In the pottery towns people were still suffering as they had from the beginning. A Medical Officer of Health found forty little girls "licking adhesive labels by the mouth at the rate of thirty gross a day. Their tongues had the polished tip characteristic of label lickers, and the rest of the tongue coated with brown

gum." In the Nottingham lace trade children were still being blinded by the double work of school and the terrible eye-strain of their employment in the lace industry.

The long monotonous hours, the drudgery and hopelessness of it all dulled them into apathy. "Can you suggest anything that anybody could do for you which would induce your master or perhaps compel him to give you a fairer or a larger wage?" one woman was asked. "If he would only time an article," she replied, "and state how long the article would take to make, and give you a certain rate of so much an hour, it would be fair, if it was only a living wage. We only want to live."

They only wanted to live! That is what so many people forgot. They did not want charity. Large, organized charities certainly existed. They were a feature of Victorian and Edwardian times. But charities are . . . little more than a sign of indifference to the fundamental problem, an effortless palliative to quieten the stirrings of conscience. The brief moment of compassion passes and is usually forgotten as quickly as the cause which aroused it.

Additional Background

These essays approach history from a sociological perspective. Sociology, the study of the origin, history, and structure of human society and its institutions, initially evolved in reaction to the cataclysmic social changes of the nineteenth century. Karl Marx, often considered to be the original "sociologist," spent years in the British Museum studying economic and social history. British philosophers John Stuart Mill and Herbert Spencer also contributed to the foundations of sociology. Contemporary sociologists study social problems, such as crime, family patterns, and the cultural adjustment of immigrants.

Interdisciplinary Activity Ideas

- Have students work in groups to prepare a multimedia sociological report on the conditions of poverty among the lower classes in the United States today. Ideas for media sources: video documentaries, popular music with political lyrics, graphs and charts, overhead projection.

- Have students reenact a British labor union negotiation. Topics on the agenda might include: higher wages, factory conditions, shift lengths, and housing conditions. Assign students to represent the factory owners, the families of the factory owners, the mediators, the workers, and the families of the workers.

BUILDING ENGLISH PROFICIENCY

Checking Comprehension

These articles contain much factual detail about the class system. You might help students evaluate their understanding by having them complete sentences such as the following:

1. In Edwardian England, _____ was the most important thing to many people. *(class)*

2. When lower-class people earned instead of inherited their wealth, they _____. *(copied the rich)*

3. Upper-class Edwardians hired servants to do such jobs as _____. *(cooking, taking care of children, other domestic duties)*

4. _____ are some of the kinds of people who were considered lower class. *(miners, farmhands, shop assistants)*

5. The upper classes thought that it was right to keep the lower classes "in their place" because _____. *(it was part of God's plan)*

Discuss the photographs on this page.

- What do the family's clothes tell you about them? *(Possible response: The people are all dressed stylishly for a summer game, implying the importance of fashion. Although the hats and parasols are intended to shield them from the sun, they also suggest additional money available to spend on accessories.)*

- Why might an employer ask his or her servants to wear uniforms? *(Possible response: to enforce the class distinction between the upper and lower classes, even in the home, or to assure that servants are dressed properly.)*

Responding

1. Possible Response Students may say that abominable conditions called society's attention to the inequity of the class system or that there was opportunity for the poor to earn money and advance into the upper class. They may also cite the exploitation of the lower class and the fact that the poor were supposed to accept their lot in life without complaint.

2. Possible Response Yes, because wealth is concentrated among a few, and there are large populations of working-class and middle-class people who do not have much discretionary income. At the bottom, many are living in abject poverty.

An upper-class family is shown on their way to the annual cricket match between Eton and Harrow, Britain's two most prestigious prep schools.

Upper-class houses required huge staffs of servants, such as the cook and house-maids shown here, to maintain them.

720

Responding

1. In your opinion, what were the best features of the British class system at the beginning of this century? the worst features?

2. Is there a class system in the United States? Why or why not?

MINI-LESSON: VISUAL LITERACY

Photography and Social Class

Teach Discuss the photographs on pages 717 and 720 as historical artifacts. Point out that before the mid-1800s, only the very rich could afford to commission painted portraits of them-selves. By the mid-1850s, however, photographic technology made small, cheap portraits available to all.

Questions

- How did the development of cheap portraits affect the self-awareness of the working class? *(Possible response: It boosted their self-image.*

They saw that they could now possess a souvenir of identity that had formerly been available only to the very rich.)*

- How did the Kodak camera affect social documentation? *(Possible response: by making it possible for people to take pictures of everyday settings and personalities.)*

Activity Idea Have students use pocket cameras to take pictures like those discussed, capturing scenes from life that would tell future generations something about life in the late 1900s.

INTERDISCIPLINARY STUDY

Popular Culture Connection
The British class system has been a staple of popular culture, from musical hall songs to television series.

Here, Julie Andrews plays Bertie in Star!, *a movie about the life of entertainer Gertrude Lawrence. First sung in 1918, this comic song about a hobo was popular in music halls, which featured vaudeville or variety acts that appealed to the middle- and working-class audiences.*

Burlington Bertie from Bow
by William Hargreaves

I'm Bert, p'raps you've heard of me,
Bert, you've had word of me,
Jogging along,
hearty and strong,
living on plates of fresh air.
I dress up in fashion,
and, when I am feeling depress'd,
I shave from my cuff
all the whiskers and fluff,
Stick my hat on and toddle up West.[1]

I'm Burlington Bertie, I rise at
    ten thirty
and saunter along like a toff,[2]
I walk down the Strand[3]
with my gloves on my hand,
then I walk down again with
    them off,
I'm all airs and graces,
correct easy paces,
without food so long I've forgot
        where my face is—
I'm Bert, Bert, I haven't a shirt,
but my people are well off,
    you know!
Nearly ev'ryone knows me,
from Smith to Lord Roseb'ry[4]

I'm Burlington Bertie from
    Bow! . . .

My pose, tho' ironical—
    shows that my monocle[5]
holds up my face,
keeps it in place,
stops it from slipping away.
Cigars—I smoke thousands,
I usually deal in the Strand,
    But you've got to take care,
    when you're getting them there
or some idiot might stand on
        your hand.

I'm Burlington Bertie, I rise at
    ten thirty
Then Buckingham Palace, I view;
I stand in the yard
while they're changing the guard,
    and the King shouts across "Toodle-oo";
    The Prince of Wales' brother,
    along with some other,
slaps me on the back, and says, "Come and
    see Mother."
I'm Bert, Bert, and Royalty's hurt;
When they ask me to dine I say, "No!
I've just had a banana
    with Lady Diana,
    I'm Burlington Bertie from Bow!"

Bow, a lower-class district in the East End of London
1. West, the fashionable West End of London.
2. toff, a fashionably dressed upper-class male. [*slang*]
3. Strand, a famous street in London.
4. Lord Rosebr'y, the Earl of Rosebery (1847–1929), British prime minister in the 1890s.

5. monocle (mon′ə kəl), *n.* an eyeglass for one eye, once considered very fashionable.

Theme Link
The British class system was an easy target for satire, and if the upper classes could look down on their "inferiors," the rest of society could make fun of the toffs.

Curricular Connection: Popular Culture
You can use the information in this article to introduce students to popular art forms that turn class struggle and social injustice into popular entertainment.

Historical Note
The word *vaudeville,* which is derived from the French, was originally a simple song with a short lyrical text, often about love. It gradually developed into a form of satire. The lyrics were usually sung to a popular melody.

In English cities during the nineteenth century, taverns often offered communal singing along with the ale. These sing-a-longs grew so in popularity that between 1850 and 1870 music halls went up all over the country and featured a variety of acts, from singing and dancing to trained animals.

BUILDING ENGLISH PROFICIENCY

ESL
LEP
ELD
SAE
LD

Drawing Conclusions

In this song, Burlington Bertie boasts of his pretended upper-class status. Have students focus on specific details in the lyrics by creating a graphic organizer such as the one shown. Partners or small groups should discuss and restate the lyrics; then they should compare their responses to form a better picture of this unique character.

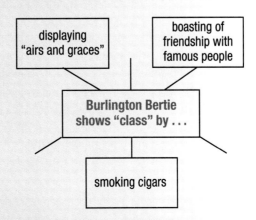

displaying "airs and graces"

boasting of friendship with famous people

Burlington Bertie shows "class" by . . .

smoking cigars

Art Study

Visual Literacy   Point out that this photograph was probably used as press copy to promote the television series *Upstairs, Downstairs,* which was produced in England and is available on video.

Question   Does seeing this photograph make you want to view the television program? Why or why not? *(Possible response: Yes, because there is a curious mixture of people. Also, many of the characters have inscrutable, almost ominous expressions on their faces, which could suggest intrigue.)*

Interdisciplinary Activity Ideas

- Have students write a song that satirizes an aspect of social structure in the United States. Suggest that they set their lyrics to the melody of a simple and well-known song.
- Make a scrapbook of Victorian and Edwardian fashions of the upper class: clothing, furniture, and architecture. Ask students to write captions that explain each cultural artifact.

Responding

1. Possible Response   The upper classes are seen as indolent, phony, and unconcerned about others.

2. Possible Response   Comical political songs are often performed in the United States. Students may be familiar with the songs of Tom Lehrer and others.

3. Possible Response   More people can identify with the lives of the working class than with the rich, but we can all dream of being wealthy and living luxuriously.

The popular, melodramatic television series *Upstairs / Downstairs* focused on the lives of the servants as well as their aristocratic employers.

Responding

1. What attitude toward the British class system is reflected in "Burlington Bertie from Bow"?

2. Could a comic song like this be popular in the contemporary United States? Why or why not?

3. Why do you think an audience would enjoy watching a drama about the lives of the poor as well as the lives of the rich?

MINI-LESSON: VISUAL LITERACY

Video: Fictional versus Factual

Teach   Have students view an episode of *Upstairs/Downstairs,* taking notes on production details like costume, dialogue, sets, accents, subject matter, and musical accompaniment.

Apply   Encourage students to research domestic life among the British upper classes at the turn of the century. Ask students to consider whether they feel that this program offers a realistic view of Edwardian life.

Questions

- What elements did the producers alter or

emphasize to make the program more interesting? *(Answers will vary.)*

- Is a fictional representation of an age more interesting than a docudrama? Why or why not? *(Possible response: The motives of the viewer determine which approach is more interesting.)*

Activity Idea   Have students view a video documentary about the same subject or era and compare and contrast the style of fictional and factual formats.

Writing Workshop

Moving Up in the World

Assignment In the time of *Pygmalion*, most people could only wonder how the upper classes really lived. Today, mass media advertising gives us a barrage of images that show what supposedly makes up an upwardly-mobile lifestyle. Analyze these images in a magazine article.

WRITER'S BLUEPRINT

Product	An article for a consumer magazine
Purpose	To educate consumers
Audience	People interested in understanding advertising
Specs	To write a successful article, you should:

❑ Imagine that you have been asked to write an article about upward mobility for a consumer magazine. Examine advertising in TV, radio, magazines, and newspapers. Try to determine what advertisers are telling us about these questions: *What should an upwardly mobile person be striving for? What defines an upwardly mobile person?* Consider things this person is urged to have, such as cars and clothing, and things this person is urged to be, such as slim and sophisticated.

❑ Begin your article with an intriguing opening that will grab your readers' interest and make them want to go on reading.

❑ Present your findings. Focus on the five most significant attributes of upward mobility promoted in the advertising you examined. Describe the messages that advertising sends to consumers about these attributes. Illustrate your conclusions with quotations and, where possible, visuals.

❑ Conclude by summarizing your findings.

❑ Write with confidence, but be reasonable and don't overstate your case.

❑ Follow the rules of grammar for correct usage, spelling, and mechanics. Use apostrophes correctly.

Writing Workshop **723**

Writing Workshop

WRITER'S BLUEPRINT
Specs

The Specs in the Writer's Blueprint address these writing and thinking skills:

- researching
- recognizing values
- identifying persuasive techniques
- making inferences
- drawing conclusions
- evaluating evidence
- summarizing
- avoiding overstatement
- using apostrophes correctly

These Specs serve as your lesson objectives, and they form the basis for the **Assessment Criteria Specs** for a superior paper, which appear on the final TE page for this lesson. You might want to read through the Assessment Criteria Specs with students when you begin the lesson.

Linking Literature to Writing

Look back at *Pygmalion* and point out to students that someone who creates topical literature, like Shaw, and someone who creates advertising are both getting at the same thing: what makes people tick, the nature of their fears and desires. But that they have differing purposes: that a writer like Shaw is trying to reveal these fears and desires, clarify them for his readers, while the advertiser is playing on these fears and desires to persuade people to buy things.

WRITING WORKSHOP OVERVIEW

Product
Expository writing: An article for a consumer magazine

Prewriting
Review the literature—Examine advertising—Discuss your findings—Identify the five attributes—Develop an intriguing opening—Plan your essay
Unit 7 Resource Book
Prewriting, pp. 43–44

Drafting
As you draft
Transparency Collection
Student Models for Writing Workshop 25, 26

Revising
Ask a partner—Strategy: Avoiding Overstatement
Unit 7 Resource Book
Revising Worksheet, p. 45

Editing
Ask a partner—Strategy: Using Apostrophes Correctly
Unit 7 Resource Book
Grammar Worksheet p. 46
Grammar Check Test p. 47

Presenting
Adding Visuals
Multimedia Presentation

Looking Back
Self-evaluate—Reflect—For Your Working Portfolio
Unit 7 Resource Book
Assessment, p. 48
Transparency Collection
Fine Art Writing Prompt 13

STEP 1 PREWRITING

Review the literature

Remind students to consider how views about class and social mobility have changed over the years. For additional support, see the worksheet referenced below.

Unit 7 Resource Book
Prewriting Worksheet, p.43

Examine advertising

Assign students to collect a wide variety of advertisements a few days before this activity. Display the advertisements in the classroom. For additional support, see the worksheet referenced below.

Unit 7 Resource Book
Prewriting Worksheet, p. 44

Discuss your findings

Students may want to create a chart that compares and contrasts the two eras.

Identify the five attributes

Encourage students to seek balance through a wide variety of subject areas.

Develop an intriguing opening

Students may want to take on a voice that borrows from the persuasive techniques of the advertising industry as part of their commentary, as in the first bulleted example.

LITERARY SOURCE
"You have no idea how frightfully interesting it is to take a human being and change her into a quite different human being by creating a new speech for her. It's filling up the deepest gulf that separates class from class and soul from soul."
from *Pygmalion* by Bernard Shaw

OR . . .
If you have time, keep a media journal. For a week or so, keep track of the advertising you see and hear on a daily basis. Transfer your notes to a chart like the one shown.

STEP 1 PREWRITING

Review the literature with a group of classmates. Look for attributes that Higgins and other characters define as essential for Eliza to become upwardly mobile. Take turns reading aloud excerpts from the play that reveal these details. Use these attributes as a jumping-off point when you move on to the next activity.

Examine advertising in television, radio, magazines, billboards, and newspapers. Record your findings in a chart like the one shown. In the second column, note both direct messages and implied messages (suggested through words or pictures) about how these attributes contribute to upward mobility. Along the way, collect illustrations to include with your article.

Attribute of Upward Mobility	Messages
luxury car	—"deep reserves of passing power" (you need to be faster) —"space-age design" (you want only the latest and the best) —picture of admiring crowds watching car drive by (you'll be moving on up, leaving the others behind)

Discuss your findings in a small group. Share the attributes and messages you charted. As you do, put things in perspective by discussing how these attributes compare and contrast with the attributes you noted in "Review the literature." Then move on to the next activity.

Identify the five attributes you'll focus on. Choose attributes that show up again and again, and that give a variety of messages about what an upwardly mobile person ought to strive for.

Develop an intriguing opening. Decide on how you'll grab your readers' attention at the beginning. Here are some ideas:

- Start with an advertisement for an upwardly-mobile lifestyle that incorporates some of your five attributes. Write as if you were trying to sell this lifestyle to your readers: "Picture yourself behind the wheel of a . . . ."

- Pose a question to the reader: "What five ingredients would you say . . . .?"

- Start as if you were telling a fairy tale: "Once upon a time there was a man who wanted all the good things in life . . . ."

724   UNIT SEVEN: THE EARLY TWENTIETH CENTURY

MINI-LESSON: PREWRITING

Research Advertising Techniques

Much has been written on the rhetoric of advertising. Students might want to compare their ideas on the subject with the ideas of people who have researched this area in depth. Encourage students to conduct research in the library, beginning their search with key words such as media studies, popular culture studies, or advertising theory.

Plan your essay, using your prewriting materials as a guide. Make notes on these categories from the Writer's Blueprint:

- An intriguing opening

- First attribute
  —messages
  —supporting quotations, visuals

- Second attribute
  —messages
  —supporting quotations, visuals

and so on . . .

- Summary of findings

STEP 2 DRAFTING

As you draft, use your ideas from "Develop an intriguing opening" to get started. Here are more drafting tips to keep in mind.

- Lay the visuals you've collected from your research out in front of you. Use them for reference and inspiration as you draft.

- If you're writing by hand, use a separate piece of paper for each attribute and write on every other line. This should give you plenty of room to revise.

- Write with confidence, but take care not to overstate your case. See the Revising Strategy in Step 3 of this lesson.

STEP 3 REVISING

Ask a partner for comments on your draft before you revise it.

✔ Have I begun with an intriguing opening?

✔ Have I dealt with five different attributes?

✔ Have I described how these attributes contribute to an upwardly mobile lifestyle?

✔ Have I been careful to avoid overstating my case?

BUILDING ENGLISH PROFICIENCY

Referring to Sources of Advertisements

As students describe advertising messages, remind them that magazine ads, billboards, and television commercials need to be given references much as print and film sources do. Offer these examples:

- for magazine ads: "in the current issue of <u>Rolling Stone</u>, . . ."

- for billboards: ". . . on both sides of the main road leading into the business district . . ."

- for TV ads: "during the nightly news on QRX, . . ."

Plan your essay

Remind students that the work spent during the planning stages can pay off in the long run with less frustration during the composing stages.

Connections to
Writer's Notebook

For selection-related prompts, refer to Writer's Notebook.

Connections to
Writer's Resource

For additional writing prompts, refer to Writer's Resource.

STEP 2 DRAFTING
The Student Models

The **transparencies** referenced below are authentic student models. Review them with the students before they draft. These questions will help:

1. How do you think the writers do in terms of supporting their conclusions with specific examples from actual advertising?

2. The writer of model 26 discusses messages in advertising but does not mention say much about upward mobility. Imagine you are this writer's editor, and suggest revisions he or she could make to address this theme.

3. Look at the Writer's Blueprint and give each writer a score on each point, from 6 (superior) to 1 (inadequate).

Transparency Collection
Student Models for Writing Workshop 25, 26

STEP 3 REVISING

Ask a partner
(Peer assessment)

Remind students to note the strengths of their partners' essays as well as the areas that need revisions.

726

Revising Strategy: Avoiding Overstatement

Have students come up with a few thesis statements that illustrate overstatement, and then tone them down.

For additional support, see the worksheet referenced below.

Unit 7 Resource Book
Revising Worksheet, p. 45

Connections to
Writer's Resource

Refer to the Grammar, Usage, and Mechanics Handbook on Writer's Resource.

STEP 4 EDITING

Ask a partner (Peer assessment)

When students discuss each other's papers, have them organize their comments so that each area—grammar, usage, mechanics, spelling—is dealt with, one at a time.

Revising Strategy

Avoiding Overstatement

Overstating your case can work against you when you're trying to reason with readers. Avoid overstatement by choosing words that accurately reflect the facts behind your claims. For example:

> Every single magazine ad has some Amazon supermodel shoving some product in your face.

The writer has a point but goes too far with it. *Every single*, *Amazon,* and *shoving some product in your face* all say that this writer is not reasoning with the reader. Here is the revised version:

> Advertisers tend to use beautiful female models to sell everything from new cars to soap.

The revised version still makes a broad claim, but this claim will ring true with many readers and can be backed up with factual examples. The use of *tend to* and *beautiful female models* give the statement a more reasonable tone than the original version.

Notice how this student has revised for overstatement.

> The mass media are ~~by far~~ *among* the most influential forces in our lives. We are ~~constantly~~ exposed to them, *every day.* ~~day in and day out.~~ They *take a part in shaping* ~~shape everything about~~ how we look, think, feel, and act. *For example, some* ~~They shape our bodies.~~ People who have anorexia and other weight-related diseases have *been influenced by* ~~them because~~ advertising *that says that you have to be thin to be happy.* ~~has convinced them that they must be thin or they have no hope of ever living a happy day in their whole lives.~~

STUDENT MODEL

STEP **4** EDITING

Ask a partner to review your revised draft before you edit. When you edit, pay special attention to using apostrophes correctly.

MINI-LESSON: GRAMMAR

Using Apostrophes Correctly

Have students edit the following sentences, paying close attention to errors with apostrophes.

According to this view, this particular advertisers (advertiser's) main goal is to sell us a lifestyle, not simply a product.

Her quality's (qualities) include perfect teeth and perfect hair, even out on the windy bayfront.

The mans (man's) domain is no longer just out in the garage, but in the fully stocked kitchen as well.

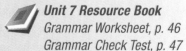

Unit 7 Resource Book
Grammar Worksheet, p. 46
Grammar Check Test, p. 47

Editing Strategy

Using Apostrophes Correctly

- Use apostrophes to form the possessives of nouns:

1. Add **'s** to form the possessive of most singular nouns: Eliza**'s** hat, the upper class**'s** manners.

2. Add only an apostrophe to form the possessive of plural nouns ending in **s**: all the girls**'** possessions, the middle and upper classes**'** lifestyles.

3. Add **'s** to form the possessive of plural nouns that do not end in **s**: the men**'s** tuxedos, the women**'s** gowns.

- Use apostrophes to form contractions, showing where letters have been omitted: can not = can**'t**, we are = we**'re**, that is = that**'s**.

> **FOR REFERENCE**
> More information on using apostrophes correctly can be found in the Language and Grammar Handbook at the back of this text.

STEP 5 PRESENTING

- Work the visuals you collected into the final copy. (See the Computer Tip.)

- Work with some classmates and prepare a multimedia presentation about the images and attributes you have examined.

> **COMPUTER TIP**
> If you have access to a scanner, try scanning your captioned pictures into your final copy to give it a true magazine-article look.

STEP 6 LOOKING BACK

Self-evaluate. Look back at the Writer's Blueprint and give yourself a score on each point, from 6 (superior) to 1 (inadequate).

Reflect. Write responses to these questions.

✔ How would you change your essay if your audience were advertisers instead of consumers?

✔ How do you think the attributes of an upwardly mobile lifestyle have changed since the time of Eliza Doolittle?

For Your Working Portfolio Add your essay and your reflection responses to your working portfolio.

Writing Workshop **727**

ASSESSMENT CRITERIA SPECS

Here are the criteria for a superior paper.

6 Superior The writer of a 6 paper impressively meets these criteria:

- Begins with an intriguing opening that grabs the reader's interest.

- Insightfully analyzes five significant attributes of upward mobility promoted in advertising in terms of the messages, both direct and implied, that advertisers want to impress upon consumers.

- Shows that the writer has done extensive research by citing specific examples from actual advertisements, both verbal and visual.

- Closes with a concise summary of the writer's conclusions.

- Maintains a confident tone that never crosses the line into overstatement.

- Makes few, if any, mistakes in grammar, usage, mechanics, and spelling. Uses apostrophes correctly.

Unit 7 Resource Book
Assessment Worksheet, p. 48

Editing Strategy: Using Apostrophes Correctly

Have students generate a list of all of the uses of apostrophes.

For additional support, see the mini-lesson at the bottom of page 726 and the worksheets referenced below.

Unit 7 Resource Book
Grammar Worksheet, p. 46
Grammar Check Test, p. 47

Connections to
Writer's Resource

Refer to the Grammar, Usage, and Mechanics Handbook on Writer's Resource.

STEP 5 PRESENTING
Adding Visuals
Multimedia Presentation

Both these suggestions would work well as interdisciplinary projects involving the media lab or computer classes at your school.

STEP 6 LOOKING BACK
Self-evaluate

The *Assessment Criteria Specs* at the bottom of this page are for a superior paper. You might want to post these in the classroom. Students can then evaluate themselves based on these criteria. For a complete scoring rubric, use the *Assessment Worksheet* referenced below.

Unit 7 Resource Book
Assessment Worksheet, p. 48

Reflect

Have students discuss how the sense of one's audience affects the form and content of the writing in general. Both of these questions could be discussed by the entire class or in small groups before students write their answers individually.

To further explore the theme, use the Fine Art Transparency referenced below.

Transparency Collection
Fine Art Writing Prompt 13

Beyond Print

Teaching Objectives

- to recognize the use of persuasion in print advertising
- to critique print advertisements
- to devise a rating system for print advertisements

Curricular Connection: Media Literacy

Use the material in this article to give students practice in evaluating print media advertising.

Introduce

Begin a class discussion about how we judge people when we see them. *(Students should mention clothes, hair style, make-up, and accessories.)* Then have students glance briefly at the two advertisements on pages 728 and 729. Ask them about their first impressions of the people in the ads. *(They are rich; members of the elite.)* Point out that the purpose of advertisements is to pursuade people to purchase products. Then have students read the article.

Beyond Print

Looking at Advertising

In *Pygmalion,* a classic story of a makeover, Professor Higgins takes a lower-class cockney woman and turns her into a high-society lady by changing the way she speaks, the way she dresses, and the way she comports herself. It's a very old story—and a very new one. In our modern world the packaging often outshines the goods. People who aspire to positions in politics and other areas hire experts to teach them how to speak in public, how to dress, and how to project a certain kind of image.

Advertising was not born in the twentieth century, but it has been developed in this century until it has reached the status of a science. Today advertisers know their target audiences down to surprisingly specific details, and they know how to reach those audiences. Earlier advertising was designed for a more general audience, but it was based on some general assumptions that still hold true today. Look at these two advertisements, a showcard (display card) from about 1900 for Pink's jams, and a display card from about 1930 for Theobroma candies. Think about the appeals that are being made.

Living the High Life Everyone wants to get ahead. That's the basic idea behind upward mobility. And it must follow—or so the advertisers would have you believe—that if you look and act rich, you will feel rich (even if you don't actually have the money to qualify otherwise). Looking rich may mean wearing the clothes that are shown in ads, wearing your hair in certain styles, using certain cosmetics. Acting rich may mean driving a certain make of car, consuming certain brands of food and drink—and treating yourself with certain luxurious goodies.

Snob Appeal No one wants to be thought a snob these days, but snobbery still has a certain

WAIT UNTIL SHE SEES INSIDE!
THEOBROMA
THE FOOD OF THE GODS
Terry's YORK
LATEST ASSORTMENT 2/ per ½ lb.

ANOTHER APPROACH

Finding Advertisements Online

Instead of analyzing print advertisements, have students critique online advertising. Have students begin by establishing criteria by which to judge such advertisements. Point out to them that online services advertise their own offerings, but there are also advertisements by companies who use the Internet to gain customers and sell products and services. Arrange a time for students to go online in small groups and see how this advertising works.

Activity Options

Activity 1   You may wish to have students bring mail-order advertisements to school so that each student gets to see a wider assortment of advertisements. Which ads appeal to the wealthy? to teens? to parents? to children? to older people? What clues are in the ads that make the target audience obvious to the reader?

Activity 2   Before students begin, have them discuss what constitutes high society in their community. Have students discuss what else they would need, besides the changes listed in the article, to enter high society in their community.

amount of appeal. People like the idea of hobnobbing with the rich and famous, and using the products they are seen (in the paid advertisements) to be using is one way to feel a little closer. In fact, testimonials by celebrities are a basic device of advertising.

Activity Options

1. Comb newspaper and magazine ads, mail-order catalogs, and other kinds of advertising to find images and descriptions of various "high-life" products. Assemble them in a scrapbook, sorted according to categories of clothing, foods, and so on. Devise your own rating system and label those items that seem to have acquired a reputation as the "best" of a large number of similar items.

2. Imagine that money's no problem, and you want to be up there among the best. Plan your own upward move. What sort of wardrobe will you need to move in high society? What sort of physical appearance do you want to present? What would you need to do in order to achieve that physical appearance? Does your general behavior need some polishing? Last, but not least—could your vocabulary and speech patterns use some improvement?

BUILDING ENGLISH PROFICIENCY

Exploring Key Concepts

You may wish to preface this activity by having students consider what the "high life" means today.

1. Ask students to imagine that a month ago they received a gift of $10 million, tax free. Ask: How has your life changed in the past month? What can you do that you couldn't do before you had the money?

2 Relate their answers to the concept of the "high life"—living at a higher level of luxury than most people. Ask questions such as the following:

- What kinds of people do you hang out with? What happened to the friends you had?
- What are your most prized possessions, and why?
- How do you spend most of your time, and why?

3. Point out that advertising styles have changed over the generations. Ask: What ads today would show the kinds of people who would give the responses that you just gave?

Part Two: War and Aftermath
Historical Overview

EXPLORING CONCEPTS

- The experiences of World War I changed the cultural concept of war.
- Technological advances in weaponry increased the horror of war.

 **Art Study**

The collage of war technology shows some of the war machines introduced in World War I.

Question   How do you think this machinery contributed to changing the conception of war? *(Possible responses: Many more people were killed in warfare; war was no longer primarily fought man-to-man, so courage, daring, and other virtues might now be less important than the amount and kinds of weapons an army had and how they deployed them; more civilians died in war.)*

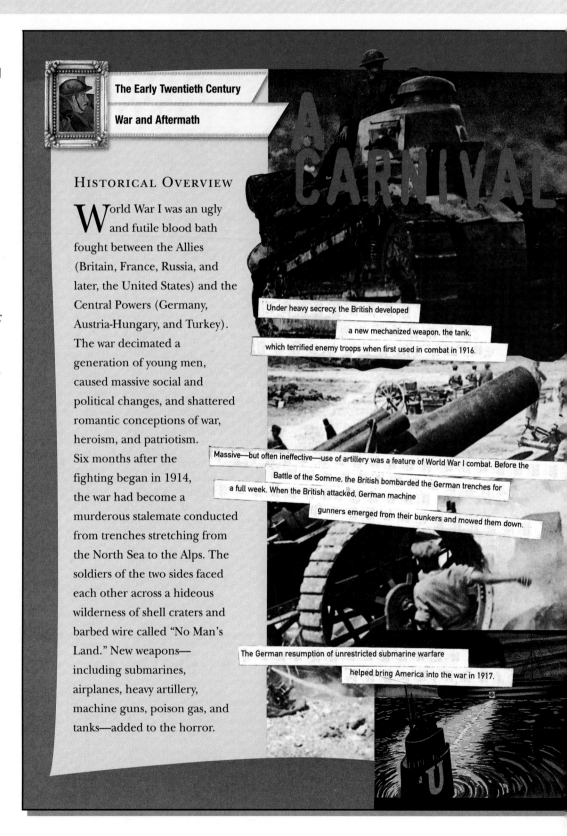

The Early Twentieth Century

War and Aftermath

HISTORICAL OVERVIEW

World War I was an ugly and futile blood bath fought between the Allies (Britain, France, Russia, and later, the United States) and the Central Powers (Germany, Austria-Hungary, and Turkey). The war decimated a generation of young men, caused massive social and political changes, and shattered romantic conceptions of war, heroism, and patriotism. Six months after the fighting began in 1914, the war had become a murderous stalemate conducted from trenches stretching from the North Sea to the Alps. The soldiers of the two sides faced each other across a hideous wilderness of shell craters and barbed wire called "No Man's Land." New weapons— including submarines, airplanes, heavy artillery, machine guns, poison gas, and tanks—added to the horror.

A CARNIVAL

Under heavy secrecy, the British developed a new mechanized weapon, the tank, which terrified enemy troops when first used in combat in 1916.

Massive—but often ineffective—use of artillery was a feature of World War I combat. Before the Battle of the Somme, the British bombarded the German trenches for a full week. When the British attacked, German machine gunners emerged from their bunkers and mowed them down.

The German resumption of unrestricted submarine warfare helped bring America into the war in 1917.

The illustrations on these pages show a few of the new types of weapons that were used in World War I.

OF DEATH

During the Battle of the Somme, British soldiers wearing gas masks fire a machine gun. Both sides used poison gas, a fearful but unpredictable weapon; a shift in the wind might send it back on those using it.

Key Dates

1914
World War I begins.

1916
Battle of the Somme; 60,000 British casualties the first day.

1917
Russian Revolution begins; United States enters the war.

1918
World War I ends.

1919
Treaty of Versailles negotiated.

1921
Irish Free State established.

1922
Joyce's Ulysses *and Eliot's* The Waste Land *are published.*

1928
British women get the vote.

1929
Great Depression begins.

WAR WEAPONS WEEK APRIL 8TH TO 13TH

The most revolutionary weapon introduced during the war was the airplane, but its full military potential would not be realized until World War II.

HELP TO PROVIDE THIS WAR WEAPON

BUY NATIONAL WAR BONDS (£5 TO £5000) AND WAR SAVINGS CERTIFICATES 15/6

731

Key Dates

1899–1907 A number of alliances between European nations attempt to create security in the region.

1898–1908 Labor strikes and assassinations create European tensions.

June 28, 1914 The assassination of Archduke Franz Ferdinand of Austria by a Serbian precipitates World War I.

1917 British poet Edward Thomas (b. 1878) dies in World War I.

April 1, 1918 British poet Isaac Rosenberg (b. 1890) dies in battle.

1918 By the end of the war, an estimated twelve million soldiers have died.

MATERIALS OF INTEREST
Books

- *The War Poets* by Robert Giddings (Random House, 1988).
- *The Great War and Modern Memory* by Paul Fussell (Oxford University Press, 1975).
- *An Illustrated Companion to the First World War* by Anthony Bruce (Viking Penguin, 1990).

Multimedia

- *All Quiet on the Western Front,* directed by Lewis Milestone (Universal Pictures, 1930).
- *Gallipoli,* directed by Peter Weir, starring Mel Gibson (1981).

 Connections to
Custom Literature Database

For further historical background, under **Background Information,** see **Modern England 1915—.**

FOR ALL STUDENTS

The literature in this section portrays the grim reality of war and challenges the assumptions about heroism and patriotism in battle.

- Why is war and dying in battle often glorified?
- How does a person lose his or her individuality during a war?

To further explore the theme, use the transparency noted below.

For At-Risk Students

View the movie *Gallipoli* and discuss with students the contrast between the ideals of glory and the senseless destruction of war's reality.

For Students Who Need Challenge

Suggest that students read and report on one of the autobiographical works of Siegfried Sassoon:

- *Memoirs of an Infantry Officer, by the author of Memoirs of a Fox-Hunting Man* (1930)
- *Siegfried's Journey, 1916–1920* (1945)

MULTICULTURAL CONNECTION

The intense nationalism in Europe contributed to the conflicts that caused World War I. Ask students to consider the effects of nationalism in a culturally diverse country and among culturally diverse nations.

- What security does nationalism hope to gain?
- What conflicts can it cause within a nation?
- What kind of nationalism can work in a culturally diverse world?

Part Two

War and Aftermath

War never involves just opposing armies. It also involves civilians, whether they are people who live where a war is being fought, whose lives may be in equal danger, or people who live back home, who may not be in personal danger but whose lives may nevertheless be forever changed.

Individuals may fight a duel; a war is fought by **groups.** As a member of a military group, it is your duty to go where you're told and do what you're ordered to do, even though you might not agree with—or even understand—what you're fighting for.

IDEAS THAT WORK

Motivating with Links to the Past

"Many youth appear to be somewhat insensitive to the causes of war and the reality of death. Unlike the characters in this literature, our youth have read about and seen news coverage of the tragedies of the Vietnam War, the war in Bosnia, and the wars fought on the streets of our cities.

Are our youth really insensitive, or is this statement just another assertion made by adults who have forgotten a younger world to which they once belonged?

I would begin with a discussion of my opening statement and allow students to compare the authors' feelings about death to young people's feelings now. I also would include some of the music from both eras that relates to war and death. I would compare the experiences of Vietnam War soldiers to those of the soldiers in this section. I would use excerpts from the novel *The Things They Carried,* by Tim O'Brien."

Anna Braziel Jackson
Carbondale, Illinois

Before Reading

The Soldier by Rupert Brooke
Suicide in the Trenches by Siegfried Sassoon

Dulce et Decorum Est by Wilfred Owen
Disabled by Wilfred Owen

Building Background

"True Poets Must Be Truthful" In the unfinished preface to the collection of war poems he hoped to publish, Wilfred Owen wrote:

"This book is not about heroes. English Poetry is not yet fit to speak of them.

"Nor is it about deeds, or lands, nor anything about glory, honor, might, majesty, dominion, or power, except War.

"Above all I am not concerned with Poetry.

"My subject is War, and the pity of War.

"The Poetry is in the pity.

"Yet these elegies are to this generation in no sense consolatory. They may be to the next. All a poet can do today is warn. That is why the true Poets must be truthful. . . ."

Throughout the course of World War I the poetry of war changed from romanticism and glory to harsh realism and bitter truth.

Literary Focus

Tone An author's attitude toward his or her subject matter or toward the audience is the **tone** of a work. Tone in writing is like tone of voice—it can alter the meaning of words. By recognizing a writer's tone, a reader can determine whether the writer views the subject with sympathy, sarcasm, affection, bitterness, or optimism. As you read these poems of war, look for clues to their tone.

Writer's Notebook

Idealism and Realism Write your definitions for the following two words: *idealism* and *realism.* What do you think are the positive characteristics of an idealist? of a realist? What are the negative characteristics of each?

The Soldier **733**

Before Reading

Building Background

Write the word *war* on the board. Invite students to brainstorm associations they have for this word and make a web.

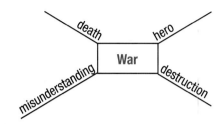

Literary Focus

Tell students that tone is the author's attitude toward the subject matter. Explain that tone is apparent in paintings, photographs, and the media, as well as in written works. Ask students to identify the tone of various TV programs or of specific characters in these programs.

Writer's Notebook

Explain to students that after reading the poems, they will categorize individual poets as realists or idealists.

Question What is the major difference between a realist and an idealist? *(Possible response: A realist sees the world as it is; an idealist sees the world as he or she would like it to be.)*

SUPPORT MATERIALS OVERVIEW

Unit 7 Resource Book
- Graphic Organizer, p. 49
- Study Guide, p. 50
- Vocabulary, p. 51
- Grammar, p. 52
- Alternate Check Test, p. 53
- Vocabulary Test, p. 54
- Selection Test, pp. 55–56

Building English Proficiency
- Selection Summaries
- Activities, p. 251

Reading, Writing & Grammar SkillBook
- Reading, pp. 71–73
- Grammar, Usage, and Mechanics, pp. 218–219

Technology
- Audiotape
- Personal Journal Software
- Custom Literature Database: Additional selections by Brooke, Sassoon, and Owen can be found on the database.
- Test Generator Software

More About the Poets

Rupert Brooke

- Much of Rupert Brooke's work shows an appreciation and affinity for the works of John Donne.
- Brooke was popular before and during the war. After the war his popularity declined.
- He became the symbol of youth that was wasted in war. Other works include "The Old Vicarage, Grantchester," "Wagner," and "John Webster and the Elizabethan Drama."

Siegfried Sassoon

- Sassoon was born into a wealthy family.
- His poems are an angry protest against war and its brutality.
- He was responsible for publishing some of Wilfred Owen's poems.
- After the war he wrote his memoirs. Other works include "Everyone Sang" and "Base Details."

Wilfred Owen

- Owen was a major influence on twentieth-century poetry.
- He produced much of his work in his first year as a soldier. Other works include "Anthem for Doomed Youth" and "Futility."

Rupert Brooke
1887–1915

For the English, handsome and gifted Rupert Brooke represented the glamor and patriotism of war. At King's College, Cambridge, he became the acknowledged leader of the literary community, and his publication of *Poems 1911* was well received. At the outbreak of World War I, Brooke hurried to enlist, urging a friend, "Come and die. It'll be great fun!" He received a commission in the Royal Navy Division. His five "War Sonnets" (1915), which included "The Soldier," contributed to his immense national popularity, which was enhanced by the posthumous publication of *1914 and Other Poems*. Ironically, Brooke attained his legendary status as a war poet without ever having engaged in actual combat. In the early stages of the war, enroute to the Dardanelles campaign, he contracted blood poisoning and died on a hospital ship anchored off the Greek island of Skyros.

Siegfried Sassoon
1886–1967

Before the war Siegfried Sassoon's life consisted of hunting, book-collecting, and writing exquisite verses. His life changed dramatically when, as "Mad Jack," he fought with exceptional bravery in France. His personal experiences also dramatically changed his attitudes toward war and toward those ignorant of the hell that soldiers were going through. By the summer of 1917, convinced that the war was being unnecessarily prolonged, he issued a statement calling for an immediate negotiated peace. Instead of being court-martialed as he had hoped, he was judged temporarily insane and hospitalized. While in the hospital he met Wilfred Owen, whom he encouraged in his writing. Sassoon was the most widely read poet of World War I.

Wilfred Owen
1893–1918

Wilfred Owen participated in some of the hardest fighting in France during the cold winter of 1917. Following a nervous collapse, Owen was hospitalized from June 1917 until September 1918 when he volunteered to return to the front. One week before the Armistice of 1918 and two weeks after being decorated for gallantry, Owen was killed by machine-gun fire. During his lifetime he had published only four poems. Through the efforts of his mother and friends, eight more poems were published in 1919. Owen's collected poems, edited by Siegfried Sassoon, appeared in 1920. Today Owen is regarded by many as the finest poet of World War I.

THE SOLDIER

Rupert Brooke

1

If I should die, think only this of me:
That there's some corner of a foreign field
That is forever England. There shall be
In that rich earth a richer dust concealed;
5 A dust whom England bore, shaped, made aware;
Gave, once, her flowers to love, her ways to roam,
A body of England's breathing English air,
Washed by the rivers, blest by suns of home.

And think, this heart, all evil shed away,
10 A pulse in the eternal mind, no less
Gives somewhere back the thoughts by England given;
Her sights and sounds; dreams happy as her day;
And laughter, learned of friends; and gentleness,
In hearts at peace, under an English heaven.

The Soldier   **735**

Selection Objectives

- to explore the theme of war and its effects
- to identify tone
- to correct dangling modifiers
- to recognize techniques of persuasion

 Unit 7 Resource Book
Graphic Organizer, p. 49
Study Guide, p. 50

Theme Link

These poems deal with war and its aftermath—from love of country to war's casualties and horrors.

Vocabulary Preview

ardent, enthusiastic, passionate
   Students can add the word and its definition to their Writer's Notebooks.

1 **Reading/Thinking Skills**
Infer

Questions

- What does "some corner of a foreign field" refer to? (*the speaker's grave*)
- Why is the corner "forever England"? (*Possible response: Since he is a British soldier who loves his country, his foreign burial site is transformed into a part of England, both physically and spiritually.*)

SELECTION SUMMARY

The Soldier; Suicide in the Trenches; Dulce et Decorum Est; Disabled

The Soldier   A soldier in a foreign land celebrates the spirit of England while contemplating his own death.

Suicide in the Trenches   A soldier changes—from a carefree youth to a frightened man. No longer able to deal with the war, he puts a bullet in his head.

Dulce et Decorum Est   The narrator describes a gas attack. All soldiers but one manage to get their masks on in time; the man who does not dies in agony. The narrator scolds the reader: "Do not lie to children that it is sweet and honorable to die for one's country."

Disabled   A veteran sits in a wheelchair and reminisces about life before he lost his legs. He was handsome, dashing—a football hero. He had no feelings about the enemy; he "joined up" for the glory, to impress a girl. Now, in his wheelchair, he watches the eyes of girls pass over him for strong men, whole men. It is cold, and no nurse comes to take him inside.

 *For summaries in other languages, see the **Building English Proficiency** book.*

SUICIDE IN THE TRENCHES

Siegfried Sassoon

2

I knew a simple soldier boy
Who grinned at life in empty joy,
Slept soundly through the lonesome dark,
And whistled early with the lark.

5 In winter trenches, cowed[1] and glum,
With crumps[2] and lice and lack of rum,
He put a bullet through his brain.
No one spoke of him again.

3

You smug-faced crowds with kindling[3] eye
10 Who cheer when soldier lads march by,
Sneak home and pray you'll never know
The hell where youth and laughter go.

---

1. **cowed** (koud), *adj.* frightened.
2. **crumps,** soldiers' slang for exploding shells, from the sound made by them.
3. **kindling** (kind′ling), *adj.* brightening.

John Nash's painting *Over the Top* (1918) shows a group of British soldiers moving up to repel a German attack on December 30, 1917. Does this image reflect a romantic view of heroism in war? Why or why not? ▼

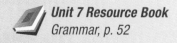

DULCE ET DECORUM EST

Wilfred Owen

4

Bent double, like old beggars under sacks,
Knock-kneed, coughing like hags, we cursed through sludge,[1]
Till on the haunting flares we turned our backs
And towards our distant rest began to trudge.

5

5 Men marched asleep. Many had lost their boots
But limped on, blood-shod.[2] All went lame; all blind;
Drunk with fatigue; deaf even to the hoots
Of tired, outstripped Five-Nines[3] that dropped behind.

Gas! GAS! Quick, boys! An ecstasy of fumbling,
10 Fitting the clumsy helmets just in time;
But someone still was yelling out and stumbling
And flound'ring like a man in fire or lime . . .
Dim, through the misty panes and thick green light,
As under a green sea, I saw him drowning.

15 In all my dreams, before my helpless sight,
He plunges at me, guttering, choking, drowning.
If in some smothering dreams you too could pace
Behind the wagon that we flung him in,
And watch the white eyes writhing[4] in his face,
20 His hanging face, like a devil's sick of sin;
If you could hear, at every jolt, the blood
Come gargling from the froth-corrupted lungs,
Obscene as cancer, bitter as the cud
Of vile, incurable sores on innocent tongues—
25 My friend, you would not tell with such high zest
To children ardent[5] for some desperate glory,
The old Lie: Dulce et decorum est

6

Pro patria mori.[6]

---

1. **sludge** (sluj), *n.* soft mud.
2. **blood-shod,** with only blood for shoes.
3. **Five-Nines,** shells containing poison gas. The use of poison gas by both sides on the Western Front was widely viewed as immoral. (See page 773.)
4. **writhe** (rīᴛʜ), *v.* twist and turn.
5. ardent (ärd′nt), *adj.* enthusiastic; passionate.
6. **Dulce . . . mori** (dŭl′chā et də kôr′əm est prō pä′trē ə môr′ē). "It is sweet and honorable to die for one's country," a quotation from one of Horace's *Odes* well known to British schoolboys. *[Latin]*

Dulce et Decorum Est   **737**

Literary Focus
4
Tone

Point out that the tone of this poem is set in the first line with the image of soldiers bent over like beggars. Discuss how the poet's use of grotesque and haunting scenes contrasts with the title.

Literary Element
5
Hyperbole

Question What does the hyperbole in lines 6, 7, and 8 tell you about the soldiers? *(Possible responses: The soldiers are overcome with exhaustion. They are so tired they don't even know what is happening behind them.)*

Reading/Thinking Skills
6
Recognize Use of Persuasion

The poet uses persuasion to get the reader to accept his ideas about war.

Question What are some ways he does this? *(Possible responses: He uses loaded words and provides vivid, shocking scenes of the war. He uses powerful words and phrases such as* haunting, blood-shod, guttering, hanging face, devil's sick of sin, obscene, cancer. *The poem is also told from a first-person point of view.)*

BUILDING ENGLISH PROFICIENCY

Relating Imagery and Language

Help students explore the language that Sassoon and Owen use to capture the horrors of war.

1. Have students set up a chart to record words and phrases that describe life on the battlefield and in the trenches.

2. Ask students to record personal responses to several of their entries, focusing on the images the words create.

3. Compare responses. Ask: Which of the images do you think readers of that time responded to the most? Why?

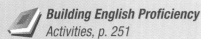
*Building English Proficiency
Activities, p. 251*

Words and Phrases	My Response
crumps and lice	
blood-shed	
white eyes writing in his face	

Questions

- What kind of life did the soldier lead before the war? *(He had girlfriends, played football, and lived a happy life.)*
- What does he do now? *(He sits in a wheelchair waiting to die.)*
- How have his thoughts changed? *(He is morbid and downtrodden; before, he was carefree and had fun.)*

8 Reading/Thinking Skills

Rcognize Cause and Effect

Point out the speaker's reference to the past when the soldier was a football hero. Discuss with students what this reveals about his motivation for becoming a soldier. *(He has a romanticized idea of heroism that he transfers to the battlefield. His enthusiasm is also fueled by alcohol.)*

Question What does the soldier think about his ideas now? *(He wonders now why he became a soldier. No one wants to know him or even cares whether he lives or dies.)*

DISABLED

Wilfred Owen

He sat in a wheeled chair, waiting for dark,
And shivered in his ghastly suit of gray,
Legless, sewn short at elbow. Through the park
Voices of boys rang saddening like a hymn,
5 Voices of play and pleasure after day,
Till gathering sleep had mothered them from him.

About this time Town used to swing so gay
When glow-lamps budded in the light blue trees,
And girls glanced lovelier as the air grew dim—
10 In the old times, before he threw away his knees.
Now he will never feel again how slim
Girls' waists are, or how warm their subtle hands;
All of them touch him like some queer disease.

There was an artist silly for his face,
15 For it was younger than his youth, last year.
Now, he is old; his back will never brace;
He's lost his color very far from here,
Poured it down shell-holes till the veins ran dry,
And half his lifetime lapsed in the hot race,
20 And leap of purple spurted from his thigh.

One time he liked a blood-smear down his leg,
After the matches, carried shoulder-high.
It was after football, when he'd drunk a peg,[1]
He thought he'd better join—He wonders why.
25 Someone had said he'd look a god in kilts,[2]
That's why; and may be, too, to please his Meg;
Aye, that was it, to please the giddy jilts[3]
He asked to join. He didn't have to beg;
Smiling they wrote his lie; aged nineteen years.

---

1. **peg,** an alcoholic drink.
2. **kilt** (kilt), *n.* a plaid pleated skirt, worn especially by Scottish soldiers or men in the Scottish Highlands.
3. **jilts,** girls.

MINI-LESSON: LITERARY FOCUS

Tone

Owen uses imagery, figurative language, and specific words to convey his attitude toward war.

Teach Tone is the attitude a writer has toward his or her subject. To identify the writer's tone, ask yourself what the writer means by the words and what the images convey. Also read the poem aloud and listen to the sounds. What do they tell you about the tone? What is Owen's attitude toward the disabled soldier? *(sympathy)* toward war? *(revulsion, horror, disgust)*

Question Wilfred Owen experienced the war firsthand. How might knowing this help you determine the tone of the poem? *(Generally, when you experience something yourself, you are able to tell about it in a more realistic manner.)*

Activity Ideas

- Have students look at Owen's other poem, "Dulce et Decorum Est," and compare its tone to that of "Disabled." *(Possible response: Both have a tone tinged with the grotesque. "Dulce et Decorum Est" contains a more haunting tone, questioning the reasoning behind dying for one's country. "Disabled" is more pitiful and hopeless.)*
- Have students write sentences that demonstrate these tones: sincerity, despair, horror, optimism.

30 Germans he scarcely thought of; all their guilt,
   And Austria's, did not move him. And no fears
   Of Fear came yet. He thought of jewelled hilts
   For daggers in plaid socks; of smart salutes;
   And care of arms; and leave; and pay arrears;[4]
35 *Esprit de corps;*[5] and hints for young recruits.
   And soon, he was drafted out with drums and cheers.

   Some cheered him home, but not as crowds cheer Goal.
   Only a solemn man who brought him fruits
   Thanked him; and then inquired about his soul.
40 Now, he will spend a few sick years in Institutes,
   And do what things the rules consider wise,
   And take whatever pity they may dole.[6]
   Tonight he noticed how the women's eyes
   Passed from him to the strong men that were whole.
45 How cold and late it is! Why don't they come
   And put him into bed? Why don't they come?

---

4. **arrears** (ə rirz′), *n. pl.* money due but not yet paid.
5. *Esprit de corps* (e sprē′ də kôr′), group spirit;
   morale. *[French]*
6. **dole** (dōl), *v.* give in charity.

Disabled   **739**

9 Reader's Response
Making Personal Connections

The young man makes a rash decision, which he later regrets.

Question   Have you ever made a hasty decision about something important? What were the consequences? With hindsight, what would you say to someone facing a similar decision? *(Answers require thoughtful reflection.)*

10 Literary Element
Point of View

Questions

- Who is the speaker in the poem? *(an outside observer)*

- How does the use of a third-person narrator contribute to the tone of the poem? *(It adds detachment.)*

- How might the tone have been different if the poem had been told from the first-person point of view? *(It might have been more self-pitying and less detached.)*

Check Test

1. In "The Soldier," what feelings does the poet express toward England? *(patriotism and love)*

2. What advice does the speaker in "Suicide in the Trenches" give the watching crowds? *(to go home and hope they never have to experience war or death)*

3. What is the meaning of "Dulce et Decorum Est"? *(It is sweet and honorable to die for one's country.)*

4. In "Disabled," what was the "lie" they wrote for the young recruit? *(that he was 19)*

5. Which is the only poem presenting a positive picture of war? *("The Soldier")*

 Unit 7 Resource Book
Alternate Check Test, p. 53

BUILDING ENGLISH PROFICIENCY

ESL
LEP
ELD
SAE
LD

Linking Past and Present

Help students realize that the bitter despair of Owen's disabled veteran is not confined to a distant time.

Activity Ideas

- Invite students to research and report on the effects of Agent Orange (used in Vietnam) and of Gulf War Syndrome.

- Encourage students who know a Vietnam or Gulf War veteran to interview the veteran about government treatment of veterans and his or her feelings about that treatment. Work with students to prepare a format for sharing what they learn.

After Reading

MAKING CONNECTIONS

1. Students' responses will vary depending on their personal viewpoints. Some may select "The Soldier" because it is less depressing and does not depict the horrors of war as vividly as the other poems.

2. Possible response: He is able to do so because he hopes his death will ensure him a peaceful place "under an English heaven."

3. Possible responses: England has given the speaker gentleness, peace, friendship, love of home and nature, and happiness. The speaker hopes to return to England everything he has received.

4. Possible responses: simple soldier boy; grinned at life

5. Possible response: The boy kills himself because being in the war is too overwhelming and frightening.

6. Possible response: The soldiers in "Dulce et Decorum Est" are both physically and mentally exhausted. They seem to be in a trance.

7. Possible response: Owen's vivid, shocking images include "Come gargling from the froth-corrupted lungs," "Obscene as cancer," "vile, incurable sores."

8. Possible response: It provides the ironic discrepancy between glorious images of the soldier and the actual horrors of war.

9. Possible response: young, happy, carefree *vs.* destroyed and joyless

10. Some students may say he is waiting to go to bed; others will think he wants to die.

11. Possible response: Brooke had a romantic view of war; Sassoon and Owen viewed it more realistically and exposed its brutality.

12. Possible response: War, anywhere and anytime, causes unnecessary death and destruction.

After Reading

Making Connections

Shaping Your Response

1. Which of the four war poems most closely reflects your personal attitude toward war? Explain your response.

Analyzing the Poems

2. In "The Soldier" why do you think the speaker is able to anticipate and accept the possibility of his death with such a positive and peaceful attitude?

3. Compare what England has given the speaker (in the first eight lines of this **sonnet**) with what the speaker's spirit will return in death (in the last six lines).

4. What words in the first stanza of "Suicide in the Trenches" indicate to you that the boy is innocent and naive?

5. Judging from the few details given, why do you think the boy kills himself?

6. In "Dulce et Decorum Est" what about the physical and mental conditions of the soldiers make them easy prey for a gas attack?

7. How does Owen's use of **figurative language** emphasize the horror of the situation surrounding the gas attack?

8. What do you think is the purpose of the quotation that ends the poem?

9. In "Disabled" contrast the young man's life before the war with his life after serving his country.

10. In what different ways might you interpret the last two lines of the poem?

Extending the Ideas

11. 🖉 What similarities in thought do you think may be caused by the **group** membership of these three soldier / poets? What differences do you find?

12. What makes these poems, written by Englishmen reflecting on England at war, universally applicable?

Literary Focus: Tone

An author's attitude toward his or her subject matter or toward the audience is the **tone** of a work. The ways an author manipulates words, chooses images, and describes characters and events are clues to a work's tone. For each of the poems in this group identify the tone and discuss which words, phrases, and images contribute to that tone.

LITERARY FOCUS: TONE

Possible Responses

- "The Soldier"—Tone: serene, hopeful, peaceful. Contribute to tone: her flowers to love; blest by suns of home; dreams happy; In hearts at peace

- "Suicide in the Trenches"—Tone: depressing, despairing. Contribute to tone: empty joy; lonesome dark; smug-faced crowds; hell where youth and laughter go

- "Dulce et Decorum Est"—Tone: grotesque, horrifying, meaningless. Contribute to tone: Bent double; haunting flares; limped on, blood-shod; helpless sight; smothering dreams; Obscene as cancer; vile, incurable sores; The old Lie

- "Disabled"—Tone: grotesque, pitiful, hopeless, detached. Contribute to tone: ghastly suit of gray; sewn short at elbow; threw away his knees; Why don't they come

Vocabulary

What other adjectives come to mind when you think of *ardent?* Create a word map of at least five adjectives that could be used as synonyms for *ardent.*

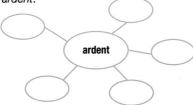

ardent

Expressing Your Ideas

Writing Choices

Writer's Notebook Update Label each poet in this group as an idealist or a realist. Would you prefer to be called an idealist or a realist? Explain your choice in a sentence or two.

The "Glory" of War Write an **essay** of comparison and contrast in which you discuss the treatment of death in war as presented by Brooke, Sassoon, and Owen. Consider especially the differences in tone, word choice, and patriotic feeling. In your conclusion try to account for the differences you have found.

Join My Cause At the beginning of World War I, when love of country was at its height in England, young men expressed their patriotism by enlisting to fight in "the Great War." If you wanted to express your patriotism and love for your country today, what method of expression would you choose? Write an **editorial** for your school newspaper urging other students to join you in your patriotic endeavor.

Other Options

Tones of War Select one of the four war poems and choose a musical composition that you think reflects the tone of the poem. Prepare an **oral reading** of the poem using the musical piece as background.

Types of Therapy Imagine that a wounded soldier such as the speaker in "Disabled" is taking therapy to deal with his feelings about the war. Draw a **picture** or create a **sculpture** that you think the soldier might work on as part of his therapy for confronting what happened to him in the war. Or, if the soldier you imagine is too disabled to draw or sculpt, demonstrate some **physical exercises** that he might undergo to maintain his health.

War on Display Prepare a **bulletin board display** on an aspect of World War I. Include pictures, charts, and maps. Choose from one of the following topics or select your own subject: Causes of World War I, Allied Powers and Central Powers, The Western Front, Types of Warfare, Great Battles, U. S. Involvement, British Losses, The Treaty of Versailles.

Disabled **741**

Building Background

Diaries and memoirs of young people can give insight into the personal side of events that may seem larger than life. You may want to discuss other such works they may have read, such as *The Diary of Anne Frank*, *The Autobiography of Malcolm X*, *The Basketball Diaries* by Jim Carroll, or Richard Wright's *Black Boy*.

Literary Focus

Suggest that as they read, students make a list of words and descriptions that evoke mood. They may note colors, temperatures, light and darkness, and passage of time.

Writer's Notebook

Students may have differing opinions about whether women should engage in combat duty. Allow time for discussion.

More About Vera Brittain

During World War I, Brittain was on duty during air-raids and aided families made homeless by bombings. Other works by Vera Brittain include

- *Testament of Friendship*
- *Testament of Experience*
- *Envoy Extraordinary*
- *Humiliation with Honour*
- *The Dark Tide*

Before Reading

from Testament of Youth

by Vera Brittain

Vera Brittain
1893–1970

The daughter of middle-class parents, Vera Brittain spent her youth sheltered and chaperoned. Her parents believed that only boys should seek higher education, but Brittain persuaded them to allow her to prepare for the rigorous entrance examinations for Oxford. When war broke out, she had just received her acceptance to Oxford. With her fiancé, Roland Leighton; her brother, Edward; and various of their friends at war, Brittain joined the war effort herself by serving for four years as a Red Cross nurse. After the Armistice she completed her studies at Oxford and became a writer and social activist. In 1933 Brittain completed *Testament of Youth,* an autobiography set against the larger background of war and social change.

Building Background

To Enlighten the Old; to Console the Young These words from Vera Brittain's foreword to her personal diary explain why she valued her diary and wanted it and her later reflections on it to be widely read:

"I belong to the few who believe in all sincerity that their own lives provide the answers to some of the many problems which puzzle humanity. I should like to help the experienced, who think they understand youth, to realize how easy it is to mistake illusion for conviction, bewilderment for weakness, enthusiasm for indiscretion or self-will. It is in the hope that these records of my own ardors, absurdities, weaknesses, and failures will enlighten the old who are puzzled about the young, and console the young who are confused about themselves, that I venture to expose them to the searchlight of public criticism."

Literary Focus

Mood The **mood** of a literary work is the prevailing emotion or overall atmosphere. An author creates mood partly through the description of the setting and partly through the people and events being described. In the following selection, look for changes in mood and the reasons for these changes.

Writer's Notebook

Women in War What role or roles do you think women should assume if their country is involved in a war? Should women serve in the same ways as men? Jot down a few thoughts on these questions.

SUPPORT MATERIALS OVERVIEW

Unit 7 Resource Book
- Graphic Organizer, p. 57
- Study Guide, p. 58
- Vocabulary, p. 59
- Grammar, p. 60
- Alternate Check Test, p. 61
- Vocabulary Test, p. 62
- Selection Test, pp. 63–64

Building English Proficiency
- Selection Summaries
- Activities, p. 252

Reading, Writing & Grammar SkillBook
- Writing, pp. 113–114
- Grammar, Usage, and Mechanics, pp. 209–210

The World of Work
- Nurse, p. 27
- Activity, p. 28

Technology
- Audiotape
- Custom Literature Database: For other selections dealing with War and Aftermath, see works by Edward Thomas on the database.
- Personal Journal Software
- Test Generator Software

Testament of Youth

Vera Brittain

When the Great War broke out, it came to me not as a superlative tragedy, but as an interruption of the most exasperating kind to my personal plans. . . .

It would not, I think, be possible for any present-day girl of the same age even to imagine how abysmally ignorant, how romantically idealistic, and how utterly unsophisticated my more sensitive contemporaries and I were at that time. The naiveties of the diary which I began to write consistently soon after leaving school, and kept up until more than half way through the War, must be read in order to be believed. My "Reflective Record, 1913," is endorsed on its title page with the following comprehensive aspirations:

1 "To extend love, to promote thought, to lighten suffering, to combat indifference, to inspire activity."

"To know everything of something and something of everything."

My diary for August 3rd, 1914, contains a most incongruous[1] mixture of war and tennis.

The day was Bank Holiday,[2] and a tennis tournament had been arranged at the Buxton[3] Club. I had promised to play with my discouraged but still faithful suitor, and did not in the least want to forgo the amusement that I knew this partnership would afford me—particularly as the events reported in the newspapers seemed too incredible to be taken quite seriously. "I do not know," I wrote in my diary, "how we all managed to play tennis so calmly and take quite an interest in the result. I suppose it is because we all know so little of the real meaning of war that we are so indifferent. B. and I had to owe 30. It was good handicapping as we had a very close game with everybody." . . .

---

1. incongruous (in kong'grü əs), *adj.* out of place; inconsistent.
2. **Bank Holiday,** any weekday on which banks are legally closed. August 3, 1914, was a Monday.
3. **Buxton,** Brittain's home town, an attractive tourist town in Derbyshire, England.

Testament of Youth **743**

During Reading

Selection Objectives

- to explore the theme of war and its aftermath
- to identify mood in a literary work
- to learn about the use of indefinite pronouns in writing

 Unit 7 Resource Book
Graphic Organizer, p. 57
Study Guide, p. 58

Theme Link

The diaries that Vera Brittain kept throughout World War I convey the theme of war and aftermath. She records how she went from being a happy young woman to being exhausted and bereaved.

Vocabulary Preview

incongruous, out of place; inconsistent
pandemonium, wild uproar, lawlessness
inquisitive, curious, prying
rendezvous, secret meeting place.
inexpedient, unwise
taut, tense
amenable, responsive; agreeable
irrepressible, uncontrollable
suppurating, oozing
despondency, discouragement

Students can add the words and definitions to their Writer's Notebooks.

1 Reader's Response
Making Personal Connections

Question What personal aspirations would you record on the title page of *your* memoirs? *(Possible responses: Some students may cite idealistic aspirations like Brittain's; others may have more practical goals.)*

SELECTION SUMMARY

Testament of Youth

As the excerpt from *Testament of Youth* begins, Vera Brittain is a young woman preoccupied with social life. After England enters the war in 1914, her brother, Edward, wants to "join up," but their father forbids it. Vera falls in love with Roland Leighton, Edward's schoolmate. Leighton secures a commission to go to the front. After a year at Oxford, Vera leaves to become a nurse. Leighton sends horror-filled, disillusioned letters; he is scheduled to return on leave at Christmas, 1915, but is killed. Vera is deeply disturbed when shown the bloody clothes he was killed in. Edward, now a soldier, is sent to the front, and Vera, as a nurse, goes to France, where she witnesses the terrible effects of mustard gas. When her mother has a breakdown, Vera's father demands that she return to England. Edward is killed in 1918. The excerpt ends with Vera lamenting the horrors that Edward was forced to experience.

 *For summaries in other languages, see the **Building English Proficiency** book.*

Questions

- What mood does Brittain create in the paragraph? (*Possible responses: frantic, panicked, chaotic*)
- What are some words she uses to build this mood? (*Possible responses: panic, rushed, wild, rumors, upset, hysterical, hurriedly*)

☙ MULTICULTURAL NOTE

English *public schools* are what we in the U.S. refer to as private schools. They are privately endowed, old (some from medieval times), and require tuition. There are two other kinds of English schools: *comprehensive schools*, which correspond to U.S. public schools, are government run and free; *grammar schools*, state or charity run, are somewhat exclusive and quite old.

3 Reading/Thinking Skills
Synthesize

You might encourage students to recall literature and movies that describe military experiences of young people—for example, *The Red Badge of Courage*, *The Young Lions*, *The Naked and the Dead*. Help them recognize connections between war and the themes of initiation and coming of age.

After that[4] events moved, even in Buxton, very quickly. The German cousins of some local acquaintances left the town in a panic. My parents rushed over in the car to familiar shops in Macclesfield and Leek, where they laid in stores of cheese, bacon, and butter under the generally shared impression that by next week we might all be besieged by the Germans. Wild rumors circulated from mouth to mouth; they were more plentiful than the newspapers, over which a free fight broke out on the station platform every time a batch came by train from London or Manchester. Our elderly cook, who had three Reservist sons, dissolved into continuous tears and was too much upset to prepare the meals with her usual competence; her young daughter-in-law, who had had a baby only the previous Friday, became hysterical and had to be forcibly restrained from getting up and following her husband to the station. One or two Buxton girls were hurriedly married to officers summoned to unknown destinations. Pandemonium[5] swept over the town. Holiday trippers wrestled with one another for the *Daily Mail;* habitually quiet and respectable citizens struggled like wolves for the provisions in the food-shops, and vented upon the distracted assistants their dismay at learning that all prices had suddenly gone up. . . .

My father vehemently[6] forbade Edward, who was still under military age, to join anything whatsoever. Having himself escaped immersion in the public-school tradition, which stood for militaristic heroism unimpaired by the damping exercise of reason, he withheld his permission for any kind of military training, and ended by taking Edward daily to the mills to divert his mind from the War. Needless to say, these uncongenial expeditions entirely failed of their desired effect, and constant explosions—to which, having inherited so many of my father's characteristics, I seemed only to add by my presence—made our house quite intolerable. A new one boiled up after each of Edward's tentative efforts at defiance, and these were numerous, for his enforced subservience[7] seemed to him synonymous with ever-lasting disgrace. One vague application for a commission which he sent to a Notts and Derby regiment actually was forwarded to the War Office—"from which," I related with ingenuous optimism, "we are expecting to hear every post."

*W*hen my father discovered this exercise of initiative, his wrath and anxiety reached the point of effervescence.[8] Work of any kind was quite impossible in the midst of so much chaos and apprehension, and letters to Edward from Roland, describing his endeavors to get a commission in a Norfolk regiment, did nothing to ease the perpetual tension. Even after the result of my Oxford Senior[9] came through, I abandoned in despair the Greek textbooks that Roland had lent me. I even took to knitting for the soldiers, though only for a very short time; utterly incompetent at all forms of needlework, I found the simplest bed-socks and sleeping-helmets altogether beyond me. "Oh, how I wish I could wake up in the morning," concludes one typical day's entry describing these commotions, "to find this terrible war the dream it seems to me to be!"

At the beginning of 1915 I was more deeply and ardently in love than I have ever been or am ever likely to be, yet at that time Roland and I had hardly been alone together, and never at all without the constant possibility of observation and interruption. In Buxton our occasional walks had always been taken either through the town in full view of my family's inquisitive[10]

---

4. **that,** August 4, when at midnight, since the Germans had not responded to an English ultimatum that they withdraw from Belgium, the English entered the war.
5. pandemonium (pan′də mō′nē əm), *n.* wild uproar; lawlessness.
6. **vehemently** (vē′ə mənt lē), *adv.* forcefully.
7. **subservience** (səb sėr′vē əns), *n.* slavish obedience.
8. **effervescence** (ef′ər ves′ns), *n.* boiling over.
9. **Oxford Senior,** an entrance exam.
10. inquisitive (in kwiz′ə tiv), *adj.* curious; prying.

MINI-LESSON: VOCABULARY

Using a Thesaurus

Teach A thesaurus is a type of dictionary that contains synonyms and antonyms for words. It can be a useful tool for enriching students' vocabularies. One can use a thesaurus for finding both concise and unusual synonyms and antonyms of a word.

Activity Idea Have students use a thesaurus to identify synonyms and antonyms for these words: *testament, ardent, extinguish, apparent, duty, envy, rejoice, interval.*

Suggest to students that they record what they think of as the most obvious synonyms and antonyms and the most unusual ones. Have them share their results with the class and compare and contrast their choices.

acquaintances, or as one half of a quartet whose other members kept us continually in sight. At Uppingham[11] every conversation that we had was exposed to inspection and facetious[12] remark by schoolmasters or relatives. In London we could only meet under the benevolent but embarrassingly interested eyes of an aunt. Consequently, by the middle of January, our desire to see one another alone had passed beyond the bounds of toleration.

In my closely supervised life, a secret visit to London was impossible even en route for Oxford; I knew that I should be seen off by a train which had been discussed for days and, as usual, have my ticket taken for me. But Leicester was a conceivable rendezvous,[13] for I had been that way before, even though from Buxton the obvious route was via Birmingham. So for my family's benefit, I invented some objectionable students, likely to travel by Birmingham, whom I wanted to avoid. Roland, in similar mood, wrote that if he could not get leave he would come without it.

When the morning arrived, my mother decided that I seemed what she called "nervy," and insisted upon accompanying me to Miller's Dale, the junction at which travelers from Buxton change to the main line. I began in despair to wonder whether she would elect to come with me all the way to Oxford, but I finally escaped without her suspecting that I had any intention other than that of catching the first available train from Leicester. The usual telegram was demanded, but I protested that at Oxford station there was always such a rush for a cab that I couldn't possibly find time to telegraph until after tea.

At Leicester, Roland, who had started from Peterborough soon after dawn, was waiting for me with another sheaf of pale pink roses. He looked tired, and said he had had a cold; actually, it was incipient influenza and he ought to have been in bed, but I did not discover this till afterwards.

4

To be alone with one another after so much observation was quite overwhelming, and for a time conversation in the Grand Hotel lounge moved somewhat spasmodically. But constraint disappeared when he told me with obvious pride that he had asked his own colonel for permission to interview the colonel of the 5th Norfolks, who were stationed some distance away and were shortly going to the front, with a view to getting a transfer.

"Next time I see the C. O.,"[14] he announced, "I shall tell him the colonel of the 5th was away. I shall say I spent the whole day looking for him—so after lunch I'm coming with you to Oxford."

I tried to subdue my leaping joy by a protest about his cold, but as we both knew this to be insincere it was quite ineffective. I only stipulated that when we arrived he must lose me at the station; "chap. rules,"[15] even more Victorian than the social code of Buxton, made it inexpedient[16] for a woman student to be seen in Oxford with a young man who was not her brother.

5

6

> CONNECT: Compare and contrast the rules of courtship that Vera and Roland had to observe with those followed in today's society.

So we found an empty first-class carriage and traveled together from Leicester to Oxford. It was a queer journey; the memory of its profound unsatisfactoriness remains with me still. I had not realized before that to be alone together would bring, all too quickly, the knowledge that being alone together was not enough.

---

11. **Uppingham**, the private school attended by Edward Brittain and his friends. In 1913 there were about 400 boys in the school. The school's First World War Memorial lists 449 names.
12. **facetious** (fə sē′shəs), *adj.* slyly humorous.
13. rendezvous (rän′də vü), *n.* secret meeting place.
14. **C. O.,** commanding officer.
15. **"chap. rules,"** chaperone rules. A chaperone (shap′ə-rōn′) is an older person appointed to make sure that proper behavior is observed.
16. inexpedient (in′ik spē′dē ənt), *adj.* unwise.

BUILDING ENGLISH PROFICIENCY

ESL
LEP
ELD
SAE
LD

Planning a Reading Strategy

Use a K-W-L chart to help students organize their knowledge as they read this selection.

1. Before reading, have the class brainstorm what they already know about World War I and English society during the era.

2. Have students add these facts to the chart and then jot down questions that they hope Brittain's memoir might answer.

3. After reading, students can share responses to the selection in small groups and work together to record on their K-W-L charts what they learned.

What We **K**now	What We **W**ant to Know	What We **L**earned

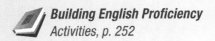

Building English Proficiency
Activities, p. 252

Art Study

Response to Caption Question   As an actively engaged wartime nurse, Brittain is no longer "abysmally ignorant," "romantically idealistic," or "utterly unsophisticated." Now her aspiration "to lighten suffering" is a real accomplishment.

7 Reading/Thinking Skills
Infer

Question   What do you think Roland means by this statement? *(Students may recognize that he is referring to their marrying, that it is a subtle proposal.)*

8 Literary Element
Symbolism

This image of the sunset suggests beauty on an awesome scale, bigger than both of them. At the same time, the color crimson foreshadows blood, and the setting sun suggests death.

EDITORIAL NOTE   This excerpt has been shortened for length. Parts of the full-length memoir are summarized in shaded passages such as this one.

▲ Compare this image of Vera Brittain as a wartime nurse with the picture she gives of herself at the beginning of the war (page 743).

he had only his pay, and we were both so distressingly young.

Thus a new constraint arose between us which again made it difficult to talk. We tried to discuss impersonally the places that we wanted to see when it was possible to travel once more; we'd go to Florence together, he said, directly the War was over.

"But," I objected—my age-perspective being somewhat different from that of today—"it wouldn't be proper until I'm at least thirty."

"Don't worry," he replied persuasively. "I'm sure I can arrange for it to be 'proper' before you get to that age!"

And then, somehow, we found ourselves suddenly admitting that each had kept the other's letters right from the beginning. We were now only a few miles from Oxford, and it was the first real thing that we had said. As we sat together silently watching the crimson sun set over the flooded land, some quality in his nearness became so unbearable that, all unsophisticated as I was, I felt afraid. I tried to explain it to myself afterwards by a familiar quotation: "There is no beauty that hath not some strangeness in the proportion...."

Like so many of the idealistic but naive young men of his generation, Roland Leighton regarded going to war as a duty, a test of heroism, and a potentially glamorous adventure. In a letter to Brittain describing his determination to secure a commission, he wrote: "I feel that I am meant to take an active part in this War. It is to me a very fascinating thing— something, if very horrible, yet very ennobling and very beautiful, something whose elemental reality raises it above the reach of all cold theorizing." On Wednesday, March 31, 1915, Vera saw Roland off to the front and returned home to the dreary realization that the war was beginning to overshadow everything in her life—school, personal relationships, ambitions, and dreams.

It was an intolerable realization, for I knew too that death might so easily overtake us before there could be anything more. I was dependent,

The next day I saw him off, although he had said that he would rather I didn't come. In the early morning we walked to the station beneath

MINI-LESSON: GRAMMAR

Using Indefinite Pronouns

Teach   A pronoun is a word used in place of a noun. An indefinite pronoun is one that does not refer to a specific person, place, or thing, such as *anybody, none, several, either.* The possessives for indefinite pronouns present two main problems:

- Gender: Unless the gender is specifically implied in a sentence, an indefinite pronoun takes a singular masculine possessive pronoun. (You may want to discuss the popular usage of *his or her, his/her,* and the plural *their* as possessive pronouns in sentences with singular indefinite pronouns. Explain that, while standard usage still employs the masculine possessive pronoun, some publications and writers use both masculine and feminine pronouns or the plural *their* in the interest of

gender equality.) Examples: Has *anyone* lost *his* mittens? Did *everyone* in the girls' gym class remember *her* sneakers?

- Singular versus plural: The possessive pronoun must always match the singular or plural indefinite pronoun. Example: *Several* went to *their* favorite restaurants.

Activity Idea   Suggest that pairs of students make up four more sentences that use indefinite pronouns.

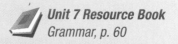

Unit 7 Resource Book
Grammar, p. 60

a dazzling sun, but the platform from which his train went out was dark and very cold. In the railway carriage we sat hand in hand until the whistle blew. We never kissed and never said a word. I got down from the carriage still clasping his hand, and held it until the gathering speed of the train made me let go. He leaned through the window looking at me with sad, heavy eyes, and I watched the train wind out of the station and swing round the curve until there was nothing left but the snowy distance, and the sun shining harshly on the bright, empty rails.

*W*hen I got back to the house, where everyone mercifully left me to myself, I realized that my hands were nearly frozen. Vaguely resenting the physical discomfort, I crouched beside the morning-room fire for almost an hour, unable to believe that I could ever again suffer such acute and conscious agony of mind. On every side there seemed to be cause for despair and no way out of it. I tried not to think because thought was intolerable, yet every effort to stop my mind from working only led to a fresh outburst of miserable speculation. I tried to read; I tried to look at the gaunt white hills across the valley, but nothing was any good, so in the end I just stayed huddled by the fire, immersed in a mood of blank hopelessness in which years seemed to have passed since the morning.

At last I fell asleep for some moments, and awoke feeling better; I was, I suppose, too young for hope to be extinguished for very long. Perhaps, I thought, Wordsworth or Browning or Shelley would have some consolation to offer; all through the War poetry was the only form of literature that I could read for comfort, and the only kind that I ever attempted to write. So I turned at once to Shelley's "Adonais,"[17] only to be provoked to new anguish by the words:

> O gentle child, beautiful as thou wert,
> Why didst thou leave the trodden paths of
>   men

Too soon, and with weak hands though
    mighty heart
Dare the unpastured dragon in his den?

But the lovely cadences[18] stirred me at last to articulateness; there was no one to whom I wanted to talk, but at least I could tell my diary a good deal of the sorrow that seemed so fathomless. . . .

With that Easter vacation began the wearing anxiety of waiting for letters which for me was to last, with only brief intervals, for more than three years, and which, I think, made all non-combatants feel more distracted than anything else in the War. Even when the letters came they were four days old, and the writer since sending them had had time to die over and over again. My diary, with its long-drawn-out record of days upon days of miserable speculation, still gives a melancholy impression of that nerve-racking suspense.

"Morning," it observes, "creeps on into afternoon, and afternoon passes into evening, while I go from one occupation to another, in apparent unconcern—but all the time this gnawing anxiety beneath it all."

Ordinary household sounds became a torment. The clock, marking off each hour of dread, struck into the immobility of tension with the shattering effect of a thunderclap. Every ring at the door suggested a telegram, every telephone call a long-distance message giving bad news. With some of us the effect of this prolonged apprehension still lingers on; even now I cannot work comfortably in a room from which it is possible to hear the front-door bell.

Having successfully competed her first-year exams at Oxford, Vera dropped all studies to commence training as a Red Cross nurse in Devonshire Hospital. In August, Roland returned home on leave, a strained reunion for the young lovers, despite their becoming officially engaged. Frustrated and depressed by lack of

---

17. **Shelley's "Adonais,"** the pastoral elegy composed in 1821 by Percy Shelley in honor of John Keats.
18. **cadence** (kād′ns), *n.* rising and falling sound.

Testament of Youth **747**

9 Reading/Thinking Skills
Visualize

Question How do you think Vera Brittain would appear if this were a scene from a movie? *(Students may imagine her as a tiny figure in a long-distance shot with her back to them; they may imagine her in a close-up shot that focuses on the anxiety in her face.)*

10 Reading/Thinking Skills
Analyze

Question How do these lines apply to Roland? *(Students may answer that he is very brave, though young, and has gone to fight an "unpastured dragon"—the enemy.)*

11 Literary Focus
Mood

A new mood creeps into these paragraphs. Brittain's term "prolonged apprehension" describes it well. Discuss with students how she effectively builds this mood with sounds—the clock, the doorbell, the telephone.

The World of Work
Nurse
For the real-life experiences of a nurse use the pages referenced below

The World of Work pp. 27–28

BUILDING ENGLISH PROFICIENCY

ESL LEP ELD SAE LD

Exploring Character

On page 746, the author refers to Roland and herself as "distressingly young." Use a web like the one shown here to help students clarify a portrait of the young Vera Brittain. Some responses may be words and phrases from the selection itself; others may express students' own inferences and conclusions as they read. Afterward, invite students to compare their webs in small groups and see how well their responses match.

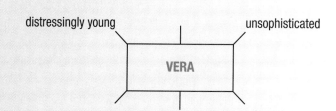

distressingly young   unsophisticated

VERA

12 Reading/Thinking Skills
Compare and Contrast

Question How is Roland similar to or different from the person he was before he went to the front? *(Students may say he is still courageous. However, he no longer has romantic ideas about fighting and questions the ultimate need to win.)*

13 Literary Element
Theme

Question How does this quoted hymn reflect the theme of this section? *(Students may point out that appealing to God to stop violence highlights a theme of human helplessness in the midst of war.)*

14 Historical Note
The Stresses of War

As a nurse, Brittain most likely encountered men with "shell shock"—a term coined during World War I. It was the first time that the terrible emotional and mental effects of war on soldiers were classified as a mental illness. Use of the term is now much less frequent. Eventually this condition came to be known as battle fatigue or post-traumatic stress disorder.

privacy and the brevity of their time together, they parted in a mood of despair and foreboding that was to persist in the grim weeks that followed.

As September wore on and the Battle of Loos came nearer, an anxious stillness seemed to settle upon the country, making everyone taut[19] and breathless. The Press and personal letters from France were alike full of anticipation and suspense. Roland wrote vaguely but significantly of movements of troops, of great changes impending, and seemed more obsessed with the idea of death than ever before. One letter, describing how he had superintended the reconstruction of some old trenches, was grim with a disgust and bitterness that I had never known him put into words:

"The dugouts have been nearly all blown in, the wire entanglements are a wreck, and in among the chaos of twisted iron and splintered timber and shapeless earth are the fleshless, blackened bones of simple men who poured out their red, sweet wine of youth[20] unknowing, for nothing more tangible than Honor or their Country's Glory or another's Lust of Power. Let him who thinks War is a glorious, golden thing, who loves to roll forth stirring words of exhortation,[21] invoking Honor and Praise and Valor and Love of Country with as thoughtless and fervid[22] a faith as inspired the priests of Baal[23] to call on their own slumbering deity, let him but look at a little pile of sodden gray rags that cover half a skull and a shinbone and what might have been Its ribs, or at this skeleton lying on its side, resting half crouching as it fell, perfect but that it is headless, and with the tattered clothing still draped round it; and let him realize how grand and glorious a thing it is to have distilled all Youth and Joy and Life into a fetid[24] heap of hideous putrescence![25] Who is there who has known and seen who can say that Victory is worth the death of even one of these?"

Had there really been a time, I wondered, when I believed that it was?

"When I think of these things," I told him in reply, "I feel that awful Abstraction, the Unknown God, must be some dread and wrathful deity before whom I can only kneel and plead for mercy, perhaps in the words of a quaint hymn of George Herbert's[26] that we used to sing at Oxford:

Throw away Thy wrath!
Throw away Thy rod!
O my God
Take the gentle path!"

In October, Vera received orders to report to First London General Hospital, Camberwell, an army hospital to which she had applied, lying about her age. Here she experienced miserable living conditions, twelve-hour workdays, and daily exposure to grisly wounds in the surgical wards, in addition to incessant anxiety over Roland's safety and the possible weakening of their love by separation and war. The last week of 1915 she spent in nervous, yet ecstatic anticipation of Roland's leave on December 25, Christmas Day.

Certainly the stage seemed perfectly set for his leave. Now that my parents had at last migrated temporarily to the Grand Hotel at Brighton, our two families were so near; the Matron had promised yet again that my own week's holiday should coincide with his, and even Edward wrote cheerfully for once to say that as soon as the actual date was known, he and Victor[27] would both be able to get leave at the same time.

---

19. **taut** (tôt), *adj.* tense.
20. **red, sweet wine of youth.** Here Leighton quotes a famous line from Rupert Brooke's poem, "The Dead." See The Language of Heroism, page 777.
21. **exhortation** (eg′zôr tā′shən), *n.* earnest advice.
22. **fervid** (fėr′vid), *adj.* spirited.
23. **priests of Baal,** those who worshiped a false god.
24. **fetid** (fet′id), *adj.* stinking.
25. **putrescence** (pyü tres′ns), *n.* rottenness.
26. **hymn of George Herbert's,** "Discipline," by the religious poet George Herbert (1593–1633).
27. **Victor,** another school friend of Edward Brittain's.

MINI-LESSON: SPEAKING AND LISTENING

Using Multimedia

Teach When students make an oral presentation on a topic, using multimedia options can enhance the audience's interest and understanding.

Activity Idea Divide the class into small groups. To each group, assign one of the following report topics or a topic of your own choosing:

- the use of mustard gas in World War I
- Count Leopold von Berchtold, the foreign minister of Austro-Hungary
- the use of tanks by both sides in World War I

Have each group prepare a three- to five-minute presentation, using multimedia support. Suggest they bring in photographs, make maps and charts for use with an overhead projector, or show videotapes of documentaries or dramatized films which contain footage pertinent to the topics. After each presentation, discuss with the class how the multimedia materials enhanced or distracted from it.

"Very wet and muddy and many of the communication trenches are quite impassable," ran a letter from Roland written on December 9th. "Three men were killed the other day by a dugout falling in on top of them and one man was drowned in a sump hole. The whole of one's world, at least of one's visible and palpable world, is mud in various stages of solidity or stickiness. . . . I can be perfectly certain about the date of my leave by tomorrow morning and will let you know."

And, when the final information did come, hurriedly written in pencil on a thin slip of paper torn from his Field Service notebook, it brought the enchanted day still nearer than I had dared to hope.

"Shall be home on leave from 24th Dec.—31st. Land Christmas Day. R."

Even to the unusual concession of a leave which began on Christmas morning after night-duty the Matron proved amenable,[28] and in the encouraging quietness of the winter's war, with no Loos in prospect, no great push in the west even possible, I dared to glorify my days—or rather my nights—by looking forward. In the pleasant peace of Ward 25, where all the patients, now well on the road to health, slept soundly, the sympathetic Scottish Sister teased me a little for my irrepressible[29] excitement. . . .

Directly after breakfast, sent on my way by exuberant good wishes from Betty and Marjorie and many of the others, I went down to Brighton. All day I waited there for a telephone message or a telegram, sitting drowsily in the lounge of the Grand Hotel, or walking up and down the promenade, watching the gray sea tossing rough with white surf-crested waves, and wondering still what kind of crossing he had had or was having.

When, by ten o'clock at night, no news had come, I concluded that the complications of telegraph and telephone on a combined Sunday and Christmas Day had made communication impossible. So, unable to fight sleep any longer after a night and a day of wakefulness, I went to bed a little disappointed, but still unperturbed. Roland's family, at their Keymer cottage, kept an even longer vigil; they sat up till nearly midnight over their Christmas dinner in the hope that he would join them, and, in their dramatic, impulsive fashion, they drank a toast to the Dead.

The next morning I had just finished dressing, and was putting the final touches to the pastel-blue crêpe-de-Chine blouse, when the expected message came to say that I was wanted on the telephone. Believing that I was at last to hear the voice for which I had waited for twenty-four hours, I dashed joyously into the corridor. But the message was not from Roland but from Clare;[30] it was not to say that he had arrived home that morning, but to tell me that he had died of wounds at a Casualty Clearing Station on December 23rd. . . .

Plunged into anguish and nightmarish confusion by the death of Roland, Brittain suffered through months of loneliness, strained communication with family and friends, and unresolved perplexity about the meaning of Roland's death.

Whenever I think of the weeks that followed the news of Roland's death, a series of pictures, disconnected but crystal clear, unroll themselves like a kaleidoscope through my mind.

A solitary cup of coffee stands before me on a hotel breakfast-table; I try to drink it, but fail ignominiously. . . .

It is Sunday, and I am out for a solitary walk through the dreary streets of Camberwell before going to bed after the night's work. In front of me on the frozen pavement a long red worm wriggles slimily. I remember that, after our death, worms destroy this body—however lovely, however beloved—and I run from the obscene thing in horror.

It is Wednesday, and I am walking up the Brixton Road on a mild, fresh morning of early

---

28. amenable (ə mē′nə bəl), *adj.* responsive; agreeable.
29. irrepressible (ir′i pres′ə bəl), *adj.* uncontrollable.
30. **Clare,** Roland Leighton's sister.

BUILDING ENGLISH PROFICIENCY

Tracking Narrative Events

The selection includes many of the most important and traumatic events in Vera's wartime experience. Help students follow Vera's story by using a time line, as shown. If necessary, place one or two events on the time line to get the class started.

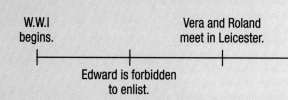

W.W.I begins.

Vera and Roland meet in Leicester.

Edward is forbidden to enlist.

18 Reader's Response
Making Personal Connections

Question Do you agree or disagree that it is wrong of Vera to feel joy for a moment? Why? *(Possible responses: Students may agree because she should be mourning Roland longer and should not be affected by the change in seasons; others may disagree because she needs to start enjoying life again, she's young, and she should look toward the future.)*

19 Active Reading
Clarify

Possible response These ruined clothes are all that is left of Roland and his patriotism.

20 Reading/Thinking Skills
Apply

You might have students compare these lines by John Masefield to lines in the poems of Brooke, Sassoon, or Owen on pages 735–739. Ask which lines most closely reflect students' ideas of war.

---

spring. Half-consciously I am repeating a line from Rupert Brooke: "The deep night, and birds singing, and clouds flying . . ." For a moment I have become conscious of the old joy in rain-washed skies and scuttling, fleecy clouds, when suddenly I remember—Roland is dead and I am not keeping faith with him; it is mean and cruel, even for a second, to feel glad to be alive.

In Sussex, by the end of January, the season was already on its upward grade; catkins hung bronze from the bare, black branches, and in the damp lanes between Hassocks and Keymer the birds sang loudly. How I hated them as I walked back to the station one late afternoon, when a red sunset turned the puddles on the road into gleaming pools of blood, and a new horror of mud and death darkened my mind with its dreadful obsession. Roland, I reflected bitterly, was now part of the corrupt clay into which war had transformed the fertile soil of France; he would never again know the smell of a wet evening in early spring.

I had arrived at the cottage that morning to find his mother and sister standing in helpless distress in the midst of his returned kit, which was lying, just opened, all over the floor. The garments sent back included the outfit that he had been wearing when he was hit. I wondered, and I wonder still, why it was thought necessary to return such relics—the tunic torn back and front by the bullet, a khaki vest dark and stiff with blood, and a pair of blood-stained breeches slit open at the top by someone obviously in a violent hurry. Those gruesome rags made me realize, as I had never realized before, all that France really meant. Eighteen months afterwards the smell of Etaples village, though fainter and more diffused, brought back to me the memory of those poor remnants of patriotism.

19 CLARIFY: Why do you think Vera calls Roland's blood-stained garments "poor remnants of patriotism"?

"Everything," I wrote later to Edward, "was damp and worn and simply caked with mud. And I was glad that neither you nor Victor nor anyone who may some day go to the front was there to see. If you had been, you would have been overwhelmed by the horror of war without its glory. For though he had only worn the things when living, the smell of those clothes was the smell of graveyards and the Dead. The mud of France which covered them was not ordinary mud; it had not the usual clean pure smell of earth, but it was as though it were saturated with dead bodies—dead that had been dead a long, long time. . . . There was his cap, bent in and shapeless out of recognition—the soft cap he wore rakishly on the back of his head—with the badge thickly coated with mud. He must have fallen on top of it, or perhaps one of the people who fetched him in trampled on it."

What actually happened to the clothes I never knew, but, incongruously enough, it was amid this heap of horror and decay that we found, surrounded by torn bills and letters, the black manuscript notebook containing his poems. On the flyleaf he had copied a few lines written by John Masefield[31] on the subject of patriotism:

"It is not a song in the street and a wreath on a column and a flag flying from a window and a pro-Boer under a pump.[32] It is a thing very holy and very terrible, like life itself. It is a burden to be borne, a thing to labor for and to suffer for and to die for, a thing which gives no happiness and no pleasantness—but a hard life, an unknown grave, and the respect and bowed heads of those who follow." **20**

---

31. **John Masefield** (1878–1967), English poet.
32. **a pro-Boer . . . pump.** Public opinion had been strongly divided on the subject of the Boer War (1899–1902), with a number of the British sympathetic to the Boer cause. Here Masefield alludes to the false patriotism of a mob punishing someone opposed to English imperialism by dousing them with water.

MINI-LESSON: VOCABULARY

Understanding Analogies

Teach An *analogy* is a relationship between two things that are basically different. Often, the analogy creates a comparison with another pair, for example:

- *Finger* is to *hand* as *toe* is to *foot*.
- *Steering wheel* is to *car* as *handlebars* are to *bicycle*.

Analogies often appear in vocabulary sections of multiple choice exams. It may be helpful for students to practice making model sentences that create the basis for analogies. For instance:

- Five _____ extend off each _____. *(fingers/hand)*
- I use the _____ to steer a _____. *(handlebars/bicycle)*

The blanks in these sentences would fit both pairs of words from the above respective analogies.

Activity Idea Students can complete these analogies based on this selection and then make up analogies of their own.

1. *War* is to *peace* as *noise* is to _____. *(silence)*
2. *Vein* is to *blood* as _____ is to *water*. *(pipe)*
3. *Day* is to *night* as _____ is to *depression*. *(sadness)*
4. *Soldier* is to _____ as *scholar* is to *intelligence*. *(courage)*

(Left to right) Edward Brittain, Roland Leighton, and Victor Richardson pose together at Uppingham School O.T.C. camp in July 1915. Do any of these faces suggest Wilfred Owen's schoolboys "ardent for some desperate glory" (page 737, line 26)?

The months of unrelieved pain and hopelessness following the death of Roland were further darkened by the departure of Vera's brother Edward for the front in February of 1916 and his later wounding in action, for which he earned the Military Cross. In September, Vera was assigned to eight months of duty on the island of Malta, where the remoteness of the war and exposure to daily sunshine effected a resurgence of hopefulness and personal vitality. After the death of two more of their friends, Edward wrote: ". . . we have lost almost all there was to lose and what have we gained? Truly as you say has patriotism worn very threadbare. . . ." In August of 1917 Vera went to France to begin work at No. 24 General Hospital, Etaples, caring for the wounded on both sides and exposing herself to considerable personal danger.

"Never in my life have I been so absolutely filthy as I get on duty here," I wrote to my mother on December 5th in answer to her request for a description of my work.

"Sister A. has six wards and there is no V.A.D.[33] in the next-door one, only an orderly, so neither she nor he spend very much time in here. Consequently I am Sister, V.A.D. and orderly all in one (somebody said the other day that no one less than God Almighty could give a correct definition of the job of a V.A.D.!) and after, quite apart from the nursing, I have stoked the stove all night, done two or three rounds of bed-pans and kept the kettles going and prepared feeds on exceedingly black Beatrice oil-stoves and refilled them from the steam kettles, literally wallowing in paraffin all the time, I feel as if I had been dragged through the gutter! Possibly acute surgical is the heaviest kind of work there is, but acute medical is, I think, more wearing than anything else on earth. You are kept on the go the whole time and in the end there seems nothing definite to show for it—except that one or two people are still alive who might otherwise have been dead." 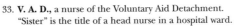 **21**

The rest of my letter referred to the effect, upon ourselves, of the new offensive at Cambrai.[34]

"The hospital is very heavy now—as heavy as when I came; the fighting is continuing very long this year, and the convoys keep coming down, two or three a night. . . . Sometimes in the middle of the night we have to turn people out of bed and make them sleep on the floor to make room for more seriously ill ones that have come down from the line. We have heaps of gassed cases at present who came in a day or two ago; there are ten in this ward alone. I wish those people who write so glibly about this being a holy War, and the orators who talk so much about going on no matter how long the War lasts and what it may mean, could see a case—to say nothing of ten cases—of mustard gas in its early stages—could see the poor things burned and blistered all over with great mustard-colored suppurating[35] blisters, with blind eyes—

---

33. **V. A. D.,** a nurse of the Voluntary Aid Detachment. "Sister" is the title of a head nurse in a hospital ward.
34. **Cambrai,** a town in France. The offensive, beginning November 20, 1917, was the first battle in which a notable use was made of tanks.
35. suppurating (sup′yə rā′ting), *adj.* oozing.

Testament of Youth **751**

 **Art Study**

Response to Caption Question
Edward Brittain appears more relaxed and optimistic than the other two young men. None, however, appears "ardent."

Literary Criticism
"At the time she began to write *(Testament of Youth),* she was the mother of a two-year-old son: the fact that she was now the mother of a potential soldier may very well have influenced her . . . The most potent and abiding image in the book is still the image of the young woman in her nurse's uniform, tending wounded men to assuage her grief because her lover has been killed. It is the classic image of women mourning husbands, sons, and lovers killed in war, and tending the survivors: an image that is not intrinsically anti-war or pro-women's emancipation . . . The book is also about survival, even resurrection . . . Like a symphony it begins with peace and calm, is succeeded by crisis and disaster, and ends with reconciliation."

Hilary Bailey
Vera Brittain

21 **Literary Element**
Tone

Question What is the tone of this letter? *(Possible responses: energetic, matter-of-fact, sympathetic)*

BUILDING ENGLISH PROFICIENCY

Using a Map

Brittain serves in a number of localities in Europe. She works in a hospital in London, vacations in Camberwell where she learns of Roland's death, and now, on this page, works in a hospital on the island of Malta and then in Etaples, France. She will move on from there. Suggest that students follow her location in Europe using a large map. If you can find a map of Europe during World War I, students will get an even better appreciation for where she is serving in relation to the battlefront.

Reader's Response
Making Personal Connections

Questions

- What are the "incompatible claims" that torment women of Brittain's generation? *(the pull between patriotic and family duties)*

- Do you think that these conflicting claims still affect females today? Explain. *(Answers may acknowledge that women today are likewise torn between conflicting duties—family, patriotic, and—now—professional.)*

Reading/Thinking Skills
Recognize Cause and Effect

Question What is the cause of Mrs. Brittain's breakdown? *(Possible responses: anxiety about her son, fear of an attack, and loss of routines)*

Reading/Thinking Skills
Recognize Values

Question What do we learn of Mr. Brittain's values from this letter? *(Students may mention that he believes a young woman should help with her family, that it is important to be at home, and that he should have the final say in what his daughter does.)*

---

sometimes temporarily, sometimes permanently—all sticky and stuck together, and always fighting for breath, with voices a mere whisper, saying that their throats are closing and they know they will choke. The only thing one can say is that such severe cases don't last long; either they die soon or else improve—usually the former; they certainly never reach England in the state we have them here, and yet people persist in saying that God made the War, when there are such inventions of the Devil about. . . .

While enduring the front-line hardship in an understaffed and besieged camp hospital, Vera was simultaneously forced to deal with the complaints and crises of her parents, who were becoming increasingly incapable of coping with wartime stress and her extended absence.

The despondency[36] at home was certainly making many of us in France quite alarmed: because we were women we feared perpetually that, just as our work was reaching its climax, our families would need our youth and vitality for their own support. One of my cousins, the daughter of an aunt, had already been summoned home from her canteen work in Boulogne; she was only one of many, for as the War continued to wear out strength and spirits, the middle-aged generation, having irrevocably yielded up its sons, began to lean with increasing weight upon its daughters. Thus the desperate choice between incompatible claims—by which the women of my generation, with their carefully trained consciences, have always been tormented—showed signs of afflicting us with new pertinacity. . . .[37]

Early in April a letter arrived from my father to say that my mother had "crocked up" and had been obliged, owing to the inefficiency of the domestic help then available, to go into a nursing-home. What exactly was wrong remained unspecified, though phrases referred to "toxic heart" and "complete general breakdown." My father had temporarily closed the flat and moved into an hotel, but he did not, he told me, wish to remain there. "As your mother and I can no longer manage without you," he concluded, "it is now your duty to leave France immediately and return to Kensington."

I read these words with real dismay, for my father's interpretation of my duty was not, I knew only too well, in the least likely to agree with that of the Army, which had always been singularly unmoved by the worries of relatives. What was I to do? I wondered desperately. There was my family, confidently demanding my presence, and here was the offensive, which made every pair of experienced hands worth ten pairs under normal conditions. I remembered how the hastily imported V.A.D.s had gone sick at the 1st London during the rush after the Somme; a great push was no time in which to teach a tyro[38] her job. How much of my mother's breakdown was physical and how much psychological—the cumulative result of pessimism at home? It did not then occur to me that my father's sense of emergency was probably heightened by a subconscious determination to get me back to London before the Germans reached the Channel ports, as everyone in England felt certain they would. I only knew that no one in France would believe a domestic difficulty to be so insoluble; if I were dead, or a male, it would have to be settled without me. I should merely be thought to have "wind-up," to be using my mother's health as an excuse to escape the advancing enemy or the threatening air raids.

Half-frantic with the misery of conflicting obligations, I envied Edward his complete powerlessness to leave the Army whatever happened at home. Today, remembering the violent clash

---

36. **despondency** (di spon′dən sē), *n.* discouragement.
37. **pertinacity** (pėr′n as′ə tē), *n.* persistence.
38. **tyro** (tī′rō), *n.* beginner.

MINI-LESSON: STUDY SKILLS

Creating Graphic Organizers

Teach Making a chart can help readers understand the time frame of events in a piece of literature. In *Testament of Youth*, the events in people's lives are measured by the chronology of the war.

Activity Idea Write the following chart on the chalkboard. Then, divide the class into small groups and have students work together to fill in an assigned column according to chronology. The more specifically students record dates, the more complete the chart.

	War Events	Vera	Edward	Roland
1914				
1915				
1916				
1917				

between family and profession, between "duty" and ambition, between conscience and achievement, which has always harassed the women now in their thirties and forties, I find myself still hoping that if the efforts of various interested parties succeed in destroying the fragile international structure built up since the Armistice, and war breaks out on a scale comparable to that of 1914, the organizers of the machine will not hesitate to conscript all women under fifty for service at home or abroad. In the long run, an irrevocable allegiance in a time of emergency makes the decision easier for the older as well as for the younger generation. What exhausts women in wartime is not the strenuous and unfamiliar tasks that fall upon them, nor even the hourly dread of death for husbands or lovers or brothers or sons; it is the incessant conflict between personal and national claims which wears out their energy and breaks their spirit. . . .

It seemed to me then, with my crude judgments and black-and-white values, quite inexplicable that the older generation, which had merely looked on at the War, should break under the strain so much more quickly than those of us who had faced death or horror at first hand for months on end. Today, with middle-age just round the corner, and children who tug my anxious thoughts relentlessly back to them whenever I have to leave them for a week, I realize how completely I underestimated the effect upon the civilian population of year upon year of diminishing hope, diminishing food, diminishing light, diminishing heat, of waiting and waiting for news which was nearly always bad when it came. . . .

 SUMMARIZE: How do the different groups that Brittain belongs to throughout influence her attitudes and behaviors?

Nevertheless, in April 1918 Vera reluctantly returned to England to take charge of her parents' household and settle into weeks of dreary domesticity and heightened anxiety over the safety of Edward, now stationed in Italy.

For some time now, my apprehensions for Edward's safety had been lulled by the long quiescence[39] of the Italian front, which had seemed a haven of peace in contrast to our own raging vortex.[40] Repeatedly, during the German offensive, I had thanked God and the Italians who fled at Caporetto[41] that Edward was out of it, and rejoiced that the worst I had to fear from this particular push was the comparatively trivial danger that threatened myself. But now I felt the familiar stirrings of the old tense fear which had been such a persistent companion throughout the War, and my alarm was increased when Edward asked me a week or two later to send him "a funny cat from Liberty's[42] . . . to alleviate tragedy with comedy."

On Sunday morning, June 16th, I opened the *Observer*, which appeared to be chiefly concerned with the new offensive—for the moment at a standstill—in the Noyon-Montdidier sector of the Western Front, and instantly saw at the head of a column the paragraph for which I had looked so long and so fearfully:

ITALIAN FRONT ABLAZE
GUN DUELS FROM MOUNTAIN TO SEA
BAD OPENING OF AN OFFENSIVE. . . .

A day or two later, more details were published of the fighting in Italy, and I learned that the Sherwood Foresters[43] had been involved in

---

39. **quiescence** (kwī es′ns), *n.* stillness.
40. **vortex** (vôr′teks), *n.* whirlwind.
41. **Caporetto,** a town in Austria, the site of the defeat of the Italian Second Army by a combined Austrian-German attack, October 24, 1917.
42. **Liberty's,** a London department store.
43. **Sherwood Foresters,** Edward Brittain's regiment.

Testament of Youth **753**

---

25 **Active Reading**
Summarize

Students may mention that being British encouraged her patriotism, being a woman meant she could only contribute by caring for people, and being a daughter gave her perspective on the anxiety of parents during the war.

26 **Reading/Thinking Skills**
Analyze

Question Why is Vera alarmed by Edward's request? *(Students may recognize that his desire for something humorous and allusion to "tragedy" indicate that the horror around him is increasing; something familiar and British would comfort him and remind him of home, so it seems he may be despairing.)*

BUILDING ENGLISH PROFICIENCY

Responding to Autobiography

Vera Brittain's memoir gives an intimate account of a devastating time in her life. Invite students to respond in one or both of these ways:

Activity Ideas

- Have pairs of students interview each other for reactions to Vera Brittain's account of her life.

- Have students write in their journals, speculating how they might respond to the tragedies and challenges faced by Vera Brittain.

27 Literary Element

Imagery

Question   Why does Brittain include this image of delphiniums? *(Possible responses: to illustrate the experience of shock; to contrast their unearthly beauty and vitality with the death of Edward)*

28 Reader's Response

Challenging the Text

Question   Do you think this is a good ending for this excerpt? Explain. *(Answers will vary, but this question should provide an opportunity to discuss writing technique. Students should recognize a need for closure, which the reflective conclusion provides. Ending with news of Edward's death would not provide a satisfactory conclusion. Some students may wish to suggest other possible endings, but remind them that since this is a memoir, they cannot add new events.)*

Check Test

1. About what issue do Edward and his father disagree? *(Edward wants to join the military but his father forbids him.)*

2. What excuse does Vera use to take a train that goes through Leicester? *(She says that there are students she does not want to see.)*

3. In what country is Roland stationed? *(France)*

4. For what reason does Vera stop her studies after one year? *(to be an army nurse)*

5. Why does Vera leave the hospital in France? *(Her mother has had a breakdown, and her father insists she come home.)*

Unit 7 Resource Book
Alternate Check Test, p. 61

---

the "show" on the Plateau. After that I made no pretense at doing anything but wander restlessly round Kensington or up and down the flat, and, though my father retired glumly to bed every evening at nine o'clock, I gave up writing the semi-fictitious record which I had begun of my life in France. Somehow I couldn't bring myself even to wrap up the *Spectator* and *Saturday Review* that I sent every week to Italy, and they remained in my bedroom, silent yet eloquent witnesses to the dread which my father and I, determinedly conversing on commonplace topics, each refused to put into words.

By the following Saturday we had still heard nothing of Edward. The interval usually allowed for news of casualties after a battle was seldom so long as this, and I began, with an artificial sense of lightness unaccompanied by real conviction, to think that there was perhaps, after all, no news to come. I had just announced to my father, as we sat over tea in the dining-room, that I really must do up Edward's papers and take them to the post office before it closed for the week-end, when there came the sudden loud clattering at the front-door knocker that always meant a telegram.

For a moment I thought that my legs would not carry me, but they behaved quite normally as I got up and went to the door. I knew what was in the telegram—I had known for a week—but because the persistent hopefulness of the human heart refuses to allow intuitive certainty to persuade the reason of that which it knows, I opened and read it in a tearing anguish of suspense.

"Regret to inform you Captain E. H. Brittain M.C. killed in action Italy June 15th."

"No answer," I told the boy mechanically, and

handed the telegram to my father, who had followed me into the hall. As we went back into the dining-room I saw, as though I had never seen them before, the bowl of blue delphiniums on the table; their intense color, vivid, ethereal,[44] seemed too radiant for earthly flowers.

Then I remembered that we should have to go down to Purley and tell the news to my mother. . . .

Long after [Father] had gone to bed and the world had grown silent, I crept into the dining-room to be alone with Edward's portrait. Carefully closing the door, I turned on the light and looked at the pale, pictured face, so dignified, so steadfast, so tragically mature. He had been through so much—far, far more than those beloved friends who had died at an earlier stage of the interminable War, leaving him alone to mourn their loss. Fate might have allowed him the little, sorry compensation of survival, the chance to make his lovely music in honor of their memory. It seemed indeed the last irony that he should have been killed by the countrymen of Fritz Kreisler,[45] the violinist whom of all others he had most greatly admired.

And suddenly, as I remembered all the dear afternoons and evenings when I had followed him on the piano as he played his violin, the sad, searching eyes of the portrait were more than I could bear, and falling on my knees before it I began to cry "Edward! Oh, Edward!" in dazed repetition, as though my persistent crying and calling would somehow bring him back. . . .

---

44. **ethereal** (i thir′ē əl), *adj.* heavenly.
45. **Fritz Kreisler** (1875–1962), Austrian violinist.

MINI-LESSON: READING/THINKING SKILLS

Relating Literature to Personal Experience

Teach   In *Testament of Youth*, Vera Brittain experiences huge philosophical and emotional changes. She is 21, an age of transition for anyone. Then war shapes how she changes and who she becomes. Suggest to students that they consider how public, historical events have affected their own personal changes.

Activity Idea   Have students write a short personal essay on one of these topics:

• How a War Has Affected My Beliefs

• How I Experienced the Last Presidential Election

• An Event That Shaped My Feelings About the Environment

• Why I Disagree with My Family/Friends About . . .

Volunteers may read their essays aloud to the class and discuss how their experiences are similar to or different from Brittain's.

After Reading

Making Connections

Shaping Your Response

1. Which death do you think was more devastating to Brittain—Roland's or Edward's? Explain your answer.

Analyzing the Memoir

2. ☺ How does Brittain characterize herself and her entire **group** of peers at the outbreak of the war?

3. What does the **imagery** she uses suggest about her feelings on the day she saw Roland off to war?

4. What contradictory feelings following Roland's death do you think contribute to Brittain's personal torment?

5. Brittain expresses the hope that, in any future war, women will be able to serve in the same ways as men. What do you think causes her to feel this way?

6. In what ways do you see Brittain in conflict with her parents? Do you think her complaints are justified? How do her views of the "older generation" change when she herself reaches middle age?

7. Brittain wrote this memoir fifteen years after the end of the war. What effect on her writing might this delay have had?

Extending the Ideas

8. Compare Roland's description of the suffering of the men at the front and his attack on idealistic attitudes toward war with Wilfred Owen's "Dulce et Decorum Est" (page 737). What similarities do you find?

Literary Focus: Mood

Mood is the prevailing atmosphere of a literary work.

1. What do you believe is the overall emotional mood of the excerpts from *Testament of Youth?*

2. Contrast the mood in the periods immediately before and after Christmas, 1915.

3. What is the mood of Brittain's description of learning of Edward's death?

LITERARY FOCUS: MOOD

Possible Responses

1. tragic, passionate, anger at injustice

2. Students may point out that the mood before Christmas is hopeful and calm; after Christmas it is lonely and full of grief.

3. Students may describe the mood as one of shock, heightened awareness, or overwhelming despair.

Suggest to students that they go back to their lists of words and images that create mood (see p. 742). Invite students to share the strongest examples with the class.

MAKING CONNECTIONS

1. Students may feel that Roland's death was more devastating because she was in love with him; others may feel that Edward's death was more devastating because he was her brother and experienced more of the horrors of war.

2. Possible response: She characterizes them as young, self-centered, naive, and patriotic.

3. Possible response: The imagery suggests that she feels as though Roland is disappearing, being carried off into nothingness.

4. Possible response: She is angry and disillusioned about the war, but she still supports the British people fighting it.

5. Possible response: She feels that women are torn between their private and public duties. She feels that serving in the same ways as men would ease pressures to stay home and would add to women's independence and equality.

6. Brittain's family duties conflicted with her patriotic ones. Students may differ on which duties should take precedence. Later, she recognizes the tremendous strain war has on the older generation, who are fighting their own battles against despair and deprivation.

7. Possible response: Time may have given her perspective on different points of view; it may have made her able to write without being overcome by the emotions and allowed her to structure the story coherently.

8. Students may mention the horror of being surrounded by dying men and corpses, the disillusionment with war, or the sense of wasted youth.

VOCABULARY STUDY

1. incongruous
2. pandemonium
3. inexpedient
4. inquisitive
5. rendezvous
6. irrepressible
7. taut
8. suppurating
9. amenable
10. despondency

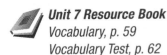
Unit 7 Resource Book
Vocabulary, p. 59
Vocabulary Test, p. 62

WRITING CHOICES
Writer's Notebook Update

Students may write that they believe women should participate fully in combat or that they should provide support. Some may feel service should be required, as Brittain does. Some students may feel that *no one* should be required to participate in wars.

It's Pandemonium

Suggest students focus on images and powerful words to vividly describe the setting, mood, sounds, and people involved. They may want to use some of the vocabulary words in their descriptions.

Selection Test

Unit 7 Resource Book
pp. 63–64

Vocabulary Study

Write the word from the list that is most clearly related to the situation being described.

amenable
despondency
incongruous
inexpedient
inquisitive
irrepressible
pandemonium
rendezvous
suppurating
taut

1. the unlikely mixture of war and tennis
2. the wild reactions of the people after war is declared
3. the unwise decision of a girl to travel unchaperoned in 1914
4. her mother's prying questions about Vera's trip to Oxford
5. Vera and Roland's secret meeting
6. Edward's uncontrollable attempts to join the war effort
7. Vera's tense feelings after she sees Roland off to the front
8. the oozing blisters that soldiers suffer because of poison gas
9. the agreeable attitude of the Sister who gives Vera leave
10. Vera's discouraged emotional state as she waits for Roland's arrival

Expressing Your Ideas

Writing Choices

Writer's Notebook Update Jot down a few ideas about how Brittain's opinion about women and war compares with your own.

It's Pandemonium Brittain describes the uproar that sweeps over the town when war is declared. Write a **description** of another kind of pandemonium: a victory celebration for a winning team, a bombing of a public building in a major city, the crash of the stock market, for example.

For Comfort's Sake Brittain says that "all through the War poetry was the only form of literature that I could read for comfort." What kind of literature do you read—or what other activity do you do—for comfort? Write a personal **journal entry** in which you explain what gives you comfort and consolation when you are tense or worried or unhappy.

Other Options

In Memoriam Compose and perform a **musical piece** that you think Edward, if he had survived, might have written in honor of the friends he lost in the war. You might want to use some words or phrases from Brooke, Sassoon, Owen, or one of the poems quoted in Brittain's memoir as inspiration for your composition.

A Conversation About Women Imagine a conversation among Mary Wollstonecroft, Elizabeth Browning, Vera Brittain, and a modern woman of your choice about women in society: their education, their relationships with men, their contributions to the world. With three of your classmates write a **script** of this conversation and present it as a dramatic reading.

OTHER OPTIONS
In Memoriam

It may be helpful for their compositions for students to listen to the music of the day. Some English composers from the World War I era are Ralph Vaughan Williams, Edward Elgar, Frederick Delius, Malcolm Arnold, Arnold Bax, and Frank Bridge.

A Conversation About Women

Students may choose either a modern woman they know personally or someone of prominence. In general, all the women may agree that while much has changed since the eighteenth century, women are still trapped in old ideas of femininity. Also, in some ways it is harder now, because women in society are expected to be both career dynamos *and* supportive wives and mothers.

Before Reading

Tickets, Please

by D. H. Lawrence

D. H. Lawrence
1885–1930

David Herbert Lawrence was born in an English coal-mining town, the son of an uneducated miner and an ambitious mother. Lawrence taught school for a few years before establishing himself as a writer. In 1912 he eloped with the aristocratic wife of one of his professors. In 1913 Lawrence's reputation began to spread with the publication of a volume of poems and the novel *Sons and Lovers*, a fictional portrait of Lawrence as an artist struggling to break free from his mother. Since most of his work is an exploration of the primitive and sexual in human nature, Lawrence was constantly in trouble with the censors, most notably for his novel, *Lady Chatterley's Lover* (1928), which was not published in Great Britain until 1960.

Building Background

Love and Power

"I told you there were two urges—two great life-urges, didn't I? There may be more. But it comes on me so strongly, now, that there are two: love and power."

In these lines from his novel *Aaron's Rod* Lawrence sets up the tension between men and women that was to form the thematic basis of almost all of his prose and poetry: power relationships in love. Smothered by an overly possessive mother, Lawrence craved the attention of women, yet often rejected them when they demanded too much of him or became too personal. He was critical of women for wanting to be loved, for being too intelligent, for desiring to conquer men. The critic Lionel Trilling suggests that it is Lawrence's "equal recognition of both the antagonism [between the sexes] and the reciprocal need, and of the interplay between the two, that gives his writing about love its unique air of discovery and truth."

Literary Focus

Idiom An **idiom** is an expression whose meaning cannot be understood from the ordinary, literal meanings of the words within the expression. For example, the idiomatic phrase "hold your tongue" means "be quiet" and the expression "get the lead out" means "start moving." Look for Lawrence's use of idiomatic expressions, particularly in the dialogue of the characters.

Writer's Notebook

Getting Even—Again Think of a situation in your life when you were so hurt by someone's actions that you wanted to do something to strike back, to get revenge. Jot down a few sentences to describe the situation that made you feel so terrible.

Tickets, Please **757**

Before Reading

Building Background

Ask students to reflect on the relationship between men and women as they read this story. You might write the words *power* and *love* on the board, asking them to keep these words in mind during their reading.

Literary Focus

Explain to students that writers often use idioms to create a casual, familiar tone in conversation.

Writer's Notebook

Students may want to describe a time when they actually struck back to get revenge or a time when they merely fantasized about what they would do.

More About D. H. Lawrence

- Lawrence was often prosecuted for what was considered obscenity in his works.
- Lawrence's wife, who was of German heritage, was harassed by war-time British authorities. Partly because of his wife's treatment, Lawrence was vehemently opposed to World War I.
- The banning of his books and the persecution of his wife prompted him into virtual self-exile.

Connections to
AuthorWorks

D. H. Lawrence is a featured author in the AuthorWorks CD-ROM series.

SUPPORT MATERIALS OVERVIEW

Unit 7 Resource Book
- Graphic Organizer, p. 65
- Study Guide, p. 66
- Vocabulary, p. 67
- Grammar, p. 68
- Alternate Check Test, p. 69
- Vocabulary Test, p. 70
- Selection Test, pp. 71–72

Building English Proficiency
- Selection Summaries
- Activities, p. 253

Reading, Writing & Grammar SkillBook
- Writing, pp. 123–124
- Grammar, Usage, and Mechanics, pp. 165–166

Technology
- Audiotape
- Personal Journal Software
- Test Generator Software

During Reading

Selection Objectives

- to explore male/female conflicts against the background of war
- to identify examples of idioms
- to recognize compound-complex sentences

 Unit 7 Resource Book
Graphic Organizer, p. 65
Study Guide, p. 66

Theme Link

Set in war-time England, the story relates how a group of women get even with a young man; the aftermath, their violent retribution, offers little satisfaction.

Vocabulary Preview

precipitous, very steep
sordid, filthy
abashed, ashamed
peremptory, decisive; dictatorial
comely, attractive
complaisant, gracious; courteous
nocturnal, nighttime
vindictive, bearing a grudge, wanting revenge
averted, turned away
prostrate, overcome; helpless

Students can add the words and definitions to their Writer's Notebooks.

 **Art Study**

Response to Caption Question The work, which appears dreary and repetitive, might nonetheless be considered a heroic attempt to support the war effort.

1 **Literary Element**
Setting

What do you learn about the setting in the opening paragraph? *(This is a factory town—"an ugly place of industry"—in central England, populated by miners.)*

758

TICKETS, PLEASE

D. H. Lawrence

◄ Does this World War I fund-raising poster make women's work in war factories seem heroic? glamorous? dreary?

There is here in the Midlands[1] a single-line tramway system[2] which boldly leaves the county town and plunges off into the black, industrial countryside, up hill and down dale, through the long ugly villages of workmen's houses, over canals and railways, past churches perched high and nobly over the smoke and shadows, through stark, grimy cold little marketplaces, tilting away in a rush past cinemas and shops down to the hollow where the collieries[3] are, then up again, past a little rural church, under the ash trees, on in a rush to the terminus,[4] the last little ugly place of industry, the cold little town that shivers on the edge of the wild, gloomy country beyond. There the green and creamy colored tram-car seems to pause and purr with curious satisfaction. But in a few minutes—the clock on the turret of the Cooperative Wholesale Society's shops gives the time—away it starts once more on the adventure. Again there are the reckless swoops downhill, bouncing the loops: again the chilly wait in the hilltop marketplace: again the breathless slithering round the precipitous[5] drop under the church: again the patient halts at the loops, waiting for the outcoming car: so on and on, for two long hours, till at last the city looms beyond the fat gasworks, the narrow factories draw near, we are in the sordid[6] streets of the great town, once more we sidle to a standstill at our terminus, abashed[7] by the great crimson and cream-colored city cars, but still perky, jaunty, somewhat dare-devil, green as a jaunty sprig of parsley out of a black colliery garden.

To ride on these cars is always an adventure. Since we are in war-time, the drivers are men unfit for active service: cripples and hunchbacks. So they have the spirit of the devil in them. The ride becomes a steeplechase.[8] Hurray! we have leapt in a clear jump over the canal bridges—now for the four-lane corner. With a shriek and a trail of sparks we are clear again. To be sure, a tram often leaps the rails—but what matter! It sits in a ditch till other trams come to haul it out. It is quite common for a car, packed with one solid mass of living people, to come to a dead halt in the midst of unbroken blackness, the heart of nowhere on a dark night, and for the driver and the girl conductor to call: "All get off—car's on fire!" Instead, however, of rushing out in a panic, the passengers stolidly[9] reply: "Get on—get on! We're not coming out. We're stopping where we are. Push on, George." So till flames actually appear.

1

---
1. **Midlands,** the central part of England.
2. **tramway system,** streetcar tracks.
3. **colliery** (kol′yər ē) *n.* coal mine.
4. **terminus** (tėr′mə nəs), *n.* the end of the line.
5. **precipitous** (pri sip′ə təs), *adj.* very steep.
6. **sordid** (sôr′did), *adj.* filthy.
7. **abashed** (ə basht′), *adj.* ashamed.
8. **steeplechase** (stē′pəl chās′), *n.* a horse race over an obstacle course.
9. **stolidly** (stol′id lē), *adv.* unemotionally; dully.

758 Unit Seven: The Early Twentieth Century

SELECTION SUMMARY

Tickets, Please

In World War I England, young, civilian males are scarce, and John Thomas, an attractive and charming tram inspector, finds no end of young women, especially among his co-workers, who are eager to keep company with him. Not interested in long-term commitment, John exchanges one female companion for another. A woman named Annie, who is worldly wise and wise to John, falls in love with him nonetheless and deludes herself into thinking he will change. When he shatters her fantasy, she conspires with several of his former girlfriends for revenge. Leading John to a waiting room, Annie delivers him into the hands of former girlfriends. After toying with him mentally, they assault him physically. Beaten to the point where his resolve is broken, he "chooses" Annie, but she does not choose him. As he is finally allowed to leave, the women show signs not of victory but of remorse.

 *For summaries in other languages, see the **Building English Proficiency** book.*

The reason for this reluctance to dismount is that the nights are howlingly cold, black, and windswept, and a car is a haven of refuge. From village to village the miners travel, for a change of cinema, of girl, of pub. The trams are desperately packed. Who is going to risk himself in the black gulf outside, to wait perhaps an hour for another tram, then to see the forlorn notice "Depot Only," because there is something wrong! Or to greet a unit of three bright cars all so tight with people that they sail past with a howl of derision.[10] Trams that pass in the night.

This, the most dangerous tram-service in England, as the authorities themselves declare, with pride, is entirely conducted by girls, and driven by rash young men, a little crippled, or by delicate young men, who creep forward in terror. The girls are fearless young hussies.[11] In their ugly blue uniform, skirts up to their knees, shapeless old peaked caps on their heads, they have all the *sang-froid*[12] of an old non-commissioned officer. With a tram packed with howling colliers, roaring hymns downstairs and a sort of antiphony[13] of obscenities upstairs, the lasses are perfectly at their ease. They pounce on the youths who try to evade their ticket-machine. They push off the men at the end of their distance. They are not going to be done in the eye—not they. They fear nobody—and everybody fears them.

"Hello, Annie!"

"Hello, Ted!"

"Oh, mind my corn, Miss Stone. It's my belief you've got a heart of stone, for you've trod on it again."

"You should keep it in your pocket," replies Miss Stone, and she goes sturdily upstairs in her high boots.

"Tickets, please."

She is peremptory,[14] suspicious, and ready to hit first. She can hold her own against ten thousand. The step of that tram-car is her Thermopylae.[15]

Therefore, there is a certain wild romance aboard these cars—and in the sturdy bosom of Annie herself. The time for soft romance is in the morning, between ten o'clock and one, when things are rather slack: that is, except marketday and Saturday. Thus Annie has time to look about her. Then she often hops off her car and into a shop where she has spied something, while the driver chats in the main road. There is very good feeling between the girls and the drivers. Are they not companions in peril, shipmates aboard this careering vessel of a tram-car, forever rocking on the waves of a stormy land.

Then, also, during the early hours, the inspectors are most in evidence. For some reason, everybody employed in this tram-service is young: there are no grey heads. It would not do. Therefore the inspectors are of the right age, and one, the chief, is also good-looking. See him stand on a wet, gloomy morning, in his long oilskin, his peaked cap well down over his eyes, waiting to board a car. His face ruddy, his small brown moustache is weathered, he has a faint impudent[16] smile. Fairly tall and agile, even in his waterproof, he springs aboard a car and greets Annie.

"Hello, Annie! Keeping the wet out?"

"Trying to."

There are only two people in the car. Inspecting is soon over. Then for a long and impudent chat on the foot-board, a good, easy, twelve-mile chat.

The inspector's name is John Thomas Raynor—always called John Thomas, except sometimes, in malice,[17] Coddy. His face sets in fury when he is addressed, from a distance, with this abbreviation. There is considerable scandal

---

10. **derision** (di rizh′ən), *n.* ridicule.
11. **hussy** (huz′ē), *n.* bad-mannered girl.
12. *sang-froid* (sang frwä′), *n.* calmness; composure; literally "cold blood." *[French]*
13. **antiphony** (an tif′ə nē), *n.* hymn sung or chanted in alternate parts.
14. **peremptory** (pə remp′tər ē), *adj.* decisive; dictatorial.
15. **Thermopylae** (thər mop′ə lē), a narrow mountain pass in Greece where in 480 B.C. a small force of Greeks held off a huge army of Persians.
16. **impudent** (im′pyə dənt), *adj.* bold; rude.
17. **malice** (mal′is), *n.* spite; ill will.

Tickets, Please **759**

2 Reading/Thinking Skills
Draw Conclusions

Lawrence packs a good deal of information about the lives of the miners into this paragraph.

Questions   What do these miners do for recreation? *(Possible response: They drink, date, and go to movies. Trams are their source of transportation.)* What are their surroundings like? *(Possible response: cold, black, stark, and windswept)*

3 Literary Element
Style

Lawrence is a master of style. Have students note that in this short paragraph, he employs hyperbole ("She can hold her own against ten thousand") and allusion (Thermopylae) as means to characterize Annie.

Question   How would you characterize Annie? *(Possible response: She is self-sufficient, decisive, and tough. She is not someone to be taken lightly.)*

4 Literary Element
Characterization

What inferences can you make about John Thomas from this description? *(He is self-assured and smug.)*

BUILDING ENGLISH PROFICIENCY

Relating Setting and Mood

Help students see how Lawrence quickly but carefully establishes a mood of casual danger, passion, and adventure.

1. Discuss with students the opening descriptive passages of the story. Ask: How does the author describe the countryside? What words does he use? *("black, industrial countryside . . . smoke and shadows . . . stark, grimy cold little marketplaces")*

2. Ask students to go back over page 758 and write in their journals other words and phrases that describe the setting. Students should look up the meanings of any words that they do not know.

3. Have students write or dictate a short paragraph about their responses to these words. Ask: How do you think this setting is meant to make you feel? What kind of story do you think will follow, based on this opening description?

Building English Proficiency
Activities, p. 253

5 Active Reading
Connect

Possible response   They have been scandalized and/or hurt by their association with John Thomas.

6 Literary Element
Setting

The lack of coconuts is a subtle reminder that a war is going on.

Question   Although this is not really a war story, there are other reminders that a war is taking place. Where do such reminders occur? *(Paragraph 1, page 758 and paragraph 2, page 759 mention that tram drivers are unfit for active service.)*

7 Reading/Thinking Skills
Make Analogies

Question   What analogy can be made between the setting of Annie and John's first date and their relationship? *(Possible response: Both are exciting, temporary, and a bit tawdry and superficial.)*

---

about John Thomas in half a dozen villages. He flirts with the girl conductors in the morning, and walks out with them in the dark night, when they leave their tram-car at the depot. Of course, the girls quit the service frequently. Then he flirts and walks out with the newcomer: always providing she is sufficiently attractive, and that she will consent to walk. It is remarkable, however, that most of the girls are quite comely,[18] they are all young, and this roving life aboard the car gives them a sailor's dash and recklessness. What matter how they behave when the ship is in port? Tomorrow they will be aboard again.

5   CONNECT: Why do you think girls quit the service frequently?

Annie, however, was something of a Tartar,[19] and her sharp tongue had kept John Thomas at arm's length for many months. Perhaps, therefore, she liked him all the more: for he always came up smiling, with impudence. She watched him vanquish[20] one girl, then another. She could tell by the movement of his mouth and eyes, when he flirted with her in the morning, that he had been walking out with this lass, or the other, the night before. A fine cock-of-the-walk he was. She could sum him up pretty well.

In this subtle antagonism[21] they knew each other like old friends, they were as shrewd with one another almost as man and wife. But Annie had always kept him sufficiently at arm's length. Besides, she had a boy of her own.

The Statutes fair, however, came in November, at Bestwood. It happened that Annie had the Monday night off. It was a drizzling ugly night, yet she dressed herself up and went to the fairground. She was alone, but she expected soon to find a pal of some sort.

The roundabouts[22] were veering round and grinding out their music, the side-shows were making as much commotion as possible. In the coconut shies[23] there were no coconuts, but artificial wartime substitutes, which the lads declared

6

---

were fastened into the irons. There was a sad decline in brilliance and luxury. None the less, the ground was muddy as ever, there was the same crush, the press of faces lighted up by the flares and the electric lights, the same smell of naphtha[24] and a few fried potatoes, and of electricity.

Who should be the first to greet Miss Annie on the showground but John Thomas. He had a black overcoat buttoned up to his chin, and a tweed cap pulled down over his brows, his face between was ruddy and smiling and handy as ever. She knew so well the way his mouth moved.

She was very glad to have a "boy." To be at the Statutes without a fellow was no fun. Instantly, like the gallant he was, he took her on the Dragons, grim-toothed, roundabout switchbacks. It was not nearly so exciting as a tram-car actually. But, then, to be seated in a shaking, green dragon, uplifted above the sea of bubble faces, careering in a rickety fashion in the lower heavens, whilst John Thomas leaned over her, his cigarette in his mouth, was after all the right style. She was a plump, quick, alive little creature. So she was quite excited and happy.

John Thomas made her stay on for the next round. And therefore she could hardly for shame repulse[25] him when he put his arm round her and drew her a little nearer to him, in a very warm and cuddly manner. Besides, he was fairly discreet, he kept his movement as hidden as possible. She looked down, and saw that his red, clean hand was out of sight of the crowd. And they knew each other so well. So they warmed up to the fair.

After the dragons they went on the horses. John Thomas paid each time, so she could but

7

---

18. comely (kum′lē), *adj.* attractive.
19. **Tartar** (tär′tər), *n.* bad-tempered person, from *Tartar,* a fierce Mongolian warrior.
20. **vanquish** (vang′kwish), *v.* conquer.
21. **antagonism** (an tag′ə niz′əm), *n.* hostility.
22. **roundabout,** merry-go-round.
23. **coconut shy,** a carnival game in which one throws coconuts at a target.
24. **naphtha** (naf′thə), *n.* liquid fuel.
25. **repulse** (ri puls′), *v.* reject.

MINI-LESSON: GRAMMAR

Compound-Complex Sentences

Teach   Remind students that at its most basic, a sentence is an independent clause, that is, a group of words that contains a subject and a predicate and expresses a complete thought. An example of this is "I will go." A complex sentence consists of an independent clause and one or more dependent clauses, the latter containing a subject and a predicate that do not constitute a complete thought; "I will go so that I can get some groceries" is an example of a complex sentence. A compound-complex sentence contains two or more independent clauses and one or more dependent clauses. "When it has stopped raining, I will go to get some groceries, and I will go to the post office" is a compound-complex sentence.

Apply   Have students look at the last sentence of the partial paragraph that begins page 761. Ask them why it is a compound-complex sentence. *(It has three independent clauses—"He was perfectly happy," "she was afraid," and "she was excited"—and one dependent clause—"[that] her hat was on one side.")*

Activity Idea   Have students write five compound-complex sentences that express their ideas or feelings about the story, underline the independent clauses, and double-underline the dependent clauses.

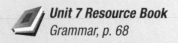
Unit 7 Resource Book
Grammar, p. 68

be complaisant.[26] He, of course, sat astride on the outer horse—named "Black Bess"—and she sat sideways towards him, on the inner horse—named "Wildfire." But of course John Thomas was not going to sit discreetly on "Black Bess," holding the brass bar. Round they spun and heaved, in the light. And round he swung on his wooden steed, flipping one leg across her mount, and perilously tipping up and down, across the space, half lying back, laughing at her. He was perfectly happy; she was afraid her hat was on one side, but she was excited.

He threw quoits[27] on a table, and won for her two large, pale blue hat-pins. And then, hearing the noise of the cinemas, announcing another performance, they climbed the boards and went in.

Of course, during these performances pitch darkness falls from time to time, when the machine goes wrong. Then there is a wild whooping, and a loud smacking of simulated kisses. In these moments John Thomas drew Annie towards him. After all, he had a wonderfully warm, cozy way of holding a girl with his arm, he seemed to make such a nice fit. And, after all, it was pleasant to be so held: so very comforting and cozy and nice. He leaned over her and she felt his breath on her hair; she knew he wanted to kiss her on the lips. And, after all, he was so warm and she fitted into him so softly. After all, she wanted him to touch her lips.

But the light sprang up; she also started electrically, and put her hat straight. He left his arm lying nonchalantly[28] behind her. Well, it was fun, it was exciting to be at the Statutes with John Thomas.

When the cinema was over they went for a walk across the dark, damp fields. He had all the arts of love-making. He was especially good at holding a girl, when he sat with her on a stile[29] in the black, drizzling darkness. He seemed to be holding her in space, against his own warmth and gratification. And his kisses were soft and slow and searching.

So Annie walked out with John Thomas, though she kept her own boy dangling in the distance. Some of the tram-girls chose to be huffy. But there, you must take things as you find them in this life.

There was no mistake about it, Annie liked John Thomas a good deal. She felt so rich and warm in herself whenever he was near. And John Thomas really liked Annie, more than usual. The soft, melting way in which she could flow into a fellow, as if she melted into his very bones, was something rare and good. He fully appreciated this.

But with a developing acquaintance there began a developing intimacy. Annie wanted to consider him a person, a man: she wanted to take an intelligent interest in him, and to have an intelligent response. She did not want a mere nocturnal[30] presence, which was what he was so far. And she prided herself that he could not leave her.

Here she made a mistake. John Thomas intended to remain a nocturnal presence; he had no idea of becoming an all-round individual to her. When she started to take an intelligent interest in him and his life and his character, he sheered off. He hated intelligent interest. And he knew that the only way to stop it was to avoid it. The possessive female was aroused in Annie. So he left her.

It is no use saying she was not surprised. She was at first startled, thrown out of her count. For she had been so *very* sure of holding him. For a while she was staggered, and everything became uncertain to her. Then she wept with fury, indignation, desolation, and misery. Then she had a spasm of despair. And then, when he came, still impudently, on to her car, still familiar, but letting her see by the movement of his head that he had gone away to somebody else for the time being, and was enjoying pastures new, then she determined to have her own back.

---

26. complaisant (kəm plā′sənt), *adj.* gracious; courteous.
27. quoits (kwoits), *n. pl.* a game in which a ring is tossed over a peg.
28. nonchalantly (non′shə lənt lē), *adv.* indifferently; casually.
29. stile (stīl), *n.* step for getting over a fence or wall.
30. nocturnal (nok tėr′nl), *adj.* nighttime.

Tickets, Please **761**

761

---

8 Literary Element
Alliteration

Point out the poetic quality of Lawrence's prose. Review that alliteration is the repetition of consonant sounds.

Question What examples of alliteration can you find in this paragraph? *(Possible responses: went, walk; dark, damp, drizzling, darkness; kisses soft, slow, searching)*

9 Literary Focus
Idioms

Question What is meant by the idiom "walked out"? by "kept her own boy dangling"? *(They were dating or going out; she was still seeing her old boyfriend.)*

10 Reading/Thinking Skills
Point of View

Draw attention to the third-person omniscient point of view, which allows the narrator to observe information about the couple that they themselves would not admit.

Question Why does Annie's "intelligent interest" and wish for John Thomas to be an "all-round individual" cause him to leave her? *(Possible response: She becomes possessive and demands more of him than merely a physical relationship—the only kind he is willing to have.)*

BUILDING ENGLISH PROFICIENCY

Noticing Character Details

Students may be able to follow "Tickets, Please" more easily if they pick out the most important character details as they read. Encourage them to complete a chart like the one shown for each main character. Students should try to use descriptive words from the story in their choices. You may wish to have students work in cooperative groups.

Who	Annie, a "fearless" tram conductor
What	collects fares, keeps order
How	Peremptory, suspicious, and ready "to hit first"

Alert students to the final sentence of this paragraph, which reminds readers of the wartime setting.

Question   What do you think will happen? *(Possible responses: Maybe something dark and lawless will happen here; these girls have all been dumped by John Thomas, so they will probably take revenge in some way.)*

12 **Literary Focus**

Characterization

Question   What does John Thomas's behavior since he poked his head in the door indicate about him? *(Possible responses: The fact that he intrudes indicates his self-confidence among his old girlfriends; his request for tea indicates his superior feelings and his expectation to be waited on.)*

13 **Literary Element**

Diction

Make sure students know *perishing* refers to the brutal weather. Be alert to any other problems that Briticisms and dialect may cause. Explain, for example, that *ay* means "yes," *tha* means "you," and *'un* means "one."

She had a very shrewd idea what girls John Thomas had taken out. She went to Nora Purdy. Nora was a tall, rather pale, but well-built girl, with beautiful yellow hair. She was rather secretive.

"Hey!" said Annie, accosting[31] her; then softly: "Who's John Thomas on with now?"

"I don't know," said Nora.

"Why, tha does," said Annie, ironically lapsing into dialect. "Tha knows as well as I do."

"Well, I do, then," said Nora. "It isn't me, so don't bother."

"It's Cissy Meakin, isn't it?"

"It is, for all I know."

"Hasn't he got a face on him!" said Annie. "I don't half like his cheek. I could knock him off the foot-board when he comes round at me."

"He'll get dropped on one of these days," said Nora.

"Ay, he will, when somebody makes up their mind to drop it on him. I should like to see him taken down a peg or two, shouldn't you?"

"I shouldn't mind," said Nora.

"You've got quite as much cause to as I have," said Annie. "But we'll drop on him one of these days, my girl. What? Don't you want to?"

"I don't mind," said Nora.

But as a matter of fact, Nora was much more vindictive[32] than Annie.

One by one Annie went the round of the old flames. It so happened that Cissy Meakin left the tramway service in quite a short time. Her mother made her leave. Then John Thomas was on the *qui vive*.[33] He cast his eyes over his old flock. And his eyes lighted on Annie. He thought she would be safe now. Besides, he liked her.

She arranged to walk home with him on Sunday night. It so happened that her car would be in the depot at half-past nine: the last car would come in at 10:15. So John Thomas was to wait for her there.

At the depot the girls had a little waiting-room of their own. It was quite rough, but cozy, with a fire and an oven and a mirror, and table and wooden chairs. The half-dozen girls who knew John Thomas only too well had arranged to take service this Sunday afternoon. So, as the cars began to come in, early, the girls dropped into the waiting-room. And instead of hurrying off home, they sat around the fire and had a cup of tea. Outside was the darkness and lawlessness of wartime.   11

John Thomas came on the car after Annie, at about a quarter to ten. He poked his head easily into the girls' waiting-room.

"Prayer-meeting?" he asked.

"Ay," said Laura Sharp. "Ladies only."

"That's me!" said John Thomas. It was one of his favorite exclamations.

"Shut the door, boy," said Muriel Baggaley.

"Oh, which side of me?" said John Thomas.

"Which tha likes," said Polly Birkin.

He had come in and closed the door behind him. The girls moved in their circle, to make a place for him near the fire. He took off his greatcoat and pushed back his hat.

"Who handles the teapot?" he said.

Nora Purdy silently poured him out a cup of tea.

"Want a bit o' my bread and drippin'?" said Muriel Baggaley to him.

"Ay, give us a bit."

And he began to eat his piece of bread.

"There's no place like home, girls," he said.   12

They all looked at him as he uttered this piece of impudence. He seemed to be sunning himself in the presence of so many damsels.

"Especially if you're not afraid to go home in the dark," said Laura Sharp.

"Me! By myself I am."

They sat till they heard the last tram come in. In a few minutes Emma Houselay entered.

"Come on, my old duck!" cried Polly Birkin.

"It *is* perishing," said Emma, holding her fingers to the fire.   13

---

31. **accost** (ə kôst′), *v.* approach and speak to.
32. **vindictive** (vin dik′tiv), *adj.* bearing a grudge; wanting revenge.
33. **on the *qui vive*** (kē vēv′), on the alert. *[French]*

MINI-LESSON: LITERARY FOCUS

Idioms

Teach   Point out that when Annie says in column 1 "I don't half like his cheek," she is using an idiom that means "I don't like his brazen talk and attitude very much." Remind students that the main difficulty in deciphering idioms is that they often express something different from the literal meaning of their component words. Suggest that, just as they use context clues when faced with an unfamiliar English word, they can usually use context clues to stretch the literal meaning of the puzzling word or combination of words to unlock the meaning of idioms.

Activity Idea   The speech of young men and women is full of idioms and idiomatic expressions. Invite students to challenge you: translate idioms they volunteer. Challenge them to provide you with meaningful context for these idioms so you can model the mental process discussed above.

"But—I'm afraid to, go home in, the dark," sang Laura Sharp, the tune having got into her mind.

"Who're you going with to-night, John Thomas?" asked Muriel Baggaley coolly.

"To-night?" said John Thomas. "Oh, I'm going home by myself to-night—all on my lonely-o."

"That's me!" said Nora Purdy, using his own ejaculation.[34]

The girls laughed shrilly.

"Me as well, Nora," said John Thomas.

"Don't know what you mean," said Laura.

"Yes, I'm toddling," said he, rising and reaching for his overcoat.

"Nay," said Polly, "We're all here waiting for you."

"We've got to be up in good time in the morning," he said, in the benevolent official manner.

They all laughed.

"Nay," said Muriel, "Don't leave us all lonely, John Thomas. Take one!"

"I'll take the lot, if you like," he responded gallantly.

"That you won't, either," said Muriel. "Two's company; seven's too much of a good thing."

"Nay—take one," said Laura. "Fair and square, all above board and say which."

"Ay," cried Annie, speaking for the first time. "Pick, John Thomas; let's hear thee."

"Nay," he said. "I'm going home quiet tonight. Feeling good, for once."

"Whereabouts?" said Annie. "Take a good 'un, then. But tha's got to take one of us!"

"Nay, how can I take one," he said, laughing uneasily. "I don't want to make enemies."

"You'd only make *one*," said Annie.

"The chosen *one*," added Laura.

"Oh, my! Who said girls!" exclaimed John Thomas, again turning, as if to escape. "Well—goodnight."

"Nay, you've got to make your pick," said Muriel. "Turn your face to the wall, and say which one touches you. Go on—we shall only just touch your back—one of us. Go on—turn your face to the wall, and don't look, and say which one touches you."

He was uneasy, mistrusting them. Yet he had not the courage to break away. They pushed him to a wall and stood him there with his face to it. Behind his back they all grimaced, tittering. He looked so comical. He looked around uneasily.

"Go on!" he cried.

"You're looking—you're looking!" they shouted.

He turned his head away. And suddenly, with a movement like a swift cat, Annie went forward and fetched him a box in the side of the head that sent his cap flying and himself staggering. He started round.

But at Annie's signal they all flew at him, slapping him, pinching him, pulling his hair, though more in fun than in spite or anger. He, however, saw red. His blue eyes flamed with strange fear as well as fury, and he butted through the girls to the door. It was locked. He wrenched at it. Roused, alert, the girls stood round and looked at him. He faced them, at bay. At that moment they were rather horrifying to him, as they stood in their short uniforms. He was distinctly afraid.

"Come on, John Thomas! Come on! Choose!" said Annie.

"What are you after? Open the door," he said.

"We shan't—not till you've chosen!" said Muriel.

"Chosen what?" he said.

"Chosen the one you're going to marry," she replied.

He hesitated a moment.

"Open the blasted door," he said, "and get back to your senses." He spoke with official authority.

"You've got to choose!" cried the girls.

14 Reading/Thinking Skills

Clarify

Question What is the significance of Laura Sharp's words? *(Possible response: It ironically expresses her "fears" and sets up the interrogation of John Thomas.)*

15 Literary Element

Tone

Questions

- How would you describe the change of tone since John Thomas arrived? *(Possible responses: The young women are now in control and clearly on the attack; they are making fun of him; they are firm and will not allow him to leave without choosing one of them.)*

- What does Annie mean when she says, "You'd only make one"? *(She conducts a personal attack on him by suggesting that whomever he chooses would end up not liking him.)*

16 Reader's Response

Making Personal Connections

Question Do you think that this is a fair confrontation? *(Possible response: Yes, this is fair retribution for John Thomas's irresponsibility in romantic relationships; no, this is clearly physical abuse and sexual harassment.)*

BUILDING ENGLISH PROFICIENCY

Dramatizing Key Events

The section that begins "One by one Annie went the round of the old flames" (at the break in the first column on page 762) introduces the story's climax. Challenge students to enact the climax.

1. Have volunteers take the parts of John Thomas, Annie, Laura, Muriel, Polly, Nora, and Emma.

2. Give this "cast" time to read through and discuss the scene (which ends with Laura's question "Who wants him" at the end of column 1 on page 765 and the girls' reply).

3. Have them enact it in reader's theater format or an improvisational paraphrase.

4. Afterward, ask: How did it feel to be John Thomas? Annie? the other girls? Do you think that his "crime" deserved such "punishment"?

17 Multicultural Note

Group

Possible response It removes their inhibitions, heightens their already strong feelings, and diminishes their sense of individual responsibility.

18 Reading/Thinking Skills

Synthesize

Question What suggests that this incident mirrors the war? *(John Thomas is described as "at the mercy of the captor." He has been taken prisoner. Several paragraphs later, Annie says, "You ought to be killed.")*

19 Reader's Response

Making Personal Connections

If these young women were tried today in a court of law, what do you think would be the outcome? *(Possible responses: At the very least, John Thomas should be awarded damages; the young women should be punished. No one was seriously hurt, and John Thomas deserved to be taught a lesson, so no one should be punished.)*

"Come on!" cried Annie, looking him in the eye. "Come on! Come on!"

He went forward, rather vaguely. She had taken off her belt, and swinging it, she fetched him a sharp blow over the head with the buckle end. He sprang and seized her. But immediately the other girls rushed upon him, pulling and tearing and beating him. Their blood was now thoroughly up. He was their sport now. They were going to have their own back, out of him. Strange, wild creatures, they hung on him and rushed at him to bear him down. His tunic was torn right up the back. Nora had hold at the back of his collar, and was actually strangling him. Luckily the button burst. He struggled in a wild frenzy of fury and terror, almost mad terror. His tunic was simply torn off his back, his shirtsleeves were torn away, his arms were naked. The girls rushed at him, clenched their hands on him, and pulled at him: or they rushed at him and pushed him, butted him with all their might: or they struck him wild blows. He ducked and cringed and struck sideways. They became more intense.

17   **EVALUATE: What effect does being together in a group seem to have on the girls' behavior?**

At last he was down. They rushed on him, kneeling on him. He had neither breath nor strength to move. His face was bleeding with a long scratch, his brow was bruised.

Annie knelt on him, the other girls knelt and hung on to him. Their faces were flushed, their hair wild, their eyes were all glittering strangely. He lay at last quite still, with face averted,[35] as an animal lies when it is defeated **18** and at the mercy of the captor. Sometimes his eye glanced back at the wild faces of the girls. His breast rose heavily, his wrists were torn.

"Now, then, my fellow!" gasped Annie at length. "Now then—now—"

At the sound of her terrifying, cold triumph, he suddenly started to struggle as an animal

might, but the girls threw themselves upon him with unnatural strength and power, forcing him down.

"Yes—now, then!" gasped Annie at length.

And there was a dead silence, in which the thud of heart-beating was to be heard. It was a suspense of pure silence in every soul.

"Now you know where you are," said Annie.

The sight of his white, bare arm maddened the girls. He lay in a kind of trance of fear and antagonism. They felt themselves with supernatural strength.

Suddenly Polly started to laugh—to giggle wildly—helplessly—and Emma and Muriel joined in. But Annie and Nora and Laura remained the same, tense, watchful, with gleaming eyes. He winced away from these eyes.

"Yes," said Annie, in a curious low tone, secret and deadly. "Yes! You've got it now. You know what you've done, don't you? You know what you've done."

He made no sound nor sign, but lay with bright, averted eyes, and averted, bleeding face.

"You ought to be *killed,* that's what you ought," said Annie, tensely. "You ought to be *killed.*" And there was a terrifying lust in her voice.

Polly was ceasing to laugh, and giving long-drawn Oh-h-hs and sighs as she came to herself.

"He's got to choose," she said vaguely.

"Oh, yes, he has," said Laura, with vindictive decision.

"Do you hear—do you hear?" said Annie. And with a sharp movement, that made him wince, she turned his face to her.

"Do you hear?" she repeated, shaking him.

But he was quite dumb. She fetched him a sharp slap on the face. He started, and his eyes widened. Then his face darkened with defiance **19** after all.

"Do you hear?" she repeated.

He only looked at her with hostile eyes.

---

35. averted (ə vėr′tid), *adj.* turned away.

MINI-LESSON: LITERARY ELEMENT

Foreshadowing

Teach   Inform students that authors give readers clues in various ways about what is to come in a story. They may create a mood or describe some aspect of a setting or characterization of a person that suggests what will happen next. In this way, foreshadowing can create suspense or foreboding. It can also add predictability to a story by depicting well-known character types and their archetypal motivations and conflicts.

Activity Idea   Have students reread page 758 and the first two paragraphs on page 759 and point out eight to ten images that foreshadow the mood and types of characters and conflicts that pervade the story.

"Speak!" she said, putting her face devilishly near his.

"What?" he said, almost overcome.

"You've got to *choose!*" she cried, as if it were some terrible menace, and as if it hurt her that she could not exact more.

"What?" he said, in fear.

"Choose your girl, Coddy. You've got to choose her now. And you'll get your neck broken if you play any more of your tricks, my boy. You're settled now."

There was a pause. Again he averted his face. He was cunning in his overthrow. He did not give in to them really—no, not if they tore him to bits.

"All right, then," he said. "I choose Annie." His voice was strange and full of malice. Annie let go of him as if he had been a hot coal.

"He's chosen Annie!" said the girls in chorus.

"Me!" cried Annie. She was still kneeling, but away from him. He was still lying prostrate,[36] with averted face. The girls grouped uneasily around.

"Me!" repeated Annie, with a terrible bitter accent.

Then she got up, drawing away from him with strange disgust and bitterness.

"I wouldn't touch him," she said.

But her face quivered with a kind of agony, she seemed as if she would fall. The other girls turned aside. He remained lying on the floor, with his torn clothes and bleeding, averted face.

"Oh, if he's chosen—" said Polly.

"I don't want him—he can choose again," said Annie, with the same rather bitter hopelessness.

"Get up," said Polly, lifting his shoulder. "Get up."

He rose slowly, a strange, ragged, dazed creature. The girls eyed him from a distance, curiously, furtively,[37] dangerously.

"Who wants him?" cried Laura, roughly.

"Nobody," they answered, with contempt.

Yet each one of them waited for him to look at her, hoped he would look at her. All except Annie, and something was broken in her.

He, however, kept his face closed and averted from them all. There was a silence of the end. He picked up the torn pieces of his tunic, without knowing what to do with them. The girls stood about uneasily, flushed, panting, tidying their hair and their dress unconsciously, and watching. He looked at none of them. He espied his cap in a corner, and went and picked it up. He put it on his head, and one of the girls burst into a shrill, hysterical laugh at the sight he presented. He, however, took no heed, but went straight to where his overcoat hung on a peg. The girls moved away from contact with him as if he had been an electric wire. He put on his coat and buttoned it down. Then he rolled his tunic-rags into a bundle, and stood before the locked door, dumbly.

"Open the door, somebody," said Laura.

"Annie's got the key," said one.

Annie silently offered the key to the girls. Nora unlocked the door.

"Tit for tat, old man," she said. "Show yourself a man, and don't bear a grudge."

But without a word or sign he had opened the door and gone, his face closed, his head dropped.

"That'll learn him," said Laura.

"Coddy!" said Nora.

"Shut up, for God's sake!" cried Annie fiercely, as if in torture.

"Well, I'm about ready to go, Polly. Look sharp!" said Muriel.

The girls were all anxious to be off. They were tidying themselves hurriedly, with mute, stupefied faces.

---

36. **prostrate** (pros′trāt), *adj.* overcome; helpless.
37. **furtively** (fėr′tiv lē), *adv.* secretly; slyly.

Tickets, Please   **765**

20

Reading/Thinking Skills

Infer

Question   What do you think "was broken in her" as a result of the incident? *(Possible response: Annie might still care for John Thomas, but now that she has unleashed her fury and turned against him, she cannot take him back. Maybe her heart is broken; maybe her spirit.)*

Literary Criticism

His most characteristic writings are essentially a record in symbolic terms of his exploration of human individuality and of all that hindered it and all that might fulfill it, whether in the natural world or in the world of other individuals . . . Lawrence had vision; he had a poetic sense of life; he had a keen ear and a piercing eye for every kind of vitality and color and sound . . . he looked at the world freshly, with his own eyes, avoiding formulas and clichés, and he forged for himself a new kind of utterance which, at his best, was able to convey powerfully and vividly what his fresh, original vision showed him.

The Norton Anthology of Literature

Check Test

1. In what geographical location does the story take place? *(the midlands, or center of England)*

2. Who are the drivers of the trams? *(men who have been rejected for army service)*

3. What position does John Thomas hold with the tram service? *(chief inspector)*

4. Where does the first date between Annie and John Thomas take place? *(a fair)*

5. Why did Annie want revenge against John Thomas? *(He didn't want a serious relationship.)*

Unit 7 Resource Book
Alternate Check Test, p. 69

BUILDING ENGLISH PROFICIENCY

Exploring Motivation

The story depicts an outbreak of sudden anger and violence. Ask students to use their journals to jot down notes about what the women feel and why they behave as they do. Ask them to consider the following:

• the new social customs of wartime (i.e., women doing work generally performed by men)

• the effect of "mob psychology" on the women

• why John chooses Annie and how she feels about being chosen

After Reading

MAKING CONNECTIONS

1. Look for answers that are well-grounded in the characters and facts presented, rather than students' preconceived ideas about sex roles.

2. Possible responses: Annie is described as fearless, preemptory, suspicious, resourceful, unafraid, and formidable to others. John Thomas is impudent, self-assured, good-looking, scandalous, and a lady's man.

3. Students may cite the lack of eligible men, the breakdown of ordinary decorum, or the implied background of violence.

4. Some students may feel John Thomas gets what he deserves for using women for his own pleasure; others may observe that he has always been honest about his lack of commitment and doesn't merit this abuse. He is probably never in any real danger.

5. Possible responses: When the mob passion dissipates, the women realize they have acted shamefully and have achieved nothing. They are embarrassed in front of each other.

6. Possible responses: Her demand that he choose is not based on a desire to be chosen, but meant to humiliate him and make him feel the kind of rejection the women have felt.

7. Possible responses: At the end of the opening paragraph, the collective "we" are described as "perky, jaunty, somewhat dare-devil, green," suggesting they are young, hopeful, and innocent. At the end, the girls are exhausted, mute, and stupefied—older, wiser, and perhaps hardened by their cruel acts.

8. Look for responses well-grounded in sound reasoning and examples.

9. The girls' recognition of their collective power and their willingness to use aggression foreshadows some strands of contemporary feminism.

After Reading

Making Connections

Shaping Your Response

1. For which character—Annie or John Thomas—do you feel the greater sympathy? Why?

Analyzing the Story

2. What indications are given that, in each other, John Thomas and Annie have met their match?

3. In what ways do you think the wartime **setting** influences the events of the story?

4. Do you think John Thomas deserves the harsh treatment he endures at the hands of his former girlfriends? Is he ever in real danger?

5. At the end of the story why do you think the girls behave so strangely after they have succeeded in humiliating John Thomas?

6. Why do you think Annie refuses John Thomas after he selects her?

7. Contrast the **mood** of the opening paragraphs with the mood of the closing episode.

Extending the Ideas

8. Do you think revenge is ever justified? Explain your answer.

9. 🐾 How do the characters and events of the story reflect the changing status of women in twentieth-century life? What, in your opinion, do Annie, Nora Purdy, and the other girls have in common with militant feminist **groups** today?

Literary Focus: Idiom

A phrase or expression whose meaning cannot be understood from the ordinary, literal meanings of the words is called an **idiom.** Look back at the following idioms in Lawrence's story and translate what you think each idiom means. Add other idioms that you find in the story.

• "a fine cock-of-the-walk" (page 760)
• "thrown out of her count" (page 761)
• "enjoying pastures new" (page 761)
• "to have her own back" (page 761)
• "taken down a peg or two" (page 762)
• "old flames" (page 762)
• "fair and square, all above board" (page 763)
• "he . . . saw red" (page 763)
• "their blood was . . . up" (page 764)

766   UNIT SEVEN: THE EARLY TWENTIETH CENTURY

LITERARY FOCUS: IDIOM

Possible Responses

1. a proud, strutting lady's man
2. thrown off guard, caught unexpectedly
3. dating and exploiting new women
4. to get revenge, recoup her dignity
5. humbled
6. former lovers, girlfriends
7. just, with no favoritism or subterfuge
8. he was very angry
9. they were angry, perhaps angry enough to commit violence

Among other idioms students may find are "Who's John Thomas on with now" (p. 762), "I'm toddling" (p. 763), and "You've got it now" (p. 764).

Vocabulary Study

Select the word that best completes each sentence. Use your Glossary, if necessary.

1. Riding on the tramway system could be dangerous because there were many dangerous curves and (peremptory, precipitous) hills.

2. At first, Annie feels (averted, complaisant) at the thought of having a "boy."

3. Annie's (vindictive, nocturnal) nature is evident in her plan for revenge on John Thomas.

4. For a time John Thomas is so defeated by the girls' attack that he can do nothing but lie (prostrate, sordid) on the ground.

5. After they have time to think about their savage attack on John Thomas, several of the girls may be (abashed, comely) by their actions.

Expressing Your Ideas

Writing Choices

Writer's Notebook Update Look back at the situation that made you want to get revenge. Write a few sentences about how you felt either about taking revenge or about not being able to strike back.

What Makes Annie Tick Write an **expository essay** explaining what you think is Annie's strongest motive—love, revenge, self-interest, hate, or a combination of these. Defend your explanation with quotations from the story.

The Verb's the Word D. H. Lawrence uses strong verbs in portraying action. Write several **descriptive paragraphs** in which you portray a scene of intense action, such as a sporting event, a rock concert, a street brawl. First describe the setting of the action. Then describe the event itself, using strong, active verbs.

Other Options

The Morning After Prepare a **dramatic monologue** that Annie might have with herself

or that John Thomas might have with himself the morning after the attack. What would be the emotional state of this character? Would Annie be embarrassed? frightened? ashamed? Would John Thomas be angry? humbled? revengeful? In your monologue, review the events of the previous night and think about the future. How will the past evening's events affect the relationship between Annie and John Thomas?

 Mob Psychology The scene in which the girls take revenge on John Thomas shows how a **group** can get out of control and become a mob. Research an historical situation—for example, the Haymarket Riot of 1886 or the disorder at the Democratic Convention in Chicago in 1968—in which a group became a mob and prepare an **oral report**. Include the events leading up to the action, what seemed to trigger it, and what the final outcome was.

VOCABULARY STUDY

1. precipitous
2. complaiscent
3. vindictive
4. prostrate
5. abashed

 Unit 7 Resource Book
Vocabulary, p. 67
Vocabulary Test, p. 70

WRITING CHOICES
Writer's Notebook Update

Remind students that they should try to capture their feelings at the time of the incident, rather than present the incident and feelings from their older, more mature vantage point.

What Makes Annie Tick

Students might refer to descriptions of Annie in the paragraphs at the bottom of column 1 on page 759 and the middle of column 1 on page 760 for insights into her character.

The Verb's the Word

You might direct students to powerful verbs that appear in the first paragraph of the story: *plunges, shivers, purr, swoops, looms.*

Selection Test

Unit 7 Resource Book
pp. 71–72

OTHER OPTIONS
The Morning After

Remind students that this assignment has two parts: a dramatic writing element and a dramatic presentation element. Encourage them by suggesting that the transformation of short stories and novels into plays and films has a long and largely successful history.

Mob Psychology

To support students in this activity, you may wish them to use historical abstracts to find articles about the situation they wish to research. Remind students of the basic elements of a good presentation: good preparation, use of 3 x 5 cards or other materials for an outline or summary of vital points, oral practice, vocal projection and clarity, and an absence of fidgeting.

Building Background

Explain that in "The Hollow Men," T. S. Eliot describes the emptiness of the modern soul by juxtaposing prayers, literary works, nursery rhymes, and allusions to history, culture, myth, and religion. Once students recognize his "patchwork" technique and identify some sources, the poem will be easier to understand.

Literary Focus

Ask students what effects free verse might achieve that structured verse could not.

Writer's Notebook

Encourage students to brainstorm ideas about their topic before writing their poem. You may want to review the conventions of structured poetry, such as rhyme and rhythmic patterns.

More About T. S. Eliot

T. S. Eliot was a pivotal leader among writers and served as the conscience of his generation. Other works by the author include

- *Murder in the Cathedral* (1935)
- *Four Quartets* (1936–1942)
- *The Family Reunion* (1939)
- *The Cocktail Party* (1950)

The Hollow Men

by T. S. Eliot

T. S. Eliot
1888–1965

Born in St. Louis, Missouri, and educated at Harvard, Thomas Stearns Eliot attended Oxford and settled in London in 1914, becoming a naturalized British subject in 1917. Beginning with "The Love Song of J. Alfred Prufrock," Eliot's works attracted considerable critical attention. From *The Waste Land* (1922), in which he expresses the despair of life without faith, to *Ash Wednesday* (1930), in which he professes an acquired Christianity, Eliot's work reflects disillusionment with contemporary values and hunger for spiritual rebirth. His collection *Old Possum's Book of Practical Cats* (1939) reached a wide audience in 1981 through the success of Andrew Lloyd Webber's musical *Cats*. Eliot was awarded the Nobel Prize in 1948.

Building Background

Defining the "Lost Generation" T. S. Eliot called his eight years at Smith Academy in St. Louis the most important of his education. There he studied classical and modern languages, classical literature and history, English and American history. Eliot turned to this classical education again and again in his roles as critic, editor, publisher, and, most importantly, poet. Many of his themes and images are references to classical works. Eliot's poetry often presents difficulties to readers who frequently must consult footnotes in order to grasp his many **metaphors, symbols,** and **allusions** to Shakespeare and other writers. His dominant influence was Dante's *Divine Comedy,* which provided a metaphor for the hell that Eliot saw in the lives of the "lost generation" following World War I. He viewed the 1920s as a time in which traditional beliefs and values were abandoned in the search for immediate pleasure and personal enjoyment.

Literary Focus

Free Verse The form known as **free verse** differs from conventional verse forms because it is free from a fixed pattern of rhythm and rhyme. Yet free verse may be highly rhythmic and may utilize a wide variety of sound devices and poetic techniques. As you read "The Hollow Men," look for the devices that indicate you are reading poetry, not prose.

Writer's Notebook

Structured Verse Choose one of the following subjects—or a subject of your own choice—and write an eight-line poem that has a definite rhyme and rhythmic pattern.

- my hero
- a pitiful sight
- holiday memories
- a painful experience
- a beautiful day

SUPPORT MATERIALS OVERVIEW

Unit 7 Resource Book
- Graphic Organizer, p. 73
- Study Guide, p. 74
- Vocabulary, p. 75
- Grammar, p. 76
- Alternate Check Test, p. 77
- Vocabulary Test, p. 78
- Selection Test, pp. 79–80

Building English Proficiency
- Selection Summaries
- Activities, p. 254

Reading, Writing & Grammar SkillBook
- Reading, pp. 20–21, 22–25

Technology
- Personal Journal Software
- Test Generator Software

The Hollow Men

T. S. Eliot

Mistah Kurtz—he dead.[1]
A penny for the Old Guy[2]

1

We are the hollow men
We are the stuffed men
Leaning together
Headpiece filled with straw. Alas!
5 Our dried voices, when
We whisper together
Are quiet and meaningless
As wind in dry grass
Or rats' feet over broken glass
10 In our dry cellar

Shape without form, shade without color,
Paralyzed force, gesture without motion;

Those who have crossed
With direct eyes,[3] to death's other
        Kingdom[4]
15 Remember us—if at all—not as lost
Violent souls, but only
As the hollow men
The stuffed men.

2

Eyes[5] I dare not meet in dreams
20 In death's dream kingdom
These do not appear:
There, the eyes are
Sunlight on a broken column
There, is a tree swinging
25 And voices are
In the wind's singing
More distant and more solemn
Than a fading star.

Let me be no nearer
30 In death's dream kingdom
Let me also wear
Such deliberate disguises
Rat's coat, crowskin, crossed staves
In a field[6]
35 Behaving as the wind behaves
No nearer—

Not that final meeting
In the twilight kingdom

---

1. **Mistah Kurtz—he dead.** In Joseph Conrad's novella *Heart of Darkness*, Kurtz, a European trader, goes into "the heart of darkness"—the central African jungle. He brings with him European standards of conduct but no moral or spiritual strength, and he soon turns into a barbarian. However, he is not paralyzed, as Eliot's "hollow men" are; he commits acts of overwhelming evil. He is not blind as they are, but at his death glimpses the nature of his actions when he exclaims, "The horror! The horror!" Kurtz is thus one of the "lost / Violent souls" mentioned in lines 15–16.
2. **A penny . . . Guy,** traditional cry of English children begging money for fireworks to celebrate Guy Fawkes Day, November 5. This commemorates the prevention of the Gunpowder Plot of 1605 in which Guy Fawkes and other conspirators planned to blow up both Houses of Parliament. On this day straw-stuffed images of Fawkes called *guys* are burned.
3. **those . . . direct eyes,** those who have represented something positive (direct), either for good or evil.
4. **death's other Kingdom,** the afterlife; eternity.
5. **eyes,** the eyes of those in the afterworld who had confident faith; those who represent positive spiritual force as opposed to the spiritual stagnation or paralysis of the "hollow men."
6. **rat's coat . . . field,** a scarecrow decorated with dead rats and crows.

The Hollow Men   769

During Reading

Selection Objectives

- to explore certain attitudes after World War I
- to identify the elements of free verse
- to understand the conventions of sentence punctuation
- to obtain insights into T. S. Eliot's view of life
- to identify how figurative language reinforces theme

 Unit 7 Resource Book
Graphic Organizer, p. 73
Study Guide, p. 74

Theme Link

"The Hollow Men" are people who have become stagnant and believe in nothing. The poem reflects the anxiety and doubts of the Lost Generation, which lived through war and its aftermath.

Vocabulary Preview

grope, search blindly

Students can add the word and its definition to their Writer's Notebooks.

1 Reading/Thinking Skills

Recognize Values

Questions

- What is the paradox suggested in lines 1 and 2? *(These people are hollow because they are empty and live lives without meaning; they are "stuffed," like scarecrows, with nothing of value— just filler.)*
- What words and phrases in the first two sections suggest meaningless lives? *(dried, dry, broken, hollow, stuffed, fading)*

SELECTION SUMMARY

The Hollow Men

Who are the hollow men? They are the members of society who sit and are paralyzed, unable to do anything because they believe in nothing and are filled with nothing but "straw." Unlike the men referred to in the epigraph who were strong, if misguided, the hollow men wait. They do not take part in life, and they will not die. They merely exist, try to shirk all responsibility, and hide among the other hollow men, hoping fate will take them where they should go.

*For summaries in other languages, see the **Building English Proficiency** book.*

Question What effects does Eliot achieve with repetition? Cite some examples. *(He reinforces meaning by repeating words like broken, hollow, stuffed, death, dream; he creates a mood of futility by creating lines that sound like mantras or meaningless rhymes: The eyes are not here / There are no eyes here; Here we go round the prickly pear. . . .)*

3 Literary Element

Figurative Language

Question What figures of speech reinforce the idea of futility and meaninglessness? *(Answers may include "hollow men," "stuffed men," "dried voices," "broken glass," "fading star," "rat's coat," "cactus land," "broken jaw.")*

Check Test

1. Describe the mood of this poem *(bleak, despairing, hopeless, empty)*

2. Who are "those who have crossed" in line 13? *(the faithful, who have died and are enjoying the afterlife)*

3. To what does the speaker compare the hollow men in lines 33–34—those with "crowskin" and "crossed staves in a field"? *(scarecrows)*

4. What is the name of the verse form of "The Hollow Men"? *(free verse)*

5. How does the world end, according to this poem? *(with a whimper, not a bang)*

Unit 7 Resource Book
Alternate Check Test, p. 77

770

3
This is the dead land
40 This is cactus land
Here the stone images
Are raised, here they receive
The supplications[7] of a dead man's hand
Under the twinkle of a fading star.
45 Is it like this
In death's other kingdom
Waking alone
At the hour when we are
Trembling with tenderness
50 Lips that would kiss
Form prayers to broken stone.

4
The eyes are not here
There are no eyes here
In this valley of dying stars
55 In this hollow valley
This broken jaw of our lost kingdoms

In this last of meeting places
We grope[8] together
And avoid speech
60 Gathered on this beach of the tumid[9] river

Sightless, unless
The eyes reappear
As the perpetual star
Multifoliate rose[10]
65 Of death's twilight kingdom
The hope only
Of empty men.

5
Here we go round the prickly pear
Prickly pear prickly pear
2 70 *Here we go round the prickly pear*
At five o'clock in the morning.[11]

Between the idea
And the reality
Between the motion
75 And the act
Falls the Shadow
For Thine is the Kingdom[12]

Between the conception
And the creation
80 Between the emotion
And the response
Falls the Shadow
Life is very long

Between the desire
85 And the spasm
Between the potency
And the existence
Between the essence
And the descent
90 Falls the Shadow
For Thine is the Kingdom

For Thine is
Life is
For Thine is the
95 *This is the way the world ends*
This is the way the world ends
This is the way the world ends
Not with a bang but a whimper.

3

---

7. **supplication** (sup′lə kā′shən), *n.* humble prayer.
8. **grope** (grōp), *v.* search blindly.
9. **tumid** (tü′mid), *adj.* swollen.
10. **Multifoliate rose,** in Dante's *Divine Comedy* a symbol of Paradise, in which the saints are the many petals of the rose.
11. **Here we go . . . morning,** a parody of the children's rhyme "Here we go round the mulberry bush."
12. **For Thine . . . Kingdom,** a phrase from the Lord's Prayer (Matthew 6:9–13).

MINI-LESSON: GRAMMAR

Standard Sentence Punctuation

Teach Eliot has used punctuation sparingly in this free verse. Punctuation makes it easier for readers to understand what they are reading. Remind students that a period (.) ends a statement, a period (.) ends a command, a question mark (?) ends a question, and an exclamation mark (!) ends an exclamation, a sentence of surprise, fear, or excitement. Ask how the use of standard punctuation might have affected "The Hollow Men." *(Possible response: Lines that now have a continuity of thought would be separate and broken. If the reader had to pause when reading, the poem would seem more disjointed.)*

Activity Idea Students can choose one section of "The Hollow Men" and rewrite it using standard punctuation. They can discuss how using standard punctuation affects the meaning of the poem.

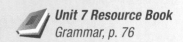
Unit 7 Resource Book
Grammar, p. 76

After Reading

Making Connections

Shaping Your Response

1. What about Eliot's poem presented the most difficulty for you?

Analyzing the Poem

2. What conclusion can you draw from the many comparisons of the hollow men to scarecrows?

3. In section 1, what do you see as the difference between those who have crossed to eternity "With direct eyes" and "the hollow men"?

4. What indication is there in section 2 that the speaker, like the other hollow men, has given up the struggle to give new meaning to his life?

5. In sections 3 and 4, what elements of the **setting** do you think reflect the emotional and spiritual emptiness of the hollow men?

6. What effect do you think the "Shadow" has on such human actions as thinking, creating, and feeling?

7. What do you think the fragments of the Lord's Prayer and the **parody** of "Here we go round the mulberry bush" suggest about the spiritual condition of the hollow men?

8. How are the hollow men shown to be unlike Mistah Kurtz and the Old Guy?

9. Why do you think the speaker suggests that the world will end "Not with a bang but a whimper"?

Extending the Ideas

10. Eliot portrayed people of the post-World War I era as "hollow men." Do you think that Eliot, if he were writing today, would hold a similar view of society or of any **group** of people in today's society?

Literary Focus: Free Verse

Free verse contains no standard rhyme and no fixed rhythmic pattern, but it does contain other sound devices, as well as figurative language. Give an example of each of the following poetic devices that contribute to the poetic quality of this verse.

- alliteration
- consonance
- simile
- imagery
- parallel structure

The Hollow Men **771**

BUILDING ENGLISH PROFICIENCY

Improving Comprehension

Many students will find Eliot's poetry difficult to understand. The following activity may be helpful.

1. Go back to Rupert Brooke's "The Soldier" on page 735 and compare it with "The Hollow Men." Point out that between the two poems, a world has been destroyed. Ask: What was that world? What has the world become? What has been lost in "The Hollow Men"?

2. Working slowly through Eliot's poem with the whole class, encourage students to share the images that come to mind in response to Eliot's images. Ask: Do you see "hollow men" today?

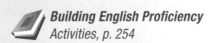
Building English Proficiency Activities, p. 254

After Reading

MAKING CONNECTIONS

1. Some students may have trouble with the figurative elements and the imagery; others may find the structure and free verse difficult; still others may find the many illusions troublesome.

2. Possible response: They are empty, passive beings, lacking substance, vitality, and the ability to communicate and live meaningful lives.

3. Possible response: Those who have crossed have lived purposeful lives and found peace.

4. Possible response: The speaker prefers to wear "deliberate disguises," like that of a scarecrow, rather than risk confrontations with confident people of faith.

5. Possible responses: "dead land," "cactus land," "hollow valley," "broken stone," " dying stars"

6. Possible responses: The "Shadow" paralyzes all human actions, feelings, and creativity. It suggests a mysterious spiritual malaise.

7. Possible response: They suggest a condition in which religious meaning has become trivialized. Prayers are no more meaningful than childish jingles.

8. Possible response: Kurtz and the Old Guy were violent men who challenged destiny; the hollow men are incapable of action and instead submit to fate.

9. Possible response: The world will be destroyed, not through violence, but through inactivity, lack of communication, and despair.

10. Possible response: Some students will say yes because they feel there exists a similar spiritual void today. Others may have a more optimistic view of the contemporary world.

LITERARY FOCUS: FREE VERSE

Possible Responses

- alliteration: shape, shade (line 11), coat, crowskin, crossed (line 33), Trembling, tenderness (line 49), prickly pear (lines 68–70)

- consonance: end of lines 7–9
- simile: As wind in dry grass (line 8)
- imagery: "death's other Kingdom" (line 14), "supplications of a dead man's hand" (line 43), "This broken jaw of our lost kingdoms" (line 56), "death's twilight kingdom" (line 65)
- parallel structure: lines 11–12; lines 72–76; lines 78–82; lines 84–90

VOCABULARY STUDY

Vocabulary words, as used in context, should reflect correct meanings and connotations. Following are some sample sentences.

They will **examine** the report for any inaccuracies.

Scientists **explore** the universe hoping to find signs of life.

The colonel will **inspect** our barracks thoroughly.

The police took a long time to **investigate** the theft.

I must **probe** further for the answer.

Did you **rummage** through the attic for the books?

Seek and you shall find.

Unit 7 Resource Book
Vocabulary, p. 75
Vocabulary Test, p. 78

Selection Test

Unit 7 Resource Book
pp. 79–80

Transparency Collection
Fine Art Writing Prompt 14

Vocabulary Study

examine
explore
inspect
investigate
probe
rummage
seek

The verb *grope* means "to search blindly and uncertainly." Each of the listed words also means "to search," but each carries a slightly different **connotation.** Choose five of these words and use each in a sentence that shows that you understand the subtle difference in meaning. Use a dictionary if you need help.

Expressing Your Ideas

Writing Choices

Writer's Notebook Update Using the same subject you chose for your rhyming poem, write an eight-line poem in free verse. Which poem do you like better? Why?

A Sense of Loss A recurrent theme in Eliot's poetry is the sense of loss; in the words of one critic, "the lost vision, the lost purpose, the lost meaning, the lost sense of fellowship, the lost sense of self." Do you see any similar sense of loss, any similar hollowness in today's society? In an **informal essay** discuss the particular sense of loss you see. Try to account for the cause and try to suggest a resolution to that loss.

Better Violent Than Hollow? The French poet Charles Baudelaire, a favorite author of Eliot's, wrote: "So far as we are human, what we do must be either evil or good; . . . and it is better, in a paradoxical way, to do evil than to do nothing: at least we exist." Do you agree with Baudelaire and Eliot that it is better to be evil than to be "hollow men"? Write your response in the form of a **letter** to Eliot in which you reinforce your position with examples from modern day society.

Other Options

"Our Dried Voices . . ." T. S. Eliot's poems lend themselves especially well to reading aloud. As a group, prepare a **choral reading** of "The Hollow Men." Start by determining which lines should be read by solo voices and which by combined voices or the entire chorus. Work to capture the multiple rhythms of the poem and vary tempos and vocal tones to match the shifting moods. After rehearsal, make a tape recording to play for other classes.

Thoroughly Modernist After World War I, many poets moved away from traditional forms and techniques and developed new forms of poetry. Likewise, painters and composers experimented with techniques that led some critics to say, "That's not art" or "That's not music." Select one of these *modernist* artists like Pablo Picasso, Joan Miro, or Paul Klee, or composers like Igor Stravinsky, Arnold Schoenberg, or Bela Bartok. Prepare an **illustrated oral report** for your class in which you show how this artist or composer is representative of the modernist movement.

WRITING CHOICES

Writer's Notebook Update

Suggest that students review the characteristics of free verse.

A Sense of Loss

Students may want to use quotations from "The Hollow Men" to reinforce their ideas. This writing assignment could lead to a debate.

OTHER OPTIONS

"Our Dried Voices . . . "

Suggest that students work in groups and carefully choose which member will say each part. Students should be encouraged to rehearse until the lines flow in a kind of sing-song pattern.

War and Aftermath

The Wasteland

History Connection

With the use of modern weapons on a mammoth scale, World War I achieved levels of horror and destructiveness unparalled in human history. The following passages explore two aspects of the frightful man-made wasteland of the Western Front.

At 5:00 on the afternoon of April 22, 1915, shelling at Langemarck near the Belgian village of Ypres had stopped. The front was quiet.

The World War I Allied soldiers were tired after the daylong shelling bout with the Germans, and they lay heavily in their trenches during the respite.

Suddenly the Germans began another deafening round of shelling from their position in the south. Seconds later the Allied soldiers noticed two greenish yellow clouds a few hundred yards in front of them. Hanging low on the horizon, the clouds were rapidly approaching them from the German line, and within one minute the clouds had reached the first Allied troops. The men quickly fell into a state of confusion; they were completely unprepared and unprotected for what was to be a devastating poison gas attack.

The gas instantly caused severe burning in their throats and lungs. The men clutched at their chests, coughed, and gasped for breath. Attempts to shield themselves from the gas were largely futile. Many tried to burrow their noses and mouths, or to cover them with cloth, but the moist, dense poison penetrated everything. Others tried to outrun the clouds, inevitably receiving lethal doses as running made them inhale even more deeply. Most fell, choking, their panic turning to agony.

The gas causing these profound, immediate effects upon the Allied troops was chlorine. The Germans, having waited for the appropriate change in wind direction, had released 160 tons of liquid chlorine from nearly 6,000 pressurized cylinders. On release the chlorine formed a thick, odorous gas cloud. Because of its form, it was impossible to control the direction of the weapon. The Germans had waited for days to release the chlorine, but at 5:00 on April 22, the breeze began to blow toward the Allied lines.

Chlorine, a poison, begins by irritating the eyes, nose, and throat. It quickly scorches the lining of the windpipe and the lungs, resulting in severe—often fatal—coughing bouts. In an extreme dose, such as was used that horrific day at Ypres, chlorine causes massive amounts of a yellowish fluid to develop in the lungs. Many of the men who died during or soon after the April 22 attack actually choked to death from the heavy liquid in their chests and throats.

After the Allied front had fallen silent, the Germans, wearing crude gas masks, advanced to survey the effects of the day's battle and of their new weapon. Even they were amazed at what they found. In all, more than 5,000 had died as a result of the poisonings. Over 10,000 were injured. Four miles of the Allied line had collapsed, and the gap was several miles deep. Yet the Germans, lacking sufficient reserves in that sector, were unable to capitalize on the Allies' fallen defenses. Indeed, they were not prepared for such a significant victory with their fledgling weapon, or they might have marched through to the English Channel and soon attempted the capture of the French city of Calais. Had that occurred, the course of World War I might have been drastically altered.

THE HORROR AT YPRES

by L. B. Taylor, Jr. and C. L. Taylor

Interdisciplinary Study

Theme Link

The horrors of World War I remained in the lives and minds of people long after the battles ended. The war that turned much of Europe into a graveyard also created an emotional and spiritual wasteland.

Curricular Connection: History

Use the information in this interdisciplinary study to discuss with students the advent and development of modern warfare and the impact it has on today's world.

Terms to Know

front, the advanced line, or the whole area, of contact between opposing sides in warfare; battleground.

respite (res′pit), time of relief and rest; lull.

futile, useless; hopeless.

sullen, gloomy, dismal; depressing.

extrude, to push or force out; expel.

shard, a broken piece; fragment.

dour, sullen, gloomy; stern.

incise, to cut into with a sharp tool; engrave.

Unit 7 Resource Book
Interdisciplinary Study Guide, p. 81

BUILDING ENGLISH PROFICIENCY

Relating to a Modern Context

The fear and horror of chemical warfare was raised once again during the Gulf War in 1990–1991. Ironically, media coverage also masked some of the other horrors of war that were very real at that time.

Activity Idea   Ask students to find articles from newspapers and news magazines that showed images from cameras mounted on the heads of missiles. Ask students to evaluate this coverage and to consider the following questions.

- What was the intended purpose of showing these images?
- How do these images mask the kind of destruction that these weapons caused?
- What other perspective could the media have taken to discuss the use of these weapons?

Art Study

The photo of the soldiers blinded by the gas portrays the kind of imagery that Siegfried Sassoon and Wilfred Owen used in their war poems. To address this photo, you could ask students to imagine how these two poets might have described this scene and what imagery they would have used. You might also suggest that the students write a letter or journal entry that one of the soldiers might have asked a friend to transcribe for him.

Additional Background

In his book *I Hear America Talking: An Illustrated History of American Words and Phrases,* Stuart Berg Flexner points out that the terms *to gas, gas alert, gas bomb,* and *gas mask* became familiar to Americans through the newspapers after the fighting at Ypres in 1915.

In addition to the chlorine gas described in this interdisciplinary study, both sides used chemical weapons, such as *sneezing gas, vomiting gas,* and the deadly *mustard gas,* or *blister gas.*

The Geneva Protocol of 1925 prohibited the use of chemical weapons, but most countries continued to stockpile them.

THE HORROR AT YPRES

GUIDING THEMSELVES BY HOLDING ONTO THE MAN IN FRONT OF THEM, SOLDIERS BLINDED BY POISON GAS WAIT FOR TREATMENT IN APRIL 1918.

The Germans did, however, follow up with a second chlorine attack two days later. Again at Ypres, they were battling Canadian regiments called in to seal the gap caused by the initial gas attack. The Canadians, still without sufficient protection against the chlorine, held fabric soaked with urine to their faces in an attempt to escape the effects of the gas. The ensuing panic was similar to that of two days before, and over 5,000 Allied men died from the combination artillery/gas attack. Still, the Germans lacked the aggressiveness to follow up on their attack, allowing the Canadian soldiers eventually to force them to retreat. These initial German poison gas attacks, however, marked the onset of modern chemical warfare—a method that was to play a significant and devastating role during the rest of World War I.

MINI-LESSON: VISUAL LITERACY

Analyzing Documentaries

Teach   Remind students that a documentary is a visual presentation that shows or analyzes news events, social conditions, and so on, with little or no fictionalization. Documentary photographs, like the World War I image on this page, are an invaluable source of information not only to those who live through the events but also to those who come after.

Because a documentary purports to tell the truth, viewers should carefully analyze the filmmaker's or photographer's purpose, degree of objectivity, and biases.

Activity Ideas

• Students can find a photographic documentary on any subject and analyze it for purpose and degree of objectivity.

• Students can view a filmed documentary on any subject and compare it to a fictionalized account of the same event.

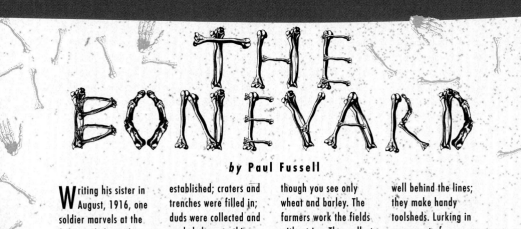

THE BONEYARD

by Paul Fussell

Writing his sister in August, 1916, one soldier marvels at the fantastic holes and ditches which scar the whole landscape and wonders, "How ever will they get it smoothed out again is more than I can imagine." The work of smoothing it out continues to this day. At first, some thought restoration of the area impossible and advised that it simply be abandoned. In 1919 the battlefields were still much as 1918 had left them, but a tourist could visit them, assisted by a series of *Illustrated Michelin Guides to the Battlefields* (1914-1918) written in English and printed in England. Gradually the road network was re-established; craters and trenches were filled in; duds were collected and exploded; nasty things were collected and buried; and villagers began returning and rebuilding, often exactly reproducing a leveled town on its original site.

Today the Somme[1] is a peaceful but sullen place, unforgetting and unforgiving. The people, who work largely at raising vegetables and grains, are "correct" but not friendly. To wander now over the fields destined to extrude their rusty metal fragments for centuries is to appreciate in the most intimate way the permanent rever-berations of July 1916. When the air is damp you can smell rusted iron everywhere, even though you see only wheat and barley. The farmers work the fields without joy. They collect the duds, shell-casings, fuses, and shards of old barbed wire as the plow unearths them and stack them in the corners of their fields. Some of the old barbed wire, both British and German, is used for fencing. Many of the shell craters are still there, though smoothed out and grown over. The mine craters are too deep to be filled and remain much as they were. When the sun is low in the afternoon, on the gradual slopes of the low hills you see the traces of the zig-zag of trenches. Many farmhouses have out in back one of the little British wooden huts that used to house soldiers well behind the lines; they make handy toolsheds. Lurking in every spot of undergrowth just off the beaten track are eloquent little things: rusted buckles, rounds of corroded small-arms ammunition, metal tabs from ammunition boxes, bits of Bully tin[2], buttons.

Albert[3] today is one of the saddest places in France. It has all been restored to its original ugliness. The red-brick Basilica is as it was before the war, with the gilded virgin back up on top of the tower, quite erect. But despite an appearance of adequacy, everything human in Albert seems to have been permanently defeated. The inhabitants are dour. Everywhere there

---

1. **Somme** (sôm), area in northern France that was the scene of a series of massive battles in late 1916.
2. **Bully tin**, container for canned meat used as rations.
3. **Albert**, town in northern France almost completely destroyed by shelling in 1918.

Historical Note

The Notorious Western Front   The Western Front was the line of contact between the Allies and the Germans, extending about six hundred miles from Switzerland to the English Channel. Because of the long drawn-out nature of trench warfare, the front did not change frequently or rapidly.

The Germans used the name *Siegfried line* to describe the Western Front, and the Allies often called it the *Hindenburg line* since it was the line to which German Field Marshal Paul von Hindenburg withdrew after the Battle of the Somme.

As Stuart Berg Flexner has pointed out, the expression "all quiet on the western front" was used frequently in official military reports and was picked up by journalists of the time. However, to the men suffering and dying in the trenches, the front was anything but "all quiet." In 1929, Erich Maria Remarque published one of the greatest anti-war novels of all time, ironically entitled *All Quiet on the Western Front*. Remarque introduced his gripping novel with a bitterly realistic sentence that sums up the consciousness of the world after World War I: "This book is to be neither an accusation nor a confession, and least of all an adventure, for death is not an adventure to those who stand face to face with it."

BUILDING ENGLISH PROFICIENCY

Irony

At the end of the article, Fussell describes the cross with the inscription *Friede* that stands at the summit of a hill in Somme. The contrast of this image to the other images in this article creates a grim irony.

Activity Idea   To help the students understand the incongruity of these images in the same place and the subsequent ambiguity of the message, ask the students to create a collage incorporating the following elements:

• translations of the word *peace* in several languages

• photos of people affected by the battles of World War I

• excerpts from memoirs, letters, poetry, and works of fiction

• religious emblems that suggest reconciliation

After completing this collage, discuss with students the irony of these images in juxtaposition. You may want to draw conclusions about what the irony teaches about war.

Responding

1. Possible Response Attempting to legislate "rules of war" is a futile exercise. The laws avoid the real problem of war itself and become empty words designed to make some nations feel they are taking a positive moral stance. On the other hand, persistently attempting to contain the fury and ferocity of war may be the only chance to eliminate it completely.

2. Possible Response Battlefields that have been turned into memorials serve a useful purpose for those who survive the battles and wars. They provide an opportunity for people to assuage their sorrow, and they stand as permanent reminders of the real price that warring nations pay.

Interdisciplinary Activity Ideas

- Students can divide into groups and create their own documentaries about a war and its aftermath. The documentaries may be presented in still photographs, on videotape, or even in multimedia. Students should include as much primary source material as possible.

- Students can organize and present a mock United Nations debate on the topic of a current world conflict. Speakers can focus on such topics as the effects of the conflict on the combatants, the effects on civilians, and the effects on other nations.

---

is an air of bitterness about being passed over by the modernity, sophistication, and affluence of modern France. Everywhere one senses a quiet fury at being condemned to live in this boneyard and backwater, where even the crops contend with soil once ruined by gas.

And a boneyard it is. Every week bones come to light. Depending on one's mood one either quietly buries them again, or flings them into the nearby brush, or saves them to turn over to the employees of the Commonwealth (formerly "Imperial") War Graves Commission, which

supervises the 2,500 British military cemeteries from offices in the main cities. The cemeteries are both pretty and bizarre, fertile with roses, projecting an almost unendurably ironic peacefulness. They memorialize not just the men buried in them, but the talents for weighty public rhetoric of Rudyard Kipling. He was called on to devise almost all the verbal formulas employed by the Imperial War Graves Commission, from "Their Name Liveth For Evermore," carved on the large "Stone of Remembrance" in each cemetery, to the words incised on headstones

over the bodies of the unidentified: "A Soldier of the Great War/Known unto God." The unforgettable, infinitely pathetic inscriptions are not Kipling's but those which the families of the dead were allowed—after long debate within the Commission about "uniformity"—to place on their stones. In addition to the still hopeful ones about dawn and fleeing shadows we find some which are more "modern," that is, more personal, particular, and hopeless:

*Our dear Ted.
He died for us.*

. . .

Our Dick

. . .

*If love could have
saved him
he would
not have died.*

And some read as if refusing to play the game of memorial language at all:

*A sorrow too deep
for words.*

The notorious Butte of Warlencourt, a fifty-foot knoll on the road to Bapaume from which the Germans strenuously held the British advance in the autumn and winter of 1916, is overgrown and silent. Crops grow right to its foot, dipping here and there to betray the persistent shapes of shell holes and mine craters. Tens of thousands of men simply disappeared here. The sticky Somme mud makes large unwieldy spheres of your shoes as you climb to the top through the thick undergrowth. At the top you can picnic, if you have the heart for it, and inspect the large weathered wooden cross erected by the Germans at the summit and apparently renewed at the end of the Second World War. On it is carved the word *Friede.*[4]

4. Friede (frē′də), peace. [*German*]

IN HIS PAINTING *Oppy Wood* (1917), BRITISH ARTIST JOHN NASH CAPTURES THE FRIGHTFUL DEVASTATION OF THE WESTERN FRONT IN WORLD WAR I.

776 UNIT SEVEN: THE EARLY TWENTIETH CENTURY

Responding

1. After World War I, an attempt was made to outlaw chemical weapons. Do you think to try to legislate "rules of warfare" makes sense? Why or why not?
2. Do you think battlefields should be turned into memorials? Why or why not?

MINI-LESSON: STUDY SKILLS

Using Primary and Secondary Sources

Teach Remind students that most of the research papers they write will use both primary and secondary sources. Primary sources include the texts of literary works, historical documents, and statistics. Secondary sources include articles and books that other researchers have produced. In other words, secondary sources are studies of primary sources.

If, for example, students quote the text of Woodrow Wilson's war message—"It is a fearful thing to lead this great peaceful people into war"—they are using a primary source. If, however, they quote Robert H. Ferrell's study *Woodrow Wilson and World War I: 1917–1921*, they are using a secondary source.

Activity Idea For practice, have students write a paragraph about an aspect of the aftermath of World War I, including and identifying at least one primary source quotation or reference and one secondary source quotation or reference.

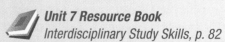

Unit 7 Resource Book
Interdisciplinary Study Skills, p. 82

Language History

The Language of Heroism

These laid the world away; poured out the red
Sweet wine of youth; gave up the years to be
Of work and joy . . . .
Rupert Brooke, "The Dead" (1914)

In his book *The Great War and Modern Memory,* literary historian Paul Fussell observes that one of the casualties of World War I was the system of "high" diction relating to warfare to which several generations of readers had become accustomed. "The tutors in this special diction had been the boys' books of George Alfred Henty; the male romances of Rider Haggard; the poems of Robert Bridges; and especially the Arthurian poems of Tennyson and the pseudo-medieval romances of William Morris." As examples of this "high" diction, Fussell offers a series of equivalents:

friend / *comrade*	obedient soldiers / *the brave*
horse / *steed* or *charger*	warfare / *strife*
enemy / *foe* or *host*	die / *perish*
danger / *peril*	draft notice / *the summons*
conquer / *vanquish*	enlist / *join the colors*
earnestly brave / *gallant*	death / *fate*
cheerfully brave / *plucky*	sky / *heavens*
stolidly brave / *staunch*	contemptible / *base*
front / *field*	legs and arms of young men / *limbs*
dead / *the fallen*	bodies / *ashes* or *dust*

How different from the elevated diction of Rupert Brooke's "red / Sweet wine of youth" was Wilfred Owen's forthright "the blood / Come gargling from the froth-corrupted lungs, / Obscene as cancer . . . ." Rejecting high-sounding abstractions that no longer held any meaning for them, Owen and other soldier poets adopted a colloquial, concrete, realistic style, bitter and deeply ironic in tone. It was a transformation that would have a profound effect on the language used by the common people for the rest of the century.

Language History **777**

Teaching Objectives

- to recognize the connection between a culture's perception of war and the language used to describe it
- to understand the difference between elevated diction and concrete, colloquial diction
- to understand the relationship between diction and tone

Introduce

Discuss the differences between a romantic view of war and a realistic view of war. How might people with these differing views use language differently to express their conceptions of war? *(Possible response: It might be reflected in their word choice and their tone, or it might be reflected in the details they choose to leave out.)*

Follow Up

After students have read the article, give them the opportunity to look through books of poetry and find other war poems that reflect either a romantic or realistic view. Ask them to create lists of paired words, such as the ones Fussell provides.

Students can experiment with the effect of diction on the tone of a work of literature by substituting words in a poem with their paired, contrasting words. Ask them to explain how the substitution affects the tone of the poem and, subsequently, the meaning of the poem.

CONTENT AREA READING

Euphemisms

Teach   Explain to students that one meaning of *diction* is "word choice" and that our choice of words affects how a message is received. Using the word *strife* instead of the word *warfare* is not only an example of high diction but also a euphemism. *Strife* is less offensive and unpleasant. We often use euphemisms when we talk about a sensitive or controversial issue in order to make the subject more palatable.

Apply   Ask students to list as many euphemisms as possible, such as *passing away* instead of

dying. Use the following discussion questions to analyze their use.

- Why is each euphemism used?
- When is using this euphemism appropriate and inappropriate?
- How might using the euphemism create misunderstandings in communication?

Activity Idea   Ask students to look for examples of euphemisms in news stories, advertising, and textbooks.

Writing Workshop

WRITER'S BLUEPRINT
Specs

The Specs in the Writer's Blueprint address these writing and thinking skills:

- creating characters
- developing setting
- plotting
- summarizing
- using teleplay format
- writing dialogue
- persuading
- using a professional tone

These Specs serve as your lesson objectives, and they form the basis for the **Assessment Criteria Specs** for a superior paper, which appear on the final TE page for this lesson. You might want to read through the Assessment Criteria Specs with students when you begin the lesson.

Linking Literature to Writing

Have volunteers pick passages from the literature that seem especially visual. Ask them to visualize the scene as it might be depicted on the screen and describe what they visualize.

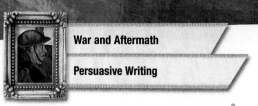

War and Aftermath

Persuasive Writing

Writing Workshop

Selling an Idea

Assignment You have read about war and its aftermath from different perspectives. Now the producer of a TV series about World War I titled *Homefront / Battlefront* has asked you and a partner to submit a proposal for an hour-long episode. See the Writer's Blueprint for details.

WRITER'S BLUEPRINT

Product	A proposal for an episode of a TV series
Purpose	To sell an idea
Audience	A TV producer
Specs	As the creator of a persuasive proposal, you and your partner should:

❑ Develop an intriguing plot, appealing main characters, and vivid settings, using the literature in this part of the unit for inspiration.

❑ Begin your proposal by briefly summarizing the plot.

❑ Describe the main characters and settings in your episode and provide a scene-by-scene outline of the plot. Make sure that at least one scene takes place on each front and that the characters on the two fronts are connected in some significant way.

❑ Present two of the scenes—one set on each front—in teleplay form.

❑ End by urging the producer to accept your proposal by giving persuasive reasons why. Address your audience in a tone enthusiastic and assured but not overly informal: one professional to another.

❑ Follow the rules of grammar, usage, spelling, and mechanics. Use a consistent teleplay format for your scenes.

WRITING WORKSHOP OVERVIEW

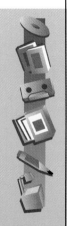

Product
Persuasive Writing: A proposal for an episode of a TV series

Prewriting
Review the literature—Brainstorm ideas—Outline the plot—Try a quickwrite—List persuasive reasons—Plan your proposal
Unit 7 Resource Book
Prewriting Worksheets pp. 83–84

Drafting
Before you write—As you draft
Transparency Collection
Student Models for Writing Workshop 27, 28

Revising
Ask another pair of writers—Strategy: Using an Appropriate Tone
Unit 7 Resource Book
Revising Worksheet p. 85

Editing
Ask another pair of writers—Strategy: Using a Consistent Teleplay Format
Unit 7 Resource Book
Grammar Worksheet p. 86
Grammar Check Test p. 87

Presenting
Tape the Episode
Perform It Live

Looking Back
Self-evaluate—Reflect—For Your Working Portfolio
Unit 7 Resource Book
Assessment Worksheet p. 88
Transparency Collection
Fine Art Writing Prompt 14

Review the literature to get ideas for your episode. For example, what ideas for plot or setting does the Literary Source suggest? Record the details you find in a chart like this.

Main Characters	Setting	Plot
boy lying about his age to join army ("Disabled")	recruiting office	wants to impress his girlfriend/ romanticizes going to war
Vera Brittain and Roland *(Testament of Youth)*	train station	saying goodbye as he goes off to war

LITERARY SOURCE
"In the early morning we walked to the station beneath a dazzling sun, but the platform from which his train went out was dark and very cold. In the railway carriage we sat hand in hand until the whistle blew."
from *Testament of Youth* by Vera Brittain

Brainstorm ideas for plots, characters, and settings. Refer to your literature review chart for inspiration. Characters and settings could be directly from the literature, completely new, or a combination. After you've finished, decide with your partner which ideas to use in your episode.

Outline the plot of your episode with your partner. You might draw a time line for the entire episode and fill it in with notes about each scene. Refer to your character and setting notes as you plan. Make sure that you set some scenes on the homefront and some on the battlefront.

Try a quickwrite. With your partner, review your plot outline and choose two scenes—one from the homefront and one from the battlefront—to develop in detail. Discuss the action in each scene. Then, take one scene each and write for five minutes about it. Consider how your scene advances the plot. What has happened before this scene? What will happen after? How is the scene linked to the one your partner is writing? How do the characters know each other?

List persuasive reasons. With your partner, brainstorm a list of reasons why a producer should accept your proposal. Consider all the strengths of the episode you've planned. Find reasons that persuasively answer the questions on the next page.

OR . . .
Instead of outlining the plot, create a storyboard for each scene. Sketch a key moment in the scene and add notes about narration, dialogue, and stage directions.

OR . . .
Instead of quickwriting, you and your partner could improvise the two scenes, acting them out loud together. After each scene, quickly jot down notes about the parts that worked well.

Writing Workshop **779**

STEP 1 PREWRITING
Review the literature

To help students get started on the chart, have the class brainstorm a list of the different settings from the selections. These settings, and others, can be placed on the chart to trigger details about the main characters and the plot.

Brainstorm ideas

Remind students that in brainstorming, some of the ideas may be general while others may be more specific, and that no ideas should be rejected until later, after all ideas are jotted down.

Outline the plot

Partners might write each episode of the plot on a separate card. Then they can arrange the cards freely until they agree on the basic outline. After they agree, details can be added to each card. For additional support, see the worksheets referenced below.

Unit 7 Resource Book
Prewriting Worksheet, p. 83
Prewriting Worksheet, p. 84

Try a quickwrite

Encourage students to write rapidly without stopping during the five minute period. Tell them to forget about punctuation and spelling for the moment and concentrate on getting their thoughts down on paper.

List persuasive reasons

After partners have finished brainstorming, have them individually circle what they consider the three most persuasive reasons. The partners can then compare their choices and work out any differences between them.

BUILDING ENGLISH PROFICIENCY
Making Real-Life Connections

Preface the prewriting for this assignment by having students consider a TV series they already enjoy.

1. Have students use the chart on page 779 to list the main characters, setting, and plot of a recent episode of the series.

2. Urge students to meet with partners or in small groups to discuss their responses and determine what made that episode enjoyable. Ask: How did it hold the viewers' attention? What were the characters like? How did each scene advance the plot?

3. Ask students to imagine the original proposal for that series. Ask: How do you think the creators "sold" their proposal?

Plan your proposal

Have partners give special attention to the two scenes—the homefront and the battlefront. Partners must include enough details about each setting and the characters in that location for readers to grasp the connection between the scenes.

Connections to
Writer's Notebook

For selection-related prompts, refer to Writer's Notebook.

Connections to
Writer's Resource

For additional writing prompts, refer to Writer's Resource.

STEP 2 DRAFTING
Before you write

Suggest that partners start by volunteering to do the sections that most appeal to them. Remind them to keep in mind when assigning the drafting that some sections will require much more time and effort than others.

As you draft

Make sure students review the Guidelines for Teleplay Format at the top of page 781.

The Student Models

The **transparencies** referenced below are authentic student models. Review them with the students before they draft. These questions will help:

1. Carefully read model 27 for plot development. Notice how the writer has topped one surprise with another.

2. What do you think of the tone of model 28? Is it appropriate for the subject matter? Why or why not?

3. Which model do you prefer and why?

Transparency Collection
Student Models for Writing Workshop 27, 28

- Why will viewers want to watch your episode instead of, say, a situation comedy or a crime drama?
- What is appealing about the characters? What is it about them that viewers will identify with?
- What basic human emotions will your episode appeal to, and how?
- What will it show viewers about the nature of war that they may not have realized before?
- What makes it different from other dramas they've seen about war?

Review your list and circle the three strongest reasons. Try to sell your proposal by emphasizing these points.

Plan your proposal, using your prewriting materials for inspiration. You might use a plan like this one, which takes into account the points in the Writer's Blueprint.

- Cover page (series title, episode title, writer's names)
- Brief plot summary
- Major issues plot will address
- Characters
- Settings
- Scene-by-scene plot outline
- Homefront scene (setting, characters, action)
- Battlefront scene (setting, characters, action)
- Persuasive reasons

STEP 2 DRAFTING

Before you write, review the Writer's Blueprint and plan. Then decide how to divide the drafting responsibilities with your partner.

As you draft, keep in mind that the two scenes you've chosen will be written as teleplays. On the next page are some guidelines and a model to help you.

MINI-LESSON: WRITING STYLE

Using an Appropriate Tone

Teach Ask students to brainstorm a list of different types of tones they have heard used in communication between people. For example: an angry tone, a critical tone, a sincere tone, a businesslike tone, a loving tone, a sarcastic tone.

Activity Idea Ask student volunteers to write a sentence in language that expresses one particular tone. Then have volunteers rewrite that sentence to express a different tone, and so on.

Discuss how the differences in tone might affect the meaning and the way it is heard by the listener.

Apply Remind students to look for the appropriate tone in their own writing. Using an appropriate tone will enhance the effectiveness of the message.

Guidelines for Teleplay Format

- Names of characters and technical directions, such as camera moves and sound effects, are in SMALL CAPITAL LETTERS.

- Other stage directions are in *italic type,* which you can create on a computer. If you're writing by hand, you can underline the stage directions to set them off from the dialogue. (Stage directions within dialogue passages should also be enclosed in parentheses.)

INTERIOR. THE PARLOR. CAMERA FOLLOWS MOM AS SHE ENTERS AND CROSSES TO UNCLE ALBERT.

MOM *(running across the room waving a letter in her hand).* Albert,

it's here. Thomas has written. Oh, I've been waiting for an

eternity!

UNCLE ALBERT *(lying on a cot, buried under wool blankets and an*

intricate homemade quilt). Oh, yes, that's wonderful, Please read

it to me, Anna.

CLOSEUP ON UNCLE ALBERT, WHO MAKES A WEAK ATTEMPT TO SIT UP IN BED, THEN LIES BACK

WITH A SIGH.

STUDENT MODEL

 **STEP 3 REVISING**

Ask another pair of writers for comments on your draft before you revise it. Use this checklist as a guide.

✔ Have we described the main characters, settings, and plot of our episode?

✔ Have we written two scenes, one set at the homefront and one at the battlefront?

✔ Have we given three persuasive reasons why our proposal should be accepted?

✔ Have we addressed our audience, the producer, in an appropriate tone?

Writing Workshop   **781**

STEP 3 REVISING

Ask another pair of writers (Peer assessment)

Remind students that their comments focus on two elements: the teleplay itself and the presentation to the producer. Have students work on the first element for a predetermined period of time (maybe ten minutes) and then announce that it is time to move to the second element.

BUILDING ENGLISH PROFICIENCY

Using Revising Helps

Draw attention to some of the revising questions offered in "Ask another pair of writers. "

- Students may be able to assess the power of their teleplays if they have friends act out the scenes. Videotaping the enactment also can help students look at their work more objectively.

- To choose the best order for their persuasive reasons, students can jot down each reason on a slip of paper. Then they can experiment until they choose the sequence that they find most compelling. Urge students to discuss their persuasive plan with a partner before revising the persuasive part of the proposal.

Revising Strategy: Using an Appropriate Tone

As they review the feature, encourage students to put themselves in the place of a producer who is presented with each of the two models and imagine how this professional would react.

For additional support, see the mini-lesson at the bottom of page 780 and the worksheet referenced below.

Unit 7 Resource Book
Revising Worksheet, p. 85

Connections to
Writer's Resource

Refer to the Grammar, Usage, and Mechanics Handbook on Writer's Resource.

STEP 4 EDITING
Ask another pair of writers (Peer assessment)

Make sure students review the guidelines for a teleplay format given in Step 2 of this lesson.

Revising Strategy

Using an Appropriate Tone

Since you're communicating with another professional, you'll want to establish a confident, businesslike tone. You can accomplish this through your choice of words, details, and sentence structure. What changes in the revised model that follows make it more appropriate than the first version?

FIRST DRAFT

Check out this idea. It's all about a family's money problems while the dad's away at war. We could show how Mom's knocking herself out on the homefront to keep the family going while Dad's knocking himself out to stay alive on the battlefront. Get the contrast? We'd show how bummed he is that he can't help his family and how bummed she is that she can't help him.

REVISED

Our episode contrasts the problems one family faces on the homefront and battlefront. On both fronts they struggle to survive. On the homefront, the mother struggles to provide for her family, while on the battlefront, the father struggles just to survive each day. Our episode focuses on the helpless anguish that the father and mother feel because they can't help one another.

STEP 4 EDITING

Ask another pair of writers to review your revised draft before you edit. When you edit, watch for errors in grammar, usage, spelling, and mechanics. Pay special attention to errors in using the correct form for a teleplay.

MINI-LESSON: GRAMMAR

Using a Consistent Teleplay Format

Review with students the Guidelines for Teleplay Format given in Step 2: Drafting. Then, from the literary selections, choose a prose passage that contains a great deal of dialogue. Write the selection on the board or on a transparency. Have students rewrite the prose in teleplay format. They will use the dialogue as given, but add the names of characters, technical directions, and stage directions.

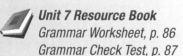
Unit 7 Resource Book
Grammar Worksheet, p. 86
Grammar Check Test, p. 87

Editing Strategy

Using a Consistent Teleplay Format

Check your scenes for consistency when you edit. Notice how the writer of the student model made changes to clear up confusion between screen directions and dialogue.

> ○ MOM (with great relief). Teddy! Where have you been? I've
> been worried sick!
>
> ○ TEDDY. I was delivering groceries and I lost track of the
> time. (Holding out a coin.) But look! (Brightening.) Look
> how much I earned!

STUDENT MODEL

STEP 5 PRESENTING

- Make a videotape or audiotape of your scenes, using classmates as cast members.

- With your partner, do a live presentation of your proposal. Have classmates comment on how persuasive they find it.

COMPUTER TIP
If your school has a computer with multimedia capabilities, you could create a short presentation that includes the text of your screenplay and a video of parts of your scenes, using student actors.

STEP 6 LOOKING BACK

Self-evaluate. Look back at the Writer's Blueprint and give your paper a score on each point, from 6 (superior) to 1 (inadequate).

Reflect. Write your responses to these questions.

✔ Which part did you enjoy writing more: the teleplay or the persuasive appeal to the producer? Why?

✔ What did you learn about the changes that war brings in the daily lives of people involved on the homefront and battlefront?

For Your Working Portfolio Add your proposal and reflection responses to your working portfolio.

Writing Workshop **783**

ASSESSMENT CRITERIA SPECS

Here are the criteria for a superior paper. A full six-level rubric for this paper appears on the Assessment Worksheet referenced below.

6 Superior The writer of a 6 paper impressively meets these criteria:

- Presents a clear, concise, scene-by-scene summary of the plot, which includes settings and characters from the period that are realistic, vivid, and intriguing.

- Fully develops two scenes from this plot in a consistent teleplay format, one set on the battlefront and one on the homefront, with the two scenes clearly linked.

- Presents persuasive reasons why the producer should accept the idea, using a professional tone throughout.

- Makes few, if any, mistakes in grammar, usage, mechanics, and spelling.

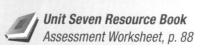
Unit Seven Resource Book
Assessment Worksheet, p. 88

Editing Strategy: Using a Consistent Teleplay Format

Have partners read through the papers one time looking only for consistency of teleplay format.

For additional support, see the mini-lesson at the bottom of page 782 and the worksheets referenced below.

Unit 7 Resource Book
Grammar Worksheet, p. 86
Grammar Check Test, p. 87

Connections to **Writer's Resource**

Refer to the Grammar, Usage, and Mechanics Handbook on Writer's Resource.

STEP 5 PRESENTING
Tape the Episode

Encourage students to bring props if they intend to videotape the episode and to bring any items needed for sound effects if they intend to audiotape it.

STEP 6 LOOKING BACK
Self-evaluate

The *Assessment Criteria Specs* at the bottom of this page are for a superior paper. You might want to post these in the classroom. Students can then evaluate themselves based on these criteria. For a complete scoring rubric, use the *Assessment Worksheet* referenced below.

Unit 7 Resource Book
Assessment Worksheet, p. 88

Reflect

Before students start writing individually, the class might discuss their impressions of changes that war brings in the daily lives of the people involved, based on current TV and news reporting of war-torn areas of the world.

To further explore the theme, use the Fine Art Transparency referenced below.

Transparency Collection
Fine Art Writing Prompt 14

Beyond Print

Teaching Objectives

- to introduce students to criteria for evaluating television news
- to have students consider the issues involved in broadcasting news about war

Curricular Connection: Visual Literacy

Although we base much of our reactions to news stories on the words themselves, we need to learn to "read" and "listen" to the visual clues that can affect our understanding of events. The images we see, the setting of a live report, and the images that are edited out of a story have a persuasive element.

Introduce

Ask students to recall a war report that they saw on the evening news. Have them tell what aspects of war were shown, how the anchor was used, and whether or not they thought the report was objective. Then have students read the article.

War and Aftermath

Media Literacy

Beyond Print

Looking at Television News

One of the reasons World War I made people change their minds about the glory of war is that, before the war, people in general had no way to experience—or even imagine—its horrors. In World War I the technology made news impossibly slow; people in the United States were even more removed from the events. By the time of World War II, radio was able to carry live accounts of many of the most important moments, and movie newsreels could give people an unprecedented visual impression of events.

The most dramatic change in war coverage came with Vietnam. Now the technology allowed nightly battlefield coverage on the national news programs. This unending stream of death and destruction brought in living color to the homes of the United States helped make Vietnam the

This ABC News photo shows a film crew at work in the combat area of Vietnam. ▼

ANOTHER APPROACH

Listening to the News

Have students listen to newscasts on the radio and analyze how they are similar to and different from television newscasts. Then have them draw up a set of criteria to evaluate radio news and use them to evaluate two different "top of the hour" radio newscasts.

You may also wish to have students compare news broadcasts on commercial stations with broadcasts on public radio stations.

Students may also listen to news from the Canadian Broadcasting Company—often aired on public radio in the U.S.—to hear a different perspective on U.S. news. The comparison may help students to analyze biases in news reporting.

most unpopular war in history. Wars can no longer be fought without considering the power of the media. The ability to understand television news is arguably the most important media knowledge you can develop. Here are some criteria to consider.

The Anchor An anchorperson introduces and concludes a newscast and reads much of the news. Anchors are very carefully chosen because they must be able to relay bad news yet still give a sense of confidence; they must appear intelligent without being threateningly intelligent; they must be good-looking without being removed from everyday people.

Production Features Although news is not considered entertainment, it is still produced like a show. Notice how the anchor is dressed, and what impression the set conveys. Notice how news boxes are used to focus attention on images and how graphics help understanding. Notice how music is used to set a tone.

The Story Lineup The stories at the beginning are the most important of the day, while those at the end are "softer." Notice how anchors introduce the stories and how later stories are "teased" through promos at the beginning of the newscast.

Editing All television requires editing. This means that speeches are cut, shots are carefully selected and spliced together, and reporters' words are thoughtfully chosen. Only CSPAN shows uninterrupted feed. Notice how the news is put together, as crafted as a movie.

Commercials News programs need to attract advertising just as other shows do, and newspeople have to consider their audience. Notice the type of ads that are shown on a news program and think about what they tell you about the business side of the news.

Activity Options

1. Work with a partner to tape-record at least two early evening national news programs. Watch them both and compare them in terms of the above criteria.

2. Imagine that you are the producer of a network newscast. The United States is about to send troops to another country to help the government protect itself from rebels. Develop a plan to cover this action, including how many reporters you will send, rules for them to follow, how you will report on the enemy, which U. S. politicians to interview, and what you will or won't show on your news program.

Beyond Print   **785**

Activity Options

Activity 1   As an alternative, you may wish to have students compare a commercial network broadcast with cable news like CNN or public television broadcasts. Students may want to add sensational "tabloid" television news programs to their comparisons.

Activity 2   Before students begin, have them interview local broadcasters to find out what constraints the government puts on news broadcasts during a war.

BUILDING ENGLISH PROFICIENCY

Checking Comprehension

The details in this feature are not difficult to understand, but there are a lot of details to consider. After students have read and discussed the feature, you might have them evaluate their understanding by creating a "pyramid" of details that make an effective television news program. Have students put what they consider to be the least important details on the bottom and the most important at the top. Students can use the following categories:

- helpful, interesting graphics
- "teasing" promos
- good ads
- articulate anchorperson
- thorough reporters

Historical Overview

EXPLORING CONCEPTS

- Social scientists and artists believed that dreams held a key to the subconscious and an understanding of identity.
- The devastation of World War I caused disillusionment and a need to reevaluate both a national and an individual identity in a drastically changed world.

Question Why might a personal identity based on an understanding of the subconscious be more valuable than an identity based on the traditional class system? *(Possible response: An identity based on an understanding of the subconscious would be based on the assumption that all people are equal. Therefore, such an identity comes from within, rather than being imposed from the outside, as in an identity based on a class system.)*

 **Art Study**

Surrealism, a movement in art during the 1920s and 1930s, was to some extent a response to Freud's writing about dreams. Through images representing dreams, nightmares, hallucinations, the Surrealists attempted to express the power of the subconscious in shaping people's identity.

Question What differences are there between the background in the painting and the image reflected in the mirror, and what do those differences suggest? *(Students might note that the background is mostly blue and very natural looking, while the reflection is red and destructive. It may imply a fear of destruction in the future or a fear of looking at ourselves.)*

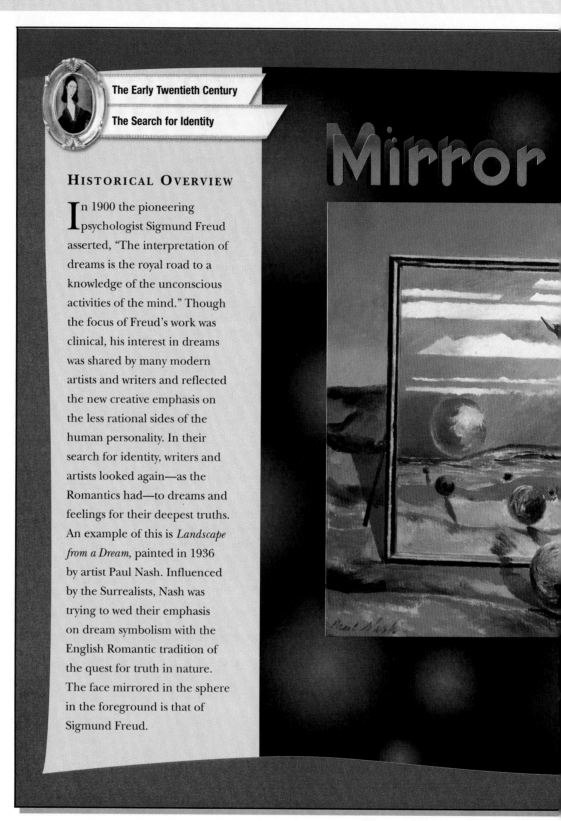

The Early Twentieth Century

The Search for Identity

HISTORICAL OVERVIEW

In 1900 the pioneering psychologist Sigmund Freud asserted, "The interpretation of dreams is the royal road to a knowledge of the unconscious activities of the mind." Though the focus of Freud's work was clinical, his interest in dreams was shared by many modern artists and writers and reflected the new creative emphasis on the less rational sides of the human personality. In their search for identity, writers and artists looked again—as the Romantics had—to dreams and feelings for their deepest truths. An example of this is *Landscape from a Dream,* painted in 1936 by artist Paul Nash. Influenced by the Surrealists, Nash was trying to wed their emphasis on dream symbolism with the English Romantic tradition of the quest for truth in nature. The face mirrored in the sphere in the foreground is that of Sigmund Freud.

Mirror

of Dreams

Key Dates

1879
Ibsen's A Doll's
House *is
produced.*

1900
Freud's The
Interpretation
of Dreams *marks
the beginning of
psychoanalysis.*

1905
*Einstein
announces his
Special Theory
of Relativity.*

1914
*World War I
begins.*

1922
Eliot's The Waste
Land *and Joyce's*
Ulysses *are
published.*

1924
*The Surrealist
movement is
founded.*

787

Key Dates

1906–1930 The Bloomsbury Group—including Virginia Woolf, T. S. Eliot, and E. M. Forster—meet in London.

1921 The Irish Free State gains limited autonomy as a dominion of the British Commonwealth.

1926 The labor unions join the General Strike in support of the mine workers.

1936 George V dies; Edward VIII abdicates the throne to marry American Wallis Warfield Simpson; George VI succeeds to the throne.

1939 Great Britain declares war on Germany.

MATERIALS OF INTEREST
Books

- *The Auden Generation: Literature and Politics in England in the 1930s* by Samuel Hynes (Princeton University Press, 1982).

- *The Bloomsbury Group: A Collection of Memoirs and Commentary,* edited by S. P. Rosenbaum (University of Toronto Press, 1995).

- *W. H. Auden and the Other Oxford Group of Poets by* B. K. Bhattacharya (Advent Books, 1990).

Multimedia

- *James Joyce's Dublin* (Carousel Film & Video).

- *The Dead,* directed by John Huston, based on the short story by James Joyce (Vestron Pictures, 1987).

Connections to
Custom Literature Database

For further historical background, under **Background Articles,** see **Modern England 1915–.**

FOR ALL STUDENTS

- To what extent is an individual's identity based on outside influences?
- How do past experiences shape a present identity?
- What happens when an individual's sense of identity contradicts an expected role?

To further explore the theme, use the transparency noted below.

Transparency Collection
Fine Art Writing Prompt 15

For At-Risk Students

- Ask students to identify a fictional character who has a secret identity.
- How do the two identities create conflict for the character?

For Students Who Need Challenge

Students could read Evelyn Waugh's social and political satires *Scoop* or *Decline and Fall* and report on his interpretation of the British identity in the 1920s and 1930s.

MULTICULTURAL CONNECTION

In every culture, individuality exists in balance with an identity defined by gender, social class, race, creed, and education. This sense of identity is further complicated when one culture dominates another one, particularly if the dominant culture, such as the British, is experiencing its own changes. Ask students to identify the various layers that may have contributed to the identity of an individual in the British Empire.

Part Three

The Search for Identity

Who am I? Through much of history, that question for most people was answered by others—family, community, church, monarch. You didn't think to question your identity because you were told who you were and what your duties were. The freedom and the ability to ask that question, to search for your identity, may be seen by some as a blessing, by others as a curse.

Multicultural Connection **Individuality** may arise either from accepting or rejecting different cultural norms or group standards. It can sometimes be a fragile thing, paradoxically needing confirmation by various groups in order to flourish.

IDEAS THAT WORK

Motivating with Personal Connections

"To make the concept of identity more tangible I will challenge my students to "cube" it: can they describe identity? compare it? associate it? analyze it? apply it? argue for or against it? As the students try to answer these questions, we will consider several modern contexts in which to ask them.

Alternative music is very popular, and identity is *de rigueur*. Ask your students to find songs that relate to the gist of any of the texts in this section.

Bring up the issue of "Generation X." Ask them to consider how their answers to the six questions change when they apply them to this issue.

Stir up some divergent thinking. What do Auden's "The Unknown Citizen" and Generation X have in common? What about an updated variation of the "Unknown Citizen" a la Generation X? How is the identity of women in "Eveline," "A Cup of Tea," and "Shakespeare's Sister" like the identity of women in Generation X?"

Jacinto Jesus Cardona
San Antonio, Texas

Before Reading

Eveline

by James Joyce

James Joyce
1881–1941

In form and content, most of James Joyce's work was controversial, and during his lifetime some of his works were banned, burned, and confiscated. Born in Dublin, the eldest of ten children, Joyce attended a Jesuit boarding school until increasing family poverty forced him to leave. He later attended University College in Dublin. He and Nora Barnacle then lived together in various places—Italy, Switzerland, and, after World War I, in France. His semi-autobiographical work, *A Portrait of the Artist as a Young Man* appeared in 1916. His novels *Ulysses* (1922) and *Finnegans Wake* (1940) greatly influenced the development of the stream-of-consciousness technique, the re-creation of a character's flow of thought.

Building Background

The Center of Paralysis Joyce said that his purpose in writing the short stories collected in *Dubliners* (1914), which includes "Eveline," was to produce "a chapter of the moral history of my country, and I chose Dublin for the scenes because the city seemed to me the center of paralysis." The style of *Dubliners* marks a sharp break with nineteenth-century fiction. Joyce locates the center of the action in the minds of the characters, and plot is not as important as psychological revelation. He also said that he wanted to give "the Irish people . . . one good look at themselves in my nicely polished looking glass."

Literary Focus

Epiphany An **epiphany** (i pif′ə nē) is a moment of enlightenment in which the underlying truth, essential nature, or meaning of something is suddenly made clear. In a mystery story, for example, an epiphany occurs when the detective discovers the identity of a murderer. In other types of stories an epiphany may occur when a character achieves insight into the reasons for his or her feelings or becomes aware of another character's motivations. In a short work, an epiphany may occur at the moment of climax or turning point in the plot. The climax does not always involve an epiphany, however. As you read "Eveline," look for the epiphany.

Writer's Notebook

Setting a Mood Details of **setting** strongly influence the mood of "Eveline." Jot down some words or phrases that describe the setting of your home and that, taken together, would help to describe the general mood or atmosphere of your surroundings. For example, consider what mood the following details would convey when taken together: polished furniture, sagging sofa, thriving plants, old television set, whir of a sewing machine, catcher's mitt on chair, pair of shoes under kitchen table, large dog asleep in the hallway.

Before Reading

Building Background

You might note that Joyce, like many people, held conflicting attitudes about "home." He both loved and reviled his family, city of birth, and country. While all of his works are set in Dublin, Joyce lived, after 1904, outside of Ireland and returned home only twice.

Literary Focus

You might point out that the literary term *epiphany* was coined by Joyce to mean those moments when the real truth of a person or object is revealed. The standard definition is "the manifestations, by gods, of their divinities to mortal eyes."

Writer's Notebook

You might suggest that student descriptions appeal to sight, taste, smell, touch, and hearing.

More About James Joyce

Although Joyce divorced himself from his homeland as well as from the Roman Catholic Church, he drew literary inspiration from his early life in Dublin and from the Jesuit schools he attended. Joyce's career as a novelist was complicated by his near-blindness. He underwent many operations to restore his sight but was forced to wear an eye patch.

Eveline **789**

SUPPORT MATERIALS OVERVIEW

Unit 7 Resource Book
- Graphic Organizer, p. 89
- Study Guide, p. 90
- Vocabulary, p. 91
- Grammar, p. 92
- Alternate Check Test, p. 93
- Vocabulary Test, p. 94
- Selection Test, pp. 95–96

Building English Proficiency
- Selection Summaries
- Activities, p. 255
- "Eveline" in Spanish

Reading, Writing & Grammar SkillBook
- Grammar, Usage, and Mechanics, pp. 243–244

Technology
- Audiotape
- Personal Journal Software
- Test Generator Software

- to explore the theme of searching for identity
- to recognize the literary representation of an epiphany
- to apply conventions of standard usage to semicolons

Unit 7 Resource Book
Graphic Organizer, p. 89
Study Guide, p. 90

Theme Link

The search for identity theme is explored in Eveline's desperate attempt to change her life in the midst of stifling oppression.

1 Literary Element
Mood

Question   What are some words or phrases that the author uses in the first two paragraphs to suggest the mood of this story? *(Possible responses: dusty, tired, clacking along the concrete, crunching on the cinder path, used to play, little Keogh the cripple, blackthorn stick, dead, everything changes)*

2 Active Reading
Summarize

Possible response   The exterior of the house is brown and dull; the interior is dusty with a yellowing photo and a broken harmonium.

Eveline
James Joyce

She sat at the window watching the evening invade the avenue. Her head was leaned against the window curtains and in her nostrils was the odor of dusty cretonne.[1] She was tired.

Few people passed. The man out of the last house passed on his way home; she heard his footsteps clacking along the concrete pavement and afterwards crunching on the cinder path before the new red houses. One time there used to be a field there in which they used to play every evening with other people's children. Then a man from Belfast bought the field and built houses in it—not like their little brown houses but bright brick houses with shining roofs. The children of the avenue used to play together in that field—the Devines, the Waters, the Dunns, little Keogh the cripple, she and her brothers and sisters. Ernest, however, never played: he was too grown up. Her father used often to hunt them in out of the field with his blackthorn stick; but usually little Keogh used to keep nix[2] and call out when he saw her father coming. Still they seemed to have been rather happy then. Her father was not so bad then; and besides, her mother was alive. That was a long time ago; she and her brothers and sisters were all grown up; her mother was dead. Tizzie Dunn was dead, too, and the Waters had gone back to England. Everything changes. Now she was going to go away like the others, to leave her home.

1 Home! She looked round the room, reviewing all its familiar objects which she had dusted once a week for so many years, wondering where on earth all the dust came from. Perhaps she would never see again those familiar objects from which she had never dreamed of being divided. And yet during all those years she had never found out the name of the priest whose yellowing photograph hung on the wall above the broken harmonium beside the colored print of the promises made to Blessed Margaret Mary Alacoque.[3] He had been a school friend of her father. Whenever he showed the photograph to a visitor her father used to pass it with a casual word: "He is in Melbourne now."

SUMMARIZE: What details so far suggest the condition of the home?   **2**

She had consented to go away, to leave her home. Was that wise? She tried to weigh each side of the question. In her home anyway she had shelter and food; she had those whom she had known all her life about her. Of course she had to work hard, both in the house and at business. What would they say of her in the Stores when they found out that she had run away with a fellow? Say she was a fool, perhaps; and her place would be filled up by advertisement. Miss Gavan would be glad. She had always had an edge on her, especially whenever there were people listening.

"Miss Hill, don't you see these ladies are waiting?"

"Look lively, Miss Hill, please."

---

1. **cretonne** (kri ton′), *n.* a strong cotton, linen, or rayon cloth with designs printed in colors.
2. **nix** (niks), *n.* watch. *[slang]*
3. **Blessed . . . Alacoque** (1647–1690), a French nun who experienced visions of Jesus.

Does the use of color in Spencer Gore's painting *Woman in a Flowered Hat* (about 1907) convey an impression of warmth or coolness?

SELECTION SUMMARY

Eveline

Eveline, a young Irish woman, sits by her window and thinks back to her childhood and to the children with whom she once played. She remembers her deceased mother and thinks of her siblings who are now grown; she is the only one who remains at home. Eveline has decided to leave home to explore a new life in Buenos Aires with Frank, a sailor, whom she intends to marry. Her father, who disapproves of the match, has forbidden them to speak, but they continue to meet in secret. As she sits by the window, her dilemma emerges. She thinks her father will miss her and fondly recalls the good times. If she stays at home, she knows her life will be like her mother's and in a moment of terror believes that Frank is her only hope. As she stands by the ship that she and Frank are to sail on, she prays for direction and discovers in this final moment that she cannot go away.

For summaries in other languages, see the Building English Proficiency book.

Eveline **791**

Response to Caption Question Most students will respond that the painting conveys an impression of coolness.

Visual Literacy The young lady, who seems very self-contained and alone, appears to exist in an interior world of black and grays; only the flowers on her hat suggest the light and colors of the outside world, but these flowers are not real. She is composed of circles and curves, while the background, particularly the window, is all verticals and horizontals. She is ready for the outside world, but can she go out?

Questions What does the contrast between interior and exterior colors suggest? *(Possible response: that her life is colorless, dreary)* What might the verticals and horizontals of the window suggest? *(Possible response: bars, like the bars of a jail)* If the window suggests jail bars, what is the artist suggesting about the life of this woman who is "ready" to go out? *(She may be ready, but for whatever reason, she is barred from the light and color of the outside world, as well as from companionship [suggested by the figure of the man].)* You might ask students to brainstrom story lines that explain why she is "barred" from a fuller life (e.g., she is a maid or an only child who cares for an elderly parent).

BUILDING ENGLISH PROFICIENCY

Analyzing Reasons

Help students focus on the decision Eveline is reconsidering.

1. Have groups of students share cultural attitudes and their own ideas about living at home as adults. Ask: What conflict is going on in Eveline's mind? When is the "right" time to leave home?

2. Suggest that each group begin a T-chart listing Eveline's reasons for staying home and for leaving.

 Building English Proficiency
Activities, p. 255
"Eveline" in Spanish

Reasons for Staying	Reasons for Leaving
has shelter and food	everyone else has left
knows everyone	has to work hard
has happy memories	scolded often by Miss Gavan

Draw Conclusions

Questions Based on what you know about Eveline, do you think she will do better if she moves to another country? *(Possible responses: Yes, she will be away from her domineering father and oppressive upbringing; no, she'll be completely lost in a foreign country.)*

4 Geographical Note

Patagonia

Patagonia is a vast semiarid plateau—mainly in Argentina—in the southern part of South America. It is approximately 260,000 square miles in extent and is bordered by the Rio Colorado to the north and the Straits of Magellan to the south. Sparsely settled, it is basically a cattle-and sheep-raising region with petroleum as its chief natural resource.

She would not cry many tears at leaving the Stores.

But in her new home, in a distant unknown country, it would not be like that. Then she would be married—she, Eveline. People would treat her with respect then. She would not be treated as her mother had been. Even now, though she was over nineteen, she sometimes felt herself in danger of her father's violence. She knew it was that that had given her the palpitations.[4] When they were growing up he had never gone for her, like he used to go for Harry and Ernest, because she was a girl; but latterly he had begun to threaten her and say what he would do to her only for her dead mother's sake. And now she had nobody to protect her. Ernest was dead and Harry, who was in the church decorating business, was nearly always down somewhere in the country. Besides, the invariable squabble for money on Saturday nights had begun to weary her unspeakably. She always gave her entire wages—seven shillings—and Harry always sent up what he could but the trouble was to get any money from her father. He said she used to squander the money, that she had no head, that he wasn't going to give her his hard-earned money to throw about the streets, and much more, for he was usually fairly bad on Saturday night. In the end he would give her the money and ask her had she any intention of buying Sunday's dinner. Then she had to rush out as quickly as she could and do her marketing, holding her black leather purse tightly in her hand as she elbowed her way through the crowds and returning home late under her load of provisions. She had hard work to keep the house together and to see that the two young children

She was about to explore another life with Frank.

who had been left to her charge went to school regularly and got their meals regularly. It was hard work—a hard life—but now that she was about to leave it she did not find it a wholly undesirable life. **3**

She was about to explore another life with Frank. Frank was very kind, manly, open-hearted. She was to go away with him by the night boat to be his wife and to live with him in Buenos Aires where he had a home waiting for her. How well she remembered the first time she had seen him; he was lodging in a house on the main road where she used to visit. It seemed a few weeks ago. He was standing at the gate, his peaked cap pushed back on his head and his hair tumbled forward over a face of bronze. Then they had come to know each other. He used to meet her outside the Stores every evening and see her home. He took her to see *The Bohemian Girl*[5] and she felt elated as she sat in an unaccustomed part of the theater with him. He was awfully fond of music and sang a little. People knew that they were courting and, when he sang about the lass that loves a sailor, she always felt pleasantly confused. He used to call her Poppens out of fun. First of all it had been an excitement for her to have a fellow and then she had begun to like him. He had tales of distant countries. He had started as a deck boy at a pound a month on a ship of the Allan Line going out to Canada. He told her the names of the ships he had been on and the names of the different services. He had sailed through the Straits of Magellan and he told her stories of the terrible Patagonians.[6] He had fallen on his feet in Buenos Aires, he said, and had come over to the old country just for a holiday. Of course, her father had found out the affair and had forbidden her to have anything to say to him. **4**

---

4. **palpitation** (pal′pə tā′shən), *n.* a very rapid beating of the heart.
5. *The Bohemian Girl,* an opera by the Irish-born composer Michael Balfe (1808–1870).
6. **Patagonians,** people living in Patagonia in the extreme south of South America.

MINI-LESSON: GRAMMAR

Using Semicolons

Teach Teach students these uses for semicolons:

- Use a semicolon to join independent clauses when coordinating conjunctions such as *and, or,* or *but* are not used.

- In a compound sentence, it is preferable to use semicolons when the two independent clauses express closely related ideas. (Some authors' style is to use semicolons even if the independent clauses are *not* closely related.)

- In a series of phrases, normally connected by commas, there are sometimes commas used for other reasons; to avoid confusion, use semicolons rather than commas to connect the items in the series.

Apply Have students point out semicolons in the selection. Ask students why the author chose to separate the independent clauses by a semicolon rather than a period.

Activity Idea Have students use semicolons in a few paragraphs that compare and contrast their lives today with the way they were a few years ago. They should proofread to see if they have correctly used semicolons to join independent clauses that express closely related ideas.

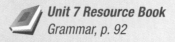

Unit 7 Resource Book
Grammar, p. 92

CLARIFY: Why might Eveline have been attracted to Frank?

"I know these sailor chaps," he said.

One day he had quarreled with Frank and after that she had to meet her lover secretly.

The evening deepened in the avenue. The white of two letters in her lap grew indistinct. One was to Harry; the other was to her father. Ernest had been her favorite but she liked Harry too. Her father was becoming old lately, she noticed; he would miss her. Sometimes he could be very nice. Not long before, when she had been laid up for a day, he had read her out a ghost story and made toast for her at the fire. Another day, when their mother was alive, they had all gone for a picnic to the Hill of Howth. She remembered her father putting on her mother's bonnet to make the children laugh.

Her time was running out but she continued to sit by the window, leaning her head against the window curtain, inhaling the odor of dusty cretonne. Down far in the avenue she could hear a street organ playing. She knew the air. Strange that it should come that very night to remind her of the promise to her mother, her promise to keep the home together as long as she could. She remembered the last night of her mother's illness; she was again in the close dark room at the other side of the hall and outside she heard a melancholy air of Italy. The organ player had been ordered to go away and given sixpence. She remembered her father strutting back into the sickroom saying: "Damned Italians! coming over here!"

As she mused the pitiful vision of her mother's life laid its spell on the very quick of her being—that life of commonplace sacrifices closing in final craziness. She trembled as she heard again her mother's voice saying constantly with foolish insistence: "Derevaun Seraun! Derevaun Seraun!"[7]

She stood up in a sudden impulse of terror.

Escape! She must escape! Frank would save her. He would give her life, perhaps love, too. But she wanted to live. Why should she be unhappy? She had a right to happiness. Frank would take her in his arms, fold her in his arms. He would save her.

She stood among the swaying crowd in the station at the North Wall. He held her hand and she knew that he was speaking to her, saying something about the passage over and over again. The station was full of soldiers with brown baggages. Through the wide doors of the sheds she caught a glimpse of the black mass of the boat, lying in beside the quay wall, with illumined portholes. She answered nothing. She felt her cheek pale and cold and, out of a maze of distress, she prayed to God to direct her, to show her what was her duty. The boat blew a long mournful whistle into the mist. If she went, tomorrow she would be on the sea with Frank, steaming toward Buenos Aires. Their passage had been booked. Could she still draw back after all he had done for her? Her distress awoke a nausea in her body and she kept moving her lips in silent fervent prayer.

A bell clanged upon her heart. She felt him seize her hand:

"Come!"

All the seas of the world tumbled about her heart. He was drawing her into them: he would drown her. She gripped with both hands at the iron railing.

"Come!"

No! No! No! It was impossible. Her hand clutched the iron in frenzy. Amid the seas she sent a cry of anguish.

"Eveline! Evvy!"

He rushed beyond the barrier and called to her to follow. He was shouted at to go on but he still called to her. She set her white face to him, passive, like a helpless animal. Her eyes gave him no sign of love or farewell or recognition.

---

7. **"Derevaun Seraun,"** possibly, corrupt Gaelic (the original language of the Irish) for "the end of pleasure is pain."

Eveline **793**

BUILDING ENGLISH PROFICIENCY

Exploring Key Statements

One or both of the following activities will help students relate to this statement in column 2, page 792: "She was about to explore another life with Frank."

Activity Ideas

• Have pairs of students role-play a phone call between Eveline and her best friend (or Eveline and Harry). Eveline calls to say she is leaving, and the friend or Harry gives her good advice.

• Have students imagine Eveline's life if she had left home. Ask: What might have happened in Buenos Aires? Invite students to write a letter from Eveline to her father, brother, or best friend, telling about her life there.

---

5 Active Reading

Clarify

Possible Response Students may say that he represents a worldliness and a sophistication that is foreign to her. Frank tells her about his travels, introduces her to opera, and gives her the attention that she craves.

6 Literary Element

Imagery

Questions Point out that the imagery describes Eveline's emotional turmoil. What images convey Eveline's distress? Why are they so powerful? *(The image of the tumbling sea and the ship's bell clanging upon her heart evoke the emotions of a disturbed woman with a terrible dilemma, a picture all the more powerful because it derives from the huge and unknown sea that she is not prepared to cross.)*

7 Literary Focus

Epiphany

Question What is the epiphany of "Eveline"? *(Possible response: The moment when she [and the reader] knows the truth about herself is when she thinks, "No! No! No!")*

Check Test

1. What is Eveline doing at the beginning? *(sitting by a window thinking about her childhood)*

2. What memories does she recall? *(memories of her deceased mother and her grown siblings)*

3. With whom does Eveline live now? *(her father)*

4. What has Eveline decided to do? *(leave the country and marry)*

5. Why does Eveline choose not to go with Frank in the end? *(She realizes that she can't leave her family and what is familiar.)*

Unit 7 Resource Book
Alternate Check Test, p. 93

MAKING CONNECTIONS

1. Possible responses: Some may say they were surprised that Eveline did not go with Frank because this was her only chance to break away from her oppressive home life. Others may say that it was too difficult for Eveline to start a new life, that staying in a bad situation sometimes feels safer than venturing into the unknown.

2. Possible response: Yes. Eveline has given her life over to her family who do not appreciate and value her, but her fear of the unknown is worthy of sympathy.

3. Possible response: The mood is somber as Eveline recalls memories of happier times. The word *swaying* evokes slow motion. Although she is aware of movement, it is secondary to her inner turmoil.

4. Possible response: If the point of view were omniscient, the thoughts and feelings of all characters would be known. By using a limited point of view, the author creates a more personal connection between Eveline and the reader.

5. Possible response: She seems paralyzed. If she were to show emotion, she might lose the control she desperately needs to maintain.

6. Possible response: No, because she has never been allowed to express herself. People need love and support from those closest to them. If a person is encouraged to share feelings and feels valued, then he or she has a better chance of trusting him- or herself and others.

7. The story suggests that Irish culture discouraged individuality and self-expression, particularly for women.

After Reading

Making Connections

Shaping Your Response	**1.** Were you surprised at the ending?
	2. Are you sympathetic to Eveline? Explain.
Analyzing the Story	**3.** What **mood** is established in the first three paragraphs? What is the mood in the paragraph beginning "She stood among the swaying crowd . . ."?
	4. How might this story have changed if it had been told from an omniscient rather than a limited **point of view?**
	5. What do you suppose causes Eveline to send Frank away without a "sign of love or farewell or recognition"?
Extending the Ideas	**6.** American author Ralph Waldo Emerson wrote, "Trust thyself: every heart vibrates to that iron string." Does Eveline trust herself? What do you think are some things that have to happen before a person can trust herself or himself?
	7. 👣 What does this story tell you about how much the culture Joyce writes about prizes **individuality?**

Literary Focus: Epiphany

When the underlying truth, essential nature, or meaning of something is suddenly made clear in a literary work, this moment is called an **epiphany.**

1. Where does the epiphany occur in "Eveline"?

2. Who or what is responsible for Eveline's final decision?

LITERARY FOCUS: EPIPHANY

Possible Responses

1. At the end when the author writes, "No! No! No! It was impossible." It is here that Eveline and the reader knows she is not able to leave.

2. She is responsible for her final decision, but she bases that decision on her sense of duty and her promise to her mother not to break up the home.

Expressing Your Ideas

Writing Choices

Writer's Notebook Update Combine some of the words or phrases that describe the setting of your home into a single paragraph. Ask a partner to identify the mood you have created.

Eveline's Role How much do expectations about women and women's roles in Eveline's culture influence her life and her actions? Write an **essay** analyzing this question. Consider her relationships with her mother, father, and brothers, and her childhood and work.

On the Aisle "The Dead," a long story by Joyce from *Dubliners,* was made into a 1987 move directed by John Huston and starring Anjelica Houston, Rachel Dowling, and Dan O'Herlihy. View and write a **review** of the film.

Other Options

No Sign of Love Create an **illustration** for this story. Since there is little action, how will you depict the mood or atmosphere or Eveline's psychological state? Will you illustrate the setting? Will you show other characters mentioned in the story? Think about what technique or colors might be suitable before beginning your work.

Research Nations as well as individuals seek identity, and Ireland is no exception. Joyce's story, which tells in part about a search for identity, was published in 1914, just two years before the Easter uprising in Dublin in 1916. Research this historic event, including reasons for the uprising and the results, and give an **oral report** to the class.

In Performance John Millington Synge (1871–1909), an Irish playwright, was one of the founders of the famous Abbey Theatre, which opened in Dublin in 1904. His one-act play "Riders to the Sea" takes place on an island off the west coast of Ireland. Read this short play for another glimpse of Irish life and, with one or more partners, choose and **perform a section** from it for the class.

WRITING CHOICES
Writer's Notebook Update

Invite students to share their descriptions of their homes with the class. Ask volunteers to identify the mood created by their descriptions.

Eveline's Role

You might lead a discussion on why women living in the latter part of the twentieth century have so many more options than those who lived in the early part of this century.

On the Aisle

The film, *The Dead,* is available on videocassette. Discuss with students their reviews of the film and encourage them to share their opinions of Irish society in the early part of the twentieth century.

Selection Test

Unit 7 Resource Book
pp. 95–96

OTHER OPTIONS
No Sign of Love

Arrange to have an exhibition in the classroom of the students' art work. Organize a class discussion and talk about the feelings that are evoked by the different illustrations.

Research

Students might also focus on some of the prominent figures of the Easter Uprising, like Michael Collins of the Irish Republican Brotherhood and Eamon de Valera, who eventually became prime minister.

In Performance

Sean O'Casey is a playwright whose plays also focus on the Irish struggle for independence from the British. You might also choose a scene to read aloud from O'Casey's *Shadow of a Gunman* or *Juno and the Paycock* so that students may develop a sense of Irish diction and dialect.

Building Background

You might ask students to discuss the following questions: Why might people of different social classes find it awkward to socialize? Are there social classes in the United States? If so, how binding are they?

Literary Focus

Point out that stereotypes originate in a society's preconceptions. Ask students for examples of words that stereotype people (e.g., *jock, nerd, bum, bimbo*). Ask what traits tend to be associated with each word.

Writer's Notebook

You might suggest that good writers are "students of human nature" who can determine a great deal by simply observing people. Ask what clothing and personal appearance can reveal about background, personality, or state of mind.

More About Katherine Mansfield

Although from a wealthy family, Mansfield spent her childhood in rural New Zealand, where she attended school with children from humble backgrounds. The adult Mansfield often struggled to make a living. Her empathy with the poor is apparent in such stories as "The Doll's House" and "Life of Ma Parker."

Before Reading

A Cup of Tea

by Katherine Mansfield

Katherine Mansfield
1888–1923

Katherine Mansfield was born in New Zealand and educated, along with her sisters, in London. Although she studied at the Royal Academy of Music, she soon realized that writing was her true calling. Her life was somewhat unconventional for the times in which she lived, and her several affairs embarrassed her family and resulted in her mother cutting Mansfield from her will. Soon after her marriage in 1918 to John Middleton Murry, a literary critic and editor, she became a virtual invalid from tuberculosis, and she died in France in 1923. Her stories depend more on atmosphere, character, and effects of language than on plot and can be found in *Collected Stories of Katherine Mansfield.*

Building Background

"Ah! but to write better!" Katherine Mansfield's journals include accounts of her daily life, the weather, and her feelings. They also show how she longed to be better at her craft:

"Jan. 2, 1922. I have not done the work I should have done. I shirk the lunch party [a part of the story 'The Dove's Nest']. This is very bad. In fact I am disgusted with myself. There must be a change from now on.

"Jan. 7. It ceased snowing, and a deep, almost gentian blue sky showed. The snow lay heaped on the trees, big blobs of snow like whipped cream . . . I wrote at my story, but did not finish the lunch party as I ought have to [sic] done. How very bad this is!

"Jan. 10. Dreamed I was back in New Zealand . . .

"Jan. 11. In bed again. Heard from Pinker *The Dial* had taken "The Doll's House." Wrote and finished "A Cup of Tea." It took about 4–5 hours . . . There is no feeling to be compared with the feeling of having written and finished a story.

"Jan. 12. I don't feel so sinful this day as I did, because I have written something and the tide is still high . . . Ah! but to write better! Let me write better, more deeply, more largely. Baleful icicles hang in a frieze outside our window pane. . . ."

Literary Focus

Stereotype A **stereotype** is a conventional character, plot, or setting that has little or no individuality. Stereotypical characters are based on fixed, generalized ideas about people or groups of people. An author may use a stereotype as background for a main character or as a contrast to that character. As you read "A Cup of Tea," decide which character if any seems to be a stereotype.

Writer's Notebook

Making It Up As You Go Think of someone you don't know but have seen—perhaps on a bus, at a mall, or at a sporting event. Jot down some ideas for a story involving that person.

796 UNIT SEVEN: THE EARLY TWENTIETH CENTURY

SUPPORT MATERIALS OVERVIEW

Unit 7 Resource Book
- Graphic Organizer, p. 97
- Study Guide, p. 98
- Vocabulary, p. 99
- Grammar, p. 100
- Alternate Check Test, p. 101
- Vocabulary Test, p. 102
- Selection Test, pp. 103–104

Building English Proficiency
- Selection Summaries
- Activities, p. 256

Reading, Writing & Grammar SkillBook
- Vocabulary, pp. 13–14
- Grammar, Usage, and Mechanics, pp. 149–152

Technology
- Audiotape
- Personal Journal Software
- Test Generator Software

A Cup of Tea

BY KATHERINE MANSFIELD

 In what ways does the young woman in William McGregor Paxson's painting *Pretty Girl* (1926) resemble Rosemary Fell?

ROSEMARY FELL was not exactly beautiful. No, you couldn't have called her beautiful. Pretty? Well, if you took her to pieces . . . But why be so cruel as to take anyone to pieces? She was young, brilliant, extremely modern, exquisitely[1] well dressed, amazingly well read in the newest of the new books, and her parties were the most delicious mixture of the really important people and . . . artists—quaint creatures, discoveries of hers, some of them too terrifying for words, but others quite presentable and amusing.

Rosemary had been married two years. She had a duck[2] of a boy. No, not Peter—Michael.

---

1. exquisitely (ek′skwi zit lē), *adv.* beautifully; admirably.
2. **duck,** a term of endearment. *[slang]*

A Cup of Tea   **797**

During Reading

Selection Objectives

- to understand origins of stereotypes and their role in literature
- to analyze an egocentric character
- to use context clues to determine meaning and connotation of vocabulary words

 *Unit 7 Resource Book*
Graphic Organizer, p. 97
Study Guide, p. 98

Theme Link

The search for identity theme is developed as Rosemary embraces a new role, benefactor to the poor, until an essential part of her identity—her sense of superiority—is threatened.

Vocabulary Preview

exquisitely, beautifully; admirably

glaze, smooth, glossy coating

cherub, an angel in the form of a child with wings

discreet, careful and sensible; proper

ply, supply with in a pressing manner

languor, lack or energy; weariness

listless, seeming too tired to care about anything

vile, very bad

ghastly, very bad

exotic, from a foreign country; strange or different

Students can add the words and definitions to their Writer's Notebooks.

Art Study

Response to Caption Question
Students might respond that the subject of the painting is, like Rosemary Fell, young, brilliant, modern, and exquisitely dressed. Unlike Rosemary, the subject of the painting is pretty.

SELECTION SUMMARY

A Cup of Tea

In this short story, a wealthy, shallow, and spoiled woman named Rosemary is returning from a shopping trip when a destitute young woman asks her for the price of a cup of tea. For Rosemary, the woman's desperation is romantic, "like something out of a novel by Dostoevski." Intrigued by the image of herself as savior, Rosemary invites the woman home. But when Rosemary's husband arrives and remarks to Rosemary that the woman is "astonishingly pretty," Rosemary's interest in her charitable adventure quickly dissolves. She sends the woman on her way.

 *For summaries in other languages, see the **Building English Proficiency** book.*

1

Literary Element

Diction

You might note to the class that, while Rosemary is not the narrator, the narrator uses words and expressions that mimic the way Rosemary thinks and speaks.

Question What are examples of "Rosemary diction" in the first two paragraphs? *(Possible responses: "newest of the new"; "most delicious mixture"; "really important people"; "quaint creaures"; "too terrifying for words"; "quite presentable and amusing"; "duck of a boy"; "rich, really rich"; "odious and stuffy and sounds like one's grandparents")*

Literary Criticism

Miss Mansfield had no affection for the modern metropolitan young woman. Almost without exception the young women she presents are callous, temperamental, selfish, and unreasonable. They demand the servile, undeviating attention of their men; their hypersensitive nerves cannot endure the slightest strain.

Sylvia Berkman
Katherine Mansfield: A Critical Style

And her husband absolutely adored her. They were rich, really rich, not just comfortably well off, which is odious[3] and stuffy and sounds like one's grandparents. But if Rosemary wanted to shop she would go to Paris as you and I would go to Bond Street.[4] If she wanted to buy flowers, the car pulled up at that perfect shop in Regent Street, and Rosemary inside the shop just gazed in her dazzled rather exotic way, and said: "I want those and those and those. Give me four bunches of those. And that jar of roses. Yes. I'll have all the roses in the jar. No, no lilac. I hate lilac. It's got no shape." The attendant bowed and put the lilac out of sight, as though this was only too true; lilac was dreadfully shapeless. "Give me those stumpy little tulips. Those red and white ones." And she was followed to the car by a thin shopgirl staggering under an immense white paper armful that looked like a baby in long clothes. . . .

1

One winter afternoon she had been buying something in a little antique shop in Curzon Street. It was a shop she liked. For one thing, one usually had it to oneself. And then the man who kept it was ridiculously fond of serving her. He beamed whenever she came in. He clasped his hands; he was so gratified he could scarcely speak. Flattery, of course. All the same, there was something . . .

"You see, madam," he would explain in his low respectful tones, "I love my things. I would rather not part with them than sell them to someone who does not appreciate them, who has not that fine feeling which is so rare. . . ." And, breathing deeply, he unrolled a tiny square of blue velvet and pressed it on the glass counter with his pale finger-tips.

Today it was a little box. He had been keeping it for her. He had shown it to nobody as yet. An exquisite little enamel box with a glaze[5] so fine it looked as though it had been baked in cream. On the lid a minute creature stood under a flowery tree, and a more minute creature still had her arms around his neck. Her hat, really no bigger than a geranium petal, hung

from a branch; it had green ribbons. And there was a pink cloud like a watchful cherub[6] floating above their heads. Rosemary took her hands out of her long gloves. She always took off her gloves to examine such things. Yes, she liked it very much. She loved it; it was a great duck. She must have it. And, turning the creamy box, opening and shutting it, she couldn't help noticing how charming her hands were against the blue velvet. The shopman, in some dim cavern of his mind, may have dared to think so too. For he took a pencil, leaned over the counter, and his pale bloodless fingers crept timidly towards those rosy, flashing ones, as he murmured gently: "If I may venture to point out to madam, the flowers on the little lady's bodice."

"Charming!" Rosemary admired the flowers. But what was the price? For a moment the shopman did not seem to hear. Then a murmur reached her.

"Twenty-eight guineas, madame."

"Twenty-eight guineas." Rosemary gave no sign. She laid the little box down: she buttoned her gloves again. Twenty-eight guineas. Even if one is rich . . . She looked vague. She stared at a plump tea-kettle like a plump hen above the shopman's head, and her voice was dreamy as she answered: "Well, keep it for me—will you? I'll . . ."

But the shopman had already bowed as though keeping it for her was all any human being could ask. He would be willing, of course, to keep it for her for ever.

The discreet[7] door shut with a click. She was outside on the step, gazing at the winter afternoon. Rain was falling, and with the rain it

---

3. **odious** (ō′dē əs), *adj.* hateful; offensive.
4. **Bond Street.** Like Regent Street (mentioned later), Bond Street is in an elegant shopping area in London.
5. glaze (glāz), *n.* smooth, glossy coating.
6. cherub (cher′əb), *n.* here, an angel in the form of a child with wings.
7. discreet (dis krēt′), *adj.* careful and sensible; proper.

MINI-LESSON: GRAMMAR

Recognizing Phrases

Teach Remind students that, while it is important to use complete sentences in most formal writing, in creative writing authors often use phrases to imitate spontaneous human speech. Ask students to identify the sentence and the phrase in the following passage from page 798.

(1) He had shown it to nobody as yet. (2) An exquisite little enamel box with a glaze so fine it looked as though it had been baked in cream. *(Item 1 is a sentence; item 2 is a phrase.)*

A complete sentence must contain a subject and a predicate and express a complete thought. (To help students see that *it looked as though it had been baked in cream* is not an independent clause, add the understood conjunction *that* before it.) Ask students how they could make

item 2 into a sentence. *(Put the phrase It was at the beginning.)*

Activity Ideas

- Have students work in small groups to find other incomplete sentences in the story and turn them into complete sentences.
- Have students write a paragraph of narration or a brief dialogue with both complete and incomplete sentences to capture the rhythms of speech. Ask them to underline the incomplete sentences.

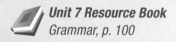

Unit 7 Resource Book
Grammar, p. 100

seemed the dark came too, spinning down like ashes. There was a cold bitter taste in the air, and the new-lighted lamps looked sad. Sad were the lights in the houses opposite. Dimly they burned as if regretting something. And people hurried by, hidden under their hateful umbrellas. Rosemary felt a strange pang. She pressed her muff to her breast; she wished she had the little box, too, to cling to. Of course, the car was there. She'd only to cross the pavement. But still she waited. There are moments, horrible moments in life, when one emerges from shelter and looks out, and it's awful. One oughtn't to give way to them. One ought to go home and have an extra-special tea. But at the very instant of thinking that, a young girl, thin, dark, shadowy—where had she come from?—was standing at Rosemary's elbow and a voice like a sigh, almost like a sob, breathed: "Madame, may I speak to you a moment?"

"Speak to me?" Rosemary turned. She saw a little battered creature with enormous eyes, someone quite young, no older than herself, who clutched at her coat-collar with reddened hands, and shivered as though she had just come out of the water.

"M-madam," stammered the voice. "Would you let me have the price of a cup of tea?"

"A cup of tea?" There was something simple, sincere in that voice; it wasn't in the least the voice of a beggar. "Then have you no money at all?" asked Rosemary.

"None, madam," came the answer.

"How extraordinary!" Rosemary peered through the dusk, and the girl gazed back at her. How more than ordinary! And suddenly it seemed to Rosemary such an adventure. It was like something out of a novel by Dostoevski,[8] this meeting in the dusk. Supposing she took the girl home? Supposing she did do one of

Supposing she did do one of those things she was always reading about or seeing on the stage . . . ?

those things she was always reading about or seeing on the stage, what would happen? It would be thrilling. And she heard herself saying afterwards to the amazement of her friends: "I simply took her home with me," as she stepped forward and said to that dim person beside her: "Come home to tea with me."

The girl drew back startled. She even stopped shivering for a moment. Rosemary put out a hand and touched her arm. "I mean it," she said, smiling. And she felt how simple and kind her smile was. "Why won't you? Do. Come home with me now in my car and have tea."

"You—you don't mean it, madam," said the girl, and there was pain in her voice.

"But I do," cried Rosemary. "I want you to. To please me. Come along."

The girl put her fingers to her lips and her eyes devoured Rosemary. "You're—you're not taking me to the police station?" she stammered.

"The police station!" Rosemary laughed out. "Why should I be so cruel? No, I only want to make you warm and to hear—anything you care to tell me."

Hungry people are easily led. The footman held the door of the car open, and a moment later they were skimming through the dusk.

"There!" said Rosemary. She had a feeling of triumph as she slipped her hand through the velvet strap. She could have said, "Now I've got you," as she gazed at the little captive she had netted. But of course she meant it kindly. Oh, more than kindly. She was going to prove to this

---

8. **Dostoevski** (dos′tə yef′ skē), Feodor (1821–1881), Russian novelist. (See from *Crime and Punishment* on page 194.)

---

2 Reading/Thinking Skills

Find the Main Idea

You might point out to students that this passage operates on two levels of meaning, one literal and one symbolic.

Question What does the phrase "one emerges from shelter and looks out, and it's awful" mean literally? symbolically? *(Possible response: Literally, the "shelter" she has emerged from is the store and what is "awful" is the dark, damp weather; symbolically, what is "awful" is her occasional glimpse of reality, from which she is usually "sheltered" by wealth.)*

---

3 Literary Focus

Stereotype

You might point out to students that the girl reminds Rosemary of a general type of character she has come across in stories and plays—in other words, Rosemary sees her as a stereotype.

Questions What stereotype does the girl seem to fit, in most respects? *(Possible response: a beggar or pauper, such as the kind that often appears in fairy tales and other children's stories)* Which details reinforce this stereotype? *(She looks thin, cold, and bedraggled; she asks for money; she behaves meekly.)*

BUILDING ENGLISH PROFICIENCY

Exploring Symbols

Help students understand Mansfield's use of symbols.

1. Show pictures of any traditional symbols that you can find easily—for example, a lamb, lion, dove, peace sign, crown, or rainbow. Ask volunteers what each one represents; elicit that a symbol stands for or suggests something beyond itself.

2. Explain that some symbols mean the same thing to many people, but other symbols may be invented by writers to suggest several meanings. In this story, for instance, winter is a traditional symbol for death. The little box is Mansfield's symbol for Rosemary's expensive, empty life.

3. Ask students to think of some things that have symbolic meaning to them (such as an old teddy bear, a "lucky" shirt, a first car, or a diploma). Have them draw the symbol and write a sentence that explains what it means.

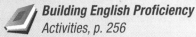
Building English Proficiency Activities, p. 256

Irony

Question   What is ironic about Rosemary congratulating herself on being natural? *(Possible responses: She congratulates herself on being simple, while the reader sees that her behavior is perfectly unnatural for her.)*

Evaluate

Possible response   The reader learns that Rosemary lacks the imagination and sensitivity to perceive why the girl doesn't help; Rosemary's response is typical, "People need to learn to help themselves."

---

girl that—wonderful things did happen in life, that—fairy god-mothers were real, that—rich people had hearts, and that women *were* sisters. She turned impulsively, saying: "Don't be frightened. After all, why should-n't you come back with me? We're both women. If I'm the more for-tunate, you ought to expect . . ."

But happily at that moment, for she didn't know how the sen-tence was going to end, the car stopped. The bell was rung, the door opened, and with a charm-ing, protecting, almost embrac-ing movement, Rosemary drew the other into the hall. Warmth, softness, light, a sweet scent, all those things so familiar to her she never even thought about them, she watched that other receive. It was fascinating. She was like the little rich girl in her nursery with all the cupboards to open, all the boxes to unpack.

"Come, come upstairs," said Rosemary, long-ing to begin to be generous. "Come up to my room." And, besides, she wanted to spare this poor little thing from being stared at by the servants; she decided as they mounted the stairs she would not even ring for Jeanne, but take off her things by herself. The great thing was to be natural!

And "There!" cried Rosemary again, as they reached her beautiful big bedroom with the curtains drawn, the fire leaping on her wonder-ful lacquer furniture, her gold cushions and the primrose and blue rugs.

The girl stood just inside the door; she seemed dazed. But Rosemary didn't mind that.

"Come and sit down," she cried, dragging her big chair up to the fire, "in this comfy chair. Come and get warm. You look so dread-fully cold."

"I daren't, madam," said the girl, and she edged backwards.

"Oh, please,"—Rosemary ran forward—"you mustn't be frightened, you mustn't, really. Sit

To be quite sincere, she looked rather stupid. But Rosemary wouldn't acknowledge it.

down, and when I've taken off my things we shall go into the next room and have tea and be cosy. Why are you afraid?" And gently she half pushed the thin figure into its deep cradle.

But there was no answer. The girl stayed just as she had been put, with her hands by her sides and her mouth slightly open. To be quite sincere, she looked rather stupid. But Rosemary wouldn't acknowledge it. She leaned over her, saying: "Won't you take off your hat? Your pretty hair is all wet. And one is so much more comfortable without a hat, isn't one?"

There was a whisper that sounded like "Very good, madam," and the crushed hat was taken off.

"Let me help you off with your coat, too," said Rosemary.

The girl stood up. But she held on to the chair with one hand and let Rosemary pull. It was quite an effort. The other scarcely helped her at all. She seemed to stagger like a child, and the thought came and went through Rosemary's mind, that if people wanted helping they must respond a little, just a little, otherwise it became very difficult indeed. And what was she to do with the coat now? She left it on the floor, and the hat too. She was just going to take a cigarette off the mantelpiece when the girl said quickly, but so lightly and strangely: "I'm very sorry, madam, but I'm going to faint. I shall go off, madam, if I don't have something."

EVALUATE: What do you learn about Rosemary from her response to the fact that the girl doesn't help remove her own coat?

5

MINI-LESSON: VOCABULARY

Using Context Clues

Teach   Remind students that one way to figure out the meaning of an unfamiliar word while reading is to substitute a word or phrase that makes sense in the context.

Apply   Point out the sentence that begins "She plied the poor little crea-ture with everything . . ." (column 1, p. 801). A word that would make sense in place of *plied* is *provided*. Explain that since "provided" is not the exact meaning of *plied*, the reader must use other context clues to refine his or her understanding of the word. Discuss with students how the rest of the sentence helps to clarify the meaning of *plied*. *(By filling the girl's cup every time it is empty, Rosemary not only provides food but urges her to continue eating.)*

Activity Idea   With partners, students can practice determining word definitions and connotations from context clues by

- leafing through literature selections to find words that are unfamiliar to both
- substituting a word or phrase that makes sense in the context
- taking a closer look at the context to determine finer shades of meaning
- looking up the word in a dictionary to find out how accurate the predicted definition was

"Good heavens, how thoughtless I am!" Rosemary rushed to the bell.

"Tea! Tea at once! And some brandy immediately!"

The maid was gone again, but the girl almost cried out. "No, I don't want no brandy. I never drink brandy. It's a cup of tea I want, madam." And she burst into tears.

It was a terrible and fascinating moment. Rosemary knelt beside her chair.

"Don't cry, poor little thing," she said. "Don't cry." And she gave the other her lace handkerchief. She really was touched beyond words. She put her arm round those thin, birdlike shoulders.

Now at last the other forgot to be shy, forgot everything except that they were both women, and gasped out: "I can't go on no longer like this. I can't bear it. I shall do away with myself. I can't bear no more."

"You shan't have to. I'll look after you. Don't cry any more. Don't you see what a good thing it was that you met me? We'll have tea and you'll tell me everything. And I shall arrange something. I promise. *Do* stop crying. It's so exhausting. Please!"

The other did stop just in time for Rosemary to get up before the tea came. She had the table placed between them. She plied[9] the poor little creature with everything, all the sandwiches, all the bread and butter, and every time her cup was empty she filled it with tea, cream and sugar. People always said sugar was so nourishing. As for herself she didn't eat; she smoked and looked away tactfully so that the other should not be shy.

And really the effect of that slight meal was marvelous. When the tea-table was carried away a new being, a light, frail creature with tangled hair, dark lips, deep, lighted eyes, lay back in the big chair in a kind of sweet languor,[10] looking at the blaze. Rosemary lit a fresh cigarette; it was time to begin.

"And when did you have your last meal?" she asked softly.

But at the moment the door-handle turned.

"Rosemary, may I come in?" It was Philip.

"Of course."

He came in. "Oh, I'm so sorry," he said, and stopped and stared.

"It's quite all right," said Rosemary smiling. "This is my friend, Miss—"

"Smith, madam," said the languid figure, who was strangely still and unafraid.

"Smith," said Rosemary. "We are going to have a little talk."

"Oh, yes," said Philip. "Quite." and his eye caught sight of the coat and hat on the floor. He came over to the fire and turned his back to it. "It's a beastly afternoon," he said curiously, still looking at that listless[11] figure, looking at its hands and boots, and then at Rosemary again.

"Yes, isn't it?" said Rosemary enthusiastically. "Vile."[12]

Philip smiled his charming smile. "As a matter of fact," said he, "I wanted you to come into the library for a moment. Would you? Will Miss Smith excuse us?"

The big eyes were raised to him, but Rosemary answered for her. "Of course she will." And they went out of the room together.

"I say," said Philip, when they were alone. "Explain. Who is she? What does it all mean?"

Rosemary, laughing, leaned against the door and said: "I picked her up in Curzon Street. Really. She's a real pick-up. She asked me for the price of a cup of tea, and I brought her home with me."

"But what on earth are you going to do with her?" cried Philip.

"Be nice to her," said Rosemary quickly. "Be frightfully nice to her. Look after her. I don't know how. We haven't talked yet. But show her—treat her—make her feel—"

---

9. **ply** (plī), *v.* supply with in a pressing manner.
10. **languor** (lang′gər), *n.* lack of energy; weariness.
11. **listless** (list′lis), *adj.* seeming too tired to care about anything.
12. **vile** (vīl), *adj.* very bad.

A Cup of Tea **801**

6 Literary Element
Dialect

Question What does the contrast between the girl's "I can't bear no more" and Rosemary's "Don't cry any more" suggest? *(Possible response: the girl's background; the nonstandard double negative accurately portrays the dialect of people of her class)*

7 Reading/Thinking Skills
Compare and Contrast

Questions In what ways does Philip seem to be similar to Rosemary in his attitude toward the girl? Which details helped to form your impression? *(Possible response: Both Rosemary and Philip regard the girl as less than human. Philip looks at "the figure" curiously and stares at "its" hands and feet.)* How is Philip's attitude different than Rosemary's? *(Possible response: Philip's shocked "But what on earth are you going to do with her" shows that he is more practical.)*

BUILDING ENGLISH PROFICIENCY

Responding to Characters

Help groups of students relate to how they feel about Mansfield's distinctive characters.

Activity Ideas

• Ask students to mark the dialogue lightly with a pencil (for later erasure) and then read the dialogue together in a way that reveals their impression of the three characters.

• Have each group select one adjective that describes each character. Have them compare the three words they chose with the words of other groups.

• Ask each group to discuss (without looking ahead to p. 802) how they think the story might end. Have them work together at predicting, and then summarizing in writing, an ending that develops from their impressions of the characters.

ESL
LEP
ELD
SAE
LD

Question Do you agree with Philip? *(Some students may feel that, while Rosemary's motives are suspect, there is nothing wrong with a wealthy person "adopting" a poor one. Other students may find something distasteful about one person "acquiring" another.)*

9 Active Reading

Clarify

Possible responses To Rosemary, the girl is a stereotype of the poor, and the poor can not be pretty.

10 Reading/Thinking Skills

Synthesize

Question Do you see a connection between Rosemary's interest in the girl and the antique box? *(Possible response: Both are acquisitions.)*

11 Reading/Thinking Skills

Infer

Question What can you infer from Rosemary's "am I pretty?" *(Insecure, Rosemary gets rid of a possible rival.)*

Check Test

1. Why did the girl approach Rosemary? *(for money for food)*

2. Where does Rosemary take the girl? *(home)*

3. When the girl begins to cry, what does Rosemary promise? *(to look after her)*

4. What does Philip say that shocks Rosemary? *(that the girl is astonishing pretty)*

5. At the end of the story, what does Rosemary ask Philip? *(if he thinks she is pretty)*

 Unit 7 Resource Book
Alternate Check Test, p. 101

802

---

8 "My darling girl," said Philip, "you're quite mad, you know. It simply can't be done."

"I knew you'd say that," retorted Rosemary. "Why not? I want to. Isn't that a reason? And besides, one's always reading about these things. I decided—"

"But," said Philip slowly, and he cut the end of a cigar, "she's so astonishingly pretty."

"Pretty?" Rosemary was so surprised that she blushed. "Do you think so? I—I hadn't thought about it."

9 **CLARIFY: Why is Rosemary surprised?**

"Good Lord!" Philip struck a match. "She's absolutely lovely. Look again, my child. I was bowled over when I came into your room just now. However . . . I think you're making a ghastly[13] mistake. Sorry, darling, if I'm crude and all that. But let me know if Miss Smith is going to dine with us in time for me to look up *The Milliner's Gazette.*"

"You absurd creature!" said Rosemary, and she went out of the library, but not back to her bedroom. She went to her writing-room and sat down at her desk. Pretty! Absolutely lovely! Bowled over! Her heart beat like a heavy bell. Pretty! Lovely! She drew her check book towards her. But no, checks would be no use, of course. She opened a drawer and took out five pound notes, looked at them, put two back, and holding the three squeezed in her hand, she went back to her bedroom.

Half an hour later Philip was still in the library, when Rosemary came in.

"I only wanted to tell you," said she, and she leaned against the door again and looked at him with her dazzled exotic[14] gaze, "Miss Smith won't dine with us tonight."

Philip put down the paper. "Oh, what's happened? Previous engagement?"

Rosemary came over and sat down on his knee. "She insisted on going," said she, "so I gave the poor little thing a present of money. I couldn't keep her against her will, could I?" she added softly.

Rosemary had just done her hair, darkened her eyes a little, and put on her pearls. She put up her hands and touched Philip's cheeks.

"Do you like me?" said she, and her tone, sweet, husky, troubled him.

"I like you awfully," he said, and he held her tighter. "Kiss me."

There was a pause.

Then Rosemary said dreamily, "I saw a fascinating little box today. It cost twenty-eight guineas. May I have it?"

10 Philip jumped her on his knee. "You may, little wasteful one," said he.

But that was not really what Rosemary wanted to say.

11 "Philip," she whispered, and she pressed his head against her bosom, "am I *pretty*?"

---

13. ghastly (gast′lē), *adj.* very bad. *[informal]*
14. exotic (eg zot′ik), *adj.* from a foreign country; strange or different.

MINI-LESSON: READING/THINKING SKILLS

Analyzing a Character

Teach Remind students that authors can reveal the inner qualities of their characters through many different kinds of details:

- the character's appearance
- the character's behavior and speech
- the character's thoughts and feelings
- how other characters behave toward the character
- what other characters say about the character

Ask students to skim page 802 for different kinds of details that help to reveal Rosemary's inner qualities. Discuss with them what each detail signifies.

Activity Idea Ask students to choose one of Rosemary's traits and to search through the story for details that help to reveal that trait. (For example, the trait of vanity might be supported by details such as her enjoying the clerk's flattery and admiring her own hands.)

After Reading

Making Connections

Shaping Your Response

1. If invited, would you attend one of Rosemary's parties, with its "most delicious mixture of the really important people"? Why or why not?

Analyzing the Story

2. Part of the **characterization** of Rosemary is the description of her feelings immediately after leaving the antique shop. What does this description tell about her?

3. How do we learn Rosemary's true motives in inviting the girl home?

4. Where does the **climax** come in the story?

5. In your opinion, what is Rosemary's chief purpose in life? Support your answer with evidence from the story.

Extending the Ideas

6. If you had asked for the price of a cup of tea and received several times more than you asked for, would you feel grateful? embarrassed? demeaned? ashamed? something else? Discuss.

7. Do you think Mansfield is criticizing the values of the society in which Rosemary and her husband live, or is she merely representing it?

Literary Focus: Stereotype

A **stereotype** is based on a conventional idea, and stereotypical characters are based on fixed, generalized notions about people or groups of people. Stereotypical characters often serve as foils; that is they point up the strengths or weaknesses of another character.

1. Does Rosemary seem to consider Miss Smith a type or an individual?

2. Do you think the author intended the character of Rosemary to help portray Miss Smith, or is Miss Smith created to help portray Rosemary?

3. 👁 Miss Smith is allowed one mark of **individuality.** What is it?

Vocabulary Study

Decide whether the italicized words are used correctly in the sentences. On your paper write *Correct* or *Incorrect* for each one.

1. Stephanie liked to shop on Plum Drive, where the shops were full of *exotic* imported merchandise.

2. Yesterday she found a beautiful and *listless* pearl ring.

3. Alex found a *langour* in a shop nearby.

4. Later the two of them *plied* onto a bus and went to an art gallery.

5. There, Stephanie saw an *exquisitely* painted bowl.

After Reading

MAKING CONNECTIONS

1. Some students might feel that they would enjoy the opulence and the colorful mix of people at such a party. Others might object to being used by the hostess for status or amusement.

2. Rosemary was determined to live superficially and never to deal with pain or sorrow. She counted on material comforts to serve as her shield against the darker side of life.

3. Rosemary's true motive is revealed mainly through her thoughts: She regards the idea of taking the girl home as a thrilling adventure; she envisions her friends' reactions; she sees the girl as her "captive"; she finds it "fascinating" to show the girl her wealth and to see her burst into tears.

4. The climax of the story comes when Philip remarks on the girl's beauty. After this point, Rosemary's interest in her new role as do-gooder quickly dissolves, and the story comes to an end.

5. Rosemary's chief purpose in life is to be ornamental and to acquire things. She acquires odd people to amuse her friends and odd things to ornament her environment.

6. Some students might feel fortunate and grateful, while others might feel embarrassed or even angry. Most will probably express a combination of these feelings.

7. Mansfield is clearly criticizing society's values. She gives Rosemary neither redeeming qualities nor justification for her lack of them. Both Rosemary and Philip are consistently callous and self-serving.

LITERARY FOCUS: STEREOTYPE

1. Rosemary sees Miss Smith as a type, as evidenced by the following:

- She wants to "do one of those things she was always reading about or seeing on the stage."

- She pictures herself as a "fairy godmother."

- Lacking any genuine empathy for the girl, Rosemary fails to notice that the girl is starving.

- She fails to notice that the girl is pretty.

2. The character of Miss Smith is intended to help portray Rosemary. The reader learns very little about Miss Smith, but Rosemary's reactions to her teach us a great deal about Rosemary.

3. Miss Smith's one mark of individuality is her beauty.

VOCABULARY STUDY

1. correct
2. incorrect
3. incorrect
4. incorrect
5. correct
6. correct
7. correct
8. correct
9. correct
10. incorrect

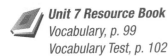

Unit 7 Resource Book
Vocabulary, p. 99
Vocabulary Test, p. 102

WRITING CHOICES
Writer's Notebook Update

Remind students of the different kinds of details authors use to reveal character: appearance; behavior and speech; thoughts and feelings; how other characters behave toward the character; and what other characters say about the character.

A Weird Experience

Students might prepare to write the letter by dividing into pairs and role-playing what could have happened.

Two Fictional Women

Suggest to students that they review "Eveline," pages 790–793, and the discussion of epiphany on page 789. Remind students to base their comparisons on the thoughts and perceptions of the characters as well as on external circumstances and behavior.

Selection Test

Unit 7 Resource Book
pp. 103–104

6. Alex, however, was more interested in an antique painting of a *cherub.*
7. He made a *discreet* inquiry about the price.
8. Stephanie thought the painting was *ghastly.*
9. She explained that she was in a *vile* mood.
10. Perhaps the *glaze* she was wearing affected her judgment.

Expressing Your Ideas

Writing Choices

Writer's Notebook Update Review the ideas you jotted down for a character based on someone you have seen but do not know. Now write a character sketch or a short short story based on that character.

A Weird Experience Assume that you are Miss Smith, and write a **letter** to a friend describing your experience with Rosemary and her husband Philip, including what happened just before you left their home.

Two Fictional Women In an **essay** compare and contrast Rosemary and Eveline in James Joyce's story. Consider their relationships with others, their economic situations, and their personalities. Does Rosemary have an epiphany too?

Other Options

The Rattle of Teacups With a small group, adapt "A Cup of Tea" into a one-act **radio play.** Use dialogue from the story, and make up the rest. You will need lines for Rosemary, Philip, the clerk, Miss Smith, the maid, and perhaps a narrator. If you can, include some sound effects—such as the sound of rain and of Rosemary's car, the crackling of a fire, the sound of teacups rattling, and the closing of a door. Record your production and play it for the class.

Artistic Values Look carefully at the painting that accompanies this story on page 797. With a partner, plan an **interview** with questions and answers about the artist's decisions regarding the subject, the pose, colors, shapes, and artistic style of the work. You might include some comments about the young woman who posed for the picture. With you playing the interviewer and your partner playing the artist, practice the interview and present it to the class.

OTHER OPTIONS
The Rattle of Teacups

Students could choose to "fill in" the scene in which Rosemary sends Miss Smith away, or they might leave it to the imagination of the audience as Mansfield did.

Artistic Values

Students who have an interest in art history might enjoy doing research on the life of William McGregor Paxson, trends in art that influenced his work, and possible social conditions that helped foster those trends.

Before Reading

The Unknown Citizen
Musée des Beaux Arts
Who's Who by W. H. Auden

W. H. Auden
1907–1973

W. H. Auden, the youngest of three brothers, was born in York and lived in Birmingham until he attended boarding school. He graduated from Oxford in 1928, spent a year in Germany, and taught school in England and Scotland in the early 1920s. In 1939 Auden settled in the U. S., becoming an American citizen in 1946. Later he spent his summers abroad, first in Italy and then in Austria, where he lived with American poet Chester Kallman. Auden became a poetry professor at Oxford in 1956 and died suddenly in Vienna in 1973. His works include the libretto for Igor Stravinsky's opera, *The Rake's Progress* (1949, 1951) with Kallman; criticism in *The Dyer's Hand* (1962), and *Collected Poems* (1976).

Building Background

Poetry's Role For more than four decades Auden's poetry succeeded in capturing the horrors, hopes, and anxieties of the time. He characterized the 1930s as a "low, dishonest decade," and the title of one of his works, *The Age of Anxiety* (1948), a long dramatic poem, came to characterize the post-World War II period for many. Auden delighted in playing with words, in employing a variety of rhythms, and in creating striking literary effects. But he was also insistent that poetry must fulfill a moral function, principally that of dispelling hate and promoting love. "Poetry is not concerned with telling people what to do," he once wrote, "but with extending our knowledge of good and evil . . . leading us to the point where it is possible for us to make a rational moral choice."

Literary Focus

Satire The technique that uses wit to ridicule a subject is called **satire.** Its focus is usually some social institution or human foible, and the intention is to inspire reform. What aspects of twentieth-century society does Auden satirize in "The Unknown Citizen"?

Writer's Notebook

Who's Who Today? Who are the most widely known people in the world today? Make a list of at least ten of these people. Where did you learn about them in the first place?

Before Reading

Building Background

The title, *The Age of Anxiety*, was used to describe the Cold War era of nuclear proliferation. You might lead a discussion about whether the title remains a fitting description of the "post-modern" era.

Literary Focus

Remind students that they read an example of satire in Swift's "A Modest Proposal." You might ask students to recall what reforms Swift hoped to inspire.

Writer's Notebook

You might suggest that students begin by thinking about categories of famous people: e.g., entertainer, athlete, political leader, religious leader, and "other."

More About W. H. Auden

In his early teens, Auden attended a boarding school where boys were forced to inform on each other for breaking rules. Years later, he wrote that his best reason for opposing fascism was the experience of having lived at a school where moral behavior was based on fear and distrust. Works by Auden include

- *Look Stranger!* (1936)
- *Another Time* (1940)
- *City Without Walls* (1969)

SUPPORT MATERIALS OVERVIEW

Unit 7 Resource Book
- Graphic Organizer, p. 105
- Study Guide, p. 106
- Vocabulary, p. 107
- Grammar, p. 108
- Alternate Check Test, p. 109
- Vocabulary Test, p. 110
- Selection Test, pp. 111–112

Building English Proficiency
- Selection Summaries
- Activities, p. 257

Reading, Writing & Grammar SkillBook
- Reading, pp. 77–78
- Writing, pp. 127–128
- Grammar, Usage, and Mechanics, pp. 239–242

Technology
- Audiotape
- Personal Journal Software
- Test Generator Software

Selection Objectives

- to relate Auden's poetry to the twentieth-century search for identity
- to understand satire
- to apply standard usage to commas

Unit 7 Resource Book
Graphic Organizer, p. 105
Study Guide, p. 106

Theme Link

Each of the three poems develops the search for identity theme by depicting the isolation of the individual within society.

1 Reading/Thinking Skills

Infer

Questions What does this line suggest about the narrator's view of religion? *(that religion is outdated)* In the old-fashioned sense, is the "unknown citizen" a saint? *(No; he is very ordinary.)* How is he a saint in the modern sense of the word? *(Possible responses: He doesn't cause trouble; he behaves exactly as society wishes for him to behave.)*

2 Literary Focus

Satire

Question What do you think Auden is satirizing in "The Unknown Citizen"? *(Possible responses: society's faith in statistical information; the premium society places on normalcy, and its repression of individuality; the individual who does not question, who fits in and gets by)*

THE *Unknown Citizen*

W. H. Auden

1
He was found by the Bureau of Statistics to be
One against whom there was no official complaint,
And all the reports on his conduct agree
That, in the modern sense of an old-fashioned word, he
     was a saint,
5 For in everything he did he served the Greater Community.
Except for the War till the day he retired
He worked in a factory and never got fired,
But satisfied his employers, Fudge Motors Inc.
Yet he wasn't a scab[1] or odd in his views,
10 For his Union reports that he paid his dues,
(Our report on his Union shows it was sound)
And our Social Psychology workers found
That he was popular with his mates and liked a drink.
The Press are convinced that he bought a paper every day
15 And that his reactions to advertisements were normal in every way.
Policies taken out in his name prove that he was fully insured,
And his Health-card shows he was once in hospital but
     left it cured.
Both Producers Research and High-Grade Living declare
He was fully sensible to the advantages of the Installment Plan
20 And had everything necessary to the Modern Man,
A phonograph, a radio, a car and a frigidaire.
Our researchers into Public Opinion are content
That he held the proper opinions for the time of year;
When there was peace, he was for peace; when there was war,
     he went.
25 He was married and added five children to the population,
Which our Eugenist[2] says was the right number for a parent of
     his generation.
And our teachers report that he never interfered with
     their education.
Was he free? Was he happy? The question is absurd:
2 Had anything been wrong, we should certainly have heard.

---

1. **scab,** worker who will not join a labor union or who takes a striker's job.
2. **Eugenist,** eugenicist, an expert in eugenics, the science of improving the human race by a careful selection of parents in order to breed healthier and more intelligent children.

806   UNIT SEVEN: THE EARLY TWENTIETH CENTURY

Is the **tone** of W. H. Auden's poem "The Unknown Citizen" similar to that of René Magritte's painting *Reproduction Prohibited* (1937)? Why or why not? ➤

SELECTION SUMMARY

The Unknown Citizen; Musée des Beaux Arts; Who's Who

The Unknown Citizen A bureaucrat eulogizes an ideal citizen for his perfect conformity to the government's standard of normalcy, citing the findings of various departments within the bureau, such as Social Psychology, Producers Research, High-Grade Living, and Public Opinion.

Musée des Beaux Arts The narrator notes that the Old Masters understood the true nature of suffering. To illustrate his point, he describes several details from paintings by Pieter Brueghel, each demonstrating that suffering is a solitary experience, endured amidst the oblivion or indifference of others.

Who's Who In the first eight lines of this sonnet, the courage, passion, and achievements of a hero are depicted. In the final six lines, a side of the hero that shocked his public—his love for a very ordinary person—is revealed.

*For summaries in other languages, see the **Building English Proficiency** book.*

The Unknown Citizen **807**

Responses to Caption Questions
The tones of the poem and of the painting are similar. Both offer a portrait of an unknown man.

Visual Literacy A man looks in a mirror. It reflects not his face, but the back of his head. There seem to be no details to offer clues. There is a book, but the viewer can barely make out the writing, and there is the title, *Reproduction Prohibited.*

Questions If you accept the mirror's reflection at "face value," what is suggested? *(Possible response: The figure has no face; he is all back and, therefore, has no cover to read.)* What might this suggest? *(The figure is without individuality.)* What does the title, *Reproduction Prohibited,* suggest? *(Possible response: The reflection of a "faceless society" is faceless; a society in which individuality is discouraged leaves no reflection of itself because there is nothing to reflect upon.)*

BUILDING ENGLISH PROFICIENCY

Making Real-Life Connections

Auden subtly suggests that what was true of the Unknown Citizen is true of us, the readers. Encourage students to make that connection.

1. Ask students to create a web of numbers around their name. These should be numbers that describe them or that are assigned to them, such as birthdate (for example, 7-7-80), telephone, ZIP code, social security, driver's license, passport, library card, medical insurance, and height. Tell them not to add private numbers such as ATM access codes.

2. Ask students to write one sentence that tells something important about them that all the numbers cannot reveal.

3. As students share responses, ask: How does it feel to be defined by numbers? How do you think the Unknown Citizen felt about it?

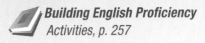 *Building English Proficiency*
Activities, p. 257

You might note to the class that Auden alludes to three Breughel paintings.

- Lines 5–8 refer to *The Numbering in at Bethlehem,* which depicts the arrival of Joseph and pregnant Mary in Bethlehem. The couple, shown as only a small detail, go unnoticed by villagers caught up in the bustle of everyday life.
- Lines 10–13 allude to *The Massacre of the Innocents,* which depicts the biblical story of King Herod's campaign to murder all boys under the age of two as a means of eliminating the newborn Christ.
- Lines 14–21 refer to *The Fall of Icarus,* shown at right.

MUSÉE DES

Beaux Arts

W. H. Auden

About suffering they were never wrong,
The Old Masters;[1] how well they understood
Its human position; how it takes place
While someone else is eating or opening a
    window or just walking dully along;
5 How, when the aged are reverently,
    passionately waiting
For the miraculous birth, there always must be
Children who did not specially want it to
    happen, skating
On a pond at the edge of the wood:
They never forgot
10 That even the dreadful martyrdom must run
    its course
Anyhow in a corner, some untidy spot
Where the dogs go on with their doggy life
    and the torturer's horse
Scratches its innocent behind on a tree.

In Bruegel's *Icarus,*[2] for instance: how
    everything turns away
15 Quite leisurely from the disaster; the
    ploughman may
Have heard the splash, the forsaken cry,
But for him it was not an important failure;
    the sun shone
As it had to on the white legs disappearing
    into the green
Water; and the expensive delicate ship that
    must have seen
20 Something amazing, a boy falling out of the sky,
Had somewhere to get to and sailed calmly on.

808   UNIT SEVEN: THE EARLY TWENTIETH CENTURY

Musée des Beaux Arts (mū zā′ dā bō zār′), the Royal Museum of Fine Arts in Brussels, Belgium.
1. **Old Masters,** any great painters before 1700.
2. **Bruegel's *Icarus*** (ik′ər əs). The painting *The Fall of Icarus* by Pieter Bruegel (pē′tər broi′gəl) was inspired by the Greek myth that relates how Daedalus made wings of feathers and wax for his son Icarus and himself in order to escape imprisonment. Despite his father's warnings, Icarus flew too near the sun; the wax holding together the feathers of his wings melted, and he fell into the sea and drowned.

MINI-LESSON: GRAMMAR

Commas

Teach   Remind students that commas are used to make writing easier to read and understand. Commas separate items in a series and set off an introductory word from the rest of the sentence. Tell students that another common use for commas is to set apart a phrase that precedes or interrupts the main idea of a sentence. Ask them to find an example of this use of commas in the poem. *(In lines 5–6, "when the aged are reverently, passionately waiting/For the miraculous birth," interrupts the sentence.)* Yet another use for commas is to set apart a phrase that modifies a noun or pronoun. Ask students to find an example of this. *(In lines 20, "a boy falling out of the sky" modifies "something.")*

Activity Idea   Have students supply the missing commas.

- While teaching at a boys' school Auden delighted his students with his eccentricity boundless energy and sense of fun. *(While teaching at a boys' school, Auden delighted his students with his eccentricity, boundless energy, and sense of fun.)*
- Auden wanting his students to write poetry initiated a school magazine. *(Auden, wanting his students to write poetry, initiated a school magazine.)*

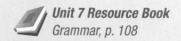
Unit 7 Resource Book
Grammar, p. 108

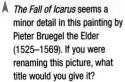 *Art Study*

Response to Caption Question
While students responses will vary, titles should reflect the idea that suffering, tragedy, and even triumph usually goes unnoticed.

▲ *The Fall of Icarus* seems a minor detail in this painting by Pieter Bruegel the Elder (1525–1569). If you were renaming this picture, what title would you give it?

Musée des Beaux Arts   **809**

BUILDING ENGLISH PROFICIENCY

Linking Past and Present

Help students compare Auden's conclusion about past events to their own about the present.

1. Ask groups of students to read "Musée des Beaux Arts" and summarize what Auden concludes about suffering.

2. Bring in newspapers, one for each group. Ask the groups to find and summarize three stories about suffering and tell whether people ignored or tried to help the one in need. Have them write a conclusion based on their research.

Story 1 (summary)	Story 2 (summary)	Story 3 (summary)
ignored?/Helped?	ignored?/Helped?	ignored?/Helped?

Conclusion:

"Who's Who" was probably inspired by T. E. Lawrence, better known as Lawrence of Arabia, a famous British hero of World War I. Lawrence played a critical role in organizing the Arab revolt against the Turks, Germany's allies, and later wrote an acclaimed account of his experiences, *The Seven Pillars of Wisdom*. His literary reputation was further enhanced by his translation of the *Odyssey* and by his enormous correspondence, to which Auden alludes in the last line.

5

Reading/Thinking Skills
Analyze

Question How did the image you formed of the subject while reading the first eight lines change after you read the last six lines? *(Possible response: The first eight lines paint him as a dashing adventurer and superhero; in the last six lines, the depiction of his lover as a very ordinary person makes the hero seem more ordinary and human.)*

Check Test

1. In "The Unknown Citizen," why is the citizen called a saint? *(He does everything expected of him by the state and by industry; he conforms without questioning.)*

2. In "Musée des Beaux Arts," what did the Old Masters understand? *(human suffering)*

3. In "Musée des Beaux Arts," how do people react when a boy drowns? *(They ignore it.)*

4. What acts make the subject of "Who's Who" a hero? *(He fought, fished, hunted, worked, climbed mountains, and named a sea.)*

5. In "Who's Who," what astonishes the critics? *(The hero loved an ordinary person, who doesn't return the love.)*

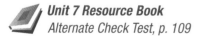
Unit 7 Resource Book
Alternate Check Test, p. 109

4

WHO'S *Who*

W. H. Auden

A shilling life[1] will give you all the facts:
How Father beat him, how he ran away,
What were the struggles of his youth, what acts
Made him the greatest figure of his day:
5 Of how he fought, fished, hunted, worked all night,
Though giddy, climbed new mountains; named a sea;
Some of the last researchers even write
Love made him weep his pints like you and me.

With all his honors on, he sighed for one
10 Who, say astonished critics, lived at home;
Did little jobs about the house with skill
And nothing else; could whistle; would sit still
Or potter round the garden; answered some
Of his long marvellous letters but kept none.

5

---

1. **shilling life,** an inexpensive biography, one costing a shilling, a former British coin worth about 25 cents when Auden wrote this poem.

MINI-LESSON: LITERARY FOCUS

Satire

Teach Ask students to reread the definition of *satire* on page 805. Point out that when comedians on TV make fun of current trends and societal attitudes, their skits and monologues are forms of satire. Invite students to describe some examples they have seen and to identify the aspect of society that was being satirized.

Activity Ideas

• Students can decide whether or not "Musée des Beaux Arts" and "Who's Who?" are examples of satire. Is something or someone being ridiculed? Is something extraordinary being contrasted with the ordinary? What should be reformed? *("Musée . . . " may be satire; "Who's Who?" is not.)*

• Groups can create satires. They should: (1) choose a social institution or human foible to satirize; (2) choose a form for the satire—for example, skit, editorial, cartoon, song; (3) create the satire; (4) present it to the class.

After Reading

Making Connections

Shaping Your Response

1. From these three poems, what can you **infer** was Auden's view of life?

Analyzing the Poems

2. Explain the double meaning of *unknown* in the title of the poem

3. The **rhyme scheme** of "The Unknown Citizen" is not quite regular. Chart it. Why do you think Auden didn't choose to make it completely regular?

4. The title "The Unknown Citizen" may be an **allusion** to the unknown soldier honored in several graveyards around the world. What might such a connection add to the overall effect of the poem?

5. In "Musée des Beaux Arts," what truth about human suffering does the speaker feel the Old Masters understood, and how does Bruegel's painting illustrate this truth?

6. Explain why the critics mentioned in "Who's Who" are astonished (line 10).

Extending the Ideas

7. If you had a choice, would you rather be an unknown or a known citizen? Explain.

8. Auden thought poetry should extend our knowledge of good and evil (see page 805). Explain whether or not "Musée des Beaux Arts" achieves this aim.

Literary Focus: Satire

Satire uses wit to ridicule a subject, usually a human trait such as envy, greed, or stupidity, or a social institution such as government, business, religion, or the family. Usually the intent is to inspire reform.

1. For what kinds of behavior is the Unknown Citizen praised?

2. What kind of world did the Unknown Citizen inhabit?

3. In the next-to-last line of "The Unknown Citizen" the speaker asks two questions. Judging by the tone of the speaker's answer, do you think the poet endorses the speaker's views?

4. What human traits and what social institutions are satirized in "The Unknown Citizen"?

Who's Who **811**

After Reading

MAKING CONNECTIONS

1. Possible response: Auden seemed to see life as a lonely experience. In "The Unknown Citizen," the subject goes through life playing a role, never sharing his thoughts or feelings; "Musée des Beaux" deals with the isolation of the sufferer; and in "Who's Who," even fame and glory can't protect the subject from the loneliness of loving in vain.

2. Possible response: The citizen is "unknown" to the statisticians, who keep the records, and is perhaps unknown to himself.

3. Possible response: The rhyme scheme of the first 13 lines is *ababaccdeeffd.* The irregular scheme may reflect the poet's distaste for conformity.

4. Possible response: The "unknown soldier" is honored as a symbol of all who died in a war. The "unknown citizen" is honored for conforming to society.

5. Possible response: According to the speaker, the Old Masters understood that much suffering goes unnoticed or ignored. In *The Fall of Icarus*, the ploughman and the sailors were too absorbed in their own pursuits to care about the drowning boy.

6. Possible response: They are astonished that such a remarkable man would love an ordinary person, who did not seem to appreciate the hero or his greatness.

7. Possible response: Some students may prefer the privacy of being unknown; others may prefer being connected, which requires communication.

8. Possible response: Auden shows that the most common evil is people's everyday indifference to the suffering of others.

LITERARY FOCUS: SATIRE

Possible Responses

1. He is praised for working in one factory, being liked by his peers, having no health problems, buying modern "necessities," holding "proper opinions," getting married and having the "right" number of children, and never challenging authority.

2. He inhabited a world in which everything was measured by statistics. Normalcy was the ideal, and conformity was required.

3. Auden sees the assumptions of the speaker, not the questions posed to the speaker, as absurd. He has shown that the citizen was probably not happy and certainly not free, because every aspect of his life was monitored for signs of deviation from the norm.

4. "The Unknown Citizen" satirizes society's faith in statistical information, the premium society places on conformity, and its repression of individuality.

Expressing Your Ideas

Writing Choices

Writer's Notebook Update Look over the list you made of well-known people today. Now add their occupations or claims to fame.

Who're You? Study an entry from a biographical work such as *Who's Who,* and following this model write your own **biographical entry** as you would wish it to be ten years from now.

Auden's Use of Satire Develop your answers to the questions under Literary Focus: Satire into an **analytical essay** in which you discuss how Auden uses satire in "The Unknown Citizen." Quote lines from the poem to support your statements. If Auden's intent was to inspire reform, what sort of reform do you think he had in mind?

Wealth and Fame	
Rock Musicians	𝅅𝅅𝅅𝅅𝅅𝅅 𝅅𝅅𝅅𝅅
Movie Stars	𝅅𝅅𝅅𝅅 𝅅𝅅𝅅𝅅𝅅
Politicians	𝅅 𝅅

Other Options

Private Lives Many people are concerned about the amount of personal information stored on computers and the resulting decrease in privacy. With a partner, develop an argument for each side of this issue: People have less privacy than they once had. Consider some of these questions and any others you think of: Does lack of privacy matter? Can stored computer information about private matters be put to illegal or immoral use? Is the matter serious enough to warrant some kind of action—either personal or legal? Present your **debate** to the class.

Rich and Famous? Take another look at the list you made of well-known people and each person's claim to fame. Compare your list with others in the class, and prepare a **statistical report** showing the number of times individuals are listed, the types of occupations shown, the number of women versus men, and any other statistics the lists bring to mind. Create one or more graphic organizers to illustrate your report. What if anything can you conclude about famous people and reasons for fame?

Before Reading

Shakespeare's Sister from A Room of One's Own

by Virginia Woolf

Virginia Woolf
1882–1941

Virginia Woolf was born into a literary and artistic family and educated at home by her father Leslie Stephen. After his death in 1904 she, with her brothers and her sister Vanessa, a painter, formed what came to be known as the Bloomsbury Group, an informal association of writers and artists. One member was Leonard Woolf, whom Virginia married in 1912. Her novels, which include *Mrs. Dalloway* (1925), *To the Lighthouse* (1927), and *The Waves* (1931), were increasingly experimental. She also wrote literary criticism and short stories, and her now-published letters and diaries contain fascinating insights. Frequently troubled by periods of mental illness, she drowned herself near her Sussex home.

Building Background

Critical Reception *A Room of One's Own,* from which the following excerpt is taken, has become in the words of one critic "a classic of the feminist movement." It is a book-length essay based on two lectures given by Woolf in 1928. Asked to speak about women and fiction to women at Cambridge University, Woolf began by expressing the view that "a woman must have money and a room of her own if she is to write fiction." When the essay was published, critic Arnold Bennett commented on Woolf's main theme:

". . . I beg to state that I have myself written long and formidable novels in bedrooms whose doors certainly had no locks, and in the full dreadful knowledge that I had not five hundred a year of my own—nor fifty. And I beg to state further that from the moment when I obtained possession of both money and a lockable door all the high-brows in London conspired together to assert that I could no longer write."

Before this excerpt, Woolf tells of visiting the British Museum library to research the lives of some men and women in history.

Literary Focus

Paradox A **paradox** is a statement that seems to say two opposite things, such as this Robert Browning line often quoted: "Less is more." A paradox can also be a person, thing, or situation that is full of contradictions. In her essay, Woolf writes of a paradox.

Writer's Notebook

Distinguishing the Sexes At one time, many English nouns had "feminine" suffixes to distinguish males from females. Although many of these have almost disappeared from the language, some are still in use. Place the following words into two lists: (1) words that have virtually disappeared; (2) words still in use: actress, aviatrix, countess, executrix, giantess, huntress, laundress, lioness, majorette, mistress, princess, seamstress, shepherdess, songstress, sorceress, suffragette, temptress, tigress, usherette, waitress.

Shakespeare's Sister **813**

Before Reading

Building Background

Susan Faludi writes, "The meaning of the word feminist has not really changed since it first appeared in the *Athenaeum* of April 27, 1895, describing a woman who 'has in her the capacity of fighting her way back to independence.'" Ask if students agree with this definition. Those who disagree might brainstorm a better definition.

Literary Focus

Ask students if they can relate a paradox from their lives.

Writer's Notebook

Students might discuss words on their lists that blur the distinction between genders; e.g., it is becoming more common to use the word *actor* for women as well as men.

More About Virginia Woolf

Virginia Woolf's husband, Leonard, associated her mental problems with her genius and noted a relationship between the completion of a literary work and the onset of depression. In 1941, four weeks after she finished her last work, *Between the Acts,* she committed suicide.

Connections to
AuthorWorks

Doris Lessing, another writer who explores the search for identify theme, is a featured author in the AuthorWorks CD-ROM series.

SUPPORT MATERIALS OVERVIEW

Unit 7 Resource Book
- Graphic Organizer, p. 113
- Study Guide, p. 114
- Vocabulary, p. 115
- Grammar, p. 116
- Alternate Check Test, p. 117
- Vocabulary Test, p. 118
- Selection Test, pp. 119–120

Building English Proficiency
- Selection Summaries
- Activities, p. 258

Reading, Writing & Grammar SkillBook
- Reading, pp. 42–44, 93–94
- Grammar, Usage, and Mechanics, pp. 211–213, 218–219, 239–242

Technology
- Audiotape
- Personal Journal Software
- Test Generator Software

Unit 7 Resource Book
Graphic Organizer, p. 113
Study Guide, p. 114

Theme Link

Virginia Woolf raises questions as to the true identity of women whose lives were recorded only by the men in whose imaginations they lived. In the past, most women were not allowed time to search for their identities.

Vocabulary Preview

perennial, lasting for a very long time; enduring

incorporeal, not made of any material substance; spiritual

prosaically, in an ordinary way

impropriety, improper conduct

agog, full of expectation; eager

servile, slavelike

inglorious, shameful; disgraceful

thwart, prevent from doing something

asunder, in pieces or separate parts

anonymity, condition of being unknown

Students can add the words and definitions to their Writer's Notebooks.

Art Study

Response to Caption Question The portrait suggests a thoughtful, introspective person.

1 **Active Reading**

Clarify

Possible response However complex, fiction, like a spider's web, must be attached to something real, that is, to life.

814

SHAKESPEARE'S SISTER

Virginia Woolf

I t was disappointing not to have brought back in the evening some important statement, some authentic fact. Women are poorer than men because— this or that. Perhaps now it would be better to give up seeking for the truth, and receiving on one's head an avalanche of opinion hot as lava, discolored as dishwater. It would be better to draw the curtains; to shut out distractions; to light the lamp; to narrow the inquiry and to ask the historian, who records not opinions but facts, to describe under what conditions women lived, not throughout the ages, but in England, say in the time of Elizabeth.

For it is a perennial[1] puzzle why no woman wrote a word of that extraordinary literature when every other man, it seemed, was capable of song or sonnet. What were the conditions in which women lived, I asked myself; for fiction, imaginative work that is, is not dropped like a pebble upon the ground, as science may be; fiction is like a spider's web, attached ever so lightly perhaps, but still attached to life at all four corners. Often the attachment is scarcely perceptible; Shakespeare's plays, for instance, seem to hang there complete by themselves. But

◄ Does Hans Holbein's portrait of *Mrs. Pemberton* (1556) suggest that she was a confident, outgoing person or a thoughtful, introspective one?

when the web is pulled askew, hooked up at the edge, torn in the middle, one remembers that these webs are not spun in midair by incorporeal[2] creatures, but are the work of suffering human beings, and are attached to grossly material things, like health and money and the houses we live in.

CLARIFY: Explain Woolf's simile comparing fiction and a spider's web.

1

I went, therefore, to the shelf where the histories stand and took down one of the latest, Professor Trevelyan's *History of England*.[3] Once more I looked up Women, found "position of," and turned to the pages indicated. "Wife-beating,"

---

1. perennial (pə ren′ē əl), *adj.* lasting for a very long time; enduring.
2. incorporeal (in′kôr pôr′ē əl), *adj.* not made of any material substance; spiritual.
3. **Professor . . . England.** British historian G. M. Trevelyan published a one-volume history in 1926.

SELECTION SUMMARY

Shakespeare's Sister

In this excerpt from Virginia Woolf's *A Room of One's Own,* the author finds that the great female characters of the 1500s and 1600s are primarily figments of the imaginations of men and have no basis in real life. The women who dominate the lives of kings in the pages of literature bear no resemblance to the real-life oppressed females of the Elizabethan period. Woolf looks to a historian, Professor Trevelyan, for an explanation of this disparity and finds that he too ignores the historical significance of women. Woolf invents the charac-ter of Shakespeare's sister to emphasize the different attitudes that prevailed toward men and women. Men were educated and valued members of society; women were their servants. Woolf concludes her essay with the belief that we must all work toward, and honor, every woman's right to express herself.

*For summaries in other languages, see the **Building English Proficiency** book.*

I read, "was a recognized right of man, and was practiced without shame by high as well as low. . . . Similarly," the historian goes on, "the daughter who refused to marry the gentleman of her parents' choice was liable to be locked up, beaten, and flung about the room, without any shock being inflicted on public opinion. Marriage was not an affair of personal affection, but of family avarice,[4] particularly in the 'chivalrous' upper classes. . . . Betrothal often took place while one or both of the parties was in the cradle, and marriage when they were scarcely out of the nurses' charge." That was about 1470, soon after Chaucer's time. The next reference to the position of women is some two hundred years later, in the time of the Stuarts. "It was still the exception for women of the upper and middle class to choose their own husbands, and when the husband had been assigned, he was lord and master, so far at least as law and custom could make him. Yet even so," Professor Trevelyan concludes, "neither Shakespeare's women nor those of authentic seventeenth-century memoirs, like the Verneys and the Hutchinsons,[5] seem wanting in personality and character." Certainly, if we consider it, Cleopatra must have had a way with her; Lady Macbeth, one would suppose, had a will of her own; Rosalind,[6] one might conclude, was an attractive girl. Professor Trevelyan is speaking no more than the truth when he remarks that Shakespeare's women do not seem wanting in personality and character. Not being a historian, one might go even further and say that women have burned like beacons in all the works of all the poets from the beginning of time—Clytemnestra, Antigone, Cleopatra, Lady Macbeth, Phedre, Cressida, Rosalind, Desdemona, the Duchess of Malfi, among the dramatists; then among the prose writers: Millamant, Clarissa, Becky Sharp, Anna Karenina, Emma Bovary, Madame de Guermantes[7]—the names flock to mind, nor do they recall women "lacking in personality and character." Indeed, if woman had no existence save

in the fiction written by men, one would imagine her a person of the utmost importance; very various; heroic and mean; splendid and sordid; infinitely beautiful and hideous in the extreme; as great as a man, some think even greater. But this is woman in fiction. In fact, as Professor Trevelyan points out, she was locked up, beaten, flung about the room.

A very queer, composite being thus emerges. Imaginatively she is of the highest importance; practically she is completely insignificant. She pervades poetry from cover to cover; she is all but absent from history. She dominates the lives of kings and conquerors in fiction; in fact she was the slave of any boy whose parents forced a ring upon her finger. Some of the most inspired words, some of the most profound thoughts in literature fall from her lips; in real life she could hardly read, could scarcely spell, and was the property of her husband.

It was certainly an odd monster that one made up by reading the historians first and the poets afterwards—a worm winged like an eagle; the spirit of life and beauty in a kitchen chopping up suet. But these monsters, however amusing to the imagination, have no existence in fact. What one must do to bring her to life

---

4. **avarice** (av′ər is), *n.* greed for wealth.
5. **Verneys . . . Hutchinsons,** two families of the 1600s. Lucy Hutchinson wrote a biography of her husband after his death.
6. **Cleopatra . . . Rosalind,** leading characters in Shakespeare's *Antony and Cleopatra, Macbeth,* and *As You Like It.*
7. **Clytemnestra . . . Madame de Guermantes.** Clytemnestra is in Aeschylus' *Agamemnon;* Antigone is in Sophocles' *Antigone;* Phedre is in Racine's *Phedre;* Cressida is in Shakespeare's *Troilus and Cressida;* Desdemona is in his *Othello; The Duchess of Malfi* is a play by Webster; Millamant is in Congreve's *The Way of the World; Clarissa Harlowe* is a novel by Richardson; Becky Sharp is the heroine in Thackeray's *Vanity Fair; Anna Karenina* is a novel by Tolstoy; Emma Bovary is in Flaubert's *Madame Bovary;* and Madame de Guermantes is in Proust's *Remembrance of Things Past.*

Shakespeare's Sister **815**

Elizabeth and Mary

Elizabeth, known as the Virgin Queen, was 25 years old when she became Queen of England in 1558. The golden period of her reign is called the Elizabethan Age. Mary Queen of Scots, a Roman Catholic, vied for Elizabeth's Protestant throne and was eventually beheaded at Elizabeth's behest. Mary's son James became King of England when Elizabeth died 16 years later.

5 Reading/Thinking Skills

Find the main Idea

Question What point is Woolf making here? (*Possible response: She finds it shocking that there is no history of women before the eighteenth century, and the history that is written is incomplete and lopsided without recording women's contributions.*)

was to think poetically and prosaically[8] at one and the same moment, thus keeping in touch with fact—that she is Mrs. Martin, aged thirty-six, dressed in blue, wearing a black hat and brown shoes; but not losing sight of fiction either—that she is a vessel in which all sorts of spirits and forces are coursing and flashing perpetually. The moment, however, that one tries this method with the Elizabethan woman, one branch of illumination fails; one is held up by the scarcity of facts. One knows nothing detailed, nothing perfectly true and substantial about her. History scarcely mentions her. And I turned to Professor Trevelyan again to see what history meant to him. I found by looking at his chapter headings that it meant—

"The Manor Court and the Methods of Open-Field Agriculture . . . The Cistercians and Sheep-Farming . . . The Crusades . . . The University . . . The House of Commons . . . The Hundred Years' War . . . The Wars of the Roses . . . The Renaissance Scholars . . . The Dissolution of the Monasteries . . . Agrarian and Religious Strife . . . The Origin of English Sea-Power . . . The Armada . . ." and so on. Occasionally an individual woman is mentioned, an Elizabeth, or a Mary; a queen or a great lady. But by no possible means could middle-class women with nothing but brains and character at their command have taken part in any one of the great movements which, brought together, constitute the historian's view of the past. Nor shall we find her in any collection of anecdotes. Aubrey[9] hardly mentions her. She never writes her own life and scarcely keeps a diary; there are only a handful of her letters in existence. She left no plays or poems by which we can judge her. What one wants, I thought—and why does not some brilliant student at Newnham or Girton[10] supply it?—is a mass of information; at what age did she marry; how many children had she as a rule; what was her house like; had she a room to herself; did she do the cooking; would she be likely to have a servant? All these facts lie somewhere, presumably, in parish registers and

account books; the life of the average Elizabethan woman must be scattered about somewhere, could one collect it and make a book of it. It would be ambitious beyond my daring. I thought, looking about the shelves for books that were not there, to suggest to the students of those famous colleges that they should rewrite history, though I own that it often seems a little queer as it is, unreal, lopsided; but why should they not add a supplement to history? calling it, of course, by some inconspicuous name so that women might figure there without impropriety?[11] For one often catches a glimpse of them in the lives of the great, whisking away into the background, concealing, I sometimes think, a wink, a laugh, perhaps a tear. And, after all, we have lives enough of Jane Austen; it scarcely seems necessary to consider again the influence of the tragedies of Joanna Baillie[12] upon the poetry of Edgar Allen Poe; as for myself, I should not mind if the homes and haunts of Mary Russell Mitford[13] were closed to the public for a century at least. But what I find deplorable, I continued, looking about the bookshelves again, is that nothing is known about women before the eighteenth century. I have no model in my mind to turn about this way and that. Here am I asking why women did not write poetry in the Elizabethan age, and I am not sure how they were educated; whether they were taught to write; whether they had sitting rooms to themselves; how many women had children before they were twenty-one; what, in short, they did from eight in the morning till

---

8. prosaically (prō zā′ik lē) *adv.* in an ordinary way.
9. **Aubrey,** John Aubrey (1626–1697), English biographer chiefly known for his *Brief Lives* of eminent people.
10. **Newnham or Girton,** two women's colleges at Cambridge University.
11. impropriety (im′prə prī′ə tē), *n.* improper conduct.
12. **Joanna Baillie** (1762–1851), Scottish dramatist and poet.
13. **Mary Russell Mitford** (1787–1855), English poet and dramatist. She is chiefly remembered for *Our Village: sketches of rural life, character, and scenery.*

MINI-LESSON: GRAMMAR

Punctuating Multiple Adjectives

Teach Two or more adjectives modifying the same noun should be separated by commas if they are coordinate in thought—that is, if the word *and* placed between them would not change the meaning. However, if a compound is formed by multiple adjectives that are included in thought with the noun modified, an adjective modifying this compound should not be separated from it by a comma. Examples are *hot corned beef; cool, refreshing water.*

Hyphenate a compound or multiple adjective when it *precedes* the word it modifies. Examples are *well-liked person;* (but) *That person is well liked.*

Activity Idea Have students read through the selection and write down examples of coordinated multiple adjectives that are separated by commas, adjectives that are included in thought with the noun modified and are not separated by commas, and those that are hyphenated as modifiers.

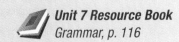

Unit 7 Resource Book
Grammar, p. 116

eight at night. They had no money evidently; according to Professor Trevelyan they were married whether they liked it or not before they were out of the nursery, at fifteen or sixteen very likely. It would have been extremely odd, even upon this showing, had one of them suddenly written the plays of Shakespeare, I concluded, and I thought of that old gentleman, who is dead now, but was a bishop, I think, who declared that it was impossible for any woman, past, present, or to come, to have the genius of Shakespeare. He wrote to the papers about it. He also told a lady who applied to him for information that cats do not as a matter of fact go to heaven, thought they have, he added, souls of a sort. How much thinking those old gentlemen used to save one! How the borders of ignorance shrank back at their approach! Cats do not go to heaven. Women cannot write the plays of Shakespeare.

6 Be that as it may, I could not help thinking, as I looked at the works of Shakespeare on the shelf, that the bishop was right at least in this; it would have been impossible, completely and entirely, for any woman to have written the plays of Shakespeare in the age of Shakespeare. Let me imagine, since facts are so hard to come by, what would have happened had Shakespeare had a wonderfully gifted sister, called Judith, let us say. Shakespeare himself went, very probably—his mother was an heiress—to grammar school, where he may have learned Latin—Ovid, Virgil, **7** and Horace[14]—and the elements of grammar and logic. He was, it is well known, a wild boy who poached rabbits, perhaps shot a deer, and had, rather sooner than he should have done, to marry a woman in the neighborhood, who bore him a child rather quicker than was right. That escapade sent him to seek his fortune in London. He had, it seemed, a taste for the theater; he began by holding horses at the stage door. Very soon he got work in the theater, became a successful actor, and lived at the hub of the universe, meeting everybody, knowing

everybody, practicing his art on the boards, exercising his wits in the streets, and even getting access to the palace of the queen. Meanwhile his extraordinarily gifted sister, let us suppose, remained at home. She was as adventurous, as imaginative, as agog[15] to see the world as he was. But she was not sent to school. She had no chance of learning grammar and logic, let alone of reading Horace and Virgil. She picked up a book now and then, one of her brother's perhaps, and read a few pages. But then her parents came in and told her to mend the stockings or mind the stew and not moon about with books and papers. They would have spoken sharply but kindly, for they were substantial people who knew the conditions of life for a woman and loved their daughter—indeed, more likely than not she was the apple of her father's eye. Perhaps she scribbled some pages up in an apple loft on the sly, but was careful to hide them or set fire to them. Soon, however, before she was out of her teens, she was to be betrothed to the son of a neighboring wool-stapler.[16] She cried out that marriage was hateful to her, and for that she was severely beaten by her father. Then he ceased to scold her. He begged her instead not to hurt him, not to shame him in this matter of her marriage. He would give her a chain of beads or a fine petticoat, he said; and there were tears in his eyes. How could she **8** disobey him? How could she break his heart? The force of her own gift alone drove her to it. She made up a small parcel of her belongings, let herself down by a rope one summer's night, and took the road to London. She was not seventeen. The birds that sang in the hedge were not more musical than she was. She had the quickest fancy, a gift like her brother's, for the tune of words. Like him, she had a taste for the

---

14. **Ovid, Virgil, and Horace,** Latin poets.
15. agog (ə gog′), *adj.* full of expectation or excitement; eager.
16. **wool-stapler,** a dealer who buys, grades, and sells wool.

BUILDING ENGLISH PROFICIENCY

Expanding Vocabulary Notebooks

Encourage students to add new words to their vocabulary notebooks as they read Woolf's essay.

1. Suggest the following words from pages 816–817: *substantial, deplorable, poached, inconspicuous, heiress, escapade.* You may also want students to locate others.

2. Challenge students not to just define the words but also to use each one in an original sentence that illustrates its meaning.

inconspicuous	easy to overlook
Embarrassed by his torn jacket, David kept his back to the wall and tried to stay inconspicuous.	

ESL LEP ELD SAE LD

Geographical Note
Elephant and Castle

Urban historians believe that the South London crossroads called the Elephant and Castle was originally named *Infanta de Castile*, for a Spanish princess betrothed to an English prince. Mispronounced by generations of Londoners, *Infanta de Castile* was gradually transposed into Elephant and Castle.

---

10 Active Reading
Summarize

Possible response   She had no education, few social ties, no encouragement to make a better life for herself, and basically functioned in servitude to men.

---

11 Reading/Thinking Skills
Infer

Question   Why does Woolf refer to some women who were thought to be witches or possessed by spirits as simply frustrated and suppressed writers? *(Possible response: Perhaps these women had no creative outlets in which to express themselves and to channel their energies, and in acting out their frustrations at their lack of independence, or in asserting independence, they were labeled as strange, evil, and dangerous.)*

---

theater. She stood at the stage door: she wanted to act, she said. Men laughed in her face. The manager—a fat, loose-lipped man—guffawed. He bellowed something about poodles dancing and women acting—no woman, he said, could possibly be an actress. He hinted—you can imagine what. She could get no training in her craft. Could she even seek her dinner in a tavern or roam the streets at midnight? Yet her genius was for fiction and lusted to feed abundantly upon the lives of men and women and the study of their ways. At last—for she was very young, oddly like Shakespeare the poet in her face, with the same gray eyes and rounded brows—at last Nick Greene the actor-manager took pity on her; she found herself with child by that gentleman and so—who shall measure the heat and violence of the poet's heart when caught and tangled in a woman's body?—killed herself one winter's night and lies buried at some crossroads where the omnibuses now stop outside the Elephant and Castle![17]

SUMMARIZE: What would have prevented Shakespeare's sister from writing?

That, more or less, is how the story would run, I think, if a woman in Shakespeare's day had had Shakespeare's genius. But for my part, I agree with the deceased bishop, if such he was—it is unthinkable that any woman in Shakespeare's day should have had Shakespeare's genius. For genius like Shakespeare's is not born among laboring, uneducated servile[18] people. It was not born in England among the Saxons and the Britons. It is not born today among the working classes. How, then, could it have been born among women whose work began, according to Professor Trevelyan, almost before they were out of the nursery, who were forced to it by their parents and held to it by all the power of law and custom? Yet genius of a sort must have existed among women as it must have existed among the working classes. Now and again an Emily Brontë

or a Robert Burns blazes out and proves its presence. But certainly it never got itself on to paper. When, however, one reads of a witch being ducked, of a woman possessed by devils, of a wise woman selling herbs, or even of a very remarkable man who had a mother, then I think we are on the track of a lost novelist, a suppressed poet, of some mute and inglorious[19] Jane Austen, some Emily Brontë who dashed her brains out on the moor or mopped and mowed about the highways crazed with the torture that her gift had put her to. Indeed, I would venture to guess that Anon, who wrote so many poems without signing them, was often a woman. It was a woman Edward FitzGerald, I think, suggested who made the ballads and the folk songs, crooning them to her children, beguiling her spinning with them, or the length of the winter's night.

This may be true or it may be false—who can say?—but what is true in it, so it seemed to me, reviewing the story of Shakespeare's sister as I had made it, is that any woman born with a great gift in the sixteenth century would certainly have gone crazed, shot herself, or ended her days in some lonely cottage outside the village, half witch, half wizard, feared and mocked at. For it needs little skill in psychology to be sure that a highly gifted girl who had tried to use her gift for poetry would have been so thwarted[20] and hindered by other people, so tortured and pulled asunder[21] by her own contrary instincts, that she must have lost her health and sanity to a certainty. No girl could have walked to London and stood at a stage door and forced her way into the presence of actor-managers without doing herself a violence and suffering an anguish which may have been irrational—for chastity may

---

17. **crossroads . . . Elephant and Castle.** Suicides were often buried at crossroads; the Elephant and Castle is a common name for a tavern.
18. servile (sėr′vəl), *adj.* slavelike.
19. inglorious (in glôr′ē əs), *adj.* shameful; disgraceful.
20. thwart (thwôrt), *v.* prevent from doing something.
21. asunder (ə sun′dər), *adv.* in pieces or separate parts.

MINI-LESSON: LITERARY FOCUS

Paradox

Teach   Point out that a paradox is a tenet that is seemingly contradictory and opposed to common sense but is probably true. Virginia Woolf exposes the paradox of the fictional Elizabethan woman as opposed to her real-life counterpart. Discuss the importance of analyzing the fantasized female characters of Elizabethan literature versus the reality of the actual women who lived during that time period.

Question   Do you think Woolf's essay has relevance to the women of today? *(Possible response: Yes. A typical example of a modern-day para-dox would be the equality of the sexes. It is guaranteed under the law; however, there is very often an inequality in the salaries paid to men and women for the same job—a man, frequently, is paid more.)*

Activity Idea   Have students write their own essays that expose a modern-day paradox experienced by them or by someone they know. Invite volunteers to share their essays with the class.

be a fetish invented by certain societies for unknown reasons—but were none the less inevitable. Chastity had then, it has even now, a religious importance in a woman's life, and has so wrapped itself round with nerves and instincts that to cut it free and bring it to the light of day demands courage of the rarest. To have lived a free life in London in the sixteenth century would have meant for a woman who was poet and playwright a nervous stress and dilemma which might well have killed her. Had she survived, whatever she had written would have been twisted and deformed, issuing from a strained and morbid imagination. And undoubtedly, I thought, looking at the shelf where there are no plays by women, her work would have gone unsigned. That refuge she would have sought certainly. It was the relic of the sense of chastity that dictated anonymity[22] to women even so late as the nineteenth century. Currer Bell, George Eliot, George Sand,[23] all the victims of inner strife as their writings prove, sought ineffectively to veil themselves by using the name of a man. Thus they did homage to the convention, which if not implanted by the other sex was liberally encouraged by them (the chief glory of a woman is not to be talked of, said Pericles,[24] himself a much-talked-of man), that publicity in women is detestable. Anonymity runs in their blood. The desire to be veiled still possesses them. . . .

> **CLARIFY:** Why did these women deny their individuality to choose anonymity?

I told you in the course of this paper that Shakespeare had a sister; but do not look for her in Sir Sidney Lee's life of the poet. She died young—alas, she never wrote a word. She lies buried where the omnibuses now stop, opposite the Elephant and Castle. Now my belief is that this poet who never wrote a word and was buried at the crossroads still lives. She lives in you and in me, and in many other women who are not here tonight, for they are washing up the dishes and

putting the children to bed. But she lives; for great poets do not die; they are continuing presences; they need only the opportunity to walk among us in the flesh. This opportunity, as I think, it is now coming within your power to give her. For my belief is that if we live another century or so—I am talking of the common life which is the real life and not of the little separate lives which we live as individuals—and have five hundred a year each of us and rooms of our own; if we have the habit of freedom and the courage to write exactly what we think; if we escape a little from the common sitting room and see human beings not always in their relation to each other but in relation to reality; and the sky, too, and the trees or whatever it may be in themselves; if we look past Milton's bogey,[25] for no human being should shut out the view; if we face the fact, for it is a fact, that there is no arm to cling to, but that we go alone and that our relation is to the world of reality and not only to the world of men and women, then the opportunity will come and the dead poet who was Shakespeare's sister will put on the body which she has so often laid down. Drawing her life from the lives of the unknown who were her forerunners, as her brother did before her, she will be born. As for her coming without that preparation, without that effort on our part, without that determination that when she is born again she shall find it possible to live and write her poetry, that we cannot expect, for that would be impossible. But I maintain that she would come if we worked for her, and that so to work, even in poverty and obscurity, is worth while.

---

22. **anonymity** (an′ə nim′ə tē), *n.* condition of being unknown.
23. **Currer Bell, George Eliot, George Sand,** male pen names of the English novelists Charlotte Brontë and Mary Ann Evans, and the French novelist Amandine-Aurore Dupin.
24. **Pericles** (per′ə klēz′), Greek statesman and orator (495–429 B.C.).
25. **Milton's bogey.** In *Paradise Lost*, Milton portrays Eve as inferior to Adam. A bogey is a person or thing feared without reason.

Shakespeare's Sister **819**

12

13

BUILDING ENGLISH PROFICIENCY

Making Cultural Connections

Invite students to discuss opportunities for women in the United States and in countries from which their families came. Have students share ideas in small groups on such questions as these:

- Why do some people resist the idea that men and women should have equal opportunities?
- What, if anything, limits a woman's ability to be successful in all areas?

Follow up by asking students to list (anonymously, but indicating whether from a male or a female) the five things they most want out of life, in the order in which they want them. Have a group of students tally the results and report them to the class.

After Reading

MAKING CONNECTIONS

1. Answers will vary. Some students may suggest that there is still inequality between men and women and that men still control many personal and professional aspects of a woman's life.

2. By discussing these fictional female characters, Woolf effectively shows the disparity between these imagined women and their real-life counterparts. It is an effective technique because she is able to demonstrate the enormous differences between the two.

3. By inventing a female sibling of Shakespeare's, Woolf is able to show the inequality of the typical upbringing of a male and female from the same household. Whereas Shakespeare attended school, his sister did not. Where he was encouraged, she was stymied.

4. To have a space of one's own and a little money to survive is to have some independence from others and the opportunity to explore one's creative instincts.

5. Woolf speaks with a great deal of passion on the subject of women. A woman's status was rarely challenged in Woolf's time. She championed an unpopular cause, raised questions, and made her voice heard.

6. Possible response: People who feel threatened by the progress made by women in this century often are fearful of change, and prefer the security of the familiar rather than the upheaval they might experience through change.

After Reading

Making Connections

Shaping Your Response

1. Do you find this essay relevant to your life? Why or why not?

Analyzing the Essay

2. Why do you suppose Woolf mentions so many fictional female characters? Is this technique effective, in your opinion?

3. What does Woolf achieve through her invention of a character she calls Shakespeare's sister?

4. Woolf says that it is necessary for women to "have five hundred a year . . . and rooms of our own" to succeed artistically. Why does she say this? Do you agree?

5. 👆 The struggle for **individuality** often means that a person cannot be a conformist. What aspects of this essay mark Woolf as a nonconformist?

Extending the Ideas

6. Some people seem to feel threatened by changing roles for women, by women's achievements outside the home, and by women who achieve. Why do you think they have these feelings?

Literary Focus: Paradox

A statement that may be valid but that seems to say two different and contradictory things is a **paradox.** A paradox can also be a person, thing, or situation that is full of contradictions.

1. Woolf says that a "composite being . . . emerges" when one considers women in the 1500s and 1600s. What makes this "being" a paradox?

2. What does Professor Trevelyan have to do with this paradox?

Vocabulary Study

Choose the word from the list that most closely describes each idea or event.

agog
anonymity
asunder
impropriety
incorporeal
inglorious
perennial
prosaically
servile
thwart

1. Stories about that crumbling pile of stonework known as Hoxley Hall were enduring in our small town.

2. Over the years the previous owner had acquired a reputation that was shameful.

3. Had he become rich through some kind of improper conduct?

4. It was known that he had treated his servants in a way to make them feel like slaves.

5. Whatever the truth, it seemed that he had not lived his life in a plain, unexciting fashion.

820   UNIT SEVEN: THE EARLY TWENTIETH CENTURY

LITERARY FOCUS: PARADOX

Possible Responses

1. The composite being to which Woolf refers is the ideal woman who is conceived in men's minds. Beautiful, smart, and loaded with wisdom, she is everything any man could possibly want, but she is fictional and never existed in the 1500s and 1600s.

2. Professor Trevelyan points out these paradoxes and informs the reader of some general facts pertaining to women's lives at this time but goes no further. He focuses on events primarily dominated by men, and, except for the occasional mention of the queens Mary or Elizabeth, ignores the common woman.

6 Hoxley Hall, too, had hardly become an unknown and forgotten building.

7. Now Brian, Rosemary, and I approached the mansion, all extremely eager to learn its secrets.

8. At first we were prevented from entering because of an iron chain through the handles of the front double doors.

9. Brian had thoughtfully brought a tool to snap the chain, however, and soon the links fell to the porch.

10. Imagine our surprise when, as we opened the front door, we witnessed a ghostly, translucent figure gliding down the stairway.

Expressing Your Ideas

Writing Choices

Reader's Log Update Review your lists of feminine endings, and in a paragraph explain whether you think such endings are useful and why or why not.

I Want to Be Me Finding your identity or striving to become an individual is part of growing up. Have you ever felt that people or circumstances were working to prevent you from finding your identity? In an **informal essay** describe one such episode in your life and what the outcome was.

Dear Ms. Woolf Write a **letter** to Virginia Woolf describing major events in women's rights today. You may want to do some research on the status of women's rights and on events of the last few years before starting your letter.

Other Options

Uncovering the Past Woolf has some insights into the writing of history that ignores women, but how *is* history written? In a small group, review the school year or the last semester, and discuss how you will decide which events in your school would be suitable for a history of that time. Who or what defines a "major" event? Is a major happening one that affects a few people or many? Should a controversial matter be included? Should you consider the relevance of an event to the community as a whole? Will you include more than one viewpoint in your history? Summarize the **discussion** and present the **summary** to the rest of the class.

Picture the Past Design a **mural** showing major events in the history of women's rights. If you want to include words or quotations in your mural, you might review Daniel Defoe's essay "The Education of Women" (page 306) and the excerpt from Mary Wollstonecraft's *A Vindication of the Rights of Woman* (page 456).

Shakespeare's Sister **821**

Before Reading

Building Background

You might begin by playing recordings of Dylan Thomas reading his own work. Both "Do Not Go Gentle into That Good Night" and "A Child's Christmas in Wales" are available.

Literary Focus

Suggest that as students read the selection they write down words and phrases that are particularly rich in imagery and that give a clear mental picture of what the author is trying to convey.

Writer's Notebook

Ask volunteers to share their words and phrases with the class.

More About Dylan Thomas

Thomas was equally famous as a boisterous, hard-drinking man as he was as a poet. He died in St. Vincent's Hospital in New York City, while on a lecture tour. His death was attributed to acute alcoholic intoxication. Other works by Dylan Thomas include

- *The World I Breathe* (1939)
- *New Poems* (1942)
- *In Country Sleep* (1952)

Before Reading

Do Not Go Gentle into That Good Night
A Child's Christmas in Wales by Dylan Thomas

Dylan Thomas
1914–1953

Dylan Thomas's fame—based in part on his exuberant lifestyle and popular public readings—threatened to overshadow his poetry. He was born in Swansea, Wales, left school at sixteen to work as a newspaper reporter, and published his first volume of poetry at nineteen. *Portrait of the Artist as a Young Dog,* a collection of stories about his childhood and youth, appeared in 1940. He married Caitlin Macnamara in 1937, and they and their children were often partly supported by friends. *Deaths and Entrances* (1946) is his most famous poetry collection. *Quite Early One Morning* (1954), another book of boyhood reminiscences, and a verse play, *Under Milk Wood* (1954) were published after his death in New York during his fourth lecture tour.

Building Background

Galloping Words Dylan Thomas's father was a schoolteacher who read to Dylan when the boy was young. Thomas described "the colors the words cast on my eyes . . . and though what the words meant was, in its own way, often deliciously funny enough, so much funnier seemed to me, at that almost forgotten time, the shape and shade and size and noise of words as they hummed, strummed, jigged, and galloped along." Thomas wrote "Do Not Go Gentle into That Good Night" just before the death of his father. "A Child's Christmas in Wales" is an expanded version of a talk Thomas gave on the BBC radio station. It was first published in *Harper's Bazaar* and then recorded, becoming one of the most famous works Thomas ever read for the public.

Literary Focus

Imagery Details that appeal to the senses and provide vividness in a literary work or tend to arouse emotions or feelings in a reader are called **imagery.** Effective imagery often appeals to more than one sense at a time, as in this passage from Dylan Thomas's *Portrait of the Artist as a Young Dog.*

"On windy October nights, dry leaves scraped across the sidewalk, and the dust of them caught in our throats. Already the air nipped at our noses, and our breath hung for an instant in the icy air and vanished. Always, the shadow of a cat crossed the alley behind Mrs. Wiley's house, and the bushes were full of strange and fearful shapes."

Notice the imagery in these selections by Thomas.

Writer's Notebook

Remember When? Think of your favorite holiday, and under headings for the five senses (sight, hearing, taste, smell, and touch) jot down several words or phrases that appeal to these senses and help to describe the holiday. For example, under *hearing,* you might write "murmur of voices"; under *sight,* you might describe a burning candle.

SUPPORT MATERIALS OVERVIEW

Unit 7 Resource Book
- Graphic Organizer, p. 121
- Study Guide, p. 122
- Vocabulary, p. 123
- Grammar, p. 124
- Alternate Check Test, p. 125
- Vocabulary Test, p. 126
- Selection Test, pp. 127–128

Building English Proficiency
- Selection Summaries
- Activities, p. 259

Reading, Writing & Grammar SkillBook
- Reading, pp. 51–52, 53–54
- Writing, pp. 123–124
- Grammar, Usage, and Mechanics, pp. 243–244

Technology
- Audiotape
- Personal Journal Software
- Test Generator Software

DO NOT GO GENTLE INTO THAT GOOD NIGHT

DYLAN THOMAS

1

Do not go gentle into that good night,
Old age should burn and rave at close of day;
Rage, rage against the dying of the light.

Though wise men at their end know dark is right,
5 Because their words had forked no lightning they
Do not go gentle into that good night.

Good men, the last wave by, crying how bright
Their frail deeds might have danced in a green bay,
Rage, rage against the dying of the light.

10 Wild men who caught and sang the sun in flight,
And learn, too late, they grieved it on its way,
Do not go gentle into that good night.

Grave men, near death, who see with blinding sight
Blind eyes could blaze like meteors and be gay,
15 Rage, rage against the dying of the light.

And you, my father, there on the sad height,
Curse, bless, me now with your fierce tears, I pray.
Do not go gentle into that good night.
Rage, rage against the dying of the light.

2

Do Not Go Gentle into That Good Night   **823**

Selection Objectives

- to recognize imagery
- to understand the differences between literal and figurative language
- to learn to use colons properly

 Unit 7 Resource Book
Graphic Organizer, p. 121
Study Guide, p. 122

Theme Link

Dylan Thomas's search for identity is explored in memories of his father's death and of Christmases past.

Vocabulary Preview

sidle, move sideways
daft, without sense or reason; silly
catapult, slingshot
judiciously, wisely; sensibly
tread, set the foot down; walk; step
constitutional, walk taken for one's health
  Students can add the words and definitions to their Writer's Notebooks.

1 | Reading/Thinking Skills
Literal and Figurative Language

Questions   "Good night" is repeated several times. To what does the phrase refer? *(death)* What is ironic about its use? *(The narrator finds little "good" in death; also, the reader is obviously meant to recall "good night" used as a parting phrase for "sleep well," not "die well.")*

2 | Reading/Thinking Skills
Find the Main Idea

Question   It is usually thought to be a blessing to "go gentle into that good night." Why does the poet ask that his father rage? *(Possible response: All manner of men should regret what they didn't do, accomplish, attempt, or understand in their lifetimes.)*

SELECTION SUMMARY

Do Not Go Gentle into That Good Night;
A Child's Christmas in Wales

Do Not Go Gentle into That Good Night   A young man demands that his father not surrender to death but fiercely hold on to his will to live.

A Child's Christmas in Wales   The narrator reflects on Christmas memories: of the Protheros whose house catches fire on Christmas Eve; of snow and the mail man; of useless and useful presents; of unnamed uncles eating and smoking cigars; of tall tales told by the fire; of light streaming from the windows and smoke curling from the chimneys of all the houses of the town; of fiddle playing and singing and music rising up from the town as the night grew older; and finally of bed, "words to the close and holy darkness," and then sleep.

 *For summaries in other languages, see the **Building English Proficiency** book.*

Art Study

A Child's Christmas in Wales

DYLAN THOMAS

▲ *Snow Scene* was painted in 1879 by an amateur artist identified as W. Park. In its depiction of childhood, what qualities does it share with Dylan Thomas's memoir?

MINI-LESSON: LITERARY FOCUS

Imagery

Teach   Remind students that imagery is details that provide vividness in a literary work. When students have read the poem, ask them what "that good night" is a metaphor for. Point out that Thomas's words about light and darkness in this poem create powerful images of going into "that good night."

Activity Idea   Have students complete a chart with three words or phrases in this poem that describe light and three that describe darkness. Invite students to choose and read aloud the ones they consider most vivid.

One Christmas was so much like another, in those years around the sea-town corner now and out of all sound except the distant speaking of the voices I sometimes hear a moment before sleep, that I can never remember whether it snowed for six days and six nights when I was twelve or whether it snowed for twelve days and twelve nights when I was six. All the Christmases roll down toward the two-tongued sea, like a cold and headlong moon bundling down the sky that was our street; and they stop at the rim of the ice-edged, fish-freezing waves, and I plunge my hands in the snow and bring out whatever I can find. In goes my hand into that wool-white bell-tongued ball of holidays resting at the rim of the carol-singing sea, and out come Mrs. Prothero and the firemen.

It was on the afternoon of the day of Christmas Eve, and I was in Mrs. Prothero's garden, waiting for cats, with her son Jim. It was snowing. It was always snowing at Christmas. December, in my mem-

ory, is white as Lapland, though there were no reindeers. But there were cats. Patient, cold and callous, our hands wrapped in socks, we waited to snowball the cats. Sleek and long as jaguars and horrible-whiskered, spitting and snarling, they would slink and sidle[1] over the white back-garden walls, and the lynx-eyed hunters, Jim and I, fur-capped and moccasined trappers from Hudson Bay, off Mumbles Road, would hurl our deadly snowballs at the green of their eyes. The wise cats never appeared. We were so still, Eskimo-footed arctic marksmen in the muf-fling silence of the eternal snows—eternal, ever since Wednesday—that we never heard Mrs. Prothero's first cry from her igloo at the bottom of the garden. Or, if we heard it at all, it was, to us, like the far-off challenge of our enemy and

. . . Mrs. Prothero was announcing ruin like a town crier in Pompeii.

prey, the neighbour's polar cat. But soon the voice grew louder.

"Fire!" cried Mrs. Prothero, and she beat the dinner-gong.

And we ran down the garden, with the snow-balls in our arms, toward the house; and smoke, indeed, was pouring out of the dining-room, and the bong was bombilating,[2] and Mrs. Prothero was announcing ruin like a town crier in Pompeii.[3] This was better than all the cats in Wales standing on the wall in a row. We bounded into the house, laden with snowballs, and stopped at the open door of the smoke-filled room. Something was burning all right; perhaps it was Mr. Prothero, who always slept there after midday dinner with a new paper over his face. But he was standing in the middle of the room, saying, "A fine Christmas!" and smack-ing at the smoke with a slipper.

"Call the fire brigade," cried Mrs. Prothero as she beat the gong.

"They won't be there," said Mr. Prothero, "It's Christmas."

There was no fire to be seen, only clouds of smoke and Mr. Prothero standing in the middle of them, waving his slipper as though he were conducting.

"Do something," he said.

And we threw all our snowballs into the smoke—I think we missed Mr. Prothero—and ran out of the house to the telephone box.

"Let's call the police as well," Jim said.

"And the ambulance."

"And Ernie Jenkins, he likes fires."

But we only called the fire brigade, and soon

---

1. sidle (sī′dl), v. move sideways.
2. bombilate (bom′bə lāt), v. hum; boom.
3. Pompeii (pom pā′), city in ancient Italy buried by an eruption of the volcano Mount Vesuvius in A.D. 79.

A Child's Christmas in Wales **825**

Geographical Note
Lapland

Lapland stretches across Arctic Norway, Sweden, Finland, and includes the Kola Peninsula of Russia. The Lapps' name for themselves is Sami. The traditional way of life for most Sami is reindeer herding, and they are imagined here to be a nomadic people who live in a landscape of perpet-ual winter.

Literary Element
Alliteration

Question   Thomas uses alliteration here for a humorous effect. What do you hear and see with "the bong was bombilating"? *(Possible response: a large gong with a deep resonant sound ringing in everyone's ears)*

BUILDING ENGLISH PROFICIENCY

Exploring Style

Direct students' attention to one distinctive element of Thomas's style in this memoir—his use of hyphenated adjectives.

1. Read aloud the first sentence on page 825; then point out the expression *sea-town corner.* Invite comments.

2. Have students locate other hyphenated adjectives in which one of the words is a noun. Work with them to locate the word that each one describes and to make a personal response to it.

Building English Proficiency Activities, p. 259

Hyphenated Adjective	Describes	My Response
ice-edged	waves	That's <u>cold</u>!
lynx-eyed	hunters	Did they plan to be cruel?

Question These two paragraphs express in images what snow means to the author. What senses are appealed to here? Explain. *(Possible response: smell, touch, sight, hearing; you can smell the snow, feel the cold, see the snow growing, and hear the muffled sounds produced by it.)*

6

Literary Element
Alliteration

Question What was the postman doing when he "mittened on them manfully"? *(knocking on the door; ringing the bell)*

7

Active Reading
Clarify

Possible Response The town was covered, bundled, and wrapped in snow, like a head or an arm in a bandage.

8

Literary Element
Figurative Language

Question Can you identify examples of metaphor and simile in the description of the postman? *(Possible responses: metaphor—"making ghosts with his breath"; simile—"jogged . . . like small boys wanting to do out"; "He went . . . like a man on fishmonger's slabs"; "He wagged his bag like a frozen camel's hump.")*

---

the fire engine came and three tall men in helmets brought a hose into the house and Mr. Prothero got out just in time before they turned it on. Nobody could have had a noisier Christmas Eve. And when the firemen turned off the hose and were standing in the wet, smoky room, Jim's aunt, Miss Prothero, came downstairs and peered in at them. Jim and I waited, very quietly, to hear what she would say to them. She said the right thing, always. She looked at the three tall firemen in their shining helmets, standing among the smoke and cinders and dissolving snowballs, and she said: "Would you like anything to read?"

5

Years and years and years ago, when I was a boy, when there were wolves in Wales, and birds the color of red-flannel petticoats whisked past the harp-shaped hills, when we sang and wallowed all night and day in caves that smelt like Sunday afternoons in damp front farmhouse parlors, and we chased, with the jawbones of deacons, the English and the bears, before the motor car, before the wheel, before the duchess-faced horse when we rode the daft[4] and happy hills bareback, it snowed and it snowed. But here a small boy says: "It snowed last year, too. I made a snowman and my brother knocked it down and I knocked my brother down and then we had tea."

"But that was not the same snow," I say. "Our snow was not only shaken from whitewash buckets down the sky, it came shawling out of the ground and swam and drifted out of the arms and hands and bodies of the trees; snow grew overnight on the roofs of the houses like a pure and grandfather moss, minutely white-ivied the walls and settled on the postman, opening the gate, like a dumb, numb thunderstorm of white, torn Christmas cards."

"Were there postmen then, too?"

6

"With sprinkling eyes and wind-cherried noses, on spread, frozen feet they crunched up to the doors and mittened on them manfully. But all that the children could hear was a ringing of bells."

"You mean that the postman went rat-a-tat-tat and the doors rang?"

"I mean that the bells that the children could hear were inside them."

"I only hear thunder sometimes, never bells."

"There were church bells, too."

"Inside them?"

"No, no, no, in the bat-black, snow-white belfries, tugged by bishops and storks. And they rang their tidings over the bandaged town, over the frozen foam of the powder and ice-cream hills, over the crackling sea. It seemed that all the churches boomed for joy under my window; and the weathercocks[5] crew for Christmas, on our fence."

CLARIFY: Why might Thomas use the word *bandaged* to describe the town?

7

"Get back to the postmen."

"They were just ordinary postmen, fond of walking and dogs and Christmas and the snow. They knocked on the doors with blue knuckles. . . ."

"Ours has got a black knocker. . . ."

"And then they stood on the white Welcome mat in the little, drifted porches and huffed and puffed, making ghosts with their breath, and jogged from foot to foot like small boys wanting to go out."

"And then the Presents?"

"And then the Presents, after the Christmas box.[6] And the cold postman, with a rose on his button-nose, tingled down the tea-tray-slithered run of the chilly glinting hill. He went in his ice-bound boots like a man on fishmonger's slabs. He wagged his bag like a frozen camel's hump, dizzily turned the corner on one foot, and, by God, he was gone."

8

---

4. daft (daft), *adj.* without sense or reason; silly.
5. **weathercock,** vane to show which way the wind is blowing, especially one in the shape of a rooster.
6. **Christmas box,** Christmas gift given to the postman.

MINI-LESSON: GRAMMAR

Using Colons

Teach A colon generally means that something is about to follow. Remind students of these uses for a colon:

- before a list of items
- after expressions such as *as follows* and *the following*
- before a long, formal statement or quotation
- between two independent clauses when the second clause explains or restates the idea of the first
- between the hour and the minute when time is written (1:00 P.M.)
- after the salutation of a formal letter (Sirs:)

- after the chapter number when a reference to a Bible passage includes the verse (Isaiah 53:5)

Have students state the reason for the use of colons on these pages: all column interrupters; line 14, page 826 *(a stylistic use of a colon instead of a comma);* line 2, page 827; line 2, page 828; top of column 2, page 829

Activity Idea Ask students to write a paragraph using colons for several reasons, such as the time of departure for a trip and preceding the items they will pack.

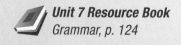

Unit 7 Resource Book
Grammar, p. 124

"Get back to the Presents."

"There were the Useful Presents: engulfing mufflers of the old coach days, and mittens made for giant sloths; zebra scarfs of a substance like silky gum that could be tug-o'-warred down to the galoshes, blinding tam-o'-shanters like patchwork tea cozies and bunny-suited busbies and balaclavas[7] for victims of head-shrinking tribes; from aunts who always wore wool next to the skin there were mustached and rasping vests that made you wonder why the aunts had any skin left at all; and once I had a little crocheted nose bag from an aunt now, alas, no longer whinnying with us. And pictureless books in which small boys, though warned with quotations not to, *would* skate on Farmer Giles' pond and did and drowned; and books that told me everything about the wasp, except why."

"Go on to the Useless Presents."

"Bags of moist and many-colored jelly babies and a folded flag and a false nose and a tram-conductor's cap and a machine that punched tickets and rang a bell; never a catapult;[8] once, by mistake that no one could explain, a little hatchet; and a celluloid duck that made, when you pressed it, a most unducklike sound, a mewing moo that an ambitious cat might make who wished to be a cow; and a painting book in which I could make the grass, the trees, the sea and the animals any color I pleased, and still the dazzling sky-blue sheep are grazing in the red field under the rainbow-billed and pea-green birds. Hard-boileds, toffee, fudge and allsorts, crunches, cracknels, humbugs, glaciers, marzipan, and butterwelsh for the Welsh. And troops of bright tin soldiers who, if they could not fight, could always run. And Snakes-and-Families and Happy Ladders. And Easy Hobbi-Games for Little Engineers, complete with instructions. Oh, easy for Leonardo![9] And a whistle to make the dogs bark to wake up the old man next door to make him beat on the wall with his stick to shake our picture off the wall. And a packet of cigarettes: you put one in your mouth and you stood at the corner of the street and you waited for hours, in vain, for an old lady to scold you for smoking a cig-

arette, and then with a smirk you ate it. And then it was breakfast under the balloons."

"Were there Uncles, like in our house?"

"There are always Uncles at Christmas. The same Uncles. And on Christmas mornings, with dog-disturbing whistle and sugar fags, I would scour the swatched town for the news of the little world, and find always a dead bird by the white Post Office or by the deserted swings; perhaps a robin, all but one of his fires out. Men and women wading or scooping back from chapel, with taproom noses and wind-bussed cheeks, all albinos, huddled their stiff black jarring feathers against the irreligious snow. Mistletoe hung from the gas brackets in all the front parlors; there was sherry and walnuts and bottled beer and crackers[10] by the dessertspoons; and cats in their furabouts watched the fires; and the high-heaped fire spat, all ready for the chestnuts and the mulling pokers.[11] Some few large men sat in the front parlors, without their collars, Uncles almost certainly, trying their new cigars, holding them out judiciously[12] at arms' length, returning them to their mouths, coughing, then holding them out again as though waiting for the explosion; and some few small aunts, not wanted in the kitchen, nor anywhere else for that matter, sat on the very edges of their chairs, poised and brittle, afraid to break, like faded cups and saucers."

CLARIFY: The Uncles are given no individual identity. Why?

---

7. **busby** (buz′bē) *n.* . . . **balaclava** (bal′ə klä′və), *n.* two kinds of hats.
8. **catapult** (kat′ə pult), *n.* slingshot.
9. **Leonardo,** Leonardo da Vinci (1452–1519), Italian painter, architect, engineer, and scientist.
10. **cracker,** party favor containing jokes or gifts that pops when the ends are pulled.
11. **mulling pokers,** fireplace pokers used to heat and stir a mulled drink. To *mull* is to heat, sweeten, and spice ale, wine, cider, and so on.
12. **judiciously** (jü dish′əs lē), *adv.* wisely; sensibly.

A Child's Christmas in Wales   **827**

9 | Reading/Thinking Skills
Visualize

Ask students to visualize what the Useful Presents look like, then describe what the author is communicating. *(Possible responses: mufflers that are very long; mittens that are way too big; scarves that are too long and made from some nasty material; too-large woolen caps and too-small hats; woolly underwear that itches; a crocheted device to cover the nose; and books of a moral and uplifting nature)*

10 | Active Reading
Clarify

Possible response   It is an overview of what Christmas was like for Thomas's family and other families. The notion that "there are always uncles at Christmas" is a statement about what it was like to be part of a large extended family. The individual and specifics aren't important. It's a general feeling of a Christmas gathering in an old-fashioned family that the author wants to capture.

BUILDING ENGLISH PROFICIENCY

Exploring Compound Words

To expand students' vocabulary, show them that many English words are made by joining shorter words together. These are called compound words.

1. Ask pairs of students to find and list 10 compound words on pages 826–827. (Limit them to closed compounds.) Have them write the shorter words that make up the compound.

2. Invite students to make 10 new words, using one of the short words in each compound word to make the new words.

Compound Word	Words Joined Together	New Word
snowball	snow + balls	snowflake
grandfather	grand + father	godfather

Ask students to read through this paragraph again to identify different kinds of figurative language that Thomas uses. *(Possible responses: metaphor—"the spit of myself"; hyperbole—"cheeks bulged with goose"; simile—"cocky as a bullfinch"; "singing like a big-bosomed thrush"; "uncles breathed like dolphins, like snow descending")*

12 Active Reading
Clarify

Possible Response The narrator and Jim, Dan, and Jack are speaking.

Not many those mornings trod[13] the piling streets: an old man always, fawn-bowlered,[14] yellow-gloved and, at this time of year, with spats[15] of snow, would take his constitutional[16] to the white bowling green and back, as he would take it wet or fine on Christmas Day or Doomsday; sometimes two hale young men, with big pipes blazing, no overcoats and wind-blown scarfs, would trudge, unspeaking, down to the forlorn sea, to work up an appetite, to blow away the fumes, who knows, to walk into the waves until nothing of them was left but the two curling smoke clouds of their inextinguishable briars. Then I would be slapdashing home, the gravy smell of the dinners of others, the bird smell, the brandy, the pudding and mince, coiling up to my nostrils, when out of a snow-clogged side lane would come a boy the spit of myself, with a pink-tipped cigarette and the violet past of a black eye, cocky as a bullfinch, leering all to himself. I hated him on sight and sound, and would be about to put my dog whistle to my lips and blow him off the face of Christmas when suddenly he, with a violet wink, put *his* whistle to *his* lips and blew so stridently, so high, so exquisitely loud, that gobbling faces, their cheeks bulged with goose, would press against their tinseled windows, the whole length of the white echoing street. For dinner we had turkey and blazing pudding, and after dinner the Uncles sat in front of the fire, loosened all buttons, put their large moist hands over their watch chains, groaned a little and slept. Mothers, aunts and sisters scuttled to and fro, bearing tureens.[17] Auntie Bessie, who had already been frightened, twice, by a clock-work mouse, whimpered at the sideboard and had some elderberry wine. The dog was sick. Auntie Dosie had to have three aspirins, but Auntie Hannah, who liked port, stood in the middle of the snow-bound back yard, singing like a big-bosomed thrush. I would blow up balloons to see how big they would blow up to; and when they burst, which they all did, the Uncles jumped and rumbled. In the rich and heavy afternoon, the Uncles breathing like dolphins and the snow descending, I would sit

among festoons and Chinese lanterns and nibble dates and try to make a model man-o'-war,[18] following the Instructions for Little Engineers, and produce what might be mistaken for a sea-going tramcar. Or I would go out, my bright new boots squeaking, into the white world, on to the seaward hill, to call on Jim and Dan and Jack and to pad through the still streets, leaving huge deep footprints on the hidden pavements.

CLARIFY: Who is speaking here? **12**

"I bet people will think there's been hippos."

"What would you do if you saw a hippo coming down our street?"

"I'd go like this, bang! I'd throw him over the railings and roll him down the hill and then I'd tickle him under the ear and he'd wag his tail."

"What would you do if you saw *two* hippos?"

Iron-flanked and bellowing he-hippos clanked and battered through the scudding snow toward us as we passed Mr. Daniel's house.

"Let's post Mr. Daniel a snowball through his letter box."

"Let's write things in the snow."

"Let's write, 'Mr. Daniel looks like a spaniel' all over his lawn."

Or we walked on the white shore. "Can the fishes see it's snowing?"

The silent one-clouded heavens drifted on to the sea. Now we were snow-blind travelers lost on the north hills, and vast dewlapped dogs, with

---

13. tread (tred), *v.* trod, trodden or trod, treading, set the foot down; walk; step.
14. **bowlered,** wearing a bowler, a stiff felt hat with a narrow brim.
15. **spats** (spats), *n. pl.* short gaiters, outer coverings for the lower leg or ankle made of cloth or leather and worn over the instep, reaching just above the ankle.
16. constitutional (kon′stə tü′shə nəl), *n.* walk or other exercise taken for one's health.
17. **tureen** (tə rēn′), *n.* deep, covered dish for serving soup.
18. **man-o'-war,** warship used in past wars.

MINI-LESSON: LITERARY FOCUS

Imagery

Teach By definition, an image is a word or phrase that appeals to one or more of the five senses. (Imagery is also the term for details that tend to arouse emotions and feelings.) Have students draw five boxes and label each one with a sense. Ask them to read through the selection again and write in the appropriate box words or phrases that evoke imagery involving the senses.

Activity Ideas

- Have students write a few paragraphs about a favorite holiday. Ask them to include images that appeal to the five senses.
- Ask volunteers to research other poems by Dylan Thomas that are rich in imagery. Have students share the poems with the class.

flasks round their necks, ambled and shambled up to us, baying "Excelsior."[19] We returned him through the poor streets where only a few children fumbled with bare red fingers in the wheel-rutted snow and catcalled after us, their voices fading away, as we trudged uphill, into the cries of the dock birds and the hooting of ships out in the whirling bay. And then, at tea the recovered Uncles would be jolly; and the ice cake loomed in the center of the table like a marble grave. Auntie Hannah laced her tea with rum, because it was only once a year.

> The wind through the trees made noises as of old and unpleasant and maybe webfooted men wheezing in caves.

Bring out the tall tales now that we told by the fire as the gaslight bubbled like a diver. Ghosts whooed like owls in the long nights when I dared not look over my shoulder; animals lurked in the cubbyhole under the stairs where the gas meter ticked. And I remember that we went singing carols once, when there wasn't the shaving of a moon to light the flying street. At the end of a long road was a drive that led to a large house, and we stumbled up the darkness of the drive that night, each one of us afraid, each one holding a stone in his hand in case, and all of us too brave to say a word. The wind through the trees made noises as of old and unpleasant and maybe webfooted men wheezing in caves. We reached the black bulk of the house.

"What shall we give them? Hark, the Herald?"

"No," Jack said, "Good King Wenceslas. I'll count three."

One, two, three, and we began to sing, our voices high and seemingly distant in the snow-felted darkness round the house that was occupied by nobody we knew. We stood close together, near the dark door.

Good King Wenceslas looked out
On the Feast of Stephen . . .

And then a small, dry voice, like the voice of someone who has not spoken for a long time, joined our singing: a small, dry, eggshell voice from the other side of the door: a small dry voice through the keyhole. And when we stopped running we were outside *our* house; the front room was lovely; balloons floated under the hot-water-bottle-gulping gas; everything was good again and shone over the town.

"Perhaps it was a ghost," Jim said.

"Perhaps it was trolls,"[20] Dan said, who was always reading.

"Let's go in and see if there's any jelly left," Jack said. And we did that.

Always on Christmas night there was music. An uncle played the fiddle, a cousin sang "Cherry Ripe," and another uncle sang "Drake's Drum." It was very warm in the little house. Auntie Hannah, who had got on to the parsnip wine, sang about Bleeding Hearts and Death, and then another in which she said her heart was like a Bird's Nest; and then everybody laughed again; and then I went to bed. Looking through my bedroom window, out into the moonlight and the unending smoke-colored snow, I could see the lights in the windows of all the other houses on our hill and hear the music rising from them up the long, steadily falling night. I turned the gas down, I got into bed. I said some words to the close and holy darkness, and then I slept.

---

19. **excelsior** (ek sel′sē ôr), *adj.* ever upward; higher. [*Latin*]
20. **troll** (trōl), *n.* in Scandinavian folklore, an ugly dwarf or giant with supernatural powers living underground or in a cave.

A Child's Christmas in Wales **829**

---

13 Literary Element
Mood

Question What is the mood that Dylan Thomas is creating in this paragraph? (*Possible responses: scared, dark, ghostly, fearful with nervous anticipation*)

14 Reader's Response
Making Personal Connections

Question How does the last paragraph make you feel? (*Possible responses: safe, protected, happy, contented*)

Check Test

1. What does the son want his father to do in "Do Not Go Gentle"? (*He wants him to hold on to his will to live.*)

2. What is *A Child's Christmas in Wales* about? (*fond memories of many Christmases*)

3. What happens to the Protheros? (*Their house catches fire on Christmas Eve.*)

4. According to the author, what are the two kinds of presents? (*useful and useless*)

5. What are some other memories that he writes about? (*snow, tall tales told by the fire, unnamed uncles who sang and smoked*)

 Unit 7 Resource Book
Alternate Check Test, p. 125

BUILDING ENGLISH PROFICIENCY

Making Personal Connections

Use one or more of these activities to help students relate to the selection.

Activity Ideas

- Bring old magazines (such as libraries give away) to class. Invite students to make a collage, using pieces cut from magazine pictures, showing a child's view of a favorite holiday.

- Ask several students of the same culture to show the class how one of their holidays is celebrated. Have them decide what to present—e.g. music, dance, or traditional foods.

- Have a group of students present a reading of this selection while others provide musical background.

After Reading

MAKING CONNECTIONS

1. The speaker demands a struggle against dying and feels that the will to live should triumph over the mere acceptance of death.

2. Answers will vary. Yes; the sights and sounds like the snow, the presents, the postman, and the ringing bells are all familiar. No; the village is a very different environment, and the people are eccentric.

3. Yes, the speaker says "Curse, bless, me," and desperately wants a response from the person to whom he is talking. It doesn't matter what form that response takes.

4. He refers to Christmas in general terms, as a collective concept. He uses phrases like "One Christmas was so much like another"; "There were always uncles at Christmas"; "Years and years ago when I was a young boy." He connects specific recollections and makes it into a whole, which represents the Christmas of his memory.

5. The author introduces the small boy so that the reader may experience Christmas through the eyes of a child and also to make it more personal.

6. It is a sweet, tender, and loving remembrance, vivid in imagery and comical in characterization.

7. Answers will vary.

After Reading

Making Connections

Shaping Your Response

1. In "Do Not Go Gentle . . ." why do you think the speaker urges resistance to instead of acceptance of death?

2. Is there anything in "A Child's Christmas in Wales" with which you can identify, or is the reminiscence too foreign or too dated? Explain.

Analyzing the Selections

3. Does line 17 of the poem contain a **paradox?** Why, or why not?

4. Explain how Thomas combines many Christmases into this one essay. How does he signal the reader what he is doing?

5. For what purpose do you think Thomas introduces the small boy who speaks in the essay?

6. How would you describe the **mood** of this essay?

Extending the Ideas

7. Name some presents that you have received or given that would fit into either of the two categories of presents Thomas mentions in "A Child's Christmas in Wales."

Literary Focus: Imagery

Details that tend to arouse emotions or feelings in a reader or that appeal to the senses and provide vividness in a literary work are called **imagery.**

1. In "Do Not Go Gentle . . ." what contrasting and repeated images appeal to the sense of sight?

2. Why are images appealing to the sense of sight particularly appropriate in this poem?

3. What images in "A Child's Christmas in Wales" seem most vivid to you?

LITERARY FOCUS: IMAGERY

Possible Responses

1. the "dying light" and "good night"

2. Images appealing to the sense of sight are appropriate because the sense of sight is also used to refer to mental or spiritual perception. It is sometimes said that the eyes are windows to the world as well as passageways to the soul.

3. Responses will vary, but may include the snow, the family, the postman, and of course, the presents.

Vocabulary Study

catapult
constitutional
daft
sidle
tread

Using context clues, fill in each blank with the most appropriate word from the list.

After an enormous Thanksgiving dinner, Grandfather decided to take his usual ____. He stepped across an icy street, making an effort to ____ carefully. He was just reaching the curb when he felt a small object, evidently shot from a ____, strike him lightly between his shoulder blades. He turned around just in time to see a small boy ____ between two buildings. "Are you ____?" shouted Grandfather after the disappearing shape. "You might have hurt someone!"

Expressing Your Ideas

Writing Choices

Writer's Notebook Update Describe your favorite holiday, and include some of the images you jotted down before reading Dylan Thomas. Try to create a particular mood such as reverence, joy, nostalgia, contentment, humor, or excitement.

Brain-Stretching Lists Thomas makes use of compound words like "fish-freezing waves," which are similar to the kennings used in *Beowulf.* Point out several examples of these compounds and then devise your own **list of compounds** to describe waves, sand, sky, clouds, or people in a warm climate.

Relatively Speaking When Thomas describes uncles and aunts in his reminiscence they often, but not always, tend to be types, not individuals. Write a **description** of a relative, such as an uncle or an aunt, in a few paragraphs. Make an effort to demonstrate the **individuality** of this person by exactly describing physical characteristics and by detailing this person's actions.

Write a Villanelle "Do Not Go Gentle . . ." is a **villanelle** (vil′ə nel′), a verse form consisting of five three-line stanzas and a final quatrain. The rhyme scheme is *aba* in every stanza except the last, which is *abaa.* Lines 1 and 3 repeat alternatively as refrains. Although this is a challenging verse form, many poets have used it successfully. Work with a partner, if you wish, to write a poem in this verse form.

Other Options

Season's Greetings Design and illustrate a **greeting card** based on "A Child's Christmas in Wales," perhaps using a short quotation from the essay.

And the Winner Is . . . Hold a **photo competition** for black-and-white or color photographs of holiday celebrations. Work with a group to set a deadline for entries, assign judges, decide how many and what prizes you will award, and where winning photos will be displayed.

A Child's Christmas in Wales **831**

Building Background

You might ask students to share their experiences of trying to study, to really concentrate, under difficult conditions. You might note that difficult conditions can be external, such as background noise, or internal, for example, the inability to keep one's mind focused.

Literary Focus

You might note how Desai's similes make her writing more personal, more alive: "I felt like a gatecrasher at a party or a visitor to a public library trying to control a sneeze."

Writer's Notebook

Students might work as a class or in groups to brainstorm similes.

More About Anita Desai

Desai grew up in a home where three languages were spoken—Hindi, English, and German. She considers English her "literary language," because it was the language she read and in which she was taught to write. As soon as the young Anita was taught the alphabet, she "went home and started to write, wanting passionately to create books of my own and so belong to the world of books." She started contributing to children's magazines when she was nine or ten and has never stopped writing.

Before Reading

Studies in the Park

by Anita Desai

Anita Desai
born 1937

Anita Desai was born in Mussorie, India. She was educated at Queen Mary's School in Delhi and received her B. A. degree from the University of Delhi. She married Ashvin Desai in 1952; they have two sons and two daughters. In the United States she has taught writing at Smith College and at Mount Holyoke, and in 1993 became a professor of writing at the Massachusetts Institute of Technology. Desai's works include short stories, children's books, and several novels for adults, including *In Custody* (1984), recently made into a film by Merchant Ivory Productions, *Baumgartner's Bombay* (1989), which one critic called "a wonder of exquisitely crafted prose," and *Journey to Ithaca* (1995).

Building Background

India India is a complex country containing several religions and over 1,600 languages and dialects. Fifteen of these are recognized in India's Constitution, but Hindi is the official language, spoken by a little over thirty percent of the population. English is spoken by more than fifteen million people in India, however. In fact, all students are required to be bilingual, and many are trilingual, speaking Hindi, English, and their mother tongue.

The English language is a legacy from the days of British dominance over India, a legacy that also extended to banking, the judicial system, a network of railroads and roads, and education. In general, students who attend school have six years of primary school, three years of secondary school, and three years of upper secondary school. The narrator in the following story is in secondary school, but he soon finds other avenues of interest—to the dismay of his father.

Literary Focus

Simile A **simile** is a kind of figurative language, usually signaled by the words *like* or *as*. It is a comparison between two unlike things that have something in common. For example, the narrator says his father's voice "came out of his nose like the whistle of a punctual train," a comparison of two sounds. Similes help to make writing more vivid. Watch for them in the following story.

Writer's Notebook

Devising Similes Try your hand at creating some similes by completing the following phrases. Be as original as you can.

car engine sounded like . . .

eyes as bright as . . .

sweater as red as . . .

breeze smelled like . . .

weather as hot as . . .

SUPPORT MATERIALS OVERVIEW

Unit 7 Resource Book
- Graphic Organizer, p. 129
- Study Guide, p. 130
- Vocabulary, p. 131
- Grammar, p. 132
- Alternate Check Test, p. 133
- Vocabulary Test, p. 134
- Selection Test, pp. 135–136

Building English Proficiency
- Selection Summaries
- Activities, p. 260

Reading, Writing & Grammar SkillBook
- Grammar, Usage, and Mechanics, pp. 245–246

The World of Work
- Yoga Instructor, p. 29
- Activity, p. 30

Technology
- Audiotape
- Personal Journal Software
- Test Generator Software

STUDIES IN THE PARK

Anita Desai

Turn it off, turn it off, turn it off! First he listens to the news in Hindi. Directly after, in English. Broom—brroom—brrroom—the voice of doom roars. Next, in Tamil. Then in Punjabi. In Gujarati.[1] What next, my god, what next? Turn it off before I smash it onto his head, fling it out of the window, do nothing of the sort of course, nothing of the sort.

—And my mother. She cuts and fries, cuts and fries. All day I hear her chopping and slicing and the pan of oil hissing. What all does she find to fry and feed us on, for God's sake? Eggplants, potatoes, spinach, shoe soles, newspapers, finally she'll slice me and feed me to my brothers and sisters. Ah, now she's turned on the tap. It's roaring and pouring, pouring and roaring into a bucket without a bottom.

—The bell rings. Voices clash, clatter and break. The tin-and-bottle man? The neighbors? The police? The Help-the-Blind man? Thieves and burglars? All of them, all of them, ten or twenty or a hundred of them, marching up the stairs, hammering at the door, breaking in and climbing over me—ten, twenty or a hundred of them.

—Then, worst of all, the milk arrives. In the tallest glass in the house. "Suno, drink your milk. Good for you, Suno. You need it. Now, before the exams. Must have it, Suno. Drink." The voice wheedles its way into my ear like a worm. I shudder. The table tips over. The milk runs. The tumbler clangs on the floor. "Suno, Suno, how will you do your exams?"

—That is precisely what I ask myself. All very well to give me a room—Uncle's been pushed off on a pilgrimage to Hardwar to clear a room for me—and to bring me milk and say, "Study, Suno, study for your exam." What about the uproar around me? These people don't know the meaning of the word Quiet. When my mother fills buckets, sloshes the kitchen floor, fries and sizzles things in the pan, she thinks she is being Quiet. The children have never even heard the word, it amazes and puzzles them. On their way back from school they fling their satchels in at my door, then tear in to snatch them back before I tear them to bits. Bawl when I pull their ears, screech when mother whacks them. Stuff themselves with her fries and then smear the grease on my books.

So I raced out of my room, with my fingers in my ears, to scream till the roof fell down about their ears. But the radio suddenly went off, the door to my parents' room suddenly opened and my father appeared, bathed and shaven, stuffed and set up with the news of the world in six different languages—his white *dhoti*[2] blazing, his white shirt crackling, his patent leather pumps glittering. He stopped in the doorway and I stopped on the balls of my feet and wavered. My fingers came out of my ears, my hair came down over my eyes. Then he looked away from me, took his watch out of his pocket and inquired, "Is the food ready?" in a voice that came out of his nose like the whistle of a punctual train. He skated off towards his meal, I turned and slouched back to my room. On his way to work, he looked in to say, "Remember, Suno, I expect good results from you. Study hard, Suno." Just behind him, I saw all the rest of them standing,

---

1. **Hindi** (hin′dē) . . . **Tamil** (tam′əl) . . . **Punjabi** (pun-jä′bē) . . . **Gujarati** (gu̇j′ə rät′ē). Four of the languages spoken in India.
2. *dhoti* (dō′tē), *n.* a loincloth worn by Hindu men in India.

Studies in the Park   **833**

SELECTION SUMMARY

Studies in the Park

Suno is studying for the exams that will earn him an intermediate degree. There is great pressure from his family to receive a "first," that is, the highest grade, in order to get a job after the exam. Finding it impossible to study at home, surrounded by his noisy family, Suno begins going each day to King Edward's Park, where he joins other students "who escaped their city flats and families like mine to come and study." He studies his books and at the same time observes the other denizens of the park. When he reaches the point where he can't study another word, he observes a tender scene in the park between an old man and a dying, young woman. This glimpse of what it means to be truly "alive" changes Suno, possibly forever.

*For summaries in other languages, see the **Building English Proficiency** book.*

During Reading

Selection Objectives

- to consider the search for identity through the eyes of a student
- to identify and appreciate similes
- to consider the role of setting in plot
- to apply conventional standards of usage to quotation marks

Unit 7 Resource Book
Graphic Organizer, p. 129
Study Guide, p. 130

Theme Link

The search for identity theme is explored through the story of a teenage boy, who discovers that he can only be happy by rejecting family expectations and seeking what is best for him.

Vocabulary Preview

subjugate, subdue; conquer

insinuate, act or speak to gain favor in an indirect way

imbibe, drink in; absorb

supine, lazily inactive; listless

parasite, person who lives on others without making any fitting returns

Students can add the words and definitions to their Writer's Notebooks.

1 **Literary Element**
Setting

Questions Where is the action taking place at this point in the story? (in the narrator's house) How is the setting a problem? *(Suno needs quiet to study for his exam, but he has a large, noisy family.)*

2 **Literary Focus**
Simile

Question To what does Suno compare the nasal quality of his father's voice? *(to the whistle of a punctual train)*

Multicultural Note
National Examinations

In many countries, including India, national examinations must be passed to graduate from high school (or its equivalent). Such exams do not test minimum skills, such as many states in the U.S. now require, but require students to demonstrate comprehensive knowledge of subject matter. Scores from such tests often determine one's future—a high score means acceptance into a college and, eventually, a higher standard of living.

Literary Element
Point of View

Questions From whose point of view is the story told? *(Suno's; first-person)* What limitations does this point of view impose? *(Possible response: The reader only knows what Suno is thinking and feeling. Other characters are known only through his thoughts and reactions.)* What advantages does this point of view provide? *(Possible response: First-person point of view is highly realistic; it duplicates the way one sees the world; it provides a sense of immediacy and often offers in-depth characterization of the principal character, the narrator.)*

---

peering in, silently. All of them stared at me, at the exam I was to take. At the degree I was to get. Or not get. Horrifying thought. Oh study, study, study, they all breathed at me while my father's footsteps went down the stairs, crushing each underfoot in turn. I felt their eyes on me, goggling, and their breath on me, hot with earnestness. I looked back at them, into their open mouths and staring eyes.

I snarled at him but he only smiled, determined to be friendly

"Study," I said, and found I croaked. "I know I ought to study. And how do you expect me to study—in this madhouse? You run wild, *wild*. I'm getting out," I screamed, leaping up and grabbing my books, "I'm going to study outside. Even the street is quieter," I screeched and threw myself past them and down the stairs that my father had just cowed and subjugated[3] so that they still lay quivering, and paid no attention to the howls that broke out behind me of "Suno, Suno, listen. Your milk—your studies—your exams, Suno!"

At first I tried the tea shop at the corner. In my reading I had often come across men who wrote at cafe tables—letters, verse, whole novels—over a cup of coffee or a glass of absinthe.[4] I thought it would be simple to read a chapter of history over a cup of tea. There was no crowd in the mornings, none of my friends would be there. But the proprietor would not leave me alone. Bored, picking his nose, he wandered down from behind the counter to my table by the weighing machine and tried to pass the time of day by complaining about his piles, the new waiter and the high prices. "And sugar," he whined. "How can I give you anything to put in

your tea with sugar at four rupees[5] a kilo? There's rationed sugar, I know, at two rupees, but that's not enough to feed even an ant. And the way you all sugar your tea—*hai, hai,*" he sighed, worse than my mother. I didn't answer. I frowned at my book and looked stubborn. But when I got rid of him, the waiter arrived. "Have a biscuit?" he murmured, flicking at my table and chair with his filthy duster. "A bun? Fritters? Make you some hot fritters?" I snarled at him but he only smiled, determined to be friendly. Just a boy, really, in a pink shirt with purple circles stamped all over it—he thought he looked so smart. He was growing sideburns, he kept fingering them. "I'm a student, too," he said, "sixth class, fail. My mother wanted me to go back and try again, but I didn't like the teacher—he beat me. So I came here to look for a job. Lala-*ji* had just thrown out a boy called Hari for selling lottery tickets to the clients so he took me on. I can make out a bill . . ." He would have babbled on if Lala-*ji* had not come and shoved him into the kitchen with an oath. So it went on. I didn't read more than half a chapter that whole morning. I didn't want to go home either. I walked along the street, staring at my shoes, with my shoulders slumped in the way that makes my father scream, "What's the matter? Haven't you bones? A spine?" I kicked some rubble along the pavement, down the drain, then stopped at the iron gates of King Edward's Park.

"Exam troubles?" asked a *gram*[6] vendor who sat outside it, in a friendly voice. Not insinuating,[7] but low, pleasant. "The park's full of boys like you," he continued in that sympathetic voice. "I see them walk up and down, up and down with their books, like mad poets. Then I'm glad I was

---

3. subjugate (sub′jə gāt′), *v.* subdue; conquer.
4. **absinthe** (ab′sinth), *n.* a bitter, green alcoholic drink flavored with anise, or other herbs.
5. **rupee** (rü pē′), *n.* monetary unit of India and some other countries.
6. *gram* (gram), *n.* any of various beans grown for food in India and often served roasted.
7. insinuate (in sin′yü āt), *v.* act or speak to gain favor in an indirect way.

MINI-LESSON: GRAMMAR

Quotation Marks and Dialogue

Teach Quotation marks serve several purposes:

- to enclose a direct quotation:
  As Charles Dickens once wrote, "Let sleeping dogs lie."

- to set off any quoted or emphasized word or short phrase:
  All items marked "out" should be deleted.

- to indicate the ironical use of words:
  Debbie's sister often "borrowed" Debbie's favorite clothes.

- to enclose the titles of articles, poems, stories, speeches, and parts of whole printed works:
  "The Yellow Eye" was printed in *The New England Review*.

If necessary, review the following rules of punctuation:

- With the comma and the period, quotation marks go outside:
  "She was a good actress," said Sean, "and a good friend."

- With the semicolon and the colon, quotation marks go inside:
  Sara thanked us "for always being there when I needed you"; she was very grateful for our support.

Activity Idea Have pairs find examples in this story of at least two uses for quotation marks. *(Hint: See p. 840 for the third use above.)*

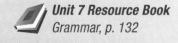

Unit 7 Resource Book
Grammar, p. 132

never sent to school," and he began to whistle, not impertinently but so cheerfully that I stopped and stared at him. He had a crippled arm that hung out of his shirt sleeve like a leg of mutton dangling on a hook. His face was scarred as though he had been dragged out of some terrible accident. But he was shuffling hot *gram* into paper cones with his one hand and whistling like a bird, whistling the tune of, "We are the *bul-buls*[8] of our land, our land is Paradise." Nodding at the greenery beyond the gates, he said, "The park's a good place to study in," and, taking his hint, I went in.

I wonder how it is I never thought of the park before. It isn't far from our house and I sometimes went there as a boy, if I managed to run away from school, to lie on a bench, eat peanuts, shy stones at the chipmunks that came for the shells, and drink from the fountain. But then it was not as exciting as playing marbles in the street or stoning rats with my school friends in the vacant lot behind the cinema. It had straight paths, beds of flapping red flowers—cannas, I think—rows of palm trees like limp flags, a dry fountain and some green benches. Old men sat on them with their legs far apart, heads dropping over the tops of sticks, mumbling through their dentures or cackling with that mad, ripping laughter that makes children think of old men as wizards and bogey-men. Bag-like women in gray and fawn *saris* or black *borkhas*[9] screamed, just as gray and fawn and black birds do, at children falling into the fountain or racing on rickety legs after the chipmunks and pigeons. A madman or two, prancing around in paper caps and bits of rags, munching banana peels and scratching like monkeys. Corners behind hibiscus bushes stinking of piss. Iron rails with rows of beggars contentedly dozing, scratching, gambling, with their sackcloth backs to the rails. A city park.

What I hadn't noticed, or thought of, were all the students who escaped from their city flats and families like mine to come and study here. Now, walking down a path with my history book tucked under my arm, I felt like a gatecrasher at a party or a visitor to a public library trying to control a sneeze. They all seemed to belong here, to be at home here. Dressed in loose pajamas, they strolled up and down under the palms, books open in their hands, heads lowered into them. Or they sat in twos and threes on the grass, reading aloud in turns. Or lay full length under the trees, books spread out across their faces—sleeping, or else imbibing[10] information through the subconscious. Opening out my book, I too strolled up and down, reading to myself in a low murmur.

CLARIFY: Why does Suno feel like a gatecrasher?

In the beginning, when I first started studying in the park, I couldn't concentrate on my studies. I'd keep looking up at the boy strolling in front of me, reciting poetry in a kind of thundering whisper, waving his arms about and running his bony fingers through his hair till it stood up like a thorn bush. Or at the chipmunks that fought and played and chased each other all over the park, now and then joining forces against the sparrows over a nest or a paper cone of *gram*. Or at the madman going through the rubble at the bottom of the dry fountain and coming up with a rubber shoe, a banana peel or a piece of glittering tin that he appreciated so much that he put it in his mouth and chewed it till blood ran in strings from his mouth.

It took me time to get accustomed to the ways of the park. I went there daily, for the

---

8. *bul-bul* (bŭl′bŭl), *n.* song bird of southern Asia and Africa, of the same family as the thrush.
9. *sari . . . borkha.* A sari (sär′ē) is the outer garment of Hindu women, a long piece of cotton or silk wrapped around the body, with one end falling nearly to the feet and the other end thrown over the head or shoulder. A borkha (bùr′kə) is a garment worn by Muslim women that covers the head and face.
10. imbibe (im bīb′), *v.* drink in; absorb.

Studies in the Park 835

5 Literary Focus
Simile

Questions What similes does Desai use to describe the vendor? *("a crippled arm that hung out of his shirt sleeve like a leg of mutton dangling on a hook"; "face was scarred as though he had been dragged out of some terrible accident")* How do the similes affect your image of the vendor? *(Possible response: The similes evoke a stronger, more compelling image, allowing the reader to view the vendor through Suno's eyes.)*

6 Active Reading
Clarify

Possible response The other students all seem to belong in the park, "to be at home here."

7 Reader's Response
Challenging the Text

Question Why do you think the author included this image of a madman chewing on a piece of tin until "blood ran in strings from his mouth"? *(Possible responses: The incident may foreshadow something; the park seems to be Suno's first attempt to establish a measure of independence from his family, and he sees both the good and the bad in his new world.)*

BUILDING ENGLISH PROFICIENCY

ESL
LEP
ELD
SAE
LD

Exploring Synonyms

Help students use Desai's story to expand their knowledge of synonyms.

1. Point out this sentence from the first column on page 834: "Oh study, study, study, they all breathed at me . . ." Explain that Desai could have used the word said. She chose breathed, an unusual synonym for said, because it is a strong, vivid verb that expresses exactly what she means.

2. Ask pairs of students to hunt for other strong verbs that are used instead of said on these pages. (Answers include *croaked, screamed, screeched, sighed, murmured, snarled,* and *babbled.*)

3. Challenge students to think of five synonyms for walked. (Many appear in the story.) Have them list their synonyms and then exchange lists with partners. Together, partners can create original sentences for the verb synonyms that they like best.

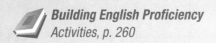

Building English Proficiency
Activities, p. 260

Literary Focus

Simile

Question   In what way is the park like a hotel or a hospital? *(Possible response: Like these institutions, the park has its own order and routine. Certain events happen regularly, such as the early morning yoga class.)*

Reader's Response

Making Personal Connections

Questions   What does Suno mean by his question, "What's the body compared to the soul, the mind"? Do you agree or disagree? *(Possible response: Suno believes that the mind and the soul are much more important than physical things. Students' responses to this comment will vary, but some might point out that in most religions, the body is only a temporary home for the soul, which is eternal.)*

Multicultural Note

Hinduism

Among the oldest of world religions, Hinduism is unique in that it had no single founder but grew over a period of 4,000 years. In general, most Hindus accept the Vedas as the most sacred of scriptures. Over time, the practice of yoga was included in Hinduism, and the doctrine of *karma* was introduced, according to which the individual reaps the results of good and bad actions through a series of lifetimes.

whole day, and soon I got to know it as well as my own room at home and found I could study there, or sleep, or daydream, as I chose. Then I fell into its routine, its rhythm, and my time moved in accordance with its time. We were like a house-owner and his house, or a turtle and its shell, or a river and its bank—so close. I resented everyone else who came to the park—I thought they couldn't possibly share my feeling for it. Except, perhaps, the students.

The park was like a hotel, or a hospital, belonging to the city but with its own order and routine, enclosed by iron rails, laid out according to prescription in rows of palms, benches and paths. If I went there very early in the morning, I'd come upon a yoga class. It consisted of young bodybuilders rippling their muscles like snakes as well as old crack-pots determined to keep up with the youngest and fittest, all sitting cross-legged on the grass and displaying *hus-mukh*[11] to the sun just rising over the palms; the Laughing Face pose it was called, but they looked like gargoyles[12] with their mouths torn open and their thick, discolored tongues sticking out. If I were the sun, I'd feel so disgusted by such a reception I'd just turn around and go back. And that was the simplest of their poses—after that they'd go into contortions that would embarrass an ape. Once their leader, a black and hirsute[13] man like an aborigine, saw me watching and called me to join them. I shook my head and ducked behind an oleander. . . . I despise all that body-beautiful worship anyway. What's the body compared to the soul, the mind?

I'd stroll under the palms, breathing in the cool of the early morning, feeling it drive out, or wash clean, the stifling dark of the night, and try to avoid bumping into all the other early morning visitors to the park—mostly aged men sent by their wives to fetch the milk from the Government dairy booth just outside the gates. Their bottles clinking in green cloth bags and newspapers rolled up and tucked under their arms, they strutted along like stiff puppets and mostly they would be discussing philosophy. "Ah but in Vedanta[14] it

is a different matter," one would say, his eyes gleaming fanatically, and another would announce, "The sage Shanakaracharya showed the way," and some would refer to the Upanishads or the Bhagavad Puranas,[15] but in such argumentative, hacking tones that you could see they were quite capable of coming to blows over some theological argument. Certainly it was the mind above the body for these old coots but I found nothing to admire in them either. I particularly resented it when one of them disengaged himself from the discussion long enough to notice me and throw me a gentle look of commiseration.[16] As if he'd been through exams, too, long long ago, and knew all about them. So what?

Worst of all were the athletes, wrestlers, Mr. Indias and others who lay on their backs and were massaged with oil till every muscle shone and glittered. The men who massaged them huffed and puffed and cursed as they climbed up and down the supine[17] bodies, pounding and pummeling the men who lay there wearing nothing but little greasy clouts, groaning and panting in a way I found obscene and disgusting. They never looked up at me or at anyone. They lived in a meaty, sweating world of their own—massages, oils, the body, a match to be fought and won—I kicked up dust in their direction but never went too close.

The afternoons would be quiet, almost empty. I would sit under a tree and read, stroll and study, doze too. Then, in the evening, as the sky softened from its blank white glare and took

---

11. **hus-mukh** (hus′mùk), *n.* a cheerful or laughing face. [*Hindi*]
12. **gargoyle** (gär′goil), *n.* figure in the shape of a grotesque animal or human being, often draining water from the gutter of a building.
13. **hirsute** (hėr′sūt), *adj.* hairy.
14. **Vedanta** (vi dan′tə), *n.* a system of philosophy founded on the Vedas, sacred writings of the ancient Hindus.
15. **Upanishads** (ü pan′ə shadz) . . . **Bhagavad Puranas** (bug′ə vəd pù rä′nəz), *n. pl.* ancient commentaries and Hindu epics, myths, and other literature.
16. **commiseration** (kə miz′ə rā′shən), *n.* feeling of sympathy for another's trouble.
17. supine (sū pīn′), adj. lazily inactive; listless.

MINI-LESSON: VOCABULARY

Recognizing Multiple-meaning Words

Teach   Many words have multiple meanings. The ability to distinguish and use a word's various meanings can increase students' vocabularies. Many times the correct meaning of such a word can be inferred from the context; at other times the word must be looked up in a dictionary and the various meanings tried before finding one that is correct in the context.

Activity Idea   Divide students into small groups, and assign one of these words from the selection to each group: *study, prescription, philosophy, parasite, vision, patient.*

Ask each group to

- find its word in the dictionary and record all the word's meanings
- write a paragraph, using several of the word's meanings; or write a word play or pun that derives its humor from the word's multiple meanings
- share its results with the class

Head of a Woman (1937) was painted by the Nobel Prize-winning Indian poet and dramatist Rabindranath Tagore (1861–1941). What is the chief feeling conveyed by this image?

The World of Work

Yoga Instructor

For a real-life discussion of yoga and its connection to Hinduism, use the pages referenced below.

The World of Work
pp. 29–30

Art Study

Response to Caption Question   The image conveys both the feeling of intrigue and mystery and a sense of inner calm.

BUILDING ENGLISH PROFICIENCY

Exploring Connotation

Help students understand the idea that words can carry meanings that go beyond their dictionary definitions.

1. Explain that many words connote, or suggest, positive or negative feelings. To show how Suno despises people, the writer uses words and phrases on page 836 with negative connotations, such as *crack-pots, hacking tones,* and *greasy clouts.*

2. Ask students to create two webs, one (with words from p. 836) connoting negative feelings, the other (their own words) connoting positive feelings to describe a bodybuilder.

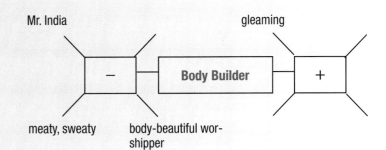

Mr. India   gleaming

─   **Body Builder**   +

meaty, sweaty   body-beautiful wor-
shipper

837

12 **Reader's Response**
Making Personal Connections

Questions Have you ever felt like Suno after studying for a difficult exam? What would you advise him to do? *(Responses will vary. Students might note that Suno obviously needs a break from his studies; he has probably reached the point where he can absorb no more information.)*

13 **Literary Focus**
Simile

Question To what does Suno compare his father's advice, "get a first"? *(to the chugging of a railroad engine)* Earlier in the story, the father's voice is compared to a train. What do these two similes suggest about the father/son relationship? *(Possible response: that the relationship is "mechanical"; that the father "runs" on track, relentlessly; that Suno feels chased, about to be run down by the forces around him.)*

on shades of pink and orange and the palm trees rustled a little in an invisible breeze, the crowds would begin to pour out of Darya Ganji, Mori Gate, Chandni Chowk and the Jama Masjid bazaars and slums. Large families would come to sit about on the grass, eating peanuts and listening to a transistor radio placed in the center of the circle. Mothers would sit together in flocks like screeching birds while children jumped into the dry fountains, broke flowers and terrorized each other. There would be a few young men moaning at the corners, waiting for a girl to roll her hips and dart her fish eyes in their direction, and then start the exciting adventure of pursuit. The children's cries would grow more piercing with the dark; frightened, shrill and exalted with mystery and farewell. I would wander back to the flat.

The exams drew nearer. Not three, not two, but only one month to go. I had to stop daydreaming and set myself tasks for every day and remind myself constantly to complete them. It grew so hot I had to give up strolling on the paths and staked out a private place for myself under a tree. I noticed the tension tightening the eyes and mouths of other students—they applied themselves more diligently to their books, talked less, slept less. Everyone looked a little demented from lack of sleep. Our books seemed attached to our hands as though by roots, they were a part of us, they lived because we fed them. They were 11 parasites[18] and, like parasites, were sucking us dry. We mumbled to ourselves, not always consciously. Chipmunks jumped over our feet, mocking us. The *gram* seller down at the gate whistled softly "I'm glad I never went to school, I am a *bul-bul*, I live in Paradise . . ."

12 My brains began to jam up. I could feel it happening, slowly. As if the oil were all used up. As if everything was getting locked together, rusted. The white cells, the gray matter, the springs and nuts and bolts. I yelled at my mother—I think it was my mother—"What do you think I am? What do you want of me?" and crushed a glass of milk between my hands. It was

sticky. She had put sugar in my milk. As if I were a baby. I wanted to cry. They wouldn't let me sleep, they wanted to see my light on all night, they made sure I never stopped studying. Then they brought me milk and sugar and made clicking sounds with their tongues. I raced out to the park. I think I sobbed as I paced up and down, up and down, in the corner that stank of piss. My head ached worse than ever. I slept all day under the tree and had to work all night.

My father laid his hand on my shoulder. I knew I was not to fling it off. So I sat still, slouching, ready to spring aside if he lifted it only slightly. "You must get a first,[19] Suno," he said through his nose, "must get a first, or else you won't get a job. Must get a job, Suno," he sighed and wiped his nose and went off, his patent leather pumps squealing like mice. I flung myself back in my chair and howled. Get a first, get a first, get a first—like a railway engine, it 13 went charging over me, grinding me down, and left me dead and mangled on the tracks.

Everything hung still and yellow in the park. I lay sluggishly on a heap of waste paper under my tree and read without seeing, slept without sleeping. Sometimes I went to the water tap that leaked and drank the leak. It tasted of brass. I spat out a mouthful. It nearly went over the feet of the student waiting for his turn at that dripping tap. I stepped aside for him. He swilled the water around his mouth and spat, too, carefully missing my feet. Wiping his mouth, he asked, "B.A.?"

"No, Inter.[20]"

"Hu," he burped. "Wait till you do your B.A. Then you'll get to know." His face was like a gray bone. It was not unkind, it simply had no expression. "Another two weeks," he sighed and slouched off to his own lair.

I touched my face. I thought it would be all

---

18. parasite (par′ə sit), *n.* person who lives on others without making any useful or fitting returns.
19. **first,** the highest grade.
20. **Inter,** intermediate degree, taken during high school and before the B. A. (Bachelor of Arts) or college degree.

MINI-LESSON: CRITICAL THINKING

Infer

Teach "Studies in the Park" is told entirely from Suno's point of view. Other people and events are seen only through his eyes. But strategic readers can make inferences based on the information Suno provides and on their own experiences.

Activity Idea Have students choose various scenes, then make inferences about the characters or events beyond what Suno tells us. For example, in the scene on page 838 when Suno's father tells him he "must get a first," the reader might infer that

- Suno's father knows others who did not get a first and so did not get a job. (Clue: The father says Suno "must get a first, or else you won't get a job.")
- Suno's father loves him and knows he's under a lot of pressure, but he also knows Suno must do well on the exam to succeed in life. (Clue: The father places a hand on Suno's shoulder as if to comfort him, but at the same time reminds Suno that he "must get a job.")

bone, like his. I was surprised to find a bit of skin still covering it. I felt as if we were all dying in the park, that when we entered the examination hall it would be to be declared officially dead. That's what the degree was about. What else was it all about? Why were we creeping around here, hiding from the city, from teachers and parents, pretending to study and prepare? Prepare for what? We hadn't been told. Inter, they said, or B.A. or M.A. These were like official stamps—they would declare us dead. Ready for a dead world. A world in which ghosts went about, squeaking or whining, rattling or rustling. Slowly, slowly we were killing ourselves in order to join them. The ball-point pen in my pocket was the only thing that still lived, that still worked. I didn't work myself any more—I mean physically, my body no longer functioned. I was constipated, I was dying. I was lying under a yellow tree, feeling the dust sift through the leaves to cover me. It was filling my eyes, my throat. I could barely walk. I never strolled. Only on the way out of the park, late in the evening, I crept down the path under the palms, past the benches.

15

PREDICT: Do you think Suno will pass the exam?

Then I saw the scene that stopped it all, stopped me just before I died.

Hidden behind an oleander was a bench. A woman lay on it, stretched out. She was a Muslim, wrapped in a black *borkha*. I hesitated when I saw this straight, still figure in black on the bench. Just then she lifted a pale, thin hand and lifted her veil. I saw her face. It lay bared, in the black folds of her *borkha*, like a flower, wax-white and composed, like a Persian lily or a tobacco flower at night. She was young. Very young, very pale, beautiful with a beauty I had never come across even in a dream. It caught me and held me tight, tight till I couldn't breathe and couldn't move. She was so white, so still, I saw she was very ill—with anemia, perhaps, or T.B.[21] Too pale, too white—I could see she was dying. Her head—so still and

white it might have been carved if it weren't for this softness, this softness of a flower at night—lay in the lap of a very old man. Very much older than her. With spectacles and a long gray beard like a goat's, or a scholar's. He was looking down at her and caressing her face— so tenderly, so tenderly, I had never seen a hand move so gently and tenderly. Beside them, on the ground, two little girls were playing. Round little girls, rather dirty, drawing lines in the gravel. They stared at me but the man and the woman did not notice me. They never looked at anyone else, only at each other, with an expression that halted me. It was tender, loving, yes, but in an inhuman way, so intense. Divine, I felt, or insane. I stood, half-hidden by the bush, holding my book, and wondered at them. She was ill, I could see, dying. Perhaps she had only a short time to live. Why didn't he take her to the Victoria Zenana Hospital, so close to the park? Who was this man—her husband, her father, a lover? I couldn't make out although I watched them without moving, without breathing. I felt not as if I were staring rudely at strangers, but as if I were gazing at a painting or a sculpture, some work of art. Or seeing a vision. They were still and I stood still and the children stared. Then she lifted her arms above her head and laughed. Very quietly.

I broke away and hurried down the path, in order to leave them alone, in privacy. They

> **Then I saw the scene that stopped it all, stopped me just before I died.**

---

21. **anemia** (ə nē′mē ə) **. . . TB.** Anemia is a condition resulting from an insufficiency of red blood cells and characterized by weakness and pallor. *TB* is short for *tuberculosis,* an infectious disease most often of the lungs.

Studies in the Park **839**

14
Reading/Thinking Skills
Literal and Figurative Language

Questions   Suno has concluded that the exam will "kill" him. What does he mean by that? Is he really going to die? (*Possible response: Perhaps he means that his personality is being killed; he is forced to what others want so that his creativity and ingenuity wither and die.*)

15
Active Reading
Predict

Possible response   Predictions will vary. Students should base their predictions on clues, such as Suno's state of mind or how hard he has studied.

16
Reading/Thinking Skills
Draw Conclusions

Question   What do you think the beautiful, dying woman represents to Suno? (*Possible response: how fragile and beautiful life is*)

BUILDING ENGLISH PROFICIENCY

ESL
LEP
ELD
SAE
LD

Summarizing a Story

To help students describe story elements, have them work together in groups to make a story triangle, following these directions:

1. Name the main character.

2. Write two words describing the main character.

3. Write three words describing the setting.

4. Write four words stating the main problem.

5. Write five words describing the second problem.

6. Write six words telling how the problem is resolved (on page 840).

One possible response:

1. Suno
2. young   man
3. lives   in   India
4. worries   about   taking   exams
5. daydreams   and   hates   the   world
6. finally   sees   what   being   human   means

Possible response   Suno has found a new kind of individuality. He has chosen his own path, rather than that set out for him by his parents.

Question   What is the theme of "Studies in the Park"? (*Possible response: We each must find our own path. When one is forced into a course of action against one's nature, the soul withers and one becomes sick at heart.*)

Check Test

1. What is Suno's task? (*to study for his upcoming "Inter" exam*)

2. Why does he have trouble studying at home? (*His family is too noisy and interfering.*)

3. Other than at home, where else does Suno attempt to study? (*a tea shop and a park*)

4. Why is the park a good place to study? (*It seems a bit quieter than Suno's home or the tea shop. Also, there are many other students studying in the park, and it probably helps to have other students nearby for moral support.*)

5. What scene causes Suno to refuse to take the exam? (*He sees a beautiful, but dying woman with her head in the lap of an old man. The two are looking at each other in a tender, intense way, and Suno realizes that this is "what being alive means."*)

Unit 7 Resource Book
Alternate Check Test, p. 133

---

weren't a work of art, or a vision, but real, human and alive as no one else in my life had been real and alive. I had only that glimpse of them. But I felt I could never open my books and study or take degrees after that. They belonged to the dead, and now I had seen what being alive meant. The vision burned the surfaces of my eyes so that they watered as I groped my way up the stairs to the flat. I could hardly find my way to the bed.

It was not just the examination but everything else had suddenly withered and died, gone lifeless and purposeless when compared with this vision. My studies, my family, my life—they all belonged to the dead and only what I had seen in the park had any meaning.

Since I did not know how to span the distance between that beautiful ideal and my stupid, dull existence, I simply lay still and shut my eyes. I kept them shut so as not to see all the puzzled, pleading, indignant faces of my family around me, but I could not shut out their voices.

"Suno, Suno," I heard them croon and coax and mourn.

"Suno, drink milk."

"Suno, study."

"Suno, take the exam."

And when they tired of being so patient with me and I still would not get up, they began to crackle and spit and storm.

"Get up, Suno."

"Study, Suno."

"At once, Suno."

Only my mother became resigned and gentle. She must have seen something quite out of the ordinary on my face to make her so. I felt her hand on my forehead and heard her say, "Leave him alone. Let him sleep tonight. He is tired out, that is what it is—he has driven himself too much and now he must sleep."

Then I heard all of them leave the room. Her hand stayed on my forehead, wet and smelling of onions, and after a bit my tears began to flow from under my lids.

"Poor Suno, sleep," she murmured.

I went back to the park of course. But now I was changed. I had stopped being a student—I was a "professional." My life was dictated by the rules and routine of the park. I still had my book open on the palms of my hands as I strolled but now my eyes strayed without guilt, darting at the young girls walking in pairs, their arms linked, giggling and bumping into each other. Sometimes I stopped to rest on a bench and conversed with one of the old men, told him who my father was and what examination I was preparing for, and allowing him to tell me about his youth, his politics, his philosophy, his youth and again his youth. Or I joked with the other students, sitting on the grass and throwing peanut shells at the chipmunks, and shocking them, I could see, with my irreverence and cynicism about the school, the exam, the system. Once I even nodded at the yoga teacher and exchanged a few words with him. He suggested I join his class and I nodded vaguely and said I would think it over. It might help. My father says I need help. He says I am hopeless but that I need help. I just laugh but I know that he knows I will never appear for the examination, I will never come up to that hurdle or cross it—life has taken a different path for me, in the form of a search, not a race as it is for him, for them.

> **EVALUATE: Do you think that Suno has lost his individuality or that he has found a new kind of individuality?**

Yes, it is a search, a kind of perpetual search for me and now that I have accepted it and don't struggle, I find it satisfies me entirely, and I wander about the park as freely as a prince in his palace garden. I look over the benches, I glance behind the bushes, and wonder if I shall ever get another glimpse of that strange vision that set me free. I never have but I keep hoping, wishing.

After Reading

After Reading

Making Connections

MAKING CONNECTIONS

Shaping Your Response

1. Are you sympathetic to Suno? Why or Why not?

Analyzing the Story

2. What are the **conflicts** in this story?

3. If Suno is the **protagonist** in this story, does he have an **antogonist?** If so, who—or what?

4. Trace the changes in Suno's feelings about himself throughout the story.

5. Why do you think Suno is so affected by the man and woman he sees in the park?

6. Discuss whether or not Suno undergoes an **epiphany.** Do you think he will be permanently changed?

Extending the Ideas

7. In a different time and place, Suno might be called a dropout. Yet he now refers to himself as a "professional." What do you think he means?

8. 👣 People have their own personal ways of responding to group pressures to achieve, such as getting a first in an exam. Do you think that such pressures are harmful to **individuality,** or do they test it and improve it?

Literary Focus: Simile

A **simile** is a figurative comparison between two unlike things that have something in common. It is usually signaled by the words *like* or *as.*

1. The narrator says that he and the park "were like a house-owner and his house, or a turtle and its shell, or a river and its bank—so close." Later he compares the park to a hotel or a hospital. What is the effect of these similes?

2. The body builders ripple their muscles "like snakes" and Suno's father's shoes squeal "like mice." How do these similes reveal the narrator's state of mind?

Vocabulary Study

Write the letter of the word that is not related in meaning to the other words in the set.

imbibe
insinuate
parasite
subjugate
supine

1. **a.** sleep   **b.** imbibe   **c.** drink   **d.** absorb
2. **a.** subjugate **b.** subtract   **c.** defeat   **d.** enslave
3. **a.** supine   **b.** active   **c.** lively   **d.** energetic
4. **a.** hanger-on **b.** partner   **c.** parasite   **d.** dependent
5. **a.** insinuate **b.** hint   **c.** ask   **d.** imply

Studies in the Park   **841**

LITERARY FOCUS: SIMILE

Possible Responses

1. We see that the park has become something of a home and something of a theater of life for Suno.

2. Snakes and mice are considered rather unpleasant creatures by most people, indicating that Suno is agitated and repelled by those around him.

MAKING CONNECTIONS

1. Many teenagers feel overwhelmed at one time or another by adults' expectations. Students might also empathize with Suno's difficulty in concentrating on his studies.

2. Possible responses: between Suno and his family, between Suno and his studies, between Suno's inertia and his desire to pass his exam

3. Yes; the antagonist is the exam or his family's wishes for him.

4. Suno begins by wondering how he will do on his exams, but he seems committed to studying hard and doing as well as he can. As the exams draw nearer, he studies more diligently until his brain begins to "jam up." He realizes that for him, the exams mean a death of sorts. Then he sees a loving couple and realizes that for him, life is in such moments, not in books. He feels his existence is "stupid, dull." He decides to study the denizens of the park instead and hints that he will never take the exam.

5. The beautiful young woman is obviously dying; she and the old man are devoted to each other. Upon seeing them, Suno realizes that life is not learned in books.

6. Possible response: Yes; Suno recognizes a truth about life and himself when he observes the young woman in the park. He appears to have been changed permanently; he says that "life has taken a different path for me, in the form of a search, not a race as it is for (his father)."

7. that he has found what he is meant to do in life—studying and learning about other people, i.e., about life.

8. Students might note that some people are challenged by pressure and withstand it well; others are cowed by pressure and so react poorly to stressful situations.

VOCABULARY STUDY

1. a
2. b
3. a
4. b
5. c

Unit 7 Resource Book
Vocabulary , p. 131
Vocabulary Test, p. 134

WRITING CHOICES
Writer's Notebook Update

You might divide the class into two to four groups and hold a simile contest: each simile receives one point; particularly humorous or creative similes receive two points; the winning team is awarded a preset amount of extra-credit points.

Great Expectations

Before writing, students might organize their thoughts in a chart such as the one below:

Expectations	
How You Feel About Them	How You Will Achieve Them

Urban Space

Students who do not have access to a city park might choose another space about which to write; for example, their favorite place to study.

Selection Test

Unit 7 Resource Book
pp. 135–136

Transparency Collection
Fine Art Writing Prompt 15

Expressing Your Ideas
Writing Choices

Writer's Log Update Compare the similes you wrote before reading "Studies in the Park" with those of others in your class, and have someone put them on the chalkboard. How many red things were suggested to compare with a red sweater, for example? (an apple? blood? a rose? a sunset?) Which seem most appropriate?

Great Expectations "Remember, Suno, I expect good results from you," Suno's father says. What are some expectations other people have for you? What are your expectations for yourself? In a short **essay** write about them, how you feel about them, and how you think you will achieve them.

Urban Space If you live near a city park or often visit one, describe the people, animals, and plants you see there in a **column** suitable for a daily newspaper. Include your feelings about the place. Does it seem hospitable? safe? clean? Or is it just the opposite?

Other Options

On the Aisle View one of the films described here and give an **oral review** for the class. The 1984 movie *A Passage to India* is based on E. M. Forster's novel of the same name and depicts India under British rule and the consequences of racial prejudice. *Gandhi* (1982), an Academy-Award winning film starring Ben Kingsley as Mohandas K. Gandhi (1869–1948), is the story of the work and the death of this Hindu political, social, and religious leader.

Good Listening Find and **play a recording** of the music of Ravi Shankar (pictured here) for the class. Shankar plays the sitar (si tär′), an Indian instrument with a long neck and two sets of strings, one beneath the other. What else can you learn about this unique instrument and the music it produces?

OTHER OPTIONS
On the Aisle

Remind students that a review generally contains a plot summary and the reviewer's opinion of the work. Opinions should be supported specific examples from the film.

The Search For Identity

Modern Faces

Fine Art Connection
In a famous observation, Virginia Woolf stated, "In or about December, 1910, human character changed." The portraits in this section were created by artists who were contemporaries of Woolf's.

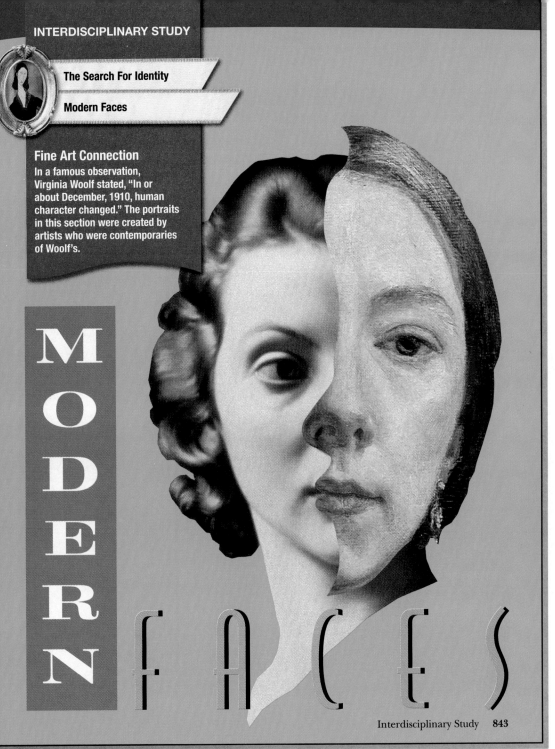

MODERN FACES

Interdisciplinary Study   843

Theme Link

Students can consider whether identity is an internal or external quality (or both) as they examine these portraits of Woolf's contemporaries.

Curricular Connection: Fine Art

You can use this interdisciplinary study to discuss with students how portraiture does not necessarily intend to capture an exact likeness of an individual but to communicate a sense of the individual's personality.

Interdisciplinary Activity Ideas

• Students can search for portraits of the authors in this unit and create a gallery of literary figures.

• Students can draw or paint portraits of the authors or characters in this unit.

• Students can compare the portraits on these pages with contemporary portraits and discuss changes that have taken place in the art of portraiture.

 Unit 7 Resource Book
Interdisciplinary Study Guide, p. 137

BUILDING ENGLISH PROFICIENCY

ESL
LEP
ELD
SAE
LD

Linking Past and Present

Students may better understand what would have been considered "modern" in 1910 by thinking about what is considered "modern" today. You might use the following activity to preface "Modern Faces."

1. Divide the class into groups of three to five students each; give each group five strips of tagboard, each strip measuring 4" x 12".

2. Explain that groups should write on their strips five characteristics of a "modern look." Answers may relate to standards of fashion, tastes in entertainment, personal values, household amenities, and so on.

3. Have each group arrange its characteristics in order, from what they think is the most important to the least important.

4. Invite groups to examine and comment upon the others' responses.

Art Study

Additional Background

Lytton Strachey An English biographer and member of the Bloomsbury Group, Lytton Strachey (1880–1932) is best known for his style of biographies, which did not follow the Victorian practice of idealizing the subject.

(top left) Gwen John, *Self-Portrait* (1900)
Gwen John spent most of her artistic career in Paris, living as a recluse, often in great poverty. Does this self–portrait reflect a timid nature?

(above) Meredith Frampton
Portrait of a Young Woman (1935)
A painstaking craftsman, Frampton worked very slowly at his portraits. Why do you think he grouped these objects around his subject?

(left) Henry Lamb, *Portrait of Lytton Strachey* (1914)
Lytton Strachey was famous for the satiric biographical sketches in his book *Eminent Victorians.* Do you think Henry Lamb was attempting satire in his portrait of Strachey?

MINI-LESSON: TECHNOLOGY

Do Multimedia Presentations

Teach Scanning graphics into a computer in order to colorize, modify, or simply include them in a presentation can add valuable detail to a report. As long as you make sure that you do not violate copyright laws (check with your school's technology adviser) you can juxtapose works of art so viewers can compare and contrast, see development or change over time, or observe contrasting perspectives on a single subject.

Activity Idea Have students choose a topic related to the writings in this cluster and assemble works of art that they could use to create a multimedia presentation. If a scanner is available, give them the opportunity to create a presentation using scanned art.

Unit 7 Resource Book
Study Skill Activity, p. 138

Art Study

(top left) Simon Bussy, *Lady Ottoline Morrell* (1920) Lady Ottoline Morrell was an upper-class hostess famous for her gatherings of artists, writers, and other cultural figures. Does her portrait suggest a self-confident person?

(above) Ann Rice, *Portrait of Katherine Mansfield* Mansfield's fiction ranged from sympathetic studies of the victimized to sharp social satire. Which quality — sympathy or satire — seems to be most reflected in Ann Rice's portrait?

(left) Percy Wyndham Lewis *Portrait of Stephen Spender* (1938) Lewis's paintings show the influence of cubism, with its attempt to interpret the world in terms of geometric forms. What shapes can you see in his portrait of poet Stephen Spender?

Responding

1. Which of these painters would you commission to do a portrait of you?

2. Are there qualities shared by all these faces? If so, what are they?

Writing Workshop

WRITER'S BLUEPRINT
Specs

The Specs in the Writer's Blueprint address these writing and thinking skills:

- analyzing character
- composing a thesis statement
- drawing conclusions
- predicting
- comparing and contrasting
- using quotations
- avoiding sentence fragments

These Specs serve as your lesson objectives, and they form the basis for the **Assessment Criteria Specs** for a superior paper, which appear on the final TE page for this lesson. You might want to read through the Assessment Criteria Specs with students when you begin the lesson.

Linking Literature to Writing

Ask students to discuss ways in which a writer can show a character's moods, intentions, and reactions indirectly. Have volunteers read short passages in which they think the writer is hinting at a character's feelings and discuss what the writer seems to be getting at.

The Search for Identity

Expository Writing

Writing Workshop

Turning Points

Assignment In James Joyce's "Eveline" and Anita Desai's "Studies in the Park," the main characters seem to change in some significant way, but the authors never directly define the change. Try to get into the mind of one of these characters and identify this change.

WRITER'S BLUEPRINT

Product — An interpretive essay

Purpose — To interpret how a character changes

Audience — Readers who are familiar with these stories

Specs — As the writer of a successful essay, you should:

❏ Choose either Joyce's Eveline or Desai's Suno as your subject.

❏ Begin your essay with a thesis statement that summarizes your views on how this character has changed and why. The rest of your essay will amplify and explain this thesis. Then give a brief profile of your character.

❏ Identify the point in the story when the character changes by experiencing an epiphany—a moment of heightened awareness that signals a turning point in her or his life—and explain how you think this turning point comes about.

❏ End by describing how the character's life will be different as a result of this heightened awareness, how the character's behavior will change.

❏ Use quotations from the story to support your conclusions.

❏ Follow the rules of grammar, usage, spelling, and mechanics. Avoid sentence fragments.

WRITING WORKSHOP OVERVIEW

Product
Expository writing: An interpretive essay

Prewriting
Choose a character—Define the epiphany—Profile your character—Compose your thesis statement—Plan your essay
Unit 7 Resource Book
Prewriting Worksheets pp. 139–140

Drafting
Start writing
Transparency Collection
Student Models for Writing Workshop 29, 30

Revising
Ask a partner—Strategy: Writing an Effective Thesis Statement
Unit 7 Resource Book
Revising Worksheet p. 141

Editing
Ask a partner—Strategy: Avoiding Sentence Fragments
Unit 7 Resource Book
Grammar Worksheet p. 142
Grammar Check Test p. 143

Presenting
Read Aloud and Discuss
Illustrate

Looking Back
Self-evaluate—Reflect—For Your Working Portfolio
Unit 7 Resource Book
Assessment Worksheet p. 144
Transparency Collection
Fine Art Writing Prompt 15

STEP 1 PREWRITING
Choose a character

Students will probably want to revisit the literature before making this choice. Students may want to jot down quick answers to the questions as you read them aloud.

Choose a character. Joyce's Eveline or Desai's Suno—which character intrigues you more? Does either character's situation remind you of an experience in your own life? Which character do you find more sympathetic? The answers to these questions should help you decide which character you'll write about.

Define the epiphany—the moment that you think the author means to signal a turning point in the character's life, after which the character's behavior will change. Reread this part of the story carefully and make notes on the character's reactions.

Profile your character to find out how this epiphany comes about. Look over the character traits listed below. Which ones strike you as particularly fitting for your character? Note these, as well as any other traits that come to mind:

OR . . .
Plot your character's progression on a time line. Indicate and illustrate with brief quotations the moment at which your character experiences an epiphany.

> independent, dependent, passive, aggressive, logical, illogical, happy, unhappy, hard-working, lazy, self-confident, uncertain, kind, cruel, decisive, indecisive, strong, weak, brave, cowardly, patient, impatient, lively, dull

Compose your thesis statement—your argument, which the rest of your essay will prove. For this essay, your thesis statement will focus on how your character has changed. It should:

- consist of a sentence or two
- state the claim you intend to prove (how your character has changed)
- raise questions that your essay must answer

Look ahead to the Revising Strategy in Step 3 of this lesson for more detailed information on what goes into an effective thesis statement. Look closely at the examples you'll find there. Then look back at your character profile notes and fill in a chart like the one that follows:

Before: Character at Start of Story	After: Character at End of Story	Differences Between Before and After	Insights Character Has Gained

Define the epiphany

Discuss with students what an epiphany is. Some students may have experienced a turning point in their own lives that could be shared as an example.

Profile your character

Ask students if they can see any of these character traits reflected in the character's physical being—his or her clothes, posture, or patterns of speech. For additional support, see the worksheet referenced below.

 Unit 7 Resource Book
Prewriting Worksheet, p. 139

Compose your thesis statement

Encourage students to spend time narrowing down and fine-tuning their thesis statement. This prewriting work can help the writer stay focused during the drafting stages. For additional support, see the worksheet referenced below.

Unit 7 Resource Book
Prewriting Worksheet, p. 140

Writing Workshop **847**

BUILDING ENGLISH PROFICIENCY

Using Prewriting Helps

Draw attention to some of the prewriting helps provided on page 847.

- For the "Choose a character" activity, encourage students to make the comparisons between the characters and themselves by creating Venn diagrams. Model an example, as needed.

- In the "Profile your character" activity, some students may be more successful if they use a web to brainstorm character traits. Encourage them to add incidents from the story for support.

Plan your essay

Students may want to begin with a rhetorical question about change and personal identity.

Connections to Writer's Notebook

For selection-related prompts, refer to Writer's Notebook.

Connections to Writer's Resource

For additional writing prompts, refer to Writer's Resource.

STEP 2 DRAFTING
The Student Models

The **transparencies** referenced below are authentic student models. Review them with the students before they draft. These questions will help:

1. Find the thesis statement of model 29. What questions does it raise? Does the essay go on to answer them?

2. How well does the writer of model 30 do at predicting how the character's behavior will change as a result of this heightened awareness?

3 Look at both models in terms of intended audience. Do you think either writer spends too much time summarizing the plot?

Transparency Collection
Student Models for Writing Workshop 29, 30

Ask a partner (Peer assessment)

Have students find the thesis statement in their partner's essay. If they cannot locate it exactly, revisions may be needed to make the main argument more explicit.

From your chart, compose your thesis statement: a sentence or two that states your claim.

Plan your essay. Consider using a writing plan like this one:

Introduction
- Thesis statement
- Questions it raises
- A brief profile of your character

Body
- Your character's epiphany
  —supporting quotations
- Analysis of how character's change occurs
  —supporting quotations

Conclusion
- Summary of argument: how you have answered questions raised by the thesis statement
- How you think the character's life will be different in the future

STEP **2** DRAFTING

Start writing. Here are some drafting tips.

- Drafting is a process of discovery. Be prepared to refine and restate your thesis as your argument develops.

- Remember that your audience is familiar with the literature. Avoid a long, detailed plot summary. Concentrate on your character.

STEP **3** REVISING

Ask a partner for comments on your draft before you revise it.

✔ Have I identified the point in the story when the character has an epiphany?

✔ Have I analyzed how this turning point comes about?

✔ Does my conclusion describe how I think the character's life will be different as a result of this heightened awareness?

✔ Does my thesis raise questions?

MINI-LESSON: WRITING STYLE
Writing an Effective Thesis Statement

Teach   A simple formula will help students who have trouble developing a thesis statement.

SPECIFIC SUBJECT (Eveline's joyless life) + SPECIFIC FEELING OR CLAIM (she prefers it that way) = AN EFFECTIVE THESIS STATEMENT (Eveline's life is joyless, but she realizes that she prefers it that way.)

Activity Idea   Have students work in pairs to critique and rewrite the following thesis statements to make them more bold and likely to spark questions for the reader. Have them use the formula above if they have difficulty.

These stories are about very human characters.

The characters in these stories have a lot to learn.

These writers are interested in character more than plot.

Apply   Have students read each other's thesis statements and then list the questions the statement raises. If not many questions come to mind, the writer will probably want to consider revisions.

Revising Strategy

Writing an Effective Thesis Statement

A thesis statement in an essay like this one must make a claim that raises questions—questions that demand answers. If the thesis statement raises no questions, the essay has nowhere to go.

> Eveline lives a sad and depressing life.

This claim raises no questions for the essay to answer. It gives us nothing to disagree with or wonder about. Here is a revised example:

> Eveline's life is joyless, but at the end of the story she realizes that she actually prefers it that way.

How could someone *prefer* a joyless life, and why? This is an effective thesis statement because it makes a claim that raises questions. Make sure your thesis statement raises questions that your essay goes on to answer.

LITERARY SOURCE
"He rushed beyond the barrier and called to her to follow. He was shouted at to go on but he still called to her. She set her white face to him, passive, like a helpless animal. Her eyes gave him no sign of love or farewell or recognition."
from "Eveline" by James Joyce

Ask a partner to review your revised draft before you edit. Look closely for errors with sentence fragments.

Editing Strategy

Avoiding Sentence Fragments

A sentence fragment is a group of words that is punctuated as a sentence but is not a complete thought. It leaves the reader wondering.

> Because Eveline lacked the courage to take a chance. (*Because she lacked the courage—what?*)

> At the station while the boat pulled away. (*What happened* at the station while the boat pulled away?)

You can correct a sentence fragment either by pulling it into an adjacent sentence or by adding words. See the model on the next page.

FOR REFERENCE
More advice on avoiding and correcting sentence fragments can be found in the Language and Grammar Handbook at the end of this book.

STEP 3 REVISING

Revising Strategy: Writing an Effective Thesis Statement

Have students read the examples and explanations and then note the questions that their peer's thesis sparks for them.

For additional support, see the mini-lesson at the bottom of page 848 and the worksheet referenced below.

Unit 7 Resource Book
Revising Worksheet, p. 141

Connections to
Writer's Resource

Refer to the Grammar, Usage, and Mechanics Handbook on Writer's Resource.

STEP 4 EDITING

Ask a partner (Peer assessment)

Remind students to give specific, constructive feedback rather than general comments.

Editing Strategy: Avoiding Sentence Fragments

Have students read the essays out loud, listening for any sentences that do not quite sound complete.

For additional support, see the mini-lesson at the bottom of this page and the worksheets referenced below.

Unit 7 Resource Book
Grammar Worksheet, p. 142
Grammar Check Test, p. 143

Connections to
Writer's Resource

Refer to the Grammar, Usage, and Mechanics Handbook on Writer's Resource.

MINI-LESSON: GRAMMAR

Avoiding Sentence Fragments

A complete sentence contains a subject and a predicate. Have students underline the subjects and circle the predicates in the following sentences. If one or the other is lacking, rewrite the fragment to make it a complete sentence. Remind students, however, that at times writers do purposefully include fragments for a desired effect.

She looked stunning in her new dress. A fashionable and expensive sequined evening gown. But she had dribbled raspberry sauce on the sleeve. An unforgiveable error. The tabloids reported this the next morning. Because she had belittled them. The waiters and waitresses had the last laugh.

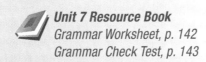
Unit 7 Resource Book
Grammar Worksheet, p. 142
Grammar Check Test, p. 143

STEP 5 PRESENTING
Read Aloud and Discuss

As they discuss, have students consider reasons outside of the text for disagreements in meaning. Should your background influence your interpretations of a text, or should a writer's work have a single meaning for all readers?

Illustrate

Encourage students to be creative with their illustrations. The illustration can be an impressionistic representation that does not actually show the character himself or herself.

STEP 6 LOOKING BACK
Self-evaluate

The *Assessment Criteria Specs* at the bottom of this page are for a superior paper. You might want to post these in the classroom. Students can then evaluate themselves based on these criteria. For a complete scoring rubric, use the *Assessment Worksheet* referenced below.

Unit 7 Resource Book
Assessment Worksheet, p. 144

Reflect

Encourage students to discuss how their ideas changed as they began to write. It is not unusual for writers to change their ideas or concepts as they write.

Have students discuss their moment of epiphany with the rest of the class, if the moment is not too private.

To further explore the theme, use the Fine Art Transparency referenced below.

Transparency Collection
Fine Art Writing Prompt 15

850

She remembers A promise she made to her mother years before. She promised to keep the home together. As long as she could. However, she fears that she will become like her mother.

STEP **5** PRESENTING

Here are a few suggestions for sharing your essay.

- Read your essay to a small group of classmates who chose the same character. Have them comment on whether your views agree or disagree with theirs.

- To illustrate your essay, create a piece of visual art that depicts your character at the moment of insight. Place him or her in the setting as you imagine it and with an expression that you imagine he or she might have at that moment.

STEP **6** LOOKING BACK

Self-evaluate. How would you evaluate your work? Look back at the Writer's Blueprint and give yourself a score for each item, from 6 (superior) to 1 (inadequate).

Reflect. Write responses to these questions.

- In what ways did your ideas about your thesis change during drafting and revising?

- Have you ever experienced an epiphany? If so, what was it? If not, try to imagine a moment like this occurring in your life, and describe what it might be like.

For Your Working Portfolio Add your essay and your reflection responses to your working portfolio.

ASSESSMENT CRITERIA SPECS

6 Superior The writer of a 6 paper impressively meets these criteria:

- Begins with an effective thesis statement which makes a specific claim that raises intriguing questions about how a character changes, and which the rest of the essay goes on to amplify and explain.

- Profiles this character in terms of character traits that directly contribute to that change.

- Clearly identifies a specific point in the story when the character experiences an epiphany and what the writer thinks went through the character's mind at that moment.

- Explains in detail how this turning point came about and convincingly predicts how the character's behavior will change as a result.

- Cites appropriate quotations from the literature to support the explanation and predictions.

- Makes few, if any, mistakes in grammar, usage, spelling, and mechanics. Avoids sentence fragments.

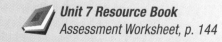
Unit 7 Resource Book
Assessment Worksheet, p. 144

Beyond Print

Looking at a Portrait

Portrait pointers can capture the complexities of a person at the same time that they convey their own impressions and feelings about their subject. Explain which of the portraits on pages 844–845 you consider flattering. Which do you find unflattering? Why? What insights do these portraits give you about each subject? Use the following guidelines to analyze a portrait, or any work of art.

Try to determine the artist's purpose. Does the painter seem more concerned with artistic style and composition than with the subject? Is the artist conveying a message? What, for example, might Henry Lamb's portrait of Lytton Strachey on page 844 suggest about its subject?

Remember that every artist has a point of view. Does the painter appear to be sympathetic? appreciative? critical? How might culture shape the artist's attitudes? Does the artist espouse a special idea or philosophy? From whose vantage point are subjects seen?

Note details that lead to the big picture. Look for patterns in shapes, colors, lines, and textures. Is there a focal point that draws your attention? Do things such as color, facial expressions, shadows, surroundings, and print provide clues to what's going on? Look at the background. Note, for example, the objects surrounding the woman in Frampton's portrait on page 844. What impressions do they convey about his subject? What do her hands and body language suggest?

Be an active viewer. Think about what appeals to you and why. How do these modern portraits differ from older ones such as the *Mona Lisa*? Viewing art is a personal experience, and individuals react differently to a piece of art. If you view art actively, knowledgeably, and with an open mind, you can enrich your experience.

Activity Option

You have commissioned someone to paint your portrait. Decide the following: What will you wear? What setting and details will you choose? How will you wear your hair? What features do you want highlighted? What impression about yourself do you wish to convey?

Beyond Print

Teaching Objectives

- to analyze portraits
- to understand the painter's and the subject's contribution to a portrait

Curricular Connection: Visual Literacy

This article can help students understand the creative and interpretive nature of portraiture. Discuss with students the similarities between the techniques in painting and the techniques writers use to develop characters, such as figurative language.

Introduce

Use the first paragraph to introduce the subject of the portraits. Discuss whether or not viewers who do not know what the subjects looked like in real life can judge whether or not the portrait is flattering. Then have the class work in small groups to read and discuss the questions on the rest of the page.

Activity Option

You may wish to have a "portrait" day at which students appear in class as they would wish to be painted. If possible, arrange to take a photograph of the class to preserve the assemblage.

ANOTHER APPROACH

Portraits By Comparison

Another way that students can focus on the features of painted portraits is to compare these portraits with photographs of the subjects. This will help students focus on the unique features and decisions that belong to the realm of portrait painting.

Activity Idea   Students can create portrait albums of British writers from the early twentieth century by following these guidelines.

- Locate both a photograph and a painted portrait for each author.

- Read biographical materials about the authors and create captions for the portraits and photos.

- Provide interpretations of the portraits based on their research.

   For ambitious students, you can recommend writing to the National Portrait Gallery, which sells postcards of many of the works in its collection: National Portrait Gallery, St. Martin's Place, London, WC2H 0HE, United Kingdom.

Unit Wrap-Up

🐾 MULTICULTURAL CONNECTION

The following ideas may facilitate discussion of the interrelationship of communication, group values, and individuality, all of which are explored in Unit 7.

Communication

An individual's communication skills reflects his or her personality, ethnic traditions, and educational background. We often make faulty assumptions about other people's character and abilities based on someone's communication skills.

Possible Response   People's communication skills certainly affect how they are perceived in the job market and in the world of education. Unfortunately, judgments are sometimes based on accents and regional dialects.

Groups

The security of a group identity and the desire for an individual identity create a tension that is perhaps never completely resolved.

Possible Response   Answers may depend on how closely the group ideals match the student's personal values.

Individuality

In spite of the portrayals of doubts about clearly defining or communicating one's identity, the literature suggests that this identity is somehow discovered in dialogue between people.

Possible Responses   The greatest obstacles may be the lack of opportunities, the prejudices of other people, or a fear of losing a group identity. The greatest obstacle to communicating an identity may be the refusal of other people to listen.

Activities

Activity 1   Students can work in groups to list assumptions they make about various groups based on communication skills.

🐾 Multicultural Connections

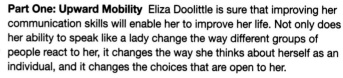

Communication

Part One: Upward Mobility Eliza Doolittle is sure that improving her communication skills will enable her to improve her life. Not only does her ability to speak like a lady change the way different groups of people react to her, it changes the way she thinks about herself as an individual, and it changes the choices that are open to her.

■ Do you think changing a person's communication skills could possibly have such drastic results in today's world?

Groups

Part Two: War and Aftermath The individuality of each of these authors was changed profoundly and forever by their identities as group members in time of war. A saving grace—perhaps—lay in their abilities to communicate their experiences.

■ How would you hold on to your individuality if you were being pressured to join a group such as an army or an excited mob?

Individuality

Part Three: The Search for Identity The question "Who am I?" is one that no other individual or member of your group can answer for you, as these fictional characters all learn. And if you do find an answer, you can never be sure of communicating it clearly to anyone else.

■ In your opinion, what is the greatest obstacle to any individual's learning his or her true identity? What is the greatest obstacle to communicating that knowledge, once found?

Activities

1. Discuss specific ways you might improve your communication skills—with members of your own group or other groups.

2. Write a letter either applying for membership in a group or resigning membership in a group. The group may be real, such as a student activity club or a business association, or it may be abstract, such as adults or curly-haired people. Be sure to explain your reasons for wanting in or out.

3. Create a graphic image or a symbol that in your own mind represents the individual that is *you*.

Activity 2   Students can suggest external ways to represent changes in their personalities. They may suggest items of clothing, hair styles, and various accessories that they feel express their identities.

Independent and Group Projects

Research

Women United In the early twentieth century, women intensified their already longstanding campaigns in England and the United States to obtain the right to vote. Their efforts included meetings, marches, vandalism, and hunger strikes. Research the views for and against the women's suffrage movement and the actions that women were taking. Give an **oral presentation**—illustrated, if possible—of the women's suffrage movement during this time.

Art

Plans for Peace Prepare an advertising campaign for a world without war. Develop an eye-catching logo and a forceful slogan (keep it simple). Adapt your design to posters, key chains, greeting cards, calendars, mugs, tee shirts, or anything else you can think of that will help you spread the word of world peace. Display your work for the class.

Language

Many Accents Research several languages to find out their ways of saying everyday expressions such as *hello, good-bye, please, thank you, happy birthday,* and the designations for family members such as *mother, father, sister, brother, aunt,* and *uncle.* Or, if you have access to a variety of language speakers, write a brief message for them all to translate. Create a bulletin board, using a large world map as a centerpiece, of languages around the world. If possible, include photos of people from the different countries who are saying these things.

Media

You Are There Work with a group to prepare a **multimedia overview** of the early twentieth century. Use bits of dialogue, lines of poetry, excerpts from the prose in this unit, and any other bits of writing you can cull from old magazines, newspapers, letters, and so on. Add popular World War I songs; photographs of people, objects, and events; and cartoons or paintings. Figure out how best to organize these various things for easy accessibility, and link them with a voice-over narration.

853

UNIT 7 OPTIONS
Research

You may wish to have students focus on the suffrage movement in England. Encourage them to use unusual reference sources, such as the movie *Mary Poppins,* in which Mrs. Banks is portrayed as a suffragette.

Art

Students may wish to work together in groups to create articles such as calendars, quilts, or other large-scale works.

Language

Students who do not have access to foreign language speakers may be able to find foreign language tapes in a library and use these to find out the correct pronunciation of simple words and phrases.

Media

Students might consider choosing a title or theme that will help them focus the variety of materials they select and to create a cohesive narration.

Selection Test

Unit 7 Resource Book
New Selection, pp.
Test 1
Test 2

Planning Unit 8: The Later Twentieth Century

Literature

Integrated Language Arts

	Literary	Writing/Grammar, Usage and Mechanics	Reading, Thinking, Listening, Speaking	Vocabulary/Spelling
Shooting an Elephant *by George Orwell* Essay *(average)* p. 860	Irony, theme Genre, diction Metaphor Symbolism	Descriptive words Write a letter Short story Editorial Using affixes	Infer Draw conclusions	Paragraph

Wartime Speeches
by Winston Churchill
Speech
(average)
p. 869
	Theme
	Repetition
	Simile
	Style
	Parallelism
	Imagery
		Characteristics of a great
		  speech
		List of crimes
		Short story
		Using commas correctly
				Words with multiple
				  meanings

Homage to a Government *by Philip Larkin* Poem *(average)* p. 876 **Two Poems on the Passing of an Empire** *by Derek Walcott* Poem *(challenging)* p. 877	Repetition Diction Irony	Advantages and disadvan- tages of colonialism Poem Feature story Using apostrophes correctly	Compare and contrast	
from In the Ditch *by Buchi Emecheta* Novel Excerpt *(easy)* p. 881	Dialogue, metaphor Stereotype Character, theme Stream of consciousness	List of obstacles Dialogue Letter of advice Expressions of time Writing dialogue	Generalize Recognize values Infer	

Meeting Individual Needs

Multi-modal Activities	Mini-Lessons
Artistic creation	Using affixes
Discussion and debate	Making decisions
Photo essay	
Analyzing motivation	
Linking character and conflict	
Analyzing a key thematic passage	

Speech excerpts	Using commas
Pictorial time line	correctly
Videotaped interview	Words with multiple
Exploring contrasting images	meanings

Bulletin board display	Using apostrophes
Fabric design	correctly
Persuasive speech	
Linking literature and history	

Illustrated recipe book	Expressions of time
Choreograph or design	Dialogue
Relating causes and effects	Writing dialogue
Bringing a narrative to life	Planning your time
Making cultural connections	

Interdisciplinary Studies
Effects of Empire

Format	Content Area	Highlights	Skill
Article: **South Africa**	History	This selection is a time line of South Africa's socio-political situation over the past 300 years.	Creating a time line
Interview: **The Pulse of Village Life**	Career	An American diplomat discusses economic distress of a west African country granted independence by the British.	Interviewing

Writing Workshop

Mode	Writing Format	Writing Focus	Proofreading Skills
Expository writing	A literary analysis	Being concise	Using commas correctly

Program Support Materials

For Every Selection	For Every Writing Workshop
Unit Resource Book	**Unit Resource Book**
Graphic Organizer	Prewriting Worksheet
Study Guide	Revising Strategy Worksheet
Vocabulary Worksheet	Editing Strategy Worksheet
Grammar Worksheet	Presentation Worksheet
Spelling, Speaking and Listening, or Literary Language Worksheet	Writing Rubric
Alternate Check Test	**Transparency Collection**
Vocabulary Test	Fine Art Transparency
Selection Test	Student Writing Model Transparencies

For Every Interdisciplinary Study	Assessment
Unit Resource Book	**Unit Resource Book**
Study Guide	TE Check Tests
Mini-Lesson Skill Worksheet	Alternate Check Test (blackline master)
	Vocabulary Test (blackline master)
	Selection Test (blackline master)
	Test Generator Software
	Assessment Handbook

Planning Unit 8: The Later Twentieth Century

Literature

Integrated Language Arts

	Literary	Writing/Grammar, Usage and Mechanics	Reading, Thinking, Listening, Speaking	Vocabulary/Spelling
Eve to Her Daughters *by Judith Wright* Poem *(average)* p. 906 **The Frog Prince** *by Stevie Smith* Poem *(easy)* p. 909 **Not Waving but Drowning** *by Stevie Smith* Poem *(average)* p. 911 **The Explorers** *by Margaret Atwood* Poem *(average)* p. 911	Allusion Free verse	Poem Journal entry Letter to Eve Indefinite and definite articles	Connect Clarify Recognize multiple meanings Visualize Understanding idioms and puns Infer	
The Truly Married Woman *by Abioseh Nicol* Short Story *(average)* p. 916	Point of view Foreshadowing Dramatic irony	Paragraph on physical punishment Article Character sketch Appositives	Infer Recognize propaganda Generalize	
A Shocking Accident *by Graham Greene* Short Story *(average)* p. 926	Tone Irony Stereotype	Dialogue Opening paragraph Description Parentheses	Compare and contrast	
The Courtship of Mr. Lyon *by Angela Carter* Short Story *(average)* p. 933	Magic realism Foreshadowing Imagery, mood Hyperbole and simile Character Style	Paragraph Modern fairy story The Beast's story Recognize sentence fragments	Analyze Infer Draw conclusions Main idea and supporting details	Meaning within context

Meeting Individual Needs

Multi-modal Activities	Mini-Lessons
Perform a song	Indefinite and definite
Create an artwork	articles
Tall tale	Allusion
Exploring verbs and verbals	Analyze
Exploring vocabulary	
Exploring folklore	

Cartoon strip	Appositives
Wedding gift	Recognize cause and
Understanding characters	effect
Keeping track of story events	Point of view
Exploring a key passage	

Film review	Parentheses
Five important things learned	
Tall tale	
Distinguishing between fantasy	
and reality	
Making real-life connections	

Illustrate a scene	Magic realism
Prepare a bibliography	Meaning within
Present a puppet play	context
Linking language and imagery	Recognize sentence
Analyzing rhetorical questions	fragments
Exploring style	

Interdisciplinary Studies
Myth Under a Microscope

Format	Content Area	Highlights	Skill
Article: **Some Biomythology** *by Lewis Thomas*	Science	A scientific examination of mythological creatures.	Analyze how art reflects culture and belief Use vocabulary appropriate to audience

Writing Workshop

Mode	Writing Format	Writing Focus	Proofreading Skills
Narrative writing	A monologue	Ending with a humorous touch Using sensory details	Using sentence fragments

Program Support Materials

For Every Selection	For Every Writing Workshop
Unit Resource Book	**Unit Resource Book**
Graphic Organizer	Prewriting Worksheet
Study Guide	Revising Strategy Worksheet
Vocabulary Worksheet	Editing Strategy Worksheet
Grammar Worksheet	Presentation Worksheet
Spelling, Speaking and Listening, or Literary Language Worksheet	Writing Rubric
Alternate Check Test	**Transparency Collection**
Vocabulary Test	Fine Art Transparency
Selection Test	Student Writing Model Transparencies

For Every Interdisciplinary Study	Assessment
Unit Resource Book	**Unit Resource Book**
Study Guide	TE Check Tests
Mini-Lesson Skill Worksheet	Alternate Check Test (blackline master)
	Vocabulary Test (blackline master)
	Selection Test (blackline master)
	Test Generator Software
	Assessment Handbook

Part One Selections

Shooting an Elephant

Audiotape An unabridged reading of *Animal Farm*, 3 hours, is available from Books on Tape, 1981.

Videotape *George Orwell*, 52 minutes, Films for the Humanities & Sciences, is a documentary biography. Consider showing the film version of George Orwell's *Animal Farm*, 72 minutes, Library Video Company, 1955, an award-winning animated version.

Home Connection At some time or other, most people let those around them pressure them into doing something they knew they shouldn't. For an at-home activity, students might discuss with family members the dynamics of peer pressure and techniques for resisting it.

Wartime Speeches

Videotape *Speeches of Winston Churchill*, 60 minutes, from the In Their Own Words Series, is offered through Library Video Company. *World War II: When Lions Roared*, 186 minutes, PBS

Home Video, 1994, from the NBC miniseries, is a behind-the-scenes true story of how Roosevelt, Churchill, and Stalin led their countries against Hitler.

Home Connection "We will never surrender!" Winston Churchill's eloquence helped the British people to resist relentless German bombing during World War II. For an at-home activity, students might ask family members who they thought was the most eloquent person to whom they had ever listened and what contributed to the power of this individual's words.

Homage to a Government/Two Poems on the Passing of an Empire

Audiotape The author reads excerpts from several of his works in *Derek Walcott Reads,* 1 hour 30 minutes, Harper Audio, 1994.

Videotape *Derek Walcott: A World of Ideas*, 30 minutes, PBS Video, is an interview with the poet by Bill Moyers.

Community Resources Students might use the resources of the local library to research the history of the the process by which one of the countries that were once British colonies or pro-

tectorates—such as India, Pakistan, Burma, Nigeria, Ghana, Kenya, Israel, and Jordan—became independent.

from In the Ditch

Community Resources Immigrants have a variety of problems in adjusting to their new homelands, which may include learning a new language, finding adequate housing, learning new job skills, securing education, and adjusting to a whole range of cultural differences. You might invite someone who helps such newcomers with their problems to visit the class and discuss their work.

Connections to
Custom Literature Database

For Part One "The Passing of Empire" Selections with Lessons

- "Mary Postgate" by Rudyard Kipling
- An Iron Curtain Has Descended by Winston Churchill

Additional theme-based selections can be accessed on the ScottForesman database.

Connections to
AuthorWorks

Information about the life and times of George Orwell and Derek Walcott is available on ScottForesman's AuthorWorks CD-ROM.

Part Two Selections

Eve to Her Daughters/The Frog Prince/Not Waving but Drowning/The Explorers

Audiotape *Anthology of 20th Century English Poetry*, 3 audiocassettes, Folkways/Smithsonian, highlights many important contemporary poets.

The author reads her work in *Margaret Atwood Reads*, 45 minutes, American Audio Prose Library.

Videotape *Stevie*, 102 minutes, Sultan Entertainment, features Glenda Jackson portraying the role of the poet Stevie Smith.

Community Resources Students might be interested in hearing the experiences of someone whose daily work involves administering first aid to those who are sick or injured. Such people might include police personnel, firefighters, paramedics, and lifeguards, doctors, nurses, emergency room personnel, and so on.

The Truly Married Woman

Community Resources The degree of involvement of family members, particularly parents, in decisions about marriage varies widely in countries around the world. While in many places the modern Western notion of couples deciding for themselves has taken hold, arranged marriages are still the

norm in many cultures. Students might use the resources of the local library to do a comparative study of marriage in today's world.

A Shocking Accident

Videotape *A Shocking Accident*, 25 minutes, Direct Cinema, 1983, is a film adaptation of the story. *Graham Greene: Brighton Rock,* 26 minutes, Films for the Humanities & Sciences, includes the author discussing his life and work.

Home Connection In this story, Graham Greene

introduces a cartoonish bit of humor into a realistic story. Is it funny? Everyone's definition of humor differs. For an at-home activity, students might discuss with family members what makes something funny.

The Courtship of Mr. Lyon

Community Resources With its roots as far back as the classical tale of Cupid and Psyche, the story of Beauty and the Beast is one of the oldest and most widespread of folktale motifs. Students might use the resources of the local library to research some of the different treatments of this familiar story.

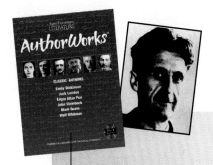

Connections to
NovelWorks

An audiotape of *Animal Farm*, a novel by George Orwell, is among the many teaching tools included in the ScottForesman NovelWorks Kit.

Connections to
Custom Literature Database

For Part Two "The Slant View" Selections with Lessons

- "The Lantern-Bearers" by Robert Louis Stevenson
- from *Idle Days in Patagonia*, Chapter XII by W. H. Hudson

Additional theme-based selections can be accessed on the ScottForesman database.

The Later Twentieth Century

🎨 Art Study

Mr. and Mrs. Clark and Percy, pages 856–857, was painted in 1970–1971 by David Hockney. The acrylic on canvas is one of a series of large double portraits (seven feet by ten feet) which Hockney painted of his friends. This portrait shows fashion designer Ossie Clark and his wife, fabric designer Celia Birtwell, in their London home with Percy, one of their two white cats. The image on the wall at the left is one of Hockney's own etchings from a series called "The Rake's Progress."

Hockney painted the final work not only from firsthand observations of the scene but also from many small detailed drawings and from many photographs of his friends and their room. He deliberately left out many objects in order to create an effect of simplicity.

Question How does this portrait differ from the Gainsborough portrait of Mr. and Mrs. Andrews on page 209? (*It differs in setting, the degree of formality, both in the sitters' postures and in dress, and in the palette.*)

Question Do you think the Clarks were pleased with this depiction of themselves? Why or why not? (*Students might suggest that the subjects were pleased because the portrait presents them as relaxed yet dignified, intelligent, and stylish.*)

UNIT **8**

The Late Twentieth Century

The Passing of Empire
Part One, pages 856–901

The Slant View
Part Two, pages 902–954

THEMES IN ENGLISH LITERATURE

The Absurd Person
Theme Portfolio, pages 955–965

855

THEMATIC CONNECTIONS

Britons had no sooner recovered from World War II than the British empire began to disintegrate. The literature of Britain itself began to include the voices of many former colonials, however. It remains to be seen whether the arrival of people from different cultures will prove as influential as the influx of Normans to English shores over nine hundred years earlier.

Part One
The Passing of Empire

Part One features selections that explore attitudes about war and colonialism.

Ideas to Explore

- How does a life-and-death struggle to guarantee the survival of civilization itself affect a nation?
- How do a nation's forms of expression change when it acquires a global point of view?

Part Two
The Slant View

The literature in Part Two raises some questions about whether we need to cultivate new ways of thinking about old topics.

Ideas to Explore

- How has the relationship between men and women changed in the twentieth century?
- How has the style of literary expression changed?

 *Art Study*

The photo of a Royal Horse Guard conveys the British imperial spirit. A detail of *Buste D'Homme au Chapeau* by Pablo Picasso is in a style of painting called cubism.

EXPLORING CONCEPTS

- The breakup of the British empire led to the rise of new, independent nations in Africa, Asia, and elsewhere.
- The political shape of Africa was transfigured, with the change from a continent of colonies before World War II to a continent of over 50 independent nations by 1980.

Research Activity   Have students start with the key dates and work in small groups to compile a list of the colonies that became nations after World War II. They can display their findings on a time line or on a map.

Research Activity   Small groups of students might use library or online resources to find out about and report on any of the people on this page or any of the countries listed under key dates on the next page.

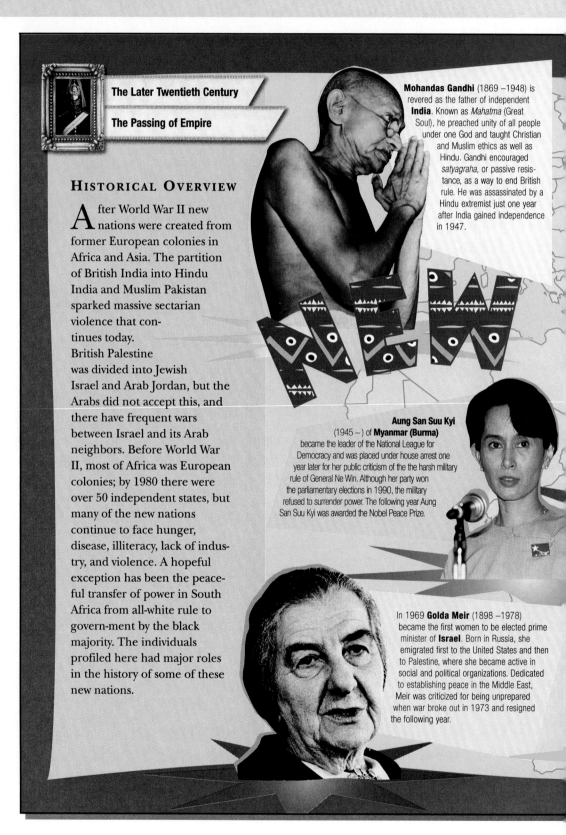

The Later Twentieth Century

The Passing of Empire

HISTORICAL OVERVIEW

After World War II new nations were created from former European colonies in Africa and Asia. The partition of British India into Hindu India and Muslim Pakistan sparked massive sectarian violence that continues today. British Palestine was divided into Jewish Israel and Arab Jordan, but the Arabs did not accept this, and there have frequent wars between Israel and its Arab neighbors. Before World War II, most of Africa was European colonies; by 1980 there were over 50 independent states, but many of the new nations continue to face hunger, disease, illiteracy, lack of industry, and violence. A hopeful exception has been the peaceful transfer of power in South Africa from all-white rule to govern-ment by the black majority. The individuals profiled here had major roles in the history of some of these new nations.

Mohandas Gandhi (1869 –1948) is revered as the father of independent **India**. Known as *Mahatma* (Great Soul), he preached unity of all people under one God and taught Christian and Muslim ethics as well as Hindu. Gandhi encouraged *satyagraha*, or passive resistance, as a way to end British rule. He was assassinated by a Hindu extremist just one year after India gained independence in 1947.

Aung San Suu Kyi (1945 –) of **Myanmar (Burma)** became the leader of the National League for Democracy and was placed under house arrest one year later for her public criticism of the the harsh military rule of General Ne Win. Although her party won the parliamentary elections in 1990, the military refused to surrender power. The following year Aung San Suu Kyi was awarded the Nobel Peace Prize.

In 1969 **Golda Meir** (1898 –1978) became the first women to be elected prime minister of **Israel**. Born in Russia, she emigrated first to the United States and then to Palestine, where she became active in social and political organizations. Dedicated to establishing peace in the Middle East, Meir was criticized for being unprepared when war broke out in 1973 and resigned the following year.

Kwame Nkrumah (1909–1972) was prime minister of the Gold Coast when it became the independent country of **Ghana** in 1957. Elected president of Ghana in 1960, Nkrumah was a controversial leader who introduced a number of social and economic reforms but was strongly criticized for the dictatorial methods he used.

Jomo Kenyatta (1890?–1978) became the first president of an independent **Kenya** in 1964. He was imprisoned by the British from 1953 to 1961 for his political activities. As president, Kenyatta worked to unite the disparate cultures of Kenya's Africans, Asians, Arabs, and Europeans, and to modernize the economy.

In 1994 **Nelson Mandela** (1918 –) was elected the first black president of **South Africa**. This was the first election in which the country's black majority were allowed to vote. Between 1962 and 1990, Mandela had been imprisoned by South Africa because of his opposition to the government policy of *apartheid* (racial segregation).

Key Dates

1945
World War II ends; United Nations established.

1947
British India partitioned; Palestine partitioned.

1948
Gandhi assassinated; Israel becomes independent.

1949
South African policy of apartheid goes into effect.

1952
Mau Mau uprising begins in Kenya.

1957
Ghana becomes independent.

1963
Kenya becomes independent.

1964
Mandela imprisoned in South Africa.

1991
Aung San Suu Kyi wins Nobel Peace Prize.

1994
Mandela elected president of South Africa.

857

Key Dates

Some countries that achieved independence from Britain:

1961 Sierra Leone

1962 Trinidad and Tobago; Jamaica

1964 Malta

1965 Republic of Maldives (formerly the Maldive Islands)

1966 Barbados

1970 Tonga

1973 Bahamas

1974 Grenada

1978 Tuvalu (formerly the Ellice Islands)

1979 St. Lucia

1981 Belize (formerly British Honduras)

MATERIALS OF INTEREST
Books

- *The Collected Essays, Journalism and Letters of George Orwell* edited by Sonia Orwell and Ian Angus (Harcourt, 1968).

- *Omeros* by Derek Walcott (Farrar, Strauss,1992).

Multimedia

- *The Jewel in the Crown* [videotape] a made-for-television movie based on *The Raj Quartet* by Paul Scott. 5 cassettes, 774 min., color, VHS. Paramount Home Video, order #12100.

- *A Passage to India* [videotape] based on the novel by E. M. Forster. VHS, PG. RCA/Columbia Pictures Home Video, order 60485.

Connections to
Custom Literature Database

For further historical background, under **Background Articles,** see **Modern England 1915–.**

Transparency Collection
Fine Art Transparency 16

FOR ALL STUDENTS

- What rights and burdens come with being a citizen of a free country?
- What responsibilities does a nation have toward those who have formerly been its colonial subjects?

  To further explore the theme, use the transparency referenced below.

For At-Risk Students

Recall movies about World War II and about the British colonial presence in Asia and Africa.

For Students Who Need Challenge

Have students research and report on the imperial ventures of other nations, such as Spain, Portugal, China, and Russia.

For Auditory Learners

- Play an excerpt from a recorded speech by Winston Churchill and ask students to comment on the national spirit the recording evokes.
- Play an excerpt from the folk music of a nation once under British domination, such as India or the West Indies, and ask students to comment on the national spirit the recording evokes.

✍ MULTICULTURAL CONNECTION

Interactions between people of diverse cultural backgrounds are especially difficult when one or both groups is not able to express itself fully and honestly. Ask students to discuss how literature can be one of the fundamental bridges between cultural groups.

Part One

The Passing of Empire

The British Empire at its peak had been widespread and powerful, but now, after World War II, the empire was fast diminishing. For a country that had largely defined itself by its influence abroad the change was not an easy one. The people who had been in control for so many years now found control slipping from their grasp.

✍ Multicultural Focus **Interactions** Encounters between people of diverse cultural backgrounds are heightened under conditions of colonialism. Who gains, and who loses in these encounters? George Orwell observed that when one person rules another, he "wears a mask, and his face grows to fit it." What might that face look like once the mask comes off?

IDEAS THAT WORK

Motivating with Research and Discussion

"Start with the question, 'What does the title tell you?' Since there is a lot of history involved, have students do some library research on the history of their country or interview someone who has experienced the horrors of war. The speeches are difficult; offer some historical background or assign students to do mini-research on that period.

The last two selections touch on the immigrant experiences—compare and contrast the students' experiences with those in the selection. Allow students in pairs or small groups to discuss themes like discrimination, racism, diversity. Encourage students to predict what they would have done if they were the person in "Shooting an Elephant."

Nancy Duke S. La[
New York, New Yor[

with mud, the eyes wide open, the teeth bared and grinning with an expression of unendurable agony. (Never tell me, by the way, that the dead look peaceful. Most of the corpses I have seen looked devilish.) The friction of the great beast's foot had stripped the skin from his back as neatly as one skins a rabbit. As soon as I saw the dead man I sent an orderly to a friend's house nearby to borrow an elephant rifle. I had already sent back the pony, not wanting it to go mad with fright and throw me if it smelled the elephant.

The orderly came back in a few minutes with a rifle and five cartridges, and meanwhile some Burmans had arrived and told us that the elephant was in the paddy fields below, only a few hundred yards away. As I started forward practically the whole population of the quarter flocked out of their houses and followed me. They had seen the rifle and were all shouting excitedly that I was going to shoot the elephant. They had not shown much interest in the elephant when he was merely ravaging their homes, but it was different now that he was going to be shot. It was a bit of fun to them, as it would be to an English crowd; besides, they wanted the meat. It made me vaguely uneasy. I had no intention of shooting the elephant—I had merely sent for the rifle to defend myself if necessary—and it is always unnerving to have a crowd following you. I marched down the hill, looking and feeling a fool, with the rifle over my shoulder and an ever-growing army of people jostling at my heels. At the bottom, when you got away from the huts, there was a metalled road and beyond that a miry waste of paddy fields a thousand yards across, not yet ploughed but soggy from the first rains and dotted with coarse grass. The elephant was standing eighty yards from the road, his left side towards us. He took not the slightest notice of the crowd's approach. He was tearing up bunches of grass, beating them against his knees to clean them and stuffing them into his mouth.

I had halted on the road. As soon as I saw the elephant I knew with perfect certainty that I ought not to shoot him. It is a serious matter to shoot a working elephant—it is comparable to destroying a huge and costly piece of machinery—and obviously one ought not to do it if it can possibly be avoided. And at that distance, peacefully eating, the elephant looked no more dangerous than a cow. I thought then and I think now that his attack of "must" was already passing off; in which case he would merely wander harmlessly about until the mahout came back and caught him. Moreover, I did not in the least want to shoot him. I decided that I would watch him for a little while to make sure that he did not turn savage again, and then go home.

> **SUMMARIZE: What are the reasons Orwell gives for not wanting to kill the elephant?** [6]

But at that moment I glanced round at the crowd that had followed me. It was an immense crowd, two thousand at the least and growing every minute. It blocked the road for a long distance on either side. I looked at the sea of yellow faces above the garish clothes—faces all happy and excited over this bit of fun, all certain that the elephant was going to be shot. They were watching me as they would watch a conjuror[14] about to perform a trick. They did [7] not like me, but with the magical rifle in my hands I was momentarily worth watching. And suddenly I realized that I should have to shoot the elephant after all. The people expected it [8] of me and I had got to do it; I could feel their two thousand wills pressing me forward, irresistibly. And it was at this moment, as I stood there with the rifle in my hands, that I first grasped the hollowness, the futility of the white man's dominion in the East. Here was I, the

---

14. **conjuror** (kon′jər ər), *n.* magician.

Shooting An Elephant **863**

BUILDING ENGLISH PROFICIENCY

Linking Character and Conflict

Help students better understand the narrator's conflict by creating a web of words and phrases that describe or give clues to his emotions. If appropriate, students also can jot down causes for the emotions. (You can use this activity on its own or as an extension of the Building English Proficiency activity on p. 861.)

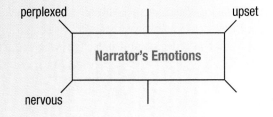

perplexed   upset

Narrator's Emotions

nervous

Metaphor

Questions What metaphor does the narrator use to describe his situation? Why do you think this metaphor is appropriate? *(Possible response: The narrator uses a theater metaphor when he says that he was supposed to be the leading actor but instead had become a puppet, even a hollow dummy. The theater metaphor points up the narrator's belief that colonialism was largely dependent upon image, display, masks, and artificial show.)*

10 **Literary Focus**

Irony

Point out to students that the narrator deliberately uses a common expression of polite society—"that would never do"—to emphasize the absurdity of his feelings at the time. The situation is forcing him to commit a violent act with serious consequences merely to avoid being the subject of laughter.

11 **Active Reading**

Evaluate

Possible Response The narrator feels he must shoot in order to uphold the image of the white imperialist; he cannot display fear or become an object of ridicule.

---

white man with his gun, standing in front of the unarmed native crowd—seemingly the leading actor of the piece; but in reality I was only an absurd puppet pushed to and fro by the will of those yellow faces behind. I perceived in this moment that when the white man turns tyrant it is his own freedom that he destroys. He becomes a sort of hollow, posing dummy, the conventionalized figure of a sahib.[15] For it is the condition of his rule that he shall spend his life in trying to impress the "natives" and so in every crisis he has got to do what the "natives" expect of him. He wears a mask, and his face grows to fit it. I had got to shoot the elephant. I had committed myself to doing it when I sent for the rifle. A sahib has got to act like a sahib; he has got to appear resolute,[16] to know his own mind and do definite things. To come all that way, rifle in hand, with two thousand people marching at my heels, and then to trail feebly away, having done nothing—no, that was impossible. The crowd would laugh at me. And my whole life, every white man's life in the East, was one long struggle not to be laughed at.

But I did not want to shoot the elephant. I watched him beating his bunch of grass against his knees, with that preoccupied grandmotherly air that elephants have. It seemed to me that it would be murder to shoot him. At that age I was not squeamish[17] about killing animals, but I had never shot an elephant and never wanted to. (Somehow it always seems worse to kill a *large* animal.) Besides, there was the beast's owner to be considered. Alive, the elephant was worth at least a hundred pounds; dead, he would only be worth the value of his tusks—five pounds, possibly. But I had to act quickly. I turned to some experienced-looking Burmans who had been there when we arrived, and asked them how the elephant had been behaving. They all said the same thing: he took no notice of you if you left him alone, but he might charge if you went too close to him.

It was perfectly clear to me what I ought to do. I ought to walk up to within, say, twenty-five yards of the elephant and test his behavior. If he charged I could shoot, if he took no notice of me it would be safe to leave him until the mahout came back. But also I knew that I was going to do no such thing. I was a poor shot with a rifle and the ground was soft mud into which one would sink at every step. If the elephant charged and I missed him, I should have about as much chance as a toad under a steam-roller. But even then I was not thinking particularly of my own skin, only the watchful yellow faces behind. For at that moment, with the crowd watching me, I was not afraid in the ordinary sense, as I would have been if I had been alone. A white man mustn't be frightened of "natives"; and so, in general, he isn't frightened. The sole thought in my mind was that if anything went wrong those two thousand Burmans would see me pursued, caught, trampled on and reduced to a grinning corpse like that Indian up the hill. And if that happened it was quite probable that some of them would laugh. That would never do. There was only one alternative. I shoved the cartridges into the magazine and lay down on the road to get a better aim.

EVALUATE: What do you think is the real reason Orwell decides to shoot the elephant?

The crowd grew very still, and a deep, low, happy sigh, as of people who see the theater curtain go up at last, breathed from innumerable throats. They were going to have their bit of fun after all. The rifle was a beautiful German thing with cross-hair sights. I did not then know that in shooting an elephant one should shoot to cut an imaginary bar running from ear-hole to ear-hole. I ought therefore, as the elephant was side-

---

15. **sahib** (sä′ib), *n.* in British India, a European.
16. resolute (rez′ə lŭt), *adj.* determined.
17. **squeamish** (skwē′mish), *adj.* easily shocked; nauseated.

MINI-LESSON: READING/THINKING SKILLS

Making Decisions

Teach The narrator of "Shooting an Elephant" is painfully aware of the interplay of rational and emotional factors in his decision-making. Remind students that good decision-making often includes the following preparatory steps:

- gathering evidence
- considering alternatives
- seeking expert advice
- applying values

Questions Which of the listed steps did the narrator follow? Which of the steps proved to be the most significant? *(The narrator gathered evidence and considered alternatives but did not seek advice. The imperialist values he applied proved to be the most significant in his decision.)*

Activity Idea Have students

- imagine a situation in which they become aware that a crime had been committed secretly
- decide what action to take based upon gathering the evidence, considering alternatives, obtaining advice, and applying values

ways on, to have aimed straight at his ear-hole; actually I aimed several inches in front of this, thinking the brain would be further forward.

When I pulled the trigger I did not hear the bang or feel the kick— one never does when a shot goes home—but I heard the devilish roar of glee that went up from the crowd. In that instant, in too short a time, one would have thought, even for the bullet to get there, a mysterious, terrible change had come over the elephant. He neither stirred nor fell, but every line of his body had altered. He looked suddenly stricken, shrunken, immensely old, as though the frightful impact of the bullet had paralyzed him without knocking him down. At last, after what seemed a long time—it might have been five seconds, I dare say—he sagged flabbily to his knees. His mouth slobbered. An enormous senility[18] seemed to have settled upon him. One could have imagined him thousands of years old. I fired again into the same spot. At the second shot he did not collapse but climbed with desperate slowness to his feet and stood weakly upright, with legs sagging and head dropping. I fired a third time. That was the shot that did for him. You could see the agony of it jolt his whole body and knock the last remnant of strength from his legs. But in falling he seemed for a moment to rise, for as his hind legs collapsed beneath him he seemed to tower upwards like a huge rock toppling, his trunk reaching skyward like a tree. He trumpeted, for the first and only time. And then down he came, his belly towards me, with a crash that seemed to shake the ground even where I lay.

I got up. The Burmans were already racing past me across the mud. It was obvious that the elephant would never rise again, but he was not dead. He was breathing very rhythmically with long rattling gasps, his great mound of a side painfully rising and falling. His mouth was wide open—I could see far down into caverns of pale pink throat. I waited a long time for him to die, but his breathing did not weaken. Finally I fired my two remaining

HE WAS DYING, VERY SLOWLY AND IN GREAT AGONY . . .

shots into the spot where I thought his heart must be. The thick blood welled out of him like red velvet, but still he did not die. His body did not even jerk when the shots hit him, the tortured breathing continued without a pause. He was dying, very slowly and in great agony, but in some world remote from me where not even a bullet could damage him further. I felt that I had got to put an end to that dreadful noise. It seemed dreadful to see the great beast lying there, powerless to move and yet powerless to die, and not even to be able to finish him. I sent back for my small rifle and poured shot after shot into his heart and down his throat. They seemed to make no impression. The tortured gasps continued as steadily as the ticking of a clock.

In the end I could not stand it any longer and went away. I heard later that it took him half an hour to die. Burmans were arriving with dahs[19] and baskets even before I left, and I was told they had stripped his body almost to the bones by the afternoon.

Afterwards, of course, there were endless discussions about the shooting of the elephant. The owner was furious, but he was only an Indian and could do nothing. Besides, legally I had done the right thing, for a mad elephant has to be killed, like a mad dog, if its owner fails to control it. Among the Europeans opinion was divided. The older men said I was right, the younger men said it was a damn shame to shoot an elephant for killing a coolie, because an elephant was worth more than any damn Coringhee coolie. And afterwards I was very glad that the coolie had been killed; it put me legally in the right and it gave me a sufficient pretext for shooting the elephant. I often wondered whether any of the others grasped that I had done it solely to avoid looking a fool.

_____

18. **senility** (sə nil′ə tē), _n._ mental and physical deterioration associated with old age.
19. **dah** (dä), _n._ a heavy Burmese knife.

12 Literary Element
Symbolism

Question What do you think the elephant might symbolize in this essay? Give reasons from the text to support your answer. (Possible responses: The elephant symbolizes the British Raj, the imperial domination of the Far East. The elephant is described in terms that the narrator wants the reader to apply to the Empire—old, stricken, shrunken, senile, dying a slow and agonizing death.)

13 Literary Focus
Irony

Point out that the narrator saves his most horrific irony for the end of the essay. He admits that he was "very glad" the coolie had been trampled by the elephant because it justified the shooting. The irony lies in the dehumanizing effect of the imperialist venture, reducing the narrator to rejoicing in the death of another human being.

Check Test

1. Why is the narrator hated by the Burmese? (He is an official representative of the white imperial government.)

2. What "crimes" had the elephant committed? (destroyed a hut, killed livestock, overturned a van, trampled a Dravidian man)

3. What did the narrator intend to do when he first saw the elephant? (watch it for a while and then go home)

4. What forces the narrator to shoot? (his position as a white imperialist and his fear of being ridiculed)

5. Why doesn't the elephant die quickly? (The narrator does not shoot accurately.)

 *Unit 8 Resource Book*
Alternate Check Test, p. 5

BUILDING ENGLISH PROFICIENCY

Analyzing a Key Thematic Passage

Read aloud the sentence at the top of the first column on page 864: "I perceived in this moment that when the white man turns tyrant it is his own freedom that he destroys." Point out that in this paragraph, the narrator presents the theme of this selection—that tyranny destroys the tyrant's freedom. To lead students to a clearer understanding of the theme, ask questions such as the following:

• What things does Orwell compare himself to as he looks at the elephant?

• Why does Orwell insist that he has been forced into a position of shooting the elephant?

• Do you think the desire to avoid being laughed at is universal? Why do you think this?

After Reading

MAKING CONNECTIONS

1. Students' responses will vary, but most will probably assert the absurdity of shooting the animal and the wisdom of pursuing alternatives.

2. Students are likely to focus on the hostility that arises whenever any one group of people dominates another, imposes political and cultural restrictions on another, or does not recognize the dignity and independence of another.

3. Possible response: His mixed feelings grew out of his position as enforcer of foreign laws imposed on the Burmese, his growing awareness of the evils of imperialism, and the distance he has to maintain between himself and the Burmese.

4. Possible response: As the narrator explains, he felt pressured by his position and his image as a white imperialist.

5. The narrator feels the episode reveals that the real motives of despotic government officials are maintaining face and upholding an image of themselves as proud, fearless, and always in control.

6. The reactions of the younger Europeans reveal the extent to which they have been dehumanized by imperialism; they prefer the elephant to the trampled man.

7. Possible response: Orwell might attack such abuses as economic oppression by industrial powers, cultural imperialism by Western nations, and racial prejudice.

866

After Reading

Making Connections

Shaping Your Response

1. Do you think Orwell should have shot the elephant? Explain your response.

Analyzing the Essay

2. 🐾 Why do you think the **interactions** between the Burmese people and the Europeans are so hostile?

3. As a member of the Imperial Police in Burma, Orwell found himself hating both the empire he served and the Burmese. What do you think accounts for the mixed feelings he describes?

4. Orwell's better judgment tells him not to kill the elephant. Why, then, do you think he decides to kill it after all?

5. What lesson does Orwell feel this episode offers into the "real nature of imperialism—the real motives for which despotic governments act"?

6. How do the reactions of the younger Europeans to the incident support Orwell's criticism of British imperialism?

Extending the Ideas

7. Judging from this selection, what abuses of power in the modern world would Orwell be likely to attack if he were living today?

Literary Focus: Irony

Irony is a term used to describe the contrast between what appears to be and what really is. What do you find ironic about the following situations?

1. Orwell is an important police officer.

2. Orwell secretly favors the Burmese people.

3. Orwell decides to kill the elephant.

4. When he is shot, the elephant is calmly grazing in a field.

5. The white man is dominant in the East.

LITERARY FOCUS: IRONY

Possible Responses

1. Orwell is a responsible police officer, yet he is fearful of ridicule and manipulated by his position into committing an act he actually deplores.

2. Orwell favors the Burmese, yet he is also full of anger and irritation toward them. Nor is he able to voice his true feelings.

3. Orwell decides to kill the elephant, but the decision is not made through free will.

4. The elephant is shot even though his temporary frenzy has clearly ended.

5. The white man was politically and economically dominant, yet the narrator feels he is a puppet manipulated by the facts of his race and status.

Vocabulary Study

despotic
imperialism
oppressor
resolute
tyranny

Each of the listed words can be used to discuss the actions of a government that has extended its authority over another country. Using these five words, write a paragraph describing the actions of an agent of the government taking control of a group of people. Your paragraph should demonstrate that you understand the meaning of each word.

Expressing Your Ideas

Writing Choices

Writer's Notebook Update Look back at the situation you described in your writer's notebook. As you think about that situation now, jot down several words to describe your feelings about the event.

The Dirty Work of Empire In "Shooting an Elephant," Orwell states that, in a job like that he held in Burma, "you see the dirty work of Empire at close quarters." Write a **letter** such as Orwell might have written home to a close friend or relative about the evils of imperialism as he has come to know them first hand.

(S)he Was Only . . . Orwell tells us that the owner of the elephant could do nothing because "he was only an Indian." Write a **short story** of a modern injustice which can be explained in part because "he or she was only . . . ." You might choose, for example, "he was only a child," or "she was only a woman," or "he was only a freshman."

Obvious Targets Orwell states, "As a police officer I was an obvious target and was baited whenever it seemed safe to do so." Why do you think officers of the law are so often the targets of people's antagonism? Write an **editorial** for your school newspaper in which you discuss this predicament and offer solutions for correcting the situation.

Other Options

Tyranny Destroys Freedom The theme of Orwell's essay can best be described in his own words: "When the white man turns tyrant it is his own freedom that he destroys." Use that quotation as the theme of an **artistic creation**—a painting, a sculpture, a collage, or whatever art form you are best at.

Should Have / Shouldn't Have Join with two classmates and prepare a script of the **discussion and debate** that might have taken place among Europeans in the town square after the shooting of the elephant. One classmate can present the position of the older Europeans, one can speak for the younger men, and one can be Orwell himself. Perform your script for the class.

Guilt, Shame, and Outrage Orwell felt a strong sense of guilt, shame, and outrage at the effects of imperialism on the Burmese people. Is there something in American society today that makes you feel guilty or ashamed or outraged? Prepare a **photo essay,** using photographs that you have taken yourself and/or that you have clipped from newspapers and magazines, to explain why you feel as you do.

Shooting an Elephant **867**

Possible Response

The new Commissioner knew he had to be resolute and not allow the slightest resistance to the tyranny and imperialism he represented. He enjoyed playing the role of the cruel oppressor and keeping an entire nation prostrate at his feet. Not once did he think of the eventual consequences of his despotic behavior.

Unit 8 Resource Book
Vocabulary, p. 3
Vocabulary Test, p.6

WRITING CHOICES
Writer's Notebook Update

Encourage students to record both their feelings at the time of the event and their present feelings about it. They might also comment about the difference between feelings they expressed publicly and feelings they kept secret.

The Dirty Work of Empire

The personal letter about imperialism might be a good opportunity for students to demonstrate their understanding of irony.

(S)he Was Only . . .

Because students are writing fiction, not nonfiction, they should avoid didactic statements and essayistic analyses of prejudice.

Obvious Targets

Students might include an anecdote or an example to support their opinions.

Selection Test

Unit 8 Resource Book
pp. 7–8

OTHER OPTIONS
Tyranny Destroys Freedom

Students might literally include the quotation in the work of art, build it into the title, or simply let it inspire their efforts.

Guilt, Shame, and Outrage

Encourage students to maintain a clear focus on a single topic as they prepare their collages. They might ask of each photograph, "Does this image relate directly to my particular topic?"

Building Background

You might ask students of their prior knowledge of World War II—the combatants, leaders, major defeats and victories.

Literary Focus

Students should note that a work of literature—whether fiction, nonfiction, poetry, or drama—may have multiple themes. Not only do authors build multiple themes into their works, but readers also extract different themes as they read. Remind students that a theme is not a topic; a theme is a central idea, not merely the subject of a work.

Writer's Notebook

Encourage students to consider whether a great speech need be about a great topic or whether a trivial or even distasteful topic can be the subject of magnificent oratory.

More About Winston Churchill

Despite his heroic stature during World War II, Churchill earned many political enemies and was unceremoniously voted from office after the war. When he returned to power in 1951, he did his best to smooth out old political rivalries and unify his nation. Churchill, whose mother was born an American, received an Honorary Citizenship of the United States in April, 1963.

Before Reading

Wartime Speeches

by Winston Churchill

Winston Churchill
1874–1965

Eldest son of Lord Randolph Churchill and American heiress Jennie Jerome, Winston Churchill first served with the cavalry. A correspondent during the Boer War, he was first elected to Parliament in 1900. When Great Britain declared war on Germany in 1939, he returned to the Admiralty. In 1940 Churchill became Prime Minister. Throughout World War II he coordinated military strategies to defeat Hitler. His conferences with U. S. President Franklin Delano Roosevelt and Soviet leader Josef Stalin helped shape postwar Europe. He served again as Prime Minister from 1951 to 1955. Churchill wrote many outstanding historical works, most notably *The Second World War* and *A History of the English-Speaking Peoples.* He was knighted in 1953, the same year he received the Nobel Prize for literature.

Building Background

"Their Finest Hour" In the early months of his prime ministry Winston Churchill inspired the English people with words of hope and undying spirit. His opening speech, delivered in the House of Commons on May 13, 1940, just three days after receiving his appointment from King George VI, set an optimistic tone. Just three weeks later, on June 4, 1940, an ever-confident Churchill told of the great military feat at Dunkirk in which 335,000 Allied soldiers were evacuated by naval vessels and small civilian craft that were under continual German attack. The frightened people of Britain, fully aware that a German invasion of their island was possible, rejoiced with Churchill as he praised the strong young airmen who would defend their country. How their attitude might have been different had they heard Churchill's remark made with his hand covering the microphone: "And we will hit them over the head with beer bottles, which is all we have really got." Two weeks later, when France had fallen, Churchill again bolstered English morale by calling for full attention to the duty ahead, for the people's "finest hour." Churchill's memorable phrases kept the English people hopeful through the bitter summer weeks of 1940.

Literary Focus

Theme A **theme** is a main idea or an underlying meaning of a literary work. A theme may be stated directly or it may be implied. As you read these excerpts from Churchill's speeches, look for common themes that run through all the speeches.

Writer's Notebook

A Great Speech What do you think makes a great speech? What makes a great speaker? Write down characteristics of each.

SUPPORT MATERIALS OVERVIEW

Unit 8 Resource Book
- Graphic Organizer, p. 9
- Study Guide, p. 10
- Vocabulary, p. 11
- Grammar, p. 12
- Alternate Check Test, p. 13
- Vocabulary Test, p. 14
- Selection Test, pp. 15–16

Building English Proficiency
- Selection Summaries
- Activities, p. 262

Reading, Writing & Grammar SkillBook
- Reading, pp. 85–86, 87–88
- Grammar, Usage, and Mechanics, pp. 239–242

Technology
- Audiotape
- Personal Journal Software
- Test Generator Software

Richard Eurich's *Evacuation of Duinkirk* depicts a British flotilla of small boats rescuing Allied troops trapped by German forces at Dunkirk in May 1940. What qualities of this famous episode does the painting emphasize?

WARTIME SPEECHES

WINSTON CHURCHILL

BLOOD, TOIL, TEARS, AND SWEAT

. . . In this crisis[1] I hope I may be pardoned if I do not address the House[2] at any length today. I hope that any of my friends and colleagues, or former colleagues, who are affected by the political reconstruction,[3] will make all allowance for any lack of ceremony with which it has been necessary to act. I would say to the House, as I said to those who have joined this Government: "I have nothing to offer but blood, toil, tears, and sweat."

We have before us an ordeal of the most grievous[4] kind. We have before us many, many long months of struggle and of suffering. You ask what is our policy? I will say: It is to wage war, by sea, land, and air, with all our might and with all the strength that God can give us: to wage war

---

1. **this crisis.** Great Britain was fully engaged in World War II with fighting going on in several different countries and with threats of invasion at home.
2. **the House,** the House of Commons, a part of the British Parliament.
3. **political reconstruction.** Three days before this speech King George VI had asked Churchill to form a new administration.
4. **grievous** (grē′vəs), *adj.* severe; causing great pain and suffering.

Wartime Speeches **869**

During Reading

Selection Objectives

- to explore the theme of the British national struggle and heroic spirit during World War II
- to recognize and analyze the literary concept of theme
- to identify the qualities of a great speech, including figurative language, word choice, and tone
- to practice using commas correctly in dates, addresses, places, and numbers

 Unit 8 Resource Book
Graphic Organizer, p. 9
Study Guide, p. 10

Theme Link

Churchill's speeches exemplify a heroic spirit, despite the passing of empire.

Vocabulary Preview

buoyancy, tendency to be hopeful and cheerful

protracted, drawn out; prolonged

vindicate, uphold; justify

abate, decrease; reduce

sinister, threatening

Students can add the words and definitions to their Writer's Notebooks.

 **Art Study**

Response to Caption Question The painting brings out the sense of urgency during the evacuation, the fear and the heroism of a life-and-death drama, and the unified participation of military and civilians in the war effort.

SELECTION SUMMARY

Churchill's Wartime Speeches

from Blood, Toil, Tears, and Sweat Churchill directs the English to face the future squarely. He foresees "blood, toil, tears, and sweat"—suffering, grief, and hard work—for victory to be won. He identifies British policy as total war and the aim as victory.

from A Miracle of Deliverance Churchill praises all involved in the Dunkirk evacuation. He singles out the Air Force, without whom the sea rescue would have been a disaster. He is confident that victory is possible if all do their duty.

from The Finest Hour Churchill recalls, just after the fall of France, that the first years of World War I were filled with defeat, and yet victory was achieved. He says that defeat of the Allies would mean the onset of a new Dark Age. He urges all to act so that people in the future will call this Britain's "finest hour."

 For summaries in other languages, see the Building English Proficiency book.

Point out to students that repetition can be one of an orator's most powerful weapons. By repeating the word *victory,* Churchill emphasizes his central theme and leaves his audience with a unified impression.

2 **Active Reading**
Clarify

Possible Response The tone may be described as resolute, realistic, hopeful.

3 **Literary Element**
Simile

Questions What simile does Churchill use? Why is it appropriate? *(Possible responses: Churchill compares the movement of the German army to the swinging of a scythe cutting down grain. The simile suggests the traditional personification of Death as the Grim Reaper.)*

4 **Literary Element**
Style

Point out that Churchill's speeches are not simply long strings of empty rhetorical flourishes. He provides facts, figures, and details that give a sense of authority to all of his subsequent comments and evaluations. By using specific names and numbers, Churchill helped to erase some of the anxieties his people felt.

---

1 against a monstrous tyranny, never surpassed in the dark, lamentable[5] catalog of human crime. That is our policy. You ask, What is our aim? I can answer in one word: Victory—victory at all costs, victory in spite of all terror, victory, however long and hard the road may be; for without victory, there is no survival. Let that be realized; no survival for the British Empire; no survival for all that the British Empire has stood for, no survival for the urge and impulse of the ages, that mankind will move forward towards its goal. But I take up my task with buoyancy[6] and hope. I feel sure that our cause will not be suffered to fail among men. At this time I feel entitled to claim the aid of all, and I say, "Come, then, let us go forward together with our united strength."

2 **CLARIFY: What tone do you think Churchill is trying to set for the English people?**

A MIRACLE OF DELIVERANCE

3 . . . The German eruption swept like a sharp scythe around the right and rear of the armies of the north. Eight or nine armored divisions, each of about four hundred armored vehicles of different kinds, but carefully assorted to be complementary[1] and divisible into small self-contained units, cut off all communications between us and the main French armies. It severed our own communications for food and ammunition, which ran first to Amiens and afterward through Abbeville, and it shored its way up the coast to Boulogne and Calais, and almost to Dunkirk.[2] Behind this armored and mechanized onslaught came a number of German divisions in lorries,[3] and behind them again there plodded comparatively slowly the dull brute mass of the ordinary Germany Army and German people, always so ready to be led to the trampling down in other lands of liberties and comforts which they have never know in their own. . . .

Meanwhile, the Royal Air Force, which had already been intervening in the battle, so far as its range would allow, from home bases, now used part of its main metropolitan fighter strength, and struck at the German bombers and at the fighters which in large numbers protected them. This struggle was protracted[4] and fierce. Suddenly the scene has cleared, the crash and thunder has for the moment—but only for the moment—died away. A miracle of deliverance, achieved by valor, by perseverance, by perfect discipline, by faultless service, by resource, by skill, by unconquerable fidelity, is manifest[5] to us all. The enemy was hurled back by the retreating British and French troops. He was so roughly handled that he did not hurry their departure seriously. The Royal Air Force engaged the main strength of the German Air Force, and inflicted upon them losses of at least four to one; and the navy, using nearly one thousand ships of all kinds, carried over **4** 335,000 men, French and British, out of the jaws of death and shame, to their native land and to the tasks which lie immediately ahead. We must be very careful not to assign to this deliverance the attributes of a victory. Wars are not won by evacuations. But there was a victory inside this deliverance, which should be noted. It was gained by the air force. Many of our soldiers coming back have not seen the air force at work; they saw only the bombers which escaped its protective attack. They underrate its achievements. I have heard much talk of this; that is

---

5. **lamentable** (lam′ən tə bəl), *adj.* deplorable; to be regretted or pitied.
6. buoyancy (boi′ən sē), *n.* tendency to be hopeful and cheerful.

1. **complementary** (kom′plə men′tər ē), *adj.* formed together as a complete unit.
2. **Amiens . . . Dunkirk.** Towns in northern France under attack by German forces.
3. **lorry** (lôr′ē), *n.* truck.
4. protracted (prō trak′tid), *adj.* drawn out; prolonged.
5. **manifest** (man′ə fest), *adj.* clear.

MINI-LESSON: GRAMMAR

Using Commas Correctly

Teach Remind students that accuracy requires following conventional usage and putting commas in their right places. Historical writing in particular affords many cases of commas needed in dates, addresses, places, and numbers. Show students the chart.

Activity Ideas

- Have students write a paragraph describing one battle or event of World War II, using commas in dates, addresses, places, and numbers.
- Invite students to write a postcard as if they were writing from a favorite vacation spot; they should use commas correctly.

Examples of Comma Usage	
Dates	June 1940
	June 4, 1940
Addresses	10 Downing Street
	London, England
Places	Abbeville, France
Numbers	335,000 troops

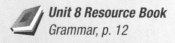

Unit 8 Resource Book
Grammar, p. 12

why I go out of my way to say this. I will tell you about it.

This was a great trial of strength between the British and German air forces. Can you conceive a greater objective for the Germans in the air than to make evacuation from these beaches impossible, and to sink all these ships which were displayed, almost to the extent of thousands? Could there have been an objective of greater military importance and significance for the whole purpose of the war than this? They tried hard, and they were beaten back; they were frustrated in their task. We got the army away; and they have paid fourfold for any loses which they have inflicted. Very large formations of German airplanes—and we know that they are a very brave race—have turned on several occasions from the attack of one quarter of their number of the Royal Air Force, and have dispersed in different directions. Twelve airplanes have been hunted by two. One airplane was driven into the water and cast away by the mere charge of a British airplane, which had no more ammunition. All of our types—the Hurricane, the Spitfire, and the new Defiant—and all our pilots have been vindicated[6] as superior to what they have at present to face.

When we consider how much greater would be our advantage in defending the air above this island against an overseas attack, I must say that I find in these facts a sure basis upon which practical and reassuring thoughts may rest. I will pay my tribute to these young airmen. The great French Army was very largely, for the time being, cast back and disturbed by the onrush of a few thousands of armored vehicles. May it not also be that the cause of civilization itself will be defended by the skill and devotion of a few thousand airmen? There never has been, I suppose, in all the world, in all the history of war, such an opportunity for youth. The Knights of the Round Table, the Crusaders, all fall back into the past—not only distant but prosaic;[7] these young men, going forth every morn to guard their native land and all that we stand for, holding in their hands these instruments of colossal and shattering power, of whom it may be said that

> Every morn brought forth a noble chance,
> And every chance brought forth a noble knight,[8]

deserve our gratitude, as do all of the brave men who, in so many ways and on so many occasions, are ready, and continue ready, to give life and all for their native land. . . .

Turning once again, and this time more generally, to the question of invasion, I would observe that there has never been a period in all these long centuries of which we boast when an absolute guarantee against invasion, still less against serious raids, could have been given to our people. In the days of Napoleon the same wind which would have carried his transports across the Channel might have driven away the blockading fleet. There was always the chance, and it is that chance which has excited and befooled[9] the imaginations of many Continental tyrants. Many are the tales that are told. We are assured that novel methods will be adopted, and when we see the originality of malice, the ingenuity of aggression, which our enemy displays, we may certainly prepare ourselves for every kind of novel stratagem and every kind of brutal and treacherous maneuver. I think that no idea is so outlandish that it should not be considered and viewed with a searching, but at the same time, I hope, with a steady eye. We must never forget the solid assurances of sea power and those which belong to air power if it can be locally exercised.

I have, myself, full confidence that if all do their duty, if nothing is neglected, and if the best arrangements are made, as they are being made, we shall prove ourselves once again able to defend our island home, to ride out the storm of

5

---

6. **vindicate** (vin′də kāt), v. uphold; justify.
7. **prosaic** (prō zā′ik), adj. ordinary; not exciting.
8. **Every . . . knight.** These lines, slightly misquoted, are from "The Passing of Arthur" in Tennyson's *Idylls of the King.*
9. **befool** (bi fūl′), v. deceive.

Wartime Speeches **871**

Literary Criticism

One of Churchill's biographers summarizes the 22-year-old orator's essay "The Scaffolding of Rhetoric": "Churchill laid out the guidelines for the successful public speaker. First, a striking presence. As long as he is invested with 'a personal significance,' it matters not whether he be small, ugly, or deformed. 'Sometimes,' he thought, building on his own experience, 'a slight and not unpleasing stammer or impediment has been of some assistance in securing the attention of the audience.' The orator must employ the right word, the striking phrase, the colorful analogy, a wild extravagance of language, constructing sentences that are 'long, rolling, and sonorous,' molding them into a rhythmic whole, 'a rapid succession of waves of sound and vivid pictures,' thereby electrifying the audience and preparing for the great climax when his final words would fall 'amid a thunder of assent.'"

Norman Rose
Churchill: The Unruly Giant

5 ## Literary Focus

Theme

You might note to the class that each person's responsibility to do his or her duty is a theme of many of Churchill's speeches. In conveying this theme, Churchill emphasizes both the specific actions that must be taken—the practical "arrangements"—as well as each individual's willingness to perform to the "utmost."

BUILDING ENGLISH PROFICIENCY

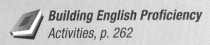

Exploring Contrasting Images

In the excerpt titled "A Miracle of Deliverance," Churchill's choice of language forces a mental picture of a battle between a huge, mindless lumbering beast—German ground troops—and a slight, gallant, intrepid creature—the RAF. Lead students to an appreciation of how Churchill "builds" these images by having students construct a T-chart of contrasting vocabulary. As students share responses, encourage them to see how the images arouse emotions of pride and courage.

Germans	RAF
armored and mechanized onslaught	miracle
plodded	valor
dull	

*Building English Proficiency
Activities, p. 262*

war, and to outlive the menace of tyranny, if necessary for years, if necessary alone. At any rate, that is what we are going to try to do. That is the resolve of His Majesty's Government—every man of them. That is the will of Parliament and the nation. The British Empire and the French Republic, linked together in their cause and in their need, will defend to the death their native soil, aiding each other like good comrades to the utmost of their strength. Even though large tracts of Europe and many old and famous states have fallen or may fall into the grip of the Gestapo[10] and all the odious[11] apparatus of Nazi rule, we shall not flag or fail. We shall go on to the end, we shall fight in France, we shall fight on the seas and oceans, we shall fight with growing confidence and growing strength in the air, we shall defend our island, whatever the cost may be, we shall fight on the beaches, we shall fight on the landing grounds, we shall fight in the fields and in the streets, we shall fight in the hills; we shall never surrender, and even if, which I do not for a moment believe, this island or a large part of it were subjugated[12] and starving, then our Empire beyond the seas, armed and guarded by the British fleet, would carry on the struggle, until, in God's good time, the New World,[13] with all its power and might, steps forth to the rescue and the liberation of the old.

THEIR FINEST HOUR

During the first four years of the last war the Allies experienced nothing but disaster and disappointment. . . . We repeatedly asked ourselves the question, "How are we going to win?" and no one was ever able to answer it with much precision, until at the end, quite suddenly, quite unexpectedly, our terrible foe collapsed before us, and we were so glutted with victory that in our folly we threw it away.

However matters may go in France or with the French government or other French governments, we in this island and in the British

Empire will never lose our sense of comradeship with the French people. . . . If final victory rewards our toils they shall share the gains—aye, and freedom shall be restored to all. We abate[1] nothing of our just demands; not one jot or tittle do we recede. . . . Czechs, Poles, Norwegians, Dutch, Belgians, have joined their causes to our own. All these shall be restored.

What General Weygand[2] called the Battle of France is over. I expect that the Battle of Britain is about to begin. Upon this battle depends the survival of Christian civilization. Upon it depends our own British life, and the long continuity of our institutions and our Empire. The whole fury and might of the enemy must very soon be turned on us. Hitler knows that he will have to break us in this island or lose the war. If we can stand up to him, all Europe may be free and the life of the world may move forward into broad, sunlit uplands. But if we fail, then the whole world, including the United States, including all that we have known and cared for, will sink into the abyss[3] of a new Dark Age, made more sinister,[4] and perhaps more protracted, by the lights of perverted[5] science. Let us therefore brace ourselves to our duties, and so bear ourselves that, if the British Empire and its Commonwealth last for a thousand years, men will say, "This was their finest hour."

CLARIFY: What do you think Churchill means by "perverted science"?

---

10. **Gestapo** (gə stä′pō), the secret police in Nazi Germany.
11. **odious** (ō′dē əs), *adj.* hateful; offensive.
12. **subjugate** (sub′jə gāt), *v.* conquer.
13. **New World,** the United States.

1. abate (ə bāt′), *v.* decrease; reduce.
2. **General Weygand,** commander in chief of the French army.
3. **abyss** (ə bis′), *n.* lowest depth.
4. sinister (sin′ə stər), *adj.* threatening.
5. **perverted** (pər vėr′tid), *adj.* used for wrong purposes.

MINI-LESSON: VOCABULARY
Words with Multiple Meanings

Teach Point out to students that many words have more than one meaning, particularly those that can function as more than one part of speech. Here are some that occur in Churchill's speeches. By using the context, students can know which meaning Churchill was giving to the word.

Activity Idea Ask students to write an account of a hero or recent heroic act, using at least three words with multiple meanings.

suffer	verb	to experience pain
	verb	to allow
flag	noun	a pennant or standard
	verb	to signal
	verb	to run out of energy
cast	noun	a mold or form
	verb	to throw
tract	noun	a treatise or pamphlet
	noun	a wide expanse of land

After Reading

Making Connections

Shaping Your Response

1. What characteristic of Churchill's speeches impresses you the most?
2. Do you think Churchill wrote his own speeches? Why or why not?

Analyzing the Speeches

3. When he says he has "nothing to offer but blood, toil, tears, and sweat," what message do you think Churchill is sending to the English people?
4. What distinction, if any, do you draw between the *policy* and the *aim* Churchill defines for his administration?
5. What do Churchill's comments about the German Army indicate about his opinions of the German people?
6. Why do you think Churchill spends so much time talking about the air war?
7. Why do you think Churchill mentions the New World at the end of his speech "A Miracle of Deliverance"?
8. 👣 What does Churchill conclude about Britain's **interactions** with the nations of the world?

Extending the Ideas

9. If Churchill were alive today, what advice do you think he might give to the President of the United States?

Literary Focus: Theme

A **theme** is a main idea or an underlying meaning of a literary work. In a few words tell what you think is the theme of each speech excerpt. What do you think is the common theme that runs through all three speeches?

Vocabulary Study

Use your understanding of the italicized word to write the letter of the word or phrase that best completes each sentence. Use your Glossary if necessary.

1. If you were looking at *sinister* clouds, you might predict ___.

   a. a warm, balmy day **b.** a light drizzle **c.** a heavy thunderstorm

2. The man with a *protracted* illness would ___.

   a. return to work the next day **b.** face a lengthy hospital stay
   c. die in the near future

3. The test grade that would most likely lead to a feeling of *bouyancy* is ___.

   a. an *A* **b.** a *C* **c.** an *F*

Wartime Speeches **873**

MAKING CONNECTIONS

1. Responses will vary, but students might cite Churchill's expressions of strength of purpose, his fierce hope for victory, his clarity, word choice, repetitions, and rhythms.

2. Possible response: He must have written his own speeches because each exhibits the same style, which is so individualistic that it has come to be referred to as Churchillian.

3. The message he is sending is one of harsh reality—that the people should expect suffering, grief, and hard labor.

4. Students might respond that the policy is *how* the government will proceed and the aim is *what* the government intends to achieve.

5. He appears to believe that Germans are a "dull brute mass," eager to destroy the civilized world.

6. Students might respond that he wants to reinforce the one aspect of the war that is positive—air defense.

7. Possible response: He wants to give his people as much hope and comfort as possible, and he would like the United States to enter the war.

8. Churchill emphasizes a global sense of comradeship among the nations of the world.

9. Responses will vary, but students might focus on the theme of duty, encouraging the President to persuade Americans to do what is expected of them in all cultural, intellectual, financial, and military ways.

LITERARY FOCUS: THEME

Possible Responses

- The theme of the first excerpt might be the firm resolve of the people to achieve victory at any cost.
- The theme of the second excerpt might be the justifiable pride and confidence that Britons should have in themselves and their fighting forces.
- The theme of the third excerpt might be the vital necessity of preserving civilization from destruction.
- Themes that run through all three excerpts include the call to duty, the necessity of endurance and self-sacrifice, and the intense hope of victory.

VOCABULARY STUDY

1. c
2. b
3. a
4. c
5. c

Unit 8 Resource Book
Vocabulary, p. 11
Vocabulary Test, p. 14

WRITING CHOICES
Writer's Notebook Update

Students might now add such characteristics as clarity of thought, rousing emotion, precise word choice, vivid imagery, repetition, rhythm, memorable phrases, and the overall character and self-confidence of the speaker.

A Lamentable Catalog

Students' lists will vary, but encourage them to note whether the crimes have remained basically the same over the centuries or whether they have changed. They might find common elements among the motivations of the crimes as well as in the crimes themselves.

Prepare for Invasion

Some students may be familiar with science fiction movies and stories in which such preparations take place. Encourage them to use their prior knowledge, their common sense, and their imaginations as they write their stories.

Selection Test

Unit 8 Resource Book
pp. 15–16

---

4. When the flood waters *abated* ___.
   a. more of the land was covered with water
   b. trees and houses were knocked down with its force
   c. more of the land was left exposed

5. The defendant felt *vindicated* when the jury ___.
   a. could not reach a verdict b. declared him guilty
   c. declared him innocent

Expressing Your Ideas

Writing Choices

Writer's Notebook Update Which of the characteristics of a great speech do you find in the Churchill excerpts? Are there additional characteristics you would add after reading Churchill?

A Lamentable Catalog Churchill says that Hitler's tyranny is the darkest in the "lamentable catalog of human crime." Make a **list of crimes** that you would place in the catalog of human crime. Then write a brief summary of the common elements you find among the crimes on your list.

Prepare for Invasion The people of the United States have never experienced invasion of their own country. Imagine how you would need to prepare yourself if you received word that your town was going to be invaded by a hostile force. (You can decide what that force will be.) Write a **short story** in which you describe your preparations for invasion.

Other Options

Inspirational Speakers Study the speeches of another great inspirational speaker. (You can find such speeches in anthologies; ask your teacher or librarian for help.) Select several excerpts from your chosen speaker's famous speeches and study his or her style of expression. If you can, listen to a recording of the speeches to get a sense of his or her style of delivery. Present your **speech excerpts** to your class.

A Pictorial Time Line Work with a small group to prepare a **pictorial time line** of what you have researched to be the key events of World War II. Remember to consider not only the war itself but also the events that led up to the war and the events that followed the end of the war. Be sure to include pictures of the people who influenced and were influenced by the events.

I Remember It Well Find someone who has vivid memories of World War II. You might, for example, find a soldier who served in the war, a mother who was left alone to raise small children, a victim of the Holocaust, a citizen who recalls F. D. Roosevelt's fireside chats. Videotape an interview of remembrances. If your school has a media lab, edit your interview to the best ten minutes or so. Play your **videotaped interview** for your class.

OTHER OPTIONS
Inspirational Speakers

Students should not assume that the recorded version of a speech is the only way it can be delivered. A speech reflects its context and the character of the speaker, but many speeches, like pieces of music, can be given new interpretations by new performers. Ask students to deliver the excerpts in their own style, adding their own character and emotions.

A Pictorial Time Line

Students might also add quotations from famous speeches to the time line, linking each quote to a particular major event.

Before Reading

Homage to a Government by Philip Larkin
Two Poems on the Passing of an Empire by Derek Walcott

Philip Larkin
1922–1985

Born in Coventry and educated at Oxford, Larkin became a university librarian in 1943. His first collection of poetry was *The North Ship* (1945); his last was *High Windows* (1974). From 1961 to 1971 Larkin was jazz critic for the London *Daily Telegraph*.

Derek Walcott
Born 1930

Born on the Caribbean island of St. Lucia, Walcott attended University College of West Indies. He taught at schools and colleges in several countries and in 1959 founded the Trinidad Theatre Workshop. Poet, playwright, reviewer, art critic, Walcott received the Nobel Prize for literature in 1992.

Building Background

Reflections on Colonialism As the British government gradually relinquished its power throughout the world, it met with diverse reactions. Many people at home demanded that British dominance continue; most of the people in dominated countries struggled with how to gain their freedom or how to handle their new-found independence. Derek Walcott reflects on attitudes in the West Indies: "The whole idea of America, and the whole idea of everything on this side of the world . . . is imported; we're all imported, black, Spanish. When one says one is American, that's the experience of being American—that transference of whatever color, or name, or place. The difficult part is the realization that one is part of the whole idea of colonization. Because the easiest thing to do about colonialism is to refer to history in terms of guilt or punishment or revenge, or whatever. Whereas the rare thing is the resolution of being where one is and doing something positive about that reality."

Literary Focus

Repetition The use of the same word or phrase in two or more places to achieve a particular effect is **repetition.** Sometimes the words repeated are exactly the same; at other times the author may vary a word or phrase slightly. Look for Larkin's use of repetition in "Homage to a Government."

Writer's Notebook

Advantages and Disadvantages Fill in a chart like the one below with what you think might be the advantages and the disadvantages of colonialism, both for the country in power and for the colony.

	The Country in Power	The Colony
Advantages		
Disadvantages		

Homage to a Government **875**

Before Reading

Building Background

Ask students what they think the history of the U.S. reveals about the pros and cons of being a colony?

Literary Focus

Students might note that repetition is one of a writer's most versatile tools. A repeated phrase can comfort or terrify, inspire or depress. Discuss the effects that are achieved in music when a beat, a melody, or a lyric is repeated.

Writer's Notebook

Encourage students to explore the advantages and disadvantages of colonialism from several different aspects: political, cultural, racial, religious, and economic.

More About Philip Larkin and Derek Walcott

- Although Larkin was praised by Auden as "a master of the English language," he wrote comparatively few poems. He once said he wrote about four poems a year—"of which one is no good."

- In a brilliant 1965 essay, Walcott described the figure of the contemporary West Indian poet as a new kind of Robinson Crusoe. His poet/Crusoe is, he said, like Adam creating names in paradise, like Columbus discovering a new world by accident, and at the same time a figure "that supplies the anguish of authority, of the conscience of empire."

SUPPORT MATERIALS OVERVIEW

Unit 8 Resource Book
- Graphic Organizer, p. 17
- Study Guide, p. 18
- Vocabulary, p. 19
- Grammar, p. 20
- Alternate Check Test, p. 21
- Vocabulary Test, p. 22
- Selection Test, pp. 23–24

Building English Proficiency
- Selection Summaries
- Activities, p. 263

Reading, Writing & Grammar SkillBook
- Grammar, Usage, and Mechanics, pp. 175–177

Technology
- Audiotape
- Personal Journal Software
- Test Generator Software

Selection Objectives

- to explore the passing of empire in the works of twentieth-century poets
- to identify the effects of repetition
- to practice correct use of apostrophes

📕 **Unit 8 Resource Book**
Graphic Organizer, p. 17
Study Guide, p. 18

Theme Link

In these poems, the narrators explore the political, financial, and personal effects of the passing of empire.

 Literary Focus
Repetition

Question   Why do you think the narrator repeats the phrase "all right"? *(Possible response: By inserting the phrase like a dramatic aside, the speaker draws attention to it. The reader, however, realizes that the speaker "doth protest too much" and that the situation is, ironically, far from all right.)*

 🎨 *Art Study*

Response to Caption Question
Responses will vary, some foreseeing a rejection of pride in wartime actions and others asserting that war memories unite veterans whatever their political outlooks.

HOMAGE TO A GOVERNMENT
PHILIP LARKIN

Next year we are to bring the soldiers home
For lack of money, and it is all right.
Places they guarded, or kept orderly,
Must guard themselves, and keep themselves orderly.
5   We want the money for ourselves at home
Instead of working. And this is all right.

It's hard to say who wanted it to happen,
But now it's been decided nobody minds.
The places are a long way off, not here,
10   Which is all right, and from what we hear
The soldiers there only made trouble happen.
Next year we shall be easier in our minds.

Next year we shall be living in a country
That brought its soldiers home for lack of money.
15   The statues will be standing in the same
Tree-muffled squares, and look nearly the same.
Our children will not know it's a different country.
All we can hope to leave them now is money.

———————————

homage (hom′ij), *n.* dutiful respect.

Their jackets draped with medals, World War II veterans attend a British celebration of the anniversary of VE (Victory in Europe) Day, May 8, 1945. Do you think that, years from now, veterans of recent American military actions like the Persian Gulf War will gather in this way? Why or why not? ▼

SELECTION SUMMARY

Homage to a Government; Two Poems on the Passing of Empire

Homage to a Government   The speaker states that the government will recall its soldiers because the money is needed for people at home. No one minds, and the soldiers only caused trouble anyway. This new situation is "all right." The nation's children will not realize how the country has changed and that their only legacy will be money.

Two Poems on the Passing of Empire   The speaker of the first poem notes that a heron on a stump is like the eagle on a Roman standard, recalling the trampling armies of that fallen empire. The speaker of the second poem describes a poor pensioner, a veteran wounded for his country. The pensioner hears children singing "Rule, Britannia" and wonders what they think of the ideals for which he fought.

 For summaries in other languages, see the Building English Proficiency book.

TWO POEMS ON THE PASSING OF AN EMPIRE

DEREK WALCOTT

1

A heron flies across the morning marsh and brakes
its teetering wings to decorate a stump
                    (thank God
that from this act the landscape is complete
and time and motion at a period
as such an emblem[1] led Rome's trampling feet,
pursued by late proconsuls[2] bearing law)
and underline this quiet with a caw.

2

In the small coffin of his house, the pensioner,[3]
A veteran of the African campaign,
Bends, as if threading an eternal needle;
One-eyed as any grave, his skull, cropped wool,
Or lifts his desert squint to hear
The children singing, "Rule, Britannia, rule,"
As if they needed practise to play dead.
Boys will still pour their blood out for a sieve[4]
Despite his balsam[5] eye and doddering[6] jaw;
And if one eye should weep, would they believe
In such a poor flag as an empty sleeve?

---

1. **such an emblem,** the Roman eagle on a standard—a
   flag or a symbol—carried before Roman armies.
2. **proconsul** (prō kon′səl), *n.* governor of an ancient
   Roman province; governor of a colony or other
   dependent territory during British colonial expansion.
3. **pensioner** (pen′shə nər), *n.* retired or disabled person who receives a regular payment.
4. **sieve** (siv), *n.* utensil with holes that let liquids, but
   not large pieces, pass through.
5. **balsam** (bôl′səm), *adj.* running, as sap from a tree.
6. **doddering** (dod′ər ing), *adj.* trembling.

Two Poems on the Passing of an Empire   **877**

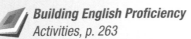
877

After Reading

MAKING CONNECTIONS

1. Students might prefer the Larkin poem for its irony, plain word choice, or concern for future generations. Students might prefer the Walcott poems for their graphic imagery, human sympathy, or curiosity about future generations.

2. The soldiers might be leaving less industrialized nations.

3. The speaker sees the evacuation as defeat, abandonment, and robbery of the future's inheritance.

4. The tone is ironic, not because the government's action is bad but because it has been forced upon the nation by weakness and failure.

5. He may see the drawbacks of imperialism for the colonies, but still regrets loss of national pride.

6. The heron is resting peacefully; the eagle was being carried in a military onslaught.

7. The heron might represent peace, undisturbed nature, or timelessness.

8. The coffin suggests that the pensioner is enduring a living death.

9. The tone might be described as meditative, ironic, or cynical. The contributing images include the heron/eagle, the coffin/house, the singing children, and empty sleeve.

10. Responses will vary, but most students will see interactions fraught with tension, dishonesty, and conflict.

LITERARY FOCUS: REPETITION

Possible Responses

Repetitive word sets: "it is all right," "lack of money," "next year we shall be" Effect: It has been said that if something is repeated often enough, people will begin to believe it. The citizens are repeating these words, hoping that they are (or will be) true.

878

After Reading

Making Connections

Shaping Your Response

1. Which of these poems expressing attitudes toward imperialism do you prefer? Why?

Analyzing the Poems

2. What kinds of places do you think the soldiers are leaving in "Homage to a Government"?

3. What seems to be the reaction of the speaker in the poem to the evacuation process?

4. What is the **tone** of the poem? Does the speaker really intend an "homage"?

5. What do you **infer** is the speaker's attitude toward imperialism?

6. In "Two Poems on the Passing of an Empire" how does the heron on the stump differ from the eagle carried before advancing Roman armies?

7. If the heron is a **symbol,** what do you think the heron represents?

8. What seems to be suggested by comparing the pensioner's house to a coffin?

9. What is the **tone** of "Two Poems . . ."? What **images** contribute to that tone?

Extending the Ideas

10. What is your attitude toward the **interactions** of people that characterize colonialism? Is it appropriate for one country to have power and control over another country—even if both countries benefit from it in some way?

Literary Focus: Repetition

Repetition is the use of the same word or phrase in exactly the same way or with a slight variation. Identify the three repetitive word sets that Larkin uses in "Homage to a Government." What effect do you think this repetition has?

Vocabulary Study

Study the dictionary entry shown here for *homage*.

1. Why are two pronunciations given? Which is the preferred pronunciation? How do you know?

> **hom age** (hom′ij, om′ij), *n.* **1** dutiful respect; reverence: *Everyone paid homage to the great leader.* See **honor** for synonym study. **2** (in the Middle Ages) a pledge of loyalty and service by a vassal to a lord. **3** thing done or given to show such acknowledgement. [< Old French < Medieval Latin *hominaticum* < Latin *hominem* human being, man]

MINI-LESSON: GRAMMAR

Using Apostrophes Correctly

Teach Remind students of basic rules for apostrophes in contractions and possessives.

- Use an apostrophe in place of letters omitted in contractions: *isn't* for *is not, it's* for *it is*

- Use an apostrophe and *-s* for the possessive of most singular nouns: Rome's armies, Keats's poems

- Use an apostrophe alone for the possessive of plural nouns ending in *-s*: fathers' smiles

- Use an apostrophe and *-s* for the possessive of

plural nouns not ending in *-s*: women's sports, men's voices

- Use an apostrophe and *-s* with the last word of a possessive compound noun: sister-in-law's cat, great-aunt's house

Activity Idea For practice, have students write a paragraph about the theme of change, using apostrophes correctly.

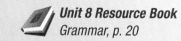

Unit 8 Resource Book
Grammar, p. 20

2. What special meaning did the word have during the Middle Ages that it doesn't have now?

3. Explain the derivation of the word.

4. *Honor* is named as a synonym for *homage*. List at least three other words that could be used as synonyms for *homage*.

5. If you needed to hyphenate *homage* in a paper, where should you break it?

Expressing Your Ideas

Writing Choices

Writer's Notebook Update In your chart you listed advantages and disadvantages of colonialism for the countries. Add to your consideration the individual people in those countries. What are the advantages and disadvantages for the common man or woman?

Repeat for Emphasis In "Homage to a Government" Philip Larkin repeats variations of "and it is all right" to emphasize his attitude that it *wasn't* all right. Write a **poem** on a subject of your choice. Repeat a phrase—or a variation of that phrase—several times so that its use becomes ironic.

Feature the Poet These Larkin and Walcott poems express their individual attitudes toward British colonialism and imperialism. The complete collections of each poet deal with many other subjects as well. Select either Larkin or Walcott and read at least five other poems by that author. Write a **feature story** for a literary magazine in which you introduce a range of your chosen author's poetry.

Other Options

Honoring the Winners Derek Walcott is the most recent writer featured in this book to receive the Nobel Prize for literature (1992). Work with other class members to prepare a **bulletin board display** that features the Nobel Prize for literature in general and concentrates on several of the specific Nobel winners you have studied this year.

Caribbean Color Walcott has been called the poet of the Caribbean people. In his verse he attempts to capture the color, the culture, the music, the spirit of the islands. Create a **fabric design** that captures your impression of the Caribbean islands and people. (You might want to do some research in books on art or design before you create your own design.)

Speak Your Mind Larkin and Walcott used poetry to express their attitudes toward the British government's imperialism. Select one of the following United States governmental policy issues—national educational goals, continued space exploration, a balanced national budget, foreign policy—or a governmental issue of your choice, and prepare a **persuasive speech** in which you support your personal feelings with documented facts.

Two Poems on the Passing of an Empire   **879**

Before Reading

Building Background

What examples can students give of contemporary cultural conflicts?

Literary Focus

Point out to students that dialogue is the literary element that makes fiction most like drama. You might discuss how the writer's craft and the reader's imagination combine to create a character's voice.

Writer's Notebook

Encourage students to consider many different types of obstacles for their lists: political, religious, cultural, physical, linguistic, psychological, intellectual, and racial. Remind them that different family members are likely to face different obstacles.

More About Buchi Emecheta

In Emecheta's Ibo family, the oldest woman had the role of "big mother." Her father's sister took this role, and the family gathered around her after dinner to hear tales of their origins and ancestors. Emecheta recalled that she thought no life could be more essential than that of a storyteller and that she always wanted to become one. Other works by the author include

- *Second-Class Citizen* (1974)
- *The Slave Girl* (1977)
- *Adah's Story* (1983)
- *Head Above Water* (1984)

---

from In the Ditch

by Buchi Emecheta

Buchi Emecheta
born 1945

Born in Lagos, Nigeria, Buchi Emecheta (bü′chē em′ə-chē′tə) was married at age 16 and had five children by age 22. In England she supported the family while her husband studied. When they divorced—because her husband objected to her personal educational and writing ambitions—she became a single parent struggling to raise children and earn a college degree. Her first novel, *In the Ditch,* originally appeared as a series of magazine columns, and later it served as her master's thesis in sociology. In addition to novels drawn from her own life, Emecheta has written several novels about life in Nigeria. Today Emecheta continues to lecture, teach, and write. Her works are published by her own publishing company, Ogugwu Afor.

Building Background

Struggling for Position With over one hundred million people, including more than fifty ethnic groups, Nigeria is the most populous country in Africa. A British colony since 1906, Nigeria became an independent country in 1960, just two years before Emecheta and her husband moved to England. Emecheta had lived in the southeastern part of Nigeria where the Ibo people are the dominant culture. Most prominent in the Ibo society is a respect for personal achievement and a strong sense of community spirit. However, Ibo women are clearly subordinate to Ibo men. In her personal struggle for position, Emecheta was dealing not only with her Ibo background, but also with her status as a black woman in white society.

Literary Focus

Dialogue A conversation between two or more people in a literary work is called **dialogue.** Dialogue can serve many purposes; among them are characterization, creation of mood, advancement of the plot, and development of a theme. As you read this selection, look for Emecheta's purpose in using dialogue.

Writer's Notebook

Pick Up and Pack Out Imagine a move you might make to a foreign country. Make a list of the obstacles you think you and your family might have to overcome in order to feel comfortable in a different land. What obstacles would you add to your list if you were very poor?

SUPPORT MATERIALS OVERVIEW

Unit 8 Resource Book
- Graphic Organizer, p. 25
- Study Guide, p. 26
- Vocabulary, p. 27
- Grammar, p. 28
- Alternate Check Test, p. 29
- Vocabulary Test, p. 30
- Selection Test, pp. 31–32

Building English Proficiency
- Selection Summaries
- Activities, p. 264

Reading, Writing & Grammar SkillBook
- Grammar, Usage, and Mechanics, pp. 245–246

The World of Work
- Housing Authority Program Supervisor, p.31
- Activity, p. 32

Technology
- Audiotape
- Personal Journal Software
- Test Generator Software

IN THE DITCH

BUCHI EMECHETA

1

QUALIFYING FOR THE MANSIONS

There was a crik, and a crack, then another crik, then crack, crack, cra. . . . Adah pulled herself up with a start and sat in the hollow of the large double bed. It had a gradual valley-like hollow, which gave it a sort of *U* look. On both sides of her the mattress rose gently, just like two table-lands sheltering her in a hollow valley. The crik and the crack sounds came once more and she grabbed her four-month-old baby from its carry-cot. The cot was lying on one of the table-lands.

The sleepy baby was cross, her little face twisted in anger. Adah held the wet bundle to her breast and stared at her roommate, the Great Rat. The rat was by now used to Adah's fright, he had long sensed that Adah was terrified of his sharp piercing eyes, long mouth, and his big brown body. He stood

 Consuelo Kanaga's 1950 photograph of a black woman and her children is titled *She Is a Tree of Life to Them.* Does this seem an appropriate title? Why or why not?

In the Ditch **881**

During Reading

Selection Objectives

- to recognize a character's values and motivations
- to identify the purposes and techniques of dialogue
- to practice correct written expressions of time

Unit 8 Resource Book
Graphic Organizer, p. 25
Study Guide, p. 26

Theme Link

The the passing of empire theme is developed in the story of a strong and independent Nigerian woman, struggling alone in London to provide decent housing for her family of five children.

Vocabulary Preview

effrontery, shameless boldness
incoherent, confused; having no logical connection of ideas
coveted, strongly desired
pacify, quiet down
simultaneously, at the same time
reluctantly, slowly and unwillingly

Students can add the words and definitions to their Writer's Notebooks.

 *Art Study*

Response to Caption Question It is an appropriate title: The woman stands above the children, sheltering them like a tree.

The World of Work

Public Housing Authority Program Supervisor

For a discussion of public housing, use the pages referenced below.

The World of Work
pp. 31–32

SELECTION SUMMARY

In the Ditch

Adah, a Nigerian separated from her husband, awakes in her shabby London apartment having to protect her baby from a rat. Her landlord, also a Nigerian, again pressures her to move out with her five children. Ignoring her complaints, the landlord has made life miserable for her. One day, he tries juju (traditional magic) to force her out, but she is not frightened. Instead, the landlord and his wife are embarrassed in public. Later, Adah is informed that temporary public housing has been found for her nearby. Adah's neighbor protests that the place is "rough," but Adah jumps at the chance, moving in that very night. She considers the new place "not bad " and a symbol of greater independence, freedom, and peace of mind.

 For summaries in other languages, see the **Building English Proficiency** *book.*

there, relaxed but watchful, wondering what trick Adah was up to now.

She was always too scared to shout. Her mouth was dry and she was too frightened even to move. The rat got bored with watching her, started to hop from one table to another, happily enjoying its night play. Adah's eyes followed its movements in the dim candlelight, then carefully and noiselessly she stretched out to reach the small reading-table by the big bed, picked up one of the library books she had piled on the table, aimed carefully at the hopping rat, and flung. The rat, for once, was scared. It ran right into the broken wardrobe at the end of the room, disturbing a group of sleeping cockroaches. One of the frightened cockroaches ran into Adah's hollow for maternal protection.

She had been told the week before that the Council[1] would soon have them rehoused.

She put the baby back in her cot, but did not dare go to sleep again. She was happy in her victory over the rat; at least she might now get some peace for a few nights. Another crashing noise jarred into her happy thoughts from the outside. "Oh, not *again!*" she moaned to herself, nearly in tears.

This time it was her landlord. He had long given her notice to quit the premises with her five young children. But unfortunately for Adah, she was black, separated from her husband, and, with five kids all under six, there were few landlords who would dream of taking the like of her into their houses.

Her landlord, a Nigerian, like herself, being aware of Adah's predicament, was, of course, taking the best advantage of the situation. The rent he charged was double what was normally asked for rooms in such houses. He now wanted her to leave because she had had the effrontery[2] to ask him to do something about the rats, the cockroaches, and the filth. When he had failed to do anything about them, she had been to the Town Hall and, because there was no other place for her to live just then, the Council had stepped in.

They had asked the landlord to do some repairs, and even asked him to give Adah a rent-book.

To give Adah a rent-book would have put him in trouble because, being a council tenant, he had pretended to the authorities that Adah was a relative and only a guest. He had begged Adah to withdraw her application for a flat from the Council but it was too late. There were, however, still lots of things he could do to make her life miserable. He would thunder at her kids for any of the slightest childish noises; this happened so frequently that one of her boys would run at the sight of any black man, and she dared not leave them alone in the flat for fear of what might happen to them. She could not leave any piece of food or drink in the filthy shared kitchen for fear of it being poisoned. All their food had to be kept under her bed, so it was hardly surprising that the number of rats had increased. The man was desperate and would stop at nothing. He had switched off the electricity so that she had to keep a candle burning all night, conscious of the terrible fire risk to the children, but even more afraid of what accidents could happen in utter darkness. But now there was something new: he was trying magic.

CLARIFY: Why would her landlord get in trouble for giving Adah a rent-book?

The poor man, instead of sleeping like everybody else, would wake up very early in the morning, round three or four, drape himself in colorful African material, just like juju masqueraders in Lagos,[3] and start moving to and fro to the music of his low-toned mournful songs. When Adah had first seen this figure she could

---

1. **the Council,** in Britain, a local government that provides low-rent housing for low-income families.
2. effrontery (ə frun′tər ē), *n.* shameless boldness.
3. **juju masqueraders in Lagos.** In Adah's hometown of Lagos, the capital of Nigeria, medicine men used fetishes or charms (jujus) to cast magic spells.

MINI-LESSON: GRAMMAR

Expressions of Time

Teach Remind students of some of the conventions of standard usage for expressions of time, such as centuries, dates, and hours.

- Capitalize B.C. (before Christ) and B.C.E. (before the common era) and place after the date: 1050 B.C., 1050 B.C.E.
- Capitalize A.D. (*anno Domini*, "in the year of the Lord") and place before the date: A.D. 850.
- When expressing decades, use numerals followed by -*s*: the 1990s.
- Use numerals to express years and exact dates: February 14, 1996.
- Capitalize A.M. (*ante meridiem*), "before noon," and P.M. (*post meridiem*), "after noon".

Activity Ideas

- Students can write the correct forms of centuries and dates of 10 major events in British history.
- Have students write a paragraph about moving from one country or home to another, using at least five correct expressions of time.

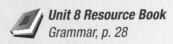

Unit 8 Resource Book
Grammar, p. 28

not believe her eyes. She was on the verge of screaming, but when she looked closer and saw it was only her landlord, she could feel only pity and contempt for him. Adah was more afraid of the rat than the juju landlord.

This morning she simply stared at him, not knowing what to do next; then, amused, she decided to join in his songs which, of course, she had known from childhood. Why was it that she was not afraid? she wondered. Was it because here in England one's mind was always taken up with worrying about the things that really matter? But juju mattered to her at home in Nigeria all right; there, such a scene in the middle of the night could even mean death for some. Probably, she thought, it was because there it was the custom, the norm, and what everybody believed in. The people not only believed in juju but such beliefs had become internalised[4] and it would not occur to anyone to think otherwise. But here, in north-west London, how could she think of the little man who was so familiar to her by day in his greasy second-hand lounge suit as a medicine man? She had heard rumors, and read in the papers of other Africans in London being "terrorised" by juju. *But I am tough and free,* she thought, *free,* she repeated to herself. In England she was free to keep her job, keep her kids, do her studies; she felt safe to ignore the juju man and his pranks. No, the juju trick would not work in England, it was out of place, on alien ground. God dammit, juju, in England, where you're surrounded by walls of unbelief!

On that particular morning, the landlord had either slept late or was very tired, or both, for Adah soon heard the rattling of the milkman's van; it must be six A.M. Mrs. Devlin, the Irish woman living in the top flat, padded down with her empty bottles rattling, the milkman came up the road with his merry whistle, and the landlord stood on the pavement, just outside Adah's ground-floor window, like a statue, apprehensive[5] of the rattle and whistle. Adah watched from the window, fascinated. What would happen now? she wondered.

Mrs. Devlin gave such a scream that the poor milkman had to lean against his van for support. The landlord could not push the old lady away, for she blocked the only doorway leading into the house. He simply did not know how to begin to explain what he had been doing, and stared at them all, his eyes looking ridiculously white in his black face. Adah did not want to miss the show so, tying a *lappa*[6] over her nightdress, went out. The landlord's wife also came out, and so did the other Nigerians living down the road. How could the landlord explain to this group of Londoners why at such an early hour he had tied a red cloth round his naked body and arranged an ostrich feather sticking up at the back of his head, looking to them like a television Red Indian who had had a shot too many?

The milkman fixed his gaze on him, silently demanding an explanation. The face of the landlady was another picture. It was still unmade-up and she still had her hair threaded (like many African women, she "threaded" her hair before going to bed, in small pleats, so that when the thread was taken out, the hair would lie on the head in attractive coils and not stick out), and in her haste she had not remembered to cover it with her wig. Mrs. Devlin, who was on good speaking terms and neighborly with Adah, looked appealingly to her to explain. Just then the landlady's face turned to her, saying without words, "Please don't say anything, please don't."

Adah started to stare at the ceiling by the doorway to avoid looking at any more faces. Then she thought of the picture they, the Nigerians, must present to their neighbors. The plaits[7] on the landlady's head would definitely

---

4. **internalised** (in tèr′nl īzd), *adj.* incorporated into one's own personality.
5. **apprehensive** (ap′ri hen′siv), *adj.* fearful; anxious about the future.
6. *lappa* (lap′ə), *n.* dressing gown.
7. **plait** (plāt), *n.* braid.

In the Ditch **883**

Point out that the juju landlord attempts to apply some ancient Nigerian beliefs and values to life in contemporary London. However, Adah analyzes why those particular values no longer affect her.

Questions Do you agree with Adah that a change of setting can effect a change of values? Why or why not? *(Possible response: A change of setting—particularly one as radical as a change of continent—can change individual values because the values of the surrounding community, the people who live in the setting, are different.)*

4 Literary Element
Metaphor

Questions What metaphor does Adah use to describe the belief system that surrounds her? Why is it an appropriate metaphor? *(Possible responses: She says juju in England is surrounded by "walls of unbelief," suggesting a prison or a fortress. The metaphor is appropriate because of Adah's own struggle to escape the prison-like walls of poverty that confine her.)*

5 Literary Element
Stereotype

Question Point out that Emecheta deliberately describes the neighbors' impression of the juju landlord—a stereotyped African—with another stereotype: an intoxicated "Red Indian." What is the key word in this passage? *(television, which presents simplified and distorted images of many different groups of people)*

BUILDING ENGLISH PROFICIENCY

Relating Causes and Effects

Emecheta provides a wealth of details that give the reader a sensually "dense" portrait of the setting, characters, and story events—and their impact on Adah. To keep track of details, as well as to "sort out" the plot's events, students may find it helpful to complete the graphic begun here.

Building English Proficiency
Activities, p. 264

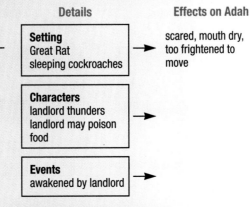

Details	Effects on Adah
Setting Great Rat sleeping cockroaches	scared, mouth dry, too frightened to move
Characters landlord thunders landlord may poison food	
Events awakened by landlord	

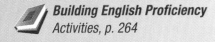

ESL
LEP
ELD
SAE
LD

remind any foreign person of the pictures of black devils they knew from their childhoods, for her plaits stood out straight, just like four horns. The landlord with the feather looked like the Devil's servant. Adah too was part of the picture. Her *lappa* with yellow and red splashes provided a good background.

Blast these illustrators! Who told them that the Devil was black? Who told them that angels are always white? Had it never occurred to them that there might be black angels and a white devil?

The milkman recovered first from the shock. "Were you going to *her* room?" he asked, deliberately, with accusation in every word, pointing at Adah's room.

Adah did nothing to help the landlord's dilemma but was quite regretting coming out in the first place. She did not know why she was so keen on keeping her landlord's secret. Patriotism? After all, one did not like to have one's dirty linen washed in public. Whatever happened, they were all originally from the same country, the same color, both caught in the entangled web of an industrial society. He wanted to make money from his house to pay for his studies. Adah wanted the proper value for the rent she paid. In their own country, the situation would never have occurred in the first place. Ibo people seldom separate from their husbands after the birth of five children. But in England, anything could be tried, and even done. It's a free country.

The landlady started scolding her husband in Yoruba.[8] The other Nigerians agreed with her. Why should he take it upon himself to frighten a lonely woman? Did he not fear God? The whole race of men were beasts. She had always said that, in fact her mother told her so at home when she was little. He had made a fool of himself. God only knew what these whites were going to do.

7 EVALUATE: What do you think the landlord's wife means when she says that God only knew what these whites were going to do?

To Adah she said nothing, but her frank speech was meant as an apology. It was very funny really, because everybody knew that everything the landlord had done had been planned by the two of them.

When the landlady started her speech in the Yoruba language, which Adah understood perfectly, the white people started to move away. The milkman swore, so did Mr. Devlin and his two sons, who by now had joined the party. Mrs. Devlin would go to the "Town 'all, Monday."

2

DRIFTING TO THE MANSIONS

After a cold and rainy night, the day was warm. It was early spring. Adah found a space on a bench beside two women who were talking about death, and sat down. It seemed very odd to be talking about death on such a beautiful afternoon, and in such a beautiful park. She looked at the two women momentarily and decided that the day was too fresh, too pure and too lovely to listen to death-talk.

The blue sky was liberally dotted with white clouds. The flats opposite had window-boxes displaying the first flowering shrubs. There were daffodils everywhere. Daffodils in the park, daffodils in the front and back gardens of houses, daffodils edging the park's footpaths, all planted with the type of carelessness that has a touch of calculation.

She inhaled the pure fresh air around her and said under her breath, "I feel so happy I could burst." A group of pigeons wobbled towards her as she unpacked her fish sandwich. She broke one slice of bread into pieces and threw it at them. They pecked at the crumbs agitatedly. Why was it that pigeons were always hun-

---

8. **Yoruba** (yor′ù bə), people from the southwest of Nigeria and the language they speak.

---

gry? Eating as quickly as they did must give them stomach ache.

It was a Friday, and her half-day. She would have her sandwich and spend a couple of hours in the library, then she would cook, then what, she would clean the flat, then bed. Q.E.D.!⁹

But the warmth of the sun was caressing and, after the sort of nights she had been having lately, the lure to doze off was too much of a temptation. The last bit of resistance to sleep was removed when the two women talking about death decided to leave. So she could snore if she liked.

Africans say that it is possible to have four seasons in one day in England, and indeed when Adah woke it might have been any winter day. The park was empty, even the pigeons had taken shelter from the icy cold rain. She got up quickly, looked at the clock on the tower and realised that she had slept the two hours she had saved for reading. Not to worry . . . she had enough fresh air in her lungs to face her choky¹⁰ flat. She hurried home.

Mrs. Devlin was at the door of their house when she got home. She was excitedly talking to her friend Mrs. Marshall, who was, as usual, holding the lead of her black dog. The two women turned to look in Adah's direction when they saw her coming. She was sure they were still talking of the juju episode which had been so spiced to flavor that she was already the heroine of a rather dramatic story. But heroines, being human like everybody else, do get bored of being praised. Not being in the mood to listen to any more new versions of the juju episode, she decided to dash past them, without greeting, to the nursery.

"Hey, what do you think *you're* doing? Come 'ere, we've good news for yer."

Adah wondered what good news there could be for her. She seldom got any news, but good news—well, she might as well listen.

"They've got a flat for yer. The manager was 'ere a minute ago, he said he would come back in thirty minutes to see if you were back."

"Me? A council flat for me? Are you sure he was asking for me? I can't believe it. Are you quite sure? I mean . . ." Adah was becoming incoherent¹¹ in her excitement. Her voice was loud and panicky.

"Yes, of course, dear, he came for you. Aahr, dear, don't cry, it's going to be all right now. He's coming soon," Mrs. Devlin assured her.

Adah did not realise that her eyes were watering. She wiped her face, peered at the thin face of Mrs. Marshall to make sure she was not dreaming, and in response Mrs. Marshall pulled her dog to herself, nodding intermittently. "It is true, it is true."

Yes, it must be true, but she still had to fetch her babies from the nursery. The day was too good to be ruined by Matron's anger. The matron of her kids' nursery had become a friend, but was very keen on punctuality. She never hid the fact that she too had children of her own who would be waiting for her at home. So mothers were usually begged to come for their babies on time. Though she was so happy about Mrs. Devlin's announcement, though she was dying to see the manager himself and get all the particulars, she would rather have taken the risk of missing all these than face an angry matron. She had a frightening anger, that matron had.

Aloud she said, "I must get the children first, otherwise I'll get told off by the matron."

"That's all right, you run along and get them; we'll wait for him when he comes. I am so happy for yer."

She thanked Mrs. Devlin and ran excitedly to the nursery. She picked up the baby from the pram¹² where she had been left in the clean hospital-like room. The babies' room was painted

---

9. **Q.E.D.,** "which was to be proved" [for Latin *quod erat demonstrandum*].
10. **choky** (chō′kē), *adj.* suffocating.
11. **incoherent** (in′kō hir′ənt), *adj.* confused; having no logical connection of ideas.
12. **pram** (pram), *n.* baby carriage.

In the Ditch **885**

BUILDING ENGLISH PROFICIENCY

Bringing a Narrative to Life

The narrative's mood begins to change in Section 2. Let students enjoy and explore Adah's sense of exhilaration by encouraging them to read aloud the scene and the dialogue between Adah, Mrs. Devlin, and Mrs. Marshall.

1. Separate students into four or five small groups. Let each group decide who will take what characters and how the rest of the text will be divided.

2. Give the groups enough time to read the passage several times, to discuss and choose intonations and gestures, and to practice reading aloud.

3. Invite groups to present their interpretations. Afterward, discuss variations, particularly any that were widely divergent, and how groups arrived at their presentation styles.

The Author Speaks

In an interview, Buchi Emecheta said: "What I am trying to do is get our profession back. Women are born storytellers. We keep the history. We are the true conservatives—we conserve things and we never forget. What I do is not clever or unusual. It is what my aunt and my grandmother did, and their mothers before them."

blue with blue and pink teddies painted all over the blue furniture. Even the drinking mugs had teddies drawn on them. Did babies, when only four months old, really take notice of all those teddies, or were the teddies for the delight of the plump nurses with merry faces and fixed smiles? Her baby was gurgling at nothing in the pram. She even gave a smile of recognition when she saw her mother. Adah did not have much time to talk to her as she was supposed to be doing. It took her a long time to learn this ritual of talking to a baby who either did not understand or in most cases did not know what to make of it. In England they said it was very good to chatter to your child, even when it was a few hours old, so she too started doing it, but would make sure that none of her people were around. They might well think her a witch, talking to something that did not answer back.

In the toddlers' room there was always noise and clatter. Shrill repetitive and nerve-racking voices piped in the air. The nurses clad in their shapeless flowered overalls moved about in the confusion, soothing, separating, yelling and laughing alternately. The floor was cluttered with children's litter. Toys of all shapes—kangaroos, lizards, ducks—all sorts. Some were very good, soft and cuddly, though in most cases the little devils would rather throw them at one another than play with them.

One of the nurses, on seeing Adah, made several attempts to call her children away from the confusion, but the kids found it funny to pretend not to hear her. Adah, annoyed, marched into the confusion, pulled Bubu, one of her two boys, by the collar, but he jerked away and she had to let him go for fear of dropping the baby. Triumphant, Bubu laughed and invited his mother to "chase me, Mummy, you can't catch me, you can't catch me." Luckily for Adah, a nurse saw her predicament and, marching in like a sergeant-major, took Bubu and his younger sister Dada by the hand to the cloakroom for their coats. The kids protested fiercely, "I don't want to go home, I want to play."

"You'll come back tomorrow, then if the weather is nice we'll go to the park, we'll go by bus, we'll . . ." The nurse went on and on, telling them what they were going to do "tomorrow." To kids tomorrow is always a long time away and they would scarcely remember what it was the nurse had said the day before. She went on cooing to them in that sugary tone some people reserve for kids. They eventually came out of the nursery.

The next argument was who was to be on the right or the left of the baby's pram. Bubu said he had been on the right of the pram in the morning, and would now stay on the left. Dada said she took the left first, and was not going to give it up. She looked determined, clutching the coveted[13] side with her little hands, and leaning her head against it. Bubu tried to pull her away, and Adah commanded him to stop. "Tomorrow you'll be on the left." Bubu was pacified,[14] especially as Adah agreed with him that Dada was a naughty girl and would not have sweets tomorrow.

S he hurried them home as fast as she could in the circumstances. Coming into her street, she could see that the man was already waiting for her. She quickened her pace and the children on either side of her started to trot, just like horses, their unworn gloves dangling lifelessly from the sleeves of their coats.

The man who was waiting for her was in his mid-thirties, with his belly slightly protruding. With a belly like that he must watch his diet, his beer . . . "Hello," she said breathless.

The man seemed unsure of what he should do next. He had glasses, his gray top coat was unbuttoned, revealing a very clean shirt. The glasses he had on gave him a highly intelligent look, but he ruined the effect by keeping his mouth open most of the time. With his mouth

13. coveted (kuv′ə tid), *adj.* strongly desired.
14. pacify (pas′ə fī), *v.* quiet down.

MINI-LESSON: WRITING STYLE

Writing Dialogue

Teach Point out to students that the placement of the attributions in a dialogue should have the following characteristics:

- **clarity** Be sure each speaker can be easily identified by the reader. Dialogue becomes confusing if the reader mistakes one character's words for another's.

- **variety** Don't begin or end every speech with "he said" or "she said." Avoid monotony in dialogue by using a variety of verbs *(declared, screamed, whispered)* and carefully chosen adverbs *(softly, hissingly, slyly)*.

- **naturalness** Place the attribution where the speaker might naturally pause to take a breath or stop to think. "I'd better not," she said, "or I'll pay the price."

Activity Idea For practice, have students write a dialogue about raising children; the dialogue should be between any two or more characters they know from literature or the movies, using attributions clearly, naturally, and with variety.

opened like that he looked both intelligent and stupid simultaneously.[15]

He decided to come to the point. "Are you Mrs. Obi?"

"Of course."

She wondered why professionals ask this sort of question. What exactly was she supposed to do, wear a label? Of course she was Mrs. Obi. She was beginning to hate the suspense. "Have you a flat for me?" She might as well know the worst. This man now managed to look like both a sharp plain-clothes detective and a mere clerk.

He cleared his throat. There was nothing to clear—he was just embarrassed or something. "Yes, we've got temporary accommodation for you at the Pussy Mansions, not very far, just around the corner."

"Come now, that's unfair," Mrs. Devlin cried. "Why do you put a girl like her in such a Godforsaken place? Her children are very young, and she's very hard working. It's not fair at all. Why, she might as well stay where she is now!"

"Huh?" cried Adah wondering whether Mrs. Devlin had gone mad. "Stay here? You must be joking. Any hole is better than this filth."

This pleased the man in the gray coat, and he gave Mrs. Devlin a why-don't-you-shut-your-mouth sort of look. Mrs. Devlin went on protesting.

"It's a rough place to put a girl like that."

The gray-coated man felt that he had to volunteer an explanation as Adah was beginning to look at him dubiously.[16] "You see, we have to rehouse you rather quickly because we were  told about the kind of bitter experiences you are being subjected to and gather that this place is not very safe for your children. You are going to stay at the Mansions for a short while—just a temporary arrangement, nothing permanent at all. Of course you can reject the offer if you don't particularly like it."

He started to dangle two keys in front of Adah's face as if tantalising her. "Take it or leave it!" his attitude seemed to be saying.

His cuff links were real gold, and his wrist-watch was golden too. He probably was the manager after all. The keys kept on dangling in front of her. Should she refuse the offer to save Mrs. Devlin the humiliation of being slighted? Should she accept the offer just to move away from the oppressive situation she was in? *Poor Mrs. Devlin, you don't know the gripping fears I go through every time I leave my children indoors to do some shopping, you don't know what it is like to realise that all your letters are being opened and read before you lay your hands on them, and you cannot dream what independence it is to have your own front door, your own toilet and bath, just for you and your family.*

Her feelings were transparent,[17] and Mrs. Devlin started to shuffle her way inside. Adah took the keys from the man very quickly. The man's mouth opened wider, surprised. He collected himself with a jerk, and said, "You'll let us know tomorrow if you are going to accept it, won't you, so that the flat could be redecorated for you?"

It had taken Adah nine months of court-going, letter-writing and tribunal-visiting to get her this much. Now this man wanted her to approve first of all, then wait for redecoration before moving in; he must be out of his mind.

"I'm moving in tonight!"

"What?" The man jumped to attention as if giving a military salute. "Are you quite sure, madam? We don't want to rush you, and we always want our tenants to move into clean flats, you know, we could have it done over for you."

"Is there any law preventing me from moving in today? Is there any law preventing you and your people from decorating when we've already moved in?"

"Of course not, madam." The man began to look over his shoulder as if he was about to sell Adah some stolen goods. "In that case, er, I do

---

15. **simultaneously** (sī′məl tā′nē əs lē), *adv.* at the same time.
16. **dubiously** (dü′bē əs lē), *adv.* doubtfully.
17. **transparent** (tran sper′ənt), *adj.* easily seen through.

In the Ditch   **887**

Question Based on Adah's personality and the goals she has for herself and her children, what would you say is the theme of this novel excerpt? *(Possible response: The theme might be summed up in the last line of this excerpt—her personal journey towards "independence, freedom, and peace of mind.")*

16 Active Reading
Predict

Possible response Adah might be able to forge a better life for her family. Free from at least some of the pressures (the Great Rat, the juju landlord), she might be able to read and study and perhaps break out of the poverty that imprisons her.

Check Test

1. Who is Adah's roommate? *(the Great Rat)*

2. What unusual tactic does Adah's landlord try to force her to move out? *(juju magic)*

3. Who first tells Adah about her new apartment? *(Mrs. Devlin)*

4. When does Adah move into her new apartment? *(that very night)*

5. What three important things does Adah feel she acquired after the move? *(independence, freedom, peace of mind)*

 *Unit 8 Resource Book*
Alternate Check Test, p. 29

---

wish you a happy stay at the Mansions. Er . . . if you want anything, we will do the best we can. Goodbye."

He turned around, walked quickly round the corner and disappeared, leaving Adah with the keys, and a hollow in her stomach, as if she had not eaten for days. She was going to take the flat and move out of this horrible place. She couldn't care less if in doing so she was offending a friend like Mrs. Devlin—it was her own life. Why couldn't people leave her to make her own mistakes? She was going to take the flat. She must move, and move that very night.

Having collected her two older youngsters from school, Adah avoided Mrs. Devlin for the rest of the evening. She did not wish to sing her joy aloud in case the landlord and landlady should guess that she was up to something. With suppressed[18] excitement she told her children, the ones who were old enough to understand. "We can't believe it," they had chorused. She sped to the news-agent round the corner, and the man agreed to move her few possessions to the Mansions for her for thirty shillings. It was then the thought occurred to her that she had not even seen the flat. She sped down the road to the block. So this was the block of flats.

The outside looked like a prison, red bricks with tiny yellow windows. The shape of the whole block was square, with those tiny windows peeping into the streets. The block looked dependable, solid. The outside look was not too encouraging, but she must not despair. She went round in circles looking for an opening into the block, found one eventually, but it was so dark that she was not at first sure that she was not walking into a cave. She emerged into an open space, with a crowd of children playing.

She looked on both sides of her, feeling lost. She saw a little boy with a friendly face and asked him where flat number *X* was.

The boy looked at her and said, "They moved yesterday, they've moved to Hampstead."

Adah thanked him, and told him that she was going to be the new tenant, and asked him could he please show her where the flat was. The boy did not look too happy at this question. He seemed to consider it for a while, shrugged his little shoulders as if to say, "After all, what must be, must be." He got up reluctantly[19] and took her up what seemed to Adah to be ten flights of stone steps. She had never climbed such steep steps in her life, and at that speed too.

When they got to the top, the boy pointed to a door by a gaping shute. "There it is." He waited for Adah to open the door. She did, and the boy peeped inside just once and ran away, his mind already preoccupied with something else.

Adah went in, gingerly at first, inspecting one room after the other. It was not bad at all compared to what she had. She was very pleased with the bath in particular. All these rooms, just for her—well, God was wonderful. He had heard her prayers. Oh, yes, they were going to spend the night there. She went down the stairs quickly, ran down to her old house, calling on the news agent on her way, picked up her odds and ends, and two hours later she was a tenant of the Mansions.

On that first night they had no beds, no curtains and no floor coverings, but Adah made do with an oil heater and piles of old blankets and bed sheets. There were three important things she knew she had acquired that night, her independence, her freedom, and peace of mind.

> **PREDICT: What kind of a life do you think Adah will make for the children and herself in the Mansions?**

15
16

---

18. **suppressed** (sə prest′), *adj.* held back; subdued.
19. reluctantly (ri luk′tənt lē), *adv.* slowly and unwillingly.

MINI-LESSON: STUDY SKILLS

Planning Your Time

Teach Point out that Adah carefully budgets her time in order to fulfill her commitments to her family and still have time for her personal development. On her half day, for example, she allows herself two hours for reading.

Questions What is your study schedule? Do you write it out or rely on keeping it in your head? Is your schedule the same every day? What are the variables that affect when and how long you study? *(Ideally, students will have a basically stable study schedule, including such variables as long-term projects and examinations.)*

Activity Idea Have students (1) produce a written version of their study schedules, (2) keep a written record for five consecutive days of how closely they adhere to the schedule, and (3) compare their records and discuss what changes they need to make in order to make the schedule even more useful.

After Reading

Making Connections

Shaping Your Response

1. Why do you think Emecheta might have chosen *In the Ditch* as the title of her book?

2. What actress would you choose to play Adah in a film version of *In the Ditch*?

Analyzing the Novel Excerpt

3. Why do you think the landlord wants to make Adah's life miserable?

4. Why might Adah agree to protect her landlord by keeping quiet in front of the Londoners?

5. What commentary on cultural differences is suggested by Adah's thoughts about the colors of the devil and angels?

6. 👣 Compare and contrast Adah's **interactions** with the Nigerians with her interactions with the Londoners.

7. Why do you think Adah feels freer in London than she had in Nigeria?

8. What beliefs and values seem to govern Adah's life?

Extending the Ideas

9. Do you think that a woman today in circumstances similar to Adah's would have the same experiences that Adah does?

Literary Focus: Dialogue

With two classmates read aloud the two dialogue scenes from "Drifting to the Mansions" on pages 885 and 887. For each scene determine what purpose or purposes the dialogue serves:

Dialogue Purposes	Adah and Mrs. Devlin (page 885)	Adah, Mrs. Devlin, and the manager (page 887)
Characterization		
Creation of Mood		
Plot Advancement		
Theme Development		

Vocabulary Study

coveted
effrontery
incoherent
pacify
reluctantly
simultaneously

Select the vocabulary word that is most clearly related to the situation conveyed in the sentence. You will not use all the words.

1. So excited was she—far beyond being tense—
   That her words sounded crazy: they didn't make sense.

2. How she envies big diamonds (say, set in a ring);
   Her wish list is quite long; she just wants everything!

LITERARY FOCUS: DIALOGUE

Possible Responses

Page 885   The dialogue might be said to focus primarily on helping to fill out Adah's and Mrs. Devlin's characters and to help create the mood by describing Adah's surprise and tension.

Page 887   The dialogue might be said to focus primarily on further developing Adah's character, advancing the plot by setting up the move itself, and conveying the theme of Adah's struggle against a variety of social and economic obstacles.

After Reading

MAKING CONNECTIONS

1. Possible responses: Emecheta may have felt that she had been symbolically thrown into a ditch when she and her husband separated. Her life was "below grade," and she had to climb out of a difficult situation.

2. Responses will vary; students might suggest Whoopi Goldberg as a believable Adah.

3. If the landlord can force her out, he can rent the apartment for more money to someone else.

4. Adah feels some sympathy for her landlord as a fellow Nigerian struggling in an industrialized country.

5. Adah's comment points up the difficulty of reconciling many cultural differences, which have been thousands of years in the making. It points out that racial stereotypes afflict all races.

6. Adah's interactions with the Nigerians have a hidden layer based upon their shared heritage. Adah seems to have a simpler relationship with her white neighbors based on their shared immediate experiences.

7. In Nigeria, women were subject to men, and in London Adah is free to forge her own existence—with all the burdens that entails.

8. Above all, Adah seems to believe in a brighter future for herself and her family. She believes she can better her financial condition, particularly through study, assert her independence, and approach a greater peace of mind.

9. Responses will vary, but students might assert that Adah's experiences could very well be replicated in other cities today around the world.

VOCABULARY STUDY

1. incoherent
2. covet
3. effrontery
4. reluctantly
5. pacify

Unit 8 Resource Book
Vocabulary, p. 27
Vocabulary, Test, p. 30

WRITING CHOICES
Writer's Notebook Update

In addition to noting all of the obstacles in their notebooks, students might also list all of the weapons and resources that can be used to confront and overcome those obstacles. Encourage them to consider personal, intellectual, emotional, physical, and community resources.

You Won't Believe What I Saw

Students might also consider writing a dialogue between two of Adah's Nigerian neighbors who know and understand what took place and either approve or disapprove.

Advice from Adah

Students might prewrite a list of advantages and disadvantages before attempting the letter itself. They may also want to create a comparison-and-contrast graphic organizer to help organize their thoughts.

Selection Test

Unit 8 Resource Book
pp. 31–32

Transparency Collection
Fine Arts Writing Prompt, p. 16

---

3. With an attitude bold—no, I'll even say brash—
   Their behavior is shocking and shameless and rash.
4. He was very unwilling, did not want to go;
   When at last he consented, his movements were slow.
5. He was true to his form, he was reckless and wild,
   But a cookie from Grandma becalmed the small child.

Expressing Your Ideas

Writing Choices

Writer's Notebook Update Review the obstacles you listed in your notebook. Put a check by each obstacle that matches Adah's problems in England. List additional obstacles that Adah confronts.

You Won't Believe What I Saw Write the **dialogue** that you imagine might take place between the milkman and his wife when he returns from his workday to tell her about the strange scene he observed early in the morning. Remember that he is unfamiliar with the landlord's Ibo culture and may well be suspicious of anyone who looks different and acts in a strange manner.

Advice from Adah Write a **letter of advice** that Adah might send to a young woman from her country who wishes to move to London. Include both warnings and encouragements. Emphasize also how important it is to understand and cope with cultural differences.

Other Options

Cooking with Adah Research the food of Nigeria and prepare an **illustrated recipe book** containing recipes for several dishes that Adah might serve to her children to celebrate their new life in the Mansions. If you can, prepare one or more of the recipes for your class.

Imagine the Ritual Imagine the music, the dance, and the ritual that might surround the masquerader wearing this traditional African mask that comes from the country of Liberia. Select appropriate music and choreograph a ritualistic **dance**. Perform your dance for your class. Or, if you wish, you might design a colorful **costume** that you think a juju masquerader might wear. You may design it on paper or, if you can sew, you might want to stitch it up and model it for your class.

OTHER OPTIONS
Cooking with Adah

Students might also research the lives of Africans in England and report on other aspects of the interaction of the cultures: fashion, art, entertainment, language, education, holidays, and politics.

The Passing of Empire

Effects of Empire

History Connection

The story of South Africa for over three hundred years has been a story of European domination. Not until the 1980s did the black majority of the country begin to win the rights that had been denied them for centuries.

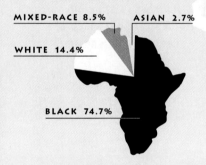

SOUTH AFRICA

LOSS OF FREEDOM

1652 THE FIRST EUROPEANS TO SETTLE IN SOUTHERNMOST AFRICA ARRIVE. WORKERS OF THE DUTCH EAST INDIA COMPANY, HEADED BY JAN VAN RIEBEECK, ESTABLISH A COMPANY OUTPOST NEAR THE CAPE OF GOOD HOPE. PEOPLE WHO LEAVE THE COMPANY START FARMS IN THE AREA. THEY CALL THEMSELVES AFRIKANERS (af′rə kä′nərz), AND OVER TIME THEY SPEAK A FORM OF DUTCH CALLED AFRIKAANS, WHICH IS INFLUENCED BY AFRICAN LANGUAGES.

1795 BRITAIN SEIZES THE CAPE COLONY. BRITISH SETTLERS AND OFFICIALS LOOK DOWN ON THE AFRIKANERS, WHO ALSO ARE CALLED BOERS (bôrz), A DUTCH WORD FOR FARMERS.

1873 AFRIKANERS MOVE HUNDREDS OF MILES INLAND TO ESCAPE BRITISH DOMINATION. DURING THIS MIGRATION, CALLED THE GREAT TREK, HOSTILITIES INCREASE BETWEEN THE AFRIKANERS AND BLACK AFRICANS, WHOSE LANDS THE DUTCH DESCENDANTS ENTER. THE BOERS SETTLE IN AREAS THAT THEY TAKE FROM ZULUS, XHOSAS, AND OTHER AFRICAN PEOPLES.

1879 THE ZULU WAR BEGINS WITH BRITISH INVASION OF ZULULAND. AFTER AN INITIAL DISASTER AT ISANDHLWANA, THE BRITISH ARMY DEFEATS ZULU FORCES, FINALLY CAPTURING ZULU KING CETEWAYO.

1899 BRITAIN ATTEMPTS TO ADD INLAND REGIONS, INCLUDING GOLD-PRODUCING LANDS, TO ITS EMPIRE. THE BOER WAR BEGINS. THE BOERS SURRENDER IN 1902. BRITAIN TURNS OVER AUTHORITY FOR COLONIES— NATAL, THE CAPE COLONY, THE TRANSVAAL, AND THE ORANGE FREE STATE—TO THEIR EUROPEAN SETTLERS. MOST OF THE POPULATION, WHO ARE BLACK PEOPLE, HOLD NO POLITICAL POWER.

1910 THE UNION OF SOUTH AFRICA IS FORMED. AS IN THE COLONIES, BLACK AFRICANS ARE NOT ALLOWED TO VOTE, CONTROL ANY APPRECIABLE WEALTH, OR SHARE THE RIGHTS HELD BY WHITE SOUTH AFRICANS.

1912 THE AFRICAN NATIVE NATIONAL CONGRESS IS FORMED TO FIGHT AGAINST RACIAL INEQUALITY. THE GROUP LATER IS KNOWN AS THE AFRICAN NATIONAL CONGRESS, OR ANC.

PERCENT OF POPULATION BY RACE

MIXED-RACE 8.5%   ASIAN 2.7%

WHITE 14.4%

BLACK 74.7%

Even though blacks have always been in the majority in South Africa, whites have controlled the political system for most of the last 350 years.

(*Source:* Countries of the World and Their Leaders Yearbook 1994)

Interdisciplinary Study   **891**

Interdisciplinary Study

Theme Link

South Africa was colonized by whites in stages, despite resistance of black Africans. Eventually, racism became public policy, with heartbreaking results.

Curricular Connection: History

Use the historical information in this interdisciplinary study to explore the long struggle of blacks in South Africa. To emphasize the long history of racial tension there you may want to point out what was happening elsewhere during some of the early dates cited. For example, the year 1795 was twenty-two years after the Boston Tea Party in 1773.

Additional Background

The Dutch East India Company was chartered by the Dutch government to control trade in Asia and other places. It was one of the world's first joint stock companies, with many stockholders sharing profits and losses. Although it was not officially part of the Dutch government, the company was given extensive political power, and established several colonies. Its headquarters in Indonesia were established in 1619. The company was finally absorbed into the government in 1798.

Unit 8 Resource Book
Study Guide, p. 33

BUILDING ENGLISH PROFICIENCY

Responding to Information

Encourage students to use their dialogue journals as they examine the time line and think about what it reveals about the history of South Africa. For example, in the left-hand column of a T-chart, they could note specific details about a particular year or event; in the right-hand column, they could express an opinion about it, jot down a question for discussion, and so on. Afterward, invite volunteers to share their comments.

Fact/Detail	My Response
1795: Britain takes control of the Cape colony away from the Dutch.	How did that happen?
The Union of South Africa allows little participation to black Africans.	It doesn't seem like much of a union if most of the people in it are discriminated against!

Research Topics

- Tensions between the ANC and other black independence groups
- Changes in South Africa during Nelson Mandela's presidency
- The role and presence of the Zulus in South Africa

MULTICULTURAL CONNECTION

In South Africa, a distinction is made between "black" and "colored" people. Blacks are considered fully African, and are divided into ten ethnic groups. Colored people are those of mixed race, descended from the indigenous people of the Cape of Good Hope and early Dutch settlers. During apartheid, with its complex system of racial categories, colored people were treated less brutally than blacks.

You may discuss with students how the classification of and varied discrimination against people who are oppressed leads to resentments and divisions that can weaken a struggle for independence and equality in any part of the world.

STRUGGLE FOR FREEDOM

1948 THE NATIONAL PARTY, DOMINATED BY AFRIKANERS, COMES TO POWER. THE TRADITIONAL PRACTICES OF APARTHEID (ə pärt´hāt), A SYSTEM OF RACIAL SEPARATION AND WHITE SUPREMACY, BECOMES LAW. BLACK AFRICANS IN SOUTH AFRICA ARE FORCED TO LIVE IN CROWDED, UNPRODUCTIVE "HOMELANDS," WHILE WHITE PEOPLE ARE GIVEN ADDITIONAL PRODUCTIVE LANDS. THREE QUARTERS OF THE POPULATION ARE FORCED TO MOVE ONTO THIRTEEN PERCENT OF THE LAND.

1962 NELSON MANDELA, A LEADER OF THE AFRICAN NATIONAL CONGRESS, IS IMPRISONED. THE GOVERNMENT CONTINUALLY ACTS TO WEAKEN ATTEMPTS TO ORGANIZE OR UNIFY BLACK SOUTH AFRICANS.

1976 AFTER THE GOVERNMENT MANDATES THE TEACHING OF AFRICAN CHILDREN IN AFRIKAANS, BLACK STUDENTS IN THE TOWNSHIP OF SOWETO PROTEST, AND DISTURBANCES ARISE IN VARIOUS COMMUNITIES. THE GOVERNMENT BRUTALLY SUPPRESSES THE "SOWETO UPRISING," KILLING MORE THAN 600 PEOPLE.

1977 CHARISMATIC BLACK ACTIVIST STEVEN BIKO IS TORTURED WHILE IN POLICE CUSTODY. HE DIES, AND THE MOVEMENT FOR FREEDOM AMONG BLACK SOUTH AFRICANS GAINS SUPPORT. INTERNATIONAL REACTIONS AGAINST SOUTH AFRICAN GOVERNMENT POLICIES GROW. INVESTMENT IN SOUTH AFRICA DECLINES.

IN DETENTION

He fell from the ninth floor
He hanged himself
He slipped on a piece of
soap while washing
He hanged himself
He slipped on a piece of soap
while washing
He fell from the ninth floor
He hanged himself while washing
He slipped from the ninth floor
He hung from the ninth floor
He slipped on the ninth floor
while washing
He fell from a piece of soap
while slipping
He hung from the ninth floor
He washed from the ninth
floor while slipping
He hung from a piece of
soap while washing

This poem by South African Christopher van Wyk gives a cynical view of official explanations for deaths in detention.

Hector Peterson, 13, was the first child killed in the Soweto uprising of 1976. Students were protesting a mandate that required classes to be taught in Afrikaans when police opened fire.

892   UNIT EIGHT: THE LATE TWENTIETH CENTURY

MINI-LESSON: STUDY SKILLS

Creating a Time Line

A time line can be a useful tool for organizing events and understanding their relationships to each other.

Activity Idea   Divide the class into small groups. Each group will create a time line, first making a rough pencil draft, then drawing a finished one on a large piece of poster board with markers. The time lines will trace local events, national events, and world events, and may be organized with three parallel lines as follows:

	1700s	1800s	1900's
Local_____			
National_____			
World_____			

Groups may fill in specific dates. They may choose to focus on political events, natural occurrences, technological advances, social change, and so on. Display the time lines in the classroom and lead a discussion of what students learned from this activity.

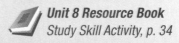

Unit 8 Resource Book
Study Skill Activity, p. 34

ACHIEVEMENT OF FREEDOM

1986 SOUTH AFRICA BEGINS TO REPEAL APARTHEID LAWS, A PROCESS THAT CONTINUES UNTIL 1991.

1990 NELSON MANDELA IS RELEASED FROM PRISON. HIS LEADERSHIP IS HAILED AROUND THE WORLD.

1994 THE FIRST NATIONAL ELECTIONS IN WHICH PEOPLE OF ALL RACES CAN VOTE ARE HELD. NELSON MANDELA IS ELECTED PRESIDENT.

> During my lifetime I have dedicated myself to this struggle of the African people. I have fought against white domination and I have fought against black domination. I have cherished the idea of a democratic and free society in which all persons live together in harmony and with equal opportunities. It is an ideal which I hope to live for and achieve. But if needs be, it is an ideal for which I am prepared to die.
> --Nelson Mandela

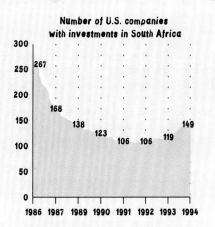

Number of U.S. companies with investments in South Africa

Year	Number
1986	267
1987	168
1989	138
1990	123
1991	106
1992	106
1993	119
1994	149

Responding

What parallels do you see between the struggle of blacks in South Africa during the 1970s and '80s and that of blacks in the U.S. during the 1960s? what differences?

During the late 1980s public disapproval of apartheid among people throughout the world caused many businesses to limit their investments in South Africa. The number of U.S. companies with investments in South Africa declined until reforms took effect in the 1990s. (No data is available for 1988.)

Interdisciplinary Activity Ideas

- Students can organize a "South African Awareness Day" at the school. Students may visit other classes to teach about the history of South Africa, show a video of the film *Biko*, or set up a booth to hand out copies of newspaper and magazine articles.
- Students may read the book *Burger's Daughter* (1973) by Nadine Gordimer. Then, they may write personal essays about the emotional effects of apartheid.

Responding

Possible responses   Students may cite as parallels that blacks in both places were socially and economically disadvantaged and were struggling for equality. Differences mentioned may be that by the 1960s in America, segregation was already being made illegal, there was already a noticeable population of successful blacks, and the federal government, on the whole, supported equal rights for blacks. In South Africa in the 1970s and 1980s, blacks struggled for official rights, while in the U.S. in the 1960s, blacks fought for the enforcement of civil rights, many of which they already had on paper. In both places, people died in the struggle for justice.

BUILDING ENGLISH PROFICIENCY

Responding to Illustrations

Encourage students to respond to one or more of the verbal and visual features that shed light upon the time line information.

Activity Ideas

- Have a group of volunteers present a skit in which a South African official tries to explain the death of a jailed black African to the man's family, using the words of "In Detention."
- Invite pairs or groups of students to watch a videotape of the movie *Sarafina!* (1992) and share what they learn from it about the Soweto uprising.

- Urge students to respond to the quotation from Nelson Mandela— by reading it aloud with expression or by interpreting it through art, music, or drama.
- Have students use the graph on page 893 to draw and share conclu-sions about the history of relations between the United States and South Africa.

Citizens in newly independent countries can fall prey to political corruption, suffer inadequate social services, and succumb to profound discontent.

Curricular Connection: Career

Mention various careers that involve helping others and working abroad and discuss with students the difficulties of working to help people without interfering with their cultures or governments.

Interdisciplinary Activity Ideas

In small groups, students may research and report on the Peace Corps, its history, or its work in Asia, Africa, Eastern Europe, or South America.

Responding

1. Possible Responses Students may believe that independence is always good for a country, even if there is a difficult period of adjustment. Others may believe that independence can be a bad thing because some tiny countries have no way to survive economically.

2. Possible Responses Some similarities are that the Gambians retained British customs and that a new elite grew quickly. Differences include that the United States fought for independence, while Britain voluntarily freed The Gambia; the Gambians were indigenous to the country, while in the U.S., independence was gained by immigrants and their descendants.

INTERDISCIPLINARY STUDY

Career Connection
Achieving independence, a glorious development to many nations and peoples, to others seems a mixed blessing. An American diplomat encountered uneasy feelings and economic distress in a west African country granted independence by the British.

THE PULSE OF VILLAGE LIFE

INTERVIEW WITH DR. EDWARD BRYNN

When Dr. Edward Brynn arrived in The Gambia, in western Africa, in April 1984 to start a short tour as Chief of Mission for the United States, most African states had been independent for twenty years. However, in the British Empire, not every colony was equally eager for that independence. The Gambia, an approximately 200-mile-long sliver of a country that cuts into Senegal, was one of the reluctant ones. Foreign Service officer Dr. Brynn wrote, "Britain forced independence on to this mini-colony more than the Gambians demanded it. In 1984 nostalgia for olden times remained very lively. Judges sweltered under wigs as they heard cases and issued judgments. Photos of the Queen graced the walls of villagers throughout the country. All news emanated from the BBC. . . .

"My days were not so pressed with work to preclude travel. Despite the heat I found a bike and pedaled down dozens of dusty roads through villages little changed over the centuries. My ambition was to seek our Peace Corps Volunteers and to hear their thoughts on development and the role of Americans. . . .

"In Sub-Saharan Africa per capita income levels are on average about 50 percent of what they were at independence. In The Gambia all the indexes are down: people are less healthy, hungrier, more crowded, less content with their lives. Independence was sold to them as a panacea, a way to escape a heritage of poverty, inequality, even slavery. The reality was quite different: the firm, unfeeling, distant hand of colonial administrators was supplanted by an indigenous elite which tended toward corruption or, at least, favoritism of kith and kin. Sitting in a small village, my bike leaning heavily against a frail tree, I found myself feeling keenly the pulse of village life on the banks of one of Africa's grand rivers.

Drama in the pounding of the drums, sorrow in the soft crying of a mother seeing her malnourished baby at death's door, a ubiquitous silence induced by intense, enervating heat—all of these made up a rural African evening.

"Back in the capital, I entertained the elite at a fancy table. I engaged senior ministers, whose own ties to the village down the road had almost disappeared, as they sought to do good and often did well—for themselves and their families. They were amused, and sometimes embarrassed, to see that I spent so much time with their poorest cousins. Their hearts and minds were in London and New York. Another generation would have to pass before real independence came to The Gambia."

Responding
1. Is independence always a good thing for a country? Why or why not?

2. The U.S. and The Gambia are both former colonies of Britain. From what you have read in this article, what similarities and differences do you see in their achievement of independence?

MINI-LESSON: SPEAKING AND LISTENING

Interviewing Interviewing may seem pretty simple: one person asks questions and the other person answers. However, journalists, TV talk-show hosts, and other professionals know that a good interview is the result of skill, rapport, and spontaneity.

Apply Show the class examples of interviews, either printed in magazines or newspapers, or taped from TV. Discuss the role of research, personality, and humor in these examples.

Activity Idea The class can divide into pairs or small groups. Each group can plan to interview
- a member of the school community
- a person active in local government
- someone who contributes to the local community
- an entertainer in the community

After this person has agreed to an interview, the groups can prepare by:
- researching the person's life, starting perhaps with information in back issues of a school or local newspaper
- learning about the person's specialty—for instance, the history of local politics if he or she is in government, or the local theater scene if he or she is an actor or entertainer.

Students can decide whether they will conduct a video or audio only interview.

Language History

The Language of the Twentieth Century

 War is peace. Freedom is slavery. Ignorance is strength.
George Orwell, *Nineteen Eighty-four* (1948)

The English language has continued to grow and change during the twentieth century, as it has throughout its long and rich history. Two world wars have provided such terms as *zeppelin, U-boat, blitzkrieg, jeep, concentration camp,* and *A-bomb;* from science and technology came *neurosis, antibiotic, radio, television, videotape,* and *megabyte;* from the arts came *montage, surrealism,* and *absurdist.* As the language continued to change, words took on new meanings. *Scan* once meant to study with great care; now it means to glance at hastily. *Sophistication,* once a term of condemnation, now signifies approval.

The widespread use of manipulative language by propagandists and advertisers has disturbed many people. Probably the best-known analyst of the corruption of English by politicians and salespeople in the recent past was George Orwell (see page 859). In essays like "Politics and the English Language," he protested against bad language habits that corrupt thinking: "Modern writing at its worst does not consist in picking out words for the sake of their meaning and inventing images in order to make the meaning clearer. It consists in gumming together long strips of words which have already been set in order by someone else, and making the results presentable by sheer humbug."

Orwell's novel *Nineteen Eighty-four* depicts a slave society ruled by a self-perpetuating elite. The official language is called *Newspeak.* Each year words are eliminated from its vocabulary. The purpose of impoverishing the language is to narrow the range of thought of the citizens, so that it will become increasingly difficult for them to express, or even to form, an unorthodox concept. Ultimately, they will cease to think altogether. In order to create more mental confusion in the citizens, the elite promote the practice of *doublethink,* the ability to hold two contradictory beliefs simultaneously. Perhaps Orwell's bleak fantasy should be seen more as a warning than a prediction. But in a world full of official euphemism, in which murder is referred to as "termination with extreme prejudice," Orwell's admonition to rid ourselves of bad language habits seems more relevant than ever before.

Language History   **895**

CONTENT AREA READING

Retaining Information

Some students may be able to read quickly, but have trouble retaining information. Students who have more trouble reading may be focused on getting through the material and not really learning it. Retaining what you read is more than memorizing—it means processing the information and making sure you understand it.

Give students the following pointers for effectively retaining information:

- At the end of each paragraph, ask yourself, "What was the main point?"
- At the end of each page, ask yourself, "Where is the writer taking me?"
- At the end of each chapter, ask yourself, "What was proved?"

They might practice using these photos on another Orwell essay or with an article in any current news magazine.

Writing Workshop

WRITER'S BLUEPRINT

Specs

The Specs in the Writer's Blueprint address these writing and thinking skills:

- researching
- recognizing values
- composing a thesis statement
- drawing conclusions
- using specific examples
- taking a position
- reasoning
- being concise
- using commas correctly

These Specs serve as your lesson objectives, and they form the basis for the **Assessment Criteria Specs** for a superior paper, which appear on the final TE page for this lesson. You might want to read through the Assessment Criteria Specs with students when you begin the lesson.

Linking Literature to Writing

Since students are going to produce a literary analysis of an author's attitudes, you might lead a short discussion on the element of tone.

Conclusions About Colonialism

Assignment Authors from former colonies of the British Empire have expressed their attitudes toward colonialism in their works. Analyze one of these author's attitudes.

WRITER'S BLUEPRINT

Product   A literary analysis

Purpose   To explore an author's attitudes toward colonialism

Audience   A British literary magazine

Specs   As the writer of a successful analysis, you should:

❑ Imagine that you are writing for a British literary magazine on the theme Attitudes Toward Colonialism. Focus on one of the six writers from "Choose an author," on the next page.

❑ Read at least two of this author's stories, poems, articles, or essays. Draw conclusions about the author's attitudes toward the influence of British colonial rule on the life of the colony. Also, look for biographical information that might help.

❑ Begin with a thesis statement that sums up the author's attitudes toward colonialism. It will serve as the guiding force in your paper. Go on to explain how you arrived at this statement. Support your conclusions with examples from the author's works, including quotations.

❑ End by summing up your personal reactions to these attitudes.

❑ Be concise. Avoid empty words and phrases.

❑ Follow the rules of grammar, usage, spelling, and mechanics. Use commas correctly.

 STEP  PREWRITING

Look for clues about attitudes toward colonialism. Before you look at your chosen author, practice finding clues in another author's work. Review George Orwell's "Shooting an Elephant" on pages 860–865 with

---

WRITING WORKSHOP OVERVIEW

Product
Expository writing: A literary analysis

Prewriting
Look for clues about attitudes—Choose an author—Read—Compose a thesis statement—Plan your essay
Unit 8 Resource Book
Prewriting Worksheets pp. 35–36

Drafting
Start writing
Transparency Collection
Student Models for Writing Workshop 31, 32

Revising
Ask a partner—Strategy: Being Concise
Unit 8 Resource Book
Revising Worksheet p. 37

Editing
Ask a partner—Strategy: Using Commas Correctly
Unit 8 Resource Book
Grammar Worksheet p. 38
Grammar Check Test p. 39

Presenting
Read Aloud
Locate Media

Looking Back
Self-evaluate—Reflect—For Your Working Portfolio
Unit 8 Resource Book
Assessment Worksheet p. 40
Transparency Collection
Fine Art Writing Prompt 16

a small group. Add entries to the first column of the chart shown and fill in the second column with your own conclusions and questions.

Orwell's "Shooting an Elephant"	Conclusions and Questions
When a Burman tripped him on the football field, "the crowd yelled with hideous laughter."	Orwell sees that the Burmese hate the British. But how does he, himself, feel about the situation?
"I perceived in this moment that when the white man turns tyrant it is his own freedom that he destroys."	

Choose an author to focus on from the six shown in the author web. Read about your author in encyclopedias or other sources such as the *Contemporary Author* series before making your choice.

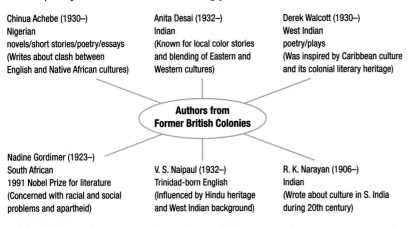

Chinua Achebe (1930–)
Nigerian
novels/short stories/poetry/essays
(Writes about clash between
English and Native African cultures)

Anita Desai (1932–)
Indian
(Known for local color stories
and blending of Eastern and
Western cultures)

Derek Walcott (1930–)
West Indian
poetry/plays
(Was inspired by Caribbean culture
and its colonial literary heritage)

**Authors from
Former British Colonies**

Nadine Gordimer (1923–)
South African
1991 Nobel Prize for literature
(Concerned with racial and social
problems and apartheid)

V. S. Naipaul (1932–)
Trinidad-born English
(Influenced by Hindu heritage
and West Indian background)

R. K. Narayan (1906–)
Indian
(Wrote about culture in S. India
during 20th century)

Read at least two stories, poems, or essays by the author you've chosen. Make notes on the author's attitudes, using a chart like the one you made in "Look for clues about attitudes." As you proceed, search for answers to any questions you posed in the second column.

Don't be surprised if your conclusions reveal mixed feelings on the author's part toward both the British and native peoples. These authors are dealing with complex political and social issues.

Compose a thesis statement to serve as the guiding force for your essay. It should consist of a sentence or two that sums up your author's attitudes toward colonialism and should be specific and limited enough to provide well-defined boundaries for your essay. Use your chart as a

OR . . .
Read something by several other authors on the list as well to get an idea of their attitudes toward colonialism. This will give you insight on the attitudes of the author you chose.

Writing Workshop   897

STEP 1 PREWRITING
Look for clues about attitudes

Discuss with students the types of clues they may look for. How are attitudes revealed through literature? For additional support, see the worksheets referenced below.

 Unit 8 Resource Book
Prewriting Worksheet, p. 35
Prewriting Worksheet, p. 36

Choose an author

Work with school and community librarians to have plenty of materials available for students in the classroom.

Read

Remind students to keep track of references and sources for later citations.

Compose a thesis statement

Have each student write his or her thesis statement on a single sheet of paper, then pass it around the group. Group members should then write a comment or question on the back of each paper. This should help students revise their statements.

BUILDING ENGLISH PROFICIENCY

Exploring Key Concepts

The interpretation of an author's attitudes toward colonialism will be influenced by students' reactions to the readings in this section. Have students review their journal entries for these readings and then create a semantic web arising from colonialism. They then can compare their interpretations with those of the writer they have chosen.

Plan your essay

Students may want to build their essays around their favorite quotes. Encourage students to use a different plan from the one shown if they wish, but remind them that a plan will enable them to write a more organized essay.

Connections to
Writer's Notebook

For selection-related prompts, refer to Writer's Notebook.

Connections to
Writer's Resource

For additional writing prompts, refer to Writer's Resource.

STEP 2 DRAFTING
Start writing

Ask students to reflect on how the writing of this essay has influenced their thoughts on this issue before they write their conclusions.

The Student Models

The **transparencies** referenced below are authentic student models. Review them with the students before they draft. These questions and suggestions will help:

1. Which writer does a better job of ful-filling the Specs in the Writer's Blueprint and why?

2. What are the writers' thesis statements? How well do they work as guiding forces for the essays?

3. Have students read both models aloud; then suggest ways to make the language more concise.

Transparency Collection
Student Models for Writing Workshop 31, 32

898

OR . . .
Before you compose your thesis statement, discuss your ideas with a partner and make notes on your partner's comments. After you compose it, ask your partner for comments on the result.

guide. Here are two examples of thesis statements. Notice how vague and ill-defined the first version is when compared with the second, revised version:

> In "Shooting an Elephant," Orwell shows that he does not approve of what goes on between the British and the native peoples in Burma.

> In "Shooting an Elephant," Orwell sees the colonial process as a mutual loss of freedom. Each side, in its own way, enslaves the other.

Plan your essay. Here is one way to organize your ideas. Make notes on each category.

- **Introduction**
  Author and works to be discussed
  Thesis statement (author's attitudes toward colonialism)

- **Body**
  First conclusion
  —examples from text
  Second conclusion
  —examples from text
  and so on . . .

- **Conclusion**
  Personal reaction to author's attitudes
  —agree or disagree
  —reasons why

Start writing. Consider these suggestions:

- Write your thesis statement on an index card and keep it in front of you while you draft to help you stay focused.

- Begin with a quotation or a provocative question that leads into your thesis statement. For example: *When does the slave become the master and the master the slave?*

- When you finish the introduction and body, reread them and make a fresh set of notes on your reactions before you write the ending.

MINI-LESSON: WRITING STYLE
Being Concise

Teach   Make sure students understand that writing clean, concise prose takes revising, that it takes time to whittle away all of the excess to get at the exact right words.

Activity Idea   Have students work in pairs to create a focused piece of writing out of the following group of sentences. Then have them generate a list of "warning signs" to look for in their own writing that signal imprecise language and unnecessary words and phrases.

> I guess the very best way to sum up all of these important points is to say that it just isn't very fair. Each person's culture is very, very important and so they all have things to say. If we all have things to say, don't we all deserve respect? Or should we let power determine whose culture is or isn't the norm?

Apply   As students critique each other's essays, have them highlight any words that are not pulling much weight.

Ask a partner for comments on your draft before you revise it.

✔ Have I begun with a thesis statement about the author's attitudes toward colonialism?

✔ Does the rest of my essay relate to this thesis?

✔ Have I supported my conclusions with evidence from the literature?

✔ Have I given my personal reactions to the author's attitudes?

✔ Is my writing concise?

Revising Strategy

Being Concise

One goal in revising is to eliminate unnecessary words and phrases that slow the reader down, such as the ones in italics.

WORDY *The reason that* this author is critical of colonialism is because it supports apartheid.

REVISED This author is critical of colonialism because it supports apartheid.

WORDY *In my opinion, it seems to me that* Desai is highly critical of the British.

REVISED Desai seems highly critical of the British.

When you revise, make every word count.

STEP **4** EDITING

Ask a partner to review your revised draft before you edit. When you edit, watch for errors in grammar, usage, spelling, and mechanics. Pay special attention to errors with commas. See the Editing Strategy and student model on the next page.

Writing Workshop   **899**

STEP 3 REVISING
Ask a partner (Peer assessment)

Have students create a checklist from the questions given in the text. Partners can make notes on the checklist to indicate strengths and weaknesses in the essay.

Revising Strategy: Being Concise

Ask your students to discuss how they feel as readers when they have to work through wordy or padded prose. You might have volunteers bring in examples of published writing they feel is wordy, and try revising it.

For additional support, see the mini-lesson at the bottom of page 898 and the worksheet referenced below.

Unit 8 Resource Book
Revising Worksheet, p. 37

Connections to
Writer's Resource

Refer to the Grammar, Usage, and Mechanics Handbook on Writer's Resource.

STEP 4 EDITING
Ask a partner (Peer assessment)

You might have students edit in groups, with each group member reading all the papers in the group, but concentrating on one aspect of correctness only, such as spelling or punctuation.

MINI-LESSON: GRAMMAR

Using Commas Correctly

Have students edit the following sentences for mistakes in comma usage. Ask students to explain why each comma is necessary or should be eliminated.

Of course culture, (eliminate) is transmitted in many ways—through the stories we tell, (necessary) the songs we sing, (necessary) and the events we celebrate. It is difficult to destroy a heritage, (eliminate) through laws, (necessary) though many have tried. I feel a very strong sense of my own culture not because of state laws, (necessary) but because of, (eliminate) my grandparents, (eliminate) and my friends in the neighborhood.

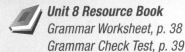
Unit 8 Resource Book
Grammar Worksheet, p. 38
Grammar Check Test, p. 39

Editing Strategy: Using Commas Correctly

Be sure to review the student model. You might begin by reading the passage aloud without pausing for the inserted commas, then read it again, pausing for each comma. For additional support, see the mini-lesson at the bottom of page 899 and the worksheets referenced below.

Unit 8 Resource Book
Grammar Worksheet, p. 38
Grammar Check Test, p. 39

Connections to
Writer's Resource

Refer to the Grammar, Usage, and Mechanics Handbook on Writer's Resource.

STEP 5 PRESENTING
Read Aloud

You might arrange for writers to lead discussions on colonialism after reading their work.

STEP 6 LOOKING BACK
Self-evaluate

The *Assessment Criteria Specs* at the bottom of this page are for a superior paper. You might want to post these in the classroom. Students can then evaluate themselves based on these criteria.

For a complete scoring rubric, use the *Assessment Worksheet* referenced below.

Unit 8 Resource Book
Assessment Worksheet, p. 40

Reflect

Remind students that the United States was a British colony and have them compare the American experience with British colonialism to the other examples they've read about.

To further explore the theme, use the Fine Art Transparency referenced below.

Transparency Collection
Fine Art Writing Prompt 16

900

Editing Strategy

Using Commas Correctly

Without commas, elements of sentences may run together, causing confusion. Notice how this writer paid close attention to commas during editing.

The authors of these works, all from former colonies of the British Empire, have expressed their attitudes toward colonialism in their stories, poems, articles, and essays. One of these authors, Derek Walcott, conveys his attitudes through poetry.

STUDENT MODEL

FOR REFERENCE
You'll find more rules for using commas in the Language and Grammar Handbook at the back of this text.

STEP 5 PRESENTING

- Read your analysis to a world history class that's studying colonialism.
- Locate and share with your classmates art, film, and music that represents the period and culture your author writes about.

STEP 6 LOOKING BACK

Self-evaluate. What grade would you give your paper? Look back at the Writer's Blueprint and give yourself a score on each point, from 6 (superior) to 1 (inadequate).

Reflect. Write answers to these questions.

✔ Put yourself in the place of the colonized people you read about. How would you have felt in their situation?

✔ Compare your writing plan and your final draft. What kinds of changes did you make? What do they tell you about how to use a writing plan?

For Your Working Portfolio Add your analysis and your reflection responses to your working portfolio.

ASSESSMENT CRITERIA SPECS

Here are the criteria for a superior paper.

6 Superior The writer of a 6 paper impressively meets these criteria:

- Begins with a thesis statement that is specific and limited enough to serve as the guiding force for the paper.
- Characterizes the author's attitudes toward colonialism by drawing insightful conclusions based on a careful reading of the author's works.
- Supports these conclusions with pointed examples and quotations from these works.

- Evaluates the author's attitudes toward colonialism by citing the writer's own personal reactions based on specific, relevant reasons.
- Writes concisely throughout, avoiding empty words and phrases.
- Makes few, if any, errors in grammar, usage, mechanics, and spelling. Uses commas correctly.

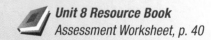

Unit 8 Resource Book
Assessment Worksheet, p. 40

Beyond Print

Propaganda

Propaganda is a systematic effort to spread opinions or beliefs. Advertising uses propaganda techniques to convince us that we need, or want, a product or service. Propaganda can also be used for the public good, such as the nationwide effort to ban smoking in public places. In his wartime speeches, Winston Churchill was a master at convincing people of his viewpoint. Equally adept was his adversary, Adolph Hitler, who used propaganda to incite the Germans to action. Use the following criteria to evaluate ads, articles, and speeches.

Fact and Opinion Examine words and phrases like *clearly*, *everybody knows,* and *without question.* Look at the rest of the statement. Is it a fact that expansion of an airport will improve a community or that building low-income housing will ruin the area?

Authoritative Sources Are speakers qualified to offer an opinion on a given subject? Educational background, professional experience, and personal knowledge are just a few of the factors that make sources reliable. An experienced statesman such as Winston Churchill, for example, would have informed opinions about how to conduct World War II.

Loaded Words Be on the lookout for words designed to appeal to your emotions. In "Shooting an Elephant," George Orwell uses words like *oppressors* and *tyranny* to convey his strong feelings about imperialism and to sway the emotions of his readers.

Testimonial Authority figures or celebrities are often used to support or oppose something. Watch out! A man in a white coat is not necessarily a doctor. An NBA player may not be the best judge of orange juice.

Bandwagon An ad that urges us to buy a book because it is a best seller, or campaign literature urging us to vote for a candidate who is leading in the polls is an example of the bandwagon technique.

Activity Option

Examine these selections, listing words and phrases designed to sway your emotions—for or against the British Empire. Based on biographical information, which authors do you consider authoritative?

Beyond Print **901**

EXPLORING CONCEPTS

- As Britain became a multicultural society, people struggled to find their place in that society.

- As the British Commonwealth disbanded, Britain had to decide how closely to connect to the rest of Europe.

The captions that identify the pieces of the puzzle represent some of the important events in Britain in recent years.

Research Activity   Small groups of students might use the library or online sources to find out the current situation in Northern Ireland, the state of the Royal Family, and the political successes or failures of the current prime minister.

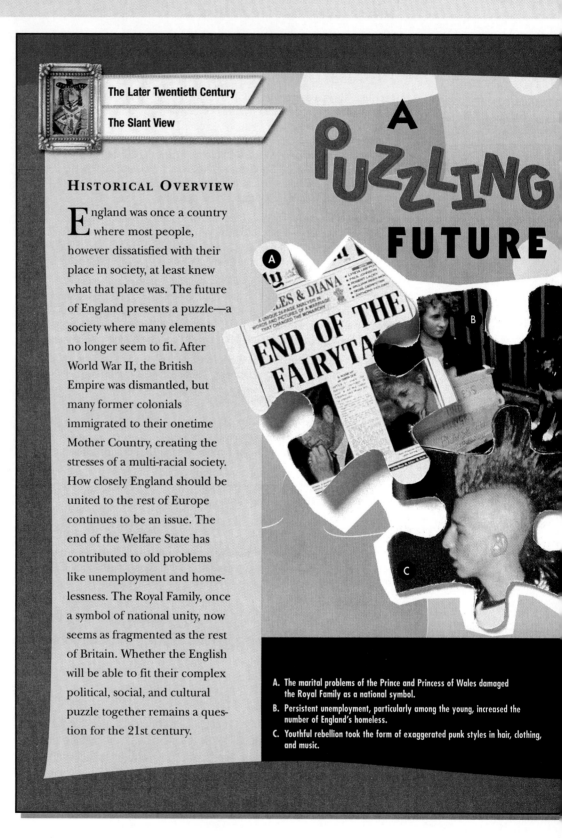

The Later Twentieth Century

The Slant View

A PUZZLING FUTURE

HISTORICAL OVERVIEW

England was once a country where most people, however dissatisfied with their place in society, at least knew what that place was. The future of England presents a puzzle—a society where many elements no longer seem to fit. After World War II, the British Empire was dismantled, but many former colonials immigrated to their onetime Mother Country, creating the stresses of a multi-racial society. How closely England should be united to the rest of Europe continues to be an issue. The end of the Welfare State has contributed to old problems like unemployment and home-lessness. The Royal Family, once a symbol of national unity, now seems as fragmented as the rest of Britain. Whether the English will be able to fit their complex political, social, and cultural puzzle together remains a question for the 21st century.

A. The marital problems of the Prince and Princess of Wales damaged the Royal Family as a national symbol.

B. Persistent unemployment, particularly among the young, increased the number of England's homeless.

C. Youthful rebellion took the form of exaggerated punk styles in hair, clothing, and music.

Key Dates

1972 British troops kill 13 in Northern Ireland on "Bloody Sunday."

1973 England joins the Common Market.

1976 Punk rock becomes popular with British working class youth.

1978 Margaret Thatcher becomes Prime Minister.

1980 Unemployment reaches highest level since 1930s Depression.

1982 England defeats Argentina in the Falklands War.

1984 Widespread strike begins by British miners.

1985 Racial violence breaks out in Brixton.

1994 Channel Tunnel completed.

D. The Channel Tunnel between England and France physically linked the island nation to the European mainland.

E. England's victory over Argentina in the brief Falklands War marked a brief return of British imperialism.

F. Miners were no longer central to a British economy moving away from heavy industry.

G. The erection of Europe's largest Hindu temple indicated England's growing multiculturalism.

H. A hopeful sign was movement in the negotiations to end decades of violence in Northern Ireland.

903

Key Dates

1972 The British government begins direct rule of Northern Ireland.

1979 Lord Mountbatten is assassinated in Ireland by IRA terrorists.

1981 Belize gains independence from Britain; Charles, the Prince of Wales, marries Lady Diana Spencer.

1984 Britain signs treaty with China to return Hong Kong in 1997; Brunei gains independence from Britain.

1990 Margaret Thatcher resigns; John Major becomes Prime Minister.

1991 The Provisional IRA claims responsibility for bombing the British Prime Minister's residence.

Feb. 9, 1996 The IRA ends a seventeen-month cease fire, resuming terrorist activities.

MATERIALS OF INTEREST
Books

- *Disenchantments: An Anthology of Modern Fairy Tale Poetry* edited by Wolfgang Mieder (University Press of New England, 1985).

- *The Norton Anthology of Literature by Women: The Tradition in English* edited by Sandra M. Gilbert and Susan Gubar (Norton, 1985).

Multimedia

The Rise and Fall of the British Empire [videotape], 35 min., b/w and color, VHS. Educational Audio Visual, Order J7VH 0189.

Connections to
Custom Literature Database

For further historical background, under **Background Articles,** see **Modern England 1915–**.

904

Part Two

The Slant View

How are we supposed to regard a world that—as we are told more and more—is not what it appears to be? Modern physics and mathematics have created new dimensions to aid in thinking about the world, and modern philosophy and psychology have their counterparts.

Multicultural Connection **Perspective** It may be that the best way to view an increasingly confusing world is from new **perspectives.** Perspective involves seeing people and events from diverse viewpoints; yet a person's culture has a great influence on the ways that person views such basic and universal aspects of life as youth, time, love, and death.

IDEAS THAT WORK

Motivating with Brainstorming

"**I think it is essential to spend time before reading introducing the basic themes presented.** I begin by having students individually brainstorm similar events in their lives. After this initial step, they share in small groups before sharing as a whole class. They then reflect on any common or central ideas they recognize. Now I finally have them read the selections.

To demonstrate their understanding of the readings and the larger ideas developed during class sharing, I might have them write a personal narrative about one important event, write an essay comparing/contrasting their feelings or memories with those of one of the authors or characters, or allow for them to demonstrate their understanding through art, music, or some other alternative. How the understanding is demonstrated is not really the big issue. What is important is that my students understand the universality of feelings."

Dennis Szymkowiak
Crystal Lake, Illinois

Before Reading

Eve to Her Daughters by Judith Wright
The Frog Prince by Stevie Smith

Not Waving but Drowning by Stevie Smith
The Explorers by Margaret Atwood

Building Background

Poetry's Sources In "Eve to Her Daughters," Judith Wright's inspiration comes from the Genesis account of the first humans to be created. In her poetry, Stevie Smith made use of nursery rhymes, fairy tales, history, and popular songs, employing clever twists and witty verbal maneuvers to create verse that is fresh and engaging. Margaret Atwood says that when she was in high school and college she was writing "borderline literary material" and that she "even wrote an opera about synthetic fabrics for . . . Home Economics class. It was about that time," she says, "I realized I didn't want to be a home economist." The work of these poets proves that the wellsprings of literature are deep and varied, and that artists always bring their own special slant to their work.

Literary Focus

Allusion A brief reference to a person, event, or place, real or fictitious, or to a piece of music or work of art is called an **allusion.** An allusion can concisely convey much information. In the title of his novel, *For Whom the Bell Tolls,* Ernest Hemingway alludes to John Donne's essay (page 228), for example. Edward Albee's play, *Who's Afraid of Virginia Woolf?,* is obviously an allusion, though an obscure one, to the author. Two of the four poems that follow contain allusions.

Writer's Notebook

Yesterdays Writers often recall events from their childhood in their work. In fact, Dylan Thomas based "A Child's Christmas in Wales" (page 824) on such memories. Can you recall a story read to you as a child? childhood games? childhood superstitions? Make a list of some of these memories in your notebook for possible use in a poem, paragraph, or essay.

Eve to Her Daughters   905

Before Reading

Building Background

Ask students to supply the names of famous nursery rhymes and fairy tales—for example, the story of Cinderella—that have become models for contemporary literature and films. Discuss how these stories have been recast with a modern twist. Then explain that the poems students are about to read are reworkings of stories and recognizable situations—with a spin.

Literary Focus

Explain that an allusion is a brief reference to a person, event, or place, real or fictitious, or to a work of art. Have students imagine that someone called them a Judas, a Romeo, or a Michael Jordan. Ask a volunteer to explain the source of each allusion and tell what quality it indicates.

Writer's Notebook

Suggest that students recall a dramatic moment or event from their childhood, perhaps something that made them extremely happy, sad, or frustrated. Encourage them to quickwrite a list of words they associate with the memory. Remind them that they may use these notes for the writing assignment on page 914.

SUPPORT MATERIALS OVERVIEW

Unit 8 Resource Book
- Graphic Organizer, p. 41
- Study Guide, p. 42
- Vocabulary, p. 43
- Grammar, p. 44
- Alternate Check Test, p. 45
- Vocabulary Test, p. 46
- Selection Test, pp. 47–48

Building English Proficiency
- Selection Summaries
- Activities, p. 265

Reading, Writing & Grammar SkillBook
- Reading, pp. 79–80

The World of Work
- Lifeguard, p. 34
- Activities, p. 35

Technology
- Audiotape
- Personal Journal Software
- Test Generator Software

More About Judith Wright

After college, Wright worked in an advertising agency, and as a secretary, a clerk, and a statistician. Later, she was a part-time lecturer at various Australian universities and a literary editor. Although best known as a poet, Wright published a book of short stories in 1966 titled *The Nature of Love* and has written several children's books.

More About Stevie Smith

The British film *Stevie,* starring Glenda Jackson in the title role, is based on the life of Stevie Smith. Smith's poetry, which is often preoccupied with death, includes nursery rhymes, popular songs, even hymns, and employs clever twists and witty wordplay. Other works by Smith include

- *Novel on Yellow Paper* (1936)
- *The Collected Poems of Stevie Smith* (1975)

More About Margaret Atwood

Atwood's works explore, among other things, the tensions between art and life. Some of her best-known works, including *The Handmaid's Tale,* focus on women— their suffering and isolation, along with their resourceful measures to improve their lives. Other works by Atwood include

- *The Circle Game* (1966)
- *The Edible Woman* (1969)
- *Cat's Eye* (1989)

Judith Wright
born 1915

Born in Armidale, New South Wales, Australia, Wright was educated at New England Girls' School in Armidale and the University of Sydney. She has written poetry, children's stories, literary criticism, and works based on the life of her grandfather, who first settled in Australia. Her books of poetry include *Fourth Quarter and Other Poems* (1976) and *The Double Tree: Selected Poems* (1978). She is active in the conservation movement in Australia.

Stevie Smith
1902–1971

Stevie Smith lived most of her life in a London suburb, although she was born in the Yorkshire city of Hull. Christened Florence Margaret, she acquired her nickname when she was horseback riding with a friend, and some boys called to her, "Come on Steve," after a famous jockey. After attending the North London Collegiate School for Girls, she went to work for a magazine publishing company, for whom she worked for thirty years. Her first book of poetry was *A Good Time Was Had by All* (1937). She published three novels and seven more books of poetry, including *Not Waving, but Drowning* (1957) and *The Frog Prince and Other Poems* (1966). *Me Again* (1981) is a collection of some of her short stories, essays, reviews, and letters.

Margaret Atwood
born 1939

Margaret Atwood writes poems, novels, and short stories. She has also written children's books and plays. Born in Ottawa, Canada, she moved to Toronto with her family in 1946 and spent many summers with her parents in the north woods of Canada, resulting in experiences that, according to critic Jerome H. Rosenberg, "have contributed to both the imagery and the vision of her works." Atwood graduated from the University of Toronto and received a master's degree in English from Harvard. She has taught literture and creative writing. Her works include *Lady Oracle* (1976); *Bluebeard's Egg* (1982), a collection of stories; *The Handmaid's Tale* (1985), a novel that won a Governor General's Award; and *Wilderness Trips* (1991), a book of poetry.

SELECTION SUMMARY

Poems

Eve to Her Daughters   Eve says that Adam has reasoned that God, who can't be demonstrated, doesn't exist. She concludes that maybe the only thing that does exist is our faults—they are demonstrable.

The Frog Prince   An enchanted frog says he is content but wants the spell broken anyway, which he thinks would be "heavenly."

Not Waving but Drowning   Acquaintances of a man who has drowned say he was probably

clowning around in cold water and had heart failure. But the dead man says he was "not waving but drowning."

The Explorers   The explorers who come to a tiny island will find the speaker and a companion—who are two skeletons.

 *For summaries in other languages, see the **Building English Proficiency** book.*

Eve to Her Daughters

Judith Wright

> It was not I who began it.
> Turned out into draughty caves,
> hungry so often, having to work for our bread,
> hearing the children whining,
> 5 I was nevertheless not unhappy.
> Where Adam went I was fairly contented to go.
> I adapted myself to the punishment: it was my life.
>
> But Adam, you know . . . !
> He kept on brooding over the insult,
> 10 over the trick They had played on us, over the scolding.
> He had discovered a flaw in himself
> and he had to make up for it.
> Outside Eden the earth was imperfect,
> the seasons changed, the game was fleet-footed,
> 15 he had to work for our living, and he didn't like it.
> He even complained of my cooking
> (it was hard to compete with Heaven).
>
> So, he set to work.
> The earth must be made a new Eden
> 20 with central heating, domesticated animals,
> mechanical harvesters, combustion engines,
> escalators, refrigerators,
> and modern means of communication
> and multiplied opportunities for safe investment
> 25 and higher education for Abel and Cain
> and the rest of the family.
> You can see how his pride has been hurt.

Eve to Her Daughters   **907**

BUILDING ENGLISH PROFICIENCY

Exploring Verbs and Verbals

You can use this page to help students explore English verbs and verb forms.

1. Analyze the first four lines of the poem. Explain that *was* and *began* are the only true verbs in those lines. The verb forms *turned out* and *having* are verbals—specifically, participles (verb forms that act as adjectives). *To work* also is a verbal—an infinitive (in this case, acting as a noun).

2. Have students work in groups to identify the other verb forms on page 907. Encourage them to try to identify each one as a *verb* (e.g., *went, had played,* and *has been hurt*) or a *verbal* (e.g., *hearing, brooding, to compete,* and *multiplied*).

3. As groups share responses, help students with problematic verb forms.

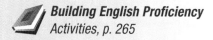
Building English Proficiency
Activities, p. 265

During Reading

Selection Objectives

- to analyze the different perspectives in four modern poems
- to identify allusions in the poems
- to recognize indefinite and definite articles

Unit 8 Resource Book
Graphic Organizer, p. 41
Study Guide, p. 42

Theme Link

The speakers in the poems present the slant view on old stories.

1 **Historical Note**
Eve and Adam

Ask students to recall the creation story in Genesis (pp. 268–271). Review that Adam and Eve—the first man and woman—were tempted by Satan in the form of a serpent. Once they disobeyed God and tasted the fruit of knowledge, they were cast out of Eden. The world outside was one of pain and strife—a world where people had to work and suffer.

2 **Reading/Thinking Skills**
Connect

Draw attention to the first sentence and explain that because of Eve, women have traditionally been blamed for causing discord and the misfortunes of humanity.

Questions

- What other women from the Bible or mythology cause dissension and suffering? *(Possible responses: Eris, Pandora, the Maenads, and Delilah)*
- What in Wright's poem suggests that it is Adam, not Eve, who causes human misery? *(Possible response: He is dissatisfied and set on creating a new Eden.)*

3 Reading/Thinking Skills
Clarify

These two stanzas present a paradox. Here is a possible interpretation:

- Adam has discovered how the world works, probably by applying principles of modern science and physics.

- With this knowledge, he determines that God cannot be demonstrated and therefore doesn't exist.

- Because Adam understands the mechanics of the world, he feels he has invented it (that is, he is God).

- But because Adam/God cannot be demonstrated, he does not exist—a conclusion that Adam refuses to accept.

4 Literary Focus
Allusion

Questions

- Who is "the Other"? *(Satan or the devil)* Cain and Abel? *(the sons of Adam and Eve)*

- What do you think *fallout* (line 44) alludes to? *(probably to nuclear fallout—one more example of the disastrous effects of Adam's tampering with the world)*

In the process he had to unravel everything,
because he believed that mechanism

30 was the whole secret—he was always mechanical-minded.
He got to the very inside of the whole machine
exclaiming as he went, So this is how it works!
And now that I know how it works, why, I must have
          invented it.
As for God and the Other, they cannot be demonstrated,

3 35 and what cannot be demonstrated
doesn't exist.
You see, he had always been jealous.

Yes, he got to the center
where nothing at all can be demonstrated.
40 And clearly he doesn't exist; but he refuses
to accept the conclusion.
You see, he was always an egotist.

4 It was warmer than this in the cave;
there was none of this fallout.
45 I would suggest, for the sake of the children,
that it's time you took over.

But you are my daughters, you inherit my own faults
          of character;
you are submissive, following Adam
even beyond existence.
50 Faults of character have their own logic
and it always works out.
I observed this with Abel and Cain.

Perhaps the whole elaborate fable
right from the beginning
55 is meant to demonstrate this; perhaps it's the whole secret.
Perhaps nothing exists but our faults?

But it's useless to make
such a suggestion to Adam.
He has turned himself into God,
60 who is faultless and doesn't exist.

Does this illustration by Ken Joudry have a humorous or serious **tone**? Explain. ➤

MINI-LESSON: GRAMMAR

Indefinite and Definite Articles

Teach   Ask students to recall what the definite and indefinite articles are. *(The definite article is* the *and the indefinite articles are* a *and* an.*)* Definite articles introduce a particular or exemplary person, place, or thing. Indefinite articles introduce any one of a class of persons, places, or things. Ask students when the article *an* is used. *(before words that begin with vowels or vowel sounds: an egotist, a suggestion, an honor)*

Activity Ideas

- Suggest that students locate a brief stanza or paragraph from another selection in their textbook, copy it onto a sheet of paper, and identify the definite and indefinite articles by circling them in two different

colors of ink. Students should provide a color key for their pages (e.g., black=definite, blue=indefinite).

- Challenge students to compose a sentence that contains five definite articles and three indefinite articles. Ask authors of the most amusing or creative sentences to write them on the board.

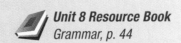
Unit 8 Resource Book
Grammar, p. 44

Questions What is the lesson of this "elaborate fable" (line 53)? How does it tie in with the final two lines of Wright's poem? *(Possible responses: Men should recognize their flaws, temper their knowledge with humility, and not aspire to be God; if women can overcome their tendency to be submissive, they can take over things and improve the world.)*

Art Study

Response to Caption Question The tone appears to be humorous, judging from the jaunty angle of the man's hat and the romantic graffiti in the lower right corner.

Visual Literacy The falling apples and serpent are visual allusions to the biblical story of Adam and Eve. The fact that evil, as represented by the snake, is catching the man off guard adds to the light tone of the picture. If possible, show students a traditional depiction of the temptation of Adam and Eve and invite them to make comparisons.

Questions Do you think it is necessary to know the story of Adam and Eve in order to appreciate this picture? *(Possible responses: Yes, knowing this allusion makes the picture more meaningful; no, even those who don't know the allusion can enjoy the humor.)*

BUILDING ENGLISH PROFICIENCY

Expanding Vocabulary

Encourage students to increase their vocabulary by discussing the many relatively advanced, sophisticated words that Wright employs.

1. Point out the word *unravel* (line 28). Invite any student who may be familiar with the word to explain its meaning. Explain that the word's meaning has been "stretched" (expanded, amplified) to machines. The poet may be speaking metaphorically, likening the tubes, wires, and other "innards" of the machines to knitting or intertwined materials.

2. Discuss the meanings of additional words and phrases on page 908 that may be difficult or unfamiliar. Consider these possibilities: *mechanism, egotist, submissive, mechanical-minded, fallout, logic, demonstrated, inherit, elaborate, jealous, faults of character.*

Reader's Response

Making Personal Connections

Initiate discussion about how people can stay in a bad situation because they fear change or have grown accustomed, perhaps even comfortable, in that situation.

Question Why do you think people are resistant to change? *(Possible response: because they fear the unknown or get accustomed to routine and the familiar)*

Reading/Thinking Skills

Recognize Multiple Meanings

Lead students to recognize and discuss the different meanings of *disenchantment.* *(freedom from false notions; freedom from a magic spell)* and *heavenly* *(divine or holy; happy or excellent)*

Question How do you interpret the final phrase, "Only disenchanted people/Can be heavenly"? *(Possible responses: Only people who face reality can be happy.)*

🎨 Art Study

Response to Caption Question
Students may think that the frog looks more nervous than contented or that his facial expression and body position indicate distress.

The FROG PRINCE

Stevie Smith

I am a frog
I live under a spell
I live at the bottom
Of a green well

5 And here I must wait
Until a maiden places me
On her royal pillow
And kisses me
In her father's palace.

10 The story is familiar
Everybody knows it well
But do other enchanted people feel as
    nervous
As I do? The stories do not tell,

Ask if they will be happier
15 When the changes come,
As already they are fairly happy
In a frog's doom?

I have been a frog now
For a hundred years
20 And in all this time
I have not shed many tears.

I am happy, I like the life,
Can swim for many a mile
(When I have hopped to the river)
25 And am for ever agile.

And the quietness,
Yes, I like to be quiet
I am habituated

To a quiet life,

30 But always when I think these thoughts
As I sit in my well
Another thought comes to me and says:
It is part of the spell

To be happy
35 To work up contentment
To make much of being a frog
To fear disenchantment

Says, It will be *heavenly*
To be set free
40 Cries, *Heavenly* the girl who disenchants
And the royal times, *heavenly*,
And I think it will be.

Come then, royal girl and royal times,
Come quickly,
45 I can be happy until you come
But I cannot be heavenly,
Only disenchanted people
Can be heavenly.

MINI-LESSON: LITERARY FOCUS

Allusion

Teach Remind students that many of Stevie Smith's poems allude to childhood stories and nursery rhymes. Point out that "The Frog Prince" alludes to a fairy tale. Call on a volunteer to briefly summarize the fairy tale about the princess and the frog. *(The main points to bring out are the princess must kiss the frog so that the spell cast on him is broken and he can turn back into a handsome prince, but it is difficult to find anyone who would kiss a frog.)*

Questions What is the poem's allusion to a "spell" in lines 2 and 33 and to "enchanted people" in line 12, "disenchantment" in line 37, and "disenchanted people" in line 47? *(All these lines allude to the spell, or*

enchantment, that has turned the prince into a frog.) Might the words *disenchantment* and *disenchanted* have other meanings? *(They also can mean disillusionment and disillusioned in the sense of disappointment and disappointed.)*

Activity Idea Invite students to write a response to the frog prince in which they allude to other fairy tales or stories they know where the spell of an enchanted person has been broken. What became of the people in those stories?

NOT WAVING BUT DROWNING

Stevie Smith

Nobody heard him, the dead man,
But still he lay moaning:
I was much farther out than you thought
And not waving but drowning.

5 Poor chap, he always loved larking
And now he's dead
It must have been too cold for him his heart gave way,
They said.

O no no no, it was cold always
10 (Still the dead one lay moaning)
I was much too far out all my life
And not waving but drowning.

◄ The Frog Prince in Stevie Smith's poem says he feels
both nervous and contented. Does her drawing of him
suggest either feeling?

---

7 Reading/Thinking Skills
Visualizing

Ask students to visualize the scene described here. Invite them to explain how someone in this situation could be misunderstood to be waving instead of drowning.

8 Reading/Thinking Skills
Understanding Idioms and Puns

Draw attention to Stevie Smith's use of the terms "farther out" and "far out" in the poem. Invite discussion about what "far out" means both literally *(at a great distance)* and figuratively *(departing from the conventional).*

Question   How do you interpret line 3, "I was much farther out than you thought"? *(Possible response: The drowning man was literally in deep water—too far out from shore; perhaps he was also "far out" figuratively because he was wild, "loved larking," and consequently not taken seriously, even when he was calling for help.)*

9 Literary Criticism
Who's Waving?

Some critics think that the title and poem provide a metaphor for the creative artist, whose works are considered "far out" and misinterpreted by the public. Other critics think the poem refers to all those people living on the periphery—nonconformists and individuals who are rejected, misinterpreted, and ignored by mainstream society.

BUILDING ENGLISH PROFICIENCY

ESL
LEP
ELD
SAE
LD

Exploring Folklore

Use one or both of these activities to enhance students' appreciation of "The Frog Prince."

Activity Ideas

• Provide students with a variety of print and video versions of this classic fairy tale. Have student pairs or small groups read or watch a version of their choice and then share their impressions with the class. Encourage discussion of that version and how the version supports or differs from Smith's poem.

• Encourage students to share similar fairy tales from their native cultures. Ask them to determine if differences that exist between the English versions and theirs is cultural or geographical. For example, if another version has an animal other than a frog, is it because the animal has a certain symbolism in their country?

The World of Work

Lifeguard
For the real-life experiences of a lifeguard, use—

The World of Work
pp. 33–34

911

912

10 Literary Element
Free Verse

Remind students that free verse is written without a regular metrical pattern and seldom uses rhymes at the ends of lines. It is regarded as poetry because of its rhythm and its use of poetic devices such as alliteration, internal rhyme, repetition, imagery, and concentrated language.

11 Reading/Thinking Skills
Infer

Questions Who do you think is the speaker in the poem? Do you think this speaker is a survivor or not? *(Possible responses: The speaker appears to be someone narrating thoughts just before dying. This may be the person who survived longer than his or her partner, but who will be one of two skeletons once the explorers come ashore. Some students may think that the speaker is a third party, another castaway who has survived the two skeletons.)*

Check Test

1. In "Eve to Her Daughters," to what story does the poem allude? *(to the biblical story of Adam and Eve being expelled from Eden)*

2. Why does Adam decide that God does not exist? *(because He cannot be demonstrated)*

3. What kind of people can be heavenly, according to the title character in "The Frog Prince"? *(disenchanted people)*

4. In "The Explorers," what do the explorers find? *(two skeletons)*

5. Which poem contains an allusion to a fairy tale? *("The Frog Prince")*

Unit 8 Resource Book
Alternate Check Test, p. 45

The Explorers

Margaret Atwood

10

The explorers will come
in several minutes
and find this island.

5 (It is a stunted island,
rocky, with room
for only a few trees, a thin
layer of soil; hardly
bigger than a bed.
That is how they've missed it
10 until now)

Already their boats draw near,
their flags flutter,
their oars push at the water.

They will be jubilant
15 and shout, at finding
that there was something
they had not found before,

although this island will afford
not much more than a foothold:
20 little to explore;

but they will be surprised

(we can't see them yet;
we know they must be
coming, because they always come
25 several minutes too late)

(they won't be able
to tell how long
we were cast away, or why,
or, from these
30 gnawed bones,
which was the survivor)

11 at the two skeletons

MINI-LESSON: READING/THINKING SKILLS

Analyzing

Teach Tell students that to analyze something is to notice details, see possible interrelationships, and think them through. This poem may be straightforward, but it may have a more complex interpretation.

Questions Who is speaking in this poem? *(a dead person, one of two skeletons on an island)* Who are the explorers? *(Answers will vary.)* Reexamine lines 23–25. About whom do people often say that they always come too late? *(the police)* What clue in the poem suggests that the speaker may be somewhere other than on a real island? (The size of the island is "hardly bigger than a bed.") If the explorers are really the police, then who might the two skeletons be? *(Accept logically supported interpretations.)*

Activity Idea Invite students to think of other defensible interpretations. *(Another is rescuers arriving too late at a cave-in.)*

After Reading

Making Connections

Shaping Your Response

1. Which one of these poems seems most modern to you?

2. What things do you associate with being "cast away"?

Analyzing the Poems

3. What can you **infer** is the "secret" Adam was trying to discover in "Eve to Her Daughters"?

4. If Adam has "turned himself into God, / Who . . . doesn't exist," where does this leave Adam?

5. How do the last four lines of "The Frog Prince" explain why he is eager for the "royal girl" to arrive?

6. What can you infer is the social criticism implied in the title and the **repetition** of the line "not waving but drowning"?

7. What is **ironic** about the fact that the explorers of Atwood's poem will find two skeletons?

8. Do you think the speaker in "The Explorers" is the survivor? Discuss.

Extending the Ideas

9. In Wright's poem, Adam thought that "what cannot be demonstrated doesn't exist." Do you think that everything in this world can be demonstrated? Explain.

Literary Focus: Allusion

An **allusion** is a brief reference to a person, event, or place, real or fictitious, or to a piece of music or work of art. Much information can be conveyed concisely in an allusion.

1. Wright refers to a "new Eden." What do you have to know to understand this allusion?

2. Is there a connection between Wright's reference to Adam's character and modern people? Explain.

3. To what traditional literary form does Smith allude in "The Frog Prince"?

The Explorers   913

LITERARY FOCUS: ALLUSION

1. To understand this allusion to a "new Eden," students must know what the "old" Eden was like.

2. Responses will vary, but students should infer that the poet may be comparing Adam to modern people because most of Adam's inventions are modern inventions; examples include central heating, escalators, and refrigerators (lines 20–25).

3. In "The Frog Prince," Smith is alluding to the traditional literary form of the fairy tale.

After Reading

MAKING CONNECTIONS

1. Before students answer, you might elicit discussion on what constitutes "modern" poetry. (free verse? satiric tone? multiple interpretations? contemporary subject matter?)

2. Answers may include items such as shipwrecks, debris, trash, and useless objects. Students might also mention emotions such as alienation, loneliness, and rejection.

3. Possible responses: the key to the universe; scientific answers

4. Possible response: If Adam becomes God, who doesn't exist, then Adam likewise doesn't exist.

5. The frog prince is content with his present state of enchantment, but he has a chance for a "heavenly" future with the princess once the spell is lifted.

6. Possible responses: Society often misunderstands or ignores the requests for help of unconventional people; society often rejects its artists.

7. Possible responses: The explorers, who expect to be the first people to find the island, will discover that others (the skeletons) have found the island earlier; the explorers arrive "several minutes too late"; they had expected to find something valuable but find death instead.

8. Accept any reasonable inference. Perhaps the speaker is one of the skeletons, who died just before the explorers came; perhaps the speaker is a third party who survives.

9. Responses will vary and may depend on students' personal beliefs, but they should be supported with clear explanations.

 Unit Resource Book
Vocabulary, p. 43
Vocabulary Test, p. 46

913

Expressing Your Ideas

Writing Choices

Writer's Notebook Update Compare your lists of childhood memories with a partner and collaborate on a poem using some of these remembrances.

The *Real* Story Think of a character in a fairy tale, fable, or old story that you know well, and give that character a new point of view. Maybe Cinderella didn't want to marry the prince? Maybe Dorothy's dog, Toto, didn't really like being carried all over Oz? Write your version as a **journal entry** made by the character you choose.

Dear Mom Assume that you are one of the daughters to whom Eve has addressed her remarks in Judith Wright's poem. In a **letter** to Eve, react to your mother's analysis and criticism of your father, Adam.

Other Options

Composing Set "Not Waving but Drowning" to music. Think about the tempo, whether it will be in a major or minor key, and whether it will have a refrain. You may have to rewrite the poem slightly to make it into a lyric. Perform your **song** for the class.

A Perfect Place Using any medium you wish, create an **artwork** depicting a "new Eden." Consider whether it will contain people (if so, who?), where it will be situated, and whether it will contain buildings, animals, and /or natural surroundings. You may wish to review the description in Genesis (pages 268–271), and then decide what would make your new place "perfect."

You Won't Believe What I Tell You Take on the character of an explorer and tell the story of how you discovered an island or other surprising place—but tell it as a **tall tale.** Imagine that your audience is gathered for a luncheon at a natural history museum and that you're their entertaining speaker. Exaggerate as wildly as you please, but remember that a tall tale is always told with a completely straight face. If you like, illustrate your talk with some "snapshots" or "slides" that you have taken.

Before Reading

The Truly Married Woman

by Abioseh Nicol

Abioseh Nicol
1924–1994

Dr. Davidson Sylvester Hector Willoughby Nicol—Abioseh (ab ē ō′sə) was a pen name—was born in Freetown, Sierra Leone. He earned B.A., M.A., M.D., and Ph.D degrees and was ambassador from Sierra Leone to the United Nations from 1968 to 1971. He was also Under Secretary General of the United Nations and the executive director of the United Nations Institute for Training and Research until his retirement in 1982. He taught at the University of South Carolina and the Center of International Studies at Cambridge University in England, published many articles on medicine, education, and politics, and wrote poetry and short stories. His story collections include *The Truly Married Woman and Other Stories* and *Two African Tales*, both published in 1965.

Building Background

The Lure of Tradition Tradition plays an important part in this story, and though the beliefs, customs, and opinions may not be quite the same as those in your family, you may find many similarities. While it is true that the couple in the story at first have a somewhat unconventional lifestyle, they are fully aware that their arrangement is not acceptable in their church or their families, though it seems acceptable to many of their neighbors. The author explores the effect of tradition on the lives of his characters, and in an ironic twist shows how, finally, adherence to tradition results in a nontraditional outcome, illustrating once again that there is no one **perspective** on how to live one's life.

Literary Focus

Point of View The vantage point from which an author presents the actions and characters in a story is called **point of view.** The story may be related by a character (*first-person* point of view), or by a narrator who does not participate in the actions (*third-person* point of view). The third-person narrator may be *omniscient*—able to see into the minds of all characters; *limited*—confined to a single character's perception; or *objective*—describing only what can be seen. Decide the point of view as you read the following story.

Writer's Notebook

Crime and Punishment Have you ever been punished unjustly, either for something you didn't know was wrong or for something you didn't do? Write about the situation in your notebook, telling about the incident and how you feel about it now.

The Truly Married Woman **915**

Before Reading

Building Background

Ask students to mention traditions in their families and cultures. Ask how such traditions came to be. Which traditions will students be expected to carry on? What would happen if they rejected such traditions?

Literary Focus

Remember that the narrator of a story presents facts from his or her point of view. To determine how important point of view can be, try looking at something from an aerial view, through a magnifying glass, or upside down.

Writer's Notebook

Ask students if they have ever heard the maxim: "Spare the rod and spoil the child"? Help them determine what it means and ask if they agree.

More About Abioseh Nicol

Nicol was a diplomat, physician, and medical researcher. He was also principal of Fourah Bay College in Sierra Leone from 1960 to 1967 and vice-chancellor of the University of Sierra Leone. Other works by Nicol include

- *Africa, A Subjective View* (1964)
- *West African Verse* (1967)
- *Creative Women in Changing Societies* (1982)

SUPPORT MATERIALS OVERVIEW

Unit 8 Resource Book
- Graphic Organizer, p. 49
- Study Guide, p. 50
- Vocabulary, p. 51
- Grammar, p. 52
- Alternate Check Test, p. 53
- Vocabulary Test, p. 54
- Selection Test, pp. 55–56

Building English Proficiency
- Selection Summaries
- Activities, p. 266

Reading, Writing & Grammar SkillBook
- Vocabulary, pp. 79–80
- Grammar, Usage, and Mechanics, pp. 171–172

Technology
- Audiotape
- Personal Journal Software
- Test Generator Software

Selection Objectives

- to analyze the significance of perspectives in the story
- to identify point of view
- to examine traditions of another culture as depicted in the story
- to recognize the use of appositives

Unit 8 Resource Book
Graphic Organizer, p. 49
Study Guide, p. 50

Theme Link

The cosmopolitan Abioseh Nicol offers a unique perspective, a slanting view, on his culture and explores the effect of traditions on the lives of his characters.

Vocabulary Preview

officiously, too readily offering services or advice; meddling

tirade, long, scolding speech

ostentatious, showing off

deterrent, something that discourages or hinders

abode, place of residence; house or home

mien, manner of holding the head and body; way of acting and looking

anomaly, something deviating from the rule; something abnormal

disparage, speak slightingly of; belittle

trepidation, fear; fright

Students can add the words and definitions to their Writer's Notebooks.

1 ### Geographical Note
Where Is Sierra Leone?

Although we cannot be sure of exactly where this story takes place, we know that it is an African town similar to those in Sierra Leone, where Nicol was born. Locate Sierra Leone on a map or globe. *(the west coast of Africa, bordered on the south by Liberia, and on the west by the Atlantic Ocean)*

916

THE TRULY MARRIED WOMAN

Abioseh Nicol

1 AJAYI stirred for a while and then sat up. He looked at the cheap alarm clock on the chair by his bedside. It was six-fifteen, and light outside already; the African town was slowly waking to life. The night-watchmen roused from sleep by the angry crowing of cockerels were officiously[1] banging the locks of stores and houses to assure themselves and their employers, if near, of their efficiency. Village women were tramping through the streets to the market place with their wares, arguing and gossiping.

Ajayi sipped his cup of morning tea. It was as he liked it, weak and sugary, without milk. With an effort of will, he got up and walked to the window, and standing there he took six deep breaths. This done daily, he firmly believed, would prevent tuberculosis. He walked through his ramshackle compound to an outhouse and took a quick bath, pouring the water over his head from a tin cup with which he scooped water from a bucket.

By then Ayo had laid out his breakfast. Ayo was his wife. Not really one, he would explain to close friends, but a mistress. A good one. She had borne him three children and was now three months gone with another. They had been together for twelve years. She was a patient, handsome woman. Very dark with very white teeth and open sincere eyes. Her hair was always carefully plaited. When she first came to him—to the exasperation of her parents—he had fully intended marrying her as soon as she had shown satisfactory evidence of fertility, but he had never quite got round to it. In the first year or so she would report to him in great detail the splendor of the marriage celebrations of her friends, looking at him with hopeful eyes. He would close the matter with a tirade[2] on the sinfulness of ostentation.[3] She gave up after some

---

1. officiously (ə fish′əs lē), *adv.* too readily offering services or advice; meddling.
2. tirade (tī′rād), *n.* long, scolding speech.
3. ostentation (os′ten tā′shən), *n.* showing off.

916 Unit Eight: The Later Twentieth Century

SELECTION SUMMARY

The Truly Married Woman

Ajayi has been living with Ayo for 12 years in their African village where he works as a government clerk. He has "never quite got round" to marrying her. She has had his three children and is pregnant. Ayo gets up at 5:00 every morning to make his tea and breakfast.

Three missionaries arrive at Ajayi's office looking for him. On an impulse he invites them and his boss to his house. Thinking Ajayi is married, one takes a picture of Ajayi and his family as a "saved and happy African family." After they leave, Ajayi asks Ayo to marry him.

The morning after their wedding, Ajayi finds Ayo still in bed, not in the kitchen making his tea. He asks if she is ill; she replies, "Now I am a truly married woman you must treat me with a little more respect. . . . make yourself a cup of tea."

 *For summaries in other languages, see the **Building English Proficiency** book.*

time. Her father never spoke to her again after she had left home. Her mother visited her secretly and attended the baptismal ceremonies of all her children. The Church charged extra for illegitimate children as a deterrent;[4] two dollars instead of fifty cents. Apart from this, there was no other great objection. Occasionally, two or three times a year, the pastor would preach violently against adultery, polygamy, and unmarried couples living together. Ajayi and Ayo were good church-people and attended regularly, but sat in different pews.

After such occasions, their friends would sympathize with them and other couples in similar positions. There would be a little grumbling and the male members of the congregation would say that the trouble with the Church was that it did not stick to its business of preaching the Gospel, but meddled in people's private lives. Ajayi would indignantly absent himself from Church for a few weeks but would go back eventually because he liked singing hymns and because he knew secretly that the pastor was right.

Ayo was a good mistress. Her father was convinced she could have married a high-school teacher at least, or a pharmacist, but instead, she had attached herself to a junior Government clerk. But Ayo loved Ajayi, and was happy in her own slow, private way. She cooked his meals and bore him children. In what spare time she had she either did a little petty trading, visited friends, or gossiped with Omo, the woman next door. **2**

With his towel round his waist, Ajayi strode back to the bedroom, dried himself and dressed quickly but carefully in his pink tussore[5] suit. He got down the new bottle of patent medicine which one of his friends who worked in a drug store had recommended to him. Ajayi believed that to keep healthy, a man must regularly take a dose of some medicine. He read the label of this one. It listed about twenty diseased conditions of widely differing pathology[6] which the contents of the bottle were reputed to cure if the patient persevered in its daily intake. Ajayi underlined in his own mind at least six from which he believed he either suffered or was on the threshold of suffering: dizziness, muscle pain, impotence, fever, jaundice, and paralytic tremors. Intelligence and courage caused him to skip the obviously female maladies and others

---

4. **deterrent** (di tėr′ənt), *n.* something that discourages or hinders.
5. **tussore** (tus′ōr), *adj.* made from *tussah*, a coarse, Asian silk.
6. **pathology** (pa thol′ə jē), *n.* unhealthy conditions and processes caused by a disease.

The Truly Married Woman   **917**

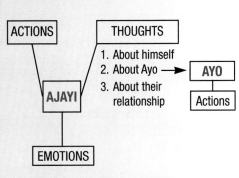
BUILDING ENGLISH PROFICIENCY

Understanding Characters

Nicol reveals Ajayi's character by presenting Ajayi's thoughts, actions, and emotions. Ayo's character is revealed through her own actions and through Ajayi's thoughts. Help students examine both characters by using a diagram such as the one shown. Encourage them to use the diagrams in answering the After Reading questions and to pinpoint statements that indicate Ajayi's underestimation or complete misunderstanding of Ayo.

ACTIONS — AJAYI — EMOTIONS

THOUGHTS
1. About himself
2. About Ayo → AYO
3. About their relationship → Actions

Building English Proficiency
Activities, p. 266

Response to Caption Question
These painted figurines reflect qualities of African folk art, while at the same time depicting a contemporary Western bridal party. Further, the men with cameras are capturing the scene on film, which suggests another perspective.

Visual Literacy   One of the many things that makes this work of art interesting is the fact that we as viewers are looking at a scene as it is being photographed. We are witnesses to a significant moment in people's lives, "frozen" both by the cameras and the artist.

Question   What form of art would you choose to capture a memorable moment in your life—for example, high school graduation, first car, or marriage?

---

2   **Reading/Thinking Skills**
Infer

In the first few paragraphs, we learn a lot about the lives of Ajayi and Ayo.

Question   Based on information provided, what can you infer about the following:

- their union *(It seems happy; even though she is expected to wait on him; they are compatible.)*
- the church's view of their union *(It half-heartedly tries to deter such unions with extra charges and occasional tirades but doesn't object strenuously.)*
- Ayo's relationship with her parents *(Her father has disowned her, but her mother visits her and attends the children's baptisms.)*
- their way of life *(They live in a ramshackle compound, she waits on him and trades and gossips in her spare time.)*

Reader's Response

Making Personal Connections

Questions

- Do you think that Ayo's argument against beating their son is a good one? Would you add anything to her words? *(Possible response: The argument seems logical and convincing.)*

- Do you think Ajayi has found her argument convincing? *(Apparently so; he seems proud of her and decides he will not beat his son again.)*

- Does it surprise you that, given her culture, Ayo speaks up to Ajayi and acts independently? *(Possible responses: Yes, at first she seemed submissive; no, she has already shown her independence by defying her parents and living with Ajayi.)*

4 Literary Element

Foreshadowing

Ayo's feminist leanings make Ajayi proud. He considers her an asset.

Question   Given what you know about Ajayi, do you think her support of women's issues and groups will turn out to be an asset to him? *(Possible responses: Yes, he likes her spirit; no, he is too much a chauvinist.)*

---

such as nervous debility or bladder pains. It said on the label too that a teaspoonful should be taken three times a day. But since he only remembered to take it in the morning and in any case believed in shock treatment, he took a swig and two large gulps. The medicine was bitter and astringent. He grimaced but was satisfied. It was obviously a good and strong medicine or else it would not have been so bitter.

He went in to breakfast. He soon finished his maize porridge, fried beans, and cocoa. He then severely flogged his eldest son, a ten-year-old boy, for wetting his sleeping-mat last night. Ayo came in after the boy had fled screaming to the backyard.

"Ajayi, you flog that boy too much," she said. "He should stop wetting the floor, he is a big boy," he replied. "In any case, no one is going to instruct me on how to bring up my son." "He is mine too," Ayo said. She seldom opposed him unless she felt strongly about something. "He has not stopped wetting, although you beat him every time he does. In fact, he is doing it more and more now. Perhaps if you stopped whipping him he might get better." "Did I whip him to begin doing it?" Ajayi asked. "No." "Well, how will stopping whipping him stop him doing it?" Ajayi asked triumphantly. "Nevertheless," Ayo said, "our own countrywoman Bimbola, who has just come back from England and America studying nursing, told us in a women's group meeting that it was wrong to punish children for such things." "All right, I'll see," he said, reaching for his sun-helmet.

All that day at the office he thought about this and other matters. So Ayo had been attending women's meetings. Well, what do you know. She would be running for the Town Council next. The sly woman. Always looking so quiet and meek and then quoting modern theories from overseas doctors at him. He smiled with pride. Indeed Ayo was an asset. Perhaps it was wrong to beat the boy. He decided he would not do so again.

Towards closing-time the chief clerk sent for him. Wondering what mistake he had made that day, or on what mission he was to be sent, he hurried along to the forward office. There were three white men sitting on chairs by the chief clerk, who was an aging African dressed with severe respectability. On seeing them, Ajayi's heart started thudding. The police, he thought; heavens, what have I done?

"Mr. Ajayi, these gentlemen have inquired for you," the chief clerk said formally. "Pleased to meet you, Mr. Ajayi," the tallest said, with a smile. "We represent the World Gospel Crusading Alliance from Minnesota. My name is Jonathan Olsen." Ajayi shook hands and the other two were introduced.

"You expressed an interest in our work a year ago and we have not forgotten. We are on our way to India and we thought we would look you up personally."

It transpired that the three Crusaders were *en route* and that their ship had stopped for refueling off the African port for a few hours. The chief clerk looked at Ajayi with new respect. Ajayi tried desperately to remember any connection with W.G.C.A. (as Olsen by then had proceeded to call it) whilst he made conversation with them a little haltingly. Then suddenly he remembered. Some time ago he had got hold of a magazine from his sub-tenant who worked at the United States Information Service. He had cut a coupon from it and posted it to W.G.C.A. asking for information, but really hoping that they would send illustrated Bibles free which he might give away or sell. He hoped for at least large reproductions of religious paintings which, suitably framed, would decorate his parlor or which he might paste up on his bedroom wall. But nothing had come of it and he had forgotten. Now here was W.G.C.A. as large as life. Three lives. Instantly and recklessly he invited all three and the chief clerk to come to his house for a cold drink. They all agreed.

"Mine is a humble abode,"[7] he warned them.

---

7. abode (ə bōd′), *n.* place of residence; house or home.

MINI-LESSON: GRAMMAR

Appositives

Teach   An appositive is a noun or noun phrase placed right after another and giving more information about the first. Appositives are set off by commas. Either one of the nouns or noun phrases could be omitted without seriously changing the meaning or the grammar of the sentence. Example: Prince Charles, the heir to the throne of England, arrived early.

To demonstrate, have a student rewrite this sentence so that it contains an appositive: The chief clerk, who was an aging and well-dressed African, sat near three white men. *(The chief clerk, an aging and well-dressed African, sat near three white men.)*

Activity Idea   Suggest that students locate in a newspaper article a sentence containing appositives, highlight or underline the sentence, and bring it to class. Post the sentences in the classroom. Discuss any sentences that are incorrectly identified as containing appositives.

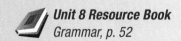

Unit 8 Resource Book
Grammar, p. 52

"No abode is humble that is illumined[8] by Christian love," Olsen replied. "His is illumined all right, I can assure you," the chief clerk remarked dryly.

Olsen suggested a taxi, but Ajayi neatly blocked that by saying the roads were bad. He had hurriedly whispered to a fellow clerk to rush home on a bicycle and tell Ayo he was coming in half an hour with white men and that she should clean up and get fruit drinks. Ayo was puzzled by the message as she firmly imagined all white men drank only whisky and iced beer. But the messenger had said that there was a mixture of friendliness and piety in the visitors' mien,[9] which made him suspect that they might be missionaries. Another confirmatory point was that they were walking instead of being in a car. That cleared up the anomaly[10] in Ayo's mind and she set to work at once. Oju, now recovered from his morning disgrace, was dispatched with a basket on his head to buy soft drinks. Ayo whisked off the wall all their commercial calendars with suggestive pictures. She propped up family photographs which had fallen face downwards on the table. She removed the Wild West novels and romance magazines from the parlor and put instead an old copy of Bunyan's *Pilgrim's Progress* [11] and a prayer-book which she believed would add culture and religious force to the decorations. She remembered the wine glasses and the beer-advertising table-mats in time and put those under the sofa. She just had time to change to her Sunday frock and borrow a wedding ring from her neighbor when Ajayi and the guests arrived. The chief clerk was rather surprised at the changes in the room—which he had visited before—and in Ayo's dress and ring. But he concealed his feelings. Ayo was introduced and made a little conversation in English. This pleased Ajayi a great deal. The children had been changed too into Sunday suits, faces washed and hair brushed. Olsen was delighted and insisted on taking photographs for the Crusade journal. Ayo served drinks and then

modestly retired, leaving the men to discuss serious matters. Olsen by then was talking earnestly on the imminence[12] of Christ's Second Coming and offering Ajayi ordination[13] into deaconship.

EVALUATE: What is Ayo assuming by making all the changes in her house?

The visit passed off well and soon the missionaries left to catch their boat. Ajayi had been saved from holy orders by the chief clerk's timely explanation that it was strictly against Government regulations for civil servants to indulge in non-official organisations. To help Ajayi out of his quandary, he had even gone further and said that contravention[14] might result in a fine or imprisonment. "Talk about colonial oppression," the youngest of the missionaries had said, gloomily.

The next day Ajayi called at the chief clerk's office with a carefully wrapped bottle of beer as a present for his help generally on the occasion. They discussed happily the friendliness and interest the white men had shown.

This incident and Ayo's protest against flagellation[15] as a specific against enuresis[16] made Ajayi very thoughtful for a week. He decided to marry Ayo. Another consideration which added weight to the thought was the snapshot Olsen took for

---

8. **illumine** (i lü′mən), *v.* make bright.
9. mien (mēn), *n.* manner of holding the head and body; way of acting and looking.
10. anomaly (ə nom′ə lē), *n.* something deviating from the rule; something abnormal.
11. **Bunyan's *Pilgrim's Progress*,** a long, prose allegory by John Bunyan, published in 1678 and 1684, that tells of a Christian's progress from this world to Heaven.
12. **imminence** (im′ə nəns), *n.* likeliness; probability of happening soon.
13. **ordination** (ôrd′n ā′shən), *n.* act or ceremony of making a person a member of the clergy.
14. contravention (kon′trə ven′shən), *n.* conflict; opposition.
15. **flagellation** (flaj′ə lā′shən), *n.* a whipping.
16. **enuresis** (en′yù rē′sis), *n.* bed-wetting.

The Truly Married Woman **919**

Questions

- What biases and propaganda does the phrase "one saved and happy African family" suggest? *(Possible response: It implies that an entire cultural group must be "saved" and made respectable by white missionaries.)*

- Look again at the picture on page 916. Do you think it is a good accompaniment to this story? *(Possible response: Yes, the concept of public image comes through both in the art and in this passage.)*

9 **Literary Element**

Dramatic Irony

When Ajayi finally proposes, Ayo cautions him, "Do not say I forced you into it." Remind students that dramatic irony occurs when the reader sees something about characters that they themselves do not recognize.

Questions

- In this passage, why does Ayo's rejection of Ajayi seem ironic? *(She rejects his advances, saying they should wait until the marriage, although they have been living together 12 years.)*

- What suggests that Ayo now has the upper hand in their relationship? *(She is determined; he is obedient.)*

his magazine. In some peculiar way Ajayi felt he and Ayo should marry, as millions of Americans would see their picture—Olsen had assured him of this—as "one saved and happy African family." He announced his intention of marrying her to Ayo one evening, after a particularly good meal and a satisfactory bout of belching. Ayo at once became extremely solicitous and got up looking at him with some anxiety. Was he ill? she asked. Was there anything wrong at the office? Had anyone insulted him? No, he answered, there was nothing wrong with his wanting to get married, was there? Or had she anyone else in mind? Ayo laughed, "As you will," she said; "let us get married, but do not say I forced you into it."

They discussed the wedding that night. Ajayi wanted to have a white wedding with veil and orange blossom. But Ayo with regret decided it would not be quite right. They agreed on gray. Ayo particularly wanted a corset to strap down her obvious bulge; Ajayi gave way gallantly to this feminine whim, chucking her under the chin and saying, "You women with your vanity!" But he was firm about no honeymoon. He said he could not afford the expense and that one bed was as good as another. Ayo gave way on that. They agreed, however, on a church wedding and that their children could act as bridal pages to keep the cost of clothes within the family.

That evening Ajayi, inflamed by the idea and arrangements for the wedding, pulled Ayo excitedly to him as they lay in bed. "No," said Ayo, shyly, pushing him back gently, "you mustn't. Wait until after the marriage." "Why?" said Ajayi, rather surprised, but obedient. "Because it will not somehow be right," Ayo replied seriously and determinedly.

Ayo's father unbent somewhat when he heard of the proposed marriage. He insisted, however, that Ayo move herself and all her possessions back home to his house. The children were sent to Ayo's married sister. Most of Ajayi's family were in favor of the union, except his sister, who, moved by the threat implicit in Ayo's improved social position, had advised Ajayi to

see a soothsayer first. As Ayo had got wind of this through friends met at market on Saturday, she saw the soothsayer first and fixed things. When Ajayi and his sister called at night to see him, he had, after consulting the oracles, pronounced future happiness, avoiding the sister's eye. The latter had restrained herself from scratching the old man's face and had accepted defeat.

The only other flaw in a felicitous situation had been Ayo's neighbor Omo, who had always on urgent occasions at short notice loaned Ayo her wedding ring. She had suddenly turned cold. Especially after Ayo had shown her the wedding presents Ajayi intended to give her. The neighbor had handled the flimsy nylon articles with a mixture of envy and rage.

"Do you mean you are going to wear these?" she had asked. "Yes," Ayo had replied simply. "But, my sister," she had protested, "you will catch cold with these. Suppose you had an accident and all those doctors lifted your clothes in hospital. They will see everything through these." "I never have accidents," Ayo answered, and added, "Ajayi says all the Hollywood cinema women wear these. It says so there. Look— 'Trademark Hollywood.'" "These are disgraceful; they hide nothing, it is extremely fast of you to wear them," the jealous girl said, pushing them back furiously over the fence to Ayo.

"Why should I want to hide anything from my husband when we are married?" Ayo said triumphantly, moving back to her own kitchen and feeling safe in future from the patronizing way the wedding ring had always been lent her.

The arrangements had to be made swiftly, since time and the corset ribs were both against them; Ajayi's domestic routine was also sorely tried, especially his morning cup of tea which he badly missed. He borrowed heavily from a moneylender to pay the dowry and for the music, dancing, and feasting, and for dresses of the same pattern which Ayo and her female relations would wear after the ceremony on the wedding day.

The engagement took place quietly, Ajayi's

MINI-LESSON: READING/THINKING SKILLS

Recognizing Cause and Effect

Teach Remind students that an effect is something that happens because of something else, which is called the cause. Ask: Have you ever had a friend who seemed to like you only when you were unhappy or in trouble? Some people can remain friends with you only as long as they have the "upper hand"—have some control over you. Sometimes we lose these friends when we show them we are no longer dependent on them.

Question Why do you think Ayo's neighbor Omo has suddenly turned cold toward her? Why does she act with envy, jealousy, and rage toward Ayo when shown Ayo's wedding gifts from her husband-to-be? *(Omo's*

jealousy and anger toward Ayo are caused by her learning that Ayo will soon marry and will no longer need to borrow Omo's wedding ring to appear respectable. Omo will no longer have the upper hand because she and Ayo will be equals.)

Activity Idea Ask each student to make a list of five other causes and effects in the story. Then have students share their lists and, omitting duplicates, see how many causes and effects the class has recognized in the story.

uncle and other relations taking a Bible and a ring to Ayo's father and asking for her hand in marriage, the day before the wedding. They took with them two small girls carrying on their heads large hollow gourds. These contained articles like pins, farthings, fruit, kola nuts, and cloth. The articles were symbolic gifts to the bride from the bridegroom, so that she might be precluded in future marital disputes from saying, "Not a pin or a farthing has the black-guard given me since we got married."

On arrival at Ayo's father's house, the small procession passed it first as if uncertain, then returned to it. This gave warning to the occupants. Ajayi's uncle then knocked several times. Voices from within shouted back and ordered him to name himself, his ancestry, and his mission. He did this. Argument and some abuse followed on either side. After his family credentials had been seriously examined, questioned, doubted, and disparaged,[17] Ajayi's uncle started wheedling and cajoling. This went on for about half an hour to the enjoyment and mock trepidation[18] of Ajayi's relations. He himself had remained at home, waiting. Finally, Ayo's father opened the door. Honor was satisfied and it was now supposed to be clearly evident to Ajayi's relations, in case it had not been before, that they were entering a family and a household which was distinguished, difficult, and jealous of their distinction.

"What is your mission here?" Ayo's father then asked sternly.

Ajayi's uncle answered humbly:

"We have come to pluck a red, red rose
That in your beautiful garden grows.
Which never has been plucked before,
So lovelier than any other."

"Will you be able to nurture our lovely rose well?" another of Ayo's male relations asked.

Ajayi's family party replied:

"So well shall we nurture your rose
"Twill bring forth many others."

They were finally admitted; drinks were served and prayers offered. The gifts were accepted and other given in exchange.

Conversation went on for about thirty minutes on every conceivable subject but the one at hand. All through this, Ayo and her sisters and some young female relations were kept hidden in an adjoining bedroom. Finally with some delicacy, Ajayi's uncle broached the subject after Ayo's father had given him an opening by asking what, apart from the honor of being entertained by himself and his family, did Ajayi's relations seek. They had heard, the latter replied, that in this very household there was a maiden chaste, beautiful, and obedient, known to all by the name of Ayo. This maiden they sought as wife for their kinsman Ajayi. Ayo's father opened the bedroom door and brought forth Ayo's sister. Was this the one? he asked, testing them. They examined her. No it was not this one they replied, this one was too short to be Ayo. Then a cousin was brought out. Was this she? No, this one is too fat, the applicants said. About ten women in all were brought out. But none was the correct one. Each was too short or too fat or too fair, as the case was, to suit the description of the maiden they sought. At this point, Ajayi's uncle slapped his thigh, as if to show that his doubts were confirmed; turning to his party, he stated that it was a good thing they had insisted on seeing for themselves the bride demanded, or else the wrong woman would have been foisted on them. They agreed, nodding. All right, all right, Ayo's father had replied, there was no cause for impatience. He wanted to be sure they knew whom they wanted. Standing on guard at the bedroom door, he turned his back to the assembly, and with tears in his eyes beckoned to Ayo sitting on the bed inside. He kissed her lightly on the forehead to forgive the past years. Then he led her forth and turned fiercely to the audience. Was this then the girl they wanted, he asked them sternly.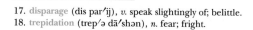

---

17. **disparage** (dis par′ij), *v.* speak slightingly of; belittle.
18. **trepidation** (trep′ə dā′shən), *n.* fear; fright.

The Truly Married Woman   **921**

10 **Multicultural Note**

Marriage Rituals

Encourage students to observe both similarities and differences between the marriage rituals mentioned here and the rituals in their own country. You might encourage them to make charts such as those below, adding details as they finish the story.

Similarities
ring given
gifts exchanged
expenses involved
engagement takes place
bride's father is asked for her hand
symbolic gifts exchanged
music, dancing, feasting

Differences
soothsayer consulted
oracles consulted
groom's family stages a dramatic dialogue at bride's house
groom pays dowry

BUILDING ENGLISH PROFICIENCY

Exploring a Key Passage

Help students understand and appreciate the engagement ritual that Nicol details.

1. Divide students into two or three groups and invite the groups to present their interpretation of the scene. Tell them to begin with the very last sentence on page 920 and end after the first paragraph on page 922.

2. After each group has presented its scenario, discuss differences in interpretations. Ask student groups to support their interpretation with information from the text.

3. Have students explain the symbolism of each step of the engagement ceremony.

4. Invite students to share engagement and marriage customs from their native culture. If they can, have students compare the symbolism in the ceremonies from their cultures with those in the story.

Active Reading

Clarify

References to Ayo's age, graying hair, and pregnancy suggest that he sees the humor in this situation.

Reading/Thinking Skills

Generalize

Question Generalize about what Ayo thinks a "truly married woman" is entitled to. *(Possible response: to be independent, respected, and equal in marriage to her mate)*

Check Test

1. Why hadn't Ajayi married Ayo after living with her for 12 years? *(He had "never quite got round to it"; he is lazy.)*

2. Over what does the couple argue concerning their oldest son? *(Ayo does not want Ajayi to beat their son for wetting his sleeping-mat.)*

3. How do the three Crusaders first hear about Ajayi? *(He had filled out a coupon from a magazine and sent it to their organization.)*

4. What general changes does Ayo make to the house before the three white men arrive? *(She cleans up and tries to make things look more respectable by hiding objectionable items and replacing them with family photos and religious materials.)*

5. What does Ajayi request that Ayo do the morning after the wedding? *(make him a cup of tea)*

Unit 8 Resource Book
Alternate Check Test, p. 53

CLARIFY: In your opinion, what is the author's perspective on all this ceremony?

"This *is* the very one," Ajayi's uncle replied with joy. "Hip, hip, hip, hooray," everybody shouted, encircling Ayo and waving white handkerchiefs over her head. The musicians smote their guitars instantly; someone beat an empty wine bottle rhythmically with a corkscrew; after a few preliminary trills the flutes rose high in melody; all danced round Ayo. And as she stood in the center, a woman in her mid-thirties, her hair slightly streaked gray, undergoing a ceremony of honor she had often witnessed and long put outside her fate, remembering the classic description of chastity, obedience, and beauty, she wept with joy and the unborn child stirred within her for the first time.

The next morning she was bathed by an old and respected female member of her family, and her mother helped her to dress. Her father gave her away at the marriage service at church. It was a quiet wedding with only sixty guests or so. Ajayi looked stiff in dinner jacket with buttonhole, an ensemble which he wore only on special occasions. Afterwards they went to Ayo's family home for the wedding luncheon. At the door they were met by another of Ayo's numerous elderly aunts, who held a glass of water to their lips for them to sip in turn, Ajayi being first. The guests were all gathered outside behind the couple. The aunt made a conveniently long speech until all the guests had foregathered. She warned Ayo not to be too friendly with other women as they would inevitably steal her husband; that they should live peaceably and not let the sun go down on a quarrel between them. Turning to Ajayi, she told him with a twinkle in her eye that a wife could be quite as exciting as a mistress, and also not to use physical violence against their daughter, his wife.

After this they entered and the western part of the ceremony took place. The wedding cake (which Ayo had made) was cut and speeches made. Then Ajayi departed to his own family home where other celebrations went on. Later he changed into a lounge suit and called for Ayo. There was weeping in Ayo's household as if she was setting off on a long journey. Her mother in saying goodbye, remarked between tears, that although she would not have the honor next morning of showing the world evidence of Ayo's virginity, yet in the true feminine powers of procreation none except the blind and deaf could say Ayo had lacked zeal.

They called on various relations on both sides of the family and at last they were home. Ayo seemed different in Ajayi's eyes. He had never really looked at her carefully before. Now he observed her head held erectly and gracefully through years of balancing loads on it in childhood; her statuesque neck with its three natural horizontal ridges—to him, signs of beauty; her handsome shoulders. He clasped her with a new tenderness.

The next morning, as his alarm clock went off, he stirred and reached for his morning cup of tea. It was not there. He sprang up and looked. Nothing. He listened for Ayo's footsteps outside in the kitchen. Nothing. He turned to look beside him. Ayo was there and her bare ebony back was heaving gently. She must be ill, he thought; all that excitement yesterday.

"Ayo, Ayo," he cried, "are you ill?" She turned round slowly still lying down and faced him. She tweaked her toes luxuriously under the cotton coverlet and patted her breast slowly. There was a terrible calm about her. "No, Ajayi," she replied, "are you?" she asked him. "Are your legs paralysed?" she continued. "No," he said. He was puzzled and alarmed, thinking that her mind had become unhinged under the strain.

"Ajayi, my husband," she said, "for twelve years I have got up every morning at five to make tea for you and breakfast. Now I am a truly married woman you must treat me with a little more respect. You are now a husband and not a lover. Get up and make yourself a cup of tea."

MINI-LESSON: LITERARY FOCUS

Point of View

Teach Point of view is the perspective from which a story is told—the eyes and mind of the storyteller. Ask what point of view this story is told from. *(third-person limited)* Ask whose mind generally we know in the story. *(Ajayi's)* We hear Ayo speak to Ajayi in only four places—pages 918, 920 twice, and 922 at the end. Ask: Why do you think the author chose the third-person limited point of view for this story, allowing us into Ajayi's mind often but seldom allowing us to hear from Ayo? *(Students should note that the author can create the surprise at the end only by limiting our knowledge of Ayo's mind. By telling us Ajayi's thoughts and feelings all along, the author leads us to view the story's ending from his point of view, thus making us as surprised as Ajayi is by Ayo's closing attitude.)*

Activity Idea Have students speculate on differences had the story been told in third-person limited from Ayo's perspective.

After Reading

Making Connections

Shaping Your Response

1. Do you think Ajayi will regret having married Ayo? Will she regret having married him?

Analyzing the Story

2. What methods does the author use to **characterize** Ajayi and Ayo?

3. Who is the **protagonist** in the story, in your opinion?

4. What is the **climax** or turning point in the story?

5. Do you find the author's **perspective** sympathetic? ironic? humorous? something else?

6. Why, in your opinion, has marriage changed Ayo's morning routine?

7. Do Ajayi and Ayo have an equal partnership before they are married? Explain.

Extending the Ideas

8. Are marriage partners usually equal, in your opinion? Should they be, or is it better if one partner makes most of the decisions?

Literary Focus: Point of View

Point of view is the vantage point from which an author presents the actions and characters in a story. "The Truly Married Woman" is told from the third-person point of view.

1. Is the third-person narrator *omniscient*—able to see into the minds of all the characters?

2. Is the narrator *objective*—describing only what can be seen?

3. Is the point of view *limited*—confined to a single character's perception? If so, who is that character?

Vocabulary Study

Use your understanding of the meaning of the italicized word to choose the word or phrase that best completes each sentence.

1. You would expect a *tirade* to be ___.
   a. whispered   **b.** sung   **c.** shouted

2. The person most likely to act *officiously* would be a ___.
   a. guitar player   **b.** government clerk   **c.** television weatherperson

3. The best example of an *anomaly* is a ___.
   a. billionaire wearing rags   **b.** dog wearing a collar
   c. cyclist wearing a helmet

4. A common *deterrent* to overweight is ___.
   a. having clothes that are too tight   **b.** watching chefs on television
   c. eating junk food

The Truly Married Woman   **923**

MAKING CONNECTIONS

1. Student responses should reflect an understanding of the couple. The fact that Ajayi takes pride in Ayo's independence suggests he may be able to adjust to the changes in their relationship.

2. The author shows Ajayi and Ayo in a variety of circumstances (their daily household routines; his workplace; their relationships with friends, relatives, neighbors, and the church), thereby demonstrating what they are like as people; the author can see inside Ajayi's mind but not Ayo's.

3. Possible responses: Ajayi is the protagonist because his actions move the story along; Ayo, the wiser and stronger of the two, is the protagonist.

4. Possible responses: The turning point in the story—where their relationship begins to change—is when Ajayi proposes marriage to Ayo and she refuses his romantic overtures; the climax occurs at the end when she refuses to make him a cup of tea.

5. Accept all well-documented and thoughtful answers. Students should note the author's humorous tone.

6. Possible responses: She is now legally on a par and has the security of marriage bonds.

7. Most students will not think the couple had an equal partnership before marriage, since Ayo had to wait on Ajayi; evidence to support this fact is the difference between Ayo's morning routine before and after the wedding.

8. Responses will vary according to students' personal beliefs but should be supported by sound reasoning.

VOCABULARY STUDY

1. c   **2.** b   **3.** a   **4.** a   **5.** a

6. c   **7.** b   **8.** a   **9.** c   **10.** a

Unit 8 Resource Book
Vocabulary, p. 51
Vocabulary Test, p. 54

LITERARY FOCUS: POINT OF VIEW

. No, the narrator of the story is not omniscient ecause he cannot see into the minds of all the haracters.

. No, the narrator is not objective because he tells s more than just what is visible.

3. Yes, the point of view is limited because the narrator is able to see into the mind only of Ajayi. He tells us only the words and actions of the other characters.

WRITING CHOICES
Writer's Notebook

You may wish to allow volunteers to stage a brief debate on the affirmative and negative views toward physical punishment, basing their arguments on their notebook writings.

Can This Marriage Work?

Call on volunteers to read their articles aloud to the class. Collect all articles and post them around the classroom.

Your Ideal

Invite students to illustrate their descriptions of their ideal mates with drawings or collages of pictures clipped from magazines and/or newspapers.

Selection Test

Unit 8 Resource Book
pp. 55–56

---

5. Many people feel *trepidation* at the sound of ___.
   a. a police siren   **b.** rain on a roof   **c.** a robin's song

6. If you described someone's *mien*, you would include his ___.
   a. singing voice   **b.** terrible temper   **c.** way of holding his body

7. If you wanted help in designing your *abode,* you might consult ___.
   a. a rabbi   **b.** an architect   **c.** a gardener

8. If you found yourself involved in a *contravention,* you might try___.
   a. to avoid the conflict
   b. to vote for the best candidate
   c. to be considerate to your loved one

9. If someone were to *disparage* your athletic ability, you would probably feel ___.
   a. proud   **b.** flattered   **c.** dejected

10. To many people, an example of *ostentation* would be ___.
    a. bragging about your parents' income
    b. collecting money for the homeless
    c. hitchhiking on an expressway

Expressing Your Ideas

Writing Choices

Writer's Notebook Update In the story, Ajayi beats his eldest son. Write a paragraph telling how you feel about physical punishment for a child. Does it help a child to learn the right way to live, or does it make the child resentful?

Can This Marriage Work? Will the marriage of Ajayi and Ayo be a success? If you were a marriage counselor, how would you rate their chances? In an **article** that might appear in a popular magazine, analyze their past life together, their personalities, their community of friends and relatives, and propose any changes you feel will be necessary for success.

Your Ideal Many people have a type of person in mind with whom they would like to spend their lives. What is your ideal? In a **character sketch,** describe that person. Consider the factors most important to you—looks? education? kindliness? something else?—and tell why they are important.

Other Options

Cartoon Art Create a **cartoon strip** showing the main events in the story. How many panels will it take to tell the whole story? Make the cartoons black and white or in color (for Sunday editions). Display them in the classroom or submit them to your school newspaper.

Congratulations! Assume that you must buy a **wedding gift** for the newly married couple. What will you buy? Find or draw a picture of the gift you think will be most appropriate.

OTHER OPTIONS
Cartoon Art

You may want to tell students that stick figures will be fine for their cartoons if they are unable to draw rounded cartoon figures. Most cartoons have simple art and a simple, clear story line uncluttered by details.

Congratulations

Should a wedding gift be practical and useful or should it be a luxury that the couple might not buy for themselves? Suggest that students discuss these questions before drawing the gift they think appropriate for Ajayi and Ayo.

A Shocking Accident

by Graham Greene

Graham Greene
1904–1991

Graham Greene classified his fiction into "entertainments" and "novels." The former are thrillers and detective stories, including *The Ministry of Fear* (1943); *The Third Man* (1950), originally written as a screenplay; and *Our Man in Havana* (1958), filmed in 1959. Greene was educated at Berkhamsted School, where his father was headmaster, and then at Balliol College. He married in 1927, and after four years at *The Times* in London, he left to try to earn his living as a writer. He converted to Catholicism, and his religious convictions often influenced his writing, especially in such works as *The Quiet American* (1955), set in Vietnam; and *A Burnt Out Case* (1961), set in a leper colony. He also wrote plays, essays, short stories, and many travel books.

Building Background

The Role of the Subconscious In the Foreword to his book titled *A World of My Own,* published after Greene's death, editor Yvonne Cloetta wrote about his method of working: "It is well known that Graham was always very interested in dreams, and that he relied a great deal on the role played by the subconscious in writing. He would sit down to work straightway after breakfast, writing until he had five hundred words (which in the last while he reduced to approximately two hundred). He was in the habit of then rereading, every evening before going to bed, the section of the novel or story he had written in the morning, leaving his subconscious to work during the night. Some dreams enabled him to overcome a 'blockage'; others provided him on occasion with material for short stories or even an idea for a new novel. . . ."

Literary Focus

Tone An author's attitude toward his or her subject matter is called **tone.** By recognizing tone a reader can determine whether a writer views the subject with sympathy, humor, affection, or disapproval. Any of the following might provide a clue to the tone of a work: word choice, style, choice of images, treatment of events and characters. How does tone play an important part in "A Shocking Accident"?

Writer's Notebook

Jot down some words to describe the feelings you would have on discovering that you have taken the wrong bus, train, or plane and are headed in the direction opposite to the one you had planned.

A Shocking Accident **925**

Before Reading

Building Background

Ask students if they have ever had an uncontrollable urge to laugh at something at an inappropriate time? Was it nervousness or something else that made them feel this way? Why do old comedy skits in which someone slips on a banana peel or gets a pie in the face still delight viewers?

Literary Focus

An author's tone, or attitude toward a subject, influences how readers react. Imagine you were reading about a "shocking accident" as written by a reporter for a respected newspaper or a writer for *Mad Magazine.* How might the tones differ?

Writer's Notebook

Students might get creative juices flowing by acting out this scene.

More About Graham Greene

After trying to run away from school (where his father was headmaster), Greene was sent to a psychiatrist. He enjoyed psychoanalysis but still was so bored with school that he played Russian roulette!

 Connections to
NovelWorks

Novelworks: Lord of the Flies by William Golding another major contemporary British novelist, offers unique materials for teaching the novel.

SUPPORT MATERIALS OVERVIEW

Unit 8 Resource Book
- Graphic Organizer, p. 57
- Study Guide, p. 58
- Vocabulary, p. 59
- Grammar, p. 60
- Alternate Check Test, p. 61
- Vocabulary Test, p. 62
- Selection Test, pp. 63–64

Building English Proficiency
- Selection Summaries
- Activities, p. 267

Reading, Writing & Grammar SkillBook
- Reading, pp. 71–73
- Grammar, Usage, and Mechanics, pp. 247–248

Technology
- Audiotape
- Personal Journal Software
- Test Generator Software

Selection Objectives

- to recognize the significance of perspectives in the selection
- to identify tone in literature
- to examine the use of parentheses in standard written English

Unit 8 Resource Book
Graphic Organizer, p. 57
Study Guide, p. 58

Theme Link

Although Graham Greene was well known for writing about serious themes, such as religion, espionage, and political unrest, his story "A Shocking Accident" provides a lighter perspective, and a slant view, on human nature.

Vocabulary Preview

apprehension, expectation of misfortune; dread of impending danger

embark, begin an undertaking

ricochet, move with a bounce or jump

intrinsically, essentially; belonging to a thing by its very nature

brevity, shortness in time

appease, to put an end to

Students can add the words and definitions to their Writer's Notebooks.

1 Reading/Thinking Skills
Compare and Contrast

Questions

- How has Jerome "re-created" his father? *(Possible response: He has imagined that this "restless, widowed author" is actually a mysterious adventurer.)*

- How does his imagined father differ from his real one? *(Possible response: He is more exciting and lives dangerously.)*

926

A Shocking Accident

GRAHAM GREENE

Jerome was called into his house master's room in the break between the second and third class on a Thursday morning. He had no fear of trouble, for he was a warden—the name that the proprietor and headmaster of a rather expensive preparatory school had chosen to give to approved, reliable boys in the lower forms[1] (from a warden one became a guardian and finally before leaving, it was hoped for Marlborough or Rugby,[2] a crusader). The house master, Mr. Wordsworth, sat behind his desk with an appearance of perplexity and apprehension.[3] Jerome had the odd impression when he entered that he was a cause of fear.

"Sit down, Jerome," Mr. Wordsworth said. "All going well with the trigonometry?"

"Yes, sir."

"I've had a telephone call, Jerome. From your aunt. I'm afraid I have bad news for you."

"Yes, sir?"

"Your father has had an accident."

"Oh."

Mr. Wordsworth looked at him with some surprise. "A serious accident."

"Yes, sir?"

Jerome worshipped his father: the verb is exact. As man re-creates God, so Jerome re-created his father—from a restless widowed author into a mysterious adventurer who traveled in far places—Nice, Beirut, Majorca, even the Canaries. The time had arrived about his eighth birthday when Jerome believed that his father either "ran guns" or was a member of the British Secret Service. Now it occurred to him that his father might have been wounded in "a hail of machine-gun bullets."

Mr. Wordsworth played with the ruler on his desk. He seemed at a loss how to continue. He said, "You know your father was in Naples?"

"Yes, sir."

"Your aunt heard from the hospital today."

"Oh."

Mr. Wordsworth said with desperation, "It was a street accident."

"Yes sir?" It seemed quite likely to Jerome that they would call it a street accident. The police of course had fired first; his father would not take human life except as a last resort.

"I'm afraid your father was very seriously hurt indeed."

"Oh."

"In fact, Jerome, he died yesterday. Quite without pain."

"Did they shoot him through the heart?"

"I beg your pardon. What did you say, Jerome?"

"Did they shoot him through the heart?"

"Nobody shot him, Jerome. A pig fell on him." An inexplicable[4] convulsion took place in the nerves of Mr. Wordsworth's face; it really looked for a moment as though he were going to laugh. He closed his eyes, composed his features and said rapidly as though it were necessary to expel the story as quickly as possible, "Your father was walking along a street in Naples when a pig fell on him. A shocking accident. Apparently in the poorer quarters of Naples they keep pigs on their balconies. This one was on the fifth floor. It had grown too fat. The balcony broke. The pig fell on your father."

Mr. Wordsworth left his desk rapidly and

---

1. **lower forms,** lower grades.
2. **Marlborough or Rugby,** two well-known boarding schools.
3. apprehension (ap′ri hen′shən), *n.* expectation of misfortune; dread of impending danger.
4. **inexplicable** (in′ik splik′ə bəl), *adj.* mysterious.

SELECTION SUMMARY

A Shocking Accident

When he is just a schoolboy, Jerome is told of his father's death. Although Jerome idolizes his father, the man is a rather dull travel writer; and while walking in Naples, Italy, he was killed by a pig falling on him from an apartment balcony. Growing up, Jerome learns that other people find the story of his father's death humorous, especially the way his aunt tells it. Jerome, still very fond of his father's memory, tries to think of ways he can tell people the story without causing them to laugh. When he grows up, Jerome becomes an accountant and plans to marry Sally. But will Sally laugh when she hears how his father died? And if she does, will he still want to marry her? Sally's reaction leaves no doubt in Jerome's mind—she doesn't laugh. She takes the story very seriously, in the same way Jerome did as a boy.

For summaries in other languages, see the Building English Proficiency book.

went to the window, turning his back on Jerome. He shook a little with emotion.

Jerome said, "What happened to the pig?"

2

CLARIFY: What "emotion" do you imagine Mr Wordsworth is shaking with?

This was not callousness on the part of Jerome, as it was interpreted by Mr. Wordsworth to his colleagues (he even discussed with them whether, perhaps, Jerome was yet fitted to be a warden). Jerome was only attempting to visualize the strange scene to get the details right. Nor was Jerome a boy who cried; he was a boy who brooded, and it never occurred to him at his preparatory school that the circumstances of his father's death were comic—they were still part of the mystery of life. It was later, in his first term at his public school, when he told the story to his best friend, that he began to realize how it affected others. Naturally after that disclosure he was known, rather unreasonably, as Pig.

Unfortunately his aunt had no sense of humor. There was an enlarged snapshot of his father on the piano; a large sad man in an unsuitable dark suit posed in Capri with an umbrella (to guard him against sunstroke), the Faraglione rocks forming the background. By the age of sixteen Jerome was well aware that the portrait looked more like the author of *Sunshine and Shade* and *Rambles in the Balearics* than an agent of the Secret Service. All the same he loved the memory of his father:

he still possessed an album filled with picture-postcards (the stamps had been soaked off long ago for his other collection), and it pained him when his aunt embarked⁵ with strangers on the story of his father's death.

"A shocking accident," she would begin, and the stranger would compose his or her features into the correct shape for interest and commiseration. Both reactions, of course, were false, but it was terrible for Jerome to see how suddenly, midway in her rambling discourse, the interest would become genuine. "I can't think how such things can be allowed in a civilized country," his aunt would say. "I suppose one has to regard Italy as civilized. One is prepared for all kinds of things abroad, of course, and my brother was a great traveler. He always carried a water-filter with him. It was far less expensive,

---

5. embark (em bärk′), v. begin an undertaking.

British artist Fred Aris chose a famous example of Georgian architecture, the Royal Crescent at Bath, as the background for his painting *Pigs in Bath* (1981). How does the setting affect the **perspective** of this work of fantasy? ▼

3

2

Active Reading
Clarify

Mr. Wordsworth appears to be laughing. Point out that throughout Jerome's life, others who hear the story will have the same reaction.

3

Literary Element
Irony

Questions

- Judging from the aunt's description, what kind of man does Jerome's father appear to have been? *(Possible response: fond of travel, foresighted, and careful)*

- How is the fact that he was "a careful man" ironic? *(Possible response: because no foresight or precaution he could have taken would have prevented this bizarre accident)*

Art Study

Response to Caption Question The fact that this is a real setting with flying pigs superimposed makes the perspective doubly humorous.

Visual Literacy The formal architecture that serves as a backdrop for this absurd scene provides contrast that enhances the humor. Even the pig is smiling. The man, who appears to pop right out of the picture, seems to be daring the viewer to laugh.

BUILDING ENGLISH PROFICIENCY

Distinguishing Between Fantasy and Reality

Some students may experience difficulty in recognizing the connection between reality and Jerome's fantasy interpretation of events. Suggest that, as they read, they create a chart such as the one shown. You may wish to check at the end of each page to ensure that students have correctly interpreted the real and the make-believe.

Fact	Jerome's Interpretation	Clue
"a restless widowed author"	"a mysterious adventurer"	"Jerome re-created his father"

Building English Proficiency
Activities, p. 267

4 Literary Focus
Tone

Jerome's obsession with his father's unlikely biographers, and his concern about how to present the story of the accident, help reinforce Greene's tone.

- What word would you use to describe Greene's tone in this paragraph? *(Possible responses: humorous, light, or ironic)*

- How does he feel about Jerome? *(Possible response: He is gently mocking Jerome for maintaining his childhood fantasies.)*

5 Reader's Response
Making Personal Connections

Jerome thinks of two ways of telling the story of his father's death that will not cause his listeners to laugh. One is a long method and the other is a brief method.

Question Which method would you be less likely to laugh at? *(Answers will vary but should be supported rationally; some students may find both methods ineffectual at warding off laughter.)*

6 Literary Element
Stereotype

Stereotypes are generalizations about people based on limited information.

Questions

- What stereotype is associated here with accountants? *(Possible response: They are rather dull people, more concerned with numbers than with emotional matters.)*

- What other jobs can you think of that might be associated with stereotypical behavior? *(Possible responses: librarians—quiet and intellectual; athletes—macho; scientists—antisocial)*

3 you know, than buying all those bottles of mineral water. My brother always said that his filter paid for his dinner wine. You can see from that what a careful man he was, but who could possibly have expected when he was walking along the Via Dottore Manuele Panucci on his way to the Hydrographic Museum that a pig would fall on him?" That was the moment when the interest became genuine.

4 Jerome's father had not been a very distinguished writer, but the time always seems to come, after an author's death, when somebody thinks it worth his while to write a letter to the *Times Literary Supplement* announcing the preparation of a biography and asking to see any letters or documents or receive any anecdotes from the friends of the dead man. Most of the biographies, of course, never appear—one wonders whether the whole thing may not be an obscure form of blackmail and whether many a potential writer of a biography or thesis finds the means in this way to finish his education at Kansas or Nottingham. Jerome, however, as a chartered accountant, lived far from the literary world. He did not realize how small the menace really was, or that the danger period for someone of his father's obscurity had long passed. Sometimes he rehearsed the method of recounting his father's death so as to reduce the comic element to its smallest dimensions—it would be of no use to refuse information, for in that case the biographer would undoubtedly visit his aunt who was living to a great old age with no sign of flagging.

5 It seemed to Jerome that there were two possible methods—the first led gently up to the accident, so that by the time it was described the listener was so well prepared that the death came really as an anti-climax. The chief danger of laughter in such a story was always surprise. When he rehearsed this method Jerome began boringly enough.

"You know Naples and those high tenement buildings? Somebody once told me that the Neapolitan always feels at home in New York just as the man from Turin feels at home in London because the river runs in much the same way in both cities. Where was I? Oh, yes. Naples, of course. You'd be surprised in the poorer quarters what things they keep on the balconies of those sky-scraping tenements—not washing, you know, or bedding, but things like livestock, chickens or even pigs. Of course the pigs get no exercise whatever and fatten all the quicker." He could imagine how his hearer's eyes would have glazed by this time. "I've no idea, have you, how heavy a pig can be, but these old buildings are all badly in need of repair. A balcony on the fifth floor gave way under one of those pigs. It struck the third floor balcony on its way down and sort of ricocheted[6] into the street. My father was on the way to the Hydrographic Museum when the pig hit him. Coming from that height and that angle it broke his neck." This was really a masterly attempt to make an intrinsically[7] interesting subject boring.

The other method Jerome rehearsed had the virtue of brevity.[8]

"My father was killed by a pig."

"Really? In India?"

"No, in Italy."

"How interesting. I never realized there was pig-sticking[9] in Italy. Was your father keen on polo?"

6 In course of time, neither too early nor too late, rather as though, in his capacity as a chartered accountant, Jerome had studied the statistics and taken the average, he became engaged to be married: to a pleasant fresh-faced girl of twenty-five whose father was a doctor in Pinner. Her name was Sally, her favorite author

---

6. **ricochet** (rik′ə shā′), *v.* move with a bounce or jump.
7. **intrinsically** (in trin′sik lē), *adv.* essentially; belonging to a thing by its very nature.
8. **brevity** (brev′ə tē), *n.* shortness in time.
9. **pig-sticking,** the hunting of wild boars with a spear, especially in India.

MINI-LESSON: GRAMMAR

Parentheses

Teach The word *parenthesis* comes from a Greek word meaning "a placing between." Parentheses are paired punctuation marks used to enclose incidental information that is added to a sentence but is not essential to it. Refer students to the top of column 2 on page 927: "(the stamps had been soaked off long ago for his other collection)." Point out that the statement within the parentheses, although informative, is not essential to the sentence.

Activity Idea Ask students to find another sentence that includes parentheses from another story in their textbook. Ask volunteers to copy the sentences on the board. Point out that whenever the parenthetical material is a complete thought requiring punctuation, the punctuation goes within the parentheses.

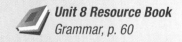

Unit 8 Resource Book
Grammar, p. 60

was still Hugh Walpole,[10] and she had adored babies ever since she had been given a doll at the age of five which moved its eyes and made water. Their relationship was contented rather than exciting, as became the love-affair of a chartered accountant; it would never have done if it had interfered with the figures.

CLARIFY: Why wouldn't an accountant have an exciting relationship?

One thought worried Jerome, however. Now that within a year he might himself become a father, his love for the dead man increased; he realized what affection had gone into the picture-postcards. He felt a longing to protect his memory, and uncertain whether this quiet love of his would survive if Sally were so insensitive as to laugh when she heard the story of his father's death. Inevitably she would hear it when Jerome brought her to dinner with his aunt. Several times he tried to tell her himself, as she was naturally anxious to know all she could that concerned him.

"You were very small when your father died?"

"Just nine."

"Poor little boy," she said.

"I was at school. They broke the news to me."

"Did you take it very hard?"

"I can't remember."

"You never told me how it happened."

"It was very sudden. A street accident."

"You'll never drive fast, will you, Jemmy?" (She had begun to call him "Jemmy.") It was too late then to try the second method—the one he thought of as the pig-sticking one.

They were going to marry quietly in a registry-office and have their honeymoon at Torquay. He avoided taking her to see his aunt until a week before the wedding, but then the night came, and he could not have told himself whether his apprehension was more for his father's memory or the security of his own love.

The moment came all to soon. "Is that Jemmy's father?" Sally asked, picking up the portrait of the man with the umbrella.

"Yes dear. How did you guess?"

"He has Jemmy's eyes and brow, hasn't he?"

"Has Jerome lent you his books?"

"No."

"I will give you a set for your wedding. He wrote so tenderly about his travels. My own favorite is *Nooks and Crannies*. He would have had a great future. It made that shocking accident all the worse."

"Yes?"

Jerome longed to leave the room and not see that loved face crinkle with irresistible amusement.

"I had so many letters from his readers after the pig fell on him." She had never been so abrupt before.

And then the miracle happened. Sally did not laugh. Sally sat with open eyes of horror while his aunt told her the story, and at the end, "How horrible," Sally said. "It makes you think, doesn't it? Happening like that. Out of a clear sky."

Jerome's heart sang with joy. It was as though she had appeased[11] his fear for ever. In the taxi going home he kissed her with more passion than he had ever shown and she returned it. There were babies in her pale blue pupils, babies that rolled their eyes and made water.

"A week today," Jerome said, and she squeezed his hand. "Penny for your thoughts, my darling."

"I was wondering," Sally said, "what happened to the poor pig?"

"They almost certainly had it for dinner," Jerome said happily and kissed the dear child again.

10. **Hugh Walpole** (1884–1941), popular English novelist of the 1920s and 1930s. Greene is suggesting that Sally is a person of conventional taste.

11. appease (ə pēz′), *v.* put an end to.

The narrator assumes that an accountant would not have an exciting love relationship because he is too concerned with figures and statistics.

8 Literary Criticism

Jerome and Sally

Both Jerome and Sally reflect a concern for conventionality and the opinions of others. Jerome's whole life seems to be a reaction to the oddness of his father's death. He chooses a stereotypically conventional occupation, that of a chartered accountant, and selects a conventional young woman to marry. Although Jerome reveres his father, his own life seems an attempt to escape the unusual.

Question Do you think this is a fair appraisal of this story? Are Jerome and Sally well matched as mates? *(Allow any interpretations that display a thoughtful reading of the text.)*

Check Test

1. How does Jerome's father die? *(a pig falls on him)*

2. How do most people react to the story of the accident? *(They laugh.)*

3. What is Jerome's profession? *(accountant)*

4. Why does Jerome delay taking Sally to meet his aunt? *(He fears Sally will hear about his father and laugh.)*

5. What "miracle" happens that makes Jerome's heart "sing with joy"? *(Sally hears the story and does not laugh.)*

Unit 8 Resource Book
Alternate Check Test, p. 61

BUILDING ENGLISH PROFICIENCY

Making Real-Life Connections

On these pages, Jerome considers various ways to tell the story of his father's "shocking accident." Invite students to explore his thinking by attempting a similar process.

1. Have students choose a real or imaginary event from their own lives. Give them a few minutes to jot down notes about the event.

2. Point out Jerome's *second* method of telling the story—a one-sentence summary (page 928). Call on volunteers to tell their stories in one sentence each.

3. Point out that Jerome's *first* storytelling method is to make the story seem boring (so that he won't be laughed at). Have students write or dictate a "boring" version of their stories and share comments about the amount of work it took to do so.

ESL
LEP
ELD
SAE
LD

After Reading

MAKING CONNECTIONS

1. Student's ideas about Jerome's response may vary, but the response seems logical for a young boy who is both shocked and curious.

2. Jerome's perspective on his father is unrealistic: he has reinvented his father from a "restless, widowed author" into a "mysterious adventurer."

3. The story is told from the third-person limited point of view.

4. Student responses will vary but should demonstrate logical reasoning.

5. Possible responses: They seem well suited. Both are conventional and humorless. Sally's concern about what happened to the pig echoes Jerome's question when he first heard the news of the accident.

6. Accept all thoughtful answers. Greene may have portrayed Jerome's father as dull and slightly comical as a way of satirizing himself and his fellow travel writers.

After Reading

Making Connections

Shaping Your Response	**1.** Does Jerome's response to the report of his father's death—"What happened to the pig?"—seem insensitive or logical to you?
Analyzing the Story	**2.** 👣 How is Jerome's **perspective** on his father different from a true one? Why?
	3. From what **point of view** is the story told?
	4. Which of Jerome's two versions of his father's death, the brief or the boring, seems more likely to achieve Jerome's desired result in your opinion?
	5. In what ways is Sally an ideal mate for Jerome?
Extending the Ideas	**6.** Graham Greene was himself a travel writer. What do you think his **purpose** may have been in portraying Jerome's father the way he did?

Literary Focus: Tone

An author's attitude toward his or her subject matter is called **tone.**

1. Do you think the author thought he was writing a humorous story? How can you tell?

2. How would you express the tone of the story?

3. Is the title of the story appropriate in your opinion? Explain.

Vocabulary Study

Choose the word from the list that is most clearly related to the situation conveyed in each sentence. You will not use all of the words.

appease
apprehension
brevity
embark
intrinscally
ricochet

1. You might feel this when alone at night;
It's akin to terror and close to fright.

2. The shot had gone wild, for the bullet, they found,
Had bounced off of a car and gone into the ground.

3. When an answer machine tells you, "Wait for the beep,"
Keep it short, to the point—don't put someone to sleep.

4. The bus is too slow, and you're sure to be late;
You will have to do this to a friend who's irate.

5. Now it's time to set out on our cross-country tour;
Let's be sure that the doors are all locked and secure.

LITERARY FOCUS: TONE

1. Students should perceive that Greene knew he was writing a humorous story. Clues to this fact might include the following: Mr. Wordsworth's turning his back on Jerome to hide the fact that he was laughing; the ironic title of the story; the laughable circumstances of Jerome's father's death and how others react to it.

2. tongue-in-cheek or ironic

3. Students should understand that because the irony of the title indicates the author's tone, it is therefore appropriate.

Expressing Your Ideas

Writing Choices

Writer's Notebook Update Look back at the words you wrote to express the emotions you would feel on taking the wrong bus, train, or plane. Then write a dialogue between you and a fellow passenger who seems uninterested in your plight. Try to convey by the words you choose and by sentence length or stucture the feelings of both yourself and the other passenger.

Beginnings The opening paragraph of any short story is extremely important. Often it indicates the point of view, introduces an important character, establishes the setting, and may suggest the direction of the plot. Recall some episode from your own life that might be expanded into a short story. Then write the **opening paragraph**. (Review the first paragraph of Greene's story and of some of the other short stories in units 7 and 8.)

Adding Details Greene provides no details about Jerome's appearance. Imagine how he looks and dresses, and write a **description** that could be inserted into the story at some point.

Other Options

On the Aisle *The Third Man* is probably the best film of Graham Greene's works which were made into films, although many other of his works, including *Our Man in Havana,* deserve viewing. With a partner, view one of his films and **review** it as if the two of you were on your own television show. Briefly describe the plot, without giving away too much; then analyze the acting and photography, and conclude with your rating. How many stars will you give it?

It's Already Happened? American author Willa Cather once wrote, "Most of the basic material a writer works with is acquired before the age of fifteen." Prefacing your remarks with the title, "Everything I Need to Know I Learned Before I Was Fifteen," tell a partner **five important things** that you have learned.

It Happened Like This . . . What other bizarre and—let's face it—funny ways can you think of for a person to die? Make up a **tall tale** to share with the class or a group of storytellers about someone's death in another "shocking accident." Remember, a tall tale is funnier if it's told with a straight face. Who can tell the tallest, most outlandish tale?

VOCABULARY STUDY

1. apprehension
2. ricochet
3. brevity
4. appease
5. embark

Unit 8 Resource Book
Vocabulary, p. 59
Vocabulary Test, p. 62

WRITING CHOICES
Writer's Notebook

Call on pairs of volunteers to act out their dialogues before the rest of the class. Call on other volunteers to critique each of the dialogues, using the following criteria: content of script, acting ability of the presenters, entertainment value of the dialogue, realism of the dialogue.

Beginnings

Collect all opening paragraphs and challenge students to write an entire story based on their openings. You may wish to read some of the more entertaining paragraphs to the class, maintaining the anonymity of the authors.

Selection Test

Unit 8 Resource Book
pp. 63–64

OTHER OPTIONS
On the Aisle

Allow time for volunteers to perform their film reviews before the class as if they were on television. You may wish to suggest that volunteers make a sound recording and/or a videotape of these performances.

It's Already Happened?

Collect students' lists headed "Everything I Need to Know I Learned Before I Was Fifteen" and bind them into book form. Make the book available in the classroom for students to peruse at their leisure. You may wish to submit some of the lists for publication in the school newspaper.

Building Background

The best-known version of the fairy tale "Beauty and the Beast" was written by Madame de Villeneuve in the mid-1700s. After reviewing the plot of this story, lead students to speculate on why its theme—the transforming power of love—is perennially popular.

Literary Focus

Discuss with students the ability of magic realism to combine elements of dreams, magic, myths, and fairy tales with realistic elements. Elicit names of books, television programs, movies, or video games that contain elements of magic realism.

Writer's Notebook

Suggest that students exchange their word webs with several classmates to add to their idea banks.

More About Angela Carter

Carter's works, which have been called *Gothic* and *surreal,* often blend eroticism and violence, horror and comedy. Other works by Carter include

- *The Passion of New Eve* (1977)
- *Black Venus's Tale* (1980)
- *Nights at the Circus* (1984)
- *Black Venus and Come Unto These Yellow Sands* (1985)

The Courtship of Mr. Lyon

by Angela Carter

Angela Carter
1940–1992

A novelist, short-story writer, teacher, and critic, Angela Carter lived in England, the United States, and Australia. She was born in London and received her B. A. degree from Bristol University. She taught at Sheffield University from 1976 to 1978. Her first novel, *Shadow Dance,* was published in 1965 and her last, *Wise Children,* in 1992. She also wrote screenplays based on her works for *The Magic Toyshop* (1968), and *The Company of Wolves* (1984). She published three collections of short stories, including *The Bloody Chamber* (1979), a collection of adult fairy tales which contains "The Courtship of Mr. Lyon." Her work has elements of fantasy and sensuality, and Joyce Carol Oates, writing in the *New York Times,* called Carter "gifted and inventive."

Building Background

A Tale Retold The story of Beauty and the Beast has fascinated children, artists, musicians, moviemakers, and writers for decades. Probably of French origin, the tale tells of Beauty, the daughter of a merchant who has suffered financial misfortune. On his return from an unsuccessful journey to try to recover his losses, he discovers a rose in a deserted garden and plucks it for Beauty. The Beast, who owns the garden and the adjoining palace, threatens him with death unless he gives him his daughter. To save her father, Beauty agrees to live with the Beast. If you know the story, or similar ones (which appear in many of the world's languages), you know the ending—an ending that Angela Carter preserves in her story. However, she introduces new plot elements, expands the characterizations, and devises an unexpected setting, so that her story is as mysterious and satisfying as the original.

Literary Focus

Magic Realism Stories and novels that combine elements of dreams, magic, myths, and fairy tales, along with realistic elements are often labeled **magic realism**. In magic realist works, inexplicable events and dreamlike settings may exist with everyday happenings and ordinary characters. Or fantastic characters who do the unexpected may exist in quite realistic settings. The themes of magic realism are related to everyday life as most people know it, however.

Writer's Notebook

Up, Up, And Away! Recall some of the fantastic events or settings or characters you have read about, seen in films, or dreamed about, such as people (you?) who can fly. On your paper make a web like the one that follows.

SUPPORT MATERIALS OVERVIEW

Unit 8 Resource Book
- Graphic Organizer, p. 65
- Study Guide, p. 66
- Vocabulary, p. 67
- Grammar, p. 68
- Alternate Check Test, p. 69
- Vocabulary Test, p. 70
- Selection Test, pp. 71–72

Building English Proficiency
- Selection Summaries
- Activities, p. 268

Reading, Writing & Grammar SkillBook
- Grammar, Usage, and Mechanics, pp. 143–144, 149–152

Technology
- Audiotape
- Personal Journal Software
- Test Generator Software

 One of the most famous treatments of the story of Beauty and the Beast is the 1946 movie version by French film maker Jean Cocteau. What aspects of the Beast does Cocteau's make-up and costuming emphasize?

The Courtship of Mr. Lyon

ANGELA CARTER

Outside her kitchen window, the hedgerow glistened as if the snow possessed a light of its own; when the sky darkened towards evening, an unearthly, reflected pallor remained behind upon the winter's landscape, while still the soft flakes floated down. This lovely girl, whose skin possesses that same inner light so you would have thought she, too, was made all of snow, pauses in her chores in the mean kitchen to look out at the country road. Nothing has passed that way all day; the road is white and unmarked as a spilled bolt of bridal satin.

The Courtship of Mr. Lyon **933**

SELECTION SUMMARY

The Courtship of Mr. Lyon

In this modern version of "Beauty and the Beast," Beauty's father, almost bankrupt, gets his car stuck in a rut in snow and becomes the guest of the Beast, who appears to be a huge lion. Because her father picks a white rose for Beauty, the Beast requires him to bring her back for dinner. She stays with the Beast out of a sense of obligation, until her father calls for her to come home. The Beast insures that her father prospers, and Beauty forgets about the Beast until it is almost spring, when the Beast's dog comes to her house. She recalls the Beast, rushes to his house, and finds him dying. Overcome with pity and love for him, Beauty flings herself at the Beast. Suddenly, he begins to change into human form. The story ends with Beauty and the Beast, now Mr. and Mrs. Lyon, happily walking in their garden.

 *For summaries in other languages, see the **Building English Proficiency** book.*

During Reading

Selection Objectives

- to recognize the different slant a modern author can give an old story
- to identify magic realism
- to identify sentence fragments

Unit 8 Resource Book
Graphic Organizer, p. 65
Study Guide, p. 66

Theme Link

"The Courtship of Mr. Lyon" demonstrates Carter's ability to give an old story a fresh slant or interpretation by planting it in a modern setting.

Vocabulary Preview

petrol, gasoline

reticent, reserved; quiet

benign, gracious; gentle

impecunious, having little or no money

leonine, of or like a lion

gravity, seriousness

herbivore, any of a large group of animals that feed chiefly on plants

unguent, ointment; cream

hirsute, hairy

petulant, likely to have little fits of bad temper

Students can add the words and definitions to their Writer's Notebooks.

 **Art Study**

Response to Caption Question The animal makeup stresses his bestial nature, while his elegant clothes indicate his wealth and refinement.

Question What clues do the Beast's furrowed brow and the woman's body language provide about their relationship? *(Possible responses: He is pensive and concerned about how she regards him; she is repulsed and guarded.)*

Questions

- Why are these three sentences set off this way? *(They express Beauty's thoughts and concerns.)*

- What indicates that this will not be the traditional story of Beauty and the Beast? *(Possible responses: the telephone wires; also, the title)*

1

Father said he would be home before nightfall.

The snow brought down all the telephone wires; he couldn't have called, even with the best of news.

The roads are bad. I hope he'll be safe.

But the old car stuck fast in a rut, wouldn't budge an inch; the engine whirred, coughed and died and he was far from home. Ruined once; then ruined again, as he had learned from his lawyers that very morning; at the conclusion of the lengthy, slow attempt to restore his fortunes, he had turned out his pockets to find the cash for petrol[1] to take him home. And not even enough money left over to buy his Beauty, his girl child, his pet, the one white rose she said she wanted; the only gift she wanted, no matter how the case went, how rich he might once again be. She had asked for so little and he had not been able to give it to her. He cursed the useless car, the last straw that broke his spirit; then, nothing for it but to fasten his old sheepskin coat around him, abandon the heap of metal and set off down the snow-filled lane to look for help.

Behind wrought-iron gates, a short, snowy drive performed a reticent[2] flourish before a miniature, perfect, Palladian[3] house that seemed to hide itself shyly behind snow-laden skirts of an antique cypress. It was almost night; that house, with its sweet, retiring, melancholy grace, would have seemed deserted but for a light that flickered in an upstairs window, so vague it might have been the reflection of a star, if any stars could have penetrated the snow that whirled yet more thickly. Chilled through, he pressed the latch of the gate and saw, with a pang, how, on the withered ghost of a tangle of thorns, there clung, still, the faded rag of a white rose.

2

The gate clanged loudly shut behind him; too loudly. For an instant, that reverberating clang seemed final, emphatic, ominous, as if the gate, now closed, barred all within it from the world outside the walled, wintry garden. And,

from a distance, though from what distance he could not tell, he heard the most singular sound in the world: a great roaring, as of a beast of prey.

In too much need to allow himself to be intimidated, he squared up to the mahogany door. This door was equipped with a knocker in the shape of a lion's head, with a ring through the nose; as he raised his hand towards it, it came to him this lion's head was not, as he had thought at first, made of brass, but, instead, of solid gold. Before, however, he could announce his presence, the door swung silently inward on well-oiled hinges and he saw a white hall where the candles of a great chandelier cast their benign[4] light upon so many, many flowers in great, free-standing jars of crystal that it seemed the whole of spring drew him into its warmth with a profound intake of perfumed breath. Yet there was no living person in the hall.

The door behind him closed as silently as it had opened, yet, this time, he felt no fear although he knew by the pervasive atmosphere of a suspension of reality that he had entered a place of privilege where all the laws of the world he knew need not necessarily apply, for the very rich are often very eccentric and the house was plainly that of an exceedingly wealthy man. As it was, when nobody came to help him with his coat, he took it off himself. At that, the crystals of the chandelier tinkled a little, as if emitting a pleased chuckle, and the door of a cloakroom opened of its own accord. There were, however, no clothes at all in this cloakroom, not even the statutory[5] country-house garden mackintosh to greet his own squirearchal sheepskin, but when he emerged again into the hall, he found a greeting waiting for him at last—there was, of all things, a liver-and-white King Charles spaniel

3

1. petrol (pet′rəl), *n.* gasoline. *[British]*
2. reticent (ret′ə sənt), *adj.* reserved; quiet.
3. **Palladian,** in the style of Andrea Palladio, an Italian architect who lived in the 1500s.
4. benign (bi nīn′), *adj.* gracious; gentle.
5. statutory (stach′ù tôr′ē), *adj.* required by a statute or law; here, so common as to seem required.

MINI-LESSON: LITERARY FOCUS

Magic Realism

Teach   Magic realism came to Britain by way of South America and the Caribbean. The term was first applied in literature to the work of Spanish-speaking novelists. (The term *magic realism,* coined by Franz Roh, a German art critic, was first applied to the works of certain German artists in the 1920s.) Magic realists of Latin America whose novels and stories have influenced British writers, including Angela Carter, are

- Alejo Carpentier (b. 1904) of Cuba
- Jorge Luis Borges (1899–1987) of Argentina
- Gabriel García Márquez (b. 1928) of Colombia
- Isabel Allende (b. 1942) of Chile.

Students may wish to explore works by some of the preceding writers.

Activity Idea   Create a large chart (on the board) with the headings "Everyday Elements" and "Magical Elements." Tell students that as they read the story, they may take turns filling in the chart as they come upon details in the story that fit these categories. After students have read the story, have them finish the chart; then discuss the elements listed.

crouched, with head intelligently cocked, on the Kelim[6] runner. It gave him further, comforting proof of his unseen host's wealth and eccentricity to see the dog wore, in place of a collar, a diamond necklace.

The dog sprang to its feet in welcome and busily shepherded him (how amusing!) to a snug little leather-paneled study on the first floor, where a low table was drawn up to a roaring log fire. On the table, a silver tray; round the neck of the whisky decanter, a silver tag with the legend *Drink me*, while the cover of the silver dish was engraved with the exhortation *Eat me*, in a flowing hand. This dish contained sandwiches of thick-cut roast beef, still bloody. He drank the one with soda and ate the other with some excellent mustard thoughtfully provided in a stoneware pot, and when the spaniel saw to it he had served himself, she trotted off about her own business.

All that remained to make Beauty's father entirely comfortable was to find, in a curtained recess, not only a telephone, but the card of a garage that advertised a twenty-four-hour rescue service; a couple of calls later and he had confirmed, thank God, there was no serious trouble, only the car's age and the cold weather. . . . Could he pick it up from the village in an hour? And directions to the village, but half a mile away, were supplied, in a new tone of deference,[7] as soon as he described the house from where he was calling.

And he was disconcerted but, in his impecunious[8] circumstances, relieved to hear the bill would go on his hospitable if absent host's account; no question, assured the mechanic. It was the master's custom.

Time for another whisky as he tried, unsuccessfully, to call Beauty and tell her he would be late; but the lines were still down, although, miraculously, the storm had cleared as the moon rose and now a glance between the velvet curtains revealed a landscape as of ivory with an inlay of silver. Then the spaniel appeared again, with his hat in her careful mouth, prettily wagging her tail, as if to tell him it was time to be gone, that this magical hospitality was over.

As the door swung to behind him, he saw the lion's eyes were made of agate.[9]

Great wreaths of snow now precariously curded the rose trees, and when he brushed against a stem on his way to the gate, a chill armful softly thudded to the ground to reveal, as if miraculously preserved beneath it, one last, single, perfect rose that might have been the last rose left living in all the white winter, and of so intense and yet delicate a fragrance it seemed to ring like a dulcimer[10] on the frozen air.

How could his host, so mysterious, so kind, deny Beauty her present?

Not now distant but close at hand, close as that mahogany front door, rose a mighty, furious roaring; the garden seemed to hold its breath in apprehension. But still, because he loved his daughter, Beauty's father stole the rose.

At that, every window of the house blazed with furious light and a fugal[11] baying, as of a pride of lions, introduced his host.

There is always a dignity about great bulk, an assertiveness, a quality of being more *there* than most of us are. The being who now confronted Beauty's father seemed to him, in his confusion, vaster than the house he owned, ponderous yet swift, and the moonlight glittered on his great, mazy head of hair, on the eyes green as agate, on the golden hairs of the great paws that grasped his shoulders so that their claws pierced the sheepskin as he shook him like an angry child shakes a doll.

This leonine[12] apparition[13] shook Beauty's

---

6. **Kelim** (kə lēm′), also spelled Kilim, a woven carpet, without pile, made in Turkey, Kurdistan, and elsewhere.
7. **deference** (def′ər əns), *n.* great respect.
8. **impecunious** (im′pi kyü′nē əs), *adj.* having little or no money.
9. **agate** (ag′it), *n.* a variety of quartz, a very hard mineral.
10. **dulcimer** (dul′sə mər), *n.* musical instrument with metal strings.
11. **fugal** (fyü′gəl), *adj.* in the style of a fugue, a musical composition based on one or more short themes.
12. **leonine** (lē′ə nīn), *adj.* of or like a lion.
13. **apparition** (ap′ə rish′ən), *n.* the appearance of something strange, remarkable, or unexpected.

The Courtship of Mr. Lyon **935**

6

Reading/Thinking Skills
Infer

One meaning of the word *surmise* is "the formation of an idea."

Question   What do you think is happening to the Beast, as indicated by the phrase "almost the dawning of surmise"? *(Possible responses; He is falling in love; he is planning a courtship.)*

7

Historical Note
Queen Anne Style

The Queen Anne style of English furniture was first created in the early 1700s. The wood furniture, usually dark in finish, was characterized by simple and graceful curves, notably the cabriole leg. Chairs were upholstered and had shaped backs. Fabrics used were fine linens, velvets, damasks, brocades, and leather. Among the accessories, usually made of iron or brass, were candlesticks, lighting fixtures, and drapery rods.

8

Reading/Thinking Skills
Draw Conclusions

One feature that distinguishes this modern version of the fairy tale from the original rendering is the psychological insight provided into the characters.

Questions

• What details indicate that Beauty is both frightened and a bit fascinated by the Beast? *(Possible responses: She finds his difference bewildering; she feels a pressure in his house "as if it lay under water"; she feels like a sacrificial lamb; she is fixated on his great paws and smiles with both her mouth and her eyes.)*

• What acts and feelings humanize the Beast? *(He offers to aid Beauty's father; he is shy and fears rejection.)*

---

father until his teeth rattled and then dropped him sprawling on his knees while the spaniel, darting from the open door, danced round them, yapping distractedly, like a lady at whose dinner party blows have been exchanged.

"My good fellow—" stammered Beauty's father; but the only response was a renewed roar.

"Good fellow? I am no good fellow! I am the Beast, and you must call me Beast, while I call you Thief!"

"Forgive me for robbing your garden, Beast!"

Head of a lion; mane and mighty paws of a lion; he reared on his hind legs like an angry lion yet wore a smoking jacket of dull red brocade and was the owner of that lovely house and the low hills that cupped it.

"It was for my daughter," said Beauty's father. "All she wanted, in the whole world, was one white, perfect rose."

The Beast rudely snatched the photograph her father drew from his wallet and inspected it, first brusquely, then with a strange kind of wonder, almost the dawning of surmise. The camera had captured a certain look she had, sometimes, of absolute sweetness and absolute gravity,[14] as if her eyes might pierce appearances and see your soul. When he handed the picture back, the Beast took good care not to scratch the surface with his claws.

"Take her the rose, then, but bring her to dinner," he growled; and what else was there to be done?

Although her father had told her of the nature of the one who waited for her, she could not control an instinctual shudder of fear when she saw him, for a lion is a lion and a man is a man, and though lions are more beautiful by far than we are, yet they belong to a different order of beauty and, besides, they have no respect for us; why should they? Yet wild things have a far more rational fear of us than is ours of them, and some kind of sadness in his agate eyes, that looked almost blind, as if sick of sight, moved her heart.

He sat, impassive as a figurehead, at the top of the table; the dining room was Queen Anne,[15] tapestried, a gem. Apart from an aromatic soup kept hot over a spirit lamp, the food, though exquisite, was cold—a cold bird, a cold soufflé, cheese. He asked her father to serve them from a buffet and, himself, ate nothing. He grudgingly admitted what she had already guessed, that he disliked the presence of servants because, she thought, a constant human presence would remind him too bitterly of his otherness, but the spaniel sat at his feet throughout the meal, jumping up from time to time to see that everything was in order.

How strange he was. She found his bewildering difference from herself almost intolerable; its presence choked her. There seemed a heavy, soundless pressure upon her in his house, as if it lay under water, and when she saw the great paws lying on the arm of his chair, she thought: They are the death of any tender herbivore.[16] And such a one she felt herself to be, Miss Lamb, spotless, sacrificial.

Yet she stayed, and smiled, because her father wanted her to do so; and when the Beast told her how he would aid her father's appeal against the judgment, she smiled with both her mouth and her eyes. But when, as they sipped their brandy, the Beast, in the diffuse, rumbling purr with which he conversed, suggested, with a hint of shyness, of fear of refusal, that she should stay here, with him, in comfort, while her father returned to London to take up the legal cudgels again, she forced a smile. For she knew with a pang of dread, as soon as he spoke, that it would be so and her visit to the Beast must be, on some magically reciprocal scale, the price of her father's good fortune.

Do not think she had no will of her own; only, she was possessed by a sense of obligation

---

14. gravity (grav′ə tē), *n.* seriousness.
15. **Queen Anne**, of or having to do with a style of English architecture and furniture first popular in the early 1700s, during the reign of Queen Anne.
16. herbivore (hėr′bə vôr), *n.* any of a large group of animals that feed chiefly on plants.

MINI-LESSON: VOCABULARY
Meaning Within Context

Teach   When the father shows the Beast a photograph of Beauty, the Beast snatches it rudely (middle of column 1 above). The author tells us that he "inspected it, first brusquely, then with a strange kind of wonder, almost the dawning of surmise." To understand the significance of the Beast's reaction to the photograph, students must know the meaning of the word *surmise* as used in this context. Have them look up in a dictionary the meanings of the word *surmise* and decide which definition best suits the word as used in this sentence. *(It is used in the sentence as a noun: "a thought or idea based on scanty evidence.")*

Activity Idea   Have students hypothesize about the meaning of other difficult words they come to in this story. They can then verify their proposed meaning by looking up each word in a dictionary.

to an unusual degree and, besides, she would gladly have gone to the ends of the earth for her father, whom she loved dearly.

Her bedroom contained a marvelous glass bed; she had a bathroom, with towels thick as fleece and vials of suave unguents;[17] and a little parlor of her own, the walls of which were covered with an antique paper of birds of paradise and Chinamen, where there were precious books and pictures and the flowers grown by invisible gardeners in the Beast's hothouses. Next morning, her father kissed her and drove away with a renewed hope about him that made her glad, but all the same, she longed for the shabby home of their poverty. The unaccustomed luxury about her she found poignant, because it gave no pleasure to its possessor, and himself she did not see all day as if, curious reversal, she frightened him, although the spaniel came and sat with her, to keep her company. Today the spaniel wore a neat choker of turquoises.

Who prepared her meals? Loneliness of the Beast; all the time she stayed there, she saw no evidence of another human presence but the trays of food that arrived on a dumbwaiter inside a mahogany cupboard in her parlor. Dinner was eggs Benedict and grilled veal; she ate it as she browsed in a book she had found in the rosewood revolving bookcase, a collection of courtly and elegant French fairy tales about white cats who were transformed princesses and fairies who were birds. Then she pulled a sprig of muscat grapes from a fat bunch for her dessert and found herself yawning; she discovered she was bored. At that, the spaniel took hold of her skirt with its velvet mouth and gave it a firm but gentle tug. She allowed the dog to trot before her to the study in which her father had been entertained and there, to her well-disguised dismay, she found her host, seated beside the fire with a tray of coffee at his elbow from which she must pour.

The voice that seemed to issue from a cave full of echoes, his dark, soft rumbling growl—after her day of pastel-colored idleness, how could she converse with the possessor of a voice that seemed an instrument created to inspire the terror that the chords of great organs bring? Fascinated, almost awed, she watched the firelight play on the gold fringes of his mane; he was irradiated, as if with a kind of halo, and she thought of the first great beast of the Apocalypse, the winged lion with his paw upon the Gospel, Saint Mark.[18] Small talk turned to dust in her mouth; small talk had never, at the best of times, been Beauty's forte, and she had little practice at it.

But he, hesitantly, as if he himself were in awe of a young girl who looked as though she had been carved out of a single pearl, asked after her father's law case; and her dead mother; and how they, who had been so rich, had come to be so poor. He forced himself to master his shyness, which was that of a wild creature, and so she contrived to master her own—to such effect that soon she was chattering away to him as if she had known him all her life. When the little cupid in the gilt clock on the mantelpiece struck its miniature tambourine, she was astonished to discover it did so twelve times.

"So late! You will want to sleep," he said.

At that, they both fell silent, as if these strange companions were suddenly overcome with embarrassment to find themselves together, alone, in that room in the depths of the winter's night. As she was about to rise, he flung himself at her feet and buried his head in her lap. She stayed stock-still, transfixed; she felt his hot breath on her fingers, the stiff bristles of his muzzle grazing her skin, the rough lapping of his tongue, and then, with a flood of compassion, understood: All he is doing is kissing my hands.

He drew back his head and gazed at her with his green, inscrutable eyes, in which she saw her

---

17. **unguent** (ung′gwənt), *n.* ointment; cream.
18. **Apocalypse . . . Saint Mark.** Revelation, the last book of the New Testament in the Bible, is sometimes called The Apocalypse. The symbol of St. Mark, author of one of the four Gospels, is a winged lion.

The Courtship of Mr. Lyon **937**

BUILDING ENGLISH PROFICIENCY

Analyzing Rhetorical Questions

Draw students' attention to the rhetorical question as a storytelling device.

1. Read aloud the short paragraph in column 1 of page 936 that begins, "Take her the rose . . ." Point out the question at the end ("what else was there to be done?").

2. Explain that this is a *rhetorical* question, a question to which an answer is not really expected. Writers often use rhetorical questions as a variation to stating an obvious fact. Point out that this rhetorical question interests the reader much more than the statement "He knew there was nothing else to do."

3. Have students locate the other rhetorical questions throughout these pages and suggest what statements they might replace.

4. Challenge students to find two or three other places in the selection where a rhetorical question might fit and to suggest an appropriate rhetorical question.

face repeated twice, as small as if it were in bud. Then, without another word, he sprang from the room and she saw, with an indescribable shock, he went on all fours.

Next day, all day, the hills on which the snow still settled echoed with the Beast's rumbling roar. Has master gone a-hunting? Beauty asked the spaniel. But the spaniel growled, almost bad-temperedly, as if to say that she would not have answered, even if she could have.

Beauty would pass the day in her suite reading or, perhaps, doing a little embroidery; a box of colored silks and a frame had been provided for her. Or, well wrapped up, she wandered in the walled garden, among the leafless roses, with the spaniel at her heels, and did a little raking and rearranging. An idle, restful time; a holiday. The enchantment of that bright, sad, pretty place enveloped her and she found that, against all her expectations, she was happy there. She no longer felt the slightest apprehension at her nightly interviews with the Beast. All the natural laws of the world were held in suspension here, where an army of invisibles tenderly waited on her, and she would talk with the lion, under the patient chaperonage of the brown-eyed dog, on the nature of the moon and its borrowed light, about the stars and the substances of which they were made, about the variable transformations of the weather. Yet still his strangeness made her shiver; and when he helplessly fell before her to kiss her hands, as he did every night when they parted, she would retreat nervously into her skin, flinching at his touch.

The telephone shrilled; for her. Her father. Such news!

The Beast sunk his great head on his paws. You will come back to me? It will be lonely here, without you.

She was moved almost to tears that he should care for her so. It was in her heart to drop a kiss upon his shaggy mane, but though she stretched out her hand towards him, she could not bring herself to touch him of her own free will, he was so different from herself. But, yes, she said; I will come back. Soon, before the winter is over. Then the taxi came and took her away.

You are never at the mercy of the elements in London, where the huddled warmth of humanity melts the snow before it has time to settle; and her father was as good as rich again, since his hirsute[19] friend's lawyers had the business so well in hand that his credit brought them nothing but the best. A resplendent hotel; the opera, theaters; a whole new wardrobe for his darling, so she could step out on his arm to parties, to receptions, to restaurants, and life was as she had never known it, for her father had ruined himself before her birth killed her mother.

Although the Beast was the source of the newfound prosperity and they talked of him often, now that they were so far away from the timeless spell of his house it seemed to possess the radiant and finite quality of dream and the Beast himself, so monstrous, so benign, some kind of spirit of good fortune who had smiled on them and let them go. She sent him flowers, white roses in return for the ones he had given her; and when she left the florist, she experienced a sudden sense of perfect freedom, as if she had just escaped from an unknown danger, had been grazed by the possibility of some change but, finally, left intact. Yet, with this exhilaration, a desolating emptiness. But her father was waiting for her at the hotel; they had planned a delicious expedition to buy her furs and she was as eager for the treat as any girl might be.

Since the flowers in the shop were the same all year round, nothing in the window could tell her that winter had almost gone.

Returning late from supper after the theater, she took off her earrings in front of the mirror: Beauty. She smiled at herself with satisfaction. She was learning, at the end of her adolescence,

---

19. **hirsute** (hėr′sūt), *adj.* hairy.

MINI-LESSON: GRAMMAR

Recognizing Sentence Fragments

Teach Remind students that a sentence fragment is a group of words that does not express a complete thought. Standard usage requires that a group of words must have a subject and a verb in order to be a complete sentence. This is a rule that some modern authors choose to break occasionally, as Angela Carter does several times in this selection. For example, in the second new paragraph on page 938, after the second sentence (ending with "rearranging"), we find this fragment: "An idle, restful time; a holiday."

Question Why is this a fragment? *(There is no verb on either side of the semicolon.)*

Activity Idea Challenge students to find another sentence fragment in the story and identify its missing part or parts. *(Possible responses: p. 937, column 1, paragraph 2, first line, "Loneliness of the Beast;" [no verb]; p. 937, column 2, second new paragraph, "So late!" [no subject or verb]; p. 938, third new paragraph, "Her father." [no verb] and "Such news!" [no subject or verb])*

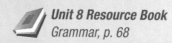

Unit 8 Resource Book
Grammar, p. 68

how to be a spoiled child and that pearly skin of hers was plumping out, a little, with high living and compliments, a certain inwardness was beginning to transform the lines around her mouth, those signatures of the personality, and her sweetness and her gravity could sometimes turn a mite petulant[20] when things went not quite as she wanted them to go. You could not have said that her freshness was fading, but she smiled at herself in mirrors a little too often these days, and the face that smiled back was not quite the one she had seen contained in the Beast's agate eyes. Her face was acquiring, instead of beauty, a lacquer of the invincible prettiness that characterizes certain pampered, exquisite, expensive cats.

The soft wind of spring breathed in from the nearby park through the open windows; she did not know why it made her want to cry.

There was a sudden, urgent, scrabbling sound, as of claws, at her door.

Her trance before the mirror broke; all at once, she remembered everything perfectly. Spring was here and she had broken her promise. Now the Beast himself had come in pursuit of her! First, she was frightened of his anger; then, mysteriously joyful, she ran to open the door. But it was his liver-and-white spotted spaniel who hurled herself into the girl's arms in a flurry of little barks and gruff murmuring, of whimpering and relief.

Yet where was the well-brushed, jeweled dog who had sat beside her embroidery frame in the parlor with birds of paradise nodding on the walls? This one's fringed ears were matted with mud, her coat was dusty and snarled, she was thin as a dog that has walked a long way, and if she had not been a dog, she would have been in tears.

After that first, rapturous greeting, she did not wait for Beauty to order her food and water; she seized the chiffon hem of her evening dress, whimpered and tugged. Threw back her head, howled, then tugged and whimpered again.

There was a slow, late train that would take her to the station where she had left for London three months ago. Beauty scribbled a note for her father, threw a coat round her shoulders. Quickly, quickly, urged the spaniel soundlessly; and Beauty knew the Beast was dying.

In the thick dark before dawn, the station-master roused a sleepy driver for her. Fast as you can.

It seemed December still possessed his garden. The ground was hard as iron, the skirts of the dark cypress moved on the chill wind with a mournful rustle and there were no green shoots on the roses, as if, this year, they would not bloom. And not one light in any of the windows, only, in the topmost attic, the faintest smear of radiance on a pane, the thin ghost of a light on the verge of extinction.

The spaniel had slept a little, in her arms, for the poor thing was exhausted. But now her grieving agitation fed Beauty's urgency, and as the girl pushed open the front door, she saw, with a thrust of conscience, how the golden door knocker was thickly muffled in black crepe.

The door did not open silently, as before, but with a doleful groaning of the hinges and, this time, onto perfect darkness. Beauty clicked her gold cigarette lighter; the tapers in the chandelier had drowned in their own wax and the prisms were wreathed with drifting arabesques of cobwebs. The flowers in the glass jars were dead, as if nobody had had the heart to replace them after she was gone. Dust, everywhere; and it was cold. There was an air of exhaustion, of despair, in the house and, worse, a kind of physical disillusion, as if its glamor had been sustained by a cheap conjuring trick and now the conjurer, having failed to pull the crowds, had departed to try his luck elsewhere.

Beauty found a candle to light her way and followed the faithful spaniel up the staircase, past the study, past her suite, through a house

20. **petulant** (pech′ə lənt), *adj.* likely to have little fits of bad temper.

The Courtship of Mr. Lyon **939**

12 Literary Element
Style

Draw students' attention to stylistic elements that Carter uses to create a sense of urgency:

- powerful verbs *(whimpered, howled, tugged, scribbled, threw)*
- sentence fragments *("Threw back her head, howled, then tugged and whimpered again." "Fast as you can.")*

13 Literary Element
Mood

Questions

- How does the mood of these paragraphs contrast to the mood described in the second column of page 934? *(Possible response: It is dark; the golden door knocker is muffled in black crepe; the door does not open silently but with groaning hinges; the chandelier is dark and full of cobwebs; there are no flowers; and there is a cold, bleak atmosphere rather then the springlike warmth in the first scene.)*

- What signs of death and decay are apparent? *(Possible responses: no green shoots on the roses; "a thin ghost of a light"; black crepe on the knocker; tapers that have drowned in their wax; cobwebs, dead flowers, dust, cold, and an air of exhaustion and despair)*

BUILDING ENGLISH PROFICIENCY

Exploring Style

Continue to make students aware of "tools" that Carter employs to add interest to her prose.

1. Point out that in addition to the literary device of the rhetorical question (see page 937 of this Teacher's Guide), this author also uses sentence fragments, the second person *you*, and indirect discourse.

2. Share the following examples with students: fragment—"An idle, restful time; a holiday" (page 938, second new paragraph); second person—"You are never at the mercy of the elements in London" (page 938, column 2, first paragraph); indirect discourse—You will come back to me? (page 938, column 1, fourth new paragraph)

3. Divide students into three groups; assign a device to each group. Allow groups time to locate more examples of each and then share their findings.

4. Invite volunteers to read aloud prose segments containing these devices. Discuss with students how the various devices add interest and a certain rhythm, as well as enhance the fairy-tale quality of the prose.

Art Study

Response to Caption Question This colored wood engraving portrays Beauty, who loves and is caring for the dying Beast—a scene from the end of the story. The black-and-white still from Cocteau's film depicts a horrified Beauty and a perplexed Beast from the early part of the story.

14 Reading/Thinking Skills
Find the Main Idea

Questions

• How do you interpret this sentence: "Was it because she had only looked at her own face, reflected there?" *(Possible response: Not until now has Beauty recognized him as a person whom she loves.)*

• What causes the Beast's transformation? *(Beauty's kisses and declaration of love)*

• What theme do you find in this story? *(Possible response: Love has the power to transform us.)*

Check Test

1. What causes Beauty's father to seek help at Mr. Lyon's estate? *(His car breaks down.)*

2. When is the first time during his visit that the father sees his host? *(when he takes the rose for Beauty from the Beast's garden)*

3. Why doesn't Mr. Lyon keep servants? *(They remind him of his "otherness.")*

4. Who summons Beauty to aid the dying Mr. Lyon? *(his pet spaniel)*

5. At the end of the story, how do readers know what becomes of Beauty and Mr. Lyon? *(They marry, as indicated in the final sentence.)*

Unit 8 Resource Book
Alternate Check Test, p. 69

echoing with desertion up a little back staircase dedicated to mice and spiders, stumbling, ripping the hem of her dress in her haste.

What a modest bedroom! An attic, with a sloping roof, they might have given the chambermaid if the Beast had employed staff. A night light on the mantelpiece, no curtains at the windows, no carpet on the floor and a narrow, iron bedstead on which he lay, sadly diminished, his bulk scarcely disturbing the faded patchwork quilt, his mane a grayish rat's nest and his eyes closed. On the stick-backed chair where his clothes had been thrown, the roses she had sent him were thrust into the jug from the washstand, but they were all dead.

The spaniel jumped up on the bed and burrowed her way under the scanty covers, softly keening.

"Oh, Beast," said Beauty. "I have come home."

His eyelids flickered. How was it she had never noticed before that his agate eyes were equipped with lids, like those of a man? Was it because she had only looked at her own face, reflected there?

"I'm dying, Beauty," he said in a cracked whisper of his former purr. "Since you left me, I have been sick. I could not go hunting, I found

This wood engraving of Beauty discovering the dying Beast was based on a watercolor drawing done in 1874 by British artist Walter Crane. How does Crane 's image of the Beast differ from Cocteau's?

I had not the stomach to kill the gentle beasts, I could not eat. I am sick and I must die; but I shall die happy because you have come to say goodbye to me."

She flung herself upon him, so that the iron bedstead groaned, and covered his poor paws with her kisses.

"Don't die, Beast! If you'll have me, I'll never leave you."

When her lips touched the meat-hook claws, they drew back into their pads and she saw how he had always kept his fists clenched but now, painfully, tentatively, at last began to stretch his fingers. Her tears fell on his face like snow and, under their soft transformation, the bones showed through the pelt, the flesh through the wide, tawny brow. And then it was no longer a lion in her arms but a man, a man with an unkempt mane of hair and, how strange, a broken nose, such as the noses of retired boxers, that gave him a distant, heroic resemblance to the handsomest of all the beasts.

"Do you know," said Mr. Lyon, "I think I might be able to manage a little breakfast today, Beauty, if you would eat something with me."

Mr. and Mrs. Lyon walk in the garden; the old spaniel drowses on the grass, in a drift of fallen petals.

After Reading

After Reading

Making Connections

Shaping Your Response

1. Why do you think the author chose the title she did, instead of calling the story "Beauty and the Beast"?

Analyzing the Story

2. The Beast wears a brocade smoking jacket, a somewhat strange article of clothing for a lion. What are some other examples of the combination of realism with unreality?

3. What do we learn of the Beast from the **setting?**

4. How does the author elicit sympathy for the Beast?

5. Where does the **climax** of the story occur, in your opinion?

Extending the Ideas

6. 🐾 How might this story have changed if it had been told from the Beast's **perspective**?

7. What truths about life do you think are evident in this story, fantasy though it may be?

Literary Focus: Magic Realism

Stories and novels that combine elements of dreams, magic, myths, and fairy tales, along with realistic elements, are often labeled **magic realism.**

1. What kinds of magic do you find in "The Courtship of Mr. Lyon"?

2. Carter often places a realistic detail, such as the Beast's Queen Anne dining room, alongside the mystery of how the food gets prepared. Yet Beauty never asks the Beast about this mystery, though she wonders about it. What does this reveal about Beauty?

3. Many old myths and tales tell of women who marry and thus transform animals (think also of "The Frog Prince" on page 909), but almost none tell about men who do so. Why do you think this might be true?

Vocabulary Study

benign
gravity
herbivore
hirsute
impecunious
leonine
petrol
petulant
reticent
unguent

Choose the word that best answers each question. Use a dictionary if you need help.

1. What is the first word that describes how the Beast looks?

2. Which word can mean both "seriousness" and "a natural force that causes objects to move toward the center of the earth"?

3. *Pecunia* is the Latin word for money. Which word means "having no money"?

The Courtship of Mr. Lyon **941**

LITERARY FOCUS: MAGIC REALISM

1. Responses will vary but should include the transformation of Mr. Lyon from a beast into a man.

2. Possible responses: Beauty is too polite or sensitive or afraid to ask rude questions; Beauty is not intelligent enough to ask questions; Beauty herself is enchanted while at the house of the Beast.

3. Responses will vary but might include that people have long thought of men as tending toward wildness or beastly behavior, in need of "taming" or being transformed by the "civilizing influence" of women.

MAKING CONNECTIONS

1. Possible responses: The title suggests that this is a love story; it provides a modern slant on the fairy tale.

2. Possible responses: the spaniel, which wears various jeweled collars and acts as a house servant; doors that open and close by themselves; food that seems to be prepared by invisible hands

3. Possible response: He is wealthy and isolated, has elegant taste, and is a thoughtful host.

4. He does not keep human servants because they remind him of his "otherness"; Beauty notices his sad eyes and his loneliness; he pathetically kisses Beauty's hands; he goes out to the hills and roars with frustration and torment; and finally, when beauty returns to him, he is dying.

5. Accept all well-documented and thoughtful answers; most students will say that the climax occurs when Beauty returns to the beast and openly declares her love for him.

6. Accept all well-considered answers. If the story were told from the beast's perspective, we would not learn of his longings, since he would be guarded about expressing his feelings. We would also not be given insights into Beauty's personality. Only an omniscient narrator could provide all this information.

7. Answers should indicate understanding that some people behave in a "beastly" manner when they feel lonely and unloved but that they can be transformed into the best version of themselves by love and attention from a person for whom they care.

VOCABULARY STUDY

1. hirsute
2. gravity
3. impecunious
4. reticent
5. petrol
6. petulant
7. herbivore
8. benign
9. unguent
10. leonine

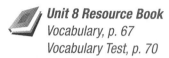

Unit 8 Resource Book
Vocabulary, p. 67
Vocabulary Test, p. 70

WRITING CHOICES

Writer's Notebook

Allow time for class discussion of the story's elements of magic realism and whether students could accept the story's mysterious details without wishing for more explanation. Make a web of the mysterious details on the board as students contribute to it from their notes.

The Mane Problem

Make sure students use *I, my, me,* and *mine* in the story. They might want to incorporate elements of magic realism to enliven their narration. Have them consider adopting a humorous or satiric tone rather than a serious one. Ask students to revise their stories and add them to their notebooks.

Selection Test

Unit 8 Resource Book
pp. 71–72

---

4. Which word means the opposite of "loud and effusive"?
5. Which word is related to *petroleum?*
6. Which word describes Beauty, when she can't get her way?
7. A *carnivore* eats meat. What word names an animal that eats plants?
8. Which word has the same root as *benefit?*
9. Which word names something to put on a burn?
10. What is the second word that describes how the Beast looks?

Expressing Your Ideas

Writing Choices

Writer's Notebook Update Review the web you made, and make additions to it, if you wish, based on your reading of "The Courtship of Mr. Lyon." In a paragraph, tell your feelings about this type of story. Do you find yourself accepting the many unexplainable details, or do you want more explanation for some of the happenings?

Goldilocks And the Chicago Bears? Read a fairy tale and outline what you might do to update the characters, the setting, and the plot. Then write a **modern fairy story** that is at least recognizable as coming from its source.

The Mane Problem How did the Beast get to be a beast? Was he under an evil spell, and if so, who cast the spell and why? Write **the Beast's story** in the first person from his **perspective,** explaining how you as the Beast were originally transformed from a man into an animal and why.

Other Options

Illustration The illustrations on page 933 and 940 show how two different artists have interpreted the Beast; many others have done so over the years. Try your hand at creating an **illustration** for one or two scenes of Angela Carter's story: perhaps the Beast's Palladian house (you may need to do some research on architectural history), the door knocker, the King Charles spaniel, Beauty, or Mr. Lyon.

Other Versions After doing the necessary research, prepare a **bibliography** of other works (picture books, operas, films, musicals, television programs, and so on) based on Beauty and the Beast, and distribute it to the class.

Roar Like a Lion With a small group, write a script based on the original story of Beauty and the Beast and, using hand puppets which you and your partners have made, present a **puppet play** of the story for a group of young children.

OTHER OPTIONS

Illustration

Make any necessary arrangements to display students' illustrations in a school display case or an appropriate hallway near the classroom, or in the classroom.

Other Versions

Choose a volunteer to go through all the students' "Beauty and the Beast" bibliographies and compile a master bibliography that includes all listings but avoids duplications. If your class has Internet access, suggest that students add this bibliography to the class home page.

Roar Like a Lion

If possible, suggest that students videotape their puppet plays as they are performed before a group of young children, including the children's response to the show. Allow volunteers to show their videotapes to the class.

The Slant View

Myth Under a Microscope

Science Connection
In the following essay, biologist Lewis Thomas examines several mythological creatures from the perspective of science.

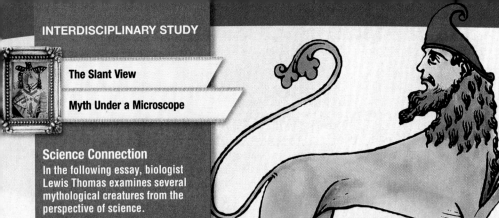

Griffon

SOME BIOMYTHOLOGY

by Lewis Thomas

The mythical animals cataloged in the bestiaries[1] of the world seem, at a casual glance, nothing but exotic nonsense. The thought comes that Western civilized, scientific, technologic society is a standing proof of human progress, in having risen above such imaginings. They are as obsolete as the old anecdotes in which they played their puzzling, ambiguous roles, and we have no more need for the beasts than for the stories. The Griffon, Phoenix, Centaur, Sphinx, Manticore, Ganesha, Ch'i-lin, and all the rest are like recurrent bad dreams, and we are well rid of them. So we say.

The trouble is that they are in fact like dreams, and not necessarily bad ones, and we may have a hard time doing without them. They may be as essential for society as mythology itself, as loaded with symbols, and as necessary for the architecture of our collective unconscious. If Levi-Strauss[2] is right, myths are constructed by a universal logic that, like language itself, is as characteristic for human beings as nest-building is for birds.

The stories seem to be different stories, but the underlying structure is always the same, in any part of the world, at any time. They are like engrams,[3] built into our genes. In this sense, bestiaries are part of our inheritance.

There is something basically similar about most of these crazy animals. They are all unbiologic, but unbiologic in the same way. Bestiaries do not contain, as a rule, totally novel creatures of the imagination made up of parts that we have never seen before. On the contrary, they are made up of parts that are entirely familiar. What is novel, and startling, is that they are mixtures of species.

It is perhaps this characteristic that makes the usual bestiary so outlandish to the twentieth-century mind. Our most powerful story, equivalent in its way to a universal myth, is evolution. Never mind that it is true whereas myths are not; it is filled with symbolism, and this is the way it has influenced the mind of society. In our latest enlightenment, the fabulous beasts are worse than improbable—

---

1. **bestiary** (bes′tē er ē), *n.* collection of natural history and animal tales popular in the Middle Ages.
2. **Lévi-Strauss,** Claude Lévi-Strauss (born 1908), French anthropologist who has written extensively on mythology.
3. **engram** (en′gram), *n.* whatever happens to the brain when a memory is formed, thought by scientists to be some change in brain cells.

Interdisciplinary Study   **943**

Interdisciplinary Study

Theme Link
The fabulous beasts of mythology provide an imaginative "slant view" of the natural world, yet such mythological creatures can also suggest other extraordinary evolutionary combinations with an actual scientific basis.

Curricular Connection: Science

Use the material in this interdisciplinary study to help students understand that living members of Thomas's microbestiary are every bit as odd as mythical beasts.

Terms to Know

collective unconscious, a group psyche, proposed by psychologist Carl Gustav Jung, consisting of inherited ideas and predispositions

benignity (bi nig′n tē), something kindly, favorable, or beneficial

postulate, to assume, without proof, that something is true, real, or necessary

replicate, exactly reproduce; duplicate

fallibility, ability to be mistaken or deceived

cytoplasm, the protoplasm of a cell, outside of the nucleus

Unit 8 Resource Book
Study Guide, p. 73

BUILDING ENGLISH PROFICIENCY

ESL
LEP
ELD
SAE
LD

Exploring Key Terms

To grasp what Thomas is saying in this essay, students must understand what is meant by the word *myth.* Guide students toward that understanding.

1. Before they begin reading, present the term and invite students to comment on what it means or what they associate with it. (For example, they might equate *myth* with terms such as *make-believe* or *fairy tale,* name mythological characters such as Hercules, or recount myths from various cultures.)

2. Point out the second sentence of the second paragraph. Discuss some of the symbolic elements that specific myths might contain and the fact that a myth may be so familiar that we can make reference to it without realizing it. Ask: Do you agree that a myth is essential for society? Why or why not?

3. As students continue to read and discuss the essay, help them to conclude that in a broader sense, myths are stories or story elements that help define a culture's values and beliefs.

Art Study

A medieval bestiary was more than a widely read form of natural history. Although its purpose was ostensibly the presentation of factual information about animals, it was also a vehicle for literary and artistic expression. In addition, most bestiaries included moral, ethical, and religious lessons based on the talks of the fabulous beasts they "documented."

As Richard H. Randall, Jr., points out in *A Cloisters Bestiary* (The Metropolitan Museum of Art, 1960), none of the many versions of the medieval bestiary can be assigned to a single author. However, much of the information in bestiaries can be traced back to a single anonymous book, the *Physiologus*, which summarized classical knowledge of animals. The *Physiologus* included observations by such ancients as Herodotus, Aristotle, Pliny the Elder, and later, Saint Ambrose and Saint Isidore. As time passed, each new scribe added new information, based on a combination of faith, experience, and imagination.

PHOENIX

they are impossible, because they violate evolution. They are not species, and they deny the existence of species.

The Phoenix comes the closest to being a conventional animal, all bird for all of its adult life. It is, in fact, the most exuberant, elaborate, and ornamented of all plumed birds. It exists in the mythology of Egypt, Greece, the Middle East, and Europe, and is the same as the vermilion bird of ancient China. It lives for five hundred triumphant years, and when it dies it constructs a sort of egg-shaped cocoon around itself. Inside, it disintegrates and gives rise to a wormlike creature, which then develops into the new Phoenix, ready for the next five hundred years. In other versions the dead bird bursts into flames, and the new one arises from the ashes, but the worm story is very old, told no doubt by an early biologist.

There are so many examples of hybrid beings in bestiaries that you could say that an ardent belief in mixed forms of life is an ancient human idea, or that something else, deeply believed in, is symbolized by these consortia.[4] They are disturbing to look at, nightmarish, but most of them, oddly enough, are intended as lucky benignities. The Ch'i-lin, for instance, out of ancient China, has the body of a deer covered with gleaming scales, a marvelous bushy tail, cloven hooves, and small horns. Whoever saw a Ch'i-lin was in luck, and if you got to ride one, you had it made.

The Ganesha is one of the oldest and most familiar Hindu deities, possessing a fat human body, four human arms, and the head of a cheerful-looking elephant. Prayers to Ganesha are regarded as the quickest way around obstacles.

Not all mythical beasts are friendly, of course, but even the hostile ones have certain amiable redeeming aspects. The Manticore has a lion's body, a

man's face, and a tail with a venomous snake's head at the end of it. It bounds around seeking prey with huge claws and three rows of teeth, but it makes the sounds of a beautiful silver flute.

Some of the animal myths have the ring of contemporary biologic theory, if you allow for differences in jargon. An ancient idea in India postulates an initial Being, the first form of life on the earth, analogous to our version of the earliest procaryotic[5] arrangement of membrane-limited nucleic acid, the initial cell, born of lightning and methane. The Indian Being, undefined and indefinable, finding itself alone, fearing death, yearning for company, began to swell in size, rearranged itself inside, and then split into two identical halves. One of these changed into a cow, the other a bull, and they mated, then changed again to a mare and stallion, and so on, down to the ants, and thus the earth was populated. There is a lot of oversimplification here, and too much short-hand for modern purposes, but the essential myth is recognizable.

The serpent keeps recurring through the earliest cycles of mythology, always as a central symbol for the life of the universe and the continuity of creation. There are two great identical snakes on a Levantine libation vase of around 2000 B.C., coiled around each other in a double helix, representing the original generation of life. They are the replicated parts of the first source of living, and they are wonderfully homologous.[6]

There is a Peruvian deity, painted on a clay pot dating from around A.D. 300, believed

---

4. consortia (kən sôr′shē ə), *n. pl.* of **consortium** (kən sôr′shē əm), partnership; association.
5. procaryotic (prō kar′ē ot′ik), *adj.* referring to a type of single-celled organism.
6. homologous (hō mol′ə gəs), *adj.* corresponding in structure and origin but not in function, like the wing of a bird and the foreleg of a horse.

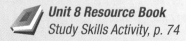

SPHINX

944

MINI-LESSON: VISUAL LITERACY

Analyze How Art Reflects Culture and Belief

Teach   Point out to students that medieval bestiaries often included moral and religious lessons to accompany each of the amazing creatures they pictured. The lessons reflected the religious beliefs as well as the cultural heritages of the writers.

For example, the unicorn was said to be a beautiful horse-like beast with a single long horn in the middle of his forehead. The unicorn could supposedly be captured in only one way: He had to be lured by a virgin girl to whom he would surrender. The writers compared the unicorn to Jesus Christ, who appeared on earth through a virgin mother and was then betrayed.

Activity Idea   Have students

- choose a fabulous beast (such as the phoenix or the griffon) and write a moral to accompany the story of the creature
- choose a fabulous beast and speculate about what the creature reveals about the culture that originated it

Unit 8 Resource Book
Study Skills Activity, p. 74

to be responsible for guarding farms. His hair is made of snakes, entwined in braids, with wings for his headdress. Plants of various kinds are growing out of his sides and back, and a vegetable of some sort seems to be growing from his mouth. The whole effect is wild and disheveled but essentially friendly. He is, in fact, an imaginary version of a genuine animal, symbiopholus, described in *Nature* several years back, a species of weevil in the mountains of northern New Guinea that lives symbiotically[7] with dozens of plants, growing in the niches and clefts in its carapace,[8] rooted all the way down to its flesh, plus a whole ecosystem of mites, rotifers, nematodes, and bacteria attached to the garden. The weevil could be taken for a good-luck omen on its own evidence; it is not attacked by predators, it lives a long, untroubled life, and nothing else will eat it, either because of something distasteful in the system or simply because of the ambiguity. The weevil is only about thirty millimeters long, easily overlooked; but it has the makings of a myth.

MANTICORE

Perhaps we should be looking around for other candidates. I suggest the need for a new bestiary, to take the place of the old ones. I can think of several creatures that seem designed for this function, if you will accept a microbestiary, and if you are looking for metaphors.

First of all, there is Myxotricha paradoxa. This is the protozoan,[9] not yet as famous as he should be, who seems to be telling us everything about everything, all at once. His cilia[10]

are not cilia at all, but individual spirochetes,[11] and at the base of attachment of each spirochete is an oval organelle,[12] embedded in the myxotricha membrane, which is a bacterium. It is not an animal after all—it is a company, an assemblage.

The story told by myxotricha is as deep as any myth, as profoundly allusive. This creature has lagged behind the rest of us, and is still going through the process of being assembled. Our cilia gave up any independent existence long ago, and our organelles are now truly ours, but the genomes[13] controlling separate parts of our cells are still different genomes, lodged in separate compartments; doctrinally, we are still assemblages.

There is another protozoan, called blepharisma, telling a long story about the chanciness and fallibility of complex life. Blepharisma is called that because of a conspicuous fringe of ciliated membranes around the oral cavity, which evidently reminded someone of eyelashes (blepharidos). The whole mythlike tale has been related in a book by Giese. Blepharisma has come much further along than myxotricha, but not far enough to be free of slip-ups. There are three different sets of self-duplicating nuclei,

CH'I-LIN

---

7. **symbiotically** (sim′bē ot′i kal lē), *adj.* referring to the relationship of two unlike organisms that live together for mutual benefit.
8. **carapace** (kar′ə pās), *n.* shell or bony covering on the back of an animal.
9. **protozoan** (prō′tə zō′ən), *n.* a microscopic animal that reproduces by dividing itself.
10. **cilia** (sil′ē ə), *n. pl.* of **cilium** (sil′ē əm), in microrganisms, very small, hairlike projections used to propel them through water.
11. **spirochete** (spī′rə kēt′), *n.* a kind of bacterium.
12. **organelle** (ôr′gə nel′), *n.* in microrganisms, a minute, specialized part of a cell.
13. **genome** (jē′nōm), *n.* the total genetic structure of a cell or organism.

MULTICULTURAL NOTE

In 1967, the Argentine writer Jorge Luis Borges published *El libro de los seres imaginarios*, one of the few twentieth-century bestiaries and perhaps the greatest. The book was later expanded and translated into English by Borges and Norman Thomas di Giovanni as *The Book of Imaginary Beings*.

In his preface, Borges refers to the book as "a handbook of the strange creatures conceived through time and space by the human imagination." He remarks, however, that his title is so broad that "imaginary beings" could logically include Prince Hamlet, the point, the line, all generic terms, and perhaps "each one of us."

The Book of Imaginary Beings ranges across cultures, and one of its effects is to reveal the universality of the fabulous-beast-making faculty. In addition to the more commonly known beasts such as the centaur, the chimera, the minotaur, and so on, the book tells the tales of such creatures as

- the Arabian Bahamut, or Behemoth, a fish at the base of the world
- the Islamic Burak, a horse's body with a man's face and a peacock's wings and tail
- the Indian Naga, a serpent or dragon that can take the form of a man
- the Chinese T'ao T'ieh, a creature with the single huge head of a dragon, tiger, or person, connected to two separate bodies

---

BUILDING ENGLISH PROFICIENCY

ESL
LEP
ELD
SAE
LD

Improving Comprehension

Both the argument and the vocabulary in this essay may pose a challenge. One or more of the following activities may help.

Activity Ideas

- Team-teach the essay with a science teacher—someone who can tell a little more about Thomas and his work, explain unfamiliar vocabulary, and simplify the information about the real-life creatures that Thomas describes.
- Encourage students to use their vocabulary notebooks, and make a dictionary available. Have students record and define unfamiliar words that are not explained in the footnotes.

- Use a jigsaw approach. Assign each of several groups of students a topic within the essay (for example, the various mythological beasts and real-life creatures); have each group focus on what Thomas says about that topic and then share its findings with the class.

Responding

1. Possible Response Creating genetic mutations in a laboratory can benefit the human race. Scientists can develop disease-resistant strains that can be raised for food to solve the world's hunger problems. On the negative side, however, human beings might set off genetic chain reactions that could prove harmful and uncontrollable.

2. Possible Response Students' composite fantasy creatures will vary, but each should combine recognizable parts or features from real animals. Suggest that students be as creative in naming their creatures as they are in constructing them.

Interdisciplinary Activity Ideas

- Students can divide into groups and create a modern bestiary based on composites of human beings and machines. Each group can be responsible for researching, designing, describing, and depicting one such creature, such as a cyborg, a bionic person, a human computer, or a virtual reality creature.

- Groups of students can organize a presentation on how Hollywood special effects teams design and create the amazing creatures of science-fiction movies. Students can include in each presentation an analysis of how such creatures combine the real and the imagined.

GREEK HERO FIGHTING A CENTAUR

with the DNA in each set serving different purposes: a large macronucleus, governing the events in regeneration after injury, a set of eight or more micronuclei containing the parts of the genome needed for reproduction, and great numbers of tiny nuclei from which the cilia arise.

One part of the organism produces a pinkish pigment, now called blepharismin, which is similar to hypericin and certain other photosensitizing plant pigments. Blepharismin causes no trouble unless the animal swims into sunlight, but then the pigment kills it outright. Under certain circumstances, the membrane surrounding blepharisma disintegrates and comes independently loose, like a cast-off shell, leaving the creature a transient albino. At times of famine, a single blepharisma will begin eating its neighbors; it then enlarges to an immense size and turns into a cannibalistic giant, straight out of any Norse fable. Evidently, this creature still has trouble getting along with the several parts of itself, and with the collective parts of other blepharismae.

There are innumerable plant-animal combinations, mostly in the sea, where the green plant cells provide carbohydrate and oxygen for the animal and receive a share of energy in return. It is the fairest of arrangements. When the paramecium bursaria runs out of food, all he needs to do is stay in the sun and his green endosymbionts will keep him supplied as though he were a grain.

Bacteria are the greatest of all at setting up

946 UNIT EIGHT: THE LATE TWENTIETH CENTURY

joint enterprises, on which the lives of their hosts are totally dependent. The nitrogen-fixing rhizobia in root nodules, the mycetomes of insects, and the enzyme-producing colonies in the digestive tracts of many animals are variations of this meticulously symmetrical symbiosis.

The meaning of these stories may be basically the same as the meaning of a medieval bestiary. There is a tendency for living things to join up, establish linkages, live inside each other, return to earlier arrangements, get along, whenever possible. This is the way of the world.

The new phenomenon of cell fusion, a laboratory trick on which much of today's science of molecular genetics relies for its data, is the simplest and most spectacular symbol of the tendency. In a way, it is the most unbiologic of all phenomena, violating the most fundamental myth of the last century, for it denies the importance of specificity, integrity, and separateness in living things. Any cell—man, animal, fish, fowl, or insect—given the chance and under the right conditions, brought into contact with any other cell, however foreign, will fuse with it. Cytoplasm will flow easily from one to the other, the nuclei will combine, and it will become, for a time anyway, a single cell with two complete, alien genomes, ready to dance, ready to multiply. It is a Chimera, a Griffon, a Sphinx, a Ganesha, a Peruvian god, a Ch'i-lin, an omen of good fortune, a wish for the world.

Responding
1. Thomas seems to feel that the ability to create genetic mutations in the laboratory is a good thing. Do you agree? Why or why not?

2. Using any medium you like, create a composite fantasy creature of your own that combines different features from two or more real animals.

MINI-LESSON: SPEAKING AND LISTENING

Use Vocabulary Appropriate to Audience

Teach Point out to students that "Some Biomythology" reads like an illustrated lecture and that the vocabulary used by Lewis Thomas is mature and scientific but not obscure, pretentious, or intimidating. Thomas assumes that his audience has

- a basic knowledge of scientific terms (such as *protozoan* and *nuclei*)
- a familiarity with formal terms, such as *libation*
- the ability to understand the definitions he provides for the more complex terms (such as *symbiopholus* and *blepharismin*)

Activity Ideas

- Ask one or more students to read aloud one of Thomas's paragraphs from the second half of the essay and then read it as if they were reading to an audience of eighth-grade students. What explanations or changes do they have to make to fit the new audience?

- Have students make a list of basic scientific words that they think should be in the working vocabulary of the average adult American. They might consider such words as *amoeba, cell, chromosome, watt, ecosystem, black hole*, and so on.

Writing Workshop

Life from Odd Angles

Assignment You have read several selections in which the characters see things from unique viewpoints. Now tell a story of your own from a unique viewpoint.

WRITER'S BLUEPRINT

Product	A monologue
Purpose	To get into the mind of a character who sees things from a unique viewpoint
Audience	Readers whom your character is addressing directly
Specs	As the writer of a successful monologue, you should:

❏ Choose a narrator, living or nonliving, who sees things from a unique viewpoint and an appropriate event for this narrator to describe. For example:

—a picnic as seen by an ant

—a rush-hour ride across a big city as seen by a taxicab

—the arrival home of a new baby as seen by the baby

—a morning in the life of a bathroom mirror

❏ Present your monologue as a series of incidents in time order, from first to last.

❏ Use the first-person ("I") point of view, with the narrator telling readers what's going through his or her (or its) mind as the event unfolds. Don't reveal your narrator's identify directly but hint at it along the way, so that your audience can discover it for themselves.

❏ Begin with a mysterious or startling detail to grab your reader's attention. Include information about sensory details, feelings, and thoughts that run through the narrator's mind as the event unfolds.

❏ End with a humorous touch.

❏ Follow the rules of grammar, usage, spelling, and mechanics—with one exception. Use sentence fragments if they realistically portray the way your narrator thinks and speaks.

Writing Workshop   **947**

WRITER'S BLUEPRINT
Specs

The Specs in the Writer's Blueprint address these writing and thinking skills:

• creating a character

• organizing events

• foreshadowing

• using first-person point of view

• using sensory details

• writing humor

• writing realistic dialogue

These Specs serve as your lesson objectives, and they form the basis for the **Assessment Criteria Specs** for a superior paper, which appear on the final TE page for this lesson. You might want to read through the Assessment Criteria Specs with students when you begin the lesson.

Linking Literature to Writing

Interesting storytelling often grows out of a unique perspective and an observant eye. Have students discuss authors, comedians, and filmmakers whom they feel work from a slant view.

WRITING WORKSHOP OVERVIEW

Product
Narrative writing: A monologue

Prewriting
Review the literature—Brainstorm ideas for characters and events—Define your narrator's viewpoint—Brainstorm sensory details—Plan your opening—Break down your event—Plan your monologue
Unit 8 Resource Book
Prewriting Worksheets pp. 83–84

Drafting
Start writing
Transparency Collection
Student Models for Writing Workshop 33, 34

Revising
Ask a partner—Strategy: Ending with a Humorous Touch
Unit 8 Resource Book
Revising Worksheet p. 85

Editing
Ask a partner—Strategy: Using Sentence Fragments
Unit 8 Resource Book
Grammar Worksheet p. 86
Grammar Check Test p. 87

Presenting
Read Aloud
Identify Narrator

Looking Back
Self-evaluate—Reflect—For Your Working Portfolio
Unit 8 Resource Book
Assessment Worksheet p. 88
Transparency Collection
Fine Art Writing Prompt 17

STEP 1 PREWRITING
Review the literature

Encourage students to create more categories for their charts.

Brainstorm ideas for characters and events

Challenge students to come up with at least ten interesting perspectives to choose from. For additional support, see the worksheet referenced below.

Unit 8 Resource Book
Prewriting Worksheet, p. 83

Define your narrator's viewpoint

Some students might find a web chart will allow them to be more flexible or creative.

Brainstorm sensory details

Instruct students to write sensory details as quickly as they come to mind. Remind them not to try to write complete sentences, use capitalization, or even think about spelling. If students have difficulty recognizing the sensory details in their quickwrites, have them exchange papers with a partner who can underline the details. For additional support, see the worksheet referenced below.

Unit 8 Resource Book
Prewriting Worksheet, p. 84

Plan your opening

Some movies open with a unique or enigmatic perspective that intrigues the audience. Show clips of the first minutes of a few movies and discuss the techniques used.

LITERARY SOURCE
"But you are my daughters,/ you inherit my own faults/of character;/you are submissive, following Adam/even beyond existence."
from "Eve to Her Daughters" by Judith Wright

Review the literature in this part of the unit. Meet with a group to discuss the main characters. Make notes in charts like the one shown. Think of each category as contributing to the character's unique viewpoint.

Eve in "Eve to Her Daughters"

Location	Desires, Goals	Problems, Fears, Complaints	Limitations, Restrictions
outside Eden	to have her daughters take over for her	Adam's discontent and egotism	submissive, subject to Adam's will and God's punishment

Brainstorm ideas for characters and events. List characters who experience life from a unique viewpoint. These characters may be living or nonliving (see the examples in the Writer's Blueprint). Choose the character and event that you feel would interest readers most.

Define your narrator's viewpoint in a chart like the one you made in "Review the literature." For example:

a morning in the life of a bathroom mirror

Location	Desires, Goals	Problems, Fears, Complaints	Limitations, Restrictions
bathroom of a house, on wall above sink	—to be able to give grooming tips to sloppy family members —to be able to see more of world	—afraid they'll break me —They never look at <u>me</u>, only themselves!	—can't move, can't look around —full of ideas but can't communicate, can't express myself

OR . . .
Take on your character's voice and improvise a monologue about what you see, feel, and smell. Audiotape it and make notes on sensory details as you play it back.

Brainstorm sensory details in a quickwrite. Visualize yourself in the position of your narrator. How do things look and sound and feel and smell? Write for a few minutes about everything your senses pick up. When you finish, underline the sensory details you've come up with.

Plan your opening. You'll want to grab your readers' attention by hinting at your narrator's identity. Jot down some ideas. For example:

> In a moment the door will open and the first of them will stagger in, rub the sleep from her eyes, and stare at me as if I held the answer to the riddle of life itself.

948   UNIT EIGHT: THE LATER TWENTIETH CENTURY

MINI-LESSON: PREWRITING
Using Sensory Details

Give students practice writing detailed description by having them create a verbal still life.

Start by having students make a frame by cutting a square out of a sheet of notebook paper. Then send them outside or around the school to find a place to frame and describe in vivid detail. For example, students may frame a bathroom sink and describe the water draining, or they might frame an ant bed and describe the actions of the ants.

Finally, have students read their paragraphs to the class to see if their peers can figure out what was described.

Not you again. I've seen your face so many times I'd know it like the back of my hand—if I had a hand.

Break down your event into a series of incidents in time order, from first to last. List them or arrange them in a time line.

Plan your monologue by making notes in a plan like the one shown. Use your prewriting materials to guide you.

Narrator
Event
Mysterious or startling detail to begin

Incident #1
—Sights
—Sounds
—Smells
—Feelings
—Thoughts

Incident #2
and so on . . .

Humorous touch to close (see the Revising Strategy in Step 3)

 OR . . .
Make your plan in the form of a storyboard. On a separate piece of paper, sketch a key moment from each incident and on the back make notes on sights, sounds, smells, feelings, and thoughts.

STEP 2 DRAFTING

Start writing. Use your prewriting materials as a guide, but be flexible. Here are some tips that may help you as you draft.

- Close your eyes and visualize the setting as your monologue begins. Then begin writing.

- As you write, keep in mind that you'll be hinting at your narrator's identity all along without ever stating it directly.

- End with a humorous touch. See the Revising Strategy in Step 3.

STEP 3 REVISING

Ask a partner for comments on your draft before you revise it. Use the checklist on the next page to guide your comments.

Break down your event

Encourage students to work towards building a structured plot line.

Plan your monologue

Assure students that they needn't necessarily make notes for every single "Incident" category.

 Connections to
Writer's Notebook

For selection-related prompts, refer to Writer's Notebook.

Connections to
Writer's Resource

For additional writing prompts, refer to Writer's Resource.

STEP 2 DRAFTING
Start writing

Encourage students to freewrite material that can be pared down later.

The Student Models

The **transparencies** referenced below are authentic student models. Review them with the students before they draft.

1. After reading model 33, can you think of a more mysterious or startling detail that the writer could use at the beginning?

2. Find the sentence fragments in each model. Do they add to or detract from the monologue? Explain.

 Transparency Collection
Student Models for Writing Workshop 33, 34

STEP 3 REVISING
Ask a partner
(Peer assessment)

Have students read their papers aloud to get a feel for the narrator's voice.

BUILDING ENGLISH PROFICIENCY

Using Prewriting Helps

Draw attention to some of the prewriting helps provided on pages 948–949.

- After students read the "Literary Source" note, discuss Eve's unique viewpoint—that is, what gives her a slant view. Offer students the option of creating a monologue in which they speak as the first of their kind (for example, the first movie theater or the first personal computer).

- Encourage students who are interested in the "Or . . ." activity on page 948 to spend a few hours walking about taping comments in the voice of their character as new situations arise. Urge them to review the tape several times, taking notes that might be useful to their monologues.

Revising Strategy: Ending with a Humorous Touch

Have students share monologues, stories, or commercials they have seen or heard that end with a humorous twist.

For additional support, see the worksheet referenced below.

Unit 8 Resource Book
Revising Worksheet, p. 85

Connections to
Writer's Resource

Refer to the Grammar, Usage, and Mechanics Handbook on Writer's Resource.

STEP 4 EDITING

Ask a partner (Peer assessment)

Ask students to consider differences in editing fiction as opposed to nonfiction.

✔ Did I begin with a startling or mysterious detail to hook the reader?

✔ Have I effectively hinted at the narrator's identity without directly revealing it?

✔ Have I ended with a humorous touch?

Revising Strategy

Ending with a Humorous Touch

One way is to end a monologue like this one is with a humorous touch, a little joke or anecdote. Here are two examples of humorous closings (a pun and a reference to a popular fairy tale), using the idea of a morning in the life of a bathroom mirror:

> No! Don't walk out, don't leave me again! Oh well, I guess I'll do what I do every day after they leave for work, sit here on the wall and reflect on the morning's events.

> If only you could hear me, my sweet Angela, I would tell you, and you would know, that you and you alone are the fairest of them all. Perhaps someday, somehow, I will find a way to tell you.

Notice how this writer, who wrote from the point of view of a television set, adds a line to bring his monologue to a clever close.

What I need is a change of scenery. I've been sitting in this same spot for what seems like years now. My view isn't so bad, though. I can look out the window and watch cars go by. That's a good thing. But I feel like I have no control over my life. *If only I could reach the remote control.* ∧

 STUDENT MODEL

STEP EDITING

Ask a partner to review your revised draft before you edit. When you edit, watch for errors in grammar, and leave them in your monologue if they help show how your character thinks and speaks.

MINI-LESSON: GRAMMAR

Using Sentence Fragments

Have students discuss the strengths and weaknesses of the following versions of a monologue spoken by a self-absorbed cabdriver. Which version sounds more interesting, more true to life? Why?

They never thank me for the ride. Never. Just hop into my cab. Pay me no mind. Expect me to just silently take them wherever their impulses dictate. Such ingrates.

They never thank me for the ride. They just hop into my cab, pay me no mind, and expect me to just silently take them wherever their impulses dictate. They are such ingrates.

Unit 8 Resource Book
Grammar Worksheet, p. 86
Grammar Check Test, p. 87

Editing Strategy

Using Sentence Fragments

Sentence fragments are to be avoided in most writing. But since people often think and speak in fragments, they're acceptable when they appear in a monologue. Notice how this writer uses fragments to give his narrator's thoughts a realistic structure.

FOR REFERENCE
More information about sentence fragments can be found in the Language and Grammar Handbook at the back of this text.

> He stares at me. Really stares. Bores a hole right through me. I can't look him in the eye. I bet it gives him great pleasure to watch me squirm.

 STUDENT MODEL

STEP 5 PRESENTING

- Create a unique *voice* for your narrator before reading your monologue to classmates.
- Share your monologue with a small group and have them talk about when they figured out the narrator's identity and how.

STEP 6 LOOKING BACK

Self-evaluate. Look back at the Writer's Blueprint and give yourself a score on each point, from 6 (superior) to 1 (inadequate).

Reflect. Write answers to these questions.

✔ Was this particular assignment fun to write? Why or why not?

✔ If you were to make this monologue part of a longer story, what are some other events that might happen in the story?

For Your Working Portfolio Add your monologue and reflection responses to your working portfolio.

ASSESSMENT CRITERIA SPECS

Here are the criteria for a superior paper. A full six-level rubric for this paper appears on the Assessment Worksheet referenced below.

6 Superior   The writer of a 6 paper impressively meets these criteria:

- Narrates the monologue from a unique viewpoint that is both startling and amusing.
- Organizes events within a well-planned structure.
- Uses first-person point of view, featuring a narrator whose identity is not immediately

apparent but is cleverly hinted at for the reader to discover along the way.

- Gets deep into the narrator's mind, revealing intimate sensations, thoughts, and feelings.
- Ends with a humorous touch.
- Makes few, if any, mistakes in grammar, usage, mechanics, and spelling—but may use sentence fragments for the sake of realism.

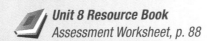
Unit 8 Resource Book
Assessment Worksheet, p. 88

Editing Strategy: Using Sentence Fragments

For additional support, see the mini-lesson at the bottom of page 950 and the worksheets referenced below.

Unit 8 Resource Book
Grammar Worksheet, p. 86
Grammar Check Test, p. 87

Connections to
Writer's Resource

Refer to the Grammar, Usage, and Mechanics Handbook on Writer's Resource.

STEP 5 PRESENTING
Read Aloud

Advise students to practice their delivery at home, in front of a mirror.

Identify Narrator

Writers will benefit from knowing exactly which clues readers picked up, and from seeing that details they didn't realize were clues turned out to be clues.

STEP 6 LOOKING BACK
Self-evaluate

The *Assessment Criteria Specs* at the bottom of this page are for a superior paper. You might want to post these in the classroom. Students can then evaluate themselves based on these criteria. For a complete scoring rubric, use the *Assessment Worksheet* referenced below.

Unit 8 Resource Book
Assessment Worksheet, p. 88

Reflect

After students discuss why they did or didn't like this assignment, ask them to describe the kind of projects they would assign if they were English teachers.

To further explore the theme, use the Fine Art Transparency referenced below.

Transparency Collection
Fine Art Writing Prompt 17

Beyond Print

Teaching Objectives

- to understand the concept of cause and effect
- to understand simple cause and effect relationships and cause-effect chains
- to identify cause-effect relationships in short stories
- to diagram cause-effect relationships

Curricular Connection: Critical Thinking

Use the material in this article to give students practice in recognizing and diagramming cause-effect relationships.

Introduce

Have students read the first paragraph. Then have them give examples of simple cause-effect relationships. Next, have them read the rest of the article. Point out that cause-effect relationships can also have multiple causes and multiple effects.

Question Why are cause-effect relationships easier to predict in any scientific field than they are in politics, government, or education, for example? *(Possible answer: Although humans are frequently predictable in their actions and reactions, quite often they are unpredictable, which explains why elections are upset. In botany, physics, and chemistry, for example, cause-effect relationships, if not subject to human interference, are usually predictable.)*

Activity Options

Activity 1 Encourage students to look for complex as well as simple cause-effect relationships.

Activity 2 Allow students to use a software program with animation if they wish.

Activity 3 You may wish to have students diagram the relationships they find first before beginning the discussion.

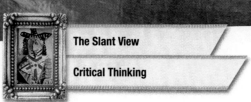
Beyond Print

Cause and Effect

Any person, thing, or event that produces an effect is a *cause*. It is the reason something happens. The result of an event, idea, or action is an *effect*. It is whatever is produced or made to happen by a cause. In simple cause-effect relationships, one cause has one effect; for example, you turn on the TV set, and a picture appears.

Cause-effect relationships, however, are usually more complex than those in which a single cause produces a single effect. One type of complex cause-effect relationship occurs when a single cause produces a chain of effects. For example, in Graham Greene's story "A Shocking Accident," a pig falls from a balcony and kills Jerome's father. Classmates who hear the story laugh and call Jerome "Pig," making him self-conscious and fearful that others will learn about the mishap and laugh. Later, when his fiancée hears the story, however, she delights him with her serious, thoughtful reaction.

Drawing a diagram can help you understand this kind of chain of causation:

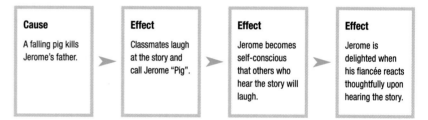

Cause	Effect	Effect	Effect
A falling pig kills Jerome's father.	Classmates laugh at the story and call Jerome "Pig".	Jerome becomes self-conscious that others who hear the story will laugh.	Jerome is delighted when his fiancée reacts thoughtfully upon hearing the story.

Activity Options

1. Diagram cause-effect relationships in either "The Truly Married Woman" or "The Courtship of Mr. Lyon."

2. Create a cause-effect diagram in the form of a storyboard illustrating key events in one of the other stories in this book.

3. With a group of students, select a movie that exhibits complex cause-effect relationships and discuss how they contribute to the film's theme.

ANOTHER APPROACH

Kinesthetic Demonstration of Cause and Effect

Use two dominoes to demonstrate a simple one cause/one effect relationship. Then use a group of four dominoes, labeling each one appropriately to demonstrate the cause-and-effect chain shown in the diagram. Have students label and set up the dominoes to demonstrate the cause-and-effect chains they identify in "The Truly Married Woman" or "The Courtship of Mr. Lyon."

Multicultural Connections

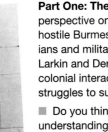

Interactions

Part One: The Passing of Empire George Orwell acquires a unique perspective on imperialism when his job forces him to interact with hostile Burmese. Winston Churchill oversees the interactions of civilians and military personnel as England battles for its existence. Philip Larkin and Derek Walcott comment from their own perspectives on colonial interactions, and Buchi Emecheta's character, Adah, struggles to survive in a world she has inherited from others.

■ Do you think that rulers and their subjects can ever interact with understanding, or are their perspectives so influenced by their positions that they cannot?

Perspective

Part Two: The Slant View The perspective from which a story is told may drastically alter the participants' views of each other and of their interactions. Each of the characters in these selections responds to a situation in a way that is not quite expected.

■ What advantages are there in being able to look at life from different perspectives?

Activities

1. Choose a selection from this unit and stage the interactions—the conflicts and the resolutions—as a series of "frozen moments" in pantomime. Use as many students as there are main characters and plan in advance exactly what poses (and how many) are needed to tell the story. Practice your pantomime before staging it for the class.

2. Choose a selection and retell it briefly from the perspective of another character; for example, recount the events in "Eveline" from Frank's point of view or the soldier in "Disabled" from the point of view of a nurse.

953

Unit Wrap-Up

MULTICULTURAL CONNECTION

Unusual perspectives can result from cultural interaction, societal change, people's unique personalities, and other factors that shape the perspectives revealed in Parts One and Two of Unit 8. The following ideas and questions may facilitate discussion.

Interactions

- Differences in cultural perspectives can strain interactions among people.
- Rulers and those they rule necessarily have different perspectives.

Possible Response Students may cite historical examples in which the ruled and their ruler(s) interacted with understanding. Such examples will be found in nations that have a democratic form of government. In dictatorships such examples are extremely rare or nonexistent.

Perspective

People are often at a loss to understand perspectives that are based on values different from their own.

Possible Responses Looking at life from different persepctives can free one from stereotypical responses. It can open up new understandings and result in a deeper appreciation of life.

Activities

Activity 1 Students may want to refer to their cause-effect analysis for ideas about some of the important moments.

Activity 2 Have students consider which of the following will change with the new perspective, and how they will be different: diction, tone, style, content.

953

UNIT 1 OPTIONS
Media

Encourage students to use a wide variety of sources such as these:

- the television interview of Princess Diana in 1996
- British tabloid newspapers
- *People* magazine
- Biographies of the royal family
- history texts

Graphic Arts

Make sure students use up-to-date sources, or the data may be wrong. For example, Hong Kong is due to be returned to Chinese rule in 1997.

Music

- Encourage students to interview people who lived at the height of the group's fame, or people who continue to admire them.
- Help students locate local radio stations that play their group's hits so they can hear them firsthand.

Popular Culture

- Inform students that some of these shows are available on video and some may be found on their local PBS affiliate.
- In order to understand what makes humor specifically British, students may need to identify the traits found in American humor for contrast.

Unit Test

Unit 8 Resource Book
New Selection
Test 1
Test 2

Independent and Group Projects

Media

The British Monarchy The British monarchy has always been a dominant force in the lives of the British people. Working with several other members of your class, prepare a **television documentary** about British rulers. Using appropriate time lines and illlustrations, briefly trace the history of the monarchy. Place your greatest emphasis on the roles of British rulers in the twentieth century. Conclude your show with a panel discussion in which you and your colleagues attempt to predict the future of the monarchy.

Graphic Arts

The Commonwealth of Nations The Commonwealth of Nations is an association of forty-nine nations and dependencies that give allegiance, real and symbolic, to the British crown. It is what the British Empire has evolved into in the later twentieth century. Prepare a **map of the world** that identifies all the members of the Commonwealth of Nations. Include a caption for each nation telling briefly its history and its present relationship to England.

Music

Monkeeing with Beatlemania Beginning with the release of the Beatles' first album in 1963, British rock groups invaded the musical world with new sounds and styles. Select one of the following British groups—the Beatles, the Rolling Stones, the Monkees, Herman's Hermits, the Animals—or a group of your choice, and prepare an **interactive museum exhibit** (select from audio, video, graphics, and computer "hands-on" activities) designed to explain the influence of your chosen rock group to a teenage audience in the year 2025.

Popular Culture

Boundless British Humor British humor abounds on American television. With a group of classmates, view several British comedy shows. You might choose from *Monty Python's Flying Circus* (see pages 961–962), *Dr. Who, Fawlty Towers, Are You Being Served?,* or *Absolutely Fabulous,* for example. Try to determine what special qualities of humor are present in these shows. Working together, write a **humorous script** that attempts to capture some elements of British humor. Perform your script for your class.

954

THE ABSURD PERSON

THEMES *in*
ENGLISH
LITERATURE

About
Theater of the Absurd

The absurd as a stated philosophy is very much a twentieth-century phenomenon, and yet elements of the absurd can be found in most periods of literature. The Theater of the Absurd came into focus with plays such as *Waiting for Godot* and *Endgame* by Samuel Beckett and *The Bald Soprano* by Eugène Ionesco. Plays by Harold Pinter, such as *The Birthday Party*, *The Dumb Waiter*, and *A Slight Ache*, added to the canon. In the U.S., Arthur Kopit contributed *Oh Dad, Poor Dad, Momma's Hung You In the Closet and I'm Feelin' So Sad*. Tom Stoppard carried on the tradition with plays like *Rosencrantz and Guildenstern are Dead*, *Albert's Bridge*, and *If You're Glad I'll Be Frank*.

THE
ABSURD PERSON

Edward Lear, caricature of himself (1870s)

from **The Theater of the Absurd**

Absurd means "ridiculous," but in the later twentieth century it has come to be used also for a philosophy and an artistic movement. Theater of the Absurd, as it has come to be called, relies in part on theatrical effects, such as are seen in the work of jugglers, acrobats, bullfighters, or mimes; clowning, fooling, and mad scenes; verbal nonsense; and elements of dream and fantasy. None of these is new, of course—they go back untold centuries. What *is* new is the term (coined by theater critic Martin Esslin) and its application to a philosophy of life, to a sense that life in the late 1900s doesn't have the same kind of meaning—or doesn't have meaning in the same way—as life seemed to have in earlier, simpler times.

The hallmark of this attitude is its sense that the certitudes and unshakable basic assumptions of former ages have been swept away, that they have been tested and found wanting, that they have been discredited as cheap and somewhat childish illusions. The decline of religious faith was masked until the end of the Second World War by the substitute religions of faith in progress, nationalism, and various totalitarian fallacies. All this was shattered by the war. By 1942, Albert Camus[1] . . . tried to diagnose the human situation in a world of shattered beliefs:

"A world that can be explained by reasoning, however faulty, is a familiar world. But in a universe that is suddenly deprived of illusions and of light, man feels a stranger. His is an irremediable[2] exile, because he is deprived of memories of a lost homeland as much as he lacks the hope of a promised land to come. This divorce between man and his life, the actor and his setting, truly constitutes the feeling of Absurdity."

Theme Link to the Literature

Some other selections in the text that deal with the theme of the absurd are listed here.

- "Get Up and Bar the Door" (p. 28)
- "Song" (p. 226)
- from *The Rape of the Lock* (p. 314)
- "A Mad Tea-Party" from *Alice's Adventures in Wonderland* (p. 547)
- "Not Waving but Drowning" (p. 911)
- "A Shocking Accident" (p. 926)

Nicely
Nicely
Clive

Absurd originally means "out of harmony," in a musical context. Hence its dictionary definition: "out of harmony with reason or propriety; incongruous, unreasonable, illogical." In common usage, *absurd* may simply mean "ridiculous," but this is not the sense in which Camus uses the word, . . . [Eugène] Ionesco[3] defined his understanding of the term as follows: "Absurd is that which is devoid of purpose. . . . Cut off from his religious, metaphysical, and transcendental roots, man is lost; all his actions become senseless, absurd, useless."

Martin Esslin (1961)

To Clive Barrow it was just an ordinary day nothing unusual or strange about it, everything quite novel, nothing outstanley just another day but to Roger it was something special, a day amongst days . . . a red lettuce day . . . because Roger was getting married and as he dressed that morning he thought about the gay batchelor soups he'd had with all his pals. And Clive said nothing. To Roger everything was different, wasn't this the day his Mother had told him about, in his best suit and all that, grimming and shakeing hands, people tying boots and ricebudda on his car.

To have and to harm . . . till death duty part . . . he knew it all off by hertz. Clive Barrow seemed oblivious. Roger could visualise Anne in her flowing weddy drag, being wheeled up the aisle, smiling a blessing. He had butterfield in his stomarce as he fastened his bough tie and brushed his hairs. "I hope I'm doing the right thing" he thought looking in the mirror, "Am I good enough for her?" Roger need not have worried because he was. "Should I have flowers all round the spokes?" said Anne polishing her foot rest. "Or should I keep it syble?" she continued looking down on her grain haired Mother.

"Does it really matter?" repaid her Mother wearily wiping her sign. "He won't be looking at your spokes anyway." Anne smiled the smile of someone who's seen a few laughs.

Then luckily Anne's father came home from sea and cancelled the husband.

John Lennon (1964)

Life's But a Walking Shadow

LIFE'S BUT A WALKING SHADOW, A POOR PLAYER
THAT STRUTS AND FRETS HIS HOUR UPON THE STAGE
AND THEN IS HEARD NO MORE; IT IS A TALE
TOLD BY AN IDIOT, FULL OF SOUND AND FURY,
SIGNIFYING NOTHING.

William Shakespeare (about 1606)

---

1. **Albert Camus** (àl ber´ ka´ mʏ´) (1913–1960), French novelist and essayist.
2. **irremediable** (ir´i mē´dē ə bəl), *adj.* incurable.

3. **Eugène Ionesco** (œ zhen´ yo nes´kō), born 1912, French playright, born in Romania.

957

About John Lennon

Known to the world as one-fourth of the legendary British rock group The Beatles, John Lennon (1940–1980) was also a writer. In addition to music and lyrics for some of the Beatles' songs, Lennon wrote two books of nonsense, *In His Own Write* and *A Spaniard in the Works*, both characterized by puns, homonyms, and bizarre word substitutions.

About the Shakespeare Quote

This quote is from *Macbeth*, Act Five, Scene 5. Macbeth speaks these lines upon hearing of Lady Macbeth's death (see p. 184).

BUILDING ENGLISH PROFICIENCY

Exploring Key Concepts

To help students grasp the concept of the absurd, have them decide what elements contribute to the absurdity of each of the following episodes:

1. A man dreams he is a butterfly; on waking, he can't decide whether he is a man who has dreamed he was a butterfly or a butterfly dreaming he is a man.

2. A mapmaker creates a map of a country that is the same size as the country.

3. A poor young couple want to buy Christmas presents for each other: The man sells his pocket watch to buy hair combs for his wife; the wife sells her hair to buy him a watch chain.

4. A group of people put out to sea in a sieve.

5. Gardeners are ordered to paint roses red.

About Edward Lear

Edward Lear (1812–1888) was an English artist and poet known mostly for his nonsense poetry concerning the immortal Jumblies, the Yonghy-Bonghy-Bò, the Owl and the Pussycat, and other characters beloved of children. He did much to popularize the limerick, and some of his word inventions, such as the famous "runcible" spoon, have remained in the language.

About William Blake

William Blake (see p. 401), profoundly religious yet fiercely individualistic, considered that the degree of historical validity of the Bible was irrelevant; it represented to him the Great Code of Art, the total form of what he called the Divine Vision, which he believed to have been so obscured by the nightmare of history as to be all but totally darkened in his own time.

Incidents in the Life of My Uncle Arly

O my agèd Uncle Arly!
Sitting on a heap of Barley
    Through the silent hours of night,
Close beside a leafy thicket:
In his hat a Railway-Ticket.
      (But his shoes were far too tight.)

Long ago, in youth, he squandered
All his goods away, and wandered
    To the Tiniskoop-hills afar.
There on golden sunsets blazing,
Every evening found him gazing,
Singing, "Orb! you're quite amazing!
    How I wonder what you are!"

Like the ancient Medes and Persians,
Always by his own exertions
    He subsisted on those hills;
Whiles—by teaching children spelling—
Or at times by merely yelling—
Or at intervals by selling
    "Propter's Nicodemus Pills."

Later in his morning rambles
He perceived the moving brambles
    Something square and white disclose.
'Twas a First-Class Railway-Ticket;
But, on stooping down to pick it
Off the ground, a pea-green Cricket
    Settled on my uncle's Nose.

Never—never more—oh! never,
Did that Cricket leave him ever,
    Dawn or evening, day or night;
Clinging as a constant treasure,
Chirping with a cheerious measure,
Wholly to my uncle's pleasure.
    (Though his shoes were far too tight.)

So for three-and-forty winters,
Till his shoes were worn to splinters,
    All those hills he wandered o'er—
Sometimes silent; sometimes yelling;
Till he came to Borley-Melling,
Near his old ancestral dwelling.
    (But his shoes were far too tight.)

On a little heap of Barley
Died my agèd uncle Arly,
    And they buried him one night
Close beside the leafy thicket;
There—his hat and Railway-Ticket;
There—his ever faithful Cricket.
    (But his shoes were far too tight.)

Edward Lear (1895)

TO NOBODADDY

Why art thou silent & invisible,
Father of Jealousy?
Why dost thou hide thyself in clouds
From every searching Eye?

Why darkness & obscurity
In all thy words & laws,
That none dare eat the fruit but from
The wily serpent's jaws?
Or is it because Secrecy
Gains female's loud applause?

William Blake (1863)

nobodaddy. The speaker is suggesting that God the Father is actually nobody's daddy.

MINI-LESSON: READING/THINKING SKILLS

Recognize Values

Recognizing values is identifying statements based on deeply held beliefs or philosophies.

Teach Point out to students that this passage from William Blake presents a very negative version of the orthodox Christian conception of God. Ask students what characteristics Blake attributes to this God. *(silence, invisibility, jealousy, obscurity, secrecy)*

Activity Idea Have one student play the role of Blake, working up his or her conception of the poet from this poem and the material on pages 401–407. Have several other students serve as a panel to question Blake about his views on religion.

from
The Crack in the Teacup

There is no doubt the post-war period has seen the intensification of the gloom that characterizes influential twentieth-century art. This is the time of the bomb, of the spread of dictatorships and torture, of forces of destruction unleashed against innocent people, of the collapse of the rich societies of the west. Such ideas are not cheerful, they are painful to hear, and impossible to solve. Therefore, the larger audiences gravitate to escapist culture, and in spite of huge resources deployed[1] to foster it, art is still the domain[2] of a small élite, and its predominant theme is despair. Man's immense powers for self-destruction are contrasted to the littleness of his spiritual capacities; the accessibility of riches and power is compared to the emotional emptiness of the individual; the vast organized fabric of society is shown to engulf the people within it. But futility and the sense of meaninglessness have penetrated all modern European literature so deeply that the case cannot be said to be peculiarly British. It certainly belongs to Britain, too, though, for some of the most articulate[3] voices of contemporary goallessness have come from Britain.

Marina Warner (1979)

1. **deploy** (di ploiʹ), *v.* use.
2. **domain** (dō mānʹ), *n.* area of activity or control.
3. **articulate** (är tikʹyə lit), *adj.* able to put into words easily and clearly.

SOLOMON GRUNDY

Solomon Grundy,
Born on a Monday,
Christened on Tuesday,
Married on Wednesday,
Took ill on Thursday,
Worse on Friday,
Died on Saturday,
Buried on Sunday,
This is the end
Of Solomon Grundy.

Mother Goose rhyme (1700s)

Ronald Searle,
The Greedy Carpet *(1972)*

959

About Marina Warner

Novelist and cultural critic, Marina Warner (born 1946) is best known for her books dealing with female myths and symbols, such as *Alone of All Her Sex: The Myth and Cult of the Virgin Mary* (1976), *Joan of Arc: The Image of Female Heroism* (1981), and *Monuments and Maidens: The Allegory of Female Form* (1986).

About Solomon Grundy

This rhyme was first collected by J. O. Halliwell in *The Nursery Rhymes of England* (1842). In *The Oxford Dictionary of Nursery Rhymes*, folklore scholars Peter and Iona Opie note that "this rhyme was sufficiently well known in Britain in 1945 to be parodied in an advertisement issued by the National Savings Committee."

Art Study

Visual Literacy   Ronald Searle has a distinctive style. One of the great graphic satirists, he has exerted considerable influence on pictorial humor. This ink and watercolor picture is typical of his bizarre choice of subject and whimsical distortion of reality.

Question   How does the title contribute to the surprise and the humor in this picture? *(Possible response: The situation is not an accident; the carpet has apparently been lying in wait for a victim to walk on it.)*

BUILDING ENGLISH PROFICIENCY

Exploring Key Concepts

Students may need help with the passage from Marina Warner's "The Crack in the Teacup." Point out that she is tracing the sense of absurdity, the "futility and meaninglessness," that mark much modern culture to the impact of events and trends in twentieth-century history. Ask students what is "absurd" about the following:

1. Human beings have created stockpiles of weapons capable of destroying the earth.

2. Modern societies are so complex that those who must live in them cannot understand them.

Then ask students to provide examples of aspects of contemporary life that strike them as "absurd."

Art Study

Visual Literacy In the exclusively Scottish sport of tossing the caber, a tapered fir pole about 17 feet long and about 90 pounds in weight must be thrown so that it turns end over end and comes to rest with the small end pointing away from the thrower. Here the artist has substituted Anglican priests for cabers, resulting in a humorous, surrealistic image.

Question How do the physical attitudes of the clergymen being tossed add to the humor and surrealism of this picture? *(Possible response: Instead of being alarmed, they seem to regard this activity as normal, and they even cooperate with the sportsmen by standing on their heads.)*

James Grainger, Clergy Tossing *(1981)*

T H E
D E A D   P A R R O T
S K E T C H

Mr. Praline walks into a pet shop carrying a dead parrot in a cage. He walks to counter where shopkeeper tries to hide below cash register.

PRALINE. Hello, I wish to register a complaint . . . Hello? Miss?

SHOPKEEPER. What do you mean, miss?

PRALINE. Oh, I'm sorry, I have a cold. I wish to make a complaint.

SHOPKEEPER. Sorry, we're closing for lunch.

PRALINE. Never mind that, my lad, I wish to complain about this parrot what I purchased not half an hour ago from this very boutique.

SHOPKEEPER. Oh yes, the Norwegian Blue. What's wrong with it?

PRALINE. I'll tell you what's wrong with it. It's dead, that's what's wrong with it.

SHOPKEEPER. No, no, it's resting. Look!

PRALINE. Look my lad, I know a dead parrot when I see one, and I'm looking at one right now.

SHOPKEEPER. No, no sir, it's not dead. It's resting.

PRALINE. Resting?

SHOPKEEPER. Yeah, remarkable bird the Norwegian Blue, beautiful plumage, innit?

PRALINE. The plumage don't enter into it—it's stone dead.

SHOPKEEPER. No, no—it's just resting.

PRALINE. All right then, if it's resting I'll wake it up. *(Shouts into cage.)* Hello Polly! I've got a nice cuttlefish for you when you wake up, Polly Parrot!

SHOPKEEPER *(jogging cage).* There, it moved.

PRALINE. No he didn't. That was you pushing the cage.

SHOPKEEPER. I did not.

PRALINE. Yes, you did. *(Takes parrot out of cage, shouts.)* Hello Polly, Polly! *(Bangs it against counter.)* Polly Parrot, wake up. Polly. *(Throws it in the air and lets it fall to the floor.)* Now that's what I call a dead parrot.

SHOPKEEPER. No, no—it's stunned.

PRALINE. Look my lad, I've had just about enough of this. That parrot is definitely deceased. And when I bought it not half an hour ago, you assured me that its lack of movements was due to it being tired and shagged out after a long squawk.

SHOPKEEPER. It's probably pining for the fiords.[1]

PRALINE. Pining for the fiords, what kind of talk is that? Look, why did it fall flat on its back the moment I got it home?

SHOPKEEPER. The Norwegian Blue prefers kipping[2] on its back. Beautiful bird, lovely plumage.

PRALINE. Look, I took the liberty of examining that parrot, and I discovered that the only reason that it had been sitting on its perch in the first place was that it had been nailed there.

SHOPKEEPER. Well of course it was nailed there. Otherwise it would muscle up to those bars and voom.

PRALINE. Look matey *(picks up parrot)*, this parrot wouldn't voom if I put four thousand volts through it. It's bleeding demised.

SHOPKEEPER. It's not, it's pining.

PRALINE. It's not pining, it's passed on. This

---

1. **fiord** (fyôrd), *n.* a long, narrow bay of the sea bordered by steep cliffs, such as found in Norway.
2. **kip,** sleep.

961

About
Monty Python's Flying Circus
Monty Python's Flying Circus was the collective name of a group of writers and actors: Graham Chapman, John Cleese, Terry Gilliam, Eric Idle, Terry Jones, and Michael Palin, as well as the name of their television series, which they created for the BBC.

BUILDING ENGLISH PROFICIENCY

Exploring National Games

Caber-tossing is one of a number of traditional Scottish sporting events sometimes collectively referred to as "Highland games." Students might be interested in discussing games that are characteristic of other parts of the world. *(Some examples might include boccie, jai-alai, kendo, and cricket.)*

About Richard Corbet

Bishop first of Oxford and then of Norwich, Richard Corbet (1582–1635) wrote verse on a variety of topics. In his sketch of Corbet in *Brief Lives*, John Aubrey records the following anecdote: "[Corbet's] conversation was extreme[ly] pleasant. Dr. Stubbins was one of his cronies; he was a jolly fat Dr and a very good house-keeper; as Dr Corbet and he were riding in Lob Lane in wet weather ('tis an extraordinar[il]y deep, dirty lane) the coach fell; and Dr Corbet said that Dr Stubbins was up to the elbows in mud, [and] he was up to the elbows in Stubbins."

parrot is no more. It has ceased to be. It's expired and gone to meet its maker. This is a late parrot. It's a stiff. Bereft of life, it rests in peace. If you hadn't nailed it to the perch, it would be pushing up the daisies. It's rung down the curtain and joined the choir invisible. This is an ex-parrot.

SHOPKEEPER. Well, I'd better replace it then.

PRALINE *(to camera)*. If you want to get anything done in this country you've got to complain till you're blue in the mouth.

SHOPKEEPER. Sorry guv, we're right out of parrots.

PRALINE. I see. I see. I get the picture.

SHOPKEEPER. I've got a slug.

PRALINE. Does it talk?

SHOPKEEPER. Not really, no.

PRALINE. Well, it's scarcely a replacement then, is it?

SHOPKEEPER. Listen, I'll tell you what *(handing over a card)*, tell you what, if you go to my brother's pet shop in Bolton he'll replace your parrot for you.

PRALINE. Bolton, eh?

SHOPKEEPER. Yeah.

PRALINE. All right.

(He leaves, holding the parrot.
Caption: A similar pet shop in Bolton, Lancs.
Closeup of sign on door reading: "Similar Pet Shops Ltd." Pull back from sign to see same pet shop. Shopkeeper now has mustache. Praline walks into shop. He looks around with interest, noticing the empty parrot cage still on the floor.)

PRALINE. Er, excuse me. This is Bolton, is it?

SHOPKEEPER. No, no it's, er, Ipswich.

PRALINE *(to camera)*. That's Inter-City Rail for you. *(Leaves.)*

Monty Python's Flying Circus (1989)

Epilogus Incerti Authoris

Like to the mowing tones of unspoke speeches

Or like two lobsters clad in logic breeches;

Or like the gray fleece of a crimson cat,

Or like the mooncalf[1] in a slipshod hat;

Or like the shadow when the sun is gone,

Or like a thought that never was thought upon;

Even such is man who never was begotten

Until his children were both dead and rotten. . . .

Richard Corbet (1600s)

Delight in nonsense has its root in the feeling of freedom we enjoy when we are able to abandon the straitjacket of logic.

Sigmund Freud (1905)

Epilogus . . . Authoris (ep'i lō'gəs in ker'tē ow thôr'əs), Epilogue of a Doubtful Author. *[Latin]*

1. **mooncalf** (mün'kaf'), *n.* a foolish person; dolt.

MINI-LESSON: READING/THINKING SKILLS

Fantasy and Reality

Distinguishing between fantasy and reality is understanding the difference between something that could happen in real life and something that could not.

Teach   Point out to students that although literary treatments of the absurd often contain fantastic elements, fantasy is not a necessary ingredient of absurdity. Ask students whether "The Dead Parrot Sketch" is fantasy or reality. *(While full of nonsense elements, the sketch is not a fantasy.)*

Activity Idea   Have students revise "The Dead Parrot Sketch," introducing elements of fantasy into it (for example, the parrot might abruptly be brought to life).

from THE PERILS OF INVISIBILITY

W. S. Gilbert, drawing from
The Bab Ballads *(1869)*

Old PETER led a wretched life—
Old PETER had a furious wife;
Old PETER, too, was truly stout,
He measured several yards about.

The little fairy PICKLEKIN
One summer afternoon looked in,
And said, "Old PETER, how-de-do?
Can I do anything for you?

"I have three gifts—the first will give
Unbounded riches while you live;
The second, health where'er you be;
The third, invisibility."

"O, little fairy PICKLEKIN,"
Old PETER answered, with a grin,
"To hesitate would be absurd—
Undoubtedly I choose the third."

"'Tis yours," the fairy said; "be quite
Invisible to mortal sight
Whene'er you please. Remember me
Most kindly, pray, to MRS. P."

Old MRS. PETER overheard
Wee PICKLEKIN'S concluding word,
And, jealous of her girlhood's choice,
Said, "That was some young woman's voice!"

Old PETER let her scold and swear—
Old PETER, bless him, didn't care.

"My dear, your rage is wasted quite—
Observe, I disappear from sight!"

A well-bred fairy (so I've heard)
Is always faithful to her word:
Old PETER vanished like a shot,
But then—*his suit of clothes did not.*

For when conferred[1] the fairy slim
Invisibility on him,
She popped away on fairy wings,
Without referring to his "things."

So there remained a coat of blue,
A vest and double eyeglass too,
His tail, his shoes, his socks as well,
His pair of—no, I must not tell.

---

1. **confer** (kən fër′), *v.* award; bestow.

963

Art Study

Visual Literacy John Tenniel, a cartoonist on the staff of the British humor magazine *Punch*, worked closely with Lewis Carroll to illustrate both *Alice's Adventures in Wonderland* (see p. 547) and *Through the Looking Glass*. His interpretations of the characters have visualize them.

Question How does this illustration help to define Looking Glass Land as a place where strange and unusual things take place? *(Possible response: Humpty Dumpty is a large egg, personified as an argumentative human.)*

Old MRS. PETER soon began
To see the failure of his plan,
And then resolved (I quote the bard)
To "hoist him with his own petard."[2]

Old PETER woke next day and dressed,
Put on his coat and shoes and vest,
His shirt and stock—*but could not find
His only pair of—*never mind!

Old PETER was a decent man,
And though he twigged[3] his lady's plan,
Yet, hearing her approaching, he
Resumed invisibility.

"Dear Mrs. P., my only joy,"
Exclaimed the horrified old boy;
"Now give them up, I beg of you—
You know what I'm referring to!"

But no; the cross old lady swore
She'd keep his—what I said before—
To make him publicly absurd;
And MRS. PETER kept her word. . . .

W. S. Gilbert (1870)

John Tenniel, drawing
of Alice and Humpty
Dumpty, from
Through the Looking
Glass *(1872)*

G L O R Y

"There's glory for you!" [*said Humpty Dumpty.*]

"I don't know what you mean by 'glory,'" Alice said.

Humpty Dumpty smiled contemptuously. "Of course you don't—till I tell you. I meant there's a 'nice knock-down argument for you!'"

"But 'glory' doesn't mean 'a nice knock-down argument,'" Alice objected.

"When I use a word," Humpty Dumpty said, in rather a scornful tone, "it means just what I choose it to mean—neither more nor less."

"The question is," said Alice, "whether you can make words mean so many different things."

"The question is," said Humpty Dumpty, "which is to be master—that's all."

Lewis Carroll (1872)

2. **"hoist . . . petard,"** destroy him with his own weapon, as an artilleryman blown up with his own explosives. From Shakespeare's *Hamlet* (act 3, scene 4, line 207).

3. **twig,** understand. *[slang]*

MINI-LESSON: LITERARY ELEMENT

Characterization

Characterization is the methods—including physical and behavioral description, speech, thoughts, and feelings—that an author uses to develop the personality of a character in a literary work.

Teach Point out that there are two basic types of characters—*flat* and *round*. Flat characters—sometimes called *stereotypes*—are, like cartoon characters, one-dimensional and lack complexity. Round characters are fully developed, realistic individuals, who act according to complex and believable patterns of emotion, motivation, and behavior. Ask students whether Old Peter is a round or flat character. (flat)

Activity Idea Have students write a brief sketch of Old Peter that provides a fuller characterization.

Terry Clark, Sergeant Pilot *(1990)*

from   Tom   o'   Bedlam

From the hag and hungry goblin
   That into rags would rend ye,
   The spirit that stands by the naked man
   In the Book of Moons[1] defend ye,
That of your five sound senses
You never be forsaken,
Nor wander from yourselves with Tom
Abroad to beg your bacon,
   While I do sing, Any food, any feeding,
   Feeding, drink, or clothing;
   Come dame or maid, be not afraid,
   Poor Tom will injure nothing. . . .

Anonymous (about 1620)

Bedlam (bed′ləm), old name for the
Hospital of St. Mary of Bethlehem, an
insane asylum in London. By custom, certain patients were turned out to become
wandering beggars.
1. **Book of Moons,** an astrological treatise
for fortune-telling.

RESPONDING

1. Which of these selections contain
theatrical effects? Which contain
clowning and verbal nonsense?
Which contain elements of dream
and fantasy?
2. Which selections seem to support
the notion that life is meaningless?
Did they convince you?
3. Which selection did you find the
most humorous? Why?
4. List other works you are familiar
with that contain similar elements.
(You might find them in stories,
poems, songs, movies, television,
videos, comic strips, and elsewhere.)
Discuss just how widespread are
elements of the absurd in today's art
and popular culture.

965

Art Study

Question   What is strangely logical
about this situation? *(Either the pilots are
their own planes, or the planes are their
own pilots.)*

About Tom o' Bedlam

This haunting poem, from a manuscript
commonplace—or literary scrapbook—is
an example of the mad song, the dramatic
expression of a conventionalized view of
insanity. Tom is an out-patient from the
madhouse, a wandering beggar, asking for
alms and insisting he is harmless.

Responding

1. "The Dead Parrot Sketch" and the
excerpt from "The Perils of Invisibility"
contain theatrical effects. "Nicely Nicely
Clive," "Incidents in the Life of My Uncle
Arly," "Epilogus Incerti Authoris," and the
excerpt from *Through the Looking Glass*
contain clowning and verbal nonsense.
Incidents from "The Life of My Uncle Arly,"
Ronald Searle's "The Greedy Carpet,"
James Grainger's "Clergy Tossing," the
excerpt from *The Perils of Invisibility*, John
Tenniel's illustration and the excerpt from
Through the Looking Glass, and Terry
Clark's "Sergeant Pilot" contain elements
of dream and fantasy.

2. "Life's But a Walking Shadow" and
"Solomon Grundy"

3. Students might find the visual selections the most obviously humorous, along
with "Nicely Nicely Clive" and "The Dead
Parrot Sketch."

4. Students will probably have little trouble in providing many examples drawn
from contemporary popular culture that
reflect both silly and serious treatments
of the absurd.

Glossaries, Handbooks, and Indexes

Glossary of Literary Terms

Words within entries in SMALL CAPITAL LETTERS refer to other entries in the Glossary of Literary Terms.

allegory (al′ə gôr′ē), a NARRATIVE either in VERSE or prose, in which characters, action, and sometimes SETTING represent abstract concepts apart from the literal meaning of the story. The underlying meaning may have moral, social, religious, or political significance, and the characters are often PERSONIFICATIONS of abstract ideas such as charity, hope, greed, or envy. Edmund Spenser used allegory in his long poem, *The Faerie Queene,* which was dedicated to Queen Elizabeth I.

alliteration (ə lit′ə rā′ shən), the REPETITION of consonant sounds at the beginnings of words or within words, particularly in accented syllables. It can be used to reinforce meaning, to unify thought, or simply to produce a musical effect. "Grim and greedy the gruesome monster . . ." (*Beowulf,* page 8) is an example.

allusion (ə lü′zhən), a brief reference to a person, event, or place, real or fictitious, or to a work of art. Auden's "Musée des Beaux Arts" (page 808) alludes to *The Fall of Icarus,* a painting by Bruegel, and to the Greek MYTH that inspired the painting.

analogy (ə nal′ə jē), a comparison made between two objects, situations, or ideas that are somewhat alike but unlike in most respects. Frequently an unfamiliar or complex object or idea will be explained through comparison to a familiar or simpler one. For example, Blake refers to Jesus as the meek and mild "Lamb of God" (page 404).

anapest (an′ə pest), a three-syllable metrical FOOT consisting of two unaccented syllables followed by an accented syllable (‿ ‿ ′), as in *interfere.* In the following lines, anapestic feet combine with iambic feet.

> It was in/and about/the Mar-/tinmas time,/
> When the green/leaves were/a falling. . . .
>
> from "Bonny Barbara Allan"

anastrophe (ə nas′trə fē)
See INVERSION.

antagonist (an tag′ə nist), a character in a story or play who opposes the chief character or PROTAGONIST. In *Beowulf* (page 8) Grendel is an antagonist, as is Satan in Milton's *Paradise Lost* (page 255).

aphorism (af′ə riz′əm), a brief saying embodying a moral, such as Pope's "Know then thyself, presume not God to scan; / The proper study of mankind is Man."

apostrophe (ə pos′trə fē), a figure of speech in which an absent person, an abstract concept, or an inanimate object is directly addressed. "Milton! thou shouldst be living at this hour . . ." from Wordsworth's "London, 1802" is an example of the first; "Death, be not proud . . ." from Donne's Holy Sonnet 10 is an example of the second; and "O sylvan Wye! thou wanderer through the woods . . ." from Wordsworth's "Tintern Abbey" (page 409) is an example of the third.

archetype (är′kə tīp), an image, story pattern, or character type that recurs frequently in literature and evokes strong, often unconscious, associations in the reader. For example, the wicked witch and the enchanted prince are character types widely dispersed throughout folk tales and literature. The story of a hero who undertakes a dangerous quest, as in *Beowulf* (page 8) or *Sir Gawain and the Green Knight* (page 61), is a recurrent story pattern.

assonance (as′n əns), the REPETITION of similar vowel sounds followed by different consonant sounds in stressed syllables or words. It is often used instead of RHYME. In this line from Tennyson's "Ulysses" (page 531), the words *sleep, feed,* and *me* are assonant.

> . . . That hoard, and sleep, and feed, and know not me.

autobiography See BIOGRAPHY.

ballad, a NARRATIVE song or poem passed on in the oral tradition. It often makes use of REPETITION and DIALOGUE. An example is "Edward" (page 26). If the author of a ballad is unknown, it is called a *folk ballad;* if the author is known, it is called a *literary ballad.*

ballad stanza, a STANZA usually consisting of four alternating lines of iambic TETRAMETER and TRIMETER and rhyming the second and fourth lines.

> The wind sae cauld blew south and north,
> And blew into the floor;
> Quoth our goodman to our goodwife,
> "Gae out and bar the door."
>
> from "Get Up and Bar the Door" (page 28)

See IAMB.

biography, an account of a person's life. An example is Boswell's *The Life of Samuel Johnson, L L. D.* (page 361). AUTOBIOGRAPHY is the story of all or part of a person's life written by the person who lived it. Brittain's *Testament of Youth* (page 743) is an autobiography.

blank verse, unrhymed iambic PENTAMETER.

> I may/assert/Eter-/nal Prov/idence,
> And jus/tify/the ways/of God/to men.
>> Milton, from *Paradise Lost* (page 255)

Macbeth (page 118) and "Ulysses" (page 531) are also written in blank verse.

> *See* IAMB.

cacophony (kə kof′ə nē), a succession of harsh, discordant sounds in either poetry or prose, used to achieve a specific effect. Note the harshness of sound and difficulty of articulation in these lines:

> Light thickens, and the crow
> Makes wing to the rooky wood. . . .
>> Shakespeare, from *Macbeth* (page 118)

caesura (si zhür′ə), a pause in a line of VERSE, usually near the middle. It most often reflects the sense of the line and is frequently greater than a normal pause. It is used to add variety to regular METER and therefore to add emphasis to certain words. A caesura can be indicated by punctuation, the grammatical construction of a sentence, or the placement of lines on a page. For purposes of study, the mark indicating a caesura is two short, vertical lines.

> Born but to die, ‖ and reasoning but to err:
> Alike in ignorance, ‖ his reason such,
> Whether he thinks too little, ‖ or too much . . .
>> Pope, from *An Essay on Man*

The caesura is a particularly important device in Anglo-Saxon poetry.

caricature (kar′ə kə chür), exaggeration of prominent features of appearance or character.

carpe diem (kär′pe dē′əm), Latin for "seize the day," or enjoy life's pleasures while you are able. The term is applied to a THEME frequently found in LYRIC poetry, as in Herrick's "To the Virgins, to Make Much of Time" (page 233).

Cavalier poetry, a type of LYRIC poetry of the late Renaissance period, influenced by poet Ben Jonson and the Elizabethan court poets, and consisting mostly of love poems. Supporters of Charles I (1625–1649) were called Cavaliers and included Robert Herrick (page 233).

characterization, the methods an author uses to develop a character in a literary work. A character's physical traits and personality may be described, as are those of John Thomas in Lawrence's "Tickets, Please" (page 758). A character's speech and behavior may be described, as are those of the Beast in "The Courting of Mr. Lyon" (page 933). The thoughts and feelings of a character or the reactions of other characters to an individual may be shown, as in Greene's "A Shocking Accident" (page 926). Any or all of these methods may be used in the same work.

classicism (klas′ə siz′əm), a style of literature characterized by attention to form and influenced by the classical writers of Greece and Rome. Many authors have been influenced by classicism, and it flourished especially during the Age of Reason.

climax, the decisive point in a story or play when the action changes course and begins to resolve itself. In *Macbeth,* the banquet scene in act 3 (page 148) when the ghost of Banquo appears to Macbeth is often regarded as the climax. Not every story or play has this kind of dramatic climax. Sometimes a character may simply resolve a problem in his or her mind. At times there is no resolution of the PLOT; the climax then comes when a character realizes that a resolution is impossible.

> *See also* PLOT.

comedy, a play written primarily to amuse. In addition to arousing laughter, comic writing often appeals to the intellect. Thus the comic mode has often been used to "instruct" the audience about the follies of certain social conventions and human foibles, as in Shaw's *Pygmalion* (page 662). When used in this way, the comedy tends toward SATIRE.

comic relief, an amusing episode in a serious or tragic literary work, especially a drama, that is introduced to relieve tension. The drunken porter's scene in *Macbeth,* act 2, scene 3 is an example of comic relief.

conceit, an elaborate and surprising figure of speech comparing two very dissimilar things. It usually involves intellectual cleverness and ingenuity. In the last three STANZAS of "A Valediction: Forbidding Mourning" (page 227), Donne compares his soul and that of his love to the two legs or branches of a draftsman's compass used to make a circle. The previously unseen likeness as developed by the poet helps us to understand the subject described (the relationship of the lovers' souls) more clearly.

Glossary of Literary Terms **969**

conflict, the struggle between two opposing forces. The four basic kinds of conflict are these: 1. a person against another person or ANTAGONIST, as in *Beowulf* (page 8); 2. a person against nature; 3. a person against society, as in Desai's "Studies in the Park" (page 833); and 4. two elements within a person struggling for mastery, as in Joyce's "Eveline" (page 790).

connotation, the emotional associations surrounding a word, as opposed to the word's literal meaning or DENOTATION. Some connotations are fairly universal, others quite personal. Many of the words in Shakespeare's "Sonnet 18" (page 111) suggest associations that cluster around the idea of summer.

consonance (kon′sə nəns), the repetition of consonant sounds that are preceded by different vowel sounds:

> For*l*orn! the very word is like a be*ll*
> To to*ll* me back from thee to my so*l*e se*lf*!
>   Keats, from "Ode to a Nightingale" (page 426)

Consonance (also called SLANT RHYME) is an effective device for linking sound, MOOD, and meaning. In the lines above, the *l* sounds reinforce the melancholy mood.

couplet, a pair of rhyming lines with identical METER:

> True wit is Nature to advantage dressed,
> What oft was thought, but ne′er so well expressed.
>   Pope, from *An Essay on Criticism* (page 325)

dactyl (dak′tl), a three-syllable metrical FOOT consisting of an accented syllable followed by two unaccented syllables ($′ ⌣ ⌣$) as in *settlement.* The following line is basically in dactylic HEXAMETER:

> Loosing his/arms from her/waist he flew/upward,
> a-/waiting the/sea beast.
>   Charles Kingsley, from *Andromeda*

denotation the strict, literal meaning of a word.
> *See also* CONNOTATION.

denouement (dā′nü mäɴ′), the resolution of the PLOT. The word is derived from a French word meaning "to untie."

dialect, a form of speech characteristic of a particular region or class, differing from the standard language in pronunciation, vocabulary, and grammatical form. Burns's poems (pages 450–452) are written in Scottish dialect. In Shaw's *Pygmalion* (page 662), Eliza Doolittle, as a flower girl, speaks in the cockney dialect characteristic of a certain part of London.

dialogue, conversation between two or more people in a literary work. Dialogue can help develop CHARACTERIZATION of those speaking and those spoken about, create MOOD, advance PLOT, and develop THEME.

diary, a record of daily happenings written by a person for his or her own use. The diarist is moved by a need to record daily routine and confess innermost thoughts. The diary makes up in immediacy and frankness what it lacks in artistic shape and coherence. An example is *The Diary* of Pepys (page 340).
> *See also* JOURNAL.

diction, the author's choice of words and phrases in a literary work. This choice involves both the CONNOTATION and DENOTATION of a word as well as levels of usage. For example, the diction of the characters in Shaw's *Pygmalion* (page 662) indicates their education, background, and social standing.

drama, a literary work in verse or prose, written to be acted, that tells a story through the speech and actions of the characters. A drama may be a TRAGEDY, such as *Macbeth* (page 118), or a COMEDY, such as *Pygmalion* (page 662).

dramatic convention, any of several devices that the audience accepts as reality in a dramatic work. For instance, the audience accepts that an interval between acts may represent hours, days, weeks, months, or years; that a bare stage may be a meadow or an inner room; or that audible dialogue is supposed to represent whispered conversation.

dramatic monologue (mon′l ôg), a LYRIC poem in which the speaker addresses someone whose replies are not recorded. Sometimes the one addressed seems to be present, sometimes not. Examples are Robert Browning's "Porphyria's Lover" (page 539) and "My Last Duchess" (page 542).

elegy (el′ə gē), a solemn, reflective poem, usually about death, or about someone who has died, written in a formal style.

end rhyme, the rhyming of words at the ends of lines of poetry, as in Housman's "Loveliest of Trees" (page 601).

end-stopped line, a line of poetry that contains a complete thought, thus necessitating the use of a semicolon, colon, or period at the end:

> Great lord of all things, yet a prey to all;

Sole judge of truth, in endless error hurled:
The glory, jest, and riddle of the world!

                      Pope, from *An Essay on Man*

See also RUN-ON LINE.

epic, a long NARRATIVE poem (originally handed down in oral tradition—later a literary form) dealing with great heroes and adventures; having a national, world-wide, or cosmic setting; involving supernatural forces; and written in a deliberately ceremonial STYLE. Examples are *Beowulf* (page 8) and Milton's *Paradise Lost* (page 255).

epigram, any short, witty VERSE or saying, often ending with a wry twist:

'Tis with our judgments as our watches; none
Go just alike, yet each believes his own.

            Pope, from *An Essay on Criticism* (page 325)

Compare with MAXIM *and* PROVERB.

epigraph, a motto or quotation at the beginning of a book, poem, or chapter, often indicating the THEME. An example is found at the beginning of Eliot's "The Hollow Men" (page 769).

epiphany (i pif′ə nē), a moment of enlightenment in which the underlying truth, essential nature, or meaning of something is suddenly made clear. Each of James Joyce's stories builds to an epiphany. In "Eveline" (page 790), it is the moment when she realizes she cannot go away with Frank.

epitaph (ep′ə taf), a brief statement commemorating a dead person, often inscribed on a tombstone. Malory's "Day of Destiny" (page 79) concludes with King Arthur's epitaph.

epithet (ep′ə thet), a descriptive expression, usually mentioning a quality or attribute of the person or thing being described. In *Beowulf* (page 8) the epithet *Spear-Danes* is used for the Danes. Often the epithet *Lion-Hearted* is applied to King Richard I (1157–1199).

essay, a brief composition that presents a personal viewpoint. An essay may present a viewpoint through formal analysis and argument, as in Defoe's "The Education of Women" (page 306), or it may be more informal in style, as in Orwell's "Shooting an Elephant" (page 860).

exposition, the beginning of a work of fiction, particularly a play, in which the author sets the amosphere and TONE, explains the SETTING, introduces the characters, and provides the reader with any other information needed in order to understand the PLOT.

extended metaphor, a comparison that is developed at great length, often through a whole work or a great part of it. It is common in poetry but is used in prose as well. Sir Walter Raleigh develops an extended metaphor comparing life to a play in his poem "What Is Our Life?" the first four lines of which appear here:

What is our life? a play of passion;
Our mirth, the music of division,
Our mothers' wombs the tiring-houses be
Where we are dressed for this short comedy.

See also METAPHOR.

fable, a brief TALE in which the characters are often animals, told to point out a moral truth.

falling action, the RESOLUTION of a dramatic PLOT, which takes place after the CLIMAX.

fantasy, a work that takes place in an unreal world, concerns incredible characters, or employs fictional scientific principles, as in "A Mad Tea Party" (page 547).

See also SCIENCE FICTION.

fiction, a type of literature drawn from the imagination of the author that tells about imaginary people and happenings. NOVELS and SHORT STORIES are fiction.

figurative language, language used in a nonliteral way to express a suitable relationship between essentially unlike things in order to furnish new effects or fresh insights. The more common figures of speech are SIMILE, METAPHOR, PERSONIFICATION, HYPERBOLE, and SYNECDOCHE.

flashback, interruption of a NARRATIVE to show an episode that happened before that particular point in the story.

foil, a character whose traits are the opposite of those of another character, and who thus points up the strengths or weaknesses of the other character. Henry Higgins and Liza Doolittle are foils in Shaw's *Pygmalion* (page 662).

folk literature, a type of early literature that was passed orally from generation to generation, and only written down after centuries. The authorship of folk literature is unknown. Folk literature includes MYTHS, FABLES, fairy tales, EPICS, and LEGENDS. Examples are *Beowulf* (page 8) and the Folk Ballads (pages 25–28).

foot, a group of syllables in VERSE usually consisting of one accented syllable and one or more unaccented syllables. A foot may occasionally, for variety, have two accented syllables (a SPONDEE) or two unaccented syllables. In the following lines the feet are separated by slanted lines.

> Come live/with me/and be/my Love,
> And we/will all/the plea-/sures prove. . . .
>> Marlowe, from "The Passionate
>> Shepherd to His Love"

The most common line lengths are five feet (PENTAMETER), four feet (TETRAMETER), and three feet (TRIMETER). The lines quoted above are iambic tetrameter.

> *See also* ANAPEST, DACTYL, IAMB *and* TROCHEE.

foreshadowing, a hint given to the reader of what is to come.

frame, a NARRATIVE device presenting a story or group of stories within the frame of a larger narrative. In Chaucer's *The Canterbury Tales* (page 47), the pilgrimage is the frame unifying and providing continuity for the stories told by the pilgrims.

free verse, a type of poetry that differs from conventional VERSE forms in being "free" from a fixed pattern of METER and RHYME, but using RHYTHM and other poetic devices. An example is Eliot's "The Hollow Men" (page 769).

gothic novel, a NOVEL written in a STYLE characterized by mystery, horror, and the supernatural, and usually having a medieval or other period SETTING. An example is Mary Shelly's *Frankenstein* (page 492).

heroic couplet, a pair of rhymed VERSE lines in iambic PENTAMETER:

> All human things are subject to decay,
> And when fate summons, monarchs must obey.
>> Dryden, from *Mac Flecknoe*

hexameter (hek sam′ə tər), a metrical line of six feet.

> How man-/y weep-/ing eyes/I made/to pine/with woe . . .
>> Elizabeth I, "When I was Fair and Young"

humor, in literature, writing whose purpose is to amuse or to evoke laughter. Humorous writing can be sympathetic to human nature or satirical. Some forms of humor are IRONY, SATIRE, PARODY, and CARICATURE.

hyperbole (hī pėr′bə lē), a figure of speech involving great exaggeration. The effect may be serious or comic.

> If thou be'st born to strange sights,
>> Things invisible to see,
> Ride ten thousand days and nights,
>> Till age snow white hairs on thee. . . .
>>> Donne, from "Song" (page 226)

iamb (ī′amb), a two-syllable metrical FOOT consisting of an unaccented syllable followed by an accented syllable (‿ ′), as in *until.* The following line is in iambic PENTAMETER:

> For God's/sake, hold/your tongue,/and let/me love. . . .
>> Donne, from "The Canonization"

idiom, an expression whose meaning cannot be understood from the ordinary meanings of the words in it. For example, "to give a leg up," is to provide someone assistance or encouragement; "to knuckle down" means to apply oneself or work hard.

imagery, the sensory details that provide vividness in a literary work and tend to arouse emotions or feelings in a reader that abstract language does not. Carter's "The Courtship of Mr. Lyon" (page 933) contains many sensory details.

incremental repetition, a form of REPETITION in which successive STANZAS advance the story or reveal a situation by changes in a single phrase or line. Often a question and answer form is used. An example is the ballad "Edward" (page 26).

inference, a reasonable conclusion about the behavior of a character or the meaning of an event, drawn from the limited information presented by the author. In Browning's "My Last Duchess" (page 542), the reader can infer a great deal about the character of the speaker, the Duke, from what he says.

in medias res (in mā′dē äs rās′), Latin for "in the middle of things." In a traditional EPIC the opening scene often begins in the middle of the action. Milton's *Paradise Lost* (page 255) opens with Satan and his angels already defeated and in Hell; later in the poem the story of the battle between Satan and the forces of Heaven, which led to this defeat, is told. This device may be used in any NARRATIVE form.

interior monologue, a technique used by writers to present the STREAM OF CONSCIOUSNESS of a fictional character, either directly by presenting what is passing through the character's mind or indirectly by the author's selection of and comments upon the character's thoughts. Joyce's

"Eveline" (page 790) consists largely of interior monologue.

internal rhyme, the rhyming of words or accented syllables within a line that may or may not have a RHYME at the end as well.

inversion, reversal of the usual order of the parts of a sentence, primarily for emphasis or to achieve a certain RHYTHM or RHYME. In the example that follows, lines 1, 4, and 5 contain inverted order.

> In Seville was he born, a pleasant city,
> Famous for oranges and women—he
> Who has not seen it will be much to pity,
> So says the proverb—and I quite agree;
> Of all the Spanish towns is none more pretty.
>
> Byron, from *Don Juan*

invocation the call on a deity or muse (classical goddess who inspired a poet) for help and inspiration. It is found at the beginning of traditional EPIC poems. In *Paradise Lost* (page 255) Milton invokes the "Heavenly Muse" instead of one of the traditional muses of poetry.

irony, the term used to describe a contrast between what appears to be and what really is. In *verbal irony,* the intended meaning of a statement or work is different from (often the opposite of) what the statement or work literally says, as in Swift's "A Modest Proposal" (page 296). *Understatement,* in which an idea is expressed less emphatically than it might be, is a form of verbal irony often used for humorous or cutting effect. For example, Johnson's remark in his "Letter to Chesterfield" (page 357): "To be so distinguished is an honor which, being very little accustomed to favors from the great, I know not well how to receive." *Irony of situation* refers to an occurrence that is contrary to what is expected or intended, as in Hardy's "Ah, Are You Digging on My Grave?" (page 577). *Dramatic irony* refers to a situation in which events or facts not known to a character on stage or in a fictional work are known to another character and the audience or reader. In Pope's *The Rape of the Lock* (page 314), events known to the sylph Ariel and to the reader are unknown to Belinda.

journal, a formal record of a person's daily experiences. It is less intimate or personal than a DIARY and more chronological than an AUTOBIOGRAPHY.

kenning, a metaphorical compound word used as a poetic device. In *Beowulf* (page 8) there are many examples of kennings: the king is the "ring-giver," the rough sea is the "whale-road," and the calm sea is the "swan-road."

legend, a story handed down from the past, often associated with some period in the history of a people. A legend differs from a MYTH in having some historical truth and often less of the supernatural. Malory's *Morte Darthur* (page 79) is based on legends of King Arthur and the Knights of the Round Table.

literary ballad *See* BALLAD.

lyric, a poem, usually short, that expresses some basic emotion or state of mind. It usually creates a single impression and is highly personal. It may be rhymed or unrhymed. A SONNET is a lyric poem. Other examples of lyrics are Burns's "A Red, Red Rose" (page 452) and most of the shorter poems of the Romantics.

magic realism, a fictional literary work that combines elements of dreams, magic, myths, and fairy tales, along with realistic elements. Carter's "The Courtship of Mr. Lyon" (page 933) can be described as magic realism.

maxim, a brief saying embodying a moral, such as "Look before you leap."

memoir (mem′wär), a form of AUTOBIOGRAPHY that is more concerned with personalities, events, and actions of public importance than with the private life of the writer. Orwell's "Shooting an Elephant" (page 860) is an example of memoir in the form of an essay.

metaphor, a figure of speech that makes a comparison, without *like* or *as,* between two basically unlike things that have something in common. This comparison may be stated (She was a stone) or implied (Her stony silence filled the room). In "Meditation 17" (page 228) Donne compares the individual to a chapter in a book and, later, to a piece of a continent.

See also SIMILE *and* FIGURATIVE LANGUAGE.

metaphysical poetry, poetry exhibiting a highly intellectual style that is witty, subtle, and sometimes fantastic, particularly in the use of CONCEITS. See especially the poems of Donne (pages 226–227).

meter, the pattern of stressed and unstressed syllables in POETRY. *See also* RHYTHM and FOOT.

metonymy a figure of speech in which a specific word naming an object is substituted for another word with which it is closely associated. An example is in Genesis: "In the sweat of thy face shalt thou eat bread." Here, *sweat* is used to represent hard physical labor.

mock epic, a SATIRE using the form and style of an EPIC poem to treat a trivial incident. Pope's *The Rape of the Lock* (page 314) is a mock epic.

monologue *See* SOLILOQUY *and* DRAMATIC MONOLOGUE.

mood, the overall atmosphere or prevailing emotional aura of a work. Coleridge's "Kubla Khan" (page 417) might be described as having a hypnotic, dreamlike mood or atmosphere. *See* TONE for a comparison.

moral, the lesson or inner meaning to be learned from a FABLE, TALE, or other story. The moral of "The Pardoner's Tale" in *The Canterbury Tales* (page 48), as stated by the Pardoner, is "Avarice is the root of all evil."

motif a character, incident, idea, or object that appears over and over in various works or in various parts of the same work. In Shakespeare's SONNETS (pages 111–112) the effect of time is a recurrent motif.

motivation, the process of presenting a convincing cause for the actions of a character in a dramatic or fictional work in order to justify those actions. Motivation usually involves a combination of external events and the character's psychological traits.

myth, a traditional story connected with the religion of a people, usually attempting to account for something in nature. A myth has less historical background than a LEGEND. Milton's *Paradise Lost* (page 255) has mythic elements in its attempts to interpret aspects of the universe.

narrative, a story or account of an event or a series of events. It may be told either in POETRY or in prose, and it may be either fictional or true.

narrative poetry, a poem that tells a story or recounts a series of events. It may be either long or short. EPICS and BALLADS are types of narrative poetry.

narrator, the teller of a story. The teller may be a character in the story, as in Mary Shelley's *Frankenstein* (page 492); an anonymous voice outside the story, as in Greene's "A Shocking

Accident" (page 926); or the author, as in Brittain's *Testament of Youth* (page 776). A narrator's attitude toward his or her subject is capable of much variation; it can range from one of indifference to one of extreme conviction and feeling.

See also PERSONA *and* POINT OF VIEW.

naturalism, a literary movement in the late nineteenth and early twentieth century characterized by writing that depicts events as rigidly determined by the forces of heredity and environment. The world described tends to be bleak. There are elements of naturalism in the work of Thomas Hardy.

neoclassicism, writing of a later period that shows the influence of the Greek and Roman classics. The term is often applied to English literature of the eighteenth century.

See also CLASSICISM.

nonfiction, any writing that is not FICTION; any type of prose that deals with real people and happenings. BIOGRAPHY and history are types of nonfiction. An example is the excerpt from Boswell's *The Life of Samuel Johnson, LL. D.* (page 401).

novel, a long work of NARRATIVE prose fiction dealing with characters, situations, and SETTINGS that imitate those of real life. Among the authors in this text who have written novels are Thomas Hardy, Joseph Conrad, James Joyce, Virginia Woolf, H. G. Wells, Anita Desai, Graham Greene, and Angela Carter.

ode, a long LYRIC poem, formal in STYLE and complex in form, often written in commemoration or celebration of a special quality, object, or occasion. Examples are Shelley's "Ode to the West Wind" (page 469) and Keats's "Ode to a Nightingale" (page 426).

onomatopoeia (on′ə mat′ə pē′ə), a word or words used in such a way that the sound imitates the thing spoken of. Some single words in which sound suggests meaning are *hiss, smack, buzz, and hum.* An example in which sound echoes sense throughout the whole phrase is "The murmurous haunt of flies on summer eves," from Keats's "Ode to a Nightingale"(page 426).

parable, a brief fictional work that concretely illustrates an abstract idea or teaches some lesson or truth. It differs from a FABLE in that its characters are generally people rather than animals, and it differs from an ALLEGORY in that its characters do not necessarily represent abstract qualities.

paradox, a statement, often metaphorical, that seems to be self-contradictory but that has valid meaning, as in "The child is father of the Man" from Wordsworth's poem "My Heart Leaps Up" (page 413). Woolf describes a paradoxical woman in "Shakespeare's Sister" (page 814).

parallelism, the use of phrases or sentences that are similar in structure. Churchill's words in his Blood, Toil, Tears, and Sweat speech (page 869) are an example of parallelism: "You ask, What is our aim? I can answer in one word: Victory—victory at all costs, victory in spite of all terror, victory, however long and hard the road may be. . . ."

parody, a humorous imitation of serious writing. It follows the form of the original, but often changes the sense to ridicule the writer's STYLE. Eliot's "The Hollow Men" (page 769) has a parody of the children's rhyme "Here we go round the mulberry bush."
    See also SATIRE.

pastoral, a conventional form of LYRIC poetry presenting an idealized picture of rural life.

pentameter (pen tam′ə ter), a metrical line of five feet.
    Shall I/compare/thee to/a sum-/mer's day?
    Thou art/more love-/ly and/more tem-/perate.
              Shakespeare, from Sonnet 18 (page 111)

persona (pər sō′nə), the mask or voice of the author or the author's creation in a particular work. Tennyson is the author of "Ulysses" (page 531), but the persona, in this case the SPEAKER, is Ulysses, through whom Tennyson speaks. In "A Shocking Accident" (page 926), Graham Greene has assumed a voice or persona—detached, witty, ironic—in telling the story.
    See also NARRATOR.

personification (pər son′ə fə kā′shən), the representation of abstractions, ideas, animals, or inanimate objects as human beings by endowing them with human qualities. In Shelley's "Ode to the West Wind" (page 469), the Mediterranean is personified:
    Thou who didst waken from his summer dreams
    The blue Mediterranean, where he lay,
    Lulled by the coil of his crystàlline streams. . . .
Personification is one kind of FIGURATIVE LANGUAGE.

play *See* DRAMA.

plot, a series of happenings in a literary work. The term is used to refer to the action as it is organized around a CONFLICT and builds through complication to a CLIMAX followed by a DENOUEMENT or RESOLUTION. (See the plot diagram on page 116.)

poetry, a type of literature that creates an emotional response by the imaginative use of words patterned to produce a desired effect through RHYTHM, sound, and meaning. Poetry may be RHYMED or unrhymed. Among the many forms of poetry are the EPIC, ODE, LYRIC, SONNET, BALLAD, and ELEGY.

point of view, the vantage point from which an author presents the actions and characters of a story. The story may be related by a character (the *first-person* point of view), or the story may be told by a NARRATOR who does not participate in the action (the *third-person* point of view). Further, the third-person narrator may be *omniscient* (om nish′ənt)—able to see into the minds of all characters, as in Lawrence's "Tickets, Please" (page 758). Or the third-person narrator may be *limited*—confined to a single character's perceptions, as in Joyce's "Eveline" (page 790). An author who describes only what can be seen, like a newspaper reporter, is said to use an *objective* or *dramatic* point of view.

prologue, a section preceding the main body of a work and serving as an introduction. An example is the *Prologue to The Canterbury Tales* (page 47).

protagonist (prō tag′ənist), the leading character in a literary work.
    See also ANTAGONIST.

proverb, a short, wise saying, often handed down from the past, that expresses a truth or shrewd observation about life. "Haste makes waste" is an example. There are many proverbs in the Bible.

psalm, a song or poem in praise of God. The term is most often applied to the songs or hymns in the Book of Psalms in the Bible. An example is the Twenty-third Psalm on page 272.

pun, a play on words; a humorous use of a word where it can have two different meanings (*pitcher / pitcher*) or two or more words with the same or nearly the same sound but with different meanings (*night / knight*).

quatrain, a verse STANZA of four lines. This stanza may take many forms, according to line lengths and RHYME patterns. Herrick's poem "To the Virgins, to Make Much of Time" (page 233) contains quatrains.

rationalism, a philosophy that emphasizes the role of reason rather than of sensory experience and faith in answering basic questions of human existence. It was most influential during the Age of Reason (1660–1780) and influenced such writers of that period as Swift and Pope.

realism, a way of representing life that emphasizes ordinary people in everyday experiences. The excerpt from Emecheta's *In the Ditch* (page 881) is an example of realism.

refrain, the REPETITION of one or more lines in each STANZA of a poem. The ballad "Edward" (page 26) makes use of refrain.

repetition, a poetic device in which a sound, word, or phrase is repeated for style and emphasis, as in Thomas's "Do Not Go Gentle into That Good Night" (page 823).

resolution, events that follow the climax of a PLOT in which the complications of the plot are resolved.

rhyme, the exact repetition of sounds in at least the final accented syllables of two or more words:

> Hither the heroes and the nymphs *resort,*
> To taste awhile the pleasures of a *court.*
> > Pope, from *The Rape of the Lock* (page 314)

rhyme scheme, any pattern of end rhyme in a STANZA. For purposes of study, the pattern is labeled as shown below, with the first rhyme and all the words rhyming with it labeled *a,* the second rhyme and all the words rhyming with it labeled *b,* and so on.

> Queen and huntress, chaste and fair,   *a*
> Now the sun is laid to sleep,   *b*
> Seated in thy silver chair,   *a*
> State in wonted manner keep;   *b*
> Hesperus entreats thy light,   *c*
> Goddess excellently bright.   *c*
> > Jonson, from "To Cynthia"

rhythm, the arrangement of stressed and unstressed sounds into patterns in speech or writing. Rhythm, or METER, may be regular, or it may vary within a line or work. The four most common meters are IAMB ($\smile$ $'$), TROCHEE ($'$ $\smile$), ANAPEST ($\smile$ $\smile$ $'$), and DACTYL ($'$ $\smile$ $\smile$).

rising action, the part of a dramatic PLOT that leads up to the CLIMAX. In rising action, the complication caused by the CONFLICT of opposing forces is developed.

romance, a long NARRATIVE in poetry or prose that originated in the medieval period. Its main elements are adventure, love, and magic. There are elements of the romance in the excerpts from *Morte Darthur* (page 79) and *Sir Gawain and the Green Knight* (page 61).

romanticism, a type of literature that, unlike REALISM, tends to portray the uncommon. The material selected tends to deal with extraordinary people in unusual settings having unusual experiences. In romantic literature there is often a stress on the past and an emphasis on nature. Examples are Coleridge's "Kubla Khan" (page 417) and Mary Shelley's *Frankenstein* (page 492). There are many other examples in Unit 5.

run-on line, a line in which the thought continues beyond the end of the poetic line. For example, there should be no pause after *thine* in the first line that follows:

> For sure our souls were near allied, and thine
> Cast in the same poetic mold with mine.
> > Dryden, from "To the Memory of Mr. Oldham"

satire, the technique that employs wit to ridicule a subject, usually some social institution or human foible, with the intention of inspiring reform. IRONY and sarcasm are often used in writing satire, and PARODY is closely related. Swift's "A Modest Proposal" (page 296), and Shaw's *Pygmalion* (page 662) provide examples of satire.

scansion (skan′shən), the result of *scanning,* or marking off lines of POETRY into feet and indicating the stressed and unstressed syllables.
See RHYTHM *and* FOOT.

science fiction, a fictional literary work that uses scientific and technological facts and hypotheses as a basis for stories about such subjects as extraterrestrial beings, adventures in the future or on other planets, and travel through time. Wells's "The Star" (page 612) is science fiction.

sermon, a written version of a speech on some aspect of religion, morality, conduct, or the like, meant to be delivered in a church. Donne wrote many sermons.

setting, the time (both time of day and period in history) and place in which the action of a NARRA-

TIVE occurs. The setting may be suggested through DIALOGUE and action, or it may be described by the NARRATOR or one of the characters. Setting contributes strongly to the MOOD, atmosphere, and plausibility of a work. For example, the setting of Conrad's "The Lagoon" (page 586) contributes greatly to the atmosphere of the story.

short story, a short prose NARRATIVE that is carefully crafted and usually tightly constructed. The short story form developed in the 1800s.

simile (sim′ə lē), a figure of speech involving a direct comparison, using *like* or *as,* between two basically unlike things that have something in common.

> And so I dare to hope,
> Though changed, no doubt, from what I was when first
> I came among these hills, when like a roe
> I bounded o'er the mountains. . . .
>> Wordsworth, from "Lines Composed a Few
>> Miles Above Tintern Abbey" (page 409)

In this example the narrator compares himself when a young man to a small, agile deer.

slant rhyme (also called CONSONANCE), rhyme in which the vowel sounds are not quite identical, as in the first and third lines that follow:

> And I untightened next the *tress*
>> About her neck; her cheek once more
> Blushed bright beneath my burning *kiss* . . .
>> Browning, from "Porphyria's Lover" (page 539)

soliloquy (sə lil′ə kwē), a DRAMATIC CONVENTION that allows a character alone on stage to speak his or her thoughts aloud. If someone else is on stage but cannot hear the character's words, the soliloquy becomes an *aside.*

> *Compare with* DRAMATIC MONOLOGUE.

sonnet, a LYRIC poem with a traditional form of fourteen iambic PENTAMETER lines. Sonnets fall into two groups, according to their RHYME SCHEMES. The *Italian* or *Petrarchan* sonnet, named after the Italian poet Petrarch, is usually rhymed *abbaabba cdecde* (with variations permitted in the *cdecde* rhyme scheme). It forms basically a two-part poem of eight lines *(octave)* and six lines *(sestet)* respectively. These two parts are played off against each other in a great variety of ways. The *English* or *Shakespearean* sonnet is usually rhymed *abab cdcd efef gg,* presenting a four-part structure in which an idea or theme is developed in three QUATRAINS and then brought to a conclusion in the COUPLET.

sound devices, the choice and arrangement of words to please the ear and suit meaning. RHYME, RHYTHM, ASSONANCE, CONSONANCE, ONOMATOPOEIA, and ALLITERATION are examples of sound devices.

speaker, the person or PERSONA who is speaking in a poem, as in Elizabeth Barrett Browning's "Sonnet 43" (page 539).

spondee, a metrical FOOT of two accented syllables (′′), as in *pipe dream.* It serves occasionally as a substitute to vary the meter, as in the last foot of the second line that follows:

> The sedge/has with-/ered from/the lake
> And no/birds sing!
>> Keats, from "La Belle Dame Sans Merci"
>> (page 423)

sprung rhythm, a metrical form in which the accented or stressed syllables are *scanned* without regard to the number of unstressed syllables in a FOOT. A foot may have from one to four syllables, with the accent always on the first syllable. The term was invented and the technique developed by Gerard Manley Hopkins. The following line is scanned according to Hopkins's theory:

> And for all/this,/nature is/never/spent. . . .
>> Hopkins, from "God's Grandeur"

The first foot has three syllables, the second foot one, the third foot three, the fourth foot two, and the fifth foot one, with the accent on the first syllable of each foot.

stage directions, directions given by the author of a play to indicate the action, costumes, SETTING, arrangement of the stage, and so on. For examples of stage directions, see Shaw's *Pygmalion* (page 662), where they are printed in italic type.

stanza, a group of lines that are set off and form a division in a poem, sometimes linked with other stanzas by RHYME.

stereotype (ster′ē ə tīp′), a conventional character, PLOT, or SETTING that possesses little or no individuality but that may be used for a purpose. Such situations, characters, or settings are usually predictable. Orwell, in "Shooting an Elephant" (page 860), depicts the Burmese somewhat stereotypically.

stream of consciousness, the recording or re-creation of a character's flow of thought. Raw images, perceptions, and memories come and go in seemingly random, but actually controlled, fashion, much as they do in people's minds. James Joyce and Virginia Woolf often depicted stream of consciousness in their writings.

style, the distinctive handling of language by an author. It involves the specific choices made with regard to DICTION, syntax, FIGURATIVE LANGUAGE, and so on. For a comparison of two different styles, see Coleridge's "Kubla Khan" (page 417) and Pope's *The Rape of the Lock* (page 314).

symbol, something relatively concrete, such as an object, action, character, or scene, that signifies something relatively abstract, such as a concept or idea. In Yeats's "Sailing to Byzantium" (page 608), the city of Byzantium is a symbol for the unity of all aspects of life—religious, aesthetic, practical, and intellectual.

synecdoche (si nek′də kē), a figure of speech in which a part stands for the whole, as in "hired *hands." Hands* (the part) stands for the whole (those who do manual labor; those who work with their hands). The term also refers to a figurative expression in which the whole stands for a part, as in "call the *law." Law* (the whole) represents the police (a part of the whole system of law).

tale, a simple prose or verse NARRATIVE, either true or fictitious, such as those told by Chaucer's pilgrims in *The Canterbury Tales* (page 47).

terza rima (ter′tsä rē′mä), a VERSE form with a three-line STANZA rhyming *aba bcb cdc,* and so on.

> O wild West Wind, thou breath of Autumn's being,
> Thou, from whose unseen presence the leaves
> dead
> Are driven, like ghosts from an enchanter fleeing,
>
> Yellow, and black, and pale, and hectic red,
> Pestilence-stricken multitudes: O thou,
> Who chariotest to their dark wintry bed. . . .
> Shelley, from "Ode to the West Wind" (page 469)

tetrameter (te tram′ə ter), a metrical line of four feet.

> Had we/but world/enough/and time . . . .
> Marvell, "To His Coy Mistress" (page 234)

theme, the underlying meaning of a literary work. A theme may be directly stated but more often is implied. The topic of Wilfred Owen's poem "Disabled" (page 739) is stated in the title. The theme concerns the poignant thoughts of a veteran and the bitter waste of a life once full of promise.

tone, the author's attitude, either stated or implied, toward his or her subject matter and toward the audience. Swift's tone in "A Modest Proposal" (page 296) is ironic. He pretends to be setting forth serious suggestions for alleviating the poverty of the Irish, all the while knowing that his proposal will shock even the most hardened politician or clergyman.

tragedy, dramatic or NARRATIVE writing in which the main character suffers disaster after a serious and significant struggle, but faces his or her downfall in such a way as to attain heroic stature. Shakespeare's *Macbeth* (page 118) is a tragedy.

trimeter (trim′ə ter), a metrical line of three feet.

> Down to/a sun-/less sea.
> Coleridge, from "Kubla Khan" (page 417)

trochee (trō′kē) (′‿), a metrical FOOT made up of one accented syllable followed by an unaccented syllable, as in *answer:*

> Double,/double,/toil and/trouble;
> Fire/burn and/caldron/bubble.
> Shakespeare, from *Macbeth* (page 118)

verse, in its most general sense, a synonym for POETRY. *Verse* may also be used to refer to poetry carefully composed as to RHYTHM and RHYME XSCHEME, but of inferior literary value.

villanelle (vil′ə nel′), a poetic form normally consisting of five three-line STANZAS and a final QUATRAIN, rhyming *aba aba aba aba aba abaa,* and with lines 1 and 3 repeating alternately as REFRAINS throughout. An example is Thomas's "Do Not Go Gentle into That Good Night" (page 823).

Glossary of Vocabulary Words

a	hat	ī	ice	ü	rule
ā	age	o	hot	ch	child
ä	far	ō	open	ng	long
â	care	ô	order, all	sh	she
e	let	oi	oil	th	thin
ē	equal	ou	out	ᴛH	then
ė	term	u	cup	zh	measure
i	it	ů	put		

ə { a in about / e in taken / i in pencil / o in lemon / u in circus

A

abashed (ə basht′), *adj.* ashamed.

abate (ə bāt′), *v.* decrease; reduce.

abject (ab′jekt), *adj.* miserable.

abjure (ab jür′), *v.* take back.

abode (ə bōd′), *n.* place of residence; house or home.

absolution (ab′sə lü′shən), *n.* a declaration that frees a person from guilt or punishment for sin.

abstemious (ab stē′mē əs), *adj.* moderate.

abysmal (ə biz′məl), *adj.* bottomless.

adversary (ad′vər ser′ē), *n.* opponent; enemy.

affliction (ə flik′shən), *n.* pain; misery.

agape (ə gāp′), *adj.* openmouthed with wonder.

agog (ə gog′), *adj.* full of expectation or excitement; eager.

amenable (ə mē′nə bəl), *adj.* responsive; agreeable.

anarchy (an′ər kē), *n.* absence of a system of government and law.

anomaly (ə nom′ə lē), *n.* something deviating from the rule; something abnormal.

anonymity (an′ə nim′ə tē), *n.* condition of being unknown.

apparition (ap′ə rish′ən), *n.* something strange, remarkable, or unexpected.

appease (ə pēz′), *v.* put an end to.

apprehension (ap′ri hen′shən), *n.* expectation of misfortune; dread of impending danger.

arbitrate (är′bə trāt), *v.* decide a dispute.

ardent (ärd′nt), *adj.* enthusiastic; passionate.

arduous (är′jü əs), *adj.* difficult.

artifice (är′tə fis), *n.* skillful construction.

asperity (a sper′ə tē), *n.* harshness.

aspire (ə spīr′), *v.* rise high.

asunder (ə sun′dər), *adv.* in pieces or separate parts.

audacious (ô dā′shəs), *adj.* bold.

augment (ôg ment′), *v.* increase.

avarice (av′ər is), *n.* greed for wealth.

avenge (ə venj′), *v.* revenge.

averted (ə vėr′tid), *adj.* turned away.

avouch (ə vouch′), *v.* affirm.

B

baldric (bôl′drik), *n.* a belt hung from one shoulder to the opposite side of the body, to support the wearer's sword.

baleful (bāl′fəl), *adj.* destructive.

bane (bān), *n.* destruction.

beguile (bi gīl′), *v.* trick.

benign (bi nīn′), *adj.* gracious; gentle.

bewitch (bi wich′), *v.* charm; fascinate.

blackguard (blag′ärd), *n.* scoundrel.

boon (bün), *n.* favor.

booty (bü′tē), *n.* money, especially seized illegally; gains; winnings.

bower (bou′ər), *n.* shelter.

brandish (bran′dish), *v.* wave or shake threateningly.

breach (brēch), *n.* break or gap.

brevity (brev′ə tē), *n.* shortness in time, speech, or writing; conciseness.

brougham (brüm), *n.* a closed carriage or automobile, having an outside seat for the driver.

bruit (brüt), *v.* announce by a great noise.

buoyancy (boi′ən sē), *n.* tendency to be hopeful and cheerful.

C

cadence (kād′ns), *n.* rhythm.

calumnious (kə lum′nē əs), *adj.* slanderous.

cant (kant), *n.* insincere talk.

casement (kās′mənt), *n.* window.

catapult (kat′ə pult), *n.* slingshot.

cataract (kat′ə rakt′), *n.* waterfall.

cauldron (kôl′drən), *n.* large kettle.

censure (sen′shər), *v.* criticize.

centrifugal (sen trif′yə gəl), *adj.* moving away from a center.

certitude (sėr′tə tyüd), *n.* certainty; sureness.

chasten (chā′sn), *v.* discipline.

cherub (cher′əb), *n.* an angel in the form of a child with wings.

chid (chid), past tense of **chide** (chīd), *v.* scold.

cistern (sis′tərn), *n.* reservoir for holding water.

clad (klad), *adj.* clothed.

clamorous (klam′ər əs), *adj.* noisy.

clemency (klem′ən sē), *n.* mercy or leniency.

combustible (kəm bus′tə bəl), *adj.* easily burned.

comely (kum′lē), *adj.* attractive.

commendation (kom′ən dā′shən), *n.* praise.

commiserate (kə miz′ə rāt), *v.* pity; sympathize with.

compass (kum′pəs), *v.* plot; scheme.

complaisant (kəm plā′snt), *adj.* gracious; courteous.

constitutional (kon′stə tü′shə nəl), *n.* walk or other exercise taken for one's health.

contend (kən tend′), *v.* fight; struggle.

contravention (kon′trə ven′shən), *n.* conflict; opposition.

conviction (kən vik′shən), *n.* firm belief.

copse (kops), *n.* thicket of small bushes or shrubs.

corporeal (kôr pôr′ē əl), *adj.* of or for the body.

coveted (kuv′ə tid), *adj.* strongly desired.

crypt (kript), *n.* burial vault.

D

daft (daft), *adj.* without sense or reason; silly.

darkling (därk′ling), *adv.* in the dark.

dauntless (dônt′lis), *adj.* brave.

decorum (di kôr′əm), *n.* proper behavior.

delineate (di lin′ē āt), *v.* describe in words; portray.

deluge (del′yüj), *n.* downpour; a heavy fall, as of rain.

demean (di mēn′), *v.* lower in dignity; degrade.

demeanor (di mē′nər), *n.* behavior.

deprecate (dep′rə kāt), *v.* express strong disapproval of; belittle.

desolation (des′ə lā′shən), *n.* sad loneliness.

despondency (di spon′dən sē), *n.* discouragement.

despotic (des pot′ik), *adj.* having unlimited power.

deterrent (di tėr′ənt), *n.* something that discourages or hinders.

devastating (dev′ə stā′ting), *adj.* very destructive.

diffident (dif′ə dənt), *adj.* lacking in self-confidence; shy.

diminutive (də min′yə tiv), *adj.* very small.

dire (dīr), *adj.* dreadful.

dirge (dėrj), *n.* funeral song.

disburse (dis pėrs′), *v.* pay out.

discreet (dis krēt′), *adj.* careful and sensible; proper.

disdain (dis dān′), *v.* scorn.

disparage (dis par′ij), *v.* speak slightingly of; belittle.

dissipate (dis′ə pāt), *v.* spread in different directions; scatter.

dissuade (di swād′), *v.* persuade not to do something.

dolorous (dol′ər əs), *adj.* sorrowful.

doughty (dou′tē), *adj.* brave.

drear (drir), *adj.* gloomy; sad; sorrowful.

dudgeon (duj′ən), *n.* feeling of anger or resentment.

E

ecstatic (ek stat′ik), *adj.* full of joy.

effrontery (ə frun′tər ē), *n.* shameless boldness.

embark (em bärk′), *v.* begin an undertaking; set out; start.

enmity (en′mə tē), *n.* hatred.

enthrall (en thrôl′), *v.* hold captive.

entice (en tīs′), *v.* tempt.

entreat (en trēt′), *v.* beg.

epicure (ep′ə kyùr), *n.* lover of luxury.

epithet (ep′ə thet), *n.* descriptive expression.

erratic (ə rat′ik), *adj.* irregular.

erring (ėr′ing), *adj.* wandering; straying.

essay (es′ā), *n.* trial.

esteem (e stēm′), *n.* high regard.

exhortation (eg′zôr tā′shən), *n.* strong urging to do something.

exotic (eg zot′ik), *adj.* from a foreign country; not native; fascinating or interesting because strange or different.

expedient (ek spē′dē ənt), *n.* method of bringing about desired results.

exquisitely (ek′skwi zit lē), *adv.* beautifully; admirably.

extrinsic (ek strin′sik), *adj.* external.

F

factitious (fak tish′əs), *adj.* artificial.

fallacy (fal′ə sē), *n.* false idea.

fidelity (fə del′ə tē), *n.* faithfulness.

flout (flout), *v.* treat with scorn or contempt.

folly (fol′ē), *n.* a being foolish; lack of sense.

forlorn (fôr lôrn′), *adj.* abandoned; desolate.

G

gallant (gal′ənt), *adj.* noble in spirit or in conduct.

genial (jē′nyəl), *adj.* cheerful and friendly; kindly.

genteel (jen tēl′), *adj.* polite; well-bred.

ghastly (gast′lē), *adj.* very bad. *[informal]*

gibbet (jib′it), *n.* gallows, a structure for hanging criminals.

glaze (glāz), *n.* smooth, glossy coating.

gloam (glōm), *n.* gloaming; twilight.

gravity (grav′ə tē), *n.* seriousness.

grievous (grē′vəs), *adj.* causing great.pain or suffering; severe.

grope (grōp), *v.* search blindly.

grot (grot), *n.* grotto; a cave or cavern. *[archaic]*

grovel (gruv′əl), *v.* crawl humbly on the ground.

guile (gīl), *n.* deceit.

H

harbinger (här′bən jər), *n.* forerunner.

hauberk (hô′bərk), *n.* a flexible coat of armor made of small loops of chain linked together.

hemlock (hem′lok), *n.* a poison.

herbivore (hėr'bə vôr), *n.* any of a large group of animals that feed chiefly on plants.

hirsute (hėr'süt), *adj.* hairy.

homage (hom'ij), *n.* dutiful respect.

I

imbibe (im bīb'), *v.* drink in; absorb.

imminent (im'ə nənt), *adj.* about to happen.

immortal (i môr'tl), *adj.* living forever.

impartiality (im'pär shē al'ə tē), *n.* fairness.

impecunious (im'pi kyü'nē əs), *adj.* having little or no money.

impenetrable (im pen'ə trə bəl), *adj.* unable to be passed through.

imperialism (im pir'ē ə liz'əm), *n.* policy of extending the rule or authority of one country over other countries and colonies.

impertinent (im pėrt'n ənt), *adj.* rudely bold.

impetuous (im pech'ü əs), *adj.* rash; hasty.

impotence (im'pə təns), *n.* condition of helplessness.

impropriety (im'prə prī'ə tē), *n.* improper conduct.

impudent (im'pyə dənt), *adj.* very rude.

incipient (in sip'ē ənt), *adj.* just beginning; in an early stage.

incoherent (in'kō hir'ənt), *adj.* confused; having no logical connection of ideas.

incomprehensible (in'kom pri hen'sə bəl), *adj.* impossible to understand.

incongruous (in kong'grü əs), *adj.* out of place; inconsistent.

incorporeal (in'kôr pôr'ē əl), *adj.* not made of any material substance; spiritual.

incorrigible (in kôr'ə jə bəl), *adj.* too firmly fixed in bad ways to be changed.

indignant (in dig'nənt), *adj.* angry at something unjust.

indolent (in'dl ənt), *adj.* lazy.

inexpedient (in'ik spē'dē ənt), *adj.* unwise.

inexplicable (in'ik splik'ə bəl), *adj.* mysterious; unable to be explained.

infamous (in'fə məs), *adj.* disgraceful.

infinite (in'fə nit), *adj.* endless.

ingenious (in jē'nyəs), *adj.* cleverly planned.

inglorious (in glôr'ē əs), *adj.* shameful; disgraceful.

inquisitive (in kwiz'ə tiv), *adj.* curious; prying.

insinuate (in sin'yü āt), *v.* act or speak to gain favor in an indirect way.

insolence (in'sə ləns), *n.* bold rudeness.

interfuse (in'tər fyüz'), *v.* blend; mix.

intrinsically (in trin'sik lē), *adv.* essentially; belonging to a thing by its very nature.

irrepressible (ir'i pres'ə bəl), *adj.* uncontrollable.

J

jovial (jō'vē əl), *adj.* cheerful.

judicious (jü dish'əs), *adj.* wise.

L

lamentable (lam'ən tə bəl), *adj.* sorrowful.

languish (lang'guish), *v.* become weak or worn out.

languor (lang'gər), *n.* lack of energy; weariness.

lassitude (las'ə tüd), *n.* lack of energy; weariness.

laudable (lô'də bəl), *adj.* praiseworthy.

lavish (lav'ish), *v.* give or spend freely.

leonine (lē'ə nīn), *adj.* of or like a lion.

liege (lēj), *adj.* honorable; having a right to respect and service.

lissomely (lis'əm lē), *adv.* limberly; supplely.

listless (list'lis), *adj.* seeming too tired to care about anything.

loath (lōth), *adj.* reluctant.

luminous (lü'mə nəs), *adj.* shining; bright.

M

magnanimous (mag nan′ə məs), *adj.* generous in forgiving.

malevolence (mə lev′ə ləns), *n.* ill will.

malicious (mə lish′əs), *adj.* evil.

manifest (man′ə fest), *adj.* plain; clear.

mead (mēd), *n.* meadow.

mendacity (men das′ə tē), *n.* untruthfulness; lie.

mettle (met′l), *n.* courage.

mien (mēn), *n.* manner of holding the head and body; way of acting and looking.

minion (min′yən), *n.* favorite; darling.

N

negligent (neg′lə jənt), *adj.* careless.

nocturnal (nok tėr′nl), *adj.* nighttime.

O

obdurate (ob′dər it), *adj.* stubborn.

oblivious (ə bliv′ē əs), *adj.* unmindful; forgetful.

odious (ō′dē əs), *adj.* hateful; offensive.

officiously (ə fish′əs lē), *adv.* too readily offering services or advice; meddling.

ominous (om′ə nəs), *adj.* unfavorable; threatening.

oppressor (ə pres′ər), *n.* person who is cruel or unjust.

ostentation (os′ten tā′shən), *n.* showing off.

P

pacify (pas′ə fī), *v.* quiet down.

palpable (pal′pə bəl), *adj.* definite.

paltry (pôl′trē), *adj.* worthless.

pandemonium (pan′də mō′nē əm), *n.* wild uproar; lawlessness.

parasite (par′ə sīt), *n.* person who lives on others without making any useful or fitting returns.

parsimony (pär′sə mō′nē), *n.* stinginess.

peerless (pir′lis), *adj.* without equal; matchless.

peremptory (pə remp′tər ē), *adj.* decisive; dictatorial.

perennial (pə ren′ē əl), *adj.* lasting for a very long time; enduring.

perfunctorily (pər fungk′tər i lē), *adv.* mechanically; indifferently.

pernicious (pər nish′əs), *adj.* harmful.

perplexity (pər plek′sə tē), *n.* confusion.

pestilence (pes′tl əns), *n.* epidemic disease.

petrol (pet′rəl), *n.* gasoline. [British]

petulant (pech′ə lənt), *adj.* likely to have little fits of bad temper.

piety (pī′ə tē), *n.* reverence for God.

pique (pēk), *n.* anger; wounded pride.

plaintive (plān′tiv), *adj.* mournful.

plinth (plinth), *n.* the lower, square part of the base of a column.

plunder (plun′dər), *v.* steal by force, especially during war.

ply (plī), *v.* supply with in a pressing manner.

precipitous (pri sip′ə təs), *adj.* very steep.

prerogative (pri rog′ə tiv), *n.* right or privilege that nobody else has.

presumptuous (pri zump′chü əs), *adj.* too bold; forward.

pristine (pris′tēn′), *adj.* original.

procrastinate (prō kras′tə nāt), *v.* put things off until later; delay.

prodigious (prə dij′əs), *adj.* huge.

promontory (prom′ən tôr′ē), *n.* a high point of land extending from the coast into the water.

propitiate (prə pish′ē āt), *v.* win the favor of.

propriety (prə prī′ə tē), *n.* proper behavior.

prosaically (prō zā′ik lē), *adv.* in an ordinary way.

prostrate (pros′trāt), *adj.* overcome; helpless.

protracted (prō trak′tid), *adj.* drawn out; prolonged.

provocation (prov′ə kā′shən), *n.* something that stirs up or irritates.

prowess (prou′is), *n.* bravery; daring.

prudent (prüd′nt), *adj.* sensible; discreet.

publican (pub′lə kən), *n.* tavern keeper.

purgatory (pėr′gə tôr′ē), *n.* any condition of temporary suffering.

R

ragout (ra gü′), *n.* a highly seasoned meat stew.

raiment (rā′mənt), *n.* clothing.

recompense (rek′əm pens), *n.* reward.

recourse (rē′kôrs), *n.* appeal for help or protection.

recreant (rek′rē ənt), *n.* coward.

redcoat (red′kōt′), *n.* a British soldier.

reluctantly (ri luk′tənt lē), *adv.* slowly and unwillingly.

remonstrance (ri mon′strəns), *n.* protest; complaint.

rendezvous (rän′də vü), *n.* secret meeting place.

renown (ri noun′), *n.* fame.

replenish (ri plen′ish), *v.* refill.

repudiate (ri pyü′dē āt), *v.* reject.

requiem (rek′wē əm), *n.* musical service or hymn for the dead.

requite (ri kwīt′), *v.* repay.

resolute (rez′ə lüt), *adj.* determined.

restraint (ri strānt′), *n.* limit; restriction.

reticent (ret′ə sənt), *adj.* reserved; quiet.

revelation (rev′ə lā′shən), *n.* disclosure of divine truth.

revelry (rev′əl rē), *n.* noisy partying.

ricochet (rik′ə shā′), *v.* move with a bounce or jump.

robust (rōbust′), *adj.* strong and healthy; sturdy.

S

salutary (sal′yə ter′ē), *adj.* beneficial.

sanctify (sangk′tə fī), *v.* make holy.

scruple (skrü′pəl), *n.* doubt.

sensibility (sen′sə bil′ə tē), *n.* tendency to be hurt or offended too easily.

sepulcher (sep′əl kər), *n.* tomb.

servile (sėr′vəl), *adj.* slavelike.

sidle (sī′dl), *v.* move sideways.

simultaneously (sī′məl tā′nē əs lē), *adv.* at the same time.

sinister (sin′ə stər), *adj.* threatening.

slay (slā), *v.* **slew, slain, slaying.** kill with violence.

slovenly (sluv′ən lē), *adj.* untidy.

smite (smīt), *v.* **smote, smitten** or **smote, smiting.** hit; give a hard blow to.

sordid (sôr′did), *adj.* filthy.

spate (spāt), *n.* a sudden flood.

specious (spē′shəs), *adj.* apparently good, but not really so.

specter (spek′tər), *n.* ghost.

stagnant (stag′nənt), *adj.* still; not flowing.

staid (stād), *adj.* having a settled, quiet character; sober; sedate.

stealthy (stel′thē), *adj.* secret.

steed (stēd), *n.* horse.

strew (strü), *v.* scatter or sprinkle.

stupent (stüp′nt), *adj.* dumfounded; amazed.

subdue (səb dü′), *v.* conquer.

subjective (səb jek′tiv), *adj.* existing in the mind.

subjugate (sub′jə gāt), *v.* subdue; conquer.

suborn (sə bôrn′), *v.* hire or bribe.

superfluous (sů pėr′flü əs), *adj.* needless; unnecessary.

supine (sü pīn′), *adj.* lazily inactive; listless.

suppurating (sup′yə rā′ting), *adj.* oozing.

surmise (sər mīz′), *n.* guesswork.

swoon (swün), *n., v.* faint.

sylvan (sil′vən), *adj.* of or flowing through woods.

symmetry (sim′ə trē), *n.* pleasing proportions between the parts of a whole; harmony.

T

tarry (tar′ē), *v.* delay.

taut (tôt), *adj.* tense.

tempestuous (tem pes′chü əs), *adj.* stormy; violent.

terrestrial (tə res′trē əl), *adj.* earthly.

thrall (thrôl), *n.* bondage; condition of being under some power or influence.

thwart (thwôrt), *v.* prevent from doing something.

tirade (tī′rād), *n.* long, scolding speech.

toll (tōl), *v.* ring.

tranquillity (trang kwil′ə tē), *n.* peacefulness.

transgress (trans gres′), *v.* sin against.

transitory (tran′sə tôr′ē), *adj.* passing soon or quickly.

transpire (tran spīr′), *v.* breathe out.

tread (tred), *v.* **trod, trodden** or **trod, treading.** set the foot down; walk; step.

tremulous (trem′yə ləs), *adj.* quivering.

trepidation (trep′ə dā′shən), *n.* fear; fright.

tumult (tü′mult), *n.* commotion.

turbid (tėr′bid), *adj.* confused; disordered.

tyranny (tir′ə nē), *n.* cruel or unjust use of power.

U

unabashed (un′ə basht′), *adj.* not ashamed or embarrassed.

unguent (ung′gwənt), *n.* ointment; salve; cream.

unprecedented (un pres′ə den′tid), *adj.* never done before; never known before.

upbraid (up brād′), *v.* find fault with.

V

vagrant (vā′grənt), *adj.* wandering.

valiant (val′yənt), *adj.* courageous.

vanquish (vang′kwish), *v.* defeat.

vehement (vē′ə mənt), *adj.* forceful.

verdurous (vėr′jər əs), *adj.* green and fresh.

verity (ver′ə tē), *n.* truth.

vie (vī), *v.* compete.

vile (vīl), *adj.* very bad.

vindicate (vin′də kāt), *v.* uphold; justify.

vindictive (vin dik′tiv), *adj.* bearing a grudge; wanting revenge.

vintner (vint′nər), *n.* wine merchant.

W

wantonness (won′tən nis), *n.* lack of restraint.

wrath (rath), *n.* great anger.

writhe (rīŦH), *v.* twist and turn; suffer mentally.

wrought (rôt), *v.* a past tense and a past participle of **work.** *[archaic]*

Z

zealous (zel′əs), *adj.* enthusiastic.

zephyr (zef′ər), *n.* mild breeze; gentle wind.

Language and Grammar Handbook

When your teacher returns papers, are you sometimes confused by comments such as "Incorrect subject-verb agreement" or "Unclear antecedent"? This Handbook will help you respond to such comments as you edit your writing and also provide answers to questions that arise about language during peer- and self-evaluation.

The Handbook is alphabetically arranged, with each entry explaining a certain term or concept. For example, if you can't remember when to use *good* or *well* look up the entry **good, well** and you'll find an explanation of when to use each word and a sentence using each word.

A

p. 203

active and passive voice A verb is said to be in the active voice when its subject is the doer of the action, and in the passive voice when its subject is the receiver of the action. A passive verb is a form of the verb *be* plus the past participle of the verb: *is* prepared, *had been* prepared, *will be* prepared, and so on.

> **active:** The coach *prepared* the team for the playoffs.
> **passive:** The team *was prepared* for the playoffs by the coach.

Active verbs are more natural, direct, and forceful than passive verbs. Passive verbs are useful and effective, however, when the doer of the action is unknown or unimportant, or to emphasize the receiver of the action:

◆ The soul *is placed* in the body like a rough diamond. . . .
  from "The Education of Women" by Daniel Defoe

◆ In Moulmein, in Lower Burma, I *was hated* by large numbers of people
  . . . .
  from "Shooting an Elephant" by George Orwell

p. 159
p. 211

adjective Adjectives are modifiers that describe nouns and pronouns and make their meaning more exact. Adjectives tell *what kind, which one,* or *how many.*

What kind:	*red* car	*denim* jacket	*fast* food
Which one:	*that* video	*this* computer	*those* families
How many:	*six* weeks	*several* papers	*many* years

p. 159
p. 211

adverb Adverbs modify verbs, adjectives, or other adverbs. They tell *how, when,* or *where* about verbs.

How:	quickly	fearfully	courageously
When:	soon	now	tomorrow
Where:	there	near	here

See also **comparative forms of adjectives and adverbs.**

p. 205

1. Subject-verb agreement. When the subject and verb of a sentence are both singular or both plural, they agree in number. This is called subject-verb agreement.

	Singular	**Plural**
1st person	I drive	we drive
2nd person	you drive	you drive
3rd person	he/she/it/drives	they drive

Some verbs, like *to be,* have irregular forms.

Present tense Singular	**Present tense Plural**	**Past tense Singular**	**Past tense Plural**
I am	we are	I was	we were
you are	you are	you were	you were
he/she/it is	they are	he/she/it was	they were

a. Most compound subjects joined by *and* or *both . . . and* are plural and are followed by plural verbs.

            s   s   v
Both Tomas and Matt were standing in the cafeteria line.

b. A compound subject joined by *or, either. . . or,* or *neither . . . nor* is followed by a verb that agrees in number with the closer subject.

           s   s   v
Neither Margarita nor her sisters attend that school.

           s   s   v
Neither her sisters nor Margarita attends that school.

Problems arise when it isn't obvious what the subject is. The following rules should help you with some of the most troublesome situations:

c. Phrases or clauses coming between the subject and the verb do not affect the subject-verb agreement.

           s   v
◆ The appointment of the other Ministers usually takes a little longer. . .
    from "Wartime Speeches" by Winston Churchill

           s   v
◆ Some persons of a desponding spirit are in great concern about that vast number of poor people who are aged, diseased, or maimed. . . .
    from *A Modest Proposal* by Jonathan Swift

p. 209

d. Singular verbs are used with singular indefinite pronouns—*each, every, either, neither, anyone, anybody, one, everyone, everybody, someone, somebody, nobody, no one.*

Neither of us was on time.

Everyone attends the free film on Monday.

e. Plural indefinite pronouns take plural verbs. They are *both, few, many,* and *several.*

Both of the bands travel frequently.

p. 187
f. The indefinite pronouns *all, any, more, most, none,* and *some* may take a singular or plural verb, depending on their meaning in a sentence.

Singular	**Plural**
Most of the van *is* filled.	*Most* of the buses *were* full.
All of the snow *has* melted	*All* of the clouds *have* vanished.

p. 207
g. The verb agrees with the subject regardless of the number of the predicate complement (after a form of a linking verb).

Her greatest delight was her flowers.

Flowers were her greatest delight.

h. Unusual word order does not affect agreement; the verb generally agrees with the subject, whether the subject follows or precedes it.

◆ . . . between the layers of cotton-wool were little brass figures . . . .
from "The Lumber-Room" by Saki

i. Be especially careful of sentences beginning with *There;* be sure the verb agrees with the subject.

◆ There are only two people in the car.
from "Tickets, Please" by D. H. Lawrence

2. Pronoun-antecedent agreement. An antecedent is a word, clause, or phrase to which a pronoun refers. The pronoun agrees with its antecedent in person, number, and gender.

antec.   pron.
José must let me know when he is free.

antec.   pron.
My cousins didn't know it, but their car was in the shop.

b. Singular pronouns are generally used to refer to the indefinite pronouns *one, anyone, each, either, neither, everybody, everyone, somebody, someone, nobody,* and *no one.*

> antec.   pron.
> Did anyone misplace her notes?

> antec.   pron.
> Everybody was told to bring his lunch.

The second sentence poses problems. It is clearly plural in meaning, and *everybody* may not refer to men only. To avoid the latter problem, you could write "Everybody was told to bring his or her lunch." This solution is clumsy and wordy, though. Sometimes it is best to revise: "*Students* were told to bring *their* lunches."

all right *All right* is used both as an adjective and as an adverb. The spelling *alright* is not accepted in either formal or informal writing.

ambiguity An ambiguous sentence is one that has two or more possible meanings. The most common causes of ambiguity are these:

1. Unclear pronoun reference

> Ambiguous: He told his Dad that *he* missed the plane.

Since it is not clear who missed the plane, the sentence should be revised.

> Clear: "I missed the plane, Dad," he said.
> Clear: "You missed the plane, Dad," he said.

2. Misplaced modifiers. Misplaced modifiers, because of their position in a sentence, do not clearly modify the word they are intended to modify. They are also often a source of humor that the writer does not intend.

> Ambiguous: The queen left the palace leaning on her husband.
> Clear: Leaning on her husband, the queen left the palace.
> Clear: The queen, leaning on her husband, left the palace.

3. Incomplete comparisons

> Ambiguous: Maria likes pizza as much as Kim.
> Clear: Maria likes pizza as much as Kim does.

amount, number *Amount* is used to refer to nouns which name things that can be measured or weighed: large amount of sand, small amount of gold. *Number* is used in referring to nouns which name things that can be counted: large number of rocks, small number of coins.

apostrophe (') An apostrophe is used in possessive words, both singular and plural, and in contractions. It is also used to form the plurals of letters and numbers.

women's hockey	Marta's boots	won't
P's and Q's	11's and 12's	weren't

NOTE: An apostrophe is not used in forming other plurals or in the possessive form of personal pronouns: "The tickets are theirs."

p. 247

Language and Grammar Handbook   **989**

It may be used to indicate places in words in which the speaker does not pronounce certain sounds.

◆ I went into a public-'ouse to get a pint o' beer,
The publican 'e up an' sez, "We serve no red-coats here."
from "Tommy" by Rudyard Kipling

p. 171

appositive Apposition means, literally, a "putting beside." An appositive is a noun or phrase that follows a noun and identifies or explains it more fully. It is usually set off by commas or dashes.

◆ The glorious lamp of heaven, the sun,/The higher he's a-getting. . . .
from "To the Virgins, to Make Much of Time" by Robert Herrick

If, however, the appositive is used to specify a particular person or thing, it is not set off.

◆ . . . I was in Mrs. Prothero's garden . . . with her son Jim.
from *A Child's Christmas in Wales* by Dylan Thomas

awkward writing A general term (abbreviated *awk*) sometimes used in theme correcting to indicate such faults as inappropriate word choice, unnecessary repetition, clumsy phrasing, confusing word order, or any other weakness or expression that makes reading difficult and obscures meaning.

Many writers have found that reading their first drafts aloud helps them detect clumsy or unclear phrasing in their work. Once identified, awkward construction can almost always be improved by rethinking and rewording.

bad, badly In formal English and in writing, *bad* (the adjective) is used to modify a noun or pronoun and is used after a linking verb. *Badly* (the adverb) modifies a verb.

She felt *bad* about forgetting to write to her dad. [adjective used with linking verb *felt*]

He limped *badly* after his fall. [adverb modifying the verb *limped*]

HINT: To check yourself, mentally eliminate the first term. You would never say "between *we*," you would say "between *us*," *us* being the objective form of the pronoun *we*.

between you and me After prepositions such as *between,* use the objective form of the personal pronouns: between you and *me,* between you and *her,* between you and *him,* between you and us, between you and *them.*

The contest will be between you and *us.*

◆ . . . those were the terms of the covenant made between *us* in Arthur's hall. . . .
from "Sir Gawain and the Green Knight"

p. 236

capitalization
1. Capitalize all proper nouns and adjectives.

Britain	Wales	Edward
British	Welsh	Edwardian

2. Capitalize people's names and titles.

Mister Fell	Dr. Johnson	Bishop Carr
Ms. Anita Patel	Mother	Uncle John
Senator Rodriguez	Prince Henry	Justice O'Connor

3. Capitalize the names of races, languages, religions, revered persons, deities, and religious bodies, buildings, and writings. Also capitalize any adjectives made from these names.

Indo-European	Islam	Beth Emet Synagogue
Hindu	God	Church of England
Buddha	French	the Bible

4. Capitalize geographical names (except for articles and prepositions) and any adjectives made from these names.

Canterbury	the Lake District	Stratford-on-Avon
the Thames River	North Sea	Irish stew
Loch Lomond	Yorkshire	Sherwood Forest

5. Capitalize the names of structures, public places, organizations, and bodies in the universe.

Windsor Castle	the Senate	Scotland Yard
Parliament	the Capitol	the Milky Way
Saturn	Stonehenge	Labour Party

6. Capitalize the names of historical events, times, and documents.

Battle of Hastings	Wars of the Roses	Domesday Book
Magna Carta	the Age of Reason	Gun Powder Plot

7. Capitalize the names of months, days, holidays, and time abbreviations. The seasons are not capitalized.

November	Tuesday	B.C.
Thanksgiving	A. M.	summer

8. Capitalize the first words in sentences, lines of poetry, and direct quotations.

◆ On either side the river lie
 Long fields of barley and of rye. . . .
  from "The Lady of Shalott" by Alfred, Lord Tennyson

9. Capitalize certain parts of letters, outlines, and the first, last, and all other important words in titles.

Dear Mr. O'Brien,
Sincerely yours,

I. Mary Queen of Scots
 A. Early Life
  1. Parents
  2. Cousin
 B. Adult Life

Our Mutual Friend (book)
The Times (newspaper)
Macbeth (play)
Masterpiece Theatre (TV series)
"A Shocking Accident" (short story)
The Gondoliers (operetta)
"Born in America" (song)
Time (magazine)
"Ode to a Nightingale" (poem)
The Return of the Jedi (movie)

See also **Italics.**

p. 157

clause A clause is a group of words that has a subject and a verb. A clause is independent when it can stand alone and make sense. A dependent clause has a subject and a verb, but when it stands alone it is incomplete, and the reader is left wondering about the meaning.

Independent Clause	**Dependent Clause**
Jane Austen wrote *Pride and Prejudice.*	Because Jane Austen wrote *Pride and Prejudice.*

collective nouns A collective noun is one that though singular in form names a group of people or things: *committee, mob, team, class.* When a collective noun means the group taken as a whole, use a singular verb and pronoun. When individual members of a group are meant, use a plural verb and pronoun.

The class should bring *its* petition to the study hall at noon.

The committee *were* still in disgreement about *their* purpose.

p. 243
p. 247

colon (:) A colon is often used to explain or clarify what has preceded it.

◆ Ernest, however, never played: he was too grown up.
from "Eveline" by James Joyce

A colon is also used after phrases that introduce a list or quotation.

◆ "There were the Useful Presents: engulfing mufflers of the old coach days, and mittens made for giant sloths; zebra scarfs of a substance like silky gum. . . ."
from *A Child's Christmas in Wales* by Dylan Thomas

p. 239
p. 247

comma (,) Commas are used to show a pause or separation between words and word groups in sentences and to avoid confusion in sentences.

1. Use a comma between items in a series. Words, phrases, and clauses in a series are separated by commas:

NOTE: If the items in a series are all separated by a word like *and,* no comma is necessary: Dolphins and whales and seals were the main attractions.

◆ The sun with its specks of planets, its dust of planetoids, and its impalpable comets, swims in a vacant immensity that almost defeats the imagination.
  from "The Star" by H. G. Wells

2. Use a comma after certain introductory words and groups of words such as clauses and prepositional phrases of five words or more.

◆ With his towel round his waist, Ajayi strode back to the bedroom, ...
  from "The Truly Married Woman" by Abioseh Nicol

3. Use a comma to set off nouns in direct address. The name or title by which persons (or animals) are addressed is called a noun of direct address.

◆ "Mr. Ajayi, these gentlemen have enquired for you," the chief clark said formally.
  from "The Truly Married Woman" by Abioseh Nicol

4. Use commas to set off interrupting elements and appositives. Any phrase or clause that interrupts the flow of a sentence is often set off by commas. Parenthetical expressions like *of course, after all, to be sure, on the other hand, I suppose,* and *as you know;* and words like *yes, no, oh,* and *well* are all set off by commas.

◆ The white man, turning his back upon the setting sun, looked along the empty and broad expanse of the sea-reach.
  from "The Lagoon" by Joseph Conrad

◆ "After all, why shouldn't you come back with me?"
  from "A Cup of Tea" by Katherine Mansfield

NOTE: No comma is used when the connecting words are *so that:*

5. Use a comma before a coordinating conjunction *(and, but, for, or, nor, yet, so)* in a compound sentence.

◆ They were all amazed at his color, for they saw that he was bright green all over. . . . The hood of the mantle was the same . . . and he had thrown it back off his hair so that it lay on his shoulders.
  from "Sir Gawain and the Green Knight"

6. Use a comma after a dependent clause that begins a sentence. Do not use a comma before a dependent clause that follows the independent clause.

◆ Though his imagination might incline him to a belief of the marvelous and mysterious, his vigorous reason examined the evidence with jealousy.
  from *The Life of Samuel Johnson, LL.D* by James Boswell

◆ Those were the days of darkness that followed the star and the heat.
  from "The Star" by H. G. Wells

comma splice *See* **run-on.**

p. 214 **comparative forms of adjectives and adverbs** To show a greater degree of the quality or characteristic named by an adjective or adverb, *-er* or *-est* is added to the word or *more* or *most* is put before it.

> **Positive:** Ramon is *tall.*

> **Comparative:** Ramon is *taller* than Bill.

> **Superlative:** Ramon is the *tallest* person in the class.

More and *most* are generally used with longer adjectives and adverbs, and with all adverbs ending in *-ly.*

> **Positive:** The video was *disturbing.*

> **Comparative:** The second video was *more disturbing* than the first.

> **Superlative:** That video was the *most disturbing* one I have seen.

See also **modifiers.**

p. 233 **conjunction** A conjunction is a word that links one part of a sentence to another. It can join words, phrases, or entire sentences. Coordinating conjunctions *(and, but, for, yet, or, nor, so)* connect words, phrases, and clauses of equal value. Subordinating conjunctions *(after, because, so that, unless, while, and so on)* connect dependent, or subordinate, clauses with main clauses.

> **Coordinating:** He arrived early, *yet* he left late.

> **Subordinating:** Marta spoke first *because* she had to leave.

D **dangling modifiers** A modifier that has no word in a sentence which it can logically modify is said to be dangling.

> **Dangling:** *Born in Ireland in 1950,* Ian Murphy's books have been translated into many languages. [The books weren't born in 1950.]

> **Revised:** The books of Ian Murphy, who was born in Ireland in 1950, have been translated into many languages.

> **Dangling:** *Having driven the same route for several years,* the landscape was familiar. [Who was familiar with the landscape?]

> **Revised:** *Having driven the same route for several years,* I was familiar with the landscape.

p. 247 **dash (—)** A dash is used to indicate a sudden break or change of thought in a sentence:

> ◆ For brave Macbeth—well he deserves that name— . . .
>   Like valor's minion carved out his passage . . . .
>   from *Macbeth* by William Shakespeare

dialogue Dialogue is often used to enliven many types of writing. Notice the punctuation, capitalization, and paragraphing of the following passage.

◆ But he was standing in the middle of the room, saying, "A fine
  Christmas!" and smacking at the smoke with a slipper.
  "Call the fire brigade," cried Mrs. Prothero as she beat the gong.
  "They won't be there," said Mr. Prothero, "it's Christmas."
  from *A Child's Christmas in Wales* by Dylan Thomas

See also **quotation marks.**

direct address *See* **comma 3.**

E

ellipsis (. . .) An ellipsis is used to indicate that words (or sentences or paragraphs) have been omitted. An ellipsis consists of three dots, but if the omitted portion would have completed the sentence, a fourth dot is added for the period.

◆ . . . Our labor must be to pervert that end,
  And out of good still to find means of evil. . . .
  from *Paradise Lost* by John Milton

etc. Etc. is the abbreviation for the Latin *et cetera,* meaning "and others." It is usually read *and so forth* or pronounced (et set′ər ə). It is acceptable in reference and business usage but out of place in most other writing.

 p. 247

exclamation point (!) An exclamation mark is used at the end of an exclamatory sentence——one that shows excitement or strong emotion. Exclamation points can also be used with strong interjections.

F

fragment *See* **sentence fragment.**

p. 224 **G**

gerund A verb form ending in *-ing* that is used as a noun.

◆ By the pricking of my thumbs,
  Something wicked this way comes.
  from *Macbeth* by William Shakespeare

HINT: When you are refer-
ring to health, use *well* if
the meaning is "not ill." "I
am quite well, thank you."
If the meaning is
"pleasant" or "in good
spirits," use *good.* "I feel
good today."

good, well *Good* is used as an adjective to modify a noun or pronoun. Do not use it to modify a verb. *Well* is usually used as an adverb to modify a verb.

◆ "Don't you see what a *good* thing it was that you met me?"
  from "A Cup of Tea" by Katherine Mansfield

◆ "Sit down, Jerome," Mr. Wordsworth said. "All going *well* with the trigonometry?"
  from "A Shocking Accident" by Graham Greene

H

hopefully This is often used to mean "it is hoped" or "I hope," as in the following sentence, "*Hopefully,* I may be pardoned." However, in formal writing, avoid this usage.

however Words like *however, moreover, nevertheless, therefore, consequently,* etc. (known as conjunctive adverbs) require special punctuation. If the word comes within a clause, it is generally set off by commas:

> ◆ He, however, kept his face closed and averted from them all.
> from "Tickets, Please" by D. H. Lawrence

If the conjunctive adverb separates two independent clauses, a semicolon is used preceding the word. If it begins a sentence, a comma is used after it:

> ◆ Therefore, I repeat, let no man talk to me of these . . . .
> from "A Modest Proposal" by Jonathan Swift

p. 227

infinitive The infinitive is the simple form of the verb, usually preceded by *to.* Infinitives are used as nouns, adjectives, or adverbs. In the following lines, each infinitive acts as a noun phrase:

> ◆ Good nature and good sense must ever join;
> *To error* is human, *to forgive* divine.
> from *An Essay on Criticism* by Alexander Pope

p. 235

interjection An interjection is a word or phrase used to express strong emotion.

> ◆ Ring the alarum-bell. Murder and treason!
> Banquo and Donalbain! Malcolm! awake!
> from *Macbeth* by William Shakespeare

italics Italic type is used to indicate titles of whole works such as books, magazines, newspapers, plays, films, and so on. It is also used to indicate foreign words and phrases or to emphasize a word.

> ◆ And pictureless books in which small boys, though warned with quotations not to, *would* skate on Farmer Giles' pond. . . .
> from *A Child's Christmas in Wales* by Dylan Thomas

See also **Capitalization 9** for titles that are italicized.

NOTE: In formal English the correct way to respond to a question such as, "Who's there?" is "It is I." This sounds too formal in some situations, however. While it is not correct to say, "It's them," "It's him," "it's us," or "it's her"—"It's me" is generally accepted as standard usage.

its, it's *Its* is the possessive form of the personal pronoun *it; it's* is the contraction meaning "it is."

p. 197

lay, lie This verb pair presents problems because, in addition to the similarity between the words, the past tense of *lie* is *lay.* The verb to *lay* means "to put or place something somewhere." The verb *to lie* means "to rest" or "to be at rest."

Present	Past	Past Participle	Present Participle
lay	laid	(has) laid	(is) laying
lie	lay	(has) lain	(is) lying

Notice how the verbs are used in the following sentences:

NOTE: *Lied* refers only to not telling the truth: "The jury was convinced that the defendent lied."

◆ Hark! *I laid* [placed] their daggers ready; He could not miss 'em.
from *Macbeth* by William Shakespeare

◆ Here let them *lie* [rest] / Till famine and the ague eat them up.
from *Macbeth* by William Shakespeare

M

media *Media* is the plural of *medium.* Many people use a singular verb when referring to the mass media. In formal writing it is best to use a plural verb.

All the media *are* focused on the national election.

misplaced modifier *See* **ambiguity.**

p. 218

modifier A modifier is a word or group of words that restrict, limit, or make more exact the meaning of other words. The modifiers of nouns and pronouns are usually adjectives, participles, adjective phrases, and adjective clauses. The modifiers of verbs, adjectives, and adverbs are adverbs, adverb phrases, and adverb clauses. In the following example, the italicized words modify the words in boldface type.

Besides, the *invariable* **squabble** for money on *Saturday* **nights** had begun **to weary** her *unspeakably.*
from "Eveline" by James Joyce

HINT: When trying to decide which pronoun to use, remember that you would not say, "Myself is going to the game." You would use *I.* Use *I* with a compound subject, too.

myself (and **himself, herself,** and so on) A reflexive pronoun reflects the action of the verb back to the subject. An intensive pronoun adds emphasis to the noun or pronoun just named.

◆ "I'm going to study outside. Even the street is quieter," I screeched and threw *myself* past them. . . .[reflexive]
from "Studies in the Park" by Anita Desai

◆ THE DAUGHTER. It's too tiresome. Do you expect us to go and get one *ourselves?* [intensive]
from *Pygmalion* by Bernard Shaw

Be careful not to use *myself* and the other reflexive and intensive pronouns when you simply need to use the personal pronoun *I* or its objective form *me.*

Incorrect: Ismail told Stephanie and *myself* a good story.

Correct: Ismail told Stephanie and *me* a good story.

N

p. 161
p. 173

noun A noun is a word that names a person, place, thing, or idea. Most nouns are made plural by adding *-s* or *-es* to the singular. When you are unsure about a plural form, check a dictionary.

P

parallel construction Items in a sentence that are of equal importance should be expressed in parallel (or similar) forms. These can take the form of noun phrases, verb phrases, infinitive phrases, and prepositional phrases:

Language and Grammar Handbook   **997**

◆ . . . it has been delayed till I am indifferent, and cannot enjoy it; till I am solitary, and cannot impart it; till I am known, and do not want it.
from "Letter to Chesterfield" by Samuel Johnson

◆ . . . we shall fight in France, we shall fight on the seas, we shall fight with growing confidence and growing strength in the air, . . . we shall fight in the fields and in the streets, we shall fight in the hills. . . .
from "Wartime Speeches" by Winston Churchill

parentheses ( ) Parentheses are used to enclose words that interrupt or add explanation to a sentence. They are also used to enclose references to page numbers, chapters, or dates. Punctuation marks that belong to the sentence come after the parentheses, not before.

◆ Those who are more thrifty (as I must confess the times require) may flay the carcass . . . .
from *A Modest Proposal* by Jonathan Swift

p. 222

participle A participle is a verb form used in forming various tenses of verbs. The present participle ends in *-ing: growing.* The past participle usually ends in *-ed, -t, -d, -en,* or *-n: scared, wept, said, risen, grown.* Participles are also used as adjectives, modifying nouns and pronouns.

◆ . . . when the sky darkened towards evening, an unearthly, *reflected* pallor remained. . . . [*Reflected* modifies the noun *pallor.*]
from "The Courtship of Mr. Lyon" by Angela Carter

plagiarism Using the words, ideas, or expressions of others as if they were your own is called plagiarism. Plagiarism problems usually grow from the following circumstances: 1. copying a passage from a source without giving credit; 2. paraphrasing a source so closely that only a few words or phrases are changed; 3. using someone else's ideas without giving credit. In a short paper credit is usually given directly in the text. In a longer piece of writing, you will need to footnote your sources.

p. 175
p. 178

possessive case The possessive case is formed in various ways. For singular nouns and indefinite pronouns, add an apostrophe and *-s:*

my *brother's* car   *no one's* notebook   *everybody's* children

For plural nouns ending in an *-s,* add only an apostrophe:

the *doctors'* offices   the *babies'* shoes   the *teachers'* rooms

NOTE: Apostrophes are not used with personal pronouns such as *his, hers,* or *ours* to show possession.

If the plural is irregular and does not end in *-s,* add an apostrophe and then an *-s: women's* clothing.

p. 231

prepositions Prepositions are words such as *about, between, during, from, in, of, over, under, until,* and *with* that show the relationship between a noun or pronoun and some other word in a sentence.

prepositional phrase Prepositional phrases are groups of words that begin with a preposition and end with a noun or pronoun (the object of the preposition). These phrases act as modifiers.

◆ There was a table set out under a tree in front of the house. . . .

from "A Mad Tea Party" by Lewis Carroll

p. 180
p. 183

pronoun A pronoun is a word used instead of a noun to designate a person or object. Subject pronouns are used as subjects of sentences. Object pronouns can be used as direct objects, indirect objects, or objects of prepositions.

HINT: When you are uncertain about whether to use a subject pronoun or an object pronoun, take out the first pronoun to test the sentence. (You wouldn't say "Me played yesterday" or "Tom asked I to stay.")

When a pronoun is used as the subject, it is in the nominative case. When a pronoun is used as an object, it is in the objective case.

Subject Pronouns	Object Pronouns
Singular: I; you; he, she, it	me; you; him, her, it
Plural: we; you; they	us; you; them
He and *I* played yesterday	Tom asked *her* and *me* to stay.

See also **ambiguity.**

p. 245
p. 247

quotation marks (" ") Quotation marks enclose a speaker's words. They are also used to enclose some titles. When you use someone's words in your writing, use the following rules:

1. Enclose all quoted words within quotation marks.

   Matthew Arnold wrote, "And we are here as on a darkling plain."

2. Introductory and explanatory expressions *(he said, I replied)* are set off by a comma, or if they interrupt a sentence, by two commas.

3. Periods and commas are always put inside quotation marks. Semicolons are put outside quotation marks.

   "I've read several of his poems," he said, "and liked them."

4. A question mark or exclamation point is put inside the quotation mark if it applies only to the quoted matter, outside if it applies to the complete sentence that contains the quotation.

   Didn't Matthew Arnold write "Dover Beach"?

5. When both the sentence and the quotation ending the sentence are questions or exclamations, only one mark is used—inside the quotation marks.

   Who wrote "Ah, Are You Digging On My Grave?"

Language and Grammar Handbook   **999**

6. A long quoted passage is often presented without quotation marks and indented instead, sometimes in smaller type.

See also **dialogue.**

R

real, really *Real* is used as an adjective, and *really* is used as an adverb.

We couldn't tell the *real* picture from the fake one.

The concert was *really* great. [not "real great"]

run-on sentence A run-on sentence occurs when there is only a comma (known as a comma splice) or no punctuation between two independent clauses. Separate the clauses into two complete sentences, join them with a semicolon, or use a comma and a coordinating conjunction.

Run on: The student received her schedule, then she went home.
Correct: The student received her schedule. Then she went home.
Correct: The student received her schedule; then she went home.
Correct: The student received her schedule, and then she went home.

Often, in narrative writing, authors purposely choose to use run-ons for effect, such as in the following passage:

◆ There was no mistake about it, Annie liked John Thomas a good deal.
   from "Tickets, Please" by D. H. Lawrence

See also **stringy sentences.**

S

p. 243
p. 247

semicolon (;) Use this punctuation mark to separate the two parts of a compound sentence when they are not joined by a comma and a conjunction.

◆ No man is an island, entire of itself; every man is a piece of the continent, a part of the main.
   from Meditation 17 by John Donne

NOTE: While some words or word groups are not complete sentences with a subject and a verb, they are complete in thought and are known as "minor-type sentences." Notice their use in the quoted passage.

p. 149
p. 229

sentence fragment A fragment often occurs when one sentence is finished, but another thought occurs to the writer and that thought is written and punctuated as a complete sentence.

Fragment: I loved the movie. Especially when Hamlet stages the play.
Correct: I loved the movie, especially when Hamlet stages the play.

◆ The bell rings. Voices clash, clatter, and break. The tin-and-bottle man? The neighbors? The police? The Help-the-Blind Man? Thieves and burglars?
   from "Studies in the Park" by Anita Desai

stringy sentences A stringy sentence is one in which several independent clauses are strung together with *and.* Correct a stringy sentence by breaking it into individual sentences or changing some of the independent clauses into subordinate clauses or phrases.

Stringy: Saturday morning I have to take my brother to his music lesson and pick up some dry cleaning and then I'm supposed to let Mom have the car so she can shop and I guess I'll have to walk or hitch a ride to football practice.

Correct: Saturday morning I have to take my brother to his music lesson and pick up some dry cleaning. Since I'm supposed to let Mom have the car so she can shop, I guess I'll have to walk or hitch a ride to football practice.

T

titles *See* **capitalization 2** and **9.**

V

p. 189
p. 193
p. 199

verb A verb is a word that tells about an action or a state of being. The form or tense of the verb tells whether the action occurred in the past, the present, or the future.

p. 191

verb tense Verb tenses indicate action in the past, present, future, and so on. Use the same tense to show two or more actions that occur at the same time.

Incorrect: She *brought* [past] two videos and some popcorn. Then she *talks* [present] all through the movies.

Correct: She *brought* [past] two videos and some popcorn. Then she *talked* [past] all through the movies.

When the verb in the main clause is in the present tense, the verb in the subordinate clause is in whatever tense expresses the meaning intended.

Mr. Washington *thinks* that the dinner *was* a success.

voice *See* **active and passive voice.**

W

p. 185

who, whom Use *who* as the subject of a sentence or clause:

Who is the author of this short story?

Use *whom* as a direct object or as the object of a preposition:

◆ So, thanks to all at once and to each one,
Whom we invite to see us crowned at Scone.
from *Macbeth* by William Shakespeare

◆ Any man's death diminishes me, because I am involved in mankind; and therefore never send to know for *whom* the bell tolls . . . .
from Meditation 17 by John Donne

who's, whose *Who's* is a contraction meaning "who is"; *whose* is a possessive.

Language and Grammar Handbook **1001**

After talking to everyone, decide *who's* planning to go.

◆ A knave *whose* practice it is to invite the unwary to game . . . .
from *Dictionary of the English Language* by Samuel Johnson

would of This expression is often used mistakenly because it sounds like *would've,* the contraction for *would have.* In formal writing, write out *would have,* and you won't be confused:

◆ For at that moment, with the crowd watching me, I was not afraid in the ordinary sense, as I *would have* been if I *had* been alone.
from "Shooting an Elephant" by George Orwell

 your, you're *Your* is the possessive form of the personal pronoun *you; you're* is a contraction meaning "you are."

◆ Commend to me *your* fair and gracious lady. . . .
from "Sir Gawain and the Green Knight"

Even though it's late, I hope *you're* going with me.

NOTE: In the example from "Shooting an Elephant," notice the last clause, "if I had been alone." In *if*-clauses and wishes pertaining to the past, the verb to use is *had,* not *would have.*

Index of Skills

Interdisciplinary Connections

Literary, Genres, Terms, and Techniques

Media and Technology

Multicultural Awareness and Appreciation

Reading/Thinking Strategies

■

Speaking, Listening, and Viewing

■

Vocabulary and Study Skills

Writing Forms, Modes, and Processes

Index of Fine Arts & Artists

Index of Authors and Titles

Acknowledgments

continued from page iv

599–601 "Loveliest of Trees," "When I Was One-and-Twenty," and "To An Athlete Dying Young" from *The Collected Poems Of A. E. Housman.* Copyright 1939, 1940 by Henry Holt and Co., Inc. Copyright © 1967 by Robert F. Symons. Reprinted by permission of Henry Holt and Co., Inc. and The Society of Authors as the literary representative of the Estate of A. E. Housman. **607** "The Second Coming" by W.B. Yeats from *The Poems Of W.B. Yeats: A New Edition,* edited by Richard J. Finneran. Copyright 1924 by Macmillan Publishing Company, renewed 1952 by Bertha Georgie Yeats. Reprinted with permission of Simon & Schuster, Inc. **608** "Sailing to Byzantium" by W.B. Yeats from *The Poems Of W.B. Yeats: A New Edition,* edited by Richard J. Finneran. Copyright 1928 by Macmillan Publishing Company, renewed © 1956 by Georgie Yeats. Reprinted with permission of Simon & Schuster, Inc. **612** "The Star" by H. G. Wells. Reprinted by permission of A. P. Watt on behalf of the Literary Executors of the Estate of H. G. Wells. **631** "Counting the Years" from *Time,* Fall 1992. Copyright © 1992 by Time Inc. Reprinted by permission. **648** "Stanley Meets Mutesa" by James D. Rubadiri. Reprinted by permission. **649** "England, My England" by William Ernest Henley. Reprinted by permission. **650** "England Your England" by George Orwell. Reprinted by permission. **654** From *The Crack in the Teacup* by Marina Warner. Reprinted by permission. **718** The Upper Class by Marina Warner. **718** Excerpts from *Britain—Twentieth Century: The Story of Social Conditions* by Mary Cathcart Borer. Reprinted by permission. **721** "Burlington Bertie from Bow" by William Hargreaves. Reprinted by permission. **743** From *Testament Of Youth* by Vera Brittain. Copyright 1933 by Vera Brittain. Reprinted by permission of Virago Press and Victor Gollancz Limited. **758** "Tickets, Please" from *Complete Short Stories Of D.H. Lawrence* by D. H. Lawrence. Copyright 1922 by Thomas Seltzer, Inc., renewal copyright 1950 by Frieda Lawrence. Used by permission of Viking Penguin, a division of Penguin Books USA Inc. **769** "The Hollow Men" by T.S. Eliot from *Collected Poems 1909-1962.* Copyright © 1936 by Harcourt Brace & Company; copyright © 1964, 1963 by T.S. Eliot. Reprinted by permission of the publisher and Faber and Faber Limited. **773** "The Horror at Ypres" from *Chemical And Biological Warfare* by L. B. Taylor, Jr. and C. L. Taylor. Copyright © 1985 by L. B. Taylor, Jr. and C. L. Taylor. Reprinted by permission of Franklin Watts. **775** "The Boneyard" from *The Great War And Modern Memory* by Paul Fussell, pp. 69-71. Reprinted by permission. **790** "Eveline" from *Dubliners* by James Joyce. Copyright 1916 by B.W. Heubsch. Definitive text copyright © 1967 by the Estate of James Joyce. Used by permission of Viking Penguin, a division of Penguin Books USA Inc. **797** "A Cup of Tea" from *The Short Stories Of Katherine Mansfield* by Katherine Mansfield.

Copyright 1923 by Alfred A. Knopf Inc. and renewed 1951 by John Middleton Murry. Reprinted by permission of Alfred A. Knopf Inc. **806–808** "The Unknown Citizen" and "Musée des Beaux Arts" by W.H. Auden from *W.H. Auden: Collected Poems.* Copyright 1940 and renewed © 1968 by W.H. Auden. Reprinted by permission of Random House, Inc. and Faber and Faber Limited. **810** "Who's Who" by W.H. Auden from *W.H. Auden: Collected Poems.* Copyright 1937 and renewed © 1965 by W.H. Auden. Reprinted by permission of Random House, Inc. and Faber and Faber Limited. **814** "Shakespeare's Sister" from *A Room Of One's Own* by Virginia Woolf. Copyright 1929 by Harcourt Brace & Company and renewed 1957 by Leonard Woolf. Reprinted by permission of Harcourt Brace & Company and The Society of Authors as the literary representative of the Estate of Virginia Woolf. **823** Dylan Thomas, "Do Not Go Gentle into That Good Night." Reprinted by permission. **824** Dylan Thomas, *A Child's Christmas In Wales.* Copyright 1954 by New Directions Publishing Corporation and David Higham Associates Limited. **833** "Studies in the Park" from *Games At Twilight* by Anita Desai. Copyright © 1978 by Anita Desai. Reproduced by permission of the author c/o Rogers, Coleridge & White Ltd., 20 Powis Mews, London W11 1JN. **860** "Shooting an Elephant" by George Orwell from *Shooting an Elephant and Other Essays.* Copyright 1950 by Sonia Brownell Orwell; renewed © 1978 by Sonia Pitt-Rivers. Reprinted by permission of Harcourt Brace & Company, the estate of the late Sonia Brownell Orwell and Martin Secker & Warburg Ltd **876** "Homage To a Government" from *High Windows* by Philip Larkin. Reprinted by permission. **877** "Two Poems on the Passing of an Empire" from *Collected Poems 1948-1984* by Derek Walcott. Reprinted by permission. **881** "Qualifying for the Mansions" and "Drifting to the Mansions" from *In The Ditch* by Buchi Emecheta. Copyright © 1972 by Buchi Emecheta. Reprinted by permission of the author. **907** "Eve To Her Daughters" from *Collected Poems* by Judith Wright. Reprinted by permission. **910–911** "The Frog Prince" and "Not Waving but Drowning" by Stevie Smith from *The Collected Poems of Stevie Smith.* Copyright © 1972 by Stevie Smith. Reprinted by permission of New Directions Publishing Corporation and James MacGibbon. **912** "The Explorers" by Margaret Atwood. Reprinted by permission. **916** "The Truly Married Woman" from *The Truly Married Woman And Other Stories* by Abioseh Nicol. Copyright ©1965 by Oxford University Press. Reprinted by permission of David Higham Associates Limited. **926** Graham Greene, "A Shocking Accident." Reprinted by permission. **933** Angela Carter, "The Courtship of Mr. Lyon." Reprinted by permission. **943** "Some Biomythology" from *The Lives of a Cell* by Lewis Thomas. Reprinted by permission. **956** From *The Theater of the Absurd* by Martin Esslin. Reprinted by permission. **957** "Nicely Nicely Clive" from *In His Own Write* by John Lennon. Reprinted by permission. **959**

From *The Crack In The Teacup* by Marina Warner. Reprinted by permission. **961** "The Dead Parrot Sketch" from *Monty Python's Flying Circus.* Reprinted by permission. **963** From *The Perils of Invisibility* by W.S. Gilbert. Reprinted by permission. **964** "Glory" by Lewis Carroll. Reprinted by permision.

Illustrations

Unless otherwise acknowledged, all photographs are the property of Scott, Foresman and Company. Page abbreviations are as follows: (t)top, (c)center, (b)bottom, (l)left, (r)right.

Front cover & frontispiece page ii Dante Gabriel Rossetti, "The Beloved"/Tate Gallery, London/Bridgeman Art Library, London/Superstock, Inc. **vii** William Morris and Edward Burne-Jones, "The Arming of the Knights," Birmingham Museums and Art Gallery **x** Private Collection **xii** Gerard ter Borch II, "The Suitor's Visit," (detail), c. 1658, Andrew W. Mellon Collection, © 1995 Board of Trustees, National Gallery of Art, Washington **xiv** "View of Broad Quay, Bristol," anonymous, British School, c.1735, City of Bristol Museum and Art Gallery **xxi** David Hockney, "Mr. and Mrs. Clark and Percy," 1970-1971. Acrylic, 84" x 120". © David Hockney/Tate Gallery, London/Art Resource **xxviii** "The Terrible Twins" by P. J. Crook, 1989. Courtesy Montpelier Sandelson, London **xxxvi–1** William Morris and Edward Burne-Jones, "The Arming of the Knights," (detail)/Birmingham Museums and Art Gallery **1, 42, 44, 88, 95,100(icon)** M805fol.48/The Pierpont Morgan Library/ Art Resource **2(t)** Copyright British Museum **2(bl)** Superstock, Inc. **2(br)** Erich Lessing/Art Resource **3(t)** Colchester and Essex Museum **3(bl)** Universitetets Oldsaksamling, Oslo **3(br)** Copyright British Museum **8, 13, 16–17, 21** Werner Forman/Art Resource, NY **27** Bibliothèque Nationale, Paris **31** Scala/Art Resource **32** Michael Holford **33(t)** Copyright British Museum **33(bl)** Koninklijk Instituut voor de Tropen, Amsterdam **33(br)** Hirmer Fotoarchiv, Munich **34(t)** Sonia Halliday **34(cl,cr,br)** Photofest **34(bl)** Foto Marburg/Art Resource **42(l)** Giraudon/Art Resource **42(r), 43(l)** British Library **43(c)** Reverend K. Wilkinson Riddle **43(r)** Erich Lessing/Art Resource **45** Bodleian Library, Oxford **46** British Library **51** Museum of London **53** M630fol.12/The Pierpont Morgan Library/Art Resource **54** Copyright British Museum **56** The Huntington Library, San Marino, California **61** Bridgeman/Art Resource **69** British Library **74** M805fol.48/The Pierpont Morgan Library/ Art Resource **77** E. Hugo **80** Lambeth Palace Library **84** Museo de Arte de Ponce **88** P. Kent **89** The Metropolitan Museum of Art, The Cloisters Collection, Munsey Fund, 1932 (32.130.3a) **90(t)** Bridgeman/Art Resource **90–91** Birmingham Museums and Art Gallery **90(b)** New York Public Library **91(t)** Art Resource **91(b)** Kobal Collection **92** New York Public Library **93** Illustrations by N. C. Wyeth, from *The Boy's King Arthur* by Sidney Lanier are used with the permission of Charles Scribner's Sons,

copyright renewed 1945 N. C. Wyeth **101** Richard C. Allen/The Carson Collection **102** Bridgeman/Art Resource **103(t)** Bibliothèque Nationale, Paris **103(b)** M630fol.12, The Pierpont Morgan Library/Art Resource **104–105** Private Collection **106–107** title art, Janice Clark **106(t)** Scala/Art Resource **106(b)** National Portrait Gallery, London **107(t)** Armillary sphere & telescope, Ancient Art & Architecture Collection/Ronald Sheridan Photo-Library; Books, Erich Lessing/Art Resource; da Vinci Self-Portrait, Scala/Art Resource; Sheet music, Folger Shakespeare Library; Lute, The Granger Collection **109** National Portrait Gallery, London **110, 119** Victoria & Albert Museum, London/Art Resource **128** Tate Gallery, London/Art Resource **146(t)** Copyright British Museum **147** Scale drawing by Irwin Smith from *Shakespeare's Globe Playhouse: A Modern Reconstruction in Text and Scale Drawings* by Irwin Smith. Charles Scribner's Sons, New York, 1956. Hand colored by Cheryl Kucharzak **155** Kunsthaus Zurich, © 1995, Copyright by Kunsthaus Zurich. All rights reserved. **165, 179** From the Art Collection of the Folger Shakespeare Library **192–193, 194–195** bloody backrounds, Diane Cole **192, 193** Copyright British Museum **194** Photofest **195** UPI/Corbis-Bettmann **196** Courtesy Diane Bray **205(t)** Victoria & Albert Museum, London/Art Resource **205(b)** Tate Gallery, London/Art Resource **209** Art Resource **210** Laing Art Gallery, Newcastle upon Tyne (Tyne and Wear Museums) **215(tl)** Bridgeman/Art Resource **215(tr)** Courtesy Anthony Green. R. A. c/o The Piccadilly Gallery, London, W1X 1PF **215(b)** © National Trust Photographic Library **217** Kenwood House, Hampstead/Bridgeman Art Library, London/Superstock, Inc. **220–221** Gerard ter Borch II, "The Suitor's Visit" (detail), c. 1658, Andrew W. Mellon Collection, © 1995 Board of Trustees, National Gallery of Art, Washington **222–223** ARXIU MAS **225** National Portrait Gallery, London **228** Staatliche Kunstsammlungen, Dresden. Photo: Sachische Landesbibliothek, Dresden **232(t)** Copyright British Museum **232(b)** Granger Collection **235** Courtesy Lord Sackville, Photo: Lime Tree Studios **239** UPI/Corbis-Bettmann **240(t)** Gamma-Liaison **240(b)** Gamma-Liaison **242–243** UPI/Corbis-Bettmann **244** Diltz/Gamma-Liaison **250–251(t&b)** Scala/Art Resource **250–251(c)** Bridgeman/Art Resource **253** National Portrait Gallery, London **257** Courtesy of the Fogg Art Museum, Harvard University Art Museums, Gift of W. A. White **263** Copyright British Museum **263(background)** Superstock, Inc. **268** Scala/Art Resource **276** Worcester Art Museum, Worcester, MA/Superstock, Inc. **276–277(background)** Superstock, Inc. **277** Everett Collection, Inc. **278(t)** M945fol.168v/The Pierpont Morgan Library/Art Resource **278(b)** Victoria & Albert Museum, London/Art Resource **279(tl)** Tate Gallery, London/E. T. Archives, London/Superstock, Inc. **279(b)** Museo del Prado, Madrid, Spain/A. K. G., Berlin/Superstock, Inc. **288(t)** Courtesy Lord Sackville, Photo: Lime Tree Studios **288(b)** Copyright British Museum **289** Scala/Art Resource **290–291** "View of Broad Quay, Bristol" (detail), anonymous, British School, c.1735, City of Bristol Museum and Art Gallery

291, 292, 294, 328, 331, 335(icon) T. H. Shepherd, "Arthur's Club House, St. James's Street," (detail)/Superstock, Inc. 295 National Portrait Gallery, London 297 Tate Gallery, London/Art Resource 304 Copyright British Museum 305 National Portrait Gallery, London 307 Winslow Homer, "Blackboard," Gift (Partial and Promised) of Jo Ann and Julian Ganz, Jr., in Honor of the 50th Anniversary of the National Gallery of Art, © 1995 Board of Trustees, National Gallery of Art, Washington 313 Bodleian Library, University of Oxford 328(b) Central Broadcasting 329(tr&b) Tribune Media Services 330 Jack Higgins 336(t) National Portrait Gallery, London/Superstock, Inc. 336(c) Granger Collection 336(b), 337(all) National Portrait Gallery, London/Superstock, Inc. 339 Corbis-Bettmann Archive 341 Yale Center for British Art, Paul Mellon Collection 343, 349 Pepys Library, by permission of the Master and Fellows, Magdalene College, Cambridge 350, 352–353 National Portrait Gallery, London 360 Scottish National Portrait Gallery, photo by Tom Scott 362, 370(t) Copyright British Museum 370(b) Bibliothèque Nationale, Paris 371 Scala/Art Resource 372(t) Giraudon/Art Resource 372(c) Erich Lessing/Art Resource 372–373(background) FPG International Corp. 373(t) © 1997 Andy Warhol Foundation for the Visual Arts/ARS, New York 373(l) Library of Congress 381(t) Tate Gallery, London/Art Resource 381(b) National Portrait Gallery, London 386–387(t), 390 Museum of London 386–387(b) Bridgeman/Art Resource 391(t) The Minneapolis Institute of Arts 391(b) Associated Newspapers Limited 397, 398, 400, 431, 438, 444(icon) Dante Gabriel Rossetti, "Reverie" (detail), Christie's, London/Superstock, Inc. 397, 446, 448, 475, 481, 487(icon) Edvard Munch, "Self-Portrait in Weimar," (detail)/Munch Museum, Oslo, Norway/Lerner Fine Art/Superstock, Inc. 397, 488, 490, 507, 513, 518(icon) Giovanni Stradano, "Alchemist Laboratory" (detail), Palazzo Vecchio, Florence, Italy/E. T. Archives, London/Superstock, Inc. 396–397 John Constable, "The Hay Wain," 1821 (detail) Reproduced by courtesy of the Trustees, The National Gallery, London 398(t) Victoria & Albert Museum, London/Art Resource 398–399 Superstock, Inc. 399(tl&tr) Copyright British Museum 399(b) Tate Gallery, London/Art Resource 401 National Portrait Gallery, London 403 The Metropolitan Museum of Art, The Elisha Whittelsey Collection, The Elisha Whittelsey Fund, 1967 (67.809.16) 407 Copyright British Museum 408 National Portrait Gallery, London 411 National Railway Museum/Science & Society Picture Library 416 National Portrait Gallery, London 419 Courtesy of the Arthur M. Sackler Museum, Harvard University Art Museums, Loan from Private Collection 422 National Portrait Gallery, London 424 Bridgeman/Art Resource 431 Honolulu Academy of Arts 432 Staatliche Museen Preussischer Kulturbesitz, Antikenmuseum, Berlin 433 National Museum of American History/Smithsonian Institution 434 & 435(all) Allan Hobson/SS/Photo Researchers 436 Detroit Institute of Arts, Michigan/A.K.G., Berlin/Superstock, Inc. 445 Yale Center for British Art, Paul Mellon Collection 446–447(t)

Copyright British Museum 446(c) Mansell Collection 446(b) Bulloz 447(c) Trustees of the Wedgwood Museum, Barlaston, Staffordshire, England 447(b) Library of Congress 449 National Portrait Gallery, London 451 Bridgeman/Art Resource 455 Corbis-Bettmann Archive 456 Plate 66 from Mrs. Hurst Dancing, text by Gordon Mingay, Watercolors by Diana Sperling. © Victor Gollancz Ltd. 1981 462 Granger Collection 465 Tate Gallery, London/Art Resource 468 Corbis-Bettmann Archive 472 Bequest of Mrs. Martin Brimmer, Courtesy, Museum of Fine Arts, Boston 475, 476(l) Corbis-Bettmann Archive 476(r), 478(l) Granger Collection 477(l) National Portrait Gallery, London 477(r) UPI/Corbis-Bettmann 478(r), 479(r) Sophia Smith Collection, Smith College 479(l) League of Women Voters of Japan 480 Courtesy Tanya Wallace 488–489(E)(b) Mansell Collection 489(B)(t) Museo del Prado, Madrid, Spain/Jack Novak/Superstock, Inc. 489(C)(tc) Walker Art Gallery, Liverpool 489(F)(cl) Smithsonian Institution 491 Bodleian Library, University of Oxford 492–493 diorama, Diane Cole 493 Bridgeman/Art Resource 499 Everett Collection, Inc. Hand-colored by Cheryl Kucharzak 503 Scala/Art Resource 507(background) FPG International Corp. 507 British Library 508–509(background) FPG International Corp. 508 Museum of Modern Art, Film Stills Archive 510(t) Alinari/Art Resource 510(bl) Boltin Picture Library 510(br) Everett Collection, Inc. 511(bl) Copyright British Museum 511(br) Everett Collection, Inc. 512(background) Michael Orton/Tony Stone Images 512 From A Pictorial History Of Science Fiction by David Kyle. Copyright © The Hamlyn Publishing Group Limited, 1976 519 Museum of Modern Art, Film Stills Archive 520(t) Bridgeman/Art Resource 520(b) Everett Collection, Inc. Hand-colored by Cheryl Kucharzak 521 Bridgeman/Art Resource 523, 524, 526, 559, 564, 569(icon) Illustration by John Tenniel for Alice's Adventures in Wonderland 523, 570, 572, 629, 634, 639(icon) Ernst Ludwig Kirchner, "Bildnis des Dichters Frank" (detail), Christie's London/Superstock, Inc. 523–524 George Williams Joy, "The Bayswater Omnibus," 1895 (detail)/Museum of London 524(t), 524(b), 525(b) Hulton Deutsch Collection Ltd. 524(c) International Museum of Photography/George Eastman House 525(t) Mansell Collection 527 National Portrait Gallery, London 528 Bridgeman/Art Resource 533 The Saint Louis Art Museum, Bequest of Morton D. May 538(t&b) National Portrait Gallery, London 541 Erich Lessing/Art Resource 546 Library of Congress 547 Everett Collection, Inc. 554 Corbis-Bettmann Archive 555 High Museum of Art, Atlanta, Georgia; purchase with funds from the Friends of Art 36.20 560 Brown Brothers 562(tl) Hulton Deutsch Collection Ltd. 562(tr) Edwin H. Colbert 562(cr,cl,b) Mansell Collection 563 Hulton Deutsch Collection Ltd. 570(t) National Gallery of Canada, Ottawa. Gift of the Massey Collection of English Painting, 1946 570(tc) From Punch, December 10, 1892, Hand-colored by Cheryl Kucharzak 570(bc) Newberry Library, Chicago 570(b) Museum of London 571 Mansell Collection. Hand-colored by Cheryl Kucharzak 573 National Portrait Gallery, London 575

Tate Gallery, London/Art Resource **580** National Portrait Gallery, London **581** Tate Gallery, London/Art Resource **585** Drawing by Walter Tiffle **586, 593** North Wind Picture Archives **600** Granger Collection **602** National Portrait Gallery, London **606** By courtesy of the Victoria & Albert Museum, London **611** UPI/Corbis-Bettmann **612** Vasily Kandinsky, "Several Circles No. 323," 1926. The Solomon R. Guggenheim Museum, New York, Photograph by David Heald, © The Solomon R.Guggenheim Foundation, New York (FN41.283) **623** National Portrait Gallery, London **628** Richard C. Allen/Carson Collection **639** From *A Pictorial History Of Science Fiction* by David Kyle. Copyright © The Hamlyn Publishing Group Limited, 1976 **641(t)**, Everett Collection **641(b)** Erich Lessing/Art Resource **642** Vasily Kandinsky, "Several Circles No. 323," 1926. The Solomon R. Guggenheim Museum, New York, Photograph by David Heald, © The Solomon R.Guggenheim Foundation, New York (FN41.283) **644–645** Mansell Collection **646** Hand-colored by Cheryl Kucharzak **650–651** Oriental and India Office Collections/British Library, Photo 154 f.31d neg. B6140 **653** Robert Opie Collection **655** National Army Museum, London, **657, 658, 660, 717, 723, 728(icon)** Courtesy Bassano Studios, London **657, 730, 732, 773, 778, 784(icon)** Imperial War Museum, London **657, 786, 788, 843, 846, 851(icon)** Amedeo Modigliani, "Jeanne Hebuterne au Foulard" (detail), Christie's, London/Superstock, Inc. **656–657** Charles Ginner, "Piccadilly Circus," 1912 (detail), Tate Gallery, London/Art Resource **658–659** diorama, Diane Cole **658 & 659 (A,B,C,F,G,I & 658–659(background)** Hulton Deutsch Collection Ltd. **658(D)** Museum of London **658(E)** Mary Evans Picture Library **659(H)** Copyright British Museum **661** National Portrait Gallery, London **662(r)** Kobal Collection **662(l)** Museum of Modern Art, Film Stills Archive **667, 670, 678, 690–691** Martha Swope/© Time, Inc. **696(l)** Angus McBean **696(r)** Zoe Dominic **697(l)** Mark Douet **697(r)** Photofest **705, 713** Martha Swope/Time, Inc. **717(t), 720(t&b)** Hulton Deutsch Collection Ltd. **717(b)** International Museum of Photography/George Eastman House **721** Everett Collection, Inc. **722** Photofest **728, 729** Robert Opie Collection **730(t)** National Archives **730(c)** Imperial War Museum, London **730(b) & 731(inset)** From the copy in the Bowman Gray Collection, University of North Carolina at Chapel Hill **731(t)** Imperial War Museum, London **734(t)** Culver Pictures Inc. **734(c)** Fitzwilliam Museum, University of Cambridge **734(b)** Culver Pictures Inc. **736** Imperial War Museum, London **742, 746, 751** Vera Brittain Archive/Mills Memorial Library/McMaster University, Hamilton, Ontario, Canada **757** Corbis-Bettmann Archive **758** From the copy in the Bowman Gray Collection, University of North Carolina at Chapel Hill **768** AP/Wide World **774, 776** Imperial War Museum, London **784** ABC News photo **786–787** Tate Gallery, London/Art Resource **787(br)** Corbis-Bettmann Archive **789** National Portrait Gallery, London **791** Plymouth City Museums & Art Gallery **796** Courtesy of Alfred Knopf **797** Collection of Dr. John Boreske/Vose Galleries of Boston **805** UPI/Corbis-Bettmann **807** ©1996 C. Hercovici, Brussels/Artists Rights Society (ARS), New York/Giraudon/Art Resource **808–809** Musee Royaux des Beaux-Arts de Belgique, Brussels **813** Courtesy of Harcourt, Brace **814** Victoria & Albert Museum, London/Art Resource **822** National Portrait Gallery, London **824** Bridgeman/Art Resource **837** Gallery, Vishva-Bharati University, Santiniketan, India **842** UPI/Corbis-Bettmann **843(l&r), 844(tl,tr,b), 845(tl)** Tate Gallery, London/Art Resource **845(tr)** National Art Gallery of New Zealand **845(b)** Bridgeman/Art Resource **852(t)** Martha Swope, © Time, Inc. **852(b)** Plymouth City Museums & Art Gallery **853** Imperial War Museum, London **854–855** David Hockney, "Mr. and Mrs. Clark and Percy" (detail), 1970-1971. Acrylic, 84" x 120". © David Hockney. Tate Gallery, London/Art Resource **855, 856, 858, 891, 896, 901(icon)** Superstock, Inc. **855, 902, 904, 943, 947, 952(icon)** Pablo Picasso, "Buste D'Homme au Chapeau," (detail) ©1997 Succession Picasso/Artists Rights Society (ARS), New York/Superstock, Inc. **856(t&b)** UPI/Corbis-Bettmann **856(c)** AFP/Corbis-Bettmann **857(tl&tr)** UPI/Corbis-Bettmann **857(b)** S. Ferry/Gamma-Liaison **859** AP/Wide World **860** Popperfoto **868** Brian Seed/Life Magazine, Time, Inc. **869** National Maritime Museum, London **875(t)** Rogers RBO/Camera Press/Globe Photos, Inc. **875(b)** Evan Richman/Reuters/Corbis-Bettmann **876** Diana Walker/Gamma-Liaison **880** George Braziller **881** The Brooklyn Museum, 82.65.2250, Collection of Charles and Lucille Plotz **890** The Seattle Art Museum, Gift of Katherine White and the Boeing Company, Photo: Paul Macapia **891** Corbis-Bettmann Archive **892** AP/Wide World **893(t)** Ian Berry/Magnum Photos **893(b)** Dick Arthur/*Honolulu Advertiser*, HI/Rothco **894** Courtesy Dr. Edward Brynn **902(A)** Spooner/ Gamma-Liaison **902(B)** Joe Taver/Gamma-Liaison **902(D)** Alistair Berg/Spooner/Gamma-Liaison **902(E)** Karim Daher/Gamma-Liaison **902(icon)** Superstock, Inc. **903(C)** Reuters/Corbis-Bettmann **903(F)** Katie Arkell/Gamma-Liaison **903(G)** Alistair Berg/Spooner/Gamma-Liaison **903(H)** Jacob Sutton/Gamma-Liaison **906(c)** National Portrait Gallery, London **906(b)** Laurence Acland **909** Ken Joudrey **915** New York Times/NYT Pictures **916–917** The Jean Pigozzi Collection, C. A. A. C., Ltd. **925** Corbis-Bettmann Archive **927** Portal Gallery, London **932** © Tara Heinemann 1984 **933** Everett Collection, Inc. **953** The Brooklyn Museum, 82.65.2250, Collection of Charles and Lucille Plotz **954(t)** Diana Walker/Gamma-Liaison **954(b)** Portal Gallery, London **959** Bibliothèque Nationale, Paris **960, 965** Portal Gallery, London **964** Granger Collection

Handlettering by Eliza Schulte.

Electronic Illustrations by Bruce Burdick, Steven Kiecker, Nikki Limper, and Gwen Plogman.

Custom Literature Database

The *ScottForesman Custom Literature Database* is a collection of over 1400 literary selections. Over 200 titles in the database have lessons to support students as they read. Eight indices—Title, Author, Genre, Subject, Nationality, Literary Themes, Anthology Correlations, and Lessons for Selected Titles—help you navigate through the database, allowing you to search for, view, and print the exact selection you want. The Anthology Correlations index lets you identify titles in the database correlated to *ScottForesman Literature and Integrated Studies*.

Address to the Apostles from Bible, Matthew, 10:5–42*

African Proverbs

"Aladdin, or The Wonderful Lamp" from *A Thousand and One Nights*

"Ali Baba and the Forty Thieves" from *A Thousand and One Nights*

Anglo-Saxon Riddles

Apocalyptic Utterances from Bible, Matthew 24:4–25:46

Articles of Confederation

Babylonian Law from *The Hammurabi Code*

Battle of Brunanburh, The

"Battle of Otterbourne, The"

Bhagavad Gita

Bible, Acts of the Apostles

Bible, Corinthians 1:13

Bible, Genesis 1–3

Bible, John

Bible, Luke 10:25–37*

Bible, Mark

Bible, Psalm 1

Bible, Psalm 8

Bible, Psalm 23 in Six Translations

Bible, Psalm 24

Bible, Psalm 91

Bible, Psalm 100*

Bible, Psalm 137

Bible, Ruth*

"Birth of Hatshepsut, The"

Birth of Jesus, The from Bible, Matthew 1:18–4:17

"Bonnie George Campbell"

"Bonny Barbara Allan"

Book of Jonah, The from The Hebrew Bible

"Brahman, the Tiger and the Six Judges, The"*

Brown v. *Board of Education of Topeka*

"Caedmon's Hymn"

Chinese Exclusion Act*

Civil Rights Act of 1964*

"Clementine"

Code of Manu, The

Constitution of the Confederate States of America, The

Constitution of the United States

Death of Jesus, The from Bible, Matthew 26:14–28:20

"Deep River"

"Demon Lover, The"

"Descent of Ishtar into the Underworld, The"

Dred Scott v. *Sandford*

"Egyptian Love Song"

"Emergence Song"

"Enchanted Horse, The" from *A Thousand and One Nights*

Everyman

"Experiences of a Chinese Immigrant" from *The Independent**

"Follow the Drinking Gourd"*

"Get Up and Bar the Door"

Gibbons v. *Ogden*

"Go Down, Moses"*

Hammurabi Code, The

"How Thoutii Took the Town of Joppa"

"Joshua Fit de Battle ob Jericho"

Kingdom of Heaven Parables from Bible, Matthew 13:1–52

Laws, The from Bible, Exodus 19:1–23:33

"Little Old Sod Shanty on the Claim, The"

"Lord Randal"

Magna Carta

Marbury v. *Madison*

"May Colvin"*

Mayflower Compact, The

NAACP v. *Alabama*

"Old Chisholm Trail, The"

On Humility and Forgiveness from Bible, Matthew 18:1–35

Parables from Bible, Luke*

"Pat Works on the Railway"

"Peasant and the Workman, The"

Plessy v. *Ferguson*

Preamble to the Constitution of the Knights of Labor

Prince Shotuku's Constitution

Resolution of the Stamp Act Congress

"Scheherazade" from *A Thousand and One Nights*

"Seafarer, The"

Second Shepherd's Play, The

Seneca Falls Declaration of Sentiments and Resolutions, The

Sermon on the Mount from Bible, Matthew 5:1–7:27

"Seven Voyages of Sindbad the Sailor, The" from *A Thousand and One Nights**

"Shenandoah"

"Shipwrecked Sailor, The"

Sir Gawain and the Green Knight*

"Sir Patrick Spens"*

Song of Creation

"Story of Rhampsinites, The"

"Story of the Fisherman, The" from *A Thousand and One Nights*

"Sumer is icumen in"

Sura LXXV—The Resurrection from *The Koran*

Sura LXXVI—Man from *The Koran*

"Swing Low, Sweet Chariot"

"Three Ravens, The"

Treaty of Peace with Great Britain

Trustees of Dartmouth College v. *Woodward*

"Twa Corbies, The"

Virginia Bill of Rights

Vishnu Purana

Volstead Act, The

"Wanderer, The"

"Western Wind"

"Wife of Usher's Well, The"

Adams, Henry
Education of Henry Adams, The, Chapter XXV, "The Dynamo and the Virgin"

"Prayer to the Virgin of Chartres"

Addison, Joseph
"Artifices in Tragedy" from *The Spectator*

"Party Patches" from *The Spectator*

"Sir Roger at Church" from *The Spectator*

"Westminster Abbey" from *The Spectator*

"Will Wimble" from *The Spectator**

"Wit: True, False, and Mixed"

Aelfric, Abbot
"Colloquy on the Occupations, A"

Aesop
"Crow and the Pitcher, The"

"Fox and the Crow, The"

"Fox and the Grapes, The"

*This selection includes background information, a study guide, and comprehension and critical thinking questions in a lesson on the disc.

Custom Literature Database

"Hound and the Hare, The"
"Mice and the Weasels, The"
"North Wind and the Sun, The"

Alcaeus
"Drinking Song"
"Summer"
"Winter"

Alcott, Louisa May
"Amy's Valley of Humiliation" from
    Little Women*
Hospital Sketches
"Old-Fashioned Thanksgiving, An"*
"Onawandah, Fourth Spinning Wheel
    Story"

Alighieri, Dante
Divine Comedy, The, " The Inferno,"
    Canto I
Divine Comedy, The, "The Inferno,"
    Canto III
Divine Comedy, The, "The Inferno,"
    Canto XXXIV

Alline, Henry
"The Conduct of Most Sailors"

Anacreon
"Beauty"
"Combat, The"
"Cup, The"
"Love"

Andersen, Hans Christian
"Emperor's New Clothes, The"*
"Little Mermaid, The"
"Red Shoes, The"
"Snow Queen, The"
"Steadfast Tin Soldier, The"
"Swineherd, The"
"Thumbelina"
"Tinder-Box, The"
"Ugly Duckling, The"*

Anderson, Sherwood
"Discovery of a Father"*
"Stolen Day"

Anonymous
Independent, The
"My mind to me a kingdom is"
"There is a Lady Sweet and Kind"

Anthony, Susan B.
On Woman's Right to Suffrage*
"Political Economy of Women"

Antin, Mary
"Immigrant Goes to School, An" from
    The Promised Land*

Aristotle
Poetics, The

Arnold, Matthew
"Isolation, To Marguerite"
"Last Word, The"
"Requiescat"
"Scholar-Gipsy, The"
"Self-Dependence"
"Thyrsis"

Aspinwall, Alicia
"Upsidedownians, The"

Aulnoy, Comtesse d'
"White Cat, The"
"Yellow Dwarf, The"

Aupaumut, Hendrick
A Short Narration of My Last Journey
    to the Western Contry

Babur
Babur-nama*

Bacon, Francis
"Of Studies"
"Of Truth"

Bambara, Toni Cade
"Blues Ain't No Mockin Bird"*
"Happy Birthday"*

Barbour, Ralph Henry
"Brewster's Debut"

Beach, Lewis
Clod, The*

Bede
*Ecclesiastical History of the English
    People, The,* Book II, Chapters
    9–13*
*Ecclesiastical History of the English
    People, The,* Book IV, Chapter 24

Behn, Aphra
"Lady's Looking Glass, The"
"Love in Fantastic Triumph Sat from
    Abdelazar"
Oroonoko

Bellamy, Edward
Looking Back*

Belloc, Hilaire
"Lion, The"
"Yak, The"

Benét, Stephen Vincent
"By the Waters of Babylon"

Benet, WIlliam Rose
"Skater of Ghost Lake, The"

Bennet, John
"Fritz the Master Fiddler"

Bierce, Ambrose
"Occurrence at Owl Creek Bridge,
    An"

Blackwell, Alice Stone
Indifference of Women, The*

Blake, William
"And did those feet" from *Milton*
"Chimney Sweeper, The" from *Songs
    of Experience*
"Chimney Sweeper, The," from
    Songs of Innocence
"Divine Image, The" from *Songs of
    Innocence*
"Holy Thursday" from *Songs of
    Experience*
"Holy Thursday" from *Songs of
    Innocence*
"Human Abstract, The" from *Songs
    of Experience*
"Infant Joy"
"Infant Sorrow"
Introduction ("Hear the voice of the
    Bard") from *Songs of Experience*
Introduction ("Piping down the
    valleys") from *Songs of Innocence*
"Lamb, The" from *Songs of
    Innocence*
"Nurse's Song" from *Songs of
    Experience*
"Poison Tree, A"
"Proverbs of Hell" from *The Marriage
    of Heaven and Hell*
"Sick Rose, The"
Song ("How sweet I roamed")
"Tyger, The" from *Songs of
    Experience*

Bleecker, Ann Eliza
"On the Immensity of Creation"

Boas, Franz
"Raven's Adventures"
"Sedna, Mistress of the Underworld"

Boswell, James
*Life of Samuel Johnson, LL.D, The
London Journal, 1762–1763*

Bradstreet, Anne
"Contemplations"
"Prologue, The"
"To My Dear and Loving Husband"
"Upon the Burning of Our House, July
    10th, 1666"

Brontë, Emily
"No coward soul is mine"
"Remembrance"
Song ("The linnet in the rocky dells")

Brooke, Rupert
"Peace"*

Brooks, Gwendolyn
"Pete at the Zoo"

Brothers Grimm
"Bremen Town Musicians, The"*
"Elves and the Shoemaker, The"
"Fisherman and His Wife, The"
"Frog Prince, The"
"Gallant Tailor, The"
"Hansel and Grethel"
"Juniper Tree, The"
"Rapunzel"
"Rumpelstiltskin"*
"Sleeping Beauty, The"
"Snow-white"
"Twelve Dancing Princesses, The"

Brown, Dee
"Katlian and the Iron People"*

Brown, John
Last Speech

Browning, Elizabeth Barrett
Sonnet 1 ("I thought once how
    Theocritus had sung") from
    Sonnets from the Portuguese
Sonnet 14 ("If thou must love me, let
    it be for naught") from *Sonnets
    from the Portuguese*
Sonnet 26 ("I lived with visions for
    my company") from *Sonnets from
    the Portuguese*

*This selection includes background information, a study guide, and comprehension and critical thinking questions in a lesson on the disc.

Custom Literature Database

Chopin, Kate
"Pair of Silk Stockings, A"*

Christie, Agatha
"Third-Floor Flat, The"*

Churchill, Winston
Blood, Sweat, and Tears
Dunkirk
Iron Curtain Has Descended, An*
Their Finest Hour

Clay, Henry
On the Compromise of 1850

Clough, Arthur Hugh
"Epi-Strauss-um"
"Latest Decalogue, The"
"Say not the struggle nought availeth"

Cobb, Frank I. and Walter Lippmann
Interpretation of President Wilson's Fourteen Points

Coleridge, Samuel Taylor
Biographia Literaria
"Christabel"
"Eolian Harp, The"
"Frost at Midnight"
"Kubla Khan"
"Rime of the Ancient Mariner, The"
"This Lime-Tree Bower My Prison"

Colum, Padraic
"Aegir's Feast: How Thor Triumphed"
"Baldur's Doom"
"Building of the Wall, The"
"Children of Loki, The"
"Dwarf's Hoard, and the Curse That It Brought"
"How Brock Brought Judgement on Loki"
"How Freya Gained Her Necklace and How Her Loved One Was Lost to Her"
"How Thor and Loki Be-Fooled Thrym the Giant"
"Iduna and Her Apples: How Loki Put the Gods in Danger"

"Odin Goes to Mimir's Well; His Sacrifice for Wisdom"
"Sif's Golden Hair: How Loki Wrought Mischief in Asgard"
"Sigurd's Youth" from The Children of Odin
"Thor and Loki in the Giants' City"
"Twilight of the Gods, The"
"Valkyrie, The"

Conrad, Joseph
Secret Sharer, The
Youth*

Crane, Stephen
"Bride Comes to Yellow Sky, The"
"Do not weep, maiden, for war is kind"
"Episode of War, An"
"I met a seer"
"Man saw a ball of gold in the sky, A"
"Mystery of Heroism, A"
"Open Boat, The"*
Red Badge of Courage, The
"Think as I Think"

Crevecoeur, Michel-Guillaume Jean de
Letters from an American Farmer

Curtin, Jeremiah, and Hewitt, J. N. B.
"Woman Who Fell from the Sky, The"

Curtis, Natalie
"Creation"
"Deathless One and the Wind, The"
"Morning Star and the Evening Star, The"
"Origin of Corn and Pemmican, The"
"Stories of Wak-Chung-Kaka, the Foolish One"
"Story of Gomoidema Pokoma-Kiaka, The"
"Story of the First Mother, The"
"Story of Wakiash and the First Totem-Pole, The"*
"Vision of the Earth-Maker, A"*

Davis, Jefferson
Inaugural Address of Jefferson Davis
Last Message to the People of the Confederacy
Message to Congress

Davis, Richard H.
"Midsummer Pirates"

de la Mare, Walter
"All But Blind"
"All That's Past"
"Cake and Sack"
"Dwelling Place, The"
"Flight, The"
"Listeners, The"*
"Nobody Knows"
"Silver"
"Song of the Mad Prince, The"
"Tartary"
"Up and Down"

De Quincey, Thomas
"On the Knocking at the Gate in Macbeth"
"Poetry of Pope, The"

Defoe, Daniel
Essay Upon Projects, An
Journal of the Plague Year, A

Dekker, Thomas
"Lullaby"

Delgado, Reverend Father Fray Carlos
Report Made By Reverend Father Fray Carlos Delgado

Dickens, Charles
David Copperfield
"Signalman, The"*

Dickinson, Emily
"Alter! When the Hills do"
"Apparently with no surprise"
"Because I could not stop for death"
"Bustle in a House, The"
" 'Faith' Is a fine invention"
" 'Hope' is the thing with feathers"
"I felt a Funeral, in my Brain"
"I heard a Fly buzz – when I died"
"I like to see it lap the Miles"
"I taste a liquor never brewed"
"I Years had been from Home"
"I'll tell you how the Sun rose"
"If you were coming in the Fall"
"Morns are meeker than they were, The"
"Much Madness is divinest Sense"
"Narrow Fellow in the grass, A"*

"Of all the Souls that stand create"
"Some keep the Sabbath going to Church"
"Success is counted sweetest"*
"Surgeons must be very careful"
"There's a certain Slant of light"
"This is my letter to the World"
"To make a prairie it takes a clover"
"Triumph – may be of several kinds"*

Dixon, Roland B.
"Creation, The"
"Theft of Fire, The"

Donne, John
"Bait, The"
"Ecstacy, The"
"Flea, The"
"Indifferent, The"
Meditation 17 from Devotions
"On His Mistress"
Song ("Go and catch a falling star")
Sonnet 4 ("At the round earth's imagined corners, blow") from Holy Sonnets*
Sonnet 6 ("This is my play's last scene; here heavens appoint") from Holy Sonnets
Sonnet 10 ("Death, be not proud, though some have called thee") from Holy Sonnets*
Sonnet 14 ("Batter my heart, three-personed God; for You") from Holy Sonnets
"Sun Rising, The"
"Valediction: Forbidding Mourning, A"
"Woman's Constancy"

Dorsey, George and Kroeber, Alfred L.
"Star Husband, The"

Douglass, Frederick
Life and Times of Frederick Douglass, The*
Meaning of July Fourth for the Negro, The*
Narrative of the Life of Frederick Douglass, The
Oration in Memory of Abraham Lincoln

Dowson, Ernest
"Cynara"

"They are not long"

Doyle, Sir Arthur Conan
"Adventure of the Blue Carbuncle, The"*

Hound of the Baskervilles, The*

"Man with the Twisted Lip, The"*

"Musgrave Ritual, The"

"Redheaded League, The"

"Silver Blaze"

Dryden, John
Absalom and Achitophel

Essay of Dramatic Poesy, An

"I Feed a Flame Within"

Mac Flecknoe

Preface to *Fables Ancient and Modern, The*

"Song for St. Cecilia's Day, A"

"Song Sung by Venus in Honor of Britannia"

"To the Memory of Mr. Oldham"

DuBois, W. E. B.
Behold the Land

Crisis, The

"Of the Meaning of Progress" from *The Souls of Black Folk*

"Of the Sorrow Songs" from *The Souls of Black Folk*

Dunbar, Paul Laurence
"Booker T. Washington"*

"Douglass"*

"Keep A-Pluggin' Away"*

"Life's Tragedy"*

"Love's Apotheosis"*

"We Wear the Mask"

Duncan, Sara Jeannette
Saunterings

Eastman, Charles
From the Deep Woods to Civilization*

Edwards, Jonathan
Personal Narrative

"Sarah Pierrepont"

"Sinners in the Hands of an Angry God"

Eisenhower, Dwight
Atoms for Peace

Eliot, George
"Lifted Veil, The"*

Elizabeth I
"When I was fair and young"

Emerson, Ralph Waldo
"American Scholar, The"

"Brahma"

"Concord Hymn"

"Days"

"Each and All"

"Experience"

"Fable"

Journals

"Maxims"

"Nature"

"Rhodora, The"

"Self-Reliance"

"Snowstorm, The"

Emmett, Daniel
"Dixie"*

Euripides
Medea*

Fitzgerald, Edward
Rubáiyát of Omar Khayyám, The

Forster, E. M.
"Celestial Omnibus, The"

Franklin, Benjamin
Autobiography of Benjamin Frankin, The, Franklin's Childhood

Autobiography of Benjamin Franklin, The, Seeking Moral Perfection

"Dialogue Between Franklin and the Gout"

"Edict by the King of Prussia, An"

"Ephemera, The"

Letter of November 21, 1783

"Receipt to Make a New England Funeral Elegy, A"

Speech at the Constitutional Convention

"Way to Wealth, The"

"Whistle, The"

"Witch Trial at Mount Holly, A"*

Freeman, Mary E. Wilkins
"New England Nun, A"*

Freneau, Philip
"Indian Burying-Ground, The"

"On the Memorable Victory"

"To a Caty-Did"

"Wild Honeysuckle, The"

Frost, Robert
"Death of the Hired Man, The"*

"It Bids Pretty Fair"

"Oven Bird, The"

"Pasture, The"

"Road Not Taken, The"

"Runaway, The"

"Time to Talk, A"

"Wood-Pile, The"

Fuller, Margaret
"Woman in the Nineteenth Century"

Garrison, William Lloyd
"Liberator, The"

On the Death of John Brown

Gascoigne, George
"Lullaby of a Lover"

Gilbert, W. S.
"Aesthete, The"

"Englishman, The" from *H. M. S. Pinafore*

"Let the Punishment Fit the Crime" from *The Mikado*

"Policeman's Lot, The"

"They'll None of 'Em Be Missed"

Gissing, George
"Scrupulous Father, The"*

Goddard, Pliny Earle
"Creation, The"

Goldsmith, Oliver
She Stoops to Conquer, Act One

She Stoops to Conquer, Act Two

She Stoops to Conquer, Act Three

She Stoops to Conquer, Act Four

She Stoops To Conquer, Act Five

Gray, Thomas
"Bard, The"

"Elegy Written in a Country Churchyard"*

"Ode on a Distant Prospect of Eton College"

"Sonnet on the Death of Richard West"

Gregory, Lady Augusta
"Boy Deeds of Cuchulain"

Spreading the News*

Greville, Fulke, Lord Brooke
"Chorus Sacerdotum"

"Of His Cynthia"

"You Little Stars"

Haines, Alice Calhoun
"Tenderhearted Dragon, A"

Hale, Edward Everett
"Man Without a Country, The"*

Hale, Lucretia P.
"Mrs. Peterkin's Tea-party"

"Peterkins Celebrate the Fourth of July, The"

Hancock, H. Irving
"Rip Van Winkle Man-O'-War, The"

Hardy, Thomas
"Afterwards"

"Ah, are you digging on my grave?"

"Beeny Cliff"

"Channel Firing"

"Convergence of the Twain, The"

"Darkling Thrush, The"

"Epitaph on a Pessimist"

"Hap"*

"In Tenebris"

"In Time of 'The Breaking of Nations' "*

"Man He Killed, The"

"Neutral Tones"

Our Exploits at West Poley*

"Three Strangers, The"

"Walk, The"

"When I Set Out for Lyonesse"

"Withered Arm, The"

Harper, Ellen Watkins
Colored People in America, The

On the Twenty-Fourth Anniversary of the American Anti-Slavery Society

Harris, Joel Chandler
"Creature with No Claws, The"

"Wonderful Tar-Baby Story, The"

Custom Literature Database

Harte, Bret
"Baby Sylvester"
"Brown of Calaveras"
"Iliad of Sandy Bar, The"
"Luck of Roaring Camp, The"
"Miggles"
"Outcasts of Poker Flat, The"*
"Plain Language from Truthful James"
"Tennessee's Partner"

Hawthorne, Nathaniel
"Birthmark, The"
"Dr. Heidegger's Experiment"
"Drowne's Wooden Image"
"Golden Touch, The"*
"Maypole of Merry Mount, The"
"Minister's Black Veil, The"*
"My Kinsman, Major Molineaux"
Notebooks, The
"Rappaccini's Daughter"
"Young Goodman Brown"*

Hayford, J. E. Casely
"As in a Glass Darkly" from Ethiopia Unbound
"Black Man's Burden, The" from Ethiopia Unbound
"Gold Coast Native Institutions"
"Saving the Wind" from Ethiopia Unbound

Hayne, Paul Hamilton
"Aspects of the Pines"

Hazlitt, William
"Macbeth"
My First Acquaintance with Poets
"On Going a Journey"

Heine, Heinrich
"Loreley, The"*

Henley, William Ernest
"Invictus"

Henry, Patrick
Speech in the Virginia Convention, March 23, 1775

Herbert, George
"Altar, The"
"Avarice"
"Bitter-Sweet"
"Collar, The"
"Easter Wings"*

"Love (III)"
"Man"
"Pulley, The"
"Redemption"
"Virtue"*

Heredia y Heredia, Jose Maria
"Ode to Niagara"

Herrick, Robert
"Argument of His Book, The" from Hesperides
"Corinna's Going A-Maying"
"Ode for Ben Jonson, An"
"To the Virgins, to Make Much of Time"
"Upon Julia's Clothes"

Hobbes, Thomas
Leviathan, Part I, Chapters 13–15

Holmes, Oliver Wendell
"Ballad of the Oysterman, The"
"Chambered Nautilus, The"
"Last Leaf, The"
"My Last Walk with the Schoolmistress"
"Old Ironsides"

Hoover, Herbert
Philosophy of Rugged Individualism, The

Hopkins, Gerard Manley
"Carrion Comfort"*
"Felix Randal"
"God's Grandeur"
"Habit of Perfection, The"
"No worst, there is none"*
"Pied Beauty"
"Spring and Fall"
"Thou Art Indeed Just, Lord"
"Windhover, The"

Horace
"Ad Leuconeon"
"Death of Cleopatra, The"
"Golden Mean, The"
"Ship of State, The"

Housman, A. E.
"Loveliest of trees, the cherry now"
"Night is freezing fast, The"
"Oh, when I was in love with you"

"On moonlit heath and lonesome bark"
"To an Athlete Dying Young"
"White in the moon the long road lies"

Howard, Henry, Earl of Surrey
"Alas, So All Things Now Do Hold Their Peace"
"Love, that doth reign and live within in my thought"
"Lover's Vow, A"

Howe, Julia Ward
"Battle Hymn of the Republic, The"*

Howells, William Dean
"Christmas Every Day"*
"Editha"

Hudson, W. H.
Idle Days in Patagonia, The, Chapter XII*

Hughes, Rupert
"Latest News About the Three Wishes, The"

Hunt, James Henry Leigh
"Abou Ben Adhem and the Angel"

Huxley, Thomas Henry
"Method of Scientific Investigation, The"

Irving, Washington
"Early Life in Manhattan" from A History of New York
"Legend of Sleepy Hollow, The"*
"Rip Van Winkle"
Tour on the Prairies, A

Jackson, Andrew
Second Inaugural Address

Jacobs, Harriet Ann
Incidents in the Life of a Slave Girl, Chapter I*

Jacobs, Joseph
"Dick Whittington and His Cat"*
"Jack and the Beanstalk"
"Jack the Giant-Killer"

Jacobs, W. W.
Monkey's Paw, The*

James, Henry
"Four Meetings"
"Middle Years, The"
"Real Thing, The"

James, William
"On a Certain Blindness in Human Beings"

Jefferson, Thomas
Declaration of Independence, The
Jefferson's First Inaugural Address
Virginia Statute of Religious Liberty

Jewett, Sarah Orne
"Courting of Sister Wisby, The"
"Hiltons' Holiday, The"
"Miss Tempy's Watchers"
"Native of Winby, A"*
"White Heron, A"

Johnson, Andrew
Johnson's Proclamation of Amnesty

Johnson, James Weldon
Autobiography of an Ex-Colored Man, The, Chapters 1–2*
Autobiography of an Ex-Colored Man, The, Chapters 3–4*

Johnson, Lyndon
Speech at Johns Hopkins University

Johnson, Pauline
"Corn Husker, The"
"Silhouette"

Johnson, Samuel
Dictionary of the English Language
Life of Milton, The*
London
"On Choosing Friends" from the Rambler No. 160
"On Fiction" from the Rambler No. 4
"On Forgiveness" from the Rambler No. 185
"On Self-Indulgence" from the Rambler No. 155
"On Spring" from the Rambler No. 5
"On the Death of Dr. Robert Levet"
"On the Tyranny of Parents" from the Rambler No. 148
Preface to Shakespeare, The

Jonson, Ben
"Elegy, An"
"Ode to Himself, An"
"On My First Daughter"
"On My First Son"
"Song: To Celia"
"Still to Be Neat"

---

*This selection includes background information, a study guide, and comprehension and critical thinking questions in a lesson on the disc.

Custom Literature Database

Major, Charles
"Big Bear, The"

Malory, Sir Thomas
"Arthur Marries Gwynevere"
Morte d'Arthur, Le, Book 21, Chapters 5–7

Marlowe, Christopher
"Passionate Shepherd to His Love, The"*
Tragical History of Doctor Faustus, The, Act One
Tragical History of Doctor Faustus, The, Act Two
Tragical History of Doctor Faustus, The, Act Three
Tragical History of Doctor Faustus, The, Act Four
Tragical History of Doctor Faustus, The, Act Five

Marshall, George C.
Marshal Plan, The

Marvell, Andrew
"Bermudas"
"Dialogue Between the Soul and Body, A"
"Garden, The"
"Picture of Little T. C. in a Prospect of Flowers, The"

Masefield, John
"Cargoes"*
"Sea-Fever"*

Masters, Edgar Lee
"Cooney Potter"
"Dow Kritt"
"Hortense Robbins"
"Mrs. Kessler"
"Samuel Gardner"

Mather, Cotton
Wonders of the Invisible World, The

Maupassant, Guy de
"Boule de Suif" (Ball of Fat)
"Devil, The"
"Diamond Necklace, The"
"Horla, The"
"Piece of String, The"*
"Two Friends"*

McCrae, John
"In Flanders Fields"*

McNeil, Everett
"King of the Golden Woods, The"

Melville, Herman
"Art"
"Bartleby the Scrivener"
"Maldive Shark, The"
"Portent, The"
"Shiloh"

Meredith, George
"Lucifer in Starlight"

Mill, John Stuart
Autobiography of John Stuart Mill, The
On Liberty
"Black Hero of the Ranges, The"*

Milton, John
"Il Penseroso"
"L'Allegro"
"Lycidas"
"On Shakespeare"
"On the Late Massacre in Piedmont"
Paradise Lost, Book VI
Paradise Lost, Book IX*
Paradise Lost, Book XII
"When I consider how my light is spent"

Monroe, James
Monroe Doctrine, The

Montagu, Lady Mary Wortley
"Answer to a Love-Letter in Verse, An"
"Lady's Resolve, The"
"On The Death of Mrs. Bowes"

Moore, Milcah Martha
"Female Patriots, The"

Moore, Thomas
"Harp that once through Tara's halls, The"
"Minstrel Boy, The"

More, Hannah
"Slavery, a Poem"

Morris, William
"Apology, An" from *The Earthly Paradise*
"Defence of Guenevere, The"*
"Haystack in the Floods, The"
"Love Is Enough"

Morton, Sarah Wentworth
"African Chief, The"

Nashe, Thomas
"Autumn"
"Litany in Time of Plague, A"

Nesbit, E.
"Beautiful As the Day"
"Jungle, The"
"Plush Usurper, The"*
"Pride of Perks, The" from *The Railway Children*

Newman, John Henry Cardinal
"Lead, Kindly Light"

Nightingale, Florence
Cassandra

Northup, Solomon
"Christmas on the Plantation" from *Twelve Years a Slave*
"Picking Cotton" from *Twelve Years a Slave*

O. Henry (William Sidney Porter)
"After Twenty Years"
"Cop and the Anthem, The"*
"Furnished Room, The"
"Hearts and Hands"*
"Man Higher Up, The"*
"Ransom of Red Chief, The"*
"Retrieved Reformation, A"*
"Unfinished Story, An"

Owen, Wilfred
"Anthem for Doomed Youth"*
"Strange Meeting"

Ozaki, Yei Theodora
"Momotaro, or the Story of the Son of a Peach"
"Story of Urashima Taro, the Fisher Lad, The"*
"Tongue-Cut Sparrow, The"

Paine, Thomas
American Crisis, The
Common Sense

Palou, Francisco
Life of Junípero Serra

Parris, Robert
"Refusal to Pay Taxes, A" from *The Liberator*

Peacock, Thomas Love
"War Song of Dinas Vawr, The"

Pepys, Samuel
Diary, The

Perrault, Charles
"Bluebeard"
"Cinderella"
"Little Red Ridinghood"
"Puss in Boots"

Plato
Apology
Crito
Phaedo

Po Chu-i
"After Passing the Examination"
"Chu Ch'en Village"*
"Escorting Candidates to the Examination Hall"
"Golden Bells"*
"In Early Summer Lodging in a Temple to Enjoy the Moonlight"
"Old Man with the Broken Arm, The"
"On Board Ship: Reading Yu Chen's Poems"
"Prisoner, The"
"Remembering Golden Bells"*
"Watching the Reapers"

Poe, Edgar Allan
"Annabel Lee"
"Bells, The"
"Cask of Amontillado, The"
"Eldorado"
"Fall of the House of Usher, The"*
"Hop-Frog"
"Israfel"
"Ligeia"
"Masque of the Red Death, The"
"Oval Portrait, The"
"Philosophy of Composition, The"
Poetic Principle, The
"Purloined Letter, The"*
"Tell-Tale Heart, The"
"To Helen"*
"Ulalume"
"William Wilson"

Pope, Alexander
"Eloisa to Abelard"
"Epistle to Dr. Arbuthnot"
"Epistle to Miss Blount"
"Essay on Criticism, An"
Essay on Man, An
"Rape of the Lock, The"

Pyle, Howard
"Enchanted Island, The"
"Epilogue" from *The Merry Adventures of Robin Hood*
"Good Gifts and a Fool's Folly"*
"King Richard Cometh to Sherwood Forest" from *The Merry Adventures of Robin Hood*
"King Stork"
"Prologue" from *The Merry Adventures of Robin Hood*
"Robin Hood and Allan a Dale" from *The Merry Adventures of Robin Hood*
"Robin Hood and Guy of Gisbourne" from *The Merry Adventures of Robin Hood*
"Robin Hood Seeketh the Curtal Friar" from *The Merry Adventures of Robin Hood*
"Robin Hood Turns Butcher" from *The Merry Adventures of Robin Hood*
"Shooting-Match at Nottingham Town, The" from *The Merry Adventures of Robin Hood*
"Story of Sir Gawaine, The" from *The Story of King Arthur and His Knights*
"Winning of a Queen, The" from *The Story of King Arthur and His Knights*
"Winning of a Sword, The" from *The Story of King Arthur and His Knights*
"Winning of Kinghood, The" from *The Story of King Arthur and His Knights*

Quintero, Serafin and Joaquin Alvarez
Sunny Morning, A

Raleigh, Sir Walter
"Even Such Is Time"
"Nature, that washed her hands in milk"
"Nymph's Reply to the Shepherd, The"
"Sir Walter Raleigh to His Son"
"To Queen Elizabeth"
"What Is Our Life"

Rand, Silas
"Bird Whose Wings Made the Wind, The"
"Glooscap"

Ransome, Arthur
"Baba Yaga"
"Fire-bird, the Horse of Power and the Princess Vasilissa, The"
"Fool of the World and the Flying Ship, The"

Richards, Laura E.
"Chop-Chin and the Golden Dragon"

Riley, James Whitcomb
"When the frost is on the punkin"

Robinson, Edward Arlington
"Luke Havergal"
"Miniver Cheevy"*
"Mr. Flood's Party"

Roosevelt, Franklin Delano
First Inaugural Address
Four Freedoms Speech
Japanese Relocation Order*

Roosevelt, Franklin Delano and Churchill, Winston S.
Atlantic Charter, The

Roosevelt, Theodore
Roosevelt Corollary to the Monroe Doctrine, The

Rossetti, Christina
"Birthday, A"*
"Goblin Market"
"Sleeping at last"
Song ("When I am dead, my dearest")
"Up-Hill"

Rossetti, Dante Gabriel
"Blessed Damozel, The"
"Eden Bower"
"Sestina (after Dante)"
"Silent Noon"
"Woodspurge, The"

Ruskin, John
Modern Painters
Praeterita

Ryan, Abram Joseph
"Conquered Banner, The"

Sa'di
"Old Man, The" from *Tales from the Gulistan*
"Padshah and the Hermit, The" from *Tales from the Gulistan*
"Padshah and the Slave, The" from *Tales from the Gulistan*
"Solitary Dervish, The" from *Tales from the Gulistan*
"Son of a Rich Man and The Dervish Boy, The" from *Tales from the Gulistan*
"Thief and the Pious Man, The" from *Tales from the Gulistan*

Saki (H. H. Munro)
"Esme"
"Laura"
"Mrs. Packletide's Tiger"
"Sredni Vashtar"
"Tobermory"

Sandburg, Carl
"Chicago"*
"Fog"

Sappho
"Bride, A"*
"Forgotten"
"Garlands"
"Hesperus the Bringer"
"Hymn to Aphrodite"*
"Love's Distraction"
"Ode to Anactoria"

Sarmiento, Domingo Faustino
"Portrait of Facundo, A" from *Life in the Argentine Republic in the Days of the Tyrants*

Sassoon, Siegfried
"Glory of Women"
"Rear Guard, The"
"They"

Scott, Sir Walter
"My Native Land"
"Proud Maisie"*
"Soldier, Rest! Thy Warfare O'er"

Service, Robert W.
"Shooting of Dan McGrew, The"

Seward, William H.
Irrepressible Conflict, An

Shakespeare, William
"All the world's a stage" from *As You Like It*
"Blow, blow thou winter wind!" from *As You Like It*
"Fear no more the heat o' the sun" from *Cymbeline*
Hamlet, Prince of Denmark, Act One
Hamlet, Prince of Denmark, Act Two
Hamlet, Prince of Denmark, Act Three
Hamlet, Prince of Denmark, Act Four
Hamlet, Prince of Denmark, Act Five
King Lear, Act One
King Lear, Act Two
King Lear, Act Three
King Lear, Act Four
King Lear, Act Five
Midsummer Night's Dream, A, Act One
Midsummer Night's Dream, A, Act Two
Midsummer Night's Dream, A, Act Three
Midsummer Night's Dream, A, Act Four
Midsummer Night's Dream, A, Act Five
Much Ado About Nothing, Act One
Much Ado About Nothing, Act Two
Much Ado About Nothing, Act Three
Much Ado About Nothing, Act Four

---

*This selection includes background information, a study guide, and comprehension and critical thinking questions in a lesson on the disc.

Custom Literature Database

Much Ado About Nothing, Act Five

"O Mistress Mine" from *Twelfth Night*

Othello, the Moor of Venice, Act One

Othello, the Moor of Venice, Act Two

Othello, the Moor of Venice, Act Three

Othello, the Moor of Venice, Act Four

Othello, the Moor of Venice, Act Five

"Sigh No More" from *Much Ado About Nothing*

Sonnet 1 ("From fairest creatures we desire increase")

Sonnet 3 ("Look in thy glass, and tell the face thou viewest")

Sonnet 8 ("Music to hear, why hear'st thou music sadly?")

Sonnet 12 ("When I do count the clock that tells the time")

Sonnet 15 ("When I consider everything that grows")

Sonnet 18 ("Shall I compare thee to a summer's day?")

Sonnet 22 ("My glass shall not persuade me I am old")

Sonnet 23 ("As an unperfect actor on the stage")

Sonnet 27 ("Weary with toil, I haste me to my bed")

Sonnet 29 ("When, in disgrace with fortune and men's eyes")

Sonnet 30 ("When to the sessions of sweet silent thought")*

Sonnet 33 ("Full many a glorious morning have I seen")

Sonnet 46 ("Mine eye and heart are at mortal war")

Sonnet 47 ("Betwixt mine eye and heart a league is took")

Sonnet 49 ("Against that time, if ever that time come")

Sonnet 51 ("Thus can my love excuse the slow offense")

Sonnet 54 ("O, how much more doth beauty beauteous seem")

Sonnet 55 ("Not marble nor the gilded monuments")*

Sonnet 56 ("Sweet love, renew thy force!")

Sonnet 62 ("Sin of self-love possesseth all mine eye")

Sonnet 64 ("When I have seen by Time's fell hand defaced")

Sonnet 65 ("Since brass, nor stone, nor earth, nor boundless sea")

Sonnet 71 ("No longer mourn for me when I am dead")

Sonnet 73 ("That time of year though mayst in me behold")

Sonnet 76 ("Why is my verse so barren of new pride?")

Sonnet 80 ("O, how faint when I of you do write")

Sonnet 87 ("Farewell! Thou art too dear for my possessing")

Sonnet 92 ("But do thy worst to steal thyself away")

Sonnet 93 ("So shall I live, supposing thou art true")

Sonnet 94 ("They that have power to hurt and will do none")

Sonnet 97 ("How like a winter hath my absence been")

Sonnet 98 ("From you have I been absent in the spring")

Sonnet 104 ("To me, fair friend, you never can be old")

Sonnet 106 ("When in the chronicle of wasted time")

Sonnet 107 ("Not mine own fears nor the prophetic soul")

Sonnet 109 ("O, never say that I was false of heart")

Sonnet 110 ("Alas, 'tis true, I have gone here and there")

Sonnet 113 ("Since I left you, mine eye is in my mind")

Sonnet 115 ("Those lines that I before have writ do lie")

Sonnet 116 ("Let me not to the marriage of true minds")

Sonnet 120 ("That you were once unkind befriends me now")

Sonnet 128 ("How oft, when thou, my music, music play'st")

Sonnet 129 ("Th' expense of spirit in a waste of shame")

Sonnet 132 ("Thine eyes I love, and they, as pitying me")

Sonnet 138 ("When my love swears that she is made of truth")

Sonnet 140 ("Be wise as thou art cruel")

Sonnet 144 ("Two loves I have, of comfort and despair")

Sonnet 146 ("Poor soul, the center of my sinful earth")

Sonnet 147 ("My love is as a fever, longing still")

Taming of the Shrew, The, Act One

Taming of the Shrew, The, Act Two

Taming of the Shrew, The, Act Three

Taming of the Shrew, The, Act Four

Taming of the Shrew, The, Act Five

Tempest, The, Act One

Tempest, The, Act Two

Tempest, The, Act Three

Tempest, The, Act Four

Tempest, The, Act Five

"Under the Greenwood Tree" from *As You Like It*

"Who Is Silvia?" from *Two Gentlemen of Verona*

"Winter" from *Love's Labour's Lost*

Shaw, Bernard
Epilogue from *Pygmalion*

Shelley, Mary
Frankenstein

Shelley, Percy Bysshe
"Cloud, The"

Defence of Poetry, A

"Dirge, A"

"England in 1819"

"Hymn of Pan"

"Lines: 'When the lamp is shattered' "

"Song to the Men of England"

"To a Skylark"*

"To Jane: The Invitation"

"To—" ("Music, When Soft Voices Die")

"To Wordsworth"

Sheridan, Richard Brinsley
School for Scandal, The, Act One

School for Scandal, The, Act Two

School for Scandal, The, Act Three

School for Scandal, The, Act Four

School for Scandal, The, Act Five

Sidney, Sir Philip
"My true love hath my heart" from *The Arcadia*

"Oft Have I Mused"

Sonnet 31 ("With how sad steps, Oh Moon, thou climb'st the skies") from *Astrophel and Stella*

Sonnet 39 ("Come sleep! O sleep the certain knot of peace") from *Astrophel and Stella*

Sonnet 41 ("Having this day my horse, my hand, my lance") from *Astrophel and Stella*

"Thou Blind Man's Mark"

Skinner, Alanson, and Slaterlee, John V.
"Manabozho"

Smith, John
Description of New England, A

Generall Historie of Virginia, New England, and the Summer Isles, The

Sophocles
Antigone

Electra

Oedipus at Colonus

Oedipus the King

Southey, Robert
"Cataract of Lodore, The"

"Old Man's Comforts, The"*

" 'You are old, Father William' "*

Spenser, Edmund
"Epithalamion"

Faerie Queene, The, from Canto I

Sonnet 1 ("Happy ye leaves when as those lilly hands") from *Amoretti*

Sonnet 26 ("Sweet is the rose, but grows upon a briar") from *Amoretti*

Sonnet 30 ("My love is like to ice, and I to fire") from *Amoretti*

Sonnet 34 ("Like a ship, that through the ocean wide") from *Amoretti*

Sonnet 54 ("Of this worlds theatre in which we stay") from *Amoretti*

Sonnet 67 ("Lyke as a huntsman after weary chase") from *Amoretti*

Sonnet 75 ("One day I wrote her name upon the strand") from *Amoretti*

Sonnet 79 ("Men call you fayre, and you doe credit it") from *Amoretti*

Stansbury, Joseph
"Ode for the Year 1776"

---

*This selection includes background information, a study guide, and comprehension and critical thinking questions in a lesson on the disc.

Custom Literature Database

Wheatley, Phillis
Letter to Rev. Occum
"To His Excellency General Washington"
"To S. M., A Young African Painter on Seeing His Works"
"To the Right Honourable William, Earl of Dartmouth"

Whitman, Walt
"A Child's Amaze"
"As Toilsome I Wander'd Virginia's Woods"
"Beat! Beat! Drums!"*
"Beautiful Women"
"Bivouac on a Mountain Side"
"Cavalry Crossing a Ford"
"Crossing Brooklyn Ferry"*
"For You O Democracy"*
"I saw in Louisiana a live-oak growing"
"Joy, Shipmate, Joy!"
"Noiseless patient spider, A"
"On the Beach at Night"
"On the Beach at Night Alone"
"Passage to India"
"Sight in Camp in the Daybreak Gray and Dim, A"

"Song of Myself," 1,16,17,24
"Song of Myself," 3
"Sparkles from the Wheel"
"We Two Boys Together Clinging"
"When I heard the learn'd astronomer"
"When Lilacs Last in the Dooryard Bloomed"*

Whittier, John Greenleaf
"Barbara Frietchie"*
"Hampton Beach"
"Ichabod"
"Kansas Emigrants, The"
"Telling the Bees"

Wiesel, Elie
Acceptance Speech for the Nobel Peace Prize

Wilde, Oscar
"Ballad of Reading Gaol, The"*
"Birthday of the Infanta, The"
"Canterville Ghost, The"
"De Profundis"
"Few Maxims for the Instruction of the Over-Educated, A"
"Grave of Shelley, The"
"Happy Prince, The"

Importance of Being Earnest, The, Act One*
Importance of Being Earnest, The, Act Two
Importance of Being Earnest, The, Act Three
"Phrases and Philosophies for the Use of the Young"
"Prison Reform" from the *Daily Chronicle*
"Symphony in Yellow"

Wilson, Woodrow
First Inaugural Address
Peace Without Victory

Wordsworth, William
"Composed upon Westminster Bridge"*
"Elegiac Stanzas"
"Expostualtion and Reply"
"I travelled among unknown men"
"I Wandered Lonely as a Cloud"
"It is a beauteous evening, calm and free"*
"Lines Written in Early Spring"
"London, 1802"
"Lucy Gray"
"Michael"

"Nuns fret not at their convent's narrow room"
"Ode: Intimations of Immortality from Recollections of Early Childhood"*
Preface to *Lyrical Ballads*
Prelude, The, Book 1
"Resolution and Independence"
"She Dwelt Among the Untrodden Ways"
"slumber did my spirit seal, A"
"Solitary Reaper, The"
"Strange fits of passion have I known"
"Three Years She Grew"
"To a Skylark"

Wyatt, Sir Thomas
"Divers Doth Use"
"He is not dead that sometime hath a fall"
"My lute awake!"
"They Flee from Me"
"Varium et Mutabile"
"Whoso List to Hunt"

Zimmermann, Arthur
Zimmerman Note, The

---

*This selection includes background information, a study guide, and comprehension and critical thinking questions in a lesson on the disc.